Lecture Notes in Computer Science 3441

Commenced Publication in 1973
Founding and Former Series Editors:
Gerhard Goos, Juris Hartmanis, and Jan van Leeuwen

T0223555

Vladimiro Sassone (Ed.)

Foundations of Software Science and Computation Structures

8th International Conference, FOSSACS 2005
Held as Part of the Joint European Conferences
on Theory and Practice of Software, ETAPS 2005
Edinburgh, UK, April 4-8, 2005
Proceedings

 Springer

Volume Editor

Vladimiro Sassone
University of Sussex
Dept. of Informatics
Brighton BN1 9QH, UK
E-mail: v.sassone@sussex.ac.uk

Library of Congress Control Number: Applied for

CR Subject Classification (1998): F.3, F.4.2, F.1.1, D.3.3-4, D.2.1

ISSN 0302-9743
ISBN 3-540-25388-2 Springer Berlin Heidelberg New York

Springer is a part of Springer Science+Business Media

springeronline.com

© Springer-Verlag Berlin Heidelberg 2005
Printed in Germany

Typesetting: Camera-ready by author, data conversion by Scientific Publishing Services, Chennai, India
Printed on acid-free paper   SPIN: 11402060   06/3142   5 4 3 2 1 0

Foreword

ETAPS 2005 was the eighth instance of the *European Joint Conferences on Theory and Practice of Software*. ETAPS is an annual federated conference that was established in 1998 by combining a number of existing and new conferences. This year it comprised five conferences (CC, ESOP, FASE, FOSSACS, TACAS), 17 satellite workshops (AVIS, BYTECODE, CEES, CLASE, CMSB, COCV, FAC, FESCA, FINCO, GCW-DSE, GLPL, LDTA, QAPL, SC, SLAP, TGC, UITP), seven invited lectures (not including those that were specific to the satellite events), and several tutorials. We received over 550 submissions to the five conferences this year, giving acceptance rates below 30% for each one. Congratulations to all the authors who made it to the final program! I hope that most of the other authors still found a way of participating in this exciting event and I hope you will continue submitting.

The events that comprise ETAPS address various aspects of the system development process, including specification, design, implementation, analysis and improvement. The languages, methodologies and tools which support these activities are all well within its scope. Different blends of theory and practice are represented, with an inclination towards theory with a practical motivation on the one hand and soundly based practice on the other. Many of the issues involved in software design apply to systems in general, including hardware systems, and the emphasis on software is not intended to be exclusive.

ETAPS is a loose confederation in which each event retains its own identity, with a separate program committee and proceedings. Its format is open-ended, allowing it to grow and evolve as time goes by. Contributed talks and system demonstrations are in synchronized parallel sessions, with invited lectures in plenary sessions. Two of the invited lectures are reserved for "unifying" talks on topics of interest to the whole range of ETAPS attendees. The aim of cramming all this activity into a single one-week meeting is to create a strong magnet for academic and industrial researchers working on topics within its scope, giving them the opportunity to learn about research in related areas, and thereby to foster new and existing links between work in areas that were formerly addressed in separate meetings.

ETAPS 2005 was organized by the School of Informatics of the University of Edinburgh, in cooperation with

- European Association for Theoretical Computer Science (EATCS);
- European Association for Programming Languages and Systems (EAPLS);
- European Association of Software Science and Technology (EASST).

The organizing team comprised:

- Chair: Don Sannella
- Publicity: David Aspinall
- Satellite Events: Massimo Felici
- Secretariat: Dyane Goodchild
- Local Arrangements: Monika-Jeannette Lekuse

- Tutorials: Alberto Momigliano
- Finances: Ian Stark
- Website: Jennifer Tenzer, Daniel Winterstein
- Fundraising: Phil Wadler

ETAPS 2005 received support from the University of Edinburgh.

Overall planning for ETAPS conferences is the responsibility of its Steering Committee, whose current membership is:

Perdita Stevens (Edinburgh, Chair), Luca Aceto (Aalborg and Reykjavík), Rastislav Bodik (Berkeley), Maura Cerioli (Genoa), Evelyn Duesterwald (IBM, USA), Hartmut Ehrig (Berlin), José Fiadeiro (Leicester), Marie-Claude Gaudel (Paris), Roberto Gorrieri (Bologna), Reiko Heckel (Paderborn), Holger Hermanns (Saarbrücken), Joost-Pieter Katoen (Aachen), Paul Klint (Amsterdam), Jens Knoop (Vienna), Kim Larsen (Aalborg), Tiziana Margaria (Dortmund), Ugo Montanari (Pisa), Hanne Riis Nielson (Copenhagen), Fernando Orejas (Barcelona), Mooly Sagiv (Tel Aviv), Don Sannella (Edinburgh), Vladimiro Sassone (Sussex), Peter Sestoft (Copenhagen), Michel Wermelinger (Lisbon), Igor Walukiewicz (Bordeaux), Andreas Zeller (Saarbrücken), Lenore Zuck (Chicago).

I would like to express my sincere gratitude to all of these people and organizations, the program committee chairs and PC members of the ETAPS conferences, the organizers of the satellite events, the speakers themselves, the many reviewers, and Springer for agreeing to publish the ETAPS proceedings. Finally, I would like to thank the organizer of ETAPS 2005, Don Sannella. He has been instrumental in the development of ETAPS since its beginning; it is quite beyond the limits of what might be expected that, in addition to all the work he has done as the original ETAPS Steering Committee Chairman and current ETAPS Treasurer, he has been prepared to take on the task of organizing this instance of ETAPS. It gives me particular pleasure to thank him for organizing ETAPS in this wonderful city of Edinburgh in this my first year as ETAPS Steering Committee Chair.

Edinburgh, January 2005   Perdita Stevens
                                                    ETAPS Steering Committee Chair

Preface

This volume collects the proceedings of "Foundations of Software Science and Computation Structures," FOSSACS 2005. FOSSACS is a member conference of ETAPS, the "European Joint Conferences on Theory and Practice of Software," dedicated to foundational research for software science. It invites submissions on theories and methods to underpin the analysis, integration, synthesis, transformation, and verification of programs and software systems. Topics covered usually include: algebraic models; automata and language theory; behavioral equivalences; categorical models; computation processes over discrete and continuous data; computation structures; logics of programs; modal, spatial, and temporal logics; models of concurrent, reactive, distributed, and mobile systems; models of security and trust; language-based security; process algebras and calculi; semantics of programming languages; software specification and refinement; and type systems and type theory.

FOSSACS 2005 consisted of one invited and 30 contributed papers, selected out of 108 submissions, yielding an acceptance rate of less than 28%. The quality of the manuscripts was very high indeed, and the Program Committee had to reject several deserving ones. Besides making for a strong 2005 program, this is an indication that FOSSACS is becoming an established point of reference in the international landscape of theoretical computer science. This is a trend that I believe will continue in its forthcoming editions.

Besides Marcelo Fiore's invited talk, the volume includes Ugo Montanari's invited address as an ETAPS unifying speaker. Ugo's '*Model Checking for Nominal Calculi*' reflects broadly on topics in semantics, weaving together verification via semantic equivalences and model checking, Web services, the π-calculus, and the derivation of bisimulation congruences over reactive systems. Marcelo's contribution, '*Mathematical Models of Computational and Combinatorial Structures*,' advocates a combinatorial approach to semantic models by introducing a calculus of *generalized species of structures* as a unification and generalization of models arising in several distinct areas, including his previous work on denotational models of the π-calculus and of variable-binding operators. The conference program was organized into nine sessions, each focusing on reflecting common research topics among the accepted papers. The order of presentation of the papers in this volume maintains the structure of those sessions.

I have a debt of gratitude to the Program Committee for their scholarly effort during the discussion phase; to the referees, for carrying out the reviewing task with competence, care, and precision; to the invited speakers for their inspired work; and ultimately to the authors for submitting their best work to FOSSACS. Thanks to David Aspinall and Don Sannella for the local organization, and to Martin Karusseit and Tiziana Margaria for their support with the conference electronic management system.

I hope you enjoy the volume.

Sussex, January 2005

Vladimiro Sassone
Program Chair
FOSSACS 2005

Organization

Program Committee

Luca Aceto (Aalborg, Denmark)
Luís Caires (Lisbon, Portugal)
Witold Charatonik (Wroclaw, Poland)
Robert Harper (CMU, USA)
Naoki Kobayashi (Tokyo, Japan)
Guy McCusker (Sussex, UK)
Anca Muscholl (LIAFA Paris, France)
Andrew Pitts (Cambridge, UK)
David Sands (Chalmers, Sweden)
Vladimiro Sassone (Sussex, UK)
Peter Selinger (Ottawa, Canada)
Glynn Winskel (Cambridge, UK)

Michele Bugliesi (Venice, Italy)
Giuseppe Castagna (ENS Paris, France)
Vincent Danos (PPS Paris, France)
Petr Jančar (Ostrava, Czech Republic)
Orna Kupferman (Jerusalem, Israel)
Ugo Montanari (Pisa, Italy)
Tobias Nipkow (Munich, Denmark)
Amir Pnueli (Weizmann, Israel and
          New York, USA)
Andre Scedrov (UPenn, USA)
Wolfgang Thomas (Aachen, Denmark)
Nobuko Yoshida (Imperial, UK)

Referees

Reynald Affeldt
Jonathan Aldrich
Jan Altenbernd
Torben Amtoft
Eugene Asarin
David Aspinall
Franz Baader
Christel Baier
Patrick Baillot
Sebastian Bala
Paolo Baldan
Richard Banach
Nicolas Baudru
Gerd Behrmann
Martin Berger
Ulrich Berger
Gerd Berhmann
Marco Bernardo
Alexis Bes
Stephen Bloom
Richard Blute
Viviana Bono

Ana Bove
Tomas Brázdil
Thomas Brihaye
Stephen Brookes
Franck van Breugel
Marzia Buscemi
Michael Butler
Marco Carbone
Josep Carmona
Alberto Casagrande
Ilaria Castellani
Amine Chaieb
Stefano Chessa
Corina Cirstea
Giovanni Conforti
Thierry Coquand
Silvia Crafa
Karl Crary
Federico Crazzolara
Pedro D'Argenio
Jim Davies
Josée Desharnais

Pietro Di Gianantonio
Ernst-Erich Doberkat
Marie Duflot
Martín Escardó
Alessandro Fantechi
Marcelo Fiore
Riccardo Focardi
Alain Frisch
Fabio Gadducci
Philippe Gaucher
Simon Gay
Blaise Genest
Neil Ghani
Rob van Glabbeek
Daniele Gorla
Eric Goubault
Jean Goubault-Larrecq
Susanne Graf
Erich Grädel
S. Gutierrez-Nolasco
Joshua Guttman
Peter Habermehl

Table of Contents

Algebraic Models

Games and Automata

Language Analysis

Partial Order Models

Logics

Coalgebraic Modal Logics

Computational Models

Model Checking for Nominal Calculi*

Gian Luigi Ferrari, Ugo Montanari, and Emilio Tuosto

Dipartimento di Informatica, Largo Bruno Pontecorvo 3, 56127 Pisa – Italy

Abstract. Nominal calculi have been shown very effective to formally model a variety of computational phenomena. The models of nominal calculi have often infinite states, thus making model checking a difficult task. In this note we survey some of the approaches for model checking nominal calculi. Then, we focus on *History-Dependent automata*, a syntax-free automaton-based model of mobility. History-Dependent automata have provided the formal basis to design and implement some existing verification toolkits. We then introduce a novel syntax-free setting to model the symbolic semantics of a nominal calculus. Our approach relies on the notions of reactive systems and observed borrowed contexts introduced by Leifer and Milner, and further developed by Sassone, Lack and Sobocinski. We argue that the symbolic semantics model based on borrowed contexts can be conveniently applied to web service discovery and binding.

1 Summary

Model checking has been shown very effective for proving properties of system behaviour whenever a finite model of it can be constructed. The approach is convenient since it does not require formal proofs and since the same automaton-like model can accommodate system specification languages with substantially different syntax and semantics. Among the properties which can be checked, behavioural equivalence is especially important for matching specifications and implementations, for proving the system resistant to certain attacks and for replacing the system with a simpler one with the same properties.

Names have been used in process calculi for representing a variety of different informations concerning addresses, mobility links, continuations, localities, causal dependencies, security keys and session identifiers. When an unbound number of new names can be generated during execution, the models tend to be infinite even in the simplest cases, unless explicit mechanisms are introduced to allocate and garbage collect names, allowing the same states to be reused with different name meanings.

We review some existing syntax-free models for name-passing calculi and focus on *History-Dependent automata* (HD-automata), introduced by Montanari and Pistore in 1995 [62]. HD-automata [62, 63, 71] have been shown a suitable automata-based model for representing Petri nets, CCS with causality and localities and some versions of π-calculus [59, 75].

---

* Work supported by European Union project PROFUNDIS, Contract No. IST-2001-33100.

V. Sassone (Ed.): FOSSACS 2005, LNCS 3441, pp. 1–24, 2005.

Different versions of HD-automata have been defined. The simplest version can be easily translated to ordinary automata, but possibly with a larger number of states. In a second version, the states are equipped with name symmetries which further reduce the size of the automata. Furthermore, a theory based on coalgebras in a category of "named sets" can be developed for this kind of HD-automata, which extends the applicability of the approach to other nominal calculi and guarantees the existence of the minimal automaton within the same bisimilarity class [64, 34].

HD-automata also constitute the formal basis upon which several verification toolk-its have been defined and implemented. The front end towards the π-calculus and the translation algorithm for the simplest version of HD-automata have been implemented in the HAL tool [31, 32], which relies on the JACK verification environment [7] for handling the resulting ordinary automata. The minimisation algorithm, naturally suggested by the coalgebraic framework, has been implemented in the Mihda toolkit [35, 36] within the European project PROFUNDIS. Other versions of HD-automata can be equipped with algebraic operations, and are based on a algebraic-coalgebraic theory [61].

Here we propose a further instance handling the symbolic versions of nominal calculi, where inputs are represented as variables which are instantiated only when needed. As it is the case for logic programming unification, one would like the variables to be instantiated only the least possible, still guaranteeing that all behaviours are eventually explored. The approach we follow relies on the notion of reactive system and of observable borrowed contexts introduced by Leifer and Milner [53, 52] and further developed by Sassone, Lack and Sobocinski [76, 78, 50] using G-categories and adhesive categories. The reduction semantics of reactive systems is extended in order to introduce as borrowed contexts both the variable instantiations needed in the transitions and the ordinary π-calculus actions. It is argued that the symbolic semantics model based on borrowed contexts can be conveniently applied to web service discovery and binding.

In this paper we review the main results on HD-automata setting them in the mainstream research on nominal calculi. The final part of the paper introduces a novel symbolic semantics of π-calculus based on reactive systems and observed borrowed contexts. In our approach, unification is the basic interaction mechanism. We consider this as being the first step toward the definition of a formal framework (models, proof techniques and verification toolkits) for the so-called *service oriented computing* paradigm.

2   Verification via Semantics Equivalence

In the last thirty years the application of formal methods to software engineering has generated techniques and tools to deal with the various facets of the software development process (see e.g. [19] and the references therein). One of the main advantages of exploiting formal techniques consists of the possibility of constructing *abstractions* that approximate behaviours of the system under development. Often, these abstractions are amenable to automatic verification of properties thus providing a support to the certification of software quality.

Among the different proposals, *verification via semantics equivalence* provides a well established framework to deal with the checking of behavioural properties. In this approach, checking behavioural properties is reduced to the problem of contrasting two system abstractions in order to determine whether their behaviours coincide with respect to a suitable notion of semantics equivalence. For instance, it is possible to verify whether an abstraction of the implementation is consistent with its abstract specification. Another example is provided by the *information leak* detection; in [39] the analysis of information flow is done by verifying that the abstraction of the system *P* is equivalent to another abstraction obtained by suitably restricting the behaviour of *P*. A similar idea has been exploited in [1] for the analysis of cryptographic protocols.

Bisimilarity [69] has been proved to be an effective basis for verification based on semantics-equivalence of system abstractions described in some process calculus, i.e. Milner's Calculus of Communicating Systems (CCS) [58]. Bisimilarity is a *co-inductive* relation defined over a special class of automata called *labelled transition systems*. A generic labelled transition system (LTS) describes the evolution of a system by its interactions with the external environment. The co-inductive nature of bisimulation provides an effective proof method to establish semantics equivalence: it is sufficient to exhibit a bisimulation relating the two abstractions. Bisimulation-based proof methods have been exploited to establish properties of a variety of systems such as communication protocols, hardware designs and embedded controllers. Moreover, they have been incorporated in several toolkits for the verification of properties. Indeed, finite state verification environments have enjoyed substantial and growing use over the last years. Here, we mention the Concurrency WorkBench [21], the Meije-FC2 tools [8] and the JACK toolkit [7] to cite a few. Several systems of considerable complexity have been formalised and proved correct by exploiting these semantics-based verification environments.

The advent of mobile computing and wireless communication together with the development of applications running over the Internet (*Global Computing Systems*) have introduced software engineering scenarios that are much more dynamic than those handled with the techniques discussed above. Indeed, finite state verification of global computing systems is much more difficult: in this case, even simple systems can generate infinite state spaces. An illustrative example is provided by the π-calculus [59, 75]. The π-calculus primitives are simple but expressive: channel names can be created, communicated (thus giving the possibility of dynamically reconfiguring process acquaintances) and they are subjected to sophisticated scoping rules. The π-calculus is the archetype of name passing or nominal process calculi. Nominal calculi emphasise the principle that name mechanisms (e.g. local name generation, name exchanges, etc.) provide a suitable abstraction to formally explain a wide range of phenomena of global computing systems (see e.g. [80, 41]). Moreover, nominal calculi provide a basic programming model that has been incorporated in suitable libraries or novel programming languages [22, 4]. Finally, the usefulness of names has been also emphasised in practice. For instance, Needham [66] pointed out the role of names for the security of distributed systems. The World Wide Web provides an excellent (perhaps the most important) example of the power of names and name binding/resolution.

Nominal calculi have greater expressive power than ordinary process calculi, but the possibility of dynamically generating new names leads also to a much more complicated theory. In particular, bisimilarity is not always a congruence even for the strong bisimilarity. Moreover, the ordinary, underlying LTSs are infinite-state and infinite branching, thus making verification via semantics equivalence a difficult task.

Bisimulation-based proof techniques for nominal calculi can be roughly divided into two main families. The first consists of the *syntax-based* approaches while the second refers to the *syntax-free* approaches. The former line of development represents the states of the LTS with their syntactic denotation, while in the latter the states are just items characterised by their properties and connections. We recall a few of the approaches of both families without the ambition of being exhaustive.

Among the syntax-based, the most efficient approaches for finite-state verification rely on symbolic semantics. Symbolic semantics [42, 6, 54], generalise standard operational semantics by keeping track of equalities among names: transitions are derived in the context of such constraints. The main advantage of the symbolic semantics is that it yields a smaller transition system. The idea of symbolic semantics has been exploited to provide a convenient characterisation of *open bisimilarity* [74] and in the design of the corresponding bisimulation checker, the *Mobility WorkBench* (MWB) [83]. The MWB adapts to the case of the π-calculus the *on-the-fly* approach of [30], where the bisimulation relation is constructed during the state space generation. The MWB checks for open bisimilarity in the case of (finite-control) π-calculus processes and has also been reworked to deal with the Fusion calculus [70]. To gain efficiency, the MWB has been extended in [44] with modules implementing certain bisimulation-preserving program transformations, the *up-to-techniques* (introduced in [73]). Symbolic semantics has been also exploited in the design of the MCC model checker for the π-calculus [84]. The key idea of the approach is to provide an encoding of π-calculus symbolic semantics as a logic programming system. It is important to emphasise that all the constructions of the symbolic semantics rely on an *external* metalanguage and on a theory to describe and reason about name equalities.

A different approach is the definition of semantic-based techniques where names have a central role and are explicitly dealt with. Basically, in these frameworks it is possible to allocate and garbage collect names, allowing the same names to be reused with different meanings. This alternative line of research explores models of name-passing calculi, regardless of their syntactic details and aims at providing uniform theories that can be used to handle a variety of calculi and semantics. A well studied approach is based on the so-called permutation model, whose ingredients are a set of names and an action of its group of permutations (renaming substitutions) on an abstract set [37, 40, 47, 64]. In this setting, transition systems for nominal calculi are constructed via suitable functors over the underlying category of names and permutations: the internal theory of names.

It is important to notice that these approaches are *syntax-free* and provide the abstract framework to capture the notions of name abstraction and fresh name that are needed to describe and reason about nominal calculi. The HD-automata [34, 64, 71] and indexed LTSs [17] are examples of syntax-free models of name process calculi developed following the permutation approach.

3   Model Checking

Probably, the most successful formal technique applied in practice in the verification of systems is *model checking* (we refer to [18] for a detailed introduction to this field). Roughly speaking, model checking is used to determine whether a system abstraction (expressed as an automata or a term of a process calculus) satisfies a property (expressed as a modal or temporal logic formula). In order to model check a system with respect to a given formula it is necessary to prove that the system is a model of the formula. Tools supporting model checking techniques have matured to be used in practice (e.g. the SPIN model checker [45, 46] and SMV [57]). Recently, these techniques have been adopted to verify properties of programs written in high level programming languages like C++ and Java (e.g. JavaPathFinder [10], BANDERA [23], SLAM [3] and BLAST [43]).

Model checking presents several advantages. It is completely automatic, provided that finiteness of the system (the model) is guaranteed. Usually, it provides counterexamples when a system does not satisfy the property. This gives information on the design choices that have lead to the implementation errors. Finally, it is possible to obtain very high efficiency by exploiting refined data structures (e.g. BDDs), or symbolic techniques.

While modal and temporal logics have been proved suitable to express many properties of interest of concurrent systems, similar logics for global computing systems are still lacking. Only recently a new class of modal logics, *spatial logics* [15, 16], has been introduced to address the characterising issues of global computing. In our opinion, this explains why traditionally model checking has been exploited on foundational models for global computing only for limited fields and has not been fully applied to the general setting.

Without the ambition of being exhaustive, we now review some of the approaches to model check properties of nominal calculi. The MWB provides a model checking functionality. This is based on the implementation of the tableau-based proof system [25, 26] for the π-μ calculus, an extension of the propositional μ-calculus in which it is possible to express name parameterisation and quantifications over names. The MCC system also provides a model checking facility for the π-μ calculus.

The *HD-automata Laboratory* (HAL) [32] supports verification by model checking of properties expressed as formulae of a suitable modal logic, a high level logic with modalities indexed by π-calculus actions. This logic, although expressive enough to describe interesting safety and liveness properties of π-calculus specifications, is less expressive than the π-μ calculus. The construction of the HAL model checker takes direct advantage of the finite representation of π-calculus specifications presented in [62]. In particular, a HAL module translates these logical formulae into classical modal logic formulae and the translation is driven by the finite state representation of the system (the π-calculus process) to be verified.

The most relevant examples of application of model checking techniques and nominal calculi are those of the verification of security protocols [56, 20]. Several prototypical tools based on nominal calculi have been in fact designed and implemented [60, 55, 27, 38]. Indeed, nominal calculi provide a solid formal context for expressing many facets of cryptographic protocols in natural way. For instance, many authentication protocols rely on *nonce-challenges* where a fresh sequence of bit must be generated; the correctness of these protocols relies on the uniqueness of the nonces used in a given session. This can be easily modelled in nominal calculi, e.g. the π-calculus, where freshly generated names can be expressed and dealt with. An advantage of using model checking is that, when the protocol does not satisfy the security property, then the counterexample is the attack that an intruder could perform.

The main drawback of these approaches is that they require a finite state space while, in general, the generation of fresh names easily leads to infinite state spaces, if no countermeasure for garbage-collecting and reusing names is adopted. In practice, this problem has been faced by imposing strong conditions that limit the generality of the analysis. In particular, *finitary* systems, namely systems with infinite behaviour which can be finitely represented, are not considered. For instance, the analysis are performed on instances of protocols where only a limited number of participants is *apriori* fixed and in general recursion or iteration is forbidden. Hence, model checking security properties for nominal calculi can only deal with protocol sessions where a finite number of participants run in parallel and all the participants are non-recursive processes. Recently, symbolic ad-hoc model checkers have been proposed to overcome these issues e.g., [5, 82, 9, 2]. Despite the technical differences, all these approaches check a given property by generating a "symbolic" state space, where states collect constraints over the names involved in the execution. If there is a reachable state that violates the property, but whose constraints hold, then an attack is found. The symbolic techniques exploited in these approaches enforce efficiency both in the size of the generated state space and in the visit of it, but they still require finite state space.

4 History-Dependent Automata

History Dependent automata (HD-automata in brief) are one of the proposal based on the syntax-free approach. HD-automata are an operational model for history dependent formalisms, namely those formalisms accounting for systems whose behaviour at a given time might be influenced by some "historical" information which is too expensive to be included explicitly in the states. HD-automata allow for a compact representation of agent behaviour by collapsing states differing only for the renaming of local names and encompass the main characteristics of name-passing calculi, namely creation/deallocation of names. Basically, HD-automata associate a "history" to the names of the states appearing in the computation, in the sense that it is possible to reconstruct the associations which have led to the state containing the name. Clearly, if a state is reached in two different computations, different histories could be assigned to its names. Process calculi exhibiting causality, localities and mobility, and Petri nets, can be translated (preserving bisimilarity) to HD-automata [71].

Different versions of HD-automata have been defined [71, 63, 64, 34]. When handling causality, locality and the link mobility exhibited by the synchronous π-calculus without matching, the simplest version can be easily translated to ordinary automata. However, in general, a larger number of states is necessary for representing HD-automata with ordinary automata. The front-end towards the π-calculus and the translation algorithm have been implemented in the HAL toolkit, which relies on the JACK verification environment for handling the resulting ordinary automata.

In a second version, states of HD-automata are equipped with name symmetries which further reduce the size of the automata [64] and which guarantee the existence of the minimal realization. The minimal automata are computed using a partition refinement algorithm [34]. They have a very important practical fall-out: for instance, the problem of deciding bisimilarity is reduced to the problem of computing the minimal transition system [67, 29, 49]. Moreover, the minimal automaton is indistinguishable from the original one with respect to many behavioural properties (e.g., bisimilarity) and properties expressed in most modal or temporal logics. The minimisation algorithm, naturally suggested by the coalgebraic framework, has been implemented in the Mihda toolkit [36] within the European project PROFUNDIS. Other versions of HD-automata can be equipped with algebraic operations [61], thus relying on an algebraic-coalgebraic, namely bialgebraic, theory.

Similarly to ordinary automata, HD-automata consist of states and labelled transitions, their peculiarity being that states and transitions are equipped with names which are no longer dealt with as syntactic components of labels, but become an explicit part of the operational model. Noteworthy, names in states of HD-automata have *local meaning* which requires a mechanism for describing how names correspond each other along transitions.

Graphically, we can represent such correspondences using "wires" that connect names of label, source and target states of transitions as in Figure 1, where a tran-

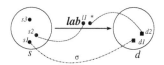

Fig. 1. A HD-automaton transition

sition from source state s to destination state d is depicted. State s has three names, $s1$, $s2$ and $s3$ while d has two names $d1$ and $d2$ which correspond to name $s1$ of s and to the new name $\star$, respectively. The transition is labelled by *lab* and exposes two names: name $l1$ and $\star$ the former corresponding to name $s2$ of s and the latter to a fresh name denoted as $\star$. Notice that name $s3$ is "deallocated" along such transition.

4.1 Minimising HD-Automata: An Informal Presentation

We report the formal definitions for *named sets* and *named functions* for representing finite HD-automata. These are the basic concepts upon which the partition refinement algorithm for HD-automata has been defined. For the sake of conciseness we give here only an incomplete definition. The interested reader is referred to [36] for a full presentation.

Definition 1 (Named Sets). *Let $\mathcal{N}$ be a denumerable set of names. A named set is a pair $\langle Q, g \rangle$ where Q is a totally-ordered set and $g : Q \to \bigcup_{N \in \wp_{fin}(\mathcal{N})} \mathrm{sym}(N)$ assigns a (finite) group of permutations over a finite set of names to elements in Q. For $q \in Q$, $|q|$ denotes the* carrier *of q defined as $\mathrm{dom}(\rho)$, where $\rho \in g(q)$.*

Definition 2 (Named Functions). *Let $\mathcal{N}^*$ be $\mathcal{N} \cup \{\star\}$ where $\star$ is an element not in $\mathcal{N}$. Given two named sets $\langle Q, g \rangle$ and $\langle Q', g' \rangle$, a named function $H : \langle Q, g \rangle \to \langle Q', g' \rangle$ consists of a pair of functions $\langle h, \Sigma \rangle$ where $h : Q \to Q'$ and $\Sigma : Q \to \wp_{\mathit{fin}}(\mathcal{N} \to \mathcal{N}^*)$ such that for all $q \in Q$ and $\sigma \in \Sigma(q)$*

- *σ is injective, $\sigma(|h(q)|) \subseteq |q| \cup \{\star\}$ and $\sigma|_{\mathcal{N} \setminus |h(q)|}$ is the identity;*
- *$\sigma; g(q) \subseteq \Sigma(q)$;*
- *$g(h(q)); \sigma = \Sigma(q)$.*

Named sets and functions form a category, **NS**, since named functions can be composed and identity named functions can be easily defined (see [36] for details). Given a set of labels L, if $\wp_{\mathit{fin}}(\_)$ is the finite power set functor on category Set, we define the functor $\wp_L$ on named sets as $\wp_L(\langle Q, g \rangle) = \langle \wp_{\mathit{fin}}(L \times Q), g' \rangle$ where $g'(B)$ contains all those permutations ρ such that $B\rho = B$ ($B\rho$ is element-wise application of ρ to B).

Definition 3. *A HD-automaton over L is a coalgebra for the functor $\wp_L$.*

The most important operation for minimising HD-automata is the *normalisation* which removes *redundant* transitions. In nominal calculi, redundancy is strictly connected to the concept of *active names*. A name n is *inactive* for an agent P if it is not used in the future behaviour of P.

In π-calculus, if P is bisimilar to $(\nu n)P$ we say that n is inactive in P (otherwise n is *active* in P) and a transition $P \xrightarrow{xn} Q$ is *redundant* (in the early semantics of π-calculus) when n is inactive in P. Deciding whether a name is active is as difficult as deciding bisimilarity. The importance of redundancy emerges when we try to establish the equivalence of states that have different numbers of free names. For instance, consider $P \stackrel{\text{def}}{=} x(u).(\nu v)(\bar{v}z + \bar{u}y)$ and $Q \stackrel{\text{def}}{=} x(u).\bar{u}y$, which differ only for a deadlocked alternative. They are bisimilar only if, for any name substituted for u, their continuations remain bisimilar. However, the input transition $P \xrightarrow{xz}$ cannot be matched by Q when considering only the *necessary* input transitions of agents, namely those where the acquired name is either a fresh name or one of the free names of the agent (as required for a finite representation of the transition system). Thus, unless the above transition of P is recognised as redundant and removed, the automata for P and Q would not be bisimilar. Redundant transitions occur when LTSs of π-calculus processes are compiled to HD-automata and are removed during the minimisation algorithm, since it is not possible to leave them out at compiling time[1].

The minimisation algorithm relies on functor T consisting of the composition of the normalisation functor and $\wp_L$. Consider a T-coalgebra $\langle D, K : D \to T(D) \rangle$, the minimisation algorithm is defined by the two equations below.

---

[1] In general, deciding whether a free input transition is redundant or not is equivalent to decide whether a name is active or not; therefore, it is as difficult as deciding bisimilarity.

$$H_{(0)} \stackrel{\text{def}}{=} \langle q \mapsto \bot, q \mapsto \emptyset \rangle, \quad \text{where dom}(H_{(0)}) = D \tag{1}$$

$$H_{(i+1)} \stackrel{\text{def}}{=} K; T(H_i). \tag{2}$$

In words, all the states of automaton K are initially considered equivalent, indeed, the kernel of H_0 gives rise to a single equivalence class containing the whole dom(K). At the generic $(i+1)$-th iteration, the image through T of the i-th iteration is composed with K as prescribed in (2). The algorithm stops when the fixpoint $\bar{H}$ of (2) is reached. Then $\bar{H}$ is the unique final coalgebra morphism and states mapped together by it are bisimilar.

Theorem 1 (Convergence [36]). *The iterative algorithm described by (1) and (2) is convergent on finite state automata.*

4.2 The PROFUNDIS Web

In the last years distributed applications over the World-Wide Web, have attained wide interest. Recently, the Web is exploited as a *service distributor* and applications are no longer monolithic but rather made of components (i.e., services). Applications over the Web are developed by combining and integrating Web services. The Web service framework has emerged as the standard and natural architecture to realize the so called *Service Oriented Computing* (SOC) [24, 68]. In [33] a Web-service infrastructure was developed integrating verification toolkits for checking properties of mobile systems and related higher-level toolkits for verifying security protocols. The development of the verification infrastructure has been performed inside the PROFUNDIS project (see URL http://www.it.uu.se/profundis) within the Global Computing Initiative of the European Union. For this reason we called it the *PROFUNDIS WEB*, PWeb for short. The current prototype implementation of the PWeb infrastructure can be exercised on-line at the URL http://jordie.di.unipi.it:8080/pweb.

Beyond the current prototype implementation, we envisage the important role that will be played by PWeb service coordination. Indeed, service coordination provides several benefits:

- *Model-based verification.* The coordination rules impose constraints on the execution flow of the verification session thus enabling a *model-based* verification methodology where several descriptions are manipulated together.
- *Modularity.* The verification of the properties of a large software system can be reduced to the verification of properties over subsystems of manageable complexity: the coordination rules reflect the semantic modularity of system specifications.
- *Flexibility.* The choice of the verification toolkits involved in the verification session may depend on the specific verification requirements.

The PWeb implementation has been conceived to support reasoning about the behaviour of systems specified in some dialect of the π-calculus. It supports the dynamic integration of different verification techniques (e.g. standard bisimulation checking and symbolic techniques for cryptographic protocols). The PWeb integrates several independently-developed toolkits, e.g., Mihda [35, 36] and several tools for verifying cryptographic protocols, like TRUST [82] and STA [5]. The PWeb has been designed by targeting also the goal of extending available verification environments (Mobility Workbench [83], HAL [31, 32]) with new facilities provided as Web services.

The core of the PWeb is a *directory service*. A PWeb directory service is a component that maps the description of the Web services into the corresponding network addresses and has two main facilities: the publish facility, invoked to make a toolkit available as Web service, and the query facility, used to discover available services. For instance, Mihda publishes the reduce service which accepts a (XML description of) HD-automaton describing the behaviour of a π-calculus agent. Once invoked, reduce performs the minimisation of the HD-automaton.

The service discovery mechanisms are exploited by the trader engine which manipulates pools of services distributed over several PWeb directory services. It can be used to obtain a Web service of a certain type and to bind it inside the application. The trader engine gives to the PWeb directory service the ability of finding and binding web services at run-time without "hard-coding" the name of the web service inside the application code. The following code describes the use of a simple trader for the PWeb directory.

```
import Trader
offers = Trader.query( "reducer" )
mihda = offers[ 0 ]
```

The code asks the trader for a reduce service and selects the first of them. The trader engine allows one to hide network details in the service coordination code. A further benefit is given by the possibility of replicating the services and maintaining a standard access modality to the Web services under coordination.

The fundamental technique enabling the dynamic integration of services is the separation between the service facilities (what the service provides) and the mechanisms that coordinate the way services interact (service coordination). An example of service coordination for checking whether a process A is a model for a formula F is as follows

```
hd = mihda.compile( A )
reduced_hd = mihda.reduce( hd )
reduced_hd_fc2 = mihda.Tofc2( reduced_hd )
aut = hal.unfold( reduced_hd_fc2 )
if hal.check( aut, F ):
    print 'ok'
else:
    print 'ko'
```

Variables mihda and hal have been linked by the trader engine to the required services (acquired as illustrated before). Now, the compile service of mihda is invoked yielding an HD-automaton (stored in hd). Next, hd is minimised by invoking the service reduce of Mihda; and afterward it is transformed into the FC2 format by a HAL service. Finally, the HAL service unfold generates an ordinary automaton from the FC2 representation of the automaton and prints a message which depends on whether the system satisfies the formula F or not. This is obtained by invoking the HAL model checking facility check.

5   A Borrowed Context Semantics for the Open π-Calculus

The version of the π-calculus implemented in the Mihda toolkit does not rely on a symbolic semantics. This fact makes unnecessary large the number of states, due to the existence of different input transitions for different instantiations of the input variable. While a symbolic semantics for a syntax-based version of HD-automata for the open π-calculus has been defined in [72], it might be convenient to define a symbolic semantics for the ordinary syntax-free HD-automata. More generally, in Service Oriented Computing (SOC) [24, 68] one would like to have more sophisticated mechanisms than service call and parameter passing for modelling the phase of service discovery and binding. The SOC paradigm is the emerging technology to design and develop global computing systems: several research activities have addressed the theoretical foundations of the SOC paradigm by exploiting formal frameworks based on process calculi [12, 51, 14, 11] (see also [81] for an informal presentation on the usefulness of nominal calculi to design workflow business processes).

When looking for a generalisation of parameter passing, logic programming unification comes to mind, or rather constraint programming, when service level agreements involve nonfunctional issues. When the binding occurs, not only the callee is instantiated, but also the caller. The instantiation that must be applied to the caller is formally analogous to a missing context that must be borrowed by a process in order to undergo a reduction. In this line of thought, some recent works about systematic methods for deriving LTSs from reduction rules look relevant. In particular, the approach we follow relies on the notion of reactive system, introduced by Leifer and Milner [53, 52], used by Jensen and Milner in [48] for deriving a LTS for bigraphs and further developed by Sassone, Lack and Sobocinski [76, 78, 50] using G-categories and adhesive categories.

In this section we will consider a simplified version of open π-calculus and we will develop a semantics for it using the notion of reactive systems. While the corresponding bisimilarity semantics turns out to be finer, we think that this exercise shows the feasibility of employing context borrowing for modelling symbolic semantics. The generality of the reactive system approach gives some hope that interesting abstractions of the SOC paradigm could also be modelled that way. Note however that the transition system which can be derived from reactive rules in our development is not really suitable for a HD-automata implementation, since new names are never forgotten, thus making the transition systems infinite in all but the most trivial cases. We comment in Section 6 about possible solutions of this problem.

5.1   Open π-Calculus

One of main peculiarities of the π-calculus is the richness of its observational semantics. Initially, it came equipped with the *early* and the *late* observational semantics [59] which differ each other in the way they deal with name instantiation. Symbolic semantics [42] generalises standard operational semantics by keeping track of equalities among names: transitions are derived in the context of such constraints. The main advantage of the symbolic semantics is that it yields a smaller transition system. The idea of symbolic semantics has been exploited to provide a finitary characterisation of *open*

Table 1. Semantics of π_-

$$
\begin{array}{ll}
(\text{PRE}) \; \alpha.p \xrightarrow{\alpha} p & (\text{SUM}) \; \dfrac{p \xrightarrow{\mu} p'}{p+q \xrightarrow{\mu} p'} \\[2em]
(\text{PAR}) \; \dfrac{p \xrightarrow{\mu} p'}{p \mid q \xrightarrow{\mu} p' \mid q} \; \text{if } bn(\mu) \cap fn(q) = \emptyset & (\text{COM}) \; \dfrac{p \xrightarrow{\bar{a}b} p' \quad q \xrightarrow{a'(c)} q'}{p \mid q \xrightarrow{a=a'} p' \mid q'\{^b/_c\}} \\[2em]
& (\text{REP}) \; \dfrac{p \mid p! \xrightarrow{\mu} q}{p! \xrightarrow{\mu} q}
\end{array}
$$

bisimilarity [74] which, differently from the early and the late semantics, is a congruence with respect to the contexts of the π-calculus.

We consider a subset of the π-calculus without neither matching nor restriction operators. Given a numerable infinite and totally ordered set of *names* $\mathcal{N} = \{a_1, a_2, \ldots\}$, the set **P** of π_- *processes* is defined by the grammar

$$p, q ::= \mathbf{0} \mid \mu.p \mid p \mid q \mid p+q \mid p! \qquad\qquad \alpha ::= \bar{a}b \mid a(b).$$

As usual, name a is free in $\bar{a}b$ and $a(b)$, while b is free just in the former case and bound in the latter. Moreover, a is called the *subject* and b the *object* of the action. Considering $a(b).p$, the occurrences of b in p are bound, *free names* are defined as usual and $fn(p)$ indicates the set of free names of process p. Differently than in the full π-calculus, only the input prefix binds names. Processes are considered equivalent up-to α-renaming of bound names.

The operational rules for the semantics of π_- are those reported in Table 1 together with the symmetric rules for (PAR) and (SUM). The rules specify an LTS whose labels (denoted as μ) are either actions or *fusions*. The only non-standard rule is (COM) which states that an output $\bar{a}b$ and an input $a'(c)$ can synchronise provided that a and a' are fused. Notice that, if a and a' are the same, $a = a'$ is the identity fusion, denoted as ε, which corresponds to the usual silent action τ.

The transition system of π_- resulting from specification rules in Table 1 is the same as the one obtained by applying the LTS rules of [74] to π_-. The only differences between the two LTSs are in the syntax of the labels and in the rule (COM). In [74] the labels are pairs (M, μ) or (M, τ) where M are sequences of fusions. It is easy to see that our label μ corresponds to (μ, τ) if μ is a fusion label and to $(\emptyset, \mu)$ if it is an action label. The communication rule of [74] is

$$
\dfrac{p \xmapsto{(M, \bar{a}b)} p' \quad q \xmapsto{(N, a'(c))} q'}{p \mid q \xmapsto{(L, \tau)} p' \mid q'\{^b/_c\}} \qquad L = \begin{cases} MN[a = a'], & \text{if } a \neq a' \\ MN, & \text{if } a = a' \end{cases}
$$

which resembles rule (COM) of Table 1. However it is considerably more complex since it must also collect the fusions due to matchings.

Proposition 1. *Under the label correspondende illustrate above, let $p \in \mathbf{P}$ be a π_- process, then $p \xrightarrow{\mu} q$ if, and only if, the same transition can be derived from the transition system in [74] (changing μ with the corresponding label of [74]).*

Proof. The ($\Rightarrow$) part trivially follows by induction on the length of the proof of $p \xrightarrow{\mu} q$. The ($\Leftarrow$) part follows by observing that the length of the fusions in labels of [74] is one, since π_- lacks the matching operator. $\qquad\square$

We recast the definition of *open bisimulation* given in [74] for π_-.

Definition 4 (Open Bisimulation). *A symmetric relation $S \subseteq \mathbf{P} \times \mathbf{P}$ is an* open bisimulation *if whenever pSq,*

- *if $p \xrightarrow{\alpha} p'$ then there is q' such that $q \xrightarrow{\alpha} q'$ and $p'Sq'$;*
- *if $p \xrightarrow{\varepsilon} p'$ then there is q' such that $q \xrightarrow{\varepsilon} q'$ and $p'Sq'$;*
- *if $p \xrightarrow{a=b} p'$ then there is q' such that $(q \xrightarrow{a=b} q' \vee q \xrightarrow{\varepsilon} q') \wedge \sigma_{a=b}(p')S\sigma_{a=b}(q')$,*

where $\sigma_{a=b}$ is a substitution that maps a to b (or viceversa*) and leaves the other names unchanged. Two processes p and q are* open bisimilar, *written $p \sim q$, when there is an open bisimulation relating them.*

In order to compare the ordinary bisimilarity $\sim$ with the one arising from the Leifer and Milner approach, it is convenient to introduce an additional bisimilarity for π_-.

Definition 5 (Syntactical Bisimilarity). *The* syntactical *bisimilarity relation $\simeq$ for π_- is obtained by simplifying the last condition of Definition 4 with*

if $p \xrightarrow{a=b} p'$ then there is q' such that $q \xrightarrow{a=b} q'$ and $\sigma_{a=b}(p')S\sigma_{a=b}(q')$.

It is immediate to see that $\simeq$ is finer than or equal to $\sim$. In fact its conditions for matching transition labels are more demanding than those for $\sim$.

Theorem 2 (Open Versus Syntactical Bisimilarity). *We have $\simeq \subseteq \sim$.*

An equivalence relation relating terms of an algebra is said a *congruence* if it is preserved by all the operation of the algebra, or, equivalently, if it is preserved in all the contexts of the language. In [74], $\sim$ has been proven to be a congruence for the π-calculus.

5.2   Reactive Systems

A systematic method for deriving bisimulation congruence from reduction rules has been proposed by Leifer and Milner in [53, 52], on turn inspired by [79], where the idea of interpreting $p \xrightarrow{c} q$ as "in the context c, p reacts and becomes q" has been proposed. Also, the approach of observing contexts imposed on agents at each step has been introduced in [65], yielding the notion of *dynamic bisimilarity*. Following [28], we will call *borrowed context* the context c. The basic idea of [53, 52] is to express "minimality" conditions for electing the context c among the (possibly infinite) ones that allow p to react. These conditions have been distilled by [53] in the notion of *relative push-out* (RPO) in categories of *reactive systems*. The RPO construction is reminiscent of the unification process of logic programming, which in fact can be given an interactive semantics in much the same style [13].

We want to apply this approach to a reduction semantics of π_- that reflects its LTS semantics, therefore, we collect here the main definitions and results of the RPO approach. We remark that Definitions 6, 7, 8 and Theorem 3 are borrowed from [53, 52] (aside from some minor notational conventions).

Let $\mathbf{C}$ be an arbitrary category whose arrows are denoted by f, g, h, k and whose objects by m, n. Hereafter, $f;g$ will indicate arrow composition.

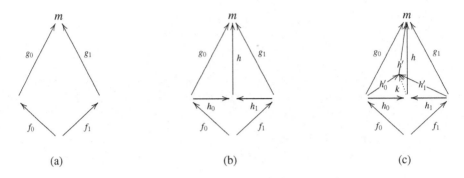

Fig. 2. Diagrams for Definitions 6

Definition 6 (Relative Push-Out and Idem Push-Out). *Consider the commuting diagram in Figure 2(a) consisting of $f_0;g_0 = f_1;g_1$. A triple $\langle h_0, h_1, h \rangle$ is an RPO if diagram in Figure 2(b) commutes and for any triple $\langle h'_0, h'_1, h' \rangle$ satisfying $f_0;h'_0 = f_1;h'_1$ and $h'_i;h' = g_i$, for $i = 0, 1$ there exists a unique k such that diagram Figure 2(c) commutes. Diagram (a) is an* idem push-out *(IPO) if $\langle g_0, g_1, id \rangle$ is an RPO.*

Definition 7 (Reactive System). *A* reactive system *is a category $\mathbf{C}$ with the following extra components:*

- *a distinguished (not necessarily initial) object $\star$;*
- *a set of pairs of arrows $(l : \star \to m, r : \star \to m)$ called* reaction rules*;*
- *a subcategory $\mathbf{D}$ of* reactive contexts *with the property that if $d;d'$ is an arrow of $\mathbf{D}$, then both d and d' are arrows in $\mathbf{D}$.*

The IPO construction yields the definition of labelled transition out of a reduction semantics and the corresponding observational semantics.

Definition 8 (Labelled Transition and Bisimulation). *We write $a \xrightarrow{\ f\ } a'$ iff there exist a reaction rule (l, r) and a reactive context d such that $\begin{smallmatrix} & f \nearrow & \nwarrow d \\ a & \searrow & \nearrow l \\ & \star & \end{smallmatrix}$ is an IPO and $a' = r;d$.*

A symmetric binary relation $S \subseteq \bigcup_m \mathbf{C}[\star, m] \times \bigcup_m \mathbf{C}[\star, m]$, where $C[x, y]$ is the set of all the arrows from x to y of category C, is a bisimulation over $\xrightarrow{\ f\ }$ *iff for $(a, b) \in S$, if $a \xrightarrow{\ f\ } a'$ then there is b' such that $b \xrightarrow{\ f\ } b'$ and $(a', b') \in S$.*

The central result of [53] can be stated as follows:

Theorem 3. *The largest bisimulation over* $\xrightarrow{\ f\ }$ *is a congruence provided that* **C** *has all* redex-RPOs.

The category **C** has all *redex-RPOs* when for all reaction rules (l,r), all arrow a, f and

all contexts d such that $a;f = l;d$ then the square $\begin{array}{c} f \nearrow \quad \nwarrow d \\ \nwarrow \quad \nearrow \\ a \quad \star \quad l \end{array}$ has an RPO.

5.3 A Reactive System for the Open π-Calculus

We shall specify a reactive system semantics for π_- taking actions and name substitutions as reactive contexts and by defining rules in such a way that the LTS will be essentially the same as the one defined in Section 5.1. However, the observational semantics resulting from the RPO approach considers labels as purely syntactical items and transitions can match only if they have identical labels. In the definition of open bisimilarity, instead, a proper fusion can be matched by an ε label. Thus it cannot be expected that the two bisimilarity relations coincide. In fact, we will show that the bisimilarity arising from the RPO approach is finer than open bisimilarity.

The reduction semantics of π_- is specified with rules of the form $P;\mu \to q$, where μ is an action or a fusion, $q \in \mathbf{P}$ and P is a *normalised process* (formally defined below). A rule $P;\mu \to q$ corresponds to a π_- transition $P \xrightarrow{\mu} q$, the only difference being that in the reactive system approach processes must be typed by (a natural number larger or equal than) the largest index of their free variables. Normalised processes can be thought of as being processes where all the occurrences of free variables are replaced by different variables $\{a_1,\ldots,a_n\}$ ordered in some standard way. Normalised processes give a logic programming flavour to the reduction semantics. In fact, they are reminiscent of predicate symbols, while processes correspond to goals: as goals are instantiations of predicate symbols, any process $p \in \mathbf{P}$ can be regarded as the instantiation of a normalised process P. This amounts to say that, whenever p and $P;\mu$ (i.e., the instance and the head of the clause) unify, then a transition for p can be deduced. They unify whenever P is the normalised process of p. Moreover, the label is the borrowed context, which turns out either to be μ whenever μ is an action or to be a fusion not implied by the substitution mapping P to p, or else to be ε if it is implied.

Let $p \in \mathbf{P}$, we assume given two functions $\hat{p}$ and σ_p such that

$$\mathrm{fn}(\hat{p}) = \{a_1,\ldots,a_n\}, \quad \hat{\hat{p}} = \hat{p}, \quad p = \sigma_p(\hat{p}), \quad p = \sigma(q) \implies \hat{p} = \hat{q} \wedge \sigma_p = \sigma \circ \sigma_q,$$

where $\sigma_p : \mathrm{fn}(\hat{p}) \to \mathrm{fn}(p)$ and $\sigma : \mathrm{fn}(q) \to \mathrm{fn}(p)$ are surjective name substitutions homomorphically extended to π_- agents ($\sigma(\_)$ stands for the extension of σ to agents). It is easy to show that $\hat{p}$ is a linear process, namely each free variable occurs exactly once. Indeed, let $x \in \mathcal{N}$ occur twice in $p \in \mathbf{P}$ and assume by absurd that $\hat{p} = p$. Now, consider $p' \in \mathbf{P}$ to be the term obtained by replacing in p the first and the second occurrence of x with y and z, respectively. Then $p = \sigma(p')$, where $\sigma = \{y \mapsto x, z \mapsto x\}$, thus by definition, $\hat{p} = \widehat{p'}$. But there is no $\sigma_{p'}$ such that $p' = \sigma_{p'}(\widehat{p'}) = \sigma_{p'}(p)$.

Notice that $\hat{\ }$ and σ_- only involve syntactical aspects of agents, therefore they can be easily defined on the syntax trees of π_-. For instance, $\hat{p}$ might be defined as the agent having the same syntax tree of p where the i-th leaf is named by a_i, assuming that leaves are ordered according to a depth-first visit: substitution σ_p is defined accordingly. The order of leaves is arbitrary and different definitions might be possible, however, all of them differ only for a permutation of (the indexes of) $\text{fn}(\hat{p})$.

Definition 9 (Normalised Processes). *The processes that are fixpoints of $\hat{}$ are the nor-malised processes and are ranged over by P.*

Before defining **PAC**, the category we work with, we specify its (basic) arrows where the underlying objects are elements of the set $\omega_\star = \omega \cup \{\star\}$ consisting of the natural numbers plus a distinguished element $\star$.

Definition 10 (Basic Arrows). *We define the following basic arrows.*
A normalised agent arrow $P_m : \star \to m$ is a pair consisting of a normalised process P and a natural number $m \in \omega$ such that, for any $a_n \in \text{fn}(P)$, $n \leq m$. We write P instead of P_m when $\text{fn}(P)$ contains exactly m names.
A fusion arrow from m to n is a surjective substitution from $\{a_1, \ldots, a_m\}$ to $\{a_1, \ldots, a_n\}$ written as $\sigma : m \to n$.
Action arrows are π_- actions parameterised on ω, more precisely

$$\bar{a}_i^m a_j : m \to m \qquad a_i^m : m \to m+1 \qquad i, j \leq m$$

that respectively correspond to output and input transitions with the object name in the latter case being a_{m+1}.
A sequence arrow $\gamma : m_0 \to m_1$ is a tuple $\langle \mu_1, \ldots, \mu_k, \sigma \rangle$ where $k \geq 0$, for each $0 < i \leq k$, $\mu_i : m_{i-1} \to m_i$ is an action arrow and $\sigma : m_k \to m'$ is a fusion arrow. In addition, we require that, if $\sigma(a_i) = \sigma(a_j)$ with $i < j$, then name a_j does not appear in actions $\mu_1, \ldots, \mu_k$. Notice that for $k = 0$ we obtain fusion arrows while for $k = 1$ and $\sigma = \text{id}_m$ we obtain action arrows.
A process arrow $p : \star \to m$ is a tuple $\langle P, \mu_1, \ldots, \mu_k, \sigma \rangle$ where $P : \star \to m_0$ is a normalised agent arrow and $\langle \mu_1, \ldots, \mu_k, \sigma \rangle$ is a sequence arrow such that $\text{dom}(\mu_1) = m_0$. Notice that for $k = 0$, and $\sigma = \text{id}_{m_0}$ we obtain normalised agent arrows.

Definition 11 (Process-Action-Context Category). *The process-action-context cate-gory **PAC** is the category having as objects elements of $\omega_\star$ and as morphisms:*

1. *the identity arrows $\text{id}_\star : \star \to \star$ and $\text{id}_m : m \to m$, the latter being the identity sub-stitution on $\{a_1, \ldots, a_m\}$;*
2. *the normalised agent arrows, the fusion arrows and the action arrows as genera-tors; and*
3. *the arrows freely generated by 2 under the composition operation $\_;\_$ subject to the usual associativity and identity axioms and, in addition, to the following axioms:*

$$\frac{\sigma : n \to m \quad a_i^m : m \to m+1}{\sigma; a_i^m = a_h^m; \sigma'}, \; h = \min_l \{\sigma(a_l) = a_i\} \quad \sigma' = \sigma[n+1 \mapsto m+1]$$

$$\frac{\sigma : n \to m \quad \bar{a}_i^m a_j : m \to m}{\sigma; \bar{a}_i^m a_j = \bar{a}_h^n a_k; \sigma}, \; h = \min_l \{\sigma(a_l) = a_i\} \quad k = \min_l \{\sigma(a_l) = a_j\}$$

($\sigma[n+1 \mapsto m+1]$ *stands for the function that behaves as* σ *for any* $a \in \{a_1,\dots,a_n\}$ *and maps* a_{n+1} *to* a_{m+1}).

The arrows of **PAC** can be given an intuitive standard representation that will be useful later in the proofs.

Proposition 2. *The arrows of* **PAC** *are exactly the process arrows, the sequence arrows and the identity arrow* $id_\star$.

Proof. First, observe that: (a) a normalised agent arrow is a process arrow with an empty sequence of actions and an identity substitution. (b) A fusion arrow σ is a sequence arrow with no action arrows and with σ as the fusion arrow; this also yields the identities id_m where $m \in \omega$. (c) Similarly, action arrows are sequence arrows with a single action arrow and the identity substitution. Now, we prove that the composition of a process (resp. sequence) arrow with a sequence arrow yields a process (resp. sequence) arrow. Consider $p : \star \to m$ and $\gamma : m \to n$ be the process arrow $\langle P, \mu_1, \dots, \mu_h, \sigma \rangle$ and the sequence arrow $\langle \mu'_1, \dots, \mu'_k, \sigma' \rangle$. By definition $p; \gamma = \langle P, \mu_1, \dots, \mu_h, \sigma, \mu'_1, \dots, \mu'_k, \sigma' \rangle$, and, observing that the two last axioms in 3 of Definition 11, allows to "exchange" a fusion arrow with an action arrow, we trivially conclude that $p; \gamma = \langle P, \mu_1, \dots, \mu_h, \mu''_1, \dots, \mu''_k, \sigma''; \sigma' \rangle$, for suitable $\mu''_1, , \dots, \mu''_k$ and σ''. We remark that if, at any stage, two names are fused, say a_i and a_j with $i < j$, then a_j is replaced by a_i by definition and this guarantees that $\langle P, \mu_1, \dots, \mu_h, \mu''_1, \dots, \mu''_k, \sigma''; \sigma' \rangle$ is a process arrow. The prove is the same when considering composition between two sequence arrows.

The proof is concluded by showing that different arrows cannot be equated by axioms. In other words, we prove that the standard representation of an arrow is unique (up to identities). Indeed, by inspecting the initial part of the proof we see that equality between two arrow can be proved only by shifting back and forth fusion arrows or introducing/cancelling identities. In the former case, any shift uniquely determines both the action and the fusion arrow of the equated arrows (Definition 11).   □

As already mentioned, in the above definitions we have introduced typed versions (the type is a natural number m) of normalised agents and actions (substitutions are already typed), such that their names are in $\{a_1, \dots, a_m\}$. This is apparently required by the "box and wires" structure of category **PAC**. We continue defining typed versions of ordinary processes and of fusions.

Given a π_- agent p and a natural number m such that $m \geq max\{k \mid a_k \in \text{fn}(p)\}$, we denote as $p_m : \star \to m$ the arrow $\hat{p}_n; \sigma$ where $n = |\text{fn}(\hat{p})| + m - |\text{fn}(p)|$ and $\sigma : n \to m$ is defined as:

- $\sigma(a_i) = \sigma_p(a_i)$, if $i \in \text{fn}(\hat{p})$,
- σ bijective and index monotone when restricted to $i \notin \text{fn}(\hat{p})$ (where σ is *index monotone* if $\sigma(a_i) = \sigma(a_h)$, $\sigma(a_j) = \sigma(a_k)$ and $i \leq j$ implies $h \leq k$).

Basically, p_m represents the agent p in terms of a normalised process with n variables. Given a fusion $a_i = a_j$ and $m \in \omega$, with $i < j \leq m$, the substitution $[a_i = a_j]_m : m \to m-1$ is defined as follows:

$$[a_i = a_j]_m(a_k) = \begin{cases} a_k, & k < j \\ a_i, & k = j \\ a_{k-1}, & j < k \leq m \end{cases}$$

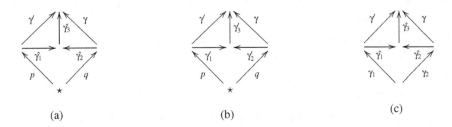

Fig. 3. Diagrams for proofs in Theorem 4

In words, $[a_i = a_j]_m$ maps the initial m names to the initial $m - 1$ by replacing a_j with a_i and mapping the names greater that a_j to their predecessors.

Definition 12 (PAC Reaction Rules). *The* reaction rules *are those generated by the following inference rules where* $m \geq |\text{fn}(P)|$:

$$\frac{P \xrightarrow{\bar{a}b} q}{P_m; \bar{a}^m b \implies q_m} \qquad \frac{P \xrightarrow{a(a_{m+1})} q}{P_m; a^m \implies q_{m+1}}$$

$$\frac{P \xrightarrow{a_i = a_j} q \quad i \neq j}{P_m; [a_i = a_j]_m \implies q_m; [a_i = a_j]_m} \qquad \frac{P \xrightarrow{\varepsilon} q}{P_m \implies q_m}$$

Definition 12 specify the reduction rules of **PAC** which rely on the LTS semantics of π_-. Take the first rule; it states that, if a normalised process P makes an output transition to q, then, in **PAC**, the corresponding arrow composed with the (output) action arrow (considered in at least $|\text{fn}(P)|$ variables m) reduces to the arrow representing q in m variables. Basically, the same can be said for the input and fusion transitions, aside that the former introduces the new variable a_{m+1} while the latter eliminates a variable. The last rule is just the special case of fusing a name with itself (i.e., $P; id$ is the lhs of the reduction).

Theorem 4. PAC *has redex relative pushouts (RPOs).*

Proof. We must prove that, given a reaction rule $q \implies r$, for any process arrow p and any sequence arrows γ, γ' such that $p; \gamma' = q; \gamma$, there exist three sequence arrows $\hat{\gamma}_1, \hat{\gamma}_2$ and $\hat{\gamma}_3$ that satisfy the following conditions:

a. the diagram in Figure 3(a) commutes, and
b. for any sequence arrows γ'_1, γ'_2 and γ'_3 such that the diagram in Figure 3(b) com-

mutes, there is a unique $\hat{\gamma}$ such that both [diagram] and [diagram] com-

mute.

Let us remark that the reduction contexts are all the arrows of **PAC**, however, for redex RPOs, γ and γ' can only be sequence arrows. Moreover, since $p;\gamma' = q;\gamma$, for Proposition 2, p and q are process arrows that are the composition of the *same* normalised linear arrow, say P with two sequence arrows. Hence, without loss of generality, it suffices to prove that there are arrows $\hat{\gamma}_1$, $\hat{\gamma}_2$ and $\hat{\gamma}_3$ forming an RPO for any diagram as in Figure 3(c).

The proof continues by case analysis.

- First assume that γ_2 is an identity fusion arrow and consider the commuting diagram below.

 We prove that $\hat{\gamma}_1 = id$, $\hat{\gamma}_2 = \gamma_1$ and $\hat{\gamma}_3 = \gamma'$ is an RPO. Indeed, condition a) trivially holds because the external square commutes by hypothesis. Consider three sequence arrows γ_1', γ_2' and γ_3' such that $\gamma' = \gamma_1';\gamma_3'$, $\gamma = \gamma_2';\gamma_3'$ and $\gamma_1;\gamma_1' = \gamma_2'$. Then, assuming $\hat{\gamma} = \gamma_3'$ we obtain that the commutativity of the triangles corresponding to condition b) holds. Finally, uniqueness of $\hat{\gamma}$ is guaranteed by observing that $\hat{\gamma}_1$ is the identity.

- Let γ_2 is a generic fusion arrow σ. By Proposition 2, there is a sequence arrow γ''

  such that $\sigma;\gamma = \gamma''$. Hence, we can equivalently prove that  has an RPO,

  which hold by the previous case.

- Finally, assume that γ_2 is an action arrow μ. By hypothesis, $\gamma_1;\gamma' = \mu;\gamma$, then, by Proposition 2,
  - either $\gamma_1 = \mu;\gamma_1'$
  - or γ_1 is the identity and $\gamma' = \mu;\gamma''$.

In the former case, the proof reduces to show that has an RPO, which hold

by the previous case. While, in the latter case, the redex diagram is and,

proceeding as before, it is easy to see that μ, id and γ constitute an RPO.

□

Definition 13 (Labelled Transitions). *The diagram in Figure 3(a) is an IPO when it is an RPO and $\hat{\gamma}_1 = \gamma'$, $\hat{\gamma}_2 = \gamma$ and $\hat{\gamma}_3 = id$. We write $p \xrightarrow{\gamma} r;\gamma$ when there is a reduction rule $q \Longrightarrow r$ and the diagram Figure 3(a) is an IPO. This defines a LTS. The corresponding bisimilarity according to Definition 8 is denoted as $\simeq$.*

The results in [53] and Theorem 12 guarantee the following corollary.

Corollary 1. *Bisimilarity relation $\simeq$ is a congruence.*

The LTS of Definition 13 is essentially the same as in Section 5.1 indeed, the states are π_- processes and it is possible to show that the IPOs of **PAC** characterise the transitions of [74]. Thus bisimilarity relation $\simeq$ essentially coincides with syntactic bisimilarity $\backsimeq$.

Theorem 5 ($\simeq$ **Is** $\backsimeq$). *Relation* $\simeq$, *which is defined on process arrows* p_m, *when restricted to those* p_m *with* $m = max\{k \mid a_k \in \text{fn}(p)\}$, *coincides with* $\backsimeq$.

Notice that, due to the missing restriction operator, two agents with different sets of free names cannot be bisimilar. Thus, observing actions or typed actions does not make a difference.

From Theorem 2 we know that $\simeq$ is finer than or equal than $\sim$. It is easy to see that it is finer from this example. Consider the following processes

$$p = (\bar{a}b \mid a'(c)) + (\bar{d}e \mid d(f)) \qquad q = \bar{a}b.a'(c) + a'(c).\bar{a}b + (\bar{d}e \mid d(f)),$$

then $p \sim q$ because the synchronisation between $\bar{a}b$ and $a'(c)$ in a context that identifies a and a' is matched by the (unique) synchronisation of q. On the contrary, $p \not\simeq q$ because the transition $p \xrightarrow{a=a'}$ cannot be matched by q. We can thus conclude the following fact.

Theorem 6. *Relation* $\simeq$ *when restricted to those* p_m *with* $m = max\{k \mid a_k \in \text{fn}(p)\}$, *is finer than* $\sim$.

6   Conclusions

In the paper we surveyed some of the approaches for model checking nominal calculi, focusing on HD-automata and on the existing toolkits for handling them. We also introduced a simplified version of open π-calculus and we proposed a bisimilarity semantics for it based on a reactive system with observed borrowed contexts. This approach has been proposed by Leifer and Milner [53, 52] and further developed by Sassone, Lack and Sobocinski [76, 78, 50] using G-categories and adhesive categories. The generality of the reactive system approach gives some hope that interesting abstractions of the SOC paradigm could also be modelled that way.

However we noticed that the transition system we obtain in this manner is not really suitable for a HD-automata implementation, since new names are never forgotten. To avoid this problem, it might be necessary to take advantage of the extended theory developed by Sassone, Lack and Sobocinski [76, 78, 50]. In particular, the actions of nominal calculi which forget names could be represented as cospans of suitable adhesive categories. In fact several expressive graph-like structures can be represented by adhesive categories and the existing theory guarantees that the categories of their cospans have the *all redex-RPOs* property [77].

Acknowledgements

The authors thank Vladimiro Sassone and Pawel Sobocinski for their helpful comments on an earlier draft of this paper.

References

1. M. Abadi and A. Gordon. A Calculus for Cryptographic Protocols: The Spi Calculus. *Inf. and Comp.*, 148(1):1–70, January 1999.
2. G. Baldi, A. Bracciali, G. Ferrari, and E. Tuosto. A Coordination-based Methodology for Security Protocol Verification. In *WISP*, ENTCS, Bologna, Italy, June 2004. Elsevier. To appear.
3. T. Ball and S. Rajamani. The SLAM Toolkit. In G. Berry, H. Comon, and A. Finkel, editors, *CAV*, volume 2102 of *LNCS*, pages 260–264. Springer, 2001.
4. N. Benton, L. Cardelli, and C. Fournet. Modern Concurrency Abstractions for C#. *TOPLAS*, 26(5):269–304, Sept. 2004.
5. M. Boreale and M. Buscemi. A Framework for the Analysis of Security Protocols. In L. Brim, P. Jančar, M. Křetinský, and A. Kučera, editors, *CONCUR*, volume 2421 of *LNCS*, pages 483–498. Springer, Aug. 2002.
6. M. Boreale and R. De Nicola. A Symbolic Semantics for the π-calculus. *Inf. and Comp.*, 126(1):34–52, April 1996.
7. A. Bouali, S. Gnesi, and S. Larosa. The Integration Project for the JACK Environment. In *EATCS Bull.*, volume 54, pages 207–223. Centrum voor Wiskunde en Informatica (CWI), 1994.
8. A. Bouali, A. Ressouche, V. Roy, and R. de Simone. The FC2TOOLS Set. In R. Alur and T. Henzinger, editors, *CAV*, volume 1102 of *LNCS*, pages 441–445, New Brunswick, NJ, USA, 1996. Springer.
9. A. Bracciali, A. Brogi, G. Ferrari, and E. Tuosto. Security Issues in Component Based Design. In U. Montanari and V. Sassone, editors, *ConCoord: International Workshop on Concurrency and Coordination*, volume 54 of *ENTCS*, Lipari Island - Italy, July 2001. Elsevier.
10. G. Brat, K. Havelund, S. Park, and W. Visser. Model Checking Programs. *Automated Software Engineering*, 10(2):203–232, 2003.
11. R. Bruni, C. Laneve, and U. Montanari. Orchestrating Transactions in Join Calculus. In L. Brim, P. Jancar, M. Kretinsky, and A. Kucera, editors, *CONCUR*, volume 2421 of *LNCS*, pages 321–336. Springer, 2002.
12. R. Bruni, H. Melgratti, and U. Montanari. Theoretical Foundations for Compensations in Flow Composition Languages. In *POPL*, 2005. To appear.
13. R. Bruni, U. Montanari, and F. Rossi. An Interactive Semantics of Logic Programming. *Theory and Practice of Logic Programming.*, 1(6):647–690, 2001.
14. M. Butler and C. Ferreira. An Operational Semantics for StAC, a Language for Modelling Long-Running Business Transactions. In R. De Nicola, G. Ferrari, and G. Meredith, editors, *COORDINATION*, volume 2949 of *LNCS*, pages 87–104. Springer, 2004.
15. L. Caires and L. Cardelli. A Spatial Logic for Concurrency (Part I). *Inf. and Comp.*, 186, 2003.
16. L. Caires and L. Cardelli. A Spatial Logic for Concurrency II. *TCS*, 322(3):517–565, Sept. 2004.
17. G. Cattani and P. Sewell. Models for Name-Passing Processes: Interleaving and Causal (Extended Abstract). *Inf. and Comp.*, 190(2):136–178, May 2004.
18. E. Clarke, O. Grumberg, and D. Peled. *Model Checking.* MIT Press, 1999.
19. E. Clarke and J. Wing. Formal Methods: State of the Art and Future Directions. *ACM Computing Surveys*, 28(4):626–643, December 1996.
20. S. Clarke, Edmund M. Jha and W. Marrero. Using State Space Exploration and a Nautural Deduction Style Message Derivation Engine to Verify Security Protocols. In *In Proc.* IFIP Working Conference on Programming Concepts and Methods (PROCOMET), 1998.

21. R. Cleaveland, J. Parrow, and B. Steffen. The Concurrency Workbench: A Semantics-Based Tool for the Verification of Concurrent Systems. *TOPLAS*, 15(1):36–72, Jan. 1993.

22. S. Conchon and F. Le Fessant. Jocaml: Mobile Agents for Objective-Caml. In *International Symposium on Agent Systems and Applications*, pages 22–29, Palm Springs, California, Oct. 1999.

23. J. Corbett, M. Dwyer, J. Hatcliff, S. Laubach, S. Corina, Robby, and H. Zheng. Bandera: Extracting Finite-state Models from Java Source Code. In *International Conference on Software Engineering*, pages 439–448, Limerick, Ireland, June 2000.

24. F. Curbera, R. Khalaf, N. Mukhi, S. Tai, and S. Weerawarana. The Next Step in Web Services. *CACM*, 46(10):29–34, 2003.

25. M. Dam. Model Checking Mobile Processes. *Inf. and Comp.*, 129(1):35–51, 1996.

26. M. Dam. Proof Systems for π-Calculus Logics. *Logic for concurrency and synchronisation*, pages 145–212, 2003.

27. G. Denker and J. Millen. CAPSL Integrated Protocol Environment. Technical report, Computer Science Laboratory, SRI International, Menlo Park, CA, 1999.

28. H. Ehrig and B. König. Deriving Bisimulation Congruences in the DPO Approach to Graph Rewriting. In I. Walukiewicz, editor, *FoSSaCS*, volume 2987, pages 151–166. LNCS, 2004.

29. J. Fernandez. An Implementation of an Efficient Algorithm for Bisimulation Equivalence. *Science of Computer Programming*, 13(2–3):219–236, May 1990.

30. J. Fernandez and L. Mounier. On-the-fly Verification of Behavioural Equivalences and Preorders. In K. Larsen and A. Skou, editors, *CAV*, volume 575 of *LNCS*, pages 181–191. Springer, July 1991.

31. G. Ferrari, G. Ferro, S. Gnesi, U. Montanari, M. Pistore, and G. Ristori. An Automata Based Verification Environment for Mobile Processes. In E. Brinksma, editor, *TACAS*, volume 1217 of *LNCS*, pages 275–289. Springer, April 1997.

32. G. Ferrari, S. Gnesi, U. Montanari, and M. Pistore. A Model Checking Verification Environment for Mobile Processes. *TOPLAS*, 12(4):1–34, 2004.

33. G. Ferrari, S. Gnesi, U. Montanari, R. Raggi, G. Trentanni, and E. Tuosto. Verification on the WEB. In J. Augusto and U. Ultes-Nitsche, editors, *VVEIS*, pages 72–74, Porto, Portugal, April 2004. INSTICC Press.

34. G. Ferrari, U. Montanari, and M. Pistore. Minimizing Transition Systems for Name Passing Calculi: A Co-algebraic Formulation. In M. Nielsen and U. Engberg, editors, *FOSSACS 2002*, volume 2303 of *LNCS*, pages 129–143. Springer, 2002.

35. G. Ferrari, U. Montanari, and E. Tuosto. From Co-algebraic Specifications to Implementation: The Mihda toolkit. In F. de Boer, M. Bonsangue, S. Graf, and W. de Roever, editors, *FMCO*, volume 2852 of *LNCS*, pages 319 – 338. Springer, November 2002.

36. G. Ferrari, U. Montanari, and E. Tuosto. Coalgebraic Minimisation of HD-automata for the π-Calculus in a Polymorphic λ-Calculus. *TCS*, 2004. To appear.

37. M. Fiore, G. Plotkin, and D. Turi. Abstract Syntax and Variable Binding (Extended Abstract). In *LICS*, pages 193–202, Trento, Italy, July 1999. IEEE.

38. P. Fiore and M. Abadi. Computing Symbolic Models for Verifying Cryptographic Protocols. In *Computer Security Foundations Workshop*, CSFW, pages 160–173, Cape Breton, Nova Scotia, Canada, June 2001. IEEE.

39. R. Focardi and R. Gorrieri. A Classification of Security Properties. *J. of Computer Security*, 3(1), 1995.

40. M. Gabbay and A. Pitts. A New Approach to Abstract Syntax Involving Binders. In G. Longo, editor, *LICS*, pages 214–224, Trento, Italy, July 1999. IEEE.

41. A. Gordon. Notes on Nominal Calculi for Security and Mobility. In R. Focardi and R. Gorrieri, editors, *FOSAD*, volume 2171 of *LNCS*, pages 262–330. Springer, September 2002.

42. M. Hennessy and H. Lin. Symbolic Bisimulations. *TCS*, 138(2):353–389, February 1995.

43. T. Henzinger, R. Jhala, R. Majumdar, and G. Sutre. Lazy Abstraction. In *POPL*, pages 58–70. ACM Press, 2002.
44. D. Hirschkoff. On the Benefits of Using the up-to Techniques for Bisimulation Verification. In W. Cleaveland, editor, *TACAS*, volume 1579 of *LNCS*, pages 285–299, Amsterdam, March 1999. Springer.
45. G. Holzmann. The Model Checker Spin. *TSE*, 23(5):279–295, May 1997.
46. G. Holzmann. *The Spin Model Checker: Primer and Reference Manual*. Addison-Wesley, Sept. 2003.
47. K. Honda. Elementary Structures in Process Theory (1): Sets with Renaming. *MSCS*, 10(5):617–663, 2000.
48. O. Jensen and R. Milner. Bigraphs and Transitions. In *POPL*, pages 38–49. ACM Press, 2003.
49. P. Kanellakis and S. Smolka. CCS Expressions, Finite State Processes and Three Problem of Equivalence. *Inf. and Comp.*, 86(1):272–302, 1990.
50. S. Lack and P. Sobociń ski. Adhesive Categories. In I. Walukiewicz, editor, *FoSSaCS*, volume 2987 of *LNCS*, pages 273–288, Barcelona, March 2004. Springer.
51. C. Laneve and G. Zavattaro. Foundations of Web Transactions. In *FoSSaCS*, LNCS, 2005. To appear.
52. J. Leifer. *Operational Congruences for Reactive Systems*. PhD thesis, Computer Laboratory, University of Cambridge, Cambridge, UK, 2001.
53. J. Leifer and R. Milner. Deriving Bisimulation Congruences for Reactive Systems. In C. Palamidessi, editor, *CONCUR*, volume 1877 of *LNCS*, pages 243–258, University Park, PA, USA, August 22-25 2000. Springer.
54. H. Lin. Complete Inference Systems for Weak Bisimulation Equivalences in the π-Calculus. *Inf. and Comp.*, 180(1):1–29, January 2003.
55. G. Lowe. Towards a Completeness Result for Model Checking of Security Protocols. In *CSFW*. IEEE, 1998.
56. W. Marrero, E. Clarke, and S. Jha. Model Checking for Security Protocols. In *Formal Verification of Security Protocols*, 1997.
57. K. McMillan. *Symbolic Model Checking*. Kluwer Academic Publisher, 1993.
58. R. Milner. *Communication and Concurrency*. Prentice Hall, 1989.
59. R. Milner, J. Parrow, and D. Walker. A Calculus of Mobile Processes, I and II. *Inf. and Comp.*, 100(1):1–40,41–77, September 1992.
60. J. Mitchell, M. Mitchell, and U. Ster. Automated analysis of cryptographic protocols using murφ. In *CSFW*, pages 141–151. IEEE, 1997.
61. U. Montanari and M. Buscemi. A First Order Coalgebraic Model of π-Calculus Early Observational Equivalence. In L. Brim, P. Jančar, M. Křetinský, and A. Kučera, editors, *CONCUR*, volume 2421 of *LNCS*, pages 449–465. Springer, Aug. 2002.
62. U. Montanari and M. Pistore. Checking Bisimilarity for Finitary π-Calculus. In I. Lee and S. Smolka, editors, *CONCUR*, volume 962 of *LNCS*, pages 42–56, Philadelphia, PA, USA, Aug. 1995. Springer.
63. U. Montanari and M. Pistore. History Dependent Automata. Technical report, Computer Science Department, Università di Pisa, 1998. TR-11-98.
64. U. Montanari and M. Pistore. π-Calculus, Structured Coalgebras, and Minimal HD-Automata. In M. Nielsen and B. Roman, editors, *MFCS*, volume 1983 of *LNCS*. Springer, 2000. An extended version will be published on Theoretical Computer Science.
65. U. Montanari and V. Sassone. Dynamic Congruence vs. Progressing Bisimulation for CCS. *Fundamenta Informaticae*, 16:171–196, 1992.
66. R. Needham. *Names*. Addison-Wesley (Mullender Ed.), 1989.
67. R. Paige and R. Tarjan. Three Partition Refinement Algorithms. *SIAM Journal on Computing*, 16(6):973–989, December 1987.

68. M. Papazoglou. Service-Oriented Computing: Concepts, Characteristics and Directions. In *Web Information Systems Engineering (WISE'03)*, LNCS, pages 3–12. Springer, 2003.
69. D. Park. Concurrency and Automata on Infinite Sequences. In *Theoretical Computer Science, 5th GI-Conf.*, volume 104 of *LNCS*, pages 167–183. Springer, Karlsruhe, March 1981.
70. J. Parrow and B. Victor. The Fusion Calculus: Expressiveness and Symmetry in Mobile Processes. In *LICS*. IEEE, 1998.
71. M. Pistore. *History Dependent Automata*. PhD thesis, Computer Science Department, Università di Pisa, 1999.
72. M. Pistore and D. Sangiorgi. A Partition Refinement Algorithm for the π-Calculus. *Inf. and Comp.*, 164(2):467–509, 2001.
73. D. Sangiorgi. On the Bisimulation Proof Method (Extended Abstract). In J. Wiedermann and P. Hájek, editors, *MFCS*, volume 969 of *LNCS*, pages 479–488, Prague, August-September 1995. Springer.
74. D. Sangiorgi. A Theory of Bisimulation for the π-Calculus. *Acta Informatica*, 33(1):69–97, 1996.
75. D. Sangiorgi and D. Walker. *The π-Calculus: a Theory of Mobile Processes*. Cambridge University Press, 2002.
76. V. Sassone and P. Sobociński. Deriving Bisimulation Congruences using 2-categories. *Nordic J. of Computing*, 10(2), 2003.
77. V. Sassone and P. Sobociński. Congruences for Contextual Graph-Rewriting. Technical Report RS-14, BRICS, June 2004.
78. V. Sassone and P. Sobociński. Locating Reaction with 2-Categories. *TCS*, 2004. To appear.
79. P. Sewell. From Rewrite Rules to Bisimulation Congruences. *LNCS*, 1466, 1998.
80. P. Sewell. Applied π – A Brief Tutorial. Technical Report 498, Computer Laboratory, University of Cambridge, Aug. 2000.
81. H. Smith and P. Fingar. Workflow is Just a Pi process. Available at http://www.bpm3.com/picalculus, 2003.
82. V. Vanackére. The TRUST protocol analyser. Automatic and Efficient Verification of Cryptographic Protocols. In *VERIFY02*, 2002.
83. B. Victor and F. Moller. The Mobility Workbench — A Tool for the π-Calculus. In D. Dill, editor, *CAV*, volume 818 of *LNCS*, pages 428–440. Springer, 1994.
84. P. Yang, C. Ramakrishnan, and S. Smolka. A Logical Encoding of the π-Calculus: Model Checking Mobile Processes Using Tabled Resolution. *STTT*, 6(1):38–66, July 2004.

Mathematical Models of Computational and Combinatorial Structures

(Invited Address)

Marcelo P. Fiore*

Computer Laboratory,
University of Cambridge
`Marcelo.Fiore@cl.cam.ac.uk`

Abstract. The general aim of this talk is to advocate a combinatorial perspective, together with its methods, in the investigation and study of models of computation structures. This, of course, should be taken in conjunction with the well-established views and methods stemming from algebra, category theory, domain theory, logic, type theory, *etc.* In support of this proposal I will show how such an approach leads to interesting connections between various areas of computer science and mathematics; concentrating on one such example in some detail. Specifically, I will consider the line of my research involving denotational models of the pi calculus and algebraic theories with variable-binding operators, indicating how the abstract mathematical structure underlying these models fits with that of Joyal's combinatorial species of structures. This analysis suggests both the unification and generalisation of models, and in the latter vein I will introduce *generalised species of structures* and their calculus. These generalised species encompass and generalise various of the notions of species used in combinatorics. Furthermore, they have a rich mathematical structure (akin to models of Girard's linear logic) that can be described purely within Lawvere's generalised logic. Indeed, I will present and treat the cartesian closed structure, the linear structure, the differential structure, *etc.* of generalised species axiomatically in this mathematical framework. As an upshot, I will observe that the setting allows for interpretations of computational calculi (like the lambda calculus, both typed and untyped; the recently introduced differential lambda calculus of Ehrhard and Regnier; *etc.*) that can be directly seen as translations into a more basic elementary calculus of interacting agents that compute by communicating and operating upon structured data.

Prologue

The process of understanding often unveils structure; and this, in turn, entails deeper understanding. In formal investigations, structure is articulated in mathematical terms. Mathematical structure typically plays a clarifying organisational role providing new insight and leading to new results. Ultimately theories are built; and then specialised,

---

* Research supported by an EPSRC Advanced Research Fellowship.

V. Sassone (Ed.): FOSSACS 2005, LNCS 3441, pp. 25–46, 2005.

generalised, or unified. It is to this general context that the present work belongs. From a specific viewpoint, however, it is part of a research programme approaching computation structure from a combinatorial perspective. By this I broadly mean the transport of ideas, methodology, techniques, questions, *etc.* between combinatorics and computer science; in particular, in regarding data type structure as combinatorial structure, and vice versa.

As an example of what such a combinatorial view intends, I will show what the notion of *bijective proof* of combinatorial identities entails on data type structure. A bijective proof of A = B consists in presenting combinatorial structures $\mathcal{A}$ and $\mathcal{B}$ that are respectively counted by A and by B together with a bijection $\mathcal{A} \cong \mathcal{B}$. The notion of bijective proof thus is nothing but that of *isomorphism of structure*, which in this view is given a fundamental role (as it is the case in many other areas of mathematics). In transporting this to the context of computation theory, for instance, one may be interested in bijections that are computable, primitive recursive, feasible, *etc.* In the context of type (or programming language) theory, the notion corresponds to the equivalence of data type structure up to isomorphism as prescribed by terms of the type theory (or programs of the programming language). Such a study has already been considered, though for entirely different reasons, under the broad heading of *type isomorphism*; see, *e.g.*, [9]. Besides applications in computer science, one interest in this subject lies in its connections to various areas of mathematics. Indeed, it is related to Tarski's high school algebra problem in mathematical logic [15], to the word problem in quotient polynomial semirings in computational algebra [16, 14], and to Thompson's groups in group theory [forthcoming joint work with Tom Leinster].

The rest of the paper provides another example of the fruitfulness of the approach advocated here. Specifically, I will first briefly review three diverse mathematical models —respectively suited for modelling name generation, combinatorial structure, and variable binding— highlighting how the various structures in each of them arise in essentially the same manner (Sect. 1). With this basis, I will then present a generalisation of the second model, putting it in the light of models of computation structures (Sect. 2). This yields connections to other areas of computer science and mathematics, and opens new perspectives for research (Sect. 3).

1   Some Computational and Combinatorial Structures

In this section I discuss in retrospective three mathematical models of computation structures in the chronological order in which I got familiar with them during my research. These are: denotational models of the pi calculus [17, 19] (Subsect. 1.1), Joyal's combinatorial species of structures [25, 26] (Subsect. 1.2), and algebraic models of equational theories with variable-binding operators [18, 19, 13] (Subsect. 1.3).[1] My intention here is not to treat any of them in full detail, but rather to give an outline of the

---

[1] Readers not familiar with the pi calculus [38] can safely skip Subsect. 1.1, or read it after Subsect. 1.3. Readers only interested in the combinatorial aspects can safely restrict their attention to Subsect. 1.2.

most relevant structures present in each model in such a way as to make explicit and apparent the similarities that run through them all.

1.1   Denotational Models of the Pi Calculus

The main ingredient leading to the construction of denotational models of the pi calculus [17, 47] was recognising that its feature allowing for the dynamic generation of names required the traditional denotational models to be indexed (or parameterised) by the set of the known names of a process. Naturally, and in the vein of previous models of store [45, 42] (see also [39–§ 4.1.4]), this was formalised by considering models in functor categories; that is, mathematical universes $\mathcal{S}^{\mathcal{V}}$ of $\mathcal{V}$-variable $\mathcal{S}$-objects (functors $\mathcal{V} \longrightarrow \mathcal{S}$) and $\mathcal{V}$-variable $\mathcal{S}$-maps (natural transformations) between them. In this context, $\mathcal{S}$ provides a basic model of denotations; whilst $\mathcal{V}$ gives an appropriate model of variation (see, $e.g.$, [30]). In the example at hand, $\mathcal{S}$ is a suitable category of domains (or simply the category of sets, if considering the finite pi calculus) and $\mathcal{V}$ is the category $\mathbf{I}$ of finite sets (or finite subsets of a fixed infinite countable set of names) and injections. Thus, a model $P \in \mathcal{S}^{\mathbf{I}}$ consists of a series of actions

$$\_[=] : P(U) \times \mathbf{I}(U, V) \longrightarrow P(V) \qquad\qquad (U, V \in \mathbf{I})$$

for which $p[\mathrm{id}_U] = p$ and $p[\imath][\jmath] = p[\imath \cdot \jmath]$ for all $p \in P(U)$ and $\imath : U \rightarrowtail V$, $\jmath : V \rightarrowtail W$ in $\mathbf{I}$. These actions allow us to regard denotations p parameterised by a set of names U as denotations $p[\imath]$ parameterised by a set of names V with respect to any injective renaming of names $\imath : U \rightarrowtail V$ in a consistent manner.

The question arises as to why the model of variation given by the category $\mathbf{I}$ in this context is the appropriate one. It was already pointed out in [17] that what it is important about $\mathbf{I}$ is its structure; namely, that it is equivalent to the free symmetric (strict) monoidal category with an initial unit on one generator. In this light, the generator stands for a generic name, whilst the tensor product allows for the creation of a new disjoint batch of generic names from two old ones. The role of the symmetry is roughly to render batches of generic names into sets, and the condition on the unit being initial allows for the ability of generating new names. This intuitive view is consistent with that of Needham's pure names [41] (see also [37]); $viz.$, those that can only be tested for equality with other ones, and indeed one can also formally recast the category $\mathbf{I}$ in these terms.

The fundamental mathematical structure of $\mathcal{S}^{\mathbf{I}}$ required for modelling the pi calculus can be now seen to arise in abstract generality. I will show this for $\mathcal{S}$ the category $\mathbf{\mathit{Set}}$ of sets and functions, but similar arguments can be made for other suitable categories.

Let $\mathbf{I}[n]$ be the free symmetric strict monoidal category with tensor product $\oplus$ and initial unit O on the (name) generator n; it can be explicitly described as the category of finite cardinals and injections (with tensor product given by addition, initial unit by the empty set, and generator by the singleton). Through the Yoneda embedding, the generator provides an object of names $N = y(n)$ in $\mathbf{\mathit{Set}}^{\mathbf{I}[n]}$ and, by Day's tensor construction [8, 23], the symmetric tensor product provides a (multiplication) symmetric tensor product $\widehat{\oplus}$ on $\mathbf{\mathit{Set}}^{\mathbf{I}[n]}$ given by

$$P \widehat{\oplus} Q = \int^{U_1, U_2 \in \mathbf{I}[n]} P(U_1) \times Q(U_2) \times \mathbf{I}[n](U_1 \oplus U_2, \_) \qquad \left(P, Q \in \mathbf{\mathit{Set}}^{\mathbf{I}[n]} \right)$$

with $y(O)$ as unit. (Note that the translation of this tensor product to Set^I has the following simple description

$$(P \widehat{\oplus} Q)(U) = \sum_{(U_1, U_2) \in SD(U)} P(U_1) \times Q(U_2) \qquad (P, Q \in Set^I, U \in I)$$

where the disjoint sum is taken over the set $SD(U)$ of sub-decompositions of U; *i.e.*, pairs (U_1, U_2) such that $U_1 \cup U_2 \subseteq U$ and $U_1 \cap U_2 = \emptyset$.) More importantly for the current discussion, we have the following situation (consult App. A)

$$
\begin{array}{ccc}
I[n]^{\circ} & \xrightarrow{\ y\ } & Set^{I[n]} \\
{\scriptstyle -\oplus n}\Big\downarrow & {\scriptstyle \overset{Lan}{\cong}} & {\scriptstyle -\widehat{\oplus}N}\Big\downarrow\ \dashv\ \delta_n\ \dashv\ \Big\uparrow \\
I[n]^{\circ} & \xrightarrow[\ y\ ]{} & Set^{I[n]}
\end{array}
$$

which yields a *name generation* operator $\delta_n = (\_ \oplus n)^*$, arising as closed structure (since $(\_ \oplus n)_! \cong \_\widehat{\oplus}N$) and simply given by

$$\delta_n P = P(\_ \oplus n) \qquad (P \in Set^{I[n]}) \ .$$

Thus, a denotation in $\delta_n P$ is nothing but a denotation in P parameterised by a new generic name.

With the aid of the cartesian closed structure of $Set^{I[n]}$ one can then model the behavioural actions of pi calculus processes: input is modelled by the exponential $(\_)^N$, free output by the product $N \times (\_)$, and bound output by the name generator $\delta_n(\_)$. For details on both the late and early behaviours consult [19].

1.2 Combinatorial Species of Structures

The theory of combinatorial species was introduced by Joyal in [25]. One of its important features is to provide a mathematical framework in which arguments in enumerative combinatorics based on generating functions acquire structural combinatorial meaning leading to bijective proofs of combinatorial identities. For instance, in [26–Chap. 2], Joyal presents a calculus of species in which structural operations on them (together with their laws) exactly correspond, modulo the process of counting, to the operations in algebras of formal power series; see also [5–Chap. 1 and 2].

The basic notion of species of structures is given by a functor $B \longrightarrow Set$, for B the category of finite sets and bijections. Naturally, the category of species is taken to be the category Set^B. Species P can be equivalently given by a series of symmetric-group actions

$$\_[=] : P[n] \times \mathfrak{S}_n \longrightarrow P[n] \qquad (n \in \mathbb{N})$$

for which $p[id] = p$ and $p[\sigma][\tau] = p[\sigma \cdot \tau]$ for all $p \in P[n]$ and $\sigma, \tau \in \mathfrak{S}_n$.

Intuitively, for a species P, the set $P(U)$ consists of the structures of type P that can be put on the set of tokens U; the action provides the abstract rule of transport of structures, which serves for describing structural equivalence (*i.e.*, when structures are the same except for a permutation of the tokens that constitute them). For instance, the species End with structures on a set of tokens U given by the endofunctions on U and action by conjugation is defined as

$$\text{End}(U) = \textbf{\textit{Set}}\,(U, U) \qquad\qquad\qquad (U \in \textbf{B})$$
$$\text{End}(\sigma)(f) = \sigma \circ f \circ \sigma^{-1} \qquad (f \in \text{End}(U, U), \sigma \in \textbf{B}(U, V))\ .$$

Two endofunctions are structurally equivalent if they are conjugate to each other.

I will now present a repertoire of operations on species: addition, multiplication, differentiation, and composition. In doing so, I will be placing emphasis in how they relate to the other structures of the paper; rather than following the standard combinatorial presentation. Nonetheless this approach is certainly known to experts.

It is important first to focus on the structure of **B**. It was already pointed out in [25–Subsect. 7.3] that it is equivalent to the free symmetric (strict) monoidal category on one generator, and we will henceforth consider it in this vein. Let $\textbf{B}[x]$ be the free symmetric strict monoidal category with tensor product $\oplus$ and unit O on the (token) generator x; it can be explicitly described as the category of finite cardinals and permutations (with tensor product given by addition, unit by the empty set, and generator by the singleton).

Addition. The addition $P + Q$ of combinatorial species P and Q is given by their categorical coproduct:

$$(P + Q)(U) = P(U) + Q(U) \qquad (P, Q \in \textbf{\textit{Set}}^{\textbf{B}}, U \in \textbf{B})\ .$$

Thus, a structure of type $P + Q$ is either a structure of type P or one of type Q together with the information of which type of structure it is.

Multiplication. By Day's tensor construction [8, 23], the symmetric tensor product on $\textbf{B}[x]$ provides a multiplication symmetric tensor product $\cdot$ on $\textbf{\textit{Set}}^{\textbf{B}[x]}$ given by

$$P \cdot Q = \int^{U_1, U_2 \in \textbf{B}[x]} P(U_1) \times Q(U_2) \times \textbf{B}[x]\,(U_1 \oplus U_2, \_) \qquad (P, Q \in \textbf{\textit{Set}}^{\textbf{B}[x]})$$

with unit $y(O)$. (Note that the translation of this tensor product to $\textbf{\textit{Set}}^{\textbf{B}}$ has the following simple description

$$(P \cdot Q)(U) \cong \sum\nolimits_{(U_1, U_2) \in D(U)} P(U_1) \times Q(U_2) \qquad (P, Q \in \textbf{\textit{Set}}^{\textbf{B}}, U \in \textbf{B})$$

where the disjoint sum is taken over the set $D(U)$ of decompositions of U; *i.e.*, pairs (U_1, U_2) such that $U_1 \cup U_2 = U$ and $U_1 \cap U_2 = \emptyset$.)

Thus, to construct a structure of type $P \cdot Q$ on a set of tokens U is to decompose U in sets of tokens U_1 and U_2, and put a structure of type P on U_1 and a structure of type Q on U_2.

Differentiation. We have the following situation (see, *e.g.*, [44])

$$
\begin{array}{ccc}
\textbf{B}[x]^\circ & \xrightarrow{\quad y \quad} & \textbf{\textit{Set}}^{\textbf{B}[x]} \\
{\scriptstyle \_\,\oplus x}\Big\downarrow & {\overset{\text{Lan}}{\scriptstyle \cong}} & {\scriptstyle \_\,\cdot x}\Big\downarrow\ \dashv d/dx \dashv\ \Big\downarrow \\
\textbf{B}[x]^\circ & \xrightarrow[\quad y \quad]{} & \textbf{\textit{Set}}^{\textbf{B}[x]}
\end{array}
$$

which yields a differentiation operator $d/dx = (\_ \oplus x)^*$, arising as closed structure (since $(\_ \oplus x)_! \cong \_ \cdot X$ for $X = y(x)$) and simply given by

$$(d/dx)P = P(\_ \oplus \mathbf{x}) \qquad\qquad (P \in \mathbf{Set}^{B[x]}) \ .$$

It follows that a structure of type $(d/dx)P$ over a set of tokens is nothing but a structure of type P over the set of tokens enlarged with a new generic one.

Composition. Using the universal properties of both $B[\mathbf{x}]$ and $\mathbf{Set}^{B[x]}$, we obtain the following situation (consult App. A)

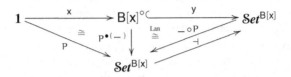

where

$$P^{\bullet}(\overbrace{\mathbf{X} \oplus \cdots \oplus \mathbf{X}}^{n \text{ times}}) = \underbrace{P \cdot \ldots \cdot P}_{n \text{ times}} \qquad\qquad (P \in \mathbf{Set}^{B[x]})$$

and

$$(Q \circ P)(\mathcal{U}) = \int^{T \in B[x]} Q(T) \times P^{\bullet T}(\mathcal{U}) \qquad\qquad (Q, P \in \mathbf{Set}^{B[x]}) \ .$$

This so-called composition (or substitution) operation $\circ$ on species yields a (highly non-symmetric) monoidal closed structure on $\mathbf{Set}^{B[x]}$ with unit $\mathbf{X} = y(\mathbf{x})$ (see also [27]). Translating it to $\mathbf{Set}^B$ we obtain, whenever $P(\emptyset) = \emptyset$, that

$$(Q \circ P)(\mathsf{U}) \cong \sum_{\mathcal{U} \in \mathrm{Part}(\mathsf{U})} Q(\mathcal{U}) \times \prod_{u \in \mathcal{U}} P(u) \qquad (Q, P \in \mathbf{Set}^B, \mathsf{U} \in \mathbf{B})$$

where the disjoint sum is taken over the set $\mathrm{Part}(\mathsf{U})$ of partitions of U. In words, a structure $q[u_1 \mapsto p_1, \ldots, u_n \mapsto p_n]$ in $(Q \circ P)(\mathsf{U})$ consists of a partition $\mathcal{U} = \{u_1, \ldots, u_n\}$ of the set of (input) tokens U, together with a structure q of type Q over the set $\mathcal{U}$ of n (place-holder) tokens for the structures p_i ($1 \leq i \leq n$) in $P(u_i)$. Monoids for this composition tensor product are known as (symmetric) operads (see, *e.g.*, [48]).

An important part of the theory of species (on which I can only refer the reader to [25] here) is that they can be equivalently seen as analytic endofunctors on $\mathbf{Set}$ (of which species are the coefficients) that embody the structure of the formal exponential power series induced by counting. From this point of view, the terminology of composition for the above operation is justified by the fact that it corresponds to the usual composition of functors.

1.3   Algebraic Theories with Variable-Binding Operators

The key to the algebraic treatment of abstract syntax with variable binding is to shift attention away from raw terms and focus on terms in context (or term judgements). This requires taking contexts seriously; considering the operations allowed on them and the structural rules that term judgements have, and building categories of contexts that reflect them. The categories of contexts so obtained provide then models of variation whose structure induces, in the associated universe of variable sets, further structure allowing for algebraic theories with variable-binding operators. These general remarks will become clear after reading the rest of the section, where the approach is exemplified.

The original approach of [18] was conceived for the framework of binding algebras [1] (see also [50]), where term judgements are subject to the admissible rules of weakening, contraction, and permutation. Thus, the natural notion of morphism between contexts is that provided by any renaming of variables. Below I will concentrate on the multi-sorted case where, of course, variable renamings should in addition be well-typed; see [13–Sect. II.1] for further details and a discussion of the syntax and semantics of the simply typed lambda calculus.

Abstractly, the category of contexts is then the free cocartesian category over the set of types. As other such free constructions, it can be explicitly described in two stages. First one considers the category F of mono-sorted (or untyped) contexts given by the free cocartesian category on one generator (with coproduct $+$, initial object 0, and generator 1); *i.e.*, the category of finite cardinals and functions (with coproduct given by addition, initial object by the empty set, and generator by the singleton). Then, for a set of types T, the category of T-sorted contexts is given by the comma construction $F \downarrow T$ (whose objects are maps $\Gamma : |\Gamma| \longrightarrow T$ with $|\Gamma| \in F$ and whose morphisms $\rho : \Gamma \longrightarrow \Gamma'$ are maps $\rho : |\Gamma| \longrightarrow |\Gamma'|$ in F such that $\Gamma = \Gamma'\rho$). The initial object $(0 \longrightarrow T)$ in $F \downarrow T$ is the empty context, whilst the coproduct

$$(|\Gamma| \xrightarrow{\Gamma} T) + (|\Gamma'| \xrightarrow{\Gamma'} T) = (|\Gamma| + |\Gamma'| \xrightarrow{[\Gamma,\Gamma']} T)$$

in $F \downarrow T$ amounts to the operation of context extension.

It is convenient to define $F[T] = (F \downarrow T)^\circ$ and identify $\tau \in T$ with its image $1 \xrightarrow{\tau} T$ in $F[T]$ under the universal embedding $T \longrightarrow F[T]$ exhibiting $F[T]$ as the free cartesian category on T.

The mathematical universe in which to consider algebraic theories is then the category $\widehat{F[T]}^T$. Informally, for $P \in \widehat{F[T]}^T$, one thinks of the sets $\{P_\tau(\Gamma)\}_{\tau \in T, \Gamma \in F[T]}$ as the τ-sorted P-elements in context Γ. As an example consider the object of variables $V = \{V_\tau\}_{\tau \in T}$ given by $V_\tau = y(\tau)$; so that

$$V_\tau(\Gamma) \cong \{x \in |\Gamma| \mid \Gamma(x) = \tau\} \qquad\qquad (\tau \in T, \Gamma \in F \downarrow T) \ .$$

Crucially, noting that $(\_ \times \tau)_! \cong \_ \times V_\tau$, the operation of context extension induces the situation below

$$
\begin{array}{ccc}
F[T] & \xrightarrow{\ \ y\ \ } & \widehat{F[T]} \\
{\scriptstyle \_ \times \tau}\Big\downarrow & {\scriptstyle \text{Lan}}_{\cong} \ \ {\scriptstyle \_ \times V_\tau}\Big\downarrow \dashv \Big\uparrow \dashv \Big\downarrow & \\
F[T] & \xrightarrow[\ \ y\ \ ]{} & \widehat{F[T]}
\end{array}
\qquad\qquad (\tau \in T)
$$

from which it follows that

$$X^{V_\tau} \cong (\_ \times \tau)^*(X) = X(\_ + \tau) \qquad\qquad (X \in \widehat{F[T]}, \tau \in T) \ .$$

Thus, the object of variables provides suitable arities for binding operators. Indeed, an operator of arity

$$\left(\tau_1^{(1)},\ldots,\tau_{n_1}^{(1)}\right)\tau_1,\ldots,\left(\tau_1^{(k)},\ldots,\tau_{n_k}^{(k)}\right)\tau_k \longrightarrow (\sigma_1,\ldots,\sigma_m)\sigma$$

that binds variables of type $\tau_1^{(i)},\ldots,\tau_{n_i}^{(i)}$ in terms of type τ_i $(1 \leq i \leq k)$ yielding a term of type σ that binds variables of type σ_j $(1 \leq j \leq m)$ corresponds to a morphism

$$\prod_{1\leq i\leq k} P_{\tau_i}^{\prod_{1\leq j\leq n_i} V_{\tau_j^{(i)}}} \longrightarrow P_\sigma^{\prod_{1\leq \ell\leq m} V_{\sigma_\ell}} \qquad \left(P \in \widehat{F[T]}^T\right)$$

in $\widehat{F[T]}$, that further corresponds to a natural family

$$\prod_{1\leq i\leq k} P_{\tau_i}\left(- + \langle\tau_1^{(i)},\ldots,\tau_{n_i}^{(i)}\rangle\right) \longrightarrow P_\sigma\left(- + \langle\sigma_1,\ldots,\sigma_m\rangle\right) \qquad \left(P \in \widehat{F[T]}^T\right)$$

associating a tuple of elements of type τ_i $(1 \leq i \leq k)$ in a context extended by new generic variables of type $\tau_j^{(i)}$ $(1 \leq j \leq n_i)$ with an element of type σ in a context extended by new generic variables of type σ_ℓ $(1 \leq \ell \leq m)$.

The framework also allows for the axiomatisation of substitution via an equational theory whose algebras correspond to Lawvere theories (see [18]). In App. B, I briefly discuss single-variable substitution in the context of algebraic theories for binding signatures. Here, as it is of direct concern to us, I will concentrate on the notion of simultaneous substitution, which arises in the same manner as operads do with respect to the composition of species. Indeed, using the universal properties of both $F[T]$ and $\widehat{F[T]}$, we have the following situation

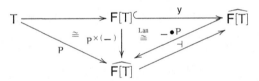

where

$$P^{\times\Delta} = \prod_{x\in|\Delta|} P_{\Delta(x)} \qquad \left(P \in \widehat{F[T]}^T, \Delta \in F[T]\right)$$

and

$$(X \bullet P)(\Gamma) = \int^{\Delta\in F[T]} X(\Delta) \times P^{\times\Delta}(\Gamma) \qquad \left(X \in \widehat{F[T]}, P \in \widehat{F[T]}^T, \Gamma \in F{\downarrow}T\right).$$

We obtain thus a (highly non-symmetric) *composition* monoidal closed structure $\circ$ on $\widehat{F[T]}^T$ given by

$$(Q \circ P)_\tau = Q_\tau \bullet P \qquad \left(Q,P \in \widehat{F[T]}^T, \tau \in T\right)$$

with unit the object of variables V.

Monoids for this composition tensor product correspond to multi-sorted Lawvere theories, and embody the structure of simultaneous substitution. To see this consider the axioms for a multiplication operation $P \circ P \longrightarrow P$ noting that, in elementary terms, $(Q \circ P)_\tau(\Gamma)$ consists of equivalence classes of pairs given by $q \in Q_\tau\langle \tau_1, \ldots, \tau_n \rangle$ together with an assignment $\langle \tau_1 \mapsto p_1, \ldots, \tau_n \mapsto p_n \rangle$ with $p_i \in P_{\tau_i}(\Gamma)$ $(1 \leq i \leq n)$ under the identification

$$q[\rho]\langle \tau_1 \mapsto p_1, \ldots, \tau_m \mapsto p_m \rangle = q\langle \sigma_1 \mapsto p_{\rho 1}, \ldots, \sigma_m \mapsto p_{\rho m} \rangle$$

for all renamings $\rho : \langle \sigma_1, \ldots, \sigma_m \rangle \longrightarrow \langle \tau_1, \ldots, \tau_n \rangle$ in $\mathbf{F} \downarrow T$, $q \in Q_\tau\langle \sigma_1, \ldots, \sigma_m \rangle$, and $p_i \in P_{\tau_i}(\Gamma)$ $(1 \leq i \leq n)$, where $q[\rho] = Q_\tau(\rho)(q) \in Q_\tau\langle \tau_1, \ldots, \tau_n \rangle$.

Finally, note that one can also consider heterogeneous notions of substitution (for which see [19]) and variations on the theme.

2   The Calculus of Generalised Species of Structures

This is the main section of the paper. In Subsect. 2.1, the notion of generalised species of structures is motivated and introduced. Afterwards, some of the structure of generalised species is presented: addition and multiplication in Subsect. 2.2; differential structure in Subsect. 2.3 and 2.6; identities and composition in Subsect. 2.4; and, the cartesian closed structure in Subsect. 2.5. Finally, Subsect. 2.7 outlines the calculus of these operations.

Somehow following the tradition in combinatorics, my emphasis here is to present generalised species as a calculus; including graphical representations that will hopefully convey the idea behind the various constructions on structures. On the other hand, however, I depart from the traditional combinatorial treatment in that the calculus is axiomatically built on top of the mathematical framework of Lawvere's generalised logic [28] (see Fig. 1 in Subsect. 2.7 for an example). This yields new algebraic proofs, even for the restriction of generalised species to their basic form recalled in Subsect. 1.2. In passing, I will remark on the relationship between the structures of this section and those of the previous one.

Generalised species have other roots in ideas of Martin Hyland and Glynn Winskel; and there is a general abstract theory, that we have developed with them and Nicola Gambino, that accounts for their bicategorical (Subsect. 2.4) and cartesian closed (Subsect. 2.5) structures. This perspective is important, for it further organises the subject (placing it, *e.g.*, in the context of models of Girard's linear logic) and guides its development.

2.1   Generalised Species

Recall that the basic notion of species of structures is given by a functor $\mathbf{B} \longrightarrow \textbf{\textit{Set}}$, for $\mathbf{B}$ the category of finite sets and bijections [25, 26]. Recall also that $\mathbf{B}$ is equivalent to the free symmetric (strict) monoidal category on one generator. Thus, writing ! for the free symmetric (strict) monoidal completion, species can be equivalently presented as functors $!\mathbf{1} \longrightarrow \textbf{\textit{Set}}$. In the spirit of Subsect. 1.3, it makes sense to consider T-sorted species, for T a set of sorts, as functors $!T \longrightarrow \textbf{\textit{Set}}$; and, even more generally, for a small category $\mathbb{T}$ of sorts and maps between them, define $\mathbb{T}$-sorted species of structures (or simply $\mathbb{T}$-species) as functors $!\mathbb{T} \longrightarrow \textbf{\textit{Set}}$.

To be able to visualise these structures we will analyse them in some detail. First, as I have already mentioned, the free symmetric strict monoidal category on one generator !1 (with tensor +, unit 0, and generator 1) can be described as the category B of finite cardinals and permutations (with tensor product given by addition, unit by the empty set, and generator by the singleton). This category, as it happens with other such free constructions, induces the free symmetric strict monoidal completion !$\mathbb{T}$ of a category $\mathbb{T}$ by the comma construction $B \Downarrow \mathbb{T}$ whose objects are maps $T : |T| \longrightarrow \mathbb{T}$ with $|T| \in B$ and whose morphisms are pairs $(\sigma, \vec{\sigma})$ as on the left below

$$
\begin{array}{c}
|T| \xrightarrow{\;\sigma\;} |T'| \\
T \searrow \;\Downarrow\; \swarrow T' \\
\mathbb{T}
\end{array}
$$

$$
(i \in |T|) \;\cdots\; T_i \;\cdots \qquad\qquad \cdots\; T_i \;\cdots\; (i \in |T|)
$$
$$
\downarrow \vec{\sigma}_i \qquad\qquad\qquad\qquad
$$
$$
(j \in |T'|) \;\cdots\; T'_{\sigma i} \;\cdots\; T'_j \;\cdots \quad = \qquad \bigg\downarrow \vec{\tau}_{\sigma i}\vec{\sigma}_i
$$
$$
\vec{\tau}_j \swarrow \qquad\qquad\qquad\qquad
$$
$$
\cdots\; T''_{\tau j} \;\cdots \qquad\qquad\qquad \cdots\; T''_{\tau \sigma i} \;\cdots
$$

with $\sigma : |T| \longrightarrow |T'|$ in B and $\vec{\sigma} : T \Longrightarrow T'\sigma$ in $\mathbb{T}^{\mathsf{T}}$. Morphisms and their composition can be drawn as on the right above. The tensor product in !$\mathbb{T}$ is given by $T \oplus T' = [T, T'] : |T| + |T'| \longrightarrow \mathbb{T}$; that is, roughly as

$$
\{\cdots T_i \cdots \mid i \in |T|\} \oplus \{\cdots T'_j \cdots \mid j \in |T'|\} = \{\cdots T_i \cdots T'_j \cdots \mid i \in |T|, j \in |T'|\},
$$

with unit $O = (0 \longrightarrow \mathbb{T})$. (Note as a remark that for what follows, and in keeping closer to the combinatorial spirit, one can equivalently take !$\mathbb{T}$ to be $B \Downarrow \mathbb{T}$.)

Henceforth, let $\{\!\![\_]\!\!\} : \mathbb{T} \longrightarrow !\mathbb{T}$ be the universal embedding exhibiting !$\mathbb{T}$ as the free symmetric strict monoidal category on $\mathbb{T}$.

It follows that a $\mathbb{T}$-species $P : !\mathbb{T} \longrightarrow Set$ describes the structures $P(T)$ of type P that can be put on bags T of tokens in $\mathbb{T}$ (given by objects in !$\mathbb{T}$) together with compatible rules of transport of structure along $\mathbb{T}$-tagged permutations (given by maps in !$\mathbb{T}$) in the form of actions

$$
\_[\_] : P(T) \times !\mathbb{T}(T, T') \longrightarrow P(T') \qquad (P : !\mathbb{T} \longrightarrow Set, T, T' \in !\mathbb{T})
$$

for which $p[\mathrm{id}_T] = p$ and $p[\sigma][\tau] = p[\sigma \cdot \tau]$ for all $p \in P(T)$ and $\sigma : T \longrightarrow T'$, $\tau : T' \longrightarrow T''$ in !$\mathbb{T}$.

Examples of generalised species in combinatorics abound: permutationals [25, 4] are **CP**-species for **CP** the groupoid of finite cyclic permutations, partitionals [40] are **B***-species for **B*** the groupoid of non-empty finite sets. Further examples are coloured permutationals [34], and species on graphs and digraphs [33].

A fundamental property of the free symmetric (strict) monoidal completion is that it comes equipped with canonical natural coherent equivalences as shown below.

$$
\mathbf{1} \xrightarrow[\cong]{O} !\mathbf{0} \;, \quad !\mathbb{C}_1 \times !\mathbb{C}_2 \xrightarrow[\cong]{\otimes} !(\mathbb{C}_1 + \mathbb{C}_2) : (C_1, C_2) \longmapsto !\amalg_1(C_1) \oplus !\amalg_2(C_2)
$$

Thus $\mathbb{T}$-species !$\mathbb{T} \longrightarrow Set$ are equivalent to functors $\mathbf{B}^{\mathsf{T}} \longrightarrow Set$, which is the notion of $\mathbb{T}$-sorted species originally introduced by Joyal [25].

Finally, it is important to generalise further; allowing for variable sets of structures. For small categories $\mathbb{A}$ and $\mathbb{B}$, an $(\mathbb{A}, \mathbb{B})$-*species of structures* is defined as a functor $!\mathbb{A} \longrightarrow \widehat{\mathbb{B}}$. The notation $P : \mathbb{A} \mathrel{!\!\longrightarrow} \mathbb{B}$ indicates that P is an $(\mathbb{A}, \mathbb{B})$-species. As before, for such a species P, we have the intuitive reading that $P(A)$ is the $\mathbb{B}^\circ$-variable set of structures of type P on the bag A of tokens in $\mathbb{A}$. However, the definition introduces an asymmetry that naturally leads to think of structures in $P(A)(b)$ as those of type P over a bag A of input tokens (or ports) in $\mathbb{A}$ and (parameterised on) an output token (or port) b in $\mathbb{B}^\circ$. As we will see in Subsect. 2.4 this interpretation is technically correct, and under it structures will be pictorially represented as on the right.

Remark. Below I will be exploiting the fact that species $P : !\mathbb{A} \longrightarrow \widehat{\mathbb{B}}$ are in duality with co-species $P^\perp : \mathbb{B}^\circ \longrightarrow \widehat{!\mathbb{A}^\circ}$ defined as $P^\perp(b)(A) = P(A)(b)$ $(b \in \mathbb{B}^\circ, A \in !\mathbb{A})$.

2.2 Commutative Rig Structure: Addition and Multiplication

The *zero* species $0 : \mathbb{A} \mathrel{!\!\longrightarrow} \mathbb{B}$ and the *addition* $P + Q : \mathbb{A} \mathrel{!\!\longrightarrow} \mathbb{B}$ of the species $P, Q : \mathbb{A} \mathrel{!\!\longrightarrow} \mathbb{B}$ are defined by

$$0(A)(b) = \emptyset, \quad (P + Q)(A)(b) = P(A)(b) + Q(A)(b) \qquad (A \in !\mathbb{A}, b \in \mathbb{B}^\circ) .$$

Representations of structures of addition and multiplication type follow. Compare them with the informal description of the addition and multiplication of structures of species given in Subsect. 1.2.

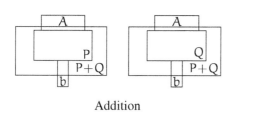

Addition

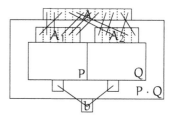

Multiplication

As in the previous section, Day's tensor construction [8, 23], provides a multiplication symmetric tensor product induced by the free symmetric strict monoidal structure. The *one* species $1 : \mathbb{A} \mathrel{!\!\longrightarrow} \mathbb{B}$ and the *multiplication* $P \cdot Q : \mathbb{A} \mathrel{!\!\longrightarrow} \mathbb{B}$ of the species $P, Q : \mathbb{A} \mathrel{!\!\longrightarrow} \mathbb{B}$ are defined as

$$1(A)(b) = !\mathbb{A}(O, A)$$
$$(P \cdot Q)(A)(b) \qquad\qquad\qquad\qquad (A \in !\mathbb{A}, b \in \mathbb{B}^\circ) .$$
$$= \int^{A_1, A_2 \in !\mathbb{A}} P(A_1)(b) \times Q(A_2)(b) \times !\mathbb{A}(A_1 \oplus A_2, A)$$

Remark. More succinctly, we have that $P + Q = +\langle P, Q \rangle$ and that $(P \cdot Q)^\perp = \widehat{\oplus}\langle P^\perp, Q^\perp \rangle$.

2.3   Differential Structure: Partial Derivatives

For $a \in \mathbb{A}$, the *partial derivative* $\frac{\partial}{\partial a}P : \mathbb{A} \,!\!\!\longrightarrow \mathbb{B}$ of the species $P : \mathbb{A} \,!\!\!\longrightarrow \mathbb{B}$ is defined as

$$\left(\tfrac{\partial}{\partial a}P\right)(A)(b) = P(A \oplus \{\!\!\{a\}\!\!\})(b) \qquad (A \in \,!\mathbb{A}, b \in \mathbb{B}^\circ) \ .$$

Structures of partial-derivative type may be represented as on the left below.

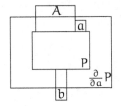

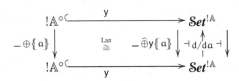

Partial Derivative

Remark. As in the previous section, the construction of partial derivatives arises from the situation on the right above. Indeed, we have that $\left(\frac{\partial}{\partial a}P\right)^\perp = (d/da)\,P^\perp$.

2.4   Bicategorical Structure: Identities and Composition

The *identity* species $I_\mathbb{C} : \mathbb{C} \,!\!\!\longrightarrow \mathbb{C}$ is defined as

$$I_\mathbb{C}(C)(c) = \,!\mathbb{C}\left(\{\!\!\{c\}\!\!\}, C\right) \qquad (C \in \,!\mathbb{C}, c \in \mathbb{C}^\circ) \ .$$

For species $P : \mathbb{A} \,!\!\!\longrightarrow \mathbb{B}$ and $Q : \mathbb{B} \,!\!\!\longrightarrow \mathbb{C}$, the *composition* $Q \circ P : \mathbb{A} \,!\!\!\longrightarrow \mathbb{C}$ is defined as

$$(Q \circ P)(A)(c) = \int^{B \in !\mathbb{B}} Q(B)(c) \times P^\#(A)(B) \qquad (A \in \,!\mathbb{A}, c \in \mathbb{C}^\circ)$$

where

$$
\begin{aligned}
&P^\#(A)(B) \\
&= \int^{X \in (!\mathbb{A})^{|B|}} \left(\textstyle\prod_{k \in |B|} P(X_k)(B_k)\right) \times \,!\mathbb{A}\left(\bigoplus_{k \in |B|} X_k, A\right)
\end{aligned}
\qquad (A \in \,!\mathbb{A}, B \in \,!\mathbb{B}^\circ) \ .
$$

One may visualise identities and composition as follows.

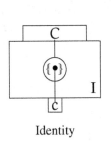

Identity

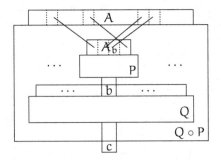

Composition

Remark. Using the universal properties of both $!(\_)$ and $\widehat{(\_)}$, we obtain the following situation

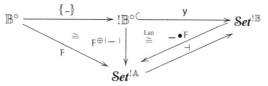

where $F^{\oplus B} = \widehat{\bigoplus}_{k \in |B|} F(B_k)$. We have that $(Q \circ P)^{\perp}$ is obtained as $(\_ \bullet P^{\perp}) Q^{\perp}$.

2.5 Cartesian Closed Structure: Product and Exponentiation

The cartesian closed structure of generalised species is presented.

There is exactly one species $\mathbb{C} \;!\!\!\rightarrow \top$ for $\top = \mathbf{0}$. More generally, for a family $P_i : \mathbb{C} \;!\!\!\rightarrow \mathbb{C}_i$ ($i \in I$), the *pairing* $\langle P_i \rangle_{i \in I} : \mathbb{C} \;!\!\!\rightarrow \sqcap_{i \in I} \mathbb{C}_i$, where $\sqcap_{i \in I} \mathbb{C}_i = \sum_{i \in I} \mathbb{C}_i$, is defined as

$$\langle P_i \rangle_{i \in I}(C)(c)$$
$$= \sum_{i \in I} \int^{z \in \mathbb{C}_i} P_i(C)(z) \times (\sqcap_{i \in I}\mathbb{C}_i)(c, \amalg_i(z)) \qquad (C \in !\mathbb{C}, c \in \sqcap_{i \in I}\mathbb{C}_i{}^{\circ}) \; .$$

For $i \in I$, the *projection* $\pi_i : \sqcap_{i \in I}\mathbb{C}_i \;!\!\!\rightarrow \mathbb{C}_i$ is defined as

$$\pi_i(C)(c) = !(\sqcap_{i \in I}\mathbb{C}_i)(\{\!| \amalg_i(c) |\!\}, C) \qquad (C \in !(\sqcap_{i \in I}\mathbb{C}_i), c \in \mathbb{C}_i{}^{\circ}) \; .$$

From the logical point of view, and using relational notation, $C \left[\langle P_i \rangle_{i \in I}\right] c$ is the extent to which there exists $i \in I$ and $c_i \in \mathbb{C}_i$ such that $C [P_i] c_i$ and c approximates $\amalg_i(c_i)$; whilst $C [\pi_i] c$ is the extent to which $\{\!| \amalg_i(c) |\!\}$ approximates C.

Pairing and projection may be depicted as follows.

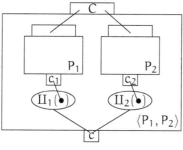

Pairing

Projection

For $P : \mathbb{C} \sqcap A \;!\!\!\rightarrow \mathbb{B}$, the *abstraction*

$$\lambda_A P : \mathbb{C} \;!\!\!\rightarrow \underline{hom}(A, \mathbb{B}) \quad \text{where } \underline{hom}(A, \mathbb{B}) = !A^{\circ} \times \mathbb{B}$$

is defined as

$$(\lambda_A P)(C)(A, b) = P(C \otimes A)(b) \qquad (C \in !\mathbb{C}, A \in !A, b \in \mathbb{B}^{\circ}) \; ,$$

where recall from Subsect. 2.1 that $C \otimes A = !\amalg_1 C \oplus !\amalg_2 A$. The *evaluation*

$$\varepsilon_{\mathbb{A},\mathbb{B}} : \underline{hom}(\mathbb{A}, \mathbb{B}) \sqcap \mathbb{A} \multimap \mathbb{B}$$

is defined as

$$\varepsilon_{\mathbb{A},\mathbb{B}}(M)(b) \qquad\qquad (M \in !(\underline{hom}(\mathbb{A}, \mathbb{B}) \sqcap \mathbb{A}), b \in \mathbb{B}^\circ)$$
$$= \int^{F \in !\underline{hom}(\mathbb{A},\mathbb{B}), \, A \in !\mathbb{A}} !\underline{hom}(\mathbb{A}, \mathbb{B})(\{[(A, b)]\}, F) \times !(\underline{hom}(\mathbb{A}, \mathbb{B}) \sqcap \mathbb{A})(F \otimes A, M) .$$

Again from the logical point of view, and using relational notation, we have that $C \, [\lambda_A P] \, (A, b)$ iff $(C \otimes A) \, [P] \, b$; whilst $M \, [\varepsilon_{\mathbb{A},\mathbb{B}}] \, b$ is the extent to which the (step) function $\{[(A, b)]\}$ approximates F, where $M = F \otimes A$ consists of a function F and an argument A.

Schematically, we have the following.

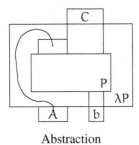

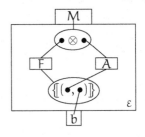

Abstraction   Evaluation

2.6   Higher-Order Differential Structure: Differentiation Operator

For a thorough treatment of differentiation one needs to introduce linear homs. In the current setting they are naturally given by

$$\underline{lin}(\mathbb{A}, \mathbb{B}) = \mathbb{A}^\circ \times \mathbb{B} .$$

With this in place, I can introduce an operator that internalises partial derivatives (and differential application) and satisfies all the basic properties of differentiation.

The *differentiation operator*

$$D_{\mathbb{A},\mathbb{B}} : \underline{hom}(\mathbb{A}, \mathbb{B}) \multimap \underline{hom}(\mathbb{A}, \underline{lin}(\mathbb{A}, \mathbb{B}))$$

is given by

$$D_{\mathbb{A},\mathbb{B}}(F)(A, a, b) = !\underline{hom}(\mathbb{A}, \mathbb{B}) \left(\{[(A \oplus \{a\}, b)]\}, F \right) \quad \begin{array}{l} (F \in !\underline{hom}(\mathbb{A}, \mathbb{B}), \\ A \in !\mathbb{A}, a \in \mathbb{A}, b \in \mathbb{B}^\circ) \end{array} .$$

2.7   Outline of the Calculus

Elsewhere I will give a formal presentation of the calculus of generalised species of structures and indicate how it is justified within the mathematical framework of generalised logic [28]. Here I will just offer an outline.

$$\left(\varepsilon \circ \langle \lambda(P) \circ \pi_1, \pi_2 \rangle\right)(D)(b) \qquad\qquad (D \in \,!(\mathbb{C} \sqcap A), b \in \mathbb{B}^\circ)$$

$$\overset{(1)}{\cong} \int^{M \in \,!(\underline{hom}(A,\mathbb{B}) \sqcap A)} \varepsilon(M)(b) \times \langle \lambda(P) \circ \pi_1, \pi_2 \rangle^\#(D)(M)$$

$$\overset{(2)}{\cong} \int^{M \in \,!(\underline{hom}(A,\mathbb{B}) \sqcap A)} \int^{F \in \,!\underline{hom}(A,\mathbb{B}), A \in \,!A} !\underline{hom}(A,\mathbb{B})\left(\{\!\!\{(A,b)\}\!\!\}, F\right) \times \,!(\underline{hom}(A,\mathbb{B}) \sqcap A)\,(!\amalg_1 F \oplus \,!\amalg_2 A, M)$$
$$\times \langle \lambda(P) \circ \pi_1, \pi_2 \rangle^\#(D)(M)$$

$$\overset{(3)}{\cong} \int^{A \in \,!A} \langle \lambda(P) \circ \pi_1, \pi_2 \rangle^\#(D)(!\amalg_1 \{\!\!\{(A,b)\}\!\!\} \oplus \,!\amalg_2 A)$$

$$\overset{(4)}{\cong} \int^{A \in \,!A} \int^{D_1, D_2 \in \,!(\mathbb{C} \sqcap A)} \langle \lambda(P) \circ \pi_1, \pi_2 \rangle^\#(D_1)(!\amalg_1 \{\!\!\{(A,b)\}\!\!\}) \times \langle \lambda(P) \circ \pi_1, \pi_2 \rangle^\#(D_2)(!\amalg_2 A)$$
$$\times \,!(\mathbb{C} \sqcap A)\,(D_1 \oplus D_2, D)$$

$$\overset{(5)}{\cong} \int^{A \in \,!A} \int^{D_1, D_2 \in \,!(\mathbb{C} \sqcap A)} (\lambda(P) \circ \pi_1)^\#(D_1)\{\!\!\{(A,b)\}\!\!\} \times \pi_2^\#(D_2)(A)$$
$$\times \,!(\mathbb{C} \sqcap A)\,(D_1 \oplus D_2, D)$$

$$\overset{(6)}{\cong} \int^{A \in \,!A} \int^{D_1, D_2 \in \,!(\mathbb{C} \sqcap A)} (\lambda(P) \circ \pi_1)(D_1)(A, b) \times \,!(\mathbb{C} \sqcap A)\,(!\amalg_2 A, D_2)$$
$$\times \,!(\mathbb{C} \sqcap A)\,(D_1 \oplus D_2, D)$$

$$\overset{(7)}{\cong} \int^{A \in \,!A} \int^{D_1 \in \,!(\mathbb{C} \sqcap A)} \int^{C \in \,!\mathbb{C}} (\lambda P)(C)(A, b) \times \pi_1^\#(D_1)(C) \times \,!(\mathbb{C} \sqcap A)\,(D_1 \oplus \,!\amalg_2 A, D)$$

$$\overset{(8)}{\cong} \int^{A \in \,!A} \int^{D_1 \in \,!(\mathbb{C} \sqcap A)} \int^{C \in \,!\mathbb{C}} P(!\amalg_1 C \oplus \,!\amalg_2 A)(b) \times \,!(\mathbb{C} \sqcap A)\,(!\amalg_1 C, D_1)$$
$$\times \,!(\mathbb{C} \sqcap A)\,(D_1 \oplus \,!\amalg_2 A, D)$$

$$\overset{(9)}{\cong} \int^{A \in \,!A} \int^{C \in \,!\mathbb{C}} P(!\amalg_1 C \oplus \,!\amalg_2 A)(b) \times \,!(\mathbb{C} \sqcap A)\,(!\amalg_1 C \oplus \,!\amalg_2 A, D)$$

$$\overset{(10)}{\cong} P(D)(b)$$

Fig. 1. An equational proof of the beta isomorphism $\varepsilon \circ \langle \lambda(P) \circ \pi_1, \pi_2 \rangle \cong P : \mathbb{C} \sqcap A \,!\!\longrightarrow \mathbb{B}$

(1) Definition of composition. (2) Definition of evaluation. (3) Density formula. (4) Law of extensions. (5) Law of extensions and definition of pairing. (6) Law of extensions and definition of projection. (7) Density formula and definition of composition. (8) Law of extensions and definitions of projection and abstraction. (9–10) Density formula and properties of the free symmetric (strict) monoidal completion.

Identities and composition come with canonical natural coherent isomorphisms establishing the unit laws of identities and the associativity of composition. Addition and multiplication yield a commutative rig structure, and commute with pre-composition.

The usual laws of pairing and projection, and of abstraction and evaluation are satisfied up to isomorphism (see Fig. 1 for a proof outline of the beta isomorphism). Thus, the closed structure *hom* comes equipped with internal identities and composition. Also the linear homs *lin* come equipped with internal identities and compositions, that actually embed in the closed structure.

Partial derivatives commute between themselves, addition, and multiplication by scalars. Moreover, they satisfy both the Leibniz (or product) and chain rules. For instance, the central reason for which the former holds is that the canonical map

(†)
$$
\begin{aligned}
&\int^{A'_1 \in !\mathbb{A}} !\mathbb{A}\left(A_1, A'_1 \oplus \{\!\{a\}\!\}\right) \times !\mathbb{A}(A'_1 \oplus A_2, A) \\
&+ \int^{A'_2 \in !\mathbb{A}} !\mathbb{A}\left(A_2, A'_2 \oplus \{\!\{a\}\!\}\right) \times !\mathbb{A}(A_1 \oplus A'_2, A) \\
&\xrightarrow{\;\;\cong\;\;} !\mathbb{A}\left(A_1 \oplus A_2, A \oplus \{\!\{a\}\!\}\right)
\end{aligned}
\qquad
\begin{aligned}
&(A_1, A_2 \in !\mathbb{A}^{\circ}, \\
&\;\; A \in !\mathbb{A}, a \in \mathbb{A})
\end{aligned}
$$

(given by tensoring and composing) is a natural isomorphism. Indeed, the definitions of multiplication and partial derivation yield

$$
\begin{aligned}
\left(\tfrac{\partial}{\partial a}(P \cdot Q)\right)(A)(b) \qquad\qquad & (a \in \mathbb{A}, P, Q : A \multimap \mathbb{B}, A \in !\mathbb{A}, b \in \mathbb{B}^{\circ}) \\
= \int^{A_1, A_2 \in !\mathbb{A}} P(A_1)(b) \times Q(A_2)(b) & \times !\mathbb{A}\left(A_1 \oplus A_2, A \oplus \{\!\{a\}\!\}\right)
\end{aligned}
$$

which by (†) above, using various distributivity and commutativity laws, and the density formula, is natural isomorphic to

$$
\begin{aligned}
&\int^{A_2, A'_1 \in !\mathbb{A}} P(A'_1 \oplus \{\!\{a\}\!\})(b) \times Q(A_2)(b) \times !\mathbb{A}(A'_1 \oplus A_2, A) \\
&+ \int^{A_1, A'_2 \in !\mathbb{A}} P(A_1)(b) \times Q(A'_2 \oplus \{\!\{a\}\!\})(b) \times !\mathbb{A}(A_1 \oplus A'_2, A) \\
&= \left(\tfrac{\partial}{\partial a}(P) \cdot Q + P \cdot \tfrac{\partial}{\partial a}(Q)\right)(A)(b) \; .
\end{aligned}
$$

Further, the differentiation operator, which internalises partial derivation, is a linear operator that is constant on linear maps.

Interestingly, a certain commutation law between abstraction and linear application (used on differentiation) entails the beta rule of the differential lambda calculus of Ehrhard and Regnier [10] as an isomorphism.

3   Concluding Remarks and Research Perspectives

I have drawn a line of investigation concerning models of computational and combinatorial structures. The general common theme of these models is that they live in mathematical universes of variable sets. My presentation here aimed at making explicit and apparent the commonalities amongst the models. In particular, I have placed emphasis in considering the various models of variation as universal constructions; showing how their structure induces relevant further structure on the associated universe of variable sets.

The models touched upon in Sect. 1 and their applications should not be considered in isolation for they are closely related. In this respect, there is a submodel of **Set$^{\mathbb{I}}$**, the so-called Schanuel topos (see, *e.g.*, [32, 24]), that occupies an interesting place. Indeed, it has been used both for giving denotational models of dynamically generated names [46, 47] and for modelling and reasoning about abstract syntax with variable binding [20]. Further, it is closely related to the category of species **Set$^{\mathbb{B}}$** [11, 35], which in turn has also been considered as a model of abstract syntax with linear variable-binding [49]. These models are by no means the only relevant for applications, and a fully systematic theory providing, for instance, constructions of models of variation that are guaranteed to properly model specific (classes of) computation structures is not yet in place.

The analysis of Sect. 1 suggests both the unification and generalisation of models, and in the latter vein I motivated and introduced generalised species of structures; see [2, 36, 7] for relevant related work. These generalised species extend various of the notions of species used in combinatorics and also their respective calculi. Indeed, they come equipped with an (heterogeneous) notion of substitution (composition) structuring them into a bicategory, which arises as from models of linear logic by a co-Kleisli construction (see [7–Sect. 9]) and supports linear and cartesian closed structure allowing for a full development of the differential calculus. Further, the setting also provides graph-like models of the lambda calculus, fixed-point operators, *etc.*

As it is the case for the basic notion of species (see [26]), generalised species of structures can be equivalently seen as generalised analytic functors (of which generalised species are the coefficients) between categories of variable sets. From this point of view, the identities and composition defined in Subsect. 2.4 respectively correspond to the usual identities and composition of functors. Interestingly, restricting attention to groupoids (which is the situation considered in combinatorics) there is an intrinsic characterisation of generalised analytic functors that places them in the context of categorical stable domain theory.

It would be important if the aforementioned structure of generalised species gave new applications in combinatorics, or could be used to tackle combinatorial problems.

I have emphasised that the calculus of generalised species can be axiomatically built on top of the mathematical framework of generalised logic. This, besides yielding new algebraic proofs, provides connections with other areas of mathematics and suggests a calculus of enriched generalised species of structures. In particular, enriching over the Sierpinski space places the subject in the context of domain theory.

As for other perspectives, motivated by a conversation with Prakash Panangaden, I was lead to consider the free symmetric (strict) monoidal completion as a symmetric Fock-space construction (see, *e.g.*, [21–Chap. 21]); and indeed, one can introduce the operators of creation and annihilation of particles in the quantum systems that these spaces model and establish their commutation laws. In this line of thought and further motivated by [6, 3], I was considering Feynman diagrams in the context of generalised species when a computational interpretation of my previous calculations became apparent. The outcome of these investigations will be reported elsewhere. Here however I would like to conclude the paper with an informal presentation of three illustrative examples.

1. The density formula

$$\int^{c \in \mathbb{C}} P(c) \times \mathbb{C}(d, c) \cong P(d) \qquad\qquad (P \in \widehat{\mathbb{C}}, d \in \mathbb{C}^\circ)$$

amounts to the basic form of action

$$(c : \mathbb{C}) \left[[P]c \rangle, \langle c[\mathbb{C}]d \rangle \right] \approx [P]d \rangle$$

with the following data flow reading: the agent P with local port c of sort $\mathbb{C}$ bound to the datum d results in the agent P with the datum d.

$\langle D\, [\varepsilon \circ \langle (\lambda P) \circ \pi_1, \pi_2 \rangle]\, b \rangle$ $\qquad\qquad$ $(D : !(\mathbb{C} \sqcap A),\, P : \mathbb{C} \sqcap A \,!\!\rightarrow \mathbb{B},\, b : \mathbb{B}^\circ)$

$\overset{(1)}{\approx}\ (M : !(\underline{hom}(A, \mathbb{B}) \sqcap A))$
$\qquad [\,\langle D\, [\langle (\lambda P) \circ \pi_1, \pi_2 \rangle^\#]\, M \rangle,\, \langle M\, [\varepsilon]\, b \rangle\,]$

$\overset{(2)}{\approx}\ (M : !(\underline{hom}(A, \mathbb{B}) \sqcap A))$
$\qquad \Big[\, \langle D\, [\langle (\lambda P) \circ \pi_1, \pi_2 \rangle^\#]\, M \rangle,$
$\qquad\quad (F : !\underline{hom}(A, \mathbb{B}),\, A : !A)$
$\qquad\qquad [\,\langle M\, [!(\underline{hom}(A, \mathbb{B}) \sqcap A)]\, !\amalg_1 F \oplus !\amalg_2 A \rangle,\, \langle F\, [!\underline{hom}(A, \mathbb{B})]\, \{\!| (A, b) |\!\} \rangle\,]\,\Big]$

$\overset{(3)}{\approx}\ (A : !A)$
$\qquad [\,\langle D\, [\langle (\lambda P) \circ \pi_1, \pi_2 \rangle^\#]\, !\amalg_1 \{\!| (A, b) |\!\} \oplus !\amalg_2 A \rangle\,]$

$\overset{(4)}{\approx}\ (A : !A,\, D_1, D_2 : !(\mathbb{C} \sqcap A))$
$\qquad [\,\langle D\, [!(\mathbb{C} \sqcap A)]\, D_1 \oplus D_2 \rangle,$
$\qquad\quad \langle D_1\, [\langle (\lambda P) \circ \pi_1, \pi_2 \rangle^\#]\, !\amalg_1 \{\!| (A, b) |\!\} \rangle,\, \langle D_2\, [\langle (\lambda P) \circ \pi_1, \pi_2 \rangle^\#]\, !\amalg_2 A \rangle\,]$

$\overset{(5)}{\approx}\ (A : !A,\, D_1, D_2 : !(\mathbb{C} \sqcap A))$
$\qquad [\,\langle D\, [!(\mathbb{C} \sqcap A)]\, D_1 \oplus D_2 \rangle,\, \langle D_1\, [((\lambda P) \circ \pi_1)^\#]\, \{\!| (A, b) |\!\} \rangle,\, \langle D_2\, [\pi_2^\#]\, A \rangle\,]$

$\overset{(6)}{\approx}\ (A : !A,\, D_1, D_2 : !(\mathbb{C} \sqcap A))$
$\qquad [\,\langle D\, [!(\mathbb{C} \sqcap A)]\, D_1 \oplus D_2 \rangle,\, \langle D_1\, [(\lambda P) \circ \pi_1]\, (A, b) \rangle,\, \langle D_2\, [!(\mathbb{C} \sqcap A)]\, !\amalg_2 A \rangle\,]$

$\overset{(7)}{\approx}\ (A : !A,\, D_1 : !(\mathbb{C} \sqcap A))$
$\qquad \Big[\,\langle D\, [!(\mathbb{C} \sqcap A)]\, D_1 \oplus !\amalg_2 A \rangle,\, (C : !\mathbb{C})[\langle D_1\, [\pi_1^\#]\, C \rangle,\, \langle C\, [\lambda P]\, (A, b) \rangle]\,\Big]$

$\overset{(8)}{\approx}\ (A : !A,\, D_1 : !(\mathbb{C} \sqcap A),\, C : !\mathbb{C})$
$\qquad [\,\langle D\, [!(\mathbb{C} \sqcap A)]\, D_1 \oplus !\amalg_2 A \rangle,\, \langle D_1\, [!(\mathbb{C} \sqcap A)]\, !\amalg_1 C \rangle,\, \langle !\amalg_1 C \oplus !\amalg_2 A\, [P]\, b \rangle\,]$

$\overset{(9)}{\approx}\ (A : !A,\, C : !\mathbb{C})$
$\qquad [\,\langle D\, [!(\mathbb{C} \sqcap A)]\, !\amalg_1 C \oplus !\amalg_2 A \rangle,\, \langle !\amalg_1 C \oplus !\amalg_2 A\, [P]\, b \rangle\,]$

$\overset{(10)}{\approx}\ \langle D\, [P]\, b \rangle$

Fig. 2. A computational interpretation of the beta isomorphism

(1) Definition of composition. (2) Definition of evaluation. (3) Laws of data flow. (4) Law of extensions. (5) Law of extensions and definition of pairing. (6) Law of extensions and definition of projection. (7) Law of data flow and definition of composition. (8) Law of extensions and definitions of projection and abstraction. (9–10) Laws of data flow.

2. The isomorphism

$$!(A \sqcap \mathbb{B})(A' \otimes B', A \otimes B) \cong !A(A', A) \times !\mathbb{B}(B', B) \qquad \begin{array}{l} (A, A' \in !A, \\ B, B' \in !\mathbb{B}) \end{array}$$

amounts to having the law of data flow

$$\langle A \otimes B\, [!(A \sqcap \mathbb{B})]\, A' \otimes B' \rangle \approx \langle A\, [!A]\, A' \rangle,\, \langle B\, [!\mathbb{B}]\, B' \rangle$$

establishing that a link between $A \otimes B$ and $A' \otimes B'$ of type $!(\mathbb{A} \sqcap \mathbb{B})$ amounts to a link of type $!\mathbb{A}$ between A and A' and one of type $!\mathbb{B}$ between B and B'.

3. The computational interpretation of the beta isomorphism in Fig. 1, translated into the informal syntax of agents used in the above two examples, is given in Fig. 2.

References

1. P. Aczel. Frege structures and the notions of proposition, truth and set. In *The Kleene Symposium*, pages 31–60. North-Holland, 1980.
2. J. Baez and J. Dolan. Higher-dimensional algebra III: n-categories and the algebra of opetopes. *Advances in Mathematics*, 135:145–206, 1998.
3. J. Baez and J. Dolan. From finite sets to Feynman diagrams. In B. Engquist and W.Schmid, editors, *Mathematics Unlimited - 2001 and Beyond*, pages 29–50. Springer-Verlag, 2001.
4. F. Bergeron. Une combinatoire du pléthysme. *Journal of Combinatorial Theory (Series A)*, 46:291–305, 1987.
5. F. Bergeron, G. Labelle, and P. Leroux. *Combinatorial species and tree-like structures*, volume 67 of *Encyclopedia of mathematics and its applications*. Cambridge University Press, 1998.
6. R. Blute and P. Panangaden. Proof nets and Feynman diagrams. Available from the second author, 1998.
7. G. Cattani and G. Winskel. Profunctors, open maps and bisimulation. BRICS Report Series RS-04-22, University of Aarhus, 2004.
8. B. Day. On closed categories of functors. In *Reports of the Midwest Category Seminar IV*, volume 137 of *Lecture Notes in Mathematics*, pages 1–38. Springer-Verlag, 1970.
9. R. Di Cosmo. *Isomorphisms of types: from λ-calculus to information retrieval and language design*. Birkhauser, 1995.
10. T. Ehrhard and L. Regnier. The differential lambda calculus. *Theoretical Computer Science*, 309:1–41, 2003.
11. M. Fiore. Notes on combinatorial functors. Draft available electronically, January 2001.
12. M. Fiore. Rough notes on presheaves. Manuscript available electronically, July 2001.
13. M. Fiore. Semantic analysis of normalisation by evaluation for typed lambda calculus. In *Proceedings of the 4th International Conference on Principles and Practice of Declarative Programming (PPDP 2002)*, pages 26–37. ACM Press, 2002.
14. M. Fiore. Isomorphisms of generic recursive polynomial types. In *Proceedings of the 31st ACM SIGPLAN-SIGACT Symposium on Principles of Programming Languages (POPL 2004)*, pages 77–88. ACM Press, 2004.
15. M. Fiore, R. Di Cosmo, and V. Balat. Remarks on isomorphisms in typed lambda calculi with empty and sum types. In *Proceedings of the 17th Annual IEEE Symposium on Logic in Computer Science (LICS'02)*, pages 147–156. IEEE, Computer Society Press, 2002.
16. M. Fiore and T. Leinster. An objective representation of the Gaussian integers. *Journal of Symbolic Computation*, 37(6):707–716, 2004.
17. M. Fiore, E. Moggi, and D. Sangiorgi. A fully-abstract model for the pi-calculus. *Information and Computation*, 178:1–42, 2002. (Extended abstract in *Proceedings of the 11th Annual IEEE Symposium on Logic in Computer Science (LICS 96)*, pages 43–54, IEEE, Computer Society Press, 1996.).
18. M. Fiore, G. Plotkin, and D. Turi. Abstract syntax and variable binding. In *Proceedings of the 14th Annual IEEE Symposium on Logic in Computer Science (LICS'99)*, pages 193–202. IEEE, Computer Society Press, 1999.

19. M. Fiore and D. Turi. Semantics of name and value passing. In *Proceedings of the 16th Annual IEEE Symposium on Logic in Computer Science (LICS'01)*, pages 93–104. IEEE, Computer Society Press, 2001.

20. M. J. Gabbay and A. Pitts. A new approach to abstract syntax with variable binding. *Formal Aspects of Computing*, 13:341–363, 2002. (See also *A new approach to abstract syntax involving binders* in *Proceedings of the 14th Annual IEEE Symposium on Logic in Computer Science (LICS'99)*, pages 214–224, IEEE, Computer Society Press, 1999.).

21. R. Geroch. *Mathematical Physics*. Chicago Lectures in Physics. The University of Chicago Press, 1985.

22. M. Hofmann. Semantical analysis of higher order abstract syntax. In *Proceedings of the 14th Annual IEEE Symposium on Logic in Computer Science (LICS'99)*, pages 204–213. IEEE, Computer Society Press, 1999.

23. G. Im and G. M. Kelly. A universal property of the convolution monoidal structure. *Journal of Pure and Applied Algebra*, 43:75–88, 1986.

24. P. Johnstone. *Sketches of an Elephant: A Topos Theory Compendium*, volume 43 of *Oxford Logic Guides*. Oxford University Press, 2002.

25. A. Joyal. Une theorie combinatoire des séries formelles. *Advances in Mathematics*, 42:1–82, 1981.

26. A. Joyal. Foncteurs analytiques et especès de structures. In *Combinatoire énumérative*, volume 1234 of *Lecture Notes in Mathematics*, pages 126–159. Springer-Verlag, 1986.

27. G. M. Kelly. Clubs and data-type constructors. In *Applications of Categories in Computer Science*, volume 177 of *London Mathematical Society Lecture Notes Series*, pages 163–190. Cambridge University Press, 1992.

28. F. W. Lawvere. Metric spaces, generalized logic and closed categories. *Rend. del Sem. Mat. e Fis. di Milano*, 43:135–166, 1973. (Also in *Reprints in Theory and Applications of Categories*, 1:1–37, 2002.).

29. F. W. Lawvere. Qualitative distinctions between some toposes of generalized graphs. In *Proceedings of the AMS 1987 Symposium on Categories in Computer Science and Logic*, volume 92 of *Contemporary Mathematics*, pages 261–299, 1989.

30. F. W. Lawvere and R. Rosebrugh. *Sets for Mathematics*. Cambridge University Press, 2001.

31. S. Mac Lane. *Categories for the Working Mathematician*. Springer-Verlag, 1971. (Revised edition 1998).

32. S. Mac Lane and I. Moerdijk. *Sheaves in Geometry and Logic: A First Introduction to Topos Theory*. Universitext. Springer-Verlag, 1992.

33. M. Méndez. Species on digraphs. *Advances in Mathematics*, 123(2):243–275, 1996.

34. M. Méndez and O. Nava. Colored species, c-monoids and plethysm, I. *Journal of Combinatorial Theory (Series A)*, 64:102–129, 1993.

35. M. Menni. About $\mathcal{H}$-quantifiers. *Applied Categorical Structures*, 11(5):421–445, 2003.

36. M. Menni. Symmetric monoidal completions and the exponential principle among labeled combinatorial structures. *Theory and Applications of Categories*, 11:397–419, 2003.

37. R. Milner. What's in a name? In *Computer Systems: Theory, Technology and Applications*, Monographs in Computer Science. Springer-Verlag, 2003.

38. R. Milner, J. Parrow, and D. Walker. A calculus of mobile processes, I and II. *Information and Computation*, 100(1):1–77, 1992.

39. E. Moggi. An abstract view of programming languages. LFCS report ECS-LFCS-90-113, University of Edinburgh, 1990.

40. O. Nava and G.-C. Rota. Plethysm, categories and combinatorics. *Advances in Mathematics*, 58:61–88, 1985.

41. R. Needham. *Distributed Systems*, chapter 12, pages 315–328. Addison-Wesley, second edition, 1993.

42. F. Oles. Type algebras, functor categories and block structure. In *Algebraic Methods in Semantics*. Cambridge University Press, 1985.

43. F. Pfenning and C. Elliot. Higher-order abstract syntax. In *Proceedings of the ACM SIG-PLAN'88 Symposium on Language Design and Implementation*, 1988.

44. D. Rajan. The adjoints to the derivative functor on species. *Journal of combinatorial theory (Series A)*, 62:93–106, 1993.

45. J. Reynolds. The essence of Algol. In *Proceedings of the International Symposium on Algorithmic Languages*, pages 345–372. North-Holland, 1981.

46. I. Stark. *Names and Higher-Order Functions*. Ph.D. thesis, University of Cambridge, 1994.

47. I. Stark. A fully abstract domain model for the pi-calculus. In *Proceedings of the 11th Annual IEEE Symposium on Logic in Computer Science (LICS'96)*, pages 36–42. IEEE, Computer Society Press, 1996.

48. R. Street. The role of Michael Batanin's monoidal globular categories. In *Higher Category Theory*, volume 230 of *Contemporary Mathematics*, pages 99–116. A.M.S., 1998.

49. M. Tanaka. Abstract syntax and variable binding for linear binders. In *Proceedings of the 25th International Symposium on Mathematical Foundations of Computer Science (MFCS'00)*, volume 1893 of *Lecture Notes in Computer Science*, pages 670–679. Springer-Verlag, 2000.

50. S. Yong. *A Framework for Binding Operators*. Ph.D. thesis (LFCS report ECS-LFCS-92-207), University of Edinburgh, 1992.

A   Fundamental Adjunctions Between Categories of Variable Sets

As it is customary, I write $\widehat{\mathbb{V}}$ for the functor category $\mathbf{Set}^{\mathbb{V}^{\circ}}$ of so-called $\mathbb{V}^{\circ}$-variable sets (or presheaves). Recall that there is a universal Yoneda embedding $y : \mathbb{V} \hookrightarrow \widehat{\mathbb{V}}$ given by $y(v) = \mathbb{V}(\_, v)$.

For small categories $\mathbb{V}$ and $\mathbb{W}$, we have the following important adjoint situations (see, *e.g.*, [29, 12])

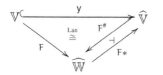 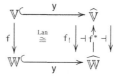

obtained by left Kan extension, where

$$F^{\#}(P) = \int^{v \in \mathbb{V}} P(v) \times Fv(\_) , \quad F_*(Q) = \widehat{\mathbb{W}}(F\_, Q) \qquad (P \in \widehat{\mathbb{V}}, Q \in \widehat{\mathbb{W}})$$

and

$$f_!(P) = \int^{v \in \mathbb{V}} P(v) \times \mathbb{W}(\_, fv) , \quad f^*(Q) = Q(f\_) \qquad (P \in \widehat{\mathbb{V}}, Q \in \widehat{\mathbb{W}}) .$$

(See, *e.g.*, [31–Chap. IX] for the above notion $\int$ of coend.)

B   Substitution Algebras and Algebraic Theories

A substitution algebra structure on $P = \{P_\tau\}_{\tau \in T}$ in $\widehat{\mathbb{F}[T]}^{\mathsf{T}}$ is given by operators

$$\eta_\tau : \longrightarrow (\tau)\tau , \quad \sigma_{\tau,\tau'} : (\tau)\tau', \tau \longrightarrow \tau' \qquad\qquad (\tau, \tau' \in T) ,$$

giving rise to morphisms

$$\eta_\tau : 1 \longrightarrow P_\tau{}^{V_\tau} , \quad \sigma_{\tau,\tau'} : P_{\tau'}{}^{V_\tau} \times P_\tau \longrightarrow P_{\tau'} \qquad\qquad (\tau, \tau' \in T)$$

in $\widehat{F[T]}$, subject to the following axioms, where we write $t[x^\tau \mapsto u]_{\tau'}$ as a shorthand for $\sigma_{\tau,\tau'}(\lambda x : V_\tau.t, u)$:

$$\eta_\tau(x)[x^\tau \mapsto u]_\tau = u \qquad\qquad\qquad\qquad (u : P_\tau) ,$$

$$t[x^\tau \mapsto u]_{\tau'} = t \qquad\qquad\qquad\qquad (t : P_{\tau'}) ,$$

$$t(x,y)[y^\tau \mapsto \eta_\tau(x)]_{\tau'} = t(x,x) \qquad\qquad (t : P_{\tau'}{}^{V_\tau \times V_\tau}, x : V_\tau) ,$$

$$\begin{aligned}&\big(t(y,x)\big[y^{\tau'} \mapsto u(x)\big]_{\tau''}\big)[x^\tau \mapsto v]_{\tau''} \\&= \big(t(y,x)[x^\tau \mapsto v]_{\tau''}\big)\big[y^{\tau'} \mapsto u(x)[x^\tau \mapsto v]_{\tau'}\big]_{\tau''}\end{aligned} \qquad \begin{aligned}&(t : P_{\tau''}{}^{V_{\tau'} \times V_\tau}, \\&\ u : P_{\tau'}{}^{V_\tau}, v : P_\tau) .\end{aligned}$$

These substitution structures can be incorporated to algebraic theories; see [18] for details. For instance, for the simply typed lambda calculus (see also [13]), where the set of types T is the closure under the arrow type constructor $\Rightarrow$ of a set of base types, this yields substitution algebras $(P, \mathsf{var}, \mathsf{sub})$ with binding operators

$$\begin{array}{lll}\text{(Application)} & \mathsf{app}_{\tau,\tau'} : & \tau \Rightarrow \tau', \tau \longrightarrow \tau' \\ \text{(Abstraction)} & \mathsf{abs}_{\tau,\tau'} : & (\tau)\tau' \longrightarrow \tau \Rightarrow \tau' \end{array} \qquad (\tau, \tau' \in T)$$

that are required to be compatible in the sense of satisfying the following axioms

$$\begin{aligned}&\big(\mathsf{app}_{\tau',\tau''}(t(x), u(x))\big)[x^\tau \mapsto u]_{\tau'} \\&= \mathsf{app}_{\tau',\tau''}\big(t(x)[x^\tau \mapsto u]_{\tau' \Rightarrow \tau''}, u(x)[x^\tau \mapsto u]_{\tau'}\big)\end{aligned} \qquad (t : P_{\tau' \Rightarrow \tau''}{}^{V_\tau}, u : P_\tau)$$

$$\begin{aligned}&\big(\mathsf{abs}_{\tau',\tau''}(\lambda y : V_{\tau'}.t(y,x))\big)[x^\tau \mapsto u]_{\tau' \Rightarrow \tau''} \\&= \mathsf{abs}_{\tau',\tau''}\big(\lambda y : V_{\tau'}.t(y,x)[x^\tau \mapsto u]_{\tau''}\big)\end{aligned} \qquad (t : P_{\tau''}{}^{V_{\tau'} \times V_\tau}, u : P_\tau)$$

where $t[x^\tau \mapsto u]_{\tau'}$ stands for $\mathsf{sub}_{\tau,\tau'}(\lambda x : V_\tau.t, u)$.

The initial algebra for this theory can be, of course, described as the simply typed lambda terms (modulo alpha conversion) with the usual capture-avoiding single-variable substitution operation (which in this setting can be shown to arise by structural recursion; again see [18] for details).

Further, beta and eta equality can be easily incorporated as the following axioms:

$$\text{(beta)} \quad \mathsf{app}_{\tau,\tau'}\big(\mathsf{abs}_{\tau,\tau'}(t), u\big) = \mathsf{sub}_{\tau,\tau'}(t, u) \qquad (t : P_{\tau'}{}^{V_\tau}, u : P_\tau)$$

$$\text{(eta)} \quad \mathsf{abs}_{\tau,\tau'}\big(\lambda x : V_\tau.\mathsf{app}_{\tau,\tau'}(t, \mathsf{var}_\tau(x))\big) = t \qquad (t : P_{\tau \Rightarrow \tau'}) .$$

(Note that the metatheory accounts for the usual side condition required in the eta equality axiom, as in higher-order abstract syntax [43] (see also [22]).)

Congruence for Structural Congruences

MohammadReza Mousavi and Michel A. Reniers

Department of Computer Science,
Eindhoven University of Technology,
NL-5600MB Eindhoven, The Netherlands

Abstract. Structural congruences have been used to define the semantics and to capture inherent properties of language constructs. They have
been used as an addendum to transition system specifications in Plotkin's
style of Structural Operational Semantics (SOS). However, there has
been little theoretical work on establishing a formal link between these
two semantic specification frameworks. In this paper, we give an interpretation of structural congruences inside the transition system specification framework. This way, we extend a number of well-behavedness
meta-theorems for SOS (such as well-definedness of the semantics and
congruence of bisimilarity) to the extended setting with structural congruences.

1 Introduction

Structural congruences were introduced in [12, 13] in the operational semantics specification of the π-calculus. There, structural congruences are a set of
equations defining an equality and congruence relation on process terms. These
equations are used as an addendum to the transition system specification, in
the Structural Operational Semantics (SOS) style of [17]. The two specifications
(structural congruences and SOS) are linked using a deduction rule dedicated to
the behavior of congruent terms, stating that if a process term can perform a
transition, all congruent process terms can mimic the same behavior.

The combination of structural congruences and SOS rules may simplify SOS
specifications and make them look more compact. They can also capture inherent (so-called *spatial*) properties of composition operators (e.g., commutativity,
associativity and zero element). Perhaps, the latter has been the main reason
for using them in combination with SOS. However, as we argue in this paper,
the interaction between the two specification styles is not as trivial as it seems.
Particularly, well-definedness and well-behavedness meta-theorems for SOS such
as those mentioned in [1] do not carry over trivially to this mixed setting. As
an interesting example, we show that the addition of structural congruences to
a set of safe SOS rules (e.g., tyft rules of [8]) can put the congruence property
of bisimilarity in jeopardy. This result shows that a standard congruence format cannot be used, as is, for the combination of structural congruences and
SOS rules. As another example, we show that well-definedness criteria defined

V. Sassone (Ed.): FOSSACS 2005, LNCS 3441, pp. 47–62, 2005.

by [5, 6] for SOS with negative premises do not necessarily hold in the setting with structural congruences.

Three solutions can be proposed to deal with the aforementioned problems. The first is to avoid using structural congruences and use "pure" SOS specifications for defining operational semantics. In this approach, there is a conceptual distinction between the transition system semantics (as the model of the algebra) and the equational theory (cf. [2], for example). This way, one may lose the compactness and the intuitive presentation of the operational semantics, but in return, one will be able to benefit from the existing theories of SOS. This solution can be recommended as a homogenous way of specifying semantics. The second solution is to use structural congruences in combination with SOS rules and prove the well-behavedness theorems (e.g., well-definedness of the semantics and congruence of the notion of equality) manually. By taking this solution, all the tedious proofs of congruence, as a typical example, have to be done manually and re-done or adapted in the case of any single change in the syntax and semantics. Although this solution is a common practice, it does not seem very promising. The third solution is to extend meta-theorems of SOS to this mixed setting. In this paper, we pursue the third solution.

The rest of this paper is structured as follows. By reviewing the related work in Section 2, we position our work within the body of research in formal semantics. Then, in Section 3, we present basic definitions about transition system specifications, bisimilarity and congruence. Subsequently, Section 4 is devoted to accommodating structural congruences in the SOS framework. In Section 5, we study structural congruences from the congruence point of view. There, we propose a syntactic format for structural congruences that induces congruence for strong bisimilarity, if they are accompanied by a set of safe SOS rules. We show, by several abstract counter-examples, that our syntactic format cannot be relaxed in any obvious way and dropping any of the syntactic restrictions may destroy the congruence property in general. In Section 6, we extend our format to allow for SOS rules with negative premises and set the respective well-definedness criteria. To illustrate our congruence format with a concrete example, in Section 7, we apply it to a CCS-like process algebra. Finally, Section 8 concludes the paper and points out possible extensions of our work. For the sake of brevity and due to space restrictions, we omit the proofs. A detailed version of this paper (containing additional results) with proofs can be consulted in [15].

2   Related Work

Structural congruences find their origin in the chemical models of computation [3]. The Chemical Abstract Machine (Cham) of [4] is among the early instances of such models. In Cham, parallel agents are modelled by molecules floating around in a chemical solution. The solution is constantly stirred using a *magical mechanism*, in the spirit of the *Brownian motion* in chemistry, that allows for possible contacts among reacting molecules.

Inspired by the magical mechanism of Cham, structural congruences were introduced in [12, 13] in the semantic specification of the π-calculus and since then, the practice of using structural congruences for the specification of operational semantics has continued. As stated in [14], structural congruences were also inspired by a curious difference between lambda-calculi and process calculi; in lambda-calculi, interacting terms are always placed adjacently in the syntax, while in process calculi, interacting agents may be dispersed around the process term due to syntactic restrictions. Thus, part of the idea is to bring interacting terms together by considering terms modulo structural changes. However, the application of structural congruences is not restricted to this concept. Structural congruence have also been used to define the semantics of new operators in terms of previously defined ones (e.g., defining the semantics of the parallel replication operator in terms of parallel composition in [12, 13] and Section 7 of this paper).

There have been a number of recent works devoted to the fundamental study of formal semantics with structural congruences. Among these, we can refer to [10, 18, 19]. Lack of a congruent notion of bisimilarity for the semantics of the π-calculus has been known since [12] (which is not only due to structural congruences), but most attempts (e.g., [10, 14, 18, 19]) were focused on deriving a suitable transition system (e.g., *contexts as labels* approach of [10]) or a notion of equivalence (e.g., barbed congruence of [14]) that induces congruence. The works of [10, 18, 19] deviate from the traditional interpretation of SOS deduction rules and establish a new semantic framework close to the reduction (reaction) rules of lambda calculus [9]. In [19], it is emphasized that the relation between this framework and the known congruence results for SOS remains to be established and the present paper realizes this goal (at least partially). Our results to date do not apply to SOS containing variable binding or name passing operators. Also, the kind of structural congruences that can be dealt with is quite limited; it is for example, not possible to consider structural congruences expressing properties such as associativity and zero elements.

To conclude, compared to the above approaches, we take a different angle to the problem, that is, to characterize the set of specifications that induce a reasonable transition relation in its commonly accepted meaning. In other words, we extend the notion of *structured operational semantics* [8, 7] to cater for structural congruences. In particular, we extend the meta-theorems concerning congruence of bisimilarity [1, 8] and well-definedness of the induced transition relation [5, 6, 7] to the setting with structural congruences.

3   Preliminaries

We assume that the set of process terms, denoted by $T(\Sigma)$ with typical members $t, t', t_0, \ldots$, is inductively defined on a set of variables $V = \{x, y, \ldots\}$ and a signature Σ. The signature contains a number of function symbols (composition operators: $f, g, \ldots$) with fixed arities $(ar(f), ar(g), \ldots)$. Function symbols with arity 0 are called constants and are typically denoted by $a, b, \ldots$. Closed terms, denoted by $C(\Sigma)$ with typical members $p, q, p_0, \ldots$, are terms that do not contain variables. A substitution σ replaces variables in a term with other terms. The set of variables appearing in term t is denoted by $vars(t)$. A transition system specification, defined below, is a logical way of defining a transition relation on (closed) terms.

Definition 1. *(Transition System Specification (TSS)) A transition system specification is a tuple (Σ, L, D) where Σ is a signature, L is a set of labels (with typical members $l, l', l_0, \ldots$) and D is a set of deduction rules. For all $l \in L$, and $s, s' \in T(\Sigma)$ we define that $(t, l, t') \in \rightarrow$ is a formula. A deduction rule $dr \in D$, is defined as a tuple (H, c) where H is a set of formulae and c is a formula. The formula c is called the conclusion and the formulae from H are called premises. A rule with an empty set of premises is called an axiom.*

The notion of closed and the concept of substitution are lifted to formulae in the natural way. A formula $(t, l, t') \in \rightarrow$ is denoted by the more intuitive notation $t \xrightarrow{l} t'$, as well. We refer to t as the source and to t' as the target of the transition. A deduction rule (H, c) is denoted by $\frac{H}{c}$ in the remainder.

In the traditional setting, the transition relation induced by a transition system specification is the smallest set of provable closed formulae using a well-founded proof tree based on the deduction rules. Note that for more complicated transition systems specifications such a unique transition relation may not exist (see [1, 6] and Section 6 of the present paper for more details). Next, we define our notion of equality, namely, the notions of strong bisimulation and bisimilarity.

Definition 2. *(Bisimulation and Bisimilarity [16]) A relation $R \subseteq C(\Sigma) \times C(\Sigma)$ is a simulation relation with respect to a transition relation $\rightarrow \subseteq C(\Sigma) \times L \times C(\Sigma)$ if and only if $\forall_{p,q \in C(\Sigma)} \ (p, q) \in R \Rightarrow \forall_{l \in L} \ \forall_{p' \in C(\Sigma)} \ p \xrightarrow{l} p' \Rightarrow \exists_{q' \in C(\Sigma)} \ q \xrightarrow{l} q' \wedge (p', q') \in R$. A bisimulation relation is a symmetric simulation relation. Closed terms p and q are bisimilar with respect to $\rightarrow$ if and only if there exists a bisimulation relation R with respect to $\rightarrow$ such that $(p, q) \in R$. Two closed terms p and q are bisimilar with respect to a transition system specification tss, if and only if they are bisimilar with respect to the transition relation induced by tss. Note that bisimilarity (with respect to a transition relation or TSS) is an equivalence relation on closed terms.*

Next, we define the concept of congruence which is of central importance to our topic.

Definition 3. *(Congruence) A relation $R \subseteq T(\Sigma) \times T(\Sigma)$ is a congruent relation with respect to a function symbol $f \in \Sigma$ if and only if for all terms $p_i, q_i \in T(\Sigma)$ $(0 \le i < ar(f))$, if $(p_i, q_i) \in R$ (for all $0 \le i < ar(f))$ then $(f(p_0, \ldots, p_{ar(f)-1}), f(q_0, \ldots, q_{ar(f)-1})) \in R$. Furthermore, R is called a congruence for a transition system specification if and only if it is a congruence with respect to all function symbols of the signature.*

Bisimilarity is not in general a congruence. However, congruence is essential for the axiomatic treatment of bisimilarity. Furthermore, congruence of bisimilarity is of crucial importance in compositional reasoning. Several syntactic formats guaranteeing congruence for bisimilarity have been proposed (see [1] for an overview). Here, we choose the **tyft** format of [8] as a sufficiently general example of such formats for our purposes. Extensions to more general formats (such as the PANTH format of [20]) are discussed in Section 6.

Definition 4. *(Tyft Format [8]) A rule is in **tyft** format if and only if it has the following shape:*

$$\frac{\{t_i \xrightarrow{l_i} y_i | i \in I\}}{f(x_0, \ldots, x_{ar(f)-1}) \xrightarrow{l} t}$$

*where x_i and y_i are all distinct variables (i.e., for all $i, i' \in I$ and $0 \leq j, j' < ar(f)$, $y_i \neq x_j$ and if $i \neq i'$ then $y_i \neq y_{i'}$ and if $j \neq j'$ then $x_j \neq x_{j'}$), f is a function symbol from the signature, I is a (possibly infinite) set of indices and t and t_i's are arbitrary terms. A transition system specification is in **tyft** format if and only if all its rules are.*

Theorem 1. *(Congruence for **tyft** [8]) For a TSS in **tyft** format, bisimilarity is a congruence.*

4   Structural Congruences: An SOS Reading

Structural congruences sc on a signature Σ consist of a set of equations of the form $t \equiv t'$, where $t, t' \in T(\Sigma)$. They induce a structural congruence relation on closed terms, as defined below.

Definition 5. *(Structural Congruence Relation) A structural congruence relation induced by structural congruences sc on signature Σ, denoted by $\equiv_{sc}$, is the minimal relation satisfying the following constraints:*

1. $\forall_{p \in C(\Sigma)} \; p \equiv_{sc} p$ *(reflexivity)*;
2. $\forall_{p,q \in C(\Sigma)} \; p \equiv_{sc} q \Rightarrow q \equiv_{sc} p$ *(symmetry)*;
3. $\forall_{p,q,r \in C(\Sigma)} \; (p \equiv_{sc} q \wedge q \equiv_{sc} r) \Rightarrow p \equiv_{sc} r$ *(transitivity)*;
4. $\forall_{f \in \Sigma} \forall_{p_i,q_i \in C(\Sigma)(0 \leq i < ar(f))} \; (\forall_{0 \leq i < ar(f)} \; p_i \equiv_{sc} q_i) \Rightarrow f(p_0, \ldots, p_{ar(f)-1}) \equiv_{sc} f(q_0, \ldots, q_{ar(f)-1})$ *(congruence)*;
5. $\forall_{\sigma:V \to C(\Sigma)} \forall_{t,t' \in T(\Sigma)} \; (t \equiv t') \in sc \Rightarrow \sigma(t) \equiv_{sc} \sigma(t')$ *(structural congruences)*.

In other words, $\equiv_{sc}$ is the smallest congruence satisfying $\equiv$ on closed terms.

In the remainder, we assume that the structural congruences have the same signature as the transition system specification they are added to. To link structural congruences to a transition system specification, a special rule is used, which we call *the structural congruence rule*.

Definition 6. *(The Structural Congruence Rule [12]) The particular rule schema of the following form (which is in fact a set of deduction rules for all $l \in L$) is called the structural congruence rule:*

$$(\textbf{struct}) \frac{x \equiv y \quad y \xrightarrow{l} y' \quad y' \equiv x'}{x \xrightarrow{l} x'} (l \in L)$$

Consider a transition system specification tss $= (\Sigma, L, D)$ *and structural congruences sc on the same signature. Extension of tss with sc, denoted by tss* $\cup$ *{(struct)}, is defined by the tuple* $(\Sigma, L, D \cup \{(\textbf{struct})\})$.

There remains a problem concerning Definition 6, namely, the structural congruence rule does not fit within the notion of a deduction rule as defined in Definition 1 since structural congruences (appearing in the premises) do not fit the definition of formulae per se. In other words, $x \equiv y$ is only a syntactic notation and has no meaning associated to it as yet. In this paper, we exploit the structural congruence relation to give a meaning to $x \equiv y$ by extending the notion of proof (see [15] for other possible interpretations). Syntactically, we allow for deduction rules of the form $\dfrac{\{\chi_i | i \in I\} \quad \{t_j \equiv t'_j | j \in J\}}{\chi}$ where χ and χ_i's are formulae as defined before (in Definition 1) and t_j and t'_j are terms from the signature. This rule format, easily accommodates the structural congruence rule. Then, we extend the notion of provable transitions to the following notion.

Definition 7. *(Provable Transitions: Extended) A proof of a closed formula* ϕ *(in an extended transition system specification tss* $\cup$ *{(struct)}) is a well-founded upwardly branching tree of which the nodes are labelled by closed formulae such that*

- *the root node is labelled by* ϕ, *and*
- *if* ψ *is the label of a node* q *and* $\{\psi_i \mid i \in I\}$ *is the set of labels of the nodes directly above* q, *then there is a deduction rule* $\dfrac{\{\chi_i \mid i \in I\} \quad \{t_j \equiv t'_j | j \in J\}}{\chi}$ *(in tss* $\cup$ *{(struct)}) and a substitution* σ *such that* $\sigma(\chi) = \psi$, *for all* $i \in I$, $\sigma(\chi_i) = \psi_i$, *and for all* $j \in J$, $\sigma(t_j) \equiv_{sc} \sigma(t'_j)$.

We re-use the same notations for provability of formulae in the extended setting.

We are not able to reproduce the results of Theorem 1 (concerning congruence for tyft format) in the extended setting with structural congruences. In fact, adding structural congruences to a set of tyft rules does not preserve the congruence property of bisimilarity. The following counter-example shows this fact.

Example 1. *Consider the following structural congruence equation and transition system specification. The common signature is assumed to have a and b as constants and f as a unary operator.*

$$a \equiv f(b) \quad (\textbf{a}) \frac{}{a \xrightarrow{l_0} a} \quad (\textbf{b}) \frac{}{b \xrightarrow{l_0} a}$$

In the above specification, both a and b can perform an l_0 *transition to a due to rules* (**a**) *and* (**b**), *respectively. On one hand, using Definition 5, a is only* *structurally congruent (by means of $\equiv_{sc}$) to itself and $f(b)$. On the other hand, b is only congruent to itself. Since $f(b)$ cannot perform any new transition, neither a nor b can perform any other transition due to (**struct**). Thus, to this end, we have $a \leftrightarrow b$. However, it does not hold that $f(a) \leftrightarrow f(b)$ since $f(a)$ cannot perform any transition (it is only congruent to $f(f(b))$ which cannot perform any transition either), but $f(b)$ can perform an l_0 transition to a (using (**struct**) since it is congruent to a). This shows that bisimilarity is not a congruence in the above transition system specification, despite the fact that the original transition system specification is in* tyft *format.*

Several other counter-examples of violating congruence property by structural congruences are presented in the remainder of this paper.

5 Well-Behaved Structural Congruences

In this section, we start with proposing a syntactic format for structural congruences and stating that structural congruences conforming to this format are safe for the purpose of congruence when added to a set of tyft rules. Then, in Section 5.2, by several counter-examples, we show that none of the syntactic constraints on this format can be dropped in general and thus our syntactic format cannot be relaxed trivially.

5.1   Congruence Format for Structural Congruences (cfsc)

Our syntactic criteria on structural congruences are defined below.

Definition 8. *(Cfsc format) Structural congruences sc (added to a transition system specification tss) are in the* cfsc *format if and only if any equation in sc is of one of the following two forms.*

1. *An fx equation is of the form $f(x_0, \ldots, x_{ar(f)-1}) \equiv g(y_0, \ldots, y_{ar(g)-1})$ for function symbols f and g (which need not be different) and for variables x_i and y_j. Variables x_i and y_j are distinct among themselves (i.e., for all $i \neq j$, $x_i \neq x_j$ and $y_i \neq y_j$) but they need not form two disjoint sets (i.e., it may be that for some i and j, $x_i = y_j$).*
2. *A defining equation is of the form $f(x_0, \ldots, x_{ar(f)-1}) \equiv t$ (or similarly, $t \equiv f(x_0, \ldots, x_{ar(f)-1})$) where f is a function symbol and t is an arbitrary term. Similar to fx equations, variables x_i have to be distinct. Two more conditions have to be satisfied for this type of equations; first, all variables in t should be bound by variables $x_0, \ldots, x_{ar(f)-1}$, i.e., $vars(t) \subseteq \{x_i | 0 \leq i < ar(f)\}$ and second, f may not appear in any other structural congruence equation and source of the conclusion of any deduction rule in tss. We have no further assumption about t, thus, there may be a repetition of variables in t, occurrences of f may appear in t and it may consist of any number of constants and function symbols.*

Note that the above two categories are not disjoint; i.e., an equation may be both fx and defining. For the remainder, it does not make any difference whether such equations are taken as fx, defining, or both.

In the following theorem, we state that structural congruences conforming to the cfsc format, when added to a set of tyft rules, induce a congruent bisimilarity relation. The proof of the following theorem follows from Theorem 1 by transforming the transition system specification with structural congruences to a "pure" transitions system specification in tyft format that provably induces the same transition relation.

Theorem 2. *(Congruence Theorem for cfsc) Consider a set of deduction rules tss in tyft format. If structural congruences sc (added to tss) are in the cfsc format, then bisimilarity with respect to tss $\cup$ {(**struct**)} is a congruence.*

5.2   Impossible Relaxations of Cfsc

Next, we show that the cfsc format cannot be relaxed in any obvious way. We take every and each syntactic constraint on cfsc and by an abstract counter-example, show that removing it will result in violating the congruence. We start with a counter-example showing that variables in each side of the fx equation need to be distinct and that the variables in the $f(x_0, \ldots, x_{ar(f)})$ side of a defining equation need to be distinct.

Example 2. $f(x, x) \equiv a$ (a) $\dfrac{}{a \xrightarrow{l_0} a}$ (b) $\dfrac{}{b \xrightarrow{l_0} a}$

Similar to Example 1, it clearly holds in the above specification that $a \leftrightarrow b$. However, it does not hold that $f(a, a) \leftrightarrow f(a, b)$ since the former can perform an l_0 transition, while the latter deadlocks. Thus, bisimilarity is not a congruence. Note that the above structural congruence can be considered both an fx equation and a defining equation.

The other condition on fx equations is that they may only have one function symbol in each side of the equation. We have already shown that this constraint cannot be relaxed in Example 1 in the previous section. There, the equation $a \equiv f(b)$ had two function symbols, namely the constant b and unary function symbol f and the congruence property is shown to be violated. A similar condition forces defining equations to have only one fresh function symbol on the side to be defined. In the following example, we show that allowing more fresh function symbols also endangers congruence.

Example 3. $f(b) \equiv a$ (a) $\dfrac{}{a \xrightarrow{l_0} a}$

Suppose that our signature consists of three constants a, b and c and a unary function symbol f. Then, it immediately follows that $b \leftrightarrow c$ since none of the two constants can perform any transition. However, it does not hold that $f(b) \leftrightarrow f(c)$ since the first term can perform a transition while the latter deadlocks.

Another constraint on a defining equation $f(x_0, \ldots, x_{ar(f)-1}) \equiv t$ is that $vars(t) \subseteq \{x_i | 0 \leq i < ar(f)\}$. The following counter-example shows that we cannot drop this constraint.

Example 4. $d \equiv f(a, x)$ **(c)** $\dfrac{}{c \xrightarrow{l_0} c}$ **(f)** $\dfrac{x_1 \xrightarrow{l_0} y_1}{f(x_0, x_1) \xrightarrow{l_0} y_1}$

Suppose that the common signature consists of a, b, c and d as constants and f as a unary operator. Equation $d \equiv f(a, x)$ fits all syntactic criteria of a defining equation (for d), but the one stated above. It follows from **(f)** *that $f(a, c) \xrightarrow{l_0} c$. Since $d \equiv f(a, x)$, then $d \xrightarrow{l_0} c$ and from the same equation (in the other direction), we can deduce that $f(a, b) \xrightarrow{l_0} c$. However, it cannot be derived that $f(b, b) \xrightarrow{l_0} c$. This witnesses that bisimilarity is not a congruence, as $a \leftrightarrow b$ but it does not hold that $f(a, b) \leftrightarrow f(b, b)$.*

The last constraint on defining equations is concerned with freshness of the function symbol being defined. In the following two counter-examples, we show that neither can the defined function symbol cannot appear neither in any other structural congruence equation, nor in the source of the conclusion of a deduction rule.

Example 5. $c \equiv a$ $c \equiv f(b)$ **(a)** $\dfrac{}{a \xrightarrow{l_0} a}$ **(b)** $\dfrac{}{b \xrightarrow{l_0} a}$

Again, in the above specification, we have $a \leftrightarrow b$ but it is not true that $f(a) \leftrightarrow f(b)$ since from the structural congruences, we can derive that $a \equiv_{sc} f(b)$ and hence $f(b)$ can perform an l_0 transition to a while $f(a)$ cannot perform any transition.

Example 6. $f(x) \equiv g(a)$ **(a)** $\dfrac{}{a \xrightarrow{l_0} a}$ **(b)** $\dfrac{}{b \xrightarrow{l_0} a}$ **(f)** $\dfrac{}{f(x) \xrightarrow{l_0} f(x)}$

It follows from the above specification that $a \leftrightarrow b$ but it does not hold that $g(a) \leftrightarrow g(b)$ since the former can perform a transition due to **(struct)** *and* **(f)** *while the latter cannot perform any transition.*

6   Structural Congruences and Negative Premises

Transition system specifications are mainly used to specify transitions of process terms in terms of transitions of their subterms. Sometimes it comes handy to define a transition based on the impossibility of a transition for a particular subterm. Several instances of SOS semantics in the literature make use of this feature (e.g., for defining priority, deadlock detection, sequencing and urgency, cf. [1, 5]). Thus, it seems natural to extend transition system specifications in tyft format to account for negative premises. The following definition realizes this goal.

Definition 9. *(Ntyft Format [7]) A rule is in* ntyft *format if and only if it has the following shape.*

$$(r)\frac{\{t_i \xrightarrow{l_i} y_i | i \in I\} \quad \{t_j \xrightarrow{l_j} | j \in J\}}{f(x_0, \ldots, x_{ar(f)-1}) \xrightarrow{l} t}$$

The same conditions as of tyft *format hold for the positive premises and the conclusion. There is no particular constraint on the terms appearing in the negative premises. Set J is the (possibly infinite) set of indices of negative premises.*

However, in the presence of negative premises, the concepts of proof and provable transitions become more complicated. A proof, as defined before, can provide a reason for presence of a transition but not for its absence. Thus, we have to resort to another notion of proof that can account for absence of transitions, as well. Here, we choose the notion of *stable model* of [5] as an intuitive model of the induced transition relation. The definition is slightly adapted to cater for structural congruences and to fit our notations and past definitions.

Definition 10. *(Stable Model) A positive closed formula ϕ is provable from a set of positive formula T and a transition system specification tss, denoted by $(T, tss) \vdash \phi$, if and only if there is a well-founded upwardly branching tree of which the nodes are labelled by closed formulae such that*

- *the root node is labelled by ϕ, and*
- *if the label of a node q, denoted by ψ, is a positive formula and $\{\psi_i \mid i \in I\}$ is the set of labels of the nodes directly above q, then there is a deduction rule*
$$\frac{\{\chi_i \mid i \in I\} \{t_j \equiv t'_j | j \in J\}}{\chi}$$
in tss (N.B. χ_i can be a positive or a negative formula) and a substitution σ such that $\sigma(\chi) = \psi$, for all $i \in I$, $\sigma(\chi_i) = \psi_i$ and for all $j \in J$, $\sigma(t_j) \equiv_{sc} \sigma(t'_j)$;
- *if the label of a node q, denoted by $p \xrightarrow{l}$, is a negative formula then there exists no p' such that $p \xrightarrow{l} p' \in T$.*

A stable model, also called a transition relation, defined by a transition system specification tss is a set of formulae T such that for all closed positive formulae ϕ, $\phi \in T$ if and only if $(T, tss) \vdash \phi$.

However, not all transition system specifications in ntyft format have a stable model and even if they have, it need not be unique. The following example shows simple instances of such phenomena.

Example 7.
$$\frac{a \xrightarrow{l_0}}{a \xrightarrow{l_0} a} \quad \Big| \quad \frac{a \xrightarrow{l_0}}{b \xrightarrow{l_0} b} \quad \frac{b \xrightarrow{l_0}}{a \xrightarrow{l_0} a}$$

Consider the above two transition system specifications, both defined on a signature with a and b as constants. The left-hand-side TSS has no stable model (as for any stable model $a \xrightarrow{l_0} a$ if and only if $a \xrightarrow{l_0}$) and the right-hand-side one has two stable models, namely, $\{a \xrightarrow{l_0} a\}$, and $\{b \xrightarrow{l_0} b\}$.

To solve this problem, in [5, 7], an extra condition is imposed on transition system specifications in ntyft format. The following definition illustrates this condition.

Definition 11. *(Stratification) A stratification of a transition system specification tss in the* ntyft *format is a function S from closed positive formulae to an ordinal such that for all deduction rules of tss in* ntyft *format (in the shape of rule* (**r**) *in Definition 9) and for all substitutions σ, $\forall_{i \in I} S(\sigma(t_i \xrightarrow{l_i} y_i)) \leq S(\sigma(f(x_0, \ldots, x_{ar(f)-1}) \xrightarrow{l} t'))$ and $\forall_{j \in J, t' \in T(\Sigma)} S(\sigma(t_j \xrightarrow{l_j} t')) < S(\sigma(f(x_0, \ldots, x_{ar(f)-1}) \xrightarrow{l} t'))$. A transition system specification is called stratified if and only if there exists a stratification function for it.*

The following theorem from [5] formalizes the advantages of stratified transition system specifications.

Theorem 3. *Consider a transition system specification tss in the* ntyft *format. If tss is stratified, then it has a unique stable model. Furthermore, bisimilarity is a congruence for the stable model of a stratified transition system specification.*

Now we have enough ingredients to study the implications of negative premises on the structural congruences. Before doing so, we show that a naive treatment of structural congruences, i.e., neglecting them, may ruin the well-definedness of the induced transition relation.

Example 8.
$$\frac{a \xrightarrow{l_0} \!\!\!\!\!/}{b \xrightarrow{l_0} b} \qquad \Bigg| \qquad a \equiv b$$

First, consider the transition system specification given in the left-hand-side (with a and b as constants). It is stratified by the function S, if we define for all closed terms p, $S(a \xrightarrow{l} p) \doteq 1$ and $S(b \xrightarrow{l} p) \doteq 2$. Following Theorem 3, it defines the unique transition relation (its stable model), which is $\{b \xrightarrow{l_0} b\}$.

Then, suppose that we add the structural congruence in the right-hand-side (which is indeed in the cfsc *format) to the specification. Suddenly, the associated transition system specification loses its well-definedness. The combination of the above deduction rule and $a \equiv b$ leads to a contradiction, namely $b \xrightarrow{l_0} b$ if and only if $a \xrightarrow{l_0} \!\!\!\!\!/$ and if $b \xrightarrow{l_0} b$ then $a \xrightarrow{l_0} b$.*

To solve the above mentioned problem, we extend the notion of stratification to structural congruences as follows.

Definition 12. *(Stratification: Extended) Consider a transition system specification tss in* ntyft *format and structural congruence in the* cfsc *format. Then, $tss \cup \{(\textbf{struct})\}$ is stratified, if there exists a function S from closed formulae to an ordinal such that for all closed substitutions σ:*

1. *for all deduction rules in tss of the form* $\dfrac{\{t_i \xrightarrow{l_i} y_i | i \in I\} \quad \{t_j \xrightarrow{l_j} | j \in J\}}{f(x_0, \dots, x_{ar(f)-1}) \xrightarrow{l} t}$, *it*

   holds that $\forall_{i \in I} \mathcal{S}(\sigma(t_i \xrightarrow{l_i} y_i)) \leq \mathcal{S}(\sigma(f(x_0, \dots, x_{ar(f)-1}) \xrightarrow{l} t'))$ *and* $\forall_{j \in J, t' \in T(\Sigma)}$
   $\mathcal{S}(\sigma(t_j \xrightarrow{l_j} t')) < \mathcal{S}(\sigma(f(x_0, \dots, x_{ar(f)-1}) \xrightarrow{l} t'))$,

2. *for all fx equations of the form* $f(x_0, \dots, x_{ar(f)-1}) \equiv g(x_0, \dots, x_{ar(g)-1})$ *in sc, it holds that* $\forall_{l \in L, t \in T(\Sigma)} \; \mathcal{S}(\sigma(f(x_0, \dots, x_{ar(f)-1}) \xrightarrow{l} t)) = \mathcal{S}(\sigma(g(x_0, \dots, x_{ar(g)-1}) \xrightarrow{l} t))$,

3. *for all defining equations of the form* $f(x_0, \dots, x_{ar(f)-1}) \equiv t$ *in sc, it holds that* $\forall_{l \in L, t' \in T(\Sigma)} \; \mathcal{S}(\sigma(t \xrightarrow{l} t')) \leq \mathcal{S}(\sigma(f(x_0, \dots, x_{ar(f)-1}) \xrightarrow{l} t'))$.

Next, we extend the well-definedness theorem for the transition relation to the setting with structural congruences. The following theorem states that if a combination of a transition system specification and structural congruences is stratified, then it defines a unique transition relation.

Theorem 4. *If the combination of transition system tss in ntyft format and tss $\cup$ {(**struct**)} is stratified, then tss $\cup$ {(**struct**)} has a unique stable model. Furthermore, for this model, bisimilarity is a congruence.*

Possible extensions to the ntyft format are the addition of ntyxt rules and predicates. The ntyft-ntyxt format of [7] is a relaxation of ntyft format that allows for variables in the source of the conclusion. In [7], it is shown how to reduce the ntyft-ntyxt format to the ntyft format. Adding structural congruences to TSS's in the ntyft-ntyxt format, however, is not straightforward. The reduction of ntyft-ntyxt to ntyft requires to copy each ntyxt rule for every function symbol in the signature. This reduction thus disallows the presence of any defining equation, as the new deduction rules contain defined function symbols in the source of their conclusion. Thus, up to now, we can only guarantee congruence for a combination of structural congruences and a transition system specification with ntyxt rules if the structural congruences comprise of fx equations only. In [15], we give a solution to this problem by interpreting defining equations as conservative operational extensions to a transition system specification.

Predicates are other ingredients of transition system specifications that are used to specify concepts such as termination and divergence on process terms [20]. Unlike negative premises and ntyxt rules, addition of predicates to a transition system specification has no implication on structural congruences and the cfsc format. Predicates can be modelled as transitions with a dummy right-hand side (a dummy variable in the premises and a dummy constant in the conclusion). Thus, the results that we have proved so far easily extend to the PANTH format of [20] which allows for both ntyft-ntyxt rules and predicates.

7   Case Study

In this section, we quote an SOS semantics of CCS from [11] (with restriction of nondeterminism to finite sum and introduction of the parallel replication operator) and then introduce structural congruences, à la [12], conforming to our format. By doing this, we show how our format is able to capture a number of non-trivial structural congruences and make the presentation look more intuitive and compact. Moreover, from this specification one can still derive congruence for strong bisimilarity automatically.

The syntax of our CCS-like process algebra is given below.

$$P \quad ::= \quad 0 \mid \alpha.P \mid P + Q \mid P \parallel Q \mid P \setminus L \mid !P \mid A$$

In this syntax, constant 0 stands for the terminating process. The action prefix operator $\alpha.P$ (which is actually a class of unary operators parameterized by labels $\alpha \in \mathcal{L}$) shows α as its first step and proceeds with P. The set of labels $\mathcal{L}$ is partitioned into the set of names, typically denoted by l, and co-names, denoted by $\bar{l}$. By extending the same notation, let $\bar{\bar{l}}$ be defined as l. Restriction operator $P \setminus L$, parameterized by $L \subseteq \mathcal{L}$, defines the scope of local names (and co-names). Nondeterministic choice is denoted by $+$. Parallel composition is denoted by $P \parallel Q$. Parallel replication of process P is denoted by $!P$ which usually serves as a restricted substitute for recursion. Recursive symbols A serve as short-hands for their defining processes, denoted by $A \doteq P$ and are used to define processes hierarchically. We treat recursive symbols as constants in our signature.

The transition system specification defining the semantics of our language is given below. In this semantics, $l, \bar{l} \in \mathcal{L}$ and $\alpha \in \mathcal{L} \cup \{\tau\}$, where τ is the result of a communication ($\bar{\tau}$ is defined to be τ).

$$(\textbf{Act}) \frac{}{\alpha.x \xrightarrow{\alpha} x} \qquad (\textbf{Res}) \frac{x \xrightarrow{\alpha} y}{x \setminus L \xrightarrow{\alpha} y \setminus L}(\alpha, \bar{\alpha} \notin L) \qquad (\textbf{Con}) \frac{t \xrightarrow{\alpha} y}{A \xrightarrow{\alpha} y}(A \doteq t)$$

$$(\textbf{Sum0}) \frac{x_0 \xrightarrow{\alpha} y}{x_0 + x_1 \xrightarrow{\alpha} y} \qquad (\textbf{Sum1}) \frac{x_1 \xrightarrow{\alpha} y}{x_0 + x_1 \xrightarrow{\alpha} y} \qquad (\textbf{Rep}) \frac{x \parallel !x \xrightarrow{\alpha} y}{!x \xrightarrow{\alpha} y}$$

$$(\textbf{Com0}) \frac{x_0 \xrightarrow{\alpha} y_0}{x_0 \parallel x_1 \xrightarrow{\alpha} y_0 \parallel x_1} \quad (\textbf{Com1}) \frac{x_1 \xrightarrow{\alpha} y_1}{x_0 \parallel x_1 \xrightarrow{\alpha} x_0 \parallel y_1} \quad (\textbf{Com2}) \frac{x_0 \xrightarrow{l} y_0 \quad x_1 \xrightarrow{\bar{l}} y_1}{x_0 \parallel x_1 \xrightarrow{\tau} y_0 \parallel y_1}$$

In the above specification, rule (**Act**) defines that an action prefix operator can execute its first action and continue with the rest. Each rule in this specification should be considered as a rule schema, representing a possibly infinite number of rules for each $l \in \mathcal{L}$. Side conditions, in this particular case study, only govern presence and absence of such copies. Rule (**Res**) allows for performing actions beyond the restricted set L (i.e., blocks the rest). Rules (**Sum0**) and (**Sum1**) define the non-deterministic choice operator. Rules (**Com0**) and (**Com1**) define the interleaving behavior of parallel composition and rule (**Com2**) defines its communication (synchronization) behavior. Rule (**Con**) shows how recursive constants represent the behavior of their defining terms and finally, **(Rep)** defines the concept of replication.

By using our format, we can copy a number of structural congruences, defined in [12] for the π-calculus and thus, eliminate some of the deduction rules. The result is the following semantic specification.

$$(\textbf{Act})\frac{}{\alpha.x \xrightarrow{\alpha} x} \qquad (\textbf{Res})\frac{x \xrightarrow{\alpha} y}{x \setminus L \xrightarrow{\alpha} y \setminus L}(\alpha, \overline{\alpha} \notin L) \qquad (\textbf{NSum0})\frac{x_0 \xrightarrow{\alpha} y}{x_0 + x_1 \xrightarrow{\alpha} y}$$

$$(\textbf{NCom0})\frac{x_0 \xrightarrow{\alpha} y_0}{x_0 \parallel x_1 \xrightarrow{\alpha} y_0 \parallel y_1} \qquad (\textbf{NCom1})\frac{x_0 \xrightarrow{l} y_0 \quad x_1 \xrightarrow{\overline{l}} y_1}{x_0 \parallel x_1 \xrightarrow{\tau} y_0 \parallel y_1}$$

$$(\textbf{struct})\frac{x \equiv y \quad y \xrightarrow{l} y' \quad y' \equiv x'}{x \xrightarrow{l} x'} \qquad \begin{array}{cc} x + y \equiv y + x & x \parallel y \equiv y \parallel x \\[2mm] A \equiv P \quad (A \doteq P) & !x \equiv x \parallel !x \end{array}$$

Note that all of the SOS rules are in tyft format and the top two structural congruence equations are fx equations while the bottom ones are defining equations. Thus, one may easily deduce from Theorem 2 that strong bisimilarity with respect to the induced transition relation is a congruence. This can already be considered an achievement. However, one may argue that we could not specify some, may be more interesting, structural congruences of [12] such as those for associativity (for parallel composition and nondeterministic choice), idempotency (for nondeterministic choice) and zero element (again for both parallel composition and choice). Our answer to this criticism is that in general, the very same structural congruences (i.e, associativity, idempotency and zero element) can be harmful for congruence. Next, we give an intuitive example of an associativity equation that harms the congruence property.

Example 9. *Take the semantics of our CCS-like language defined before. Suppose that we extend our syntax and semantics with a binary operator $\bullet$. The semantic rule for this operator is given by rule* **(LMer)**$\dfrac{x_0 \xrightarrow{\alpha} y_0}{x_0 \bullet x_1 \xrightarrow{\alpha} y_0 \parallel x_1}$.

According to the above rule, this operator forces the first action to be taken by the left-hand-side argument and then turns into a normal parallel composition operator. (Up to here, this operator is similar to the left-merge operator of [2] which is usually used for finite axiomatization of parallel composition.) This operator, as defined by rule **(LMer)** *is not associative. But, suppose that we also add the equation $x_0 \bullet (x_1 \bullet x_2) \equiv (x_0 \bullet x_1) \bullet x_2$ to our set of structural congruences, to make it associative.*

Then, we can easily observe that the congruence property is ruined. For example, it holds that $0 \leftrightarrow 0 \bullet \alpha$ (where α is a shorthand for $\alpha.0$), since none of the two can perform any action. However, it does not hold that $\alpha \bullet 0 \leftrightarrow \alpha \bullet (0 \bullet \alpha)$. The left-hand term can only perform an α action and terminate (the structural congruence rule cannot help this term perform more actions since it should contain at least two left-merge operators to fit the structure of the equation). While *the right-hand-term is congruent to* $(\alpha \bullet 0) \bullet \alpha$ *and this term can perform two consecutive* α *actions after the first of which it turns into* $(0 \parallel 0) \parallel \alpha$.

8   Conclusions

In this paper, we gave an interpretation of structural congruences inside the transition system specification framework. Using this interpretation, we defined a syntactic congruence format for structural congruences. This format induces congruences for (strong) bisimilarity, once the structural congruences are used in combination with a set of standard (e.g., tyft) SOS rules. Furthermore, the relationship between negative premises in the deduction rules, structural congruences and well-definedness of the transition relation was investigated and a sufficient well-definedness criterium was established. To show the application of our format to a concrete example, we applied our syntactic format to a CCS-like process algebra.

Extending the syntactic format to other notions of equivalence and refinement is a possible extension of our work. Another important extension of our work concerns the notions of names and variable binding.

References

1. L. Aceto, W. J. Fokkink, and C. Verhoef. Structural operational semantics. In *Handbook of Process Algebra, Chapter 3*, pages 197–292. Elsevier Science, 2001.
2. J. C. M. Baeten and W. P. Weijland. *Process Algebra*, volume 18 of *Cambridge Tracts in Theoretical Computer Science*. Cambrdige University Press, 1990.
3. J.-P. Banâtre, P. Fradet, and D. Le Métayer. Gamma and the chemical reaction model: Fifteen years after. In *Multiset Processing: Mathematical, Computer Science, and Molecular Computing Points of View*, volume 2235 of *LNCS*, pages 17–44. Springer, 2001.
4. G. Berry and G. Boudol. The chemical abstract machine. *Theoretical Computer Science*, 96:217–248, 1992.
5. R. Bol and J. F. Groote. The meaning of negative premises in transition system specifications. *Journal of the ACM*, 43(5):863–914, 1996.
6. R. van Glabbeek. The meaning of negative premises in transition system specifications II. *Journal of Logic and Algebraic Programming*, 60:229–258, 2004.
7. J. F. Groote. Transition system specifications with negative premises. *Theoretical Computer Science*, 118(2):263–299, 1993.
8. J. F. Groote and F. W. Vaandrager. Structured operational semantics and bisimulation as a congruence. *Information and Computation*, 100(2):202–260, 1992.
9. K. Honda and N. Yoshida. On reduction-based process semantics. *Theoretical Computer Science*, 152(2):437–486, 1995.
10. J. J. Leifer and R. Milner. Deriving bisimulation congruences for reactive systems. In *Proceedings of CONCUR'00*, volume 1877 of *LNCS*, pages 259–274. Springer, 2000.
11. R. Milner. *Communication and Concurrency*. Prentice Hall, 1989.

12. R. Milner. Functions as processes. *Mathematical Structures in Computer Science*, 2:119–141, 1992.
13. R. Milner. The polyadic π-calculus: a tutorial. In *Logic and Algebra of Specification*, pages 203–246. Springer, 1993.
14. R. Milner and D. Sangiorgi. Barbed bisimulation. In *Proceedings of ICALP'92*, volume 623 of *LNCS*, pages 85–695. Springer, 1992.
15. M.R. Mousavi and M.A. Reniers. Structural congruences and structural operational semantics. Technical report CSR-04-28, Department of Computer Science, Eindhoven University of Technology, Eindhoven, The Netherlands, 2004.
16. D. M. Park. Concurrency and automata on infinite sequences. In *Proceedings of 5th GI Conference*, volume 104 of *LNCS*, pages 167–183. Springer, 1981.
17. G. D. Plotkin. A structural approach to operational semantics. *Journal of Logic and Algebraic Progamming*, 60:17–139, 2004.
18. V. Sassone and P. Sobociński. Deriving bisimulation congruences: 2-categories vs. precategories. In *Proceedings of FOSSACS'03*, volume 2620 of *LNCS*, pages 409–424. Springer, 2003.
19. P. Sewell. From rewrite rules to bisimulation congruences. *Theoretical Computer Science*, 274(1-2):183–230, 2002.
20. C. Verhoef. A congruence theorem for structured operational semantics with predicates and negative premises. *Nordic Journal of Computing*, 2(2):274–302, 1995.

Probabilistic Congruence for Semistochastic Generative Processes

Ruggero Lanotte and Simone Tini

Dipartimento di Scienze della Cultura, Politiche e dell'Informazione,
Università dell'Insubria, Via Valleggio 11, I-22100, Como, Italy

Abstract. We propose an SOS transition rule format for the generative model of probabilistic processes. Transition rules are partitioned in
several strata, giving rise to an ordering relation analogous to those introduced by Ulidowski and Phillips for classic process algebras. Our rule
format guarantees that probabilistic bisimulation is a congruence w.r.t.
process algebra operations. Moreover, our rule format guarantees that
process algebra operations preserve semistochasticity of processes, i.e.
the property that the sum of the probability of the moves of any process
is either 0 or 1. Finally, we show that most of operations of the probabilistic process algebras studied in the literature are captured by our
format, which, therefore, has practical applications.

1 Introduction

Probabilistic process algebras have been introduced in the literature (see, among
the others, [2, 3, 8, 9, 10, 11, 13]) to develop techniques dealing with both functional and non-functional aspects of system behavior, such as performance and
reliability. *Probabilistic transition systems* (PTSs, for short), which extend classic labeled transition systems by some mechanism to represent the probabilistic
choice, have been employed as a basic semantic model of probabilistic processes.
In order to abstract away from irrelevant information on the way that processes
compute, several notions of behavioral *equivalence* and *preorder* have been considered. *Probabilistic bisimulation* relates two processes iff they have the same
probabilistic branching structure. In the process algebras of [2, 3, 8, 9, 10, 11, 13]),
probabilistic bisimulation is a *congruence* w.r.t. all operations, which is an important property to fit it into an axiomatic framework.

Usually, PTSs are defined by means of a *structural operational semantics* [14,
15] (SOS, for short) consisting of a set of *transition rules* of the form $\frac{premises}{conclusion}$,
which, intuitively, determine how probabilistic moves of processes can be inferred
by probabilistic moves of other processes. A set of syntactical constraints on
the transition rules is called a *transition rule format* [16]. In the area of classic
(i.e., non-probabilistic) process algebras, rule formats have been widely employed
to fix results holding for classes of process algebras. For instance, several rule
formats proposed in the literature ensure that a given behavioral equivalence
is a congruence (for a survey see [1]). Other rules formats ensure that a given
property of security is preserved by process algebra operations [17, 18].

V. Sassone (Ed.): FOSSACS 2005, LNCS 3441, pp. 63–78, 2005.

An interesting issue is to develop rule formats for probabilistic process algebras. To take a step in this direction, we propose a rule format for process algebras respecting the *generative* model of probabilistic processes [11], which requires that a single probability distribution is ascribed to all moves of any process. Such a generative model differs w.r.t. the *reactive* model of probabilistic processes, which requires that the kind of action of any process is chosen nondeterministically, and that, for any action and any process, a probability distribution is ascribed to the moves of that process labeled with that action.

Our format admits transition rules of the following form:

$$\frac{\{x_i \xrightarrow{a_i,p_i} y_i \mid i \in I\} \cup \{x_j \xrightarrow{A_j,p_j'} \mid j \in J\} \cup \{x_h \xrightarrow{B_h} \mid h \in H\}}{f(\overrightarrow{x}) \xrightarrow{a, \frac{\Pi_{i \in I} \, p_i}{\Pi_{j \in J}(1-p_j')} \cdot w_\rho} t}$$

Hence, our format extends the classic *de Simone format* [16] with probability (i.e., a probability value p appears in transition labels), premises $x_j \xrightarrow{A_j,p_j'}$ meaning that the argument j of f performs actions in the set A_j with total probability p_j', and premises $x_h \xrightarrow{B_h}$ meaning that the argument h of f performs at least one action in the set B_h. Then, to give a semantics to a given process algebra, we require that the transition rules are partitioned in n *strata* $\mathcal{R}_1, \ldots, \mathcal{R}_n$, for some $n \in \mathbb{N}$. The interpretation is that the moves of a given process t can be inferred from rules in $\mathcal{R}_i$ only if no move of t can be inferred from rules in $\mathcal{R}_j$, for any $j < i$. Hence, the partitioning gives rise to an ordering relation between transition rules analogous to those introduced for classic process algebras in [19].

We prove that process algebra operations captured by our format preserve *semistochasticity* of processes, i.e. the property that the sum of the probability of the moves of any process is either 0 or 1. This is a central issue in the theory of probabilistic processes, since semistochasticity is required by most of authors, such as [3,5,8], which concentrate on so called *semistochastic languages* [11].

Then, we prove that probabilistic bisimulation is a congruence w.r.t. all operations captured by our format.

To show that our format has practical applications, we prove that it captures most of operations of the probabilistic process algebras proposed in the literature.

Finally, we prove that our format can be enriched by *double testing* as in *GSOS format* [7], and by *look ahead* as in *tyft/tyxt format* [12]. We discuss also the possibility to admit *predicates*, as in formats *path* [4] and *panth* [20].

We discuss the related work [6], where a very preliminary rule format for the reactive model of probabilistic processes is introduced.

2 Background

Let us begin with recalling the model of probabilistic transition systems.

For any set S, let $\mathcal{M}(S)$ denote the collection of multisets over S.

Definition 1. *A probabilistic transition system (PTS, for short) is a triple* $(\mathcal{S}, Act, T)$, *where* $\mathcal{S}$ *is a set of* states, Act *is a set of* actions, *and* $T \in \mathcal{M}(\mathcal{S} \times$

$Act \times (0,1] \times S)$ *is a multiset of* transitions *such that, for all states* $s \in S$, $\sum \{\!| \, p \,|\, \exists a \in Act, s' \in S : (s,a,p,s') \in T \,|\!\} \in [0,1]$.

Def. 1 respects the *generative* (or *full*) model of probabilistic processes [11], where a single probability distribution is ascribed to all moves of any process. On the contrary, we recall that the *reactive* model admits that the kind of action is chosen nondeterministically, i.e. the multiset T satisfies the following property: for all states $s \in S$ and actions $a \in Act$, $\sum \{\!| \, p \,|\, \exists s' \in S : (s,a,p,s') \in T \,|\!\} \in [0,1]$.

Definition 2. *A state* $s \in S$ *is semistochastic iff* $\sum \{\!| \, p \,|\, \exists a \in Act, s' \in S : (s,a,p,s') \in T \,|\!\} \in \{0,1\}$. *If this sum is 1 then* s *is* stochastic. *A PTS is semistochastic iff all its states are semistochastic.*

As in [3, 5, 8], we concentrate on semistochastic PTSs, which are the semantic model of the so called *semistochastic languages* [11].

We write $s \xrightarrow{a,p} s'$ to denote that $(s,a,p,s') \in T$, and we call s and s' *source* and *target* of the transition, respectively. For a set of actions $A \subseteq Act$, we write $s \xrightarrow{A,p}$ to denote that $\sum \{\!| \, q \,|\, \exists a \in A, s' \in S : s \xrightarrow{a,q} s' \,|\!\} = p$. If this multiset is empty, then we write $s \xrightarrow{A,0}$. Finally, we write $s \xrightarrow{A}$ to denote that there is at least one transition (s,a,p,s') in T with $a \in A$, for some p and s'.

Before defining probabilistic bisimulation, we need some definitions.

For an equivalence relation $\mathcal{R}$ over S, we write $S/\mathcal{R}$ to denote the set of equivalence classes induced by $\mathcal{R}$.

Definition 3. $\mu : S \times Act \times 2^S \rightarrow [0,1]$ *is the function given by:* $\forall s \in S$, $\forall a \in Act$, $\forall S \subseteq S$

$$\mu(s,a,S) = \sum \{\!| \, p \,|\, s \xrightarrow{a,p} s' \text{ and } s' \in S \,|\!\}$$

Definition 4. *An equivalence relation* $\mathcal{R} \subseteq S \times S$ *is a* probabilistic bisimulation *if* $(s_1, s_2) \in \mathcal{R}$ *implies:* $\forall S \in S/\mathcal{R}$, $\forall a \in Act$,

$$\mu(s_1, a, S) = \mu(s_2, a, S)$$

The union of all probabilistic bisimulation is, in turn, a probabilistic bisimulation. We denote it by $\approx$, and we write $s_1 \approx s_2$ for $(s_1, s_2) \in \approx$.

Let us recall now the notions of signature and term over a signature.

A *signature* is a set Σ of *operation symbols* together with an *arity* mapping that assigns a natural $ar(f)$ to every $f \in \Sigma$. If $ar(f)$ is 0, f is called a *constant*.

For a set of *variables* Var, ranged over by $x, y, \ldots$, the set of (*open*) *terms* $T(\Sigma, \text{Var})$ over Σ and Var, ranged over by $s, t, \ldots$, is the least set such that: 1) each variable $x \in$ Var is a term; 2) $f(t_1, \ldots, t_{ar(f)})$ is a term whenever $f \in \Sigma$ and $t_1, \ldots, t_{ar(f)}$ are terms. *Closed terms* are terms that do not contain variables.

A *substitution* is a mapping $\sigma : \text{Var} \rightarrow T(\Sigma, \text{Var})$. With $\sigma(t)$ we denote the term obtained by replacing all occurrences of variables x in term t by $\sigma(x)$.

The abstract syntax of probabilistic process description languages is usually given by a signature Σ, whose closed terms are called *probabilistic processes*. The semantics is usually given by a PTS, where states are probabilistic processes.

3   Definitions

In this section we introduce the notions of PB transition rule and PB transition system specification (PB stays for probabilistic bisimulation).

Definition 5. *For any operation $f \in \Sigma$ and tuple $\overrightarrow{x} = x_1, \ldots, x_{ar(f)}$ of variables, a PB transition rule ρ is of the form*

$$\frac{\{x_i \xrightarrow{a_i, p_i} y_i \mid i \in I\} \cup \{x_j \xrightarrow{A_j, p'_j} \mid j \in J\} \cup \{x_h \xrightarrow{B_h} \mid h \in H\}}{f(\overrightarrow{x}) \xrightarrow{a, \frac{\Pi_{i \in I} p_i}{\Pi_{j \in J}(1-p'_j)} \cdot w_\rho} t}$$

where:

1. *I, J, H are subsets of $\{1, \ldots, ar(f)\}$ such that $J \subseteq I$;*
2. *$a_i \in Act$ for $i \in I$, $A_j \subseteq Act$ for $j \in J$, $B_h \subseteq Act$ for $h \in H$, $a \in Act$;*
3. *for all $i \in I$ and $j \in J$ such that $i = j$, it holds that $a_i \notin A_j$;*
4. *p_i is a variable with range $(0, 1]$ for $i \in I$, p'_j is a variable with range $[0, 1)$ for $j \in J$;*
5. *t is a term over Σ and $\overrightarrow{x} \cup \{y_i \mid i \in I\}$;*
6. *w_ρ is the weight of ρ and satisfies $0 < w_\rho \leq 1$.*

Transitions $\{x_i \xrightarrow{a_i, p_i} y_i \mid i \in I\}$ are the *active premises*; variables $\{x_i \mid i \in I\}$ are the *active variables*; transitions $\{x_j \xrightarrow{A_j, p'_j} \mid j \in J\}$ are the *unneeded premises*; transitions $\{x_h \xrightarrow{B_h} \mid h \in H\}$ are the *unquantified premises*; transition $f(\overrightarrow{x}) \xrightarrow{a, \frac{\Pi_{i \in I} p_i}{\Pi_{j \in J}(1-p'_j)} \cdot w_\rho} t$ is the *conclusion*; $f(\overrightarrow{x})$ is the *source*; t is the *target* of ρ.

Given terms $\overrightarrow{t}$, values $\{q_i \mid i \in I\}$ in $(0, 1]$, and values $\{q'_j \mid j \in J\}$ in $[0, 1)$, Def. 5 says that term $f(\overrightarrow{t})$ has the move $f(\overrightarrow{t}) \xrightarrow{a, q} t[\overrightarrow{t}/\overrightarrow{x}][\overrightarrow{s}/\overrightarrow{y}]$, with $q = \frac{\Pi_{i \in I} q_i}{\Pi_{j \in J}(1-q'_j)} \cdot w_\rho$, provided that t_i has the move $t_i \xrightarrow{a_i, q_i} s_i$, for all $i \in I$, the sum of the probability of the moves of t_j with label in A_j is q'_j, for all $j \in J$, and t_h has at least one move with label in B_h, for all $h \in H$.

Notice that the conclusion is triggered by both active and unquantified premises, and does not require unneeded premises, meaning that p'_j could be 0 for some $j \in J$. Unneeded premises are used to compute the probability of the conclusion. More precisely, they permit normalization of probability, which, as we will see in next sections, is needed in several operations of process algebras, such as restriction and priority. The probability of the conclusion depends on the weight of ρ and on $\frac{\Pi_{i \in I} p_i}{\Pi_{j \in J}(1-p'_j)}$, which is the conditional probability that all x_i perform a_i under the assumption that all x_j are not allowed to perform actions in A_j. Unquantified premises do not contribute in computing the probability of the conclusion. They are "necessary conditions" for the application of ρ.

Definition 6. *A PB transition system specification (PB TSS, for short) is formed by a set $\mathcal{R}$ of PB transition rules such that:*

1. $\mathcal{R}$ is partitioned into n strata $\mathcal{R}_1, \ldots, \mathcal{R}_n$, for some $n \in \mathbb{N}$;
2. for each stratum $\mathcal{R}_u$, operation f and tuple of variables $\overrightarrow{x} = x_1, \ldots, x_{ar(f)}$
   s.t. $\mathcal{R}_u$ has at least one PB transition rule with source $f(\overrightarrow{x})$, it holds that:
   (a) All PB transition rules with source $f(\overrightarrow{x})$ in stratum $\mathcal{R}_u$ have the same
       set of unquantified premises $\{x_h \xrightarrow{B_h} \mid h \in H\}$;
   (b) All PB transition rules with source $f(\overrightarrow{x})$ in stratum $\mathcal{R}_u$ have the same
       set of unneeded premises $\{x_j \xrightarrow{A_j, p'_j} \mid j \in J\}$;
   (c) All PB transition rules with source $f(\overrightarrow{x})$ in stratum $\mathcal{R}_u$ have the same
       set of active variables $\{x_i \mid i \in I\}$;
   (d) Given actions $\{a'_i \mid i \in I\}$ such that $a'_i \notin A_j$ for all indexes i and j
       with $i = j$ and $x_j \xrightarrow{A_j, p'_j}$ an unneeded premise, then there is at least
       one PB transition rule with source $f(\overrightarrow{x})$ in $\mathcal{R}_u$ with active premises
       $\{x_i \xrightarrow{a'_i, p_i} y_i \mid i \in I\}$;
   (e) Given the PB transition rules $\rho_1, \ldots, \rho_m$ in $\mathcal{R}_u$ with source $f(\overrightarrow{x})$ having
       the same active premises, their weights satisfy $w_{\rho_1} + \cdots + w_{\rho_m} = 1$.

The meaning of clause 1 is that the rules in stratum $\mathcal{R}_u$ can be applied only if no rule in strata $\mathcal{R}_1, \ldots, \mathcal{R}_{u-1}$ can be applied (see Def. 7 below).

Let us take any $f \in \Sigma$. Clause 2a implies that unquantified premises trigger either all rules with source $f(\overrightarrow{x})$ in $\mathcal{R}_u$, or none of them. In the first case, we can prove that clauses 2b–2e ensure that, given semistochastic processes $\overrightarrow{t}$, then the sum of the probability of the moves of $f(\overrightarrow{t})$ that are derivable by the rules in $\mathcal{R}_u$ is either 0 or 1. Let us distinguish two cases. In the first case, some t_i with $i \in I$ is not stochastic. Since it is semistochastic, t_i has no move. Hence, since clause 2c implies that a move of t_i is needed to infer a move of $f(\overrightarrow{t})$, no move of $f(\overrightarrow{t})$ can be derived from the rules in stratum $\mathcal{R}_u$, and, therefore, the sum of the probability of the moves of $f(\overrightarrow{t})$ derivable from $\mathcal{R}_u$ is 0. In the second case, all t_i with $i \in I$ are stochastic. Let us assume that, for all $j \in J$, q'_j is the probability such that $t_j \xrightarrow{A_j, q'_j}$. Value $\prod_{j \in J}(1 - q'_j)$ is the probability that each t_j does not perform any action in A_j. All combinations of arbitrary moves $\{t_i \xrightarrow{a_i, q_i} t'_i \mid i \in I\}$, with $a_i \in Act$ for each $i \in I$, fall into two categories:

- Some a_i is in A_j for the index $j = i$. Clause 3 of Def. 5 ensures that no move
  of $f(\overrightarrow{t})$ is inferred by rules in $\mathcal{R}_u$ from moves $\{t_i \xrightarrow{a_i, q_i} t'_i \mid i \in I\}$.
- No a_i is such that $a_i \in A_j$ for any index $j = i$. Since t_i is semistochas-
  tic, this implies $q'_j \neq 1$ for all $j \in J$. By clause 2d of Def. 6 there exist
  rules $\rho_1, \ldots, \rho_m$ with source $f(\overrightarrow{x})$ in $\mathcal{R}_u$, for some $m \in \mathbb{N}$, with active
  premises $\{x_i \xrightarrow{a_i, p_i} y_i \mid i \in I\}$. Hence, $f(\overrightarrow{t})$ has m moves with probabilities
  $w_{\rho_1} \cdot \frac{\prod_{i \in I} q_i}{\prod_{j \in J}(1 - q'_j)}, \ldots, w_{\rho_m} \cdot \frac{\prod_{i \in I} q_i}{\prod_{j \in J}(1 - q'_j)}$. Notice that these probabilities are well
  defined, since $q'_j \neq 1$ for all $j \in J$. Now, since $w_{\rho_1} + \cdots + w_{\rho_m} = 1$ by clause
  2e of Def. 6, the sum of these probabilities is $\frac{\prod_{i \in I} q_i}{\prod_{j \in J}(1 - q'_j)}$.

Since we have assumed that all $\overrightarrow{t}$ are stochastic, and that for all $j \in J$, q'_j is the probability of $t_j \xrightarrow{A_j, q'_j}$, the overall probabilities of the combinations of moves $\{t_i \xrightarrow{a_i, q_i} t'_i \mid i \in I\}$ falling in the second category is $\prod_{j \in J}(1 - q'_j)$. Hence, if $q'_j = 1$ for some $j \in J$, $f(\overrightarrow{t})$ has no move and the sum of the probability of the moves of $f(\overrightarrow{t})$ derivable from $\mathcal{R}_u$ is 0. Otherwise, if $q'_j \neq 1$ for all $j \in J$, the sum of the probability of the moves of $f(\overrightarrow{t})$ derivable from $\mathcal{R}_u$ is $\frac{\prod_{j \in J}(1 - q'_j)}{\prod_{j \in J}(1 - q'_j)} = 1$.

We can now formalize how PTSs are generated by PB TSSs.

Definition 7. *Assume a PB TSS with strata $\mathcal{R}_1, \dots, \mathcal{R}_n$.*

1. *A transition $t \xrightarrow{a, q} s$ is provable from stratum $\mathcal{R}_u$ iff there is a closed substitution instance $\dfrac{\{t_i \xrightarrow{a_i, q_i} s_i \mid i \in I\} \cup \{t_j \xrightarrow{A_j, q'_j} \mid j \in J\} \cup \{t_h \xrightarrow{B_h} \mid h \in H\}}{t \xrightarrow{a, q} s}$ of a PB transition rule in $\mathcal{R}_u$ such that:*

   (a) *for all $i \in I$, $t_i \xrightarrow{a_i, q_i} s_i$ is a transition provable from the TSS;*

   (b) *for all $j \in J$, $q'_j = \sum \{\!\!\{q \mid \exists a \in A_j, s' : t_j \xrightarrow{a, q} s' \text{ is provable from the TSS}\}\!\!\}$;*

   (c) *for all $h \in H$, at least one transition $t_h \xrightarrow{a, q_h} u_h$ with $a \in B_h$ is provable from the TSS, for some q_h and u_h;*

2. *A transition $t \xrightarrow{a, q} s$ is provable from the TSS if it is provable from some stratum $\mathcal{R}_u$ and no transition with source t is provable from strata $\mathcal{R}_1, \dots, \mathcal{R}_{u-1}$.*

Moves of terms are proved inductively w.r.t. their structure. In fact, first of all we can prove moves of constants from strata $\mathcal{R}_1, \dots, \mathcal{R}_n$ and, then, we can prove moves of constants from the TSS. This is possible since PB transition rules having a constant as source have no premise. Then, after moves of terms $\overrightarrow{t}$ have been proved from the TSS, we can prove moves of $f(\overrightarrow{t})$ from $\mathcal{R}_1, \dots, \mathcal{R}_n$ and, then, we can prove moves of $f(\overrightarrow{t})$ from the TSS.

Let us recall that, according to the classical definition (see, e.g., [12]), a (non-probabilistic) transition $t \xrightarrow{a} t'$ is provable from a given TSS iff there exists a well-founded, upwardly branching tree whose nodes are labeled by closed transitions, whose leaves have empty label, whose root is labeled by $t \xrightarrow{a} t'$, and, whenever K is the (possibly empty) set of labels of the nodes directly above a node labeled by β, then K/β is a closed substitution instance of a transition rule in the TSS.

We need a more complicated definition since our rules have the unneeded premises and the unquantified premises that are not "pure" transitions. Hence, we cannot construct the branching tree that is considered in the classical definition. Moreover, as in [19], we have to take into account that there is an ordering relation between the transition rules, given by the partitioning in n strata.

Definition 8. *The PTS induced by a PB TSS is the PTS having as transitions the transitions that are provable from the TSS.*

4   Examples

In this section we show that most of operations offered by the probabilistic process algebras proposed in the literature can be expressed by our PB TSSs.

Example 1 (Constants). Stratum $\mathcal{R}_1$ contains the following rule, for all $a \in Act$:

$$\frac{}{a \xrightarrow{a,1} 0}$$

Term a performs action a, and, then, it behaves as the idle process 0.

Let us show now that we can express the probabilistic sum of [2, 3, 8, 9, 11].

Example 2 (Probabilistic sum). Let $0 < p < 1$. Stratum $\mathcal{R}_1$ contains the following rules, for all $a_1, a_2 \in Act$, where p and $1 - p$ are their weights:

$$\frac{x_1 \xrightarrow{a_1,p_1} y_1 \quad x_2 \xrightarrow{a_2,p_2} y_2}{x_1 +^p x_2 \xrightarrow{a_1,p_1 \cdot p_2 \cdot p} y_1} \qquad \frac{x_1 \xrightarrow{a_1,p_1} y_1 \quad x_2 \xrightarrow{a_2,p_2} y_2}{x_1 +^p x_2 \xrightarrow{a_2,p_1 \cdot p_2 \cdot (1-p)} y_2}$$

Stratum $\mathcal{R}_2$ contains the following rule, for all $a_1 \in Act$:

$$\frac{x_1 \xrightarrow{a_1,p_1} y_1}{x_1 +^p x_2 \xrightarrow{a_1,p_1} y_1}$$

Stratum $\mathcal{R}_3$ contains the following rule, for all $a_2 \in Act$:

$$\frac{x_2 \xrightarrow{a_2,p_2} y_2}{x_1 +^p x_2 \xrightarrow{a_2,p_2} y_2}$$

Let us take term $t_1 +^p t_2$. Index p means that, when both t_1 and t_2 can move, t_1 moves with probability p, and t_2 moves with probability $1 - p$. Rules in $\mathcal{R}_1$ (with weights p and $1 - p$) are applied when both t_1 and t_2 are stochastic; rules in $\mathcal{R}_2$ (with weight 1) are applied when only t_1 is stochastic; rules in $\mathcal{R}_3$ (with weight 1) are applied when only t_2 is stochastic. In the first case, since t_2 (resp. t_1) is stochastic and the sum of the probability of its moves is 1, from $t_1 \xrightarrow{a_1,p_1} t'_1$ (resp. $t_2 \xrightarrow{a_2,p_2} t'_2$) we infer moves of $t_1 +^p t_2$ labeled a_1 (resp. a_2) with total probability $p_1 \cdot p$ (resp. $p_2 \cdot (1-p)$). In the other two cases, from $t_1 \xrightarrow{a_1,p_1} t'_1$ (resp. $t_2 \xrightarrow{a_2,p_2} t'_2$), we infer $t_1 +^p t_2 \xrightarrow{a_1,p_1} t'_1$ (resp. $t_1 +^p t_2 \xrightarrow{a_2,p_2} t'_2$).

Let us consider now the interleaving operation of [3].

Example 3 (Interleaving). Let $0 < p < 1$. Stratum $\mathcal{R}_1$ contains the following rules, for all $a_1, a_2 \in Act$, where p and $1 - p$ are their weights:

$$\frac{x_1 \xrightarrow{a_1,p_1} y_1 \quad x_2 \xrightarrow{a_2,p_2} y_2}{x_1 \parallel^p x_2 \xrightarrow{a_1,p_1 \cdot p_2 \cdot p} y_1 \parallel^p x_2} \qquad \frac{x_1 \xrightarrow{a_1,p_1} y_1 \quad x_2 \xrightarrow{a_2,p_2} y_2}{x_1 \parallel^p x_2 \xrightarrow{a_2,p_1 \cdot p_2 \cdot (1-p)} x_1 \parallel^p y_2}$$

Stratum $\mathcal{R}_2$ contains the following rules, for all $a_1 \in Act$:

$$\frac{x_1 \xrightarrow{a_1,p_1} y_1}{x_1 \parallel^p x_2 \xrightarrow{a_1,p_1} y_1 \parallel^p x_2}$$

Stratum $\mathcal{R}_3$ contains the following rules, for all $a_2 \in Act$:

$$\frac{x_2 \xrightarrow{a_2,p_2} y_2}{x_1 \parallel^p x_2 \xrightarrow{a_2,p_2} x_1 \parallel^p y_2}$$

As in Ex. 2, given a term $t_1 \parallel^p t_2$, index p means that, when both t_1 and t_2 can move, t_1 moves with probability p, and t_2 moves with probability $1 - p$.

Let us consider now the synchronous product of PCCS [10, 11].

Example 4 (Synchronous product). Stratum $\mathcal{R}_1$ contains the following rules, for all $a_1, a_2 \in Act$:

$$\frac{x_1 \xrightarrow{a_1,p_1} y_1 \quad x_2 \xrightarrow{a_2,p_2} y_2}{x_1 \parallel x_2 \xrightarrow{a_1 \times a_2,p_1 \cdot p_2} y_1 \parallel y_2}$$

Here, at each computation step, term $t_1 \parallel t_2$ can move only by combining an action of t_1 and an action of t_2. Actions are composed by means of operator $\times$.

Let us consider now the probabilistic version of CCS parallel composition [3].

Example 5 (Interleaving plus synchronization). Let $0 < p, q < 1$. Stratum $\mathcal{R}_1$ contains the following rules, for all $a_1, a_2 \in Act$ such that $a_2 \neq \overline{a_1}$:

$$\frac{x_1 \xrightarrow{a_1,p_1} y_1 \quad x_2 \xrightarrow{a_2,p_2} y_2}{x_1 \parallel_q^p x_2 \xrightarrow{a_1,p_1 \cdot p_2 \cdot p} y_1 \parallel_q^p x_2} \qquad \frac{x_1 \xrightarrow{a_1,p_1} y_1 \quad x_2 \xrightarrow{a_2,p_2} y_2}{x_1 \parallel_q^p x_2 \xrightarrow{a_2,p_1 \cdot p_2 \cdot (1-p)} x_1 \parallel_q^p y_2}$$

$$\frac{x_1 \xrightarrow{a_1,p_1} y_1 \quad x_2 \xrightarrow{\overline{a_1},p_2} y_2}{x_1 \parallel_q^p x_2 \xrightarrow{a_1,p_1 \cdot p_2 \cdot p \cdot (1-q)} y_1 \parallel_q^p x_2} \qquad \frac{x_1 \xrightarrow{a_1,p_1} y_1 \quad x_2 \xrightarrow{\overline{a_1},p_2} y_2}{x_1 \parallel_q^p x_2 \xrightarrow{\overline{a_1},p_1 \cdot p_2 \cdot (1-p) \cdot (1-q)} x_1 \parallel_q^p y_2}$$

$$\frac{x_1 \xrightarrow{a_1,p_1} y_1 \quad x_2 \xrightarrow{\overline{a_1},p_2} y_2}{x_1 \parallel_q^p x_2 \xrightarrow{\tau,p_1 \cdot p_2 \cdot q} y_1 \parallel_q^p y_2}$$

Stratum $\mathcal{R}_2$ contains the following rules, for all $a_1 \in Act$:

$$\frac{x_1 \xrightarrow{a_1,p_1} y_1}{x_1 \parallel_q^p x_2 \xrightarrow{a_1,p_1} y_1 \parallel_q^p x_2}$$

Stratum $\mathcal{R}_3$ contains the following rules, for all $a_2 \in Act$:

$$\frac{x_2 \xrightarrow{a_2,p_2} y_2}{x_1 \parallel_q^p x_2 \xrightarrow{a_2,p_2} x_1 \parallel_q^p y_2}$$

Let us take $t_1 \parallel_q^p t_2$. When t_1 and t_2 intend to perform actions a_1 and a_2 with $a_2 \neq \overline{a_1}$, t_1 moves with probability p and t_2 moves with probability $1 - p$, as in the case of interleaving operator of Ex. 3. When t_1 and t_2 intend to perform actions a_1 and $\overline{a_1}$, either they synchronize with probability q, thus producing action τ, or they do not synchronize with probability $1 - q$. In this second case, t_1 moves with probability $p \cdot (1-q)$, and t_2 moves with probability $(1-p) \cdot (1-q)$.

Let us consider now the operation of sequential composition of terms of [3].

Example 6 (Sequencing). Stratum $\mathcal{R}_1$ contains the following rules, for $a_1 \in Act$:

$$\frac{x_1 \xrightarrow{a_1, p_1} y_1}{x_1 \cdot x_2 \xrightarrow{a_1, p_1} y_1 \cdot x_2}$$

Stratum $\mathcal{R}_2$ contains the following transition rules, for all $a_2 \in Act$:

$$\frac{x_2 \xrightarrow{a_2, p_2} y_2}{x_1 \cdot x_2 \xrightarrow{a_2, p_2} y_2}$$

Let us take $t_1 \cdot t_2$. If t_1 moves, then rules in $\mathcal{R}_1$ can be applied and $t_1 \cdot t_2$ moves as t_1, else, if t_2 moves, rules in $\mathcal{R}_2$ can be applied and $t_1 \cdot t_2$ moves as t_2.

Let us consider now the restriction operation of [2, 8, 9, 11]. This is the first example in which we employ unneeded premises.

Example 7 (Restriction). Let $A \subseteq Act$. Stratum $\mathcal{R}_1$ contains the following rules, for all $a_1 \in Act \setminus A$:

$$\frac{x_1 \xrightarrow{a_1, p_1} y_1 \quad x_1 \xrightarrow{A, p}}{x_1 \setminus A \xrightarrow{a_1, \frac{p_1}{1-p}} y_1 \setminus A}$$

Term $t_1 \setminus A$ behaves as t_1, but it cannot perform actions in A. Let us assume that the sum of the probability of the moves of t_1 with label in A is q, i.e. $t_1 \xrightarrow{A, q}$. If $q = 1$, then no move of $t_1 \setminus A$ can be inferred by the rules in $\mathcal{R}_1$. Hence, $t_1 \setminus A$ has no move and it is semistochastic. If t_1 has a move $t_1 \xrightarrow{a_1, q_1} t_1'$, with $a_1 \notin A$, then $t_1 \setminus A$ has the same move, but with probability $\frac{q_1}{1-q}$, which is the conditional probability that t_1 has the move $t_1 \xrightarrow{a_1, q_1} t_1'$ under the assumption that t_1 is not allowed to perform actions in A. Hence, the sum of the probability of the moves of $t_1 \setminus A$ is $\frac{1-q}{1-q} = 1$, and $t_1 \setminus A$ is stochastic.

Let us consider now the operator of priority. This is the first example in which we employ unquantified premises.

Example 8 (Priority of a over b). Let $a, b \in Act$. Stratum $\mathcal{R}_1$ contains the following rules, for all $a_1 \in Act \setminus \{b\}$:

$$\frac{x_1 \xrightarrow{a_1, p_1} y_1 \quad x_1 \xrightarrow{\{b\}, p} \quad x_1 \xrightarrow{\{a\}}}{\vartheta_b^a(x_1) \xrightarrow{a_1, \frac{p_1}{1-p}} \vartheta_b^a(y_1)}$$

Stratum $\mathcal{R}_2$ contains the following rules, for all $a_1 \in Act$:

$$\frac{x_1 \xrightarrow{a_1,p_1} y_1}{\vartheta_b^a(x_1) \xrightarrow{a_1,p_1} \vartheta_b^a(y_1)}$$

Term $\vartheta_b^a(t_1)$ behaves as t_1, but it can perform action b only if it cannot perform a. Rules in $\mathcal{R}_1$ are applied only if t_1 can perform a. In this case, if the sum of the probability of the moves of t_1 labeled b is q (i.e. $t_1 \xrightarrow{\{b\},q}$), then, from any move $t_1 \xrightarrow{a_1,q_1} t_1'$ with $a_1 \neq b$, we infer a move of $\vartheta_b^a(t_1)$ with label a_1 and probability $\frac{q_1}{1-q}$, which is the conditional probability that t_1 has the move $t_1 \xrightarrow{a_1,q_1} t_1'$ under the assumption that t_1 is not allowed to perform b. So, the sum of the probability of the moves of $\vartheta_b^a(t_1)$ is $\frac{1-q}{1-q} = 1$, and $\vartheta_b^a(t_1)$ is stochastic. Rules in $\mathcal{R}_2$ can be applied only if t_1 cannot perform a. In this case, $\vartheta_b^a(t_1)$ behaves as t_1.

5   Results

Theorem 1. *The PTS induced by any PB TSS is semistochastic.*

Proof. We have to prove that, given an arbitrary term t, the sum of the probability of the moves of t is either 0 or 1. This property follows by two facts: 1) The moves of t can be derived only by the rules that are in one stratum $\mathcal{R}_u$; 2) the sum of the probability of the moves of t derivable by the rules in any stratum $\mathcal{R}_u$ is either 0 or 1, as we have proved in the previous section.   □

Theorem 2. *The probabilistic bisimulation induced by any PB TSS is a congruence.*

Proof. Let R be the least equivalence relation over PTS states such that:

1. $s \, R \, t$ whenever $s \approx t$;
2. $f(\overrightarrow{s}) \, R \, f(\overrightarrow{t})$ whenever $s_1 \, R \, t_1, \ldots, s_{ar(f)} \, R \, t_{ar(f)}$.

Lemma 1. *Given a term u over variables $\overrightarrow{x} = x_1, \ldots, x_n$ and tuples of terms $\overrightarrow{s} = s_1, \ldots, s_n$ and $\overrightarrow{t} = t_1, \ldots, t_n$, if $s_i \, R \, t_i$ holds for all $1 \leq i \leq n$, then $u[\overrightarrow{t}/\overrightarrow{x}] \, R \, u[\overrightarrow{s}/\overrightarrow{x}]$.*

To prove the thesis, it suffices to prove that, for arbitrary terms s and t, $s \, R \, t$ implies $s \approx t$. In fact, by the two clauses of the definition of R, this property implies that R and $\approx$ coincide and that $\approx$ is a congruence.

Let us reason by induction over the definition of R. The base case where $s \, R \, t$ is due to $s \approx t$ is immediate. Let us concentrate on the inductive step, where $s \equiv f(\overrightarrow{s})$, $t \equiv f(\overrightarrow{t})$, and $s \, R \, t$ is due to $s_1 \, R \, t_1, \ldots, s_{ar(f)} \, R \, t_{ar(f)}$. We can assume, by the inductive hypothesis, that $s_1 \approx t_1, \ldots, s_{ar(f)} \approx t_{ar(f)}$.

We have to prove that, for any value $0 < q \le 1$, action $a \in Act$ and equivalence class $S \in \mathcal{S}/R$, $\mu(f(\overrightarrow{s}), a, S) = q$ iff $\mu(f(\overrightarrow{t}), a, S) = q$. We prove that $\mu(f(\overrightarrow{s}), a, S) = q$ implies $\mu(f(\overrightarrow{t}), a, S) = q$; the converse is analogous.

Since $\mu(f(\overrightarrow{s}), a, S) = q$, it holds that in some stratum $\mathcal{R}_u$ of the TSS, and for some $k \in \mathbb{N}$, there exist PB transition rules $\rho_1, \ldots, \rho_k$ such that:

1. for all $1 \le l \le k$, from rule ρ_l we infer m_l transitions $f(\overrightarrow{s}) \xrightarrow{a, q_{l,1}} u_{l,1}, \ldots,$ $f(\overrightarrow{s}) \xrightarrow{a, q_{l,m_l}} u_{l,m_l}$, for some $m_l \in \mathbb{N}$;
2. $\sum_{1 \le l \le k} \sum_{1 \le i \le m_l} q_{l,i} = q$;
3. for all $1 \le l \le k$, $u_{l,1}, \ldots, u_{l,m_l} \in S$,

and, moreover, no move of $f(\overrightarrow{s})$ is derived from rules in $\mathcal{R}_1, \ldots, \mathcal{R}_{u-1}$.

Let us consider any $1 \le l \le k$. Transition rule ρ_l has the form

$$\frac{\{x_i \xrightarrow{a_i, p_i} y_i \mid i \in I\} \cup \{x_j \xrightarrow{A_j, p'_j} \mid j \in J\} \cup \{x_h \xrightarrow{B_h} \mid h \in H\}}{f(\overrightarrow{x}) \xrightarrow{a, \frac{\prod_{i \in I} p_i}{\prod_{j \in J}(1 - p'_j)} \cdot w_{\rho_l}} t}$$

Since $f(\overrightarrow{s}) \xrightarrow{a, q_{l,1}} u_{l,1}, \ldots, f(\overrightarrow{s}) \xrightarrow{a, q_{l,m_l}} u_{l,m_l}$ are derived from ρ_l, it holds that:

1. for all $i \in I$, there are states S_i s.t. $\mu(s_i, a_i, S_i) = q_i$, for some $0 < q_i \le 1$;
2. for all $j \in J$, $s_j \xrightarrow{A_j, q'_j}$, for some $0 \le q'_j < 1$;
3. for all $h \in H$, $s_h \xrightarrow{B_h}$;
4. $q_{l,1} + \cdots + q_{l,m_l} = w_{\rho_l} \cdot \frac{\prod_{i \in I} q_i}{\prod_{j \in J}(1 - q'_j)}$.

By the inductive hypothesis, it follows that:

1. for all $i \in I$, there is a set of states S'_i such that $\mu(t_i, a_i, S'_i) = q_i$ and, for all $s' \in S'_i$, there is some state $s \in S_i$ such that $s \, R \, s'$;
2. for all $j \in J$, $t_j \xrightarrow{A_j, q'_j}$;
3. for all $h \in H$, $t_h \xrightarrow{B_h}$.

Hence, by applying ρ_l, we infer n_l moves $f(\overrightarrow{t}) \xrightarrow{a, q'_{l,1}} v_1, \ldots f(\overrightarrow{t}) \xrightarrow{a, q'_{l,n_l}} v_{n_l}$, for some $n_l \in \mathbb{N}$, where:

1. $v_1, \ldots, v_{n_l} \in S$, by Lemma 1 and the fact that for all $s' \in S'_i$ there is some state $s \in S_i$ such that $s \, R \, s'$;
2. $q'_{l,1} + \cdots + q'_{l,n_l} = q_{l,1} + \cdots + q_{l,m_l}$.

Since these arguments hold for all $1 \le l \le k$, it follows that by $\rho_1, \ldots, \rho_k$ we derive $\mu(f(\overrightarrow{t}), a, S) = q$, which implies the thesis. It remains to prove that we can apply $\rho_1, \ldots, \rho_k$, i.e. no move of $f(\overrightarrow{t})$ can be derived by any rule in any stratum $\mathcal{R}_v$ with $v < u$. This follows by the fact that no move of $f(\overrightarrow{s})$ can be derived by any rule in these strata, and that $s_i \approx t_i$ for $1 \le i \le ar(f)$. $\square$

6   Extensions

The PB transition rules of Def. 5 extend the rules matching the *de Simone format* [16] with probability, unneeded premises and unquantified premises. Here we show how we can add to our rules some features offered by other formats proposed in the literature of non probabilistic process algebras.

The *GSOS format* [7] admits *negative premises* of the form $x_i \overset{g_i}{\nrightarrow}$ in rules with source $f(\overrightarrow{x})$, meaning that the ith argument of f does not perform any action labeled a_i. In [19] a result is proved which assesses that negative premises can be simulated by suitable ordering relations between rules. Since the partitioning in strata of Def. 6 introduces ordering relations between PB transition rules that are less general than those used in [19], it would be interesting to extend Def. 6 to capture all the ordering relations of [19].

The GSOS format admits also *double testing*. Namely, rules with source $f(\overrightarrow{x})$ can have two (or more) premises $x_i \overset{a_{i_1}}{\longrightarrow} y_{i_1}$ and $x_i \overset{a_{i_2}}{\longrightarrow} y_{i_2}$ with the same variable x_i in the left side. Let us show how we can add double testing to our rules.

Definition 9. *A PB transition rule with double testing ρ is of the form*

$$\frac{\{x_i \overset{a_{i_l},p_{i_l}}{\longrightarrow} y_{i_l} \mid i \in I, l \in I_i\} \cup \{x_j \overset{A_j,p_j'}{\longrightarrow} \mid j \in J\} \cup \{x_h \overset{B_h}{\longrightarrow} \mid h \in H\}}{f(\overrightarrow{x}) \xrightarrow{a, \frac{\Pi_{i \in I} \Sigma_{l \in I_i} p_{i_l}}{\Pi_{j \in J}(1-p_j')} \cdot w_\rho} t}$$

where:

1. *clauses 1-6 of Def. 5 are respected;*
2. *for all $i \in I$, it holds that $a_{i_l} \neq a_{i_{l'}}$ for all $l, l' \in I_i$ such that $l \neq l'$;*
3. *for all $i \in I$ and $l \in I_i$, if $|I_i| > 1$ then there is an $h = i$ such that $a_{i_l} \in B_h$.*

Definition 10. *A PB TSS with double testing is defined as in Def. 6, except that clause 2d is replaced by the following clause:*

- *Given actions $\{a_i' \mid i \in I\}$ such that $a_i' \notin A_j$ for all indexes i and j with $i = j$ and $x_j \overset{A_j,p_j'}{\longrightarrow}$ an unneeded premise, then there at least one PB transition rule with source $f(\overrightarrow{x})$ in $\mathcal{R}_u$ containing the active premises $\{x_i \overset{a_i',p_i}{\longrightarrow} y_i \mid i \in I\}$.*

To explain clause 2 in Def. 9, let us take the following rule, which violates it:

$$\frac{x_1 \overset{a,p_1}{\longrightarrow} y_1 \quad x_1 \overset{a,p_2}{\longrightarrow} y_2}{f(x_1) \overset{b,p_1+p_2}{\longrightarrow} 0}$$

Let t be the PCCS term $a \cdot 0$, which has the move $t \overset{a,1}{\longrightarrow} 0$. It holds that $f(t) \overset{b,2}{\longrightarrow} 0$, and, therefore, $f(t)$ is not semistochastic. The problem is that the probability of the same move of t is summed twice when computing the probability of the move of $f(t)$. Clause 2 in Def. 9 prevents this problem, since different moves of the same argument of f can appear as premises only if they have different labels.

To explain clause 3 in Def. 9, let us take the following rules, and note that the first one violates it:

$$\frac{x_1 \xrightarrow{a,p_1} y_1 \quad x_1 \xrightarrow{b,p_2} y_2}{f(x_1) \xrightarrow{d,p_1+p_2} 0} \qquad \frac{x_1 \xrightarrow{c,p_1} y_1}{f(x_1) \xrightarrow{e,p_1} 0}$$

Let t be the PCCS term $a \cdot 0 + \frac{1}{2} c \cdot 0$, which has the moves $t \xrightarrow{a,\frac{1}{2}} 0$ and $t \xrightarrow{c,\frac{1}{2}} 0$. It holds that $f(t) \xrightarrow{e,\frac{1}{2}} 0$ is the only move of $f(t)$, which, therefore, is not semistochastic. The problem is that the probability of the move of t labeled a does not contribute in computing the probability of any move of $f(t)$, since t has no move labeled b and the premise $x_1 \xrightarrow{a,p_1} y_1$ appears only in the rule where there is also the premise $x_1 \xrightarrow{b,p_2} y_2$. Clause 3 in Def. 9 prevents this problem, since premises $x_1 \xrightarrow{a,p_1} y_1$ and $x_1 \xrightarrow{b,p_2} y_2$ are admitted only in rules that are in strata where all rules have an unquantified premise $x_1 \xrightarrow{B}$ with $a, b \in B$.

Finally, notice that the new clause of Def. 10 requires that at least one rule in $\mathcal{R}_u$ *contains* the premises $\{x_i \xrightarrow{a'_i,p_i} y_i \,|\, i \in I\}$, whereas the corresponding clause in Def. 6 requires that at least one rule in $\mathcal{R}_u$ has *exactly* the premises $\{x_i \xrightarrow{a'_i,p_i} y_i \,|\, i \in I\}$. The new clause allows double testing.

Theorem 3. *The PTS induced by any PB TSS with double testing is semistochastic. The probabilistic bisimulation induced by any PB TSS with double testing is a congruence.*

The *tyxt/tyft format* [12] admits *look ahead*. Namely, transition rules with source $f(\overrightarrow{x})$ can have premises $x_i \xrightarrow{a_i} y_i$ and $y_i \xrightarrow{b_i} z_i$, with the same variable y_i appearing in the right side of the first premise and in the left side of the second premise. Let us show how we can add look ahead to our PB TSSs.

Definition 11. *A PB transition rule with look ahead ρ is of the form*

$$\frac{\{x_i \xrightarrow{a_i,p_i} y_i | i \in I\} \cup \{y_i \xrightarrow{b_i,r_i} z_i | i \in I'\} \cup \{x_j \xrightarrow{A_j,p'_j} | j \in J\} \cup \{x_h \xrightarrow{B_h} | h \in H\}}{f(\overrightarrow{x}) \xrightarrow{a,\frac{\prod_{i \in I \setminus I'} p_i \cdot \prod_{i \in I'} p_i \cdot r_i}{\prod_{j \in J}(1 - p'_j)} \cdot w_\rho} t}$$

where:

1. *clauses 1-6 of Def. 5 are respected;*
2. $I' \subseteq I$.

Also variables y_i with $i \in I'$ are called active variables.

Definition 12. *A PB TSS with look ahead is defined as in Def. 6, except that clauses 2c and 2d are replaced by the following clauses:*

1. *All PB transition rules with source $f(\overrightarrow{x})$ in stratum $\mathcal{R}_u$ have the same set of active variables $\{x_i \,|\, i \in I\} \cup \{y_i \,|\, i \in I'\}$;*
2. *Given actions $\{a_i' \,|\, i \in I\}$ such that $a_i' \not\in A_j$ for all indexes i and j with $i = j$ and $x_j \xrightarrow{A_j, p_j'}$ an unneeded premise, and actions b_i' for all indexes $i \in I'$, then there is at least one PB transition rule with source $f(\overrightarrow{x})$ in $\mathcal{R}_u$ with active premises $\{x_i \xrightarrow{a_i', p_i} y_i \,|\, i \in I\} \cup \{y_i \xrightarrow{b_i', r_i} z_i \,|\, i \in I'\}$.*

The new clauses in Deff. 11–12 extend clauses in Deff. 5–6 to take into account that two consecutive moves of x_i are considered for all $i \in I'$.

Theorem 4. *The PTS induced by any PB TSS with look ahead is semistochastic. The probabilistic bisimulation induced by any PB TSS with look ahead is a congruence.*

Definitions of PB transition rule and PB TSS admitting both double testing and look ahead could be given immediately. By combining results of Thm. 3 and Thm. 4 we infer that the PB TSSs so obtained would induce semistochastic PTSs and probabilistic bisimulations being congruences.

Both *path format* [4] and *panth format* [20] admit *predicates*, i.e. transitions of the form $t\,P$, meaning that term t satisfies some property expressed by P. Since predicates have nothing to do with probability, they can be added to PB transitions rules and PB TSSs, without affecting results in Thm. 1 and Thm. 2.

7   Related and Future Work

In this paper we have proposed a rule format for probabilistic process algebras. We believe that our format has four main merits: 1) probabilistic bisimulation is a congruence w.r.t. process algebra operations respecting the format; 2) semistochasticity is preserved by process algebra operations respecting the format; 3) the main operations offered by the probabilistic process algebras studied in the literature are captured by the format, which, therefore, has practical applications; 4) features offered by known rule formats proposed for classic process algebras, such as look ahead and double testing, are offered by the format.

Now, let us recall that in [6] a rule format for probabilistic process algebras has been already proposed. The first difference between our paper and [6] is that we consider the generative model of probabilistic processes, whereas [6] considers the reactive model. Then, our definition of TSS requires some conditions (i.e. clauses 2c–2e in Def. 6) that guarantee semistochasticity. In [6] no syntactic constraint on transition rules guarantees semistochasticity of reactive processes, i.e. the property that the sum of the probability of the moves of any process *for the same label* is either 0 or 1. Hence, in [6] semistochasticity is not ensured by the format. In [6] neither unquantified premises nor unneeded premises nor stratification are considered. We need these features to express operations requiring redistribution of probability, such as restriction (see Ex. 7) and priority (see Ex.

8). In the reactive model restriction and priority do not require redistribution of probability, and, therefore, they can be expressed with the format in [6]. Problems in [6] arise in other operations requiring redistribution of probability, such as the relabeling operation $t[f]$, where $f : Act \longrightarrow Act$ is a relabeling functions.

Our results can be extended in several directions. We aim to develop a rule format for the reactive model of probabilistic processes that guarantees results analogous to those obtained in the present paper, i.e. bisimulation being a congruence, operations preserving semistochasticity, expressiveness. Moreover, we aim to develop rule formats for other behavioral equivalences, such as probabilistic weak bisimulation [5], and probabilistic testing equivalence [21]. Finally, we aim to develop rule formats guaranteeing that security properties for probabilistic processes, such as those defined in [2], are respected by process algebra operations, on the same line followed in [17, 18] for classic process algebras.

References

1. L. Aceto, W. J. Fokkink, and C. Verhoef: Structural Operational Semantics. Handbook of Process Algebra, Elsevier, Amsterdam, 2001, 197–292.
2. A. Aldini, M. Bravetti, and R. Gorrieri: A Process-algebraic Approach for the Analysis of Probabilistic Non-interference. J. Comput. Secur. 12, 2004, 191–245.
3. J. C. M. Baeten, J. A. Bergstra, and S. A. Smolka: Axiomatizing Probabilistic Processes: ACP with Generative Probabilities. Inf. Comput. 121, 1995, 234–255.
4. J. C. M. Baeten and C. Verhoef: A Congruence Theorem for Structured Operational Semantics with Predicates. Proc. Concurrency Theory, LNCS 715, 1993.
5. C. Baier and H. Hermanns: Weak Bisimulation for Fully Probabilistic Processes. Proc. Computer Aided Verification, LNCS 1254, 1997, 119-130.
6. F. Bartels: GSOS for Probabilistic Transition Systems. Proc. Coalgebraic Methods in Computer Science, ENTCS 65, 2002.
7. B. Bloom, S. Istrail, and A. Meyer: Bisimulation Can't Be Traced. J. Assoc. Comput. Mach. 42, 1995, 232–268.
8. M. Bravetti and A. Aldini: Discrete Time Generative-reactive Probabilistic Processes with Different Advancing Speeds. Theor. Comput. Sci. 290, 2003, 355–406.
9. P. R. D'Argenio, H. Hermanns, and J. P. Katoen: On Generative Parallel Composition. Proc. Probabilistic Methods in Verification, ENTCS 22, 1999.
10. A. Giacalone, C.C. Jou, and S.A. Smolka: Algebraic Reasoning for Probabilistic Concurrent Systems. IFIP Work. Conf. on Progr., Concepts and Methods, 1990.
11. R. J. van Glabbeek, S. A. Smolka, and B. Steffen: Reactive, Generative and Stratified Models of Probabilistic Processes. Inf. Comput. 121, 1995, 59–80.
12. J. F. Groote and F. Vaandrager: Structured Operational Semantics and Bisimulation as a Congruence. Inf. Comput. 100, 1992, 202–260.
13. B. Jonsson, K. L. Larsen, and W. Yi: Probabilistic Extensions of Process Algebras. Handbook of Process Algebra, Elsevier, Amsterdam, 2001.
14. G. Plotkin: A Structural Approach to Operational Semantics. Technical report DAIMI FN-19, University of Aarhus, 1981.
15. G. Plotkin: A Structural Approach to Operational Semantics. J. Log. Algebr. Program. 60–61, 2004, 17–139.
16. R. de Simone: Higher-level Synchronizing Devices in Meije-SCCS. Theor. Comput. Sci. 37, 1985, 245–267.

17. S. Tini: Rule Formats for Non-Interference. Proc. European Symp. on Programming, LNCS 2618, 2003, 129–143.
18. S. Tini: Rule Formats for Compositional non Interference Properties. J. Log. Algebr. Program. 60–61, 2004, 353-400.
19. I. Ulidowski and I. Phillips: Ordered SOS Process Languages for Branching and Eager Bisimulations. Inf. Comput. 178, 2002, 180–213.
20. C. Verhoef: A Congruence Theorem for Structural Operational Semantics with Predicates and Negative Premises. Nord. J. Comput. 2, 1995, 274–302.
21. S. H. Wu, S. A. Smolka, and E. W. Stark: Composition and Behaviors of Probabilistic I/O Automata. Theor. Comput. Sci. 176, 1997, 1–38.

Bisimulation on Speed: A Unified Approach

Gerald Lüttgen[1] and Walter Vogler[2]

[1] Department of Computer Science, University of York,
York YO10 5DD, U.K.
luettgen@cs.york.ac.uk
[2] Institut für Informatik, Universität Augsburg,
D–86135 Augsburg, Germany
vogler@informatik.uni-augsburg.de

Abstract. Two process–algebraic approaches have been developed for comparing two bisimulation–equivalent processes with respect to speed: the one of Moller/Tofts equips actions with lower time bounds, while the one by Lüttgen/Vogler considers upper time bounds instead.

This paper sheds new light on both approaches by testifying to their close relationship. We introduce a general, intuitive concept of "faster–than", which is formalised by a notion of *amortised faster–than preorder*. When closing this preorder under all contexts, exactly the two faster–than preorders investigated by Moller/Tofts and Lüttgen/Vogler arise. For processes incorporating both lower and upper time bounds we also show that the largest precongruence contained in the amortised faster–than preorder is not a proper preorder but a timed bisimulation. In the light of this result we systematically investigate under which circumstances the amortised faster–than preorder degrades to an equivalence.

1 Introduction

Process algebras provide a popular framework for modelling and analysing the communication behaviour of asynchronous systems. Various extensions of classic process algebras, e.g., Milner's *Calculus of Communicating Systems* (CCS) [12], are also well established in the literature, including *timed process algebras*. Timed process algebras add constructs for modelling timeouts and delays of actions, and thus enable one to reason not only about the communication, or functional, behaviour of processes but also about their timing behaviour. Despite the vast literature on timed process algebra, most of which has concentrated on capturing behaviour in terms of process equivalence and refinement, there is relatively little work on relating functionally equivalent processes with respect to speed. This is surprising since designers of distributed algorithms are very interested in knowing which one out of several possible solutions to a given problem is the most time efficient one. Indeed, time efficiency is not something that can only be decided once an algorithm is implemented — often *lower* and/or *upper time bounds* on the algorithm's actions are known at design time.

Within timed process algebra, the idea of "*faster–than*" was first addressed by Moller and Tofts [14] who studied an extension of CCS, called TACS^{lt} in this

V. Sassone (Ed.): FOSSACS 2005, LNCS 3441, pp. 79–94, 2005.

paper, that allows for specifying lower time bounds of actions. They proposed the *MT–preorder* which refines bisimulation [12] and has recently been put on firm theoretical grounds via a full–abstraction result established by us in [11]. Previously, we had also investigated an analogous approach to extending CCS with upper time bounds of actions, which resulted in the calculus TACS^{ut} and the *LV–preorder* [10]; this preorder was also justified intuitively by a full–abstraction result. That latter work complements research in various Petri–net [8, 16] and process–algebra [4] frameworks based on a testing semantics rather than a bisimulation semantics. The main shortcoming of our previous research is that the reference preorders for the two *full–abstraction results* — though similar in spirit — are quite different in detail and indeed somewhat tuned towards the desired outcomes. Also, we have not explored, and neither have others in the literature, the consequences of combining both lower and upper time bounds in a single setting.

This paper presents a unified approach to studying faster–than preorders for asynchronous processes. It unifies the previously known results on faster–than preorders in two ways. Firstly, it proposes a natural reference preorder for relating two processes with respect to speed: the *amortised faster–than preorder*. This preorder formalises the intuition that the faster process must execute each action no later than the slower process does, while both processes must be functionally equivalent in the sense of strong bisimulation [12]; here, "no later" refers to absolute time as measured from the system start, as opposed to relative time which is used in our operational semantics and describes the passing of time between actions. Although the amortised faster–than relation is more abstract than the reference preorders of [10, 11], we show that both the MT–preorder and the LV–preorder remain fully–abstract in TACS^{lt} and TACS^{ut}, respectively.

Secondly, this paper characterises the largest precongruence contained in the amortised faster–than preorder when combining the calculi TACS^{lt} and TACS^{ut}, so as to being able to specify *both* lower *and* upper time bounds of actions. This is an important open problem in the literature, and it turns out that the resulting precongruence is not a proper preorder but an equivalence relation that is a variant of *timed bisimulation* [13]. The concluding part of this paper systematically investigates under which circumstances a proper preorder is obtained, and when exactly the amortised faster–than preorder degrades to an equivalence. For example, we get a positive result as in [10] when we extend TACS^{ut} by actions that may be delayed arbitrarily long; such *lazy* actions are useful for modelling system errors that are not bound to occur within some fixed time interval.

The full–abstraction results of this paper complete the picture of faster–than preorders within bisimulation–based process algebras. On the one hand, the various published faster–than preorders can be traced back to the same notion of "faster–than", which is rooted in the concept of *amortisation*. On the other hand, the amortisation approach highlights the limits for defining a useful faster–than preorder that fully supports *compositionality*. Due to space constraints, the proofs of our results are omitted here but can be found in a technical report [9].

2 Timed Asynchronous Communicating Systems

This section presents our process algebra TACS that combines the timed process algebras TACS[lt] [11] and TACS[ut] [10], both of which extend Milner's CCS [12] by permitting the specification of *lower* and respectively *upper time bounds* for the execution of actions and processes. These time bounds will be used in the next sections for comparing processes with respect to speed. Syntactically, TACS includes two types of actions: *lazy* actions α and *urgent* actions $\underline{\alpha}$; the idea is that the former can idle arbitrarily, while the latter have to be performed immediately. It also includes one clock prefixing operator "σ.", called *must–clock prefix*, for specifying minimum delays and another "$\underline{\sigma}$.", called *can–clock prefix*, for specifying maximum delays. Semantically and as in CCS, an action a or $\underline{a}$ communicates with the complements $\bar{a}$ or $\underline{\bar{a}}$, irrespective of whether either action is urgent. This communication results in an urgent internal action, if both participating actions are urgent, and a lazy internal action otherwise. Moreover, TACS adopts a concept of global, discrete time that behaves as follows: process $\sigma.P$ *must wait* for *at least* one time unit before it can start executing process P (lower time bound), while process $\underline{\sigma}.P$ *can wait* for *at most* one time unit (upper time bound); thus, $\underline{\sigma}$ can be understood as a potential time step. Upper time bounds are technically enforced by the concept of *maximal progress* [7], such that time can only pass if no urgent internal computation can be performed.

Syntax. The syntax of TACS is identical to CCS, except that we include the two clock–prefixing operators and distinguish between lazy and urgent actions, as discussed above. Formally, let Λ be a countably infinite set of lazy actions not including the distinguished unobservable, *internal* action τ. With every $a \in \Lambda$ we associate a *complementary action* $\bar{a}$, and define $\overline{\Lambda} =_{\mathrm{df}} \{\bar{a} \mid a \in \Lambda\}$. Each lazy action $a \in \Lambda$ ($\bar{a} \in \overline{\Lambda}$, τ) has an associated urgent variant, i.e., an action $\underline{a}$ ($\underline{\bar{a}}$, $\underline{\tau}$). We define $\underline{\Lambda} =_{\mathrm{df}} \{\underline{a} \mid a \in \Lambda\}$ and $\overline{\underline{\Lambda}} =_{\mathrm{df}} \{\underline{\bar{a}} \mid a \in \Lambda\}$, and take $\mathcal{A}$ ($\underline{\mathcal{A}}$) to denote the set $\Lambda \cup \overline{\Lambda} \cup \{\tau\}$ ($\underline{\Lambda} \cup \overline{\underline{\Lambda}} \cup \{\underline{\tau}\}$). Complementation is lifted to $\Lambda \cup \overline{\Lambda}$ ($\underline{\Lambda} \cup \overline{\underline{\Lambda}}$) by defining $\bar{\bar{a}} =_{\mathrm{df}} a$ ($\overline{\underline{\bar{a}}} =_{\mathrm{df}} \underline{a}$). We let $a, b, \ldots$ ($\underline{a}, \underline{b}, \ldots$) range over $\Lambda \cup \overline{\Lambda}$ ($\underline{\Lambda} \cup \overline{\underline{\Lambda}}$) and $\alpha, \beta, \ldots$ ($\underline{\alpha}, \underline{\beta}, \ldots$) over $\mathcal{A}$ ($\underline{\mathcal{A}}$). The syntax of TACS is defined as follows:

$$P ::= \mathbf{0} \mid x \mid \alpha.P \mid \underline{\alpha}.P \mid \sigma.P \mid \underline{\sigma}.P \mid P + P \mid P|P \mid P \setminus L \mid P[f] \mid \mu x.P,$$

where x is a *variable* taken from a countably infinite set $\mathcal{V}$ of variables, $L \subseteq \mathcal{A} \setminus \{\tau\}$ is a *restriction set*, and $f : \mathcal{A} \to \mathcal{A}$ is a *finite relabelling*. A finite relabelling satisfies the properties $f(\tau) = \tau$, $f(\bar{a}) = \overline{f(a)}$, and $|\{\alpha \mid f(\alpha) \neq \alpha\}| < \infty$. The set of all terms is abbreviated by $\widehat{\mathcal{P}}$, and we define $\overline{L} =_{\mathrm{df}} \{\bar{a} \mid a \in L\}$. We use the standard definitions for the semantic *sort* $\mathsf{sort}(P) \subseteq \Lambda \cup \overline{\Lambda}$ of some term P, *open* and *closed* terms, and *contexts* (terms with a "hole"). Due to our restriction to *finite* relabellings, sorts of terms are guaranteed to be finite so that contexts such as the one needed in the proof of Thm. 13 are well–defined. A variable is called *guarded* in a term if each occurrence of the variable is within the scope of an action– or σ–prefix. Moreover, we require for terms of the form $\mu x.P$ that x is guarded in P. Note that, since $\underline{\sigma}$ only denotes a potential time step, $\underline{\sigma}.P$ can perform the actions of P immediately, whence $\underline{\sigma}$ does not count as a guard.

We refer to closed and guarded terms as *processes*, with the set of all processes written as $\mathcal{P}$, and let $\equiv$ stand for syntactic equality.

Table 1. Operational semantics for TACS (action transitions)

Act $\dfrac{-}{\alpha.P \xrightarrow{\alpha} P}$	uAct $\dfrac{-}{\underline{\alpha}.P \xrightarrow{\alpha} P}$	uPre $\dfrac{P \xrightarrow{\alpha} P'}{\underline{\sigma}.P \xrightarrow{\alpha} P'}$
Sum1 $\dfrac{P \xrightarrow{\alpha} P'}{P+Q \xrightarrow{\alpha} P'}$	Sum2 $\dfrac{Q \xrightarrow{\alpha} Q'}{P+Q \xrightarrow{\alpha} Q'}$	Rec $\dfrac{P \xrightarrow{\alpha} P'}{\mu x.P \xrightarrow{\alpha} P'[\mu x.P/x]}$
Com1 $\dfrac{P \xrightarrow{\alpha} P'}{P|Q \xrightarrow{\alpha} P'|Q}$	Com2 $\dfrac{Q \xrightarrow{\alpha} Q'}{P|Q \xrightarrow{\alpha} P|Q'}$	Com3 $\dfrac{P \xrightarrow{a} P' \quad Q \xrightarrow{\bar{a}} Q'}{P|Q \xrightarrow{\tau} P'|Q'}$
Rel $\dfrac{P \xrightarrow{\alpha} P'}{P[f] \xrightarrow{f(\alpha)} P'[f]}$	Res $\dfrac{P \xrightarrow{\alpha} P'}{P \setminus L \xrightarrow{\alpha} P' \setminus L} \ \alpha \notin L \cup \overline{L}$	

Semantics. The *operational semantics* of a TACS term $P \in \widehat{\mathcal{P}}$ is given by a labelled transition system and an urgent action set. The labelled transition system has the form $\langle \widehat{\mathcal{P}}, \mathcal{A} \cup \{\sigma\}, \longrightarrow, P \rangle$, where $\widehat{\mathcal{P}}$ is the set of states, $\mathcal{A} \cup \{\sigma\}$ the alphabet, $\longrightarrow \subseteq \widehat{\mathcal{P}} \times (\mathcal{A} \cup \{\sigma\}) \times \widehat{\mathcal{P}}$ the transition relation, and P the start state. Transitions labelled with an action α are called *action transitions* that, like in CCS, are either internal activities or local communications in which two processes may synchronise to take a joint state change together. Transitions labelled with the clock symbol σ are called *clock transitions* representing a recurrent global synchronisation that encodes the progress of time. Note that transitions are labelled by ordinary (lazy) actions only. Urgency is dealt with in an orthogonal fashion by a notion of *urgent action set*. This is defined in Table 2 and contains exactly the urgent actions in which a term can initially engage. Note: the communication of two complementary actions results in an *urgent* silent action only if the two participating actions are urgent.

Table 2. Urgent action sets

$\mathcal{U}(\alpha.P) =_{\mathrm{df}} \emptyset$	$\mathcal{U}(\underline{\alpha}.P) =_{\mathrm{df}} \{\alpha\}$	$\mathcal{U}(0) =_{\mathrm{df}} \emptyset$
$\mathcal{U}(\sigma.P) =_{\mathrm{df}} \emptyset$	$\mathcal{U}(\underline{\sigma}.P) =_{\mathrm{df}} \emptyset$	$\mathcal{U}(x) =_{\mathrm{df}} \emptyset$
$\mathcal{U}(P \setminus L) =_{\mathrm{df}} \mathcal{U}(P) \setminus (L \cup \overline{L})$	$\mathcal{U}(P[f]) =_{\mathrm{df}} \{f(\alpha) \mid \alpha \in \mathcal{U}(P)\}$	$\mathcal{U}(\mu x.P) =_{\mathrm{df}} \mathcal{U}(P)$
$\mathcal{U}(P + Q) =_{\mathrm{df}} \mathcal{U}(P) \cup \mathcal{U}(Q)$	$\mathcal{U}(P|Q) =_{\mathrm{df}} \mathcal{U}(P) \cup \mathcal{U}(Q) \cup \{\tau \mid \mathcal{U}(P) \cap \overline{\mathcal{U}(Q)} \neq \emptyset\}$	

According to our operational rules, the *action–prefix* terms $\alpha.P$ and $\underline{\alpha}.P$ may engage in action α and then behave like P. The processes $\alpha.P$ ($\alpha \in \mathcal{A}$) and $\underline{a}.P$ ($a \in \Lambda \cup \overline{\Lambda}$) may also *idle*, i.e., engage in a clock transition to themselves,

Table 3. Operational semantics for TACS (clock transitions)

tNil	$\dfrac{\overline{\quad}}{0 \xrightarrow{\sigma} 0}$	tAct	$\dfrac{\overline{\quad}}{\alpha.P \xrightarrow{\sigma} \alpha.P}$	tuAct	$\dfrac{\overline{\quad}}{\underline{a}.P \xrightarrow{\sigma} \underline{a}.P}$
tPre	$\dfrac{-}{\sigma.P \xrightarrow{\sigma} P}$	tuPre	$\dfrac{-}{\underline{\sigma}.P \xrightarrow{\sigma} P}$	tRec	$\dfrac{P \xrightarrow{\sigma} P'}{\mu x.P \xrightarrow{\sigma} P'[\mu x.P/x]}$
tSum	$\dfrac{P \xrightarrow{\sigma} P' \quad Q \xrightarrow{\sigma} Q'}{P + Q \xrightarrow{\sigma} P' + Q'}$	tCom	$\dfrac{P \xrightarrow{\sigma} P' \quad Q \xrightarrow{\sigma} Q'}{P|Q \xrightarrow{\sigma} P'|Q'} \ \tau \notin \mathcal{U}(P|Q)$		
tRel	$\dfrac{P \xrightarrow{\sigma} P'}{P[f] \xrightarrow{\sigma} P'[f]}$	tRes	$\dfrac{P \xrightarrow{\sigma} P'}{P \setminus L \xrightarrow{\sigma} P' \setminus L}$		

as process 0 does; the rationale is that even an urgent communication action may have to wait for a communication partner. Hence, an $\underline{a}$–prefix expresses *potential* urgency which becomes actual only in a synchronisation with an urgent complementary action. The *must–clock prefix* term $\sigma.P$ can only engage in a clock transition to P; thus, σ stands for a delay of exactly one time unit, and it can be used to define lower time bounds, since P may perform further time steps due to clock prefixes, lazy actions or waiting for a communication. The *can–clock prefix* term $\underline{\sigma}.P$ can additionally perform any action transition that P can engage in; in this sense, $\underline{\sigma}$ represents a delay of at most one time unit and can be used to define arbitrary upper time bounds.

The term $P|Q$ stands for the *parallel composition* of P and Q according to an interleaving semantics with synchronised communication on complementary actions resulting in the internal action τ. Time has to proceed equally on both sides of the operator. The side condition of Rule (tCom) ensures that $P|Q$ can only progress on σ, if it cannot engage in any urgent internal computation, in accordance with our notion of maximal progress. Thus, due to the urgency of the actions, $\underline{a}.P \,|\, \underline{\overline{a}}.Q$ cannot perform a time step. On the other hand, $\underline{a}.P \,|\, \underline{b}.Q$ or $\underline{a}.P \,|\, \overline{a}.Q$ can, since communication is not possible or can at least be delayed; thus, $\underline{a}$ is urgent but also *patient*. Note that predicates within structural operational rules, such as $\tau \notin \mathcal{U}(P|Q)$ in Rule (tCom), are well understood.

The *summation operator* $+$ denotes nondeterministic choice such that $P+Q$ may behave like P or Q. Again, $P+Q$ can engage in a clock transition and delay the nondeterministic choice if and only if both P and Q can. Restriction $\setminus L$, relabelling $[f]$ and recursion $\mu x.\,P$ have the usual meaning.

The rules for action transitions are the same as for CCS, with the exception of the rules for the new can–clock prefix and for recursion; however, the latter is equivalent to the standard CCS rule over guarded terms. It is important to note that both faster–than settings previously investigated by us in [10, 11] can be found within TACS. The sub–calculus obtained when considering only lazy actions (urgent actions) and only must–clock prefixing (can–clock prefixing) is exactly the calculus TACS^{lt} (TACS^{ut}) studied in [11] ([10]). For improving readability we also write $\mathcal{P}^{lt}$ ($\mathcal{P}^{ut}$) for the set of processes in TACS^{lt} (TACS^{ut}).

The operational semantics for TACS possesses several important properties [7]. Firstly, it is *time–deterministic*, i.e., progress of time does not resolve choices. Formally, $P \xrightarrow{\sigma} P'$ and $P \xrightarrow{\sigma} P''$ implies $P' \equiv P''$, for all $P, P', P'' \in \widehat{\mathcal{P}}$, which can easily be proved by induction on the structure of P. This property is very intuitive, as only actions can resolve choices, and also technically convenient. Secondly, by our variant of *maximal progress*, a guarded term P can engage in a clock transition exactly if it cannot engage in an urgent internal transition. Formally, $P \xrightarrow{\sigma}$ if and only if $\tau \notin \mathcal{U}(P)$, for all guarded terms P. In particular, processes in TACS^{lt} satisfy *laziness*: they can always engage in a clock transition. Last, but not least, we note that the sort $\mathsf{sort}(P)$ of any process P is finite. This is because we only allow *finite* relabellings.

3   Generalised Full–Abstraction Results

This section presents our unified approach to "faster–than" by introducing a very simple and intuitive preorder, the *amortised faster–than preorder*, which captures the essence of faster–than within a bisimulation–based setting, as discussed below. Using this preorder as a reference preorder, we show that the LV–preorder [10] and the MT–preorder [14] are fully–abstract within the TACS^{ut} and TACS^{lt} sub–calculi of TACS, respectively.

Definition 1 (Amortised faster–than preorder). A family $(\mathcal{R}_i)_{i \in \mathbb{N}}$ of relations over $\mathcal{P}$, indexed by natural numbers (including 0), is a *family of amortised faster–than relations* if, for all $i \in \mathbb{N}$, $\langle P, Q \rangle \in \mathcal{R}_i$, and $\alpha \in \mathcal{A}$:

1. $P \xrightarrow{\alpha} P'$ implies $\exists Q', k, l. \, Q \xrightarrow{\sigma}^k \xrightarrow{\alpha} \xrightarrow{\sigma}^l Q'$ and $\langle P', Q' \rangle \in \mathcal{R}_{i+k+l}$.
2. $Q \xrightarrow{\alpha} Q'$ implies $\exists P', k, l. \, k+l \leq i, \, P \xrightarrow{\sigma}^k \xrightarrow{\alpha} \xrightarrow{\sigma}^l P'$, and $\langle P', Q' \rangle \in \mathcal{R}_{i-k-l}$.
3. $P \xrightarrow{\sigma} P'$ implies $\exists Q', k \geq 1-i. \, Q \xrightarrow{\sigma}^k Q'$ and $\langle P', Q' \rangle \in \mathcal{R}_{i-1+k}$.
4. $Q \xrightarrow{\sigma} Q'$ implies $\exists P', k \leq i+1. \, P \xrightarrow{\sigma}^k P'$ and $\langle P', Q' \rangle \in \mathcal{R}_{i+1-k}$.

We write $P \gtrsim_i Q$ if $\langle P, Q \rangle \in \mathcal{R}_i$ for some family $(\mathcal{R}_i)_{i \in \mathbb{N}}$ of amortised faster–than relations, and call $\gtrsim_0$ the *amortised faster–than preorder*.

Here, $\xrightarrow{\sigma}^k$ stands for k consecutive clock transitions. It is easy to show that $\gtrsim_0$ is indeed a preorder. While reflexivity is obvious, transitivity follows immediately from the property $\gtrsim_i \circ \gtrsim_j \subseteq \gtrsim_{i+j}$, for any $i, j \in \mathbb{N}$. Furthermore, $(\gtrsim_i)_{i \in \mathbb{N}}$ is the (componentwise) largest family of amortised faster–than relations.

The above definition reflects our intuition that processes performing delays later along execution paths are faster than functionally equivalent ones that perform delays earlier; this is because the former processes are executing actions at earlier absolute times (as measured from the start of the processes). Consider, e.g., the processes $P =_{df} a.b.\sigma.\sigma.c.\mathbf{0}$ and $Q =_{df} \sigma.a.\sigma.b.c.\mathbf{0}$. Roughly speaking,

P executes actions a, b at absolute time 0 and action c at absolute time 2. Analogously, Q executes action a at absolute time 1 and actions b, c at absolute time 2. Hence, every action in P is executed earlier than, or at the same absolute time as in Q, whence P is strictly faster than Q. This idea is formalised in the above definition as follows: Q is permitted to match an a from P by σa; the additional time step is saved as a credit by increasing the index of $\mathcal{R}$ such that P can perform this time step when needed, i.e., after its b. Thus, in Def. 1, an action or clock transition is matched by allowing the matching process fewer or more clock transitions as far as this is allowed by the available credit; the difference in the number of clock transitions is added to or subtracted from the credit. In this sense, our definition canonically captures the idea of amortisation.

The remainder of this paper is concerned with the characterisation of the largest precongruence contained in $\gtrsim_0$, for various sub–calculi of TACS, in particular TACS^{ut} and TACS^{lt}. We will also discuss below which variants of $\gtrsim_0$ have been used for TACS^{ut} and TACS^{lt} in [10, 11], and we will write $\gtrsim_i^{\mathrm{ut}}$ and $\gtrsim_i^{\mathrm{lt}}$ when restricting $\gtrsim_i$ to processes in TACS^{ut} and TACS^{lt}, respectively.

3.1   The LV–Preorder Is Fully Abstract in TACS^{ut}

TACS^{ut} is the sub–calculus of TACS that emerges when restricting ourselves to urgent actions $\underline{\alpha}$ and can–clock prefixing $\underline{\sigma}$ only, i.e., disregarding lazy actions and must–clock prefixing. We start off by recalling some definitions from [10].

Definition 2 (LV–preorder [10]). A relation $\mathcal{R}$ over $\mathcal{P}^{\mathrm{ut}}$ is an *LV–relation* if, for all $\langle P, Q \rangle \in \mathcal{R}$ and $\alpha \in \mathcal{A}$:

1. $P \xrightarrow{\alpha} P'$ implies $\exists Q'. Q \xrightarrow{\alpha} Q'$ and $\langle P', Q' \rangle \in \mathcal{R}$.
2. $Q \xrightarrow{\alpha} Q'$ implies $\exists P'. P \xrightarrow{\alpha} P'$ and $\langle P', Q' \rangle \in \mathcal{R}$.
3. $P \xrightarrow{\sigma} P'$ implies $\mathcal{U}(Q) \subseteq \mathcal{U}(P)$ and $\exists Q'. Q \xrightarrow{\sigma} Q'$ and $\langle P', Q' \rangle \in \mathcal{R}$.

We write $P \gtrsim_{\mathrm{lv}} Q$ if $\langle P, Q \rangle \in \mathcal{R}$ for some LV–relation $\mathcal{R}$, and call $\gtrsim_{\mathrm{lv}}$ the LV–preorder.

This definition is of an elegant simplicity, since an LV–relation essentially combines bisimulation on actions with simulation on clock steps; the condition on the inclusion of urgent sets is needed to get a precongruence for parallel composition.

We also introduced in [10] an amortised variant of the LV–preorder which, in contrast to the amortised faster–than preorder of Def. 1, does not allow for leading and trailing clock transitions when matching action transitions — just as for the LV–preorder. Also, for matching clock transitions, the increase or decrease of the credit is restricted.

Definition 3 (Amortised LV–preorder [10]). A family $(\mathcal{R}_i)_{i \in \mathbb{N}}$ of relations over $\mathcal{P}^{\mathrm{ut}}$ is a *family of amortised LV–relations* if, for all $i \in \mathbb{N}$, $\langle P, Q \rangle \in \mathcal{R}_i$, and $\alpha \in \mathcal{A}$:

1. $P \xrightarrow{\alpha} P'$ implies $\exists Q'. Q \xrightarrow{\alpha} Q'$ and $\langle P', Q' \rangle \in \mathcal{R}_i$.

2. $Q \xrightarrow{\alpha} Q'$ implies $\exists P'.\, P \xrightarrow{\alpha} P'$ and $\langle P', Q' \rangle \in \mathcal{R}_i$.
3. $P \xrightarrow{\sigma} P'$ implies (a) $\exists Q'.\, Q \xrightarrow{\sigma} Q'$ and $\langle P', Q' \rangle \in \mathcal{R}_i$, or
    (b) $i > 0$ and $\langle P', Q \rangle \in \mathcal{R}_{i-1}$.
4. $Q \xrightarrow{\sigma} Q'$ implies (a) $\exists P'.\, P \xrightarrow{\sigma} P'$ and $\langle P', Q' \rangle \in \mathcal{R}_i$, or
    (b) $\langle P, Q' \rangle \in \mathcal{R}_{i+1}$.

We write $P \sqsupseteq_i^{lv} Q$ if $\langle P, Q \rangle \in \mathcal{R}_i$ for some family $(\mathcal{R}_i)_{i \in \mathbb{N}}$ of amortised LV–relations, and call $\sqsupseteq_0^{lv}$ the *amortised LV–preorder*.

Theorem 4 (Full abstraction [10]). *The LV–preorder $\sqsupseteq_{lv}$ is the largest pre-congruence contained in $\sqsupseteq_0^{lv}$.*

The next theorem is the main result of this section and, because of $\sqsupseteq_0^{lv} \subseteq \sqsupseteq_0^{ut}$, generalises the above theorem.

Theorem 5 (Generalised full abstraction in TACS^{ut}). *The LV–preorder $\sqsupseteq_{lv}$ is the largest precongruence contained in $\sqsupseteq_0^{ut}$.*

3.2   The MT–Preorder is Fully Abstract in TACS^{lt}

We turn our attention to the TACS sub–calculus TACS^{lt} in which only lazy actions α and the must–clock prefix σ are available. Although a σ–prefix corresponds to exactly one time unit, these prefixes specify lower time bounds for actions in this fragment, since actions can always be delayed arbitrarily. We first recall the faster–than preorder introduced by Moller and Tofts in [14], to which we refer as *Moller–Tofts preorder*, or *MT–preorder* for short.

Definition 6 (MT–preorder [14]). A relation $\mathcal{R}$ over $\mathcal{P}^{lt}$ is an *MT–relation* if, for all $\langle P, Q \rangle \in \mathcal{R}$ and $\alpha \in \mathcal{A}$:

1. $P \xrightarrow{\alpha} P'$ implies $\exists Q', k, P''.\, Q \xrightarrow{\sigma}{}^k \xrightarrow{\alpha} Q',\, P' \xrightarrow{\sigma}{}^k P''$, and $\langle P'', Q' \rangle \in \mathcal{R}$.
2. $Q \xrightarrow{\alpha} Q'$ implies $\exists P'.\, P \xrightarrow{\alpha} P'$ and $\langle P', Q' \rangle \in \mathcal{R}$.
3. $P \xrightarrow{\sigma} P'$ implies $\exists Q'.\, Q \xrightarrow{\sigma} Q'$ and $\langle P', Q' \rangle \in \mathcal{R}$.
4. $Q \xrightarrow{\sigma} Q'$ implies $\exists P'.\, P \xrightarrow{\sigma} P'$ and $\langle P', Q' \rangle \in \mathcal{R}$.

We write $P \sqsupseteq_{mt} Q$ if $\langle P, Q \rangle \in \mathcal{R}$ for some MT–relation $\mathcal{R}$, and call $\sqsupseteq_{mt}$ the *MT–preorder*.

It is easy to see that $\sqsupseteq_{mt}$ is indeed a preorder and that it is the largest MT–relation. We have also proved in [11] that $\sqsupseteq_{mt}$ is a precongruence for all TACS^{lt} operators. The only difficult and non–standard part of that proof concerned compositionality regarding parallel composition and was based on the following *commutation lemma*.

Lemma 7 (Commutation lemma [11]). *Let $P, P' \in \mathcal{P}^{lt}$ and $w \in (\mathcal{A} \cup \{\sigma\})^*$. If $P \xrightarrow{w} \xrightarrow{\sigma}{}^k P'$, for $k \in \mathbb{N}$, then $\exists P''.\, P \xrightarrow{\sigma}{}^k \xrightarrow{w} P''$ and $P' \sqsupseteq_{mt} P''$.*

This lemma holds as well within the slightly more general setting of Sec. 5.2, in which also can–clock prefixes are allowed. We also introduced in [11] an amortised variant of the MT–preorder, which is however less abstract than the amortised faster–than preorder of Def. 1.

Definition 8 (Amortised MT–preorder [11]). A family $(\mathcal{R}_i)_{i \in \mathbb{N}}$ of relations over $\mathcal{P}^{lt}$ is a *family of amortised MT–relations* if, for all $i \in \mathbb{N}$, $\langle P, Q \rangle \in \mathcal{R}_i$, and $\alpha \in \mathcal{A}$:

1. $P \xrightarrow{\alpha} P'$ implies $\exists Q', k.\, Q \xrightarrow{\sigma}^k \xrightarrow{\alpha} Q'$ and $\langle P', Q' \rangle \in \mathcal{R}_{i+k}$.
2. $Q \xrightarrow{\alpha} Q'$ implies $\exists P', k \leq i.\, P \xrightarrow{\sigma}^k \xrightarrow{\alpha} P'$ and $\langle P', Q' \rangle \in \mathcal{R}_{i-k}$.
3. $P \xrightarrow{\sigma} P'$ implies $\exists Q', k \geq 0.\, k \geq 1-i,\, Q \xrightarrow{\sigma}^k Q'$, and $\langle P', Q' \rangle \in \mathcal{R}_{i-1+k}$.
4. $Q \xrightarrow{\sigma} Q'$ implies $\exists P',\, k \geq 0.\, k \leq i+1,\, P \xrightarrow{\sigma}^k P'$, and $\langle P', Q' \rangle \in \mathcal{R}_{i+1-k}$.

We write $P \gtrsim^{mt}_i Q$ if $\langle P, Q \rangle \in \mathcal{R}_i$ for some family $(\mathcal{R}_i)_{i \in \mathbb{N}}$ of amortised MT–relations, and call $\gtrsim^{mt}_0$ the *amortised MT–preorder*.

When comparing Defs. 8 and 1, it is obvious that $\gtrsim^{mt}_0 \subseteq \gtrsim^{lt}_0$. While Conds. (3) and (4) coincide in Defs. 8 and 1, Conds. (1) and (2) do not allow clock transitions to trail the matching α–transition — just as it is the case in Cond. (1) in Def. 6. We recall the following full–abstraction result from [11].

Theorem 9 (Full abstraction [11]). *The MT–preorder $\gtrsim_{mt}$ is the* largest precongruence *contained in $\gtrsim^{mt}_0$.*

We generalise this full–abstraction result here by replacing $\gtrsim^{mt}_0$ by $\gtrsim^{lt}_0$.

Theorem 10 (Generalised full abstraction in TACS^{lt}). *The MT–preorder $\gtrsim_{mt}$ is the* largest precongruence *contained in $\gtrsim^{lt}_0$.*

Thms. 5 and 10 testify not only to the elegance of the amortised faster–than preorder as a very intuitive faster–than preorder, but also as a unified starting point to approaching faster–than relations on processes.

4 Full Abstraction in TACS

Having identified the largest precongruences contained in the amortised faster–than preorder for the sub–calculi TACS^{ut} and TACS^{lt} of TACS, it is natural to investigate the same issue for the full calculus.

For a calculus with must–clock prefixing and urgent actions, Moller and Tofts informally argued in [14] that a precongruence relating bisimulation–equivalent processes cannot satisfy a property one would, at first sight, expect from a faster–than preorder, namely that omitting a must–clock prefix should result in a faster process. This intuition can be backed up by a more general result within our setting, which includes must–clock prefixing and urgent actions, too. Our result is not just based on a specific property; instead, we have a semantic definition of an intuitive faster–than as the coarsest precongruence refining the amortised faster–than preorder, and we will show that this precongruence degrades to a congruence, rather than a proper precongruence. This congruence turns out to be a variant of *timed bisimulation* [13].

Definition 11 (Timed bisimulation). A relation $\mathcal{R}$ over $\mathcal{P}$ is a *timed bisimulation relation* if, for all $\langle P, Q \rangle \in \mathcal{R}$ and $\alpha \in \mathcal{A}$:

1. $P \xrightarrow{\alpha} P'$ implies $\exists Q'. Q \xrightarrow{\alpha} Q'$ and $\langle P', Q' \rangle \in \mathcal{R}$.
2. $P \xrightarrow{\sigma} P'$ implies $\exists Q'. Q \xrightarrow{\sigma} Q'$ and $\langle P', Q' \rangle \in \mathcal{R}$.
3. $Q \xrightarrow{\alpha} Q'$ implies $\exists P'. P \xrightarrow{\alpha} P'$ and $\langle P', Q' \rangle \in \mathcal{R}$.
4. $Q \xrightarrow{\sigma} Q'$ implies $\exists P'. P \xrightarrow{\sigma} P'$ and $\langle P', Q' \rangle \in \mathcal{R}$.

We write $P \sim_t Q$ if $\langle P, Q \rangle \in \mathcal{R}$ for some timed bisimulation relation $\mathcal{R}$, and call $\sim_t$ *timed bisimulation*.

It is obvious that timed bisimulation $\sim_t$ is an equivalence and that it refines the amortised faster–than preorder $\gtrsim_0$. However, $\sim_t$ is not a congruence for TACS since it is not compositional for parallel composition. To see this, consider the processes $\underline{a}.\mathbf{0} + \underline{b}.\mathbf{0} \sim_t \sigma.\underline{a}.\mathbf{0} + \underline{b}.\mathbf{0}$. When putting them in parallel with process $\overline{\underline{b}}.\mathbf{0}$ the relation $\sim_t$ is no longer preserved since $(\underline{a}.\mathbf{0} + \underline{b}.\mathbf{0}) \,|\, \overline{\underline{b}}.\mathbf{0}$ can engage in an a– transition while $(\sigma.\underline{a}.\mathbf{0} + \underline{b}.\mathbf{0}) \,|\, \overline{\underline{b}}.\mathbf{0}$ cannot, as the clock transition that would enable action $\underline{a}$ is preempted by the urgent communication on $\underline{b}$. We thus have to refine timed bisimulation and take initial urgent action sets into account.

Definition 12 (Urgent timed bisimulation). A relation $\mathcal{R}$ over $\mathcal{P}$ is an *urgent timed bisimulation relation* if, for all $\langle P, Q \rangle \in \mathcal{R}$ and $\alpha \in \mathcal{A}$:

1. $P \xrightarrow{\alpha} P'$ implies $\exists Q'. Q \xrightarrow{\alpha} Q'$ and $\langle P', Q' \rangle \in \mathcal{R}$.
2. $P \xrightarrow{\sigma} P'$ implies $\mathcal{U}(Q) \subseteq \mathcal{U}(P)$ and $\exists Q'. Q \xrightarrow{\sigma} Q'$ and $\langle P', Q' \rangle \in \mathcal{R}$.
3. $Q \xrightarrow{\alpha} Q'$ implies $\exists P'. P \xrightarrow{\alpha} P'$ and $\langle P', Q' \rangle \in \mathcal{R}$.
4. $Q \xrightarrow{\sigma} Q'$ implies $\mathcal{U}(P) \subseteq \mathcal{U}(Q)$ and $\exists P'. P \xrightarrow{\sigma} P'$ and $\langle P', Q' \rangle \in \mathcal{R}$.

We write $P \simeq_t Q$ if $\langle P, Q \rangle \in \mathcal{R}$ for some urgent timed bisimulation relation $\mathcal{R}$, and call $\simeq_t$ *urgent timed bisimulation*.

We have used set inclusion in Conds. (2) and (4) above in analogy to Def. 2. It is important to note the following: if $P \xrightarrow{\sigma} P'$, then $Q \xrightarrow{\sigma} Q'$ by Cond. (2), so that Cond. (4) becomes applicable. Therefore, we could just as well require equality of urgent sets in Conds. (2) and (4). This equality is violated for the two processes $\underline{a}.\mathbf{0} + \underline{b}.\mathbf{0}$ and $\sigma.\underline{a}.\mathbf{0} + \underline{b}.\mathbf{0}$ considered above, although both can engage in a clock transition.

Theorem 13 (Full abstraction). *Urgent timed bisimulation $\simeq_t$ is the largest congruence contained in $\sim_t$.*

Theorem 14 (Full abstraction in TACS). *Urgent timed bisimulation $\simeq_t$ is the largest (pre–)congruence contained in $\gtrsim_0$.*

5   Discussion

This section investigates when exactly the amortised faster–than preorder, when closed under all contexts, collapses from a proper precongruence to a congruence. We have shown in the TACS sub–calculus with only must–clock prefixing and lazy actions (cf. Sec. 3.1) and in the sub–calculus with only can–clock prefixing and urgent actions (cf. Sec. 3.2) that indeed proper precongruences are obtained: the MT–preorder and the LV–preorder, respectively. However, when combining both clock prefixes as well as lazy and urgent actions, then the result is a congruence: urgent timed bisimulation (cf. Sec. 4). We desire to explore where exactly this borderline lies, by characterising the largest precongruence contained in the amortised faster–than preorder for other combinations of can–/must–clock prefixes as well as urgent/lazy actions. While some of the resulting settings might not appear natural, others are clearly practically relevant, and this will be pointed out when analysing each combination in turn.

5.1   Can–Clock Prefixing and Urgent+Lazy Actions

Here we find ourselves in the sub–calculus $\mathrm{TACS}^{\mathrm{ut}}$ investigated in Sec. 3.1, where additionally lazy actions may be present. Lazy actions might be used for modelling the potential of errors: many errors in practice can occur at any moment and thus cannot be associated with maximal delays.

Corollary 15 (Full–abstraction in the can/urgent+lazy setting). *The LV–preorder $\gtrsim_{lv}$ is the* largest precongruence *contained in $\gtrsim_0$, when considering* TACS *processes with can–clock prefixes only.*

Hence, Thm. 5 of Sec. 3.1 remains valid in the presence of lazy actions; one only needs to check the proof of Thm. 5 and all the proofs of [10] on which it depends.

5.2   Must– and Can–Clock Prefixing and Lazy Actions

The setting here is the one of $\mathrm{TACS}^{\mathrm{lt}}$, where can–clock prefixes are added. This does not change the result we obtained for the $\mathrm{TACS}^{\mathrm{lt}}$ setting (cf. Thm. 10 in Sec. 3.2), when extending the definition of the MT–preorder $\gtrsim_{\mathrm{mt}}$ (cf. Def. 6) from processes in $\mathcal{P}^{\mathrm{lt}}$ to the class of processes considered here.

Theorem 16 (Full abstraction in the must+can/lazy setting). *The MT–preorder $\gtrsim_{mt}$ is the* largest precongruence *contained in $\gtrsim_0$, when considering* TACS *processes with lazy actions only.*

This statement can be deduced by inspecting the proofs of Sec. 3.2, i.e., the proof of Thm. 10 and the proofs of the underlying statements adopted from [11], in the presence of $\underline{\sigma}$–prefixes. The only parts that are not straightforward concern checking whether the MT–preorder $\gtrsim_{\mathrm{mt}}$ is also compositional for can–clock prefixes and whether the commutation lemma, Lemma 7, still holds. To do so we first need to adapt the syntactic faster–than preorder $\succ$ of [11] by adding the clause $P \succ \underline{\sigma}.P$.

Definition 17 (Syntactic Faster–Than Preorder). The relation $\succ \subseteq \widehat{\mathcal{P}} \times \widehat{\mathcal{P}}$ is defined as the smallest relation satisfying the following properties, for all $P, P', Q, Q' \in \widehat{\mathcal{P}}$.

$$
\begin{array}{ll}
\text{Always: } (1) \ P \succ P & (2) \ (a) \ P \succ \sigma.P \text{ and } (b) \ P \succ \underline{\sigma}.P \\
P' \succ P, \ Q' \succ Q: \ (3) \ P'|Q' \succ P|Q & (4) \ P' + Q' \succ P + Q \\
\qquad\qquad\qquad\quad (5) \ P' \setminus L \succ P \setminus L & (6) \ P'[f] \succ P[f] \\
P' \succ P, \ x \text{ guarded: } (7) \ P'[\mu x.\, P/x] \succ \mu x.\, P
\end{array}
$$

Lemma 18. *For any P, P', if $P \xrightarrow{\sigma} P'$ then $P' \succ P$.*

This lemma is adopted from Lemma 5(2) of the full version of [11], and its proof is by a straightforward induction on the structure of P. Also the other statements of the mentioned Lemma 5 hold under the modified syntactic faster–than preorder, in particular $P' \succ P$ implies $P' \gtrsim_{\mathrm{mt}} P$ for *processes* P', P in the TACS fragment we consider in this subsection. For the proof of Lemma 5 it is important that these processes satisfy the *laziness property*, i.e., each of them can perform a time step. We can now prove that the MT–preorder is compositional for can–clock prefixes, in the TACS sub–calculus that is restricted to lazy actions only.

Lemma 19. *Let P, Q be TACS processes with lazy actions only. Then $P \gtrsim_{\mathrm{mt}} Q$ implies $\underline{\sigma}.P \gtrsim_{\mathrm{mt}} \underline{\sigma}.Q$.*

Moreover, since the correctness of the commutation lemma is only based on Lemma 5 of the full version of [11], the laziness property as well as the time–determinism property, the commutation lemma obviously remains valid even in the presence of can–clock prefixing.

5.3   Can–Clock Prefixing and Lazy Actions

This combination is one that does not appear to be intuitive. If every action can delay its execution, additional potential delays specified by can–clock prefixes seem irrelevant and can be omitted (cf. Prop. 20). Further, if every delay specified by a clock prefix can indeed be omitted, then it appears that delays are not relevant at all and may thus be safely ignored (cf. Thm. 22).

Proposition 20. *$P \sim_t \underline{\sigma}.P$ for all TACS processes P with can–clock prefixes and lazy actions only.*

Because of the irrelevance of timed behaviour, timed bisimulation $\sim_t$ coincides with standard bisimulation $\sim$ [12] — where clock transitions are ignored — in the setting considered in this section.

Lemma 21. *$\sim \ = \ \sim_t$ on TACS processes P with can–clock prefixes and lazy actions only.*

As expected, the amortised faster–than preorder, when closed under all contexts, degrades to standard bisimulation in this setting.

Theorem 22 (Full abstraction in the can/lazy setting). *Standard bisimulation $\sim$ is the* largest *precongruence* contained in $\gtrsim_0$, *when considering* TACS *processes with can–clock prefixes and lazy actions only.*

To conclude, note that Prop. 20 does not hold in the presence of must–clock prefixes; e.g., $\underline{\sigma}.\sigma.a.\mathbf{0} \xrightarrow{\sigma} \sigma.a.\mathbf{0}$ and $\sigma.a.\mathbf{0} \xrightarrow{\sigma} a.\mathbf{0}$, but obviously $\sigma.a.\mathbf{0} \not\sim a.\mathbf{0}$.

5.4   Must–Clock Prefixing and Urgent Actions, & More

For the full algebra TACS, we have shown in Sec. 4 that the largest precongruence contained in the amortised faster–than preorder is urgent timed bisimulation (cf. Thm. 14). Full TACS combines must– and can–clock prefixing with lazy and urgent actions. When leaving out either lazy actions, or can–clock prefixes, or both, the result remains valid, as can be checked by inspecting the proofs of Sec. 4. Essentially, the reason is that the context constructed within this proof uses neither lazy actions nor can–clock prefixes.

Most interesting is the case when we are left with must–clock prefixing and urgent actions only. This setting coincides with the one of Hennessy and Regan's well–known *Timed Process Language* [7], TPL, in terms of both syntax and operational semantics, when leaving out TPL's timeout operator; we refer to this calculus as TPL$^-$. It is important to note that, for TPL$^-$, urgent timed bisimulation is the same as timed bisimulation; this is because all actions are urgent, and the bisimulation conditions on actions imply that equivalent processes have the same initial (urgent) actions.

However, adding either can–clock prefixing or lazy actions to TPL$^-$ leads to a more expressive calculus than TPL$^-$. For example, the process $\underline{\sigma}.\underline{\tau}.P$ in the setting must+can–clock prefixing and urgent actions can engage in both a clock transition and a τ–transition, and the same applies to process $\tau.P$. This semantic behaviour is incompatible with the maximal–progress property in TPL$^-$, and indeed in full TPL, bearing in mind that every action is urgent.

6   Related Work

Relatively little work has been published on theories that relate processes with respect to speed. This is somewhat surprising, given the wealth of literature on timed process algebras and the importance of time efficiency in system design.

Early research on process efficiency compares untimed CCS–like terms by counting internal actions either within a testing–based [15] or a bisimulation–based [2,3] setting. Due to interleaving, e.g., $(\tau.a.\mathbf{0} \mid \tau.\overline{a}.b.\mathbf{0}) \setminus \{a\}$ is considered to be as efficient as $\tau.\tau.\tau.b.\mathbf{0}$, whereas $(\sigma.a.\mathbf{0} \mid \sigma.\overline{a}.b.\mathbf{0}) \setminus \{a\}$ $((\underline{\sigma}.\underline{a}.\mathbf{0} \mid \underline{\sigma}.\underline{\overline{a}}.\underline{b}.\mathbf{0}) \setminus \{a\})$ is strictly faster than $\sigma.\sigma.\tau.b.\mathbf{0}$ $(\underline{\sigma}.\underline{\sigma}.\underline{\tau}.\underline{b}.\mathbf{0})$ in our setting.

The most closely related research to ours is obviously the one by Moller and Tofts on processes equipped with lower time bounds [14] and our own on processes equipped with upper time bounds [10]. The work of Moller and Tofts has recently been revisited by us [11] and completed by adding an axiomatisation for finite processes, a full–abstraction result, and a "weak" variant of the MT–preorder that abstracts from the unobservable action τ. Our work on upper time bounds [10] features similar results for the LV–preorder. In both papers [10, 11], the chosen reference preorders for the full–abstraction results are less abstract than the amortised faster–than preorder advocated here. Although a couple of these reference preorders borrowed some idea of amortisation (cf. Defs. 3 and 8), they were somewhat tweaked to fit the LV–preorder and the MT–preorder, respectively. Thus, Thms. 5 and 10 are indeed significant generalisations of the corresponding theorems in [10] and in [11] (cf. Thms. 4 and 9), respectively.

Most other published work on faster–than relations focuses on settings with upper time bounds and on preorders based on De Nicola and Hennessy's testing theory. Initially, research was conducted within the setting of Petri nets [16, 17], and later for the Theoretical–CSP–style process algebra PAFAS [4]. An attractive feature when adopting testing semantics is a fundamental result stating that the considered faster–than testing preorder based on continuous–time semantics coincides with the analogous testing preorder based on discrete–time semantics [17]. It remains to be seen whether a similar result holds for our bisimulation–based approach.

Last, but not least, Corradini et al. [5] introduced the *ill–timed–but–well–caused* approach for relating processes with respect to speed [1, 6]. This approach allows system components to attach local time stamps to actions. However, as a byproduct of interleaving semantics, local time stamps may decrease within action sequences exhibited by concurrent processes. These "ill–timed" runs make it difficult to relate the faster–than preorder of [5] to ours.

7   Conclusions and Future Work

We proposed a general amortised faster–than preorder for unifying bisimulation–based process theories [10, 11, 14] that relate asynchronous processes with respect to speed. Our amortised preorder ensures that a faster process must execute each action no later than the related slower process does, while both processes must be functionally equivalent in the sense of strong bisimulation [12].

Since the amortised faster–than preorder is normally not closed under all system contexts, we characterised the largest precongruences contained in it for a range of settings. The chosen range is spanned by a two–dimensional space, with one axis indicating whether only must–clock prefixes, only can–clock prefixes, or both are permitted, and the other axis determining whether only lazy actions, only urgent actions, or both kinds of actions are available. In this space, the settings of Moller/Tofts [14], which is concerned with lower time bounds, and of Lüttgen/Vogler [10], which is concerned with upper time bounds, can be recognised as "must/lazy" and "can/urgent" combinations, respectively. Since all reference preorders chosen in [10, 11] are less abstract than the amortised faster–than preorder, the results of this paper strengthen the ones obtained for both the Moller/Tofts and the Lüttgen/Vogler approach. The following table summarises our findings for each combination of clock prefix and action type, i.e., each entry identifies the behavioural relation that characterises the largest precongruence contained in the amortised faster–than preorder.

	Lazy	*Urgent*	*Lazy+Urgent*
Must	MT–preorder	Timed bisimulation	Urgent timed bisimulation
Can	Bisimulation	LV–preorder	LV–preorder
Must+Can	MT–preorder	Urgent timed bisimulation	Urgent timed bisimulation

The table shows that the amortised faster–than relation degrades to timed bisimulation as soon as must–clock prefixes and urgent actions come together. In this case, which includes the established process algebra TPL [7], one may express time intervals by equipping actions with both lower and upper time bounds. Moreover, when extending the Moller/Tofts approach by can–clock prefixing or the Lüttgen/Vogler approach by lazy actions, the MT–preorder and the LV–preorder, respectively, remain fully–abstract.

Future work shall investigate decision procedures for the MT– and LV–preorders, in order for them to be implemented in automated verification tools.

Acknowledgements. We would like to thank the anonymous referees for their valuable comments and suggestions.

References

[1] L. Aceto and D. Murphy. Timing and causality in process algebra. *Acta Inform.*, 33(4):317–350, 1996.

[2] S. Arun-Kumar and M.C.B. Hennessy. An efficiency preorder for processes. *Acta Inform.*, 29(8):737–760, 1992.

[3] S. Arun-Kumar and V. Natarajan. Conformance: A precongruence close to bisimilarity. In *STRICT '95*, Workshops in Comp., pp. 55–68. Springer-Verlag, 1995.

[4] F. Corradini, M. Di Berardini, and W. Vogler. PAFAS at work: Comparing the worst-case efficiency of three buffer implementations. In *APAQS 2001*, pp. 231–240. IEEE Computer Society Press, 2001.

[5] F. Corradini, R. Gorrieri, and M. Roccetti. Performance preorder and competitive equivalence. *Acta Inform.*, 34(11):805–835, 1997.

[6] R. Gorrieri, M. Roccetti, and E. Stancampiano. A theory of processes with durational actions. *TCS*, 140(1):73–94, 1995.

[7] M.C.B. Hennessy and T. Regan. A process algebra for timed systems. *Inform. and Comp.*, 117(2):221–239, 1995.

[8] L. Jenner and W. Vogler. Fast asynchronous systems in dense time. *TCS*, 254(1-2):379–422, 2001.

[9] G. Lüttgen and W. Vogler. Bisimulation on speed: A unified approach. Techn. Rep. 2004-15, Universität Augsburg, Germany, 2004.

[10] G. Lüttgen and W. Vogler. Bisimulation on speed: Worst–case efficiency. *Inform. and Comp.*, 191(2):105–144, 2004.

[11] G. Lüttgen and W. Vogler. Bisimulation on speed: Lower time bounds. *RAIRO Theoretical Informatics and Applications*, 2005. To appear.

[12] R. Milner. *Communication and Concurrency*. Prentice Hall, 1989.

[13] F. Moller and C. Tofts. A temporal calculus of communicating systems. In *CONCUR '90*, vol. 458 of *LNCS*, pp. 401–415. Springer-Verlag, 1990.

[14] F. Moller and C. Tofts. Relating processes with respect to speed. In *CONCUR '91*, vol. 527 of *LNCS*, pp. 424–438. Springer-Verlag, 1991.

[15] V. Natarajan and R. Cleaveland. An algebraic theory of process efficiency. In *LICS '96*, pp. 63–72. IEEE Computer Society Press, 1996.

[16] W. Vogler. Efficiency of asynchronous systems, read arcs, and the MUTEX-problem. *TCS*, 275(1–2):589–631, 2002.

[17] W. Vogler. Faster asynchronous systems. *Inform. and Comp.*, 184(2):311–342, 2003.

Branching Cells as Local States for Event Structures and Nets: Probabilistic Applications

Samy Abbes* and Albert Benveniste**

IRISA Campus de Beaulieu,
35042 Rennes Cedex. France

Abstract. We study the concept of choice for true concurrency models such as prime event structures and safe Petri nets. We propose a dynamic variation of the notion of cluster previously introduced for nets. This new object is defined for event structures, it is called a *branching cell*. Our aim is to bring an interpretation of branching cells as a right notion of "local state", for concurrent systems.

We illustrate the above claim through applications to probabilistic concurrent models. In this respect, our results extends in part previous work by Varacca-Völzer-Winskel on probabilistic confusion free event structures. We propose a construction for probabilities over so-called *locally finite* event structures that makes concurrent processes probabilistically independent—simply attach a dice to each branching cell; dices attached to *concurrent* branching cells are thrown independently. Furthermore, we provide a true concurrency generalization of Markov chains, called *Markov nets*. Unlike in existing variants of stochastic Petri nets, our approach randomizes Mazurkiewicz traces, not firing sequences. We show in this context the Law of Large Numbers (LLN), which confirms that branching cells deserve the status of local state.

Our study was motivated by the stochastic modeling of fault propagation and alarm correlation in telecommunications networks and services. It provides the foundations for probabilistic diagnosis, as well as the statistical distributed learning of such models.

1 Introduction

The study we present in this paper was motivated by algorithmic problems of distributed nature encountered in the area of telecommunications network and service management [4], in particular distributed alarm correlation and fault diagnosis. This problem consists in reconstructing the hidden history of the distributed system from partial observations (the alarms). The supervision architecture is distributed and comprises several supervisors acting as peers and communicating asynchronously.

---

* ISR, A. V. Williams Building, University of Maryland, College Park, MD 20742, USA; work performed while this author was with IRISA/Université de Rennes 1.
** IRISA/INRIA, benveniste@irisa.fr, http://www.irisa.fr/sigma2/benveniste/

V. Sassone (Ed.): FOSSACS 2005, LNCS 3441, pp. 95–109, 2005.
© Springer-Verlag Berlin Heidelberg 2005

True concurrency is essential in these algorithms: interleaving semantics is not adequate for such large distributed systems. States need to be local. Time is totally ordered at each network node, but only partially ordered by causality between nodes. Due to unavoidable ambiguity in diagnosis, nondeterminism is solved by seeking for the "most likely" solutions of the diagnosis problem. This requires having a probabilistic setting at hand.

While searching for existing models in the literature, we found very few approaches meeting our requirements. *Stochastic Petri nets* [6] and their variants are useful for performance evaluation. This model typically randomizes the holding time in places or the firing time at transitions. Making reference to a global time causes some probabilistic coupling to occur between subsystems that otherwise do not interact. *Probabilistic process algebras* [7] or *probabilistic automata* [11] are related to so-called Markov Decision Processes from applied probability theory, they rely on interleaving semantics and do not meet our needs either. In those models, interactions occur via synchronized actions and are subject to nondeterminism. In contrast, probabilistic choices are purely private, occur between interactions and do not conflict with these. Whereas this is perfectly adequate, e.g, for testing or security protocols [8, 9], this is not convenient for modeling the uncertain occurrence and propagation of faults and alarms in telecommunications networks.

Concurrent probabilistic models is a recent area of research meeting our requirements. Runs of concurrent systems are randomized without reference to a global clock, and with a true-concurrent semantics. Fundamental difficulties have lead to restrict to models with limited concurrency, e.g., *confusion free* event structures [14, 13]. *Distributed probabilistic event structures* and *Markov nets* are studied in [1], following an approach initiated in [3]; these approaches address event structures with confusion.

It appears that the very key for the analysis of probabilistic choice in true-concurrent models are the informal concepts of "concurrent local state" and "concurrent local choices". In this paper, we investigate these notions for safe Petri nets and prime event structures. We show that so-called *branching cells* introduced in [1] for event structures provide the answer. Informally, for an event structure, branching cells are minimal subsets of events closed under immediate conflict. Processes are *dynamically* decomposed by branching cells: in different executions, the same event can belong to different branching cells. Branching cells differ from clusters [5], which are statically defined on nets.

We apply the notion of branching cell to the definition and construction of concurrent probabilistic models. The probabilities we construct in this way satisfy the following essential requirement regarding concurrency: *parallel local processes are made independent in the probabilistic sense, conditionally on their common past.* Such probabilities deserve the name of *distributed* probabilities. They generalize to event structures with confusion the notion of *valuation with independence* from [13]. When applied to event structure obtained by unfolding safe Petri nets, this yields *Markov nets,* a probabilistic form of Petri nets compliant with true concurrency. We prove a Markov property and a Law of Large Numbers for Markov nets, in which branching cells play the role of local states.

The paper is organized as follows. Branching cells for prime event structures are introduced in Section 2, together with their properties. Their use for the definition and construction of concurrent probabilistic models is demonstrated in Section 3. In Section 4, Markov nets are introduced in order to state the Markov property and the Law of Large Numbers.

2 Branching Cells and Their Properties

A prime event structure [10] is a triple $\mathcal{E} = (E, \preceq, \#)$ satisfying the following properties. $(E, \preceq)$ is a partial order. The elements of E are called *events* and E is at most countable. $\#$ is the *conflict* relation on E; it is a binary relation that is symmetric and irreflexive, and satisfies the following axiom: $\forall x, y, z \in E$, $x \# y$ and $y \preceq z$ together imply $x \# z$. A subset $A \subseteq E$ is said to be a *prefix* if it is downwards closed: $\forall x \in E$, $\forall y \in A$, $x \preceq y \Rightarrow x \in A$. Finally, a prefix v is called a *configuration* of $\mathcal{E}$ if it is *conflict-free*, i.e., if $\# \cap (v \times v) = \emptyset$. Configurations are partially ordered by inclusion, and we denote by $\mathcal{V}_\mathcal{E}$ the poset of the *finite* configurations of $\mathcal{E}$. We denote by $\Omega_\mathcal{E}$ the set of maximal configurations of $\mathcal{E}$—this set is nonempty, due to Zorn's Lemma. A subset $F \subseteq E$ implicitly defines a sub-event structure $(F, \preceq_F, \#_F)$ of $\mathcal{E}$ with causality and conflict relations inherited by:

$$\preceq_F = \preceq \cap (F \times F), \quad \#_F = \# \cap (F \times F),$$

and we shall freely write F, $\mathcal{V}_F$, and Ω_F to denote this event structure and its set of finite and maximal configurations, respectively. For $e \in E$, $[e] \overset{\Delta}{=} \{e' \in \mathcal{E} : e' \preceq e\}$ denotes the smallest configuration containing e. For v a finite or infinite configuration of $\mathcal{E}$, we set $E^v \overset{\Delta}{=} \{e \in E \setminus v : \forall e' \in v, \neg(e \# e')\}$. We denote by $\mathcal{E}^v$ the induced event structure and we call it the *future* of v. Throughout the paper, we assume that $\mathcal{E}$ satisfies the following assumption:

Assumption 1. *Configuration* $[e]$ *is finite for every event e. For every $v \in \mathcal{V}_\mathcal{E}$,* $\text{Min}_{\preceq}(E^v)$ *contains finitely many events.*

The first part of Assumption 1 is very standard, it says that every event has finitely many causal predecessors. The second part of the assumption expresses that any finite configuration enables only finitely many events. The *concurrency* relation on E, denoted by $\|$, is defined as the reflexive closure of $(\mathcal{E} \times \mathcal{E}) \setminus (\# \cup \preceq \cup \succeq)$.

A central concept in defining probabilities is the notion of choice. Choice is therefore a key concept in this paper; it is captured by the notion of immediate conflict we recall next. The *immediate conflict* relation $\#_\mu$ on E is defined by:

$$\forall e, e' \in E, \quad e \#_\mu e' \quad \text{iff} \quad ([e] \times [e']) \cap \# = \{(e, e')\}. \tag{1}$$

Definition 1 (stopping prefix). *A prefix B of $\mathcal{E}$ is called a* stopping prefix *iff it is closed under immediate conflict.*

$\mathcal{E}$ is called *locally finite* iff for each event e of $\mathcal{E}$, there exists a finite stopping prefix B containing e. The following condition is assumed throughout this paper:

Assumption 2. $\mathcal{E}$ *is locally finite.*

Locally finite event structures have not been considered by authors so far. We shall see at the end of this section that confusion freeness implies local finiteness.

Stopping prefixes B satisfy the following property (see [1–Ch.3,I-3.1]):

$$\Omega_B = \{\omega \cap B \mid \omega \in \Omega_{\mathcal{E}}\}. \tag{2}$$

Although the inclusion $\subseteq$ always holds, not every prefix does satisfy the equality of property (2). Take for instance $E = \{a, b\}$ with $a\#b$. Consider prefix $P = \{a\}$ and maximal configuration $\omega = \{b\}$. Then $\omega \cap P = \emptyset$ is not maximal in P.

Clearly, the set of all stopping prefixes is a complete lattice. However, stopping prefixes are not stable under concatenation: if B is a stopping prefix of $\mathcal{E}$, $v \in \Omega_B$, and B^v is a stopping prefix of $\mathcal{E}^v$, then $B \cup B^v$ is generally not a stopping prefix of $\mathcal{E}$. As a consequence, the concatenation of v and of a configuration stopped in $\mathcal{E}^v$ is not stopped in $\mathcal{E}$ in general. Roughly speaking, the class of stopped configurations is not closed under concatenation, which is inconvenient. The notions of recursively stopped configuration and branching cell we introduce next overcome this drawback.

Definition 2 (stopped and recursively stopped configurations).

1. *A configuration v of $\mathcal{E}$ is said to be* stopped *if there is a stopping prefix B such that $v \in \Omega_B$.*
2. *Call* recursively stopped *a configuration v of $\mathcal{E}$ such that there exists a finite nondecreasing sequence $(v_n)_{0 \le n \le N}$ of configurations, where $v_0 = \emptyset$, $v_N = v$, and for $n < N$, $v_{n+1} \setminus v_n$ is a finite stopped configuration of the future $\mathcal{E}^{v_n}$ of v_n. The set of all finite recursively stopped configurations is denoted by $\mathcal{W}_{\mathcal{E}}$, or simply $\mathcal{W}$ if no confusion can occur.*

The class of recursively stopped configurations is the smallest class of configurations that contains stopped configurations and is closed under concatenation (see the examples at the end of this section).

Definition 3 (branching cell). *Stopping prefix B is called* initial *iff $\emptyset$ is the only stopping prefix strictly contained in B. Call* branching cell *of $\mathcal{E}$ any initial stopping prefix of $\mathcal{E}^v$, where v ranges over $\mathcal{W}$. The set of all branching cells of $\mathcal{E}$ is denoted by $X_{\mathcal{E}}$ (or simply X when no confusion can occur). Branching cells are generically denoted by the symbol x.*

Informally, branching cells are minimal subsets of events closed under immediate conflict. For $v \in \mathcal{W}$, denote by $\delta(v)$ the set of branching cells that are initial prefixes of $\mathcal{E}^v$. Clearly, branching cells of $\delta(v)$ do not overlap (in general, branching cells may overlap, see the examples at the end of this section). Consider the following map Δ, called the *covering* map of $\mathcal{E}$:

$$\text{for } v \in \mathcal{W}: \quad \Delta(v) \triangleq \overline{\Delta}(v) \setminus \delta(v), \tag{3}$$

$$\text{where } \overline{\Delta}(v) \triangleq \{x \in \delta(v') \mid v' \in \mathcal{W}, v' \subseteq v\}.$$

We list some properties of branching cells. The proof of Th. 4 is given in the Appendix, the remaining proofs are found in the extended version [2].

Theorem 1. *If B is a stopping prefix of $\mathcal{E}$, then $X_B \subseteq X_{\mathcal{E}}$ and $\mathcal{W}_B \subseteq \mathcal{W}_{\mathcal{E}}$. Furthermore, the covering maps Δ and Δ_B respectively defined on $\mathcal{W}$ and $\mathcal{W}_B$ coincide on $\mathcal{W}_B$.*

Theorem 2. *For every $v \in \mathcal{W}$, $X_{\mathcal{E}^v} \subseteq X_{\mathcal{E}}$. For $v \subseteq v'$ two finite recursively stopped configurations, $v' \setminus v$ is recursively stopped in $\mathcal{E}^v$. Denote by Δ^v the covering map (3) defined on $\mathcal{E}^v$. We have:*

$$\Delta(v') = \Delta(v) \cup \Delta^v(v' \setminus v), \quad \text{and} \quad \Delta(v) \cap \Delta^v(v' \setminus v) = \emptyset. \tag{4}$$

Theorem 3. *Branching cells recursively cover stopped configurations, i.e.:*

$$\forall v \in \mathcal{W}, \quad v = \bigcup_{x \in \Delta(v)} v \cap x, \tag{5}$$

and, for each $x \in \Delta(v)$, $v \cap x$ is an element of Ω_x.

Theorem 4. *Let ξ be a subset of $\delta(\emptyset_{\mathcal{E}})$, where $\emptyset_{\mathcal{E}}$ denotes the empty configuration of $\mathcal{E}$. The formula*

$$B_\xi \stackrel{\Delta}{=} \bigcup_{x \in \xi} x \tag{6}$$

defines a stopping prefix of $\mathcal{E}$, whose set of finite configurations $\mathcal{V}_{B_\xi}$ and maximal configurations Ω_{B_ξ} respectively decompose as:

$$\mathcal{V}_{B_\xi} = \prod_{x \in \xi} \mathcal{V}_x \quad \text{and} \quad \Omega_{B_\xi} = \prod_{x \in \xi} \Omega_x. \tag{7}$$

Call thin *a prefix of $\mathcal{E}$ of the form (6), where $\xi \subseteq \delta(\emptyset_{\mathcal{E}})$. The complete lattice of thin prefixes has finite upper bound.*

Comments. Theorem 1 expresses that recursively stopped configurations and branching cells are stable under restriction to stopping prefixes.

Theorem 2 expresses that recursively stopped configurations and branching cells are stable under restriction to the futures $\mathcal{E}^v$ of elements $v \in \mathcal{W}$. Equation (4) says that covering maps are incremental with respect to the future.

Theorem 3 is self explanatory. Remark that the property $v \cap x \in \Omega_x$ extends the property $\omega \cap B \in \Omega_B$ stated by Eqn. (2).

The product forms given in Th. 4 show that branching cells are traversed by local processes that are both *concurrent* and *independent*: in the future of v, local decisions taken in a branching cell $x \in \delta(v)$ do not influence the range of possible local decisions that can be taken in other branching cells of $\delta(v)$. In other words, choices in different concurrent branching cells are made by independent and non-communicating agents. Section 3 adds a probabilistic interpretation to this.

Theorem 4 is stated only for thin prefixes that "begin" the event structure. However, Th. 4 can be recursively applied in the futures $\mathcal{E}^v$, for $v \in \mathcal{W}$, with $\delta(v)$ playing the role of $\delta(\emptyset_{\mathcal{E}})$.

Finally, the finiteness of the above introduced objects follows from our assumptions: the finiteness of branching cells follows from Assumption 2, and the finiteness of the upper bound $\bigcup_\xi B_\xi$ of thin prefixes follows from Assumption 1 (see the proof of Th. 4 in the Appendix).

Examples. For all examples of this paper, we write (abc) to denote the configuration $\{a, b, c\}$.

The event structure $\mathcal{E}$ shown in Figure 1–left has two nonempty stopping prefixes: $\{a, b\}$ and $\{a, b, c, d, e\}$. Its stopped configurations are $\emptyset, (a), (b), (a, c, e), (b, d)$, and (b, c, e). Let us determine the recursively stopped configurations and the branching cells of $\mathcal{E}$. Since $\mathcal{E}$ has a unique initial stopping prefix $\delta(\emptyset) = \{\{a, b\}\}$, it follows that (a) and (b) are recursively stopped. The future $\mathcal{E}^{(a)}$ is the event structure $\{c, e\}$ with empty conflict and causality; it has two initial stopping prefixes: $\delta(a) = \{\{c\}, \{e\}\}$. Therefore (ac) and (ae) are recursively stopped, as well as (ace). The future of (ace) is empty. The future $\mathcal{E}^{(b)}$ is given by: $\mathcal{E}^{(b)} = c \leadsto d \leadsto e$, with a unique initial stopping prefix: $\delta(b) = \{\{c, d, e\}\}$. Therefore (bd) and (bce) are also recursively stopped. The futures of (bd) and of (bce) are empty, so we are done: $\mathcal{W} = \{\emptyset, (a), (b), (ac), (ae), (ace), (bd), (bce)\}$. Note that (ac) and (ae) are recursively stopped but *not* stopped. Note also that configurations (bc) and (be) are *not* recursively stopped. Finally, the set of all branching cells is $\{\{a, b\}, \{c\}, \{e\}, \{c, d, e\}\}$.

The event structure depicted in Figure 1–middle illustrates the concurrency of branching cells of $\delta(\emptyset)$. Note that some minimal events belong to no initial branching cell.

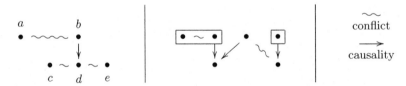

Fig. 1. Left: configuration (ac) is recursively stopped, with associated sequence $(\emptyset, (a), (ac))$ according to Definition 2; however, (ac) is not stopped. Middle: branching cells of $\delta(\emptyset)$ are depicted by frames

Local Finiteness Relaxes Confusion Freeness. Recall that event structure $\mathcal{E}$ is said to be *confusion free* if $\mathcal{E}$ satisfies the Q axiom of concrete domains [10]. Equivalently, $\mathcal{E}$ is confusion free iff [13]:

1. $\#_\mu$ is transitive,
2. for all $e, e' \in \mathcal{E}$: $e \#_\mu e' \Rightarrow [e] \setminus \{e\} = [e'] \setminus \{e'\}$.

Define, for every event $e \in E$:

$$F(e) = \{f \in E : e \,\#_\mu\, f\}, \qquad B(e) = \bigcup_{f \in [e]} F(f).$$

The second part of Assumption 1 together with point 2 above imply that every set $F(f)$ is finite. It follows that $B(e)$ is finite, and point 1 implies that $B(e)$ is a stopping prefix, that contains e. This holds for every event e, so $\mathcal{E}$ is locally finite. Moreover every finite configuration is stopped, and therefore recursively stopped. The set of branching cells is equal to $\{F(e) : e \in E\}$, which forms a partition of E. Such simple properties fail for event structures with confusion. For example, in the event structure depicted in Figure 1–left, branching cells $\{c\}$ and $\{c, d, e\}$ possess a nonempty intersection. For confusion free event structures, branching cells reduce to the *cells* defined in [13].

To summarize, confusion free event structures are locally finite, but the converse is not true. Locally finite event structures appear as event structures with "finite confusion".

3 Application to Probabilistic Event Structures

We recall that a *probabilistic event structure* is a pair $(\mathcal{E}, \mathbb{P})$ with $\mathbb{P}$ a probability measure[1] on the space Ω of maximal configurations of $\mathcal{E}$. We shall prove that a probabilistic event structure can be naturally defined from the new notion of *locally randomized* event structure (Th. 5). The construction performed below adds a probabilistic interpretation to the properties of branching cells and of recursively stopped configurations.

Definition 4 (locally randomized event structure). *A locally randomized event structure is a pair $(\mathcal{E}, (p_x)_{x \in X})$, where X is the set of branching cells of $\mathcal{E}$, and for each $x \in X$, p_x is a probability over Ω_x.*

Let $(\mathcal{E}, (p_x)_{x \in X})$ be a locally randomized event structure. For $F \subseteq E$ a sub-event structure of $\mathcal{E}$, denote by X_F the set of all branching cells of F. Call F *well formed* if it is finite and such that $X_F \subseteq X_\mathcal{E}$. Note that finite stopping prefixes are well formed according to Th. 1. For F a well formed, set:

$$\text{for } \omega_F \in \Omega_F : \quad \mathbb{P}_F(\omega_F) = \prod_{x \in \Delta(\omega_F)} p_x(\omega_F \cap x), \tag{8}$$

which is well defined since, according to Th. 3, $\omega_F \cap x \in \Omega_x$.

Lemma 1. *If $B = B_\xi$ is a thin prefix (see Th. 4), then $\mathbb{P}_B$ is the direct product of the p_x's, for x ranging over ξ. In particular, $\mathbb{P}_B$ is a probability.*

---

[1] The σ-algebra considered is the Borel σ-algebra generated by the Scott topology on Ω, see [1] for details. In the remaining of the paper, we do not mention the σ-algebras considered since they are always canonical.

Proof. This is a direct consequence of Eqn. (8) and Th. 4.   ◇

Lemma 2. *If $F \subseteq E$ is a well formed sub-event structure, then $\mathbb{P}_F$ is a probability. In particular, for each stopping prefix B, $\mathbb{P}_B$ is a probability.*

Proof. We show that $\mathbb{P}_F$ is a probability by induction on integer $n_F = \sup_{\omega_F \in \Omega_F}$ Card$\Delta(\omega_F) < \infty$. The result is a direct consequence of Lemma 1 for $n_F \leq 1$. Assume it holds until $n \geq 1$, and let F be well formed and such that $n_F \leq n+1$. Consider the (finite) upper bound D of thin prefixes of F. Applying property (2) to D yields the following decomposition for Ω_F: $\quad \Omega_F = \bigcup_{v \in \Omega_D} \{v\} \times \Omega_{F^v}$. Moreover, for each $v \in \Omega_D$ and $\omega' \in \Omega_{F^v}$, and setting $\omega = v \cup \omega'$, we obtain by Th. 2:

$$\Delta(\omega) = \Delta(v) \cup \Delta^v(\omega'), \qquad \Delta(v) \cap \Delta^v(\omega') = \emptyset. \tag{9}$$

Formulas (8) and (9) together imply:

$$\sum_{\omega \in \Omega_F} \mathbb{P}_F(\omega) = \sum_{v \in \Omega_D} \mathbb{P}_D(v) \Big(\sum_{\omega' \in \Omega_{F^v}} \mathbb{P}_{F^v}(\omega') \Big). \tag{10}$$

It follows from Th. 2 that for each $v \in \Omega_D$, the future F^v of v in F satisfies $X_{F^v} \subseteq X_F \subseteq X_\mathcal{E}$. Formula (9) implies that $n_{F^v} \leq n$. Hence we can apply the induction hypothesis to F^v and obtain $\sum_{\omega' \in \Omega_{F^v}} \mathbb{P}_{F^v}(\omega') = 1$. From Lemma 1 we get: $\sum_{v \in \Omega_D} \mathbb{P}_D(v) = 1$. This, together with Eqn. (10), implies $\sum_{\omega \in \Omega_F} \mathbb{P}_F(\omega) = 1$, which completes the induction.   ◇

Corollary 1. *Let $B \subseteq B'$ be two finite stopping prefixes of $\mathcal{E}$. The following formula holds:*

$$\forall \omega_B \in \Omega_B \; : \quad \mathbb{P}_B(\omega_B) = \sum_{\omega' \in \Omega_{B'}, \, \omega' \supseteq \omega_B} \mathbb{P}_{B'}(\omega'). \tag{11}$$

Proof. Let ω_B be an element of Ω_B, and denote by $B'' \triangleq B'^{\omega_B}$ the future of ω_B in B'. Then $\{\omega' \in \Omega_{B'} : \omega' \supseteq \omega_B\}$ is one to one with $\Omega_{B''}$. Eqn. (4) gives $\Delta(\omega') = \Delta(\omega_B) \cup \Delta^{\omega_B}(\omega' \setminus \omega_B)$, whence:

$$\sum_{\omega' \in \Omega_{B'}, \, \omega' \supseteq \omega_B} \mathbb{P}_{B'}(\omega') = \mathbb{P}_B(\omega_B) \sum_{z \in \Omega_{B''}} \mathbb{P}_{B''}(z). \tag{12}$$

From Lemma 2 applied to finite event structure B'', the sum on the right hand side of (12) equals 1, which implies (11).   ◇

Theorem 5. *Let $(\mathcal{E}, (p_x)_{x \in X})$ be a locally randomized event structure. Then there exists a unique probabilistic event structure $(\mathcal{E}, \mathbb{P})$ such that, for every finite stopping prefix B:*

$$\forall v \in \Omega_B, \quad \mathbb{P}(\{\omega \in \Omega : \omega \supseteq v) = \mathbb{P}_B(v), \tag{13}$$

where $\mathbb{P}_B$ is defined by Eqn. (8).

Proof. Corollary 1 expresses that the family $(\Omega_B, \mathbb{P}_B)$, where B ranges over the set of finite stopping prefixes, is a *projective system* of (finite) probability spaces. It is proved in [1–Ch.2] that, under Assumption 2, this projective system defines a unique probability $\mathbb{P}$ on $\Omega_\mathcal{E}$ that extends this projective system, i.e., satisfies Eqn. (13).   ◇

Probabilistic Future and Distributed Probabilities. So far we have shown how to construct probabilistic event structures from locally randomized event structures. Conversely, each probability $\mathbb{P}$ over $\mathcal{E}$, such that $\mathbb{P}(v) > 0$ for every finite configuration v, defines a family $(p_x)_{x \in X}$ of local probabilities associated to branching cells as follows, for $x \in X$ and $\omega_x \in \Omega_x$:[2]

$$p_x(\omega_x) \;\triangleq\; \frac{\mathbb{P}\left(\{\omega \in \Omega_\mathcal{E} \;:\; x \in \overline{\Delta}(\omega),\; \omega \cap x = \omega_x\}\right)}{\mathbb{P}\left(\{\omega \in \Omega_\mathcal{E} \;:\; x \in \overline{\Delta}(\omega)\}\right)}. \tag{14}$$

Of course, the following natural question arises: is it true that the family $(p_x)_{x \in X}$ conversely induces $\mathbb{P}$ through Eqn. (8) and Th. 5? Not in general. The following Th. 6, which proof is found in [1–Ch.4], provides the answer.

For $(\mathcal{E}, \mathbb{P})$ a probabilistic event structure, consider the *likelihood* function q defined on the set of finite configurations by:

$$\forall v \in \mathcal{V}_\mathcal{E}\;,\;\; q(v) \triangleq \mathbb{P}(\{\omega \in \Omega_\mathcal{E} \;:\; \omega \supseteq v\}). \tag{15}$$

For v a finite configuration, the *probabilistic future* $(\mathcal{E}^v, \mathbb{P}^v)$ is defined by

$$\mathbb{P}^v(\cdot) \triangleq \frac{1}{q(v)} \mathbb{P}(\cdot).$$

The associated likelihood q^v is given by $q^v(w) = \frac{1}{q(v)} q(v \cup w)$, for w ranging over the set of finite configurations of $\mathcal{E}^v$.

Definition 5 (distributed probability). *A probability $\mathbb{P}$ is called* distributed *iff, for each recursively stopped configuration v, and each thin prefix B^v_ξ in $\mathcal{E}^v$, the following holds:*

$$\forall \omega \in \Omega_{B^v_\xi}\;,\;\; q^v(\omega) = \prod_{x \in \xi} p_x(\omega \cap x) \tag{16}$$

where p_x is defined from $\mathbb{P}$ by using (14).

Theorem 6. *Let $(\mathcal{E}, \mathbb{P})$ be a probabilistic event structure, and let $(p_x)_{x \in X}$ be defined from $\mathbb{P}$ by using (14). The construction of Th. 5 induces again $\mathbb{P}$ iff $\mathbb{P}$ is a distributed probability. In this case, the likelihood function is given on $\mathcal{W}$ by:* $q(v) = \prod_{x \in \Delta(v)} p_x(v \cap x)$.

Remark that the likelihood given in Th. 6 extends the original formula (8). Th. 6 also shows that, for confusion-free event structures, the *valuations with independence* defined in [13] are equivalently defined as likelihoods (15) associated with distributed probabilities.

---

[2] The condition $p(v) > 0$ is stated here for simplicity, it can be removed with some more technical effort.

Comment. Eqn. (16), which characterizes distributed probabilities, has the following interpretation. Because of the absence of conflicts, and conditionally on a partial execution $v \in \mathcal{W}$, the local choices inside the different branching cells belonging to $\delta(v)$ are performed independently from one another. Eqn. (16) is the probabilistic counterpart of the concurrency of branching cells, stated by Eqn. (7) in Th. 4.

4   Markov Nets

In this section, we apply the previous results to event structures arising from the unfolding of safe and finite Petri nets. *Markov nets* are introduced and briefly studied. Proofs of the results stated in this section as well as additional results can be found in [1], Chapters 5–7.

Event structures arising from the unfolding of safe and finite Petri nets are equipped with a labelling of their events by transitions of the net. It is therefore natural to consider local randomizations of these event structures that are such that $p_x = p_{x'}$ whenever branching cells x and x' are isomorphic as labelled event structures. Finite safe Petri nets equipped with such local randomizations are called Markov nets; they generalize Markov chains to concurrent systems. We show in this section that branching cells provide the adequate concept of "local state" for Markov nets. In particular, we show that the classical Law of Large Numbers (LLN) for Markov chains properly generalizes to Markov nets, provided that the set of all equivalence classes of isomorphic branching cells is taken as state space for Markov nets. Such equivalence classes, called *dynamic clusters,* are introduced next.

Throughout this section, we assume that $\mathcal{E}$ is a locally finite event structure arising from the unfolding of a finite safe Petri net $\mathcal{N}$. Although Assumption 1 is always satisfied by the unfolding of a safe and finite Petri net, this is not necessarily the case for local finiteness (Assumption 2). Local finiteness is an important restriction, although the class of safe nets with locally finite unfolding is strictly larger than the classes of free-choice or confusion-free nets.

Let M_0 denote the initial marking of $\mathcal{N}$. For v a finite configuration of $\mathcal{E}$, we denote by $m(v)$ the marking reached in $\mathcal{N}$ after the action of configuration v. It is well known that, up to an isomorphism of labelled event structure, the future $\mathcal{E}^v$ is the unfolding of net $\mathcal{N}$ from the initial marking $m(v)$. Whence:

$$\forall v, v' \in \mathcal{V}_\mathcal{E}, \quad m(v) = m(v') \Rightarrow \mathcal{E}^v = \mathcal{E}^{v'}. \tag{17}$$

It makes thus sense to denote by $\mathcal{E}^m$ the event structure that unfolds $\mathcal{N}$ starting from the reachable marking m. Since the reachable markings are finitely many, the futures $\mathcal{E}^v = \mathcal{E}^{m(v)}$ are finitely many up to isomorphism of labelled event structures. Since each set of branching cells $\delta(v)$ is finite, it follows then from Def. 3 that branching cells of $\mathcal{E}$ are finitely many, *up to an isomorphism of labelled event structures.*

Definition 6 (dynamic cluster). *An isomorphism class of branching cells is called a* dynamic cluster *of $\mathcal{N}$. We denote by Σ the (finite) set of dynamic clusters. Dynamic clusters are generically denoted by the boldface symbol $\mathbf{s}$. The equivalence class of branching cell x is denoted by $\langle x \rangle$.*

It is shown in the extended version [2] that, if the event structure is confusion-free, branching cells can be interpreted as the events of a new event structure, called *choice structure*. The set of dynamic clusters Σ is then a finite alphabet that labels the choice structure. Under certain conditions, the labelled event structure obtained is actually itself the unfolding of a safe Petri net, called the *choice net*. The interested reader is referred to [2] for further details.

Definition 7 (Markov net). *A* Markov net *is a pair $(\mathcal{N}, (p_\mathbf{s})_{\mathbf{s} \in \Sigma})$, where $\mathcal{N}$ is a finite safe Petri net with locally finite unfolding, and $p_\mathbf{s}$ is a probability on the finite set $\Omega_\mathbf{s}$ for every $\mathbf{s} \in \Sigma$.*

Markov net $(\mathcal{N}, (p_\mathbf{s})_{\mathbf{s} \in \Sigma})$ induces a locally randomized event structure $(\mathcal{E}, (p_x)_{x \in X})$ (see Def. 4) by setting $p_x = p_{\langle x \rangle}$ for every branching cell $x \in X_\mathcal{E}$, whence a unique distributed probability $\mathbb{P}$ on Ω (Th. 5 and Th. 6). Note that, if net $\mathcal{N}$ is the product of two non interacting nets $\mathcal{N} = \mathcal{N}_1 \times \mathcal{N}_2$, then the two components $\mathcal{N}_i, i \in \{1, 2\}$ are independent in the probabilistic sense, i.e., $\mathbb{P} = \mathbb{P}_1 \otimes \mathbb{P}_2$.

Theorem 7 (Markov property). *Let $(\mathcal{N}, (p_\mathbf{s})_{\mathbf{s} \in \Sigma})$ be a Markov net, and let $\mathbb{P}$ be the associated distributed probability on Ω. For v a finite recursively stopped configuration of $\mathcal{E}$, let $m(v)$ and Σ^v denote respectively the marking reached by v and the classes of branching cells of $\mathcal{E}^v$. Then for every $v \in \mathcal{W}$, the probabilistic future $(\mathcal{E}^v, \mathbb{P}^v)$ is associated with Markov net $(\mathcal{N}^v, (p_\mathbf{s})_{\mathbf{s} \in \Sigma^v})$, where $\mathcal{N}^v$ is the same net as $\mathcal{N}$, except that $\mathcal{N}^v$ has initial marking $m(v)$. Moreover we have:*

$$\forall v, v' \in \mathcal{W}, \quad m(v) = m(v') \Rightarrow \mathbb{P}^v = \mathbb{P}^{v'}. \tag{18}$$

Eqn. (18) expresses the memoryless nature of Markov nets: the probabilistic future of a $v \in \mathcal{W}$ only depends on the final marking $m(v)$. It is the probabilistic counterpart of Eqn. (17).

The Law of Large Numbers (LLN). Call *return* to the initial marking M_0 any finite recursively stopped configuration v such that:

1. $m(v) = M_0$,
2. $\mathrm{Min}_{\preceq}(E) \cap \mathrm{Min}_{\preceq}(E^v) = \emptyset$.

Informally, Point 2 above says that all the tokens in the net have moved when we apply configuration v. It prohibits recurrent behaviors that leave a part of the initial marking unchanged. For our study of LLN, we restrict ourselves to *recurrent* Markov nets, i.e., Markov nets such that, with probability 1, $\omega \in \Omega$ contains infinitely many returns to M_0. If the considered net is indeed sequential, then our definition reduces to the classical notion of recurrence, for Markov chains [12].

For finite recurrent Markov chains, the LLN states as follows. Let Σ be the finite state space of a Markov chain $(X_k)_{k\geq 1}$, and let $f : \Sigma \to \mathbb{R}$ be a test function. The sums $S_n(f) = \sum_{k=1}^{n} f(X_k)$ are called *ergodic sums*, and the LLN studies the limit, for $n \to \infty$, of the *ergodic means*: $M_n(f) = \frac{1}{n} S_n(f)$. In extending the LLN to Markov net $\mathcal{N}$, we are faced with two difficulties:

1. What is the proper concept of state?
2. What replaces counter n, since time is not totally ordered?

Corresponding answers are:

1. The set Σ of dynamic clusters of $\mathcal{N}$ is taken as the state space.
2. For v a recursively stopped configuration, the number of branching cells contained in $\Delta(v)$ is taken as the "duration" of v.

More precisely, call *distributed function* a finite family $f = (f_s)_{s\in\Sigma}$ of real-valued functions $f_s : \Omega_s \to \mathbb{R}$. Distributed functions form a vector space of finite dimension over $\mathbb{R}$. The *concurrent ergodic sums* of f are defined as the function $S(f)$:

$$S(f) : \mathcal{W} \to \mathbb{R} , \quad \forall v \in \mathcal{W}, \; S(f)(v) = \sum_{x\in\Delta(v)} f_{\langle x\rangle}(v \cap x). \tag{19}$$

For example, if $N = (N_s)_{s\in\Sigma}$ is the distributed function given by $N_s(w) = 1$ for all $s \in \Sigma$ and $w \in \Omega_s$, then $S(N)(v)$ counts the number of branching cells contained in $\Delta(v)$. The *concurrent ergodic means* $M(f) : \mathcal{W} \to \mathbb{R}$ associated with a distributed function f are defined as the following ratios:

$$\forall v \in \mathcal{W}, \quad M(f)(v) = \frac{1}{S(N)(v)} S(f)(v) . \tag{20}$$

The LLN is concerned by the limit

$$\lim_{v\subseteq\omega, v\to\omega} M(f)(v) , \tag{21}$$

and this for each $\omega \in \Omega$, in a sense we shall make precise. The following notion of *stopping operator* will be central in this respect—stopping operators indeed generalize stopping times [12] for sequential stochastic processes:

Definition 8 (stopping operator). *A random variable* $V : \Omega \to \mathcal{W}$*, satisfying* $V(\omega) \subseteq \omega$ *for all* $\omega \in \Omega$*, is called a* stopping operator *if for all* $\omega, \omega' \in \Omega$*, we have:* $\omega' \supseteq V(\omega) \Rightarrow V(\omega') = V(\omega)$*. Say that a sequence* $(V_n)_{n\geq 1}$ *of stopping operators is* regular *if the following properties are satisfied—such sequences exist:*

1. $V_n \subseteq V_{n+1}$ *for all* n*, and* $\bigcup_n V_n(\omega) = \omega$ *for all* $\omega \in \Omega$*;*
2. *there are two constants* $k_1, k_2 > 0$ *such that, with* N *the distributed function defined above, for all* $\omega \in \Omega$ *and all* $n \geq 1$*:* $k_1 n \leq S(N)(V_n(\omega)) \leq k_2 n$*.*

Using this concept, Eqn. (21) is re-expressed as follows:

Definition 9 (convergence of ergodic means). *For f a distributed function, we say that the ergodic means $M(f)$ converge to a function $\mu : \Omega \to \mathbb{R}$ if for every regular sequence $(V_n)_{n\geq 1}$ of stopping operators,*

$$\lim_{n\to\infty} M(f)\big(V_n(\omega)\big) = \mu(\omega) \quad \text{with probability } 1. \tag{22}$$

Concurrency prevents property (22) from holding for general recurrent Markov nets, as the following particular case shows. Assume that net $\mathcal{N}$ decomposes as $\mathcal{N} = \mathcal{N}_1 \times \mathcal{N}_2$ and the two components $\mathcal{N}_1$ and $\mathcal{N}_2$ do not interact at all. In this case, regular sequences $V = (V_n)_{n\geq 1}$ of stopping operators decompose into pairs (V^1, V^2) of independent regular sequences, one for each component. For f and v decomposed as $f = (f_1, f_2)$ and $v = (v_1, v_2)$ respectively, we have $S(f)(v) = S(f_1)(v_1) + S(f_2)(v_2)$ and $S(N)(v) = S(N_1)(v_1) + S(N_2)(v_2)$. Since V_n^1 and V_n^2 are free to converge at their own speed, we cannot expect that convergence of ergodic means will hold for this case. Clearly, concurrency is the very cause for this difficulty.

For the detailed statement of the condition needed to overcome this problem, the reader is referred to [1–Ch.8]. We only give an informal explanation, in terms of Petri nets and branching cells. If, in an execution $\omega \in \Omega$, we block a token represented by some condition b in the unfolding, we measure the "loss of synchronization" of the system by counting the number of branching cells that can be traversed *without moving the blocked token.* This length defines a random variable $\Omega \to \mathbb{R}$ for each condition b of the unfolding. We say that the considered Markov net has *integrable concurrency height* if all these random variables are integrable, i.e., possess finite expectation w.r.t. probability $\mathbb{P}$, for b ranging over the set of all conditions of the unfolding. Remark that, due to the memoryless property of the system, this set of random variables is actually finite.

Theorem 8 (Law of Large Numbers). *Let $(\mathcal{N}, (p_{\mathbf{s}})_{\mathbf{s}\in\Sigma})$ be a Markov net. Assume that $\mathcal{N}$ is recurrent and has integrable concurrency height. Then:*

1. *For any distributed function $f = (f_{\mathbf{s}})_{\mathbf{s}\in\Sigma}$, the ergodic means $M(f)$ converge in the sense of Def. 9 to a function $\mu(f) : \Omega \to \mathbb{R}$.*
2. *Except possibly on a set of zero probability, $\mu(f)$ is constant and given by:*

$$\mu(f) = \sum_{\mathbf{s}\in\Sigma} p_{\mathbf{s}}(f_{\mathbf{s}})\alpha(\mathbf{s}), \quad \text{with:} \quad p_{\mathbf{s}}(f_{\mathbf{s}}) = \sum_{w\in\Omega_{\mathbf{s}}} f_{\mathbf{s}}(w)p_{\mathbf{s}}(w). \tag{23}$$

3. *In formula (23), coefficients $\alpha(\mathbf{s})$ are equal to*

$$\alpha(\mathbf{s}) = \mu(N^{\mathbf{s}}), \tag{24}$$

and satisfy $\alpha(\mathbf{s}) \in [0,1]$ and $\sum_{\mathbf{s}} \alpha(\mathbf{s}) = 1$; $\alpha(\mathbf{s})$ is the asymptotic rate of occurrence of local state $\mathbf{s}$ in a typical execution $\omega \in \Omega$.

Statement 3 is a direct consequence of statements 1 and 2: Fix $\mathbf{s} \in \Sigma$, and consider the distributed function $N^{\mathbf{s}}$ defined by $N_{\mathbf{s}}^{\mathbf{s}}(w) = 1$ for all $w \in \Omega_{\mathbf{s}}$ and $N_{\mathbf{s}'}^{\mathbf{s}} = 0$ if $\mathbf{s} \neq \mathbf{s}'$. Applying statements 1 and 2 to $N^{\mathbf{s}}$ yields $\alpha(\mathbf{s}) = \mu(N^{\mathbf{s}})$. In particular, from $N = \sum_{\mathbf{s}} N^{\mathbf{s}}$ we obtain: $\sum_{\mathbf{s}} \alpha(\mathbf{s}) = 1$.

If the net is actually sequential (i.e., reduces to a recurrent finite Markov chain), then Σ is the state space of the chain and coefficients $\alpha(\mathbf{s})$ are equal to the coefficients of the invariant measure of the chain. This again reveals that dynamic clusters play the role of local states for concurrent systems.

5   Conclusion and Perspectives

We have proposed branching cells as a form of local concurrent state for prime event structures and safe Petri nets. Our study applies to so-called locally finite event structures that significantly extend the confusion-free case. We have applied this to probabilistic event structures: for $\mathcal{E}$ an event structure with set of maximal configurations Ω, there is a one-to-one correspondence between local randomizations of the branching cells of $\mathcal{E}$ on the one hand, and the class of distributed probabilities on Ω on the other hand. Distributed probabilities yield concurrent systems in which locally concurrent random choices are taken independently in the probabilistic sense.

We have applied the construction of distributed probabilities to unfoldings of safe and finite Petri nets. This leads to the model of Markov nets, a probabilistic model of concurrent system specified by finitely many parameters. Besides the relation between causal and probabilistic independence, Markov nets bring the Markov property as a probabilistic counterpart to the memoryless nature of Petri nets. The Law of Large Numbers extends to Markov nets, with dynamic clusters taken as states. Therefore branching cells and dynamic clusters provide the adequate notion of local state, for systems with concurrency.

Acknowledgments. We wish to thank Philippe Darondeau for fruitful discussions and hints.

References

1. Abbes, S.: *Probabilistic model for concurrent and distributed systems. Limit theorems and applications.* PhD Thesis (2004), IRISA-Université de Rennes 1.
2. Abbes, S. and Benvensite, A.: *Branching cells as local states for event structures and nets: probabilistic applications.* INRIA Research Report (2004) **RR-5347**. http://www.inria.fr/rrrt/rr-5347.html
3. Benveniste, A., Haar, S. and Fabre, E.: Markov nets: probabilistic models for distributed and concurrent systems. *IEEE Trans. on Aut. Cont.* **48**:11 (2003) 1936–1950.
4. Benveniste, A., Haar, S., Fabre, E. and Jard, C.: Distributed monitoring of concurrent and asynchronous systems. *Proc. of CONCUR'03, LNCS* **2761** (2003), 1–26. Extended and improved version to appear in *Discrete Event Dynamic Systems: Theory and Application,* Kluwer, 2005.
5. Desel, J. and Esparza, R.: *Free choice Petri nets.* Cambridge University Press (1995).

6. Haas, P. J.: *Stochastic Petri nets.* Springer-Verlag (2002).
7. Hermanns, H., Herzog, U. and Katoen, J.-P.: Process algebra for performance evaluation. *T.C.S.* **274**:1 (2002) 43–88.
8. Larsen, K. G. and Skou, A.: Bisimulation through probabilistic testing. *Inf. and Comp.* **94**:1 (1991) 1–28.
9. Mateus, P., Mitchell, J. C. and Scedrov, A.: Composition of cryptographic protocols in a probabilistic polynomial-time process calculus. *Proc. of CONCURR'03, LNCS* **2761** (2003) 327–349.
10. Nielsen, M., Plotkin, G. and Winskel, G.: Petri nets, event structures and domains, part 1. *T.C.S.* **13** (1981) 85–108.
11. Segala, R. and Lynch, N.: Decision algorithms for probabilistic bisimulations. *Proc. of CONCUR'02, LNCS* **2421** (2002) 371–396.
12. Shiryaev, A. N.: *Probability.* Springer Verlag (1984).
13. Varacca, D., Völzer, H. and Winskel, G.: Probabilistic event structures and domains. *Proc. of CONCUR'04, LNCS* **3170** (2004) 481–496.
14. Völzer, H.: Randomized non-sequential processes. *Proc. of CONCUR'01, LNCS* **2154** (2001) 184–201.

A   Appendix: Proof of Th. 4.

This section presents the proof of Th. 4 of Section 2. For the other proofs of results of Section 2, the reader is referred to the extended version [2]. For the proof of the Law of large numbers, we refer to [1].

Lemma 3. *If x, y are two distinct initial stopping prefixes, then $e \parallel f$ for all pairs $(e, f) \in x \times y$.*

Proof. Follows from the definitions, and from the fact that if x, y are two events in conflict, then there are two events x', y' in *minimal* conflict and with $x' \preceq x$ and $y' \preceq y$.   ◇

Proof of Th. 4. Remark first that $\delta(\emptyset)$ is finite. Indeed, choose for each $x \in \delta(\emptyset)$ an event e_x minimal in x. All $x \in \delta(\emptyset)$ are disjoint since they are minimal, hence all the e_x are distinct, and minimal in $\mathcal{E}$. Assumption 1 (applied with $v = \emptyset$) implies that they are finitely many, and thus $\delta(\emptyset)$ is finite. Assumption 2 implies that each $x \in \delta(\emptyset)$ is a finite prefix. It follows than thin prefixes B_ξ have $\bigcup_{x \in \delta(\emptyset)} x$ as finite upper bound.

Now let ξ be a subset of $\delta(\emptyset)$, and let $B_\xi = \bigcup_{x \in \xi} x$. For each configuration v of B_ξ, and for each $x \in \xi$, $v \cap x$ is clearly a configuration of x, whence a mapping: $\phi : \mathcal{V}_{B_\xi} \to \prod_{x \in \xi} \mathcal{V}_x$. For each tuple $(v_x)_{x \in \xi}$ with $v_x \in \mathcal{V}_x$, put $v = \bigcup_{x \in \xi} v_x$. Then v is clearly a prefix of B_ξ, and it follows from Lemma 3 that v is also conflict-free, thus v is a configuration of B_ξ. The mapping $(v_x)_{x \in \xi} \to v$ defined by this way is the inverse of ϕ, thus ϕ is a bijection. Clearly, ϕ maps the set of maximal configurations of B_ξ onto $\prod_{x \in \xi} \Omega_x$, which completes the proof.

Axiomatizations for Probabilistic Finite-State Behaviors

Yuxin Deng[1,*] and Catuscia Palamidessi[2,**]

[1] INRIA Sophia-Antipolis and Université Paris 7
[2] INRIA Futurs and LIX, École Polytechnique

Abstract. We study a process calculus which combines both nondeterministic and probabilistic behavior in the style of Segala and Lynch's probabilistic automata. We consider various strong and weak behavioral equivalences, and we provide complete axiomatizations for finite-state processes, restricted to guarded definitions in case of the weak equivalences. We conjecture that in the general case of unguarded recursion the "natural" weak equivalences are undecidable.

This is the first work, to our knowledge, that provides a complete axiomatization for weak equivalences in the presence of recursion and both nondeterministic and probabilistic choice.

1 Introduction

The last decade has witnessed increasing interest in the area of formal methods for the specification and analysis of probabilistic systems [11, 3, 15, 6]. In [16] van Glabbeek *et al.* classified probabilistic models into *reactive, generative* and *stratified*. In reactive models, each labeled transition is associated with a probability, and for each state the sum of the probabilities with the same label is 1. Generative models differ from reactive ones in that for each state the sum of the probabilities of all the outgoing transitions is 1. Stratified models have more structure and for each state either there is exactly one outgoing labeled transition or there are only unlabeled transitions and the sum of their probabilities is 1.

In [11] Segala pointed out that neither reactive nor generative nor stratified models capture real nondeterminism, an essential notion for modeling scheduling freedom, implementation freedom, the external environment and incomplete information. He then introduced a model, the *probabilistic automata* (PA), where both probability and nondeterminism are taken into account. Probabilistic choice is expressed by the notion of *transition*, which, in PA, leads to a probabilistic distribution over pairs (action, state) and deadlock. Nondeterministic choice, on the other hand, is expressed by the possibility of choosing different transitions.

---

* Supported by the EU project PROFUNDIS.
** Partially supported by the Project Rossignol of the ACI Sécurité Informatique (Ministère de la recherche et nouvelles technologies).

V. Sassone (Ed.): FOSSACS 2005, LNCS 3441, pp. 110–124, 2005.

Segala proposed also a simplified version of PA called *simple probabilistic automata* (SPA), which are like ordinary automata except that a labeled transition leads to a probabilistic distribution over a set of states instead of a single state.

Figure 1 exemplifies the probabilistic models discussed above. In models where both probability and nondeterminism are present, like those of diagrams (4) and (5), a transition is usually represented as a bundle of arrows linked by a small arc. [13] provides a detailed comparison between the various models, and argues that PA subsume all other models above except for the stratified ones.

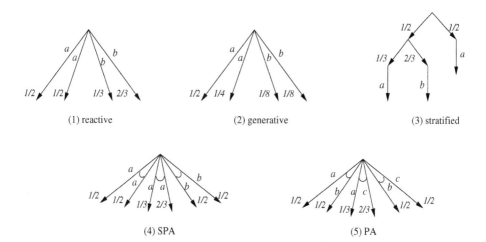

Fig. 1. Probabilistic models

In this paper we are interested in investigating axiom systems for a process calculus based on PA, in the sense that the operational semantics of each expression of the language is a probabilistic automaton[1]. Axiom systems are important both at the theoretical level, as they help gaining insight of the calculus and establishing its foundations, and at the practical level, as tools for system specification and verification. Our calculus is basically a probabilistic version of the calculus used by Milner to express finite-state behaviors [8, 10].

We shall consider the two strong and the weak behavioral equivalences common in literature, plus one novel notion of weak equivalence having the advantage of being sensitive to divergency. For recursion-free expressions we provide complete axiomatizations of all the four equivalences. For the strong equivalences we also give complete axiomatizations for all expressions, while for the weak equivalences we achieve this result only for guarded expressions.

The reason why we are interested in studying a model which expresses both nondeterministic and probabilistic behavior, and an equivalence sensitive to di-

---

[1] Except for the case of deadlock, which is treated slightly differently: following the tradition of process calculi, in our case deadlock is a state, while in PA it is one of the possible components of a transition.

vergency, is that one of the long-term goals of this line of research is to develop a theory which will allow us to reason about probabilistic algorithms used in distributed computing. In that domain it is important to ensure that an algorithm will work under any scheduler, and under other unknown or uncontrollable factors. The nondeterministic component of the calculus allows coping with these conditions in a uniform and elegant way. Furthermore, in many distributed computing applications it is important to ensure livelock-freedom (progress), and therefore we will need a semantics which does not simply ignore divergencies.

We end this section with a discussion about some related work. In [8] and [10] Milner gave complete axiomatizations for strong bisimulation and observational equivalence, respectively, for a core *CCS* [9]. These two papers serve as our starting point: in several completeness proofs that involve recursion we adopt Milner's *equational characterization theorem* and *unique solution theorem*. In Section 4 and Section 5.2 we extend [8] and [10] (for guarded expressions) respectively, to the setting of probabilistic process algebra.

In [14] Stark and Smolka gave a probabilistic version of the results of [8]. So, our paper extends [14] in that we consider also nondeterminism. Note that when nondeterministic choice is added, Stark and Smolka's technique of proving soundness of axioms is no longer usable. The same remark applies also to [1] which follows the approach of [14] but uses some axioms from iteration algebra to characterize recursion. In contrast, our probabilistic version of "bisimulation up to" technique works well when combined with the usual transition induction.

In [5] Bandini and Segala axiomatized both strong and weak behavioral equivalences for process calculi corresponding to SPA and to an alternated-model version of SPA. As their process calculus with non-alternating semantics corresponds to SPA, our results in Section 6 can be regarded as an extension of that work to PA.

For probabilistic process algebra of ACP-style, several complete axiom systems have appeared in the literature. However, in each of the systems either weak bisimulation is not investigated [4, 2] or nondeterministic choice is prohibited [4, 3].

2   Probabilistic Process Calculus

We begin with some preliminary notations. Let S be a set. A function $\eta : S \mapsto [0,1]$ is called a *discrete probability distribution*, or *distribution* for short, on S if the *support* of η, defined as $spt(\eta) = \{x \in S \mid \eta(x) > 0\}$, is finite or countably infinite and $\sum_{x \in S} \eta(x) = 1$. If η is a distribution with finite support and $V \subseteq spt(\eta)$ we use the set $\{(s_i : \eta(s_i))\}_{s_i \in V}$ to enumerate the probability associated with each element of V. To manipulate the set we introduce the operator $\uplus$ defined as follows.

$$\{(s_i : p_i)\}_{i \in I} \uplus \{(s : p)\} =$$
$$\begin{cases} \{(s_i : p_i)\}_{i \in I \setminus j} \cup \{s_j : (p_j + p)\} & \text{if } s = s_j \text{ for some } j \in I \\ \{(s_i : p_i)\}_{i \in I} \cup \{(s : p)\} & \text{otherwise.} \end{cases}$$

$$\{(s_i : p_i)\}_{i \in I} \uplus \{(t_j : p_j)\}_{j \in 1..n} =$$
$$(\{(s_i : p_i)\}_{i \in I} \uplus \{(t_1 : p_1)\}) \uplus \{(t_j : p_j)\}_{j \in 2..n}$$

Given some distributions $\eta_1, ..., \eta_n$ on S and some real numbers $r_1, ..., r_n \in [0, 1]$ with $\sum_{i \in 1..n} r_i = 1$, we define the *convex combination* $r_1 \eta_1 + ... + r_n \eta_n$ of $\eta_1, ..., \eta_n$ to be the distribution η such that $\eta(s) = \sum_{i \in 1..n} r_i \eta_i(s)$, for each $s \in S$.

We use a countable set of variables, $Var = \{X, Y, ...\}$, and a countable set of atomic actions, $Act = \{a, b, ...\}$. Given a special action τ, we let $u, v, ...$ range over the set $Act_\tau = Act \cup \{\tau\}$, and let $\alpha, \beta, ...$ range over the set $Var \cup Act_\tau$. The class of expressions $\mathcal{E}$ is defined by the following syntax:

$$E, F ::= \bigoplus_{i \in 1..n} p_i u_i.E_i \ \Big| \ \sum_{i \in 1..m} E_i \ \Big| \ X \ \Big| \ \mu_X E$$

Here $\bigoplus_{i \in 1..n} p_i u_i.E_i$ stands for a *probabilistic choice* operator, where the p_i's represent positive probabilities, i.e., they satisfy $p_i \in (0, 1]$ and $\sum_{i \in 1..n} p_i = 1$. When $n = 0$ we abbreviate the probabilistic choice as $\mathbf{0}$; when $n = 1$ we abbreviate it as $u_1.E_1$. Sometimes we are interested in certain branches of the probabilistic choice; in this case we write $\bigoplus_{i \in 1..n} p_i u_i.E_i$ as $p_1 u_1.E_1 \oplus \cdots \oplus p_n u_n.E_n$ or $(\bigoplus_{i \in 1..(n-1)} p_i u_i.E_i) \oplus p_n u_n.E_n$ where $\bigoplus_{i \in 1..(n-1)} p_i u_i.E_i$ abbreviates (with a slight abuse of notation) $p_1 u_1.E_1 \oplus \cdots \oplus p_{n-1} u_{n-1}.E_{n-1}$. The construction $\sum_{i \in 1..m} E_i$ stands for *nondeterministic choice*, and occasionally we may write it as $E_1 + ... + E_m$. The notation μ_X stands for a recursion which binds the variable X. We shall use $fv(E)$ for the set of free variables (i.e., not bound by any μ_X) in E. As usual we identify expressions which differ only by a change of bound variables. We shall write $E\{F/X\}$ for the result of substituting F for each occurrence of X in E, renaming bound variables if necessary.

Definition 1. *The variable X is* weakly guarded *(resp.* guarded*) in E if every free occurrence of X in E occurs within some subexpression $u.F$ (resp. $a.F$), otherwise X is* weakly unguarded *(resp.* unguarded*) in E.*

The operational semantics of an expression E is defined as a probabilistic automaton whose states are the expressions reachable from E and the transition relation is defined by the axioms and inference rules in Table 1, where $E \to \eta$ describes a transition that leaves from E and leads to a distribution η over $(Var \cup Act_\tau) \times \mathcal{E}$. We shall use $\vartheta(X)$ for the special distribution $\{(X, \mathbf{0} : 1)\}$. It is evident that $E \to \vartheta(X)$ iff X is weakly unguarded in E.

The behavior of each expression can be visualized by a transition graph. For instance, the expression $(\frac{1}{2}a \oplus \frac{1}{2}b) + (\frac{1}{3}a \oplus \frac{2}{3}c) + (\frac{1}{2}b \oplus \frac{1}{2}c)$ exhibits the behavior drawn in diagram (5) of Figure 1.

As in [5], we define the notion of *combined transition* as follows: $E \to_c \eta$ if there exists a collection $\{\eta_i, r_i\}_{i \in 1..n}$ of distributions and probabilities such that $\sum_{i \in 1..n} r_i = 1$, $\eta = r_1 \eta_1 + ... + r_n \eta_n$ and $E \to \eta_i$, for each $i \in 1..n$.

Table 1. Strong transitions

---

var $X \to \vartheta(X)$ psum $\bigoplus_{i\in 1..n} p_i u_i.E_i \to \biguplus_{i\in 1..n}\{(u_i, E_i : p_i)\}$

rec $\dfrac{E\{\mu_X E/X\} \to \eta}{\mu_X E \to \eta}$ nsum $\dfrac{E_j \to \eta}{\sum_{i\in 1..m} E_i \to \eta}$ for some $j \in 1..m$

We now introduce the notion of weak transitions, which generalizes the notion of *finitary weak transitions* in SPA [15] to the setting of PA. First we discuss the intuition behind it. Given an expression E, if we unfold its transition graph, we get a finitely branching tree. By cutting away all but one alternative in case of several nondeterministic candidates, we are left with a subtree with only probabilistic branches. A weak transition of E is a finite subtree of this kind, called *weak transition tree*, such that in any path from the root to a leaf there is at most one visible action. For example, let E be the expression $\mu_X(\frac{1}{2}a \oplus \frac{1}{2}\tau.X)$. It is represented by the transition graph displayed in Diagram (1) of Figure 2. After one unfolding, we get Diagram (2) which represents the weak transition $E \Rightarrow \eta$, where $\eta = \{(a, \mathbf{0} : \frac{3}{4}), (\tau, E : \frac{1}{4})\}$.

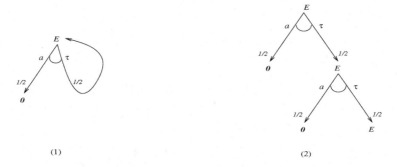

(1)   (2)

Fig. 2. A weak transition

Formally, weak transitions are defined by the rules in Table 2. Rule wea1 says that a weak transition tree starts from a bundle of labelled arrows derived from a strong transition. The meaning of Rule wea2 is as follows. Given two expressions E, F and their weak transition trees $tr(E), tr(F)$, if F is a leaf of $tr(E)$ and there is no visible action in $tr(F)$, then we can extend $tr(E)$ with $tr(F)$ at node F. If F_j is a leaf of $tr(F)$ then the probability of reaching F_j from E is pq_j, where p and q_j are the probabilities of reaching F from E, and F_j from F, respectively. Rule wea3 is similar to Rule wea2, with the difference that we can have visible actions in $tr(F)$, but not in the path from E to F. Rule wea4 allows to construct weak transitions to unguarded variables. Note that if $E \Rightarrow \vartheta(X)$ then X is unguarded in E.

Table 2. Weak transitions

$$\text{wea1} \quad \frac{E \to \eta}{E \Rightarrow \eta}$$

$$\text{wea2} \quad \frac{E \Rightarrow \{(u_i, E_i : p_i)\}_i \uplus \{(u, F : p)\} \quad F \Rightarrow \{(\tau, F_j : q_j)\}_j}{E \Rightarrow \{(u_i, E_i : p_i)\}_i \uplus \{(u, F_j : pq_j)\}_j}$$

$$\text{wea3} \quad \frac{E \Rightarrow \{(u_i, E_i : p_i)\}_i \uplus \{(\tau, F : p)\} \quad F \Rightarrow \{(v_j, F_j : q_j)\}_j}{E \Rightarrow \{(u_i, E_i : p_i)\}_i \uplus \{(v_j, F_j : pq_j)\}_j}$$

$$\text{wea4} \quad \frac{E \Rightarrow \{(\tau, E_i : p_i)\}_i \quad \forall i : E_i \Rightarrow \vartheta(X)}{E \Rightarrow \vartheta(X)}$$

For any expression E, we use $\delta(E)$ for the unique distribution $\{(\tau, E : 1)\}$, called the *virtual distribution* of E. For any expression E, we introduce a special weak transition, called *virtual transition*, denoted by $E \overset{\epsilon}{\Rightarrow} \delta(E)$. We also define a *weak combined transition*: $E \Rightarrow_c \eta$ if there exists a collection $\{\eta_i, r_i\}_{i \in 1..n}$ of distributions and probabilities such that $\sum_{i \in 1..n} r_i = 1$, $\eta = r_1 \eta_1 + ... + r_n \eta_n$ and for each $i \in 1..n$, either $E \Rightarrow \eta_i$ or $E \overset{\epsilon}{\Rightarrow} \eta_i$. We write $E \Rightarrow_c \eta$ if every component is a "normal" (i.e., non-virtual) weak transition, namely, $E \Rightarrow \eta_i$ for all $i \leq n$.

3   Behavioral Equivalences

In this section we define the behavioral equivalences that we mentioned in the introduction, namely, strong bisimulation, strong probabilistic bisimulation, divergency-sensitive equivalence and observational equivalence. We also introduce a probabilistic version of "bisimulation up to" technique to show some interesting properties of the behavioral equivalences.

3.1   Strong and Weak Equivalences

To define behavioral equivalences in probabilistic process algebra, it is customary to consider equivalence of distributions with respect to equivalence relations on processes. If η is a distribution on $S \times T$, $s \in S$ and $V \subseteq T$, we write $\eta(s, V)$ for $\sum_{t \in V} \eta(s, t)$. We lift an equivalence relation on $\mathcal{E}$ to a relation between distributions over $(Var \cup Act_\tau) \times \mathcal{E}$ in the following way.

Definition 2. *Given two distributions η_1 and η_2 over $(Var \cup Act_\tau) \times \mathcal{E}$, we say that they are equivalent w.r.t. an equivalence relation $\mathcal{R}$ on $\mathcal{E}$, written $\eta_1 \equiv_{\mathcal{R}} \eta_2$, if*

$$\forall \alpha \in Var \cup Act_\tau, \forall V \in \mathcal{E}/\mathcal{R} : \eta_1(\alpha, V) = \eta_2(\alpha, V).$$

Strong bisimulation is defined by requiring equivalence of distributions at every step. Because of the way equivalence of distributions is defined, we need to restrict to bisimulations which are equivalence relations.

Definition 3. *An equivalence relation $\mathcal{R} \subseteq \mathcal{E} \times \mathcal{E}$ is a* strong bisimulation *if $E \, \mathcal{R} \, F$ implies:*

- *whenever $E \to \eta_1$, there exists η_2 such that $F \to \eta_2$ and $\eta_1 \equiv_{\mathcal{R}} \eta_2$.*

We write $E \sim F$ if there exists a strong bisimulation $\mathcal{R}$ s.t. $E \, \mathcal{R} \, F$.

If we allow a strong transition to be matched by a strong combined transition, then we get a relation slightly weaker than strong bisimulation.

Definition 4. *An equivalence relation $\mathcal{R} \subseteq \mathcal{E} \times \mathcal{E}$ is a* strong probabilistic bisimulation *if $E \, \mathcal{R} \, F$ implies:*

- *whenever $E \to \eta_1$, there exists η_2 such that $F \to_c \eta_2$ and $\eta_1 \equiv_{\mathcal{R}} \eta_2$.*

$E \sim_c F$ if there exists a strong probabilistic bisimulation $\mathcal{R}$ s.t. $E \, \mathcal{R} \, F$.

We now consider the case of the weak bisimulation. The definition of weak bisimulation for PA is not at all straightforward. In fact, the "natural" weak version of Definition 3 would give rise to a relation which is not transitive. Therefore we only define the weak variant of Definition 4.

Definition 5. *An equivalence relation $\mathcal{R} \subseteq \mathcal{E} \times \mathcal{E}$ is a* weak probabilistic bisimulation *if $E \, \mathcal{R} \, F$ implies:*

- *whenever $E \to \eta_1$, there exists η_2 such that $F \overset{\epsilon}{\Rightarrow}_c \eta_2$ and $\eta_1 \equiv_{\mathcal{R}} \eta_2$.*

$E \approx F$ if there exists a weak probabilistic bisimulation $\mathcal{R}$ s.t. $E \, \mathcal{R} \, F$.

As usual, observational equivalence is defined in terms of weak probabilistic bisimulation.

Definition 6. *Two expressions E and F are* observationally equivalent, *written $E \simeq F$, if*

1. *whenever $E \to \eta_1$, there exists η_2 such that $F \Rightarrow_c \eta_2$ and $\eta_1 \equiv_\approx \eta_2$.*
2. *whenever $F \to \eta_2$, there exists η_1 such that $E \Rightarrow_c \eta_1$ and $\eta_1 \equiv_\approx \eta_2$.*

Often observational equivalence is criticised for being insensitive to divergency. So we introduce a variant which has not this shortcoming.

Definition 7. *An equivalence relation $\mathcal{R} \subseteq \mathcal{E} \times \mathcal{E}$ is* divergency-sensitive *if $E \, \mathcal{R} \, F$ implies:*

- *whenever $E \to \eta_1$, there exists η_2 such that $F \Rightarrow_c \eta_2$ and $\eta_1 \equiv_{\mathcal{R}} \eta_2$.*

$E \simeq F$ if there exists a divergency-sensitive equivalence $\mathcal{R}$ s.t. $E \, \mathcal{R} \, F$.

It is easy to see that $\simeq$ lies between $\sim_c$ and $\simeq$. For example, we have that $\mu_X(\tau.X + a)$ and $\tau.a$ are related by $\simeq$ but not by $\simeq$ (this shows also that $\simeq$ is sensitive to divergency), while $\tau.a$ and $\tau.a + a$ are related by $\simeq$ but not by $\sim_c$.

One can check that all the relations defined above are indeed equivalence relations and we have the inclusion ordering: $\sim \subsetneq \sim_c \subsetneq \simeq \subsetneq \simeq \subsetneq \approx$.

3.2   Probabilistic "Bisimulation up to" Technique

In the classical process algebra, the conventional approach to show $E \sim F$, for some expressions E, F, is to construct a binary relation $\mathcal{R}$ which includes the pair (E, F), and then to check that $\mathcal{R}$ is a bisimulation. This approach can still be used in probabilistic process algebra, but things are more complicated because of the extra requirement that $\mathcal{R}$ must be an equivalence relation. For example we cannot use some standard set-theoretic operators to construct $\mathcal{R}$, because, even if $\mathcal{R}_1$ and $\mathcal{R}_2$ are equivalences, $\mathcal{R}_1\mathcal{R}_2$ and $\mathcal{R}_1 \cup \mathcal{R}_2$ may not be equivalences.

To avoid the restrictive condition and at the same time to reduce the size of the relation $\mathcal{R}$, we introduce the probabilistic version of "bisimulation up to" technique.

Definition 8. *A binary relation $\mathcal{R}$ is a* strong bisimulation up to $\sim$ *if $E \,\mathcal{R}\, F$ implies:*

1. *whenever $E \to \eta_1$, there exists η_2 such that $F \to \eta_2$ and $\eta_1 \equiv_{\mathcal{R}_\sim} \eta_2$.*
2. *whenever $F \to \eta_2$, there exists η_1 such that $E \to \eta_1$ and $\eta_1 \equiv_{\mathcal{R}_\sim} \eta_2$.*

where $\mathcal{R}_\sim$ stands for the relation $(\mathcal{R} \cup \sim)^*$.

A strong bisimulation up to $\sim$ is not necessarily an equivalence relation. It is just an ordinary binary relation included in $\sim$.

Proposition 1. *If $\mathcal{R}$ is a strong bisimulation up to $\sim$, then $\mathcal{R} \subseteq \sim$.*

Similarly we can define strong probabilistic bisimulation up to $\sim_c$, weak probabilistic bisimulation up to $\approx$, etc. (some care is needed when dealing with weak equivalences). The "bisimulation up to" technique works well with Milner's transition induction technique [9], and by combining them we obtain the following results.

Proposition 2 (Properties of $\sim$ and $\sim_c$).

1. *$\sim$ is a congruence relation.*
2. *$\mu_X E \sim E\{\mu_X E/X\}$.*
3. *$\mu_X(E + X) \sim \mu_X E$.*
4. *If $E \sim F\{E/X\}$ and X weakly guarded in F, then $E \sim \mu_X F$.*

Properties 1-4 are also valid for $\sim_c$.

Proposition 3 (Properties of $\simeq$ and $\simeq$).

1. *$\simeq$ is a congruence relation.*
2. *If $\tau.E \simeq \tau.E + F$ and $\tau.F \simeq \tau.F + E$ then $\tau.E \simeq \tau.F$.*
3. *If $E \simeq F\{E/X\}$ and X is guarded in F then $E \simeq \mu_X F$.*

Properties 1-3 hold for $\simeq$ as well.

4   Axiomatizations for all Expressions

In this section we provide sound and complete axiomatizations for two strong behavioral equivalences: $\sim$ and $\sim_c$. The class of expressions to be considered is $\mathcal{E}$.

First we present the axiom system $\mathcal{A}_r$, which includes all axioms and rules displayed in Table 3. We assume the usual rules for equality (reflexivity, symmetry, transitivity and substitutivity), and the alpha-conversion of bound variables.

Table 3. The axiom system $\mathcal{A}_r$

S1 $E + \mathbf{0} = E$
S2 $E + E = E$
S3 $\sum_{i \in I} E_i = \sum_{i \in I} E_{\rho(i)}$ ρ is any permutation on I
S4 $\bigoplus_{i \in I} p_i u_i.E_i = \bigoplus_{i \in I} p_{\rho(i)} u_{\rho(i)}.E_{\rho(i)}$ ρ is any permutation on I
S5 $(\bigoplus_i p_i u_i.E_i) \oplus pu.E \oplus qu.E = (\bigoplus_i p_i u_i.E_i) \oplus (p + q)u.E$

R1 $\mu_X E = E\{\mu_X E / X\}$
R2 If $E = F\{E/X\}$, X weakly guarded in F, then $E = \mu_X F$
R3 $\mu_X(E + X) = \mu_X E$

The notation $\mathcal{A}_r \vdash E = F$ means that the equation $E = F$ is derivable by applying the axioms and rules from $\mathcal{A}_r$. The interest of $\mathcal{A}_r$ is that it characterizes exactly strong bisimulation, as shown by the following theorem.

Theorem 1 (Soundness and completeness of $\mathcal{A}_r$). $E \sim E'$ iff $\mathcal{A}_r \vdash E = E'$.

The soundness of $\mathcal{A}_r$ is easy to prove: **R1-3** correspond to clauses 2-4 of Proposition 2; **S1-4** are obvious, and **S5** is a consequence of Definition 2. For the completeness proof, the basic points are: (1) if two expressions are bisimilar then we can construct an equation set in a certain format (standard format) that they both satisfy; (2) if two expressions satisfy the same standard equation set, then they can be proved equal by $\mathcal{A}_r$. This schema is inspired by [8, 14], but in our case the definition of standard format and the proof itself are more complicated due to the presence of both probabilistic and nondeterministic dimensions.

The difference between $\sim$ and $\sim_c$ is characterized by the following axiom:

$$\mathbf{C} \quad \sum_{i \in 1..n} \bigoplus_j p_{ij} u_{ij}.E_{ij} = \sum_{i \in 1..n} \bigoplus_j p_{ij} u_{ij}.E_{ij} + \bigoplus_{i \in 1..n} \bigoplus_j r_i p_{ij} u_{ij}.E_{ij}$$

where $\sum_{i \in 1..n} r_i = 1$. We denote $\mathcal{A}_r \cup \{\mathbf{C}\}$ by $\mathcal{A}_{rc}$.

Theorem 2 (Soundness and completeness of $\mathcal{A}_{rc}$). $E \sim_c E'$ iff $\mathcal{A}_{rc} \vdash E = E'$.

5   Axiomatizations for Guarded Expressions

Now we proceed with the axiomatizations of the two weak behavioral equivalences: $\doteq$ and $\simeq$. We are not able to give a complete axiomatization for the whole set of expressions (and we conjecture that it is not possible), so we restrict to the subset of $\mathcal{E}$ consisting of *guarded expressions* only. An expression is guarded if for each of its subexpression of the form $\mu_X F$, the variable X is guarded in F (cf: Definition 1).

5.1   Axiomatizing Divergency-Sensitive Equivalence

We first study the axiom system for $\doteq$. As a starting point, let us consider the system $\mathcal{A}_{rc}$. Clearly, **S1-5** are still valid for $\doteq$, as well as **R1**. **R3** turns out to be not needed in the restricted language we are considering. As for **R2**, we replace it with its (strongly) guarded version, which we shall denote as **R2′** (see Table 4). As in the standard process algebra, we need some τ-laws to abstract from invisible steps. For $\doteq$ we use the probabilistic τ-laws **T1-3** shown in Table 4. Note that **T3** is the probabilistic extension of Milner's third τ-law ([10] page 231), and **T1** and **T2** together are equivalent, in the nonprobabilistic case, to Milner's second τ-law. However, Milner's first τ-law cannot be derived from **T1-3**, and it is actually unsound for $\doteq$. Below we let $\mathcal{A}_{gd} = \{\mathbf{R2'}, \mathbf{T1\text{-}3}\} \cup \mathcal{A}_{rc} \backslash \{\mathbf{R2\text{-}3}\}$.

Table 4. Some laws for the axiom system $\mathcal{A}_{gd}$

R2′ If $E = F\{E/X\}$, X guarded in F, then $E = \mu_X F$

T1 $\bigoplus_i p_i \tau.(E_i + X) = X + \bigoplus_i p_i \tau.(E_i + X)$

T2 $(\bigoplus_i p_i u_i.E_i) \oplus p\tau.(F + \bigoplus_j q_j \beta_j.F_j) + (\bigoplus_i p_i u_i.E_i) \oplus (\bigoplus_j pq_j \beta_j.F_j)$
$\quad = (\bigoplus_i p_i u_i.E_i) \oplus p\tau.(F + \bigoplus_j q_j \beta_j.F_j)$

T3 $(\bigoplus_i p_i u_i.E_i) \oplus pu.(F + \bigoplus_j q_j \tau.F_j) + (\bigoplus_i p_i u_i.E_i) \oplus (\bigoplus_j pq_j u.F_j)$
$\quad = (\bigoplus_i p_i u_i.E_i) \oplus pu.(F + \bigoplus_j q_j \tau.F_j)$

The rule **R2′** is shown to be sound in Proposition 3. The soundness of **T1-3**, and therefore of $\mathcal{A}_{gd}$, is evident. For the completeness proof, it is convenient to use the following saturation property, which relates operational semantics to term transformation.

Lemma 1.   *1. If $E \Rightarrow_c \eta$ with $\eta = \{(u_i, E_i : p_i)\}_i$, then $\mathcal{A}_{gd} \vdash E = E + \bigoplus_i p_i u_i.E_i$.*
   2. If $E \Rightarrow \vartheta(X)$ then $\mathcal{A}_{gd} \vdash E = E + X$.

The completeness result can be proved in a similar way as Theorem 1. The main difference is that here the key role is played by equation sets which are not only in standard format, but also saturated. The transformation of a standard equation set into a saturated one is obtained by using Lemma 1.

Theorem 3 (Soundness and completeness of $\mathcal{A}_{gd}$). *Let E and E' be two guarded expressions. Then $E \simeq E'$ iff $\mathcal{A}_{gd} \vdash E = E'$.*

5.2   Axiomatizing Observational Equivalence

In this section we focus on the axiomatization of $\simeq$. In order to obtain completeness, we can follow the same schema as for Theorem 1, with the additional machinery required for dealing with observational equivalence, like in [10]. The crucial point of the proof is to show that, if $E \simeq F$, then we can construct an equation set in standard format which is satisfied by E and F. The construction of the equation is more complicated than in [10] because of the subtlety introduced by the probabilistic dimension. Indeed, it turns out that the simple probabilistic extension of Milner's three τ-laws would not be sufficient, and we need an additional rule for the completeness proof to go through. We shall further comment on this rule at the end of Section 6.

Table 5. Two τ-laws for the axiom system $\mathcal{A}_{go}$

T4 $u.\tau.E = u.E$
T5 If $\tau.E = \tau.E + F$ and $\tau.F = \tau.F + E$ then $\tau.E = \tau.F$.

The probabilistic extension of Milner's τ-laws are axioms **T1-4**, where **T1-3** are those introduced in previous section, and **T4**, defined in Table 5, takes the same form as Milner's first τ-law [10]. In the same table **T5** is the additional rule mentioned above. We let $\mathcal{A}_{go} = \mathcal{A}_{gd} \cup \{\textbf{T4-5}\}$.

Theorem 4 (Soundness and completeness of $\mathcal{A}_{go}$). *If E and F are guarded expressions then $E \simeq F$ iff $\mathcal{A}_{go} \vdash E = F$.*

6   Axiomatizations for Finite Expressions

In this section we consider the recursion-free fragment of $\mathcal{E}$, that is the class $\mathcal{E}_f$ of all expressions which do not contain constructs of the form $\mu_X F$. In other words all expressions in $\mathcal{E}_f$ have the form: $\sum_i \bigoplus_j p_{ij} u_{ij}.E_{ij} + \sum_k X_k$.

We define four axiom systems for the four behavioral equivalences studied in this paper. Basically $\mathcal{A}_s, \mathcal{A}_{sc}, \mathcal{A}_{fd}, \mathcal{A}_{fo}$ are obtained from $\mathcal{A}_r, \mathcal{A}_{rc}, \mathcal{A}_{gd}, \mathcal{A}_{go}$ respectively, by cutting away all those axioms and rules that involve recursions.

$$\mathcal{A}_s \stackrel{\text{def}}{=} \{\textbf{S1-5}\} \qquad\qquad \mathcal{A}_{sc} \stackrel{\text{def}}{=} \mathcal{A}_s \cup \{\textbf{C}\}$$
$$\mathcal{A}_{fd} \stackrel{\text{def}}{=} \mathcal{A}_{sc} \cup \{\textbf{T1-3}\} \qquad \mathcal{A}_{fo} \stackrel{\text{def}}{=} \mathcal{A}_{fd} \cup \{\textbf{T4-5}\}$$

Theorem 5 (Soundness and completeness). *For any* $E, F \in \mathcal{E}_f$,

1. $E \sim F$ *iff* $\mathcal{A}_s \vdash E = F$;
2. $E \sim_c F$ *iff* $\mathcal{A}_{sc} \vdash E = F$;
3. $E \simeq F$ *iff* $\mathcal{A}_{fd} \vdash E = F$;
4. $E \simeq F$ *iff* $\mathcal{A}_{fo} \vdash E = F$.

Roughly speaking, all the clauses are proved by induction on the depth of the expressions. The completeness proof of $\mathcal{A}_{fo}$ is a bit tricky. In the classical process algebra the proof can be carried out directly by using Hennessy Lemma [9], which says that if $E \approx F$ then either $\tau.E \simeq F$ or $E \simeq F$ or $E \simeq \tau.F$. In the probabilistic case, however, Hennessy's Lemma does not hold. For example, let

$$E \stackrel{\text{def}}{=} a \quad \text{and} \quad F \stackrel{\text{def}}{=} a + (\frac{1}{2}\tau.a \oplus \frac{1}{2}a).$$

We can check that: (1) $\tau.E \not\simeq F$, (2) $E \not\simeq F$, (3) $E \not\simeq \tau.F$. In (1) the distribution $\{(\tau, E : 1)\}$ cannot be simulated by any distribution from F. In (2) the distribution $\{(\tau, a : \frac{1}{2}), (a, \mathbf{0} : \frac{1}{2})\}$ cannot be simulated by any distribution from E. In (3) the distribution $\{(\tau, F : 1)\}$ cannot be simulated by any distribution from E.

Fortunately, to prove the completeness of $\mathcal{A}_{fo}$, it is sufficient to use the following weaker property.

Lemma 2. *For any* $E, F \in \mathcal{E}_f$, *if* $E \approx F$ *then* $\mathcal{A}_{fo} \vdash \tau.E = \tau.F$.

It is worth noticing that rule **T5** is necessary to prove Lemma 2. Consider the following two expressions: $\tau.a$ and $\tau.(a + (\frac{1}{2}\tau.a \oplus \frac{1}{2}a))$. It is easy to see that they are observational equivalent. However, we cannot prove their equality if rule **T5** is excluded from the system $\mathcal{A}_{fo}$. In fact, by using only the other rules and axioms it is impossible to transform $\tau.(a + (\frac{1}{2}\tau.a \oplus \frac{1}{2}a))$ into an expression without a probabilistic branch $p\tau.a$ occurring in any subexpression, for some p with $0 < p < 1$. So it is not provably equal to $\tau.a$, which has no probabilistic choice.

7   Concluding Remarks

In this paper we have proposed a probabilistic process calculus which corresponds to Segala and Lynch's probabilistic automata. We have presented strong bisimulation, strong probabilistic bisimulation, divergency-sensitive equivalence and observational equivalence. Sound and complete inference systems for the four behavioral equivalences are summarized in Table 7.

Note that we have axiomatized divergency-sensitive equivalence and observational equivalence only for guarded expressions. For unguarded expressions whose transition graphs include τ-loops, we conjecture that the two behavioral

Table 6. All the axioms and rules

S1 $E + \mathbf{0} = E$

S2 $E + E = E$

S3 $\sum_{i \in I} E_i = \sum_{i \in I} E_{\rho(i)}$ ρ is any permutation on I

S4 $\bigoplus_{i \in I} p_i u_i.E_i = \bigoplus_{i \in I} p_{\rho(i)} u_{\rho(i)}.E_{\rho(i)}$ ρ is any permutation on I

S5 $(\bigoplus_i p_i u_i.E_i) \oplus pu.E \oplus qu.E = (\bigoplus_i p_i u_i.E_i) \oplus (p+q)u.E$

C $\sum_{i \in 1..n} \bigoplus_j p_{ij} u_{ij}.E_{ij} = \sum_{i \in 1..n} \bigoplus_j p_{ij} u_{ij}.E_{ij} + \bigoplus_{i \in 1..n} \bigoplus_j r_i p_{ij} u_{ij}.E_{ij}$

T1 $\bigoplus_i p_i \tau.(E_i + X) = X + \bigoplus_i p_i \tau.(E_i + X)$

T2 $(\bigoplus_i p_i u_i.E_i) \oplus p\tau.(F + \bigoplus_j q_j \beta_j.F_j) + (\bigoplus_i p_i u_i.E_i) \oplus (\bigoplus_j pq_j \beta_j.F_j)$
$= (\bigoplus_i p_i u_i.E_i) \oplus p\tau.(F + \bigoplus_j q_j \beta_j.F_j)$

T3 $(\bigoplus_i p_i u_i.E_i) \oplus pu.(F + \bigoplus_j q_j \tau.F_j) + (\bigoplus_i p_i u_i.E_i) \oplus (\bigoplus_j pq_j u.F_j)$
$= (\bigoplus_i p_i u_i.E_i) \oplus pu.(F + \bigoplus_j q_j \tau.F_j)$

T4 $u.\tau.E = u.E$

T5 If $\tau.E = \tau.E + F$ and $\tau.F = \tau.F + E$ then $\tau.E = \tau.F$.

R1 $\mu_X E = E\{\mu_X E/X\}$

R2 If $E = F\{E/X\}$, X weakly guarded in F, then $E = \mu_X F$

R2$'$ If $E = F\{E/X\}$, X guarded in F, then $E = \mu_X F$

R3 $\mu_X(E + X) = \mu_X E$

In **C**, there is a side condition $\sum_{i \in 1..n} r_i = 1$.

Table 7. All the inference systems

strong equivalences	finite expressions	all expressions
$\sim$	$\mathcal{A}_s$: **S1-5**	$\mathcal{A}_r$: **S1-5,R1-3**
$\sim_c$	$\mathcal{A}_{sc}$: **S1-5,C**	$\mathcal{A}_{rc}$: **S1-5,R1-3,C**

weak equivalences	finite expressions	guarded expressions
$\simeq$	$\mathcal{A}_{fd}$: **S1-5,C,T1-3**	$\mathcal{A}_{gd}$: **S1-5,C,T1-3,R1,R2$'$**
$\approx$	$\mathcal{A}_{fo}$: **S1-5,C,T1-5**	$\mathcal{A}_{go}$: **S1-5,C,T1-5,R1,R2$'$**

equivalences are undecidable and therefore not finitely axiomatizable. The reason is the following: in order to decide whether two expressions E and F are observational equivalent, one can compute the two sets

$$S_E = \{\eta \mid E \Rightarrow \eta\} \quad \text{and} \quad S_F = \{\eta \mid F \Rightarrow \eta\}$$

and then compare them to see whether each element of S_E is related to some element of S_F and vice versa. For guarded expressions E and F, the sets S_E and S_F are always finite and thus they can be compared in finite time. For unguarded expressions, these sets may be infinite, and so the above method does not apply. Furthermore, these sets can be infinite even when we factorize them with respect to an equivalence relation as required in the definition of probabilistic bisimulation. For example, consider the expression $E = \mu_X(\frac{1}{2}a \oplus \frac{1}{2}\tau.X)$. It can be proved that S_E is an infinite set $\{\eta_i \mid i \geq 1\}$, where

$$\eta_i = \{(a, \mathbf{0} : (1 - \frac{1}{2^i})), (\tau, E : \frac{1}{2^i})\}.$$

Furthermore, for each $i, j \geq 1$ with $i \neq j$ we have $\eta_i \not\equiv_\mathcal{R} \eta_j$ for any equivalence relation $\mathcal{R}$ which distinguishes E from $\mathbf{0}$. Hence the set S_E modulo $\mathcal{R}$ is infinite.

It should be remarked that the presence of τ-loops in itself does not necessarily cause non-decidability. For instance, the notion of weak probabilistic bisimulation defined in [11, 6] is decidable for finite-state PA. The reason is that in those works weak transitions are defined in terms of schedulers, and one may get some weak transitions that are not derivable by the (finitary) inference rules used in this paper. For instance, consider the transition graph of the above example. The definition of [11, 6] allows the underlying probabilistic execution to be infinite as long as that case occurs with probability 0. Hence with that definition one has a weak transition that leads to the distribution $\theta = \{(a, \mathbf{0} : 1)\}$. Thus each η_i becomes a convex combination of θ and $\delta(E)$, i.e. these two distributions are enough to characterize all possible weak transitions. By exploiting this property, Cattani and Segala gave a decision algorithm for weak probabilistic bisimulation in [6].

In this paper we have chosen, instead, to generate weak transitions via (finitary) inference rules, which means that only finite executions can be derived. This approach, which is also known in literature ([12]), has the advantage of being more formal, and in the case of guarded recursion it is equivalent to the one of [11, 6]. In the case of unguarded recursion, however, we feel that it would be more natural to consider also the "limit" weak transitions of [11, 6]. The axiomatization of the corresponding notion of observational equivalence is an open problem.

References

1. L. Aceto, Z. Ésik, and A. Ingólfsdóttir. Equational axioms for probabilistic bisimilarity (preliminary report). Technical Report RS-02-6, BRICS, Feb. 2002.
2. S. Andova. Process algebra with probabilistic choice. Technical Report CSR 99-12, Eindhoven University of Technology, 1999.
3. S. Andova and J. C. M. Baeten. Abstraction in probabilistic process algebra. In *Tools and Algorithms for the Construction and Analysis of Systems*, volume 2031 of *LNCS*, pages 204–219. Springer, 2001.
4. J. C. M. Baeten, J. A. Bergstra, and S. A. Smolka. Axiomatizing probabilistic processes: ACP with generative probabilities. *Information and Computation*, 121(2):234–255, 1995.
5. E. Bandini and R. Segala. Axiomatizations for probabilistic bisimulation. In *Proceedings of the 28th International Colloquium on Automata, Languages and Programming*, volume 2076 of *LNCS*, pages 370–381. Springer, 2001.
6. S. Cattani and R. Segala. Decision algorithms for probabilistic bisimulation. In *Proceedings of the 13th International Conference on Concurrency Theory*, volume 2421 of *LNCS*, pages 371–385. Springer, 2002.

7. P. R. D'Argenio, H. Hermanns, and J.-P. Katoen. On generative parallel composition. *ENTCS*, 22, 1999.
8. R. Milner. A complete inference system for a class of regular behaviours. *Journal of Computer and System Science*, 28:439–466, 1984.
9. R. Milner. *Communication and Concurrency*. Prentice-Hall, 1989.
10. R. Milner. A complete axiomatisation for observational congruence of finite-state behaviours. *Information and Computation*, 81:227–247, 1989.
11. R. Segala. Modeling and verification of randomized distributed real-time systems. Technical Report MIT/LCS/TR-676, PhD thesis, MIT, Dept. of EECS, 1995.
12. Roberto Segala and Nancy Lynch. Probabilistic simulations for probabilistic processes. In *Proceedings of the 5th International Conference on Concurrency Theory*, volume 836 of *LNCS*, pages 481–496. Springer-Verlag, 1994.
13. A. Sokolova and E. de Vink. Probabilistic automata: system types, parallel composition and comparison. In *Validation of Stochastic Systems: A Guide to Current Research*, volume 2925 of *LNCS*, pages 1–43. Springer, 2004.
14. E. W. Stark and S. A. Smolka. A complete axiom system for finite-state probabilistic processes. In *Proof, language, and interaction: essays in honour of Robin Milner*, pages 571–595. MIT Press, 2000:
15. M. Stoelinga. *Alea jacta est: verification of probabilistic, real-time and parametric systems*. PhD thesis, University of Nijmegen, 2002.
16. R. J. van Glabbeek, S. A. Smolka, and B. Steffen. Reactive, generative, and stratified models of probabilistic processes. *Information and Computation*, 121(1):59–80, 1995.

Stochastic Transition Systems for Continuous State Spaces and Non-determinism[*]

Stefano Cattani[1], Roberto Segala[2], Marta Kwiatkowska[1], and Gethin Norman[1]

[1] School of Computer Science, The University of Birmingham
Birmingham B15 2TT, United Kingdom
{stc, mzk, gxn}@cs.bham.ac.uk
[2] Dipartimento di Informatica, Università di Verona
Strada Le Grazie 15, Ca' Vignal 2 37134 Verona, Italy
roberto.segala@univr.it

Abstract. We study the interaction between non-deterministic and probabilistic behaviour in systems with continuous state spaces, arbitrary probability distributions and uncountable branching. Models of such systems have been proposed previously. Here, we introduce a model that extends probabilistic automata to the continuous setting. We identify the class of schedulers that ensures measurability properties on executions, and show that such measurability properties are preserved by parallel composition. Finally, we demonstrate how these results allow us to define an alternative notion of weak bisimulation in our model.

1 Introduction

Current trends in ubiquitous computing, such as mobility, portability, sensor and wireless ad hoc networks, place an increasing emphasis on the need to model and analyse complex stochastic behaviours. For example, network traffic demands continuously distributed durations, sensors may generate real-valued data, and the geographical mobility of agents typically involves movement in space and time with stochastic trajectories. The presence of the distributed computation scenario creates a requirement to model non-determinism, in addition to such stochastic features.

Several models capable of representing probabilistic behaviour have been proposed in the literature, see e.g. [1, 10, 13, 16, 24]. Particular attention has been paid to the nature of interaction between probabilistic and non-deterministic behaviour; though these can be seen as orthogonal, the way they interact in the model has led to fundamental distinctions. In the discrete state, discrete time model different variants have been proposed. In some models randomisation replaces non-determinism [10], while elsewhere [11] states are either probabilistic or non-deterministic, such that probabilistic and deterministic choices alternate.

---

[*] Supported in part by EPSRC grants GR/N22960, GR/S46727 and GR/S11107, MURST project CoVer and FIRB project SPY-Mod.

V. Sassone (Ed.): FOSSACS 2005, LNCS 3441, pp. 125–139, 2005.

Furthermore, one can replace conventional transitions with probabilistic transitions (transitions whose target is a distribution over states); in the resulting model of *probabilistic automata* [21, 22], both non-determinism and probabilistic choices are present at each step. Each of these variants can be endowed with appropriate relations, e.g. bisimulation, simulation or trace equivalence relations.

More recently, the analysis of probabilistic systems has been extended to continuous spaces. Such models can represent systems whose progress, for instance, depends on continuously distributed real-time or geographical position information. Stochastic process algebras [13] are an extension of process algebras in which delays are distributed according to some probability distribution over the reals. Initially, only exponential distributions were considered, as they are easier to handle because of their memoryless property. The usual convention is to replace non-determinism with race condition, leading to continuous time Markov chains, but non-determinism can be kept (e.g. interactive Markov chains [12]). Generally distributed delays have also been introduced, both in the case in which non-determinism is replaced with race conditions (e.g. generalised semi-Markov processes), and in the case in which it is retained [7, 4]. Labelled Markov processes [8] are extensions of transition systems to continuous state spaces and general distributions, but have no non-determinism, in the sense that the choice of action determines the next transition. Operational models with non-determinism have already been proposed, e.g. [7, 4, 5], and the notions of bisimulation and parallel composition have been studied for such systems; [4] also defines weak bisimulation.

When considering continuous distributions and state spaces, the notion of measurability of executions plays an important role, and a departure from pointwise consideration of behaviour is needed since the probability of reaching an individual state is often 0. This leads to the central topic of this paper: here, we investigate the measurability issues that arise from the interaction between non-determinism and continuous state spaces. By allowing the most general setting, the behaviour of a system can become mathematically intractable when studying the properties of a system over several steps of execution. We introduce a model for continuous states spaces, called *stochastic transition systems*, which can be seen as an extension of probabilistic automata to a fully continuous setting: both the set of states and the set of action labels can be continuous. This model also encapsulates labelled Markov processes by the addition of non-determinism, and it can serve as an operational model for stochastic process algebras, since states can record the passage through 3D space and/or time, and labels can include real-valued delays, as well as discrete actions.

As in the discrete case, we use the notion of scheduler as the entity that resolves non-determinism. The power of schedulers has to be restricted since arbitrary schedulers could generate executions that are not tractable from a mathematical point of view. For this reason, we define the class of *measurable* schedulers and show that it identifies the set of schedulers that generate all and only the "good" executions that are measurable. Under this restriction, we can define a probability measure on executions, thus enabling us to reason about global properties of a run of a system.

We also introduce the notion of parallel composition for stochastic transition systems and show that our measurability properties are compositional: if there exists a "good" scheduler for the composition, then there must exist two "good" schedulers on the components that give rise to the same behaviour. This property is important because it both allows for compositional reasoning and serves as a sanity check on the correctness of the definition of measurable schedulers that we have given. As a final remark, we show how we can define the notion of weak transitions for stochastic transition systems. The measurability conditions introduced in the paper are needed to define the target probability of several steps of silent transitions. Based on such transitions, we also give an alternative notion of weak bisimulation for our model.

The main contribution of this paper is the study of measurability properties of stochastic transition systems with non-determinism and continuous state spaces. We identify the class of measurable schedulers that generate tractable runs, confirming the choice originally made in [15]; this restriction enables the definition of a measure on executions. We also show that such measurability properties are preserved through parallel composition.

Structure of the Paper. In Section 2 we review the basic notions of measure theory used in this paper. Section 3 introduces the model of stochastic transition systems, and in Section 4 we study the class of schedulers that guarantees measurability of executions. Section 5 introduces a CSP-style parallel operator and analyses the compositionality properties of stochastic transition systems. In Section 6 weak transitions and weak bisimulation are defined. Finally, Section 7 discusses possible future work.

2   Preliminaries

In this section we review the basic definitions and results of measure theory that are necessary for the remainder of the paper. A basic knowledge of topology and metric spaces is assumed. Most results can be found in standard textbooks, e.g. [2]; [18] serves as a good introduction to measure theory.

Basic Definitions. Given a set X, an *algebra* over X is a family F_X of subsets of X that includes X and is closed under complementation and finite union; $\mathcal{F}_X$ is a *σ-algebra* over X if we additionally require closure under countable union. A *measurable space* is a pair $(X, \mathcal{F}_X)$, where $\mathcal{F}_X$ is a σ-algebra over X. The elements of $\mathcal{F}_X$ are called *measurable sets*. We abuse the notation and refer to X as a measurable space whenever the corresponding σ-algebra is clear from the context. The σ-algebra generated by a family G of subsets of X is the *smallest* σ-algebra including G. The *product space* of two measurable spaces $(X, \mathcal{F}_X)$ and $(Y, \mathcal{F}_Y)$ is the measurable space $(X \times Y, \mathcal{F}_X \otimes \mathcal{F}_Y)$, where $\mathcal{F}_X \otimes \mathcal{F}_Y$ is the σ-algebra generated by the *rectangles* $A \times B = \{(x, y) \mid x \in A, y \in B\}$, for all

$A \in \mathcal{F}_X$ and $B \in \mathcal{F}_Y$; we alternatively denote $\mathcal{F}_X \otimes \mathcal{F}_Y$ by $\mathcal{F}_{X \times Y}$. The union of two measurable spaces is the measurable space $(X \cup Y, \mathcal{F}_{X \cup Y})$, where $\mathcal{F}_{X \cup Y}$ is the σ-algebra generated by the union of $\mathcal{F}_X$ and $\mathcal{F}_Y$. The *Borel* σ-algebra for a topological space (X, T) is the σ-algebra generated by the open sets and is denoted by $\mathcal{B}(X)$.

Given a measurable space $(X, \mathcal{F}_X)$, a *measure* over $(X, \mathcal{F}_X)$ is a function $\mu : \mathcal{F}_X \to \mathbb{R}^{\geq 0}$ such that $\mu(\emptyset) = 0$ and, for every countable family of pairwise disjoint measurable sets $\{A_i\}_{i \in I}$, $\mu(\cup_{i \in I} A_i) = \sum_{i \in I} \mu(A_i)$; the triple $(X, \mathcal{F}_X, \mu)$ is called a *measure space*. A *probability* (resp., *sub-probability*) measure μ over $(X, \mathcal{F}_X)$ is a measure such that $\mu(X) = 1$ (resp., $\mu(X) \leq 1$). A measurable set whose complement has probability 0 is called a *support* for a measure μ. If μ is a (sub-)probability measure, $(X, \mathcal{F}_X, \mu)$ is called a *(sub-)probability space*. We denote the set of probability (resp., sub-probability) measures over $(X, \mathcal{F}_X)$ by $\mathcal{D}(X, \mathcal{F}_X)$ (resp, $sub\mathcal{D}(X, \mathcal{F}_X)$). The product probability space for two probability spaces $(X, \mathcal{F}_X, \mu_X)$ and $(Y, \mathcal{F}_Y, \mu_Y)$, is $(X \times Y, \mathcal{F}_X \otimes \mathcal{F}_Y, \mu_X \otimes \mu_Y)$, where $\mu_X \otimes \mu_Y$ is the unique probability measure such that $(\mu_X \otimes \mu_Y)(A \times B) = \mu_X(A) \cdot \mu_Y(B)$, for all $A \in \mathcal{F}_X$ and $B \in \mathcal{F}_Y$.

A function $f : (X, \mathcal{F}_X) \to (Y, \mathcal{F}_Y)$ is *measurable* if the pre-image of every measurable set is measurable, that is, if $f^{-1}(B) = \{x \in X \mid f(x) \in B\} \in \mathcal{F}_X$ for all $B \in \mathcal{F}_Y$. Given a measurable space $(X, \mathcal{F}_X)$, the indicator function for a measurable set $A \in \mathcal{F}_X$ is the measurable function $I_A(x) = 1$ if $x \in A$, 0 otherwise. Let $(X, \mathcal{F}_X, \mu)$ be a probability space, $(Y, \mathcal{F}_Y)$ a measurable space and f a measurable function from X to Y. The induced probability measure for f over $(Y, \mathcal{F}_Y)$ is given by $f(\mu)$ defined as $f(\mu)(B) = \mu(f^{-1}(B))$ for all $B \in \mathcal{F}_Y$.

We call a family S of subsets of a set X a *semi-ring* if S includes $\emptyset$, is closed under finite intersection, and if, whenever $A, B \in S$, there exists a finite family $\{A_i\}_{i \in \{0 \ldots n\}}$ of pairwise disjoint elements of S such that $A \setminus B = \cup_{i=0}^{n} A_i$.

Theorem 1. *Every sub-probability measure defined over a semi-ring S can be uniquely extended to a sub-probability measure over the σ-algebra generated by S.*

Theorem 2. *Let $(X, \mathcal{F}_X)$ and $(Y, \mathcal{F}_Y)$ be two measurable spaces and f a real-valued nonnegative measurable function on $X \times Y$. Assume we have a function $\nu : Y \times \mathcal{F}_X \to \mathbb{R}^{\geq 0}$ such that $\nu(y, \cdot)$ is a measure on $(X, \mathcal{F}_X)$ for all $y \in Y$ and $\nu(\cdot, A)$ is measurable for all $A \in \mathcal{F}_X$. Then $\int_X f(x, y) \nu(y, dx)$ exists and is a measurable function of Y.*

Regular Conditional Probabilities. As we will demonstrate later, our construction will require conditional probabilities. In the discrete case, we can define the probability of an event A given B as $P(A|B) = P(A \cap B)/P(B)$, which is defined only when $P(B) > 0$. Unfortunately, this cannot be done in general for the continuous case, as it is still meaningful to condition with respect to events of probability 0. Consider for example a measure defined on $\mathbb{R}^2$; even if the probability of a given x can be zero, it can be interesting to study the probability measure on $\mathbb{R}$ for such given x. It is therefore necessary to extend the concept of conditional probabilities.

Definition 1. *Let $(X, \mathcal{F}_X, \mu)$ be a probability space, $(Y, \mathcal{F}_Y)$ a measurable space and $f : X \to Y$ a measurable function. A* **regular conditional probability** *for μ with respect to f is a function $\nu : Y \times \mathcal{F}_X \to [0,1]$ such that:*

1. *$\nu(y, \cdot)$ is a probability measure on $\mathcal{F}_X$, for each $y \in Y$;*
2. *$\nu(\cdot, A)$ is a measurable function on $(Y, \mathcal{F}_Y)$, for each $A \in \mathcal{F}_X$;*
3. *$\mu(A \cap f^{-1}(B)) = \int_B \nu(y, A) \, f(\mu)(dy)$.*

Regular conditional probabilities do not exist for all probability spaces. It is necessary to impose restrictions on the kind of measurable spaces we consider. A *Polish space* is the topological space underlying a complete separable metric space. Given a Polish space X, $(X, \mathcal{F}_X)$ is a standard Borel space if $\mathcal{F}_X$ is the Borel σ-algebra generated by the topology. Finally, given a standard Borel space $(X, \mathcal{F}_X)$, $Y \subseteq X$ is an *analytic set* if it is the continuous image of some Polish space. The space $(Y, \mathcal{F}_Y)$ is an *analytic space* if it is measurably isomorphic to an analytic set in a Polish space, that is, if there exists a measurable bijection whose inverse is also measurable. Note that singleton sets are measurable in Polish and analytic spaces. Examples of analytic sets are the discrete spaces and any open or closed subset of the reals equipped with the Borel σ-algebra. Analytic sets are closed under union and Cartesian product. Thus, analytic sets are quite general; for instance, the semantic model of timed systems is given by the product of a discrete set (the graph-theoretic representation of a system) and the possible values of time (the real numbers).

Theorem 3. *Let $(Y, \mathcal{F}_Y)$ be an analytic spac and $f : (X, \mathcal{F}_X, \mu) \to (Y, \mathcal{F}_Y)$ a measurable function. Then there exists a regular conditional probability ν for f.*

A σ-Algebra on Probability Measures. In the following, we define probability distributions on sets of probabilistic transitions whose targets are probability measures on states. We therefore need to define a σ-algebra on sets of probability measures; we use the standard construction, due to Giry [9]. Let $(X, \mathcal{F}_X)$ be a measurable set and $\mathcal{D}(X, \mathcal{F}_X)$ the set of probability measures on X. We build a σ-algebra on the set of probability measures $\mathcal{D}(X, \mathcal{F}_X)$ as follows: for each $A \in \mathcal{F}_X$, define a function $p_A : \mathcal{D}(X, \mathcal{F}_X) \to [0,1]$ by $p_A(\nu) = \nu(A)$. The σ-algebra on $\mathcal{D}(X, \mathcal{F}_X)$, denoted by $\mathcal{F}_{\mathcal{D}(X, \mathcal{F}_X)}$ is the *least* σ-algebra such that all the p_A's are measurable. The generators of the σ-algebra are the sets of probability measures $D_{A,I} = p_A^{-1}(I) = \{\mu \in \mathcal{D}(X, \mathcal{F}_X) \mid \mu(A) \in I\}$, for all $A \in \mathcal{F}_X$ and $I \in \mathcal{B}([0,1])$.

3   Stochastic Transition Systems

In this section we introduce our model, called *stochastic transition systems*, which features both non-deterministic and probabilistic behaviour. The model can be seen as an extension of probabilistic automata [21] to continuous state and label spaces and to continuous probability measures. Stochastic transition systems are fully non-deterministic, and thus also generalise labelled Markov processes [8].

In this section we introduce the fundamental concepts of our continuous model, most of which are an adaptation of [21] to the continuous setting.

Definition 2. *A stochastic transition system (STS) S is a tuple $((Q, \mathcal{F}_Q), \bar{q}, (L, \mathcal{F}_L), \rightarrow)$, where*

- $(Q, \mathcal{F}_Q)$ *is the analytic space of states;*
- $\bar{q} \in Q$ *is the initial state;*
- $(L, \mathcal{F}_L)$ *is the analytic space of labels;*
- $\rightarrow \subseteq Q \times L \times \mathcal{D}(Q, \mathcal{F}_Q)$ *is the set of probabilistic transitions.*

We say that a transition (q, a, μ) is labelled by a and enabled from q, and denote it by $q \xrightarrow{a} \mu$; transitions are ranged over by t. We denote the set of possible transitions by $\mathcal{T} = Q \times L \times \mathcal{D}(Q, \mathcal{F}_Q)$ and define a σ-algebra on it as the product of the σ-algebras of the components, that is, $\mathcal{F}_\mathcal{T} = \mathcal{F}_Q \otimes \mathcal{F}_L \otimes \mathcal{F}_{\mathcal{D}(Q, \mathcal{F}_Q)}$. The set of transitions enabled from a state q is denoted by $\mathcal{T}(q) = \{(q', a, \mu) \in \rightarrow \mid q = q'\}$. We denote the elements of an STS S by Q, $\mathcal{F}_Q$, $\bar{q}$, L, $\mathcal{F}_L$ and $\rightarrow$ and we propagate indices when necessary; thus, the elements of S_i are Q_i, $\mathcal{F}_{Q_i}$, $\bar{q}_i$, L_i, $\mathcal{F}_{L_i}$ and $\rightarrow_i$.

Combined transitions. Following [21], since we resolve non-determinism in a randomised way, we combine the transitions leaving a state q in order to obtain a new transition. Similarly to the discrete case, this induces a probability measure on the set of transitions leaving state q, that is, a measure π on $\mathcal{T}$ with a support contained in $\mathcal{T}(q)$. Since different transitions have in general different labels, the combination of the transitions leaving a state results in a new distribution on both labels and target states.

Definition 3. *Given a state q and a sub-probability measure π over $(\mathcal{T}, \mathcal{F}_\mathcal{T})$ with a support contained in $\mathcal{T}(q)$, the **combined transition for** π **from** q is the pair (q, μ_π) (denoted by $q \rightarrow \mu_\pi$), where μ_π is the sub-probability measure over $(L \times Q, \mathcal{F}_L \otimes \mathcal{F}_Q)$ defined as follows:*

$$\mu_\pi(A \times X) = \int_{(q, a, \mu) \in \mathcal{T}} I_A(a) \mu(X) d\pi$$

The integral above is well defined for the σ-algebra $\mathcal{F}_\mathcal{T}$ on transitions. It is easy to show that μ_π is a sub-probability measure. Observe that we require π to be a sub-probability measure, therefore it is possible that no transition is scheduled with positive probability. We let this denote the probability to stop, which is defined as $\mu_\pi(\perp) = 1 - \mu_\pi(L \times Q)$.

Executions. Given an STS S, a possibly infinite alternating sequence of states and actions $\alpha = q_0 a_1 q_1 \cdots$ is called an *execution*. We denote the set of executions by *Exec*, the set of finite executions ending with a state by *Exec** and the set of infinite executions by *Exec*$^\omega$. Given a finite execution α, $\alpha[\downarrow]$ denotes its last state. The *length* of an execution α, denoted by $|\alpha|$, is the number of occurrences of actions in α; if α is infinite $|\alpha| = \infty$. We denote a finite execution α that has terminated by $\alpha\perp$, where an execution α terminates if $\perp$ is scheduled from the last state of α.

A σ-algebra on executions. We define the σ-algebra $\mathcal{F}_{Exec}$ over the set of executions. This is necessary to study the properties of system runs. In the discrete case, $\mathcal{F}_{Exec}$ is the σ-algebra generated by cones, that is, the set of executions that extend some finite prefix. This concept is generalised to the continuous case by using sets of executions called basic sets. Formally, given a non empty finite sequence of measurable sets $\Lambda = X_0 A_1 X_1 \cdots A_n X_n$, $A_i \in \mathcal{F}_L$, $i \in \{1..n\}$, and $X_i \in \mathcal{F}_Q$, $i \in \{0..n\}$, the *basic set with base Λ* is defined as:

$$C_\Lambda = \{q_0 a_1 \cdots q_n \alpha \mid \forall i \in \{0..n\}\ q_i \in X_i \text{ and } \forall i \in \{1..n\}\ a_i \in A_i \text{ and } \alpha \in Exec\}$$

The length of a basic set C_Λ is given by the number of occurrences of elements of $\mathcal{F}_L$ in Λ. Observe that basic sets form a semi-ring. $\mathcal{F}_{Exec}$ is the σ-algebra generated by basic sets.

We define the σ-algebra $\mathcal{F}_{Exec^*}$ on finite executions in a similar way as the σ-algebra generated by the sets of the form $Q_0 A_1 \cdots Q_n = \{\alpha = q_0 a_1 \cdots q_n \mid q_i \in Q_i \text{ for all } i \in \{0 \cdots n\} \text{ and } a_j \in A_j \text{ for all } j \in \{1 \cdots n\}\}$, where $Q_0 \ldots Q_n \in \mathcal{F}_Q$ and $A_1 \ldots A_n \in \mathcal{F}_L$: $(Exec^*, \mathcal{F}_{Exec^*})$ is the measurable set of finite executions. Note that $\mathcal{F}_{Exec^*}$ is the restriction of $\mathcal{F}_{Exec}$ to finite executions.

Schedulers. We use schedulers as the entities that resolve non-determinism. Given a history in the form of a sequence of states and labels that the system has visited, a scheduler chooses the next transition from the current state by assigning a sub-probability measure to the enabled transitions.

Definition 4. *A **scheduler** is a function $\eta : Exec^* \to subD(\mathcal{T})$, such that, for all $\alpha \in Exec^*$, $\mathcal{T}(\alpha[\downarrow])$ is a support for $\eta(\alpha)$.*

We denote the set of schedulers by $\mathcal{A}$. Since a scheduler η returns a distribution on transitions for each finite execution α, it induces a combined transition $(\alpha[\downarrow], \mu_{\eta(\alpha)})$ leaving the last state of each execution. Note that we use *randomised* schedulers; originally introduced for discrete systems, they have been shown to have important properties, for example the probabilistic temporal logic PCTL is preserved by bisimulation under randomised schedulers [22]. Randomised schedulers are also necessary to obtain compositionality under parallel compositions (see Section 5). Non-randomised (deterministic) schedulers can be seen as the subclass of schedulers that return a Dirac distribution after each execution.

According to the above definition, a scheduler can make arbitrary choices at each point of the computation. We define a class of schedulers whose global behaviour respects measurability properties.

Definition 5. *A scheduler η is measurable if the function $f_\eta(\alpha) = \mu_{\eta(\alpha)}$ (called the flattening of η) is a measurable function from $(Exec^*, \mathcal{F}_{Exec^*})$ to $(subD(L \times Q), \mathcal{F}_{subD(L \times Q)})$. We denote the class of measurable schedulers by $\mathcal{A}_{meas}$.*

Probabilistic executions. The interaction of an STS S and a scheduler η results in a system with no non-determinism, i.e. a purely probabilistic process. We call this object a *probabilistic execution* following [21].

Definition 6. *Given an STS S and a scheduler η, the* **probabilistic execution** *$P_{S,\eta}$ for S and η is the tuple $(Exec^*, \mathcal{F}_{L \times Q}, \mu)$, where $\mu : Exec^* \times \mathcal{F}_{L \times Q} \to [0, 1]$ such that for each $\alpha \in Exec^*$ $\mu(\alpha, \cdot)$ is a sub-probability measure over $L \times Q$ defined by $\mu_{\eta(\alpha)}$.*

A probabilistic execution defines the transitions induced by the scheduler η: given a finite execution it returns the combined transition scheduled by η. We write μ_X, $X \in \mathcal{F}_{L \times Q}$, whenever we fix X and μ is a function on $Exec^*$. Similarly, we write μ_α (or $\mu_{\eta(\alpha)}$) whenever we fix α and μ is a measure on $\mathcal{F}_{L \times Q}$.

Not all probabilistic executions are "good"; our objective is to define a measure on executions, essential to define weak transitions, and the measurability of the function μ is necessary for this purpose. In the purely probabilistic case (no non-determinism) this problem is solved by using Markov kernels (e.g. [8]). We adapt this idea to our setting by defining measurable probabilistic executions and by studying the conditions under which they are generated.

Definition 7. *A probabilistic execution $P_{S,\eta} = (Exec^*, \mathcal{F}_{L \times Q}, \mu)$ is measurable if $\mu : Exec^* \times \mathcal{F}_{L \times Q} \to [0, 1]$ is such that $\mu(\cdot, X)$ is a measurable function for each $X \in \mathcal{F}_{L \times Q}$.*

When μ has such a measurability property, we can see it as a generalisation of Markov kernels to the history-dependent case.

Related Models. As stated above, stochastic transition systems are an extension of probabilistic automata to the continuous case; the latter correspond to the subset of STSs with discrete σ-algebras on states. Labelled Markov processes (LMPs) [8] correspond to the case where there is no non-determinism on actions, that is, for every action there is exactly one distribution from each state. The measurability problem is solved in LMPs by using, for each action, a Markov kernel to denote the probability transition function. An extension of probabilistic automata with continuous distributions and real-valued time labels is proposed in [5], but measurability properties are not considered. Similar models for the continuous setting can be found in [7], proposing an alternating model, where states are either non-deterministic or probabilistic, and in [4], proposing a model where each state enables one probabilistic distribution or arbitrarily many transitions labelled with actions or time. Again, neither of these papers considers the problem of measurability of executions.

4   Measurability and Schedulers

We aim to extend the results of the discrete case to stochastic transition systems and define the measure on executions induced by a scheduler. This requires the corresponding probabilistic execution to be measurable. In this section we show that the class of measurable schedulers identifies all and only the measurable probabilistic executions. The following example shows that arbitrary schedulers

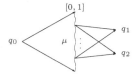

Fig. 1. A simple stochastic transition system illustrating the need for measurable schedulers

could produce "bad" executions and explains why considering the point-wise behaviour of a scheduler is not enough in the continuous setting; instead, it is necessary to consider its global behaviour.

Example 1. Consider the system of Figure 1: the initial state q_0 enables a single transition with some measure μ on the interval $[0,1]$. From each state in $[0,1]$ two Dirac transitions are enabled: one to q_1 and the other to q_2. Labels are not relevant. The probability of moving to q_1 after two steps under a scheduler η is given by $\int_{[0,1]} \mu_{\eta(q)}(\{q_1\})\mu(dq)$, that is, the probability of reaching any state q multiplied by the probability of reaching q_1 from each q. Let η be the scheduler that chooses q_1 from a non-measurable subset A of $[0,1]$, and q_2 from its complement. The integral above is not defined as $\mu_{\eta(q)}(\{q_1\})$ is not a measurable function, that is, the probabilistic execution is not measurable. We want to rule out such a probabilistic execution as "pathological" and disallow the scheduler generating it.

4.1   Measurable Schedulers and Probabilistic Executions

We restrict our analysis to measurable executions only, as they represent "well behaved", feasible, schedulers and allow us to define probability measure on paths. We think this is not an unreasonable restriction since schedulers that produce non-measurable executions represent pathological cases and thus can be discarded. A similar approach has been adopted in [15], where only the schedulers that preserve the measurability of logical formulae are considered, though without studying the nature of such schedulers.

Proposition 1. *Given an STS S, and a scheduler η, η is measurable if and only if $P_{S,\eta}$ is measurable.*

Proof outline. We prove the two directions:

– *If:* Let f_η be the flattening of η as in Definition 5. We have to show that $f_\eta^{-1}(D) \in \mathcal{F}_{Exec^*}$ for all $D \in \mathcal{F}_{subD(L \times Q)}$. Firstly, we prove it for the generators $D_{X,I}$ of $\mathcal{F}_{subD(L \times Q)}$, for all $X \in \mathcal{F}_{L \times Q}$ and $I \in \mathcal{B}([0,1])$. Consider one such $D_{X,I}$. Since $P_{S,\eta}$ is measurable, we get $\mu_X^{-1}(I) = Y \in \mathcal{F}_{Exec^*}$ by hypothesis. We show that $Y = f_\eta^{-1}(D_{X,I})$:
  - $f_\eta^{-1}(D_{X,I}) \supseteq Y$: consider $\alpha \in Y$, then $\mu(\alpha, X) \in I$; this is equivalent to $\mu_{\eta(\alpha)}(X) \in I$, which implies $\mu_{\eta(\alpha)}(X) \in D_{X,I}$. It follows that $\alpha \in f_\eta^{-1}(D_{X,I})$.

- $f_\eta^{-1}(D_{X,I}) \subseteq Y$: consider $\alpha \in f_\eta^{-1}(D_{X,I})$. Then $\mu_{\eta(\alpha)}(X) \in I$, that is, $\mu(\alpha, X) \in I$. This, of course, means that $\alpha \in \mu_X^{-1}(I) = Y$.

The result is extended to the σ-algebra $\mathcal{F}_{subD(L \times Q)}$ by standard arguments.

- Only if: consider $P_{S,\eta} = (Exec^*, \mathcal{F}_{L \times Q}, \mu)$; we have to show that for all $X \in \mathcal{F}_{L \times Q}$ and for all $I \in \mathcal{B}([0,1])$, $\mu_X^{-1}(I) \in \mathcal{F}_{Exec^*}$. It is easy to observe that $\mu_X^{-1}(I)$ corresponds to all the executions from which a distribution in the generator $D_{X,I}$ of σ-algebra on distributions (see Section 2) is scheduled. The measurability of the scheduler ensures that such set of executions is in $\mathcal{F}_{Exec^*}$, as required.   □

The proposition above shows that measurable schedulers generate all and only the measurable probabilistic executions, that is, the probabilistic executions that we are interested in. We can therefore disallow non-measurable schedulers.

4.2   Measure on Executions

We can now define the measure on $(Exec, \mathcal{F}_{Exec})$ induced by a scheduler and show that it is defined only for measurable schedulers. Being able to define such a measure is important in order to study global properties on paths, such as the extension of trace distributions [20] to our setting, or if we want to use stochastic transition systems as a model for a stochastic extension of temporal or modal logic [8, 15].

We define the measure $\delta_{\eta,q}$ on basic sets induced by a scheduler η from a start state q inductively on the length of the basic sets as follows:

$$\delta_{\eta,q}(\mathcal{C}_X) = \begin{cases} 1 & \text{if } q \in X \\ 0 & \text{otherwise} \end{cases}$$

$$\delta_{\eta,q}(\mathcal{C}_{\Lambda A X}) = \int_{\alpha \in \Lambda} \mu_{\eta(\alpha)}(A, X) \delta_{\eta,q}(d\alpha)$$

The integral above is defined when the function $f(\alpha) = \mu_{\eta(\alpha)}(A, X)$ is measurable from the measure space of finite executions to $[0,1]$. From Proposition 1, this is true whenever we deal with measurable schedulers. The measure $\delta_{\eta,q}$ extends uniquely to $\mathcal{F}_{Exec}$ since basic sets form a semi-ring (Theorem 1). We get the following Proposition.

Proposition 2. *Given an STS S and a scheduler η, the measure $\delta_{\eta,q}$ is defined for all basic sets if and only if η is measurable.*

Proof outline. The proof is a consequence of the definition of $\delta_{\eta,q}$ and of Proposition 1.   □

Using the measure defined above, and since schedulers use sub-probability distributions, we can define the probability of a set of finite executions that have terminated as the probability to stop after each execution. Formally, given a sequence $\Lambda = X_0 A_1 \cdots A_n X_n$ of measurable sets of states and actions, we define the probability to stop after Λ as $\delta_{\eta,q}(\mathcal{C}_{\Lambda\perp}) = \int_{\alpha\in\Lambda}\mu_{\eta(\alpha)}(\perp)$. The cones $\mathcal{C}_{\Lambda\perp}$ are in fact the generators of $\mathcal{F}_{Exec^*}$. The probability of eventually terminating is the probability of finite executions, which can be defined as the countable union of disjoint basic sets as follows: $Exec^* = \cup_{i\geq0}\mathcal{C}_{Q(LQ)^i\perp}$.

5   Parallel Composition and Measurability

In this section we introduce a CSP-style parallel operator [14], under which two STSs synchronise on a common interface alphabet, and study the composition-ality properties of schedulers and measurable executions.

Given an STS S, we partition its label space into two measurable sets L^p and L^i of private and interface labels, respectively. We say that two STS S_1 and S_2 are *compatible* if $L_1^p \cap L_2 = \emptyset$ and $L_2^p \cap L_1 = \emptyset$. We denote the union of the measurable spaces of labels by $(L, \mathcal{F}_L)$. We can now define the parallel composition between two compatible STSs.

Definition 8. *Let S_1 and S_2 be two compatible labelled stochastic transition systems. The **parallel composition** $S_1 \parallel S_2$ of S_1 and S_2 is the stochastic transition system $S = ((Q, \mathcal{F}_Q), \bar{q}, (L, \mathcal{F}_L), \rightarrow)$, where:*

- $(Q, F_Q) = (Q_1 \times Q_2, \mathcal{F}_{Q_1} \otimes \mathcal{F}_{Q_2})$.
- $\bar{q} = (\bar{q}_1, \bar{q}_2)$.
- $(L, \mathcal{F}_L)$ *is the union of the labels of the components.*
- $\rightarrow \subseteq Q \times L \times \mathcal{D}(Q)$ *such that $((q_1, q_2), a, \mu_1 \otimes \mu_2) \in \rightarrow$ iff, for $i \in \{1, 2\}$:*
  - *if $a \in L_i$, then $(q_i, a, \mu_i) \in \rightarrow_i$, or*
  - *if $a \notin L_i$, then $\mu_i = Dirac(q_i)$.*

Observe that $S_1 \parallel S_2$ is a well-defined STS given the closure properties of analytic spaces. Next we define two families of functions, π_1 and π_2, to be the left and right projections respectively. Given a state q of S, the projection π_i returns the i-th component of q. For an execution α of S, define the projection $\pi_i(\alpha)$ as the execution of S_i obtained from α by projecting all the states and removing all the actions not in L_i together with the subsequent state. Given a distribution μ on $Q_1 \times Q_2$, the projection $\pi_i(\mu)$ is the distribution on Q_i induced by π_i; $\pi_i(\mu)$ exists since π_i is a measurable function. Finally, given a transition $t = ((q_1, q_2), a, \mu)$, its projection $\pi_i(t)$ is $(q_i, a, \pi_i(\mu))$. If $a \notin L_i$ the projection $\pi_i(t)$ is still defined but it does not correspond to a possible transition of S_i. Note that all the variants of π_1 and π_2 are measurable functions. The following two theorems are important for compositional reasoning.

Theorem 4. *Let S_1 and S_2 be two compatible STSs and α an execution of $S_1 \parallel S_2$. Then $\pi_i(\alpha)$ is an execution of S_i, for $i \in \{1, 2\}$.*

Theorem 5. *Let S_1 and S_2 be two compatible STSs and η a measurable sched-uler for $S_1 \parallel S_2$. Then there exists a measurable scheduler η_1 such that $\delta_{\eta_1,\bar{q}_1} = \pi_1(\delta_{\eta,\bar{q}})$.*

Proof outline. We define the scheduler η_1 on the first component as follows

$$\eta_1(\alpha_1)(T) = \int_{\alpha \in \pi_1^{-1}(\alpha_1)} \eta(\alpha)(\pi_1^{-1}(T)) \, \nu(\alpha_1, d\alpha) \tag{1}$$

for all $T \in \mathcal{F}_\mathcal{T}$, where $\nu(\alpha_1, d\alpha)$ is the regular conditional probability for $\delta_{\eta,\bar{q}}$ with respect to π_1, whose existence follows from Theorem 3. It is easy to show that η_1 defines a legal scheduler for S_1 and its measurability follows from Theorem 2. In order to prove that $\delta_{\eta_1,\bar{q}_1} = \pi_1(\delta_\eta, \bar{q})$, we need to show that

$$\delta_{\eta_1,\bar{q}_1}(\mathcal{C}_\Lambda) = \delta_{\eta,\bar{q}}(\pi^{-1}(\mathcal{C}_\Lambda)) \tag{2}$$

for all basic sets $\mathcal{C}_\Lambda$. Equation (2) is proved by algebraic arguments and by exploiting the properties of regular conditional probabilities. Since the two measures agree on the basic sets, which form a semi-ring, they extend to the same measure by Theorem 1. □

Theorem 5 shows that the action of a scheduler on S can be derived from the action of the corresponding schedulers on each component since the properties of an execution can be derived from the properties of its components. This allows us to analyse systems in a compositional way. At the same time, this result also confirms that the notion of measurable schedulers and measurable executions is well-defined, since it respects the important requirement of compositionality.

Remark 1. Theorem 5 extends the analogous result for the discrete case [21]. In particular, Equation (1) can be rewritten in a more familiar form as:

$$\eta_1(\alpha_1)(t) = \sum_{\alpha \in \pi_1^{-1}(\alpha_1)} \delta(\mathcal{C}_\alpha \mid \pi_1^{-1}(\mathcal{C}_{\alpha_1})) \cdot \eta(\alpha)(\pi_1^{-1}(t)).$$

In the discrete case, we can define the probability for a single transition t. The equation above shows the intuition behind the definition of η_1: each transition is assigned the weighted probability of its inverse image under projection after each execution in the parallel composition, conditioned on being in an execution whose projection is α_1.

6   Weak Transitions and Weak Bisimulation

In this section, we show how the results of the previous sections enable us to define weak transitions and weak bisimulation in our model. A weak transition [17] abstracts from internal computation and considers sequences of actions of the form $\tau^* a \tau^*$, where τ denotes a generic internal action. In the case of probabilistic automata, this is achieved by considering sequences of transitions that form a probabilistic execution where only executions whose trace is of the form $\tau^* a \tau^*$ have positive probabilities [21]. We wish to extend such approach to stochastic transition systems. Of course, in order to do this, we must be able to define the target probability over several steps of executions and we need to restrict to measurable schedulers. Our definition of weak transitions would not be possible without the restrictions on schedulers and the construction of the measure on cones described in Section 4.

We assume the existence of another partitioning of the label space L into two measurable sets, L^e and L^τ, to denote visible and invisible actions, respectively. We denote generic internal actions by τ. A weak transition is defined as a probabilistic execution which terminates with probability 1 and with a support contained in the set of executions containing exactly one visible action. Let $\mathcal{W}_A$ denote the executions whose visible trace is exactly one action $a \in A \subseteq L^e$ and $\mathcal{W} = \mathcal{W}_L$. $\mathcal{W}_A$ is measurable as it can be constructed from basic sets and it also contains infinite executions.

Definition 9. *The pair* (q, μ), $q \in Q$ *and* $\mu \in \mathcal{D}(L \times Q)$, *is a* **weak transition** *(denoted by* $q \Rightarrow \mu$*) if there exists a measurable scheduler* η *such that* $\delta_{\eta,q}(Exec^*) = 1$, $\delta_{\eta,q}(\mathcal{W}) = 1$ *and* μ *is defined as follows:* $\mu(A, X) = \delta_{\eta,q}((\cup_{i>0} \mathcal{C}_{Q((A\cup\{\tau\})Q)^i X\perp}) \cap \mathcal{W}_A)$ *for all* $A \in \mathcal{F}_L$, $A \subseteq L^e$, *and* $X \in \mathcal{F}_Q$.

It is easy to show that, under the termination condition $\delta_{\eta,q}(Exec^*) = 1$, μ is a probability measure on $L \times Q$. Weak transitions only consider the local behaviour from one state, and therefore do not preserve measurability properties that are defined on sets of states. For this reason, we use the more general notion of weak hyper-transitions [23], defined as transitions from a distribution over states to a distribution over states and labels.

Definition 10. *Let* μ *be a probability measure on* $(Q, \mathcal{F}_Q)$ *and for each* $q \in Q$ *let* $q \Rightarrow \mu_q$ *be a weak transition. Define* $\mu'(A, X) = \int_Q \mu_q(A, X)\mu(dq)$ *if the integral is defined for all* $A \in \mathcal{F}_L$ *and* $X \in \mathcal{F}_Q$. *Then we say that* $\mu \Rightarrow \mu'$ *is a* **weak hyper-transition**.

Hyper transitions are used in the discrete case to prove linear-time properties of systems, such as the fact that bisimulation preserves trace semantics [21]. Note that, in the discrete case, a meaure defined on a set of states and a set of transitions enabled from each of such states always induce a hyper-transition, while in the continuous case this is not always true, because of the usual problems of measurability. This is the reason why we strengthen our notion of weak bisimulation and define it in terms of weak hyper-transitions.

Weak Bisimulation. We extend the notion of weak bisimulation to stochastic transition systems. Bisimulation relations, first introduced in the context of CCS [17], are fundamental relations for concurrent systems, and have been extended to the probabilistic setting, both for discrete (strong and weak bisimulation) [16, 11, 22, 3, 19] and continuous state spaces (strong bisimulation) [7, 8, 5]. A notion of weak bisimulation for the continuous setting was introduced in [4], where the problem of defining a measure on paths for weak transitions was not considered, since a weak transition was defined as a succession of τ-labelled non probabilistic transitions followed by a probabilistic transition. The notion of weak transition defined in this paper is suitable for our more general case of several probabilistic steps. Strong bisimulation could be easily defined as it does not abstract from internal computation and therefore can be defined without restrictions to measurable schedulers.

Given an equivalence relation $\mathcal{R}$ on a measurable space $(Q, \mathcal{F}_Q)$, we say that $X \in \mathcal{F}_Q$ is $\mathcal{R}$-closed if it is the union of equivalence classes. Two probability measures μ_1 and μ_2 on Q are $\mathcal{R}$-equivalent ($\mu_1 \mathcal{R} \mu_2$) if $\mu_1(X) = \mu_2(X)$ for all $\mathcal{R}$-closed $X \in \mathcal{F}_Q$, while two probability measures μ_1 and μ_2 on $Q \times L$ are $\mathcal{R}$-equivalent if $\mu_1(A, X) = \mu_2(A, X)$ for all $\mathcal{R}$-closed $X \in \mathcal{F}_Q$ and for all $A \in \mathcal{F}_L$.

Definition 11. *Let S_1 and S_2 be two STSs with the same space of labels. An equivalence relation $\mathcal{R}$ on the union of their sets of states is a* **weak bisimulation** *between S_1 and S_2 if:*

1. *$\overline{q}_1 \mathcal{R} \overline{q}_2$ and*
2. *for all μ_1 and μ_2 $\mathcal{R}$-equivalent measures on states, whenever there is a hyper-transition $\mu_1 \to \mu_1'$, there exists a weak hyper-transition $\mu_2 \Rightarrow \mu_2'$ s.t. $\mu_1' \mathcal{R} \mu_2'$.*

7   Conclusions

We have introduced an operational model for non-deterministic systems with continuous state spaces and continuous probability distributions, thus generalising existing models. We have studied a framework where it is possible to assign probabilities to sets of executions, defined weak bisimulation relation and a parallel composition operator. The relationship between our notion of bisimulation and trace distributions is currently being investigated. Stochastic transition systems are also used as a semantic model for a stochastic process algebra [6]. Further work would include a logical characterisation of our equivalence relations, approximation and metrics.

Acknowledgements. We would like to thank Prakash Panangaden for the helpful discussions.

References

1. L. d. Alfaro. *Formal Verification of Probabilistic Systems*. PhD thesis, Stanford University, 1997. Available as Technical report STAN-CS-TR-98-1601.
2. R. B. Ash. *Real Analysis and Probability*. Academic Press, 1972.
3. C. Baier and H. Hermanns. Weak bisimulation for fully probabilistic processes. In *Proc. 9th International Conference on Computer Aided Verification (CAV'97)*, volume 1254 of *Lecture Notes in Computer Science*, pages 119–130, 1997.
4. M. Bravetti. *Specification and Analysis of Stochastic Real-Time Systems*. PhD thesis, Università di Bologna, Padova, Venezia, 2002.

5. M. Bravetti and P. D'Argenio. Tutte le algebre insieme: Concepts, discussions and relations of stochastic process algebras with general distributions. In C. Baier, B. Haverkort, H. Hermanns, J.-P. Katoen, M. Siegle, and F. Vaandrager, editors, *Validation of Stochastic Systems: A Guide to Current Research*, volume 2925 of *Lecture Notes in Computer Science (Tutorial Volume)*. Springer, 2004.
6. S. Cattani. *Trace-based Process Algebras for Real-time Probabilistic Systems*. PhD thesis, School of Computer Science, The University of Birmingham, 2005. Forthcoming.
7. P. R. D'Argenio. *Algebras and Automata for Timed and Stochastic Systems*. PhD thesis, Department of Computer Science, University of Twente, Nov. 1999.
8. J. Desharnais, A. Edalat, and P. Panangaden. Bisimulation for labelled markov processes. *Information and Computation*, 179(2):163–193, 2002.
9. M. Giry. A categorical approach to probability theory. In B. Banaschewski, editor, *Categorical Aspects of Topology and Analysis*, number 915 in Lecture Notes in Mathematics, pages 68–85. Springer-Verlag, 1981.
10. R. v. Glabbeek, S. Smolka, and B. Steffen. Reactive, generative, and stratified models of probabilistic processes. *Information and Computation*, 121(1):59–80, 1995.
11. H. Hansson. *Time and Probability in Formal Design of Distributed Systems*, volume 1 of *Real-Time Safety Critical Systems*. Elsevier, 1994.
12. H. Hermanns. *Interactive Markov Chains: The Quest for Quantified Quality*, volume 2428 of *Lecture Notes in Computer Science*. Springer, 2002.
13. J. Hillston. *A Compositional Approach to Performance Modelling*. Cambridge University Press, 1996.
14. C. Hoare. *Communicating Sequential Processes*. Prentice-Hall International, Englewood Cliffs, 1985.
15. M. Kwiatkowska, G. Norman, R. Segala, and J. Sproston. Verifying quantitative properties of continuous probabilistic real-time graphs. In C. Palamidessi, editor, *Proceedings of CONCUR 2000*, volume 1877 of *Lecture Notes in Computer Science*, pages 132–137. Springer, 2000.
16. K. Larsen and A. Skou. Bisimulation through probabilistic testing. *Information and Computation*, 94(1):1–28, Sept. 1991.
17. R. Milner. *Communication and Concurrency*. Prentice-Hall International, Englewood Cliffs, 1989.
18. P. Panangaden. Measure and probability for concurrency theorists. *Theoretical Comput. Sci.*, 253(2):287–309, 2001.
19. A. Philippou, I. Lee, and O. Sokolsky. Weak bisimulation for probabilistic systems. In C. Palamidessi, editor, *Proceedings of CONCUR 2000*, volume 1877 of *Lecture Notes in Computer Science*, pages 334–349. Springer, 2000.
20. R. Segala. A compositional trace-based semantics for probabilistic automata. In I. Lee and S. Smolka, editors, *Proceedings of CONCUR 95*, volume 962 of *Lecture Notes in Computer Science*, pages 234–248. Springer-Verlag, 1995.
21. R. Segala. *Modeling and Verification of Randomized Distributed Real-Time Systems*. PhD thesis, MIT, Dept. of Electrical Engineering and Computer Science, 1995. Also appears as technical report MIT/LCS/TR-676.
22. R. Segala and N. Lynch. Probabilistic simulations for probabilistic processes. *Nordic Journal of Computing*, 2(2):250–273, 1995.
23. M. Stoelinga. *Alea jacta est: verification of probabilistic, real-time and parametric systems*. PhD thesis, University of Nijmegen, the Netherlands, Apr. 2002.
24. S. Wu, S. Smolka, and E. Stark. Composition and behaviors of probabilistic I/O automata. *Theoretical Comput. Sci.*, 176(1-2):1–38, 1999.

Model Checking Durational Probabilistic Systems

(Extended Abstract)[*]

François Laroussinie[1] and Jeremy Sproston[2]

[1]Lab. Spécification & Verification, ENS Cachan – CNRS UMR 8643, France
[2]Dipartimento di Informatica, Università di Torino, 10149 Torino, Italy
fl@lsv.ens-cachan.fr
sproston@di.unito.it

Abstract. We consider model-checking algorithms for durational probabilistic systems, which are systems exhibiting nondeterministic, probabilistic and discrete-timed behaviour. We present two semantics for durational probabilistic systems, and show how formulae of the probabilistic and timed temporal logic PTCTL can be verified on such systems. We also address complexity issues, in particular identifying the cases in which model checking durational probabilistic systems is harder than verifying non-probabilistic durational systems.

1   Introduction

Model checking is an automatic method for guaranteeing that a mathematical model of a system satisfies a formula representing a desired property [7]. Many real-life systems, such as multimedia equipment, communication protocols, networks and fault-tolerant systems, exhibit *probabilistic* behaviour, leading to the study of *probabilistic model checking* of probabilistic and stochastic models [19, 13, 8, 5, 4, 3, 14]. Similarly, it is common to observe complex *real-time* behaviour in such systems. Model checking of discrete-time systems against properties of timed temporal logics, which can refer to the time elapsed along system behaviours, has been studied extensively in, for example, [11, 6, 16].

In this paper, we aim to study model-checking algorithms for discrete-time probabilistic systems, which we call *durational probabilistic systems*. Our starting point is the work of Hansson and Jonsson [13], which considered model checking for discrete-time Markov chains (in which transitions always take duration 1) against properties of a probabilistic, timed temporal logic, and that of de Alfaro [10], which extended the approach of Hansson and Jonsson to Markov decision processes in which transitions can be of duration 0 or of duration 1. We extend this previous work by considering systems in which state-to-state transitions take arbitrary, natural numbered durations, in the style of durational transition graphs [16, 17]. We present two semantics for durational probabilistic systems: the *continuous semantics* considers intermediate states as time elapses, whereas the *jump semantics* does not consider such states. In this paper,

---

[*] Supported in part by MIUR-FIRB Perf.

V. Sassone (Ed.): FOSSACS 2005, LNCS 3441, pp. 140–154, 2005.

we restrict our attention to *strongly non-Zeno* durational probabilistic systems, in which positive durations elapse in all loops of the system.

The temporal logic that we use to describe properties of durational probabilistic systems is PTCTL (Probabilistic Timed Computation Tree Logic). The logic PTCTL includes operators that can refer to bounds on exact time, expected time, and the probability of the occurrence of events. For example, the property "a request is followed by a response within 5 time units with probability 0.99 or greater" can be expressed by the PTCTL property $request \rightarrow \mathbb{P}_{\geq 0.99}(\texttt{true}\mathsf{U}_{\leq 5}response)$. Similarly, the property "the expected amount of time which elapses before reaching an alarm state is not more than 60" can be expressed as $\mathbb{D}_{\leq 60}(alarm)$. The logic PTCTL extends the probabilistic temporal logic PCTL [13, 5], the real-time temporal logic TCTL [1], and the performance-oriented logic of de Alfaro [10] (a similar logic has also been studied in the continuous-time setting [15]).

After introducing durational probabilistic systems and PTCTL in Section 2, we present model-checking algorithms for both of the aforementioned semantics in Section 3. The novelty of these algorithms is that their running time is independent of the timing constants used in the description of the durational probabilistic system, and their *program complexity* is polynomial. Instead, to apply the previous methods of de Alfaro, Hansson and Jonsson to durational probabilistic systems, we would have to model explicitly intermediate states as time passes (even for the jump semantics), hence resulting in a blow-up of the size of the state space. The presented algorithms are restricted to temporal modalities with upper or lower time bounds; we show in Section 4 that the problem of model checking durational probabilistic systems against PTCTL formulae in which exact time bounds are used (that is, of the form $= c$) is PSPACE-hard, even for "qualitative" probabilistic properties in which the probability thresholds refer to 0 or 1 only. We also show the NP-hardness and co-NP-hardness of model checking fully probabilistic durational systems against general "quantitative" probabilistic properties including arbitrary probability thresholds and upper time bounds (of the form $\leq c$). On the positive side, model checking qualitative probabilistic properties of fully probabilistic, strongly non-Zeno durational probabilistic systems is Δ_2^p-complete and PSPACE-complete for the jump and continuous semantics, respectively, and model checking qualitative properties excluding exact time bounds is in PSPACE for general strongly non-Zeno durational probabilistic systems with the jump semantics.

2   Durational Probabilistic Systems

2.1   Syntax of Durational Probabilistic Systems

Let AP be a countable set of atomic propositions, which we assume to be fixed throughout the remainder of the paper. Let $\mathcal{I}$ be the set of finite intervals over $\mathbb{N}$. Given a set X, $\mathsf{Dist}(X)$ denotes the set of discrete probability distributions over X.

Definition 1. *A durational probabilistic system (DPS) $\mathcal{D} = (Q, q_{init}, D, L)$ comprises a finite set of states Q with an initial state $q_{init} \in Q$; a finite durational probabilistic, nondeterministic transition relation $D \subseteq Q \times \mathcal{I} \times \mathsf{Dist}(Q)$ such that, for each state $q \in Q$, there exists at least one tuple $(q, \_, \_) \in D$; and a labelling function $L : Q \rightarrow 2^{AP}$.*

Intuitively, the behaviour of a durational probabilistic system comprises of repeatedly letting time pass then taking a state-to-state transition (which we sometimes call an *action transition*). The interval ρ of some $(q, \rho, \mu) \in D$ specifies the duration of the corresponding transition. On entry to a state $q \in Q$, there is a nondeterministic choice of a triple $(q, \rho, \mu) \in D$. Then the system chooses, again nondeterministically, the amount of time that elapses, where the chosen amount must belong to ρ. Finally, the system moves *probabilistically* to a next state $q' \in Q$ with probability $\mu(q')$.

The size $|\mathcal{D}|$ of $\mathcal{D}$ is $|Q| + |D|$ plus the size of the encoding of the timing constants and probabilities used in $\mathcal{D}$. The timing constants (lower and upper bounds of transitions' intervals) are written in binary, and where, for each $(q, \rho, \mu) \in D$, the values $\mu(q')$ are written as fixed-precision binary numbers.

Durational fully probabilistic systems. A *durational fully probabilistic system* (DFPS) is a DPS where there is exactly one tuple $(q, \rho, \_) \in D$ for any state q, and where ρ is a singleton. In such a system there is no non-deterministic choice.

Strong non-Zenoness. A DPS $\mathcal{D} = (Q, q_{init}, D, L)$ is *strongly non-Zeno* if, for each state $q \in Q$, there does not exist a sequence of transitions $(q_0, \rho_0, \mu_0)...(q_n, \rho_n, \mu_n)$ of $\mathcal{D}$ such that $q_0 = q$, $\mu_i(q_{i+1}) > 0$ for all $0 \le i < n$, $\mu_n(q_0) > 0$, and ρ_i is of the form $[0; \_]$ for all $0 \le i \le n$. Note that this property can easily be checked for a DPS. The concept of strong non-Zenoness is taken from previous work for timed automata [18]. The algorithms and the complexity results we show in this paper only deal with strongly non-Zeno DPSs.

2.2   Semantics of Durational Probabilistic Systems

We give a formal semantics to durational probabilistic system in terms of *timed Markov decision processes*.

Definition 2. *A* timed Markov decision processes *(TMDP)* $\mathsf{M} = (S, s_{init}, \rightarrow, lab)$ *comprises a finite set of states S with an initial state $s_{init} \in S$; a finite timed probabilistic, nondeterministic transition relation $\rightarrow \subseteq S \times \mathbb{N} \times \mathrm{Dist}(S)$ such that, for each state $s \in S$, there exists at least one tuple $(s, \_, \_) \in \rightarrow$; and a labelling function $lab : S \rightarrow 2^{AP}$.*

A special case of a timed Markov decision process is a *timed Markov chain* (TMC), in which, for each state $s \in S$, there exists exactly one tuple $(s, \_, \_) \in \rightarrow$. The size of TMDPs and the notion of strong non-Zenoness are defined as for DPSs, because a TMDP can be regarded as a DPS for which the intervals labelling transitions are all singletons.

The transitions from state to state of a TMDP are performed in two steps: given that the current state is s, the first step concerns a nondeterministic selection of $(s, d, \nu) \in \rightarrow$, where d corresponds to the duration of the transition; the second step comprises a probabilistic choice, made according to the distribution ν, as to which state to make the transition to (that is, we make a transition to a state $s' \in S$ with probability $\nu(s')$). We often denote such a transition by $s \xrightarrow{d, \nu} s'$, and write $s \xrightarrow{d, \nu}$ to indicate that there exists $(s, d, \nu) \in \rightarrow$. If $s \xrightarrow{d, \nu} s'$ is such that $\nu(s') = 1$, then for simplicity we write $s \xrightarrow{d} s'$.

An infinite or finite *path* of the timed Markov decision process M is defined as an infinite or finite sequence of transitions, respectively, such that the target state of one transition is the source state of the next. We use $Path_{fin}$ to denote the set of finite paths of M, and $Path_{ful}$ the set of infinite paths of M. If ω is finite, we denote by $last(\omega)$ the last state of ω. For any path ω, let $\omega(i)$ be its $(i+1)$th state. Let $Path_{ful}(s)$ refer to the set of infinite paths commencing in state $s \in S$. For an infinite path $\omega = s_0 \xrightarrow{d_0,\nu_0} s_1 \xrightarrow{d_1,\nu_1} \cdots$, the accumulated duration along ω until the ith state, denoted $Time(\omega, i)$, is equal to $\sum_{0 \leq j < i} d_j$.

In contrast to a path, which corresponds to a resolution of nondeterministic and probabilistic choice, an *adversary* represents a resolution of nondeterminism *only*. Formally, an adversary of a timed Markov decision process M is a function A mapping every finite path $\omega \in Path_{fin}$ to a transition $(last(\omega), d, \nu) \in \rightarrow$. Let Adv be the set of adversaries of M. For any adversary $A \in Adv$, let $Path_{ful}^{A}$ denote the set of infinite paths resulting from the choices of distributions of A, and let $Path_{ful}^{A}(s) = Path_{ful}^{A} \cap Path_{ful}(s)$. Then, for a state $s \in S$, we define the probability measure $Prob_s^A$ over $Path_{ful}^A(s)$ in the standard way [19].

Note that, by defining adversaries as functions from finite paths, we permit adversaries to be dependent on the history of the system. Hence, the choice made by an adversary at a certain point in system execution can depend on the sequence of states visited, the nondeterministic choices taken, and the time elapsed in each state, up to that point.

As for non-probabilistic systems [17], we can define several semantics of time for DPSs. Consider a transition of duration d between two DPS states q and q'. The first semantics, called the *jump* semantics, assumes that moving from q to q' takes d time units and that there are no intermediate states: if the system is in q at time t, then it is in q' at time $t + d$ and there is no position for time $t + 1 \ldots t + d - 1$. This semantics corresponds to a kind of cost or reward automata where every transition has a weight. We will also consider the *continuous* semantics, which involves waiting in $d - 1$ intermediate positions, each corresponding to the passage of one time unit, before performing the action transition and arriving in q'. This last semantics is close to the one used for timed automata and is generally more natural to model systems; for example, it is more convenient when considering parallel composition because time progresses smoothly.

Jump semantics. The *jump* semantics of a DPS $\mathcal{D} = (Q, q_{init}, D, L)$ is defined as the TMDP $M_j(\mathcal{D}) = (S, s_{init}, \rightarrow, lab)$, where:

- $S = Q$ and $s_{init} = q_{init}$;
- $(s, d, \mu) \in \rightarrow$ if and only if there exists $(s, \rho, \mu) \in D$ and $d \in \rho$;
- $lab(s) = L(s)$ for all $s \in S$.

Continuous semantics. Let $\delta_{\max}(q)$ be the maximal delay possible in state q of a durational probabilistic system. The *continuous* semantics of a DPS $\mathcal{D} = (Q, q_{init}, D, L)$ is defined as the TMDP $M_c(\mathcal{D}) = (S, s_{init}, \rightarrow, lab)$, where:

- $S = \{(q, i) \mid 0 \leq i < \delta_{\max}(q)\}$ and $s_{init} = (q_{init}, 0)$;
- $\rightarrow$ is the smallest set of transitions satisfying the following rules:

- $(q, 0) \xrightarrow{0,\nu}$ if there exists $(q, \rho, \mu) \in D$ such that $0 \in \rho$, and where $\nu(q', 0) = \mu(q')$ for each $q' \in Q$;
- $(q, i) \xrightarrow{1} (q, i+1)$ if $i + 1 < \delta_{\max}(q)$;
- $(q, i) \xrightarrow{1,\nu}$ if there exists $(q, \rho, \mu) \in D$ such that $i+1 \in \rho$, and where $\nu(q', 0) = \mu(q')$ for each $q' \in Q$;
- for each $(q, i) \in S$, let $lab(q, i) = L(q)$.

Observe that the semantics of a DFPS is a TMC, and that the semantics of a strongly non-Zeno DPS is also strongly non-Zeno. The size of the transition relation of $\mathsf{M}_j(\mathcal{D})$ may be exponential in $|\mathcal{D}|$ because it is linearly-dependent on the magnitude of the timing constants (encoded in binary) of the DPS. However, the number of states of $\mathsf{M}_j(\mathcal{D})$ and $\mathcal{D}$ is the same. This contrasts with $\mathsf{M}_c(\mathcal{D})$, where the number of states *and* the number of transitions may be exponential in $|\mathcal{D}|$. Another difference between the semantics is that the TMDP $\mathsf{M}_c(\mathcal{D})$ only contains durations in $\{0, 1\}$.

2.3   Probabilistic Timed Temporal Logic

In this section, we recall how the branching-time temporal logic CTL can be extended with constraints on time, probability and expected time. First we recall the probabilistic temporal logic PCTL [13, 5], in which the standard universal and existential path quantifiers $\mathsf{A}\varphi$ and $\mathsf{E}\varphi$ of CTL are replaced with a probabilistic quantifier of the form $\mathbb{P}_{\bowtie\lambda}(\varphi)$, where φ is a formula interpreted over paths, $\bowtie\in \{<, \leq, \geq, >\}$ is a comparison operator and $\lambda \in [0; 1]$ is a probability. Timing constraints, expressed using subscripts on "until" path formulae (with the syntax $\mathsf{U}_{\sim c}$, where $\sim\in \{\leq, =, \geq\}$), were introduced in the temporal logics RTCTL [11] and TCTL [1]. Finally, an expected-time operator $\mathbb{D}_{\bowtie\zeta}(\Phi)$, where $\bowtie\in \{<, \leq, \geq, >\}$ is a comparison operator and $\zeta \in \mathbb{R}_{\geq 0}$ is a non-negative real, was studied in the discrete-time context by de Alfaro [10] and Andova et al. [2].

We combine the above mentioned temporal logics to obtain the temporal logic PTCTL (Probabilistic Timed Computation Tree Logic), which extends the identically-named logic of [15] with the "next" temporal modality and the expected-time operator.

Definition 3. *The formulae of* PTCTL *are given by the following grammar:*

$$\Phi ::= P \mid \Phi \wedge \Phi \mid \neg\Phi \mid \mathbb{P}_{\bowtie\lambda}(\mathsf{X}\Phi) \mid \mathbb{P}_{\bowtie\lambda}(\Phi\mathsf{U}_{\sim c}\Phi) \mid \mathbb{D}_{\bowtie\zeta}(\Phi)$$

where $P \in AP$ is an atomic proposition, $\bowtie\in \{<, \leq, \geq, >\}$, $\sim\in \{\leq, =, \geq\}$ are comparison operators, $\lambda \in [0; 1]$ is a probability, $c \in \mathbb{N}$ is a natural number, and $\zeta \in \mathbb{R}_{\geq 0}$ is a positive real.

We define PTCTL$[\leq, \geq]$ as the sub-logic of PTCTL in which subscripts of the form $= c$ are not allowed in "until" modalities $\mathsf{U}_{\sim c}$. The size $|\Phi|$ is defined in the standard way, with constants written in binary.

Given an infinite path ω of a TMDP and a PTCTL formula Φ, let $T_{\omega,\Phi} = \min\{i \mid \omega(i) \models \Phi\}$ be the index of the first state of ω which satisfies Φ, and let $T_{\omega,\Phi} = \infty$ if $\omega(i) \not\models \Phi$ for all $i \in \mathbb{N}$. Then, for a given adversary $A \in Adv$ and state $s \in S$ of the TMDP, we let $ExpectedTime_s^A(\Phi) = \mathsf{E}_s^A\{Time(\omega, T_{\omega,\Phi})\}$, where $\mathsf{E}_s^A\{\cdot\}$ is the expectation, defined in the standard way, with respect to the probability measure $Prob_s^A$.

Definition 4. *Given a TMDP* $M = (S, s_{init}, \rightarrow, lab)$ *and a* PTCTL *formula* Φ, *we define the satisfaction relation* $\models_M$ *of* PTCTL *as follows:* [1]

$$
\begin{aligned}
s \models_M P & \quad \textit{iff } P \in lab(s) \\
s \models_M \Phi_1 \wedge \Phi_2 & \quad \textit{iff } s \models_M \Phi_1 \textit{ and } s \models_M \Phi_2 \\
s \models_M \neg\Phi & \quad \textit{iff } s \not\models_M \Phi \\
s \models_M \mathbb{D}_{\bowtie\varsigma}(\Phi) & \quad \textit{iff } ExpectedTime_s^A(\Phi) \bowtie \varsigma, \ \forall A \in Adv \\
s \models_M \mathbb{P}_{\bowtie\lambda}(\varphi) & \quad \textit{iff } Prob_s^A\{\omega \in Path_{ful}^A(s) \mid \omega \models_M \varphi\} \bowtie \lambda, \ \forall A \in Adv \\
\omega \models_M X\Phi & \quad \textit{iff } \omega(1) \models_M \Phi \\
\omega \models_M \Phi_1 U_{\sim c}\Phi_2 & \quad \textit{iff } \exists i \in \mathbb{N} \textit{ s.t. } Time(\omega, i) \sim c, \ \omega(i) \models_M \Phi_2 \\
& \qquad \textit{and } \omega(j) \models_M \Phi_1 \ \forall 0 \leq j < i \ .
\end{aligned}
$$

Model checking. The model-checking problem for a PTCTL formula Φ and a TMDP M with initial state s_{init} is to decide whether $s_{init} \models_M \Phi$, which we abbreviate to $M \models \Phi$. The model-checking problem for Φ, a DPS $\mathcal{D}$ and a semantics $sem \in \{j, c\}$ is to decide whether $M_{sem}(\mathcal{D}) \models \Phi$. The complexity results will be expressed in terms of the size $|\mathcal{D}| + |\Phi|$. However, we will also consider the *program complexity* where one fixes the formula and measures the complexity as a function of the size $|\mathcal{D}|$ only. As the system is assumed to be large whereas the formula is assumed to be small, the program complexity is often considered to be a more significant estimate of the feasibility of verification in practice.

3   Model Checking for Durational Probabilistic Systems

Our approach is to introduce in Section 3.1 a model-checking algorithm for strongly non-Zeno timed Markov decision processes, which will then be used in Section 3.2 as a basis for model-checking algorithms for durational probabilistic systems.

3.1   Model Checking Timed Markov Decision Processes

Although our model-checking algorithm for TMDPs presented below uses the analogous algorithm of de Alfaro [9] in order to verify the expected-time operator, the methods and complexities for the probabilistic, time-bounded operators are new, and, for strongly non-Zeno TMDPs, improve on previous results [13, 10] as their running time is not dependent on the magnitude of the time constants used in the transitions of the TMDP. More precisely, the previous methods are defined for systems in which the maximal time duration is 1, necessitating the modelling of longer time durations via intermediate states, hence blowing-up the size of the state space.

Before presenting the algorithm, we introduce some notation. The algorithm relies on computing a topological order on the states of the TMDP, so that reachability via 0 transitions is reflected in the order: for two states $s, s' \in S$, let $s \succ_0 s'$ if and only if

---

[1] When clear from the context, we omit the M subscript from $\models_M$.

$\mathbb{P}_{\leq\lambda}(\Phi_1 \mathsf{U}_{\leq c}\Phi_2)$:   for $i := 0$ to c
　　　　　　　　for $j := 0$ to n
　　　　　　　　　　if $s_j \models \Phi_2$ then let $f(s_j, i) := 1$
　　　　　　　　　　else
　　　　　　　　　　　　if $s_j \not\models \Phi_1 \vee \Phi_2$ then let $f(s_j, i) := 0$
　　　　　　　　　　　　else let $f(s_j, i) := \max\limits_{(s_j,d,\nu)\in\to} \sum\limits_{s'\in S} \nu(s') \cdot f(s', i-d)$

$\mathbb{P}_{\leq\lambda}(\Phi_1 \mathsf{U}_{=c}\Phi_2)$:   for each $s \models \Phi_2$ let $f(s, 0) := 1$
　　　　　　　　for $i := 0$ to c
　　　　　　　　　　for $j := 0$ to n
　　　　　　　　　　　　if $s_j \not\models \Phi_1 \vee \Phi_2$ then let $f(s_j, i) := 0$
　　　　　　　　　　　　else let $f(s_j, i) := \max\limits_{(s_j,d,\nu)\in\to} \sum\limits_{s'\in S} \nu(s') \cdot f(s', i-d)$

$\mathbb{P}_{\leq\lambda}(\Phi_1 \mathsf{U}_{\geq c}\Phi_2)$:   for each $s \in S$
　　　　　　　　let $f(s, 0) := \sup\limits_{A\in Adv} Prob_s^A\{\omega \in Path_{ful}^A(s) \mid \omega \models \Phi_1 \mathsf{U}\Phi_2\}$
　　　　　　　　for $i := 0$ to c
　　　　　　　　　　for $j := 0$ to n
　　　　　　　　　　　　if $s_j \not\models \Phi_1 \vee \Phi_2$ then let $f(s_j, i) := 0$
　　　　　　　　　　　　else let $f(s_j, i) := \max\limits_{(s_j,d,\nu)\in\to} \sum\limits_{s'\in S} \nu(s') \cdot f(s', \max(0, i-d))$

Fig. 1. The algorithms for computing $\mathbb{P}_{\leq\lambda}(\Phi_1 \mathsf{U}_{\sim c}\Phi_2)$

there exists a transition $s' \xrightarrow{0,\nu}$ where $\nu(s) > 0$. Then we order the states in S according to $\succ_0$ to obtain a sequence $s_0 s_1 ... s_n$ where $n = |S| - 1$, $s_{i+j} \not\succ_0 s_i$ for each $0 \leq i < n$, $1 \leq j \leq n - i$, and each state in S appears exactly once in the sequence. The fact that such a sequence $s_0 s_1 ... s_n$ exists follows from the fact that M is strongly non-Zeno. Computing the order can be done in time $O(|S| + |\xrightarrow{0}|)$ where $|\xrightarrow{0}| = \Sigma_{(s,0,\nu)\in\to}|\nu|$ and $|\nu| = |\{s' \mid \nu(s') > 0\}|$. In the algorithm below, we will always iterate over the states of the TMDP in such a way as to respect the topological order, in order to propagate the computed probabilities correctly through the states.

Proposition 1. *Let* M $= (S, s_{init}, \to, lab)$ *be a strongly non-Zeno TMDP and Φ be a* PTCTL *formula in which the maximal constant in its time-bound subscripts is c_{max}. Deciding whether* M $\models \Phi$ *can be done in time* $O(|\Phi| \cdot ((|S| \cdot | \to | \cdot c_{max}) + poly(|\mathsf{M}|)))$.

Proof. The cases for the atomic propositions, Boolean combinations and next formulae are standard, and therefore we concentrate on the model-checking algorithm for PTCTL formulae of the form $\mathbb{P}_{\bowtie\lambda}(\Phi_1 \mathsf{U}_{\sim c}\Phi_2)$ and $\mathbb{D}_{\bowtie\zeta}(\Phi')$. We restrict our attention to the cases in which $\bowtie$ is $\leq$. The cases for $\geq$ are obtained directly by substituting min for max, and inf for sup in the following procedures, and the cases for $\bowtie\in\{<, >\}$ follow similarly. We assume that arithmetical operations can be performed in constant time.

　　Until formulae. We consider three different procedures (see Figure 1) depending on the form of $\sim$. Recall that we use a topological order for enumerating the states $s_0 s_1 ... s_n$ in order to respect $\succ_0$.

In each of the procedures, a function of the form $f : S \times \mathbb{Z} \to [0;1]$ is utilized, with the intuition that, for $0 \leq i \leq c$, the state s satisfies the path formula $\Phi_1 \mathsf{U}_{\sim i} \Phi_2$ with maximum probability $f(s,i)$. Naturally, the aim is to calculate $f(s,c)$ for each state $s \in S$. In each of the three cases, for each $i < 0$ and each $s \in S$, we assume that we have $f(s,i) = 0$. One can prove by induction over i that $f(s,i) = \sup_{A \in Adv} Prob_s^A \{\omega \in Path_{ful}^A(s) \mid \omega \models \Phi_1 \mathsf{U}_{\sim i} \Phi_2\}$ for each state $s \in S$ and each $0 \leq i \leq c$. Hence, we conclude that $s \models \mathbb{P}_{\leq \lambda}(\Phi_1 \mathsf{U}_{\sim c} \Phi_2)$ if and only if $f(s,c) \leq \lambda$. The complexity of the first two procedures, where $\sim$ is $\leq$ or $=$, is $O(c \cdot |S| \cdot | \to |)$.

When $\sim$ is $\geq$, our algorithm first requires that we compute, for each state $s \in S$, the probability $\sup_{A \in Adv} Prob_s^A \{\omega \in Path_{ful}^A(s) \mid \omega \models \Phi_1 \mathsf{U} \Phi_2\}$ (the maximum probability of satisfying the un-subscripted formula $\Phi_1 \mathsf{U} \Phi_2$). Following Bianco and de Alfaro [5], these probabilities can be computed in $O(poly(|\mathsf{M}|))$ time. Therefore, the complexity of the third procedure is $O((c \cdot |S| \cdot | \to |) + poly(|\mathsf{M}|))$.

Expected-time formulae. For formulae of the form $\mathbb{D}_{\bowtie \varsigma}(\Phi')$, we can utilize the algorithm of de Alfaro [9] (TMDPs are a special case of de Alfaro's model), which reduces to a linear programming problem, with time complexity $poly(|\mathsf{M}|)$.

Overall complexity. We obtain an overall time complexity of $O(|\Phi| \cdot (((|S| \cdot | \to | \cdot c_{max}) + poly(|\mathsf{M}|)))$. Note that the time complexity can be expressed in terms of the maximum branching degree of the transitions of the TMDP. More precisely, if $b_{max} = \max_{(-,-,\nu) \in \to} |\{s \mid \nu(s) > 0\}|$ then we can write the complexity as $O(|\Phi| \cdot ((b_{max} \cdot | \to | \cdot c_{max}) + poly(|\mathsf{M}|)))$. $\qquad \square$

3.2 Extension to Strongly Non-Zeno Durational Probabilistic Systems

We now show how the algorithms of Section 3.1 can be used to define PTCTL model-checking algorithms for DPSs. One idea would be to apply these algorithms directly to the semantic TMDP of a DPS; however, in both semantics, the corresponding TMDPs are exponential in the size of original DPS . We avoid this in the case of PTCTL$[\leq, \geq]$ by utilizing specific TMDP constructions for both of the semantics.

Proposition 2 (DPS with jump semantics). *Let* $\mathcal{D} = (Q, q_{init}, D, L)$ *be a strongly non-Zeno durational probabilistic system and* Φ *be a* PTCTL$[\leq, \geq]$ *formula in which the maximal constant in the subscripts is* c_{max}. *Deciding whether* $\mathsf{M}_j(\mathcal{D}) \models \Phi$ *can be done in time* $O(|\Phi| \cdot ((|Q| \cdot |D| \cdot c_{max}) + poly(|\mathcal{D}|)))$.

Proof (sketch). We define a TMDP $\mathsf{M}_j^r(\mathcal{D}) = (S, s_{init}, \to^r, lab)$ corresponding to a restricted version of the jump semantics of $\mathcal{D}$ where S, s_{init}, and lab are defined as for the standard jump semantics, and $(s, d, \mu) \in \to^r$ if and only if there exists $(s, [l; u], \mu) \in D$ and either $d = l$ or $d = u$. Then, for any state $s \in S$, we can show that $s \models_{\mathsf{M}_j(\mathcal{D})} \Phi$ if and only if $s \models_{\mathsf{M}_j^r(\mathcal{D})} \Phi$: the minimum and maximum probabilities and expectations depend only on the minimum and maximum durations on transitions. $\qquad \square$

Proposition 3 (DPS with continuous semantics). *Let* $\mathcal{D} = (Q, q_{init}, D, L)$ *be a strongly non-Zeno durational probabilistic system and* Φ *be a* PTCTL$[\leq, \geq]$ *formula in which the maximal constant in the subscripts is* c_{max}. *Deciding whether* $\mathsf{M}_c(\mathcal{D}) \models \Phi$ *can be done in time* $O(((|\Phi|^3 \cdot |D|^3 \cdot c_{max}) + poly(|\Phi| \cdot |D| \cdot |\mathcal{D}|)))$.

Proof (sketch). We write the continuous semantics of $\mathcal{D}$ as $M_c(\mathcal{D}) = (S, s_{init}, \rightarrow, lab)$. Our aim is to label every state (q, i) of $M_c(\mathcal{D})$ with the set of subformulae of Φ which it satisfies. For each state $q \in Q$, we construct a set $\mathsf{Sat}[q, \xi]$ of intervals such that $\alpha \in \mathsf{Sat}[q, \xi]$ if and only if $(q, \alpha) \models \xi$. For reasons of space, we explain only the general ideas behind the verification of subformulae Ψ of the form $\mathbb{P}_{\bowtie \lambda}(\Phi_1 \mathsf{U}_{\sim c} \Phi_2)$ and $\mathbb{D}_{\bowtie \zeta}(\Phi')$. For this, we assume that we have already computed the sets $\mathsf{Sat}[\_, \_]$ for Φ_1, Φ_2 and Φ'.

As in Proposition 2, we construct a restricted TMDP which represents partially the states and transitions of $M_c(\mathcal{D})$ but which will be sufficient for computing the sets $\mathsf{Sat}[q, \Psi]$. The size of the restricted TMDP will ensure a procedure running in time polynomial in $|\mathcal{D}|$.

For the interval $\rho = [l; u]$, let $\rho - 1$ be the interval $[\max(0, l-1); \max(0, u-1)]$. For each state $q \in Q$, we build the minimal set of intervals $\mathsf{Int}(q) = \bigcup_{j=1..k} [\alpha_j; \beta_j]$ such that:

- for any i, we have $i \in \mathsf{Int}(q)$ if and only if $i \in \mathsf{Sat}[q, \Phi_1] \cup \mathsf{Sat}[q, \Phi_2]$, and every interval of $\mathsf{Int}(q)$ verifies either $\Phi_1 \wedge \Phi_2$, $\Phi_1 \wedge \neg \Phi_2$ or $\neg \Phi_1 \wedge \Phi_2$;
- for any j, we have $\alpha_j < \beta_j$, and $\beta_j \leq \alpha_{j+1}$ if $j + 1 \leq k$;
- the intervals are *homogeneous for action transitions*: for any $(q, \rho, \_) \in D$, we have $[\alpha_j, \beta_j] \subseteq \rho - 1$ or $[\alpha_j, \beta_j] \cap \rho - 1 = \emptyset$;
- the interval $[0; 1)$ is treated separately: if $0 \in \mathsf{Sat}[q, \Phi_1] \cup \mathsf{Sat}[q, \Phi_2]$, then $[0; 1)$ is the first interval of $\mathsf{Int}(q)$.

Letting $D^q = \{(q, \_, \_) \mid (q, \_, \_) \in D\}$, we clearly have $|\mathsf{Int}(q)| \leq 2 \cdot (|\mathsf{Sat}[q, \Phi_1]| + |\mathsf{Sat}[q, \Phi_2]| + |D^q|) + 1$. Let ν be a *sub-distribution* on a set S if $\nu : S \rightarrow [0; 1]$ and $\sum_{s \in S} \nu(s) \leq 1$, and let $\mathsf{SubDist}(S)$ be the set of all sub-distributions on the set S. Next, we build $M_I = (Q_I, \_, \rightarrow_I, lab_I)$, which is a variant of a TMDP in which sub-distributions may be used in addition to distributions. The set of states of M_I is $Q_I = \{(q, [\alpha; \beta)) \mid q \in Q \text{ and } [\alpha; \beta) \in \mathsf{Int}(q)\}$, and the set of timed probabilistic, nondeterministic transitions $\rightarrow_I \subseteq S \times \mathbb{N} \times \mathsf{SubDist}(S)$ is the smallest set defined as follows.

(Action transition) For any $(q, \rho, \mu) \in D$ and $[\alpha; \beta) \in \mathsf{Int}(q)$, if $[\alpha; \beta) \subseteq \rho - 1$, then:

if $[\alpha; \beta) = [0; 1)$: we have the transition $(q, [\alpha; \beta)) \xrightarrow{0, \nu}_I$ if $0 \in \rho$, and the transition $(q, [\alpha; \beta)) \xrightarrow{1, \nu}_I$ if $1 \in \rho$;

if $[\alpha; \beta) \neq [0; 1)$: we have the transitions $(q, [\alpha; \beta)) \xrightarrow{1, \nu}_I$ and $(q, [\alpha; \beta)) \xrightarrow{\beta - \alpha, \nu}_I$;

where $\nu \in \mathsf{SubDist}(Q_I)$ is the (sub-)distribution such that, for each $(q', [\alpha'; \beta')) \in Q_I$, we have:

$$\nu(q', [\alpha'; \beta')) = \begin{cases} \mu(q') & \text{if } [\alpha'; \beta') = [0; 1) \text{ and } [0; 1) \in \mathsf{Int}(q') \\ 0 & \text{otherwise.} \end{cases}$$

(Time successor) For any $[\alpha; \beta)$ and $[\alpha'; \beta')$ in $\mathsf{Int}(q)$, if $\beta = \alpha'$ then we have $(q, [\alpha, \beta)) \xrightarrow{\beta - \alpha}_I (q, [\alpha'; \beta'))$.

Finally, for each $(q, [\alpha; \beta)) \in Q_I$, we let $lab_I(q, [\alpha; \beta)) \subseteq \{\Phi_1, \Phi_2\}$ depending the inclusion of $[\alpha; \beta)$ w.r.t. $\mathsf{Sat}[q, \Phi_1]$ and $\mathsf{Sat}[q, \Phi_2]$.

The TMDP M_I has the following important property: for any state $(q, [\alpha; \beta))$ of M_I, we have that $(q, \alpha) \models_{M_c(\mathcal{D})} \mathbb{P}_{\bowtie\lambda}(\Phi_1 \mathsf{U}_{\sim c}\Phi_2)$ if and only if $(q, [\alpha; \beta)) \models_{M_I} \mathbb{P}_{\bowtie\lambda}(\Phi_1 \mathsf{U}_{\sim c}\Phi_2)$. This can be shown by using the same kind of arguments we used for proving Proposition 2.

Then using the above construction of M_I, we can apply the algorithm of Section 3.1 to decide, for each $(q, [\alpha; \beta)) \in Q_I$, whether $(q, \alpha) \models_{M_c(\mathcal{D})} \mathbb{P}_{\bowtie\lambda}(\Phi_1 \mathsf{U}_{\sim c}\Phi_2)$ (the presence of sub-distributions does not affect the results of the algorithm). Now note that, for each function f considered in Section 3.1, we compute a value for each state $(q, [\alpha; \beta))$ and each $0 \leq i \leq c$. Hence we can decide whether $(q, \alpha) \models_{M_c(\mathcal{D})} \mathbb{P}_{\bowtie\lambda}(\Phi_1 \mathsf{U}_{\sim i}\Phi_2)$ also for all $0 \leq i < c$. We can use these results to compute the satisfaction sets $\mathsf{Sat}[q, \mathbb{P}_{\bowtie\lambda}(\Phi_1 \mathsf{U}_{\sim c}\Phi_2)]$ for each state $q \in Q$.

One approach would be, for each point $\alpha < \gamma < \beta$, and for each state $(q, [\alpha; \beta))$, to iterate over the individual values of γ; however, the size of intervals $[\alpha; \beta)$ in $\mathsf{Int}(q)$ for a given state q are dependent on the size of constants appearing in the time intervals ρ of the transitions $(q, \rho, \_) \in D$. We instead iterate over the size of the subscript c used in the temporal logic formula. More precisely, for each state $(q, [\alpha; \beta))$ of M_I, we have two cases.

$(q, [\alpha; \beta))$ **has a time-successor state.** (I.e. there exists a state $(q, [\beta; \beta')) \in Q_I$.) Then deciding whether $\gamma \in \mathsf{Sat}[q, \mathbb{P}_{\bowtie\lambda}(\Phi_1 \mathsf{U}_{\sim c}\Phi_2)]$ for each $\alpha < \gamma < \beta$ can depend both on whether $\mathbb{P}_{\bowtie\lambda}(\Phi_1 \mathsf{U}_{\sim c}\Phi_2)$ is satisfied in (q, α) *and* on the satisfaction of $\mathbb{P}_{\bowtie\lambda}(\Phi_1 \mathsf{U}_{\sim i}\Phi_2)$ (for some i) in (q, β). For each $1 \leq j \leq \min(c, \beta - \alpha)$, we let $\beta - j \in \mathsf{Sat}[q, \mathbb{P}_{\bowtie\lambda}(\Phi_1 \mathsf{U}_{\sim c}\Phi_2)]$ if and only if $((q, \alpha) \models_{M_c(\mathcal{D})} \mathbb{P}_{\bowtie\lambda}(\Phi_1 \mathsf{U}_{\sim c}\Phi_2)) \vee ((q, \beta) \models_{M_c(\mathcal{D})} \mathbb{P}_{\bowtie\lambda}(\Phi_1 \mathsf{U}_{\sim c-j}\Phi_2))$. Intuitively, the second conjunct corresponds to letting time pass and eventually moving to (q, β): if the formula with a subscript $c - j$ is satisfied j time units in the future, then the analogous formula with subscript c will be satisfied now. The first conjunct corresponds to taking an action transition: from the homogeneity of intervals with respect to action transitions, such a transition is available throughout the interval.
If $\beta - \alpha > c$, then for each $\alpha < j < \beta - c$ we let $j \in \mathsf{Sat}[q, \mathbb{P}_{\bowtie\lambda}(\Phi_1 \mathsf{U}_{\sim c}\Phi_2)]$ if and only if $(q, \alpha) \models_{M_c(\mathcal{D})} \mathbb{P}_{\bowtie\lambda}(\Phi_1 \mathsf{U}_{\sim c}\Phi_2)$.

$(q, [\alpha; \beta))$ **does not have a time-successor state.** In this case, for each $\alpha < j < \beta$, we let $j \in \mathsf{Sat}[q, \mathbb{P}_{\bowtie\lambda}(\Phi_1 \mathsf{U}_{\sim c}\Phi_2)]$ if and only if $(q, \alpha) \models_{M_c(\mathcal{D})} \mathbb{P}_{\bowtie\lambda}(\Phi_1 \mathsf{U}_{\sim c}\Phi_2)$.

We then merge adjacent intervals in $\mathsf{Sat}[q, \mathbb{P}_{\bowtie\lambda}(\Phi_1 \mathsf{U}_{\sim c}\Phi_2)]$. Analogously to the non-probabilistic case [17], the size of this set is bounded by $|\mathsf{Sat}[q, \Phi_1]| + |\mathsf{Sat}[q, \Phi_2]| + |D^q|$, and one can show that $|\mathsf{Sat}[q, \Psi]| \leq |\Psi| \cdot |D^q|$ for any PTCTL$[\leq, \geq]$ formula Ψ.

Observe that $|Q_I| \leq \sum_{q \in Q} |\mathsf{Int}(q)| \leq |\mathbb{P}_{\bowtie\lambda}(\Phi_1 \mathsf{U}_{\sim c}\Phi_2)| \cdot |D|$, and $| \rightarrow_I | \leq |Q_I| \cdot (1 + |D|)$. Recalling that the algorithm of Section 3.1 runs in time $O(c \cdot |Q_I| \cdot | \rightarrow_I |)$ when $\sim$ is $\leq$, we conclude that properties of the form $\mathbb{P}_{\bowtie\lambda}(\Phi_1 \mathsf{U}_{\leq c}\Phi_2)$ can be verified in time $O(c \cdot |\mathbb{P}_{\bowtie\lambda}(\Phi_1 \mathsf{U}_{\leq c}\Phi_2)|^2 \cdot |D|^3)$. Similarly, when $\sim$ is $\geq$, the corresponding algorithm of Section 3.1 runs in time $O((c \cdot |Q_I| \cdot | \rightarrow_I |) + poly(|M_I|))$. The size of the TMDP M_I is no greater than $|Q_I| \cdot 2 \cdot |\mathcal{D}|$, and hence is no greater than $|\mathbb{P}_{\leq\lambda}(\Phi_1 \mathsf{U}_{\geq c}\Phi_2)| \cdot |D| \cdot 2 \cdot |\mathcal{D}|$. Hence, the algorithm when $\sim$ is $\geq$ runs in time $O((c \cdot |\mathbb{P}_{\bowtie\lambda}(\Phi_1 \mathsf{U}_{\geq c}\Phi_2)|^2 \cdot |D|^3) + poly(|\mathbb{P}_{\bowtie\lambda}(\Phi_1 \mathsf{U}_{\geq c}\Phi_2)| \cdot |D| \cdot |\mathcal{D}|))$.

These arguments can also be adapted for formulae $\mathbb{D}_{\bowtie\zeta}(\Phi')$. For a state s of a TMDP with a set of adversaries Adv, let $e_s^+(\Phi') = \sup_{A\in Adv} ExpectedTime_s^A(\Phi')$ and let $e_s^-(\Phi') = \inf_{A\in Adv} ExpectedTime_s^A(\Phi')$. In analogy with the case of properties of the form $\mathbb{P}_{\bowtie\lambda}(\Phi_1 \mathsf{U}_{\sim c} \Phi_2)$, for each state $(q, [\alpha;\beta)) \in Q_I$, we have $e_{(q,[\alpha;\beta))}^+(\Phi') = e_{(q,\alpha)}^+(\Phi')$ and $e_{(q,[\alpha;\beta))}^-(\Phi') = e_{(q,\alpha)}^-(\Phi')$. We apply the algorithm of de Alfaro [9] to M_I to compute $e_{(q,\alpha)}^+(\Phi')$ in the case of $\mathbb{D}_{\leq\zeta}(\Phi')$ and $e_{(q,\alpha)}^-(\Phi')$ in the case of $\mathbb{D}_{\geq\zeta}(\Phi')$.

To determine the values $e_{(q,\gamma)}^+(\Phi')$ and $e_{(q,\gamma)}^-(\Phi')$ for each $\alpha < \gamma < \beta$, we have two cases as above. If $(q, [\alpha;\beta))$ has a time-successor state, then for each $1 \leq j \leq \min(c, \beta - \alpha)$, we let $e_{(q,\beta-j)}^+(\Phi') = \max(e_{(q,\alpha)}^+(\Phi'), e_{(q,\beta)}^+(\Phi') + j)$, and similarly $e_{(q,\beta-j)}^-(\Phi') = \min(e_{(q,\alpha)}^-(\Phi'), e_{(q,\beta)}^-(\Phi')+j)$. If $\beta-\alpha > c$, then for each $\alpha < j < \beta-c$ we let $e_{(q,j)}^+(\Phi') = e_{(q,\alpha)}^+(\Phi')$ and $e_{(q,j)}^-(\Phi') = e_{(q,\alpha)}^-(\Phi')$.

On the other hand, if $(q, [\alpha;\beta))$ does not have a time-successor state, then for each $\alpha < j < \beta$, we let $e_{(q,j)}^+(\Phi') = e_{(q,\alpha)}^+(\Phi')$ and $e_{(q,j)}^-(\Phi') = e_{(q,\alpha)}^-(\Phi')$.

Then we can compare the obtained values of e^+ and e^- to the threshold ζ to decide whether $j \in \mathsf{Sat}[q, \mathbb{D}_{\bowtie\zeta}(\Phi')]$. We merge adjacent intervals in $\mathsf{Sat}[q, \mathbb{D}_{\bowtie\zeta}(\Phi')]$ to obtain the final satisfaction sets; as in the non-probabilistic case [17], the size of this set is bounded by $|D^q| + |\mathsf{Sat}[q, \Phi']| + 1$.

Verification of the $\mathbb{D}_{\bowtie\zeta}(\Phi')$ operator can be done in polynomial time in the size of M_I, and therefore our procedure takes time $poly(|\mathbb{D}_{\bowtie\zeta}(\Phi')| \cdot |D| \cdot |\mathcal{D}|)$.

Overall complexity. We obtain an overall time complexity of $O((|\Phi|^3 \cdot |D|^3 \cdot c_{max}) + poly(|\Phi| \cdot |D| \cdot |\mathcal{D}|))$. □

These two propositions imply that the program complexity of model checking PTCTL$[\leq, \geq]$ for the jump and continuous semantics is in P. This contrasts with the case of timed automata (with or without probability), where algorithms are based on the region graph and are exponential in the size of the system.

4   Complexity of Model Checking Durational Probabilistic Systems

In this section we consider upper and lower bounds on the complexity of model checking strongly non-Zeno DPSs. In particular we aim at comparing these results with those obtained for (non-probabilistic) durational systems, namely durational transition graphs (DTG) [17]. A DTG consists of a state set S, initial state s_{init}, and a labelling function l; in contrast to a DPS, however, the transition relation is of the form $\rightarrow \subseteq S \times \mathcal{I} \times S$. We know that model checking TCTL over DTGs is Δ_2^p-complete (resp. PSPACE-complete) with the jump semantics (resp. continuous semantics). Furthermore, model checking TCTL$[\leq, \geq]$ can be done in polynomial time for both semantics. We now identify cases in which the addition of probability makes model checking harder than in the non-probabilistic case, even for restricted sub-logics of PTCTL.

Complexity with probabilities 0/1. First we consider PTCTL$^{0/1}$, the "qualitative" sub-logic of PTCTL in which we allow $\mathbb{P}_{\bowtie\lambda}$ operators with $\lambda \in \{0, 1\}$ only, and in which the $\mathbb{D}_{\bowtie\zeta}$ operator is excluded.

Theorem 1 (Durational fully probabilistic systems). *Model checking* PTCTL$^{0/1}$ *over a strongly non-Zeno durational fully probabilistic system is a Δ_2^p-complete (resp. PSPACE-complete) problem for the jump (resp. continuous) semantics.*

Proof. This result derives mainly from the complexity of model checking over DTGs. Indeed, the general idea is to reduce model checking of PTCTL$^{0/1}$ over a strongly non-Zeno DFPS $\mathcal{D} = (Q, q_{init}, D, L)$ to TCTL model checking over the DTG $(S, s_{init}, \rightarrow, l)$ defined as follows: $S = Q$, $s_{init} = q_{init}$, $l = L$ and $(s, \rho, s') \in \rightarrow$ iff we have $(s, \rho, \mu) \in D$ and $\mu(s') > 0$. We replace PTCTL$^{0/1}$ subformulae by TCTL counterparts in the following way: $\mathbb{P}_{>0}(\varphi)$ is replaced by $\mathsf{E}\varphi$, while $\mathbb{P}_{\geq 1}(\mathsf{X}\Phi)$ (resp. $\mathbb{P}_{\geq 1}(\Phi_1 \mathsf{U}_{\leq c}\Phi_2)$, $\mathbb{P}_{\geq 1}(\Phi_1 \mathsf{U}_{=c}\Phi_2)$) is replaced by $\mathsf{AX}\Phi$ (resp. $\mathsf{A}(\Phi_1 \mathsf{U}_{\leq c}\Phi_2)$, $\mathsf{A}(\Phi_1 \mathsf{U}_{=c}\Phi_2)$). Finally, $\mathbb{P}_{\geq 1}(\Phi_1 \mathsf{U}_{\geq c}\Phi_2)$ is replaced by $\mathsf{A}(\Phi_1 \mathsf{U}_{\geq c} P_{\Phi_1 \mathsf{U}\Phi_2})$, where $P_{\Phi_1 \mathsf{U}\Phi_2}$ is a new atomic proposition that holds for states satisfying $\mathbb{P}_{\geq 1}(\Phi_1 \mathsf{U}\Phi_2)$. The standard PCTL model-checking algorithm [5], which runs in polynomial time, can be used to label states by $P_{\Phi_1 \mathsf{U}\Phi_2}$. Note that these reductions are possible because the DFPS is strongly non-Zeno. For the remaining PTCTL$^{0/1}$ formulae, as we are considering fully probabilistic systems, we have $\mathbb{P}_{<1}(\varphi) \equiv \neg\mathbb{P}_{\geq 1}(\varphi)$ and $\mathbb{P}_{\leq 0}(\varphi) \equiv \neg\mathbb{P}_{>0}(\varphi)$. The overall transformation provides Δ_2^p-membership (resp. PSPACE-membership) for the PTCTL model checking over DPS in the jump semantics (resp. continuous semantics).

With regard to the hardness results, we adapt the proofs used for DTGs with the same transformation of formulae as described above.   □

Note that, following the results of [17] and using the translations of the proof of Theorem 1, we can find a polynomial-time algorithm for model checking DFPSs against formulae of PTCTL$^{0/1}$ without subscripts $=c$ in until modalities, both for the jump and continuous semantics.

Next, we address model checking of general, nondeterministic DPSs.

Theorem 2 (Durational probabilistic systems). *Model checking strongly non-Zeno durational probabilistic systems with the jump semantics is (1) PSPACE-hard for* PTCTL$^{0/1}$, *and (2) in PSPACE for* PTCTL$^{0/1}[\leq, \geq]$.

Proof. (1) We reduce a quantified version of the subset-sum problem, called *Q-subset-sum*, to a PTCTL$^{0/1}$ model-checking problem on strongly non-Zeno DPSs. As QBF can be reduced to Q-subset-sum, this suffices to show PSPACE-hardness. An instance I of Q-subset-sum contains a finite sequence X of integers $x_1, \ldots, x_n$, an integer G and a sequence of quantifiers $\mathcal{Q}_1, \ldots, \mathcal{Q}_n$ in $\{\exists, \forall\}$. The instance I is positive iff there exists a set Z of subsets of X s.t. (I) $\Sigma_{x \in X'} x = G$ for any $X' \in Z$ and (II) for any $Y \in Z$, if $\mathcal{Q}_i = \forall$, then there exists $Y' \in Z$ s.t. $x_j \in Y \Leftrightarrow x_j \in Y'$ for any $j < i$ and $x_i \in Y' \Leftrightarrow x_i \notin Y$. Assume w.l.o.g. that n is even and $\mathcal{Q}_{2i+1} = \forall, \mathcal{Q}_{2i+2} = \exists$ for all $0 \leq i < \frac{n}{2}$. Then we consider the DPS $\mathcal{D}_I$ described in Figure 2. The dashed lines correspond to non-deterministic choices, and the numbers in parentheses correspond to the duration of the transitions which they label.

Now assume $q_0 \models \neg\mathbb{P}_{<1}(\mathsf{F}_{=G}P)$ (where $\mathsf{F}_{\sim c^-} \equiv \mathtt{true}\mathsf{U}_{\sim c^-}$, and where q_n is the only state labelled with P): that is, there exists an adversary such that the probability of satisfying $\mathsf{F}_{=G}P$ from q_0 is 1. In terms of I, for any existential quantifier in I, it is possible to make a decision leading to a subset with exactly the sum G. Then $q_0 \models \neg\mathbb{P}_{<1}(\mathsf{F}_{=G}P)$ if and only if the instance I is positive.

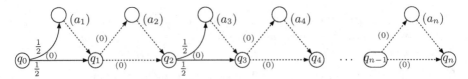

Fig. 2. The durational probabilistic system $\mathcal{D}_I$

(2) The PSPACE membership is shown as follows. For reasons of space we consider only the case $\mathbb{P}_{>0}(\Phi_1 U_{\leq c}\Phi_2)$. Because the DPS is strongly non-Zeno, it suffices to verify that for any adversary there exists a path satisfying $\Phi_1 U_{\leq c}\Phi_2$. We use the following algorithm which runs in polynomial space.

First note that $q \models \mathbb{P}_{>0}(\Phi_1 U_{\leq d}\Phi_2)$ entails $q \models \mathbb{P}_{>0}(\Phi_1 U_{\leq d+1}\Phi_2)$. For every state q we will compute the minimal d s.t. $\mathbb{P}_{>0}(\Phi_1 U_{\leq d}\Phi_2)$ holds for q. First we define $T[q]$ as 0 (resp. ∞) if $q \models \Phi_2$ (resp. $q \not\models \Phi_1$). Then, for any $j = 0, 1, \ldots, c$, we try to update $T[q]$ for $q = q_1, \ldots, q_n$ if $T[q]$ has not yet been defined (where we enumerate the states in the topological order $\succ_0$). Updating $T[q]$ to j is done if, for any $(q, \rho, \mu) \in D$, there exists at least one state q' s.t. $\mu(q') > 0$ and $T[q'] \geq j - d_\rho$ where d_ρ is the maximal duration in ρ. Finally it remains to label a state q by $\mathbb{P}_{>0}(\Phi_1 U_{\leq c}\Phi_2)$ iff $T[q] \leq c$. A similar procedure can be used to verify the other properties. □

For the continuous semantics, it is clear that model checking PTCTL is PSPACE-hard. These results show that strongly non-Zeno DFPSs are not harder to verify against PTCTL$^{0/1}$ than non-probabilistic durational systems against TCTL, and that combining probabilities and non-determinism induces a complexity blow-up for the jump semantics compared to the non-probabilistic case.

Complexity of full PTCTL. If we move from the sub-logic PTCTL$^{0/1}$ to the logic in which the operator $\mathbb{P}_{\bowtie\lambda}$ is permitted to have rational $\lambda \in [0; 1]$, we observe a complexity blow-up. It is sufficient to consider the simple formula $\mathbb{P}_{\geq\lambda}(F_{\leq c}P)$ in the fully probabilistic case with the jump semantics.

Proposition 4. *Model checking* $\mathbb{P}_{\geq\lambda}(F_{\leq c}P)$ *over durational fully probabilistic systems with the jump semantics is NP-hard.*

Proof (sketch). The proof consists in reducing the K-th largest subset problem, which is NP-hard [12–p. 225], to the problem of model checking a formula of the form $\mathbb{P}_{\geq\lambda}(F_{\leq c}P)$ on a DFPS with the jump semantics. An instance I of K-th largest subset problem is a finite set $X = \{x_1, \ldots, x_n\}$ of natural numbers and two integers K and B. The problem consists in asking whether there are at least K distinct subsets $X' \subseteq X$ s.t. $\sum_{x \in X'} x \leq B$. Consider an adaptation of the DPS of Figure 2 where we replace the non-deterministic choices in states q_{2i+1}, for $0 \leq i < \frac{n}{2}$, by distributions with probabilities $\frac{1}{2}$, and recall that q_n is the only state labelled with P. This provides a DFPS that satisfies $\mathbb{P}_{\geq\frac{K}{2^n}}(F_{\leq B}P)$ if and only if I is a positive instance. □

A corollary is that model checking PTCTL[$\leq$, $\geq$] is NP-hard and coNP-hard over durational fully probabilistic systems with the jump semantics. Note that this problem is

Table 1. Complexity results for model checking durational probabilistic systems

	Fully prob. DPS		DPS	
	jump sem.	cont. sem.	jump sem.	cont. sem.
$\textsc{Ptctl}^{0/1}[\leq,\geq]$	P-complete	P-complete	P-hard in PSPACE	P-hard in EXPTIME[†]
$\textsc{Ptctl}^{0/1}$	Δ_2^p-complete	PSPACE-complete	PSPACE-hard in EXPTIME	PSPACE-hard in EXPTIME
$\textsc{Ptctl}[\leq,\geq]$	NP-hard and coNP-hard in EXPTIME[†]			
$\textsc{Ptctl}$	Δ_2^p-hard in EXPTIME	PSPACE-hard in EXPTIME	PSPACE-hard in EXPTIME	PSPACE-hard in EXPTIME

the simplest problem within our framework referring to quantitative temporal properties. It entails that considering simple timing constraints and quantitative probabilistic properties in the same model checking problem leads to NP-hardness, whereas considering *either* simple timing constraints (as in [17]) *or* quantitative probabilistic properties (as in [5]) allows for efficient model checking.

For the general case where we have non-determinism, probabilities and $\textsc{Ptctl}$ formulae, we conjecture that model checking is EXPTIME-complete. From the algorithms of Section 3 and the complexity results for $\textsc{Ptctl}^{0/1}$, we obtain the following corollary. Note that the EXPTIME-membership comes from a direct application of the algorithm described in Proposition 1 to $\mathsf{M}_j(\mathcal{D})$ or $\mathsf{M}_c(\mathcal{D})$.

Corollary 1. *Model checking* $\textsc{Ptctl}$ *over durational probabilistic systems in the jump or continuous semantics is PSPACE-hard and it can be done in EXPTIME.*

5   Conclusion

In this paper we introduced durational probabilistic systems, a model to describe probabilistic, non-deterministic and timed systems. We showed how model checking can be done over this model, paying attention to complexity issues. Table 1 summarizes the results we presented in the paper. First, note that model checking can be done efficiently for fully probabilistic systems and qualitative $\textsc{Ptctl}^{0/1}$ properties without the exact time-bound subscript $= c$. However, as in the non-probabilistic case, adding the exact time-bound induces a complexity blow-up. This motivates the use of $\textsc{Ptctl}[\leq,\geq]$ where the subscripts in until formulae are restricted to $\leq c$ and $\geq c$ constraints. For this logic, even with quantitative properties, we have model checking algorithms running in time polynomial in $|\varPhi| \cdot |\mathcal{D}|$ and linear in c_{max}, the maximal timing constant of the formula, as described in Proposition 2 and Proposition 3, and indicated by the (†) superscripts in the table. The precise polynomial depends on the kind of DPS and the choice of semantics. The formula's time constants are encoded in binary, and hence these algorithms belong to EXPTIME; nevertheless the algorithms should be interesting in practice, because they are polynomial in $|\mathcal{D}|$. In future work, we will consider the precise complexity of the non-complete model-checking problems listed in the table.

References

1. R. Alur, C. Courcoubetis, and D. L. Dill. Model-checking in dense real-time. *Information and Computation*, 104(1):2–34, 1993.
2. S. Andova, H. Hermanns, and J.-P. Katoen. Discrete-time rewards model-checked. In *Proc. 1st Int. Workshop on Formal Modeling and Analysis of Timed Systems (FORMATS 2003)*, volume 2791 of *LNCS*, pages 88–104. Springer, 2004.
3. C. Baier, B. Haverkort, H. Hermanns, and J.-P. Katoen. Model-checking algorithms for continuous-time Markov chains. *IEEE Transactions on Software Engineering*, 29(6):524–541, 2003.
4. C. Baier and M. Kwiatkowska. Model checking for a probabilistic branching time logic with fairness. *Distributed Computing*, 11(3):125–155, 1998.
5. A. Bianco and L. de Alfaro. Model checking of probabilistic and nondeterministic systems. In *Proc. 15th Conf. on Foundations of Software Technology and Theoretical Computer Science (FSTTCS'95)*, volume 1026 of *LNCS*, pages 499–513. Springer, 1995.
6. S. Campos, E. M. Clarke, W. R. Marrero, M. Minea, and H. Hiraishi. Computing quantitative characteristic of finite-state real-time systems. In *Proc. IEEE Real-Time Systems Symposium (RTSS'94)*, pages 266–270. IEEE Computer Society Press, 1994.
7. E. M. Clarke, O. Grumberg, and D. Peled. *Model checking*. MIT Press, 1999.
8. C. Courcoubetis and M. Yannakakis. The complexity of probabilistic verification. *Journal of the ACM*, 42(4):857–907, 1995.
9. L. de Alfaro. *Formal verification of probabilistic systems*. PhD thesis, Stanford University, Department of Computer Science, 1997.
10. L. de Alfaro. Temporal logics for the specification of performance and reliability. In *Proc. 14th Annual Symp. on Theoretical Aspects of Computer Science (STACS'97)*, volume 1200 of *LNCS*, pages 165–176. Springer, 1997.
11. E. A. Emerson, A. K. Mok, A. P. Sistla, and J. Srinivasan. Quantitative temporal reasoning. *Real Time Systems*, 4(4):331–352, 1992.
12. M. R. Garey and D. S. Johnson. *Computers and Intractability: A Guide to the Theory of NP-Completeness*. Freeman, 1979.
13. H. A. Hansson and B. Jonsson. A logic for reasoning about time and reliability. *Formal Aspects of Computing*, 6(5):512–535, 1994.
14. M. Kwiatkowska. Model checking for probability and time: From theory to practice. In *Proc. 18th Annual IEEE Symposium on Logic in Computer Science (LICS'03)*, pages 351–360. IEEE Computer Society Press, 2003.
15. M. Kwiatkowska, G. Norman, R. Segala, and J. Sproston. Automatic verification of real-time systems with discrete probability distributions. *Theoretical Computer Science*, 286:101–150, 2002.
16. F. Laroussinie, N. Markey, and P. Schnoebelen. On model checking durational Kripke structures (extended abstract). In *Proc. 5th Int. Conf. Foundations of Software Science and Computation Structures (FOSSACS 2002)*, volume 2303 of *LNCS*, pages 264–279. Springer, 2002.
17. F. Laroussinie, N. Markey, and P. Schnoebelen. Efficient timed model checking for discrete time systems. Submitted, 2004.
18. S. Tripakis. Verifying progress in timed systems. In *Proc. 5th AMAST Workshop on Real-Time and Probabilistic Systems (ARTS'99)*, volume 1601 of *LNCS*, pages 299–314. Springer, 1999.
19. M. Y. Vardi. Automatic verification of probabilistic concurrent finite-state programs. In *Proc. 16th Annual Symp. on Foundations of Computer Science (FOCS'85)*, pages 327–338. IEEE Computer Society Press, 1985.

Free-Algebra Models for the π-Calculus

Ian Stark*

Laboratory for Foundations of Computer Science
School of Informatics, The University of Edinburgh, Scotland
Ian.Stark@ed.ac.uk

Abstract. The finite π-calculus has an explicit set-theoretic functor-category model that is known to be fully abstract for strong late bisimulation congruence. We characterize this as the initial free algebra for an appropriate set of operations and equations in the enriched Lawvere theories of Plotkin and Power. Thus we obtain a novel algebraic description for models of the π-calculus, and validate an existing construction as the universal such model.

The algebraic operations are intuitive, covering name creation, communication of names over channels, and nondeterminism; the equations then combine these features in a modular fashion. We work in an enriched setting, over a "possible worlds" category of sets indexed by available names. This expands significantly on the classical notion of algebraic theories, and in particular allows us to use nonstandard arities that vary as processes evolve.

Based on our algebraic theory we describe a category of models for the π-calculus, and show that they all preserve bisimulation congruence. We develop a direct construction of free models in this category; and generalise previous results to prove that all free-algebra models are fully abstract.

1 Introduction

There are by now a handful of models known to give a denotational semantics for the π-calculus [2, 3, 6, 7, 8, 10, 36]. All are fully abstract for appropriate operational equivalences, and all use functor categories to handle the central issue of names and name creation. In this paper we present a method for generating such models purely from their algebraic properties.

We address specifically the finite π-calculus model as presented by Fiore et al [8]. This uses the functor category $Set^{\mathcal{I}}$, with index $\mathcal{I}$ the category of finite name sets and injections, and is fully abstract for strong late bisimulation congruence. We exhibit this as one among a category of algebraic models for the π-calculus: all such π-algebras respect bisimulation congruence, and we give a concrete description of the free π-algebra $Pi(X)$ for any object X of $Set^{\mathcal{I}}$. We show that every free algebra is a fully-abstract model for the π-calculus, with the construction of Fiore et al. being the initial free algebra $Pi(0)$.

Our method builds on a recent line of research by Plotkin and Power who use algebraic theories in enriched categories to capture "notions of computation", in particular

---

* Research supported by an EPSRC Advanced Research Fellowship.

V. Sassone (Ed.): FOSSACS 2005, LNCS 3441, pp. 155–169, 2005.

Moggi's *computational monads* [18, 26, 27, 28]. The general idea is to describe a computational feature — I/O, state, nondeterminism — by stating a characteristic collection of operations with specified equations between them. These then induce the following suite of constructions: a notion of algebraic model for the feature; a computational monad; effectful actions to program with; and a modal logic for specification and reasoning. This approach also gives a flexible way to express interactions between features, by combining sets of operations [11, 12].

For the π-calculus, we apply and expand their technique. The enriched setting supports not only models that are objects in $Set^{\mathcal{I}}$, but also arities from $Set^{\mathcal{I}}$; so that we have operations whose arity depends on the names currently available. We use two different closed structures in $Set^{\mathcal{I}}$: the usual cartesian exponential for arities, and a monoidal function space "$\multimap$" for operations parameterised by *fresh* names. Finally, the π-calculus depends on a very particular interaction between concurrency, communication and name generation, which we can directly express in equations relating the theories for each of these features. This precision in integrating different aspects of computation is a significant benefit of the algebraic approach over existing techniques for combining computational monads [13, 15, 19, 37].

The structure of the paper is as follows. In §2 we review the relevant properties of algebraic theories and the functor category $Set^{\mathcal{I}}$. We then set out our proposed algebraic theory of π in §3. Following this, in §4 we show how models of the theory give a denotational semantics for the finite π-calculus (i.e., omitting recursion and replication), and prove that these interpretations respect bisimulation congruence (Prop. 2). Interestingly, parallel composition of processes is not in general admissible as a basic operation in the theory, although we are able to interpret it via expansion. We prove the existence of free algebras over $Set^{\mathcal{I}}$ (Thm. 3) and show that they are all fully abstract (Thm. 5). In particular, the free algebra over the empty set is exactly the model of Fiore et al., and does support an internal definition of parallel composition (Prop. 4). Finally, we identify the monad induced by the theory of π, which gives a programming language semantics for mobile communicating concurrency. We conclude in §5 by indicating possible extensions and further applications of this work.

2   Background

We outline relevant material on algebraic theories and the target category $Set^{\mathcal{I}}$. For π-calculus information, see one of the books [16, 32] or Parrow's handbook chapter [23].

2.1   Algebras and Notions of Computation

We sketch very briefly the theoretical basis for our development: for more on enriched algebraic theories see Robinson's clear and detailed exposition [31]; the link to computations and generic effects is described in [27, 28].

There is a well-established connection between algebraic theories and monads on the category Set. For example, consider the following theory, which we shall use later for an algebra A of nondeterministic computations:

$$choice : A \times A \longrightarrow A$$
$$nil : 1 \longrightarrow A$$

Operation *choice* for combining computations to be commutative, associative and idempotent with unit *nil*.

A model of this theory is a triple $\langle A, choice, nil \rangle$ of a carrier set A with two maps satisfying the relevant commuting diagrams; and these models form a category $\mathcal{ND}(\mathcal{Set})$ of "nondeterministic sets". The forgetful functor U into $\mathcal{Set}$ has a left adjoint, giving the free algebra FX over any set X.

$$\mathcal{ND}(\mathcal{Set})$$

free F $\left(\dashv \right)$ U forgetful

$$\mathcal{Set}$$

In fact, this functor F is the finite powerset $\langle \mathcal{P}_{fin}, \cup, \emptyset \rangle$, and $\mathcal{ND}(\mathcal{Set})$ is *monadic* over $\mathcal{Set}$: it is equivalent to the category of algebras for the monad $\mathcal{P}_{fin}$.

The situation here is quite general, with a precise correspondence between single-sorted algebraic theories and finitary monads on $\mathcal{Set}$ (i.e., monads that preserve filtered colimits). Kelly and Power [14, 29] extend this to an enriched setting: carriers for the algebras may be from categories other than $\mathcal{Set}$; the arities of operations can be not just natural numbers, but certain objects in a category; and equations can be replaced with other constraint systems — for example, ordered categories support inequations.

Building on this, Plotkin and Power investigate algebraic theories that induce a "computational" monad T [18]. They characterize when an operation $f : (TX)^m \to (TX)^n$ on computations is *algebraic* and hence admissible as an operation of the relevant theory. Moreover, they prove that every such algebraic operation corresponds to a computational *effect* of type $e_f : n \to Tm$ (note the reversal of indices m and n). In the example above, $\mathcal{P}_{fin}$ is the standard computational monad for finite nondeterminism, and its effects are arb : $1 \longrightarrow$ T2 and deadlock : $1 \longrightarrow$ T0. These two are enough to code up nondeterministic programming: arb() is a nondeterministic true or false, and deadlock() is the empty choice.

Thus not only do algebraic theories characterize computational monads as free algebras, but they also provide the necessary terms to program with them. They also support combining monads, a traditionally challenging area, by taking the union of theories and possibly introducing new equations describing how they interact [11, 12].

As a final example, the theory for input/output of data values from some fixed set V is:

$$in : A^V \longrightarrow A \qquad out : A \longrightarrow A^V \qquad \text{with no equations.}$$

This induces the *resumptions* monad for computations performing I/O:

$$T(-) = \mu X.(X^V + V \times X + (-))$$

as well as the effects read : $1 \longrightarrow$ TV and write : $V \to$ T1.

2.2   The Category $\mathcal{S} \rceil \sqcup^{\mathcal{I}}$

We construct our models for π over the functor category $\mathcal{Set}^{\mathcal{I}}$, where $\mathcal{I}$ is the category of finite sets and injections. Typically we treat objects $s, s' \in \mathcal{I}$ in the index category as finite sets of names. The intuition is that an object $X \in Set^{\mathcal{I}}$ is a *varying* set: if $s \in \mathcal{I}$ is the set of names available in some context, then $X(s)$ is the set of X-values using them. As the set of names available changes, so does this set of values. Functor categories of *possible worlds* like this are well established for modelling local state in programming languages [20, 22, 30] and local names in particular [17, 25, 35]. Similar categories of varying sets also appear in models for variable binding [5] and name binding (see, for example, [33] and citations there).

Category $Set^{\mathcal{I}}$ is complete and cocomplete, with limits and colimits taken pointwise. It is cartesian closed, with a convenient way to calculate function spaces using natural transformations between functors:

$$X \times Y \qquad\qquad (X \times Y)(s) = X(s) \times Y(s)$$
$$X \to Y \text{ or } Y^X \qquad\qquad Y^X(s) = Set^{\mathcal{I}}[X(s + \_), Y(s + \_)]$$

Thus elements in the varying set of functions from X to Y over names s must take account of values in $X(s + s')$, uniformly for all extended name sets $s + s'$.

There is also a symmetric monoidal closed structure $(\otimes, \multimap)$ around the *Day tensor* [4], induced by disjoint union $(s + s')$ in $\mathcal{I}$.

$$X \otimes Y = \int^{s,s' \in \mathcal{I}} X(s) \times Y(s') \times \mathcal{I}[s + s', \_]$$

All the constructions in this paper remain within the subcategory of functors in $Set^{\mathcal{I}}$ that preserve pullbacks. For such functors we can give an explicit presentation of the monoidal structure:

$$(X \otimes Y)(s) = \big\{ (x, y) \in (X \times Y)(s)$$
$$\big| \; \exists \text{disjoint } s_1, s_2 \subseteq s \, . \, x \in X(s_1), y \in Y(s_2) \big\}$$
$$(X \multimap Y)(s) = Set^{\mathcal{I}}[X(\_), Y(s + \_)]$$

Elements of $(X \otimes Y)$ denote pairs of elements from X and Y that use disjoint name sets. Elements of the monoidal function space $(X \multimap Y)$ are functions defined only at X-values that use just fresh names.

The two closed structures are related:

$$into_{X,Y} : X \otimes Y \longrightarrow X \times Y$$
$$onto_{X,Y} : (X \to Y) \longrightarrow (X \multimap Y) .$$

Where functors X and Y are pullback-preserving, these are an inclusion and surjection, respectively.

We use a variety of objects in $Set^{\mathcal{I}}$. For any fixed set S, there is a corresponding constant functor $S \in Set^{\mathcal{I}}$. The *object of names* $N \in Set^{\mathcal{I}}$ is the inclusion functor mapping any $s \in \mathcal{I}$ to the same $s \in Set$. From this we build $(N \times N \times \cdots \times N) = N^k$, the object of k-tuples of names, and $(N \otimes N \otimes \cdots \otimes N) = N^{\otimes k}$ of distinct k-tuples, with an inclusion $into : N^{\otimes k} \hookrightarrow N^k$ between them.

We have the *shift* functor δ on objects of $Set^{\mathcal{I}}$:

$$\delta : Set^{\mathcal{I}} \longrightarrow Set^{\mathcal{I}} \quad \text{defined by} \quad \delta X(\_) = X(\_ + 1) .$$

In fact $\delta(-) \cong N \multimap (-)$, and elements of δX are elements of X that may use a single fresh name, uniformly in the choice of that name. This functor is well known, for example as *dynamic allocation* in [6, 7]; it also appears as the *atom abstraction* operator $[N]X$ of FM-set theory identified by Gabbay and Pitts [9, 24]. Note that shifting the object of names gives a coproduct: $\delta N \cong (N + 1)$.

The representable objects in $Set^{\mathcal{I}}$ are $1, N, (N \otimes N), (N \otimes N \otimes N), \ldots$ The finitely presentable objects are the finite colimits of these, including in particular finite constant sets S, and all finite products of N: for example, $(N \times N) \cong N + (N \otimes N)$. These are the objects available as arities for algebraic theories over $Set^{\mathcal{I}}$.

Finally, the category $Set^{\mathcal{I}}$ is locally finitely presentable as a closed category, with respect to both cartesian and monoidal structures. This is a completeness requirement for building algebraic theories: [29–§2] and [31–§3] expand on what this involves.

3   Theory of π

The algebraic approach supports a modular presentation of theories, and we use this to manage the combination of features that come together in the π-calculus. This section presents in turn separate theories for nondeterminism, communication along channels, and dynamic name creation; followed by equations specifying exactly how these features should interact.

We assume a carrier object $A \in Set^{\mathcal{I}}$, and describe the operations and equations required for A to model the π-calculus.

3.1   Nondeterministic Choice

For nondeterminism we need a binary *choice* operation that is commutative, associative and idempotent with a unit *nil*.

$$choice : A^2 \longrightarrow A \qquad\qquad choice(p, q) = choice(q, p)$$
$$nil : 1 \longrightarrow A \qquad\qquad choice(nil, p) = choice(p, p) = p$$
$$choice(p, (choice(q, r))) = choice(choice(p, q), r)$$

In process calculus terms, *choice* captures nondeterministic sum $P + Q$ and *nil* the deadlocked process 0.

3.2   Communication

Communication in the π-calculus is along named channels, sending names themselves as data. The relevant theory is a specialised version of that for I/O given earlier.

$$out : \ A \ \longrightarrow \ A^{N \times N}$$
$$in : A^N \longrightarrow A^N \qquad \text{(No required equations)}$$
$$tau : \ A \ \longrightarrow \ A$$

These three operations correspond to the three prefixing constructions of the π-calculus: output $\bar{x}y.P$, input $x(y).P$ and silent action $\tau.P$. Argument and result arities follow the bound and free occurrences of names respectively:

- out is parameterized in the result $A^{N \times N}$ by both channel and data names;
- in accepts argument A^N parameterized by the data value, with result A^N parameterized by channel name.

The appearance of A^N and $A^{N \times N}$ here give our first nonstandard arities, N and $N \times N$, to describe operations whose arity varies according to the names currently available. We follow [27] in using formal indices to write these down: with terms like $out_{x,y}(p)$ and $in_x(q_y)$, where x and y are name parameters.

3.3   Dynamic Name Creation

Processes in the π-calculus can dynamically generate fresh communication channels: term $\nu n.P$ is the process that creates a new channel, binds it to the name n, and then becomes process P which may then use the new channel.

Our theory for this is a modification of Plotkin and Power's *block* operation for local state [27–§4]. We require a single operation *new* with a monoidal arity.

$$new : \delta A \to A \qquad\qquad new(x.p) = p \qquad \text{for } p \text{ independent of } x$$
$$\delta A \cong N \multimap A \qquad new(x.new(y.p)) = new(y.new(x.p))$$

The argument δA means that *new* is an operation of arity N in the monoidal closed structure of $Set^{\mathcal{I}}$. Recall that elements of δA are elements of A that depend on a single fresh name, uniformly in the choice of that fresh name. In the equations for *new* we write $x.p$ for the term p indexed by fresh x, borrowing Gabbay and Pitts's notation for atom abstraction [9]. (Plotkin and Power write this as $\langle p \rangle_x$.)

Strictly, all our equations are shorthand for certain diagrams in $Set^{\mathcal{I}}$ which must commute. These two state that the creation of unused fresh names cannot be observed, and computation is independent of the order in which fresh names are created. In diagram form, these are

where $up : 1 \to \delta$ and $twist : \delta^2 \to \delta^2$ are the evident natural transformations on the shift functor.

3.4   Other Operations

There are a few further constructions that might be candidates for inclusion in a theory of π.

Name testing. Some forms of the π-calculus allow direct comparison of names, with prefixes like match $[x = y]P$, mismatch $[x \neq y]Q$, or two-branched testing $(x = y) \, ? \, P : Q$. It turns out that these operations are already in the theory. The $Set^{\mathcal{I}}$ map of arities $(N \times N) \cong N + (N \otimes N) \longrightarrow 1 + 1$ induces an operation $test$ from which others follow, using nil:

$$test : A^2 \longrightarrow A^{N \times N} \qquad eq : A \longrightarrow A^{N \times N} \qquad neq : A \longrightarrow A^{N \times N} \, .$$

Bound output. The bound output prefix $\bar{x}(y).P$ for the π-calculus is equivalent to $\nu y(\bar{x}y.P)$. There is an analogous derived operation in the theory:

$$bout : \delta A \longrightarrow A^N \qquad\qquad bout_x(y.p) \overset{def}{=} new(y.out_{x,y}(p))$$

Because this is definable in terms of the operations given earlier, it can be included without affecting the induced theory or its algebras.

Parallel composition. The usual process calculus construction $(P \,|\, Q)$ is not directly admissible as an operation in our theory of π. This is because it is not *algebraic* in the sense of Plotkin and Power [28]. Informally, it does not commute with composition of computations: in a programming language, $(M \,|\, M'); N$ is not in general equivalent to $(M; N) \,|\, (M'; N)$. We shall see more on this later, in §4.

3.5   Combining Equations

To complete the theory of π we give equations to specify how the component theories interact. The algebraic approach gives us some flexibility in doing so, as investigated in [11, 12]. For example, we can assert no additional equations, giving the *sum* of theories [12–§3]; we can require that the operations from two theories commute with each other, to give the commutative combination, or *tensor*, of theories [12–§4]; or we can choose some other custom interaction. To assemble the component theories of π, we use all three methods:

- The sum of the theories of nondeterminism and communication.
- The commuting combination of nondeterminism and name creation.
- A custom set of equations for name creation and communication; mostly commuting, but some specific interaction.

These expand into three sets of equations. The first have effect by their absence:

Sum of component theories

No equations required for *choice* or *nil* with *out*, *in* or *tau*.

The commuting combination of theories says that operations act independently:

Commuting component theories

$$new(x.choice(p,q)) = choice(new(x.p), new(x.q))$$

$$new(z.out_{x,y}(p)) = out_{x,y}(new(z.p)) \qquad z \notin \{x,y\}$$
$$new(z.in_x(p_y)) = in_x(new(z.p_y)) \qquad z \notin \{x,y\}$$
$$new(z.tau(p)) = tau(new(z.p))$$

Recall that these equations with formal indices and side conditions are a shorthand for four commuting diagrams in $Set^{\mathcal{I}}$.

Finally, just two equations for interaction capture the precise flavour of the π-calculus: that the binder $\nu x.(-)$ is both creation (of new channels) and restriction (of communication on them).

Interaction between component theories

$$new(x.out_{x,y}(p)) = nil$$
$$new(x.in_x(p_y)) = nil$$

---

4   Algebraic Models for π

We now turn to look at models for the theory of π. We define what these are, and show that every such model gives a denotational semantics for the π-calculus that respects bisimulation congruence. We give a construction for free models in $Set^{\mathcal{I}}$, and prove that the category of models is monadic over $Set^{\mathcal{I}}$. We show that all free models are fully abstract for bisimulation congruence, and in particular that the initial free model is isomorphic to the construction of Fiore et al.

4.1   Categories of Algebras

Definition 1. *A π-algebra in $Set^{\mathcal{I}}$ is an object A together with maps (choice, nil, out, in, tau, new) satisfying the equations of §§3.1–3.3 and 3.5 above. These algebras form a category $\mathcal{PI}(Set^{\mathcal{I}})$, with morphisms the maps $f : A \rightarrow B$ that commute with all operations. The forgetful functor $U : \mathcal{PI}(Set^{\mathcal{I}}) \rightarrow Set^{\mathcal{I}}$ takes a π-algebra to its carrier object.*

For any π-algebra $A \in \mathcal{PI}(Set^{\mathcal{I}})$ we can build a denotational semantics of the finite π-calculus: if P is a process with free names in set s, then there is a map

$$[\![s \vdash P]\!]_A : N^{|s|} \longrightarrow A \ .$$

Here $N^{|s|}$ represents an environment instantiating the free names s.

The interpretation itself is comparatively straightforward. Process sum, nil and the π-calculus prefixes are interpreted directly by the corresponding π-algebra operations.

Binding of fresh names involves managing the monoidal structure; we use a construction $\nu(-)$ on maps into A:

$$p : N^{|s|+1} \longrightarrow A \qquad\qquad \text{Given a map } p;$$

$$N \otimes N^{|s|} \xrightarrow{into} N \times N^{|s|} \longrightarrow A \qquad\qquad \text{precompose inclusion;}$$

$$N^{|s|} \longrightarrow (N \multimap A) \qquad\qquad \text{take the monoidal transpose;}$$

$$N^{|s|} \longrightarrow \delta A \xrightarrow{new} A \qquad\qquad \text{and apply the } new \text{ operator}$$

$$\nu p : N^{|s|} \longrightarrow A \qquad\qquad \text{to get the restricted map } \nu p.$$

We then define $[\![s \vdash \nu x.P]\!]_A = \nu([\![s, x \vdash P]\!]_A)$.

As noted earlier, parallel composition is not algebraic, so we have no general map for its action on A. However, for any specific finite processes P and Q we can use the expansion law for congruence [23–Table 9] to express $(P \mid Q)$ as a sum of smaller processes, and so obtain an interpretation in the π-algebra A, recursively:

if
$$P \mid Q = \sum_{i=1}^{k} R_i \qquad \text{(canonical choice of expansion)}$$

then
$$[\![s \vdash P \mid Q]\!]_A = choice([\![s \vdash R_1]\!]_A, choice([\![s \vdash R_2]\!]_A, \dots)) : N^{|s|} \longrightarrow A .$$

This external expansion makes the translation not wholly compositional; later we shall improve on this, for one particular π-algebra, by expressing parallel composition within the algebra itself.

The interpretation $[\![s \vdash P]\!]_A$ respects weakening of the name context s, so we usually omit it and write $[\![P]\!]_A$.

Once defined, this interpretation induces a notion of equality over a model: for any π-algebra A and finite processes P, Q we write

$$A \models P = Q \quad\xLeftrightarrow{def}\quad [\![P]\!]_A = [\![Q]\!]_A$$

$$\text{and} \quad Set^{\mathcal{I}} \models P = Q \quad\xLeftrightarrow{def}\quad A \models P = Q \text{ for all } A \in \mathcal{PI}(Set^{\mathcal{I}}).$$

Proposition 2. *All π-algebra models respect (strong, late) bisimulation congruence. For any $A \in \mathcal{PI}(Set^{\mathcal{I}})$ and finite processes P, Q:*

$$P \approx Q \quad\Longrightarrow\quad A \models P = Q$$

and more generally:

$$P \approx Q \quad\Longrightarrow\quad Set^{\mathcal{I}} \models P = Q .$$

Proof. We draw on the known axiomatization of bisimulation congruence for finite processes, as given for example in [23–§8.2]. All these axioms are provable in the theory of π and hence hold in every algebra for the theory. $\qquad\square$

4.2   Free π-Algebras in $\mathcal{S}|\sqcup^{\mathcal{I}}$

The previous section proposes a theory of algebraic models for the π-calculus; but it does not yet give us any concrete π-algebras. For these we seek a free π-algebra functor $F : Set^{\mathcal{I}} \to \mathcal{PI}(Set^{\mathcal{I}})$, left adjoint to the forgetful U. Kelly and Power [14, 29] show the existence in general of such algebras for enriched theories; but there are two difficulties in our situation. First, their results are in terms of a general colimit, and for any specific theory one would also like a direct form if possible. Second, and more serious, they treat a single enrichment, while we have two together.

We can overcome both of these difficulties, in the specific case of $Set^{\mathcal{I}}$: we have an explicit description of the free π-algebras, and an accompanying proof that they are so.

Before presenting the free algebras for the full theory of π, we detour briefly through those for each of its component theories, to see how they fit together. For simplicity we present not the free functors F, but the associated monads $(U \circ F)$ on $Set^{\mathcal{I}}$.

The monad for finite nondeterminism is the finite covariant powerset, extended pointwise to $Set^{\mathcal{I}}$:

$$T_{nondet}(-) = \mathcal{P}_{fin}(-) \, .$$

The monad for communication is a version of the resumptions monad, with components for output, input and silent action:

$$T_{comm}(-) = \mu X.(N \times N \times X + N \times X^N + X + (-)) \, .$$

Here $\mu X.(-)$ is the least fixed point, which in $Set^{\mathcal{I}}$ is a straightforward pointwise union. Informally, an element of $(T_{comm}Y)(s)$ is a finite trace of π-calculus actions using names from s, finishing with a value from Y; with the refinement that at input actions the function space X^N gives a branching over possible input names, including uniform treatment of new names.

The monad for dynamic name creation is that originating with Moggi [17–§4.1.4] and investigated in [35].

$$T_{new}(-) = \mathcal{D}yn(-) = \varinjlim_{s \in \mathcal{I}} \left(N^{\otimes|s|} \multimap (-) \right) \, .$$

This is a colimit over possible sets of fresh names. In particular, the object part has $\mathcal{D}yn(X)(s) = \sum_{s' \in \mathcal{I}} X(s + s') / \sim$, where $\sim$ is an equivalence relation generated by injections between fresh name sets $s' \rightarrowtail s''$. For full element-by-element details of the $\mathcal{D}yn$ construction, see [35–§5].

Taking the approach of combining monads through monad *transformers* [15], we can try to interleave these to obtain a candidate monad for π:

$$T_{bad}(-) = \mu X.(\mathcal{P}_{fin}(\mathcal{D}yn(N \times N \times X + N \times X^N + X + (-)))) \, .$$

Working from the outside in, this asserts that: a π-calculus process is a recursive system (μX); which may have several courses of action ($\mathcal{P}_{fin}$); that each may create fresh names ($\mathcal{D}yn$); and then perform some I/O action, to give some further process.

However, this is not yet quite right: T_{bad} does not validate any of the equations of §3.5 for combining the different π-calculus effects. For example, in T_{bad} restriction *new* does not commute with *choice*; nor does it in fact restrict, as there are terms in the monad for external I/O on a *new*-bound channel.

To find the correct monad for π, we use an observation from existing operational treatments: name creation is only observable through the emission of fresh names in bound output. This leads to the following corrected definition:

$$T_\pi(-) = \mu X.(\mathcal{P}_{fin}(N \times N \times X + N \times \delta X + N \times X^N + X + \mathcal{D}yn(-))) . \quad (1)$$

This still expresses a π-calculus process as a recursive system (μX) with several courses of action ($\mathcal{P}_{fin}$); but the general application of $\mathcal{D}yn(-)$ has been replaced by a bound output term $N \times \delta X$ in the I/O expression. The core of this expression matches the functor H of Fiore et al. [8–§4.4].

The monad T_π is now a correct representation for π-calculus behaviour, and for any object $X \in Set^{\mathcal{I}}$ we can equip $T_\pi(X)$ with the six required operations to make it a π-algebra $Pi(X)$. The most interesting case is *new*; this is defined recursively by cases, using the equations from §§3.3 and 3.5, and following essentially the pattern of [36] and [8–Table 4].

We thus obtain the desired free functor $Pi : Set^{\mathcal{I}} \to \mathcal{PI}(Set^{\mathcal{I}})$, and hence a supply of concrete π-algebras. This completes the adjunction $Pi \dashv U$, with monad $U \circ Pi$ being T_π. What is more, the adjunction is monadic, so that $\mathcal{PI}(Set^{\mathcal{I}})$ is equivalent to the category of algebras for the monad T_π. To summarise:

Theorem 3.

(i) *The forgetful functor $U : \mathcal{PI}(Set^{\mathcal{I}}) \to Set^{\mathcal{I}}$ has a left adjoint Pi giving a free π-algebra $Pi(X)$ over any $X \in Set^{\mathcal{I}}$.*

(ii) *The comparison functor from $\mathcal{PI}(Set^{\mathcal{I}})$ to T_π-Alg is an equivalence of categories.*

Proof (sketch).

(i) Once we have an explicit form for Pi, it only remains to check that $Pi(X)$ is initial among π-algebras over X. Given any π-algebra A with $X \to UA$ in $Set^{\mathcal{I}}$, we must extend this to an algebra map $Pi(X) \to A$. The extension is uniquely determined by the fact that every element of $Pi(X)$ can be generated from X using operations from the theory of π.

(ii) We apply Beck's theorem to show that the adjunction is monadic. The development closely follows Power's in [29–§4], specialised to the case at hand. There is some new work to take account of the two closed structures, which is done using the properties of the function spaces $N \multimap X$ and X^N presented in §2.2. □

4.3   Fully-Abstract π-Algebras

The interpretation in §4.1 of π-calculus terms in an arbitrary π-algebra is not altogether compositional, in that we expand out parallel processes. If we specialise to the initial free π-algebra $Pi(0)$ then we can do better.

Proposition 4. *Writing $P \in \mathcal{S}et^{\mathcal{I}}$ for the carrier object of $Pi(0)$, there is a map $par : P^2 \to P$ in $\mathcal{S}et^{\mathcal{I}}$ such that for all finite π-calculus processes P, Q:*

$$[\![P \,|\, Q]\!]_{Pi(0)} = par([\![P]\!]_{Pi(0)}, [\![Q]\!]_{Pi(0)}) \,.$$

Using par instead of the expansion rule then gives a purely compositional presentation of the denotational semantics in $Pi(0)$ for finite π-calculus processes.

Proof. We decompose *par* as a sum of interleaving merge and synchronization, and then define each of these recursively by cases on the expansion (1) of $Pi(0)$ — where the base case uses the fact that $\mathcal{D}yn(0)$ is empty. This is the procedure known from existing denotational models, such as [36–§3.2] and [8–§4.6]. Note that *par* is, as expected, not a map of π-algebras. □

This semantics in $Pi(0)$ is in fact isomorphic to the fully-abstract model described by Fiore et al. in [8–Thm 6.4]. We can extend their analysis to all free π-algebras.

Theorem 5. *For any object $X \in \mathcal{S}et^{\mathcal{I}}$, the free π-algebra $Pi(X)$ is fully abstract for (strong, late) bisimulation congruence. For all finite π-calculus processes P, Q:*

$$P \approx Q \quad \Longleftrightarrow \quad Pi(X) \models P = Q$$

and hence also:

$$P \approx Q \quad \Longleftrightarrow \quad \mathcal{S}et^{\mathcal{I}} \models P = Q \,.$$

Proof. The forward direction is Prop. 2, and the reverse direction for $Pi(0)$ comes from the full abstraction result of [8]. We lift this to general $Pi(X)$ by factoring the interpretation $[\![-]\!]_{Pi(X)}$ as $[\![-]\!]_{Pi(0)}$ followed by the monomorphism $Pi(0) \rightarrowtail Pi(X)$. □

4.4 Monads and Effects for π

The operations and equations in the theory of π fit very well with a process-calculus view of concurrency. However, the monad T_π of (1) is also a "computational" monad in the style of Moggi, and gives a programming language semantics of mobile communicating systems. The operations of §3 then induce corresponding generic effects [28]:

$choice :$	$A^2 \longrightarrow A$	$arb :$	$1 \longrightarrow T2$
$nil :$	$1 \longrightarrow A$	$deadlock :$	$1 \longrightarrow T0$
$out :$	$A \longrightarrow A^{N \times N}$	$send :$	$N \times N \longrightarrow T1$
$in :$	$A^N \longrightarrow A^N$	$receive :$	$N \longrightarrow TN$
$tau :$	$A \longrightarrow A$	$skip :$	$1 \longrightarrow T1$
$new :$	$\delta A \longrightarrow A$	$fresh :$	$1 \longrightarrow TN$

For example, receive(c) fetches a value from channel c, and fresh() returns a newly allocated channel. In a suitable computational metalanguage these give a semantics for programing languages that combine higher-order functions with communicating concurrency. Alternatively, they can be used just as they stand in a language like Haskell that explicitly handles computational monads: do{x ← receive(c); send(c', x)}.

5   Extensions and Further Work

In this paper we have examined only finite π-calculus processes. We propose to give algebras for the full π-calculus, with replication and recursion, by introducing order structure with models in $Cpo^{\mathcal{I}}$. Plotkin and Power have already investigated Cpo-enrichment in work on effects for PCF: in particular, taking the least upper bound of ω-chains is then an algebraic operation of (countable) arity. Our target is the existing domain models in $Cpo^{\mathcal{I}}$, noting that Fiore et al. give a method for lifting full abstraction in $Set^{\mathcal{I}}$ up to $Cpo^{\mathcal{I}}$.

Order enrichment also offers the possibility of inequations in theories. For the *choice* operation these can distinguish between upper, lower and convex powerdomains, and we conjecture that such theories for π could characterize Hennessy's fully-abstract models for must and may-testing [10].

Alternative calculi like asynchronous π and πI can be treated by changing the arity of the *out* operation; process passing and higher-order π seem much more challenging. For different kinds of equivalence, we can follow existing models by varying arities and translation details: this is enough to capture early bisimulation congruence, early/late bisimilarity (not congruences), and bisimilarity up to name constraints. More interesting, though, is the possibility to leave the operations for π untouched and instead adjust only the equations. For example, we might add the characteristic EARLY equation of [23–§9.1] to the π-theory, and then compare this to the explicit model of early bisimulation congruence in [7]. The same approach applies to open bisimilarity and weak bisimulations, known to be challenging for categorical models: Parrow sets out equational axiomatizations for all these in [23–§9], and we now need to explore the algebraic theories they generate.

Pitts and others have championed *nominal sets* and Fraenkel-Mostowski set theory as a foundation for reasoning with names [9, 24, 34]. If we move from $Set^{\mathcal{I}}$ to its full subcategory of pullback-preserving functors then we have the Schanuel topos, which models FM set theory. As noted earlier, all of our constructions lie within this, and we conjecture that our π-calculus models are examples of universal algebra within FM set theory (given first an investigation of what that is).

Prop. 4 presented an internal *par* for $Pi(0)$, giving a fully compositional interpretation for the π-calculus. In fact we can define an internal par_μ for any free π-algebra $Pi(X)$, given an associative and commutative multiplication $\mu : X \times X \to X$. These non-initial free algebras are (fully-abstract) models for implementations of the π-calculus over a set of basic processes. For example, $Pi(1)$ models the π-calculus with an extra process "$\checkmark$" marking completion, which extends the programming language interpretation of §4.4 with a semantics for terminating threads and thread rendezvous.

More generally, the full range of π-algebras in $\mathcal{PI}(Set^{\mathcal{I}})$ may be useful to model applications of the π-calculus with domain-specific terms, equations and processes. There are many such ad-hoc extensions, notably those brought together by Abadi and Fournet under the banner of *applied* π [1].

In ongoing work, Plotkin has given a construction for modal logics from algebraic theories. Applying this to the theory of π gives a modal logic for the π-calculus up to bisimulation congruence. This can represent Hennessy-Milner logic, and also has modalities for choice and name creation; though no "spatial" modality for parallel composition.

We can extend our notion of π-algebra to other categories $\mathcal{C}$, enriched over $Set^{\mathcal{I}}$. However, we do not yet have conditions for the existence of free algebras, or for full abstraction, in general $\mathcal{C}$. This would require further investigation of the properties of algebras enriched over a doubly closed structure, as in $Set^{\mathcal{I}}$.

An alternative path, following a suggestion of Fiore, is to give a theory of name testing that exhibits $Set^{\mathcal{I}}$ as monadic over $Set^{\mathcal{F}}$, where $\mathcal{F}$ is the category of finite name sets and all maps. We have a candidate theory, and conjecture that in combination with our existing theory of π, this would allow us to generate algebraic models of π in $Set^{\mathcal{F}}$ using only cartesian closed structure.

References

[1] M. Abadi and C. Fournet. Mobile values, new names, and secure communication. In *Conf. Rec. POPL 2001*, pp. 104–115. ACM Press, 2001.

[2] G. L. Cattani and P. Sewell. Models for name-passing processes: Interleaving and causal. *Inf. Comput.*, 190(2):136–178, 2004.

[3] G. L. Cattani, I. Stark, and G. Winskel. Presheaf models for the π-calculus. In *Proc. CTCS '97*, LNCS 1290, pp. 106–126. Springer-Verlag, 1997.

[4] B. J. Day. On closed categories of functors. In *Reports of the Midwest Category Seminar IV*, Lecture Notes in Mathematics 137, pp. 1–38. Springer-Verlag, 1970.

[5] M. Fiore, G. Plotkin, and D. Turi. Abstract syntax and variable binding. In *Proc. LICS '99*, pp. 193–202. IEEE Comp. Soc. Press, 1999.

[6] M. Fiore and S. Staton. Comparing operational models of name-passing process calculi. In *Proc. CMCS 2004*, ENTCS 106, pp. 91–104. Elsevier, 2004.

[7] M. Fiore and D. Turi. Semantics of name and value passing. In *Proc. LICS 2001*, pp. 93–104. IEEE Comp. Soc. Press, 2001.

[8] M. P. Fiore, E. Moggi, and D. Sangiorgi. A fully-abstract model for the π-calculus. *Inf. Comput.*, 179(1):76–117, 2002.

[9] M. J. Gabbay and A. M. Pitts. A new approach to abstract syntax with variable binding. *Formal Asp. Comput.*, 13(3–5):341–363, 2001.

[10] M. Hennessy. A fully abstract denotational semantics for the π-calculus. *Theor. Comput. Sci.*, 278(1–2):53–89, 2002.

[11] J. M. E. Hyland, G. Plotkin, and A. J. Power. Combining computational effects: Commutativity and sum. In *Proc. TCS 2002*, pp. 474–484. Kluwer, 2002.

[12] J. M. E. Hyland, G. Plotkin, and A. J. Power. Combining effects: Sum and tensor. To appear, 2004.

[13] M. P. Jones and L. Duponcheel. Composing monads. Research Report YALEU/DCS/RR-1004, Yale University Department of Computer Science, 1993.

[14] G. M. Kelly and A. J. Power. Adjunctions whose counits are coequalizers, and presentations of finitary enriched monads. *J. Pure Appl. Algebra*, 89:163–179, 1993.

[15] S. Liang, P. Hudak, and M. P. Jones. Monad transformers and modular interpreters. In *Conf. Rec. POPL '95*, pp. 333–343. ACM Press, 1995.

[16] R. Milner. *Communicating and Mobile Systems: The Pi-Calculus*. CUP, 1999.

[17] E. Moggi. An abstract view of programming languages. Technical Report ECS-LFCS-90-113, Laboratory for Foundations of Computer Science, University of Edinburgh, 1990.

[18] E. Moggi. Notions of computation and monads. *Inf. Comput.*, 93(1):55–92, 1991.

[19] J. Newburn. All about monads, v1.1.0. http://www.nomaware.com/monads.

[20] P. W. O'Hearn and R. D. Tennent. Parametricity and local variables. *J. ACM*, 42(3):658–709, 1995. Reprinted in [21].

[21] P. W. O'Hearn and R. D. Tennent, editors. *Algol-like Languages*. Birkhauser, 1996.

[22] F. J. Oles. Functor categories and store shapes. Chapter 11 of [21].

[23] J. Parrow. An introduction to the π-calculus. In *Handbook of Process Algebra*, pp. 479–543. Elsevier, 2001.

[24] A. M. Pitts. Nominal logic, a first order theory of names and binding. *Inf. Comput.*, 186:165–193, 2003. Errata, Sept. 2004.

[25] A. M. Pitts and I. Stark. Observable properties of higher order functions that dynamically create local names, or: What's *new*? In *Proc. MFCS '93*, LNCS 711, pp. 122–141. Springer-Verlag, 1993.

[26] G. Plotkin and A. J. Power. Computational effects and operations: An overview. Submitted for publication, 2002.

[27] G. Plotkin and A. J. Power. Notions of computation determine monads. In *Proc. FoSSaCS 2002*, LNCS 2303, pp. 342–356. Springer-Verlag, 2002. Erratum, Aug. 2002.

[28] G. Plotkin and A. J. Power. Algebraic operations and generic effects. *Appl. Categ. Struct.*, 11(1):69–94, 2003.

[29] A. J. Power. Enriched Lawvere theories. *Theory Appl. Categ.*, 6(7):83–93, 1999.

[30] J. C. Reynolds. The essence of Algol. In *Proc. 1981 Int. Symp. on Algorithmic Languages*, pp. 345–372. North Holland, 1981. Reprinted in [21].

[31] E. Robinson. Variations on algebra: Monadicity and generalisations of equational theories. *Formal Asp. Comput.*, 13(3–5):308–326, 2002.

[32] D. Sangiorgi and D. Walker. *The π-Calculus: A Theory of Mobile Processes*. CUP, 2001.

[33] U. Schöpp and I. Stark. A dependent type theory with names and binding. In *Proc. CSL 2004*, LNCS 3210, pp. 235–249. Springer-Verlag, 2004.

[34] M. R. Shinwell, A. M. Pitts, and M. J. Gabbay. FreshML: Programming with binders made simple. In *Proc. ICFP 2003*, pp. 263–274. ACM Press, 2003. Erratum, May 2004.

[35] I. Stark. Categorical models for local names. *LISP Symb. Comput.*, 9(1):77–107, 1996.

[36] I. Stark. A fully abstract domain model for the π-calculus. In *Proc. LICS '96*, pp. 36–42. IEEE Comp. Soc. Press, 1996.

[37] P. Wadler and D. King. Combining monads. In *Proc. 1992 Glasgow Workshop on Functional Programming*, pp. 134–143. Springer-Verlag, 1993.

A Unifying Model of Variables and Names[*]

Marino Miculan[1] and Kidane Yemane[2]

[1] Dept. of Mathematics and Computing Science,
University of Udine, Via delle Scienze 206, I-33100 Udine, Italy
miculan@dimi.uniud.it
[2] Dept. of Information Technology, Uppsala University,
Box 337, S-751 05 Uppsala, Sweden
kidane.yemane@it.uu.se

Abstract. We investigate a category theoretic model where both "variables" and "names", usually viewed as separate notions, are particular cases of the more general notion of *distinction*. The key aspect of this model is to consider functors over the category of irreflexive, symmetric finite relations. The models previously proposed for the notions of "variables" and "names" embed faithfully in the new one, and initial algebra/final coalgebra constructions can be transferred from the formers to the latter. Moreover, the new model admits a definition of *distinction-aware* simultaneous substitutions. As a substantial application example, we give the first semantic interpretation of Miller-Tiu's $FO\lambda^\nabla$ logic.

1   Introduction

In recent years, many models for *dynamically allocable* entities, such as (bound) variables, (fresh) names, reference, etc., have been proposed. Most of (if not all) these models are based on some (sub)category of *(pre)sheaves*, i.e., functors from a suitable index category to *Set* [19, 6, 10, 8, 5, 18]. The basic idea is to stratify datatypes according to various "stages" representing different degrees of information, such as number of allocated variables. A simple example is that of set-valued functors over $\mathbb{F}$, which is the category of finite subsets $C \subset \mathbb{A}$ of a given enumerable set $\mathbb{A}$ of abstract symbols ("variable names") [6, 10]; here, the datatype of untyped λ-terms is the functor $\Lambda : \mathbb{F} \to Set$, $\Lambda_C = \{t \mid FV(t) \subseteq C\}$. Morphisms between objects of the index category describe how we can move from one stage to the others; in $\mathbb{F}$, morphisms are any function $\sigma : C \to D$, that is any variable renaming possibly with unifications. Correspondingly, $\Lambda_\sigma : \Lambda_C \to \Lambda_D$ is the usual (capture-avoiding) variable renaming $-\{\sigma\}$ on terms.

Different index categories lead to different notions of "allocable entities". The notion of *name*, particularly important for process calculi, can be modeled using the subcategory $\mathbb{I}$ of $\mathbb{F}$ of only injective functions. Thus, stages of $\mathbb{I}$ can be still "enlarged" by morphisms (which corresponds to allocation of new names), but they cannot be "contracted", which means that two different symbols can never

---

[*] Work supported by EU projects IST-2001-33100 PROFUNDIS and IST-510996 TYPES.

V. Sassone (Ed.): FOSSACS 2005, LNCS 3441, pp. 170–186, 2005.

coalesce to the same. Categories of set- and domain-valued functors over $\mathbb{I}$ have been used for modeling π-calculus, ν-calculus, etc. [19, 5].

According to this view, *variables* and *names* are quite different concepts, and as such they are rendered by different index categories. This separation is a drawback when we have to model calculi or logics where *both* aspects are present and must be dealt with at once. Some examples are: the fusion calculus, where names can be unified under some conditions; the open bisimulation of π-calculus, which is defined by closure under all (also unifying) distinction-preserving name substitutions; even, a (still unknown) algebraic model for the Mobile Ambients is supposed to deal with both variables and names (which are declared as different entities in capabilities); and finally, the logic $FO\lambda^\nabla$ [15], featuring a peculiar interplay between "global variables" and "locally scoped constants".

Why are $\mathbb{F}$ and $\mathbb{I}$ not sufficient to model these situations? The problem is that these models force the behaviour of atoms *a priori*. Atoms will always act as variables in $\mathbb{F}$, as names in $\mathbb{I}$. This is to be contrasted with the situations above, where the behaviour of an atom is not known beforehand.

A way for circumventing this problem is to distinguish *allocation* of atoms, from *specifications* of their behaviour. Behaviour of atoms is given a *symmetric, irreflexive* relation, called *distinction*: two atoms are related if and only if they cannot be unified, in any reachable stage. These relations can change dynamically, *after* that atoms are introduced. Thus a stage is a finite set of atoms, together with a distinction over it. These stages form the objects of a new index category $\mathbb{D}$, which subsumes both the idea of variables and that of names.

The aim of this paper is to give a systematic presentation of the model of set-valued functors over $\mathbb{D}$, first introduced by Ghani, Yemane and Victor for characterizing open bisimulation of π-calculus [9]. Following similar previous work about [6, 5], we focus on algebraic, coalgebraic and logical properties of this category, relating these results with the corresponding ones in $Set^\mathbb{F}$ and $Set^\mathbb{I}$.

In Section 2, we present the category $\mathbb{D}$, its properties and relations with $\mathbb{F}$ and $\mathbb{I}$. In Section 3 we study the structure of $Set^\mathbb{D}$, and its relations with $Set^\mathbb{F}$, $Set^\mathbb{I}$. In particular, due to their importance for modeling process calculi, we will study initial algebras and final coalgebras of polynomial functors over $Set^\mathbb{D}$.

In Section 4, we give a general definition of the key notions of *support* and *apartness*, and then apply and compare their instances in the cases of $Set^\mathbb{D}$, $Set^\mathbb{F}$ and $Set^\mathbb{I}$. An application of apartness is in Section 5, where we present a monoidal definition of "apartness-preserving" simultaneous substitution.

In Section 6 we turn to the logical aspects of $Set^\mathbb{D}$: restricting to the subcategory of pullback-preserving functors, we define a self-dual quantifier similar to Gabbay-Pitts' N. This quantifier, and the structure of $Set^\mathbb{D}$, will be put at work in Section 7 in giving the first denotational semantics of Miller-Tiu's $FO\lambda^\nabla$.

Final remarks and directions for future work are in Section 8.

Due to space limits, many proofs are omitted, but can be found in [14].

2   Distinctions

Let us fix an infinite, countable set of *atoms* $\mathbb{A}$. Atoms are abstract elements with no structure, intended to act both as *variables* and as *names* symbols.

We denote finite subsets of $\mathbb{A}$ as $n, m, \ldots$. Functions among these finite sets are "atom substitutions". The category of all these finite sets, and any maps among them is $\mathbb{F}$. The subcategory of $\mathbb{F}$ with only *injective* maps is $\mathbb{I}$. In fact, we can see a name essentially as an atom which must be kept apart from the others. We can formalize this concept as follows:

Definition 1. (The category $\mathbb{D}$) *The category $\mathbb{D}$ of distinctions relations is the full subcategory of Rel of irreflexive, symmetric binary relations over $\mathbb{A}$ with a finite carrier set. (Here Rel is the category of relations and monotone functions.)*

A distinction relation (n, d) is thus a finite set n of atoms and a symmetric relation $d \subseteq n \times n$ such that for all $i \in n : (i, i) \notin d$. In the following we will write (n, d) as $d^{(n)}$, possibly dropping the superscript when clear from the context. A morphisms $f : d^{(n)} \to e^{(m)}$ is any *monotone* function $f : n \to m$, that is a substitution of atoms for atoms which preserves the distinction relation (if $(a, b) \in d$ then $(f(a), f(b)) \in e$). In other words, substitutions cannot map two related (i.e., definitely distinct) atoms to the same atom of a later stage, while unrelated atoms can coalesce to a single one.

Structure of $\mathbb{D}$. The category $\mathbb{D}$ inherits from *Rel* products and coproducts. More explicitly, products and coproducts can be defined on objects as follows:

$$d_1^{(m)} \times d_2^{(n)} \triangleq (m \times n, \{((i_1, j_1), (i_2, j_2)) \mid (i_1, i_2) \in d_1 \text{ and } (j_1, j_2) \in d_2\})$$

$$d_1^{(m)} + d_2^{(n)} \triangleq (m + n, d_1 \cup \{(l + i, l + j) \mid (i, j) \in d_2\}) \qquad (l \triangleq \max(m) + 1)$$

where $m + n \triangleq m \cup \{l + i \mid i \in n\}$. Note that $\mathbb{D}$ has no terminal object, but it has initial object $(\emptyset, \emptyset)$. In fact, $\mathbb{D}$ inherits meets, joins and partial order from $\wp(\mathbb{A})$:

- $d^{(n)} \wedge e^{(m)} = (d \cap e)^{(m \cap n)}$, and $d^{(n)} \vee e^{(m)} = (d \cup e)^{(m \cup n)}$
- $d^{(n)} \leq e^{(m)}$ iff $d \wedge e = d$, that is, iff $d \subseteq e$.

For each n, let us denote $\mathbb{D}_n$ the full subcategory of $\mathbb{D}$ whose objects are all relations over n. Then, $\mathbb{D}_n$ is a complete Boolean algebra. Let $\bot^{(n)} \triangleq (n, \emptyset)$ and $\top^{(n)} \triangleq (n, n^2 \setminus \Delta_n)$ be the *empty* and *complete* distinction on n, respectively, where $\Delta : \mathbb{F} \to Rel$ is the *diagonal* functor defined as $\Delta_n = (n, \{(i, i) \mid i \in n\})$.

$\mathbb{D}$ can be given another monoidal structure. Let us define $\oplus : \mathbb{D} \times \mathbb{D} \to \mathbb{D}$ as

$$d_1^{(m)} \oplus d_2^{(n)} = (m + n, d_1 \cup d_2 \cup \{(i, j), (j, i) \mid i \in m, j \in n\}).$$

Proposition 1. $(\mathbb{D}, \oplus, \bot^{(0)})$ *is a symmetric monoidal category.*

By applying coproduct and tensor to $\bot^{(1)}$ we get two distinguished *dynamic allocation* functors $\delta^-, \delta^+ : \mathbb{D} \to \mathbb{D}$, as $\delta^- \triangleq \bot^{(1)} + \_$ and $\delta^+ \triangleq \bot^{(1)} \oplus \_$. More explicitly, the action of δ^+ on objects is $\delta^+(d^{(n)}) = d_{+1}^{(n+1)}$ where $d_{+1} = d \cup \{(*, i), (i, *) \mid i \in n\}$. Thus both δ^- and δ^+ add an extra element to the carrier, but, as the superscript $^+$ is intended to suggest, δ^+ adds in *extra* distinctions.

Embedding $\mathbb{I}$ and $\mathbb{F}$ in $\mathbb{D}$. Let $\mathbb{D}_e$ denote the full subcategory of $\mathbb{D}$ of empty distinctions $\perp^{(n)} = (n, \emptyset)$, and $\mathbb{D}_c$ the full subcategory of complete distinctions $\top^{(n)} = (n, n^2 \setminus \Delta_n)$. Notice that all morphisms in $\mathbb{D}_c$ are *mono* morphisms of $\mathbb{D}$—that is, injective maps.

Let us consider the forgetful functor $U : \mathbb{D} \to \mathbb{F}$, dropping the distinction relation. The functor $\mathsf{v} : \mathbb{F} \to \mathbb{D}_e$ mapping each n in $\mathbb{F}$ to $\perp^{(n)}$, and each $f : n \to m$ to itself, is inverse of the restriction of U to $\mathbb{D}_e$.

On the other hand, the restriction of U to $\mathbb{D}_c$ is a functor $U : \mathbb{D}_c \to \mathbb{I}$, because the only morphisms in $\mathbb{D}_c$ are the injective ones. The functor $\mathsf{t} : \mathbb{I} \to \mathbb{D}_c$ mapping each n in $\mathbb{I}$ to $\top^{(n)}$, and each $f : n \rightarrowtail m$ to itself, is inverse of U. Hence:

Proposition 2. $\mathbb{D}_e \cong \mathbb{F}$, and $\mathbb{D}_c \cong \mathbb{I}$.

Therefore, we can say that the category of $\mathbb{D}$ generalises both $\mathbb{I}$ and $\mathbb{F}$. In fact, it is easy to check that the forgetful functor $U : \mathbb{D} \to \mathbb{F}$ is the right adjoint of the inclusion functor $\mathsf{v} : \mathbb{F} \hookrightarrow \mathbb{D}$.

Remark 1. While we are on this subject, we define the functor $V : \mathbb{D} \to \mathbb{I}$ which singles out from each d the (atoms of the) largest complete distinction contained in d. More precisely, V is defined on objects as $V(d^{(n)}) = \max\{m \mid \top^{(m)} \leq d^{(n)}\}$ and on morphisms as the restriction. This defines a functor: if $f : d^{(n)} \to e^{(m)}$ is a morphism, then it preserves distinctions, and thus for $i \in V(d)$, since i is part of a complete subdistinction of d, it must be mapped in a complete subdistinction of e, and hence $f(i) \in V(e)$. However, V is not an adjoint of t. □

We recall finally that $\mathbb{F}$ has finite products (and hence also $\mathbb{D}_e$), while $\mathbb{I}$ has binary products only. Disjoint unions are finite coproducts in $\mathbb{F}$, but not in $\mathbb{I}$. Actually, disjoint union $\uplus : \mathbb{I} \times \mathbb{I} \to \mathbb{I}$ is only a monoidal structure over $\mathbb{I}$, which quite clearly corresponds to the restriction of $\oplus$ to $\mathbb{D}_c$:

Proposition 3. $\oplus \circ \langle \mathsf{t}, \mathsf{t} \rangle = \mathsf{t} \circ \uplus$, *that is, for* $n, m \in \mathbb{I}$: $\top^{(n \uplus m)} = \top^{(n)} \oplus \top^{(m)}$.

As a consequence, for Proposition 2, we have $\uplus = U \circ \oplus \circ \langle \mathsf{t}, \mathsf{t} \rangle$. On the other hand, $\oplus$ restricted to $\mathbb{D}_e$ is *not* equivalent to the coproduct $+$ in $\mathbb{F}$.

3   Presheaves over $\mathbb{D}$

$Set^{\mathbb{D}}$ is the category of functors from $\mathbb{D}$ to Set (often called *presheaves (over $\mathbb{D}^{op}$)*) and natural transformations. The structure of $\mathbb{D}$ lifts to $Set^{\mathbb{D}}$, which has:[1]

1. *Products and coproducts*, which are computed pointwise (as with all limits and colimits in functor categories); e.g. $(P \times Q)_{d^{(n)}} = P_{d^{(n)}} \times Q_{d^{(n)}}$. The terminal object is the constant functor $\mathcal{K}_1 = \mathbf{y}(\perp^{(\emptyset)})$: $\mathcal{K}_1(d) = 1$.
2. A presheaf of *atoms Atom* $\in Set^{\mathbb{D}}$, $Atom = \mathbf{y}(\perp^{(1)}) = \mathbf{y}(\top^{(1)})$. The action on objects is $Atom(d^{(n)}) = n$.

---

[1] We shall use the same symbols for the lifted structure, but ensuring the reader has enough information to deduce which category we are working in.

3. Two *dynamic allocation* functors $\delta^-, \delta^+ : Set^{\mathbb{D}} \to Set^{\mathbb{D}}$, induced by each $\kappa \in \{\delta^+, \delta^-\}$ on $\mathbb{D}$ as $\_ \circ \kappa : Set^{\mathbb{D}} \to Set^{\mathbb{D}}$.
4. Let $\wp_f$ be the finite (covariant) powerset functor on Set; then $\wp_f \circ \_ : Set^{\mathbb{D}} \to Set^{\mathbb{D}}$ is the *finite powerset* operator on $\mathbb{D}$-presheaves.
5. *Exponentials* are defined as usual in functor categories:

$$(B^A)_d \triangleq Set^{\mathbb{D}}(A \times \mathbb{D}(d, \_), B)$$
$$(B^A)_f(m) \triangleq m \circ (id_A \times (\_ \circ f)) \quad \text{for } f : d \to e \text{ in } \mathbb{D}, m : A \times \mathbb{D}(d, \_) \longrightarrow B$$

In particular, exponentials of representable functors have a nice definition:

Proposition 4. *For all $d \in \mathbb{D}$, B in $Set^{\mathbb{D}}$: $B^{\mathbf{y}(d)} \cong B_{d+\_}$.*

This allows us to point out a strict relation between *Atom* and δ^-:

Proposition 5. $(\_)^{Atom} \cong \delta^-$, *and hence* $\_ \times Atom \dashv \delta^-$.

Proof. Since $Atom = \mathbf{y}(\bot^{(1)})$, by Proposition 4 we have that $F^{Atom} \cong F_{\bot^{(1)}+\_} = F_{\delta^-(\_)} = \delta^-(F)$. The second part is an obvious consequence. □

The categories $Set^{\mathbb{F}}$ and $Set^{\mathbb{I}}$ can be embedded into $Set^{\mathbb{D}}$.

Proposition 6. *The functor $\mathsf{v} : \mathbb{F} \hookrightarrow \mathbb{D}$ induces an essential geometric morphism $\mathsf{v} : Set^{\mathbb{F}} \to Set^{\mathbb{D}}$, that is two adjunctions $\mathsf{v}_! \dashv \mathsf{v}^* \dashv \mathsf{v}_*$, where $\mathsf{v}_! \cong \_ \circ U$, $\mathsf{v}^* = \_ \circ \mathsf{v}$, and $\mathsf{v}_*(F)(d^{(n)}) = F_n$ if $d^{(n)} = \bot^{(n)}$, 1 otherwise.*

Proof. The existence of the essential geometric morphism, and that the inverse image is $\_ \circ \mathsf{v}$, is a direct application of [12–VII.2, Theorem 2]. Let us prove that $\mathsf{v}_! \cong \_ \circ U$. $\mathsf{v}_!$ can be defined as the left Kan extension along $\mathbf{y} : \mathbb{F}^{op} \hookrightarrow Set^{\mathbb{F}}$ of the functor $T : \mathbb{F}^{op} \to Set^{\mathbb{D}}$, $T(n) = \mathbb{D}(\bot^{(n)}, \_) = \mathbf{y} \circ \mathsf{v}^{op}$. Hence:

$$\mathsf{v}_!(F) = (\mathrm{Lan}_{\mathbf{y}}(T))(F) = \int^{m \in \mathbb{F}} Set^{\mathbb{F}}(\mathbf{y}(m), F) \cdot \mathbb{D}(\bot^{(m)}, \_)$$
$$= \int^{m \in \mathbb{F}} F_m \cdot \mathbb{F}(m, U(\_)) = \left(\int^{m \in \mathbb{F}} F_m \cdot \mathbb{F}(m, \_) \right) \circ U = F \circ U \quad □$$

Proposition 7. $\mathsf{v} : Set^{\mathbb{F}} \to Set^{\mathbb{D}}$ *is an embedding, that is: $\mathsf{v}^* \circ \mathsf{v}_* \cong Id$.*

As a consequence, by [12–VII.4, Lemma 1] we have also $\mathsf{v}^* \circ \mathsf{v}_! \cong Id$, and hence both v_* and $\mathsf{v}_!$ are full and faithful.

A similar result holds also for $\mathsf{t} : \mathbb{I} \hookrightarrow \mathbb{D}$, although the adjoints have not a neat description as in the previous case.

Proposition 8. t *induces an essential geometric morphism $\mathsf{t} : Set^{\mathbb{I}} \to Set^{\mathbb{D}}$, that is two adjunctions $\mathsf{t}_! \dashv \mathsf{t}^* \dashv \mathsf{t}_*$, where for all $G : \mathbb{I} \to Set$, and $d \in \mathbb{D}$, it is $\mathsf{t}_*(G)(d) = Set^{\mathbb{I}}(\mathbb{D}(d, \mathsf{t}(\_)), G)$.*

Proposition 9. $\mathsf{t} : Set^{\mathbb{I}} \to Set^{\mathbb{D}}$ *is an embedding, that is: $\mathsf{t}^* \circ \mathsf{t}_* \cong Id$.*

This means that also $\mathsf{t}^* \circ \mathsf{t}_! \cong Id$, and hence both t_* and $\mathsf{t}_!$ are full and faithful.

Algebras and Coalgebras of Polynomial Functors. It is well-known that any polynomial functor over Set (i.e., defined only by constant functors, finite products/coproducts and finite powersets) has initial algebra. This result has been generalized to $Set^{\mathbb{F}}$ [6, 10] in order to deal with signatures with *variable bindings*; in this case, polynomials can contain also Var, the functor of *variables*, and a dynamic allocation functor $\delta_{\mathbb{F}} : Set^{\mathbb{F}} \to Set^{\mathbb{F}}$. For instance, the datatype of λ-terms up-to α-conversion can be defined as the initial algebra of the functor

$$\Sigma_\Lambda(X) = Var + X \times X + \delta_{\mathbb{F}}(X) \tag{1}$$

A parallel generalization for dealing with *name generation* use the category $Set^{\mathbb{I}}$ (and its variants) [10, 8, 5], which provides the functor of *names* N and a dynamic allocation functor $\delta_{\mathbb{I}} : Set^{\mathbb{I}} \to Set^{\mathbb{I}}$. The domain for late semantics of π-calculus [5] can be defined as the final coalgebra of the functor $B : Set^{\mathbb{I}} \to Set^{\mathbb{I}}$

$$BP \triangleq \wp_f(N \times P^N + N \times N \times P + N \times \delta_{\mathbb{I}}P + P) \tag{2}$$

In $Set^{\mathbb{D}}$, we can generalize a step further. We say that a functor $F : Set^{\mathbb{D}} \to Set^{\mathbb{D}}$ is *polynomial* if it be defined by using only $Atom$, constant functors, finite products/coproducts, dynamic allocations δ^+ and δ^- and finite powersets.

There is a precise relation among initial algebras of polynomial functors on $Set^{\mathbb{F}}$ and $Set^{\mathbb{D}}$. Let us recall a general result (see e.g. [10]):

Proposition 10. *Let $\mathcal{C}, \mathcal{D}$ be two categories and $f : \mathcal{C} \longrightarrow \mathcal{D}$, $T : \mathcal{C} \longrightarrow \mathcal{C}$ and $T' : \mathcal{D} \longrightarrow \mathcal{D}$ be three functors such that $T' \circ f \cong f \circ T$ for some natural isomorphism $\phi : T' \circ f \longrightarrow f \circ T$.*
1. *If f has a right adjoint f^*, and $(A, \alpha : TA \to A)$ is an initial T-algebra in $\mathcal{C}$, then $(f(A), f(\alpha) \circ \phi_A : T'(f(A)) \to f(A))$ is an initial T'-algebra in $\mathcal{D}$.*
2. *If f has a left adjoint f^*, and $(A, \alpha : A \to TA)$ is a final T-coalgebra in $\mathcal{C}$, then $(f(A), \phi_A^{-1} \circ f(\alpha) : f(A) \to T'(f(A)))$ is a final T'-coalgebra in $\mathcal{D}$.*

For a polynomial functor $T : Set^{\mathbb{D}} \to Set^{\mathbb{D}}$, let us denote $\bar{T} : Set^{\mathbb{F}} \to Set^{\mathbb{F}}$ the functor obtained by replacing $Atom$ with Var and δ^+, δ^- with $\delta_{\mathbb{F}}$ in T.

Theorem 1. *The polynomial functor $T : Set^{\mathbb{D}} \to Set^{\mathbb{D}}$ has initial algebra, which is (isomorphic to) $F \circ U$, where (F, α) is the initial $\bar{T}$-algebra in $Set^{\mathbb{F}}$.*

Proof. The functor $\bar{T}$ has initial algebra (see e.g. [6, 10]); let us denote it by (F, α). In order to prove the result, we apply Proposition 10(1), where $f : \mathcal{C} \longrightarrow \mathcal{D}$ is the functor $v_! = {}_- \circ U : Set^{\mathbb{F}} \to Set^{\mathbb{D}}$ of Proposition 6, whose right adjoint is v^*. Then $v_!(F) = F \circ U$. We have only to prove that $T \circ v_! \cong v_! \circ \bar{T}$. It is easy to see that this holds for products, coproducts, constant functors and finite powersets. It is also trivial to see that $Atom \cong Var \circ U$.

It remains to prove that $\kappa \circ v_! \cong v_! \circ \delta_{\mathbb{F}}$, for $\kappa = \delta^+, \delta^-$. For F a functor in $Set^{\mathbb{F}}$, we prove that there is a natural isomorphism $\phi : \kappa(v_!(F)) = \kappa(F \circ U) \longrightarrow v_!(\delta_{\mathbb{F}}(F)) = \delta_{\mathbb{F}}(F) \circ U$. This is trivial, because for $d^{(n)}$ a distinction in $\mathbb{D}$, it is $\kappa(F \circ U)_d = (F \circ U)_{\kappa d} = F_{U(\kappa d)} = F_{n+1} = \delta_{\mathbb{F}}(F)_n = (\delta_{\mathbb{F}}(F) \circ U)_d$. $\square$

Therefore, initial algebras of polynomial functors in $Set^{\mathbb{D}}$ are exactly initial algebras of the corresponding functors in $Set^{\mathbb{F}}$. This means that $Set^{\mathbb{D}}$ can be used in place of $Set^{\mathbb{F}}$ for defining datatypes with variable binding, as in e.g. [9].

There is a similar connection between $Set^{\mathbb{I}}$ and $Set^{\mathbb{D}}$, about final coalgebras.

Lemma 1. $\delta^+ \circ \mathsf{t}_* \cong \mathsf{t}_* \circ \delta_{\mathbb{I}}$ and $\delta^- \circ \mathsf{t}_* \cong \mathsf{t}_* \circ (\_)^N$.

Let $T : Set^{\mathbb{I}} \to Set^{\mathbb{I}}$ be a polynomial functor. Let us denote by $\tilde{T} : Set^{\mathbb{D}} \to Set^{\mathbb{D}}$ the functor obtained by replacing in (the polynomial of) T, every occurrence of N with $\mathsf{t}_*(N)$, δ with δ^+, $(\_)^N$ with δ^-. Then, we have the following:

Theorem 2. The functor $\tilde{T} : Set^{\mathbb{D}} \to Set^{\mathbb{D}}$ has final coalgebra, which is (isomorphic to) $\mathsf{t}_*(F)$, where (F, β) is the final T-coalgebra in $Set^{\mathbb{I}}$.

Therefore, in $Set^{\mathbb{D}}$ we can define coalgebrically all the objects definable by polynomial functors in $Set^{\mathbb{I}}$, like that for late bisimulation [5]. Moreover, $Set^{\mathbb{D}}$ provides other constructors, such as $Atom$, which do not have a natural counterpart in $Set^{\mathbb{I}}$. An example of application of these distinctive constructors, following [9], is the characterization of open semantics of π-calculus as the final coalgebra of the functor $B_o : Set^{\mathbb{D}} \to Set^{\mathbb{D}}$:

$$B_o P \triangleq \wp_f(Atom \times \delta^- P + Atom \times Atom \times P + Atom \times \delta^+ P + P) \quad (3)$$

Notice that, although similar in shape, B_o is not the lifting of the functor B of strong late bisimulation in $Set^{\mathbb{I}}$ (Equation 2), nor can be defined on $Set^{\mathbb{I}}$.

4   Support and Apartness

A key feature of categories for modeling names is to provide some notion of *support* of terms/elements, and of *non-interference*, or "apartness" [19, 8]. In this section, we first introduce a general definition of *support* and *apartness*, and then we examine these notions in the case of $Set^{\mathbb{D}}$, and related categories.

Definition 2 (support). Let $\mathcal{C}$ be a category, $F : \mathcal{C} \to Set$ be a functor. Let C be an object of $\mathcal{C}$, and $a \in F_C$. A subobject $i : D \rightarrowtail C$ of C supports a (at C) if there exists a (not necessarily unique) $b \in F_D$ such that $a = F_i(b)$.

A support is called proper iff it is a proper subobject.

We denote by $\mathrm{Supp}_{F,C}(a)$ the set of subobjects of C supporting a. The intuition is that D supports $a \in F_C$ if D is "enough" for defining a. It is clear that the definition does not depend on the particular subobject representative. As a consequence, a is affected by what happens to elements in D only:

Proposition 11. For all $D \in \mathrm{Supp}_{F,C}(a)$, and for all $h, k : C \to C'$: if $h_{|D} = k_{|D}$ then $F_h(a) = F_k(a)$.

Notice that in general, the converse of Proposition 11 does not hold.

Remark 2. When $\mathcal{C} = \mathbb{F}, \mathbb{I}$, the supports of $a \in F_n$ can be seen as *approximations at stage n* of the free variables/names of a—that is, the free variables/names which are observable from n. For instance, let us consider $t \in \Lambda_n$, where Λ is the algebraic definition of untyped λ-calculus in equation 1. It is easy to prove by induction on t that for all $m \subseteq n$: $m \in \mathrm{Supp}_{\Lambda,n}(t) \iff FV(t) \subseteq m$.

Supports are viewed as "approximations" because elements may have not any proper support, at any stage. For example, consider the presheaf *Stream* :

$\mathbb{F} \rightarrow Set$ constantly equal to the set of all *infinite* lists of variables. The stream $s = (x_1, x_2, x_3, \dots)$, which has infinite free variables, belongs to $Stream_n$ for all n, but also $\text{Supp}_{Stream,n}(s) = \{n\}$. $\square$

$\text{Supp}_{F,C}(a)$ is a poset, inheriting its order from $\text{Sub}(a)$, and C itself is always its top, but it may be that there are no proper supports, as shown in the remark above. Even in the case that an element has some finite (even proper) support, still it may be that it does not have a *least* support. (Consider, e.g., $G : \mathbb{F} \rightarrow Set$ such that $G_n = \emptyset$ for $|n| < 2$, and $= \{x\}$ otherwise; then $x \in G_{\{x,y,z\}}$ is supported by $\{x, y\}$ and $\{x, z\}$ but not by $\{x\}$ alone.) However, we can prove the following:

Proposition 12. *Let C have pullbacks, $F : C \rightarrow Set$ be pullback-preserving, C be in C, and $x \in F_C$. If both C_1, C_2 support x at C, then $C_1 \wedge C_2$ supports x.*

Remark 3. In the case that $C = \mathbb{I}$, pullback-preserving functors correspond to sheaves with respect to the atomic topology, that is the Schanuel topos [12]. This subcategory of $Set^{\mathbb{I}}$ has been extensively used in previous work for modeling names and nominal calculi; see [10, 4] among others, and ultimately also the FM techniques by Gabbay and Pitts [8, 17], since the category of nominal sets with finite support is equivalent to the Schanuel topos [8–Section 7].
    We will use pullback-preserving functors over $\mathbb{D}$ in Section 6 below. $\square$

In the rest of the paper, we focus on the case when C is one of $\mathbb{F}, \mathbb{I}, \mathbb{D}$, which do have pullbacks and initial object ($\emptyset$, $\emptyset$ and $\perp^{(\emptyset)}$ respectively). As one may expect, the support in $\mathbb{D}$ is a conservative generalization of those in $\mathbb{F}$ and $\mathbb{I}$:

Proposition 13.   *1. Let $n, m \in \mathbb{F}$, and $F : \mathbb{F} \rightarrow Set$. For all $a \in F_n$: $m \in$ $\text{Supp}_{F,n}(a) \iff \text{v}(m) \in \text{Supp}_{\text{v}_!(F),\text{v}(n)}(a)$.* [2]
 2. Let $n, m \in \mathbb{I}$, and $F : \mathbb{I} \rightarrow Set$. For all $a \in F_n$: $m \in \text{Supp}_{F,n}(a) \iff \text{t}(m) \in$ $\text{Supp}_{\text{t}_*(F),\text{t}(n)}(a)$.

We can now give the following general key definition, generalizing that used sometimes in $Set^{\mathbb{I}}$ (see e.g. [19]).

Definition 3 (Apartness). *Let C be a category with pullbacks and initial object. For $A, B : C \rightarrow Set$, the functor $A \#_C B : C \rightarrow Set$ ("A apart from B") is defined on objects as follows:*

$$(A \#_C B)_C = \{(a, b) \in A_C \times B_C \mid \text{for all } f : C \rightarrow D :$$
$$\text{there exist } s_1 \in \text{Supp}_{A,D}(A_f(a)), s_2 \in \text{Supp}_{B,D}(B_f(b)) \text{ s.t. } s_1 \wedge s_2 = 0\} \quad (4)$$

For $f : C \rightarrow D$, it is $(A \#_C B)_f \triangleq A_f \times B_f$.

As a syntactic shorthand, we will write pairs $(a, b) \in (A \#_C B)_c$ as $a \# b$. In the following, we will drop the index $_C$ when clear from the context.
    Let us now apply this definition to the three categories $Set^{\mathbb{I}}$, $Set^{\mathbb{F}}$, and $Set^{\mathbb{D}}$.

---

[2] Recall that $\text{v}_!(F)_{\text{v}(n)} \cong F_n$, and hence it is consistent to consider $a \in \text{v}_!(F)_{\text{v}(n)}$.

$\mathcal{C} = \mathbb{F}$ In this case we have that $a \# b$ iff at least one of a, b is closed, i.e., it is supported by the empty set: if both a and b have only non-empty supports, then some variable can be always unified by a suitable morphism. So the definition above simplifies as follows:

$$(A \#_{\mathbb{F}} B)_n = \{(a, b) \in A_n \times B_n \mid \emptyset \in \operatorname{Supp}_{A,n}(a) \text{ or } \emptyset \in \operatorname{Supp}_{B,n}(b)\} \quad (5)$$

$\mathcal{C} = \mathbb{I}$ In this case, names are subject only to injective renamings, and therefore can be never unified. So it is sufficient to look at the present stage, that is, the definition above simplifies as follows:

$$(A \#_{\mathbb{I}} B)_n = \{(a, b) \in A_n \times B_n \mid$$
$$\text{there exist } n_1 \in \operatorname{Supp}_{A,n}(a), n_2 \in \operatorname{Supp}_{B,n}(b) \text{ s.t. } n_1 \cap n_2 = \emptyset\} \quad (6)$$

which corresponds to say that $a \# b$ iff a, b do not share any free name.

$\mathcal{C} = \mathbb{D}$ This case subsumes both previous cases: informally, $(a, b) \in (A \# B)_d$ means that if i is an atom appearing free in a, then any j occurring free in b can never be unified with i, that is $(i, j) \in d$:

$$(A \#_{\mathbb{D}} B)_{d^{(n)}} = \{(a, b) \in A_d \times B_d \mid$$
$$\text{there exist } s_1 \in \operatorname{Supp}_{A,d}(a), s_2 \in \operatorname{Supp}_{B,d}(b) \text{ s.t. } s_1 \oplus s_2 \le d\} \quad (7)$$

Actually, all these tensors arise from the monoidal structures $\oplus$ and $\uplus$ of the categories $\mathbb{I}$ and $\mathbb{D}$, via the following general construction due to Day [3]:

Proposition 14. *Let* $(\mathcal{C}, \star, I)$ *be a (symmetric) monoidal category. Then,* $(Set^{\mathcal{C}}, \star_{\mathcal{C}}, \mathbf{y}(I))$ *is a (symmetric) closed monoidal category, where*

$$(A \star_{\mathcal{C}} B)_C = \int^{C_1} A_{C_1} \times \int^{C_2} B_{C_2} \times \mathcal{C}(C_1 \star C_2, C) \quad (8)$$

Theorem 3. *The monoidal structure* $(\mathbb{D}, \oplus, \perp^{(\emptyset)})$ *induces, via equation 8, the monoidal structure* $(Set^{\mathbb{D}}, \#_{\mathbb{D}}, \mathbf{y}(\perp^{(0)}) = \mathcal{K}_1 = 1)$ *of equation 7.*

Proof. Let $A, B : \mathbb{D} \to Set$, and $d^{(n)} \in \mathbb{D}$; by applying Proposition 14 and since products preserves coends, we have

$$(A \star_{\mathbb{D}} B)_d = \iint^{d_1, d_2} A_{d_1} \times B_{d_2} \times \mathbb{D}(d_1 \oplus d_2, d)$$

$$= \left(\coprod_{d_1, d_2 \in \mathbb{D}} A_{d_1} \times B_{d_2} \times \mathbb{D}(d_1 \oplus d_2, d) \right)_{/\approx} \quad (9)$$

where the equivalence $\approx$ is defined on triples as follows

$$(a, b, f : d_1 \oplus d_2 \to d) \approx (a', b', g : d_1' \oplus d_2' \to d)$$
$$\iff A_{foinl}(a) = A_{goinl}(a') \text{ and } B_{foinr}(b) = B_{goinr}(b')$$

For each class $[(a, b, f : d_1 \oplus d_2 \to d)] \in (A \star_{\mathbb{D}} B)_d$ we can associate a unique pair $(A_{foinl}(a), B_{foinr}(b)) \in (A \#_{\mathbb{D}} B)_d$; the definition does not depend on the particular representative we choose.

On the converse, let us consider a pair $(a, b) \in (A \#_{\mathbb{D}} B)_d$; this means that

- there exists $f_1 : s_1 \rightarrowtail d$, $a' \in A_{s_1}$ such that $a = A_{f_1}(a')$
- there exists $f_2 : s_2 \rightarrowtail d$, $b' \in B_{s_2}$ such that $b = B_{f_2}(b')$

and such that $[f_1, f_2] : s_1 \oplus s_2 \rightarrowtail d$. We can associate this pair (a, b) to the equivalence class of the triple $(a', b', [f_1, f_2])$ in the coend 9. The class defined in this way does not depend on the particular a' and b' we choose.

It is easy to check that these two mappings are inverse of each other.   □

A similar constructions applies also to $Set^{\mathbb{I}}$, as observed e.g. in [19]:

Proposition 15. *The monoidal structure* $(\mathbb{I}, \uplus, 0)$ *induces, via equation 8, the monoidal structure* $(Set^{\mathbb{I}}, \#_{\mathbb{I}}, \mathbf{y}(0) = 1)$ *of equation 6.*

Using Theorem 3, we can show that $\#_{\mathbb{F}}$ is a particular case of $\#_{\mathbb{D}}$:

Proposition 16. $\#_{\mathbb{F}} = \mathsf{v}^* \circ \#_{\mathbb{D}} \circ \langle \mathsf{v}_*, \mathsf{v}_* \rangle.$

Proof. Let us prove that for $F, G : \mathbb{F} \to Set$, it is $(\mathsf{v}_*(F) \#_{\mathbb{D}} \mathsf{v}_*(G))_{\perp^{(n)}} \cong (F \#_{\mathbb{F}} G)_n$. By applying Theorem 3, we have

$$(\mathsf{v}_*(F) \#_{\mathbb{D}} \mathsf{v}_*(G))_{\perp^{(n)}} = \left(\coprod_{d_1^{(n_1)}, d_2^{(n_2)} \in \mathbb{D}} \mathsf{v}_*(F)_{d_1} \times \mathsf{v}_*(G)_{d_2} \times \mathbb{D}(d_1 \oplus d_2, \perp^{(n)}) \right)_{/\approx}$$

$$= \left(\coprod_{d_1^{(n_1)}, d_2^{(n_2)} \in \mathbb{D}} F_{n_1} \times G_{n_2} \times \mathbb{D}(d_1 \oplus d_2, \perp^{(n)}) \right)_{/\approx}$$

Let us consider the set $\mathbb{D}(d_1 \oplus d_2, \perp^{(n)})$. If $d_1 \oplus d_2 = \perp^{(m)}$ for some m, then $\mathbb{D}(d_1 \oplus d_2, \perp^{(n)}) = \mathbb{F}(m, n)$. Otherwise, $\mathbb{D}(d_1 \oplus d_2, \perp^{(n)}) = \emptyset$.

Now, the only way for having $d_1 \oplus d_2 = \perp^{(m)}$ is that both d_1 and d_2 are empty relations $\perp^{(n_1)}, \perp^{(n_2)}$, and at least one of them has no atoms at all (otherwise the $\oplus$ would add a distinction in any case). Therefore, the equivalence above can be continued as follows:

$$\dots = \left(\left(\coprod_{n_1 \in \mathbb{F}} F_{n_1} \times G_{\emptyset} \times \mathbb{F}(n_1, n) \right) + \left(\coprod_{n_2 \in \mathbb{F}} F_{\emptyset} \times G_{n_2} \times \mathbb{F}(n_2, n) \right) \right)_{/\approx}$$

This means that the triples are either of the form $(a \in F_{\emptyset}, b \in G_{n_2}, f : n_2 \to n)$, or of the form $(a \in F_{n_1}, b \in G_{\emptyset}, f : n_1 \to n)$. The first is equivalent to the pair $(F_?(a), G_f(b))$, the second to the pair $(F_f(a), G_?(b))$, both in $(F \#_{\mathbb{F}} G)_n$.   □

The next corollary is a consequence of Theorem 3 and Proposition 14:

Corollary 1. *The functor* $A \# \_ : Set^{\mathbb{D}} \to Set^{\mathbb{D}}$ *has a right adjoint* $[A]\_$, *defined on objects by* $([A]B)_d = Set^{\mathbb{D}}(A, B_{d \oplus \_})$.

Remark 4. Let us consider the counit $ev_{A,B} : A \# [A]B \longrightarrow B$ of this adjunction. For $d \in \mathbb{D}$, the component $ev_d : (A \# [A]B)_d \longrightarrow B_d$ maps an element $a \in A_d$ and a natural transformation $\phi : A \to B_{d \oplus \_}$, *apart from each other*, to an element in B_d, which can be described as follows. Let $s_1, s_2 \in \text{Sub}(d)$ supporting ϕ and a, respectively, and such that $s_1 \oplus s_2 \le d$. By the definition of support, let $\phi' : A \to B_{s_1 \oplus \_}$ and $a' \in A_{s_2}$ be the witnesses of ϕ and a at s_1 and s_2, respectively. Then, $\phi'_{s_2}(a') \in B_{s_1 \oplus s_2}$, which can be mapped to an element in B_d by the inclusion $s_1 \oplus s_2 \le d$.   □

Finally, for $A = Atom$ we have the counterpart of Proposition 5:

Proposition 17. $[Atom]\_ \cong \delta^+$, *and hence* $\_ \# Atom \dashv \delta^+$.

5   Substitution Monoidal Structure of $Set^{\mathbb{D}}$

Let us define a tensor product $\bullet : Set^{\mathbb{D}} \times Set^{\mathbb{D}} \to Set^{\mathbb{D}}$ as follows:

$$\text{for } A, B \in Set^{\mathbb{D}} : \qquad A \bullet B \triangleq \int^{e \in \mathbb{D}} A_e \cdot B^e$$

$$\text{that is, for } d \in \mathbb{D} : \qquad (A \bullet B)_d = \int^{e \in \mathbb{D}} A_e \times (B^e)_d$$

where, for $e^{(n)}$ in $\mathbb{D}$, $B^e : \mathbb{D} \to Set$ is the functor defined by

$$(B^e)_d = \{(b_1, \ldots, b_n) \in (B_d)^n \mid \text{if } (i,j) \in e \text{ then } (b_i, b_j) \in (B \# B)_d\}$$
$$(B^e)_f = (B_f)^n \qquad \text{for } f : d^{(m)} \to d'^{(m')}$$

Unfolding the coend, we obtain the following explicit description of $A \bullet B$:

$$(A \bullet B)_d = \left(\coprod_{e \in \mathbb{D}} A_e \times (B^e)_d \right)_{/\approx}$$

where $\approx$ is the equivalence relation defined by

$$(a; b_{\rho(1)}, \ldots, b_{\rho(n)}) \approx (A_\rho(a); b_1, \ldots, b_{n'}) \quad \text{for } \rho : e^{(n)} \to e'^{(n')}.$$

Actually, $B^{(\cdot)}$ can seen as a functor $B^{(\cdot)} : \mathbb{D}^{op} \to Set^{\mathbb{D}}$, adding the "reindexing" action on morphisms: for $\rho : e^{(n)} \to e'^{(n')}$, define $B^f : B^{e'} \longrightarrow B^e$ as the natural transformation with components $B^f_d : (B^{e'})_d \longrightarrow (B^e)_d$, $B^f_d(b_1, \ldots, b_{n'}) = (b_{f(1)}, \ldots, b_{f(n)})$. It is easy to check that B^f is well defined: if $(i,j) \in e'^{(n')}$, then $(f(i), f(j)) \in e^{(n)}$ and hence $(b_{f(i)}, b_{f(j)}) \in (B \# B)_d$. The functor $B^{(\cdot)}$ is a generalization of Cartesian extension; for instance, $B^{\perp^{(2)}} = B \times B$, $B^{\top^{(2)}} = B \# B$.

We can give now a more abstract definition of $\_ \bullet B : Set^{\mathbb{D}} \to Set^{\mathbb{D}}$, for all $B \in Set^{\mathbb{D}}$. In fact, $\_ \bullet B$ arises as the left Kan extension of the functor $B^{(\_)}$:

$$
\begin{array}{ccc}
1 \xrightarrow{\;\perp^{(1)}\;} & \mathbb{D}^{op} \xrightarrow{\;\mathbf{y}\;} & Set^{\mathbb{D}} \\
& \Big\downarrow{\scriptstyle B^{(\_)}} \;\;{\scriptstyle \text{Lan}}\;\cong & \\
B \searrow & \Big\downarrow{\scriptstyle \_\bullet B} & \nearrow {\scriptstyle \langle B,\_\rangle} \\
& Set^{\mathbb{D}} &
\end{array}
\tag{10}
$$

where $\langle B, \_\rangle$ is the right adjoint of $\_ \bullet B$, defined as $\langle B, A\rangle_d = Set^{\mathbb{D}}(B^d, A)$.

Proposition 18. $(Set^{\mathbb{D}}, \bullet, Atom)$ *is a (non-symmetric) monoidal category.*

Monoids in $Set^{\mathbb{D}}$ satisfy the usual properties of clones. In particular, the multiplication $\sigma : A \bullet A \to A$ of a monoid (A, σ, v) can be seen as a *distinction-preserving* simultaneous substitution: for every $d^{(n)} \in \mathbb{D}$, σ_d maps (the class of) $(a; a_1, \ldots, a_m) \in A_e \times (A^e)_d$ to an element in A_d, making sure that distinct atoms are "replaced by" elements which are apart (if $(i, j) \in e$, then $(a_i, a_j) \in (A \# A)_d$).

As in [6, 18], the monoidal structure of $Set^{\mathbb{D}}$ can be used for characterizing presheaves coherent with apartness-preserving substitution; in particular, presheaves generated by binding signatures with constructors for distinctions, such as the signature of D-Fusion [2]. Details will appear elsewhere.

6   Self-Dual Quantifier

In this section we define a *self-dual* quantifier, in a suitable subcategory of $Set^{\mathbb{D}}$. We begin with a standard construction of categorical logic. For $A, B \in Set^{\mathbb{D}}$, let us consider the morphism $\theta : A \# B \hookrightarrow A \times B \xrightarrow{\pi} B$, given by inclusion in the cartesian product. We can define the *inverse image* of θ, $\theta^* : \mathrm{Sub}(B) \to \mathrm{Sub}(A \# B)$: for $U \in \mathrm{Sub}(A)$, the subobject $\theta^*(U) \in \mathrm{Sub}(A \# B)$ is the pullback of $U \rightarrowtail B$ along θ: $\quad \theta^*(U)_d = \{(x, y) \in (A \# B)_d \mid y \in U_d\}$.

By general and well-known results [16, 12], θ^* has both left and right adjoints, denoted by $\exists_\theta, \forall_\theta : \mathrm{Sub}(A \# B) \to \mathrm{Sub}(B)$, respectively. (If $\#$ is replaced by $\times$, these are the usual existential and universal quantifiers $\exists, \forall : \mathrm{Sub}(A \times B) \to \mathrm{Sub}(B)$.) Our aim is to prove that, under some conditions, it is $\exists_\theta = \forall_\theta$.

The condition is suggested by the following result, stating that if a property of a "well-behaved" type holds for a fresh atom, then it holds for *all* fresh atoms:

Proposition 19. *Let $B : \mathbb{D} \to Set$ be a pullback preserving functor, and let U a subobject of $Atom \# B$. Let $d \in \mathbb{D}$, and $(a, x) \in U_d$. Then for all $b \in Atom_d$ such that $b \# x$: $(b, x) \in U_d$.*

Then, we have to restrict our attention to a particular class of subobjects:

Definition 4. *Let $A : \mathbb{D} \to Set$ be an object of $Set^{\mathbb{D}}$. A subobject $U \leq A$ is closed if for all $d \in \mathbb{D}$, $f : d \to e$, $x \in A_d$: if $A_f(x) \in U_e$ then $x \in U_d$.*
The lattice of closed subobjects of A is denoted by $\mathrm{ClSub}(A)$.

However, pullback-preserving subobjects of pullback-preserving functors are automatically closed, so this requirement is implied by the first one:

Proposition 20. *Let $A : \mathbb{D} \to Set$ be a pullback preserving functor, and $U \leq A$ be a subobject of A. If also U is pullback preserving, then it is closed.*

Let us denote by $\mathcal{D}$ the full subcategory of $Set^{\mathbb{D}}$ of pullback preserving functors. By above, for all $A \in \mathcal{D}$, the lattice $\mathrm{Sub}(A)$ of pullback-preserving subobjects is $\mathrm{ClSub}(A)$, but we will keep writing $\mathrm{ClSub}(A)$ for avoiding confusions.

For "well-behaved" types, θ^* restricts to closed subobjects:

Proposition 21. *For all $A, B \in \mathcal{D}$ and $U \in \mathrm{ClSub}(A) : \theta^*(U) \in \mathrm{ClSub}(A \# B)$.*

Its left and right adjoints $\exists_\theta, \forall_\theta : \mathrm{ClSub}(A \# B) \to \mathrm{ClSub}(A)$ have the following explicit descriptions: for $U \leq A \# B$:

$$\exists_\theta(U)_d = \{y \in B_d \mid \text{there exist } f : d \to e, x \in A_e,$$
$$\text{such that } x \# B_f(y) \text{ and } (x, B_f(y)) \in U_e\}$$
$$\forall_\theta(U)_d = \{y \in B_d \mid \text{for all } f : d \to e, x \in A_e, \text{ if } x \# B_f(y) \text{ then } (x, B_f(y)) \in U_e\}$$

Proposition 22. *For all B in $\mathcal{D}$: $\theta^* \circ \exists_\theta = id_{\mathrm{ClSub}(Atom \# B)}$*

Proof. For $U \in \mathrm{ClSub}(Atom \# B)$, we have to prove that $\theta^*(\exists_\theta(U)) = U$. Inclusion $\supseteq$ is trivial. Let us prove $\subseteq$. If $(a, y) \in \theta^*(\exists_\theta(U))_d$, then $a \# y$, and by definition of $\exists_\theta$ there exist $f : d \to e$, $b \in Atom_e$ such that $(b, B_f(y)) \in U_e$ (and hence $b \# B_f(y)$). But also $f(a) \# B_f(y)$, and therefore by Proposition 19, this means that also $(f(a), B_f(y)) \in U_e$. By closure of U, it must be $(a, y) \in U_d$. $\square$

Proposition 23. *Let $B \in \mathcal{D}$, and $U \in \mathrm{ClSub}(B)$; then, for all $x \in U_d$, there exist $f : d \to e$ and $a \in Atom_e$ such that $a \# B_f(x)$.*

Proposition 24. *For all B in $\mathcal{D}$: $\exists_\theta \circ \theta^* = id_{\mathrm{ClSub}(B)}$.*

Proof. Let $U \in \mathrm{ClSub}(B)$ be a closed subobject. For any $d \in \mathbb{D}$, we have

$$\exists_\theta(\theta^*(U))_d = \{x \in B_d \mid \text{there exist } f : d \to e, a \in Atom_e,$$
$$\text{s.t. } a \# B_f(x) \text{ and } (a, B_f(x)) \in \theta^*(U)_e\}$$
$$= \{x \in B_d \mid \text{there exist } f : d \to e, a \in Atom_e, \text{ s.t. } a \# B_f(x) \text{ and } B_f(x) \in U_e\}$$
$$= \{x \in U_d \mid \text{there exist } f : d \to e, a \in Atom_e, \text{ s.t. } a \# B_f(x)\}$$

For Proposition 23 above, this is exactly equal to U_d, hence the thesis. $\square$

Corollary 2. *For $A \in \mathcal{D}$, the inverse image $\theta^* : \mathrm{ClSub}(A) \to \mathrm{ClSub}(Atom \# A)$ is an isomorphism, and hence $\theta^* \dashv \exists_\theta = \forall_\theta \dashv \theta^*$*

Let us denote by $\mathsf{И} : \mathrm{ClSub}(Atom \# A) \to \mathrm{ClSub}(A)$ any of $\exists_\theta$ and $\forall_\theta$. There is a close connection between this quantifier and Gabbay-Pitts' (hence the notation); in fact, both quantifiers enjoy the following inclusions:

Proposition 25. *Let $i : A \# B \hookrightarrow A \times B$ be the inclusion map, and $i^* : \mathrm{ClSub}(A \times B) \to \mathrm{ClSub}(A \# B)$ its inverse image. Then: $\forall \leq \mathsf{И} \circ i^* \leq \exists$, that is, for all $U \in \mathrm{ClSub}(A \times B)$: $\forall U \leq \mathsf{И}(i^*(U)) \leq \exists U$.*

7   A Model for $FO\lambda^\nabla$

In this section we apply the structure of $\mathcal{D}$ for giving a semantic interpretation of the logic $FO\lambda^\nabla$ [15]. $FO\lambda^\nabla$ is a proof theory of *generic judgments*. Terms and typing judgments $\Sigma \vdash t : \tau$ of $FO\lambda^\nabla$ are as usual for simply typed λ-calculus, signatures Σ are sets $x_1:\tau_1, \ldots, x_m:\tau_m$. Sequents have the form

$$\Sigma : \sigma_1 \rhd B_1, \ldots, \sigma_n \rhd B_n \longrightarrow \sigma_0 \rhd B_0$$

where Σ is the *global* signature, and each σ_i is a *local* signature. A judgment $\sigma_i \rhd B_i$ is called *generic*; each B_i can use variables of the global signature Σ or in the local signature σ_i (formally: $\Sigma, \sigma_i \vdash B_i : o$). See [15] for further details.

Variable symbols in $FO\lambda^\nabla$ play two different roles. Those declared in global signatures act as variables of λ-calculus; instead, variables of local signatures act as "locally scoped constants", much like restricted names of π-calculus. A model of $FO\lambda^\nabla$ must account for both aspects *at once*, and this is the reason for neither $Set^{\mathbb{F}}$ nor $Set^{\mathbb{I}}$ (and their subcategories) can suffice. We can give an interpretation of both aspects in $\mathcal{D}$, taking advantage of its structure which subsumes those of $Set^{\mathbb{F}}$ and $Set^{\mathbb{I}}$: as we will see, the dynamic allocation functor δ^-, the apartness tensor (right adjoint to δ^+) and the $\boldsymbol{\mathsf{M}}$ quantifier will come into play.

The interpretation of types and terms is standard: each type τ is interpreted as a functor $[\![\tau]\!]$ in $\mathcal{D}$; the interpretation is extended to global signatures using the cartesian product. A well-typed term $\Sigma \vdash t : \gamma$ is interpreted as a morphism (i.e., a natural transformation) $[\![t]\!] : [\![\Sigma]\!] \longrightarrow [\![\gamma]\!]$ in $\mathcal{D}$. Notice that here, "local" signatures do not have any special rôle, so that terms are simply typed λ-terms without any peculiar "freshness" or "scoping" constructor.[3]

On the other hand, in the interpretation of generic judgments we consider variables in local signatures as *distinguished* atoms. A declaration y appearing in a local signature σ, is intended as a "fresh, local" atom.

Remark 5. A correct model for $FO\lambda^\nabla$ would require a distinguished functor of atoms for each type (which can occur in local signatures) of the term language. Although it is technically possible to develop a typed version of the theory of $Set^{\mathbb{D}}$ (along the lines of [13] for $Set^{\mathbb{F}}$), it does not add anything substantial to our presentation; so in the following we assume variables of local signatures, or bound by ∇, can be only of one type (denoted by α). Hence, local signatures σ are of the form $(y_1:\alpha, \ldots, y_n:\alpha)$, or better $(y_1, \ldots, y_n)$ leaving α's implicit.   □

The distinguished type of propositions, o, is interpreted as the classifier of *(closed) subobjects*: $[\![o]\!]_d = \mathrm{ClSub}(\mathbf{y}(d)) = \mathrm{ClSub}(\mathbb{D}(d, \_))$. A generic judgment $(y_1, \ldots, y_n) \rhd B$ in Σ (i.e., $\Sigma, y_1 : \alpha, \ldots y_n : \alpha \vdash B : o$) is interpreted as a closed subobject $[\![(y_1, \ldots, y_n) \rhd B]\!]_{[\![\Sigma]\!]} \leq [\![\Sigma]\!]$. More precisely, $[\![\sigma \rhd B]\!]_A \in \mathrm{ClSub}(A)$ is defined first by induction on the length of the local context σ, and then by structural induction on B. Local declarations and the ∇ quantifier are rendered by the functor $\boldsymbol{\mathsf{M}} : \mathrm{ClSub}(A \# Atom) \to \mathrm{ClSub}(A)$ above. Some interesting cases:

---

[3] As Miller and Tiu say, this is a precise choice in the design of $FO\lambda^\nabla$, motivated by the fact that standard unification algorithms still work unchanged.

$$[\![(y,\sigma) \triangleright B]\!]_A \triangleq \mathsf{M}([\![\sigma \triangleright B]\!]_{A\#Atom}) \qquad [\![\triangleright B_1 \wedge B_2]\!]_A \triangleq [\![\triangleright B_1]\!]_A \wedge [\![\triangleright B_2]\!]_A$$

$$[\![\triangleright \nabla y.B]\!]_A \triangleq \mathsf{M}([\![\triangleright B]\!]_{A\#Atom}) \qquad [\![\triangleright \forall_\gamma x.B]\!]_A \triangleq \forall([\![\triangleright B]\!]_{A\times[\![\gamma]\!]})$$

It is easy to prove by induction on σ that $[\![(\sigma,y) \triangleright B]\!]_A = [\![\sigma \triangleright \nabla y.B]\!]_A$.

Finally, a sequent $\Sigma : \mathcal{B}_1,\ldots,\mathcal{B}_n \longrightarrow \mathcal{B}_0$ is *valid* if $\bigwedge_{i=1}^n [\![\mathcal{B}_i]\!]_{[\![\Sigma]\!]} \leq [\![\mathcal{B}_0]\!]_{[\![\Sigma]\!]}$. A rule $\frac{\mathcal{S}_1\ldots\mathcal{S}_n}{\mathcal{S}}$ is *sound* if, whenever all $\mathcal{S}_1,\ldots,\mathcal{S}_n$ are valid, also $\mathcal{S}$ is valid.

Using this interpretation, one can check that the rules of $FO\lambda^\nabla$ are sound. In particular, the rules $\nabla\mathcal{L}$ and $\nabla\mathcal{R}$ are trivial consequence of above. The verification of $\forall\mathcal{R}$, and $\exists\mathcal{L}$ requires some work. Here, we have to give a categorical account of a particular encoding technique, called *raising*, used to "gain access" to local constants from "outside" their scope. A simpler (i.e., monadic) application of raising occurs, in the following equivalence, which is provable in $FO\lambda^\nabla$:

$$\nabla x \forall_\gamma y.B \equiv \forall_{\alpha\to\gamma} h \nabla x.B[(h\ x)/y] \qquad \text{where } \Sigma, x : \alpha, y : \gamma \vdash B : o \qquad (11)$$

We show first how to represent (monadic) raising as in the equation 11; interestingly, it is here where the δ^- comes into play. Referring to equation 11, let us denote $A = [\![\Sigma]\!]$ and $C = [\![\gamma]\!]$. By the definition above, the interpretation of B is a subobject of $(A \# Atom) \times C$, while $B[(h\ x)/y]$ corresponds to a subobject of $(A \times C^{Atom}) \# Atom$. Now, notice that $C^{Atom} = \delta^- C$ (Proposition 5); thus, $h : \alpha \to \gamma$ is actually a term $[\![h]\!] \in \delta^- C$, that is a term which can make use of a locally declared *variable*. We can define the *raising* morphism

$$\mathsf{r} : (A \times \delta^- C) \# Atom \to (A \# Atom) \times C \quad \text{mapping} \quad (x,h,a) \mapsto (x,a,h(a))$$

The inverse image of r is $\mathsf{r}^* : \mathrm{ClSub}((A \# Atom) \times C) \to \mathrm{ClSub}((A \times \delta^- C) \# Atom)$, defined by the following pullback:

$$
\begin{array}{ccc}
\mathsf{r}^*(U) & \longrightarrow & U \\
\downarrow & & \downarrow \\
(A \times \delta^- C) \# Atom & \xrightarrow{\ \mathsf{r}\ } & (A \# Atom) \times C
\end{array}
$$

This morphism r^* is the categorical counterpart of the syntactic raising:

Proposition 26. *Let* $\Sigma, x{:}\alpha, y{:}\gamma \vdash B : o$. *Let us denote* $A = [\![\Sigma]\!]$, $C = [\![\gamma]\!]$. *Then,* $\mathsf{r}^*([\![y \triangleright B]\!]_C) = [\![y \triangleright B[(h\ y)/x]]\!]_{A\times\delta^- C}$.

Then, quite obviously, the equation 11 states that $\mathsf{M} \circ \forall_\gamma = \forall_{\alpha\to\gamma} \circ \mathsf{M} \circ \mathsf{r}^*$, that is, the following diagram commutes:

$$
\begin{array}{ccc}
\mathrm{ClSub}((A \# Atom) \times C) \xrightarrow{\ \mathsf{r}^*\ } \mathrm{ClSub}((A \times \delta^- C) \# Atom) \longrightarrow \mathrm{ClSub}(A \times \delta^- C) \\
\downarrow{\scriptstyle\forall_\gamma} \qquad\qquad\qquad\qquad\qquad\qquad\qquad\qquad\qquad \downarrow{\scriptstyle\forall_{\alpha\to\gamma}} \\
\mathrm{ClSub}(A \# Atom) \longrightarrow\qquad\qquad\qquad\qquad\qquad\qquad \mathrm{ClSub}(A)
\end{array}
$$

which can be checked by calculation. The raising morphism can be easily generalized to the polyadic case (recall that $B^{\top^{(n)}} = B \# \cdots \# B$, n times):

$$r : (A \times \delta^{-n}C) \# Atom^{\top^{(n)}} \to (A \# Atom^{\top^{(n)}}) \times C$$
$$(x, h, a_1, \ldots, a_n) \mapsto (x, a_1, \ldots, a_n, h(a_1, \ldots, a_n))$$

Then, the soundness of the rule $\forall \mathcal{R}$ is equivalent to the following:

Proposition 27. *Let $A, C \in \mathcal{D}$ be functors, and $n \in \mathbb{N}$. Let $\pi : A \times \delta^{-n}C \to A$ be the projection, and $r : (A \times \delta^{-n}C) \# Atom^{\top^{(n)}} \longrightarrow (A \# Atom^{\top^{(n)}}) \times C$ the raising morphism. For all $G \in \mathrm{ClSub}(A)$, and $U \in \mathrm{ClSub}((A \# Atom^{\top^{(n)}}) \times C)$, if $\pi^*(G) \leq \mathsf{N}^n(r^*(U))$ then $G \leq \mathsf{N}^n(\forall_\gamma(U))$.*

8   Conclusions

In this paper, we have studied a new model for dynamically allocable entities, based on the notion of *distinction*. Previous models for variables and for names can be embedded faithfully in this model, and also results about initial algebras/final coalgebras and simultaneous substitutions are extended to the more general setting. In a suitable subcategory of the model, it is possible to define also a self-dual quantifier, similar to Gabbay-Pitts' "N". This rich structure has allowed us to define the first denotational model for the logic $FO\lambda^\nabla$.

Future work. The rich structure of $Set^{\mathbb{D}}$ can be useful also for modeling process calculi featuring both variables and names at once, like e.g. ambients. Actually, the intuition behind distinctions is also at the base of the *D-Fusion* calculus [2]; in fact, we think that the two binders λ, ν of D-Fusion can be modeled precisely by δ^- and δ^+ in $Set^{\mathbb{D}}$, respectively. Details will appear elsewhere.

$FO\lambda^\nabla$ is not complete with respect to the model presented in this paper: the N quantifier enjoys properties which are not derivable in $FO\lambda^\nabla$ (e.g., $\forall x.B \supset \nabla x.B$ and $\nabla x.B \supset \exists x.B$). One main reason is that $FO\lambda^\nabla$ does not admit *weakening on local signature*; for instance, the sequent $\Sigma : \sigma \triangleright B \longrightarrow (\sigma, y) \triangleright B$ is not derivable. This has been already noticed by Gabbay and Cheney, in their interpretation of $FO\lambda^\nabla$ into *Fresh Logic* [7], another first-order logic with a self-dual quantifier. Actually, we think that the N quantifier of $\mathcal{D}$ is closer to the N quantifier of Fresh Logic, than to the ∇ of $FO\lambda^\nabla$. For this reason, it should be possible to model Fresh Logic in $\mathcal{D}$ quite easily—another future work.

Acknowledgments. The authors wish to thank Dale Miller and Alwen Tiu for useful discussions about $FO\lambda^\nabla$, and Neil Ghani for hints about Kan extensions.

References

1. J. Adamek, editor. *Coalgebraic Methods in Computer Science*, ENTCS. 2004.
2. M. Boreale, M. G. Buscemi, and U. Montanari. D-fusion: A distinctive fusion calculus. In *Proc. APLAS'04*, LNCS 3302, pages 296–310. Springer, 2004.

3. B. J. Day. On closed categories of functors. In *Reports of the Midwest Category Seminar*, volume 137 of *Lecture Notes in Mathematics*, pages 1–38. Springer, 1970.

4. M. Fiore and S. Staton. Comparing operational models of name-passing process calculi. In Adamek [1].

5. M. Fiore and D. Turi. Semantics of name and value passing. In H. Mairson, editor, *Proc. 16th LICS*, pages 93–104, 2001.IEEE.

6. M. Fiore, G. Plotkin, and D. Turi. Abstract syntax and variable binding. In [11].

7. M. Gabbay and J. Cheney. A sequent calculus for nominal logic. In *Proc. LICS'04*, pages 139–148. IEEE Computer Society, 2004.

8. M. J. Gabbay and A. M. Pitts. A new approach to abstract syntax with variable binding. *Formal Aspects of Computing*, 13:341–363, 2002.

9. N. Ghani, K. Yemane, and B. Victor. Relationally staged computation in calculi of mobile processes. In Adamek [1].

10. M. Hofmann. Semantical analysis of higher-order abstract syntax. In Longo [11].

11. G. Longo, editor. *Proc. 14th Symp. of Logic in Computer Science*, 1999. IEEE.

12. S. Mac Lane and I. Moerdijk. *Sheaves in Geometry and Logic*. Springer, 1994.

13. M. Miculan and I. Scagnetto. A framework for typed HOAS and semantics. In *Proc. PPDP'03*, pages 184–194. ACM Press, 2003.

14. M. Miculan and K. Yemane. A unifying model of variables and names. TR UDMI/15/2004/RR, Dept. of Mathematics and Computing Science, Univ. of Udine, 2004. http://www.dimi.uniud.it/miculan/Papers/UDMI152004.pdf.

15. D. Miller and A. F. Tiu. A proof theory for generic judgments: An extended abstract. In *LICS 2003*, pages 118–127, 2003. IEEE.

16. A. M. Pitts. Categorical logic. In *Handbook of LICS*, vol. 5. OUP, 2000.

17. A. M. Pitts. Nominal logic, a first order theory of names and binding. *Information and Computation*, 186:165–193, 2003.

18. J. Power and M. Tanaka. Binding signatures for generic contexts. In *Proc. TLCA'05*, LNCS ?. Springer, 2005.

19. I. Stark. A fully abstract domain model for the π-calculus. In *Proc. LICS'96*.

A Category of Higher-Dimensional Automata

Ulrich Fahrenberg

Dept. of Mathematical Sciences, Aalborg University, Denmark
uli@math.aau.dk

Abstract. We show how parallel composition of higher-dimensional automata (HDA) can be expressed categorically in the spirit of Winskel & Nielsen. Employing the notion of computation path introduced by van Glabbeek, we define a new notion of bisimulation of HDA using open maps. We derive a connection between computation paths and carrier sequences of dipaths and show that bisimilarity of HDA can be decided by the use of geometric techniques.

Keywords: Higher-dimensional automata, bisimulation, open maps, directed topology, fibrations.

1   Introduction

In his invited talk at the 2004 EXPRESS workshop, van Glabbeek [11] put higher-dimensional automata (HDA) on top of a hierarchy of models for concurrency. In this article we develop a categorical framework for expressing constructions on HDA, building on work by Goubault in [12, 13].

Following up on a concluding remark in [13], we introduce a notion of bisimulation of HDA, both as a relation and using open maps [19]. Our notion differs from the ones introduced by van Glabbeek [10] and Cattani-Sassone [4].

Employing recent developments by Fajstrup [8], we show that bisimilarity of HDA is equivalent to a certain dipath-lifting property, which can be attacked using (directed) homotopy techniques. This confirms a prediction from [13].

Due to space limitations, we had to omit some of the more technical points in this paper. An extended version is published in [6].

The author is indebted to Eric Goubault and Emmanuel Haucourt for many valuable discussions during his visit at CEA in Paris, and to Lisbeth Fajstrup and Martin Raussen at the Department of Mathematical Sciences in Aalborg.

2   Cubical Sets

Cubical sets were introduced by Serre in [22] and have a variety of applications in algebraic topology, both in homology, cf. [20], and in homotopy theory, cf. [2, 5, 18]. Compared to the more well-known simplicial sets, they have the distinct advantage that they have a natural sense of (local) direction induced by the order

V. Sassone (Ed.): FOSSACS 2005, LNCS 3441, pp. 187–201, 2005.

on the unit interval. This makes them well-suited for applications in concurrency theory, cf. [9].

A *precubical set* is a graded set $X = \{X_n\}_{n \in \mathbb{N}}$ together with mappings $\delta^\nu_{i(n)}$: $X_n \to X_{n-1}$, $i = 1, \ldots, n$, $\nu = 0, 1$, satisfying the *precubical identity*

$$\delta^\nu_i \delta^\mu_j = \delta^\mu_{j-1} \delta^\nu_i \quad (i < j) \tag{1}$$

These are called *face maps*, and if $x = \delta^{\nu_1}_{i_1} \cdots \delta^{\nu_n}_{i_n} y$ for some cubes x, y and some (possibly empty) sequences of indices, then x is called a *face* of y. If all $\nu_i = 0$, x is said to be a *lower face* of y; if all $\nu_i = 1$, x is an *upper face* of y.

As above, we shall omit the subscript (n) in $\delta^\nu_{i(n)}$ whenever possible. Elements of X_n are called *n-cubes*.

A *cubical set* is a precubical set X together with mappings $\epsilon_{i(n)} : X_n \to X_{n+1}$, $i = 1, \ldots, n+1$, such that

$$\epsilon_i \epsilon_j = \epsilon_{j+1} \epsilon_i \quad (i \le j) \qquad \delta^\nu_i \epsilon_j = \begin{cases} \epsilon_{j-1} \delta^\nu_i & (i < j) \\ \epsilon_j \delta^\nu_{i-1} & (i > j) \\ \text{id} & (i = j) \end{cases} \tag{2}$$

These are called *degeneracies*, and equations (1) and (2) together form the *cubical identities*.

The standard example of a cubical set is the singular cubical complex of a topological space, cf. [20]: If X is a topological space, let $S_n X = \mathsf{Top}(I^n, X)$, the set of all continuous maps $I^n \to X$, where I is the unit interval. If the maps δ^ν_i and ϵ_i are given by

$$\delta^\nu_i f(t_1, \ldots, t_{n-1}) = f(t_1, \ldots, t_{i-1}, \nu, t_i, \ldots, t_{n-1})$$
$$\epsilon_i f(t_1, \ldots, t_n) = f(t_1, \ldots, \hat{t}_i, \ldots, t_n)$$

(the notation $\hat{t}_i$ means that t_i is omitted) then $SX = \{S_n X\}$ is a cubical set.

Morphisms of (pre)cubical sets are required to commute with the structure maps, i.e. if X, Y are two (pre)cubical sets, then a morphism $f : X \to Y$ is a sequence of mappings $f = \{f_n : X_n \to Y_n\}$ that fulfill the first, respectively both, of the equations

$$\delta^\nu_i f_n = f_{n-1} \delta^\nu_i \qquad \epsilon_i f_n = f_{n+1} \epsilon_i$$

This defines two categories, pCub and Cub, both of which are presheaf categories over certain small categories of *elementary cubes*, cf. [17], hence they are Cartesian closed, complete, and cocomplete. The forgetful functor

$$\mathsf{Cub} \longrightarrow \mathsf{pCub}$$

has a left adjoint, providing us with a "free" functor in the opposite direction which we shall denote F.

A (pre)cubical set $X = \{X_n\}$ is said to be *k-dimensional* if $X_n = \emptyset$ for $n > k$. The full subcategories of k-dimensional objects in our cubical categories are denoted pCub^k respectively Cub^k. The free-forgetful adjunction above passes to the k-dimensional categories.

3   Product and Tensor Product

The *product* of two (pre)cubical sets is given by

$$(X \times Y)_n = X_n \times Y_n$$

with face maps and degeneracies defined component-wise. This is a product in the categorical sense. A *(pre)cubical relation* between (pre)cubical sets X, Y is a (pre)cubical subset of the product $X \times Y$.

The *tensor product* of two *precubical* sets $Z = X \otimes Y$ is given by

$$Z_n = \bigsqcup_{p+q=n} X_p \times Y_q$$

with face maps

$$\delta_i^\alpha(x, y) = \begin{cases} (\delta_i^\alpha x, y) & (i \leq p) \\ (x, \delta_{i-p}^\alpha y) & (i \geq p+1) \end{cases} \qquad (x, y) \in X_p \times Y_q$$

The category Cub inherits this tensor product, however some identifications have to be made to get well-defined degeneracy maps, cf. [3]. The tensor product of two *cubical* sets $Z = X \otimes Y$ is then given by

$$Z_n = \left(\bigsqcup_{p+q=n} X_p \times Y_q \right) \Big/ \sim_n$$

where $\sim_n$ is the equivalence relation generated by, for all $(x, y) \in X_r \times Y_s$, $r + s = n - 1$, letting $(\epsilon_{r+1} x, y) \sim_n (x, \epsilon_1 y)$. If $x \otimes y$ denotes the equivalence class of $(x, y) \in X_p \times Y_q$ under $\sim_n$, the face maps and degeneracies of Z are given by

$$\delta_i^\alpha(x \otimes y) = \begin{cases} \delta_i^\alpha x \otimes y & (i \leq p) \\ x \otimes \delta_{i-p}^\alpha y & (i \geq p+1) \end{cases} \qquad \epsilon_i(x \otimes y) = \begin{cases} \epsilon_i x \otimes y & (i \leq p+1) \\ x \otimes \epsilon_{i-p} y & (i \geq p+1) \end{cases}$$

4   Transition Systems

We shall construct our category of higher-dimensional automata as a special arrow category in Cub. To warm up, we include a section on how *transition systems* can be understood as an arrow category in Cub^1, the category of *digraphs*. Though our exposition differs considerably from the standard one, see e.g. [23], the end result is basically the same.

A *digraph* is a 1-dimensional cubical set, i.e. a pair of sets (X_1, X_0) together with face maps $\delta^0, \delta^1 : X_1 \to X_0$ and a degeneracy mapping $\epsilon = \epsilon_1 : X_0 \to X_1$ such that $\delta^0 \epsilon = \delta^1 \epsilon = \mathrm{id}$. Morphisms of digraphs (X_1, X_0), (Y_1, Y_0) are thus mappings $f = (f_1, f_0)$ commuting with the face and degeneracy mappings. A *predigraph* is a 1-dimensional precubical set. Note that we allow both loops and multiple edges in our digraphs.

The category of digraphs has a terminal object $*$ consisting of a single vertex and the degeneracy edge on that vertex. A *transition system* is a digraph which is freely generated by a predigraph together with a specified initial point, hence the category of transition systems is $\langle * \downarrow F\mathsf{pCub}^1 \rangle$, the comma category of digraphs freely generated by predigraphs under $*$. In the spirit of [23], passing from a predigraph to the digraph freely generated by it means that we add *idle loops* to each vertex, hence allowing for transition system morphisms which collapse transitions.

As for labeling transition systems, we note that there is an isomorphism between the category of finite sets and the full subcategory of pCub^1 induced by finite one-point predigraphs, given by mapping a finite set Σ to the one-point predigraph with edge set Σ. Identifying finite sets with the digraphs freely generated by their associated predigraphs, we define a *labeled transition system* over Σ to be a digraph morphism $\lambda : \langle * \downarrow F\mathsf{pCub}^1 \rangle \rightarrow \Sigma$ which is induced by a predigraph morphism. This last convention is to ensure that idle loops are labeled with the *idle label* $\epsilon *$.

Say that a morphism $\lambda \in \mathsf{Cub}^1$ is *non-contracting* if $\lambda a = \epsilon *$ implies $a = \epsilon \delta^0 a$ for all edges a, and note that if the source and target of λ are freely generated by precubical sets, then λ is non-contracting if and only if it is in the image of the free functor $\mathsf{pCub}^1 \rightarrow \mathsf{Cub}^1$.

For morphisms between labeled transition systems we need to allow functions that map labels to "nothing," i.e. *partial* alphabet functions. The category of finite sets with partial mappings is isomorphic to the full subcategory Σ of Cub^1 induced by digraphs freely generated by finite one-point predigraphs. Hence we can define the category of labeled transition systems to be the *non-contracting comma-arrow category* $\langle * \downarrow F\mathsf{pCub}^1 \rightrightarrows \Sigma \rangle$, with objects pairs of morphisms—the second one non-contracting

$$* \longrightarrow X \Longrightarrow \Sigma$$

and morphisms pairs of arrows making the following square commute:

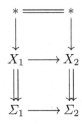

We shall always visualise non-contracting morphisms by double arrows.

Note that our transition systems have the special feature that there can be more than one transition with a given label between a pair of edges; in the terminology of [23] they are not *extensional*. Except for that, our definition is in accordance with the standards.

To express parallel composition of transition systems, we follow the approach of [23] and use a combination of product, relabeling and restriction. In our context, the product of two transition systems $* \rightarrow X_1 \rightarrow \Sigma_1$, $* \rightarrow X_2 \rightarrow \Sigma_2$ is the transition system $* \longrightarrow X_1 \times X_2 \xrightarrow{\lambda} \Sigma_1 \times \Sigma_2$, where the arrow λ is given by the universal property of the product $\Sigma_1 \times \Sigma_2$. We note that, indeed, the product of two one-point digraphs with edge sets Σ_1 respectively Σ_2 is again a one-point digraph, with edge set

$$\{(a, b), (a, \epsilon*), (\epsilon*, b) \mid a \in \Sigma_1, b \in \Sigma_2\}$$

One easily shows λ to be non-contracting, and the so-defined product is in fact the categorical product in the category $\langle * \downarrow FpCub^1 \Rightarrow \Sigma \rangle$.

A relabeling of a transition system is a non-contracting alphabet morphism under the identity, i.e. an arrow in $\langle * \downarrow FpCub^1 \Rightarrow \Sigma \rangle$ of the form

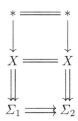

Restriction of transition systems is defined using pullbacks; given a transition system $* \to X_2 \to \Sigma_2$ and a mapping $\sigma : \Sigma_1 \to \Sigma_2$, we define the restriction of X_2 to Σ_1 by the pullback

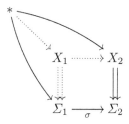

where the mapping $* \to \Sigma_1$ is uniquely determined as Σ_1 is a one-point digraph. It is not difficult to show that the so-defined morphism $X_1 \to \Sigma_1$ is in fact non-contracting.

5   Higher-Dimensional Automata

The category Cub has a terminal object $*$ consisting of a single point and all its higher-dimensional degeneracies. The category of higher-dimensional automata is the comma category $\langle * \downarrow FpCub \rangle$, with objects cubical sets freely generated by precubical sets with a specified initial 0-cube.

For labeling HDA, we follow the approach laid out in [12, 13]. We assume the finite set Σ of labels to be *totally ordered* and define a precubical set $!\Sigma'$ as follows: $!\Sigma'_0 = \{*\}$, $!\Sigma'_n$ is the set of (not necessarily strictly) increasing sequences of length n of elements of Σ, and

$$\delta^{\alpha}_{i(n)}(x_1, \ldots, x_n) = (x_1, \ldots, \hat{x}_i, \ldots, x_n)$$

Then we let $!\Sigma$ be the free cubical set on $!\Sigma'$.

Let $!\Sigma$ be the full subcategory of Cub induced by the cubical sets $!\Sigma$ as above. We show in [6] that $!\Sigma$, like the category Σ in the preceding section, is isomorphic to the category of finite sets and partial (and not necessarily order-preserving) mappings.

Define a morphism $f : X \to Y$ of cubical sets to be *non-contracting* if $f(x) = \epsilon_i \delta_i^0 f(x)$ implies $x = \epsilon_i \delta_i^0 x$ for all $x \in X_n$, $n \in \mathbb{N}$, $i = 1, \dots, n$. Note again that if the cubical sets X, Y are freely generated by precubical sets, then a morphism $f : X \to Y$ is non-contracting if and only if it is the image of a precubical morphism under the free functor.

The category of *labeled higher-dimensional automata* is then defined to be $\langle * \downarrow F\mathsf{pCub} \rightrightarrows !\Sigma \rangle$, with objects $* \longrightarrow X \rightrightarrows !\Sigma$ and morphisms commutative diagrams

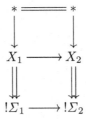

Note that by this construction, the label of an n-cube is the ordered n-tuple of the labels of all its 1-faces.

6   Constructions on HDA

As in [12], we replace the product of transition systems by the *tensor product* of higher-dimensional automata. The tensor product of two HDA $* \to X_1 \xrightarrow{\lambda} !\Sigma_1$, $* \to X_2 \xrightarrow{\mu} !\Sigma_2$ is defined to be

$$* \longrightarrow X_1 \otimes X_2 \xrightarrow{\lambda \otimes \mu} !\Sigma_1 \otimes !\Sigma_2$$

The following lemma, where $\Sigma_1 \uplus \Sigma_2$ denotes the disjoint union of Σ_1 and Σ_2 with the order induced by declaring $\Sigma_1 < \Sigma_2$, ensures that this in fact a HDA:

Lemma 1. *Given alphabets Σ_1, Σ_2, then $!\Sigma_1 \otimes !\Sigma_2 = !(\Sigma_1 \uplus \Sigma_2)$.*

For relabeling HDA we use non-contracting morphisms under the identity, and we note that if g is defined by the diagram

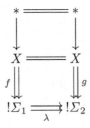

then non-contract ability of g follows from f and λ being non-contracting.

If we want to express the tensor product of two HDA $* \to X \to !\Sigma_1$, $* \to Y \to !\Sigma_2$ with *non-disjoint* alphabets Σ_1, Σ_2, we can do so by following the tensor product above with a relabeling $!\Sigma_1 \otimes !\Sigma_2 \to !(\Sigma_1 \cup \Sigma_2)$ induced by the natural projection $\Sigma_1 \uplus \Sigma_2 \to \Sigma_1 \cup \Sigma_2$ (which is not necessarily order-preserving). This projection is a *total* alphabet morphism, hence the relabeling map is indeed non-contracting.

For restrictions we again use pullbacks:

Proposition 1. *Given a higher-dimensional automaton $* \to X_2 \to !\Sigma_2$ and an injective mapping $!\Sigma_1 \to !\Sigma_2$, then $* \to X_1 \to !\Sigma_1$ as defined by the pullback diagram*

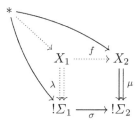

is again a higher-dimensional automaton.

The arrow $* \to !\Sigma_1$ is uniquely determined as $!\Sigma_1$ has only one cube in dimension zero. We will need the injectivity of σ later, to show that our to-be-defined notion of bisimilarity is respected by restrictions.

7   Bisimulation

In this section we fix a labeling cubical set L and work in the non-contracting double comma category $\langle * \downarrow \mathsf{FpCub} \Downarrow L \rangle$ of HDA over L. The morphisms

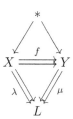

in this category respect labelings, hence they are non-contracting themselves: If $f(x) = \epsilon_i \delta_i^0 f(x)$ for some $x \in X$ and some i, then $\lambda(x) = \mu(f(x)) = \epsilon_i \delta_i^0 \lambda(x)$ and thus $x = \epsilon_i \delta_i^0 x$.

A *computation path*, cf. [10], in a precubical set X is a finite sequence $(x_1, \ldots, x_n)$ of cubes of X such that for each $k = 1, \ldots, n-1$, either $x_k = \delta_i^0 x_{k+1}$ or $x_{k+1} = \delta_i^1 x_k$ for some i. A computation path $(x_1, \ldots, x_n)$ is said to be *acyclic* if there are no other relations between the x_i than the ones above. A *rooted* computation path in a HDA $* \xrightarrow{i} X$ is a computation path $(i*, \ldots, x_n)$, and a

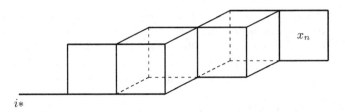

Fig. 1. An acyclic rooted computation path which ends in a 2-cube x_n

cube x of the HDA is said to be *reachable* if there is a rooted computation path $(i*, \ldots, x)$. Figure 1 shows an example of an acyclic rooted computation path.

We say that a precubical set X *is* a computation path if there is a computation path $(x_1, \ldots, x_n)$ of cubes in X such that all other cubes in X are faces of one of the x_i, and similarly for acyclic computation paths. An *elementary computation step* is an inclusion $(x_1, \ldots, x_n) \hookrightarrow (x_1, \ldots, x_n, x_{n+1})$ of computation paths.

Let CPath be the full subcategory of the category of HDA induced by the acyclic rooted computation paths, then it is not difficult to see that any morphism in CPath is a finite composite of elementary computation steps and isomorphisms.

Following the terminology of [19], we say that a morphism $f : X \to Y$ is CPath-open if it has the right-lifting property with respect to morphisms in CPath. That is, we require that for any morphism $m : P \to Q \in$ CPath and any commutative diagram as below, there exists a morphism r filling in the diagram

Lemma 2. *A morphism $f : X \to Y$ is CPath-open if and only if it satisfies the property that for any reachable $x \in X$ and for any $z' \in Y$ such that $f(x) = \delta_i^0 z'$ for some i, there is a $z \in X$ such that $x = \delta_i^0 z$ and $z' = f(z)$.*

Following established terminology, this could be called a "higher-dimensional zig-zag property."

This suggests the following definition of bisimulation of HDA: Given two HDA $* \xrightarrow{i} X \xrightarrow{\lambda} L$, $* \xrightarrow{j} Y \xrightarrow{\mu} L$ over the same alphabet, then a bisimulation of X and Y is a cubical relation $R \subseteq X \times Y$ which respects initial states and labelings, i.e. $(i*, j*) \in R_0$, and if $(x, y) \in R$ then $\lambda x = \mu y$; and for all reachable $x \in X$, $y \in Y$ such that $(x, y) \in R$,

- if $x = \delta_i^0 z$ for some z, then $y = \delta_i^0 z'$ for some z' so that $(z, z') \in R$,
- if $y = \delta_i^0 z'$ for some z', then $x = \delta_i^0 z$ for some z so that $(z, z') \in R$.

Note that bisimilarity is indeed an equivalence relation.

Proposition 2. *Two HDA Y, Z are bisimilar if and only if there is a span of CPath-open maps $Y \leftarrow X \rightarrow Z$.*

Note that when restricted to labeled transition systems, bisimulation of HDA is equivalent to strong bisimulation [21], the only difference being that strong bisimulation requires the *existence* of corresponding transitions, whereas HDA-bisimulation actually *specifies* a correspondence.

8 Bisimulation is a Congruence

We show that bisimulation is a congruence with respect to the constructions on HDA introduced in Section 6. For relabelings this is clear, and for tensor product we have the following lemma.

Lemma 3. *Given CPath-open morphisms $f \in \langle * \downarrow F\mathsf{pCub} \Downarrow L \rangle$, $g \in \langle * \downarrow F\mathsf{pCub} \downarrow \downarrow M \rangle$, then $f \otimes g \in \langle * \downarrow F\mathsf{pCub} \Downarrow L \otimes M \rangle$ is again CPath-open.*

Hence if we have spans of CPath-open morphisms $Y_1 \xleftarrow{f_1} X_1 \xrightarrow{g_1} Z_1$, $Y_2 \xleftarrow{f_2} X_2 \xrightarrow{g_2} Z_2$, then $Y_1 \otimes Y_2$ and $Z_1 \otimes Z_2$ are bisimilar via the span of CPath-open morphisms $Y_1 \otimes Y_2 \xleftarrow{f_1 \otimes f_2} X_1 \otimes X_2 \xrightarrow{g_1 \otimes g_2} Z_1 \otimes Z_2$.

Congruency of bisimilarity with respect to restriction is implied by the next lemma.

Lemma 4. *Given a CPath-open morphism $f : X \rightarrow Y \in \langle * \downarrow F\mathsf{pCub} \Downarrow L \rangle$ and a non-contracting injective morphism $\sigma : L' \rightarrow L$, then the unique morphism $f' : X' \rightarrow Y'$ defined by the double pullback diagram*

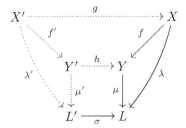

is again CPath-open.

Hence if $Y, Z \in \langle * \downarrow F\mathsf{pCub} \Downarrow L \rangle$ are bisimilar via a span of CPath-open maps $Y \leftarrow X \rightarrow Z$, the above lemma yields a span of CPath-open maps $Y' \leftarrow X' \rightarrow Z'$ of their restrictions to L'.

9 Geometric Realisation of Precubical Sets

We want to relate CPath-openness of a morphism of higher-dimensional automata to a *geometric* property of the underlying precubical sets. In order to do that, we need to recall some of the technical apparatus developed in [9, 8].

The *geometric realisation* of a precubical set X is the topological space

$$|X| = \bigsqcup_{n \in \mathbb{N}} X_n \times [0,1]^n / \equiv$$

where the equivalence relation $\equiv$ is induced by identifying

$$(\delta_i^\nu x; t_1, \ldots, t_{n-1}) \equiv (x; t_1, \ldots, t_{i-1}, \nu, t_i, \ldots, t_{n-1})$$

for all $x \in X_n$, $n \in \mathbb{N}$, $i = 1, \ldots, n$, $\nu = 0, 1$, $t_i \in [0,1]$. Geometric realisation is turned into a functor from pCub to Top by mapping $f : X \to Y \in$ pCub to the function $|f| : |X| \to |Y|$ defined by

$$|f|(x; t_1, \ldots, t_n) = (f(x); t_1, \ldots, t_n)$$

This is similar to the well-known geometric realisation functor from *simplicial* sets to topological spaces, cf. [1].

Given $x \in X_n \in X$, we denote its image in the geometric realisation by $|x| = \{(x; t_1, \ldots, t_n) \mid t_i \in [0,1]\} \subseteq |X|$. The *carrier*, carr z, of a point $z \in |X|$ is z itself if $z \in X_0$, or else the unique cube $x \in X$ such that $z \in$ int $|x|$, the interior of $|x|$. The *star* of z is the open set

$$\mathrm{St}\, z = \{z' \in |X| \mid \mathrm{carr}\, z \triangleleft \mathrm{carr}\, z'\}$$

There is a natural order on the cubes $[0,1]^n$ which is "forgotten" in the transition pCub $\longrightarrow$ Top. One can recover some of this structure by instead defining functors from pCub to the *d-spaces* or the *spaces with distinguished cubes* of M. Grandis [14, 15, 16], however here we take a different approach as laid out in [9].

Given a precubical set X and $x, y \in X$, we write $x \triangleleft y$ if x is a face of y. This defines a preorder $\triangleleft$ on X. If x is a lower face of y we write $x \triangleleft^- y$, if it is an upper face we write $x \triangleleft^+ y$. The precubical set X is said to be *locally finite* if the set $\{y \in X \mid x \triangleleft y\}$ is finite for all $x \in X_0$.

Define a precubical set X to be *non-selflinked* if $\delta_i^\nu x = \delta_j^\mu x$ implies $i = j$, $\nu = \mu$ for all $x \in X$, $i, j \in \mathbb{N}_+$, $\nu, \mu \in \{0, 1\}$. Note [9–Lemma 6.16]: If $x \triangleleft y$ in a non-selflinked precubical set, then there are *unique* sequences $\nu_1, \ldots, \nu_\ell$, $i_1 < \cdots < i_\ell$ such that $x = \delta_{i_1}^{\nu_1} \cdots \delta_{i_\ell}^{\nu_\ell} y$.

The geometric realisation of a non-selflinked precubical set contains no self-intersections; if $(x, s_1, \ldots, s_n) \equiv (x, t_1, \ldots, t_n)$, then $s_i = t_i$ for all $i = 1, \ldots, n$. By [9–Thm. 6.27], the geometric realisation of a non-selflinked precubical set is a *local po-space*; a Hausdorff topological space with a relation $\leq$ which is reflexive, antisymmetric, and *locally* transitive, i.e. transitive in each U_α for some collection $\mathcal{U} = \{U_\alpha\}$ of open sets covering X. In our case, the relation $\leq$ is induced by the natural partial orders on the unit cubes $[0,1]^n$, and a covering $\mathcal{U}$ is given by the stars $\mathrm{St}|x|$ of all vertices $x \in X_0$.

A *dimap* between local po-spaces $(X, \leq_X)$, $(Y, \leq_Y)$ is a continuous mapping $f : X \to Y$ which is *locally increasing*: for any $x \in X$ there is an open neighbourhood $U \ni x$ such that for all $x_1 \leq_X x_2 \in U$, $f(x_1) \leq_Y f(x_2)$. Local po-spaces and dimaps form a category IpoTop, and by [9–Prop. 6.38], geometric realisation is a functor from non-selflinked precubical sets to local po-spaces.

Let $\vec{I}$ denote the unit interval $[0, 1]$ with the natural (total) order, and define a *dipath* in a local po-space $(S, \leq)$ to be a dimap $p : \vec{I} \to S$. We recall [8–Def. 2.17]: Given a locally finite precubical set X and a dipath $p : \vec{I} \to |X|$, then there exists a partition of the unit interval $0 = t_1 \leq \cdots \leq t_{k+1} = 1$ and a unique sequence $x_1, \ldots, x_k \in X$ such that

- $x_i \neq x_{i+1}$
- $t \in [t_i, t_{i+1}]$ implies $p(t) \in |x_i|$
- $t \in]t_i, t_{i+1}[$ implies carr $p(t) = x_i$
- carr $p(t_i) \in \{x_{i-1}, x_i\}$

The sequence $(x_1, \ldots, x_k)$ is called the *carrier sequence* of the dipath p, and we shall denote it by carrs p. It can be shown, cf. [8–Lemma 3.2], that for all $i = 2, \ldots, n$, either $x_{i-1} \vartriangleleft^- x_i$ or $x_i \vartriangleleft^+ x_{i-1}$. Note that the definition in [8] makes an extra assumption on X which, in fact, is not necessary. Figure 2 shows an example of a carrier sequence.

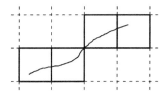

Fig. 2. A dipath and its carrier sequence

In general we call a sequence of cubes $(x_1, \ldots, x_n)$ a carrier sequence if $x_{i-1} \vartriangleleft^- x_i$ or $x_i \vartriangleleft^+ x_{i-1}$ for all $i = 2, \ldots, n$. Note that computation paths are carrier sequences, and conversely, that carrier sequences can be turned into computation paths by adding in some intermediate cubes. The next lemma shows that any carrier sequence actually is the carrier sequence of a dipath.

Lemma 5. *Given a carrier sequence $(x_1, \ldots, x_n)$ in a locally finite non-selflinked precubical set X and $z \in$ int $|x_n|$, there exists a dipath $p : \vec{I} \to |X|$ such that carrs $p = (x_1, \ldots, x_n)$ and $p(1) = z$.*

We can similarly fix $z \in$ int $|x_1|$ and get a dipath p with $p(0) = z$, but we will only need the former case. We shall also need the following two technical lemmas.

Lemma 6. *Given locally finite non-selflinked precubical sets X, Y, a morphism $f : X \to Y$, and a dipath $p : \vec{I} \to |X|$, then carrs$(|f| \circ p) = f(\text{carrs } p)$.*

Note that, taking p to be a constant dipath, the lemma implies that carr $|f|(z) = f(\text{carr } z)$ for any $z \in |X|$.

Lemma 7. *Given locally finite non-selflinked precubical sets X, Y, a morphism $f : X \to Y$, a dipath $q : \vec{I} \to |Y|$, and a carrier sequence $(x_1, \ldots, x_n)$ in X such that* $\operatorname{carrs} q = (f(x_1), \ldots, f(x_n))$, *then there exists a dipath $p : \vec{I} \to |X|$ such that* $\operatorname{carrs} p = (x_1, \ldots, x_n)$ *and* $q = |f| \circ p$.

Note again the implication of the lemma for constant dipaths: If $x \in X$ and $z' \in |Y|$ are such that $\operatorname{carr} z' = f(x)$, then there exists $z \in |X|$ such that $\operatorname{carr} z = x$ and $z' = |f|(z)$.

10   Bisimulation and Dipaths

In this final section we again fix a labeling cubical set L and work in the category of higher-dimensional automata over L. Recall that in this category, all morphisms are non-contracting.

First we note the following stronger variant of Lemma 2, which follows by an easy induction argument.

Lemma 8. *A morphism $f : X \to Y$ is CPath-open if and only if it satisfies the property that for any reachable $x_1 \in X$ and for any computation path $(y_1, \ldots, y_n)$ in Y with $y_1 = f(x_1)$, there is a computation path $(x_1, \ldots, x_n)$ in X such that $y_i = f(x_i)$ for all $i = 1, \ldots, n$.*

We call a HDA $* \xrightarrow{i} X$ *special* if the cubical set X is freely generated by a locally finite non-selflinked precubical set, and for the rest of this section we assume our HDA to be special. Note that this is not a severe restriction: Local finiteness is hardly an issue, and the requirement on a precubical set to be non-selflinked is a natural one which is quite standard in algebraic topology, cf. [1–Def. IV.21.1].

A point $z \in |X|$ in the geometric realisation of a HDA $* \xrightarrow{i} X$ is said to be *reachable* if there exists a dipath $p : \vec{I} \to |X|$ with $p(0) = |i*|$ and $p(1) = z$. This notion of "geometric" reachability is closely related to the one of computation path reachability defined in Section 7:

Proposition 3. *A point $z \in |X|$ in the geometric realisation of a special HDA $* \xrightarrow{i} X$ is reachable if and only if $\operatorname{carr} z$ is reachable.*

We can now prove the main result of this article, linking bisimulation of HDA with a dipath-lifting property of their geometric realisations:

Theorem 1. *Given a morphism $f : X \to Y$ of two special HDA, then f is CPath-open if and only if, for any reachable $z \in |X|$ and for any dipath $q : \vec{I} \to |Y|$ such that $q(0) = |f|(z)$, there is a dipath $p : \vec{I} \to |X|$ filling in the diagram*

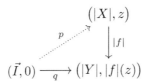

In the special case that all cubes in X are reachable, we can identify z with the mapping $z : 0 \mapsto z \in |X|$ and draw the above diagram in a more familiar fashion as

$$
\begin{array}{ccc}
0 & \xrightarrow{\;z\;} & |X| \\
\downarrow & {\scriptstyle p}\;\nearrow & \downarrow {\scriptstyle |f|} \\
\vec{I} & \xrightarrow{\;q\;} & |Y|
\end{array}
$$

That is, a morphism f from a reachable special HDA X to a special HDA Y is CPath-open if and only if its realisation has the right-lifting property with respect to the inclusion $0 \hookrightarrow \vec{I}$.

Proof. The morphism f is non-contracting, hence it is the image of a precubical morphism, also denoted f, under the free functor. Assume first f to be CPath-open, let $z \in |X|$ be reachable and $q : \vec{I} \to |Y|$ a dipath with $q(0) = |f|(z)$. Turn carrs q into a computation path $(y_1, \ldots, y_n)$. Let $x_1 = \operatorname{carr} z$, then x_1 is reachable, and $y_1 = \operatorname{carr} |f|(z) = f(x_1)$.

We can invoke Lemma 8 to get a computation path $(x_1, \ldots, x_n)$ in X such that $(y_1, \ldots, y_n) = f(x_1, \ldots, x_n)$. Lemma 7 then provides a dipath $p : \vec{I} \to |X|$ such that $q = |f| \circ p$. The construction in the proof of Lemma 7 implies that $p(0) = z$.

For the other direction, assume $|f|$ to have the dipath lifting property of the theorem, let $x_1 \in X$ be reachable, $y_1 = f(x_1) \in Y$, and let $(y_1, \ldots, y_n)$ be a computation path in Y.

Let $q : \vec{I} \to |Y|$ be the dipath associated with $(y_1, \ldots, y_n)$ as given by Lemma 5. Then $\operatorname{carr} q(0) = f(x_1)$, thus we have $z \in |X|$ such that $\operatorname{carr} z = x_1$ and $q(0) = |f|(z)$. By Proposition 3 the point z is reachable, implying that we have a dipath $p : \vec{I} \to X$ such that $q = |f| \circ p$ and $p(0) = z$.

Let $(x_1, \ldots, x_n) = \operatorname{carrs} p$, then $y_i = f(x_i)$ by Lemma 6. We show that $(x_1, \ldots, x_n)$ is actually a computation path; this will finish the proof. Assume $x_i \triangleleft^- x_{i+1}$, i.e. $x_i = \delta^0_{j_1} \cdots \delta^0_{j_\ell} x_{i+1}$ for some sequence of indices. Then $y_i = \delta^0_{j_1} \cdots \delta^0_{j_\ell} y_{i+1}$, but $(y_1, \ldots, y_n)$ is a computation path, hence as Y is non-selflinked, the sequence of indices contains only one element j_ℓ, and $x_i = \delta^0_{j_\ell} x_{i+1}$. Similar arguments apply to the other case. $\qquad\square$

11   Conclusion and Future Work

We have in this article introduced some synchronisation operations for higher-dimensional automata, notably tensor product, relabeling, and restriction.

Whether these operations capture the full flavour of HDA synchronisation remains to be seen; some other primitives might be needed. Recent work by Worytkiewicz [24] suggests some directions.

We have also defined a notion of bisimulation for HDA which is closely related to van Glabbeek's [10] computation paths. The notion of bisimulation also defined in [10] appears to be weaker than ours, and their relation should be worked out in detail.

The notions of computation paths defined in Cattani-Sassone's [4] and in [24] differ considerably from van Glabbeek's, and as a consequence they arrive at different concepts of bisimulation and even simulation. These differences need to be worked out, and also the apparent similarities between [4] and [24].

We have shown that our notion of bisimulation has an interpretation as a dipath-lifting property of morphisms, making the problem of deciding bisimilarity susceptible to some machinery from algebraic topology. In topological language, a dipath-lifting morphism is a weak kind of *fibration*, hinting that fibrations (well-studied in algebraic topology) could have applications, as well. This also suggests that a general theory of directed fibrations should be developed.

We believe that our bisimulation notion should be weakened, also taking equivalence of computation paths [10] into account. We plan to elaborate on this in a future paper, and we conjecture that this bisimulation-up-to-equivalence has a topological interpretation as a property of lifting dipaths *up to directed homotopy*. This weaker bisimulation looks to be closely related to van Glabbeek's, and there appears to be a strong connection between his unfoldings of HDA and directed coverings of local po-spaces [7].

References

1. Glen E. Bredon. *Topology and Geometry*. Springer-Verlag, 1993.
2. Ronald Brown and Philip J. Higgins. On the algebra of cubes. *Journal of Pure and Applied Algebra*, 21:233–260, 1981.
3. Ronald Brown and Philip J. Higgins. Tensor products and homotopies for ω-groupoids and crossed complexes. *Journal of Pure and Applied Algebra*, 47:1–33, 1987.
4. Gian Luca Cattani and Vladimiro Sassone. Higher dimensional transition systems. In *Proc. LICS'96*, pages 55–62. IEEE Press, 1996.
5. Sjoerd Crans. *On Combinatorial Models for Higher Dimensional Homotopies*. PhD thesis, Utrecht University, 1995.
6. Ulrich Fahrenberg. A category of higher-dimensional automata. Technical Report R-2005-01, Department of Mathematical Sciences, Aalborg University, 2005. http://www.math.aau.dk/research/reports/R-2005-01.ps.
7. Lisbeth Fajstrup. Dicovering spaces. *Homology, Homotopy and Applications*, 5(2):1–17, 2003.
8. Lisbeth Fajstrup. Dipaths and dihomotopies in a cubical complex. Report R-2003-22, Department of Mathematical Sciences, Aalborg University, 2003. http://www.math.aau.dk/research/reports/R-2003-22.ps. Submitted to *Advances in Applied Mathematics*.

9. Lisbeth Fajstrup, Eric Goubault, and Martin Raussen. Algebraic topology and concurrency. Report R-99-2008, Department of Mathematical Sciences, Aalborg University, 1999. `http://www.math.aau.dk/research/reports/R-99-2008.ps`. Conditionally accepted for publication in *Theoretical Computer Science*.

10. Robert Jan van Glabbeek. Bisimulations for higher dimensional automata. Email message, 1991. `http://theory.stanford.edu/~rvg/hda`.

11. Robert Jan van Glabbeek. On the expressiveness of higher dimensional automata. Preprint, 2004. `http://www.cse.unsw.edu.au/~rvg/hda.pdf`.

12. Eric Goubault. *The Geometry of Concurrency*. PhD thesis, Ecole Normale Supérieure, Paris, 1995. `http://www.di.ens.fr/~goubault/papers/these.ps.gz`.

13. Eric Goubault. Labelled cubical sets and asynchronous transition systems: an adjunction. In *Preliminary Proceedings CMCIM'02*, 2002. `http://www.di.ens.fr/~goubault/papers/cmcim02.ps.gz`.

14. Marco Grandis. Directed homotopy theory I. *Cahiers de Topologie et Géométrie Différentielle Catégoriques*, 44:281–316, 2003. Preprint available as `http://arxiv.org/abs/math.AT/0111048`.

15. Marco Grandis. Directed homotopy theory II. *Theory and Applications of Categories*, 14:369–391, 2002.

16. Marco Grandis. Directed combinatorial homology and noncommutative tori. *Math. Proc. Cambridge Philos. Soc.*, 2004. to appear. Preprint available as `http://www.dima.unige.it/~grandis/Bsy.pdf`.

17. Marco Grandis and Luca Mauri. Cubical sets and their site. *Theory and Applications of Categories*, 11(8):185–211, 2003.

18. J. F. Jardine. Cubical homotopy theory: a beginning. Preprint, 2002.

19. André Joyal, Mogens Nielsen, and Glynn Winskel. Bisimulation from open maps. *Information and Computation*, 127(2):164–185, 1996.

20. William S. Massey. *A Basic Course in Algebraic Topology*, volume 127 of *Graduate Texts in Mathematics*. Springer-Verlag, 1991.

21. Robin Milner. *Communication and Concurrency*. Prentice Hall, 1989.

22. Jean-Pierre Serre. *Homologie singulière des espaces fibrés*. PhD thesis, Ecole Normale Supérieure, 1951.

23. Glynn Winskel and Mogens Nielsen. Models for concurrency. In Samson Abramsky, Dov M. Gabbay, and Thomas S.E. Maibaum, editors, *Handbook of Logic in Computer Science*, volume 4, pages 1–148. Clarendon Press, Oxford, 1995.

24. Krzysztof Worytkiewicz. Synchronization from a categorical perspective. Preprint, 2004. `http://arxiv.org/abs/cs.PL/0411001`.

Third-Order Idealized Algol with Iteration Is Decidable

Andrzej S. Murawski[1],[*] and Igor Walukiewicz[2],[**]

[1] Oxford University Computing Laboratory, Parks Road,
Oxford OX1 3QD, UK
[2] LaBRI, Université Bordeaux-1, 351, Cours de la Libération,
33 405, Talence, France

Abstract. The problems of contextual equivalence and approximation are studied for the third-order fragment of Idealized Algol with iteration (IA_3^*). They are approached via a combination of game semantics and language theory. It is shown that for each IA_3^*-term one can construct a pushdown automaton recognizing a representation of the strategy induced by the term. The automata have some additional properties ensuring that the associated equivalence and inclusion problems are solvable in PTIME. This gives an EXPTIME decision procedure for contextual equivalence and approximation for β-normal terms. EXPTIME-hardness is also shown in this case, even in the absence of iteration.

1   Introduction

In recent years game semantics has provided a new methodology for constructing fully abstract models of programming languages. By definition, such models capture the notions of contextual equivalence and approximation and so offer a semantic framework in which to study these two properties. In this paper we focus on the game semantics of Idealized Algol, a language proposed by Reynolds as a synthesis of functional and imperative programming [1]. It is essentially the simply-typed λ-calculus extended with constants for modelling arithmetic, assignable variables and recursion. This view naturally determines fragments of the language when the typing framework is constrained not to exceed a particular order. Many versions of Algol have been considered in the literature. Typically, for decidability results, general recursion has to be left out completely or restricted to iteration, e.g. in the form of while-loops as will be the case in this paper. For similar reasons, base types are required to be finite.

In game models, terms of a programming language are modelled by strategies. These in turn can sometimes be represented by formal languages, i.e. sets of finite words, such that equivalence and approximation are established by verifying respectively equality and inclusion of the induced languages. This approach to

---

[*] Supported by British EPSRC (GR/R88861) and St John's College, Oxford.
[**] Supported by the European Community Research Training Network GAMES.

V. Sassone (Ed.): FOSSACS 2005, LNCS 3441, pp. 202–218, 2005.

modelling semantics is interesting not only because it gives new insights into the semantics but also because it opens up the possibility of applying existing algorithms and techniques developed for dealing with various families of formal languages [2]. Therefore, it is essential that the class of languages one uses is as simple as possible – ideally its containment problem should be decidable and of relatively low complexity.

In this paper we show how to model terms of third-order Idealized Algol with iteration (IA_3^*) using variants of visibly pushdown automata [3]. One of the advantages of taking such specialized automata is that the instances of the containment problem relevant to us will be decidable in PTIME. Another is the relative simplicity of the inductive constructions of automata for the constructs of the language. We give the constructions only for terms in β-normal form taking advantage of the fact that each term can be effectively normalized. The automata constructed by our procedure have exponential size with respect to the size of the term, which leads to an exponential-time procedure for checking approximation and equivalence of such terms. We also provide the matching lower bound by showing that equivalence of third-order terms, even without iteration, is EXPTIME-hard.

Ghica and McCusker [4] were the first to show how certain strategies can be modelled by languages. They have defined a procedure which constructs a regular language for every term of second-order Idealized Algol with iteration. Subsequently, Ong [5] has shown how to model third-order Idealized Algol without iteration using deterministic pushdown automata. Our work can be seen as an extension of his in two directions: a richer language is considered and a more specialized class of automata is used (the latter is particularly important for complexity issues). In contrast to the approach of [5], we work exclusively with the standard game semantics and translate terms directly into automata, while the translation in [5] relies on an auxiliary form of game semantics (with explicit state) in which strategies are determined by *view-functions*. In the presence of iteration these functions are no longer finite and the approach does not work any more (in yet unpublished work Ong proposes to fix this deficiency by considering view-functions whose domains are regular sets and which act uniformly with respect to the regular expressions representing these sets). It should also be noted that our construction yields automata without pushdowns for terms of order two, hence it also subsumes the construction by Ghica and McCusker.

Our results bring us closer to a complete classification of decidable instances of Idealized Algol and their complexity. Since the fourth-order fragment without iteration was shown undecidable in [6], the only unresolved cases seem to be those of second- and third-order fragments with recursively defined terms of base types (of which iteration is a special case). Recursive functions lead to undecidability at order two as shown in [5].

The outline of the paper is as follows. We present Idealized Algol and its third-order fragment IA_3^* in Section 2. Then we recapitulate the game model of the language. Next the class of *simple* terms is defined. These are terms that induce plays in which pointers can be safely omitted which makes it possible to represent their game semantics via languages. In Section 4 we introduce our particular class of automata and give an inductive construction of such an automaton for every simple term in β-normal form. In Section 5 we show how to deal with terms that are not simple. The last section concerns the EXPTIME lower bound for the complexity of equivalence in IA_3^*.

2   Idealized Algol

We consider a finitary version IA_f of Idealized Algol with active expressions [7]. It can be viewed as a simply typed λ-calculus over the base types com, exp, var (of commands, expressions and variables respectively) augmented with the constants

$skip : com$	$i : exp \quad (0 \leq i \leq max)$	$\Omega_\mathcal{B} : \mathcal{B}$
$\mathbf{succ} : exp \to exp$	$\mathbf{pred} : exp \to exp$	$\mathbf{ifzero}_\mathcal{B} : exp \to \mathcal{B} \to \mathcal{B} \to \mathcal{B}$
$\mathbf{seq}_\mathcal{B} : com \to \mathcal{B} \to \mathcal{B}$	$\mathbf{deref} : var \to exp$	$\mathbf{assign} : var \to exp \to com$
$\mathbf{cell}_\mathcal{B} : (var \to \mathcal{B}) \to \mathcal{B}$	$\mathbf{mkvar} : (exp \to com) \to exp \to var$	

where $\mathcal{B}$ ranges over base types and $exp = \{\, 0, \cdots, max \,\}$. Each of the constants corresponds to a different programming feature. For instance, sequential composition of M and N is expressed as $\mathbf{seq}_\mathcal{B} MN$, assignment of N to M is represented by $\mathbf{assign} MN$ and $\mathbf{cell}_\mathcal{B}(\lambda x.M)$ amounts to creating a local variable x visible in M. Other features can be added in a similar way, e.g. **while**-loops will be introduced via the constant $\mathbf{while} : exp \to com \to com$. In order to gain control over multiple occurrences of free identifiers during typing (cf. Definition 9) we shall use a linear form of the application rule and the contraction rule:

$$\frac{\Gamma \vdash M : T \to T' \quad \Delta \vdash N : T}{\Gamma, \Delta \vdash MN : T'} \qquad \frac{\Gamma, x_1 : T, x_2 : T \vdash M : T'}{\Gamma, x : T \vdash M[x/x_1, x/x_2] : T'}.$$

The linear application simply corresponds to composition: in any cartesian-closed category $[\![\Gamma, \Delta \vdash MN : T']\!]$ is equal (up to currying) to

$$\begin{array}{cc} [\![\Delta \vdash N : T]\!] \; ; \; [\![\vdash \lambda x^T.\lambda\Gamma.Mx : T \to (\Gamma \to T')]\!] \\ [\![\Delta]\!] \Rightarrow [\![T]\!] \qquad\quad [\![T]\!] \Rightarrow ([\![\Gamma]\!] \Rightarrow [\![T']\!]). \end{array}$$

Thanks to the applicative syntax and the above decomposition the process of interpreting the language can be divided into simple stages: the modelling of base constructs (free identifiers and constants), composition, contraction and currying.

The operational semantics of IA_f can be found in [7]; we will write $M \Downarrow$ if M reduces to $skip$. We study the induced equivalence and approximation relations.

Definition 1. *Two terms $\Gamma \vdash M_1, M_2 : T$ are equivalent ($\Gamma \vdash M_1 \cong M_2$) if for any context $C[-]$ such that $C[M_1], C[M_2]$ are closed terms of type com, we have $C[M_1] \Downarrow$ if and only if $C[M_2] \Downarrow$. Similarly, M_1 approximates M_2 ($\Gamma \vdash M_1 \lesssim M_2$) iff for all contexts satisfying the properties above whenever $C[M_1] \Downarrow$ then $C[M_2] \Downarrow$.*

In general, equivalence of $\mathsf{IA_f}$ terms is not decidable [6]. To obtain decidability one has to restrict the order of types, which is defined by:

$$\mathsf{ord}(\mathcal{B}) = 0 \quad \text{and} \quad \mathsf{ord}(\mathcal{T} \to \mathcal{T}') = \max(\mathsf{ord}(\mathcal{T}) + 1, \mathsf{ord}(\mathcal{T}')).$$

Definition 2. *An $\mathsf{IA_f}$ term $\Gamma \vdash M : T$ is an ith-order term provided its typing derivation uses sequents in which the types of free identifiers are of order less than i and the type of the term has order at most i. The collection of ith-order $\mathsf{IA_f}$ terms will be denoted by IA_i.*

To establish decidability of program approximation or equivalence of ith-order terms it suffices to consider ith-order terms in β-normal form. To type such terms, one only needs a restricted version of the application rule in which the function term M is either a constant or a term of the form $fM_1 \cdots M_k$, where $f : T$ is a free identifier (and so $\mathsf{ord}(T) < i$).

   In this paper we will be concerned with IA_3 enriched with **while**, which we denote by IA_3^* for brevity.

3   Game Semantics

Here we recall the basic notions of game semantics and discuss how to code strategies in terms of languages. To that end we investigate when it is not necessary to represent pointers in plays and obtain the class of simple terms for which pointers can be disregarded. We use the game semantics of Idealized Algol as described in [7]. The games are defined over arenas which specify the available moves and the relationship between them.

Definition 3. *An* arena *A is a triple $\langle M_A, \lambda_A, \vdash_A \rangle$, where M_A is the set of moves, $\lambda_A : M_A \to \{O, P\} \times \{q, a\}$ indicates whether a move is an O-move or a P-move and whether it is a question or an answer, and $\vdash_A \subseteq (M_A + \{\star\}) \times M_A$ is the* enabling *relation which must satisfy the following two conditions.*

- *For all $m, n \in M_A$ if $m \vdash_A n$ then m and n belong to different players and m is a question.*
- *If $\star \vdash_A m$ then m is an O-question which is not enabled by any other move. Such moves are called* initial; *the set containing them will be denoted by I_A.*

The permitted scenarios in a given arena are required to be *legal justified sequences* of moves. A justified sequence s over an arena A is a sequence of moves from M_A equipped with pointers so that every non-initial move n (in the sense of Definition 3) in s has a pointer to an earlier move m in s with $m \vdash_A n$ (m is then called the *justifier* of n). Given a justified sequence s, its O-view $\llcorner s \lrcorner$ and P-view $\ulcorner s \urcorner$ are defined as follows, where o and p stand for an O-move and a P-move respectively:

$$\llcorner \epsilon \lrcorner = \epsilon \quad \llcorner so \lrcorner = \llcorner s \lrcorner o \qquad\qquad \llcorner so \,\widehat{}\, t\, p \lrcorner = \llcorner s \lrcorner o \,\widehat{}\, p$$
$$\ulcorner \epsilon \urcorner = \epsilon \quad \ulcorner so \urcorner = o \quad (\text{if } o \text{ is initial}) \qquad \ulcorner sp \urcorner = \ulcorner s \urcorner p \quad \ulcorner sp \,\widehat{}\, t\, o \urcorner = \ulcorner s \urcorner p \,\frown o.$$

Definition 4. *A justified sequence s is* legal *if it satisfies the following:*

- *players alternate (O begins),*
- *the* visibility *condition holds: in any prefix tm of s if m is a non-initial O-move then its justifier occurs in* $\llcorner t \lrcorner$ *and if m is a P-move then its justifier is in* $\ulcorner t \urcorner$,
- *the* bracketing *condition holds: for any prefix tm of s if m is an answer then its justifier must be the last unanswered question in t.*

The set of legal sequences over arena A is denoted by L_A.

Formally, a game will be an arena together with a subset of L_A. This makes it possible to define different games over the same arenas.

Definition 5. *A* game *is a tuple* $\langle M_A, \lambda_A, \vdash_A, P_A \rangle$ *such that* $\langle M_A, \lambda_A, \vdash_A \rangle$ *is an arena and* P_A *is a non-empty, prefix-closed subset of* L_A *(called the set of* positions *or* plays *in the game)*[1].

Games can be combined by a number of constructions, notably $\times, \otimes, !, \multimap, \Rightarrow$. We describe them briefly below. In the first three cases the enabling relation is simply inherited from the component games. As for plays, we have $P_{A \times B} = P_A + P_B$ in the first case. In contrast, each play in $P_{A \otimes B}$ is an interleaving of a play from A with a play from B (and only O can switch between them). Similarly, positions in $P_{!A}$ are interleavings of a finite number of plays from P_A (again only O can jump between them). The $\multimap$ construction is more complicated: we have $M_{A \multimap B} = M_A + M_B$ but the ownership of A moves in $M_{A \multimap B}$ is reversed. The enabling relation is defined by $\vdash_{A \multimap B} = \vdash_A + \vdash_B + \{ (b, a) \mid b \in I_B \wedge a \in I_A \}$ and plays of $A \multimap B$ are interleavings of single plays from A and B. This time, however, each such play has to begin in B and only P can switch between the interleaved plays. The game $A \Rightarrow B$ is defined as $!A \multimap B$.

Example 1. The underlying arena of $((\llbracket com \rrbracket \Rightarrow \llbracket com \rrbracket) \Rightarrow \llbracket com \rrbracket) \Rightarrow \llbracket com \rrbracket$ has the following shape:

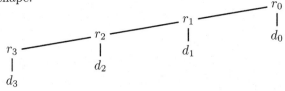

Definition 6. *In arenas corresponding to* IA_f *types we can define the* order *of a move inductively (we denote it by* $\mathrm{ord}_A(m)$*). The initial O-questions have order 0. For all other questions q we define* $\mathrm{ord}_A(q)$ *to be* $\mathrm{ord}_A(q') + 1$ *where* $q' \vdash q$ *(this definition is never ambiguous for the arenas in question). Answers inherit their order from the questions that enable them. The* order *of an arena is the maximal order of a question in it.*

---

[1] P_A also has to satisfy a closure condition [7] which we omit here.

For instance, in the example above r_3 is a third-order move. We will continue to use subscripts to indicate the order of a move.

The next important definition is that of a strategy. Strategies determine unique responses for P (if any) and do not restrict O-moves.

Definition 7. *A* strategy *in a game A (written as $\sigma : A$) is a prefix-closed subsets of plays in A such that: (i) whenever $sp_1, sp_2 \in \sigma$ and p_1, p_2 are P-moves then $p_1 = p_2$; (ii) whenever $s \in \sigma$ and $so \in P_A$ for some O-move o then $so \in \sigma$. We write* comp(σ) *for the set of non-empty complete plays in σ, i.e. plays in which all questions have been answered.*

An $\mathsf{IA_f}$ term $\Gamma \vdash M : T$, where $\Gamma = x_1 : T_1, \cdots, x_n : T_n$, is interpreted by a strategy (denoted by $[\![\Gamma \vdash M : T]\!]$) for the game

$$[\![\Gamma \vdash T]\!] = [\![T_1]\!] \times \cdots \times [\![T_n]\!] \Rightarrow [\![T]\!] =!([\![T_1]\!]) \otimes \cdots \otimes !([\![T_n]\!]) \multimap [\![T]\!].$$

Remark 1. From the definitions of the $\otimes$ and $\multimap$ constructions we can deduce the following *switching properties*. A play in $[\![\Gamma \vdash T]\!]$ always starts with an initial O-question in $[\![T]\!]$. Subsequently, whenever P makes a move in $[\![T_i]\!]$ or $[\![T]\!]$, O must also follow with a move in $[\![T_i]\!]$ or $[\![T]\!]$ respectively. We also note that the arenas used to interpret ith-order terms are of order i.

The interpretation of terms presented in [7] gives a fully abstract model in the sense made precise below.

Theorem 1. $\Gamma \vdash M_1 \precsim M_2$ *iff* comp$([\![\Gamma \vdash M_1]\!]) \subseteq$ comp$([\![\Gamma \vdash M_2]\!])$. *Consequently, $\Gamma \vdash M_1 \cong M_2$ iff* comp$([\![\Gamma \vdash M_1]\!]) =$ comp$([\![\Gamma \vdash M_2]\!])$.

In the sections to follow we will show how to represent strategies defined by β-normal $\mathsf{IA_3^*}$-terms via languages. The simplest, but not always faithful, representation consists in taking the underlying set of moves.

Definition 8. *Given $P \subseteq P_G$ we write $\mathcal{L}(P)$ for the language over the alphabet M_G consisting of the sequences of moves of the game G underlying positions in P.*

While in $\mathcal{L}(P)$ we lose information about pointers, the structure of the alphabet M_G remains unchanged; in particular each letter has an order as it is a move from M_G.

Some β-normal $\mathsf{IA_3^*}$ terms define strategies σ for which $\mathcal{L}(\sigma)$ constitutes a faithful representation. This will be the case if pointers are uniquely reconstructible. To identify such terms it is important to understand when pointers can be ignored in positions over third-order arenas and when they have to be represented explicitly in some way. Due to the well-bracketing condition, pointers from answer-moves always lead to the last unanswered question, hence they are uniquely determined by the underlying sequence of moves. The case of questions is more complicated. Initial questions do not have pointers at all, however all non-initial ones do, which is where ambiguities might arise. Nevertheless it turns out that in the positions of interest pointers leading from first-order and second-order questions are determined uniquely, because only one unanswered enabler will occur in the respective view. Third-order questions do need pointers though, the standard example [8] being $\lambda f.f(\lambda x.f(\lambda y.x))$ and $\lambda f.f(\lambda x.f(\lambda y.y))$. The terms define the following positions respectively:

$$q_0 \; q_1 \; q_2 \; q_1 \; q_2 \; q_3 \qquad q_0 \; q_1 \; q_2 \; q_1 \; q_2 \; q_3 \, .$$

Here pointers from third-order questions cannot be omitted, because several potential justifiers occur in the P-view. To get around the difficulties we will first focus on terms where the ambiguities for third-order questions cannot arise.

Definition 9. *A β-normal IA_3^*-term will be called* simple *iff it can be typed without applying the contraction rule to identifiers of second-order types.*

Clearly, the two terms above are not simple.

Lemma 1. *Suppose $\Gamma \vdash M : T$ is simple and $sq_3 \in [\![\Gamma \vdash M : T]\!]$. Then $\ulcorner s \urcorner$ contains exactly one unanswered occurrence of an enabler of q_3.*

Consequently, the justifiers of all third-order moves in positions generated by simple terms are uniquely determined so, if σ denotes a simple term, $\mathcal{L}(\sigma)$ uniquely determines σ. In the next section we focus on defining automata accepting $\mathcal{L}(\mathsf{comp}(\sigma))$.

4   Automata for Simple Terms

This section presents the construction of automata recognizing the languages defined by simple terms. The construction proceeds by induction on the term structure. The only difficult case is application. We have chosen to pass through the intermediate step of linear composition to make the technical details more transparent.

4.1   Automata Model

The pushdown automata we are going to use to capture simple terms are specialized deterministic visibly pushdown automata [3]. Their most important feature is the dependence of stack actions on input letters. Another important point in the following definitions is that the automata will use the stack only when reading third-order moves.

Definition 10. *A* strategy automaton *is a tuple*

$$\mathcal{A} = \langle \, Q, M_{push}, M_{pop}, M_{noop}, \Gamma, i, \delta_{push}, \delta_{pop}, \delta_{noop}, F \, \rangle$$

where Q is a finite set of states; $(M_{push}, M_{pop}, M_{noop})$ is the partition of the input alphabet into push, pop and noop (no stack change) letters; Γ is the stack alphabet; i is the initial state and $F \subseteq Q$ is the set of final states. The transitions are given by the partial functions:

$$\delta_{push} : Q \times M_{push} \dashrightarrow Q \times \Gamma \quad \delta_{pop} : Q \times M_{pop} \times \Gamma \dashrightarrow Q \quad \delta_{noop} : Q \times M_{noop} \dashrightarrow Q.$$

Observe that while doing a push or a noop move the automaton does not look at the top symbol of the stack. We will sometimes use an arrow notation for transitions: $s \xrightarrow{a/x} s'$ for $\delta_{push}(s, a) = (s', x)$, $s \xrightarrow{a,x} s'$ for $\delta_{pop}(s, a, x) = s'$, and $s \xrightarrow{a} s'$ for $\delta_{noop}(s, a) = s'$.

The definitions of a configuration and a run of a strategy automaton are standard. A *configuration* is a word from $Q\Gamma^*$. The *initial configuration* is i (the initial state and the empty stack). The transition functions define transitions between configurations, e.g. the transition $s \xrightarrow{a/x} s'$ of the automaton gives transitions $sv \xrightarrow{a} s'xv$ for all $v \in \Gamma^*$. A *run* on a word $w = w_1 \ldots w_n$ is a sequence of configurations: $c_0 \xrightarrow{w_1} c_1 \xrightarrow{w_2} \ldots \xrightarrow{w_n} c_n$ where $c_0 = i$ is the initial configuration. A run is *accepting* if the state in c_n is from F. We write $L(\mathcal{A})$ for the set of words accepted by $\mathcal{A}$.

Since we want to represent sequences that are not necessarily positions, notably interaction sequences, we make the next definition general enough to account for both cases.

Definition 11. *Let ρ be a prefix-closed subset of sequences over a set of moves M, and let $\mathsf{comp}(\rho)$ be the subset of ρ consisting of non-empty sequences with an equal number of question- and answer-moves[2]. We say that a strategy automaton $\mathcal{A}$ is proper for ρ if the following conditions hold.*

(A1) $L(\mathcal{A}) = \mathsf{comp}(\rho)$.
(A2) *Every run of $\mathcal{A}$ corresponds to a sequence from ρ (as $\mathcal{A}$ is deterministic each run uniquely specifies the input sequence).*
(A3) *The alphabets M_{push} and M_{pop} consist of third-order questions and answers from M respectively.*

$\mathcal{A}$ is almost proper for ρ if $L(\mathcal{A}) = \{\epsilon\} \cup \mathsf{comp}(\rho)$ and **(A2)** is satisfied.

Remark 2. If $\mathcal{A}$ is proper or almost proper for $\rho = \mathcal{L}(\sigma)$ then thanks to **(A2)** we can then make a number of useful assumptions about its structure.

1. If there is a transition on a P-move from a state, then it is either the unique transition from this state or it is a pop transition and the other transitions are pop transitions on different stack letters. This is because strategies are deterministic and the push and noop moves do not look at the contents of the stack.

---

[2] Note that this coincides with the concept of a complete play when $\rho = \mathcal{L}(\sigma)$ for some strategy σ.

2. If the game in question is well-opened, i.e. none of its plays contains two initial moves, then $\mathcal{A}$ will never return to the initial state. Otherwise σ would contain just such a play. Hence, we can assume that the initial state does not have any incoming transitions and that it does not have any outgoing pop transitions.

Our first goal will be to model simple terms. The following remark summarizes what needs to be done.

Remark 3. Recall the linear application rule from Section 2. Whenever it is applied when typing β-normal IA_3^* terms we have $\mathrm{ord}(T) \leq 1$ and if $\mathrm{ord}(T) = 1$ then M is $\mathbf{cell}_\mathcal{B}$, $\mathbf{mkvar}$ or a term of the shape $f M_1 \cdots M_k$ where the order of f's type is at most 2. Consequently, the corresponding instances of composition are restricted accordingly. To sum up, the following semantic elements are needed to model β-normal simple IA_3^*-terms.

- A strategy for each of the constants.
- Identity strategies $\mathrm{id}_{[\![T]\!]}$ ($\mathrm{ord}(T) \leq 2$).
- Composition of $\sigma : [\![T]\!] \Rightarrow [\![T']\!]$ and $\tau : [\![T']\!] \Rightarrow [\![T'']\!]$ where $\mathrm{ord}(T) \leq 2$, $\mathrm{ord}(T') \leq 1$ and $\mathrm{ord}(T'') \leq 3$; moreover, if $\mathrm{ord}(T') = 1$ then either $\tau = [\![\mathbf{cell}_\mathcal{B}]\!]$, or $\tau = [\![\mathbf{mkvar}]\!]$, or $\tau = [\![\lambda x.\lambda \Gamma.f M_1 \cdots M_k x]\!]$.
- A way of modelling contraction up to order 1.

We have not included (un)currying in the list because in the games setting they amount to identities (up to the associativity of the disjoint sum).

The strategies for the constants and identities up to order 1 do not contain third-order moves and it is easy to construct finite automata (without stack) which are proper for each of them. The strategy automata for identity strategies at order 2 can be constructed using the $\dagger$ construction (to be introduced shortly) and the equality $\mathrm{id}_{A \Rightarrow B} = \mathrm{id}_A^\dagger \multimap \mathrm{id}_B$. Contraction up to order 1 can be interpreted simply by relabelling, so in the remainder of this section we concentrate on composition.

4.2   Composition

Let $\sigma : A \Rightarrow B$ and $\tau : B \Rightarrow C$. Recall that $A \Rightarrow B = !A \multimap B$ and $B \Rightarrow C = !B \multimap C$. In order to compose the strategies, one first defines $\sigma^\dagger : !A \multimap !B$ by

$$\sigma^\dagger = \{\, s \in L_{!A \multimap !B} \mid \text{for all initial } m,\ s \upharpoonright m \in \sigma \,\},$$

where $s \upharpoonright m$ stands for the subsequence of s (pointers included) whose moves are hereditarily justified by m. Then $\sigma; \tau : A \Rightarrow C$ is taken to be $\sigma^\dagger;_{\mathrm{lin}} \tau$, where $;_{\mathrm{lin}}$ is discussed below.

The *linear composition* $\sigma;_{\mathrm{lin}} \tau : A \multimap C$ of two strategies $\sigma : A \multimap B$ and $\tau : B \multimap C$ is defined in the following way. Let u be a sequence of moves from arenas A, B and C with justification pointers from all moves except those initial in C. The set of all such sequences will be denoted by $\mathrm{int}(A, B, C)$. Define $u \upharpoonright B, C$

to be the subsequence of u consisting of all moves from B and C (pointers between A-moves and B-moves are ignored). $u \upharpoonright A, B$ is defined analogously (pointers between B and C are then ignored). Finally, define $u \upharpoonright A, C$ to be the subsequence of u consisting of all moves from A and C, but where there was a pointer from a move $m_A \in M_A$ to an initial move $m_B \in M_B$ extend the pointer to the initial move in C which was pointed to from m_B. Then given two strategies $\sigma : A \multimap B$ and $\tau : B \multimap C$ the composite strategy $\sigma ;_{\text{lin}} \tau : A \multimap C$ is defined in two steps:

$$\sigma \| \tau = \{ u \in \text{int}(A, B, C) \mid u \upharpoonright A, B \in \sigma,\ u \upharpoonright B, C \in \tau \},$$
$$\sigma ;_{\text{lin}} \tau = \{ u \upharpoonright A, C \mid u \in \sigma \| \tau \}.$$

Thus in order to carry out the composition of two strategies we will study separately: the dagger construction $\sigma^\dagger$, interaction sequences $\sigma \| \tau$, and finally the hiding operation leading to $\sigma ;_{\text{lin}} \tau$.

4.3   Dagger

Recall from Remark 3 that to model β-normal IA_3^*-terms we only need to apply $\dagger$ for $B = [\![T]\!]$ where $\text{ord}(T) \leq 1$. It is possible to describe precisely what this construction does in this case; we will write q_i, a_i to refer to any ith-order question and answer from B ($i = 0, 1$). The definition of $\sigma^\dagger$ describes it as an interleaving of plays in σ but much more can be said about the way the copies of σ are intertwined thanks to the switching conditions, cf. Remark 1, controlling the play on $!A \multimap !B$. For instance, only O will be able to switch between different copies of σ and this can only happen after P plays in B. Consequently, if $\text{ord}(T) = 0$ (no q_1, a_1 is available then) a new copy of σ can be started only after P plays a_0, i.e. when the previous one is completed. Thus $\sigma^\dagger$ in this case consists of iterated copies of σ. If $\text{ord}(T) = 1$ then a new copy of σ can be started by O each time P plays q_1 or a_0. An old copy of σ can be revisited with a_1, which will then answer some unanswered occurrence of q_1. However, due to the bracketing condition, this will be possible only after all questions played after that q_1 have been answered, i.e. when all copies of σ opened after q_1 are completed. Thus, $\sigma^\dagger$ contains "stacked" copies of σ. Thanks to this we can then characterize $K = \{ \epsilon \} \cup \text{comp}(\sigma^\dagger)$ by the (infinite) recursive equation

$$K = \{\varepsilon\} \cup \bigcup \{ q_0 \square q_1 K a_1 \square \ldots q_1 K a_1 \square a_0 K : q_0 \square q_1 a_1 \square \ldots q_1 a_1 \square a_0 \in \text{comp}(\sigma) \},$$

where $\square$'s stand for (possibly empty and possibly different) segments of moves from A. Note that q_1 is always followed by a_1 in a position of σ due to switching conditions and the fact that B represents a first-order type.

Lemma 2. *Let $T' = B_k \to \cdots \to B_1 \to B_0$ be a type of order at most 1. If there exists a proper automaton $\mathcal{A}$ for $\sigma : ![\![T]\!] \multimap [\![T']\!]$ then there exists an almost proper automaton $\mathcal{A}^\dagger$ for $\sigma^\dagger$. In this automaton the questions and answers from $M_{[\![B_k]\!]}, \cdots, M_{[\![B_1]\!]}$ become push and pop letters respectively.*

Proof. We will refer to the questions and answers of $[\![B_0]\!]$ by q_0, a_0 respectively and to those from $[\![B_i]\!]$ ($i > 0$) by q_1 and a_1. Let $L = \mathsf{comp}(\sigma)$ and $K = \{\epsilon\} \cup \mathsf{comp}(\sigma^\dagger)$. Recall that K satisfies the equation given above.

Let i and f be the initial and final states of $\mathcal{A}$ respectively. As $\mathcal{A}$ is proper for σ, we can assume that there are no transitions to i (Remark 2(2.)). Because $\mathcal{A}$ accepts only well-opened plays we can assume that all the transitions to f are of the form $s \xrightarrow{a_0} f$ and there are no transitions from f. In order to define $\mathcal{A}^\dagger$ we first "merge" f with i or, more precisely, change each transition as above to $s \xrightarrow{a_0} i$ and make i the final state. This produces an automaton accepting L^* (observe that $L^* \subseteq K$). Then we make the following additional modifications:

$$\text{replace } s \xrightarrow{q_1} s' \text{ by } s \xrightarrow{q_1/s'} i \qquad \text{and} \qquad \text{replace } s' \xrightarrow{a_1} s'' \text{ by } i \xrightarrow{a_1,s'} s''.$$

The intuition behind the construction of $\mathcal{A}^\dagger$ is quite simple. When $\mathcal{A}^\dagger$ reads q_1 it goes to the initial state and stores the return state s' on the stack (the return state is the state $\mathcal{A}$ would go to after reading q_1). After this $\mathcal{A}^\dagger$ is ready to process a new copy of K. When finished with this copy it will end up in the state i. From this state it can read a_1 and at the same time the return state from the stack which will let it continue the simulation of $\mathcal{A}$. Consequently, it is not difficult to see that $\mathcal{A}^\dagger$ satisfies **(A2)**.

Next we argue that $\mathcal{A}^\dagger$ is deterministic. Because $\mathcal{A}$ was, the modifications involving a_0 could not introduce nondeterminism. Those using q_1 and a_1 might, if $\mathcal{A}$ happened to have an outgoing noop transition from i on a_1. However, since $![\![T]\!] \multimap [\![T']\!]$ is well-opened, by Remark 2 (2.) we can assume that this is not the case.

Finally, observe that $\mathcal{A}^\dagger$ currently accepts a superset of K. To be precise, it accepts a word from K iff both a final state is entered and the stack is empty. Thus, in order to accept by final state only, we have to make the automaton aware of whether the stack is empty. The solution is quite simple. The automaton starts with the empty stack. When it wants to put the first symbol onto the stack it actually puts this symbol with a special marker. Now, when popping, the automaton can realize that there is a special marker on the symbol being popped and learn this way that the stack becomes empty. This information will then be recorded in the state. The solution thus requires doubling the number of stack symbols (one normal copy and one marked copy) and doubling the number of states (information whether stack is empty or not is kept in the state).

Note that by **(A3)** $\mathcal{A}$ does not change the stack when reading q_1 and a_1 (which are first-order moves). In $\mathcal{A}^\dagger$ these letters become push and pop letters respectively. □

4.4   Interaction Sequences: $\sigma^\dagger \| \tau$

The next challenge in modelling composition is to handle the interaction of two strategies. Recall from Remark 3 that in all instances of composition that we need to cover we have $B = [\![T]\!]$, where either $\mathsf{ord}(T) = 0$ or $\mathsf{ord}(T) = 1$ and $\tau = [\![\mathbf{cell}_\mathcal{B}]\!], [\![\mathbf{mkvar}]\!], [\![\lambda x.\lambda \Gamma.f M_1 \cdots M_k x]\!]$.

Lemma 3. *Suppose* τ :!$B \multimap C$ *is as above. Let* q_1, a_1 *denote any first-order question and answer from* B *respectively (note that in* !$B \multimap C$ *they are second-order moves). If* $\tau = [\![\mathbf{cell}_B]\!], [\![\mathbf{mkvar}]\!]$ *then, in positions from* τ, q_1 *is always followed by* a_1 *and* a_1 *is always preceded by* q_1. *In the remaining case,* q_1 *will be followed by a third-order question from* C *and each third-order answer to that question will be followed immediately by* a_1.

Lemma 4. *Suppose there exist proper automata for* σ :!$A \multimap B$ *and* τ :!$B \multimap C$. *If* τ *is as before then there exists a proper automaton* $\mathcal{A}_{||}$ *for* $\sigma^\dagger || \tau$. *Moreover, if there is a transition on a* B *move from a state of* $\mathcal{A}_{||}$ *then it is a noop transition and there is no other transition from that state.*

Proof. Let $\mathcal{A}_1$ be the almost proper automaton for $\sigma^\dagger$:!$A \multimap$!B constructed in Lemma 2 and let $\mathcal{A}_2$ be proper for τ :!$B \multimap C$. We use indices 1 and 2 to distinguish between the components of $\mathcal{A}_1$ and $\mathcal{A}_2$. The set of states and the stack alphabet of $\mathcal{A}_{||}$ will be given by

$$Q = (Q_1 \times Q_2) \cup (\{i_1\} \times Q_1 \times Q_2) \quad \text{and} \quad \Gamma = \Gamma_1 \cup \Gamma_2 \cup (\Gamma_2 \times Q_1).$$

$i = (i_1, i_2)$ and $F = F_1 \times F_2$ will be respectively the initial state and the set of final states. The alphabet of $\mathcal{A}_{||}$ will be partitioned in the following way.

$$M_{push} = (M_{push}^1 - M_B) \cup M_{push}^2 \qquad M_{pop} = (M_{pop}^1 - M_B) \cup M_{pop}^2$$
$$M_{noop} = M_{noop}^1 \cup M_{noop}^2$$

The definitions are not symmetric because first-order moves from B are push or pop letters for $\mathcal{A}_1$ and noop letters for $\mathcal{A}_2$. Note that moves from B are in M_{noop}. Finally, we define the transitions of $\mathcal{A}_{||}$ in several stages starting from those on A- and C-moves:

$$(s_1, s_2) \xrightarrow{m\square} (s_1', s_2) \qquad \text{if } m \in M_A \text{ and } s_1 \xrightarrow{m\square} s_1',$$
$$(s_1, s_2) \xrightarrow{m\square} (s_1, s_2') \qquad \text{if } m \in M_C \text{ and } s_2 \xrightarrow{m\square} s_2'.$$

$\square$ denotes an arbitrary stack action (push, pop or noop). Intuitively, for the letters considered above $\mathcal{A}_{||}$ just simulates the move of the appropriate component.

Next we deal with moves from B. Moves of order 0 are noop letters both for $\mathcal{A}_1$ and $\mathcal{A}_2$. So, we can simulate the transitions componentwise:

$$(s_1, s_2) \xrightarrow{m} (s_1', s_2') \qquad \text{if } s_1 \xrightarrow{m} s_1', s_2 \xrightarrow{m} s_2', m \in M_B \text{ and } \mathsf{ord}_B(m) = 0.$$

First-order moves from B are noop letters in $\mathcal{A}_2$ but push or pop letters in $\mathcal{A}_1$. We want them to be noop letters in $\mathcal{A}_{||}$, so we memorize the push operation in the state:

$$(s_1, s_2) \xrightarrow{q_1} (i_1, s, s_2') \qquad \text{if } q_1 \in M_B, \mathsf{ord}_B(q_1) = 1, s_1 \xrightarrow{q_1/s} i_1 \text{ and } s_2 \xrightarrow{q_1} s_2',$$
$$(i_1, s, s_2) \xrightarrow{a_1} (s_1', s_2') \qquad \text{if } a_1 \in M_B, \mathsf{ord}_B(a_1) = 1, i_1 \xrightarrow{a_1, s} s_1' \text{ and } s_2 \xrightarrow{a_1} s_2'.$$

Observe that we know that the transition on q_1 in $\mathcal{A}_1$ is a push transition leading to the initial state i_1, because $\mathcal{A}_1$ comes from Lemma 2. In order for the construction to work the information recorded in the state has to be exploited by the automaton in future steps. By Lemma 3, q_1 is always followed either by a_1 or by a third-order question from C. The above transitions take care of the first case. In the second case we will arrange for the symbol to be preserved on the stack together with the symbol pushed by the third-order question. Dually, when processing third-order answers we should be ready to process the combined symbols and decompress the information back into the state to be used by the following a_1. Thus we add the following transitions

$$(i_1, s, s_2) \xrightarrow{q_3/(X,s)} (i_1, s_2') \qquad \text{if } q_3 \in M_C \text{ and } s_2 \xrightarrow{q_3/X} s_2',$$

$$(i_1, s_2) \xrightarrow{a_3,(X,s)} (i_1, s, s_2') \qquad \text{if } a_3 \in M_C \text{ and } s_2 \xrightarrow{a_3,X} s_2',$$

which complete the definition of $\mathcal{A}_{||}$. It is not difficult to verify that $\mathcal{A}_{||}$ is proper for $\sigma^\dagger || \tau$. Note that for each state (s_1, s_2) with an outgoing transition on a B-move m there is no other transition, because m is always a P-move either for $\mathcal{A}_1$ or for $\mathcal{A}_2$ and we can then appeal to Remark 2 for that automaton. $\qquad \square$

4.5   Rounding Up

We are now ready to interpret the linear application rule introduced in Section 2. Assuming we have proper automata for $\sigma = [\![\Delta \vdash N : T]\!] : [\![\Delta]\!] \Rightarrow [\![T]\!]$ and $\tau = [\![\lambda x^T.\lambda\Gamma.Mx]\!] : [\![T]\!] \Rightarrow ([\![\Gamma]\!] \Rightarrow [\![T']\!])$ respectively, we would like to find an automaton $\mathcal{A}_{\mathrm{lin}}$ which is proper for $\sigma^\dagger ;_{\mathrm{lin}} \tau = [\![\Gamma, \Delta \vdash \lambda\Gamma.MN : \Gamma \to T']\!]$. To that end it suffices to consider the automaton $\mathcal{A}_{||}$ from Lemma 4 and hide the moves from $[\![T]\!]$. Recall that by Lemma 4 if there exists a transition on a move from $[\![T]\!]$ from a state of $\mathcal{A}_{||}$ then it is a noop transition and no other transitions leave that state. Hence, the automaton for $\sigma^\dagger ;_{\mathrm{lin}} \tau$ can be obtained by "collapsing" the sequences of $[\![T]\!]$ transitions in $\mathcal{A}_{||}$. This can be done by first replacing each transition $s_0 \xrightarrow{m\square} s_1$ by $s_0 \xrightarrow{m\square} s_{k+1}$ when there is a sequence of transitions in $\mathcal{A}_{||}$ of the form:

$$s_0 \xrightarrow{m\square} s_1 \xrightarrow{m_1} s_2 \xrightarrow{m_2} \ldots \xrightarrow{m_k} s_{k+1}$$

where m is not from $[\![T]\!]$, $m_1, \ldots, m_k$ are from $[\![T]\!]$, and s_{k+1} does not have an outgoing transition on a move from $[\![T]\!]$ (note that k is bounded by the number of states in $\mathcal{A}_{||}$). After this it is enough to remove all the transitions on letters from $[\![T]\!]$. It is easy to see that the resulting automaton $\mathcal{A}_{\mathrm{lin}}$ is proper for $\sigma^\dagger ;_{\mathrm{lin}} \tau$.

This completes the description of the construction of automata for simple terms. It remains to calculate the size of the resulting automata. For us the size of an automaton, denoted $|\mathcal{A}|$, will be the sum of the number of states and the number of stack symbols. We ignore the size of the alphabet because it is determined by types present in a sequent and hence is always linear in the size of the sequent. The number of transitions is always bounded by a polynomial in the size of the automaton.

The strategy automata for simple terms have been constructed from automata for base strategies using composition and contraction (λ-abstraction being the identity operation). Contraction does not increase the size of the automaton so it remains to calculate the increase due to composition. Suppose we have two automata $\mathcal{A}_\sigma$ and $\mathcal{A}_\tau$. Let Q_σ, Γ_σ (Q_τ, Γ_τ) stand for the sets of states and stack symbols of $\mathcal{A}_\sigma$ ($\mathcal{A}_\tau$). Examining the dagger construction we have that $|Q_\sigma^\dagger| = 2|Q_\sigma|$ and $|\Gamma_\sigma^\dagger| = 2(|\Gamma_\sigma| + |Q_\sigma|)$. For $\mathcal{A}_{||}$ we have $|Q_{||}| = 2|Q_\sigma^\dagger \times Q_\tau|$ and $|\Gamma_{||}| = |\Gamma_\sigma^\dagger| + |\Gamma_\tau| + |\Gamma_\tau \times Q_\sigma|$. Putting the two together and approximating both the number of states and stack symbols with $|\mathcal{A}_\sigma|$ and $|\mathcal{A}_\tau|$ we obtain: $|Q_{\text{lin}}| \leq 4|\mathcal{A}_\sigma||\mathcal{A}_\tau|$ and $|\Gamma_{\text{lin}}| \leq 5|\mathcal{A}_\sigma||\mathcal{A}_\tau|$. Thus $|\mathcal{A}_{\text{lin}}| \leq 9|\mathcal{A}_\sigma||\mathcal{A}_\tau|$ which gives us:

Lemma 5. *For every simple term $\Gamma \vdash M : T$ there exists an automaton which is proper for $[\![\Gamma \vdash M : T]\!]$ and whose size is exponential in the size of $\Gamma \vdash M : T$.*

5 Beyond Simple Terms

In this section we address the gap between simple terms and other β-normal IA_3^*-terms.

Lemma 6. *Any IA_3^*-term $\Gamma \vdash M : T$ in β-normal form can be obtained from a simple term $\Gamma' \vdash M' : T'$ by applications of the contraction rule for second-order identifiers followed by λ-abstractions.*

Hence, in order to account for all β-normal terms we only need to show how to interpret contraction at second order, because λ-abstraction is easy to interpret by renaming. As already noted at the end of Section 3, interpreting contraction will require an explicit representation scheme for pointers from third-order moves. Given a position sq_3 ending in a third-order move q_3 let us write $\alpha(s)$ (resp. $\alpha(s, q_3)$) for the number of open second- and third-order questions in s (resp. between q_3 and its justifier in s; if the justifier occurs immediately before q_3 then $\alpha(s, q_3) = 0$).

Definition 12. *Suppose $\sigma = [\![\Gamma \vdash M : T]\!]$, where $\Gamma \vdash M : T$ is an IA_3^*-term. The languages $\mathcal{P}(\sigma)$ and $\mathcal{P}'(\sigma)$ over $M_{[\![\Gamma \vdash T]\!]} + \{$ check, hit $\}$ are defined as follows:*

$$\mathcal{P}(\sigma) = \{\, s \, check^{\alpha(s,q_3)} \, hit \, check^{\alpha(s)-\alpha(s,q_3)-1} \mid sq_3 \in \mathcal{L}(\sigma) \,\}$$
$$\mathcal{P}'(\sigma) = \{\, s \, check^{\alpha(s,q_3)} \, hit \, check^{\alpha(s)-\alpha(s,q_3)-1} \mid \exists s'. \, sq_3s' \in \mathcal{L}(\mathsf{comp}(\sigma)) \,\}.$$

Note that q_3 is always a P-move, so s uniquely determines q_3. Clearly, $\mathcal{L}(\sigma) \cup \mathcal{P}(\sigma)$ represents σ faithfully in the sense that equality of representations coincides with equality of strategies. The subtlety is that we should compare only complete positions in strategies. This is why we introduce $\mathcal{P}'(\sigma)$. Using the results from the previous section, we first show how to construct automata recognizing $\mathcal{L}(\mathsf{comp}(\sigma)) \cup \mathcal{P}(\sigma)$ and $\mathcal{L}(\mathsf{comp}(\sigma)) \cup \mathcal{P}'(\sigma)$, where σ denotes a simple term. For this we will need to consider the nondeterministic version of strategy automata defined in the obvious way by allowing transition relations in place of functions.

By Lemma 1, in any position from σ the pointer from a third-order move q_3 points to the unique unanswered enabler visible in the P-view and hence is uniquely determined. Below we give a different characterization of the justifier relative to the whole position rather than to its P-view.

Lemma 7. *If $sq_3 \in [\![\Gamma \vdash M : T]\!]$, where $\Gamma \vdash M : T$ is simple, and q_3 is a third-order question then q_3's justifier in sq_3 is the last open enabler of q_3 in s.*

Lemma 8. *For any simple term $\Gamma \vdash M : T$ let $\sigma = [\![\Gamma \vdash M : T]\!]$. Then there exist a strategy automaton recognizing $\mathcal{L}(\mathsf{comp}(\sigma)) \cup \mathcal{P}(\sigma)$ and a nondeterministic strategy automaton accepting $\mathcal{L}(\mathsf{comp}(\sigma)) \cup \mathcal{P}'(\sigma)$ such that the push and pop letters are respectively questions and answers of order at least 2 and check, hit are pop letters. Their sizes are exponential in the size of $\Gamma \vdash M : T$.*

Proof. By Lemma 5 there exists a proper automaton $\mathcal{A}$ for $\mathcal{L}(\sigma)$. First we modify $\mathcal{A}$ so that second-order questions are pushed on the stack when read and taken off the stack when the corresponding second-order answers are processed. Note that the resulting automaton, let us call it $\mathcal{A}'$, still accepts $\mathcal{L}(\mathsf{comp}(\sigma))$, because σ satisfies the bracketing condition. Due to the modification above, the symbols present on the stack during a run of $\mathcal{A}'$ will correspond exactly to the unanswered second- and third-order questions in the sequence of moves read by the automaton (of course in the case of second-order questions these symbols are the questions themselves).

Next we modify $\mathcal{A}'$ to recognize $\mathcal{L}(\mathsf{comp}(\sigma)) \cup \mathcal{P}(\sigma)$. We add new transitions so that when the new automaton sees a *check* letter while being in state s it enters into a special mode. If $\mathcal{A}'$ could not read a third-order question q_3 from s, the new automaton rejects immediately. Otherwise there is precisely one question q_3 that can be read from s (Remark 2 (1.)). By Lemma 7 it suffices to make the new automaton read *check* letters and pop the stack as long as the stack symbol is not an enabler of q_3. When the first one comes, the automaton should read *hit* and subsequently continue accepting *check* as long as the stack is not empty.

The construction of a nondeterministic automaton accepting $\mathcal{L}(\mathsf{comp}(\sigma)) \cup \mathcal{P}'(\sigma)$ is similar except that while reading *check* and *hit* the automaton will need to guess how to extend sq_3 to a complete position accepted by $\mathcal{A}$. For this the automaton uses a pre-calculated table of triples (s_1, x, s_2) such that there is a computation of $\mathcal{A}$ from the state s_1 with only x on the stack to the state s_2 with the empty stack. The nondeterministic automaton uses this table during the last phase to guess a possible extension of the computation of $\mathcal{A}$.

As all these modifications increase the size of the automaton only by a linear factor we obtain the complexity bound required by the lemma. $\square$

Lemma 8 can be extended to all IA_3^*-terms in β-normal form. By Lemma 6, it suffices to be able to interpret λ-abstraction and contraction. Both can now be done by a suitable relabelling. Note that by identifying moves originating from the two distinguished copies of T in the contraction rule we do not lose information about pointers any more, because these are now represented explicitly.

Theorem 2. *For any* IA_3^**-term* $\Gamma \vdash M : T$ *in* β*-normal form there exist a strategy automaton accepting* $\mathcal{L}(\mathsf{comp}(\sigma)) \cup \mathcal{P}(\sigma)$ *and a nondeterministic strategy automaton accepting* $\mathcal{L}(\mathsf{comp}(\sigma)) \cup \mathcal{P}'(\sigma)$, *where* $\sigma = [\![\Gamma \vdash M : T]\!]$. *Their sizes are exponential in the size of the term.*

Suppose the strategies σ_1, σ_2 denote two β-normal IA_3^*-terms. Observe that $\mathsf{comp}(\sigma_1) \subseteq \mathsf{comp}(\sigma_2)$ is equivalent to $\mathcal{L}(\mathsf{comp}(\sigma_1)) \cup \mathcal{P}'(\sigma_1) \subseteq \mathcal{L}(\mathsf{comp}(\sigma_2)) \cup \mathcal{P}(\sigma_2)$. We can verify the containment in the same way as for deterministic finite automata using complementation and intersection. Because the strategy automaton representing the rhs is deterministic, complementation does not incur an exponential increase in size. For intersection we can construct a product automaton in the obvious way because stack operations are determined by the input and, for a given input letter, will be of the same kind in both automata. From this observation and the above theorem we obtain our main result.

Corollary 1. *The problems of contextual equivalence and approximation for* IA_3^* *terms in* β*-normal form are in* EXPTIME.

6   Lower Bound

We show EXPTIME-hardness of the equivalence problem for IA_3^* terms in β-normal form. This implies EXPTIME-hardness of the approximation problem. We use a reduction of the equivalence problem of nondeterministic automata on binary trees [9].

Labelled binary trees will be represented by positions of the game $[\![exp \rightarrow ((com \rightarrow com) \rightarrow com) \rightarrow com]\!]$. The sequence of moves $\mathcal{S}(t)$ corresponding to a given binary tree t is defined as follows

$$\mathcal{S}(x) = r_2\, q\, x\, d_2 \qquad \mathcal{S}(y(t_1, t_2)) = r_2\, q\, y\, r_3\, \mathcal{S}(t_1)\, d_3 r_3\, \mathcal{S}(t_2)\, d_3\, d_2$$

where x, y range over nullary and binary labels respectively. Observe that $\mathcal{S}(t)$ corresponds to a left-to-right depth-first traversal of t. Note that the term $\lambda f.f(\lambda x.x; x)$ defines complete positions of the shape $r_0 r_1 U d_1 d_0$ where $U ::= \epsilon \mid r_2 r_3 U d_3 r_3 U d_3 d_2$, i.e. $\lambda f.f(\lambda x.x; x)$ generates all possible sequences of r_i, d_i $(0 \leq i \leq 3)$ corresponding to trees. In order to represent a given tree automaton we can decorate the term with code that asks for node labels and prevents the positions incompatible with trees from developing into complete ones.

Lemma 9. *For any tree automaton* $\mathcal{A}$ *there exists a* β*-normal* IA_3 *term* $M_{\mathcal{A}}$ *such that* $\mathsf{comp}([\![M_{\mathcal{A}}]\!]) = \{\, r_0\, r_1\, \mathcal{S}(t)\, d_1\, d_0 \mid t \in T(\mathcal{A})\,\}$, *where* $T(\mathcal{A})$ *is the set of trees accepted by* $\mathcal{A}$.

Corollary 2. *The contextual equivalence and approximation problems for* β*-normal* IA_3*-terms are* EXPTIME*-hard. Thus the two problems for* IA_3^* *terms in* β*-normal form are* EXPTIME*-complete.*

References

1. Reynolds, J. C.: The essence of Algol. In: Algorithmic Languages. North Holland (1981) 345–372
2. Abramsky, S., Ghica, D. R., Murawski, A. S., Ong, C.-H. L.: Applying game semantics to compositional software modelling and verification. In Proc. of TACAS, LNCS **2988** (2004) 421–435
3. Alur, R., Madhusudan, P.: Visibly pushdown languages. Proc. of STOC (2004) 202–211
4. Ghica, D. R., McCusker, G.: Reasoning about Idealized Algol using regular expressions. Proc. of ICALP, LNCS **1853** (2000) 103–115
5. Ong, C.-H. L.: Observational equivalence of 3rd-order Idealized Algol is decidable. Proc. of LICS (2002) 245–256
6. Murawski, A. S.: On program equivalence in languages with ground-type references. In Proc. of LICS (2003) 108–117
7. Abramsky, S., McCusker, G.: Linearity, sharing and state: a fully abstract game semantics for Idealized Algol with active expressions. In: Algol-like languages. Birkhaüser (1997) 297–329
8. Hyland, J. M. E., Ong, C.-H. L.: On full abstraction for PCF. Information and Computation **163(2)** (2000) 285–408
9. Seidl, H.: Deciding equivalence of finite tree automata. SIAM J. Comput. **19(3)** (1990) 424–437

Fault Diagnosis Using Timed Automata

Patricia Bouyer[1,*], Fabrice Chevalier[1,*], and Deepak D'Souza[2,**]

[1] LSV – CNRS UMR 8643 & ENS de Cachan
61, avenue du Président Wilson, 94230 Cachan, France
`bouyer, chevalie@lsv.ens-cachan.fr`
[2] Dept. of Computer Science & Automation
Indian Institute of Science, Bangalore, India
`deepakd@csa.iisc.ernet.in`

Abstract. Fault diagnosis consists in observing behaviours of systems, and in detecting *online* whether an error has occurred or not. In the context of discrete event systems this problem has been well-studied, but much less work has been done in the timed framework. In this paper, we consider the problem of diagnosing faults in behaviours of timed plants. We focus on the problem of synthesizing fault diagnosers which are realizable as deterministic timed automata, with the motivation that such diagnosers would function as efficient online fault detectors. We study two classes of such mechanisms, the class of deterministic timed automata (DTA) and the class of event-recording timed automata (ERA). We show that the problem of synthesizing diagnosers in each of these classes is decidable, provided we are given a bound on the resources available to the diagnoser. We prove that under this assumption diagnosability is 2EXPTIME-complete in the case of DTA's whereas it becomes PSPACE-complete for ERA's.

1   Introduction

The problem of fault diagnosis involves detecting whether a given system (which we call a *plant*) has undergone a fault, based on a particular external observation of an execution of the plant [SSL$^+$95, SSL$^+$96]. More precisely we are given a detailed model of the plant – say as a finite state machine – based on internal unobservable events as well as externally observable events of the plant. Some of the internal actions correspond to *faults*. A *diagnoser* for such a plant is a function which given a sequence of observable events generated by the plant, tells us whether an internal fault happened or not. Not all plants are *diagnosable* (in the sense that such a function may not exist) – for example a plant which produces the two behaviours aub and afb, where u and f are internal events with f being the faulty one, and a and b are observable events, is *not* diagnosable since from the observable sequence ab it is impossible to tell whether f happened or not.

Our interest in this paper lies in the fault diagnosis problem for *timed* plants. Here we are given a plant modelled as a timed automaton. The timed automata of Alur and

---

* Work partly supported by ACI Cortos, a program of the french ministry of research.
** Part of this work was done during a visit to LSV, ENS Cachan.

Dill [AD94] are a popular model for time-dependent systems that extend classical finite state machines with real-time clocks. These clocks can record the passage of time in states, and can be used to guard the occurrence of transitions. A timed automaton generates timed sequences of events – *i.e.* an alternating sequence of real-valued delays and events. The fault diagnosis problem for timed plants is thus to detect faulty behaviours from a given timed sequence of observable events of the plant.

This problem is considerably more difficult in the timed case than in the discrete case. In the discrete case one deals with classical regular languages which have robust closure properties and relatively efficient algorithms for determinization and checking emptiness. Thus one can obtain a diagnoser by essentially determinizing the model of the plant. In the timed setting the problem is compounded by the fact that timed automata are a very expressive formalism. While their language emptiness problem is decidable, they are not determinizable, nor closed under complementation [AD94].

The problem in the timed setting has been studied by Tripakis in [Tri02] where a variety of results have been shown. In particular, it is shown to be decidable to check whether a given timed plant is diagnosable or not, and a diagnoser can be constructed as an online algorithm whenever the plant is indeed diagnosable. The diagnosis algorithm in [Tri02] is based on state estimation; it is somewhat complex, since it involves keeping track of several possible control states and *zones* that the clock values can be in, with every observable action or time delay of the plant. A natural question that one may ask here is: when is there a diagnoser which is realizable as a *deterministic* timed automaton (DTA)? Such a DTA would lead to a more efficient online diagnosis algorithm, since with each observable event or time delay there is a *single* deterministic move in the DTA.

In this paper we consider two deterministic mechanisms namely general DTA's and Event Recording automata (ERA) [AFH94]. For general DTA's we show that it is decidable to check whether a given timed plant has a diagnoser realizable as a DTA, *provided* we are given a bound on the resources (*i.e.* the number of clocks and set of constants) available to the diagnoser. Whenever such a diagnoser exists, we are able to synthesize one. The technique used is to relate the existence of a DTA diagnoser to a winning strategy for a player in a classical state-based two player game.

The decision procedure runs in 2EXPTIME in the size of the plant. We show that this high complexity is unavoidable in that the problem is 2EXPTIME-complete. The completeness argument is based on a reduction from the halting problem of an alternating Turing machine which uses exponential space.

We also look at the problem for a restricted class of DTA's called Event Recording Automata [AFH94]. These are a determinizable subclass of timed automata, in which there is an implicit clock attached to each action. We show that the problem of deciding whether there is a diagnoser realizable as an ERA – again given a bound on the resources we allow for the diagnoser – is decidable in PSPACE. Once again the problem is shown to be complete for PSPACE.

Other recent works show an increasing interest in partial observability (e.g. learning [GJL04]); this increases complexity of systems as several control problems become undecidable under partial observability [DM02, BDMP03] . However it seems useful to combine this issue with on-the-fly analysis (for example monitoring [KT04] or run-time model-checking [KPA03]). This work puts together these two aspects: the framework is fault diagnosis of partially observable systems and the deterministic mechanisms we consider fit the online constraint.

The plan of the paper is as follows. After introducing notations and definitions in section 2, we will present the problem of fault diagnosis (section 3), starting with results from [Tri02] and going on to the problem we look at. We then present our result on the class of deterministic timed automata (section 4) and then on the class of event-recording automata (section 5). The paper contains only sketches of proof. Detailed proofs can be found in [Che04] (written in french).

2   Preliminaries

For a set Γ, let Γ^* be the set of *finite* sequences of elements in Γ.

Timed Words. We consider a finite set of *actions* Σ and as time domain the set $\mathbb{Q}_{\geq 0}$ of non-negative rationals. A *timed word* over Σ is a sequence in $(\Sigma \cup \mathbb{Q}_{\geq 0})^*$, *i.e.* a finite sequence $\rho = \gamma_1, \gamma_2, \ldots$ where each γ_i is either an event in Σ or a delay in $\mathbb{Q}_{\geq 0}$.[1] A set of timed words will be called a *timed language*. If ρ is a timed word, we define time(ρ) to be the sum of all delays in ρ. If $\Sigma' \subseteq \Sigma$ and if ρ is a timed word, we denote by $\pi_{\Sigma'}(\rho)$ its projection over the alphabet Σ', which means that we erase actions not in Σ'. For example, if $\Sigma' = \{a, c\} \subseteq \{a, b, c\} = \Sigma$, then $\pi_{\Sigma'}(0.5, a, 0.7, b, 0.3, c) = 0.5, a, 0.7, 0.3, c$ which reduces naturally to the timed word $0.5, a, 1, c$. This operation extends in a natural way to timed languages.

Clocks, Operations on Clocks. We consider a finite set X of variables, called *clocks*. A *clock valuation* over X is a mapping $v : X \to \mathbb{Q}_{\geq 0}$ that assigns to each clock a time value. We use $\mathbf{0}$ to denote the valuation which sets each clock $x \in X$ to 0. If $t \in \mathbb{Q}_{\geq 0}$, the valuation $v + t$ is defined as $(v + t)(x) = v(x) + t$ for all $x \in X$. If Y is a subset of X, the valuation $v[Y \leftarrow 0]$ is defined as: for each clock x, $(v[Y \leftarrow 0])(x) = 0$ if $x \in Y$ and is $v(x)$ otherwise.

The set of *constraints* (or *guards*) over a set of clocks X, denoted $\mathcal{G}(X)$, is given by the syntax "$g ::= (x \sim c) \mid (g \wedge g)$" where $x \in X$, $c \in \mathbb{Q}_{\geq 0}$ and $\sim$ is one of $<$, $\leq$, $=$, $\geq$, or $>$. We write $v \models g$ if the valuation v satisfies the clock constraint g, and is given by $v \models (x \sim c)$ if $v(x) \sim c$ and $v \models (g_1 \wedge g_2)$ if $v \models g_1$ and $v \models g_2$. The set of valuations over X which satisfy a guard $g \in \mathcal{G}(X)$ is denoted by $[\![g]\!]_X$, or just $[\![g]\!]$ when X is clear from the context.

Symbolic Alphabet and Timed Automata. Let Σ be an alphabet of actions, and X a finite set of clocks. A *symbolic alphabet* Γ based on (Σ, X) is a finite subset of $\mathcal{G}(X) \times \Sigma \times 2^X$. As used in the framework of timed automata [AD94], a symbolic word $\gamma = (g_i, b_i, Y_i)_{1 \leq i \leq k} \in \Gamma^*$ gives rise to a set of timed words, denoted $tw(\gamma)$. We interpret the symbolic action (g, b, Y) to mean that action b can happen if the guard g is satisfied,

---

[1] Following [Tri02], we use this definition of timed words, a more classical definition of timed words as in [AD94] could be used as well.

with the clocks in Y being reset after the action. Formally, let $\rho = d_0, a_1, d_1, a_2, \ldots$ be a timed word. Then $\rho \in tw(\gamma)$ if there exists a sequence $v = (v_i)_{i \geq 1}$ of valuations such that for all $i \geq 1$, $a_i = b_i$, $v_{i-1} + d_{i-1} \models g_i$ and $v_i = (v_{i-1} + d_{i-1})[Y_i \leftarrow 0]$ (with the convention $v_0 = \mathbf{0}$).

A *timed automaton* (TA for short) is a tuple $\mathcal{A} = (\Sigma, X, Q, q_0, F, \longrightarrow, Inv)$ where Σ is a finite alphabet of actions, X is a finite set of clocks, Q is a finite set of states, $q_0 \in Q$ is the initial state, $F \subseteq Q$ is the set of final states, $\longrightarrow \subseteq Q \times \Gamma \times Q$ is a finite set of transitions over some symbolic alphabet Γ based on (Σ, X), and $Inv : Q \to \mathcal{G}(X)$ is an invariant function. The timed automaton $\mathcal{A}$ is said to be *deterministic* if, for every state, the set of symbolic actions enabled at that state is time-deterministic, *i.e.* do not contain distinct symbolic actions (g, a, Y) and (g', a, Y') with $[\![g]\!] \cap [\![g']\!] \neq \emptyset$. The class of deterministic timed automata is denoted DTA. An *event-recording automaton* (ERA for short) [AFH94] is a timed automaton $(\Sigma, X, Q, q_0, F, \longrightarrow, Inv)$ where $X = \{x_a \mid a \in \Sigma\}$ and $q \xrightarrow{g,a,Y} q'$ implies $Y = \{x_a\}$. Informally the clock x_a stores the time elapsed since the last occurrence of action a. We extend the above definitions to allow ε-transitions (or silent transitions) in our timed automata [BDGP98].

For convenience, we will assume that all guards in timed automata are compatible with invariants in the following sense. If $q \xrightarrow{g,a,Y} q'$ is a transition, we want that $[\![g]\!]$ be included in $[\![Inv(q)]\!]$, and $[Y \leftarrow 0][\![g]\!]$ be included in $[\![Inv(q')]\!]$. If it is not the case, it is easy to transform the timed automaton so that this condition holds.

A *path* in a TA $\mathcal{A}$ is a finite sequence of consecutive transitions:

$$q_0 \xrightarrow{g_1, a_1, Y_1} q_1 \ldots q_{k-1} \xrightarrow{g_k, a_k, Y_k} q_k, \text{ s.t } \forall 1 \leq i \leq k, \ (q_{i-1}, g_i, a_i, Y_i, q_i) \in \longrightarrow$$

The path is said to be *accepting* in $\mathcal{A}$ if it ends in a final state $q_k \in F$.

A timed automaton $\mathcal{A}$ can then be interpreted as a classical finite automaton on the symbolic alphabet Γ. Viewed as such, $\mathcal{A}$ accepts (or generates) a language of symbolic words, $L_{sym}(\mathcal{A}) \subseteq \Gamma^*$, constituted by the labels of the accepting paths in $\mathcal{A}$. We will be more interested in the timed language generated by $\mathcal{A}$, denoted $L(\mathcal{A})$, and defined by $L(\mathcal{A}) = tw(L_{sym}(\mathcal{A}))$.

Synchronized Product. Let $\mathcal{A}_i = (\Sigma_i, X_i, Q_i, q_0^i, F_i, \longrightarrow_i, Inv_i)$ be two timed automata. Without loss of generality we assume that X_1 and X_2 are disjoint. The *synchronized product* of $\mathcal{A}_1$ and $\mathcal{A}_2$ is defined as the timed automaton $\mathcal{A}_1 \parallel \mathcal{A}_2 = (\Sigma, X, Q, q_0, F, \longrightarrow, Inv)$ where $\Sigma = \Sigma_1 \cup \Sigma_2$, $X = X_1 \cup X_2$, $Q = Q_1 \times Q_2$, $q^0 = (q_1^0, q_2^0)$, $F = F_1 \times F_2$ and $(q_1, q_2) \xrightarrow{g,a,Y} (q_1', q_2')$ whenever one of the following conditions holds:

- $a \in \Sigma_1 \cap \Sigma_2$ and there exist $q_1 \xrightarrow{g_1, a, Y_1}_1 q_1'$ and $q_2 \xrightarrow{g_2, a, Y_2}_2 q_2'$ with $g = g_1 \wedge g_2$ and $Y = Y_1 \cup Y_2$
- $a \in \Sigma_i \setminus \Sigma_j$ (with $i \neq j$), there exists $q_i \xrightarrow{g,a,Y}_i q_i'$ and $q_j' = q_j$

This synchronized product is the classical composition where both components synchronize on common actions.

Region Automata. Region automata have been proposed in [AD94] for abstracting timed behaviours. Regions are classes of an equivalence relation over valuations which satisfy the nice property that two equivalent valuations have equivalent (time and discrete) successors. The region automaton construction is the core of the decidability proof for checking emptiness of timed automata. We will make use of the region automaton in Lemma 2. In the following if $\mathcal{A}$ is a timed automaton, we will denote its region automaton by $\mathcal{R}(\mathcal{A})$.

Granularity. In the following, we will consider models with bounded resources, for example the subclass of DTA's using 5 clocks and integer constants smaller than 7. Fixing resources of models has been frequently done in the past in several contexts: satisfiability of timed μ-calculus [LLW95], controller synthesis [DM02, BDMP03], testing [KT04]. In all cases, fixing the resources helps in getting decidability results, and it is quite natural when our aim is to synthesize a system (with given physical resources).

We formalize this notion by defining a measure of the clocks and constants used in a set of constraints. A *granularity* is a tuple $\mu = (X, m, max)$ where X is a set of clocks, m is a positive integer and $max : X \longrightarrow \mathbb{Q}_{\geq 0}$ a function which associates with each clock of X a positive rational number. The granularity of a finite set of constraints is the tuple (X, m, max) where X is the exact set of clocks mentioned in the constraints, m is the least common multiple of the denominators of the constants mentioned in the constraints, and max records for each $x \in X$ the largest constant it is compared with. A granularity $\nu = (X', m', max')$ is said to be *finer* than a granularity $\mu = (X, m, max)$ (or equivalently μ is said to be *coarser* than ν) if $X \subseteq X'$, m divides m' and for all $x \in X$ $max'(x) \geq max(x)$. A constraint g is called μ-*granular* if it belongs to some set of constraints of granularity μ (note that a μ-granular constraint is also ν-granular for any granularity ν finer than μ). We denote the set of all μ-granular constraints by $\mathcal{G}(\mu)$. A constraint $g \in \mathcal{G}(\mu)$ is called μ-*atomic* if for all $g' \in \mathcal{G}(\mu)$, either $[\![g]\!]_X \subseteq [\![g']\!]_X$ or $[\![g]\!]_X \cap [\![g']\!]_X = \emptyset$. Let $atoms_\mu$ denote this set of μ-atomic constraints. By the granularity of a timed automaton, we will mean the granularity of the set of constraints used in it. For such an automaton, the granularity μ represents its *resources* in terms of clocks and constants. We denote by DTA$_\mu$ (resp. ERA$_\mu$) the class of DTA's (resp. ERA's) whose granularity is coarser than μ. Let $\mu = (X, m, max)$ be a granularity over Σ, we denote by Γ_μ the symbolic alphabet over μ (*i.e.* the set $atoms_\mu \times \Sigma \times 2^X$) and $\mathcal{U}_\mu$ the universal single-state automaton over symbolic alphabet Γ_μ.

Let $\mu = (X, m, max)$ be a granularity over the alphabet Σ and $\nu = (X', m', max')$ be a granularity finer than μ over $\Sigma' \supseteq \Sigma$. For $(g', a', Y') \in atoms_\nu \times \Sigma' \times X'$ a symbolic letter over ν, we define the projection $(g', a', Y') \lceil \mu$ as follows: let g be the unique μ-atomic constraint such that $[\![g']\!]_{X'} \subseteq [\![g]\!]_{X'}$, $Y = Y' \cap X$, then $(g', a', Y') \lceil \mu$ is defined to be (g, a', Y) if $a' \in \Sigma$ and ε (the empty word) if $a' \notin \Sigma$. If μ is a granularity and $\mathcal{A}$ a TA whose granularity is finer than μ, we denote by $\mathcal{A} \lceil \mu$ the TA in which every transition label is replaced by its projection on μ.

3   The Fault Diagnosis Problem

In this section, we present the problem of fault diagnosis for timed systems. First we recall basic definitions and existing work and then we present our approach which involves fault diagnosis by timed automata.

3.1   Existing Work

In this section we present the basic notions and the main results from [Tri02].

For the rest of the paper, Σ_o denotes an alphabet of *observable* events while Σ_u denotes an alphabet of *unobservable* events. We assume that Σ_o and Σ_u are disjoint. Given a timed word ρ, its *observation* is its projection over Σ_o, *i.e.* $\pi_{\Sigma_o}(\rho)$. In what follows, we will simply write π instead of π_{Σ_o}. A run $\rho = \beta_1, \beta_2, \ldots, \beta_p$ is called *faulty* if there exists $i \in \mathbb{N}$ such that $\beta_i = f$. It is called Δ-*faulty* if for one such i, $\mathrm{time}(\beta_{i+1}, \ldots, \beta_p) \geq \Delta$.

A *plant* is a tuple $\mathcal{P} = (\Sigma_o, \Sigma_u, Q, q_0, \longrightarrow, X, \mathit{Inv})$ where $(\Sigma_o \cup \Sigma_u, X, Q, q_0, Q, \longrightarrow, \mathit{Inv})$ is a TA (thus a plant has all states final). A *run* of the plant is simply a timed word generated by the plant. Given a plant $\mathcal{P}$, we denote by $L_{\Delta f}(\mathcal{P})$ the set of Δ-faulty runs of $\mathcal{P}$ and $L_{\neg f}(\mathcal{P})$ the set of non-faulty runs of $\mathcal{P}$. From now on, when there is no ambiguity, $L_{\Delta f}(\mathcal{P})$ (resp. $L_{\neg f}(\mathcal{P})$) will be denoted $L_{\Delta f}$ (resp. $L_{\neg f}$).

Fault diagnosis aims at computing a function which, given an observation, decides if a fault has occurred or not, and which always announces faults at most Δ time units after it has occurred. Such a function should announce a fault on all Δ-faulty runs and should not announce a fault on non-faulty runs; this is captured by the next definition, which is an equivalent reformulation of Tripakis' notion of diagnosability.

Definition 1. *A plant $\mathcal{P}$ is called Δ-diagnosable if there exists a recursive language L such that*

$$\pi(L_{\Delta f}) \subseteq L \subseteq \pi(L_{\neg f})^c .$$

This definition raises the following computational problem where $\Delta \in \mathbb{Q}_{\geq 0}$:

Problem 1 (Δ-diagnosability) *Given a plant $\mathcal{P}$, decide whether $\mathcal{P}$ is Δ-diagnosable or not.*

This problem is solved in [Tri02]:

Theorem 1 ([Tri02]). *Δ-diagnosability is PSPACE-complete.*

3.2   Diagnosability by Automata

The problem solved in [Tri02] is very general: the diagnoser is only supposed to be recursive, which, in practice, may be a complex algorithm. The algorithm proposed in [Tri02] is based on state estimation in a TA with ε-transitions, its complexity to diagnose faults from an observation is doubly exponential in the size of the plant and in the size of the observation, though an algorithm based on regions (and no more on zones) with a complexity exponential in both the size of the plant and of the observation could be proposed as well.

This high complexity in the size of the observation is not satisfactory if we want to perform "*online diagnosis*", *i.e.* if we want the diagnoser to detect faults from real-time observations of the system.

This has motivated the definition of diagnosability using timed automata: we are no more looking for a diagnoser which may be a general algorithm but for a diagnoser which will be a timed automaton. With such a diagnoser, the complexity of detecting faults *online* will no more be (doubly) exponential in the length of the observation since after each observable action the diagnoser has just to make a single deterministic move. We formalize this notion of diagnosability using timed automata as follows.

Definition 2. *Let C be a class of timed automata. Let $\mathcal{P}$ be a plant. We say that $\mathcal{P}$ is Δ-C-diagnosable whenever there exists some $\theta \in C$ such that*

$$\pi(L_{\Delta f}) \subseteq L(\theta) \subseteq \pi(L_{\neg f})^c \ .$$

We call such a θ a Δ-C-diagnoser for $\mathcal{P}$.

The sets of diagnosers which will be of interest to us are deterministic mechanisms like DTA's and ERA's. In the sequel we will study the following problem, where $\Delta \in \mathbb{Q}_{\geq 0}$ and C is a class of automata:

Problem 2 (Δ-C-diagnosability) *Given a plant $\mathcal{P}$, decide whether $\mathcal{P}$ is Δ-C-diagnosable or not.*

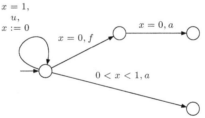

Fig. 1. Plant diagnosable but not DTA-diagnosable

We first notice that this problem is distinct from problem 1: every DTA-diagnosable plant is diagnosable, but some diagnosable plants are not DTA-diagnosable as illustrated by the plant in Fig. 1. Indeed, a diagnoser will announce a fault if action a happens at an integer date (this can not be expressed by a DTA, as shown in [BDGP98]).

4   Diagnosability with Deterministic Timed Automata

We do not consider the general problem of Δ-DTA-diagnosability but we restrict ourselves to the case when the resources of the diagnoser are fixed. We thus consider in this section the Δ-DTA$_\mu$-diagnosability problem: we aim at constructing diagnosers which are DTA's with a fixed granularity μ over Σ_o. In this framework, our main theorem is the following.

Theorem 2. *Let μ be a granularity over observable events and $\Delta \in \mathbb{Q}_{\geq 0}$. The Δ-DTA_μ-diagnosability problem is 2EXPTIME-complete.*

Before presenting the proof of this theorem, let us first state the two following useful lemmas: the first lemma states that we can construct timed automata recognizing non-faulty and Δ-faulty runs while the second one explains how behaviours of the plant can be seen "through" the granularity μ.

Lemma 1. *Let $\mathcal{P}$ be a plant and $\Delta \in \mathbb{Q}_{\geq 0}$. We can construct in polynomial time timed automata with ε-transitions $\mathcal{P}_{\neg f}$ and $\mathcal{P}_{\Delta f}$ such that $L(\mathcal{P}_{\neg f}) = \pi(L_{\neg f})$ and $L(\mathcal{P}_{\Delta f}) = \pi(L_{\Delta f})$.*

Proof (Sketch). $\mathcal{P}_{\neg f}$ is constructed from $\mathcal{P}$ as follows: erase transitions labelled by f (to prevent $\mathcal{P}$ from making faults), replace all transitions labelled by $u \in \Sigma_u$ by ε-transitions and make all states final.

Before constructing $\mathcal{P}_{\Delta f}$, we modify the plant $\mathcal{P}$, and construct a new plant $\mathcal{P}'$, which has the same observations as $\mathcal{P}$, and in which information on whether the current run is Δ-faulty or not is stored in the current state of $\mathcal{P}'$. $\mathcal{P}'$ is constructed as three copies of $\mathcal{P}$, say $\mathcal{P}_1, \mathcal{P}_2$ and $\mathcal{P}_3$: doing a fault in $\mathcal{P}_1$ leads to $\mathcal{P}_2$; in $\mathcal{P}_2$ the automaton behaves like $\mathcal{P}$ for Δ time units before switching to $\mathcal{P}_3$ by an unobservable action u. This can easily be formalized using a fresh clock z which is reset when a fault is done in $\mathcal{P}_1$ (leading to plant $\mathcal{P}_2$), adding an invariant $z \leq \Delta$ in all locations of $\mathcal{P}_2$ and as soon as $z = \Delta$, a transition labelled by u leads to $\mathcal{P}_3$. In the following we will assume that the plant is already given as $\mathcal{P}'$ and will call states of $\mathcal{P}_1$ "non-faulty" and states of $\mathcal{P}_3$ "Δ-faulty".

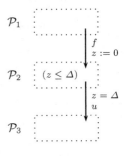

To get $\mathcal{P}_{\Delta f}$, we just replace transitions labelled by $u \in \Sigma_u$ by ε-transitions in $\mathcal{P}'$ and mark all states of $\mathcal{P}_3$ as final. It is not difficult to check that this automaton recognizes $\pi(L_{\Delta f})$. $\qquad\square$

The following lemma is a consequence of the region automata construction:

Lemma 2. *Let $\mathcal{A}$ be a timed automaton and μ a granularity. The region automaton $\mathcal{R}(\mathcal{A} \parallel \mathcal{U}_\mu){\restriction}\mu$ recognizes the set*

$$L_{sym}\left(\mathcal{R}(\mathcal{A} \parallel \mathcal{U}_\mu){\restriction}\mu\right) = \{\gamma \in \Gamma_\mu^* \mid \exists \rho \in L(\mathcal{A}) \text{ s.t. } \pi(\rho) \in tw(\gamma)\}$$

4.1 Δ-DTA$_\mu$-Diagnosability is in 2EXPTIME

In [BDMP03], the control problem under partial observability is proved to be in 2EXPTIME using a timed game construction. A similar construction can be carried out, but we present here a direct construction which gives more intuition.

Lemma 3. *Δ-DTA$_\mu$-diagnosability is in 2EXPTIME.*

Proof (Sketch). Let $\mathcal{P} = (\Sigma_o, \Sigma_u, Q, q_0, \longrightarrow, X, \mathit{Inv})$ be a plant and $\mu = (Y, m, max)$ a granularity over Σ_o. We will construct a classical (untimed) safety game $\mathcal{G}_{\mathcal{P},\mu,\Delta}$: it is a two-player turn-based perfect information game over a finite graph where one player wants to stay in the "safe" states, whereas the other player wants to enforce an "unsafe" state. We refer to [GTW02] for basics results on games. In our case, the two players are the "*diagnoser*" and the "*environment*", and player "*diagnoser*" will have a winning strategy in game $\mathcal{G}_{\mathcal{P},\mu,\Delta}$ if and only if $\mathcal{P}$ is Δ-DTA$_\mu$-diagnosable.

The arena of the game is constructed as follows: we first compute the region automaton $\mathcal{R}$ of $\mathcal{P}_{\Delta f} \parallel \mathcal{U}_\mu$. Its granularity is finer than μ, because it takes into account clocks and constraints from $\mathcal{U}_\mu$. To express that not everything can be observed, we project this automaton over the granularity μ to get $\mathcal{R}{\upharpoonright}\mu$ (intuitively this represents how runs can be seen "through" the granularity μ). This automaton (considered as a finite automaton over the alphabet Γ_μ) is not deterministic and has ε-transitions, we thus determinize it as a classical finite automaton by the usual subset construction and denote $\mathcal{K}$ the result. A state of $\mathcal{K}$ is a set $\{(q_1, R_1), \cdots, (q_k, R_k)\}$ where q_i's are states of $\mathcal{P}$ and R_i's regions; being in such a state means that according to the observation the plant can be in a state (q_i, v_i) with $v_i \in R_i$.

Finally $\mathcal{G}_{\mathcal{P},\mu,\Delta}$ is obtained from $\mathcal{K}$ by splitting every transition $q \xrightarrow{g,a,Y} q'$ of $\mathcal{K}$ into two transitions $q \xrightarrow{g,a} (q, g, a)$ and $(q, g, a) \xrightarrow{Y} q'$ where (q, g, a) is a new state. The intuition behind this split is that player "*environment*" chooses which action is done and at what time this action is done (state q will thus be an "*environment*" state) whereas player "*diagnoser*" chooses which clocks are reset (the state (q, g, a) is a "*diagnoser*" state). The forbidden states of this safety game are those states of $\mathcal{K}$ which contain both "non-faulty" and "Δ-faulty" states of $\mathcal{R}{\upharpoonright}\mu$.

Using lemma 2, we can prove that player "*diagnoser*" has a winning strategy in the game $\mathcal{G}_{\mathcal{P},\mu,\Delta}$ to avoid the forbidden states if and only if $\mathcal{P}$ is Δ-DTA$_\mu$-diagnosable. $\mathcal{G}_{\mathcal{P},\mu,\Delta}$ is a simple untimed game with a safety objective, it is easy to synthesize positional winning strategies when some exist. Such a winning strategy can be obtained from $\mathcal{G}_{\mathcal{P},\mu,\Delta}$ by erasing some of the reset transitions (*i.e.* transitions labelled by some subset Y). From this automaton, we can easily synthesize a diagnoser for $\mathcal{P}$ (by taking as final those states where all regions are Δ-faulty and merging $q \xrightarrow{g,a} (q, g, a)$ with $(q, g, a) \xrightarrow{Y} q'$ into $q \xrightarrow{g,a,Y} q'$).

The complexity of extracting winning strategies from safety (untimed) games is linear in the size of the arena, the complexity of deciding whether a Δ-DTA$_\mu$-diagnoser exists (and constructing it) is thus doubly exponential because the size of $\mathcal{R}$ is exponential in the size of $\mathcal{P}$ and μ (see [AD94]) and the size of $\mathcal{K}$ is exponential in the size of $\mathcal{R}$ thus doubly exponential in the size of $\mathcal{P}$ and μ. □

Example 1. We illustrate the proof on a small example: consider the following plant, the granularity $\mu = (\{y\}, 1, 0)$ and the delay $\Delta = 0$.

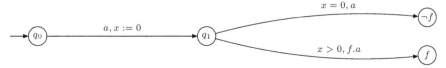

The notation $f.a$ is for an action f immediately followed by an a. This plant is Δ-DTA$_\mu$-diagnosable: a diagnoser resetting his clock when reading the first a will be able to diagnose $\mathcal{P}$ simply by checking the value of his clock when reading the second a.

The game constructed in the previous proof is depicted on the next picture:

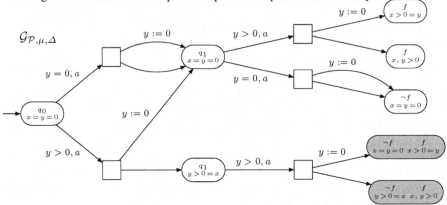

The states that player diagnoser must avoid in the above game are the gray states which contain both faulty and non-faulty regions (informally states in which the diagnoser cannot know if the run of the plant is faulty or not). In the game, "circle"-states belong to the "environment" player while "square"-states belong to the "diagnoser" player. In the game-graph, it is easy to see that "diagnoser" has a winning strategy. The problematic state is the bottom-left-most square-state: if "diagnoser" plays action "$y := 0$", he wins; if he chooses the other transition, player "environment" can win by next playing "$y > 0, a$". This confirms what we have noticed: if a diagnoser resets his clock when reading the first a, he can diagnose correctly; but if he does not reset his clock, he will be unable to diagnose the plant.

4.2 Δ-DTA$_\mu$-Diagnosability Is 2EXPTIME-Hard

The proof uses a reduction from the halting problem of alternating Turing machines using exponential space. We only sketch the reduction, details can be found in [Che04].

Let $\mathcal{M}$ be an alternating Turing machine using exponential space and let w_0 be an input for $\mathcal{M}$. We will construct a plant $\mathcal{P}$ such that there is a Δ-DTA$_\mu$-diagnoser for $\mathcal{P}$ (with $\mu = (\{t\}, 2, 1)$ and $\Delta = 1$) if and only if $\mathcal{M}$ accepts w_0. We somehow want to force a potential diagnoser θ for $\mathcal{P}$ to play the sequence of configurations which accepts w_0. The role of the plant is to give inputs to the diagnoser so that it can verify that the diagnoser really plays the accepting sequence of configurations. The diagnoser will have to play a sequence of configurations $C_0 \# C_1 \# \ldots \# C_k$ where each C_i is a configuration of $\mathcal{M}$, C_{i+1} is the successor of C_i and C_0 is the initial configuration encoding the input w_0. The behaviour of $\mathcal{P}$ is depicted on Fig. 2. $\mathcal{P}$ produces a's (on the figure, one line of a's corresponds to a configuration, *i.e.* to an exponential number of a's) and checks that the diagnoser plays the configurations of $\mathcal{M}$ correctly by performing one test. As the decision to perform the test is done in a *non-observable* way (u actions are non-observable), to be correct, a diagnoser cannot cheat and has to simulate $\mathcal{M}$. #'s are observable and are indexed to represent alternation of $\mathcal{M}$ (in case of a

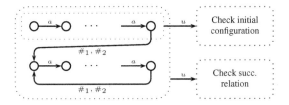

Fig. 2. Shape of the plant for the reduction

universal configuration of $\mathcal{M}$, the diagnoser has to know which transition rule the plant wants to follow). As already said, a configuration needs an exponential number of a's, as the discrete structure of $\mathcal{P}$ cannot count, we use clocks for counting this exponential number of a's. We cannot give all details here and better refer the reader to [Che04]. Note that the two checks can be encoded by 3SAT-formulae (in conjunctive normal form [Pap94]). We will now explain how such formulae can be encoded.

Given a 3SAT-formula φ we want to construct a plant $\mathcal{P}$ such that $\mathcal{P}$ is Δ-DTA$_\mu$-diagnosable if and only if φ is satisfiable. We first explain how a diag-

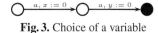

Fig. 3. Choice of a variable

noser θ will choose the truth of a propositional variable p. Consider the plant in Fig. 3. When two a's have been done, θ will know that the plant is in the black state but it will know the value of at most one of the two clocks x and y because θ is supposed to have only one clock t. The choice *true* for p will be encoded by the fact that the clock t has the same value as the clock x (we will say in this case that θ *has stored* x). We now show how we can force a diagnoser θ to set p to *true*, *i.e.* to store clock x. Fig. 4 illustrates the construction. The main idea is that if θ stores x, after three a's, if the

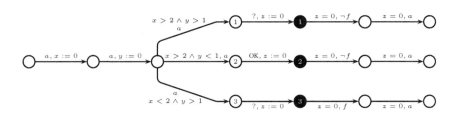

Fig. 4. Plant ensuring that p is set to *true*

constraint $x < 2$ holds he will know that $\mathcal{P}$ is in state ③ whereas if the constraint $x > 2$ holds he may not know if $\mathcal{P}$ is in state ① or in state ②. Similarly if θ stores y, he may hesitate between state ① and state ③, but if $\mathcal{P}$ is in state ②, θ knows it. To force θ storing x, $\mathcal{P}$ will give him one more information which will be an observable action "OK" or "?" with which θ will break the uncertainty between state ① and state ②, but not the uncertainty between state ① and state ③. Thus if θ stores x he will precisely know in which black state $\mathcal{P}$ is after having done four actions and will thus be able to diagnose $\mathcal{P}$ correctly, but if θ stores y he may be uncertain between states ❶ and ❸, and will thus not be able to diagnose correctly $\mathcal{P}$ because the execution after state ❶ is non-faulty ($\neg f$ represents a non-observable non-faulty action) whereas the execution after state ❸ is faulty. Of course a similar construction (breaking the uncertainty between ❸ and ❶) can be done for proposition $\neg p$, thus enforcing clock y to be stored by a diagnoser. The previous construction is extended to clauses of 3SAT by branching automata as the one on Fig. 4. It's better to explain the construction on an example. We choose the formula $p_1 \vee \neg p_3$ (thus ignoring p_2). The left-most frame of Fig. 5 corresponds to the previously

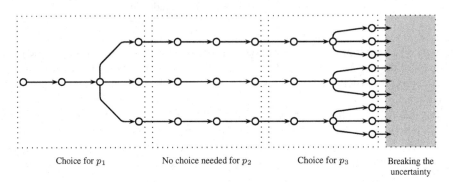

| Choice for p_1 | No choice needed for p_2 | Choice for p_3 | Breaking the uncertainty |

Fig. 5. Plant ensuring that $p_1 \vee \neg p_3$ is true

described choice for p_1, the second frame is for p_2 (p_2 is not used in the clause, thus no branching is needed, but it may be used by other clauses), there is no constraint on the choice for p_2, the third frame is for the choice for p_3. The last frame is for breaking the uncertainty between conflicting runs (adding "OK" and "?" labels followed by either a fault or no fault, as previously). It could be argued that there is no need of the frame for p_2 as p_2 is not used in the clause. However, as we have a set of clauses to be satisfied, we need to have this linear part for p_2. Indeed, for a formula $\varphi = \bigwedge_{i=1}^{n} \psi_i$ with ψ_i clause, the plant for φ will be as on Fig. 6. Non-observable action u's role is to hide what clause the plant is going to check. To be correct, θ must thus satisfy all clauses (with a unique valuation for the propositional variables). This plant can be diagnosed if and only if φ is satisfiable.

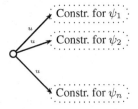

Fig. 6. Plant for a 3SAT-formula

This concludes the proof of 2EXPTIME-hardness of the Δ-DTA$_\mu$-diagnosability problem. Note that a similar construction could be done when the diagnoser can use an arbitrary (but fixed) number of clocks.   □

5   Diagnosability by Event-Recording Timed Automata

The class ERA [AFH94] appears as a natural class of automata for observing systems because clocks and thus timing information are dependent on events (thus precisely what is observed). The fundamental properties of ERA's we will use are the following:

- ERA's are *determinizable* [AFH94]
- ERA's are "*input-determined*" [DT04]: after having read a timed word, the truth of a guard is completely determined by the word itself. This implies in particular that if w is a timed word and μ a granularity for the observable events, there exists a unique symbolic word $\gamma \in \Gamma_\mu$ such that $w \in tw(\gamma)$.

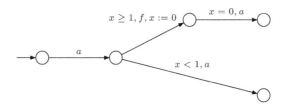

Fig. 7. Plant DTA-diagnosable but not ERA-diagnosable

As previously we restrict to ERA's with bounded resources and tackle the Δ-ERA$_\mu$-diagnosability problem for a fixed granularity μ. It is worth noticing first that ERA-diagnosability is less powerful than DTA-diagnosability as illustrated by the plant on Fig. 7: a DTA-diagnoser with one clock for this plant does not reset its clock when the first a occurs and checks the value of its clock when the second a occurs; it announces a fault only if the value is greater than 1. There is no ERA-diagnoser for this plant.

Deciding diagnosability for ERA's is much easier than for DTA's, as stated by the next theorem. Note that the PSPACE complexity is "optimal" for the diagnosability problem in the sense that there is no hope for finding interesting classes of diagnosers with a lower complexity.

Theorem 3. *Let μ be a granularity over observable events and $\Delta \in \mathbb{Q}_{\geq 0}$. The Δ-ERA$_\mu$-diagnosability problem is PSPACE-complete.*

Proof (Sketch). Let us first argue why Δ-ERA$_\mu$-diagnosability is PSPACE-hard. This can easily be shown by reducing the reachability problem in a timed automaton to Δ-ERA$_\mu$-diagnosability. Consider a timed automaton $\mathcal{A}$ over alphabet Σ and add two fresh unobservable actions u and f (the fault) which are done immediately after having reached some final state of $\mathcal{A}$. The modified automaton is noted $\mathcal{P}$. For every $\Delta > 0$, for every granularity μ, taking $\Sigma_o = \Sigma$ and $\Sigma_u = \{u, f\}$, we get that a final state is reachable in $\mathcal{A}$ if and only if there is no Δ-ERA$_\mu$-diagnoser for $\mathcal{P}$ (in case no final state is reachable, the diagnoser is trivial as it needs not accept anything).

We will now sketch the proof of PSPACE-membership of the problem. Let $\mathcal{P} = (\Sigma_o, \Sigma_u, Q, q_0, \longrightarrow, X, Inv)$ be a plant and $\mu = (Y, m, max)$ a granularity over Σ_o.

Let $S_{\Delta f} = \mathcal{R}(\mathcal{P}_{\Delta f} \parallel \mathcal{U}_\mu) \lceil \mu$ and $S_{\neg f} = \mathcal{R}(\mathcal{P}_{\neg f} \parallel \mathcal{U}_\mu) \lceil \mu$. Informally $S_{\Delta f}$ (resp. $S_{\neg f}$) recognizes all observations that may come from Δ-faulty (resp. non-faulty) runs. The result can finally be deduced from lemma 2 and from the following lemma:

Lemma 4. *The following properties are equivalent:*

(i) $\mathcal{P}$ *is* Δ-ERA_μ-*diagnosable,*
(ii) $\{\gamma \in \Gamma_\mu^* \mid \exists \rho_1 \in L_{\neg f} \text{ and } \rho_2 \in L_{\Delta f} \text{ s.t. } \pi(\rho_1), \pi(\rho_2) \in tw(\gamma)\}$ *is empty,*
(iii) $L(S_{\Delta f}) \cap L(S_{\neg f})$ *is empty.*

$\square$

Note that if $\mathcal{P}$ is Δ-ERA_μ-diagnosable, the proof provides a diagnoser: one can prove that $\pi(L_{\Delta f}) \subseteq L(S_{\Delta f}) \subseteq L(S_{\neg f})^c \subseteq \pi(L_{\neg f})^c$, $S_{\Delta f}$ is a Δ-ERA_μ-diagnoser for $\mathcal{P}$. Moreover, $S_{\Delta f}$ is an *optimal* diagnoser in the sense that it is the smallest diagnoser (for language inclusion). This property is specific to the model of ERA's; such a property does not hold for the class DTA_μ.

6   Conclusion

We have shown that diagnosability using DTA's and ERA's is a decidable problem when resources of the diagnoser are fixed. Moreover if a diagnoser exists, it is possible to construct one: the size of such a diagnoser is doubly exponential in the granularity and in the size of the plant. Thus if we assume that the diagnoser can be pre-computed, diagnosing online becomes exponential in the granularity and in the plant, but only **linear** in the length of the observation. The use of deterministic mechanisms thus allows to construct diagnosers with short response time, which is crucial in fault detection.

We have also pointed out a significant complexity jump between two classes of potential diagnosers: existence of diagnoser in the class DTA (with bounded resources) is 2EXPTIME-complete whereas it is PSPACE-complete for the class ERA (with bounded resources). The class ERA thus appears as a natural and useful class of diagnosers.

This work is related to conformance testing where the aim is to generate testers for a given specification. Such a problem has for example been considered in [KT04] where an algorithm for building small testers (with fixed resources) is proposed. We think that our approach (based on games) could be applied in such a framework as well.

As future work we aim at studying the diagnosability problem in the classes DTA and ERA but without bounding the resources of the diagnoser. We also want to explore more precisely the links between control and diagnosability: even if we can reduce diagnosability to control, the result of [BDMP03] together with our 2EXPTIME-completeness result show that diagnosability is as difficult as control for some classes of diagnosers/controllers, which may appear intriguing.

Acknowledgment. We thank Thierry Cachat for his remarks on a draft of this paper.

References

[AD94]   R. Alur and D. Dill. A theory of timed automata. *Theoretical Computer Science (TCS)*, 126(2):183–235, 1994.

[AFH94]   R. Alur, L. Fix, and T.A. Henzinger. A determinizable class of timed automata. In *Proc. 6th Int. Conf. on Computer Aided Verification (CAV'94)*, vol. 818 of *LNCS*, pp. 1–13. Springer, 1994.

[BDGP98]   B. Bérard, V. Diekert, P. Gastin, and A. Petit. Characterization of the expressive power of silent transitions in timed automata. *Fundamenta Informaticae*, 36(2–3):145–182, 1998.

[BDMP03]   P. Bouyer, D. D'Souza, P. Madhusudan, and A. Petit. Timed control with partial observability. In *Proc. 15th Int. Conf. Computer Aided Verification (CAV'2003)*, vol. 2725 of *LNCS*, pp. 180–192. Springer, 2003.

[Che04]   F. Chevalier. Détection d'erreurs dans les systèmes temporisés. Master's thesis, DEA Algorithmique, Paris, 2004.

[DM02]   D. D'Souza and P. Madhusudan. Timed control synthesis for external specifications. In *Proc. 19th Int. Symp. Theoretical Aspects of Computer Science (STACS'02)*, vol. 2285 of *LNCS*, pp. 571–582. Springer, 2002.

[DT04]   D. D'Souza and N. Tabareau. On timed automata with input-determined guards. In *Proc. Joint Conf. Formal Modelling and Analysis of Timed Systems and Formal Techniques in Real-Time and Fault Tolerant System (FORMATS+FTRTFT'04)*, vol. 3253 of *LNCS*, pp. 68–83. Springer, 2004.

[GJL04]   O. Grinchtein, B. Jonsson, and M. Leucker. Learning of event-recording automata. In *Proc. Joint Conf. Formal Modelling and Analysis of Timed Systems and Formal Techniques in Real-Time and Fault Tolerant System (FORMATS+FTRTFT'04)*, vol. 3253 of *LNCS*, pp. 379–395. Springer, 2004.

[GTW02]   E. Grädel, W. Thomas, and T. Wilke, eds. *Automata, Logics, and Infinite Games: A Guide to Current Research*, vol. 2500 of *LNCS*. Springer, 2002.

[KPA03]   K.J. Kristoffersen, C. Pedersen, and H.R. Andersen. Runtime verification of timed LTL using disjunctive normalized equation systems. In *Proc. 3rd Int. Work. Runtime Verification*, Electronic Notes in Computer Science. Elsevier, 2003.

[KT04]   M. Krichen and S. Tripakis. Real-time testing with timed automata testers and coverage criteria. In *Proc. Joint Conf. Formal Modelling and Analysis of Timed Systems and Formal Techniques in Real-Time and Fault Tolerant System (FORMATS+FTRTFT'04)*, vol. 3253 of *LNCS*, pp. 134–151. Springer, 2004.

[LLW95]   F. Laroussinie, K.G. Larsen, and C. Weise. From timed automata to logic – and back. In *Proc. 20th Int. Symp. Mathematical Foundations of Computer Science (MFCS'95)*, vol. 969 of *LNCS*, pp. 529–539. Springer, 1995.

[Pap94]   C. H. Papadimitriou. *Computational Complexity*. Addison-Wesley, 1994.

[SSL⁺95]   M. Sampath, R. Sengupta, S. Lafortune, K. Sinnamohideen, and D. C. Teneketzis. Diagnosability of discrete event systems. *IEEE Transactions on Automatic Control*, 40(9):1555–1575, 1995.

[SSL⁺96]   M. Sampath, R. Sengupta, S. Lafortune, K. Sinnamohideen, and D. C. Teneketzis. Failure diagnosis using discrete event systems. *IEEE Transactions on Control Systems Technology*, 4(2):105–124, 1996.

[Tri02]   S. Tripakis. Fault diagnosis for timed automata. In *Proc. 7th Int. Symp. Formal Techniques in Real-Time and Fault Tolerant Systems (FTRTFT'02)*, vol. 2469 of *LNCS*, pp. 205–224. Springer, 2002.

[Tri03]   S. Tripakis. Folk theorems on the determinization and minimization of timed automata. In *Proc. 1st Int. Work. on Formal Modeling and Analysis of Timed Systems (FORMATS'03)*, vol. 2791 of *LNCS*, pp. 182–188. Springer, 2003.

Optimal Conditional Reachability
for Multi-priced Timed Automata

Kim Guldstrand Larsen and Jacob Illum Rasmussen

Department of Computer Science, Aalborg University, Denmark
{kgl, illum}@cs.aau.dk

Abstract. In this paper, we prove decidability of the optimal conditional reachability problem for multi-priced timed automata, an extension of timed automata with multiple cost variables evolving according to given rates for each location. More precisely, we consider the problem of determining the minimal cost of reaching a given target state, with respect to some primary cost variable, while respecting upper bound constraints on the remaining (secondary) cost variables. Decidability is proven by constructing a zone-based algorithm that always terminates while synthesizing the optimal cost with a single secondary cost variable. The approach is then lifted to any number of secondary cost variables.

1   Introduction

Recently, research has been focused on extending the framework of timed automata (TA), [2], towards linear hybrid automata (LHA), [3], by allowing continuous variables with non-uniform rates and maintaining a decidable reachability problem.

One such class of models is that of priced (or weighted) timed automata (PTA), [9, 4], which are timed automata augmented with a single cost variable. For this class of timed automata, the minimum-cost reachability problem, i.e. finding the minimum cost of reaching some goal location, is decidable. The restriction with respect to linear hybrid automata is that the cost variable cannot be tested in guards and invariant, it cannot be reset[1], and it grows monotonically.

Ignoring the variable c_2, Figure 1 depicts a PTA for which the rate of c_1 is, respectively, 1 and 2 in locations l_1 and l_2. The type of reachability question we can ask for this model is: What is cheapest way of reaching the "happy" location. The answer, in this case, is 3 which is achieved by delaying for 1 time unit in l_1, taking the transition to l_2 and delaying for 1 time unit before proceeding to l_3.

A natural extension of PTA is to allow a secondary cost variable, thus arriving at dual-priced timed automata (DPTA), and pose reachability questions of the type: What is the cheapest primary cost of reaching the "happy" location

---

[1] Variables with these two properties are sometimes referred to as observers in the literature.

V. Sassone (Ed.): FOSSACS 2005, LNCS 3441, pp. 234–249, 2005.

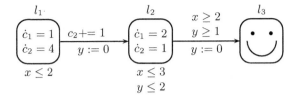

Fig. 1. Example dual-priced timed automata

under some upper bound constraint on the secondary cost? We term this *optimal conditional reachability*. There are three cases to consider, if the secondary cost is time, if the primary cost is time, and if neither the primary nor the secondary cost is time. In the first case, we can augment a PTA with time invariants corresponding to the upper bound constraint on all locations and then use minimum-cost reachability for PTA. In the second case, we can combine finding fastest traces in TA with minimum-cost reachability for PTA. The third case is the topic of this paper. Figure 1 provides a model with two cost variables for which we can pose questions of the type: What is the minimum cost for c_1 of reaching the "happy" location, while respecting $c_2 \leq 4$. The answer to this question is $\frac{11}{3}$ and is obtained by delaying for $\frac{1}{3}$ time units in l_2, then proceeding to l_2 and waiting $\frac{5}{3}$ time units before proceeding to l_3. This example illustrates that unlike minimum-cost reachability for PTA, optimal conditional reachability with two cost variables may have non-integral solutions[2].

If we generalize DPTA to allow any finite number of cost variables, we arrive at *multi-priced timed automata* (MPTA). Optimal conditional reachability for MPTA concerns minimizing the first cost variable while respecting upper bound constraints on the rest. The main contribution of this paper is the decidability of optimal conditional reachability for MPTA.

Relevant work on MPTA include the model checking problem of MPTA with respect to weighted CTL which has been studied by Brihaye et al., [6], and proven undecidable, even with discrete time.

The discrete version of conditional reachability is called multi-constrained routing and is well-known to be NP-complete, [7]. Recently, the problem has been reconsidered by Puri and Tripakis in [11] where several algorithms are proposed for solving the problem, both exactly and approximately.

For simplicity of the proofs, we prove decidability of optimal conditional reachability for MPTA, by proving the decidability for the simpler DPTA model. To show that the result can be lifted to from DPTA to MPTA, we provide, throughout the paper, descriptions of how important aspects are extended from pairs of costs to k-tuples of costs.

The rest of this paper is organized as follows. In Section 2, we give an abstract framework for symbolic optimal conditional reachability in terms of dual-priced

---

[2] The simple model in Figure 1 is acyclic, so optimal conditional reachability can be reduced to linear programming.

transition systems, including a generic algorithm for conditional optimal reachability. In Section 3, we introduce dual-priced timed automata as a syntactic model for dual-priced transition systems. In section 4, we introduce dual-priced zones as the main construct for dual-priced symbolic states. In Section 5, we define a successor operator on the constructs of the previous section. In Section 6, we discuss termination of our algorithm. Finally, we conclude the paper in Section 7 and point out directions for future research.

2   Conditional Optimal Reachability

The notation defined in this section aims at being consistent with that of [11].

The partial order, $\preceq$, over $\mathbb{R}^2_+$ defined such that $(a,b) \preceq (c,d)$ iff $a \leq c$ and $b \leq d$ is called a *domination order*. Given a set of points, $A \subseteq \mathbb{R}^2_+$, an element, $(c,d) \in A$, is said to be *redundant* if there exists another element $(a,b) \in A$ such that $(a,b) \preceq (c,d)$. We extend domination to sets, $A, B \in 2^{\mathbb{R}^2_+}$ such that $A \preceq B$ iff every $(a,b) \in B$ is redundant in A. Figure 2 depicts a set of points with black and white bullets denoting, respectively, redundant and non-redundant nodes.

A dual-priced transition system is a structure $T = (S, s_0, \Sigma, \rightarrow)$ where S is a, possibly infinite, set of states, s_0 is the initial state, Σ an alphabet of labels, and $\rightarrow$ is partial function with signature $S \times \Sigma \times S \hookrightarrow \mathbb{R}^2_+$. For brevity, we will use the notation $s \rightarrow s'$ to denote that $\exists c_1, c_2, a :\rightarrow (s, a, s') = (c_1, c_2)$, we use $s \xrightarrow[c_1,c_2]{a} s'$ whenever $\rightarrow (s, a, s') = (c_1, c_2)$, the notation $s \xrightarrow{c_1,c_2} s'$ for $\exists a \in \Sigma : s \xrightarrow[c_1,c_2]{a} s'$, and the notation $s \xrightarrow{a} s'$ for $\exists c_1, c_2 : s \xrightarrow[c_1,c_2]{a} s'$. The components of a cost pair are denoted primary, respectively, secondary costs.

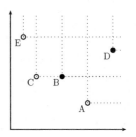

Fig. 2. Domination in $\mathbb{R}^2_+$

An execution ε of T is a sequence $\varepsilon = s_0 \xrightarrow[c_1^1,c_2^1]{a_1} s_1 \xrightarrow[c_1^2,c_2^2]{a_2} \cdots \xrightarrow[c_1^n,c_2^n]{a_n} s_n$. The cost, $\mathsf{Cost}(\varepsilon)$, of an execution ε is given as $\mathsf{Cost}(\varepsilon) = (\mathsf{Cost}_1(\varepsilon), \mathsf{Cost}_2(\varepsilon))$, where $\mathsf{Cost}_j(\varepsilon) = \sum_{i=1}^n c_j^i$ for $j \in \{1,2\}$.

The minimal primary cost of reaching a set of goal states, $G \subseteq S$, under an upper bound, p, on the secondary cost is termed the conditional optimal cost and given as:

$$\mathsf{mincost}_{\leq p}(G) = \inf\{\mathsf{Cost}_1(\varepsilon) \mid \varepsilon = s_0 \xrightarrow{c_1^1,c_2^1} \cdots \xrightarrow{c_1^n,c_2^n} s \in G, \mathsf{Cost}_2(\varepsilon) \leq p\} \quad (1)$$

In order to effectively analyze dual-priced transition systems we suggest dual-priced symbolic states of the form (A, π) where $A \subseteq S$ and $\pi : A \rightarrow 2^{\mathbb{R}^2_+}$. Intuitively, reachability of the dual-priced symbolic state (A, π) has the interpretation that all s of A are reachable with costs arbitrarily close to all $\pi(s)$.

To express successors of dual-priced symbolic states we use the Post operator $\mathsf{Post}_a(A, \pi) = (B, \eta)$ where:

$$B = \{s' \mid \exists s \in A : s \xrightarrow{a} s'\}, \text{ and} \tag{2}$$

$$\eta(s) = \{(c_1 + c, c_2 + c') \mid \exists s' \in A : s' \xrightarrow[c_1, c_2]{a} s \text{ and } \pi(s') = (c, c')\} \tag{3}$$

A symbolic execution ξ of a dual-priced transition system is a sequence $\xi = (A_0, \pi_0), \ldots, (A_n, \pi_n)$, where $A_0 = \{s_0\}$, $\pi(s_0) = (0, 0)$ and for $1 \le i \le n$ we have $(A_i, \pi_i) = \mathsf{Post}_a(A_{i-1}, \pi_{i-1})$, for some $a \in \Sigma$. The correspondence between executions and symbolic executions is captured below:

- For each execution ε of $\mathcal{T}$ ending in s there is a symbolic execution ξ ending in (A, π) such that $s \in A$ and $\mathsf{Cost}(\varepsilon) \in \pi(s)$.
- Let ξ be a symbolic execution of $\mathcal{T}$ ending in (A, π), then for each s and $(c, c') \in \pi(s)$ there is an execution ε ending in s such that $\mathsf{Cost}(\varepsilon) = (c, c')$.

From the above it follows that symbolic states accurately capture conditional optimal reachability in the sense that:

$$\mathsf{mincost}_{\le p}(G) = \inf\{minCost_{\le p}(A \cap G, \pi) \mid (A, \pi) \text{ is reachable}\}, \tag{4}$$

where $minCost_{\le p}(A, \pi)$ is defined as $\inf\{c \mid \exists s \in A : (c, c') \in \pi(s) \text{ and } c' \le p\}$. Furthermore, we define the relation $\sqsubseteq$ on dual-priced symbolic states such that $(B, \eta) \sqsubseteq (A, \pi)$ iff $A \subseteq B$ and $\eta(s) \preceq \pi(s)$ for all $s \in A$. In other words, B is bigger than A and for each state, s, in A, $\pi(s)$ is dominated by $\eta(s)$.

Based on the above result, we provide an algorithm for computing the optimal conditional reachability problem, $\mathsf{mincost}_{\le p}(G)$, in Figure 3.

$\text{COST} := \infty$
$\text{PASSED} := \emptyset$
$\text{WAITING} := \{(\{s_0\}, \pi_0)\}$
while $\text{WAITING} \ne \emptyset$ **do**
    select $(A, \pi) \in \text{WAITING}$
    if $A \cap G \ne \emptyset$ **then**
        if $minCost_{\le p}(A \cap G, \pi) \le \text{COST}$ **then**
            $\text{COST} := minCost_{\le p}(A \cap G, \pi)$ **fi**
    fi
    if $\forall (B, \eta) \in \text{PASSED} : (B, \eta) \not\sqsubseteq (A, \pi)$**then**
        $\text{PASSED} := \text{PASSED} \cup \{(A, \pi)\}$
        $\text{WAITING} := \text{WAITING} \cup \bigcup_{a \in \Sigma} \mathsf{Post}_a(A, \pi)$ **fi**
    fi
od
return COST

Fig. 3. General algorithm for computing the optimal conditional reachability cost, $\mathsf{mincost}_{\le p}(G)$

The algorithm maintains two lists, a PASSED and a WAITING list, that hold the states already explored and the states waiting to be explored, respectively. Initially, the PASSED list is empty and the WAITING list contains only the initial state. The algorithm iterates as long as the WAITING list in non-empty.

At each iteration the algorithm select a state, (A, π), from the WAITING list. The set of states, A, is checked for intersection with the set of goal states. If the intersection is non-empty, the minimum primary cost of any goal state satisfying the constraint on the secondary cost is computed and compared to COST, and if the computed cost is the smaller of the two, COST is updated appropriately.

Whether A intersects with the goal states or not, we go through the PASSED list and check whether it contains any (B, η) such that $(B, \eta) \sqsubseteq (A, \pi)$. If it does, (A, π) is discarded as it is dominated by (B, η), otherwise we add all successors of (A, π) to the WAITING list and add itself to the PASSED list.

The algorithm terminates when the WAITING list is empty and at this point, COST holds $\mathsf{mincost}_{\leq p}(G)$. Termination of the algorithm is guaranteed if $\sqsubseteq$ is a well-quasi ordering on dual-priced symbolic states.

For optimization of the algorithm, further pruning of elements in the WAITING list can be performed simultaneously with the inclusion check, $\sqsubseteq$, e.g. keeping only elements where the set of states with primary cost smaller than COST and secondary cost smaller than p. This is correct since both primary and secondary costs increase monotonically in any trace. Furthermore, for any encountered pair (A, π) with $s \in A$ we could prune $\pi(s)$ for redundant elements.

Every aspect in this section about dual-priced transition systems, including the generic algorithm, can be directly extended to multi-priced transition systems with k-tuples of cost and optimal conditional reachability of the form $\mathsf{mincost}_{\leq p_2, \ldots p_k}(G)$. That is, minimize the primary cost under individual upper bound constraints on the $k-1$ secondary costs.

The above framework may be instantiated by providing concrete syntax for dual-priced transition systems and data structures for dual-priced symbolic states that, first, allow effective computation of the Post operator and, second, have a well-quasi ordered relation, $\sqsubseteq$. In the following sections, we provide such an instantiation of the above framework.

3   Dual-Priced Timed Automata

In this section we define dual-priced timed automata which is a proper subset of linear hybrid automata, [3], and a proper superset of priced timed automata, [9], or weighted timed automata, [4], and in turn timed automata, [2]. DPTA will serve as a concrete syntax for dual-priced transition systems. First however, we recall some basic notation from the theory of timed automata.

We work with a finite set, $\mathbb{C}$, of positive, real-valued variables called clocks. $\mathcal{B}(\mathbb{C})$ is the set of formulae obtained as conjunctions of atomic constraints of the form $x \bowtie n$, where $x \in \mathbb{C}$, $n \in \mathbb{N}$, and $\bowtie \in \{\leq, =, \geq\}$[3]. We refer to the elements of $\mathcal{B}(\mathbb{C})$ as clock constraints. $\mathcal{B}(\mathbb{C})^*$ is the set of clock constraints involving only upper bounds, i.e. $\leq$.

Clock values are represented as functions from $\mathbb{C}$ to the set of non-negative reals, $\mathbb{R}_+$, called clock valuations and ranged over by u, u' etc.

For a clock valuation, $u \in (\mathbb{C} \rightarrow \mathbb{R}_+)$, and a clock constraint, $g \in \mathcal{B}(\mathbb{C})$, we write $u \in g$ when u satisfies all the constraints of g. For $t \in \mathbb{R}_+$, we define the operation $u + t$ to be the clock valuation that assigns $u(x) + t$ to all clocks, and for $R \subseteq \mathbb{C}$ the operation $u[R \rightarrow 0]$ to be the clock valuation that agrees with u for all clocks in $\mathbb{C} \backslash R$ and assigns zero to all clocks in R. $u[x \rightarrow 0]$ is shorthand for $u[\{x\} \rightarrow 0]$. Furthermore, u_0 is defined to be the clock valuation that assigns zero to all clocks.

Definition 1 (Dual-Priced Timed Automata). *A dual-priced timed automaton is a 6-tuple* $\mathcal{A} = (L, l_0, \mathbb{C}, E, I, \boldsymbol{P})$ *where* $\boldsymbol{P} = \{\mathcal{P}_1, \mathcal{P}_2\}$[4], *L is a finite set of locations,* l_0 *is the initial location,* $\mathbb{C}$ *is a finite set of clocks,* $E \subseteq L \times \mathcal{B}(\mathbb{C}) \times 2^{\mathbb{C}} \times (\mathbb{N} \times \mathbb{N}) \times L$ *is the set of edges,* $I : L \rightarrow \mathcal{B}(\mathbb{C})^*$ *assigns invariants to locations, and* $\mathcal{P}_i : L \rightarrow \mathbb{N}$ *assigns prices to locations,* $i \in \{1, 2\}$.

The concrete state semantics of a DPTA, $\mathcal{A} = (L, l_0, \mathbb{C}, E, I, \boldsymbol{P})$, is given in terms of a dual-priced transition system with state set $L \times (\mathbb{C} \rightarrow \mathbb{R}_+)$, initial state (l_0, u_0), alphabet $\Sigma = E \cup \{\delta\}$, and the transition relation, $\rightarrow$, defined as:

- $(l, u) \xrightarrow[t \cdot \mathcal{P}_1(l), t \cdot \mathcal{P}_2(l)]{\delta} (l, u + t)$ if $\forall 0 \leq t' \leq t : u + t' \in I(l)$ and

- $(l, u) \xrightarrow[c, c']{e} (l', u')$ if $e = (l, g, R, (c, c'), l') \in E, u \in g, u' = u[R \rightarrow 0]$.

We will often write concrete states as (l, u, c_1, c_2) to denote the assumption of some underlying execution, ε, ending in (l, u) with $\mathsf{Cost}(\varepsilon) = (c_1, c_2)$.

A concrete dual-priced state (l, u, c_1, c_2) is said to dominate another state (l', u', c_1', c_2') iff $l = l'$, $u = u'$, and $(c_1, c_2) \preceq (c_1', c_2')$. In such case we write $(l, v, c_1, c_2) \preceq (l', v', c_1', c_2')$.

For convenience reasons, we assume some restrictions on the structure of the DPTA in the rest of the paper. First, any DPTA should be bounded, i.e. all locations have upper bound invariants on all clocks. Second, at least one clock is reset on every transition. Note that neither restriction compromises the generality of our result, as it is well-known that any TA can be transformed into a semantically equivalent bounded TA, and that result extends directly to DPTA. Furthermore, the reset assumption can be guaranteed by introducing an extra clock which is reset on every transition.

---

[3] For simplification we do not include strict inequalities, note, however, that everything covered in this paper extends directly to strict inequalities, which is why we compute infimum costs as opposed to minimum costs.

[4] If we let $\boldsymbol{P} = \{\mathcal{P}_1, \ldots, \mathcal{P}_k\}$ we have MPTA with analogous semantics.

3.1 Relation to Linear Hybrid Automata

Any DPTA is a LHA where the value of the rate of each clock variable is one is every location, and the rates of the primary and secondary costs are $\mathcal{P}_1(l)$ and $\mathcal{P}_2(l)$, respectively, in location l.

Tools such as HYTECH, [8], can perform forward symbolic reachability analysis on LHA over a set of variables x using symbolic state structures (l, A, b) where l is a location and $A \cdot x \leq b$ defines a convex polyhedra of valid variable assignments. One of the main properties of this kind of reachability analysis is that the Post operators defined for LHA maintains convexity of the state set. However, the reachability problem for LHA is, in general, undecidable, so termination of the reachability algorithm is not guaranteed. However, a consequence of our result is that for the class of DPTA, HYTECH will terminate when performing conditional reachability.

4 Dual-Priced Zones

Now, we propose dual-priced zones as a syntactic construct for providing a symbolic semantics for the dual-priced transition system induced by DPTA.

The constructs of our proposal for dual-priced symbolic states are *zones* and *cost functions*. Zones are well-known from the analysis of timed systems and efficient implementations of zones as difference bound matrices are used in real-time verification tools such as KRONOS, [5], and UPPAAL, [10]. Briefly, zones are convex collections of clock valuations that can be described solely using difference constraints of the form $x_i - x_j \leq m$ where $m \in \mathbb{Z}$ and $x_i, x_j \in \mathbb{C} \cup \{x_0\}$, where, x_0, is a special clock whose value is fixed to zero. That way, constraints of the form $x_i \geq n$ can be written as $x_0 - x_i \leq -n$, and similarly for other constraints involving a single variable. Zones are ranged over by $Z, Z_1, Z', \ldots$. When a clock valuation, u, satisfies the difference constraints of a zone, Z, we write $u \in Z$.

The second construct is a cost function, which is an affine function over $\mathbb{C}$, i.e. a cost function, d, is a function with signature $(\mathbb{C} \to \mathbb{R}_+) \to \mathbb{R}_+$ that can be written syntactically as $a_1 \cdot x_1 + \cdots + a_n \cdot x_n + b$ where $x_i \in \mathbb{C}$, $1 \leq i \leq n$, and $a_i, b \in \mathbb{Z}$. The cost of a clock valuation, u, in a cost function, d, is given by $d(u) = a_1 \cdot u(x_1) + \cdots + a_n \cdot u(x_n) + b$. We range over cost function by d, e, d_1, e_1, d', e' etc. For ease of notation we define a number of operations on cost functions. Let $m \in \mathbb{Z}$, $p \in \mathbb{N}$ and $x_i, x_j \in \mathbb{C}$, then the substitution operation $d[x_i/\varphi]$ for $\varphi \in \{m, x_j + m\}$ is defined as $d[x_i/\varphi] = a_1 \cdot x_1 + \cdots + a_i \cdot \varphi + \cdots + a_n \cdot x_n$. The delay operation $d^{\uparrow p, x_i}$ is defined as $d^{\uparrow p, x_i} = a_1 \cdot x_1 + \cdots + (p - \sum_{j \neq i} a_j) \cdot x_i + \cdots + a_n \cdot x_n$, meaning we want the sum of the coefficients to match p by assign the correct coefficient to x_i.

Let C be a set of pairs of cost functions, i.e. $C = \{(e_1, d_1), \ldots, (e_k, d_k)\}$ and u a clock valuation, then $C(u) = \{(e_1(u), d_1(u)), \ldots (e_k(u), d_k(u))\}$ is a set of points in $\mathbb{R}_+^2$. We denote by $\lambda(C(u))$ the set of all convex combinations of $C(u)$, i.e. the convex hull.

For the construction of dual-priced symbolic states we propose dual-priced zones as given in Definition 2 below.

Definition 2 (Dual-Priced Zone). *A dual-priced zone is a pair, (Z, C), where Z is a zone and C is a set of pairs of cost functions $\{(e_1, d_1), \ldots, (e_k, d_k)\}$.*

We construct dual-priced symbolic states as structures (l, Z, C) where l is a location and (Z, C) is a dual-priced zone. A dual-priced symbolic state (l, Z, C) contains all concrete states (l', u, c_1, c_2) where $l' = l$, $u \in Z$, and $(c_1, c_2) \in \lambda(C(u))$. Not that dual-priced zones extend directly to multi-priced zones with k-tuples of cost functions and, in turn, multi-priced symbolic states.

In [9], efficient data structures for symbolic minimum-cost reachability for priced timed automata (PTA) are provided. These are so-called priced zones which effectively are zones, Z, with an associated cost function, e. For representing cost in the discrete case described in [11], subsets of $\mathbb{N} \times \mathbb{N}$ are used for representing reachability costs.

The immediate combination of the two suggest the use of zones together with sets of pairs of cost function. The following example illustrates why we also need to consider convex combinations of the cost functions.

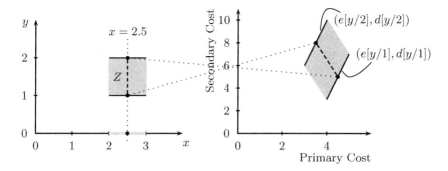

Fig. 4. The relationship between the zone, Z, defined by the constraints $2 \leq x \leq 3$ and $1 \leq y \leq 2$ with cost functions (e, d) with $e = x + y$ and $d = 4x - 3y + 1$

Consider the zone of Figure 4 described by the constraints $2 \leq x \leq 3$ and $1 \leq y \leq 2$ with the pair of cost functions (e, d) where $e = x + y$ and $d = 4x - 3y + 1$. Now, if we need to compute the projection of the zone onto the first axis due to a reset of y, what should the set of pairs of cost functions be to represent or dominate the possible cost values? The suggestion following the lines of reasoning from [9] would be to use the two pairs of cost functions $(e[y/2], d[y/2])$ and $(e[y/1], d[y/1])$. This choice, however, has a loss of information if we do not allow convex combinations. The point $(x = 2.5, y = 0)$ is obtained from Z by projection from any point satisfying $(x = 2.5, 1 \leq y \leq 2)$ corresponding to costs given by any convex combination between $(3.5, 8)$ and $(4.5, 5)$. However, maintaining only the these two points is incorrect, as neither of the points dominate any point in their convex combination.

5   Post Operator

The projection operation in the previous section serves as a first step towards a
Post operator. Consider, again, the zone in Figure 4 and assume it is, now, associated with two pairs of cost functions (e_1, d_1) and (e_2, d_2), between which we
allow arbitrary convex combinations. Now, if we perform a projection onto the
first axis we split each pair of cost functions in two, i.e. (e_i^L, d_i^L) and (e_i^U, d_i^U),
$i \in \{1, 2\}$, corresponding to the lines $L : y = 1$ and $U : y = 2$, respectively,
giving four cost functions. Originally, for any clock valuation, u, in the zone and
$0 \le \alpha \le 1$, the convex combination between $(e_1(u), d_1(u))$ and $(e_2(u), d_2(u))$ wrt.
α is a valid cost pair. However, when we split the cost functions, the cost corresponding to e.g. $(e_1(u), d_1(u))$ is given by some convex combination of (e_1^L, d_1^L)
and (e_1^U, d_1^U) for the clock valuation $u[y \to 0]$, and similarly for $(e_2(u), d_2(u))$ using the same convex combination. Contrary to the definition of dual-priced zones,
this suggests not to allow arbitrary convex combinations between (e_1^L, d_1^L) and
(e_1^U, d_1^U), (e_2^L, d_2^L) and (e_2^U, d_2^U), but rather "binary tree" convex combinations
of the form: Choose the same convex combination between (e_1^L, d_1^L), (e_1^U, d_1^U)
and (e_2^L, d_2^L), (e_2^U, d_2^U) and take any convex combination of the resulting pairs.
However, the following key lemma states that if this set is convex, it is identical
to the set of arbitrary convex combinations between the four.

Lemma 1. *Assume a set of pairs of points in* $\mathbb{R}_+^2$

$$\{(a_1, b_1), \ldots, (a_n, b_n)\}, \quad a_i \in \mathbb{R}_+^2, b_i \in \mathbb{R}_+^2, 1 \le i \le n$$

For $0 \le \alpha \le 1$, *let:*

$$A_\alpha = \{\alpha \cdot a_i + (1 - \alpha) \cdot b_i | 1 \le i \le n\} \text{ and}$$
$$B = \{a_i, b_i | 1 \le i \le n\}.$$

Now, if $\bigcup_\alpha \lambda(A_\alpha)$ *is convex (i.e.* $\bigcup_\alpha \lambda(A_\alpha) = \lambda(\bigcup_\alpha \lambda(A_\alpha))$) *then* $\bigcup_\alpha \lambda(A_\alpha) = \lambda(B)$.

Proof. We prove the lemma in two steps. First, we show that $\bigcup_\alpha \lambda(A_\alpha) \subseteq \lambda(B)$
and, secondly, that $\lambda(B) \subseteq \bigcup_\alpha \lambda(A_\alpha)$.
1. Let c be a convex combination of A_α for any $0 \le \alpha \le 1$, that is,

$$c = \lambda_1(\alpha a_1 + (1 - \alpha)b_1) + \cdots + \lambda_n(\alpha a_n + (1 - \alpha)b_n) \tag{5}$$
$$= \lambda_1 \alpha a_1 + \lambda_1(1 - \alpha)b_1 + \cdots + \lambda_n \alpha a_n + \lambda_n(1 - \alpha)b_n, \tag{6}$$

where $0 \le \lambda_i \le 1$ and $\sum_i \lambda_i = 1$. Now, (6) is a convex combination of B, thus
$c \in \lambda(B)$ and in turn $\bigcup_\alpha \lambda(A_\alpha) \subseteq \lambda(B)$.
2. Each point a_i can be given as a convex combination of A_α where $\alpha = 1$ using
$\lambda_i = 1$ and $\lambda_j = 0$ for $j \ne i$. Simililarly for b_i with $\alpha = 0$. Now, since all a_i, b_i
are included in the convex set $\bigcup_\alpha \lambda(A_\alpha)$, we know that $\lambda(B) \subseteq \lambda(\bigcup_\alpha \lambda(A_\alpha)) = \bigcup_\alpha \lambda(A_\alpha)$. □

Note, that the proof makes no mention of $\mathbb{R}_+^2$, thus the Lemma 1 is directly extendible to pairs of points in $\mathbb{R}_+^k$.

At first glance, $\bigcup_\alpha \lambda(A_\alpha)$ in Lemma 1 might seem universally convex, however, Figure 5 depicts the contrary where Lemma 1 does not hold. Let $P = \{(A, B), (C, D)\}$, now, $\bigcup_\alpha \lambda(P_\alpha)$ (the gray area with the dashed line) is not convex and not equal to $\lambda(\{A, B, C, D\})$, particularly, all points on the line from A to D are not included in the former.

Before defining the Post operator on dual-priced states of the form (l, Z, C), we need to introduce a number of definitions and operations. Let Z be a zone, then the delay operation $Z^\uparrow$ and the reset, $\{x\}Z$, with respect to a clock, $x \in \mathbb{C}$, are defined as $Z^\uparrow = \{u + t | u \in Z \text{ and } t \geq 0\}$ and $\{x\}Z = \{u[x \to 0] | u \in Z\}$. It is well-known from timed automata that both $Z^\uparrow$ and $\{x\}Z$ are representable as zones.

Given a zone, Z, if $x_i - x_j \leq m$ is a constraint in Z then $(Z \wedge (x_i - x_j = m))$ is a *facet* of Z, a *lower relative facet* of x_j, and an *upper relative facet* of x_i. The set of lower (resp. upper) relative facets of a clock, x_i, in a zone, Z, is denoted $LF_{x_i}(Z)$ (resp. $UF_{x_i}(Z)$).

The following lemma for facets is proven in [9].

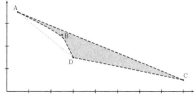

Fig. 5. Counter example

Lemma 2. *Let Z be a zone over a clock set, $\mathbb{C}$, with $x \in \mathbb{C}$, then:*

1. $Z^\uparrow = \bigcup_{F \in UF_{x_0}(Z)} F^\uparrow = Z \cup \bigcup_{F \in LF_{x_0}(Z)} F^\uparrow$ *and*
2. $\{x\}Z = \bigcup_{F \in LF_x(Z)} \{x\}F = \bigcup_{F \in UF_x(Z)} \{x\}F.$

Lemma 2.1 is most intuitively understood knowing that x_0 is fixed to zero, that way UF_{x_0} is the set of all lower bound constraints on clocks in $\mathbb{C}$ (i.e. $x \geq n$) and LF_{x_0} is the set of all upper bound constraints on clocks in $\mathbb{C}$ (i.e. $x \leq n$).

Definition 3. *Given a zone, Z, and a clock, x, $LUF_x(Z)$ is the unique, smallest collection of pairs $\{(L_1, U_1), \ldots, (L_n, U_n)\}$, such that for all $1 \leq i, j \leq n, i \neq j$ we have (i) $L_i \cap L_j = U_i \cap U_j = \emptyset$, (ii) $\{x\}L_i = \{x\}U_i$, and (iii) $L_i \subseteq F, U_i \subseteq F'$ for some $F \in LF_x(Z)$ and $F' \in UF_x(Z)$.*

We call the elements of $LUF_x(Z)$ partial relative facets with regard to x. Figure 6 illustrates the concept of partial relative facets.

Let d be a cost function and let F be a relative facet of a zone in the sense that $x_i - x_j = m$ (or $x_i = m$) is a constraint in F, then we use the shorthand notation d^F for $d[x_i/x_j + m]$ (or $d[x_i/m]$).

Definition 4 (Post Operator). *Let $\mathcal{A} = (L, l_0, \mathbb{C}, E, I, \mathbf{P})$ be a DPTA with $l \in L$ and $e = (l, g, \{x\}, (c, c'), l') \in E^5$, let Z be zone, let Z' be a zone where*

---

[5] For the general case with multiple resets, we consecutively split the pairs of cost functions for each clock that is reset.

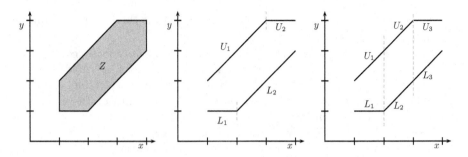

Fig. 6. From left to right (i): a zone, Z, (ii): $LF_y(Z) = \{L_1, L_2\}$ and $UF_y(Z) = \{U_1, U_2\}$ (iii): $LUF_y = \{(L_1, U_1), (L_2, U_2), (L_3, U_3)\}$

$x \in \mathbb{C}$ *is fixed at zero, and let* $C = \{(e_1, d_1), \dots, (e_k, d_k)\}$ *be a set of pairs of cost functions, then*

$$\mathsf{Post}_\delta(l, Z', C) = \left\{ \left(l, (Z' \wedge I(l))^\uparrow \wedge I(l), \{(e_i^{\uparrow \mathcal{P}_1(l), x}, d_i^{\uparrow \mathcal{P}_2(l), x}) | 1 \le i \le k\}\right) \right\}$$

$$\mathsf{Post}_e(l, Z, C) = \bigcup_{(L,U) \in LUF_x(Z \wedge g)} \left\{ (l', \{x\}(U), C') \right\}$$

where $C' = \{(e_i^L + c, d_i^L + c'), (e_i^U + c, d_i^U + c') | 1 \le i \le k\}$.

The simplification of the Post_δ operator is no restriction given the reset assumption we made in Section 3, we simply just allow Post_δ after a Post_e, which is, actually, how symbolic reachability is performed in tools such as UPPAAL and KRONOS. The Post operator as given above extends directly to multi-priced zones and the binary split in Post_e remains binary.

As shorthand notation, we write $(l, u, c_1, c_2) \in \mathsf{Post}_e(l, Z, C)$ to indicate that $(l, u, c_1, c_2) \in (l', Z', C')$ for some $(l', Z', C') \in \mathsf{Post}_e(l, Z, C)$.

Before we prove the soundness and completeness of the Post operator, we illustrate, in Figure 7, its behavior on the running example of Figure 1.

Lemma 3. *Given dual-priced symbolic state* (l, Z, C) *where* $C = \{(e_1, d_1), \dots, (e_k, d_k)\}$ *and* $a \in \{e, \delta\}$ *where* $e = (l, g, \{x\}, (c, c'), l')$ *we have*

$$(l', u', c_1', c_2') \in \mathsf{Post}_a(l, Z, C) \iff$$

$$\exists (l, u, c_1, c_2) \in (l, Z, C) : (l, u, c_1, c_2) \xrightarrow{a} (l', u', c_1', c_2')$$

Proof. We choose only to prove the lemma for Post_e as the analogous proof for Post_δ is straightforward since each concrete successor has a unique concrete predecessor, given the requirement that Post_δ is always applied after a clock reset. We prove each direction of the bi-implication separately.

$\Longleftarrow$ - *Completeness*: Let $(l, u, c_1, c_2) \in (l, Z, C)$. The costs (c_1, c_2) are given as a convex combination of $C(u)$, i.e there are $0 \le \lambda_i \le 1$ and $\sum_i \lambda_i = 1$ for $1 \le i \le k$ such that:

$$(c_1, c_2) = \sum_i \lambda_i \cdot (e_i(u), d_i(u)). \tag{7}$$

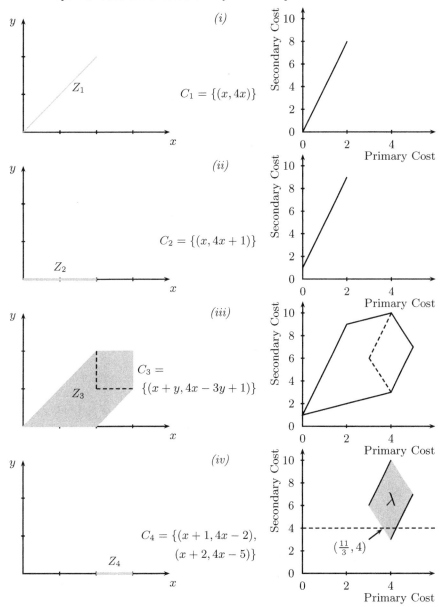

Fig. 7. Reachability analysis for $\mathsf{mincost}_{\leq 4}(\{l_3\})$ on the DPTA in Figure 1 starting from the initial state (l_1, Z_0, C_0). Areas inclosed by black lines in the cost part indicate all cost pairs computable from the cost functions. (i) $(l_1, Z_1, C_1) = \mathsf{Post}_\delta(l_1, Z_0, C_0)$ (ii) $(l_2, Z_2, C_2) = \mathsf{Post}_e(l_1, Z_1, C_1)$ where $e = (l_1, -, \{y\}, (0,1), l_2)$ (iii) $(l_2, Z_3, C_3) = \mathsf{Post}_\delta(l_2, Z_2, C_2)$. The dashed area indicates the subset of the zone satisfying the guard of $e' = (l_2, x \geq 2 \wedge y \geq 1, \{y\}, (0,0), l_3)$ (iv) $(l_3, Z_4, C_4) = \mathsf{Post}_{e'}(l_2, Z_3, C_3)$. The gray area in the cost part indicate the convex combinations between the lines describing the two cost functions. The cost pairs below the dashed line are the ones satisfying the constraint on the secondary cost. Note that $\mathsf{mincost}_{\leq 4}(\{l_3\}) = \frac{11}{3}$

The discrete successor of (l, u, c_1, c_2) with respect to e is given as $(l', u[x \to 0], c_1 + c, c_2 + c')$, which we will now prove is contained in $\mathsf{Post}_e(l, Z, C)$.

Let $(L, U) \in LUF_x(Z)$ such that $u[x \to 0] \in \{x\}L$. Given the convexity of zones there exist unique $v \in L$ and $w \in U$ where $v(x) \le u(x) \le w(x)$ and $u(y) = v(y) = w(y)$ for $y \neq x$, i.e. $u(x) = \alpha \cdot v(x) + (1 - \alpha) \cdot w(x)$ for some $0 \le \alpha \le 1$. Furthermore, the affinity of cost functions provide us with

$$(e_i(u), d_i(u)) = \alpha \cdot (e_i(v), d_i(v)) + (1 - \alpha) \cdot (e_i(w), d_i(w)), \tag{8}$$

for all $1 \le i \le k$ and the same α as above.

Now, choose $(l', u', c_1', c_2') \in \mathsf{Post}_e(l, Z, C)$ where $u' = u[x \to 0]$ and (c_1', c_2') is given by (9), which we can rewrite as:

$$\sum_i \lambda_i \cdot (\alpha \cdot (e_i^L(u') + c, d_i^L(u') + c') + (1 - \alpha) \cdot (e_i^U(u') + c, d_i^U(u') + c')) \tag{9}$$

$$= (c, c') + \sum_i \lambda_i \cdot (\alpha \cdot (e_i^L(u'), d_i^L(u')) + (1 - \alpha) \cdot (e_i^U(u'), d_i^U(u'))) \tag{10}$$

$$= (c, c') + \sum_i \lambda_i \cdot (\alpha \cdot (e_i(v), d_i(v)) + (1 - \alpha) \cdot (e_i(w), d_i(w))) \tag{11}$$

$$= (c, c') + \sum_i \lambda_i \cdot (e_i(u), d_i(u)) = (c_1 + c, c_2 + c') \tag{12}$$

The step from (10) to (11) follows from the definition of e_i^L, d_i^L, e_i^U, and d_i^U, and the step from (11) to (12) uses (8). Thus, the discrete successor of each concrete state in (l, Z, C) is contained in $\mathsf{Post}_e(l, Z, C)$.

$\Longrightarrow$ - *Soundness*: Let $(l', u', c_1', c_2') \in \mathsf{Post}_e(l, Z, C)$ such that $u' \in \{x\}L$ for some $(L, U) \in LUF_x(Z)$. Assume that:

$$(c_1', c_2') = \sum_i \lambda_i \cdot (\alpha \cdot (e_i^L(u') + c, d_i^L(u') + c') + (1 - \alpha) \cdot (e_i^U(u') + c, d_i^U(u') + c')) \tag{13}$$

for some $0 \le \alpha, \lambda_i \le 1$ and $\sum_i \lambda = 1$.

Let $v \in L$ and $w \in U$ be the unique clock valuations in Z where $u'(y) = v(y) = w(y)$ for $y \neq x$. $u \in Z$ is then the unique clock valuation with $u(y) = \alpha \cdot v(y) + (1 - \alpha) \cdot w(y)$ for all y with the same α as above. Choose the cost pair $(c_1, c_2) = \sum_i \lambda_i \cdot (e_i(u), d_i(u))$. Now, $(l, u, c_1, c_2) \in (l, Z, C)$ and the proof of completeness gives us that $(l, u, c_1, c_2) \xrightarrow{e} (l', u', c_1', c_2')$.

Now, we have that all e-successors and only e-successors of concrete states in (l, Z, C) are in the subset of $\mathsf{Post}_e(l, Z, C)$ with costs that can be written according to (13). Since DPTA are a subset of linear hybrid automata, we know that e-successors maintain convexity. So, since (l, Z, C) is, by definition, convex we know that the set of concrete states $(l', u', c_1', c_2') \in \mathsf{Post}_e(l, Z, C)$ with costs according to (13) is convex. Lemma 1 now states that this set is identical to all concrete states in $\mathsf{Post}_e(l, Z, C)$.□

If allowing k-tuples of costs as opposed to pairs, the proof of Lemma 3 is analogous, whenever we choose concrete states using α and $(1 - \alpha)$, we instead use $\alpha_1, \dots \alpha_k$ with $\sum_i \alpha_i = 1$.

Lemma 3 states that the properties of our proposed Post operator corresponds to the requirements of Post defined in Section 2.

6   Termination

In this section, we first define the ordering $\sqsubseteq$ on the structure of locations with dual-priced zones and then prove that it is a well-quasi order.

Note that given a zone, Z, with m corner points, any cost function, e, associated with Z can be represented as an element of $\mathbb{N}^m$ giving the cost at each of corner points since any corner point of a zone have integral values. Thus, we can view the set of cost function pairs, C, of a dual-priced symbolic state, (l, Z, C) as a subset of $2^{\mathbb{N}^m \times \mathbb{N}^m}$ if Z has m corner points, and whenever we refer to this representation, we write C_Z. Given a pair, $(\bar{e}, \bar{d})$, of m-vectors in C_Z, we write $\bar{e} \leq \bar{d}$, if $\bar{e}$ is component-wise less than or equal to $\bar{d}$.

Definition 5 ($\sqsubseteq$). *Given two dual-priced symbolic states (l, Z, C), (l', Z', C'), we write $(l, Z, C) \sqsubseteq (l', Z', C')$ iff (i) $l = l'$ (ii) $Z' \subseteq Z$ and (iii) for all $(\bar{e}', \bar{d}') \in C'_Z$, there exists a $(\bar{e}, \bar{d}) \in C_{Z \wedge Z'}$ such that $\bar{e} \leq \bar{e}'$ and $\bar{d} \leq \bar{d}'$.*

The order $\sqsubseteq$ on k-tuples of costs are defined analogously. Note that $(l, Z, C) \sqsubseteq (l', Z', C')$ implies that for all $u \in Z'$, $\lambda(C(u)) \preceq \lambda(C'(u))$, but not the reverse, i.e. our $\sqsubseteq$ is stronger than domination, however, the above definition suffices to guarantee termination.

Lemma 4. $\sqsubseteq$ *is a well-quasi ordering.*

The proof of Lemma 4 follows directly from the fact that $(\mathbb{N}, \leq)$ is a better-quasi ordering, [1], and better-quasi orderings are closed under Cartesian product and power sets, and, finally, better-quasi orderings imply well-quasi orderings. For k-tuples of cost, the proof is identical as we consider k Cartesian products on $\mathbb{N}^m$ instead of pairs.

Now, we have fully instantiated the framework defined in Section 2 with syntax, data structures, a Post operator, and a well-quasi order. Based on this, we can conclude that, with this instantiation, the algorithm in Figure 3 computes optimal conditional reachability for DPTA. The result is summarized in the following theorem.

Theorem 1. *Optimal conditional reachability for DPTA is decidable.*

Along with the definitions of the framework of dual-priced transitions systems, DPTA, data structure for dual-priced symbolic states, the Post operator, and $\sqsubseteq$ we have discussed the straightforward extension to k-tuples of cost, and thus MPTA. Based on this we state the following corollary of Theorem 1.

Corollary 1. *Optimal conditional reachability for MPTA is decidable.*

7   Conclusion and Future Work

We have proven the decidability of optimal conditional reachability for multi-priced timed automata. The results are obtained from a zone-based algorithm for computing optimal conditional reachability which, in turn, might lead to an efficient implementation.

The example of Figure 1 illustrates that integral solution are not guaranteed, thus the immediate discrete time semantics for MPTA will not, in general, give correct results. However, discrete analysis of MPTA can be applied, but a correct time granularity must be chosen beforehand. In the case of Figure 1 a valid time granularity is $\frac{1}{3}$. However, a valid choice of granularity is non-trivial.

Except implementation of conditional reachability in the tool UPPAAL, future research includes considering approximations along the lines of the ones proposed by Puri and Tripakis in [11]. Also, the complexity and efficiency of the algorithm in Figure 3 should be analyzed. Finally, related conditional reachability problems such as minimization under lower bound constraints and maximization under lower as well as upper bound constraints deserve investigation.

Acknowledgements. The authors would like to thank Stavros Tripakis for introducing them to multi-constrained optimization problems.

References

1. Parosh Aziz Abdulla and Aletta Nylén. Better is better than well: On efficient verification of infinite-state systems. In *Proceedings of the 15th Annual IEEE Symposium on Logic in Computer Science*, page 132. IEEE Computer Society, 2000.
2. R. Alur and D. Dill. Automata for modelling real-time systems. In *Proc. of Int. Colloquium on Algorithms, Languages and Programming*, number 443, pages 322–335, July 1990.
3. Rajeev Alur, Costas Courcoubetis, Thomas A. Henzinger, and Pei-Hsin Ho. Hybrid automata: An algorithmic approach to the specification and verification of hybrid systems. In *Hybrid Systems*, pages 209–229, 1992.
4. Rajeev Alur, Salvatore La Torre, and George J. Pappas. Optimal paths in weighted timed automata. *Lecture Notes in Computer Science*, 2034:pp. 49–??, 2001.
5. M. Bozga, C. Daws, O. Maler, A. Olivero, S. Tripakis, and S. Yovine. Kronos: A model-checking tool for real-time systems. In A. J. Hu and M. Y. Vardi, editors, *Proc. 10th International Conference on Computer Aided Verification, Vancouver, Canada*, volume 1427, pages 546–550. Springer-Verlag, 1998.
6. Thomas Brihaye, Véronique Bruyére, and Jean-François Raskin. Model-checking weighted timed automata. In *the proc. of FORMATS'04*, Lecture Notes in Computer Science. Springer-Verlag, 2004.
7. Michael R. Garey and David S. Johnson. *Computers and Intractability; A Guide to the Theory of NP-Completeness*. W. H. Freeman & Co., 1990.
8. Thomas A. Henzinger, Pei-Hsin Ho, and Howard Wong-Toi. HYTECH: A model checker for hybrid systems. *International Journal on Software Tools for Technology Transfer*, 1(1–2):110–122, 1997.

9. Kim Larsen, Gerd Behrmann, Ed Brinksma, Ansgar Fehnker, Thomas Hune, Paul Pettersson, and Judi Romijn. As cheap as possible: Efficient cost-optimal reachability for priced timed automata. *Lecture Notes in Computer Science*, 2102:pp. 493+, 2001.
10. Kim Guldstrand Larsen, Paul Pettersson, and Wang Yi. UPPAAL in a nutshell. *Int. Journal on Software Tools for Technology Transfer*, 1(1-2):134–152, 1997.
11. Anuj Puri and Stavros Tripakis. Algorithms for the multi-constrained routing problem. In *Proceedings of the 8th Scandinavian Workshop on Algorithm Theory*, pages 338–347. Springer-Verlag, 2002.

Alternating Timed Automata[*]

Sławomir Lasota[1],[**] and Igor Walukiewicz[2]

[1] Institute of Informatics, Warsaw University
Banacha 2, 02-097 Warszawa
[2] LaBRI, Université Bordeaux-1
351, Cours de la Libération, F-33 405, Talence cedex, France

Abstract. A notion of alternating timed automata is proposed. It is
shown that such automata with only one clock have decidable emptiness
problem. This gives a new class of timed languages which is closed under
boolean operations and which has an effective presentation. We prove
that the complexity of the emptiness problem for alternating timed automata with one clock is non-primitive recursive. The proof gives also
the same lower bound for the universality problem for nondeterministic
timed automata with one clock thereby answering a question asked in a
recent paper by Ouaknine and Worrell.

1 Introduction

Timed automata is a widely studied model of real-time systems. It is obtained
from finite nondeterministic automata by adding clocks which can be reset and
whose values can be compared with constants. In this paper we consider alternating version of timed automata obtained by introducing universal transitions
in the same way as it is done for standard nondeterministic automata. From
the results of Alur and Dill [2] it follows that such a model cannot have decidable emptiness problem as the universality problem for timed automata is
not decidable. In the recent paper [16] Ouaknine and Worrell has shown that
the universality problem is decidable for nondeterministic automata with one
clock. Inspired by their construction, we show that the emptiness problem for
alternating timed automata with one clock is decidable as well. We also prove
not primitive recursive lower bound for the problem. The proof implies the same
bound for the universality problem for nondeterministic timed automata with
one clock. This answers the question posed by Ouaknine and Worrell [16]. To
complete the picture we also show that an extension of our model with epsilon-
transitions has undecidable emptiness problem.

---

[*] Work reported here has been partially supported by the European Community
Research Training Network GAMES.
[**] Partially supported by the Polish KBN grant No. 4 T11C 042 25. This work was
performed in part during the author's stay at LaBRI, Université Bordeaux-1.

V. Sassone (Ed.): FOSSACS 2005, LNCS 3441, pp. 250–265, 2005.

The crucial property of timed automata models is the decidability of the emptiness problem. The drawback of the model is that the class of languages recognized by timed automata is not closed under complement and the universality question is undecidable (Π_1^1-hard) [2]. One solution to this problem is to restrict to deterministic timed automata. Another, is to restrict the reset operation; this gives the event-clock automata model [4]. A different ad-hoc solution could be to take the boolean closure of the languages recognized by timed automata. This solution does not seem promising due to the complexity of the universality problem. This consideration leads to the idea of using automata with one clock for which the universality problem is decidable. The obtained class of alternating timed automata is by definition closed under boolean operations. Moreover, using the method of Ouaknine and Worrell, we can show that the class has decidable emptiness problem. As it can be expected, there are languages recognizable by timed automata that are not recognizable by alternating timed automata with one clock. More interestingly, the converse is also true: there are languages recognizable by alternating timed automata with one clock that are not recognizable by nondeterministic timed automata with any number of clocks.

Once the decidability of the emptiness problem for alternating timed automata with one clock is shown, the next natural question is the complexity of the problem. We show a non-primitive recursive lower bound. For this we give a reduction of the reachability problem for lossy channel systems [17]. The reduction shows that the lower bound holds also for purely universal alternating timed automata. This implies non-primitive recursive lower bound for the universality problem for nondeterministic timed automata with one clock. We also point out that allowing epsilon transitions in our model permits to code perfect channel systems and hence makes the emptiness problem undecidable.

Related work. Our work is strongly inspired by the results of Ouaknine and Worrell [16]. Except for [11], it seems that the notion of alternation in the context of timed automata was not studied before. The reason was probably undecidability of the universality problem. Some research (see [5, 10, 7, 3, 6] and references within) was devoted to the control problem in the timed case. While in this case one also needs to deal with some universal branching, these works do not seem to have direct connection to our setting. Finally, let us mention that restrictions to one clock have been already considered in the context of model-checking of timed systems [12, 15].

Organization of the paper. In the next section we define alternating timed automata; we discuss their basic properties and relations with nondeterministic timed automata. In Section 3 we show decidability of the emptiness problem for alternating timed automata with one clock. In the following section we show a non-primitive recursive lower bound for the problem. Next we show the undecidability result for an extension of our model with epsilon-moves.

2   Alternating Timed Automata

In this section we introduce the alternating timed automata model and study its basic properties. The model is a quite straightforward extension of the non-deterministic model. Nevertheless some care is needed to have the desirable feature that complementation corresponds to exchanging existential and universal branchings (and final and non-final states). As can be expected, alternating timed automata can recognize more languages than their nondeterministic counterparts. The price to pay for this is that the emptiness problem becomes undecidable, in contrast to timed automata [2]. This motivates the restriction to automata with one clock. With one clock alternating automata can still recognize languages not recognizable by nondeterministic automata and moreover, as we show in the next section, they have decidable emptiness problem.

For a given finite set C of *clock variables* (or *clocks* in short), consider the set $\Phi(C)$ of clock constraints σ defined by

$$\sigma \quad ::= \quad x < c \mid x \le c \mid \sigma_1 \wedge \sigma_2 \mid \neg\sigma,$$

where c stands for an arbitrary nonnegative integer constant, and $x \in C$. For instance, note that **tt** (always true), or $x = c$, can be defined as abbreviations. Each constraint σ denotes a subset $[\sigma]$ of $(\mathbb{R}_+)^C$, in a natural way, where $\mathbb{R}_+$ stands for the set of nonnegative reals.

Transition relation of a timed automaton [2] is usually defined by a finite set of rules δ of the form

$$\delta \subseteq Q \times \Sigma \times \Phi(C) \times Q \times \mathcal{P}(C),$$

where Q is a set of *locations* (control states) and Σ is an input alphabet. A rule $\langle q, a, \sigma, q', r \rangle \in \delta$ means, roughly, that when in a location q, if the next input letter is a and the constraint σ is satisfied by the current valuation of clock variables, the next location can be q' and the clocks in r should be reset to 0. Our definition below uses an easy observation, that the relation δ can be suitably rearranged into a finite partial function

$$Q \times \Sigma \times \Phi(C) \xrightarrow{\cdot} \mathcal{P}(Q \times \mathcal{P}(C)).$$

The definition below comes naturally when one thinks of an element of the codomain as a disjunction of a finite number of pairs (q, r). Let $\mathcal{B}^+(X)$ denote the set of all positive boolean formulas over the set X of propositions, i.e., the set generated by:

$$\phi \quad ::= \quad X \mid \phi_1 \wedge \phi_2 \mid \phi_1 \vee \phi_2.$$

Definition 1 (Alternating timed automaton). *An* alternating timed automaton *is a tuple* $\mathcal{A} = (Q, q_0, \Sigma, C, F, \delta)$ *where: Q is a finite set of locations, Σ is a finite input alphabet, C is a finite set of clock variables, and $\delta : Q \times \Sigma \times \Phi(C) \xrightarrow{\cdot} \mathcal{B}^+(Q \times \mathcal{P}(C))$ is a finite partial function. Moreover $q_0 \in Q$ is an* initial state *and $F \subseteq Q$ is a set of accepting states. We also put an additional restriction:*

(Partition). *For every q and a, the set $\{[\sigma] : \delta(q, a, \sigma)$ is defined$\}$ gives a (finite) partition of $(\mathbb{R}_+)^{\mathcal{C}}$.*

The (Partition) condition does not limit the expressive power of automata. We impose it because it permits to give a nice symmetric semantic for the automata. We will often write rules of the automaton in a form: $q, a, \sigma \mapsto b$.

By a *timed word* over Σ we mean a finite sequence

$$w = (a_1, t_1)(a_2, t_2) \dots (a_n, t_n) \tag{1}$$

of pairs from $\Sigma \times \mathbb{R}_+$. Each t_i describes the amount of time that passed between reading a_{i-1} and a_i, i.e., a_1 was read at time t_1, a_2 was read at time $t_1 + t_2$, and so on. In Sections 4 and 5 it will be more convenient to use an alternative representation where t_i denotes the time elapsed since the beginning of the word.

To define an execution of an automaton, we will need two operations on valuations $\mathbf{v} \in (\mathbb{R}_+)^{\mathcal{C}}$. A valuation $\mathbf{v} + t$, for $t \in \mathbb{R}_+$, is obtained from $\mathbf{v}$ by augmenting value of each clock by t. A valuation $\mathbf{v}[r := 0]$, for $r \subseteq \mathcal{C}$, is obtained by resetting values of all clocks in r to zero.

For an alternating timed automaton $\mathcal{A}$ and a timed word w as in (1), we define the *acceptance game* $G_{\mathcal{A}, w}$ between two players Adam and Eve. Intuitively, the objective of Eve is to accept w, while the aim of Adam is the opposite. A play starts at the initial configuration $(q_0, \mathbf{v}_0)$, where $\mathbf{v}_0 : \mathcal{C} \to \mathbb{R}_+$ is a valuation assigning 0 to each clock variable. It consists of n phases. The $(k+1)$-th phase starts in $(q_k, \mathbf{v}_k)$, ends in some configuration $(q_{k+1}, \mathbf{v}_{k+1})$ and proceeds as follows. Let $\bar{\mathbf{v}} := \mathbf{v}_k + t_{k+1}$. Let σ be the unique constraint such that $\bar{\mathbf{v}}$ satisfies σ and $\delta(q_k, a_{k+1}, \sigma)$ is defined. Now the outcome of the phase is determined by the formula b. There are three cases:

- $b = b_1 \wedge b_2$: Adam chooses one of subformulas b_1, b_2 and the play continues with b replaced by the chosen subformula;
- $b = b_1 \vee b_2$: dually, Eve chooses one of subformulas;
- $b = (q, r) \in Q \times \mathcal{P}(\mathcal{C})$: the phase ends with the result $(q_{k+1}, \mathbf{v}_{k+1}) := (q, \bar{\mathbf{v}}[r := 0])$. A new phase is starting from this configuration if $k+1 < n$.

The winner is Eve if q_n is accepting ($q_n \in F$), otherwise Adam wins.

Definition 2 (Acceptance). *The automaton $\mathcal{A}$ accepts w iff Eve has a winning strategy in the game $G_{\mathcal{A}, w}$. By $L(\mathcal{A})$ we denote the language of all timed words w accepted by $\mathcal{A}$.*

To show the power of alternation we give an example of an automaton for a language not recognizable by standard (i.e. nondeterministic) timed automata (cf. [2]).

Example 1. Consider a language consisting of timed words w over a singleton alphabet $\{a\}$ that contain no pair of letters such that one of them is precisely one time unit later than the other. The alternating automaton for this language has three states q_0, q_1, q_2. State q_0 is initial. The automaton has a single clock x and the following transition rules:

$$q_0, a, \mathbf{tt} \ \mapsto \ (q_0, \emptyset) \wedge (q_1, \{x\}) \qquad\qquad q_1, a, x{\neq}1 \ \mapsto \ (q_1, \emptyset)$$

$$q_1, a, x{=}1 \ \mapsto \ (q_2, \emptyset) \qquad\qquad\qquad\qquad q_2, a, \mathbf{tt} \ \mapsto \ (q_2, \emptyset)$$

States q_0 and q_1 are accepting. Clearly, Adam has a strategy to reach q_2 iff the word is not in the language, i.e., some letter is one time unit after some other.

As one expects, we have the following:

Proposition 1. *The class of languages accepted by alternating timed automata is effectively closed under all boolean operations: union, intersection and complementation. These operations to do not increase the number of clocks of the automaton.*

The closure under conjunction and disjunction is straightforward since we permit positive boolean expressions as values of the transition function. Due to the condition (Partition) the automaton for the complement is obtained by exchanging conjunctions with disjunctions in all transitions and exchanging accepting states with non-accepting states.

Definition 3. *An alternating timed automaton $\mathcal{A}$ is called* purely universal *if the disjunction does not appear in the transition rules δ. Dually, $\mathcal{A}$ is* purely existential *if no conjunction appears in δ.*

It is obvious that every purely-existential automaton is a standard nondeterministic timed automaton. The converse is not immediately true because of the (Partition) condition. Nevertheless it is not difficult to show the following

Proposition 2. *Every standard nondeterministic automaton is equivalent to a purely-existential automaton.*

In the following sections, we consider emptiness, universality and containment for different classes of alternating timed automata. For clarity, we recall definitions here.

Definition 4. *For a class C of automata we consider three problems:*

- *Emptiness: given $\mathcal{A} \in C$ is $L(\mathcal{A})$ empty.*
- *Universality: given $\mathcal{A} \in C$ does $L(\mathcal{A})$ contain all timed words.*
- *Containment: given $\mathcal{A}, \mathcal{B} \in C$ does $L(\mathcal{A}) \subseteq L(\mathcal{B})$.*

It is well known that the universality is undecidable for non-deterministic timed automata [2] with at least two clocks. As a consequence, two other problems are also undecidable for alternating timed automata with two clocks. This is why in the rest of the paper we focus on automata with one clock only.

Proviso: In the following all automata have one clock.

Remark: The automaton from Example 1 uses only one clock. This shows that one clock alternating automata can recognize some languages not recognizable by nondeterministic automata with many clocks [2]. The converse is also true. It is enough to consider the language consisting of the words containing an appearance of a letter a at times t_1, t_2, t_1+1, t_2+1, for some $0<t_1<t_2<1$, and such that there is a at no time between t_1 and t_2 while there is one at a time between t_1+1 and t_2+1. We omit the proof.

3 Decidability

The main result of this section is that the emptiness problem for one-clock alternating timed automata is decidable. Due to closure under boolean operations, this implies the decidability of the universality and the containment problems.

Theorem 1. *Emptiness is decidable for one-clock alternating timed automata.*

Corollary 1. *The containment problem is decidable for one-clock alternating timed automata.*

The rest of this section is devoted to the proof of Theorem 1. Essentially, we have adapted the method of Ouaknine and Worrell [16] for our more general setting. We point out the differences below.

Fix a one-clock alternating timed automaton $\mathcal{A} = (Q, q_0, \Sigma, \{x\}, F, \delta)$. For readability, assume w.l.o.g. that the boolean conditions appearing in rules of δ are all in *disjunctive normal form*. In terms of acceptance games this means that each phase consists of a single move of Eve followed by a single move of Adam. Consider a labeled transition system $\mathcal{T}$ whose states are finite sets of configurations, i.e., finite sets of pairs $(q, \mathbf{v})$, where $q \in Q$ and $\mathbf{v} \in \mathbb{R}_+$. The initial position in $\mathcal{T}$ is $P_0 = \{(q_0, 0)\}$ and there is a transition $P \xrightarrow{a,t} P'$ in $\mathcal{T}$ iff P' can be obtained from P by the following nondeterministic process:

- First, for each $(q, \mathbf{v}) \in P$, do the following:
    - let $\mathbf{v}' := \mathbf{v}+t$,
    - let $b = \delta(q, a, \sigma)$ for the uniquely determined σ satisfied in $\mathbf{v}'$,
    - choose one of disjuncts of b, say

$$(q_1, r_1) \ \wedge \ \ldots \ \wedge \ (q_k, r_k) \qquad (k > 0),$$

    - let $\mathtt{Next}_{(q,\mathbf{v})} = \{(q_i, \mathbf{v}'[r_i := 0]) : i = 1 \ldots k\}$.
- Then, let $P' := \bigcup_{(q,\mathbf{v}) \in P} \mathtt{Next}_{(q,\mathbf{v})}$.

This construction is very similar to the translation from alternating to nondeterministic automata over (untimed) words: we just collect all universal choices in one set. Compared to [16], the essential difference is that we have to deal with both disjunction and conjunction, while in [16] only one of them appeared. We treat conjunction similarly to determinization in [16]. On the other hand, we leave the existential choice, i.e., nondeterminism, essentially unaffected in $\mathcal{T}$.

In what follows we will derive from $\mathcal{T}$ a finite-branching transition system $\mathcal{H}$, suitable for the decision procedure. Like in [16], the degree of the nodes of $\mathcal{H}$ will not be bounded but nevertheless finite. This is sufficient for our purposes.

A state $\{(q_1, \mathbf{v}_1), \ldots, (q_n, \mathbf{v}_n)\}$ of $\mathcal{T}$ is called *bad* iff all control states q_i are accepting ($q_i \in F$). The following proposition characterizes acceptance in $\mathcal{A}$ in terms of reachability of bad states in $\mathcal{T}$. As we consider finite words only, there are no issues concerning the quality of a strategy in the acceptance game.

Lemma 1. $\mathcal{A}$ *accepts a timed word w iff there is a path in $\mathcal{T}$, labeled by w, from P_0 to a bad state.*

Let $\widehat{\mathcal{T}}$ be a labeled transition system obtained from $\mathcal{T}$ by erasing time information from transition labels, i.e., there is a transition $P \xrightarrow{a} Q$ in $\widehat{\mathcal{T}}$ iff there is $P \xrightarrow{a,t} Q$ in $\mathcal{T}$, for some $t \in \mathbb{R}_+$. Now we cannot talk about particular timed words but still we have the following:

Lemma 2. $L(\mathcal{A})$ *is nonempty if and only if there is a path in $\widehat{\mathcal{T}}$ from P_0 to a bad state.*

Thus, the (non)emptiness problem for $\mathcal{A}$ is reduced to the reachability of a bad state in $\widehat{\mathcal{T}}$. The last difficulty is that even if each state of $\widehat{\mathcal{T}}$ is a finite set, there are uncountably many states. The following definition allows to abstract from the precise timing information in states. Let $c_{\max}$ denote the biggest constant appearing in constraints in δ. Let set $\mathtt{reg}$ of *regions* be a partition of $\mathbb{R}_+$ into $2 \cdot (c_{\max}+1)$ sets as follows:

$$\mathtt{reg} := \{\{0\}, (0,1), \{1\}, (1,2), \ldots, (c_{\max}-1, c_{\max}), \{c_{\max}\}, (c_{\max}, +\infty)\}.$$

For $\mathbf{v} \in \mathbb{R}_+$, let $\mathtt{reg}(\mathbf{v})$ denote its region; and let $\mathtt{fract}(\mathbf{v})$ denote the fractional part of $\mathbf{v}$. Below we work with finite words over the alphabet $\Lambda = \mathcal{P}(Q \times \mathtt{reg})$ consisting of finite sets of pairs $(q, \mathbf{r})$, where $q \in Q$ is a control state and $\mathbf{r} \in \mathtt{reg}$ is a region.

Definition 5. *For a state P of $\widehat{\mathcal{T}}$ we define a word $H(P)$ from Λ^* as the one obtained by the following procedure:*

- *replace each $(q, \mathbf{v}) \in P$ by a triple $\langle q, \mathtt{reg}(\mathbf{v}), \mathtt{fract}(\mathbf{v})\rangle$ (this yields a finite set of triples)*
- *sort all these triples w.r.t. $\mathtt{fract}(\mathbf{v})$ (this yields a finite sequence of triples)*
- *group together triples that have the same value of $\mathtt{fract}(\mathbf{v})$, ignoring multiple occurrences (this yields a finite sequence of finite sets of triples)*
- *forget about $\mathtt{fract}(\mathbf{v})$, i.e., replace each triple $\langle q, \mathtt{reg}(\mathbf{v}), \mathtt{fract}(\mathbf{v})\rangle$ by a pair $(q, \mathtt{reg}(\mathbf{v}))$ (this yields a finite sequence of finite sets of pairs, a word in Λ^*).*

Definition 6. *Define an equivalence relation $\sim$ over states of $\widehat{\mathcal{T}}$ as the kernel of H, i.e., $P \sim P'$ iff $H(P) = H(P')$.*

The following observations are straightforward:

Lemma 3. *Relation $\sim$ is a bisimulation over transition system $\widehat{\mathcal{T}}$.*

Lemma 4. *If P is bad and $P \sim P'$ then P' is bad.*

Let $\mathcal{H}$ denote the quotient of the transition system $\widehat{\mathcal{T}}$ by $\sim$. To put it more explicitly: states of $\mathcal{H}$ are all words $H(P)$, for a state P of $\widehat{\mathcal{T}}$; there is a transition $W_1 \xrightarrow{a} W_2$ in $\mathcal{H}$ if there is a transition $P_1 \xrightarrow{a} P_2$ in $\widehat{\mathcal{T}}$ with $H(P_1) = W_1$, $H(P_2) = W_2$. Since $\sim$ is a bisimulation, the definition does not depend on a particular choice of P_1 (and P_2). The initial state W_0 in $\mathcal{H}$ is $H(P_0)$.

By Lemma 4 it is correct to call a state W in $\mathcal{H}$ *bad* if $W = H(P)$ for a bad state P. Because $\mathcal{H}$ is a quotient of $\widehat{\mathcal{T}}$ by bisimulation, from Lemma 2 we derive:

Lemma 5. *$L(\mathcal{A})$ is nonempty iff a bad state is reachable in $\mathcal{H}$ from W_0.*

At this point, we have reduced emptiness of $L(\mathcal{A})$ to the reachability of a bad state in a countably infinite transition system $\mathcal{H}$. The rest of the proof is quite standard [1, 13] and exploits the fact that one can put an appropriate *well-quasi-order* (*wqo* in short) on states of $\mathcal{H}$. Unfortunately, we are obliged to redo the proofs as we could not find a theorem that fits precisely our setting.

Definition 7. *Let $\preceq$ denote the* monotone domination *ordering over Λ^* induced by the subset inclusion over Λ, defined as follows: $a_1 \ldots a_n \preceq b_1 \ldots b_m$ iff there exists a strictly increasing function $f : \{1, \ldots, n\} \to \{1, \ldots, m\}$ such that for each $i \leq n$, $a_i \subseteq b_{f(i)}$.*

Lemma 6 ([14]). *Relation $\preceq$ is a wqo, i.e., for arbitrary infinite sequence $W_1, W_2, \ldots$ of words over Λ, there exist indexes $i < j$ such that $W_i \preceq W_j$.*

The decision procedure for reachability of bad states will work by an exhaustive search through a sufficiently large portion of the whole reachability tree. Thus we need to know that an arbitrarily large part of that tree can be effectively constructed. Roughly, all time delays of an action a from W can be captured by a finite number of cyclic shifts of W with an appropriate change of region.

Lemma 7. *For each state W in $\mathcal{H}$, its set of successors $\{W' \in \Lambda^* : W \xrightarrow{a} W'$ for some $a\}$ is finite and effectively computable.*

The following observation is proved in the same way as Lemma 15 in [16].

Lemma 8. *The inverse of $\preceq$ relation is a simulation: whenever $W_1 \preceq W_2$ and $W_2 \xrightarrow{a} W_2'$, there is some W_1' such that $W_1 \xrightarrow{a} W_1'$ and $W_1' \preceq W_2'$.*

The next observation is more specific to our setting but fortunately very easy.

Lemma 9 (Downward closedness of badness). *Whenever $W \preceq W'$ and W' is bad then W is bad as well.*

Proof. Take a letter w_i of W. We need to show that $q \in F$ for every $(q, \mathbf{r}) \in w_i$. By the definition of $W \preceq W'$ we have $w_i \subseteq w'_j$ for some letter w'_j of W'. Hence, $(q, \mathbf{r}) \in w'_j$ and $q \in F$ as W' is bad.

Now we are ready to finally prove the following:

Lemma 10. *It is decidable whether a bad state is reachable in $\mathcal{H}$ from W_0.*

Proof. The *reachability tree* is the unraveling of $\mathcal{H}$ from W_0. The algorithm constructs a portion t of the tree conforming to the following rule: do not add a node W' to t in a situation when among its ancestors there is some $W \preceq W'$. Now, Lemma 6 guarantees that each path in t is finite. Furthermore, since the degree of each node is finite, t is a finite tree.

We need only to prove that if a bad state is reachable in $\mathcal{H}$ from W_0 then t contains at least one bad state. Let W be such a bad state reachable from W_0 in $\mathcal{H}$ by a path π of the shortest length. Assume that W is not in t, i.e., there are two other nodes in π, say W_1 and W_2 such that W_1 is an ancestor of W_2 in reachability tree and $W_1 \preceq W_2$ (i.e., W_2 was *not* added into t). Since the inverse of $\preceq$ is a simulation by Lemma 8, the sequence of transitions in π from W_2 to W can be imitated by the corresponding sequence of transitions from W_1 to some other $W' \preceq W$. W' is bad as well by Lemma 9. Moreover, the path leading to W' is strictly shorter than π, a contradiction. $\qquad\square$

Theorem 1 follows immediately from Lemma 10 and Lemma 5.

Remark: In fact, Ouaknine and Worrell showed decidability of "$L(\mathcal{A}) \subseteq L(\mathcal{B})$" in a slightly more general case, namely when automaton $\mathcal{A}$ has an arbitrary many clocks. Along the same lines one can adapt our proof for "$L(\mathcal{A}) \subseteq L(\mathcal{B})$", assumed that $\mathcal{A}$ is an arbitrary nondeterministic timed automaton and $\mathcal{B}$ is a one-clock alternating timed automaton.

4   Lower Bound

In this section we prove the following lower bound result.

Theorem 2. *The complexity of the emptiness problem for one-clock purely universal alternating timed automata is not bounded by a primitive recursive function.*

Since emptiness and universality are dual in the setting of alternating automata, as a direct conclusion we get the following:

Corollary 2. *The complexity of the universality problem for one-clock purely existential alternating (i.e., nondeterministic) timed automata is not bounded by a primitive recursive function.*

This answers the question posed by Ouaknine and Worrell [16].

The rest of this section contains the proof of Theorem 2. The proof is a reduction of the reachability problem for *lossy one-channel systems* [17].

Definition 8 (Channel system). *A* channel system *is given by a tuple* $\mathcal{S} = (Q, q_0, \Sigma, \Delta)$, *where Q is a finite set of control states, $q_0 \in Q$ is an initial state, Σ is a finite channel alphabet and $\Delta \subseteq Q \times (\{!a : a \in \Sigma\} \cup \{?a : a \in \Sigma\} \cup \{\epsilon\}) \times Q$ is a finite set of transition rules.*

A configuration of $\mathcal{S}$ is a pair (q, w) of a control state q and a channel content $w \in \Sigma^*$. Transition rules allow the system to pass from one configuration to another. In particular, a rule $\langle q, !a, q' \rangle$ allows in a state q to write to the channel and to pass to the new state q'. Similarly, $\langle q, ?a, q' \rangle$ means reading from a channel and is allowed in state q only when a is at the end of the channel. The channel is a FIFO, and by convention $\mathcal{S}$ writes at the beginning and reads at the end. Finally, a rule $\langle q, \epsilon, q' \rangle$ allows for a silent change of control state, without reading or writing.

Formally, there is a (perfect) transition $(q, w) \xrightarrow{\gamma} (q', w')$ if one of the following conditions is satisfied:

- $\gamma = \langle q, \epsilon, q' \rangle$ and $w = w'$, or
- $\gamma = \langle q, !a, q' \rangle$ for some $a \in \Sigma$, and $w' = aw$, or
- $\gamma = \langle q, ?a, q' \rangle$ for some $a \in \Sigma$, and $w = w'a$.

The *initial configuration* is (q_0, ϵ), i.e., execution of $\mathcal{S}$ starts with the empty channel. For technical convenience, we assume w.l.o.g. that there is no rule returning back to the initial state: for each rule $\langle q, x, q' \rangle \in \Delta$, $q' \neq q_0$.

A *lossy channel system* differs from the perfect one in only one respect: during the transition step, an arbitrary number of messages stored in the channel may be lost. To define lossy transitions, we need the subsequence ordering on Σ^*, denoted by $\sqsubseteq$ (e.g., `tata` $\sqsubseteq$ `atlanta`). We say that there is a lossy transition from (q, w) to (q', w'), denoted by $(q, w) \xRightarrow{\gamma} (q', w')$, iff there exists $u, u' \in \Sigma^*$ such that $u \sqsubseteq w$, $(q, u) \xrightarrow{\gamma} (q', u')$ and $w' \sqsubseteq u'$.

By a *lossy computation* of a channel system $\mathcal{S}$ we mean a finite sequence:

$$(q_0, \epsilon) \xRightarrow{\gamma_1} (q_1, w_1) \xRightarrow{\gamma_2} (q_2, w_2) \quad \dots \quad \xRightarrow{\gamma_n} (q_n, w_n). \tag{2}$$

Definition 9. *Lossy reachability problem for channel systems is: given a channel system S and a configuration (q_f, w_f), with $q_f \neq q_0$, decide whether there is a lossy computation of S ending in (q_f, w_f).*

Theorem 3 ([17]). *The lossy reachability problem for channel systems has non-primitive recursive complexity.*

The result of [17] was showed for a slightly different model. Namely, during a single transition, a finite sequence of messages was allowed to be read or written to the channel. Clearly, reachability problems in both models are polynomial-time equivalent.

In the sequel we describe a reduction from the lossy reachability for channel systems to the emptiness problem for one-clock purely-universal alternating timed automata. Given a channel system $\mathcal{S} = (Q, q_0, \Sigma, \Delta)$, and a configuration

(q_f, w_f), we effectively construct a purely-universal automaton $\mathcal{A}$ with a single clock x, and the input alphabet $\overline{\Sigma} = Q \cup \Sigma \cup \Delta$. The construction will assure that $\mathcal{A}$ accepts precisely correct encodings of lossy computations of $\mathcal{S}$ ending in (q_f, w_f). A computation as in (2) will be encoded as the following word over $\overline{\Sigma}$:

$$q_n \gamma_n w_n \quad q_{n-1} \gamma_{n-1} w_{n-1} \quad \cdots \quad q_1 \gamma_1 w_1 \quad q_0, \tag{3}$$

where $q_i \in Q$, $\gamma_i \in \Delta$, $w_i \in \Sigma^*$. Let $\mathcal{S}$ be fixed in this section.

It will be convenient here to write timed words in a slightly different way than before. From now on, whenever we write a word $w = (a_1, t_1)(a_2, t_2) \ldots (a_n, t_n)$ we mean that the letter a_i appeared t_i time units after the beginning of the word. In particular, a_{i+1} appeared $t_{i+1} - t_i$ time units after a_i. Clearly this is correct only when $t_{i+1} \geq t_i$, for $i = 1 \ldots n-1$.

Before the formal definition of encoding of a computation by a timed word we outline shortly the underlying intuition. We will require that the letter q_n appears at time 0 and then that each letter q_i appears at time $n - i$. Hence, each configuration will be placed in a unit interval. To ensure consistency of the channel contents at consecutive configurations we require that if a message survived during a step i (it was neither read nor written nor lost) then the distance in time between its appearances in the sequences w_i and w_{i-1} should be precisely 1.

We will need a new piece of notation : by $(w + 1)$ we mean the word obtained from w by increasing all t_i by one time unit, i.e., $(w + 1) = (a_1, t_1 + 1)(a_2, t_2 + 1) \ldots (a_n, t_n + 1)$.

Definition 10. *By a lossy computation encoding ending in (q_f, w_f) we mean any timed word over $\overline{\Sigma}$ of the form:*

$$(q_n, t_n)(\gamma_n, t'_n)v_n \ (q_{n-1}, t_{n-1})(\gamma_{n-1}, t'_{n-1})v_{n-1} \quad \cdots \quad (q_1, t_1)(\gamma_1, t'_1)v_1 \ (q_0, t_0),$$

where each $v_i = (a_i^1, u_i^1) \ldots (a_i^{l_i}, u_i^{l_i})$ is a timed word over Σ. Additionally we require that for each $i \leq n$ and $j = 1, \ldots, l_i$, the following conditions hold:

(P1) *Structure:*

$$q_i \in Q, \gamma_i \in \Delta, a_i^j \in \Sigma, \gamma_i = \langle q_{i-1}, x, q_i \rangle, q_n = q_f \text{ and } a_n^1 \ldots a_n^{l_n} = w_f.$$

(P2) *Distribution in time:*

$$n-i = t_i < t'_i < u_i^1 < u_i^2 < \ldots < u_i^{l_i} < t_{i+1} = n-i+1.$$

(P3a) *Epsilon move: if $\gamma_i = \langle q_{i-1}, \epsilon, q_i \rangle$ then $(v_i + 1) \sqsubseteq v_{i-1}$.*
(P3b) *Write move: if $\gamma_i = \langle q_{i-1}, !a, q_i \rangle$ then either $a_i^1 = a$ and $(a_i^2 \ldots a_i^{l_i} + 1) \sqsubseteq v_{i-1}$, or $(v_i + 1) \sqsubseteq v_{i-1}$.*
(P3c) *Read move: if $\gamma_i = \langle q_{i-1}, ?a, q_i \rangle$ then $v_{i-1} = v'(a, t)v''$ for some timed words v', v'' and $t \in \mathbb{R}_+$, such that $(v_i + 1) \sqsubseteq v'$.*

Lemma 11. $\mathcal{S}$ *has a computation of the form (2) ending in* $(q_n, w_n) = (q_f, w_f)$ *if and only if there exists a lossy computation encoding ending in* (q_f, w_f) *as in Definition 10.*

Our aim is:

Lemma 12. *A purely universal automaton* $\mathcal{A}$ *can be effectively constructed such that* $L(\mathcal{A})$ *contains precisely all lossy computation encodings ending in* (q_f, w_f).

The proof of this lemma will occupy the rest of this section. Automaton $\mathcal{A}$ will be defined as a conjunction of four automata, each responsible for some of the conditions from Definition 10:

$$\mathcal{A} := \mathcal{A}_{\text{struct}} \;\wedge\; \mathcal{A}_{\text{unit}} \;\wedge\; \mathcal{A}_{\text{strict}} \;\wedge\; \mathcal{A}_{\text{check}}.$$

All four automata will be purely universal and will use at most one clock. Automaton $\mathcal{A}_{\text{struct}}$ verifies condition *(P1)*, automata $\mathcal{A}_{\text{unit}}$ and $\mathcal{A}_{\text{strict}}$ jointly check condition *(P2)*, and $\mathcal{A}_{\text{check}}$ enforces the most involved conditions *(P3a) – (P3c)*.

We omit an obvious definition of $\mathcal{A}_{\text{struct}}$. We also omit the construction of the automaton $\mathcal{A}_{\text{unit}}$ checking that letters from Q appear precisely at times $0, 1, \ldots, n$, and automaton $\mathcal{A}_{\text{strict}}$ that accepts a timed word iff the first letter is at time 0 and no two consecutive letters appear at the same time.

Till now, all the automata were not only purely universal but also purely existential, i.e., deterministic. The power of universal choice will be only used in the last automaton $\mathcal{A}_{\text{check}}$, that checks for correctness of each transition step of $\mathcal{S}$. While analyzing definition of $\mathcal{A}_{\text{check}}$ we will comfortably assume that an input word meets all conditions verified by the other automata, otherwise the word is anyway not accepted. For conciseness, We implicitly assume that the automaton fails to accept if no rule is applicable. Moreover, when no clock is reset, we will omit writing it explicitly.

The transition rules of $\mathcal{A}_{\text{check}}$ from the initial state s_0 are as follows:

$$s_0, \Sigma \cup \Delta, \mathbf{tt} \;\mapsto\; s_0 \qquad s_0, q, \mathbf{tt} \;\mapsto\; s_0 \wedge (s_{\text{step}}, \{x\}), \quad \text{for } q \in Q \setminus \{q_0\}$$

$$s_0, q_0, \mathbf{tt} \;\mapsto\; \top.$$

Intuitively, at each $q \in Q$, except at q_0, an extra automaton is run from the state s_{step}, in order to check correctness of a single step. Symbol $\top$ on the right-hand side stands for a distinguished state that accepts unconditionally.

Now the rules $s_{\text{step}}, \gamma, \ldots \mapsto \ldots$ depend on $\gamma = \langle q, x, q' \rangle$. There are three cases, corresponding to conditions *(P3a)*, *(P3b)* and *(P3c)*, respectively. Case *(P3b)*, not much different from *(P3a)*, is omitted here.

I. Case $\gamma = \langle q, \varepsilon, q' \rangle$: $\qquad s_{\text{step}}, \langle q, \varepsilon, q' \rangle, \mathbf{tt} \mapsto s_{\text{channel}}.$

In state s_{channel}, the automaton checks the condition (P3a), i.e., whether all consecutive letters from Σ are copied one time unit later. This is done by:

$$s_{\text{channel}}, Q, \mathbf{tt} \;\mapsto\; \top \qquad s_{\text{channel}}, a, \mathbf{tt} \;\mapsto\; s_{\text{channel}} \wedge (s_a^{+1}, \{x\}), \quad \text{for } a \in \Sigma.$$

Hence, the automaton starts a check from s_a^{+1} at every letter read. Note that this is precisely here where the universal branching is essential. The task of s_a^{+1} is to check that there is letter a one time unit later:

$$s_a^{+1}, a, x = 1 \; \mapsto \; \top \qquad\qquad s_a^{+1}, \overline{\Sigma}, x < 1 \; \mapsto \; s_a^{+1}$$

II. *Case* $\gamma = \langle q, ?a, q' \rangle$: $s_{\text{step}}, \langle q, ?a, q' \rangle, \mathbf{tt} \mapsto s_{?a} \wedge (s_{\text{try}?a}, \{x\})$.

The behaviour of $s_{?a}$ is very similar to s_{channel} but additionally it will start a new copy of the automaton in the state $s_{\text{try}?a}$. The goal of $s_{\text{try}?a}$ is to check for the letter a at the end of the present configuration.

$$s_{?a}, Q, \mathbf{tt} \; \mapsto \; \top \qquad s_{?a}, b, \mathbf{tt} \; \mapsto \; s_{?a} \wedge (s_b^{+1}, \{x\}) \wedge (s_{\text{try}?a}, \{x\}), \;\; \text{for } b \in \Sigma.$$

Note the clock reset when entering to $s_{\text{try}?a}$. As we cannot know when the configuration ends we start $s_{\text{try}?a}$ at each letter read. If we realize that this was not the end (we see another channel letter) then the check just succeeds. If this was the end (we see a state) then the true check starts from the state $s_{\text{check}?a}$:

$$s_{\text{try}?a}, \Sigma, \mathbf{tt} \; \mapsto \; \top \qquad\qquad s_{\text{try}?a}, Q, \mathbf{tt} \; \mapsto \; s_{\text{check}?a}.$$

From $s_{\text{check}?a}$ we look for some a that appears more than one time unit later:

$$s_{\text{check}?a}, \overline{\Sigma}, x \le 1 \; \mapsto \; s_{\text{check}?a}$$
$$s_{\text{check}?a}, a, x > 1 \; \mapsto \; \top \qquad s_{\text{check}?a}, b, x > 1 \; \mapsto \; s_{\text{check}?a}, \;\; \text{for } b \in \Sigma \backslash \{a\}.$$

Automaton $\mathcal{A}_{\text{check}}$ has no other accepting states but $\top$.

By the very construction, $\mathcal{A}$ satisfies Lemma 12. By Lemma 11, $\mathcal{S}$ has a computation (2) ending in (q_f, w_f) if and only if $L(\mathcal{A})$ is nonempty. This completes the proof of Theorem 2.

5   Undecidability

In this section we point out that the alternating timed automata model cannot be extended with ϵ-transitions. It is known that ϵ-transitions extend the power of nondeterministic timed automata [2, 9]. Here we show some evidence that every extension of alternating timed automata with ϵ-transitions will have undecidable emptiness problem.

It turns out that there are many possible ways of introducing ϵ-transitions to alternating timed automata. To see the issues involved consider the question of whether such an automaton should be allowed to start uncountably many copies of itself or not. Facing these problems we have decided not to present any precise definition but rather to show where the problem is. We will show that the universality problem for purely existential automata with a very simple notion of ϵ-transitions is undecidable.

Timed words are written here in the same convention as in previous section: $w = (a_1, t_1)(a_2, t_2) \ldots (a_n, t_n)$ means that the letter a_i appeared at time t_i.

We consider purely existential (i.e. nondeterministic) automata with one clock. We equip them now with additional ϵ-transitions of the form $q, \epsilon, \sigma \mapsto b$. The following trick is used to shorten formal definitions.

Definition 11. *A nondeterministic timed automaton with ϵ-transitions over Σ is a nondeterministic timed automaton over the alphabet $\Sigma_\epsilon = \Sigma \cup \{\epsilon\}$.*

For convenience, we want to distinguish an automaton $\mathcal{A}$ with ϵ-transitions over Σ from the corresponding automaton over Σ_ϵ; the latter will be denoted $\mathcal{A}_\epsilon$. Given a timed word v over Σ_ϵ, by $|v|_\epsilon$ we mean the timed word over Σ obtained from w by erasing all (timed) occurrences of ϵ.

Definition 12. *A timed word over Σ is accepted by a timed automaton $\mathcal{A}$ with ϵ-transitions if there is a timed word v over Σ_ϵ accepted by $\mathcal{A}_\epsilon$ such that $w = |v|_\epsilon$.*

Note that according to the definition, an accepting run is always finite. The main result of this section is:

Theorem 4. *The universality problem for one-clock nondeterministic timed automata with ϵ-transitions is undecidable.*

The proof is by reduction of the reachability problem for perfect channel systems, defined similarly as lossy reachability in Definition 9, but w.r.t. *perfect computation* of a channel systems. Not surprisingly, a perfect computation is any finite sequence of (perfect) transitions:

$$(q_0, \epsilon) \xrightarrow{\gamma_1} (q_1, w_1) \xrightarrow{\gamma_2} (q_2, w_2) \quad \dots \quad \xrightarrow{\gamma_n} (q_n, w_n),$$

Theorem 5 ([8]). *The perfect reachability problem for channel systems is undecidable, assumed $|\Sigma| \geq 2$.*

Given a channel system $\mathcal{S} = (Q, q_0, \Sigma, \Delta)$ and a configuration (q_f, w_f), we effectively construct a one-clock nondeterministic timed automaton with ϵ-transitions $\mathcal{A}'$ over $\overline{\Sigma}$. Automaton $\mathcal{A}'$ will accept precisely the complement of the set of all *perfect computations encodings ending in* (q_f, w_f), defined by:

Definition 13. *A perfect computation encoding ending in (q_f, w_f) is defined as in Definition 10, but with the conditions* (P3a) – (P3c) *replaced by:*

(P3a) *if* $\gamma_i = \langle q_{i-1}, \epsilon, q_i \rangle$ *then* $(v_i + 1) = v_{i-1}$,
(P3b) *if* $\gamma_i = \langle q_{i-1}, !a, q_i \rangle$ *then* $(v_i + 1) = (a, t)v_{i-1}$, *for some* $t \in \mathbb{R}_+$.
(P3c) *if* $\gamma_i = \langle q_{i-1}, ?a, q_i \rangle$ *then* $(v_i(a, t) + 1) = v_{i-1}$, *for some* $t \in \mathbb{R}_+$.

Since each perfect computation encoding is a lossy one, $\mathcal{A}'$ will be defined as a disjunction, $\mathcal{A}' := \neg \mathcal{A} \vee \widehat{\mathcal{A}}$, of the complement of the automaton $\mathcal{A}$ from the previous section and another automaton $\widehat{\mathcal{A}}$. As automaton $\neg \mathcal{A}$ takes care of all timed words that are not lossy computation encodings, it is enough to have:

Lemma 13. *Automaton $\widehat{\mathcal{A}}$ accepts precisely these lossy computation encodings ending in (q_f, w_f) that are not perfect computation encodings.*

This will be enough for correctness of our reduction: $\mathcal{A}'$ will accept precisely the complement of the set of all perfect computation encodings. The construction of $\widehat{\mathcal{A}}$, omitted here, will be given in the full version of this paper.

6   Final Remarks

In this paper we have explored the possibilities opened by the observation that the universality problem for nondeterministic timed automata is decidable. We have extended this result to obtain a class of timed automata that is closed under boolean operations and that has decidable emptiness problem. We have shown that despite being decidable the problem has prohibitively high complexity. We have also considered the extension of the model with epsilon transitions which points out what makes the model decidable and what further extensions are not possible. Maybe somewhat surprisingly universality for 1-clock nondeterministic timed automata but over infinite words is undecidable. We plan to discuss this issue in the full version of the paper.

We see several topics for further work: (1) Adding event-clocks to the model. It seems that one would still obtain a decidable model. (2) Finding logical characterizations of the languages accepted by alternating timed automata with one clock. Since we have the closure under boolean operations, we may hope to find one. (3) Finding a different syntax that will avoid the prohibitive complexity of the emptiness problem. There may well be another way of presenting alternating timed automata that will give the same expressive power but for which the emptiness test will be easier.

Acknowledgments. We thank anonymous referees for valuable remarks.

References

1. P. Abdulla, K. Čerāns, B. Jonsson, and Y. Tsay. General decidability theorems for infinite state systems. In *LICS'96*, p. 313–323, 1996.
2. R. Alur and D.L. Dill. A theory of timed automata. *Theoretical Computer Science*, 126:183–235, 1994.
3. R. Alur, M. Bernadsky, and P. Madhusudan. Optimal reachability for weighted timed games. In *ICALP'04*, volume 3124 of LNCS, p. 122–133, 2004.
4. R. Alur, L. Fix, and T. Henzinger. Event-clock automata: A determinizable class of timed automata. *Theoretical Computer Science*, 204:253-273, 1999.
5. E. Asarin, O. Maler, A. Pnueli, and J. Sifakis. Controller synthesis for timed automata. In *Proc. IFAC Symp. System Structure and Control*, p. 469–474, 1998.
6. P. Bouyer, F. Cassez, E. Fleury, and K. G. Larsen. Optimal strategies in priced timed game automata. In *FSTTCS'04*, LNCS, 2004.
7. P. Bouyer, D. D'Souza, P. Madhusudan, and A. Petit. Timed control with partial observability. In *CAV'03*, volume 2725 of LNCS, p. 180–192, 2003.
8. D. Brand and P. Zafiropulo. On communicating finite-state machines. *J. ACM*, 30(2):323–342, 1983.

9. B. Bérard, V. Diekert, P. Gastin, and A. Petit. Characterization of the expressive power of silent transitions in timed automata. *Fundamenta Informaticae*, 36(2):145–182, 1998.

10. F. Cassez, T. A. Henzinger, and J.-F. Raskin. A comparison of control problems for timed and hybrid systems. In *Hybrid Systems Computation and Control (HSCC'02)*, volume 2289 of LNCS, p. 134–148, 2002.

11. M. Dickhöfer, T. Wilke. Timed alternating tree automata: the automata-theoretic solution to the TCTL model checking problem. In *ICALP'99*, volume 1644 of LNCS, p. 281-290, 1999.

12. C. Dima. Real-time automata and the Kleene algebra of sets of real numbers. In *STACS'00*, volume 1170 of LNCS, p. 279–289, 2000.

13. A. Finkel and Ph. Schnoebelen. Well structured transition systems everywhere! *Theoretical Computer Science*, 256(1-2):63–92, 2001.

14. G. Higman. Ordering by divisibility in abstract algebras. *Proc. London Math. Soc.*, 2(7):326–336, 1952.

15. F. Laroussinie, N. Markey, and Ph. Schnoebelen. Model checking timed automata with one or two clocks. In *CONCUR'04*, volume 3170 of LNCS, p. 387–401, 2004.

16. J. Ouaknine and J. Worrell. On the language inclusion problem for timed automata: Closing a decidability gap. In *LICS'04*, p. 54–63, 2004.

17. Ph. Schnoebelen. Verifying lossy channel systems has nonprimitive recursive complexity. *Information Processing Letters*, 83(5):251–261, 2002.

Full Abstraction for Polymorphic Pi-Calculus

Alan Jeffrey[1,2,*] and Julian Rathke[3]

[1] Bell Labs, Lucent Technologies, Chicago, IL, USA
[2] DePaul University, Chicago, IL, USA
[3] University of Sussex, Brighton, UK

Abstract. The problem of finding a fully abstract model for the polymorphic π-calculus was stated in Pierce and Sangiorgi's work in 1997 and has remained open since then. In this paper, we show that a slight variant of their language has a direct fully abstract model, which does not depend on type unification or logical relations. This is the first fully abstract model for a polymorphic concurrent language. In addition, we discuss the relationship between our work and Pierce and Sangiorgi's, and show that their conjectured fully abstract model is, in fact, sound but not complete.

1 Introduction

Finding sound and complete models for languages with polymorphic types is notoriously difficult. Consider the following implementation of a polymorphic 'or' function in Java 5.0 [17]:

```
static<X> X or (X t, X a, X b) {
  if (a == t) { return a; } else { return b; }
}
```

This implementation of or takes a type parameter X, which will be instantiated with the representation chosen for the booleans, together with three parameters of type X: a constant for 'true', and the values to be 'or'ed. This function can be called in many different ways, for example[1]:

```
or.<int> (1, 0, 1); or.<bool> (true, false, true);
```

In each case, there is no way for the callee to determine the exact type the caller instantiated for X, and so *no matter what implementation for* or *is used*, there is no observable difference between the above program and the following:

```
or.<int> (1, 0, 1); or.<string> ("true", "false", "true");
```

---

* This material is based upon work supported by the National Science Foundation under Grant No. 0430175.

[1] Java purists should note that this discussion assumes for simplicity that downcasting and reflection are not being used, and a particular implementation of autoboxing, for example the code or.<int> (1, 0, 1) is implemented as Integer x = new Integer(1); Integer y = new Integer(0); or.<Integer> (x, y, x).

V. Sassone (Ed.): FOSSACS 2005, LNCS 3441, pp. 266–281, 2005.

or the following:

```
or.<int> (1, 0, 1); or.<int> (2, 3, 2);
```

However, there *is* an observable difference between the above programs and:

```
or.<int> (1, 0, 1); or.<int> (1, 0, 1);
```

since we can use the following implementation of or to distinguish them:

```
static Object x=null;
static<X> X or (X t, X a, X b) {
  if (a == x) { System.out.println ("hello"); } else { x=a; }
  if (a == t) { return a; } else { return b; }
}
```

This example demonstrates some subtleties with polymorphic languages: the presence of impure features (such as mutable fields in this case) and equality testing (such as a == x in this case) can significantly impact the distinguishing power of tests. In the case of pure languages such as System F [10], the technique of *logical relations* [27, 24] can be used to establish equivalence of all of the above calls to or, which is evidently broken by the addition of impurity and equality testing.

Much of the work in finding models of pure polymorphic languages comes in finding appropriate techniques for modelling *parametricity* [26, 27] to show that programs are completely independent of the instantiations for their type parameters. Such parametricity results are surprisingly strong, and can be used to establish 'theorems for free' [31] such as the functoriality of the list type constructor. The strength of the resulting theorems, however, comes at a cost: the proof techniques required to establish them are quite difficult. In particular, even proving the existence of logical relations is problematic in the presence of recursive types [24].

In this paper, we show that providing models for impure polymorphic languages with equality testing can be surprisingly straightforward. We believe that the techniques discussed here will extend to the polymorphic features of languages such as Java 5.0 [17], and C# 2.0 [7]: F-bounded polymorphism [5], subtyping, recursive types and object features. In this paper, we will investigate a minimal impure polymorphic language with equality testing, based on Pierce and Sangiorgi's work [23] on a polymorphic extension of Milner *et al.*'s [21, 20] π-calculus.

Pierce and Sangiorgi have established a sound model for a polymorphic π-calculus, but they only conjectured completeness [23–Sec. 12.2]. In this paper, we develop a sound and complete model for a polymorphic π-calculus: the resulting model and proof techniques are remarkably straightforward. In particular, our model makes no use of type unification, which is an important feature of Pierce and Sangiorgi's model. We then compare our model to theirs, and show that ours is strictly finer: hence we have resolved their outstanding conjecture, by demonstrating their model to be sound but not complete.

This is the first sound and complete model for a polymorphic π-calculus: Pierce and Sangiorgi [23] and Honda *et al.* [3] have established soundness results, but not completeness.

$$
\begin{array}{ll}
a,b,c,d & \text{(Names)} \\
x,y,z & \text{(Variables)} \\
n,m ::= a \mid x & \text{(Values)} \\
P,Q,R ::= n(\vec{X};\vec{x}:\vec{T}).P \mid \overline{n}\langle\vec{T};\vec{n}\rangle \mid \mathbf{0} \mid P \mid Q & \text{(Processes)} \\
\quad\quad \mid v(a:T)P \mid !P \mid \text{if } n = m \text{ then } P \text{ else } Q &
\end{array}
$$

Fig. 1. Syntax

2   An Asynchronous Polymorphic Pi-Calculus

The language we investigate in this paper is an asynchronous variant of Pierce and Sangiorgi's polymorphic π-calculus. This is an extension of the π-calculus with type-passing in addition to value-passing.

2.1   Syntax

The syntax of the asynchronous polymorphic π-calculus is given in Figure 1. The syntax makes use of types (ranged over by T,U,V,W) and type variables (ranged over by X,Y,Z), which are defined in Section 2.3.

Definition 1 (Free identifiers). *Write* fn(P) *for the free names of P,* fn(n) *for the free names of n,* fv(P) *for the free variables of P,* fv(n) *for the free variables of n,* ftv(P) *for the free type variables of P and* ftv(T) *for the free type variables of T.*

Definition 2 (Substitution). *Let σ be a substitution of the form $(\vec{V}/\vec{X};\vec{n}/\vec{x})$, and let $n[\sigma]$, $T[\sigma]$ and $P[\sigma]$ be defined to be the capture-free substitution of type variables $\vec{X}$ by types $\vec{V}$ and variables $\vec{x}$ by values $\vec{n}$, defined in the normal fashion. Let the domain of a substitution* dom(σ) *be defined as* dom$(\vec{V}/\vec{X};\vec{n}/\vec{x}) = \{\vec{X},\vec{x}\}$.

Definition 3 (Process contexts). *A process context $C[\cdot]$ is a process containing one occurrence of a 'hole' $(\cdot)$. Write $C[P]$ for the process given by replacing the hole by P.*

We present an example process, following [23], in the untyped π-calculus, in which we implement a boolean abstract datatype as:

$$
v(t)v(f)v(test)(\overline{getBools}\langle t,f,test\rangle \mid !t(x,y).\overline{x}\langle\rangle \mid !f(x,y).\overline{y}\langle\rangle \mid !test(b,x,y).\overline{b}\langle x,y\rangle)
$$

This process generates new channels t, f and $test$, which it publishes on a public channel $getBools$. It then waits for input on channel t: when it receives a pair (x,y) of channels, it sends a signal on x. The same is true for channel f except that it sends the signal on y. Finally, on a test channel we wait to be sent a boolean b (which should either be t or f) together with a pair $(x.y)$ of channels, and just forwards the pair on to b, which chooses whether to signal x or signal y as appropriate. This can be typed as:

$$B_1 \stackrel{\text{def}}{=} \nu(t : Bool)\nu(f : Bool)\nu(test : Test(Bool))($$
$$\overline{getBools}\langle Bool; t, f, test\rangle \mid$$
$$!t(x : Signal, y : Signal).\overline{x}\langle\rangle \mid$$
$$!f(x : Signal, y : Signal).\overline{y}\langle\rangle \mid$$
$$!test(b : Bool, x : Signal, y : Signal).\overline{b}\langle x, y\rangle$$
$$)$$

where we define:

$$Signal \stackrel{\text{def}}{=} \updownarrow[] \quad Bool \stackrel{\text{def}}{=} \updownarrow[Signal, Signal] \quad Test(T) \stackrel{\text{def}}{=} \updownarrow[T, Signal, Signal]$$

The interesting typing is for the channel *getBools* where the implementation of booleans is published:

$$getBools : \updownarrow[X; X, X, Test(X)]$$

that is, the implementation type *Bool* is never published: instead we just publish an abstract type X together with the values $t : X$, $f : X$ and $test : Test(X)$. Since the implementing type is kept abstract, we should be entitled to change the implementation without impact on the observable behaviour of the system, for example by uniformly swapping the positions of x and y:

$$B_2 \stackrel{\text{def}}{=} \nu(t : Bool)\nu(f : Bool)\nu(test : Test(Bool))($$
$$\overline{getBools}\langle Bool; t, f, test\rangle \mid$$
$$!t(x : Signal, y : Signal).\overline{y}\langle\rangle \mid$$
$$!f(x : Signal, y : Signal).\overline{x}\langle\rangle \mid$$
$$!test(b : Bool, x : Signal, y : Signal).\overline{b}\langle y, x\rangle$$
$$)$$

As Pierce and Sangiorgi observe, as untyped processes B_1 and B_2 are easily distinguished, for example by the testing context:

$$T \stackrel{\text{def}}{=} \cdot \mid \nu(a)\nu(b)(getBools(t, f, test).\overline{t}\langle a, b\rangle \mid a().\overline{c}\langle\rangle \mid b().\overline{d}\langle\rangle)$$

However, this process does not typecheck, since when we come to typecheck T, the channel t has abstract type X, not the implementation type *Bool*. We expect any sound and complete model to consider B_1 and B_2 equivalent.

An illustrative example of a contextual inequivalence is given below. For some generative type T consider the following processes:

$$L = \nu(b : \updownarrow[T], c : \updownarrow[T], d : T)(\overline{a}\langle T, T; b, b, c, d\rangle \mid c(y : T).\overline{\text{fail}}\langle\rangle)$$
$$L' = \nu(b : \updownarrow[T], c : \updownarrow[T], d : T)(\overline{a}\langle T, T; b, b, c, d\rangle \mid c(y : T).\mathbf{0})$$

and a type environment Γ which contains only $a : \updownarrow[X, Y; \updownarrow[X], \updownarrow[Y], \updownarrow[Y], X]$ and a suitable type for fail. Now it may at first appear that L and L' should be considered equivalent with respect to the type information in Γ as the private name d is only released along channel a at some abstract type represented by X, say. And the private name c is only

$$\mu ::= \tau \mid c(\vec{U};\vec{b}) \mid v(\vec{a}:\vec{T})\overline{c}\langle\vec{U};\vec{b}\rangle \quad \text{(Untyped Labels)}$$

$$\frac{}{c(\vec{X};\vec{x}:\vec{T}).P \xrightarrow{c(\vec{U};\vec{b})} P[\vec{U}/\vec{X};\vec{b}/\vec{x}]} \text{(R-IN)} \qquad \frac{}{\overline{c}\langle\vec{U};\vec{b}\rangle \xrightarrow{\overline{c}\langle\vec{U};\vec{b}\rangle} 0} \text{(R-OUT)}$$

$$\frac{P \xrightarrow{\mu} P' \quad \mathsf{bn}(\mu)\cap\mathsf{fn}(Q)=\emptyset}{P\mid Q \xrightarrow{\mu} P'\mid Q} \text{(R-PAR)}$$

$$\frac{P \xrightarrow{c(\vec{U};\vec{b})} P' \quad Q \xrightarrow{v(\vec{a}:\vec{T})\overline{c}\langle\vec{U};\vec{b}\rangle} Q' \quad \{\vec{a}\}\cap\mathsf{fn}(P)=\emptyset}{P\mid Q \xrightarrow{\tau} v(\vec{a}:\vec{T})(P'\mid Q')} \text{(R-COM)}$$

$$\frac{P \xrightarrow{\mu} P' \quad a \notin \mathsf{fn}(\mu)\cup\mathsf{bn}(\mu)}{v(a:T)P \xrightarrow{\mu} v(a:T)P'} \text{(R-NEW)} \qquad \frac{P \xrightarrow{v(\vec{a}:\vec{T})\overline{c}\langle\vec{U};\vec{b}\rangle} P' \quad a \in \{\vec{b}\}\setminus\{c,\vec{a}\}}{v(a:T)P \xrightarrow{v(\vec{a}:\vec{T},a:T)\overline{c}\langle\vec{U};\vec{b}\rangle} P'} \text{(R-OPEN)}$$

$$\frac{!P\mid P \xrightarrow{\mu} P'}{!P \xrightarrow{\mu} P'} \text{(R-REPL)}$$

$$\frac{P \xrightarrow{\mu} P'}{\text{if } a=a \text{ then } P \text{ else } Q \xrightarrow{\mu} P'} \text{(R-TEST-T)} \qquad \frac{a\neq b \quad Q \xrightarrow{\mu} Q'}{\text{if } a=b \text{ then } P \text{ else } Q \xrightarrow{\mu} Q'} \text{(R-TEST-F)}$$

Fig. 2. Untyped Labelled Transitions $P \xrightarrow{\mu} P'$ (eliding symmetric rules for $P\mid Q$)

released as a channel which carries values of abstract type Y, say. In order to distinguish these processes a test term would need to obtain a value of type Y to send on c. However, there is a testing context which allows the name d to be cast to type Y:

$$R = a(X,Y;z:\updownarrow[X],z':\updownarrow[Y],z'':\updownarrow[Y],x:X).(\overline{z}\langle x\rangle \mid z'(y:Y).\overline{z''}\langle y\rangle)$$

It is easy to check that this process is well-typed with respect to Γ. Here, when R communicates with L and L', the vector of fresh names is received along a and the variables z and z' are aliased so that a further internal communication within R sends d as if it were of type X but receives it as if it were of type Y. It can then be sent along c to interact with the remainder of L and L' to distinguish them.

2.2 Dynamic Semantics

The untyped transition semantics for the asynchronous polymorphic π-calculus is given in Figure 2, and is the same as Pierce and Sangiorgi's. We define the free names of a label $\mathsf{fn}(\mu)$ as $\mathsf{fn}(\tau) = \emptyset$, $\mathsf{fn}(c(\vec{U};\vec{b})) = \{c,\vec{b}\}$ and $\mathsf{fn}(v(\vec{a}:\vec{T})\overline{c}\langle\vec{U};\vec{b}\rangle) = \{c,\vec{b}\}\setminus\{\vec{a}\}$. We also define the bound names of a label $\mathsf{bn}(\mu)$ as $\mathsf{bn}(\tau) = \mathsf{bn}(c(\vec{U};\vec{b})) = \emptyset$ and $\mathsf{bn}(v(\vec{a}:\vec{T})\overline{c}\langle\vec{U};\vec{b}\rangle) = \{\vec{a}\}$. The untyped semantics is useful for defining the run-time behaviour of processes, but is not immediately appropriate for defining a notion of equivalence, as it distinguishes terms such as B_1 and B_2 which cannot be distinguished by any

$$X, Y, Z \qquad \text{(Type Variables)}$$

$$T, U, V, W ::= X \mid \updownarrow[\vec{X}; \vec{T}] \quad \text{(Types: } X \text{ is non-generative, } \updownarrow[\vec{X}; \vec{T}] \text{ is generative)}$$

$$\Gamma, \Delta ::= \vec{X}; \vec{n} : \vec{T} \qquad \text{(Typing Contexts)}$$

$$\frac{X \in \Gamma}{\Gamma \vdash X} \text{ (T-TVAR)} \qquad \frac{\vec{X}, \Gamma \vdash \vec{T} \quad \{\vec{X}\} \cap \text{dom}(\Gamma) = \emptyset \quad \vec{X} \text{ disjoint}}{\Gamma \vdash \updownarrow[\vec{X}; \vec{T}]} \text{ (T-CHAN)}$$

$$\frac{\vec{X} \vdash \vec{T}}{\vec{X}; \vec{n} : \vec{T} \vdash \diamond} \text{ (T-ENV)} \qquad \frac{\Gamma \vdash \diamond \quad (n : T) \in \Gamma}{\Gamma \vdash n : T} \text{ (T-VAL)}$$

$$\frac{\Gamma \vdash n : \updownarrow[\vec{X}; \vec{T}] \quad \vec{X}, \Gamma, \vec{x} : \vec{T} \vdash P \quad \{\vec{X}, \vec{x}\} \cap \text{dom}(\Gamma) = \emptyset \quad \vec{x} \text{ disjoint}}{\Gamma \vdash n(\vec{X}; \vec{x} : \vec{T}) . P} \text{ (T-IN)}$$

$$\frac{\Gamma \vdash n : \updownarrow[\vec{X}; \vec{U}] \quad \Gamma \vdash \vec{n} : \vec{U}[\vec{T}/\vec{X}]}{\Gamma \vdash \overline{n}\langle \vec{T}; \vec{n} \rangle} \text{ (T-OUT)}$$

$$\frac{\Gamma \vdash \diamond}{\Gamma \vdash \mathbf{0}} \text{ (T-NIL)} \qquad \frac{\Gamma \vdash P \quad \Gamma \vdash Q}{\Gamma \vdash P \mid Q} \text{ (T-PAR)}$$

$$\frac{\Gamma, a : T \vdash P \quad a \notin \text{dom}(\Gamma) \quad \text{ftv}(T) \subseteq \text{dom}(\Gamma) \quad T \text{ is generative}}{\Gamma \vdash \nu(a : T)P} \text{ (T-NEW)}$$

$$\frac{\Gamma \vdash P}{\Gamma \vdash !P} \text{ (T-REPL)} \qquad \frac{\Gamma \vdash n : T \quad \Gamma \vdash m : U \quad \Gamma \vdash P \quad \Gamma \vdash Q}{\Gamma \vdash \text{if } n = m \text{ then } P \text{ else } Q} \text{ (T-TEST-W)}$$

Fig. 3. Type System, with judgements $\Gamma \vdash T$, $\Gamma \vdash \diamond$, $\Gamma \vdash n : T$ and $\Gamma \vdash P$

well-typed environment:

$$B_1 \xrightarrow{\nu(t:Bool, f:Bool, test:Test(Bool))\overline{getBools}\langle Bool; t, f, test \rangle} \xrightarrow{t(a,b)} \xrightarrow{\overline{a}\langle\rangle}$$

$$B_2 \xrightarrow{\nu(t:Bool, f:Bool, test:Test(Bool))\overline{getBools}\langle Bool; t, f, test \rangle} \xrightarrow{t(a,b)} \xrightarrow{\overline{b}\langle\rangle}$$

These behaviours correspond to the untyped test T, but do not correspond to any well-typed test, which only has access to the abstract type X and not to the concrete type *Bool*. As a result, no well-typed test can cause the action $\xrightarrow{t(a,b)}$ to be performed. We will come back to this point in Section 3.2.

2.3 Static Semantics

The static semantics for the asynchronous polymorphic π-calculus is given in Figure 3 where the domain of a typing context $\text{dom}(\Gamma)$ is $\text{dom}(\vec{X}; \vec{n} : \vec{T}) = \{\vec{X}, \vec{n}\}$, the free names of a typing context $\text{fn}(\Gamma)$ are $\text{fn}(\vec{X}; \vec{n} : \vec{T}) = \text{fn}(\vec{n})$, the free variables of a typing context $\text{fv}(\Gamma)$ are $\text{fv}(\vec{X}; \vec{n} : \vec{T}) = \text{fv}(\vec{n})$, and the free type variables of a typing context ftv(Γ) are ftv($\vec{X}; \vec{n} : \vec{T}$) = $\{\vec{X}\} \cup$ ftv($\vec{T}$). We say that a typing context Δ is closed if fv(Δ) = ftv(Δ) = $\emptyset$ and moreover for any $a : T \in \Delta$ and $a : U \in \Delta$ then $T = U$. We write $\Gamma[\sigma]$ as the typing context given by $(\vec{X}; \vec{n} : \vec{T})[\vec{W}/\vec{Y}; \vec{m}/\vec{y}] = (\vec{X} \setminus \vec{Y}; \vec{n}[\vec{m}/\vec{y}] : \vec{T}[\vec{W}/\vec{Y}])$.

This is quite a simple type system, as it does not include subtyping, bounded polymorphism, or recursive types, although we expect that such features could be added with little extra complexity.

In Section 4, we will discuss the relationship between this type system and that of Pierce and Sangiorgi. For the moment, we will just highlight one crucial non-standard point about our typing judgement: we are allowing identifiers to have more than one type in a typing context. For example:

$$X, Y; a : \updownarrow[\updownarrow[X], \updownarrow[Y]], b : \updownarrow[X], b : \updownarrow[Y] \vdash \overline{a}\langle b, b \rangle$$

To motivate the use of these mulitcontexts consider the processes

$$P \stackrel{\text{def}}{=} c(X, Y; x : \updownarrow[\updownarrow[X], \updownarrow[Y]]) . x(y : \updownarrow[X], z : \updownarrow[Y]) . \overline{x}\langle y, z \rangle$$
$$Q \stackrel{\text{def}}{=} \mathsf{v}(a : \updownarrow[\updownarrow[\text{int}], \updownarrow[\text{int}]])\mathsf{v}(b : \updownarrow[\text{int}])\overline{c}\langle \text{int}, \text{int}; a \rangle \mid \overline{a}\langle b, b \rangle$$

which can interact as follows:

$$P \mid Q \stackrel{\tau}{\longrightarrow} \mathsf{v}(a : \updownarrow[\updownarrow[\text{int}], \updownarrow[\text{int}]])(a(y : \updownarrow[\text{int}], z : \updownarrow[\text{int}]) . \overline{a}\langle y, z \rangle \mid \mathsf{v}(b : \updownarrow[\text{int}])(\overline{a}\langle b, b \rangle))$$
$$\stackrel{\tau}{\longrightarrow} \mathsf{v}(a : \updownarrow[\updownarrow[\text{int}], \updownarrow[\text{int}]])\mathsf{v}(b : \updownarrow[\text{int}])\overline{a}\langle b, b \rangle$$

This interaction comes about due to the following labelled transitions from P (with appropriate matching transitions from Q):

$$P \xrightarrow{c(\text{int}, \text{int}; a)} a(y : \updownarrow[\text{int}], z : \updownarrow[\text{int}]) . \overline{a}\langle y, z \rangle$$
$$\xrightarrow{a(b, b)} \overline{a}\langle b, b \rangle$$

Now, P typechecks as:

$$c : \updownarrow[X, Y; \updownarrow[\updownarrow[X], \updownarrow[Y]]] \vdash P$$

and we would like to find an appropriate typing for $\overline{a}\langle b, b \rangle$. The obvious typing would be to use Q's choice of concrete implementation of X and Y as int however in order to reason about P independently of Q we must choose a typing which preserves type abstraction and is independent of any choice provided by Q. To do this we use a typing which more closely resembles P's view of the interaction:

$$X, Y; c : \updownarrow[X, Y; \updownarrow[\updownarrow[X], \updownarrow[Y]]], a : \updownarrow[\updownarrow[X], \updownarrow[Y]], b : \updownarrow[X], b : \updownarrow[Y] \vdash \overline{a}\langle b, b \rangle$$

which makes a use of two different types for b in the type environment.

Pierce and Sangiorgi do not allow multiple typings for the same identifier: instead, they use *type unification* for the same purpose. In their model, the types X and Y above would be unified, and so b would just have one type $b : \updownarrow[X]$. This produces a model which is sound, but not complete, as we discuss in Section 4.

An alternative strategy to either multiple typings for variables or type unification would be subtyping with intersection types [6, 28], which ensure that meets exist in the subtype relation. Subtyping with meets are used, for example, by Hennessy and Riely [12] to ensure subject reduction. Intersection types would provide this language with pleasant properties such as principal typing, which it currently lacks, but at the cost of complexity.

3   Equivalences for Asynchronous Polymorphic Pi-Calculus

Process equivalence has a long history, including Milner's [19] bisimulation, Brookes, Hoare and Roscoe's [4] failures-divergences equivalence, and Hennessy's [11] testing equivalence. In this paper, we will follow Pierce and Sangiorgi [23] and investigate *contextual equivalence* on processes [13, 22].

Contextual equivalence has a very natural definition: it is the most generous equivalence satisfying three natural properties: *reduction closure* (that is, respecting the operational semantics), *contextuality* (that is, respecting the syntax of the language), and *barb preservation* (that is, respecting output on visible channels).

Unfortunately, although contextual equivalence has a very natural definition, it is difficult to reason about directly, due to the requirement of contextuality. Since contextuality requires processes to be equivalent in all contexts, to show contextual equivalence of P and Q, we have to show contextual equivalence of $C[P]$ and $C[Q]$ for any appropriately typed context C: moreover, attempts to show this by induction on C break down due to reduction closure.

The problem of showing processes to be contextually equivalent is not restricted to polymorphic π-calculi, for example this problem comes up in treatments of the λ-calculus [2], monomorphic π-calculus [20] and object languages [1]. The standard solution is to ask for a *fully abstract* model, which coincides with contextual equivalence, but is hopefully more tractable.

The problem of finding fully abstract models of programming languages originates with Milner [18], and was investigated in depth by Plotkin [25] for the functional language PCF. For polymorphic languages, logical relations [27] allow for the construction of fully abstract models [24] but require an induction on type, and so break down in the presence of recursive types. Sumii and Pierce have recently shown that a hybrid of context bisimulation and logical relations [30] yields a fully abstract model in the presence of recursive types.

The monomorphic first order [20] and higher-order [29] π-calculus have quite simple fully abstract models, but to date the only known models for polymorphic π-calculus have been sound but not complete [23, 3]. We will now show that a very direct treatment of type-respecting labelled transitions generates a fully abstract bisimulation equivalence which makes no use of logical relations or type unification.

3.1   Contextual Equivalence

Process contexts are typed as follows: $\Delta \vdash C[\Gamma]$ whenever $\forall(\Gamma \vdash P) . (\Delta \vdash C[P])$. A typed relation on closed processes $\mathcal{R}$ is a set of triples (Γ, P, Q) such that $\Gamma \vdash P$ and $\Gamma \vdash Q$ such that Γ is closed. We will typically write $\Gamma \vDash P \,\mathcal{R}\, Q$ whenever $(\Gamma, P, Q) \in \mathcal{R}$. Given any typed relation on closed processes $\mathcal{R}$, we can define its open extension $\mathcal{R}^\circ$ to be the typed relation on processes given by $\Gamma \vDash P \,\mathcal{R}^\circ\, Q$ whenever $\Gamma[\sigma], \Delta \vDash P[\sigma] \,\mathcal{R}\, Q[\sigma]$ for any closed typing environment of the form $(\Gamma[\sigma], \Delta)$.

Definition 4 (Reduction closure). *A typed relation $\mathcal{R}$ on closed processes is reduction-closed whenever $\Delta \vDash P \,\mathcal{R}\, Q$ and $P \overset{\tau}{\longrightarrow} P'$ implies there exists some Q' such that $Q \Longrightarrow Q'$ and $\Delta \vDash P' \,\mathcal{R}\, Q'$.*

$$\alpha ::= \tau \mid v(\vec{a} : \vec{T})c[\vec{U};\vec{b}] \mid v(\vec{a})\overline{c}\langle\vec{X};\vec{b} : \vec{V}\rangle \quad \text{(Typed Labels)}$$
$$C ::= (\Gamma \vdash [\sigma]P) \qquad\qquad\qquad \text{(Configurations)}$$

$$\frac{P \xrightarrow{\tau} P'}{(\Gamma \vdash [\sigma]P) \xrightarrow{\tau} (\Gamma \vdash [\sigma]P')} \quad \text{(TR-SILENT)}$$

$$\frac{\Gamma,\vec{a} : \vec{T} \vdash \overline{c}\langle\vec{U};\vec{b}\rangle \quad \{\vec{a}\} \cap \text{dom}(\Gamma) = \emptyset \quad \vec{T} \text{ are generative}}{(\Gamma \vdash [\sigma]P) \xrightarrow{v(\vec{a}:\vec{T})c[\vec{U};\vec{b}]} (\Gamma,\vec{a} : \vec{T} \vdash [\sigma]P \mid (\overline{c}\langle\vec{U};\vec{b}\rangle[\sigma]))} \quad \text{(TR-RECEP)}$$

$$\frac{P \xrightarrow{v(\vec{a}:\vec{T})\overline{c}\langle\vec{U};\vec{b}\rangle} P' \quad \Gamma \vdash c(\vec{X};\vec{x} : \vec{V}).\mathbf{0} \quad \{\vec{a},\vec{X}\} \cap \text{dom}(\Gamma) = \emptyset}{(\Gamma \vdash [\sigma]P) \xrightarrow{v(\vec{a})\overline{c}\langle\vec{X};\vec{b}:\vec{V}\rangle} (\vec{X},\Gamma,\vec{b} : \vec{V} \vdash [\vec{U}/\vec{X},\sigma]P')} \quad \text{(TR-OUT-W)}$$

Fig. 4. Typed Labelled Transitions $C \xrightarrow{\alpha} C'$

Definition 5 (Contextuality). *A typed relation $\mathcal{R}$ on closed processes is contextual whenever $\Gamma \vDash P \mathcal{R}^{\circ} Q$ and $\Delta \vdash C[\Gamma]$ implies $\Delta \vDash C[P] \mathcal{R}^{\circ} C[Q]$.*

Definition 6 (Barb preservation). *A typed relation $\mathcal{R}$ on closed processes is barb-preserving whenever $\Delta \vDash P \mathcal{R} Q$ and $P \xrightarrow{\overline{a}\langle\rangle}$ implies $Q \xRightarrow{\overline{a}\langle\rangle}$.*

We can now define contextual equivalence $\cong$ as the open extension of the largest symmetric typed relation on closed processes which is reduction-closed, contextual and barb-preserving. The requirement of contextuality makes it very difficult to prove properties about contextual equivalence, and so we investigate bisimulation as a more tractable proof technique for establishing contextual equivalence.

3.2   Bisimulation

As a first attempt to find a more tractable presentation of contextual equivalence, we could use *bisimulation*. Unfortunately, as we discussed in Section 2.2, our untyped labelled transition system does not respect the type system, and so gives rise to too fine an equivalence. We therefore investigate a restricted labelled transition system which respects types: this is defined in Figure 4. The transition system is given by a relation:

$$(\Gamma \vdash [\sigma]P) \xrightarrow{\alpha} (\Gamma' \vdash [\sigma']P')$$

between configurations of the form $(\Gamma \vdash [\sigma]P)$. These comprise three constituent parts:

- P is the process being observed: after the transition, it becomes process P'.
- Γ is the *external* view of the typing context P operates in. This external view may not have complete information about the types, for example P may have exported the concrete type int as an abstract type X. Only X will be recorded in the typing context. As P exports more type information, Γ may grow to become Γ'. It is here that we make use of the multiple entries in type environments.

– σ is a type substitution, mapping the external view to the internal view. This mapping provides complete information about the types exported by P, for example int/X records that external type X is internal type int. Note that this substitution is **not** applied to P, we represent that with the alternative notation $P[\sigma]$.

There are three kinds of transitions:

– *Silent transitions* $(\Gamma \vdash [\sigma]P) \xrightarrow{\tau} (\Gamma \vdash [\sigma]P')$ which are inherited from the untyped transition system.

– *Receptivity transitions* $(\Gamma \vdash [\sigma]P) \xrightarrow{v(\vec{a}:\vec{T})c[\vec{U};\vec{b}]} (\Gamma, \vec{a}:\vec{T} \vdash [\sigma]P \,|\, (\overline{c}\langle \vec{U};\vec{b}\rangle[\sigma]))$ which allow the environment to send data to the process. We require the message to type-check, and we allow the environment to generate new names, which are recorded in the type environment. We are modelling an asynchronous language, and so processes are always input-enabled. Note that the process is sending no information to the environment, so the type substitution σ does not grow. Note also that the message is typed using the external view Γ but must have the type mapping σ applied to it for it to be mapped to the internal type consistent with P.

– *Output transitions* $(\Gamma \vdash [\sigma]P) \xrightarrow{v(\vec{a})\overline{c}\langle \vec{X},\vec{b}:\vec{V}\rangle} (\vec{X},\Gamma,\vec{b}:\vec{V} \vdash [\vec{U}/\vec{X},\sigma]P')$ which allow the process to send data to the environment. The channel being used to communicate with the environment must be typed $\updownarrow[\vec{X};\vec{V}]$, so the typing context is extended with abstract types $\vec{X}$ and the new type information $\vec{b}:\vec{V}$. This may result in more than one type being given to the same name, which is why we allow duplicate entries in typing contexts. The process P must have provided concrete implementations $\vec{U}$ of the abstract types $\vec{X}$: these are recorded in the type substitution.

To demonstrate how our typed labelled transitions can be used we return to the example above of processes L and L' and type environment Γ. We show a sequence of typed transitions from $(\Gamma \vdash []L)$ which cannot be matched by $(\Gamma \vdash []L')$:

$$(\Gamma \vdash []L) \xrightarrow{v(b,c,d)\overline{a}\langle X,Y,b:\updownarrow[X],b:\updownarrow[Y],c:\updownarrow[Y],d:Y\rangle} (\Gamma' \vdash [\sigma]c(y:\updownarrow[T]).\overline{\text{fail}}\langle\rangle)$$

where σ is $[T,T/X,Y]$ and Γ' is $X,Y,\Gamma,b:\updownarrow[X],b:\updownarrow[Y],c:\updownarrow[Y],d:X$. At this point we would like to use Rule TR-RECEP to provide a message on channel c to facilitate a communication, however, there is no name of the appropriate type listed in Γ' and the restriction to generative types for the fresh names means that this cannot yet be done. However, note the following transitions:

$$(\Gamma' \vdash [\sigma]c(y:\updownarrow[T]).\overline{\text{fail}}\langle\rangle) \xrightarrow{b[d]} (\Gamma' \vdash [\sigma]c(y:\updownarrow[T]).\overline{\text{fail}}\langle\rangle \,|\, \overline{b}\langle d\rangle)$$
$$\xrightarrow{\overline{b}\langle d\rangle} (\Gamma',d:Y \vdash [\sigma]c(y:\updownarrow[T]).\overline{\text{fail}}\langle\rangle)$$
$$\xrightarrow{c[d]} (\Gamma',d:Y \vdash [\sigma]c(y:\updownarrow[T]).\overline{\text{fail}}\langle\rangle \,|\, \overline{c}\langle d\rangle)$$
$$\xRightarrow{\overline{\text{fail}}\langle\rangle}$$

in which the second type listed for b in Γ' is used to justify the $\overline{b}\langle d\rangle$ transition. These transitions serve to mimic the typecasting and subsequent use of the extruded name d by a testing context which are crucial to distinguishing L and L'.

We now formalise our notion of bisimulation equivalence. A typed relation on closed configurations $\mathcal{R}$ is a set of 5-tuples $(\Gamma, \sigma, P, \rho, Q)$ such that $\Gamma[\sigma] \vdash P$ and $\Gamma[\rho] \vdash Q$ and both $\Gamma[\sigma]$ and $\Gamma[\rho]$ are closed. For convenience we will write $\Gamma \vDash [\sigma]P \mathrel{\mathcal{R}} [\rho]Q$ whenever $(\Gamma, \sigma, P, \rho, Q) \in \mathcal{R}$.

Definition 7 (Bisimulation). *A simulation $\mathcal{R}$ is a typed relation on closed configurations such that if $\Gamma \vDash [\sigma]P \mathrel{\mathcal{R}} [\rho]Q$ and $(\Gamma \vdash [\sigma]P) \overset{\alpha}{\longrightarrow} (\Gamma' \vdash [\sigma']P')$ then we can show $(\Gamma \vdash [\rho]Q) \overset{\widehat{\alpha}}{\Longrightarrow} (\Gamma' \vdash [\rho']Q')$ for some $\Gamma' \vDash [\sigma']P' \mathrel{\mathcal{R}} [\rho']Q'$. A bisimulation is a simulation whose inverse is also a simulation. Let $\approx$ be the largest bisimulation.*

We are now in position to show full abstraction of bisimulation for contextual equivalence, and so provide a tractable model of polymorphic π-calculus.

3.3   Soundness of Bisimulation for Contextual Equivalence

The difficult property to show is that bisimulation is a congruence: from this it is routine to establish that bisimulation implies contextual equivalence. Showing congruence for bisimulation is a well-established problem for process languages, going back to Milner [19]. In the case of polymorphic π, the problem is in showing that bisimulation is preserved by parallel composition. We do this by constructing a candidate bisimulation:

$$\Gamma \vDash [\sigma]P \mid R[\sigma] \mathrel{\mathcal{R}} [\rho]Q \mid R[\rho] \text{ whenever } \Gamma \vDash [\sigma]P \approx [\rho]Q$$
$$\text{and } \Gamma \vdash R$$
$$\text{and } \sigma \text{ and } \rho \text{ are type substitutions}$$

and then showing that this is a bisimulation (up to some technicalities which we shall elide for the moment). This has a routine proof, except for one case, which is when $R[\sigma] \longrightarrow R'[\sigma]$. It is straightforward to establish that type substitutions do not influence reduction, and so we have $R[\rho] \longrightarrow R'[\rho]$, and all that remains is to show that $\Gamma \vDash [\sigma]P \mid R'[\sigma] \mathrel{\mathcal{R}} [\rho]Q \mid R'[\rho]$. Unfortunately, this is not directly possible, due to the requirement that $\Gamma \vdash R'$. If we had a subject reduction result for open processes, then this would be routine, but this result is not true due to channels with multiple types:

$$\overline{a}\langle c \rangle \mid a(x : Y).\overline{b}\langle x \rangle \longrightarrow \mathbf{0} \mid \overline{b}\langle c \rangle$$
$$X, Y; a : \updownarrow[X], a : \updownarrow[Y], b : \updownarrow[Y], c : X \vdash \overline{a}\langle c \rangle \mid a(x : Y).\overline{b}\langle x \rangle$$
$$X, Y; a : \updownarrow[X], a : \updownarrow[Y], b : \updownarrow[Y], c : X \nvdash \mathbf{0} \mid \overline{b}\langle c \rangle$$

Pierce and Sangiorgi's technique for dealing with this problem is to introduce type unification to ensure that every channel has a unique type. Unfortunately, as we will discuss in Section 4, the resulting semantics is incomplete. Instead of using such unifications, we observe that in any case where subject reduction fails, it does so because of communication on a visible channel: if the channel was hidden by a ν-binder, then it would have only one type, and so subject reduction holds. We therefore observe that in the cases where subject reduction fails to hold, there must be a pair of matching visible reductions which caused the communication.

Proposition 1 (Open subject reduction). *If* $\Gamma \vdash P$ *and* $P \xrightarrow{\tau} P''$ *then either:*

1. $\Gamma \vdash P''$, *or*
2. $P \xrightarrow{\nu(\vec{a}:\vec{T})\bar{c}\langle\vec{U};\vec{b}\rangle} \xrightarrow{c(\vec{X};\vec{b})} P'$ *where* $P'' \equiv (\nu(\vec{a}:\vec{T})P')[\vec{U}/\vec{X}]$.

In the example (up to structural equivalence):

$$\bar{a}\langle c\rangle \mid a(x:Y).\bar{b}\langle x\rangle \xrightarrow{\bar{a}\langle c\rangle} \mathbf{0} \mid a(x:Y).\bar{b}\langle x\rangle$$
$$\xrightarrow{a(c)} \mathbf{0} \mid \bar{b}\langle c\rangle$$
$$X,Y;a:\updownarrow[X],a:\updownarrow[Y],b:\updownarrow[Y],c:X \quad \vdash \quad \bar{a}\langle c\rangle \mid a(x:Y).\bar{b}\langle x\rangle$$
$$X,Y;a:\updownarrow[X],a:\updownarrow[Y],b:\updownarrow[Y],c:X,c:Y \quad \vdash \quad \mathbf{0} \mid a(x:Y).\bar{b}\langle x\rangle$$
$$X,Y;a:\updownarrow[X],a:\updownarrow[Y],b:\updownarrow[Y],c:X,c:Y \quad \vdash \quad \mathbf{0} \mid \bar{b}\langle c\rangle$$

The crucial point is that these extra transitions by the testing context correspond to complementary typed transitions by the process such that, after the visible $\bar{a}\langle c\rangle$ output action, the typing context Γ is extended with $c:Y$. The problematic residual of the test term R' ($\mathbf{0} \mid \bar{b}\langle c\rangle$ in the example) can now be typed in this extended Γ and the bisimulation argument can be completed.

Theorem 1 (Bisimulation is a congruence). *If* $\Gamma \vDash P \approx Q$ *then* $\Delta \vDash C[P] \approx C[Q]$ *for any* $\Delta \vdash C[\Gamma]$.

Theorem 2 (Soundness of bisimulation for contextual equivalence). *If* $\Gamma \vDash P \approx Q$ *then* $\Gamma \vDash P \cong Q$.

3.4   Completeness of Bisimulation for Contextual Equivalence

The proof of soundness for bisimulation required some non-standard techniques. In comparison, the proof of completeness is quite straightforward, and follows the usual *definability* argument [11, 9, 15] of showing that for every visible action α, we can find a process R which exactly tests for the ability to perform α. Once we have established definability, completeness follows in a straightforward fashion.

Theorem 3 (Completeness of bisimulation for contextual equivalence). *If* $\Gamma \vDash P \cong Q$ *then* $\Gamma \vDash P \approx Q$.

4   Comparison with Pierce and Sangiorgi

In this paper, we have shown that weak bisimulation is fully abstract for observational equivalence for an asynchronous polymorphic π-calculus. This is almost enough to settle the open problem set by Pierce and Sangiorgi [23] of finding a fully abstract semantics for their polymorphic π-calculus. There are, however, some differences between their setting and ours, most of which we believe to be routine, with one important exception: the type rule for if-then-else.

4.1   Minor Differences

The minor differences between our polymorphic π-calculus and theirs are:

1. We are considering weak bisimulation rather than strong bisimulation.
2. Since we are considering weak bisimulation, we have not included $P + Q$ in our language of processes. We expect that this could be handled in the usual fashion, by defining observational equivalence on processes in the style of Milner [19].
3. We have treated an asynchronous rather than a synchronous language, since the soundness result follows more naturally for the resulting asynchronous transition system. We expect that a fully abstract bisimulation for a synchronous language can be given by adding transitions for synchronous input as well as receptivity:

$$\frac{P \xrightarrow{c(\vec{U};\vec{b})} P' \quad \Gamma,\vec{a}:\vec{T} \vdash \bar{c}\langle\vec{U};\vec{b}\rangle}{\{\vec{a}\} \cap \mathrm{dom}(\Gamma) = \emptyset \quad \vec{T} \text{ are generative}}{(\Gamma \vdash [\sigma]P) \xrightarrow{v(\vec{a}:\vec{T})c(\vec{U};\vec{b})} (\Gamma,\vec{a}:\vec{T} \vdash [\sigma]P')} \text{ (TR-IN)}$$

Note that the label used here for synchronous input is distinct from the label used for receptivity.
4. We have used a variable-name distinction, and so have used Honda and Yoshida's definition of observational equivalence [13]. See [8] for a discussion of this issue.
5. Our type system keeps track explicitly of free type variables, rather than treating them implicitly: this makes some of the book-keeping easier, at the cost of some additional syntactic overhead.

We do not believe that these differences are substantial.

4.2   Major Difference: Typing If-Then-Else

However, there is one important difference between our language and Pierce and Sangiorgi's, even though it may appear at first sight to be a minor point: the type rule for if-then-else. In their paper, a strong type rule is given:

$$\frac{\Gamma \vdash n:T \quad \Gamma \vdash m:T \quad \Gamma \vdash P \quad \Gamma \vdash Q}{\Gamma \vdash \text{if } n = m \text{ then } P \text{ else } Q} \text{ (T-TEST-S)}$$

In our work, the weaker type rule T-TEST-W is used, which allows n and m to have different types. Note that in a language with subtyping and a top type, these rules are equivalent, since we can always choose T to be the top type, and use subsumption to derive T-TEST-W from T-TEST-S. In the absence of subtyping, however, the rule T-TEST-W allows more processes to typecheck, so raises the expressive power of tests, and hence makes observational equivalence finer. For example:

$$P \overset{\mathrm{def}}{=} v(b : \updownarrow[\mathrm{int}])v(c : \updownarrow[\mathrm{string}])\bar{a}\langle\mathrm{int}, \mathrm{string}; b, c\rangle$$
$$Q \overset{\mathrm{def}}{=} v(b : \updownarrow[\mathrm{int}])\bar{a}\langle\mathrm{int}, \mathrm{int}; b, b\rangle$$

As long as $a : \updownarrow[X, Y; \updownarrow[X], \updownarrow[Y]]$ these processes cannot be distinguished by any test which uses the type rule T-TEST-S, but they can be distinguished by:

$$R \stackrel{\text{def}}{=} a(X, Y; x : \updownarrow[X], y : \updownarrow[Y]) \,.\, \text{if } x = y \text{ then } \overline{d}\langle\rangle$$

which typechecks using type rule T-TEST-W. In fact, there is a third possible type rule for if-then-else, which makes use of type unification:

$$\frac{\Gamma \vdash n : T \quad \Gamma \vdash m : U}{\Gamma \vdash \text{if } n = m \text{ then } P \text{ else } Q} \text{ (T-TEST-U)}$$

where $\text{mgu}(T, U)$ builds the most general type substitution σ such that $T[\sigma] = U[\sigma]$. This type rule is strictly weaker than T-TEST-W, and raises the expressive power of tests even further, and hence makes observational equivalence even finer. For example:

$$P \stackrel{\text{def}}{=} \nu(c : \updownarrow[\text{int}, \text{string}]) \nu(d : \updownarrow[\text{int}]) \overline{a}\langle \text{int}, \text{string}; c, d\rangle \,.\, \overline{b}\langle \text{string}; c\rangle \,.\, d(x : \text{int}) \,.\, \overline{e}\langle x\rangle$$
$$Q \stackrel{\text{def}}{=} \nu(c : \updownarrow[\text{int}, \text{string}]) \nu(d : \updownarrow[\text{int}]) \overline{a}\langle \text{int}, \text{string}; c, d\rangle \,.\, \overline{b}\langle \text{string}; c\rangle$$

As long as $a : \updownarrow[X, Y; \updownarrow[X, Y], \updownarrow[X]], b : \updownarrow[Z; \updownarrow[\text{int}, Z]]$ and $e : \updownarrow[\text{int}]$, these processes cannot be distinguished by any test which uses T-TEST-W, but they can be distinguished by:

$$R \stackrel{\text{def}}{=} a(X, Y; x : \updownarrow[X, Y], y : \updownarrow[X]) \,.\, b(Z; z : \updownarrow[\text{int}, Z]) \,.\, \text{if } x = z \text{ then } \overline{y}\langle 5\rangle$$

which typechecks using type rule T-TEST-U. We have that:

- The type rule T-TEST-W has a matching fully abstract bisimulation equivalence $\approx$, which for purpose of this discussion we shall refer to as $\approx_w$.
- The type rule T-TEST-S has a matching fully abstract bisimulation equivalence $\approx_s$.
- The type rule T-TEST-U has a matching fully abstract bisimulation equivalence $\approx_u$.

Moreover:

- We have inclusions on these equivalences: if $\Gamma \vDash P \approx_w Q$ then $\Gamma \vDash P \approx_s Q$ for any $\Gamma \vdash_s P$ and $\Gamma \vdash_s Q$ (and similarly for $\approx_u$ and $\approx_w$).
- The above examples show that the inclusions are strict: we have $\Gamma \vDash P \not\approx_w Q$ and $\Gamma \vDash P \approx_s Q$ for some $\Gamma \vdash_s P$ and $\Gamma \vdash_s Q$ (and similarly for $\approx_u$ and $\approx_w$).
- The type rule for if-then-else used by Pierce and Sangiorgi is T-TEST-S.
- Pierce and Sangiorgi's bisimulation is the strong, synchronous version of $\approx_u$.

Hence, since synchrony and weak bisimulation play no role in the above examples, we have a resolution of Pierce and Sangiorgi's conjecture:

- Pierce and Sangiorgi's polymorphic bisimulation is sound, but not complete, for their polymorphic π-calculus.

These arguments are formalised in [16].

5   Conclusions

This paper gives the first fully abstract semantics for a polymorphic process language. Moreover the semantics is extremely straightforward: the only nonstandard part of the presentation is that names are given more than one type in a type environment. This corresponds to the ability for a polymorphic program to be sent the same channel at multiple different types. In contrast to polymorphic λ-calculi, polymorphic π-calculi have the ability to compare names for syntactic equality, and so there is an internal test which can detect when the same name has been given multiple different types.

We believe that the techniques given in this paper are quite robust (for example there are no uses of type induction) and could be scaled with little difficulty to larger type systems with features such as subtyping, F-bounded polymorphism, and recursive types. Moreover, object languages such as the ς-calculus support object equality, and so we believe that adapting our previous fully abstract semantics [14] for objects [1] to deal with generic objects would also be possible.

References

1. M. Abadi and L. Cardelli. *A Theory of Objects*. Springer-Verlag, 1996.
2. H. P. Barendregt. *The Lambda Calculus, Its Syntax and Semantics*. North Holland, 1984.
3. M. Berger, K. Honda, and N. Yoshida. Genericity and the pi-calculus. In *Proc. Int. Conf. Foundations of Software Science and Computer Structures (FoSSaCs)*, Lecture Notes in Computer Science. Springer-Verlag, 2003.
4. S. D. Brookes, C. A. R. Hoare, and A. W. Roscoe. A theory of communicating sequential processes. *J. ACM*, 31(3):560–599, 1984.
5. P. Canning, W. Cook, W. Hill, W. Olthoff, and J. C. Mitchell. F-bounded polymorphism for object-oriented programming. In *Proc. Int. Conf. Functional Programming Languages and Computer Architecture (FPCA)*, pages 273–280. ACM Press, 1989.
6. M. Coppo and M. Dezani-Ciancaglini. A new type-assignment for λ-terms. *Archiv Math. Logik*, 19:139–156, 1978.
7. Microsoft Corporation. ECMA and ISO/IEC c# and common language infrastructure standards, 2004. http://msdn.microsoft.com/net/ecma/.
8. C. Fournet and G. Gonthier. A hierarchy of equivalences for asynchronous calculi. In *Proc. Int. Conf. Automata, Languages and Programming (ICALP)*, volume 1443 of *Lecture Notes in Computer Science*. Springer-Verlag, 1998.
9. C. Fournet, G. Gonthier, J-J. Levy, L. Maranget, and D. Remy. A calculus of mobile agents. In *Proc. Int. Conf. Concurrency Theory (CONCUR)*, volume 1119 of *Lecture notes in computer science*. Springer-Verlag, 1996.
10. J-Y. Girard, P. Taylor, and Y. Lafont. *Proofs and Types*. Cambridge University Press, 1989.
11. M. Hennessy. *Algebraic Theory of Processes*. MIT Press, 1988.
12. M. Hennessy and J. Riely. Resource access control in systems of mobile agents. *Information and Computation*, 173(1):82–120, 2002.
13. K. Honda and N. Yoshida. On reduction-based process semantics. *Theoretical Computer Science*, 152(2):437–486, 1995.
14. A. S. A. Jeffrey and J. Rathke. A fully abstract may testing semantics for concurrent objects. In *Proc. IEEE Logic In Computer Science*, pages 101–112. IEEE Press, 2002. Full version to appear in *Theoretical Computer Science*.

15. A. S. A. Jeffrey and J. Rathke. Contextual equivalence for higher-order pi-calculus revisited. In *Proc. Mathematical Foundations of Programming Semantics*, Electronic Notes in Computer Science. Elsevier, 2003.

16. A. S. A. Jeffrey and J. Rathke. Full abstraction for polymorphic pi-calculus. Online edition with proofs, http://www.fabfac.org/, 2005.

17. Sun Microsystems. Release notes Java 2 platform standard edition development kit 5.0, 2004. http://java.sun.com/j2se/1.5.0/relnotes.html.

18. R. Milner. Fully abstract models of typed lambda-calculi. *Theoretical Computer Science*, 4:1–22, 1977.

19. R. Milner. *Communication and Concurrency*. Prentice-Hall, 1989.

20. R. Milner. *Communication and mobile systems: the π-calculus*. Cambridge University Press, 1999.

21. R. Milner, J. Parrow, and D. Walker. A calculus of mobile processes, Part I + II. *Information and Computation*, 100(1):1–77, 1992.

22. R. Milner and D. Sangiorgi. Barbed bisimulation. In *Proc. Int. Conf. Automata, Languages and Programming (ICALP)*, volume 623 of *Lecture Notes in Computer Science*. Springer-Verlag, 1992.

23. B. C. Pierce and D. Sangiorgi. Behavioral equivalence in the polymorphic pi-calculus. *J. ACM*, 47(3):531–584, 2000.

24. A. M. Pitts. Parametric polymorphism and operational equivalence. *Mathematical Structures in Computer Science*, 10:321–359, 2000.

25. G. D. Plotkin. LCF considered as a programming language. *Theoretical Computer Science*, 5:223–255, 1977.

26. J. C. Reynolds. Types, abstraction and parametric polymorphism. *Information Processing*, 83:513–523, 1983.

27. J. C. Reynolds. An introduction to logical relations and parametric polymorphism (abstract). In *Proc. ACM Symp. Principles of Programming Languages*, pages 155–156. ACM Press, 1993.

28. J. C. Reynolds. *Theories of Programming Languages*. Cambridge University Press, 1998.

29. D. Sangiorgi. *Expressing Mobility in Process Algebras: First-Order and Higher-Order Paradigms*. PhD thesis, University of Edinburgh, 1993.

30. E. Sumii and B. C. Pierce. A bisimulation for type abstraction and recursion. In *Proc. ACM Symp. Principles of Programming Languages*, 2005. To appear.

31. P. Wadler. Theorems for free! In *Proc. Int. Conf. Functional Programming Languages and Computer Architecture (FPCA)*, pages 347–359. ACM Press, New York, 1989.

Foundations of Web Transactions

Cosimo Laneve and Gianluigi Zavattaro

Department of Computer Science,
University of Bologna, Italy

Abstract. A timed extension of π-calculus with a transaction construct – the calculus $\mathtt{Web}\pi$ – is studied. The underlying model of $\mathtt{Web}\pi$ relies on networks of processes; time proceeds asynchronously at the network level, while it is constrained by the *local urgency* at the process level. Namely process reductions cannot be delayed to favour idle steps. The extensional model – the *timed bisimilarity* – copes with time and asynchrony in a different way with respect to previous proposals. In particular, the discriminating power of timed bisimilarity is weaker when local urgency is dropped. A labelled characterization of timed bisimilarity is also discussed.

1   Introduction

Web Services technologies intend to provide standard mechanisms for describing the interface and the services available on the web, as well as protocols for locating such services and invoking them (see e.g. WSDL [9] and UDDI [16]). To describe interfaces, services, and protocols new *web programming languages*, the so-called *orchestration* and *choreography* languages, are currently investigated. Examples of these languages are Microsoft XLANG [17] and its visual environment BizTalk, IBM WSFL [13], BPEL [2], WS-CDL [12], and WSCI [12].

Most of the web programming languages also include the notion of *web transaction*, as a unit of work involving activities that may last long periods of time. These transactions, being orthogonal to administrative domains, have the typical atomicity and isolation properties relaxed, and instead of assuming a perfect roll-back in case of failure, support the explicit programming of the compensation activity.

Despite of the great interest for web transactions, the Web Services community has not reached a common agreement on a unique notion of this form of transaction. The paper [14] gives a valuable critical comparison among three transaction protocols: BTP, WS-C/T, and WS-CAF. Other few papers (we are aware of), that discuss the formal semantics of compensable activities in this context, rely on specific proposals: the work [8] is mainly inspired by XLANG, the calculus of Butler and Ferreira [7] is inspired by BPBeans, the πt-calculus [5] considers BizTalk, the work [6] deals with short-lived transactions in BizTalk.

In this paper we follow a rather different and radical approach: we define a calculus of web transactions – the calculus $\mathtt{Web}\pi$ – that is independent of the different proposals discussed above and that allows to grab (we hope) the key

V. Sassone (Ed.): FOSSACS 2005, LNCS 3441, pp. 282–298, 2005.

concepts. Three major aspects are considered in Webπ: interruptible processes, failure handlers that are activated when the main process is interrupted, and time. Time has been considered because it is fundamental for dealing with the typical latency of web activities or with message losses. For instance, in ticketing services of airplane companies, the services should cancel reservations that are not confirmed within a certain period of time. Since Webπ is an extension of π-calculus, and the latter is emerging as one of the referring models for Web Services orchestration and choreography (it has inspired the design of languages such as XLANG and WS-CDL), we trust that the mathematical underpinnings of Webπ are digestible by the web service community.

The underlying model of Webπ includes machines and processes. The formers define networks; the latters define the computational content of locations of the networks. A location is a uniprocessor machine, written $[P]_{\widetilde{x}}$, with its own clock that is not synchronized with the clock of other locations (time progresses asynchronously between different locations). Namely, if M and N are locations, then progress of the compound machine is defined by the rule

$$\frac{\mathsf{M} \to \mathsf{M}'}{\mathsf{M}\,|\,\mathsf{N} \to \mathsf{M}'\,|\,\mathsf{N}} \tag{1}$$

Names $\widetilde{x}$ in $[P]_{\widetilde{x}}$ indicate that the location is responsible for accepting messages on such names (a name always indexes a unique location). We assume that, within a location, operations cannot be delayed in favour of idle operations – this property is called *local urgency*. For example, consider two processes running on the same location: a printer process of a warning message with a timeout and an idle process waiting for an external event. Local urgency means that, if the external event doesn't occur, then the printer process cannot be delayed. Said otherwise, the time may elapse in a location either because the process inside progresses or because no progress is possible. These two alternatives are respectively defined by the rules

$$\frac{P \to Q}{[P]_{\widetilde{x}} \to [Q]_{\widetilde{x}}} \qquad \frac{P \nrightarrow}{[P]_{\widetilde{x}} \to [\phi(P)]_{\widetilde{x}}}$$

where ϕ is a function making the time elapse of one unit. In particular, the rightmost rule permits the elapsing of one time unit only in the case when no computational step is possible inside a machine.

Processes extend the asynchronous π-calculus with *transactions* $(P \; ; \; Q)_x^n$, where P and Q are the *body* and the *compensation*, respectively, n indicates the deadline, and x is the name of the transaction. The body of a transaction executes either until termination or until the transaction fails. On failure, the compensation is activated. A transaction may fail in two different ways, either explicitly (when the abort message $\overline{x}$ is consumed, where x is the name of the transaction to be aborted) or implicitly (when the deadline is reached). The deadline may be reached either because of computational steps of the body or because of computational steps of processes in parallel. Assuming that every step costs one time slot, these two alternatives are defined by the rules

$$\frac{P \to P'}{\langle\!\langle P \,;\, Q \rangle\!\rangle_x^{n+1} \to \langle\!\langle P' \,;\, Q \rangle\!\rangle_x^n} \qquad \frac{P \to P'}{P \,|\, Q \to P' \,|\, \phi(Q)}$$

Comparing the last rule and rule (1), we obtain a model for Webπ that is locally synchronous and globally asynchronous.

Regarding time, we have been influenced by the work of Berger and Honda about π-calculus with timers [4, 3]. A timer process $\mathtt{timer}^n(P, Q)$ behaves like P, but triggers Q if P does not move within n time units. Transactions have a rather different behaviour: in $\langle\!\langle P \,;\, Q \rangle\!\rangle_x^n$ the process Q may be activated provided the execution of P is not terminated. Transactions have two interruption mechanisms: one associated to timeouts (as for the timers); the other is explicit – the abort message. Additionally, the model of time in [4, 3] is different from the one considered here. Berger and Honda have a rule

$$P \to \phi(P)$$

that allows the time elapse even if P may progress. In Webπ this rule is restricted to locations $[\,P\,]_{\widetilde{x}}$, where it is reasonable to verify $P \nrightarrow$ since P collect all the entities competing for the location processor.

The calculus Webπ is initially equipped with a reduction semantics, consisting of a reduction relation and a barbed bisimulation. The reduction relation defines reductions that take one unit of time. The barbed bisimulation, called *timed bisimilarity*, is sensible to the number of internal moves (it is a strong equivalence). Timed bisimilarity is also sensible to local urgency: its discriminating power of timed bisimilarity is weaker when local urgency is dropped.

In order to support direct proofs of equality, Webπ is also equipped with a labelled semantics. In particular, we define a labelled transition system and consider the standard notion of asynchronous bisimulation [1] that admits inputs to be also mimicked by internal moves. It turns out that asynchronous bisimulation is not a congruence because it is not substitution and time closed (this is the same as in [3]) and it is not closed by a property checking whether a process manifests an input that is not underneath a transaction. When asynchronous bisimulation is appropriately closed, the resulting equivalence, called *labelled time bisimilarity*, is equal to time bisimilarity when the discriminating power of contexts is augmented with the match operator.

The paper is structured as follows. For the sake of presentation, we separate processes and machines. The syntax and the reduction relation of Webπ processes and machines are respectively defined in Sections 2 and 5. Section 3 introduces timed bisimilarity and demonstrates that the discriminating power of timed bisimilarity is weaker when local urgency is dropped. Section 4 defines the labelled semantics, the corresponding congruence relation, and its relationship with timed bisimilarity. Section 6 draws some conclusive remarks.

2   The Calculus Webπ

The syntax relies on countable sets of *names*, ranged over by $x, y, z, u, \cdots$. Tuples of names are written $\widetilde{u}$. Natural numbers $\{0, 1, 2, 3, \cdots\}$ or ∞ are ranged over by $n, m, \cdots$. The syntax of Webπ defines *processes* P.

$$P ::= \quad \mathbf{0} \quad | \quad \overline{x}\,\widetilde{u} \quad | \quad x(\widetilde{u}).P \quad | \quad (x)P \quad | \quad P\,|\,P \quad | \quad !x(\widetilde{u}).P \quad | \quad \langle\!| P \,;\, P |\!\rangle_x^n$$

A process can be the inert process $\mathbf{0}$, a message $\overline{x}\,\widetilde{u}$ sent on a name x that carries a tuple of names $\widetilde{u}$, an input $x(\widetilde{u}).P$ that consumes a message $\overline{x}\,\widetilde{w}$ and behaves like $P\{\widetilde{w}/\widetilde{u}\}$, a restriction $(x)P$ that behaves as P except that inputs and messages on x are prohibited, a parallel composition of processes, a replicated input $!x(\widetilde{u}).P$ that consumes a message $\overline{x}\,\widetilde{w}$ and behaves like $P\{\widetilde{w}/\widetilde{u}\}\,|\,!x(\widetilde{u}).P$, or a (web) transaction $\langle\!| P \,;\, Q |\!\rangle_x^n$ that behaves as the *body* P except that, if the body does not terminate, the *compensation* Q is triggered after n steps or because of a transaction abort message $\overline{x}$. The label n, called the *time stamp* of the transaction, is a natural number or ∞. The *timeless transaction* $\langle\!| P \,;\, Q |\!\rangle_x$ is an abbreviation for $\langle\!| P \,;\, Q |\!\rangle_x^\infty$, and we assume that $\infty + 1 = \infty$. It is possible to write out-of-time transactions $\langle\!| P \,;\, Q |\!\rangle_x^0$: the semantics (in particular, the structural congruence) will simplify these processes on-the-fly. It is worth to notice that the syntax of Webπ processes extends the asynchronous π-calculus with the transaction process.

The input $x(\widetilde{u}).P$, restriction $(x)P$, and replicated input $!x(\widetilde{u}).P$ are binders of names $\widetilde{u}$, x, and $\widetilde{u}$, respectively. The scope of these binders are the processes P. We use the standard notions of α-equivalence, *free* and *bound names* of processes, noted $\mathtt{fn}(P)$, $\mathtt{bn}(P)$, respectively. In particular,

– $\mathtt{fn}(\langle\!| P \,;\, Q |\!\rangle_x^n) = \mathtt{fn}(P) \cup \mathtt{fn}(Q) \cup \{x\}$ and α-equivalence equates $(x)(\langle\!| P \,;\, Q |\!\rangle_x^n)$ with $(z)(\langle\!| P\{z/x\} \,;\, Q\{z/x\} |\!\rangle_z^n)$ provided $z \notin \mathtt{fn}(\langle\!| P \,;\, Q |\!\rangle_x^n)$;

In the following we let $\prod_{i \in I} P_i$ be the parallel composition of the processes P_i. We also let $\tau.P$ be the process $(z)(\overline{z}\,|\,z().P)$ where $z \notin \mathtt{fn}(P)$.

Remark 1. 1. The process $\langle\!| P \,;\, Q |\!\rangle_x^n$ is intended to define a "web" transaction (the keyword "web" is always omitted in the following). It has not to be confused with "database" transactions, which usually grant atomicity and isolation properties. These two properties are usually not retained by transactional activities over the web.

2. An high-level programming language using Webπ transactions should neglect names marking transactions, such as x in $\langle\!| P \,;\, Q |\!\rangle_x^n$. Our insight is that these names are process identifiers of transactions, therefore they are dynamically generated by the run-time support of the language. This design choice may be easily implemented by using a distinguished name called this. Then programmers may write $\langle\!| P \,;\, Q |\!\rangle^n$, which means $(\mathsf{this})(\langle\!| P \,;\, Q |\!\rangle_{\mathsf{this}}^n)$. A further consequence of this insight is that two different transactions always bear different names marking them. Even if we conform with this intuition in every example, we purposely do not enforce in Webπ a discipline for the use of names marking transactions.

2.1   The Reduction Relation

Following the tradition of π-calculus [15], the reduction relation of Webπ is defined by using a structural congruence that equates all agents one never wants to distinguish.

Definition 1. *The structural congruence $\equiv$ is the least congruence closed with respect to α-renaming, satisfying the abelian monoid laws for parallel (associativity, commutativity, and $\mathbf{0}$ as identity), and the following axioms:*

1. *the scope laws:*

$$(u)\mathbf{0} \equiv \mathbf{0}, \qquad (u)(v)P \equiv (v)(u)P,$$
$$P \,|\, (u)Q \equiv (u)(P \,|\, Q) \,, \quad \textit{if } u \notin \mathtt{fn}(P)$$
$$\langle\!(z)P \;;\; Q\rangle\!{}_x^n \equiv (z)\langle\!P \;;\; Q\rangle\!{}_x^n \,, \quad \textit{if } z \notin \{x\} \cup \mathtt{fn}(Q)$$
$$\langle\!P \;;\; (z)Q\rangle\!{}_x^0 \equiv (z)\langle\!P \;;\; Q\rangle\!{}_x^0 \,, \quad \textit{if } z \notin \{x\} \cup \mathtt{fn}(P)$$

2. *the repetition law:*

$$!x(\widetilde{u}).P \equiv x(\widetilde{u}).P \,|\, !x(\widetilde{u}).P$$

3. *the transaction laws:*

$$\langle\!\mathbf{0} \;;\; Q\rangle\!{}_x^n \equiv \mathbf{0}$$
$$\langle\!\langle\!P \;;\; Q\rangle\!{}_y^n \,|\, R \;;\; R'\rangle\!{}_x^m \equiv \langle\!P \;;\; Q\rangle\!{}_y^n \,|\, \langle\!R \;;\; R'\rangle\!{}_x^m$$

4. *the floating laws:*

$$\langle\!\overline{z}\,\widetilde{u} \,|\, P \;;\; Q\rangle\!{}_x^n \equiv \overline{z}\,\widetilde{u} \,|\, \langle\!P \;;\; Q\rangle\!{}_x^n$$
$$\langle\!y(\widetilde{v}).P \,|\, P' \;;\; \overline{z}\,\widetilde{u} \,|\, Q\rangle\!{}_x^0 \equiv \overline{z}\,\widetilde{u} \,|\, \langle\!y(\widetilde{v}).P \,|\, P' \;;\; Q\rangle\!{}_x^0$$

The scope laws and the repetition law are standard; let us discuss the transaction and floating laws that are unusual. The law $\langle\!\mathbf{0} \;;\; Q\rangle\!{}_x^n \equiv \mathbf{0}$ defines committed transactions, namely transactions with $\mathbf{0}$ as body. These transactions, being committed, are equivalent to $\mathbf{0}$ and, therefore, cannot fail anymore. The law $\langle\!\langle\!P \;;\; Q\rangle\!{}_y^n \,|\, R \;;\; R'\rangle\!{}_x^m \equiv \langle\!P \;;\; Q\rangle\!{}_y^n \,|\, \langle\!R \;;\; R'\rangle\!{}_x^m$ moves transactions outside parent transactions, thus flattening the nesting of transactions. Notwithstanding this flattening, parent transactions may still affect children transactions by means of transaction names. The law $\langle\!\overline{z}\,\widetilde{u} \,|\, P \;;\; R\rangle\!{}_x^n \equiv \overline{z}\,\widetilde{u} \,|\, \langle\!P \;;\; R\rangle\!{}_x^n$ floats messages outside transactions, thus modelling the fact that messages are particles that independently move towards their inputs. The intended semantics is the following. If a process emits a message, this message traverses the surrounding transaction boundaries, until it reaches the corresponding input. The law $\langle\!y(\widetilde{v}).P \,|\, P' \;;\; \overline{z}\,\widetilde{u} \,|\, Q\rangle\!{}_x^0 \equiv \overline{z}\,\widetilde{u} \,|\, \langle\!y(\widetilde{v}).P \,|\, P' \;;\; Q\rangle\!{}_x^0$ models floatings of messages from compensations of out-of-time transactions whose bodies contain an input guarded process (failed transactions, see below).

The dynamic behaviour of processes is defined by the reduction relation. The main technical difficulty of this notion is time elapsing. In web models, time of different machines does not progress synchronously. Therefore we assume that each machine of the network has its own clock that is not synchronized with other clocks. On the contrary, all the processes running in the same location, compete for the same processor time. This competition is modelled in $\text{Web}\pi$ by assuming that every reduction costs one time slot. Henceforth, when a subprocess performs a reduction, the flow of time is communicated to all the competing processes. This "flow of time" communication is a formal expedient for describing the elapse of one time slot without defining any machine clock. Should we have used a machine clock, as it happens in practice for running processes, then the time stamps of transactions could have been replaced with an absolute clock time that is compared with the machine clock when the transaction thread is executed.

The operation of decreasing by 1 the time stamps of active transactions on the same machine is modelled by the *time stepper function* below, that adapts the corresponding function in [4] to $\text{Web}\pi$. The definitions of this function and another auxiliary function are in order:

input predicate $\text{inp}(P)$**:** this predicate verifies whether a process contains an input that is not underneath a transaction. It is the least relations such that:

$$\begin{aligned}
&\text{inp}(x(\widetilde{u}).P) \\
&\text{inp}((x)P) \quad \text{if } \text{inp}(P) \\
&\text{inp}(P\,|\,Q) \quad \text{if } \text{inp}(P) \text{ or } \text{inp}(Q) \\
&\text{inp}(!x(\widetilde{u}).P)
\end{aligned}$$

time stepper function $\phi(P)$**:** this function decreases the time stamps by 1. For the missing cases, $\phi(P) = P$.

$$\begin{aligned}
\phi((x)P) &= (x)\phi(P) \\
\phi(P\,|\,Q) &= \phi(P)\,|\,\phi(Q) \\
\phi(\langle P\,;\,R\rangle_x^0) &= \begin{cases} \langle \phi(P)\,;\,\phi(R)\rangle_x^0 & \text{if } \text{inp}(P) \\ \langle \phi(P)\,;\,R\rangle_x^0 & \text{otherwise} \end{cases} \\
\phi(\langle P\,;\,R\rangle_x^{n+1}) &= \langle \phi(P)\,;\,R\rangle_x^n
\end{aligned}$$

The stepper function is defined by induction on the syntax. The critical processes are the out-of-time transactions $\langle P\,;\,R\rangle_x^0$. In this case, the input predicate is used to verify whether (a) the body P contains input-guarded processes or (b) not. In (a) the compensation is active, and the time must elapse for the transactions therein (and for transactions inside the body). In (b), since $\text{inp}(P)$ is false, the time only elapses for the transactions inside the body. In fact, this definition is sound provided the time stepper function does not modify the input predicate and preserves structural congruence. For example, if $\text{inp}(P)$ is false then $\langle P\,;\,R\rangle_x^0 \equiv P$, and since $\phi(\langle P\,;\,R\rangle_x^0) = \langle \phi(P)\,;\,R\rangle_x^0$, we must verify that $\langle \phi(P)\,;\,R\rangle_x^0$ is structurally congruent to $\phi(P)$. This is actually the case, as a consequence of the following proposition.

Proposition 1. *1.* $\text{inp}(P)$ *if and only if* $\text{inp}(\phi(P))$.
2. $P \equiv Q$ *implies* $\text{inp}(P) = \text{inp}(Q)$ *and* $\phi(P) \equiv \phi(Q)$.

The input predicate permits the formal definitions of failed and commited transactions.

Definition 2. *A transaction* $\langle P \; ; \; Q \rangle^0_x$ *is* failed *if* inp(P) *is true; it is* commit-ted *if* inp(P) *is false.*

We observe that a failed transaction $\langle P \; ; \; Q \rangle^0_x$ may be always rewritten into a structurally congruent process $(\tilde{z})\langle y(\tilde{u}).P' \,|\, P'' \; ; \; Q \rangle^0_x$, for some $\tilde{z}$, y, $\tilde{u}$, P', and P''. This "canonical form" has been used in the second floating law and is used in the definition of the following reduction relation.

Definition 3. *The* reduction relation $\rightarrow$ *is the least relation satisfying the reductions:*

(COM)
$$\overline{x}\,\tilde{v} \,|\, x(\tilde{u}).P \quad \rightarrow \quad P\{\tilde{v}/\tilde{u}\}$$

(FAIL)
$$\overline{x} \,|\, \langle z(\tilde{u}).P \,|\, Q \; ; \; R \rangle^{n+1}_x \quad \rightarrow \quad \langle z(\tilde{u}).P \,|\, \phi(Q) \; ; \; R \rangle^0_x$$

and closed under $\equiv$*,* (x)*-, and the rules:*

$$\frac{P \rightarrow Q}{P \,|\, R \rightarrow Q \,|\, \phi(R)} \qquad \frac{P \rightarrow Q}{\langle P \; ; \; R \rangle^{n+1}_x \rightarrow \langle Q \; ; \; R \rangle^n_x} \qquad \frac{P \rightarrow Q}{\langle y(\tilde{v}).R \,|\, R' \; ; \; P \rangle^0_x} \\ \rightarrow \langle y(\tilde{v}).R \,|\, \phi(R') \; ; \; Q \rangle^0_x$$

Rule (COM) is standard in process calculi and models the input-output inter-action. Rule (FAIL) models transaction failures: when a transaction abort (a message on a transaction name) is emitted, the corresponding transaction is ter-minated by turning the time stamp to 0, thus activating the compensation (see the last inference rule). On the contrary, aborts are not possible if the transac-tion is already terminated, namely every input-guarded process in the body has completed its own work (this is never the case if the body contains replicated inputs). The inference rules lift reductions to parallel and transaction contexts, updating them because a time slot is elapsed.

In order to clarify the semantics, the reductions of few sample processes are reported. The process

$$\overline{z} \,|\, \overline{x} \,|\, \langle x().\mathbf{0} \; ; \; \overline{y} \rangle^n_z$$

has the following two computations $(n > 0)$:

$$\overline{z} \,|\, \overline{x} \,|\, \langle x().\mathbf{0} \; ; \; \overline{y} \rangle^n_z \quad \equiv \quad \overline{x} \,|\, \overline{z} \,|\, \langle x().\mathbf{0} \; ; \; \overline{y} \rangle^n_z$$
$$\rightarrow \quad \overline{x} \,|\, \langle x().\mathbf{0} \; ; \; \overline{y} \rangle^0_z \quad \text{by (FAIL) and parallel closure}$$
$$\equiv \quad \overline{x} \,|\, \overline{y} \,|\, \langle x().\mathbf{0} \; ; \; \mathbf{0} \rangle^0_z$$

$$\overline{z} \,|\, \overline{x} \,|\, \langle x().\mathbf{0} \; ; \; \overline{y} \rangle^n_z \quad \rightarrow \quad \overline{z} \,|\, \langle \mathbf{0} \; ; \; \overline{y} \rangle^{n-1}_z \quad \text{by (COM) and parallel closure}$$
$$\equiv \quad \overline{z}$$

In the first computation, the message $\overline{x}$ is not consumed because the body of the transaction is cancelled on transaction failure. In the second one, the message $\overline{y}$ cannot be produced because the compensation process is garbage collected on transaction commit.

Consider now the process $P = (z, z')(\overline{x} \mid \langle x().\mathbf{0} \; ; \; \overline{y} \rangle^1_z \mid \langle x().\mathbf{0} \; ; \; \overline{y} \rangle^1_{z'})$. It evolves as follows

$$P \equiv (z, z') \left(\langle \overline{x} \mid x().\mathbf{0} \; ; \; \overline{y} \rangle^1_z \mid \langle x().\mathbf{0} \; ; \; \overline{y} \rangle^1_{z'} \right)$$
$$\rightarrow (z, z')\langle x().\mathbf{0} \; ; \; \overline{y} \rangle^0_{z'} \qquad \text{by (COMM), restriction and transaction closure}$$

and in a similar way, but with z instead of z'. We remark that the process $Q = \overline{x} \mid x().\overline{y}$ has a similar behaviour. However the processes $\phi(P)$ and $\phi(Q)$ have different behaviours. In particular $\phi(P) \equiv \overline{x} \mid \overline{y} \mid \overline{y}$, while $\phi(Q) = Q$.

In Webπ it is easy to delay a process P of n steps. To this aim, let $x \notin \mathtt{fn}(P)$ then

$$(x)\langle x().\mathbf{0} \; ; \; P \rangle^n_x$$

behaves like $\mathbf{0}$ for n time units, and evolves to P afterwards.

It is worth to notice that the reduction relation of processes does not define the dynamics of temporarily blocked transactions as the one above. Indeed, by definition $(x)\langle x().\mathbf{0} \; ; \; P \rangle^n_x \nrightarrow$ if $n > 0$. This sloppiness is due to the fact that the process reduction is defined in a compositional way and therefore cannot express the absence of a reduction, which is a global property of the processor running the process. One solution to this problem is to introduce a rule like $P \rightarrow \phi(P)$ in [4]. However this solution is at odd with local urgency: it states that a machine (processor) may idle, even if there are some actions that can be performed. We prefer to keep the present reduction (intensional) semantics and to stick to an extensional semantics that is a congruence, thus defining the meaning of a process when it is plugged in any possible context.

3 Timed Bisimilarity

The extensional semantics of Webπ – the *timed bisimilarity* – relies on the notions of barb and contexts. A process P has a *barb* x, and write $P \downarrow x$, if P manifests an output on the free name x. Formally:

$$
\begin{array}{ll}
\overline{x}\,\widetilde{u} \downarrow x & \\
(z)P \downarrow x & \text{if } P \downarrow x \text{ and } x \neq z \\
(P \mid Q) \downarrow x & \text{if } P \downarrow x \text{ or } Q \downarrow x \\
\langle P \; ; \; R \rangle^0_z \downarrow x & \text{if } P \downarrow x \text{ or } (\mathtt{inp}(P) \text{ and } R \downarrow x) \\
\langle P \; ; \; R \rangle^{n+1}_z \downarrow x & \text{if } P \downarrow x
\end{array}
$$

Therefore inputs (both simple and replicated) have no barb. This is standard in asynchronous calculi: an observer has no direct way of knowing if the message he has sent has been received.

Context processes, noted $\mathsf{C}[\cdot]$, are defined by the following grammar:

$$
\begin{array}{rcl}
\mathsf{C}[\cdot] & ::= & [\cdot] \quad \mid \quad x(\widetilde{u}).\mathsf{C}[\cdot] \quad \mid \quad (x)\mathsf{C}[\cdot] \quad \mid \quad \mathsf{C}[\cdot] \mid P \quad \mid \quad !x(\widetilde{u}).\mathsf{C}[\cdot] \\
& & \mid \quad \langle \mathsf{C}[\cdot] \; ; \; P \rangle^n_x \quad \mid \quad \langle P \; ; \; \mathsf{C}[\cdot] \rangle^n_x
\end{array}
$$

Definition 4. *A* timed barbed bisimulation *S is a symmetric relation between processes such that $P\,S\,Q$ implies*

1. *if $P \downarrow x$ then $Q \downarrow x$;*
2. *if $P \to P'$ then $Q \to Q'$ and $P'\,S\,Q'$;*

Timed bisimilarity, *denoted with $\sim_t$, is the largest timed barbed bisimulation that is also a congruence.*

As an illustration of timed bisimilar processes we discuss few examples. The following identity adapts an equation of asynchronous bisimilarity [1] to Webπ, thus suggesting that timed bisimilarity is asynchronous:

$$\langle\!| x(u).\overline{x}\,u \,|\, \tau.\mathbf{0} \,;\; P |\!\rangle_z^1 \sim_t \langle\!| \tau.(v)v().\mathbf{0} \,;\; P |\!\rangle_z^1$$

It is worth to notice that $\mathbf{0} \not\sim_t x(u).\overline{x}\,u$. For instance the context $\mathsf{C}[\cdot] = (z)([\cdot]\,|\,\overline{x}\,w\,|\,\langle\!| x(u).\mathbf{0}\,;\; \overline{v}\,|\!\rangle_z^1)$ separates the two processes. Due to local urgency, the transaction z cannot fail in $\mathsf{C}[\mathbf{0}]$ (thus the message $\overline{v}$ cannot be produced), while it can fail in $\mathsf{C}[x(\widetilde{u}).\overline{x}\,\widetilde{u}]$ (thus activating the compensation $\overline{v}$).

Timed bisimilarity may be inferred by considering only a subset of contexts and applying substitutions.

Lemma 1. *(Context Lemma) Let* timed-prime bisimilarity, *in notation $\sim_t'$, be the largest timed barbed bisimulation such that if $P \sim_t' Q$ then, for every R, x, n, S, $\widetilde{w}$, $\widetilde{z}$: $\langle\!| P\{\widetilde{w}/\widetilde{z}\} \,;\; R |\!\rangle_x^n \,|\, S \sim_t' \langle\!| Q\{\widetilde{w}/\widetilde{z}\} \,;\; R |\!\rangle_x^n \,|\, S$. Then $\sim_t\,=\,\sim_t'$.*

It is worth to notice that the corresponding lemma about π-calculus reduces contexts to those whose shape is $[\cdot]\{\widetilde{u}/\widetilde{v}\} \,|\, R$.

We conclude this section by demonstrating that the discriminating power of $\sim_t$ is weaker when local urgency is dropped. To this aim, we consider a new reduction relation of processes denoted with $\to^\phi$ defined by augmenting Definition 3 (where $\to^\phi$ is substituted for $\to$) with the idle rule:

$$\begin{array}{c}\text{(IDLE)}\\ P \to^\phi \phi(P)\end{array}$$

The (IDLE) rule allows time to pass asynchronously even when other reductions are possible. Let $\sim_t^{\text{idle}}$ be defined as $\sim_t$ considering the reduction relation $\to^\phi$ instead of $\to$. Then $(x)x().\mathbf{0} \sim_t^{\text{idle}} (x)x().\mathbf{0}\,|\,z().\overline{z}$ while $(x)x().\mathbf{0} \not\sim_t (x)x().\mathbf{0}\,|\,z().\overline{z}$. However a model of time similar to (IDLE) can be simulated with the local urgency assumption. It suffices to put in the context a process always able to perform internal synchronizations; thus letting the time to pass.

Proposition 2. *$P \sim_t Q$ implies $P \sim_t^{\text{idle}} Q$.*

Proof. (Sketch) Let τ^* be the process $(x)(\overline{x} \,|\, !x().\overline{x})$. An easy check gives that, for every P, $P \to^\phi Q$ if and only if $\tau^*\,|\,P \to \tau^*\,|\,Q$. The proposition follows directly by this property. $\qquad\square$

4   The Labelled Semantics

Even if the context lemma restricts the shape of contexts for inferring timed bisimilarity, direct proofs remain particularly difficult. A standard device to avoid such quantification consists of introducing a labelled operational model and equipping it with an (asynchronous) bisimulation.

Let μ range over input labels $\overset{\diamond}{x}(\widetilde{u})$ and $\overset{\circ}{x}(\widetilde{u})$, bound output labels $(\widetilde{z})\overline{x}\,\widetilde{u}$ where $\widetilde{z} \subseteq \widetilde{u}$, and $\overset{\diamond}{\tau}$ and $\overset{\circ}{\tau}$. Let $\star$ range over $\{\diamond, \circ\}$; we define $\overset{\star}{x}(\widetilde{u}) = \overset{\circ}{x}(\widetilde{u})$, $(\widetilde{z})\overline{x}\,\widetilde{u} = (\widetilde{z})\overline{x}\,\widetilde{u}$, and $\overset{\star}{\tau} = \overset{\circ}{\tau}$. Let also $\mathtt{fn}(\overset{\star}{\tau}) = \emptyset$, $\mathtt{fn}(\overset{\star}{x}(\widetilde{u})) = \{x\}$, $\mathtt{fn}(\overline{x}\,\widetilde{u}) = \{x\} \cup \widetilde{u}$, and $\mathtt{fn}((\widetilde{z})\overline{x}\,\widetilde{u}) = \{x\} \cup \widetilde{u} \setminus \widetilde{z}$. Finally, let $\mathtt{bn}(\mu)$ be $\widetilde{z}$ if $\mu = (\widetilde{z})\overline{x}\,\widetilde{u}$, be $\widetilde{u}$ if $\mu = \overset{\star}{x}(\widetilde{u})$, and be $\emptyset$, otherwise. We implicitly identify terms up to α-renaming $\equiv_\alpha$: that is, if $P \equiv_\alpha Q$ and $Q \overset{\mu}{\longrightarrow} P'$ then $P \overset{\mu}{\longrightarrow} P'$.

Definition 5. *The* transition relation *of* $\mathtt{Web}\pi$ *processes, noted* $\overset{\mu}{\longrightarrow}$, *is the least relation satisfying the rules:*

$$(\text{IN}) \quad x(\widetilde{u}).P \overset{\overset{\diamond}{x}(\widetilde{u})}{\longrightarrow} P$$

$$(\text{OUT}) \quad \overline{x}\,\widetilde{u} \overset{\overline{x}\,\widetilde{u}}{\longrightarrow} 0$$

$$(\text{RES}) \quad \frac{P \overset{\mu}{\longrightarrow} Q \quad x \notin \mathtt{fn}(\mu)}{(x)P \overset{\mu}{\longrightarrow} (x)Q}$$

$$(\text{OPEN}) \quad \frac{P \overset{(\widetilde{v})\overline{x}\,\widetilde{u}}{\longrightarrow} Q \quad w \neq x \quad w \in \widetilde{u} \setminus \widetilde{v}}{(w)P \overset{(w\widetilde{v})\overline{x}\,\widetilde{u}}{\longrightarrow} Q}$$

$$(\text{PAR}) \quad \frac{P \overset{\mu}{\longrightarrow} Q \quad \mathtt{bn}(\mu) \cap \mathtt{fn}(R) = \emptyset}{P \mid R \overset{\mu}{\longrightarrow} Q \mid \phi(R)}$$

$$(\text{COM}) \quad \frac{P \overset{(\widetilde{w})\overline{x}\,\widetilde{v}}{\longrightarrow} P' \quad Q \overset{\overset{\star}{x}(\widetilde{u})}{\longrightarrow} Q' \quad \widetilde{w} \cap \mathtt{fn}(Q) = \emptyset}{P \mid Q \overset{\overset{\star}{\tau}}{\longrightarrow} (\widetilde{w})(P' \mid Q'\{\widetilde{v}/\widetilde{u}\})}$$

$$(\text{REPIN}) \quad !x(\widetilde{u}).P \overset{\overset{\diamond}{x}(\widetilde{u})}{\longrightarrow} P \mid !x(\widetilde{u}).P$$

$$(\text{ABORT}) \quad \langle\!| P \;;\; R |\!\rangle^{n+1}_x \overset{\overset{\diamond}{x}()}{\longrightarrow} \langle\!| P \;;\; R |\!\rangle^0_x$$

$$(\text{SELF}) \quad \frac{P \overset{\overline{x}}{\longrightarrow} Q}{\langle\!| P \;;\; R |\!\rangle^{n+1}_x \overset{\overset{\circ}{\tau}}{\longrightarrow} \langle\!| Q \;;\; R |\!\rangle^0_x}$$

$$(\text{TRANS}) \quad \frac{P \overset{\mu}{\longrightarrow} Q \quad \mathtt{bn}(\mu) \cap (\mathtt{fn}(R) \cup \{x\}) = \emptyset}{\langle\!| P \;;\; R |\!\rangle^{n+1}_x \overset{\overset{\circ}{\mu}}{\longrightarrow} \langle\!| Q \;;\; R |\!\rangle^n_x}$$

$$(\text{TRANS-B}) \quad \frac{P \overset{\overset{\circ}{\mu}}{\longrightarrow} Q \quad \mathtt{bn}(\overset{\circ}{\mu}) \cap (\mathtt{fn}(R) \cup \{x\}) = \emptyset \quad \mathtt{inp}(P)}{\langle\!| P \;;\; R |\!\rangle^0_x \overset{\overset{\circ}{\mu}}{\longrightarrow} \langle\!| Q \;;\; \phi(R) |\!\rangle^0_x}$$

$$(\text{TRANS-C}) \quad \frac{P \overset{\overset{\circ}{\mu}}{\longrightarrow} Q \quad \mathtt{bn}(\overset{\circ}{\mu}) \cap (\mathtt{fn}(R) \cup \{x\}) = \emptyset \quad \neg\mathtt{inp}(P)}{\langle\!| P \;;\; R |\!\rangle^0_x \overset{\overset{\circ}{\mu}}{\longrightarrow} \langle\!| Q \;;\; R |\!\rangle^0_x}$$

$$(\text{TRANS-F}) \quad \frac{R \overset{\mu}{\longrightarrow} R' \quad \mathtt{bn}(\mu) \cap (\mathtt{fn}(P) \cup \{x\}) = \emptyset \quad \mathtt{inp}(P)}{\langle\!| P \;;\; R |\!\rangle^0_x \overset{\overset{\circ}{\mu}}{\longrightarrow} \langle\!| \phi(P) \;;\; R' |\!\rangle^0_x}$$

The transitions of $P \mid Q$ *have mirror cases that have been omitted.*

The first seven rules are almost standard in π-calculus. Exceptions are (replicated) inputs whose transitions are labelled with $\overset{\diamond}{x}(\widetilde{u})$, and rule (PAR) that uses the time stepper function. The symbol $\diamond$ is used to mark input transitions that are not underneath a transaction. These transitions must be blocked if they are due to bodies of failed transactions. Transitions that are underneath transactions are marked with a $\circ$ symbol: see rule (TRANS). These transitions are never blocked: see rules (TRANS-B) and (TRANS-C). We discuss the other rules. Rule (ABORT) models transaction termination due to an abort message. It amounts to turning the time stamp to 0. We remark that abort is not possible if the time stamp is already 0. The label is marked with $\circ$ because the transition is assumed to be underneath a transaction. Rule (SELF) is similar to (ABORT), taking into account the case when the abort message is raised by the body of the transaction. Rule (TRANS) lifts transitions to transaction contexts and decreases the transaction time stamp because a transition of the body is going to occur. This rule applies also to outputs transitions, thus looking at odd with the reduction relation, where messages are moved outside transaction bodies by means of a structural rule. Actually this is only apparent: in the reduction relation, the decreasing of the time stamp is performed by the contextual rules for parallel composition (by ϕ) or for transactions. Rules (TRANS-B) and (TRANS-C) lift transitions of bodies of transactions to out-of-time transaction contexts. According to this rule output transitions are always enabled because $(\widetilde{z})\overline{x}\,\widetilde{u} \overset{\circ}{=} (\widetilde{z})\overline{x}\,\widetilde{u}$. On the contrary, input and τ transitions are enabled provided they are underneath not failed transaction contexts. The two rules separate the cases whether the compensation is active or not. Rule (TRANS-F) lifts transitions of compensations to failed transaction contexts. We observe that the transition in the conclusion is labelled with a $\circ$. This means that the transition cannot be blocked by an external failed transaction boundary.

The following statement guarantees that transitions in the bodies of failed transactions preserve the input predicate. If this was not the case, a committed transaction could become failed, thus enabling transitions of the compensation.

Proposition 3. *If $P \overset{\overset{\circ}{\mu}}{\longrightarrow} Q$ and $\mathrm{inp}(P)$ then $\mathrm{inp}(Q)$.*

We are now in place for formalizing a correspondence result between the labelled and the reduction semantics.

Proposition 4. *Let P be a Webπ process. Then*

1. *$P \downarrow v$ if and only if $P \overset{(\widetilde{z})\overline{v}\,\widetilde{u}}{\longrightarrow}$, for some $\widetilde{z}$ and $\widetilde{u}$;*
2. *$P \overset{\tau}{\longrightarrow} Q$ implies $P \rightarrow Q$;*
3. *$P \rightarrow Q$ implies there is R such that $R \equiv Q$ and $P \overset{\tau}{\longrightarrow} R$.*

The labelled bisimulation that we consider recalls the asynchronous bisimulation [1] for processes. In the following definition $\star, \bullet$ range over $\{\diamond, \circ\}$

Definition 6. *An* asynchronous bisimulation *is a symmetric binary relation* $\mathcal{S}$ *between processes such that* $P\mathcal{S}Q$ *implies*

1. *if* $P \xrightarrow{\hat{\tau}} P'$ *then* $Q \xrightarrow{\hat{\tau}} Q'$ *and* $P'\mathcal{S}Q'$,
2. *if* $P \xrightarrow{(\tilde{v})\overline{x}\,\tilde{u}} P'$ *and* $\tilde{v} \cap \mathbf{fn}(Q) = \emptyset$, *then* $Q \xrightarrow{(\tilde{v})\overline{x}\,\tilde{u}} Q'$ *and* $P'\mathcal{S}Q'$;
3. *if* $P \xrightarrow{\hat{x}(\tilde{u})} P'$ *and* $\tilde{u} \cap \mathbf{fn}(Q) = \emptyset$, *then*
    (a) *either* $Q \xrightarrow{\hat{x}(\tilde{u})} Q'$ *and* $P'\mathcal{S}Q'$,
    (b) *or* $Q \xrightarrow{\hat{\tau}} Q'$ *and* $P'\mathcal{S}(Q' \,|\, \overline{x}\,\tilde{u})$.

Asynchronous bisimilarity, *in notation* $\sim_a$, *is the largest asynchronous bisimulation.*

The item 3 of the definition of asynchronous bisimulation allows to match an input transition with a τ transition. This item permits to equate the following processes, that have been already discussed in the previous Section:

$$\langle\!\langle x(u).\overline{x}\,u \,|\, \tau.\mathbf{0} \,;\, P\rangle\!\rangle_z^1 \sim_a \langle\!\langle \tau.(v)v().\mathbf{0} \,;\, P\rangle\!\rangle_z^1$$

Remark 2. Our approach is different from [3]. Berger uses a standard bisimulation definition on a transition system extended with the Honda-Tokoro rule $\mathbf{0} \xrightarrow{x(\tilde{u})} \overline{x}\,\tilde{u}$ [11]. On the contrary, we stick to the approach in [1], where a slightly modified bisimulation (with the item *3.(b)*) is applied to a standard transition system.

Asynchronous bisimulation equates structurally congruent processes:

Proposition 5. $P \equiv Q$ *implies* $P \sim_a Q$.

In contrast with asynchronous π-calculus, $\sim_a$ is not a congruence for $\mathtt{Web}\pi$ because it is not closed with respect to input, parallel composition, and transaction contexts. This may be remedied by appropriately closing the equivalence. With respect to [3], where closures regarded substitutions and time, we also need to close by the input predicate.

Definition 7. *A binary relation* $\mathcal{R}$ *over processes is*

- substitution-closed *if* $P\mathcal{R}Q$ *implies, for every substitution* σ, *$P\sigma \mathcal{R} Q\sigma$;*
- time-closed *if* $P\mathcal{R}Q$ *implies* $\phi(P)\mathcal{R}\phi(Q)$;
- input-predicate-closed *if* $P\mathcal{R}Q$ *implies* $\mathtt{inp}(P) = \mathtt{inp}(Q)$.

These are counterexamples showing that the asynchronous bisimulation $\sim_a$ is neither substitution-closed, nor time-closed, nor input-predicate-closed.

1. As regards substitution closure, we adapt a counterexample in [3]. Let

$$P \stackrel{def}{=} (a)(\overline{x}\,a \,|\, !y(u).\overline{u})$$
$$Q \stackrel{def}{=} (a)(\overline{x}\,a \,|\, !y(u).\overline{u} \,|\, (z)\langle\!\langle y(u).(\overline{u} \,|\, a().\overline{b}) \,;\, \mathbf{0}\rangle\!\rangle_z^2)$$

We have that $P \sim_a Q$ but $P\{y/x\} \not\sim_a Q\{y/x\}$ because $Q\{y/x\}$ may produce the message $\bar{b}$ while this is not the case for $P\{y/x\}$. The main difference between this counterexample and the one reported in [3] is that we do not exploit nesting of transactions. The equivalence result between P and Q relies on the fact that, in general, $!y(u).\bar{u} \mid (z)\langle y(u).(\bar{u} \mid x(\tilde{v}).P) \; ; \; \mathbf{0}\rangle_z^1) \sim_a !y(u).\bar{u}$ and $(a)(\bar{x}\,a) \sim_a (a)(\bar{x}\,a \mid (z)\langle a().\bar{b} \; ; \; \mathbf{0}\rangle_z^1)$.

2. As regards time closure, we adapt another counterexample in [3]. Let

$$P \stackrel{def}{=} (z)\langle \tau.\bar{x} \; ; \; \mathbf{0}\rangle_z^1$$
$$Q \stackrel{def}{=} (z)\langle \tau.\tau.\mathbf{0} \; ; \; \bar{x}\,\rangle_z^1$$

then $P \sim_a Q$ but $\phi(P) \not\sim_a \phi(Q)$ because $\phi(Q) \xrightarrow{\bar{x}}$ and $\phi(P)$ cannot.

3. As regards input-predicate closure, let

$$P \stackrel{def}{=} \mathbf{0}$$
$$Q \stackrel{def}{=} (z)z()$$

then $P \sim_a Q$ and $\mathtt{inp}(P) \neq \mathtt{inp}(Q)$. Since $\mathtt{inp}(P)$ is different from $\mathtt{inp}(Q)$, it is possible to separate P and Q by using contexts such as $\langle [\cdot] \; ; \; \bar{y}\,\rangle_x^0$.

Definition 8. Labelled timed bisimilarity, *in notation* $\simeq_a$, *is the greatest asynchronous bisimulation contained into* $\sim_a$ *that is also substitution-closed, time-closed, and input-predicate closed.*

Lemma 2. $\simeq_a$ *is a congruence.*

We are now in place to report the correspondence result between the labelled timed bisimilarity and the timed bisimulation congruence.

Proposition 6. $P \simeq_a Q$ *implies* $P \sim_t Q$.

Proof. By Proposition 4, $\simeq_a$ is a timed barbed bisimulation, and by Lemma 2 it is also a congruence. The statement follows because $\sim_t$ is the largest one. $\square$

The converse implication of Proposition 6 also holds in the asynchronous π-calculus (with strong semantics) [10]. The technique shows that if $P \sim_t Q$ then the bisimulation game between P and Q of $\simeq_a$ holds (the closures of the definition of $\simeq_a$ hold easily). This is obtained by means of small contexts checking that bound outputs of P and Q are the same up-to alpha-equivalence. These contexts disappear after few steps (namely, if $P \xrightarrow{\mu} P'$ then $\mathsf{C}[P] \xrightarrow{\tau} \cdots \xrightarrow{\tau} P'$). Unfortunately, this technique applies badly to Webπ because such "checking steps" make the time elapse in P and Q. Namely, if $P \xrightarrow{\mu} P'$ then $\mathsf{C}[P] \xrightarrow{\tau} \cdots \xrightarrow{\tau} \phi^n(P')$, for some n (rather than $n = 0$). Since we are missing a direct proof (even if we conjecture the equality $\simeq_a = \sim_t$), we use an alternative, weaker technique that has been proposed for the weak asynchronous bisimulation [1].

Let us extend the Webπ syntax with the rule:

$$P ::= \quad \cdots \quad | \quad [x = y]P$$

A match process $[x = y]P$ executes P provided x is equal to y. Let $[x_i = y_i]^{i \in I} P$ be the sequence of name matches $[x_i = y_i]$ followed by the process P. The semantics of name match is defined by the structural congruence rule

$$[x = x]P \equiv P .$$

Let also $\text{inp}([x = x]P) = \text{inp}(P)$. Finally, let $\sim_{t,M}$ be the largest timed barbed bisimulation that is a congruence with respect to contexts in Webπ extended with the name match (namely $\mathsf{C}[\cdot] ::= \cdots \quad | \quad [x = y]\mathsf{C}[\cdot]$). It is easy to demonstrate that $\simeq_a \subseteq \sim_{t,M} \subseteq \sim_t$ (the first containment is proved with arguments similar to Proposition 6).

Lemma 3. *If $P \sim_{t,M} Q$ then $P \simeq_a Q$.*

Proof. It is easy to verify that $\sim_{t,M}$ is substitution-closed, timed-closed, and input-predicate-closed. We demonstrate that, for any move $P \xrightarrow{\mu} P'$, there exist contexts $\mathsf{C}[\cdot]$ such that $\mathsf{C}[P] \sim_{t,M} \mathsf{C}[Q]$ implies $Q \xrightarrow{\mu'} Q'$ and one of the items 1 – 3 of Definition 6 is satisfied. We report only the two most significant cases. Let $\star, \bullet \in \{\circ, \diamond\}$.

$P \xrightarrow{\overset{\star}{x}(\tilde{u})} P'$. We consider the context $\mathsf{C}[\cdot] = \overline{x}\,\tilde{u} \mid [\cdot]$. Then $\mathsf{C}[P] \to P'$. As $P \sim_{t,M} Q$ then $\mathsf{C}[P] \sim_{t,M} \mathsf{C}[Q]$, and there is Q' such that $\mathsf{C}[Q] \to Q'$ and $P' \sim_{t,M} Q'$. There are two cases, either $Q \xrightarrow{\overset{\bullet}{x}(\tilde{u})} Q'$ (thus the item 3.(a) of the Definition 6 is satisfied) or $Q \xrightarrow{\tau} Q''$ and $P' \sim_{t,M} Q'' \mid \overline{x}\,\tilde{u}$ (thus the item 3.(b) of the Definition 6 is satisfied).

$P \xrightarrow{(\tilde{v})\overline{x}\,\tilde{u}} P'$. Let $\tilde{u} = u_1 \dots u_n$. Let also $F = \{i \mid u_i \notin \tilde{v}\}$, $B = \{i \mid u_i \in \tilde{v}\}$, $E = \{(i,j) \mid i < j \text{ and } u_i = u_j \text{ and } u_i, u_j \in B\}$, $D = \{(i,j) \mid i < j \text{ and } u_i \neq u_j \text{ and } u_i, u_j \in B\}$. Consider the context

$$\mathsf{C}_\mu[\cdot] = x(z_1 \dots z_n).\left(\prod_{i \in F}[z_i = u_i]a_i \mid \prod_{i \in B, u \in \text{fn}(P) \cup \text{fn}(Q)}[z_i = u]b_{i,u} \right.$$
$$\left. | \prod_{(i,j) \in E}[z_i = z_j]c_i \mid \prod_{(i,j) \in D}[z_i = z_j]d_i \right) \mid [\cdot]$$

where all the names $a_i, b_{i,u}, c_i, d_i$ are fresh and pairwise different. Then $\mathsf{C}_\mu[P] \to P'' \sim_{t,M} \prod_{i \in H} \overline{e_i} \mid P'$, where e_i are a subset of labels of $a_i, b_{i,u}, c_i, d_i$. As $P \sim_{t,M} Q$ are timed bisimilar, then also $\mathsf{C}_\mu[Q] \to Q''$ where $P'' \sim_{t,M} Q''$. By definition of $\mathsf{C}[\cdot]$, it must be the case that $Q'' \sim_{t,M} \prod_{i \in fi} \overline{e_i} \mid Q'$, for some Q' and $Q \xrightarrow{(\tilde{v})\overline{x}\,\tilde{u}} Q'$. An easy reasoning permits to state that, if $d \notin \text{fn}(R) \cup \text{fn}(R')$, then $\overline{d} \mid R \sim_{t,M} \overline{d} \mid R'$ if and only if $R \sim_{t,M} R'$. Applying this result we conclude that $P' \sim_{t,M} Q'$ (thus the item 2. of the Definition 6 is satisfied). $\square$

5   Machines

In this section we study the syntax and the reduction relation of Webπ machines. The extensional semantics is omitted in this contribution: a thorough analysis of the extensional semantics for machines (and the induced equality on processes) will be addressed in the full paper.

The syntax of *machines* M is defined by the following rules.

$$\text{M} ::=\quad \mathbf{0} \quad | \quad [\, P\,]_{\widetilde{x}} \quad | \quad (x)\text{M} \quad | \quad \text{M}\,|\,\text{M}$$

A machine may be empty; a location $[\, P\,]_{\widetilde{x}}$ running the process P and accepting all messages on names in the set $\widetilde{x}$; a machine (x)M with local name x; or a network of locations. The symbols $\mathbf{0}$ and $|$ are overloaded because they also denote the empty and parallel processes, respectively; the actual meaning is made clear from the context. The index $\widetilde{x}$ in the location $[\, P\,]_{\widetilde{x}}$ indicates a set $\widetilde{x}$, even if it is denoted with the same notation of tuples.

We assume that a name may index at most one machine. Formally, let $\text{ln}(\text{M})$ be defined as $\text{ln}(\mathbf{0}) = \emptyset$, $\text{ln}([\, P\,]_{\widetilde{x}}) = \widetilde{x}$, $\text{ln}((x)\text{M}) = \text{ln}(\text{M}) \setminus \{x\}$, and $\text{ln}(\text{M}\,|\,\text{N}) = \text{ln}(\text{M}) \cup \text{ln}(\text{N})$. Networks $\text{M}\,|\,\text{N}$ are constrained to satisfy the property $\text{ln}(\text{M}) \cap \text{ln}(\text{N}) = \emptyset$.

The *structural congruence* $\equiv$ is the least congruence closed with respect to α-renaming, satisfying the abelian monoid laws for parallel (associativity, commutativity and $\mathbf{0}$ as identity), and the following axioms:

1. the scope laws:

$$(u)\mathbf{0} \equiv \mathbf{0}, \qquad (x)(z)\text{M} \equiv (z)(x)\text{M},$$
$$\text{M}\,|\,(x)\text{N} \equiv (x)(\text{M}\,|\,\text{N})\,,\quad \textit{if } x \notin \text{fn}(\text{M})$$
$$[\,(x)P\,]_{\widetilde{z}} \equiv (x)[\, P\,]_{\widetilde{z}x}\,,\quad \textit{if } x \notin \widetilde{z}$$

2. the lifting law:

$$[\, P\,]_{\widetilde{x}} \equiv [\, Q\,]_{\widetilde{x}}\,,\qquad \textit{if } P \equiv Q$$

The first three scope laws are standard. The last one is used to extrude a name outside a machine; the effect is that the extruded name is added to the set of the names on which the machine is the receptor. The lifting law lifts to machines the structural congruence defined on processes.

The *reduction relation* for machines is the least relation closed under $\equiv$, (x)-, and parallel composition, and satisfying the reductions:

(INTRA)	(TIME)	(DELIV)
$\dfrac{P \to Q}{[\, P\,]_{\widetilde{x}} \to [\, Q\,]_{\widetilde{x}}}$	$\dfrac{P \nrightarrow}{[\, P\,]_{\widetilde{x}} \to [\, \phi(P)\,]_{\widetilde{x}}}$	$\begin{array}{c}[\,\overline{x}\widetilde{v}\,|\,P\,]_{\widetilde{z}}\,|\,[\, Q\,]_{\widetilde{y}x} \\ \to [\, P\,]_{\widetilde{z}}\,|\,[\,\overline{x}\widetilde{v}\,|\,Q\,]_{\widetilde{y}x}\end{array}$

As a consequence of the closure under parallel composition, time progress asynchronously between machines. Namely, if $\text{M} \to \text{M}'$ then also $\text{M}\,|\,\text{N} \to \text{M}'\,|\,\text{N}$. In particular, the time of N does not elapse. Rule (INTRA) lifts the local reductions to the machine. Rule (TIME) reflects our approach for modeling the time. In particular, as local computations are urgent, this rule permits the elapsing of one time unit – the application of ϕ – only in the case when no internal computation is possible inside a machine. Rule (DELIV) delivers a message to the unique machine having x in the index. This rule does not consume time both in the sender and in the receiver machines. This does not mean that communication takes no time. Delays of deliveries follow from asynchrony between machines and nondeterminism of reductions due to (DELIV). Alternatively, one could extend the syntax of machines by adding messages in parallel with machines and replacing (DELIV) with two rules: one putting a message outside the sender machine, the other actually delivering the message to the receiver machine. The present solution has been preferred for simplicity.

It is worth to notice that, in the present model, a message may be either consumed in the same machine in which it has been produced (see rule (COM) in the reduction relation of processes) or delivered to another machine in the network (the unique responsible for accepting that message). This appears a bit counterintuitive: a machine that is not responsible to accept messages on a given name may actually consume messages that have been produced locally. In fact, in practice this scenario never occurs. If a machine defines a name x and exports it to other machines, then the machines receiving x may use it with output capability only. Since Webπ processes are unrestricted, the present reduction relation of machines results a conservative extension of the practical scenario.

6   Conclusions

We have studied Webπ, a process calculus extending the asynchronous π-calculus with a timed transaction construct. The main theoretical contribution of this paper is the investigation of the extensional semantics of Webπ, the timed bisimilarity, and of its labelled counterpart.

A number of issues have been overlooked. We retain that the following twos are particularly significant to judge the benefits of Webπ. First of all, Webπ has been motivated by the need of assessing the proposals of web programming languages. It will be foundational if it is possible to translate these proposals in Webπ, in particular the transactional protocols that are defined therein. The techniques developed in this paper will be necessary for comparing the translations. The next step is therefore the translation in Webπ of some emerging technology, such as BPEL.

The second issue has a theoretical flavour. The identity of $\sim_t$ and $\simeq_a$ has been only conjectured because we were not able to provide a direct proof. To measure the discriminating power of $\simeq_a$, we have introduced an operator that is able to perform several tests and emit a message in one step. This expedient appears useless when machines are used because it is possible to delegate a different location to perform the tests and emit the message (the time spent by a location for a computation has no effect on the time of other locations). While this remark does not help in solving our conjecture, it prompts the investigation of the extensional semantics of machines.

References

1. R. M. Amadio, I. Castellani, and S. Sangiorgi. On bisimulations for the asynchronous π-calculus. *Theoretical Computer Science*, 195(2):291–324, 1998.
2. T. Andrews and et.al. Business Process Execution Language for Web Services. Version 1.1. Specification, BEA Systems, IBM Corp., Microsoft Corp., SAP AG, Siebel Systems, 2003.
3. M. Berger. Basic theory of reduction congruence for two timed asynchronous π-calculi. In *CONCUR '04: Proceedings of the 15th International Conference on Concurrency Theory*, volume 3170 of *LNCS*, pages 115–130. Springer-Verlag, 2004.
4. M. Berger and K. Honda. The two-phase commitment protocol in an extended pi-calculus. In *EXPRESS '00: Proceedings of the 7th International Workshop on Expressiveness in Concurrency*, volume 39.1 of *ENTCS*. Elsevier Science Publishers, 2000.
5. L. Bocchi, C. Laneve, and G. Zavattaro. A calculus for long running transactions. In *FMOODS'03, Proceedings of the 6th IFIP International Conference on Formal Methods for Open Object-based Distributed Systems*, volume 2884 of *LNCS*, pages 124–138. Springer-Verlag, 2003.
6. R. Bruni, C. Laneve, and U. Montanari. Orchestrating transactions in join calculus. In *CONCUR 2002: Proceedings of the 13th International Conference on Concurrency Theory*, volume 2421 of *LNCS*, pages 321–337. Springer Verlag, 2002.
7. M. Butler and C. Ferreira. An operational semantics for StAC, a language for modelling long-running business transactions. In *COORDINATION'04, Proceedings of the 6th International Conference on Coordination Models and Languages*, volume 2949 of *LNCS*, pages 87–104. Springer-Verlag, 2004.
8. M. Butler, T. Hoare, and C. Ferreira. A trace semantics for long-running transactions. In Proceedings of 25 Years of CSP, London, 2004.
9. E. Christensen, F. Curbera, G. Meredith, and S. Weerawarana. Web Services Description Language (WSDL 1.1). W3C Note, 2001.
10. C. Fournet and G. Gonthier. A hierarchy of equivalences for asynchronous calculi. In *ICALP '98, Proceedings of the 25th International Colloquium on Automata, Languages, and Programming*, volume 1443 of *LNCS*, pages 844–855. Springer-Verlag, 1998.
11. K. Honda and M. Tokoro. On asynchronous communication semantics. In *Proceedings of Object-Based Concurrent Computing (ECOOP '91)*, volume 612 of *LNCS*, pages 21–52. Springer Verlag, 1992.
12. N. Kavantzas, G. Olsson, J. Mischkinsky, and M. Chapman. Web Services Choreography Description Languages. Oracle Corporation, 2003.
13. F. Leymann. Web Services Flow Language (wsfl 1.0). Technical report, IBM Software Group, 2001.
14. M. Little. Web services transactions: Past, present and future. Proceedings of the XML Conference and Exposition, Philadelphia, USA, 2003.
15. R. Milner, J. Parrow, and D. Walker. A calculus of mobile processes. *Information and Computation*, 100(1):1–77, 1992.
16. OASIS. Introduction to UDDI: Important features and functional concepts. Organization for the Advancement of Structured Information Standards, 2004.
17. S. Thatte. XLANG: Web services for business process design. Microsoft Corporation, 2001.

Bridging Language-Based and Process Calculi Security*

Riccardo Focardi[1], Sabina Rossi[1], and Andrei Sabelfeld[2]

[1] Dipartimento di Informatica, Università Ca' Foscari di Venezia,
30172 Venezia, Italy
{focardi, srossi}@dsi.unive.it
[2] Dept. of Computer Science, Chalmers University of Technology,
41296 Göteborg, Sweden
andrei@cs.chalmers.se

Abstract. Language-based and process calculi-based information security are well developed fields of computer security. Although these fields have much in common, it is somewhat surprising that the literature lacks a comprehensive account of a formal link between the two disciplines. This paper develops such a link between a language-based specification of security and a process-algebraic framework for security properties. Encoding imperative programs into a CCS-like process calculus, we show that timing-sensitive security for these programs exactly corresponds to the well understood process-algebraic security property of persistent bisimulation-based nondeducibility on compositions (P_BNDC). This rigorous connection opens up possibilities for cross-fertilization, leading to both flexible policies when specifying the security of heterogeneous systems and to a synergy of techniques for enforcing security specifications.

1 Introduction

As computing systems are becoming increasingly complex, security challenges become increasingly versatile. In the presence of such challenges, we believe that practical security solutions are unlikely to emerge from a single theoretical framework, but rather need to be based on a combination of different specialized approaches. The goal of this paper is to develop a flexible way of specifying the security of heterogeneous systems—using a combination of language-based definitions and process-algebraic ones. The intention is to be able to specify security partly by language-based security models (e.g., for parts of the system that are implemented by code with no communication) and partly by process-algebraic models (e.g., communication-intensive parts of the system). This combined approach empowers us with a synergy of techniques for enforcing security properties (e.g., combining security type systems with process equivalence checking) to analyze parts of the system separately and yet establish the security of the entire system.

Language-based information security [27] and process calculus-based information security [7, 25] are well developed fields of computer security. Although process calculi are programming languages, there are different motivations and traditions in addressing information security by the two communities. While the former is concerned with

---

* This work was supported by the EU-FET project MyThS (IST-2001-32617).

V. Sassone (Ed.): FOSSACS 2005, LNCS 3441, pp. 299–315, 2005.

preventing secret data from being leaked through the execution of programs, the latter deals with preventing secret events from being revealed through the execution of communicating processes. Although these fields have much in common (e.g., both rely on *noninterference* [12] as a baseline security policy stating that secrets do not interfere with the attacker-observable behavior of the system), it is somewhat surprising that the literature lacks a comprehensive account of a formal link between the two disciplines (which in particular means that it has not been established whether the interpretations of noninterference by the two disciplines are compatible).

This paper develops a rigorous link between a language-based specification of security for imperative programs and a process-algebraic framework of security properties. More specifically, we link two compositional security properties: a timing-sensitive security characterization for a simple imperative language and a persistent security characterization for a CCS-like process calculus. We achieve this connection through the following steps: (i) we uniform the semantics of the imperative language to the standard *Labelled Transition System* semantics of process calculi, by making read/write memory actions explicitly observable as labelled transitions; (ii) based on this semantics, we formalize low level observations in the imperative language in terms of a bisimulation relation; (iii) we encode the programming language into the process calculus, ensuring a lock-step semantic relation between the source and target languages; we prove that the new bisimulation notion for the imperative language is preserved by the encoding; (iv) this tight relation reveals some unexpected uniformities allowing us to precisely identify what the program security characterization corresponds to in the process-calculus world: it turns out to be the well understood property of persistent bisimulation-based nondeducibility on compositions (or P_BNDC).

Such a link opens up various possibilities for cross-fertilization, leading to flexible policies when specifying the security of complex systems and to a rich combination of techniques for enforcing security specifications. Finding exactly what property from the family of process-algebraic properties [7, 9] corresponds to the language-based timing-sensitive security sheds valuable light on the nature of the language-based property. As a direct benefit, the results of this paper enable us to use security checkers based on process-equivalence checking (such as CoSeC [6] and CoPS [23], with the latter one based precisely on P_BNDC) for certifying language-based security.

For clarity, this paper uses a simple sequential language. However, it is a distributed setting that will enable us to fully capitalize on the formal connection. Indeed, the security specifications for both the source (imperative) and target (process algebraic) languages are compositional [28, 9]. Because the source-language security specification is suitable for both multithreaded [28] and distributed [26, 21] settings, we are confident that the formal link established in this paper can be generalized to a distributed scenario, where different components can be analyzed with specialized techniques. For example, communication-intensive parts of the system (where conservative language-based security mechanisms for the source language such as type systems are too restrictive) can be analyzed at the level of the target language, gaining on the precision of the analysis.

The paper is organized as follows. Section 2 presents the source imperative language Imp and the target process-algebraic language VSPA. Section 3 develops an encoding of the source language into the target language and demonstrates a semantic relation between Imp's programs and their VSPA's translations. Section 4 establishes a formal connection between the security properties of the two languages. The paper closes by discussing related work in Section 5 and conclusions and future work in Section 6.

The proofs of the results presented in this paper are reported in [10].

2   The Source Language and Target Calculus

In this section, we present Imp, the source imperative language, and VSPA, the target process calculus, along with security definitions for the respective languages.

2.1   The Imp Programming Language

We consider a simple sequential programming language, Imp [30], described by the following grammar:

$$B, Exp ::= F(Id, \ldots, Id)$$
$$C ::= \text{stop} \mid \text{skip} \mid Id := Exp \mid C; C \mid \text{if } B \text{ then } C \text{ else } C \mid \text{while } B \text{ do } C$$

Let $C, D, \ldots$ range over commands (programs), $Id, Id_1, \ldots$ range over identifiers (variables), $B, B_1, \ldots, Exp, Exp_1, \ldots$ range over boolean and arithmetic expressions, respectively, $F, F_1, \ldots$ range over function symbols, and, finally, $v, v_1, \ldots$ range over the set of basic values Val. For simplicity, but without loss of generality, we assume that exactly one function symbol occurs in an expression.

A *configuration* is a pair $\langle C, s \rangle$ of a command C and a state (memory) s. A *state* s is a finite mapping from variables to values. The small-step semantics are given by transitions

$$\langle \text{skip}, s \rangle \overset{\text{tick}}{\to} \langle \text{stop}, s \rangle$$

$$\frac{\langle Exp, s \rangle \downarrow v}{\langle Id := Exp, s \rangle \overset{\text{tick}}{\to} \langle \text{stop}, [Id \mapsto v]s \rangle}$$

$$\frac{\langle C_1, s \rangle \overset{\text{tick}}{\to} \langle \text{stop}, s' \rangle}{\langle C_1; C_2, s \rangle \overset{\text{tick}}{\to} \langle C_2, s' \rangle} \qquad \frac{\langle C_1, s \rangle \overset{\text{tick}}{\to} \langle C_1', s' \rangle}{\langle C_1; C_2, s \rangle \overset{\text{tick}}{\to} \langle C_1'; C_2, s' \rangle}$$

$$\frac{\langle B, s \rangle \downarrow \text{True}}{\langle \text{if } B \text{ then } C_1 \text{ else } C_2, s \rangle \overset{\text{tick}}{\to} \langle C_1, s \rangle}$$

$$\frac{\langle B, s \rangle \downarrow \text{False}}{\langle \text{if } B \text{ then } C_1 \text{ else } C_2, s \rangle \overset{\text{tick}}{\to} \langle C_2, s \rangle}$$

$$\frac{\langle B, s \rangle \downarrow \text{True}}{\langle \text{while } B \text{ do } C, s \rangle \overset{\text{tick}}{\to} \langle C; \text{while } B \text{ do } C, s \rangle}$$

$$\frac{\langle B, s \rangle \downarrow \text{False}}{\langle \text{while } B \text{ do } C, s \rangle \overset{\text{tick}}{\to} \langle \text{stop}, s \rangle}$$

Fig. 1. Small-step semantics of Imp commands

between configurations, defined by standard transition rules (see Fig. 1). Arithmetic and boolean expressions are executed atomically by $\downarrow$ transitions. The $\overset{\text{tick}}{\rightarrow}$ transitions are deterministic. The general form of a deterministic transition is $\langle C, s \rangle \overset{\text{tick}}{\rightarrow} \langle C', s' \rangle$. Here, one step of computation starting with a command C in a state s gives a new command C' and a new state s'. There are no transitions from configurations that contain the terminal program stop. We write $[Id \mapsto v]s$ for the state obtained from s by setting the image of Id to v. For example, the assignment rule describes one step of computation that leads to termination with the state updated according to the value of the expression on the right-hand side of the assignment.

Security Specification. We assume that the set of variables is partitioned into *high* and *low* security classes corresponding to high and low confidentiality levels. Note that our results are not specific to this security structure (which is adopted for simplicity)—a generalization to an arbitrary security lattice is straightforward. Variables h and l will denote typical high and low variables respectively. Two states s and t are *low-equal* $s =_L t$ if the low components of s and t are the same.

Confidentiality is preserved by a computing system if low-level observations reveal nothing about high-level data. The notion of noninterference [12] is widely used for expressing such confidentiality policies. Intuitively, noninterference means that low-observable behavior is unchanged as high inputs are varied. The indistinguishability of behavior for the attacker can be represented naturally by the notion of *bisimulation* (e.g., [7, 28]). The following definition is recalled from [28]:

Definition 1. Strong low-bisimulation $\approx_L$ is the union of all symmetric relations R such that if $C\ R\ D$ then for all states s and t such that $s =_L t$ whenever $\langle C, s \rangle \overset{\text{tick}}{\rightarrow} \langle C', s' \rangle$ then there exist D' and t' such that $\langle D, t \rangle \overset{\text{tick}}{\rightarrow} \langle D', t' \rangle$, $s' =_L t'$, and $C'\ R\ D'$.

Intuitively, two programs C and D are strongly low-bisimilar if varying the high parts of memories at any point of computation does not introduce any difference between the low parts of the memories throughout the computation. Protecting variations at any point of computation results in a rather restrictive security condition. However, this restrictiveness is justified in a concurrent setting (which is the ultimate motivation of our work) when threads may introduce secrets into high memory at any computation step. Based on this notion of low-bisimulation, a definition of security is given in [28]:

Definition 2. A program C is secure if and only if $C \approx_L C$.

Examples. Because the underlying low-bisimulation is strong, or lock-step, it captures timing-sensitive security of programs. Below, we exemplify different kinds of information flow handled by the security definition:

$l := h$ This is an example of an *explicit flow*. To see that this program is insecure according to Definition 2, take some s and t that are the same except $s(h) = 0$ and $t(h) = 1$. Since $\langle l := h, s \rangle \overset{\text{tick}}{\rightarrow} \langle \text{stop}, [l \mapsto 0]s \rangle$ and $\langle l := h, t \rangle \overset{\text{tick}}{\rightarrow} \langle \text{stop}, [l \mapsto 1]t \rangle$ hold, the resulting memories are not low-equal. Because these are the only possible transitions for both configurations, we have $l := h \not\approx_L l := h$.

if $h > 0$ **then** $l := 1$ **else** $l := 0$ This exemplifies an *implicit flow* [4] through branching on a high condition. If the computation starts with low-equal memories s and t that are the same except $s(h) = 0$ and $t(h) = 1$, then, after one step of computation (the test of the condition), the memories are still low-equal. However, after another computation step they become different in l (0 or 1, depending on the initial value of h). Because these are the only possible transitions for configurations with both s and t, the program is not self-low-similar and thus is insecure.

while $h > 0$ **do** $h := h - 1$ Assuming the worst-case scenario, an attacker may observe the timing of program execution. The attacker may learn the value of h from the timing behavior of the program above. This is an instance of a *timing covert channel* [19]. The program is rightfully rejected by Definition 2. Indeed, take some s and t that are the same except $s(h) = 1$ and $t(h) = 0$. We have $\langle$while $h > 0$ do $h := h - 1, s\rangle \overset{\text{tick}}{\rightarrow} \langle h := h - 1;$ while $h > 0$ do $h := h - 1, s\rangle \overset{\text{tick}}{\rightarrow} \langle$while $h > 0$ do $h := h - 1, [h \mapsto 0]s\rangle \overset{\text{tick}}{\rightarrow} \langle$stop, $[h \mapsto 0]s\rangle$ but $\langle$while $h > 0$ do $h := h - 1, t\rangle \overset{\text{tick}}{\rightarrow} \langle$stop, $t\rangle \overset{\text{tick}}{\not\rightarrow}$ with no transition from the latter configuration to match the transitions of the previous sequence.

The examples above are insecure. Here is an instance of a secure program:

if $h = 1$ **then** $h := h + 1$ **else skip**   Indeed, neither the low part of the memory nor the timing behavior depends on the value of h. A suitable symmetric relation that makes this program low-bisimilar to itself is, e.g., the relation $\{($if $h = 1$ then $h := h + 1$ else skip, if $h = 1$ then $h := h + 1$ else skip$), (h := h + 1,$ skip$), ($skip$, h := h + 1), (h := h + 1, h := h + 1), ($skip, skip$), ($stop, stop$)\}$.

2.2   The VSPA Calculus

The *Value-passing Security Process Algebra* (VSPA, for short) is a variation of Milner's value-passing CCS [22], where the set of visible actions is partitioned into high-level actions and low-level ones in order to specify multilevel-security systems.

Let $E, E_1, E_2, \ldots$ range over *processes*, $x, x_1, x_2, \ldots$ range over *variables*, $c, c_1, c_2, \ldots$ range over *input channels*, and $\bar{c}, \bar{c}_1, \bar{c}_2, \ldots$ range over *output channels*. As for Imp, let $B, B_1, \ldots, Exp, Exp_1, \ldots$ range over boolean and arithmetic expressions, respectively, $F, F_1, \ldots$ range over function symbols, and, finally, $v, v_1, \ldots$ range over the set of basic values Val. (The set of basic values Val, and boolean/arithmetic expressions are the same as in Imp.) The set of visible actions is $\mathcal{L} = \{c(v) \mid v \in Val\} \cup \{\bar{c}(v) \mid v \in Val\}$ where $c(v)$ and $\bar{c}(v)$ represent the input and the output of value v over the channel c, respectively. The syntax of VSPA processes is defined as follows:

$$E ::= \mathbf{0} \mid c(x).E \mid \bar{c}(Exp).E \mid \tau.E \mid E_1 + E_2 \mid E_1|E_2 \mid E \setminus R \mid E[g] \mid$$
$$A(Exp_1, \ldots, Exp_n) \mid \textbf{if } B \textbf{ then } E_1 \textbf{ else } E_2$$
$$B, Exp ::= F(x_1, \ldots, x_n)$$

Each constant A is associated with a definition $A(x_1, \ldots, x_n) \overset{\text{def}}{=} E$, where $x_1, \ldots, x_n$ are distinct variables and E is a VSPA process whose only free variables are $x_1, \ldots, x_n$. R is a set of channels and g is a function relabeling channel names which preserves the

$$c(x).E \xrightarrow{c(v)} E[v/x] \qquad \overline{c}(v).E \xrightarrow{\overline{c}(v)} E \qquad \tau.E \xrightarrow{\tau} E$$

$$\frac{E_1 \xrightarrow{a} E_1'}{E_1 + E_2 \xrightarrow{a} E_1'} \qquad \frac{E_2 \xrightarrow{a} E_2'}{E_1 + E_2 \xrightarrow{a} E_2'}$$

$$\frac{E_1 \xrightarrow{a} E_1'}{E_1|E_2 \xrightarrow{a} E_1'|E_2} \qquad \frac{E_2 \xrightarrow{a} E_2'}{E_1|E_2 \xrightarrow{a} E_1|E_2'} \qquad \frac{E_1 \xrightarrow{c(v)} E_1' \quad E_2 \xrightarrow{\overline{c}(v)} E_2'}{E_1|E_2 \xrightarrow{\tau} E_1'|E_2'}$$

$$\frac{E \xrightarrow{a} E'}{E[g] \xrightarrow{g(a)} E'[g]} \qquad \frac{E \xrightarrow{a} E' \quad a \notin R}{E \setminus R \xrightarrow{a} E' \setminus R}$$

$$\frac{E[v_1/x_1, \ldots, v_n/x_n] \xrightarrow{a} E' \quad A(x_1, \ldots, x_n) \stackrel{def}{=} E}{A(v_1, \ldots, v_n) \xrightarrow{a} E'}$$

$$\frac{E_1 \xrightarrow{a} E_1'}{\textbf{if True then } E_1 \textbf{ else } E_2 \xrightarrow{a} E_1'} \qquad \frac{E_2 \xrightarrow{a} E_2'}{\textbf{if False then } E_1 \textbf{ else } E_2 \xrightarrow{a} E_2'}$$

Fig. 2. VSPA operational semantics

complementation operator $\bar{\cdot}$. Finally, the set of channels is partitioned into *high-level* channels H and *low-level* ones L. By an abuse of notation, we write $c(v), \overline{c}(v) \in H$ whenever $c, \overline{c} \in H$, and similarly for L.

Intuitively, **0** is the empty process; $c(x).E$ is a process that reads a value $v \in Val$ from channel c assigning it to variable x; $\overline{c}(Exp).E$ is a process that evaluates expression Exp and sends the resulting value as output over c; $E_1 + E_2$ represents the nondeterministic choice between the two processes E_1 and E_2; $E_1|E_2$ is the parallel composition of E_1 and E_2, where executions are interleaved, possibly synchronized on complementary input/output actions, producing an internal action τ; $E \setminus R$ is a process E prevented from using channels in R; $E[g]$ is the process E whose channels are renamed *via* the relabeling function g; $A(Exp_1, ..., Exp_n)$ behaves like the respective definition where the variables $x_1, \cdots, x_n$ are substituted with the results of expressions $Exp_1, \cdots, Exp_n$; finally, **if** B **then** E_1 **else** E_2 behaves as E_1 if B evaluates to True and as E_2, otherwise. We implicitly equate processes whose expressions are substituted by the corresponding values, e.g., $\overline{c}(F(v_1, \ldots v_n)).E$ is the same as $\overline{c}(v).E$ if $F(v_1, \ldots v_n) = v$. This corresponds to the $\downarrow$ expression evaluation of Imp. The operational semantics of VSPA is given in Fig. 2. We denote by $\mathcal{E}$ the set of all VSPA processes and by $\mathcal{E}_H$ the set of all high-level processes, i.e., using only channels in H.

The *weak bisimulation* relation [22] equates two processes if they are able to mutually simulate each other step by step. Weak bisimulation does not care about internal τ actions. We write $E \stackrel{a}{\Longrightarrow} E'$ if $E(\xrightarrow{\tau})^* \xrightarrow{a} (\xrightarrow{\tau})^* E'$. Moreover, we let $E \stackrel{\hat{a}}{\Longrightarrow} E'$ stand for $E \stackrel{a}{\Longrightarrow} E'$ in case $a \neq \tau$, and for $E(\xrightarrow{\tau})^* E'$ in case $a = \tau$.

Definition 3 (Weak bisimulation). *A symmetric binary relation $R \subseteq \mathcal{E} \times \mathcal{E}$ over processes is a* weak bisimulation *if whenever $(E, F) \in R$ and $E \stackrel{a}{\rightarrow} E'$, then there exists F' such that $F \stackrel{\hat{a}}{\Longrightarrow} F'$ and $(E', F') \in R$.*

Two processes $E, F \in \mathcal{E}$ are *weakly bisimilar*, denoted by $E \approx F$, if there exists a weak bisimulation R containing the pair (E, F). The relation $\approx$ is the largest weak bisimulation and it is an equivalence relation [22].

Persistent BNDC Security. In [9] we give a notion of security for VSPA processes called *Persistent BNDC*, where *BNDC* stands for *Bisimulation-based Nondeducibility on Compositions*. *BNDC* [5] is a generalization to concurrent processes of noninterference [12], consisting of checking a process E against all high-level processes Π.

Definition 4 (BNDC). *Let* $E \in \mathcal{E}$. $E \in BNDC$ *iff* $\forall\, \Pi \in \mathcal{E}_H$, $E \setminus H \approx (E|\Pi) \setminus H$.

Intuitively, BNDC requires that high-level processes Π have no effect at all on the (low-level) execution of E.

To introduce *Persistent BNDC (P_BNDC)* we define a new observation equivalence where high-level actions *may* be ignored, i.e., they may be matched by zero or more τ actions. An action a is high if a is either an input $c(v)$ or an output $\bar{c}(v)$, over a high-level channel $c \in H$. Otherwise, a is low. We write $\tilde{a}$ to denote $\hat{a}$ if a is low, and a or $\hat{\tau}$ if a is high. We now define weak bisimulation up to high, by just using $\tilde{a}$ in place of $\hat{a}$, thus allowing high-level actions to be simulated by (possibly empty) sequences of τ's.

Definition 5 (Weak bisimulation up to high). *A symmetric binary relation* $R \subseteq \mathcal{E} \times \mathcal{E}$ *over processes is a* weak bisimulation up to high *if whenever* $(E, F) \in R$ *and* $E \xrightarrow{a} E'$, *then there exists* F' *such that* $F \xRightarrow{\tilde{a}} F'$ *and* $(E', F') \in R$.

We say that two processes E, F are *weakly bisimilar up to high*, written $E \approx_{\setminus H} F$, if $(E, F) \in R$ for some weak bisimulation up to high R.

Definition 6 (P_BNDC). *Let* $E \in \mathcal{E}$. $E \in P\_BNDC$ *iff* $E \setminus H \approx_{\setminus H} E$.

Intuitively, *P_BNDC* requires that forbidding any high-level activity (by restriction) is equivalent to ignoring it. For example, process $E \stackrel{\text{def}}{=} h.\bar{l} + \bar{l}$ is *P_BNDC* since the high level input h is simulated, in $E \setminus H$, by not moving. Indeed, the high level activity is not visible to the low level users who can only observe the low level output $\bar{l}$. Notice that this secure process allows some low level actions to follow high actions.

It has been proved [9] that *P_BNDC* corresponds to requiring *BNDC* over all the possible reachable states. This is why we call it *Persistent BNDC*.

Proposition 1. $E \in P\_BNDC$ *iff* $\forall\, E'$ *reachable from* E, $E' \in BNDC$.

Note that P_BNDC is similarly spirited to Imp's security definition. In particular, the Π process in $BNDC$ corresponds to the possibility for arbitrary changes in the high part of state over the computation. Further, persistence in P_BNDC corresponds to requiring strong low-bisimulation on reachable Imp commands. There are also obvious differences, highlighting the specifics of the application domains of the two security specifications: P_BNDC is concerned with protecting the occurrence of high events whereas program security protects high memories.

P_BNDC satisfies useful compositionality properties and is much easier to check than *BNDC*, since no quantification over all possible high-level processes is required.

$$\frac{s(Id) = v}{\langle C, s \rangle \xrightarrow{\overline{\texttt{eget}}_{Id}(v)} \langle C, s \rangle} \qquad \langle C, s \rangle \xrightarrow{\texttt{eput}_{Id}(v)} \langle C, [Id \mapsto v]s \rangle \qquad \frac{\langle C, s \rangle \xrightarrow{a} \langle C', s' \rangle \quad a \notin R}{\langle C, s \rangle \setminus R \xrightarrow{a} \langle C', s' \rangle \setminus R}$$

Fig. 3. Semantic rules for environment

Example. We give a very simple example of an insecure process. In particular, we show an indirect flow due to the possibility for a high-level user to lock and unlock a process:

$$E \stackrel{\text{def}}{=} \texttt{hlock.hunlock.}\overline{\texttt{l}} + \overline{\texttt{l}}$$

where `hlock` and `hunlock` are high-level channels and `l` is a low-level one. (To simplify we are not even sending values over channels.) At a first glance, process E seems to be secure as it always performs $\overline{\texttt{l}}$ before terminating, thus low-level users should deduce nothing of what is done at the high level. However, a high-level user might lock the process through `hlock` and never unlock it, thus leading to an unexpected behavior since $\overline{\texttt{l}}$ would be locked too. This ability for a high-level user to synchronize with a low-level one constitutes an indirect information flow and is detected by P_BNDC since $E \xrightarrow{\texttt{hlock}} \texttt{hunlock.}\overline{\texttt{l}}$ cannot be simulated by $E \setminus H$. In fact, $E \setminus H$ can execute neither high-level actions nor τ ones, thus the only possibility it has to simulate `hlock` is not moving. However, this simulation is fine as long as the reached states are bisimilar up to high, i.e., $\texttt{hunlock.}\overline{\texttt{l}} \approx_{\setminus H} E \setminus H$, but this is not true.

3   Mapping Imp into VSPA

With the source and target languages in place, this section develops an encoding of the former into the latter. The encoding is done in two steps: enriching Imp's semantics with process calculi-style environment interaction rules and encoding the extended version of Imp into VSPA. A lock-step relation of Imp's executions with their VSPA's translations guarantees that the encoding is semantically adequate.

3.1   Extending Imp Semantics

The original definition of strong low-bisimulation (Definition 1) implicitly takes into account an environment that is capable of both reading from and writing to the state at any point of computation. Alternatively, and rather naturally, we can represent this environment explicitly, by the semantic rules for reading and modifying the state, depicted in Fig. 3. Reading the value v of a variable Id is observable by an action $\overline{\texttt{eget}}_{Id}(v)$; writing the value v to Id is observable by an action $\texttt{eput}_{Id}(v)$. (We adopt the process calculi convention of using $\overline{}$ to denote output actions.)

Assume $a \in \{\texttt{tick}, \overline{\texttt{eget}}(\cdot), \texttt{eput}(\cdot)\}$. Action a is *high* ($a \in H$) if for some high variable Id we have either $a = \overline{\texttt{eget}}_{Id}(\cdot)$ or $a = \texttt{eput}_{Id}(\cdot)$. Otherwise, a is *low* ($a \in L$). High and low actions represent high and low environments, respectively. Similarly to VSPA's restriction, we define a restriction on actions in the semantics for

Imp, also shown in Fig. 3. For a set of actions R, an R-restricted configuration $\langle C, s \rangle \setminus R$ behaves as $\langle C, s \rangle$ except that its communication on actions from R is prohibited. The restriction is helpful for relating the extended semantics to Imp's original semantics: configuration $\langle C, s \rangle \setminus \{\overline{\texttt{eget}}_{Id}(v), \texttt{eput}_{Id}(v) \mid Id \text{ is a variable and } v \in Val\}$ behaves under the extended semantics exactly as $\langle C, s \rangle$ under the original semantics.

These extended semantics of Imp are useful for different reasons: (i) They make read/write actions on the state explicitly observable as labeled transitions in the style of *Labeled Transition System* semantics for process calculi. This helps us proving a semantic correspondence in Section 3.2. (ii) Further, the extended semantics allow us to characterize the security of Imp programs using a notion of bisimulation up to high, similar to the one defined for VSPA. As a matter of fact, in Section 4, we show how security of Imp programs can be equivalently expressed in the style of *P_BNDC*, facilitating the proof that the security of Imp programs is the same as *P_BNDC* security of their translations into VSPA.

3.2   Translation

We translate Imp into VSPA following the translation described by Milner in [22], with the following important modifications: (i) We make explicit the fact that the external (possibly hostile) environment can manipulate the shared memory but cannot directly interact with a program. This is achieved by equipping registers, i.e., processes implementing Imp variables, with read/write channels accessible by the environment. All the other channels are "internalized" through restriction operators. (ii) We use a `lock` to guarantee the atomicity of expression evaluations. In fact, Imp expressions are evaluated in one atomic step. Since expression evaluation is translated into a process which sequentially accesses registers in order to read the actual variable values, to regain atomicity we need to guarantee that variables are not modified during this reading phase.

The language we want to translate contains program variables, to which values may be assigned, and the meaning of a program variable Id is a "storage location". We therefore begin by defining a storage register holding a value v as follows:

$$Reg(v) \stackrel{\text{def}}{=} \texttt{put}x.Reg(x) + \overline{\texttt{get}}v.Reg(v)$$
$$+\overline{\texttt{lock}}.(\texttt{eput}x.\overline{\texttt{unlock}}.Reg(x) + \overline{\texttt{unlock}}.Reg(v))$$
$$+\overline{\texttt{lock}}.(\overline{\texttt{eget}}v.\overline{\texttt{unlock}}.Reg(v) + \overline{\texttt{unlock}}.Reg(v))$$

(We shall often write $\texttt{put}(x)$ as $\texttt{put}x$ etc.) Thus, via $\overline{\texttt{get}}$ the stored value v may be read from the register, and via $\texttt{put}$ a new value x may be written to the register. Actions $\overline{\texttt{eget}}$ and $\texttt{eput}$ are intended to model the interactions of an external observer with the register. Before and after such actions, $\overline{\texttt{lock}}$ and $\overline{\texttt{unlock}}$ are required to be executed in order to guarantee mutual exclusion on the memory between expression evaluations and the environment. This implements the atomic expression evaluation of Imp. We also have an (abstract) time-out mechanism, that nondeterministically unlocks the registers. This is necessary to avoid blocking the program by the environment via refusing to accept $\overline{\texttt{eget}}$ or to execute $\texttt{eput}$ after the lock has been grabbed. As a matter of fact, we want the environment to interact with the registers without interfering in any way with the program execution. The (global) lock is implemented by the process:

$$Lock \overset{\text{def}}{=} \texttt{lock.unlock}.Lock$$

For each program variable Id, we introduce a register $Reg_{Id}(y) \overset{\text{def}}{=} Reg(y)[g_{Id}]$, where g_{Id} is the relabeling function $\{\texttt{put}_{Id}/\texttt{put}, \texttt{get}_{Id}/\texttt{get}, \texttt{eput}_{Id}/\texttt{eput}, \texttt{eget}_{Id}/\texttt{eget}\}$.

This representation of registers—or program variables—as processes is fundamental to our translation; it indicates that resources like variables, as well as the programs which use them, can be thought of as processes, so that our calculus can get away with the single notion of process to represent different kinds of entity.

There is no basic notion of sequential composition in our calculus, but we can define it. To do this, we assume that processes may indicate their termination by a special channel $\overline{\texttt{done}}$. We say that a process is *well-terminating* if it cannot do any further move after performing $\overline{\texttt{done}}$; as we will see, the processes which arise from translating Imp commands are all well-terminating, since they terminate with $\overline{\texttt{done}}.\mathbf{0}$ (written $Done$) instead of just $\mathbf{0}$.

The combinator $Before$ for sequential composition is as follows:

$$P\ Before\ Q \overset{\text{def}}{=} (P[b/\texttt{done}] | b.Q) \setminus \{b\}$$

where b is a new name, so that no conflict arises with the $\texttt{done}$ action performed by Q. It is easy to see that $Before$ preserves well-termination, i.e., if P and Q are well-terminating then so is $P\ Before\ Q$.

An expression of the language will "terminate" by yielding up its results via the special channel $\overline{\texttt{res}}$, not used by processes. If P represents such an expression, then we may wish another process Q to refer to the result by using the value variable x. To this end, we define another combinator, $Into$:

$$P\ Into(x)\ Q(x) \overset{\text{def}}{=} (P|\texttt{res}(x).Q(x)) \setminus \{\texttt{res}\}$$

$Q(x)$ is parametric on x and $Into$ binds this variable to the result of the expression P. Notice that we do not need to relabel $\texttt{res}$ to a new channel, as we did with the special channel $\texttt{done}$. Indeed, $Q(x)$ is a process and not an expression, thus it does not use channel $\texttt{res}$ to communicate with sibling processes and no conflict is ever possible. Note that $Q(x)$ might use $\texttt{res}$ into a nested $Into$ combinator. In this case, however, $\texttt{res}$ would be inside the scope of a restriction thus not be visible at this external $Into$ level.

The translation function $\mathcal{T}$ of Imp commands into VSPA processes is given in Fig. 4. Each expression $F(Id_1, \ldots Id_n)$ is translated into a process which collects the values of $Id_1, \ldots Id_n$ and returns $F(x_1, \ldots, x_n)$ over channel $\texttt{res}$. A state s associating variables $Id_1, \ldots, Id_m$ to values $s(Id_1), \ldots, s(Id_m)$, respectively, is translated into the parallel composition of the relative registers. The translation of commands is straightforward. Note that before and after each expression evaluation we lock and release the global lock so that the environment cannot interact with the memory while expressions are evaluated. This achieves atomic expression evaluations as in Imp. Configurations $\langle C, s \rangle$ are translated as the parallel composition of the global $Lock$ and the translations of C and s. $ACC_s = \{\overline{\texttt{put}_{Id_1}}, \texttt{get}_{Id_1}, \ldots, \overline{\texttt{put}_{Id_m}}, \texttt{get}_{Id_m}, \texttt{lock}, \texttt{unlock}\}$ is the set of all channels used by commands to access registers, plus the lock commands. Thus, the restriction over $ACC_s \cup \{\texttt{done}\}$ aims both at internalizing all the communications

$$T[\![F(Id_1, \ldots Id_n)]\!] = \mathtt{get}_{Id_1} x_1 . \cdots . \mathtt{get}_{Id_n} x_n . \overline{\mathtt{res}}(F(x_1, \ldots, x_n)).\mathbf{0}$$
$$T[\![s]\!] = Reg_{Id_1}(s(Id_1)) | \ldots | Reg_{Id_m}(s(Id_m))$$
$$T[\![\mathsf{stop}]\!] = \mathbf{0}$$
$$T[\![\mathsf{skip}]\!] = \overline{\mathtt{lock}}.\mathtt{tick}.\overline{\mathtt{unlock}}.Done$$
$$T[\![Id := Exp]\!] = \overline{\mathtt{lock}}.T[\![Exp]\!] \ Into(x) \ (\overline{\mathtt{put}}_{Id} x.\mathtt{tick}.\overline{\mathtt{unlock}}.Done)$$
$$T[\![C_1; C_2]\!] = T[\![C_1]\!] \ Before \ T[\![C_2]\!]$$
$$T[\![\mathsf{if} \ B \ \mathsf{then} \ C_1 \ \mathsf{else} \ C_2]\!] = \overline{\mathtt{lock}}.T[\![B]\!] \ Into(x) \ (\mathsf{if} \ x \ \mathsf{then} \ \mathtt{tick}.\overline{\mathtt{unlock}}.T[\![C_1]\!]$$
$$\mathsf{else} \ \mathtt{tick}.\overline{\mathtt{unlock}}.T[\![C_2]\!])$$
$$T[\![\mathsf{while} \ B \ \mathsf{do} \ C]\!] = Z \quad \mathsf{where} \ Z \overset{\mathrm{def}}{=} \overline{\mathtt{lock}}.T[\![B]\!] \ Into(x) \ (\mathsf{if} \ x \ \mathsf{then} \ \mathtt{tick}.$$
$$\overline{\mathtt{unlock}}.T[\![C]\!] \ Before \ Z \ \mathsf{else} \ \mathtt{tick}.\overline{\mathtt{unlock}}.Done)$$
$$T[\![\langle C, s \rangle]\!] = (T[\![s]\!] \mid T[\![C]\!] \mid Lock) \setminus ACC_s \cup \{\mathtt{done}\}$$
$$T[\![\langle C, s \rangle \setminus R]\!] = T[\![\langle C, s \rangle]\!] \setminus R$$

Fig. 4. Translation of commands

between commands and registers and at removing the last done action. The environment channels $\mathtt{eput}_{Id}$ and $\mathtt{eget}_{Id}$ are not restricted and, together with $\mathtt{tick}$, they are the only observable actions of $T[\![\langle C, s \rangle]\!]$: $\mathtt{eput}_{Id}$ and $\mathtt{eget}_{Id}$ are high if the corresponding Imp variable Id is high; all the other observable actions, including $\mathtt{tick}$, are low (the security level of unobservable actions is irrelevant for the security definition).

Examples. Consider the program $l := h$ where h is a high variable and l is a low one. These variables are represented by processes $Reg_h(s(h))$ and $Reg_l(s(l))$ for a state s.

$$T[\![l := h]\!] = \overline{\mathtt{lock}}.T[\![h]\!] \ Into(x) \ (\overline{\mathtt{put}}_l x.\mathtt{tick}.\overline{\mathtt{unlock}}.Done)$$
$$= (\overline{\mathtt{lock}}.\mathtt{get}_h x.\overline{\mathtt{res}} x.\mathbf{0} \mid \mathtt{res}(x).(\overline{\mathtt{put}}_l x.\mathtt{tick}.\overline{\mathtt{unlock}}.\overline{\mathtt{done}}.\mathbf{0})) \setminus \{\mathtt{res}\}$$

(Notice that expression h can be seen as $ID(h)$ where ID is the identity function over Val.) The execution of the translation in a state s is as follows where $s' = [l \mapsto s(h)]s$:

$$T[\![\langle l := h, s \rangle]\!] = (T[\![s]\!] \mid T[\![l := h]\!] \mid Lock) \setminus ACC_s \cup \{\mathtt{done}\}$$
$$= (T[\![s]\!] \mid (\overline{\mathtt{lock}}.\mathtt{get}_h x.\overline{\mathtt{res}} x.\mathbf{0} \mid \mathtt{res}(x).(\overline{\mathtt{put}}_l x.\mathtt{tick}.\overline{\mathtt{unlock}}.\overline{\mathtt{done}}.\mathbf{0})) \setminus \{\mathtt{res}\}$$
$$\mid Lock) \setminus ACC_s \cup \{\mathtt{done}\} \qquad \qquad \qquad \text{(by definition of } T[\![l := h]\!])$$
$$\overset{\tau}{\to} (T[\![s]\!] \mid (\mathtt{get}_h x.\overline{\mathtt{res}} x.\mathbf{0} \mid \mathtt{res}(x).(\overline{\mathtt{put}}_l x.\mathtt{tick}.\overline{\mathtt{unlock}}.\overline{\mathtt{done}}.\mathbf{0})) \setminus \{\mathtt{res}\}$$
$$\mid \mathtt{unlock}.Lock) \setminus ACC_s \cup \{\mathtt{done}\} \qquad \qquad \text{(by synchronization on } \mathtt{lock})$$
$$\overset{\tau}{\to} (T[\![s]\!] \mid (\overline{\mathtt{res}} s(h).\mathbf{0} \mid \mathtt{res}(x).(\overline{\mathtt{put}}_l x.\mathtt{tick}.\overline{\mathtt{unlock}}.\overline{\mathtt{done}}.\mathbf{0})) \setminus \{\mathtt{res}\}$$
$$\mid \mathtt{unlock}.Lock) \setminus ACC_s \cup \{\mathtt{done}\} \qquad \text{(fetching the value } s(h) \text{ of } h \text{ from } Reg_h)$$
$$\overset{\tau}{\to} (T[\![s]\!] \mid (\mathbf{0} \mid (\overline{\mathtt{put}}_l s(h).\mathtt{tick}.\overline{\mathtt{unlock}}.\overline{\mathtt{done}}.\mathbf{0})) \setminus \{\mathtt{res}\}$$
$$\mid \mathtt{unlock}.Lock) \setminus ACC_s \cup \{\mathtt{done}\} \qquad \qquad \text{(passing } s(h) \text{ on } res)$$
$$\overset{\tau}{\to} (T[\![s']\!] \mid (\mathbf{0} \mid (\mathtt{tick}.\overline{\mathtt{unlock}}.\overline{\mathtt{done}}.\mathbf{0})) \setminus \{\mathtt{res}\}$$
$$\mid \mathtt{unlock}.Lock) \setminus ACC_{s'} \cup \{\mathtt{done}\} \qquad \text{(updating } Reg_l \text{ with } s(h); \text{ new state is } s')$$
$$\overset{\mathtt{tick}}{\to} (T[\![s']\!] \mid (\mathbf{0} \mid \overline{\mathtt{unlock}}.\overline{\mathtt{done}}.\mathbf{0})) \setminus \{\mathtt{res}\}$$
$$\mid \mathtt{unlock}.Lock) \setminus ACC_{s'} \cup \{\mathtt{done}\} \qquad \qquad \text{(performing } \mathtt{tick})$$

$$\xrightarrow{\tau}(\mathcal{T}[\![s']\!] \mid (0 \mid \overline{\text{done}}.0)) \setminus \{\text{res}\} \mid Lock) \setminus ACC_{s'} \cup \{\text{done}\} \qquad \text{(unlocking)}$$

$$\approx (\mathcal{T}[\![s']\!] \mid 0 \mid Lock) \setminus ACC_{s'} \cup \{\text{done}\} \qquad \text{(bisimilarity)}$$

$$= \mathcal{T}[\![\langle \text{stop}, s' \rangle]\!] \qquad \text{(definition of translation)}$$

We have demonstrated that $\mathcal{T}[\![\langle l := h, s \rangle]\!] \overset{\text{tick}}{\Longrightarrow} P$ for P such that $P \approx \mathcal{T}[\![\langle \text{stop}, s' \rangle]\!]$.
As another example, the program if $h > 0$ then $l := 1$ else $l := 0$ is translated into:

$\mathcal{T}[\![\text{if } h > 0 \text{ then } l := 1 \text{ else } l := 0]\!]$

$= \overline{\text{lock}}.\mathcal{T}[\![h > 0]\!] \, Into(x)$

$\quad (\text{if } x \text{ then } \text{tick}.\overline{\text{unlock}}.\mathcal{T}[\![l := 1]\!] \text{ else } \text{tick}.\overline{\text{unlock}}.\mathcal{T}[\![l := 0]\!])$

$= (\overline{\text{lock}}.\text{get}_h x.\overline{\text{res}}(x > 0).0 \mid \text{res}(x).$

$\quad (\text{if } x \text{ then } \text{tick}.\overline{\text{unlock}}.\mathcal{T}[\![l := 1]\!] \text{ else } \text{tick}.\overline{\text{unlock}}.\mathcal{T}[\![l := 0]\!])) \setminus \{\text{res}\}$

$= (\overline{\text{lock}}.\text{get}_h x.\overline{\text{res}}(x > 0).0 \mid \text{res}(x).$

$\quad (\text{if } x \text{ then } \text{tick}.\overline{\text{unlock}}.$

$\quad\quad (\overline{\text{lock}.\text{res}}1.0 \mid \text{res}(x).(\overline{\text{put}}_l x.\text{tick}.\overline{\text{unlock}.\text{done}}.0)) \setminus \{\text{res}\}$

$\quad \text{else } \text{tick}.\overline{\text{unlock}}.$

$\quad\quad (\overline{\text{lock}.\text{res}}0.0 \mid \text{res}(x).(\overline{\text{put}}_l x.\text{tick}.\overline{\text{unlock}.\text{done}}.0)) \setminus \{\text{res}\})) \setminus \{\text{res}\}$

Semantic Correspondence. The propositions below state the semantic correspondence between any R-restricted configuration $\langle C, s \rangle \setminus R$ and its translation $\mathcal{T}[\![\langle C, s \rangle \setminus R]\!]$. Let $Env = \{\overline{\text{eget}}.(\cdot), \text{eput}.(\cdot)\}$ denote the set of all the possible environment actions.

Proposition 2. *Given an R-restricted configuration $cfg = \langle C, s \rangle \setminus R$, with $R \subseteq Env$, if $cfg \overset{a}{\rightarrow} cfg'$ then there exists a process P' such that $\mathcal{T}[\![cfg]\!] \overset{\hat{a}}{\Longrightarrow} P'$ and $P' \approx \mathcal{T}[\![cfg']\!]$. Moreover, when $a = \text{tick}$ we have that $\mathcal{T}[\![cfg]\!] \overset{\hat{\tau}}{\Longrightarrow} \tilde{P} \overset{\text{tick}}{\longrightarrow} P'$ and $\tilde{P} \approx \text{tick}.\mathcal{T}[\![cfg']\!]$.*

Intuitively, every (possibly restricted) Imp configuration move is coherently simulated by its VSPA translation, in a way that the reached process is weakly bisimilar to the translation of the reached configuration. Moreover, for tick moves, the translation $\mathcal{T}[\![cfg]\!]$ always reaches a state equivalent to $\text{tick}.\mathcal{T}[\![cfg']\!]$ before actually performing the tick. Intuitively, this is due to the fact that the lock is released only after tick is performed. Notice that if $R = \emptyset$ there is no restriction at all.

Next proposition is about the other way around: each process which is weakly bisimilar to the translation of a (possibly restricted) Imp configuration cfg always moves to processes weakly bisimilar to either $\mathcal{T}[\![cfg']\!]$ or $\text{tick}.\mathcal{T}[\![cfg'']\!]$, where cfg' and cfg'' are reached from cfg by performing the expected corresponding actions. As for previous proposition, $\text{tick}.\mathcal{T}[\![cfg'']\!]$ represents an intermediate state reached before performing the actual tick action.

Proposition 3. *Given an R-restricted configuration $cfg = \langle C, s \rangle \setminus R$, with $R \subseteq Env$, and a process P*

- *if $P \approx \mathcal{T}[\![cfg]\!]$ and $P \overset{\tau}{\rightarrow} P'$ then either $P' \approx P$ or $P' \approx \text{tick}.\mathcal{T}[\![cfg']\!]$ and $cfg \overset{\text{tick}}{\rightarrow} cfg'$;*
- *if $P \approx \mathcal{T}[\![cfg]\!]$ and $P \overset{a}{\rightarrow} P'$ with $a \neq \tau, \text{tick}$, then either $P' \approx \mathcal{T}[\![cfg']\!]$ and $cfg \overset{a}{\rightarrow} cfg'$ or $P' \approx \text{tick}.\mathcal{T}[\![cfg'']\!]$ and $cfg \overset{a}{\rightarrow} cfg' \overset{\text{tick}}{\rightarrow} cfg''$.*

4   Security Correspondence

We study the relationship between the security of Imp programs and that of VSPA processes. First, we give a notion of weak bisimulation up to high in the Imp setting, which allows us to characterize the security of Imp programs in a *P_BNDC* style. Then, we show that this new characterization of Imp program security exactly corresponds to requiring *P_BNDC* of VSPA program translations. More specifically, we prove that a program C is secure if and only if its translation $T[\![\langle C, s\rangle]\!]$ is *P_BNDC* for all states s.

P_BNDC-Like Security Characterization for Imp. In order to define weak bisimula-tion up to high, similarly to what we have done for VSPA, we define the operation $\tilde{a}$ to be a in case a is low, and a or null (which means no action) in case a is high.

Definition 7. *A symmetric binary relation R on (possibly restricted) configurations is a bisimulation up to high if whenever cfg_1 R cfg_2 and $cfg_1 \xrightarrow{a} cfg_1'$, there exists cfg_2' such that $cfg_2 \xrightarrow{\tilde{a}} cfg_2'$ and cfg_1' R cfg_2'.*

We write $\approx_{\backslash H}$ for the union of all bisimulations up to high. This definition brings us close to the nature of the process-algebraic security specification from Section 2.2. Using bisimulation up to high and restriction we can faithfully represent the original definition of strong low-bisimulation. The following proposition states the correspondence between strong low-bisimulation (defined on the `tick` actions of the original semantics) and bisimulation up to high (defined on the extended semantics) with restriction:

Proposition 4. $C \approx_L D$ *iff* $\langle C, s\rangle \approx_{\backslash H} \langle D, s\rangle \setminus H$ *and* $\langle C, s\rangle \setminus H \approx_{\backslash H} \langle D, s\rangle$, $\forall s$.

As a direct consequence, the security of Imp can be expressed in a "*P_BNDC* style":

Corollary 1. *A program C is secure iff* $\langle C, s\rangle \approx_{\backslash H} \langle C, s\rangle \setminus H$ *for all s.*

Program Security is P_BNDC. The following theorem shows that weak bisimulation up to high is preserved in the translation from Imp to VSPA.

Theorem 1. *Let $cfg_1 = \langle C, s\rangle \setminus R$ and $cfg_2 = \langle D, t\rangle \setminus R'$, with $R, R' \subseteq H$, be two configurations (possibly) restricted over high level actions. It holds that $cfg_1 \approx_{\backslash H} cfg_2$ iff $T[\![cfg_1]\!] \approx_{\backslash H} T[\![cfg_2]\!]$.*

This theorem has the flavor of a full-abstraction result (cf. [1]) for the indistinguishability relation $\approx_{\backslash H}$. As a corollary of the theorem, we receive a direct link between program security and *P_BNDC* security:

Corollary 2. *A program C is secure iff its translation $T[\![\langle C, s\rangle]\!]$ is P_BNDC $\forall s$.*

Examples. Recall from Section 2.1 that the program $l := h$ is rejected by the security definition for Imp. Recall from Section 3.2 that

$$T[\![l := h]\!] = (\overline{\text{lock}}.\text{get}_h x.\overline{\text{res}}x.0 \mid \text{res}(x).(\overline{\text{put}}_l x.\text{tick}.\overline{\text{unlock}}.\overline{\text{done}}.0)) \setminus \{\text{res}\}$$

To see that this translation is rejected by *P_BNDC*, take a state s that, for example, maps all its variables to 0. We demonstrate that $T[\![\langle l := h, s\rangle]\!] \setminus H \not\approx_{\backslash H} T[\![\langle l := h, s\rangle]\!]$.

Varying the high variable from 0 to 1 on the right-hand side can be done by the transition $T[\![\langle l := h, s\rangle]\!] \xrightarrow{\text{eput}_h(1)} F$ for some F. If the translation were secure then this transition would have to be simulated up to H by $T[\![\langle l := h, s\rangle]\!] \setminus H$. Such a transition would have to be a $\hat{\tau}$ transition because $\text{eput}_h(1)$ is a high transition, but $T[\![\langle l := h, s\rangle]\!] \setminus H$ is restricted from high actions. Therefore, $T[\![\langle l := h, s\rangle]\!] \setminus H$ would reduce to some process E, whose register for h remains 0.

By the definition of weak bisimulation up to H, we would have $E \setminus H \approx_{\setminus H} F$. Let subsequent actions correspond to traversing the two processes passing $\overline{\text{put}}_l(0)$ and $\overline{\text{put}}_l(1)$, respectively, and reaching $\overline{\text{unlock}}$. Note that actions on internal channels $\text{lock}, \text{get}_h, \text{res}, \text{put}_l$ are hidden from the environment. However, as an effect of the latter action, the register for l will store different values. Even though the tick actions can still be simulated, this breaks bisimulation because the externally visible action $\text{get}_l(0)$ by the successor of E (after $\overline{\text{unlock}}$) cannot be simulated by the successor of F (after $\overline{\text{unlock}}$).

Further, recall from Section 2.1 that the program if $h > 0$ then $l := 1$ else $l := 0$ is rejected by Imp's security definition. In Section 3.2 we saw that

$$T[\![\text{if } h > 0 \text{ then } l := 1 \text{ else } l := 0]\!] =$$

$\quad (\overline{\text{lock}}.\text{get}_h x.\overline{\text{res}}(x > 0).0 \mid \text{res}(x).$

$\quad\quad (\text{if } x \text{ then } \text{tick}.\overline{\text{unlock}}.$

$\quad\quad\quad (\overline{\text{lock}}.\overline{\text{res}}1.0 \mid \text{res}(x).(\overline{\text{put}}_l x.\text{tick}.\overline{\text{unlock}}.\overline{\text{done}}.0)) \setminus \{\text{res}\}$

$\quad\quad else \text{ tick}.\overline{\text{unlock}}.$

$\quad\quad\quad (\overline{\text{lock}}.\overline{\text{res}}0.0 \mid \text{res}(x).(\overline{\text{put}}_l x.\text{tick}.\overline{\text{unlock}}.\overline{\text{done}}.0)) \setminus \{\text{res}\})) \setminus \{\text{res}\}$

The information flow from $h > 0$ to l is evident in the translation. The result of inspecting the expression $h > 0$ is sent on the channel res. When this result is received and checked, either it triggers the process that puts 1 in the register for l or a similar process that puts 0 to that register.

As above, the VSPA translation fails to satisfy P_BNDC. Varying the high state by a high environment action $\text{eput}_h(\cdot)$ in the beginning leads to different values in the register for l. This difference can be observed by low environment actions $\overline{\text{eget}}_l(\cdot)$.

5   Related Work

A large body of work on information-flow security has been developed in the area of programming languages (see a recent survey [27]) and process calculus (e.g., [7, 25, 24, 13, 18]). While both language-based and process calculus-based security are relatively established fields, only little has been done for understanding the connection between the two.

A line of work initiated by Honda et al. [14] and pursued by Honda and Yoshida [15, 16] develops security type systems for the π-calculus. The use of linear and affine types gives the power for these systems to soundly embed type systems for imperative multi-threaded languages [29] into the typed π-calculus. This direction is appealing as it leads to automatic security enforcement mechanisms by security type checking. Nevertheless, automatic enforcement comes at the price of lower precision. Our approach opens up possibilities for combining high-precision security verification (such as equivalence checking in process calculi [23]) with type-based verification. Steps in this direction have been made in, e.g., [17, 2, 31], however, not treating timing-sensitive security.

Giambiagi and Dam's work on *admissible flows* [3, 11] illustrates a useful synergy of an imperative language and a CCS-like process calculus. The assurance provided by admissible flows is that a security protocol implementation (written in the imperative language) leaks no more information than prescribed in the specification (written in the process calculus).

Mantel and Sabelfeld [21] have suggested an embedding of a multithreaded and distributed language into MAKS [20], an abstract framework for modeling the security of event-based systems. The translation of a program is secure (as an event system) if and only if the program itself is secure (in the sense that the program satisfies self-low-similarity). While this work offers a useful connection between language-based and event-based security, it is inherently restricted to expressing event systems as trace models. In the present work, the security of both the source and target languages is defined in terms of bisimulation. This enables us to capture additional information leaks, e.g., through deadlock behavior [7], which trace-based models generally fail to detect.

Our inspiration for handling timing-sensitive security stems from the work by Focardi et al. [8], where explicit `tick` events are used to keep track of timing in a scenario of a discrete-time process calculus.

6   Conclusion and Future Work

We have established a formal connection between a language-based and a process calculus security definition of information security. Concretely, we have shown that a timing-sensitive security definition corresponds to P_BNDC, persistent bisimulation-based nondeducibility on compositions. Thereby, we have identified a point in the space of process calculus-based definitions [7] that exactly corresponds to compositional timing-sensitive language-based security.

Drawing on Milner's work [22], we have developed a generally useful encoding of an imperative language into a CCS-like calculus. We expect that this encoding will be helpful for both future work on information security topics as well as other topics that necessitate representation of programming languages in process calculus.

This paper sets solid ground for future work in the following directions:

Security policies: We have used as a starting point a timing-sensitive language-based security specification. This choice has allowed us to establish a tight, timing-sensitive, correspondence between computation steps in the imperative language and the actions of processes. However, it is important to consider a full spectrum of attackers, including the attacker that may not observe (non)termination. Future work includes weakening security policies and investigating the relation between the two kinds of security for a termination-insensitive attacker.

Concurrency and distribution: Concurrency and distribution are out of scope for this paper for lack of space. However, the technical machinery is already in place to add multithreading and distribution to the imperative language (for example, the program security characterization is known to be compositional for Imp with dynamic thread creation [28]). We conjecture that in presence of concurrency, P_BNDC will remain to correspond to the language-based security definition. We expect parallel compositions of Imp threads to be encoded by parallel compositions of VSPA processes. In this case, the security correspondence result would be a consequence of the compositionality of the two properties. We anticipate the security correspondence to hold without major changes in the encoding. The effect of distribution features in both source and target languages is certainly a worthwhile topic for future work. An extension of the source language with channel-based communication [26] is a natural point for investigating the connection to process calculi security. As a matter of fact, P_BNDC has been specifically developed for communicating processes, thus it should be applicable even when channels are used both for communication and for manipulating memories.

Modular security: According to the vision we stated in the introduction, for the security analysis of heterogeneous systems we need heterogeneous, scalable techniques. The key to scalability is modular analysis that allows analyzing parts of a systems in isolation and plug together secure components together. That the resulting system is secure is guaranteed by compositionality results. While compositionality properties for Imp and VSPA have been studied separately, we intend to explore the interplay between the two. In particular, we expect to obtain stronger compositionality results for the image of secure imperative programs in VSPA than for regular VSPA processes.

References

1. M. Abadi. Protection in programming-language translations. In *Proc. International Collo-quium on Automata, Languages, and Programming*, volume 1443 of *LNCS*, pages 868–883. Springer-Verlag, July 1998.
2. D. Clark, C. Hankin, and S. Hunt. Information flow for Algol-like languages. *Journal of Computer Languages*, 28(1):3–28, April 2002.
3. M. Dam and P. Giambiagi. Confidentiality for mobile code: The case of a simple payment protocol. In *Proc. IEEE Computer Security Foundations Workshop*, pages 233–244, July 2000.
4. D. E. Denning and P. J. Denning. Certification of programs for secure information flow. *Comm. of the ACM*, 20(7):504–513, July 1977.
5. R. Focardi and R. Gorrieri. A Classification of Security Properties for Process Algebras. *Journal of Computer Security*, 3(1):5–33, 1994/1995.
6. R. Focardi and R. Gorrieri. The Compositional Security Checker: A Tool for the Verifica-tion of Information Flow Security Properties. *IEEE Transactions on Software Engineering*, 23(9):550–571, 1997.
7. R. Focardi and R. Gorrieri. Classification of Security Properties (Part I: Information Flow). In R. Focardi and R. Gorrieri, editors, *Foundations of Security Analysis and Design*, volume 2171 of *LNCS*, pages 331–396. Springer-Verlag, 2001.
8. R. Focardi, R. Gorrieri, and F. Martinelli. Information flow analysis in a discrete-time process algebra. In *Proc. IEEE Computer Security Foundations Workshop*, pages 170–184, July 2000.
9. R. Focardi and S. Rossi. Information Flow Security in Dynamic Contexts. In *Proc. of the IEEE Computer Security Foundations Workshop*, pages 307–319. IEEE Computer Society Press, 2002.

10. R. Focardi, S. Rossi, and A. Sabelfeld. Bridging Language-Based and Process Calculi Security. Technical Report CS-2004-14, Dipartimento di Informatica, Università Ca' Foscari di Venezia, Italy, 2004. http://www.dsi.unive.it/ricerca/TR/index.htm.
11. P. Giambiagi and M.Dam. On the secure implementation of security protocols. In *Proc. European Symp. on Programming*, volume 2618 of *LNCS*, pages 144–158. Springer-Verlag, April 2003.
12. J. A. Goguen and J. Meseguer. Security policies and security models. In *Proc. IEEE Symp. on Security and Privacy*, pages 11–20, April 1982.
13. M. Hennessy and J. Riely. Information flow vs. resource access in the asynchronous pi-calculus. *ACM TOPLAS*, 24(5):566–591, 2002.
14. K. Honda, V. Vasconcelos, and N. Yoshida. Secure information flow as typed process behaviour. In *Proc. European Symp. on Programming*, volume 1782 of *LNCS*, pages 180–199. Springer-Verlag, 2000.
15. K. Honda and N. Yoshida. A uniform type structure for secure information flow. In *Proc. ACM Symp. on Principles of Programming Languages*, pages 81–92, January 2002.
16. K. Honda and N. Yoshida. Noninterference through flow analysis. *Journal of Functional Programming*, 2005. To appear.
17. R. Joshi and K. R. M. Leino. A semantic approach to secure information flow. *Science of Computer Programming*, 37(1–3):113–138, 2000.
18. N. Kobayashi. Type-based information flow analysis for the pi-calculus. Technical Report TR03-0007, Tokyo Institute of Technology, October 2003.
19. B. W. Lampson. A note on the confinement problem. *Comm. of the ACM*, 16(10):613–615, October 1973.
20. H. Mantel. Possibilistic definitions of security – An assembly kit –. In *Proc. IEEE Computer Security Foundations Workshop*, pages 185–199, July 2000.
21. H. Mantel and A. Sabelfeld. A unifying approach to the security of distributed and multi-threaded programs. *J. Computer Security*, 11(4):615–676, September 2003.
22. R. Milner. *Communication and Concurrency*. Prentice-Hall, 1989.
23. C. Piazza, E. Pivato, and S. Rossi. CoPS - Checker of Persistent Security. In *Proc. International Conference on Tools and Algorithms for the Construction and Analysis of Systems*, volume 2988 of *LNCS*, pages 144–152. Springer-Verlag, March 2004.
24. F. Pottier. A simple view of type-secure information flow in the pi-calculus. In *Proc. IEEE Computer Security Foundations Workshop*, pages 320–330, June 2002.
25. P. Ryan. Mathematical models of computer security—tutorial lectures. In R. Focardi and R. Gorrieri, editors, *Foundations of Security Analysis and Design*, volume 2171 of *LNCS*, pages 1–62. Springer-Verlag, 2001.
26. A. Sabelfeld and H. Mantel. Static confidentiality enforcement for distributed programs. In *Proc. Symp. on Static Analysis*, volume 2477 of *LNCS*, pages 376–394. Springer-Verlag, September 2002.
27. A. Sabelfeld and A. C. Myers. Language-based information-flow security. *IEEE J. Selected Areas in Communications*, 21(1):5–19, January 2003.
28. A. Sabelfeld and D. Sands. Probabilistic noninterference for multi-threaded programs. In *Proc. IEEE Computer Security Foundations Workshop*, pages 200–214, July 2000.
29. G. Smith and D. Volpano. Secure information flow in a multi-threaded imperative language. In *Proc. ACM Symp. on Principles of Programming Languages*, pages 355–364, January 1998.
30. G. Winskel. *The Formal Semantics of Programming Languages: An Introduction*. MIT Press, Cambridge, MA, 1993.
31. N. Yoshida, K. Honda, and M. Berger. Linearity and bisimulation. In *Proc. Foundations of Software Science and Computation Structure*, volume 2303 of *LNCS*, pages 417–433. Springer-Verlag, April 2002.

History-Based Access Control with Local Policies

Massimo Bartoletti, Pierpaolo Degano, and Gian Luigi Ferrari

Dipartimento di Informatica, Università di Pisa, Italy
{bartolet, degano, giangi}@di.unipi.it

Abstract. An extension of the λ-calculus is proposed, to study history-based access control. It allows for security policies with a possibly nested, local scope. We define a type and effect system that, given a program, extracts a history expression, i.e. a correct approximation to the set of histories obtainable at run-time. Validity of history expressions is non-regular, because the scope of policies can be nested. Nevertheless, a transformation of history expressions is presented, that makes verification possible through standard model checking techniques. A program will never fail at run-time if its history expression, extracted at compile-time, is valid.

1   Introduction

Models and techniques for language-based security are receiving increasing attention [14, 16]. Among these, access control plays a relevant role [15]. Indeed, features for defining and enforcing access control policies are a main concern in the design of modern programming languages. Access control *policies* specify the rules by which principals are authorized to access protected objects and resources; while *mechanism* will implement the controls imposed by the given policy. For example, a policy may specify that a principal P can never read a certain file F. This policy can be enforced by a trusted component of the operating system, that intercepts any access to F and prevents P from reading.

Several models for access control have been proposed, among which *stack inspection*, adopted by Java and C♯. In this model, a policy grants static access rights to code, while actual run-time rights depend on the static rights of the code frames on the call stack. As access controls only rely on the current call stack, stack inspection may be insecure when trusted code depends on results supplied by untrusted code [11]. In fact, access controls are insensitive to the frame of an untrusted piece of code, when popped from the call stack. Additionally, some standard code optimizations (e.g. method inlining) may break security in the presence of stack inspection (however, it is sometimes possible to exploit static techniques, e.g. those in [4], that allow for secure optimizations).

V. Sassone (Ed.): FOSSACS 2005, LNCS 3441, pp. 316–332, 2005.

The main weaknesses of stack inspection are caused by the fact that the call stack only records a fragment of the whole execution. *History-based access control* considers instead (a suitable abstraction of) the entire execution, and the actual rights of the running code depend on the static rights of *all* the pieces of code (possibly partially) executed so far. History-based access control has been recently receiving major attention, at both levels of foundations [2, 10, 18] and of language design and implementation [1, 8].

The typical run-time mechanisms for enforcing history-based policies are *execution monitors*, which observe computations and abort them whenever about to violate the given policy. The observations are called *events*, and are an abstraction of security-relevant activities (e.g. opening a socket connection, reading and writing a file). Sequences of events, possibly infinite, are called *histories*. Usually, the security policy of the monitor is a global property: it is an invariant that must hold at any point of the execution. Execution monitors have been proved to enforce exactly the class of *safety* properties [17].

Checking each single event in a history may be inefficient. A different approach is to instrument the code with *local checks* (see e.g. Java and C♯), each enforcing its own local policy. Under certain circumstances, the two ways are equivalent [6, 7, 22]. Recently, Skalka and Smith [18] have addressed the problem of history-based access control with local checks, combining a static technique with model checking. In their approach, local checks enforce regular properties of histories. These properties are written as μ-calculus logic formulae, verified by Büchi automata. From a given program, their type and effect system extracts a history expression, i.e. an over-approximate, finite representation of all the histories the program can generate. History expressions are then model checked to (statically) guarantee that each local check will always succeed at run-time. If so, all the local checks can be safely removed from the program.

Building upon [18], we propose here $\lambda^{[]}$, an extension of the λ-calculus that allows for expressive and flexible history-based access control policies. The security properties imposed in our programs are *regular* properties of histories, and have a possibly nested, local scope. A program e protected by a policy φ is written $\varphi[e]$, called *policy framing*. During the evaluation of e, the whole execution history (i.e. the past history followed by the events generated so far by e) must respect the policy φ. This allows for safe composition of programs that are protected by different policies. For example, suppose to have an expression $\lambda x.\, \varphi[(x\, v)\, e]$ that takes as input a function for x, and applies it to the value v while enforcing the policy φ. Then, supplying the function $\lambda y.\, \varphi'[e']$, we have the following computation:

$$(\lambda x.\, \varphi[(x\, v)\, e])\, (\lambda y.\, \varphi'[e']) \;\rightarrow\; \varphi[(\lambda y.\, \varphi'[e'])\, v\, e] \;\rightarrow\; \varphi[\varphi'[e'\{v/y\}]\, e]$$
$$\rightarrow^* \varphi[\varphi'[v']\, e] \;\rightarrow\; \varphi[v'\, e]$$

Evaluating the application of e' to v must respect, at each step, both policies φ and φ'. As soon as a function v' is obtained, the scope of φ' is left, and the application of v' to e' continues under the scope of φ. Note that the first step of the computation above can be viewed as dynamically placing a program into a *sandbox* enforcing the policy φ. This programming paradigm seems difficult to express in a language with local checks or global policies, only.

Even though policies are regular properties, the nesting of policy framings may give rise to *non-regular* properties: indeed, every history η must obey the conjunction of all the policies within the scope of which the last event of η occurs. Run-time mechanisms enforcing this kind of properties need to be at least powerful as pushdown automata. Consequently, $\lambda^{[]}$ is strictly more expressive than the sub-language that only admits policy framings with single events, i.e. local checks (of course, the above holds under the assumption that the access control mechanism is not encoded in λ-expressions themselves).

We define a type and effect system for $\lambda^{[]}$. The types are standard, while the effects are *history expressions*, a finite approximation of the infinitary language of histories, together with explicit representation of the scope of policy framings. We say that a history expression is valid if all its histories are such, i.e. they represent safe executions. Considering finite histories only is sufficient, because the validity of histories is a safety property. Recall that computations not enjoying a safety property are rejected in a finite number of steps [17]. If the effect of a program is valid, then the program will never throw any security exceptions.

Even though validity of histories is a non-regular property, we show that history expressions can be model checked with standard techniques. We define a transformation that, given an history expression H, obtains an expression H' such that (i) the histories represented by H' are regular, and (ii) they respect exactly the same policies (within their scopes) obeyed by the histories represented by H. From the history expression H' we then extract a Basic Process Algebra process p and a regular formula φ such that H' is valid if and only if p satisfies φ. This satisfiability problem is known to be decidable by model checking [9].

2   The Language $\lambda^{[]}$

To study access control in a pure framework, we consider $\lambda^{[]}$, a call-by-value λ-calculus enriched with access events and security policies. An *access event* $\alpha \in \Sigma$ abstracts from a security-relevant operation; sequences η of access events are called *histories*. Security policies $\varphi \in \Pi$ are regular properties of histories. A *policy framing* $\varphi[e]$ localizes the scope of the policy φ to the expression e; framings can be nested. To enhance readability, our calculus comprises conditional expressions and named abstractions (the variable z in $e' = \lambda_z x.e$ stands for e' itself within e). The syntax of $\lambda^{[]}$ follows. We omit the definition of policies φ and of guards b, as they are not relevant for the subsequent technical development.

Syntax of $\lambda^{[]}$ Expressions

$$e, e' \quad ::= \quad x \mid \alpha \mid \text{if } b \text{ then } e \text{ else } e' \mid \lambda_z x. e \mid e\, e' \mid \varphi[e]$$

The values of $\lambda^{[]}$ are the variables and the abstractions. We write $*$ for a fixed, closed, event-free value, and $\lambda_-.\, e$ for $\lambda x.\, e$, for $x \notin fv(e)$. The following abbreviation is standard: $e; e' = (\lambda_-.\, e')e$.

We define the behaviour of $\lambda^{[]}$ expressions through the following SOS operational semantics. The configurations are pairs η, e. A transition $\eta, e \rightarrow \eta', e'$ means that, starting from a history η, the expression e may evolve to e', possibly extending the history η. We write $\eta \models \varphi$ when the history η obeys the policy φ. We assume as given a total function $\mathcal{B}$ that evaluates the guards in conditionals.

Operational Semantics of $\lambda^{[]}$

$$\frac{\eta, e_1 \rightarrow \eta', e_1'}{\eta, e_1 e_2 \rightarrow \eta', e_1' e_2} \qquad \frac{\eta, e_2 \rightarrow \eta', e_2'}{\eta, v e_2 \rightarrow \eta', v e_2'} \qquad \eta, (\lambda_z x.e)v \rightarrow \eta, e\{v/x, \lambda_z x.e/z\}$$

$$\frac{}{\eta, \alpha \rightarrow \eta\alpha, *} \qquad \frac{\eta, e \rightarrow \eta', e' \quad \eta, \eta' \models \varphi}{\eta, \varphi[e] \rightarrow \eta', \varphi[e']} \qquad \frac{\eta \models \varphi}{\eta, \varphi[v] \rightarrow \eta, v}$$

$$\frac{\mathcal{B}(b) = true}{\eta, \texttt{if } b \texttt{ then } e_0 \texttt{ else } e_1 \rightarrow \eta, e_0} \qquad \frac{\mathcal{B}(b) = false}{\eta, \texttt{if } b \texttt{ then } e_0 \texttt{ else } e_1 \rightarrow \eta, e_1}$$

It is immediate to define a semantics of $\lambda^{[]}$, equivalent to that given above, that explicitly records entering and exiting a framing $\varphi[\cdots]$, by enriching histories with special events $[_\varphi$ and $]_\varphi$. Each transition requires to verify that the current history is *valid*, roughly it satisfies all the policies φ whose scope has been entered but not exited yet, i.e. the number of $[_\varphi$ is greater then that of $]_\varphi$. Counting is not regular: therefore, validity is not a regular property.

To illustrate our approach, consider a simple web browser that displays HTML pages and runs applets. Applets can be trusted (e.g. because signed, or downloaded from a trusted site), or untrusted. The browser has a site policy φ always applied to untrusted applets. The site policy says that an applet cannot connect to the web after it has read from the local disk. After executing an untrusted applet, the browser writes some logging information to the local disk. Additionally, all applets must obey a user policy that is supplied to the browser. We define the browser as a function that processes the URL u, be it an applet or an HTML page, and the user policy φ', rendered as a framing $p = \lambda x.\, \varphi'[x*]$.

$Browser = \lambda u.\, \lambda p.\, \texttt{if } html(u) \texttt{ then } display(u) \texttt{ else}$

$\qquad\qquad\qquad\qquad \texttt{if } trusted(u) \texttt{ then } p\, u \texttt{ else } \varphi[p\, u;\, Write\, *]$

We consider three trusted applets: $Read = \lambda_-.\, \alpha_r$ to read files, $Write = \lambda_-.\, \alpha_w$ to write files, and $Connect = \lambda_-.\, \alpha_c$ to open web connections. Note that our applets are overly simplified, because we are only interested in the events they can generate, namely $\alpha_r, \alpha_w, \alpha_c$. We also have an untrusted applet, that tries to spoof the browser by executing a supplied applet z with a void user policy.

$$Untrusted \; = \; \lambda z. \lambda_-. \, Browser \, z \, (\lambda y. \, y*)$$

The behaviour of an untrusted write, executed with a user policy φ' saying that applets cannot write the local disk, is illustrated by the following trace:

$$\varepsilon, \; Browser \, (Untrusted \, Write) \, (\lambda y. \varphi'[y*])$$
$$\rightarrow^* \; \varepsilon, \; \varphi[(\lambda y. \varphi'[y*]) \, (\lambda_-. \, Browser \, Write \, (\lambda y. \, y*)); \, Write*]$$
$$\rightarrow^* \; \varepsilon, \; \varphi[\varphi'[Browser \, Write \, (\lambda y. \, y*)]; \, Write*]$$
$$\rightarrow^* \; \varepsilon, \; \varphi[\varphi'[(\lambda y. \, y*) \, Write]; \, Write*] \;\; \rightarrow^* \;\; \varepsilon, \; \varphi[\varphi'[\alpha_w]; \, Write*]$$

At this point, a security exception is thrown, because the history α_w would not satisfy the innermost policy φ'. Consider now an untrusted applet that reads the local disk and then tries to connect.

$$\varepsilon, \; Browser \, (Untrusted \, (\lambda_-. \, Read*; \, Connect*)) \, (\lambda y. \varphi'[y*])$$
$$\rightarrow^* \; \varepsilon, \; \varphi[(\lambda y. \varphi'[y*]) \, (Untrusted \, (\lambda_-. \, Read*; \, Connect*)); \, Write*]$$
$$\rightarrow^* \; \varepsilon, \; \varphi[\varphi'[Browser \, (\lambda_-. \, Read*; \, Connect*) \, (\lambda y. \, y*)]; \, Write*]$$
$$\rightarrow^* \; \varepsilon, \; \varphi[\varphi'[Read*; \, Connect*]; \, Write*] \;\; \rightarrow^* \;\; \alpha_r, \; \varphi[\varphi'[Connect*]; \, Write*]$$

Again, we have a security exception, because the history $\alpha_r \alpha_c$ does not satisfy the outermost policy φ. As a further example, consider an untrusted read:

$$\varepsilon, \; Browser \, (Untrusted \, Read) \, (\lambda y. \varphi'[y*])$$
$$\rightarrow^* \; \varepsilon, \; \varphi[(\lambda y. \varphi'[y*]) \, (Untrusted \, Read); \, Write*]$$
$$\rightarrow^* \; \varepsilon, \; \varphi[\varphi'[Browser \, Read \, (\lambda y. \, y*)]; \, Write*] \;\; \rightarrow^* \;\; \varepsilon, \; \varphi[\varphi'[Read*]; \, Write*]$$
$$\rightarrow^* \; \alpha_r, \; \varphi[\varphi'[*]; \, Write*] \;\; \rightarrow^* \;\; \alpha_r, \; \varphi[Write*] \;\; \rightarrow^* \;\; \alpha_r \alpha_w, \; \varphi[*]$$

Unlike in the first computation, the write operation has been performed, because the scope of the policy φ' has been left upon termination of the untrusted applet.

3   A Type and Effect System for $\lambda^{[\,]}$

To statically predict the histories generated by programs at run-time, we introduce *history expressions* with the following abstract syntax.

History Expressions

$$H, H' \; ::= \; \varepsilon \; | \; h \; | \; \alpha \; | \; H \cdot H' \; | \; H + H' \; | \; \varphi[H] \; | \; \mu h.H$$

History expressions include the empty history ε, events α, sequencing $H \cdot H'$, non-deterministic choice $H + H'$, policy framing $\varphi[H]$, and recursion $\mu h.H$ (μ binds the occurrences of the variable h in H). Free variables and closed expressions are defined as expected. We assume that the operator $\cdot$ has precedence over $+$, that in turn has precedence over μ.

Hereafter, we extend histories with an explicit representation of policy framings. We use special symbols $[_\varphi$ and $]_\varphi$ to denote the opening and closing of the scope of the policy φ. Formally, an *enriched history* η, or simply *history* when unambiguous, is a (possibly infinite) sequence $(\beta_1, \beta_2, \ldots)$ where $\beta_i \in \Sigma \cup \Sigma_\Pi$, $\Sigma_\Pi = \{ [_\varphi,]_\varphi \mid \varphi \in \Pi \}$, and $\Sigma \cap \Sigma_\Pi = \emptyset$.

Let $\mathcal{H}$ range over sets of histories. Then, $\mathcal{H}\mathcal{H}'$ denotes the set of histories $\{ \eta\eta' \mid \eta \in \mathcal{H}, \eta' \in \mathcal{H}' \}$, and $\varphi[\mathcal{H}]$ is the set $\{ [_\varphi \eta]_\varphi \mid \eta \in \mathcal{H} \}$. Note that, if η is infinite, then $\eta\eta' = \eta$, for each η' (in particular, $\varphi[\eta] = [_\varphi \eta]_\varphi = [_\varphi \eta)$.

The *denotational semantics* of history expressions is defined over the complete lattice $(2^{(\Sigma \cup \Sigma_\Pi)^*}, \subseteq)$. The environment ρ used below maps variables to sets of (finite) histories. We stipulate that concatenation and union of sets of histories are defined only if both their operands are defined. Hereafter, we feel free to omit curly braces, when unambiguous.

Denotational Semantics of History Expressions

$$[\![\varepsilon]\!]_\rho = \varepsilon \qquad [\![\alpha]\!]_\rho = \alpha \qquad [\![h]\!]_\rho = \rho(h) \qquad [\![\varphi[H]]\!]_\rho = \varphi[[\![H]\!]_\rho]$$

$$[\![H \cdot H']\!]_\rho = [\![H]\!]_\rho [\![H']\!]_\rho \qquad [\![H + H']\!]_\rho = [\![H]\!]_\rho \cup [\![H']\!]_\rho$$

$$[\![\mu h.H]\!]_\rho = \bigcup_{n \in \omega} f^n(\emptyset) \quad \text{where } f(X) = [\![H]\!]_{\rho\{X/h\}}$$

As an example, consider $H = \mu h. \alpha + h \cdot h + \varphi[h]$. The semantics of H consists of all the histories having an arbitrary number of occurrences of α, and arbitrarily nested framings of φ. For instance, $\alpha\varphi[\alpha], \varphi[\alpha]\varphi[\alpha\varphi[\alpha]] \in [\![H]\!]_\emptyset$.

We now introduce a type and effect system [19] for $\lambda^{[]}$, extending [18]. Types and type environments, ranged over by τ and Γ, are defined as follows.

Types and Type Environments

$$\tau ::= unit \mid \tau \xrightarrow{H} \tau \qquad \Gamma ::= \emptyset \mid \Gamma; x : \tau \quad (x \notin dom(\Gamma))$$

A typing judgment $\Gamma, H \vdash e : \tau$ means that the expression e evaluates to a value of type τ, and produces a history belonging to the effect H. The history expression H in the functional type $\tau \xrightarrow{H} \tau'$ describes the latent effect associated with an abstraction, i.e. one of the histories in $[\![H]\!]$ is generated when a value is applied to an abstraction with that type. The relation $\Gamma, H \vdash e : \tau$ is defined as the least relation closed under the following rules.

Type and Effect System for $\lambda^{[]}$

$$\Gamma, \varepsilon \vdash x : \Gamma(x) \qquad \Gamma, \alpha \vdash \alpha : unit \qquad \Gamma, \varepsilon \vdash * : unit$$

$$\frac{\Gamma; x : \tau; z : \tau \xrightarrow{H} \tau', H \vdash e : \tau'}{\Gamma, \varepsilon \vdash \lambda_z x.e : \tau \xrightarrow{H} \tau'} \qquad \frac{\Gamma, H \vdash e : \tau \xrightarrow{H''} \tau' \quad \Gamma, H' \vdash e' : \tau}{\Gamma, H \cdot H' \cdot H'' \vdash ee' : \tau'}$$

$$\frac{\Gamma, H \vdash e : \tau \quad \Gamma, H \vdash e' : \tau}{\Gamma, H \vdash \text{if } b \text{ then } e \text{ else } e' : \tau} \qquad \frac{\Gamma, H \vdash e : \tau}{\Gamma, \varphi[H] \vdash \varphi[e] : \tau} \qquad \frac{\Gamma, H \vdash e : \tau}{\Gamma, H + H' \vdash e : \tau}$$

Typing judgments are standard. The last rule allows for *weakening* of effects. The effects in the rule for application are concatenated according to the evaluation order of the call-by-value semantics. The rule for abstraction constraints the premise to equate the effect and the latent effect of functional type. Let η be a history; let $\eta^\flat$ be the subsequence of η containing only events in Σ; and let η^π be the set of all the prefixes of η. For example, if $\eta = \alpha \varphi[\alpha' \varphi'[\alpha'']]$, then $(\eta^\flat)^\pi = \{\alpha, \alpha\alpha', \alpha\alpha'\alpha''\}$. The next theorem ensures that our type and effect system does approximate the actual run-time histories (its proof, as well as others, and further technical details can be found in [3]).

Theorem 1. *If* $\Gamma, H \vdash e : \tau$ *and* $\varepsilon, e \to^* \eta, e'$, *then* $\eta \in (\llbracket H \rrbracket^\flat)^\pi$.

We now define when an access control history is valid. Intuitively, valid histories represent viable computations, while invalid ones represent computations that would have been stopped by the access control mechanism of $\lambda^{[]}$. Let $\eta = \beta_1 \cdots \beta_n$ be a history. Let $\Phi(\eta)$ be the set of the policies φ such that the number of $[_\varphi$ is greater than the number of $]_\varphi$ in η. We say that η is *valid* when $(\beta_1 \cdots \beta_k)^\flat \models \bigwedge \Phi(\beta_1 \cdots \beta_k)$, for all $k \in 1..n$. A history expression H is *valid* when all the histories in $\llbracket H \rrbracket$ are such.

For example, consider the history $\eta_0 = \alpha_r \varphi[\alpha_c]$, where φ is the property saying that no α_c occurs after α_r. Then, η_0 is *not* valid, because $(\alpha_r [_\varphi \alpha_c)^\flat = \alpha_r \alpha_c$ does not satisfy $\bigwedge \Phi(\alpha_r [_\varphi \alpha_c) = \varphi$. The history $\eta_1 = \varphi[\alpha_r]\alpha_c$ is valid, because $([_\varphi \alpha_r)^\flat = \alpha_r$ satisfies $\bigwedge \Phi([_\varphi \alpha_r) = \varphi$, and $\bigwedge \Phi(\eta_1) = \bigwedge \emptyset = true$.

We now state the type safety property. We say that e *goes wrong* when $\varepsilon, e \to^* \eta', e'$, and e' is not a value, and there is no η'', e'' such that $\eta', e' \to \eta'', e''$. For example, a computation goes wrong when attempting to execute an event forbidden by a currently active policy framing.

Theorem 2 (Type Safety). *Let $\Gamma, H \vdash e : \tau$, for e closed. If H is valid, then e does not go wrong.*

Proof (Sketch). The proof is greatly simplified by defining a new transition system with transition relation $\twoheadrightarrow$, where the special framing events $[_\varphi$ and $]_\varphi$ replace the policy framing $\varphi[\cdots]$. The original and the new transition systems do agree step by step, up to obvious transformations on expressions (to convert policy framings into framing events) and on histories (to insert framing events in histories). Similarly, we introduce a type and effect system with relation $\Gamma, H \vdash_\sharp$, much in the style of $\vdash$ above. Indeed, if $\Gamma, H \vdash e : \tau$ then $\Gamma, H \vdash_\sharp e : tau$. Then, we prove first a Subject Reduction lemma, ensuring that, if $\Gamma, H_0 \vdash_\sharp e_0 : \tau$ and $\eta_0, e_0 \twoheadrightarrow \eta_1, e_1$, for e_0 closed and well-formed, then there exists H_1 such that $\Gamma, H_1 \vdash_\sharp e_1 : \tau$ and $\eta_1 [\![H_1]\!] \subseteq \eta_0 [\![H_0]\!]$. Secondly, we prove a Progress lemma, stating that if $\Gamma, H \vdash_\sharp e : \tau$, for e closed, and let ηH is valid for some η, then, either e is a value, or there exists a transition $\eta, e \twoheadrightarrow \eta', e'$.

Now type safety follows by contradiction. Assume that $\varepsilon, e \twoheadrightarrow^* \eta, e_0$, and η, e_0 is a stuck configuration, i.e. e_0 is not a value, and there is no transition from η, e_0. By the Subject Reduction lemma, $\Gamma, H' \vdash_\sharp e_0 : \tau$, for some H' such that $\eta [\![H']\!] \subseteq [\![H]\!]$. Since H is valid by hypothesis, then $\eta [\![H']\!]$ is valid, as well as η, because validity is a prefix-closed property. We assumed that η, e_0 is stuck, then by the Progress lemma, e_0 must be a value: contradiction. □

Example 1. Consider the following expression, where b and b' are boolean guards:

$$e = \lambda_z x. \text{ if } b \text{ then } \alpha \text{ else } (\text{if } b' \text{ then } zzx \text{ else } \varphi[zx])$$

Let $\Gamma = \{z : \tau \xrightarrow{H} \tau, x : \tau\}$. Then, the following typing derivation is possible:

$$\cfrac{\cfrac{\cfrac{\Gamma, \varepsilon \vdash z : \tau \xrightarrow{H} \tau \quad \Gamma, \varepsilon \vdash x : \tau}{\Gamma, H \vdash zx : \tau}}{\cfrac{\Gamma, H \cdot H \vdash zzx : \tau}{\Gamma, H \cdot H + \varphi[H] \vdash zzx : \tau} \quad \cfrac{\Gamma, \varphi[H] \vdash \varphi[zx] : \tau}{\Gamma, H \cdot H + \varphi[H] \vdash \varphi[zx] : \tau}}{\cfrac{\Gamma, \alpha \vdash \alpha : unit \quad \Gamma, H \cdot H + \varphi[H] \vdash \text{if } b' \text{ then } zzx \text{ else } \varphi[zx] : \tau}{\Gamma, \alpha + H \cdot H + \varphi[H] \vdash \text{if } b \text{ then } \alpha \text{ else } (\text{if } b' \text{ then } zzx \text{ else } \varphi[zx]) : \tau}}}$$

To apply the rule for abstraction, the constraint $H = \alpha + H \cdot H + \varphi[H]$ must be solved. A solution is $\mu h. \alpha + h \cdot h + \varphi[h]$, thus $\emptyset, \varepsilon \vdash e : unit \xrightarrow{\mu h. \alpha + h \cdot h + \varphi[h]} unit$. Note in passing that a simple extension of the type inference algorithm of [18] suffices for solving constraints as the one above.

4   Verification of History Expressions

We now introduce a procedure to verify the validity of history expressions. Our technique is based on model checking Basic Process Algebras (BPAs) with

Büchi automata. The standard decision procedure for verifying that a BPA process p satisfies a ω-regular property φ amounts to constructing the pushdown automaton for p and the Büchi automaton for the negation of φ. Then, the property holds if the (context-free) language accepted by the conjunction of the above, which is still a pushdown automaton, is empty. This problem is known to be decidable, and several algorithms and tools show this approach feasible [9].

Recall that our notion of validity is non-regular, and that context-free languages are not closed under intersection, thus making the emptiness problem undecidable. We then need to manipulate history expressions in order to make validity a regular property. Indeed, the intersection of a context-free language and a regular language is context-free, so emptiness is decidable.

4.1 Regularization of History Expressions

History expressions can generate histories with *redundant framings*, i.e. nestings of the same policy framing. For example, the history $\eta = \varphi[\alpha\varphi'[\varphi[\alpha']]]$ has an inner redundant φ-framing around the event α'. Since α' is already under the scope of the outermost φ-framing, it happens that η is valid if and only if $\varphi[\alpha\varphi'[\alpha']]$ is valid. While removing inner redundant framings from a history preserves its validity, one needs the expressive power of a pushdown automaton, because open and closed framings are to be matched in pairs. Below, we introduce a transformation that, given a history expression H, yields an H' such that (i) H is valid if and only if H' is valid, and (ii) the histories generated by H' can be verified by a finite state automaton.

Let $h^* \in fv(H)$ be a selected occurrence of h in H. We say that h^* is guarded by $guard(h^*, H)$, defined as the smallest set satisfying the following equations.

Guards

$$guard(h^*, h) = \emptyset$$
$$guard(h^*, H_0 \ op \ H_1) = guard(h^*, H_i) \quad \text{if } h^* \in H_i, \ op \in \{\cdot, +\}$$
$$guard(h^*, \varphi[H]) = \{\varphi\} \cup guard(h^*, H)$$
$$guard(h^*, \mu h'. \ H') = guard(h^*, H') \quad \text{if } h' \neq h$$

For example, in $\mu h. \varphi[\alpha \cdot h \cdot \varphi'[h]] \cdot h$, the first occurrence of h is guarded by $\{\varphi\}$, the second one is guarded by $\{\varphi, \varphi'\}$, and the third one is unguarded.

Let H be a (possibly non-closed) history expression. Without loss of generality, assume that all the variables in H have distinct names. We define below $H \downarrow_{\Phi, \Gamma}$, the expression produced by the *regularization* of H against a set of policies Φ and a mapping Γ from variables to history expressions.

Regularization of History Expressions

$$\varepsilon \downarrow_{\Phi,\Gamma} = \varepsilon \qquad h \downarrow_{\Phi,\Gamma} = h \qquad \alpha \downarrow_{\Phi,\Gamma} = \alpha$$

$$(H \cdot H') \downarrow_{\Phi,\Gamma} = H \downarrow_{\Phi,\Gamma} \cdot H' \downarrow_{\Phi,\Gamma} \qquad (H + H') \downarrow_{\Phi,\Gamma} = H \downarrow_{\Phi,\Gamma} + H' \downarrow_{\Phi,\Gamma}$$

$$\varphi[H] \downarrow_{\Phi,\Gamma} = \begin{cases} H \downarrow_{\Phi,\Gamma} & \text{if } \varphi \in \Phi \\ \varphi[H \downarrow_{\Phi \cup \{\varphi\},\Gamma}] & \text{otherwise} \end{cases}$$

$$(\mu h. H) \downarrow_{\Phi,\Gamma} = \mu h. (H' \sigma' \downarrow_{\Phi,\Gamma\{(\mu h.H)\Gamma/h\}} \sigma)$$

where $H = H'\{h/h_i\}_i$, h_i fresh, $h \notin fv(H')$, and

$$\sigma(h_i) = (\mu h.H)\Gamma \downarrow_{\Phi \cup guard(h_i,H'),\Gamma} \qquad \sigma'(h_i) = \begin{cases} h & \text{if } guard(h_i, H') \subseteq \Phi \\ h_i & \text{otherwise} \end{cases}$$

Intuitively, $H\downarrow_{\Phi,\Gamma}$ results from H by eliminating all the redundant framings, and all the framings in Φ. The environment Γ is needed to deal with free variables in the case of nested μ-expressions, as shown by Example 3 below. We sometimes omit to write the component Γ when unneeded, and, when H is closed, we abbreviate $H \downarrow_{\emptyset,\emptyset}$ with $H \downarrow$.

The last two regularization rules would benefit from some explanation. Consider first a history expression of the form $\varphi[H]$ to be regularized against a set of policies Φ. To eliminate the redundant framings, we must ensure that H has neither φ-framings, nor redundant framings itself. This is accomplished by regularizing H against $\Phi \cup \{\varphi\}$. Consider a history expression of the form $\mu h.H$. Its regularization against Φ and Γ proceeds as follows. Each free occurrence of h in H guarded by some $\Phi' \not\subseteq \Phi$ is unfolded and regularized against $\Phi \cup \Phi'$. The substitution Γ is used to bind the free variables to closed history expressions. Technically, the i-th free occurrence of h in H is picked up by the substitution $\{h/h_i\}$, for h_i fresh. Note also that $\sigma(h_i)$ is computed only if $\sigma'(h_i) = h_i$.

As a matter of fact, regularization is a total function, and its definition can be easily turned into a terminating rewriting system.

Example 2. Let $H_0 = \mu h. H$, where $H = \alpha + h \cdot h + \varphi[h]$. Then, H can be written as $H'\{h/h_i\}_{i \in 0..2}$, where $H' = \alpha + h_0 \cdot h_1 + \varphi[h_2]$. Since $guard(h_2, H') = \{\varphi\} \not\subseteq \emptyset$:

$$H_0 \downarrow_\emptyset = \mu h. H'\{h/h_0, h/h_1\} \downarrow_\emptyset \{H_0 \downarrow_\varphi /h_2\} = \mu h. \alpha + h \cdot h + \varphi[H_0 \downarrow_\varphi]$$

To compute $H_0 \downarrow_\varphi$, note that no occurrence of h is guarded by $\Phi \not\subseteq \{\varphi\}$. Then:

$$H_0 \downarrow_\varphi = \mu h. (\alpha + h \cdot h + \varphi[h]) \downarrow_\varphi = \mu h. \alpha + h \cdot h + h$$

Since $[\![H_0 \downarrow_\varphi]\!] = \{\alpha\}^\omega$ has no φ-framings, we have that $[\![H_0 \downarrow]\!] = \left(\{\}\alpha^\omega \varphi[\{\}\alpha^\omega] \right)^\omega$ has no redundant framings.

Example 3. Let $H_0 = \mu h. H_1$, where $H_1 = \mu h'. H_2$, and $H_2 = \alpha + h \cdot \varphi[h']$. Since $guard(h, H_1) = \emptyset$, we have that:

$$H_0 \downarrow_{\emptyset,\emptyset} = \mu h. (H_1 \downarrow_{\emptyset,\{H_0/h\}})$$

Note that H_2 can be written as $H_2'\{h/h_0\}$, where $H_2' = \alpha + h \cdot \varphi[h_0]$. Since $guard(h_0, H_2') = \{\varphi\} \not\subseteq \emptyset$, it follows that:

$$\begin{aligned}
H_1 \downarrow_{\emptyset,\{H_0/h\}} &= \mu h'. H_2' \downarrow_{\emptyset,\{H_0/h, H_1\{H_0/h\}/h'\}} \{H_1\{H_0/h\} \downarrow_{\varphi,\{H_0/h\}} / h_0\} \\
&= \mu h'. \alpha + h \cdot \varphi[h_0] \{(\mu h'. \alpha + H_0 \cdot \varphi[h']) \downarrow_{\varphi,\{H_0/h\}} / h_0\} \\
&= \mu h'. \alpha + h \cdot \varphi[H_3 \downarrow_{\varphi,\{H/h\}}] \;=\; \alpha + h \cdot \varphi[H_3 \downarrow_{\varphi,\{H/h\}}]
\end{aligned}$$

where $H_3 = \mu h'. \alpha + H_0 \cdot \varphi[h']$, and the last simplification is possible because the outermost μ binds no variable. Since $guard(h', \alpha + H_0 \cdot \varphi[h']) = \{\varphi\} \subseteq \{\varphi\}$:

$$H_3 \downarrow_\varphi \;=\; \mu h'. (\alpha + H_0 \cdot \varphi[h']) \downarrow_\varphi \;=\; \mu h'. \alpha + H_0 \downarrow_\varphi \cdot h'$$

Since $\{\varphi\}$ contains both $guard(h, H_1) = \emptyset$, and $guard(h', H_2) = \{\varphi\}$, then:

$$H_0 \downarrow_\varphi = \mu h.(\mu h'.\alpha + h \cdot \varphi[h']) \downarrow_\varphi = \mu h.\mu h'.(\alpha + h \cdot \varphi[h']) \downarrow_\varphi = \mu h.\mu h'.\alpha + h \cdot h'$$

Putting together the computations above, we have that:

$$\begin{aligned}
H_0 \downarrow_\emptyset &= \mu h. \alpha + h \cdot \varphi[H_3 \downarrow_\varphi] \\
H_3 \downarrow_\varphi &= \mu h'. \alpha + (\mu h. \mu h'. \alpha + h \cdot h') \cdot h'
\end{aligned}$$

We now establish the following basic property of regularization.

Theorem 3. *$H \downarrow$ has no redundant framings.*

Regularization preserves validity. To prove that, it is convenient to introduce a *normal form* for histories. It permits to compare the histories produced by an expression H with those of the regularization of H. Note that normalization (as well as regularization) are non-regular transformations: constructing the normal form of a history requires counting the framing openings and closings (see the last equation below): a pushdown automaton is therefore needed.

Normalization of Histories

$$\varepsilon \Downarrow_\Phi = \varepsilon \qquad (\mathcal{H}\mathcal{H}') \Downarrow_\Phi = \mathcal{H}\Downarrow_\Phi \mathcal{H}'\Downarrow_\Phi \qquad (\mathcal{H} \cup \mathcal{H}') \Downarrow_\Phi = \mathcal{H}\Downarrow_\Phi \cup \mathcal{H}'\Downarrow_\Phi$$

$$\alpha \Downarrow_\Phi = \left(\bigwedge \Phi\right)[\alpha] \qquad \varphi[\mathcal{H}] \Downarrow_\Phi = \mathcal{H}\Downarrow_{\Phi \cup \{\varphi\}}$$

Intuitively, normalization transforms histories with policy framings in histories with local checks. Indeed, $\eta \Downarrow_\Phi$ is intended to record that each event in η must obey *all* the policies in Φ. This is apparent in the second and in the last equation above. We abbreviate $\mathcal{H}\Downarrow_\emptyset$ with $\mathcal{H}\Downarrow$. Note that $\mathcal{H}\Downarrow_\emptyset$ is defined if and only if $\mathcal{H}$ has balanced framings.

Example 4. Consider the history $\eta = \alpha\varphi[\alpha'\varphi'[\alpha'']]$. Its normal form is:

$$\eta\Downarrow = \alpha\Downarrow (\varphi[\alpha'\varphi'[\alpha'']])\Downarrow = \alpha\,(\alpha'\varphi'[\alpha''])\Downarrow_\varphi = \alpha\,(\alpha'\Downarrow_\varphi)\,(\varphi'[\alpha''])\Downarrow_\varphi$$
$$= \alpha\,\varphi[\alpha']\,(\alpha''\Downarrow_{\varphi,\varphi'}) = \alpha\,\varphi[\alpha']\,(\varphi \wedge \varphi')[\alpha'']$$

A history expression H and its regularization $H\downarrow$ have the same normal form.

Theorem 4. $[\![H\downarrow]\!]\Downarrow = [\![H]\!]\Downarrow$.

The next theorem states that normalization preserves the validity of histories. Summing up, a history expression H is valid iff its regularization $H\downarrow$ is valid.

Theorem 5. *A history η is valid if and only if $\eta\Downarrow$ is valid.*

4.2   Basic Process Algebras

Basic Process Algebras [5] provide a natural characterization of (possibly infinite) histories. A *BPA process* is given by the following abstract syntax:

$$p \; ::= \; \varepsilon \mid \alpha \mid p\cdot p' \mid p + p' \mid X$$

where ε denotes the terminated process, $\alpha \in \Sigma$, X is a variable, $\cdot$ denotes sequential composition, $+$ represents (nondeterministic) choice.

A BPA process p is *guarded* if each variable occurrence in p occurs in a subexpression $\alpha \cdot q$ of p. We assume a finite set $\Delta = \{X \overset{def}{=} p\}$ of guarded definitions, such that, for each variable X, there exists a single, guarded p such that $\{X \overset{def}{=} p\} \in \Delta$. As usual, we consider the process $\varepsilon \cdot p$ to be equivalent to p.

The operational semantics of BPAs is given by the following labelled transition system, in the SOS style.

Operational Semantics of BPA processes

$$\frac{}{\alpha \xrightarrow{\alpha} \varepsilon} \qquad \frac{p \xrightarrow{\alpha} p'}{p+q \xrightarrow{\alpha} p'} \qquad \frac{q \xrightarrow{\alpha} q'}{p+q \xrightarrow{\alpha} q'} \qquad \frac{p \xrightarrow{\alpha} p'}{p\cdot q \xrightarrow{\alpha} p'\cdot q} \qquad \frac{p \xrightarrow{\alpha} p' \quad X \overset{def}{=} p \in \Delta}{X \xrightarrow{\alpha} p'}$$

The set $\{ (a_i)_i \mid p_0 \xrightarrow{a_1} \cdots \xrightarrow{a_i} p_i \} \cup \{ (a_i)_i \mid p_0 \cdots \xrightarrow{a_i} \cdots \}$ is denoted by $[\![p_0, \Delta]\!]$, where $[\![p, \Delta]\!]^{fin}$ is the first set, containing the strings that label finite computations. We omit the component Δ, when empty.

We now introduce a mapping from history expressions to BPAs, in the line of [18]. Without loss of generality, we assume that all the variables in H have distinct names. The mapping takes as input a history expression H and an injective function Γ from history variables h to BPA variables X, and it outputs a BPA process p and a finite set of definitions Δ. To avoid the problem of unguarded BPA processes, we assume a standard preprocessing step, that inserts a dummy event before each unguarded occurrence of a variable in a history expression. Dummy events are eventually discarded before the verification phase.

The rules that transform history expressions into BPAs are rather standard. History events, variables, concatenation and choice are mapped into the corresponding BPA counterparts. A history expression $\mu h.H$ is mapped to a fresh BPA variable X, bound to the translation of H in the set of definitions Δ. An expression $\varphi[H]$ is mapped to the BPA for H, surrounded by the opening and closing of the φ-framing.

Mapping History Expressions to BPAs

$$BPA(\varepsilon, \Gamma) = \langle \varepsilon, \emptyset \rangle$$
$$BPA(\alpha, \Gamma) = \langle \alpha, \emptyset \rangle$$
$$BPA(h, \Gamma) = \langle \Gamma(h), \emptyset \rangle$$
$$BPA(H_0 \cdot H_1, \Gamma) = \langle p_0 \cdot p_1, \Delta_0 \cup \Delta_1 \rangle, \text{ where } BPA(H_i, \Gamma) = \langle p_i, \Delta_i \rangle$$
$$BPA(H_0 + H_1, \Gamma) = \langle p_0 + p_1, \Delta_0 \cup \Delta_1 \rangle, \text{ where } BPA(H_i, \Gamma) = \langle p_i, \Delta_i \rangle$$
$$BPA(\mu h.H, \Gamma) = \langle X, \Delta \cup \{X \overset{def}{=} p\} \rangle, \text{ where } BPA(H, \Gamma\{X/h\}) = \langle p, \Delta \rangle$$
$$BPA(\varphi[H], \Gamma) = \langle [_\varphi \cdot p \cdot]_\varphi, \Delta \rangle, \text{ where } BPA(H, \Gamma) = \langle p, \Delta \rangle$$

We now state the correspondence between history expressions and BPAs. The prefixes of the histories generated by a history expression H (i.e. $\llbracket H \rrbracket^\pi$) are all and only the finite prefixes of the strings that label the computations of $BPA(H)$. Recall that this is enough, because validity is a safety property.

Lemma 1. $\llbracket H \rrbracket^\pi = \llbracket BPA(H) \rrbracket^{fin}$.

4.3   Büchi Automata

Büchi automata are finite state automata whose acceptance condition roughly says that a computation is accepted if some final state is visited infinitely often; see [21] for details. Since we also need to establish the validity of finite histories, we use the standard trick of padding a finite string with a special symbol $. Then, each final state has a self-loop labelled with $. For brevity, we will omit these transitions hereafter.

Given a policy φ, we are interested in defining a formula $\varphi_{[]}$ to be used in verifying that a history η, with no redundant framings of φ, respects φ within its scope. Let the formula φ be defined by the Büchi automaton $A_\varphi = \langle \Sigma, Q, Q_0, \rho, F \rangle$, which we assume to have a non-final sink state. We define the formula $\varphi_{[]}$ through the following Büchi automaton $A_{\varphi_{[]}}$.

Büchi Automaton for $\varphi_{[]}$

$$A_{\varphi_{[]}} = \langle \Sigma', Q', Q_0, \rho', F' \rangle$$
$$\Sigma' = \Sigma \cup \{ [_\varphi,]_\varphi \mid \varphi \in \Pi \}$$
$$Q' = F' = Q \cup \{ q' \mid q \in F \}$$
$$\rho' = \rho \cup \{ \langle q, [_\varphi, q' \rangle \mid q \in F \} \cup \{ \langle q',]_\varphi, q \rangle \}$$
$$\cup \{ \langle q_0', \alpha, q_1' \rangle \mid \langle q_0, \alpha, q_1 \rangle \in \rho \text{ and } q_1 \in F \}$$
$$\cup \{ \langle q, [_{\varphi'}, q \rangle \cup \langle q,]_{\varphi'}, q \rangle \mid q \in Q' \text{ and } \varphi' \neq \varphi \}$$

Intuitively, $A_{\varphi_{[]}}$ has two layers. The first is a copy of A_φ, where all the states are final. This models the fact that we are outside the scope of φ, i.e. the history leading to any state in this layer has balanced framings of φ (or none). The second layer is reachable from the first one when opening a framing for φ, while closing a framing gets back. The transitions in the second layer are a copy of those connecting final states in A_φ. Consequently, the states in the second layer are exactly the final states in A_φ. Since A_φ is only concerned with the verification of φ, the transitions for opening and closing framings $\varphi' \neq \varphi$ are rendered as self-loops.

Example 5. Let φ be the policy saying that no event α_c can occur after an α_r. The Büchi automata for φ and for $\varphi_{[]}$ are in Figure 1. For example, the history $[_\varphi \alpha_r]_\varphi \alpha_c$ is accepted by $A_{\varphi_{[]}}$, while $\alpha_r [_\varphi \alpha_c]_\varphi$ is not (recall that we do not draw the self-loops labelled by $).

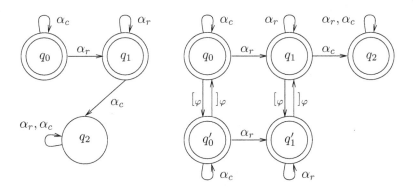

Fig. 1. Büchi automata for φ (left) and for $\varphi[]$ (right)

We now relate validity of histories with the formulae $\varphi_{[]}$. Since BPAs can generate infinite histories, we extend by continuity our notion of validity, saying that an *infinite* history is valid when all its *finite* prefixes are valid. Assuming continuity is not a limitation, because validity is a *safety* property: nothing bad can happen in any execution step [17]. The following lemma states that a history η is valid if and only if it satisfies $\varphi_{[]}$ for all the policies φ spanning over η.

Lemma 2. *Let η be a history with no redundant framings. Then, η is valid if and only if $\eta \models \varphi_{[]}$, for all φ such that $[_\varphi \in \eta$.*

Büchi automata are closed under intersection [21]: therefore, a valid history η is accepted by the intersection of the automata $A_{\varphi_{[]}}$, for all φ occurring in η.

The main result of our paper follows. Validity of a history expression H can be decided by showing that the BPA generated by the regularization of H satisfies a ω-regular formula. Together with Theorem 2, a $\lambda^{[]}$ expression never violates security if its effect is checked valid.

Theorem 6. $[\![H]\!]$ *is valid if and only if* $[\![BPA(H\downarrow)]\!] \models \bigwedge_{\varphi \in H} \varphi[]$.

Proof. By lemma 5, $[\![H]\!]$ is valid if and only if $[\![H]\!] \Downarrow$ is valid. By theorem 4, $[\![H]\!] \Downarrow = [\![H\downarrow]\!] \Downarrow$. By lemma 5, $[\![H\downarrow]\!] \Downarrow$ is valid if and only if $[\![H\downarrow]\!]$ is valid. By theorem 3, $[\![H\downarrow]\!]$ has no redundant framings. By definition, $[\![H\downarrow]\!]$ is valid if and only if $[\![H\downarrow]\!]^\pi$ is valid. By lemma 1, $[\![H\downarrow]\!]^\pi = [\![BPA(H\downarrow)]\!]^{fin}$. By continuity, $[\![BPA(H\downarrow)]\!]^{fin}$ is valid if and only if $[\![BPA(H\downarrow)]\!]$ is valid. Then, by lemma 2, $[\![BPA(H\downarrow)]\!]$ is valid if and only if $[\![BPA(H\downarrow)]\!] \models \bigwedge_{\varphi \in H} \varphi[]$. $\qquad \square$

5   Conclusions

We proposed a novel approach to history-based access control. To this aim, we have introduced $\lambda^{[]}$, an extension of the λ-calculus that allows for security policies with a local scope. Along the lines of Skalka and Smith [18], we have used a type and effect system to extract from a given program a history expression that approximates its run-time behaviour. Verifying the validity of a history expression ensures that there will be no security violations at run-time. Our security policies are regular properties of histories; however, the augmented flexibility due to nesting of scopes makes validity a non-regular property, unlike [18]. So, $\lambda^{[]}$ is expressive enough to describe and enforce security policies that cannot be naturally dealt with local checks or global policies. Non-regularity seemed to prevent us from verifying validity by standard model checking techniques, but we have been able to transform history expressions so that model checking is feasible.

Our model is less general than the resource access control framework of Igarashi and Kobayashi [12], but we provide a static verification technique, while [12] does not. We have no explicit notion of resource, as they have, but we plan to introduce it in the future.

Compared to Skalka and Smith's λ_{hist}, our $\lambda^{[]}$ features a different programming construct for access control. The programming model and the type system of [18] also allow for access events parametrized by constants, and for let-polymorphism. Although omitted for simplicity, these features can be easily recovered by using the same techniques of [18]. As a matter of fact, λ_{hist} turns out to be the sub-calculus of $\lambda^{[]}$ where the scope of policies can only include single events. Intuitively, a framing $\varphi[*]$ corresponds to a local check of the regular policy φ on the current history. It is not always possible to transform a program in $\lambda^{[]}$ into a program in λ_{hist} that obeys the same security properties, provided that the transformation is only allowed to substitute suitable local checks for policy framings. Clearly, unrestricted transformations, (e.g. security-passing style ones that record the set of active framings) can do the job, because λ_{hist} is Turing complete.

Our policy framings roughly resemble the scoped methods of [20]. This construct extends the Java source language by allowing programmers to limit the sequence of methods that may be applied to an object. A scoped method is annotated with a regular expression which describe the permitted sequences of access events. Methods must explicitly declare the sequence of events they may produce, while we infer them by a type and effect system.

Colcombet and Fradet [7] and Marriot, Stuckey and Sulzmann [13] mix static and dynamic techniques to transform programs in order to make them obey a given safety property. Compared to [7, 13], our programming model allows for local policies, while the other only considers global ones. In future work, we aim at investigating if a similar mixed approach is feasible in our programming model. This might be non-trivial, because local policies seem to make the techniques used in [7, 13] not directly exploitable.

Acknowledgments

We wish to thank the anonymous referees for their insightful comments and suggestions. This work has been partially supported by EU project DEGAS (IST-2001-32072) and FET project PROFUNDIS (IST-2001-33100).

References

1. M. Abadi and C. Fournet. Access control based on execution history. In *Proc. 10th Annual Network and Distributed System Security Symposium*, 2003.
2. A. Banerjee and D. A. Naumann. History-based access control and secure information flow. In *Workshop on Construction and Analysis of Safe, Secure and Interoperable Smart Cards (CASSIS)*, 2004.
3. M. Bartoletti. PhD thesis, Università di Pisa, Submitted.
4. M. Bartoletti, P. Degano, and G. L. Ferrari. Method inlining in the presence of stack inspection. In *Workshop on Issues in the Theory of Security*, 2004.
5. J. A. Bergstra and J. W. Klop. Algebra of communicating processes with abstraction. *Theoretical Computer Science*, 37:77–121, 1985.
6. F. Besson, T. Jensen, D. Le Métayer, and T. Thorn. Model checking security properties of control flow graphs. *Journal of Computer Security*, 9:217–250, 2001.
7. T. Colcombet and P. Fradet. Enforcing trace properties by program transformation. In *Proc. 27th ACM SIGPLAN-SIGACT Symposium on Principles of Programming Languages*, 2000.
8. G. Edjlali, A. Acharya, and V. Chaudhary. History-based access control for mobile code. In *Secure Internet Programming*, volume 1603 of *LNCS*, 1999.

9. J. Esparza. On the decidability of model checking for several μ-calculi and Petri nets. In *Proc. 19th Int. Colloquium on Trees in Algebra and Programming*, 1994.
10. P. W. Fong. Access control by tracking shallow execution history. In *IEEE Symposium on Security and Privacy*, 2004.
11. C. Fournet and A. D. Gordon. Stack inspection: theory and variants. *ACM Transactions on Programming Languages and Systems*, 25(3):360–399, 2003.
12. A. Igarashi and N. Kobayashi. Resource usage analysis. In *Proc. 29th ACM SIGPLAN-SIGACT Symposium on Principles of Programming Languages*, 2002.
13. K. Marriott, P. J. Stuckey, and M. Sulzmann. Resource usage verification. In *Proc. First Asian Programming Languages Symposium*, 2003.
14. A. Sabelfeld and A. C. Myers. Language-based information flow security. *IEEE Journal on selected areas in communication*, 21(1), 2003.
15. P. Samarati and S. de Capitani di Vimercati. Access control: Policies, models, and mechanisms. In *FOSAD Tutorial Lectures*, volume 2171 of *LNCS*. Springer, 2001.
16. F. Schneider, G. Morrisett, and R. Harper. A language-based approach to security. In *Informatics: 10 Years Back, 10 Years Ahead*. Springer, 2001.
17. F. B. Schneider. Enforceable security policies. *ACM Transactions on Information and System Security (TISSEC)*, 3(1):30–50, 2000.
18. C. Skalka and S. Smith. History effects and verification. In *Asian Programming Languages Symposium*, 2004.
19. J.-P. Talpin and P. Jouvelot. The type and effect discipline. In *Proc. 7th IEEE Symposium on Logic in Computer Science*, 1992.
20. G. Tan, X. Ou, and D. Walker. Resource usage analysis via scoped methods. In *Foundations of Object-Oriented Languages*, 2003.
21. M. Y. Vardi. An automata-theoretic approach to linear temporal logic. In *Proc. Banff Higher order workshop conference on Logics for concurrency*, 1996.
22. D. Walker. A type system for expressive security policies. In *Proc. 27th ACM SIGPLAN-SIGACT Symposium on Principles of Programming Languages*, 2000.

Composition and Decomposition in True-Concurrency

Sibylle Fröschle*

Institute of Informatics, University of Warsaw, Poland
sib@mimuw.edu.pl

Abstract. The idea of composition and decomposition to obtain computability results is particularly relevant for true-concurrency. In contrast to the interleaving world, where composition and decomposition must be considered with respect to a process algebra operator, e.g. parallel composition, we can directly recognize whether a truly-concurrent model such as a labelled asynchronous transition system or a 1-safe Petri net can be dissected into independent 'chunks of behaviour'. In this paper we introduce the corresponding concept 'decomposition into independent components', and investigate how it translates into truly-concurrent bisimulation equivalences. We prove that, under a natural restriction, history preserving (hp), hereditary hp (hhp), and coherent hhp (chhp) bisimilarity are decomposable with respect to prime decompositions. Apart from giving a general proof technique our decomposition theory leads to several coincidence results. In particular, we resolve that hp, hhp, and chhp bisimilarity coincide for 'normal form' basic parallel processes.

1 Introduction

In the finite-state world truly-concurrent problems are typically harder than their interleaving counterparts. This is demonstrated by the following examples. Model-checking CTL is well-known to be polynomial-time but model-checking CTL_P is NP-hard [1]. The problem of synthesizing controllers for discrete event systems is decidable in an interleaving setting and can be computed in polynomial-time; in a truly-concurrent setting the problem is undecidable [2]. Classical bisimilarity is polynomial-time decidable while *hereditary history preserving (hhp) bisimilarity* has been proved undecidable [3]; plain *history preserving (hp) bisimilarity* is decidable [4] but has been shown DEXPTIME-complete [5, 6].

There is, however, a positive trend for true-concurrency in the *infinite*-state world. The above effect seems reversed for *basic parallel processes (BPP)*. Under interleaving semantics a small fragment of a logic equivalent to CTL* is undecidable for *very basic* BPP; under partial order interpretation the full logic is decidable for BPP [7]. Trace equivalence on BPP is undecidable but pomset trace and location trace equivalence on BPP are shown decidable in [8]. Classical bisimilarity on BPP is PSPACE-complete [9, 10]; in contrast, for BPP, distributed bisimilarity, and with it hp bisimilarity, are polynomial-time decidable [11]. The positive trend is further confirmed by results of

---

* This work was supported by the EPSRC Grants GR/M84763 and GR/R16891, and the European Community Research Training Network 'GAMES'.

[12, 13]: hhp bisimilarity on BPP is decidable and coincides with its strengthening to *coherent hhp bisimilarity*.

We can explain this discrepancy as follows. Models such as *labelled asynchronous transition systems (lats')* [14] or *labelled 1-safe Petri nets (net systems)* faithfully capture how the transitions of a system are related concerning concurrency and conflict. The way we allow concurrency and conflict to interact will directly impact on the computational power of truly-concurrent equivalences and logics. The negative results of [2] and [3] build on the insight that truly-concurrent models have the power to encode tiling systems. If the interplay between concurrency and conflict is restricted this power can be lost [15], and a truly-concurrent concept may be particularly natural to decide. BPP are infinite-state but, under truly-concurrent semantics, they have a simple tree-like structure, which has turned out to be directly exploitable: e.g. the decidability results of [8] follow by a reduction to the equivalence problem of recognizable tree languages.

In this paper we advocate the following thesis. System classes with a restricted interplay between concurrency and conflict often have characteristic decomposition properties. These might translate into truly-concurrent equivalences or logics in a very concrete way, and thereby allow us to decide the respective concept by a 'divide and conquer' approach.

The idea of decomposition provides one of the crucial techniques to establish decidability and upper complexity bounds in infinite-state verification. For example, the polynomial-time decision procedure for classical bisimilarity on normed BPP [16] is based on the following insight:[1] any normed BPP can be expressed uniquely, up to bisimilarity, as a parallel composition of prime factors [18]. A process is *prime* if it is not the nil process and it is irreducible with respect to parallel composition, up to bisimilarity. Such a decomposition theory translates into cancellation properties of the form "$P \| Q \sim R \| Q$ implies $P \sim R$", which provide the means to reduce pairs of processes to compare into smaller pairs of processes to check. Questions about prime decomposability were first addressed by Milner and Moller in [19].

In the interleaving world, decomposition must be considered with respect to a process algebra operator, e.g. parallel composition, and the behavioural equivalence of choice: can a process term P be expressed as a process term Q of particular form, a parallel composition of prime processes, such that P and Q are bisimilar? In contrast, in true-concurrency, decomposition can be considered at the level of the semantic model: we can directly recognize whether a lats or net system can be dissected into independent 'chunks of behaviour'. Having fixed a specific decomposition view on the level of the model we can then separately investigate whether this view translates into a given equivalence. For example, we might suspect: if two parallel compositions of sequential systems, say S and S', are equivalent under a truly-concurrent bisimilarity then there is a one-to-one correspondence between the components of S and those of S' such that related components are equivalent. For classical bisimilarity this decomposition property will certainly not hold: $a \| b$ is bisimilar to $a.b + b.a$.

---

[1] Very recently this result has been improved to $O(n^3)$ by an algorithm that does not use decomposition in this sense [17].

There are two axioms of independence: (1) If two independent transitions can occur consecutively then they can also occur in the opposite order. (2) If two independent transitions are enabled at the same state then they can also occur one after the other. This indicates that decomposition is inherently connected to the shuffling of transitions: the behaviour of a system corresponds to the shuffle product of the behaviour of its independent components. Therefore, decomposition theorems provide an important tool to establish coincidence between hp, hhp, and chhp bisimilarity: proving that the three equivalences coincide amounts to proving that whenever two systems are hp bisimilar there exists a hp bisimulation that satifies specific shuffle properties, the hereditary and coherent condition.

The contribution of this paper is threefold: (1) We transfer the idea of prime decomposition to the truly-concurrent world. (2) We analyse whether this concept translates into truly-concurrent bisimulation equivalences. We show that, under a natural restriction, hp, and also, hhp and chhp bisimilarity are indeed decomposable with respect to prime decompositions. (3) We apply our decomposition theory to obtain coincidence results. In particular, this gives us several positive results for hhp bisimilarity, a concept which is renowned for being difficult to analyse. In more detail, after presenting the necessary definitions in Section 2, we proceed as follows.

In Section 3 we introduce the notion '*decomposition into independent components*' and a corresponding concept of *prime component* for the model of lats'; components are defined as concrete sub-systems of the respective lats. We show that every non-empty system uniquely decomposes into its set of prime components.

In Section 4 we show that hp, hhp, and chhp bisimilarity are *composable* with respect to decompositions in the following sense: assume two systems S_1, S_2, each decomposed into a set of independent components; whenever we can exhibit a one-to-one correspondence between the components of S_1 and those of S_2 such that related components are hp (hhp, chhp) bisimilar then S_1 and S_2 are hp (hhp, chhp) bisimilar. This is straightforward but guarantees the soundness of our decomposition approach. It is related to congruence in the process algebra world: if $P \sim P'$ and $Q \sim Q'$ then $P \| Q \sim P' \| Q'$.

Section 5 is the core of the paper: we analyse whether hp, hhp, and chhp bisimilarity are *decomposable* in the converse sense. We demonstrate that hp bisimilarity is *not* decomposable with respect to prime decompositions. However, we identify a natural restriction under which this is indeed given for hp, and also, hhp and chhp bisimilarity: for systems whose prime components are, what we shall call, *concurrent step connected* (*csc*). We obtain: whenever two *csc-decomposable systems* S_1, S_2 are hp (hhp, chhp) bisimilar then there is a one-to-one correspondence between the prime components of S_1 and those of S_2 such that related components are hp (hhp, chhp) bisimilar. The proof of this statement is non-trivial. In particular, we require the combinatorial argument of Hall's Marriage Theorem.

In Section 6 we apply our (de)composition theory to prove several coincidence results. As an immediate consequence we obtain coincidence between hp, hhp, and chhp bisimilarity for *parallel compositions of sequential systems*. Most interesting is, perhaps, that this intuitive result has turned out non-trivial to prove, and that the key insight behind it is of general significance. By employing our (de)composition theory in an inductive argument we extend the coincidence result to the class *concurrency-degree bounded communication-free net systems*.

Most importantly, we resolve that hp, hhp, and chhp bisimilarity coincide for the *simple basic parallel processes (SBPP)* of [7]. SBPP correspond to BPP in normal form, which in the interleaving world represent the entire BPP class; in true-concurrency they form a strictly smaller class. The coincidence for SBPP complements the positive results already achieved for (h)hp bisimilarity on BPP. Via [11] it follows that hhp bisimilarity on SBPP is polynomial-time decidable. Since hp and hhp bisimilarity do *not* coincide for BPP in general, the coincidence for SBPP underlines that SBPP and BPP do behave differently in the truly-concurrent world.

In Section 7 we conclude the paper and point to future research. Most of the proofs are kept informal in this extended abstract; a detailed account can be found in [20]. Our primary model is lats', but we also informally employ net systems, which can be understood as a class of lats'; for the definition of net systems we also refer to [20].

2   Preliminaries

Systems. A *labelled (coherent) asynchronous transition system* (for this paper simply *system*) is defined as a structure $S = (S_S, s_S^i, T_S, \to_S, I_S, l_S)$, where S_S is a set of *states* with *initial state* $s_S^i \in S_S$, T_S is the set of *transitions*[2], $\to_S \subseteq S_S \times T_S \times S_S$ is the *transition relation*, $I_S \subseteq T_S \times T_S$, the *independence relation*, is an irreflexive, symmetric relation, and $l_S : T_S \to Act$ is the *labelling function*, where $Act = \{a, b, \dots\}$ is a set of *actions*, such that

1. $t \in T_S \implies \exists s, s' \in S_S. \ s \xrightarrow{t}_S s'$,
2. $s \xrightarrow{t}_S s' \ \& \ s \xrightarrow{t}_S s'' \implies s' = s''$,
3. $t_1 \ I_S \ t_2 \ \& \ s \xrightarrow{t_1}_S s_1 \ \& \ s_1 \xrightarrow{t_2}_S u \implies \exists s_2. \ s \xrightarrow{t_2}_S s_2 \ \& \ s_2 \xrightarrow{t_1}_S u$, and
4. $t_1 \ I_S \ t_2 \ \& \ s \xrightarrow{t_1}_S s_1 \ \& \ s \xrightarrow{t_2}_S s_2 \implies \exists u. \ s_1 \xrightarrow{t_2}_S u \ \& \ s_2 \xrightarrow{t_1}_S u$.

We lift $\to_S$ to sequences of transitions in the usual way. We also lift I_S to sequences and sets of transitions, e.g. we write $t_1 \dots t_n \ I_S \ t'_1 \dots t'_m$ iff $t_i \ I_S \ t'_j$ for all $i \in [1, n]$, $j \in [1, m]$. In this paper we assume a further axiom:

5. $s \in S_S \implies \exists w \in T_S^*. \ s_S^i \xrightarrow{w} s$.

Axiom (1) says that every transition can occur from some state, and axiom (2) that the occurrence of a transition at a state leads to a unique state. Axioms (3) and (4) express the two axioms of independence mentioned in the introduction. Our additional axiom (5) specifies that every state is reachable from the initial state. A system S is *finite* iff S_S and T_S are finite sets. S is *empty* iff $T_S = \emptyset$, and *non-empty* otherwise.

Let S be a system, and $s \in S_S$. The transitions of $T_c \subseteq T_S$ are *concurrently enabled* at s, $T_c \in cenabl_S(s)$, iff $\forall t \in T_c. \ \exists s'. \ s \xrightarrow{t} s'$ and $\forall t, t' \in T_c. \ t \neq t' \implies t \ I_S \ t'$. We define the *smallest upper bound on the number of transitions that are concurrently*

---

[2] in the sense of Petri net boxes.

enabled at s by $cbound_S(s) = \min\{\kappa \mid \forall T_c \in cenabl_S(s). |T_c| \leq \kappa\}$. S is *concurrency-degree finite* iff for each $s \in S_S$, $cbound_S(s) \in \mathbf{N}_0$. E.g., finitely branching systems are always concurrency-degree finite. **We only consider systems that are concurrency-degree finite.**

Partial Order Runs. A *pomset* is a labelled partial order; specified via a labelled strict order, it is a tuple $p = (E_p, <_p, l_p)$, where E_p is a set of *events*, $<_p$ a strict order relation on E_p, and l_p a labelling function $l_p : E_p \rightarrow Act$. A function g is an *isomorphism* between pomset p and pomset q iff $g : E_p \rightarrow E_q$ is a bijection such that (1) $l_p = l_q \circ g$, and (2) $e <_p e'$ iff $g(e) <_q g(e')$ for all $e, e' \in E_p$.

Assume a system S. Let $r = t_1 t_2 \ldots t_n \in T_S^*$ be a sequence of transitions. We write $|r|$ for the length of r, that is $|r| = n$; for any $i \in [1, |r|]$ we denote the ith transition of r, t_i, by $r[i]$. r is a *run* of S, $r \in Runs(S)$, iff $s_S^i \xrightarrow{r} s$ for some state $s \in S_S$. The *pomset* of r, $pom(r)$, has as events the integers from 1 to n, where the label of event i is $l_S(t_i)$, and the strict ordering is the transitive closure of the following "proximate cause" relation: event i *proximately causes* event j, written $i <_r^{prox} j$, iff $i < j$ and t_i and t_j are *not* independent in S. We denote this strict ordering on [1,n] by '$<_r$'.

Hp, Hhp, and Chhp Bisimilarity. Hp bisimilarity relates two systems whose behaviour can be bisimulated while preserving the labelling of transitions and the causal dependencies between them. Technically, this can be realized by basing hp bisimulation on pairs of *synchronous runs* [5]: intuitively, two runs are *synchronous* if their induced pomsets are isomorphic, and both runs correspond to the same linearization of the associated pomset isomorphism class. Formally, this amounts to: let S_1, S_2 be two systems; $r_1 \in Runs(S_1)$ and $r_2 \in Runs(S_2)$ are synchronous, $(r_1, r_2) \in SRuns(S_1, S_2)$, iff the identity function on $[1, |r_1|]$ is an isomorphism between $pom(r_1)$ and $pom(r_2)$. A set $\mathcal{H} \subseteq SRuns(S_1, S_2)$ is *prefix-closed* iff $(r_1 t_1, r_2 t_2) \in \mathcal{H}$ implies $(r_1, r_2) \in \mathcal{H}$. As noted in [21] it is safe to restrict our attention to prefix-closed hp bisimulations.

Hhp bisimilarity is obtained from hp bisimilarity by the addition of a *backtracking* requirement, and chhp bisimilarity furthermore imposes a *padding* requirement. These conditions reflect the first and, respectively, second axiom of independence.

Definition 1. *Let S_1 and S_2 be two systems. A history preserving (hp) bisimulation relating S_1 and S_2 is a prefix-closed relation $\mathcal{H} \subseteq SRuns(S_1, S_2)$ that satisfies:*

1. $(\varepsilon, \varepsilon) \in \mathcal{H}$.
2. *If $(r_1, r_2) \in \mathcal{H}$ and $r_1 t_1 \in Runs(S_1)$ for some $t_1 \in T_1$, then there is $t_2 \in T_2$ such that $(r_1 t_1, r_2 t_2) \in \mathcal{H}$.*
3. *Vice versa.*

A hp bisimulation $\mathcal{H}$ is hereditary *(h) when it further satisfies:*

4. *If $(r_1 t_1 w_1, r_2 t_2 w_2) \in \mathcal{H}$ for some $w_1 \in T_1^*$, $w_2 \in T_2^*$, $t_1 \in T_1$, and $t_2 \in T_2$ such that $|w_1| = |w_2|$, $t_1 I_1 w_1$ (or $t_2 I_2 w_2$ equivalently), then $(r_1 w_1, r_2 w_2) \in \mathcal{H}$.*

A hhp bisimulation $\mathcal{H}$ is coherent *(c) when it further satisfies:*

5. *If $(r_1 w_1, r_2 w_2)$, $(r_1 t_1, r_2 t_2) \in \mathcal{H}$ for some $w_1 \in T_1^*$, $w_2 \in T_2^*$, $t_1 \in T_1$, and $t_2 \in T_2$ such that $|w_1| = |w_2|$, $t_1 I_1 w_1$, and $t_2 I_2 w_2$, then $(r_1 t_1 w_1, r_2 t_2 w_2) \in \mathcal{H}$.*

S_1 and S_2 are ((c)h)hp bisimilar, *written* $S_1 \sim_{((c)h)hp} S_2$, *iff there exists a ((c)h)hp bisimulation relating them. Given two systems S_1 and S_2, we also use* $\sim_{((c)h)hp}$ *to denote the set* $\bigcup\{\mathcal{H} : \mathcal{H}$ *is a ((c)h)hp bisimulation relating S_1 and $S_2\}$. (Note: chhp bisimulations are not closed under union; so,* $\sim_{chhp}$ *is not necessarily the largest chhp bisimulation.)*

Further Concepts. Let A, B be alphabets. For $r \in A^*$, if $B \subseteq A$, let $r \upharpoonright B$ denote the sequence obtained by erasing from r all occurrences of letters which are not in B. If $B = T_c$ for some system c we write $r \upharpoonright c$ short for $r \upharpoonright T_c$.

   The *shuffle* of n words $u_1, \ldots, u_n \in A^*$ is the set $u_1 \otimes \cdots \otimes u_n$ of all words of the form $u_{1,1} u_{2,1} \cdots u_{n,1} u_{1,2} u_{2,2} \cdots u_{n,2} \cdots u_{1,k} u_{2,k} \cdots u_{n,k}$ with $k \geq 0$, $u_{i,j} \in A^*$, such that $u_{i,1} u_{i,2} \cdots u_{i,k} = u_i$ for $1 \leq i \leq n$ [22]. We carry this notation over to pairs $(u, w) \in A^* \times B^*$ satisfying $|u| = |w|$, considering that such entities can be viewed as words in $(A \times B)^*$.

3   Decomposed Systems

We now introduce our notion of 'decomposition into independent components'. Components are defined as concrete sub-systems of the respective system.

   Let S be a system. A system c is a *sub-system* of S iff

1. $S_c \subseteq S_S$,
2. $s_c^i = s_S^i$,
3. $T_c \subseteq T_S$,
4. $\to_c = \to_S \cap (S_c \times T_c \times S_c)$,
5. $I_c = I_S \cap (T_c \times T_c)$, and
6. $l_c = l_S \upharpoonright_{T_c}$.

Let c_1 and c_2 be two sub-systems of S. We say c_1 and c_2 are *independent (with respect to S)*, written $c_1 \, I_S \, c_2$, iff $T_{c_1} \, I_S \, T_{c_2}$. The *empty sub-system of S* is defined by $c_{empty}^S = (\{s_S^i\}, s_S^i, \emptyset, \emptyset, \emptyset, \emptyset)$.

Definition 2. *A* decomposition *of a system S is a set* $\mathcal{D} = \{c_1, \ldots, c_n\}$, $n \in \mathbf{N}$, *of sub-systems of S such that*

   1. $\forall i, j \in [1, n]. \, (i \neq j \implies c_i \, I_S \, c_j)$, *and*
   2. $Runs(S) = \bigcup\{r_1 \otimes \cdots \otimes r_n \mid r_i \in Runs(c_i)$ *for all* $i \in [1, n]\}$.

A decomposed system *is a pair $(S, \mathcal{D})$, where $\mathcal{D}$ is a decomposition of system S.*

   Every system S has at least one decomposition: the one consisting of S itself. A system may well have many different decompositions: e.g., $P = a.0 \,\|\, b.0 \,\|\, c.0$ can be decomposed into $\{(a.0 \,\|\, b.0), c.0\}$, into $\{a.0, (b.0 \,\|\, c.0)\}$, and into $\{a.0, b.0, c.0\}$. Every non-empty system will, however, uniquely decompose into a set of *prime components*.

Definition 3. *A sub-system c of a system S is a* divisor *of S iff there exists a decomposition $\mathcal{D}$ of S such that $c \in \mathcal{D}$. A system S is* prime *iff S is non-empty, and c_{empty}^S and S are the only divisors of S.*

Theorem 1. *Each non-empty system S has a unique decomposition $\mathcal{D}$ such that for all $c \in \mathcal{D}$ c is prime.*

Proof (Sketch). This can be established following the standard proof of unique prime factorization of natural numbers (see e.g. [23]). Instead of proceeding by induction on **N**, we proceed by induction on the smallest upper bound on the number of transitions that can occur concurrently at the initial state. This is possible due to our restriction to concurrency-degree finite systems.

Definition 4. *We define the* prime components *of a system S, denoted by $PComps(S)$, as follows: if S is empty we set $PComps(S) = \emptyset$, otherwise we define $PComps(S)$ to be the decomposition associated with S by Theorem 1.*

Theorem 2. *Let S be a finite system. $PComps(S)$ is computable.*

Proof (Sketch). Let S be a non-empty finite system. We partition T_S into non-empty subsets such that each subset is a connected component with respect to the dependence relation (the complement of I_S). The sub-systems naturally induced by these sets of transitions are prime and together they form a decomposition of S.

Convention 1. *In the context of a decomposed system $(S, \mathcal{D})$ we use the following decomposition functions: $K : T_S \to \mathcal{D}$, defined by $K(t) = c_i \iff t \in T_{c_i}$, and $Ks : T_S^* \to \mathcal{P}(\mathcal{D})$, defined by $Ks(w) = \{K(t) \mid t \in w\}$. ($K$ is a function by clause (1) of the definition of decomposition, and the irreflexivity of independence.)*
If it is clear from the context that a system S is non-empty and there is no other decomposition specified, we understand S as the decomposed system $S = (S, PComps(S))$.

4   Composition

Hp, hhp, and chhp bisimilarity are composable with respect to decompositions in the following sense: whenever we can exhibit a one-to-one correspondence between the components of two decomposed systems such that related components are hp (hhp, chhp) bisimilar then the two systems are hp (hhp, chhp) bisimilar.

Theorem 3. *Let $x \in \{hp, hhp, chhp\}$; let $(S_1, \mathcal{D}_1)$ and $(S_2, \mathcal{D}_2)$ be two decomposed systems. If there exists a bijection $\beta : \mathcal{D}_1 \to \mathcal{D}_2$ such that $c_1 \sim_x \beta(c_1)$ for each $c_1 \in \mathcal{D}_1$ then we have $S_1 \sim_x S_2$.*

Proof (Sketch). Let $(S_1, \mathcal{D}_1)$ and $(S_2, \mathcal{D}_2)$ be two decomposed systems. Assume we are given a bijection $\beta : \mathcal{D}_1 \to \mathcal{D}_2$, say $\beta = \{(c_1^1, c_2^1), \ldots, (c_1^n, c_2^n)\}$, and a family $\{\mathcal{H}^i\}_{i=1}^n$ such that for all $i \in [1, n]$ $\mathcal{H}^i$ is a hp bisimulation relating c_1^i and c_2^i. We define $\mathcal{H} = \bigcup \{r^1 \otimes \cdots \otimes r^n \mid r^i \in \mathcal{H}^i \text{ for all } i \in [1, n]\}$. It is straightforward to check that $\mathcal{H}$ is a hp bisimulation relating S_1 and S_2. Furthermore, it is routine to establish: if for all $i \in [1, n]$ $\mathcal{H}^i$ is hereditary then $\mathcal{H}$ will also be hereditary; if for all $i \in [1, n]$ $\mathcal{H}^i$ is coherent then $\mathcal{H}$ will also be coherent.

5   Decomposition

It is trivial that hp, hhp, and chhp bisimilarity are *not* decomposable in the converse sense: as we saw $P = a.0 \,\|\, b.0 \,\|\, c.0$ can be decomposed into $\{(a.0 \,\|\, b.0), c.0\}$ and also into $\{a.0, (b.0 \,\|\, c.0)\}$; but certainly we cannot exhibit a bijection between the two decompositions such that related components are bisimilar. The more natural question to ask is whether a notion of equivalence is decomposable with respect to *prime decompositions*.

The example of Figure 1 demonstrates hp bisimilarity is *not* decomposable in this sense, either. On the one hand, A and B are hp bisimilar. The additional transition b_3' in B can easily be hidden by adopting the following strategy: if b_3' occurs as the first transition we will match it against b_1. Then in both systems 'parallel b' is the only remaining behaviour, and b_1' can safely be matched by b_2. If we start out with b_1' we will match it against b_1. Then the a-transition is disabled in both systems, and this time it will be safe to match b_3' by b_2. On the other hand, a bijection between the prime components of A and those of B can clearly not be found.

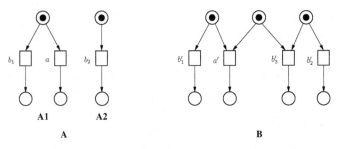

Fig. 1. The transitions of A and B are labelled as their names suggest: e.g. $l(b_1') = b$. A consists of two prime components: A_1 and A_2; B has only one prime component: B itself

A and B are *not* (c)hhp bisimilar: at $(b_1 b_2, b_1' b_3')$ we can backtrack (b_1, b_1'); then the a-transition becomes available in A but not in B. In Section 7 we will briefly discuss whether (c)hhp bisimilarity may be decomposable with respect to prime decompositions. Here we want to analyse whether there are conditions under which we do obtain decomposition for hp bisimilarity; this is important with respect to establishing coincidence results. We will find that, on systems whose prime components are, what we shall call, *concurrent step connected* (*csc*), hp, and also hhp and chhp, bisimilarity are indeed decomposable with respect to prime decompositions: whenever two *csc-decomposable systems* are hp (hhp, chhp) bisimilar then there is a one-to-one correspondence between their prime components such that related components are hp (hhp, chhp) bisimilar.

We start out by explaining two special types of runs, which will play a key role in the proof. A run r is a *concurrent step* iff all the transitions on r occur independently of each other. A run r is *maximal with respect to initial concurrency* iff whenever a further transition t is executed at r, t will occur causally dependent on some transition on r.

Definition 5. *Let S be a system, and $r \in Runs(S)$.*
r is a concurrent step *of S, written $r \in csteps(S)$, iff we have:*
$$\forall k, l \in [1, |r|]. \ (k \neq l \Rightarrow r[k] \ I_S \ r[l]).$$
r is maximal with respect to initial concurrency, *written $r \in icmax(S)$, iff we have:*
$$\forall t \in T_S. \ (rt \in Runs(S) \Rightarrow \exists i \in [1, |r|]. \ i <_{rt} |rt|).$$

Clearly, in pairs of synchronous runs, and hence in hp bisimilarity, concurrent steps are always matched against concurrent steps.

Fact 1. *Let S_1 and S_2 be two systems. For all $(r_1, r_2) \in SRuns(S_1, S_2)$ we have: $r_1 \in csteps(S_1) \iff r_2 \in csteps(S_2)$.*

With the concept 'maximal with respect to initial concurrency' it is easy to identify a scenario which, given two decomposed systems $(S_1, \mathcal{D}_1)$, $(S_2, \mathcal{D}_2)$, allows us to infer that two components $c_1 \in \mathcal{D}_1$, $c_2 \in \mathcal{D}_2$ are hp (hhp, chhp) bisimilar:

Lemma 1. *Let $x \in \{hp, hhp, chhp\}$; let $(S_1, \mathcal{D}_1)$, $(S_2, \mathcal{D}_2)$ be two decomposed systems. For any pair $c_1 \in \mathcal{D}_1$, $c_2 \in \mathcal{D}_2$ we have: if there exists $(r_1, r_2) \in \sim_x$ such that for $i = 1$, and 2 $\left\{ \begin{array}{l} c_i \notin Ks(r_i), \ and \\ \forall c_i' \in \mathcal{D}_i \backslash c_i. \ r_i \uparrow c_i' \in icmax(c_i') \end{array} \right\}$ then $c_1 \sim_x c_2$.*

Proof (Sketch). Given entities as above, we can extract a hp (hhp, chhp) bisimulation relating c_1 and c_2 from any hp (hhp, chhp) bisimulation containing (r_1, r_2). This is so because: (1) the full behaviour of c_1 and c_2 has still to be matched at (r_1, r_2), and (2) the causal dependencies will force that behaviour of c_1 has to be matched against behaviour of c_2, and vice versa.

From the example of Figure 1 it is clear that, given two hp bisimilar systems, we may never be in a position to apply this lemma. A and B are hp bisimilar but there is no $(r_1, r_2) \in \sim_{hp}$ such that, via Lemma 1, we can deduce $c_1 \sim_{hp} c_2$ for any $c_1 \in PComps(A)$, $c_2 \in PComps(B)$: if B, the only prime component of B, is not contained in $Ks(r_1)$ then $(r_1, r_2) = (\varepsilon, \varepsilon)$; but we neither have $\varepsilon \in icmax(A_1)$ nor $\varepsilon \in icmax(A_2)$.

The scenario of Lemma 1 will, however, certainly be available if for the system class under study we can show: the matching in hp bisimilarity respects prime components in that: let $(r_1, r_2) \in \sim_{hp}$; if, in (r_1, r_2), a transition of prime component c_1 is matched to a transition of prime component c_2, then, in (r_1, r_2), any other transition of c_1 is also matched to a transition of c_2, and vice versa. Then, given $(r_1, r_2) \in \sim_{hp}$, r_1 is 'maximal with respect to initial concurrency' for all but one prime component c_1 such that $c_1 \notin Ks(r_1)$ iff the analogue is true for r_2. On second thought, to guarantee the applicability of Lemma 1 it is sufficient to obtain that the matching of *concurrent steps* (rather than the matching of *all* runs) respects prime components: concurrent steps can be seen as the minimum to consider when we want to achieve maximality with respect to initial concurrency.

We now identify a system class, as large as intuitively possible, which naturally satisfies this criteria: *csc-decomposable systems*. They have the following characteristic: each of their prime components is *cstep connected* (csc) in that: whenever we have computed a concurrent step r and we compute one further concurrently enabled transition

t then there is the possibility of computing a sequence of transitions w such that the last transition of w is causally dependent on t and some transition of r. In short we may say: every concurrent step has a causal link with any further concurrently enabled transition.

Definition 6. *Let S be a system.*
Let $r \in Runs(S)$, and $k, l \in [1, |r|]$. $w \in T_S^+$ is a causal link at r between the events k and l, denoted by $w \in clinks_S(r, k, l)$, iff we have:
$$rw \in Runs(S) \ \& \ k <_{rw} |rw| \ \& \ l <_{rw} |rw|.$$
S is cstep connected (csc) iff for all $r \in csteps(S)$ with $|r| \geq 1$ we have:
$$\forall t \in T_S. \ (rt \in csteps(S) \Rightarrow \exists k \in [1, |r|]. \ \exists w \in T_S^+. \ w \in clinks_S(rt, k, |rt|)).$$
S is csc-decomposable iff every prime component of S is csc. (Note that non-empty csc systems are always prime.)

Example 1. Consider Figure 1. B is not csc: we can do b_1', and then b_3', but there is no causal link between b_1' and b_3'. *Sequential systems* ($\neg(\exists s, s', t, t'. \ t \ I_S \ t' \ \& \ s \xrightarrow{tt'}_S s')$), such as A_1 and A_2, and *initially sequential systems* ($\forall r \in csteps(S). \ |r| \leq 1$) are trivially csc.

Lemma 2. *Let S_1 and S_2 be two csc-decomposable systems. For all $(r_1, r_2) \in \sim_{hp}$ such that $r_i \in csteps(S_i)$ for $i = 1$, or 2 equivalently (Fact 1), we have:*
$$\forall k, l \in [1, |r_1|]. \ (K(r_1[k]) = K(r_1[l]) \iff K(r_2[k]) = K(r_2[l])).$$

Proof (Sketch). We proceed by induction on the length of two related concurrent steps. Let (r_1, r_2) be given as above. Assume, in (r_1, r_2), a transition of prime component c_1 is matched to a transition of prime component c_2, and we want to match a further concurrently enabled c_1-transition, t_1. There will be a causal link at $r_1 t_1$ between event $|r_1 t_1|$ and one of the previously matched c_1-events. By induction hypothesis we can assume these are all matched by c_2-events. But then t_1 has to be matched by a c_2-transition: otherwise the causal link could not be matched in a partial order preserving fashion.

It is routine to derive the following corollaries:

Corollary 1. *Let S_1 and S_2 be two csc-decomposable systems.*

1. *For all $(r_1, r_2) \in \sim_{hp}$ such that $r_i \in csteps(S_i)$ for $i = 1$, or 2 equivalently (Fact 1), we have: $|Ks(r_1)| = |Ks(r_2)|$.*
2. *If $S_1 \sim_{hp} S_2$ then $|PComps(S_1)| = |PComps(S_2)|$.*

Corollary 2. *Let S_1 and S_2 be two csc-decomposable systems, and let $(r_1, r_2) \in \sim_{hp}$ such that $r_i \in csteps(S_i)$ for $i = 1$, or 2 equivalently (Fact 1). For any pair of components $c_1 \in PComps(S_1)$, $c_2 \in PComps(S_2)$ such that $K(r_1[k]) = c_1$ and $K(r_2[k]) = c_2$ for some $k \in [1, |r_1|]$ we have: $r_1 \upharpoonright c_1 \in icmax(c_1) \iff r_2 \upharpoonright c_2 \in icmax(c_2)$.*

For hhp and chhp bisimilarity there is now a simple argument that proves, for csc-decomposable systems, the two bisimilarities are indeed decomposable with respect to prime decompositions (c.f. [20]). This argument relies on backtracking; considering hp bisimilarity it is only obvious that, given two csc-decomposable systems S_1, S_2 with $S_1 \sim_{hp} S_2$, a bijection between $PComps(S_1)$ and $PComps(S_2)$ exists, and further, for each $c_1 \in PComps(S_1)$ there is $c_2 \in PComps(S_2)$ such that $c_1 \sim_{hp} c_2$, and vice versa. To prove decomposition for hp bisimilarity we need something more sophisticated: the combinatorial argument of Hall's Marriage Theorem (e.g. see [24]).

Theorem 4. *Let $x \in \{hp, hhp, chhp\}$; let S_1, S_2 be two csc-decomposable systems. If $S_1 \sim_x S_2$ then there exists a bijection $\beta : PComps(S_1) \to PComps(S_2)$ between the prime components of S_1 and those of S_2 such that $c_1 \sim_x \beta(c_1)$ for each $c_1 \in PComps(S_1)$.*

Proof. Let x, S_1, S_2 be given as above, and assume $S_1 \sim_x S_2$. We shall prove that a bijection β exists as required. By Corollary 1(2) we have (A) $|PComps(S_1)| = |PComps(S_2)|$, and it only remains to show that an injective map can be found. For each $c_1 \in PComps(S_1)$ let $C_{2_{c_1}}$ be the set of prime components of S_2 which are x bisimilar to c_1. By Hall's Marriage Theorem the required injection exists if and only if the following condition is fulfilled:

$$(*) \quad \forall C_1 \subseteq PComps(S_1). \mid \bigcup_{c_1 \in C_1} C_{2_{c_1}} \mid \geq |C_1|.$$

Choose an arbitrary subset C_1 of $PComps(S_1)$. Let $\bar{C}_1 = PComps(S_1) \backslash C_1$, and consider $r_1 \in csteps(S_1)$ such that (B) $Ks(r_1) = \bar{C}_1$, and $\forall c_1 \in \bar{C}_1$. $r_1 \uparrow c_1 \in icmax(c_1)$; this is clearly possible. There must be r_2 such that $(r_1, r_2) \in \sim_x$; set $\bar{C}_2 = Ks(r_2)$, and $C_2 = PComps(S_2) \backslash \bar{C}_2$. By Corollary 2 we obtain $\forall c_2 \in \bar{C}_2$. $r_2 \uparrow c_2 \in icmax(c_2)$. On the other hand, (B) and Corollary 1(1) give us $|\bar{C}_1| = |\bar{C}_2|$, and considering (A) we gain (C) $|C_1| = |C_2|$. Next we show that for each remaining component $c_2 \in C_2$ there is a component $c_1 \in C_1$ such that $c_1 \sim_x c_2$. With (C) this will immediately establish $\mid \bigcup_{c_1 \in C_1} C_{2_{c_1}} \mid \geq |C_1|$, and thereby $(*)$.

Assume C_2 is non-empty, and choose any $c_2 \in C_2$. Consider r_2' such that $r_2 r_2' \in csteps(S_2)$, $Ks(r_2') = C_2 \backslash c_2$, and $\forall c_2' \in C_2 \backslash c_2$. $r_2' \uparrow c_2' \in icmax(c_2')$; this is clearly possible. Note that altogether we have (D) $Ks(r_2 r_2') = PComps(S_2) \backslash c_2$, and $\forall c_2' \in PComps(S_2) \backslash c_2$. $r_2 r_2' \uparrow c_2' \in icmax(c_2')$. There must be r_1' such that $(r_1 r_1', r_2 r_2') \in \sim_x$. Corollary 1(1) gives us $|Ks(r_1 r_1')| = |Ks(r_2 r_2')|$, and by (D), (A), and (B) this implies $Ks(r_1 r_1') = PComps(S_1) \backslash c_1$ for some $c_1 \in C_1$. By Corollary 2 we obtain $\forall c_1' \in PComps(S_1) \backslash c_1$. $r_1 r_1' \uparrow c_1' \in icmax(c_1')$. But altogether this means we can apply Lemma 1 to infer $c_1 \sim_x c_2$. Thus, c_1 provides a component exactly as required.

6   Coincidence Results

We now apply our composition and decomposition theory to prove several coincidence results on hp, hhp, and chhp bisimilarity. First of all, our theory gives us a general proof technique: whenever we consider whether (any two of) the three equivalences coincide for a class of csc-decomposable systems, we can restrict our attention to the respective class of prime components. This is immediate by the following argument:

Argument 1. Assume two csc-decomposable systems S_1 and S_2 that are hp bisimilar. By Theorem 4(hp) we obtain a bijection between the prime components of S_1 and those of S_2 such that related components are hp bisimilar. Then, provided that hp, hhp, and chhp bisimilarity coincide for the class of the prime components, by Theorem 3(chhp) we can conclude that S_1 and S_2 are chhp (and thus also hhp) bisimilar.

It is folklore that for sequential systems hp, hhp, and chhp bisimilarity all coincide with classical bisimilarity (e.g. see [13]). Furthermore, we have already mentioned that sequential systems are csc. Then, with the previous argument we obtain:

Theorem 5. *Hp, hhp, and chhp bisimilarity coincide for parallel compositions of sequential systems.* (Formally, a parallel composition of sequential systems is a system which can be decomposed into sequential components.)

Consider the following generalization of the class 'parallel compositions of sequential systems': each system S is a parallel composition of *initially sequential* components such that each component may, by performing a transition, fork into a parallel composition of initially sequential sub-components, each of which may in turn evolve into a parallel composition of initially sequential sub-components, and so on; this description is complete in that we do not allow any communication between parallel threads. This system class is best known as, and most conveniently captured by, *communication-free net systems*[3]. (Formally, a net system $\mathcal{N}$ is *communication-free* iff $\forall t \in T_N. \, |^\bullet t| = 1$.)

If a communication-free net system S is *concurrency-degree bounded* in that the smallest upper bound on the number of transitions that can be concurrently enabled in S with respect to any state, $cbound(S)$, is given by a natural number, then, for each proper component c of S, $cbound(c)$ will be strictly smaller than $cbound(S)$. With Argument 1 we then obtain coincidence for concurrency-degree bounded communication-free net systems by induction on $cbound(S)$.

Definition 7. *Let S be a system. The* smallest upper bound on the number of transitions that can be concurrently enabled in S with respect to any state, $cbound(S)$, *is defined by* $\max\{cbound_S(s) \mid s \in S_S\}$. S is concurrency-degree bounded *iff* $cbound(S) \in \mathbf{N}_0$.

Theorem 6. *Two councurrency-degree bounded communication-free net systems are hp bisimilar iff they are hhp bisimilar iff they are chhp bisimilar.*

By translating Argument 1 into a tableau system, we achieve coincidence for *simple basic parallel processes* (SBPP). These can be interpreted as an orthogonal class of communication-free net systems[3]: we lift the restriction to concurrency-degree bounded systems, but require our systems to be finitely representable. Following [7], SBPP are defined by process expressions of the grammar: $E ::= S \mid E \, \| \, E$, where '$\|$' is parallel composition and S is an *initially sequential process* expression given by: $S ::= \mathbf{0} \mid a.E \mid S + S \mid X$, where $\mathbf{0}$ is the empty process, $a.E$, where $a \in Act$, is action prefix, '$+$' is nondeterministic choice, and X is an 'initially sequential process' variable. Every SBPP can effectively be transformed into a chhp bisimilar *SBPP in normal form.*

---

[3] As their unfoldings communication-free net systems also capture the class of communication-free weighted Petri nets.

Definition 8. *Let $Vars = \{X_1, X_2, \ldots\}$ be a set of process variables, and $Vars^{\otimes} = \{\alpha, \beta, \ldots\}$ the set of finite multisets over $Vars$. We identify $\alpha = \{X, X, Y\}$ with the parallel composition $X \parallel X \parallel Y$; the empty multiset is recognized as the process $\mathbf{0}$.*
A SBPP in normal form is a pair $\mathcal{E} = (E_0, \Delta_{\mathcal{E}})$, where $E_0 \in Vars^{\otimes}$, and $\Delta_{\mathcal{E}}$ is a finite family of recursive equations $\{X_i := E_i \mid 1 \le i \le m\}$. The X_i are distinct, and the E_i are of the form: $a_1.\alpha_1 + a_2.\alpha_2 + \ldots + a_n.\alpha_n$, where $n \ge 1$, and $\forall i \in [1, n]$. $\alpha_i \in Vars^{\otimes}$. Further, $\forall i \in [0, m]$, E_i at most contains the variables $\{X_1, \ldots, X_m\}$.

Theorem 7. *Two SBPP are hp bisimilar iff they are hhp bisimilar iff they are chhp bisimilar.*

Proof (Sketch). The tableau proof system of Figure 2 gives rise to a decision procedure that decides whether two SBPP in normal form are hp bisimilar, and at the same time, whether they are chhp bisimilar. Rule **Match** provides matching for initially sequential processes; rule **Decomp** reflects our decomposition theory, and provides the means to reduce pairs of processes to check into smaller pairs of processes to compare. Theorem 4(hp) implies forward soundness of **Decomp** for hp bisimilarity, Theorem 3(chhp) gives us backwards soundness of **Decomp** for chhp bisimilarity. Finiteness, completeness for hp bisimilarity, and soundness for chhp bisimilarity of the tableau system can then be proved by using the standard arguments.

Rec $\qquad \dfrac{X = Y}{E = F} \qquad$ where $(X := E) \in \Delta_{\mathcal{E}}, (Y := F) \in \Delta_{\mathcal{F}}$

Match $\qquad \dfrac{\sum_{i=1}^{n} a_i.\alpha_i = \sum_{j=1}^{m} b_j.\beta_j}{\{\alpha_i = \beta_{f(i)}\}_{i=1}^{n} \qquad \{\alpha_{g(j)} = \beta_j\}_{j=1}^{m}}$

$\qquad\qquad$ where $f : [1, n] \to [1, m], g : [1, m] \to [1, n]$ are functions such that $\forall i \in [1, n]$. $a_i = b_{f(i)}$, and similarly for g.

Decomp $\qquad \dfrac{\alpha = \beta}{\{X = Y\}_{(X,Y)\in b}} \qquad$ where $b : \alpha \to \beta$ is a bijection (relating variable instances).

A node n is a *successful terminal* iff

$n\colon \mathbf{0} = \mathbf{0}$, or

$n\colon X = Y$, and there is a node $n_a\colon X = Y$ above n in the tableau.

A node n is an *unsuccessful terminal* iff

$n\colon \alpha = \beta$, and a bijection b as required by rule **Decomp** does not exist, or

$n\colon \sum_{i=1}^{n} a_i.\alpha_i = \sum_{j=1}^{m} b_j.\beta_j$, and f and g as required by rule **Match** do not exist.

Fig. 2. A tableau system with respect to two SBPP in normal form $\mathcal{E}$ and $\mathcal{F}$

7   Conclusions

There are further applications of our decomposition theory. In analogy to Argument 1 decidability of hp (hhp, chhp) bisimilarity on a class of finite-state csc-decomposable systems reduces to decidability on the respective class of prime components (recall Theorem 2). Further, if a system is specified in terms of csc components, our decomposition theory is profitable with respect to tackling the state explosion problem: we do not need to check hp (hhp, chhp) bisimilarity on the global state space but we can proceed by checking the respective equivalence on pairs of components.

One might speculate that (c)hhp bisimilarity is decomposable with respect to prime decompositions for systems in general: with the help of backtracking one might be able to prove a general version of Lemma 2; though this may be hard, or at least technically tedious, to carry through. Furthermore, as pointed out to me by Lasota, in the formulation of a general version of Lemma 2 and the decomposition theorem, one will have to address the issue of (c)hhp bisimilar choices: let $P = (P_1 \parallel P_2) + (P_1 \parallel P_2)$ and $Q = P_1 \parallel P_2$; clearly $P \sim_{(c)hhp} Q$ but since P is prime there is no bijection between the prime components of P and those of Q.

It is, of course, also possible to investigate whether a truly-concurrent equivalence satisfies the unique decomposition property usually investigated in the interleaving setting. (Given some class of process terms, is each of them uniquely, up to the equivalence, represented as a parallel composition of primes?) Indeed, unique decomposition with respect to distributed bisimilarity has been proved for BPP [25]. Note, however, that decomposition in this sense is *not* sufficient to establish the results of Section 6.

We hope this paper motivates the particular significance of composition and decomposition for true-concurrency: decomposition characteristics of a system class may translate into truly-concurrent equivalences or logics in a very concrete way, and thereby lead us to decision procedures and/or coincidence results. In this spirit, the ideas of the paper can be taken further: one could investigate whether a similar approach is possible with respect to temporal logics, and, orthogonally, whether our decomposition theory can be generalized by integrating a concept of synchronization. Indeed, the latter idea stands behind the result that (c)hhp bisimilarity is decidable for a class of live free-choice systems [13]. This is so far the only positive result on hhp bisimilarity for a class that admits a flexible form of synchronization. ([26] presents that hhp bisimilarity is decidable for trace-labelled systems but the proof turned out to be incomplete [15].)

Acknowledgements. I would like to thank Walter Vogler: he has provided crucial help by pointing out to me that Hall's Marriage Theorem has to be applied in the proof of an earlier version of Theorem 4. I thank Javier Esparza, Mogens Nielsen, Damian Niwinski, and the anonymous referees for their valuable comments on this work. I thank Monika Maidl, who has helped to clarify a question related to Theorem 2. Finally, I would like to thank Slawomir Lasota for pointing out to me the issue of (c)hhp bisimilar choices.

References

1. Penczek, W., Kuiper, R.: Traces and logic. In: The Book of Traces. World Scientific (1995) 307–381
2. Madhusudan, P., Thiagarajan, P.S.: Controllers for discrete event systems via morphisms. In: CONCUR'98. Volume 1466 of LNCS. (1998) 18–33

3. Jurdziński, M., Nielsen, M., Srba, J.: Domino hereditary history preserving bisimilarity is undecidable. Inform. and Comput. **184** (2003) 343–368

4. Vogler, W.: Deciding history preserving bisimilarity. In: ICALP'91. Volume 510 of LNCS. (1991) 495–505

5. Jategaonkar, L., Meyer, A.R.: Deciding true concurrency equivalences on safe, finite nets. TCS **154** (1996) 107–143

6. Montanari, U., Pistore, M.: Minimal transition systems for history-preserving bisimulation. In: STACS'97. Volume 1200 of LNCS. (1997) 413–425

7. Esparza, J., Kiehn, A.: On the model checking problem for branching time logics and basic parallel processes. In: CAV'95. Volume 939 of LNCS. (1995) 353–366

8. Sunesen, K., Nielsen, M.: Behavioural equivalence for infinite systems—partially decidable! In: ICATPN'96. Volume 1091 of LNCS. (1996) 460–479

9. Jančar, P.: Strong bisimilarity on basic parallel processes is PSPACE-complete. In: LICS'03, IEEE (2003) 216–??.

10. Srba, J.: Strong bisimilarity and regularity of basic parallel processes is PSPACE-hard. In: STACS'02. Volume 2285 of LNCS. (2002) 535–546

11. Lasota, S.: A polynomial-time algorithm for deciding true concurrency equivalences of basic parallel processes. In: MFCS'03. Volume 2747 of LNCS. (2003) 521–530

12. Fröschle, S.: Decidability of plain and hereditary history-preserving bisimulation for BPP. In: EXPRESS'99. Volume 27 of ENTCS. (1999)

13. Fröschle, S.: Decidability and Coincidence of Equivalences for Concurrency. PhD thesis, University of Edinburgh (2004)

14. Winskel, G., Nielsen, M.: Models for concurrency. In: Handbook of logic in computer science, Vol. 4. Oxford Univ. Press (1995) 1–148

15. Fröschle, S.: The decidability border of hereditary history preserving bisimilarity. Information Processing Letters (to appear)

16. Hirshfeld, Y., Jerrum, M., Moller, F.: A polynomial-time algorithm for deciding bisimulation equivalence of normed basic parallel processes. Mathematical Structures in Computer Science **6** (1996) 251–259

17. Jančar, P., Kot, M.: Bisimilarity on normed basic parallel processes can be decided in time $o(n^3)$. In: AVIS'04. ENTCS (2004)

18. Christensen, S., Hirshfeld, Y., Moller, F.: Decomposability, decidability and axiomatisability for bisimulation equivalence on basic parallel processes. In: LICS'93, IEEE (1993) 386–396

19. Milner, R., Moller, F.: Unique decomposition of processes. TCS **107** (1993) 357–363

20. Fröschle, S.: Composition and decomposition in true-concurrency. Technical Report 276, Institute of Informatics, University of Warsaw (2004)

21. Fröschle, S., Hildebrandt, T.: On plain and hereditary history-preserving bisimulation. In: MFCS'99. Volume 1672 of LNCS. (1999) 354–365

22. Pin, J.E.: Syntactic semigroups. In: Handbook of formal languages, Vol. 1. Springer (1997) 680–746

23. Norman, C.W.: Undergraduate Algebra. Oxford Science Publications (1986)

24. Truss, J.K.: Discrete Mathematics for Computer Scientists. Addison-Wesley (1991)

25. Christensen, S.: Decidability and Decomposition in Process Algebras. PhD thesis, University of Edinburgh (1993)

26. Mukund, M.: Hereditary history preserving bisimulation is decidable for trace-labelled systems. In: FST TCS'02. Volume 2556 of LNCS. (2002) 289–300

Component Refinement and CSC Solving for STG Decomposition*

Mark Schaefer and Walter Vogler

University of Augsburg, Germany
{schaefer, vogler}@informatik.uni-augsburg.de

Abstract. STGs (Signal Transition Graphs) give a formalism for the description of asynchronous circuits based on Petri nets. To overcome the state explosion problem one may encounter during circuit synthesis, a nondeterministic algorithm for decomposing STGs was suggested by Chu and improved by one of the present authors.

We study how CSC solving (which is essential for circuit synthesis) can be combined with decomposition. For this purpose the correctness definition for decomposition is enhanced with internal signals and it is shown that speed-independent CSC solving preserves correctness. The latter uses a more general result about correctness of top-down decomposition. Furthermore, we apply our definition to give the first correctness proof for the decomposition method of Carmona and Cortadella.

1   Introduction

Signal Transition Graphs (STG) are a formalism for the description of asynchronous circuit behaviour. An STG is a labelled Petri net where the labels denote signal changes between logical high and logical low. The synthesis of circuits from STGs is supported by several tools, e.g. PETRIFY [5], and it often involves the generation of the reachability graph, which may have a size exponential in the size of the STG (state explosion). To cope with this problem, Chu suggested a nondeterministic method for decomposing an STG (without internal signals) into several smaller ones [4], see also [10]. While there are strong restrictions on the structure and labelling of STGs in [4], the improved decomposition algorithm of Vogler, Wollowski and Kangsah [12, 11] works under – comparatively moderate – restrictions on the labelling only.

Roughly, this decomposition algorithm works as follows. Initially, a partition of the output signals has to be chosen, and for each set in this partition a component producing the respective output signals will be constructed as follows.

For each component, our algorithm finds a set of signals that (at least initially) can be regarded as irrelevant for the output signals under consideration;

---

* This work was partially supported by the DFG-project 'STG-Dekomposition' Vo615/7-1.

V. Sassone (Ed.): FOSSACS 2005, LNCS 3441, pp. 348–363, 2005.

then, it takes a copy of the original STG and turns each transition corresponding to an irrelevant signal into a dummy (λ-labelled) transition; finally, it tries
to remove all dummy transitions by so-called secure transition contractions and
deletions of (structurally) redundant places or redundant transitions.

In general, our algorithm might find during this process that additional signals are relevant; then, it has to start anew from a suitably modified copy of the
original STG – which eventually gives a correct component as proven in [12, 11].

Complete state coding (CSC) is an important property for STGs and must
be achieved before an asynchronous circuit can be synthesized; e.g. PETRIFY
can *solve CSC*, i.e. modify an STG on the basis of its reachability graph such
that CSC holds. While some decomposition methods [2, 13] have to assume that
the original STG satisfies CSC, our decomposition algorithm is more general
since it does not presuppose this; on the other hand, the methods in [2, 13]
construct components with CSC, while our components might not have CSC.
For each such component one can solve CSC and synthesize a separate circuit
e.g. by using PETRIFY; compared to solving CSC for the original STG (with
its potentially huge reachability graph) and synthesizing one circuit, this can be
much faster, see experimental results in [12, 11].

One would expect that the components generated by our decomposition algorithm are still correct when they have been modified to achieve CSC, and in
fact it would also be very interesting in what sense CSC-solving with PETRIFY
is correct – independently of the issue of decomposition; it seems that no correctness for this has been proven so far. For such correctness results, one needs
a correctness definition that takes *internal signals* into account.

The purpose of this paper is to enhance the correctness definition of [12] and
[11] appropriately, to study its properties and give applications in the area of
decomposition and CSC-solving.

As the main property of the new correctness notion, we show that it is preserved when decomposition is performed stepwise. While this correctness of top-
down decomposition is of interest in itself, it can in particular be used to improve
the efficiency of our decomposition algorithm. Then we prove that CSC-solving
for speed-independent circuits as performed by PETRIFY is correct in our sense.
With our result on the correctness of top-down decomposition, we then conclude that speed-independent CSC-solving can indeed be combined with the
decomposition algorithm of [12, 11]. As another contribution, we prove that the
decomposition method in [2] is correct in the sense of our enhanced correctness
definition; in [2] itself, no correctness proof is given.

The paper is organized as follows. In the next section, Petri Nets, STGs
and their basic notions are introduced. Furthermore the correctness definition
is enhanced with internal signals. In Section 3, we prove top-down decomposition correct in terms of our enhanced correctness definition; the succeed-
ing section studies correctness of speed-independent CSC solving on its own
and in combination with decomposition. Section 5 shows the correctness for
the approach of [2]. We conclude with Section 6. Due to lack of space we
omit all proofs; they can be found at www.informatik.uni-augsburg.de/forschung
/techBerichte/reports/2004-13.html.

2   Basic Definitions

This section provides the basic notions for Petri nets and STGs, for a more detailed explanation cf. e.g. [6]. A *Petri net* is a 4-tuple $N = (P, T, W, M_N)$ where P is a finite set of *places* and T a finite set of *transitions* with $P \cap T = \emptyset$. $W : P \times T \cup T \times P \to \mathbb{N}_0$ is the *weight function* and M_N the *initial marking*, where a *marking* is a function $P \to \mathbb{N}_0$. A *node* is a place or a transition and a Petri net can be considered as a bipartite graph with weighted and directed edges between its nodes. A marking is a function which assigns a number of *tokens* to each place. Whenever a Petri net N, N', N_1, etc. is introduced, the corresponding tuples $(P, T, W, M_N), (P', T', W', M_{N'})$, (P_1, T_1, W_1, M_{N_1}) etc. are introduced implicitly and the same applies to STGs later on.

The *preset* of a node x is denoted as ${}^\bullet x$ and defined by ${}^\bullet x = \{y \in P \cup T \mid W(y, x) > 0\}$, the *postset* of a node x is denoted as $x^\bullet$ and defined by $x^\bullet = \{y \in P \cup T \mid W(x, y) > 0\}$. We write ${}^\bullet x^\bullet$ as shorthand for ${}^\bullet x \cup x^\bullet$. All these notions are extended to sets as usual. We say that there is an *arc* from each $y \in {}^\bullet x$ to x.

Given a *sequence* $x \in X^*$, and a set $X' \subseteq X$, $x{\downarrow}_{X'}$ denotes the *projection of x onto X'* and is obtained from x by omitting all elements not in X'. This is extended to sets of sequences as usual, i.e. elementwise.

A transition t is *enabled under a marking M* if $\forall p \in {}^\bullet t : M(p) \geq W(p, t)$, which is denoted by $M[t\rangle$. An enabled transition can *fire* or *occur* yielding a new marking M', written as $M[t\rangle M'$, if $M[t\rangle$ and $M'(p) = M(p) - W(p, t) + W(t, p)$ for all $p \in P$.

A transition sequence $v = t_0 t_1 \ldots t_n$ is *enabled under a marking M* (yielding M') if $M[t_0\rangle M_0[t_1\rangle M_1 \ldots M_{n-1}[t_n\rangle M_n = M'$, and we write $M[v\rangle$, $M[v\rangle M'$ resp.; v is called *firing sequence* if $M_N[v\rangle$. The empty transition sequence λ is enabled under every marking.

M' is called *reachable from M* if a transition sequence v with $M[v\rangle M'$ exists. The set of all markings reachable from M is denoted by $[M\rangle$. $[M_N\rangle$ is the set of *reachable markings* (of N), and we only deal with N where this set is finite (i.e. N is *bounded*).

An *STG* is a tuple $N = (P, T, W, M_N, In, Out, Int, l)$ where (P, T, W, M_N) is a Petri net and In, Out and Int are disjoint sets of *input*, *output* and *internal* signals. We define the set of all signals $Sig := In \cup Out \cup Int$, the set of *locally controlled* or just *local signals* $Loc := Out \cup Int$ and the set of all *external signals* $Ext := In \cup Out$. $l : T \to Sig \times \{+, -\}$ is the *labelling function*. In this paper we do not have to consider λ-labelled *dummy transitions*, which play an important role in the decomposition algorithm of [12,11].

An STG can be taken as a formalism for *asynchronous circuits*. Such a circuit has input signals, which are under the control of its environment, and local signals, whose values are changed by the circuit. The STG describes which output and internal signals should be performed; at the same time, it describes assumptions about the environment, which should perform input signals only if this is specified by the STG.

$Sig \times \{+, -\}$ or short $Sig\pm$ is the set of *signal changes* or *signal transitions*; its elements are denoted as $a+$, $a-$ resp. instead of $(a, +)$, $(a, -)$ resp. A plus sign denotes that a signal value changes from *logical low* (written as 0) to *logical high* (written as 1), and a minus sign denotes the other direction. We write $a\pm$ if it is not important or unknown which direction takes place; if such a term appears more than once in the same context, it always denotes the same direction.

Some of the results of this paper do not depend on the fact that transition labels are of the form $a+$ or $a-$, i.e. they can be applied in any setting where actions can be regarded as inputs, outputs or internal.

We lift the notion of enabledness to transition labels: We write $M[a\pm\rangle\rangle M'$ if $M[t\rangle M'$ and $l(t) = a\pm$. This is extended to sequences as usual. A sequence $v \in (Sig\pm)^*$ is called a *trace of a marking* M if $M[v\rangle\rangle$, and a *trace* of N if $M = M_N$. The *language of* N is the set of all traces of N and denoted by $L(N)$.

The *reachability graph* RG_N of an STG N is an edge-labelled directed graph on the reachable markings with M_N as root; there is an edge from M to M' labelled $s\pm \in Sig\pm$ whenever $M[s\pm\rangle\rangle M'$. RG_N can be seen as a finite automaton (where all states are final), and $L(N)$ is the language of this automaton. N is *deterministic* if its reachability graph is a deterministic automaton, i.e. if for each reachable marking M and each signal transition $s\pm$ there is at most one M' with $M[s\pm\rangle\rangle M'$.

The identity of the transitions or places of an STG, as well as the names of the internal signals are not relevant for us; hence, we regard STGs N and N' as equal if they are *externally isomorphic*, i.e. if they have the same input and output signals, and we can rename the internal signals of N and then map the transitions (places resp.) of the resulting STG bijectively onto the transitions (places resp.) of N' such that the weight function, the marking and the labelling are preserved. (Altogether, the external signals are preserved while the internal signals might be renamed.)

For the modular construction of STGs, the operations *hiding*, *relabelling* and *parallel composition* are of interest.

Given an STG N and a set H of signals with $H \cap In = \emptyset$, the *hiding of H* results in the STG $N/H = (P, T, W, M_N, In, Out \setminus H, Int \cup H, l)$.

Given a bijection ϕ defined for all external signals of N, the *relabelling* of N is $\phi(N) = (P, T, W, M_0, \phi(In), \phi(Out), Int, \phi \circ l)$; this assumes that, if necessary, the internal signals of N are renamed such that $Int \cap (\phi(In) \cup \phi(Out)) = \emptyset$ and ϕ is extended to be the identity on the internal signals.

Observe that hiding and relabeling preserve determinism as defined above and the same will apply for parallel composition. In particular hiding does not change the identity of signals or removes them completely from the STG as it is done in other settings.

In the following definition of *parallel composition* $\|$, we will have to consider the distinction between input, output and internal signals. The idea of parallel composition is that the composed systems run in parallel synchronising on common signals. Since a system controls its outputs, we cannot allow a signal to be an output of more than one component; input signals, on the other hand, can be shared. An output signal of one component can be an input of one or several others, and in any case it is an output of the composition. Internal signals of one component are not shared with other components (this can be achieved with a suitable renaming) and they become internal signals of the composition.

A composition can also be ill-defined due to what e.g. Ebergen [8] calls computation interference; this is a semantic problem, and we will not consider it here, but later in the definition of correctness.

The *parallel composition* of STGs N_1 and N_2 is defined if $Loc_1 \cap Loc_2 = \emptyset$ and $Int_1 \cap In_2 = Int_2 \cap In_1 = \emptyset$. Then, let $A = Sig_1 \cap Sig_2$ be the set of common signals; observe that A contains no internal signals. If e.g. s is an output of N_1 and an input of N_2, then an occurrence of s in N_1 is 'seen' by N_2, i.e. it must be accompanied by an occurrence of s in N_2. Since we do not know a priori which $s\pm$-labelled transition of N_2 will occur together with some $s\pm$-labelled transition of N_1, we have to allow for each possible pairing. Thus, the *parallel composition* $N = N_1 \parallel N_2$ is obtained from the disjoint union of N_1 and N_2 by combining each $s\pm$-labelled transition t_1 of N_1 with each $s\pm$-labelled transition t_2 from N_2 if $s \in A$. In the formal definition of parallel composition, $*$ is used as a dummy element, which is formally combined e.g. with those transitions that do not have their label in the synchronisation set A. (We assume that $*$ is not a transition or a place of any net.) Thus, N is defined by

$$P = P_1 \times \{*\} \cup \{*\} \times P_2$$
$$T = \{(t_1, t_2) \mid t_1 \in T_1, t_2 \in T_2, l_1(t_1) = l_2(t_2) \in A\pm\}$$
$$\cup \{(t_1, *) \mid t_1 \in T_1, l_1(t_1) \notin A\pm\}$$
$$\cup \{(*, t_2) \mid t_2 \in T_2, l_2(t_2) \notin A\pm\}$$
$$W((p_1, p_2), (t_1, t_2)) = \begin{cases} W_1(p_1, t_1) & \text{if } p_1 \in P_1, \ t_1 \in T_1 \\ W_2(p_2, t_2) & \text{if } p_2 \in P_2, \ t_2 \in T_2 \end{cases}$$
$$W((t_1, t_2), (p_1, p_2)) = \begin{cases} W_1(t_1, p_1) & \text{if } p_1 \in P_1, \ t_1 \in T_1 \\ W_2(t_2, p_2) & \text{if } p_2 \in P_2, \ t_2 \in T_2 \end{cases}$$
$$l((t_1, t_2)) = \begin{cases} l_1(t_1) & \text{if } t_1 \in T_1 \\ l_2(t_2) & \text{if } t_2 \in T_2 \end{cases}$$
$$M_N = M_{N_1} \dot\cup M_{N_2}, \text{ i.e.}$$
$$M_N((p_1, p_2)) = \begin{cases} M_{N_1}(p_1) & \text{if } p_1 \in P_1 \\ M_{N_2}(p_2) & \text{if } p_2 \in P_2 \end{cases}$$
$$Int = Int_1 \cup Int_2 \qquad Out = Out_1 \cup Out_2 \qquad In = (In_1 \cup In_2) - (Out_1 \cup Out_2)$$

It is not hard to see that parallel composition is associative and commutative up to external isomorphism and $\parallel_{i \in I} N_i$ is defined if each $N_i \parallel N_j$ is defined. Furthermore, one can consider the place set of the composition as the disjoint union of the place sets of the components; therefore, we can consider markings of the composition (regarded as multisets) as the disjoint union of markings of the components; the latter makes clear what we mean by the restriction $M\big|_{P_i}$ for a marking M of the composition.

STGs together with the three operations defined above form a *circuit algebra* as defined in Dill's PhD thesis [7], when regarding externally isomorphic STGs as equal. For our further considerations we will use the properties

$$(C6) : (N/H_1)/H_2 = N/(H_1 \cup H_2) \text{ and}$$

$$(C8) : N_1/H_1||N_2/H_2 = (N_1||N_2)/(H_1 \cup H_2) \text{ if } H_i \cap Sig_{3-i} = \emptyset, i = 1, 2$$

satisfied by a circuit algebra.[1]

Let RG be the reachability graph of an STG N. A *state vector* is a function $sv : Sig \rightarrow \{0, 1\}$ where '0' means logical low and '1' logical high. A *state assignment* assigns a state vector to each marking M of RG denoted by sv_M.

A state assignment must satisfy for every signal $x \in Sig$ and every pair of markings $M, M' \in [M_N\rangle$:

$$M[x+\rangle\rangle M' \text{ implies } sv_M(x) = 0, sv_{M'}(x) = 1$$

$$M[x-\rangle\rangle M' \text{ implies } sv_M(x) = 1, sv_{M'}(x) = 0$$

$$M[y\pm\rangle\rangle M' \text{ for } y \neq x \text{ implies } sv_M(x) = sv_{M'}(x)$$

If such an assignment exists, it is uniquely defined by these properties,[2] and the reachability graph (and also the underlying STG) is called *consistent*. From an *inconsistent* STG, one cannot synthesize a circuit.

Another necessary condition for synthesis is *complete state coding (CSC)*. We say that a consistent RG (and N) *has CSC* if:

$$\forall x \in Loc, \ M, M' \in [M_N\rangle : sv_M = sv_{M'} \Rightarrow (M[x\pm\rangle\rangle \Leftrightarrow M'[x\pm\rangle\rangle)$$

If RG *violates CSC*, no asynchronous circuit can be synthesized because a circuit determines the next local signal changes only from the current state of its signals (the state vector); hence, the circuit cannot distinguish the two markings with the same state vector and the same local signals must be enabled. It is possible that different input signals are enabled in M and M' because these are not controlled by the circuit.

As mentioned in the introduction, PETRIFY can modify an STG such that CSC is satisfied. If one is interested in speed-independent circuits, as we are in this paper, one can require that PETRIFY preserves the following important property.

---

[1] There are 7 additional laws a circuit algebra must fulfil (in our setting): (C1) $(N_1||N_2)||N_3 = N_1||(N_2||N_3) = N_1||N_2||N_3$, (C2): $N_1||N_2 = N_2||N_1$; (C3): $\phi_2(\phi_1(N)) = (\phi_2 \circ \phi_1)(N)$, (C4): $\phi(N_1||N_2) = \phi(N_1)||\phi(N_2)$, (C5): $id(N) = N$, (C7): $N/\emptyset = N$, (C9): $\phi(N/H) = \phi'(N)/\phi'(H)$. These properties are satisfied for our definitions, where (C4) and (C9) only have to hold if both sides are defined.

[2] At least for every signal $s \in Sig$ which actually occurs, i.e. $M[s\pm\rangle\rangle$ for some reachable marking M.

Definition 1 (Input Properness). An *STG* is *input proper* if no input signal becomes enabled by the occurrence of an internal signal, i.e. $M_1[t\rangle M_2$ with M_1 a reachable marking, $\neg M_1[a\rangle\rangle$ and $M_2[a\rangle\rangle$, $a \in In$, implies $l(t) \notin Int\pm$.   □

Recall that an STG also specifies which inputs the environment may perform; if the environment performs an input that is not enabled in the current marking of the STG, then such an unexpected input may lead to a malfunction of the circuit. To meet this assumption, the environment must "know" whether an input is expected or not. But if input properness is violated, the environment cannot see whether the respective input is already allowed, since internal signal transitions cannot be observed from the outside.

Actually, the implementation of non-input-proper STGs is still possible, but one has to make *timing assumptions* about the relative order of signal transitions, e.g. one might assume that an input is slower than an internal signal if both are triggered by the same output. Such assumptions are not necessary for input proper STGs, and *speed-independent* implementations are possible.

Now we give our improved correctness definition, which considers internal signals; afterwards, we will explain its specific properties and why they are sound.

Definition 2 (Correct Decomposition). A collection of deterministic components $(C_i)_{i \in I}$ is a *correct decomposition* of (or simply *correct w.r.t.*) a deterministic STG N – also called *specification* – when hiding H, if the parallel composition $C' = \|_{i \in I} C_i$ is defined, $C = C'/H$, $In_C \subseteq In_N$, $Out_C \subseteq Out_N$ and there is an *STG-bisimulation* $\mathcal{B}$ between the markings of N and those of C with the following properties:

1. $(M_N, M_C) \in \mathcal{B}$
2. For all $(M, M') \in \mathcal{B}$, we have:
   (N1) If $a \in In_N$ and $M[a\pm\rangle\rangle M_1$, then either $a \in In_C$, $M'[a\pm\rangle\rangle M_1'$ and $(M_1, M_1') \in \mathcal{B}$ for some M_1' or $a \notin In_C$ and $(M_1, M') \in \mathcal{B}$.
   (N2) If $x \in Out_N$ and $M[x\pm\rangle\rangle M_1$, then $M'[vx\pm\rangle\rangle M_1'$ and $(M_1, M_1') \in \mathcal{B}$ for some M_1' with $v \in (Int_C\pm)^*$.
   (N3) If $u \in Int_N$ and $M[u\pm\rangle\rangle M_1$, then $M'[v\rangle\rangle M_1'$ and $(M_1, M_1') \in \mathcal{B}$ for some M_1' and $v \in (Int_{C'}\pm)^*$.
   (C1) If $x \in Out_C$ and $M'[x\pm\rangle\rangle M_1'$, then $M[vx\pm\rangle\rangle M_1$ and $(M_1, M_1') \in \mathcal{B}$ for some M_1 with $v \in (Int_N\pm)^*$.
   (C2) If $x \in Out_i$ for some $i \in I$ and $M'|_{P_i}[x\pm\rangle\rangle$, then $M'[x\pm\rangle\rangle$. (no *computation interference*)
   (C3) If $u \in Int_C$ and $M'[u\pm\rangle\rangle M_1'$, then $M[v\rangle\rangle M_1$ and $(M_1, M_1') \in \mathcal{B}$ for some M_1 and $v \in (Int_N\pm)^*$.

Here, and whenever we have a collection $(C_i)_{i \in I}$ in the following, P_i stands for P_{C_i}, Out_i for Out_{C_i} etc.

In the most simple case, $(C_i)_{i \in I}$ consists of just one component C_1 and H is empty; in this case we say that C_1 is a *(correct) implementation* of N, and (C2) is always trivially true.   □

$\mathcal{B}$ describes how behaviour of N and C closely match each other, similar to ordinary bisimulation. As in [12, 11], we allow Out_C to be a proper subset of Out_N for the case that there are output signals, which are in fact never produced by the specification. Our decomposition algorithm actually only produces components C_i where $Out_C = Out_N$; in any case, if equality is desired, it can be achieved by formally adding the missing output signals $Out_N \setminus Out_C$ to some set Out_i.

For a different reason we allow In_C to be a proper subset of In_N; there are cases where some inputs are just *irrelevant* for the behaviour of a circuit, but they were possibly included by some design error. The decomposition algorithm might detect such signals, since they are not needed for any component. Because of this possibility, in (N1) an input signal transition of the specification does not have to be matched by the implementation.

(C2) ensures that no computation interference (mentioned before the definition of parallel composition) occurs; i.e. if a component produces an output (which is under the control of this component), then the other components expect this signal if it belongs to their inputs, and no malfunction of these other components must be feared. (C2) is actually also satisfied for $x \in Int_i$, since internal signals of one component are by definition unknown to the other components.

Remarkably, there is no condition that requires a matching for an input occurring in the implementation. On the one hand, if also the specification allows such an input in a matching marking, then the markings after the input must match again by (N1) due to determinism. On the other hand, there are very natural decompositions which allow additional inputs compared to the specification, and it does no harm to include these decompositions in our definition: since the specification also describes which inputs are or are not allowed for the environment, the additional inputs will actually never occur if the decomposition runs in an environment it is meant for. (The additional input leads to a marking which in a way corresponds to a don't-care entry in a Karnaugh-diagram.)

As a consequence, the components might have behaviour and markings that never turn up if the components run in an appropriate environment; also, these markings do not appear in $\mathcal{B}$. A subtle property of our correctness definition is that it allows e.g. computation interference for such markings, which is perfectly reasonable since such an interference will not occur in practical use.

The features discussed so far are taken from [12], where some more explanations can be found. The new features deal with internal signals; they extend the definition of [12] conservatively: for STGs without internal signals, the two correctness notions coincide. The consequence will be that the result about top-down decomposition in the next section also applies in the setting of our decomposition algorithm, where we have not considered internal signals so far.

First of all, we allow the hiding of some output signals in the parallel composition of the components; this concerns additional signals to enable communication between the components. It is no problem that we allow hiding at the "top-level" only: by way of an example, assume that the components C_1 and

C_2 communicate via a signal x which should not be visible to the other components; this would be modelled by $\left(((C_1\|C_2)/\{x\}) \ \| \ (\|_{i\in I\setminus\{1,2\}}C_i)\right)/H$. Now this equals $\|_{i\in I}C_i/(H \cup \{x\})$ by the properties (C8) and (C6) of a circuit algebra, where (C8) is applicable since x is internal to $(C_1\|C_2)/\{x\}$ and hence not a signal of $\|_{i\in I\setminus\{1,2\}}C_i$. We will use similar reasoning in Section 3 where a component will be replaced by a decomposition of its own.

In (N2) and (C1) outputs do not have to be matched directly; (N2) allows the components to prepare the production of this output by some internal signals, e.g. to achieve CSC or to inform other components about this event; (C1) allows the specification to perform superfluous internal signals. In any case, from an external point of view each output is matched by the same output.

In contrast, input signals must be matched directly; if the implementation could precede the input by some internal signals, the environment could produce the input as specified in N at a stage where the implementation is not ready yet to receive it, which could lead to malfunction as discussed above in connection with input properness. As for computation interference, the absence of this malfunction is only checked for markings appearing in $\mathcal{B}$, since only for these the problem is practically relevant.

In fact, the direct matching of inputs implies that the implementation is in a sense input proper, at least in its "reachable behaviour": assume that $M_1[u\pm\rangle\rangle M_2$ with $u \in Int_C$, M_1 a reachable marking of C, and $M_2[a\pm\rangle\rangle$ for some $a \in In_C$; then either there is no pair (M, M_1) in the STG-bisimulation (hence, M_1 will not be reached if C works in a proper environment) or $\neg M[a\rangle\rangle$ (a proper environment will not produce a) or $M_1[a\rangle\rangle$ by (N1).

Finally, (N3) and (C3) prescribe the matching of an internal signal by a sequence of internal signals – just as in ordinary weak bisimulation. Note that we have several internal signals, since these have to be implemented physically; but regarding external behaviour, the identity of an internal signal does not matter. In principle, performing an internal signal could make a choice, e.g. by disabling an output; according to these clauses, this choice has to be matched.

Translating the treatment of internal signals in the definition of the somewhat related notion of I/O-compatibility [1] to our setting, one would require that e.g. in (N3) $(M_1, M') \in \mathcal{B}$ without involving any u – and analogously in (C3); the idea is that internal signals cannot make decisions in digital circuits. There are several reasons not to follow this idea. First of all, this concerns a property one might like all STGs to have and it is not related to comparing STGs or to the communication between circuits – in contrast to e.g. computation interference; if one wants this property to ensure physical implementability, it has to hold also for markings not appearing in $\mathcal{B}$. Therefore, this property has no adequate place in a correctness definition and should be required separately. Secondly, one might want to use so-called ME-elements , which can make decisions; the respective signals could be internal to the parallel composition. We see it as an advantage that we can cover such cases. Finally, the alternative definition turned out to be technically inconvenient.

Observe that the alternative definition coincides with ours if the specification does not have internal signals; then, (N3) is never applicable, and in (C3) we have $v = \lambda$ and $M = M_1$.

Another important comment: our correctness definition concerns the correctness of a decomposition, but it also covers the question whether one STG is an implementation of another. With this notion, we will prove below that speed-independent CSC-solving with PETRIFY produces a correct implementation.

One would like this implementation relation to be a preorder. Reflexivity is obvious (choose $\mathcal{B}$ as the identity), and transitivity will follow from our first main result in the next section. One would also like it to be a precongruence for the operations of interest. This is obvious for relabelling and easy for hiding (use the same STG-bisimulation). The much more important case of parallel composition will be discussed in the next section.

Also, a more general result for hiding follows easily: (*) if $(C_i)_{i \in I}$ is correct w.r.t. N when hiding H, then $(C_i)_{i \in I}$ is also correct w.r.t. N/H' when hiding $H \cup H'$. As a consequence, we can apply our decomposition algorithm [12, 11] also to an STG N_1 with internal signals as follows. Since the algorithm can only decompose STGs without internal signals, we change the internal signals of N_1 to outputs obtaining an STG N_2 with $N_1 = N_2/H$ for a suitable set H. Then we decompose N_2, obtaining a correct decomposition $(C_i)_{i \in I}$ of N_2. After that, the formerly internal signals are hidden in N_2 and in $\|_{i \in I} C_i$ and from (*) we get that $(C_i)_{i \in I}$ is a correct decomposition of $N_1 = N_2/H$ when hiding H.

3   Decomposition of Subcomponents

In this section we will show that correctness is preserved when we decompose a component of an STG decomposition into *subcomponents*. This result makes it possible to design and implement STGs in a top-down fashion.

In particular, such top-down decomposition can be useful for efficiency of our decomposition algorithm. For example, consider a case where only one component C_i of a decomposition needs a specific input signal a, which therefore will be removed from every other one by the decomposition algorithm (cf. Section 1). Alternatively, the algorithm could first construct a component C_j which generates every output signal that is not produced by C_i, and afterwards decompose it into smaller components. This way, the signal a will only be removed from one component (C_j), which can improve performance.

Stepwise decomposition is possible under two minor conditions stated in the following theorem: the composition of the subcomponents must have all output signals of the decomposed component and its internal signals must be unknown to the other components. The first condition is often automatically true or can be achieved easily as mentioned after the definition of correctness, the latter one is an obvious restriction required by our definition of parallel composition and can trivially be fulfilled renaming internal signals. The proof of this theorem requires a careful and detailed case analysis.

Theorem 3 (Correctness of Top-down Decomposition).

1. *Let N be an STG and $(C_i)_{i \in I}$ a correct decomposition of N when hiding H_C. Furthermore let $(C_k)_{k \in K}$ be a correct decomposition of some C_j when hiding H_K ($j \in I$, $I \cap K = \emptyset$). Then $(C_i)_{i \in I'}$ with $I' := I \cup K \setminus \{j\}$ is a correct decomposition of N when hiding $H_C \cup H_K$ if $\bigcup_{k \in K} Out_{C_k} \setminus H_K = Out_{C_j}$ and $(\bigcup_{k \in K} Int_{C_k} \cup H_K) \cap \bigcup_{i \in I \setminus \{j\}} Sig_{C_i} = \emptyset$.*
2. *The implementation relation is a preorder.*

Remark: One might expect that refining a component C_j of $(\|_{i \in I} C_i)/H_C$ with $(\|_{k \in K} C_k)/H_K$ would give the STG $(\|_{i \in I \setminus \{j\}} C_i \| (\|_{k \in K} C_k/H_K))/H_C$, where there is not just one hiding on the top-level as in the theorem. But with the same reasoning already used in the discussion of Definition 2, we can derive from the properties (C8) (use the second assumption on H_K) and (C6) of a circuit algebra that for $H = H_C \cup H_K$:

$$\left(\|_{i \in I \setminus \{j\}} C_i \| (\|_{k \in K} C_k/H_K)\right)/H_C = \left(\left((\|_{i \in I'} C_i)/H_K\right)/H_C = \|_{i \in I'} C_i/H\right.$$

As explained after Definition 2, our correctness definition coincides with the one of [12, 11] if we only consider STGs without internal signals; hence, Theorem 3 also holds in this setting (where of course no hiding is applied, i.e. the hiding sets are taken to be empty). Therefore, the theorem can indeed be used to improve the decomposition of [12, 11] as explained at the beginning of this section. It is an open problem how to group the output signals for optimal efficiency.

Surprisingly, the theorem has also an impact on the question whether the implementation relation between STGs is a precongruence for parallel composition, which we will now show under some mild restrictions. Recall that, for some $N_1 \| N_2$ to be defined, we only had some syntactic requirements regarding the signal sets; but the composition only makes sense in the area of circuits, if we also ensure absence of computation interference; for the following definition cf. the discussion on condition (C2) of Definition 2.

Definition 4 (Interference-free). A parallel composition $N_1 \| N_2$ is *interference-free* if, for all its reachable markings $M_1 \,\dot{\cup}\, M_2$, $i \in \{1, 2\}$ and $x \in Out_i$, $M_i[x\pm\rangle\rangle$ implies $M_1 \,\dot{\cup}\, M_2[x\pm\rangle\rangle$. □

Corollary 5. *If N_2 is a correct implementation of N_1, N_1 and N_2 have the same output signals, and $N_1 \| N$ is a well-defined and interference-free parallel composition, then $N_2 \| N$ is a correct implementation of $N_1 \| N$.*

Note that each of our operations hiding, renaming and parallel composition with another STG changes the set of output signals in the same way, such that equality of these sets is preserved.

Corollary 6 (Implementation Relation as Precongruence). *The implementation relation is a precongruence for hiding, relabelling and parallel composition when restricted to STGs with the same output signals.*

We will see another application of the theorem in the next section.

4   CSC-Solving for Components of a Decomposition

In this section we will prove that CSC-solving fits into our correctness definition, i.e. that it leads to a correct implementation. Theorem 3 then implies that CSC-solving can be combined with our decomposition algorithm. The latter could be shown directly without this theorem, but its use makes the following proof much easier, because we have to consider only one component. First, we will introduce an operation that the tool PETRIFY uses to achieve CSC.

Given an STG without CSC, PETRIFY can (in many cases) insert internal signals into the STG such that their values distinguish between the markings with equal state vectors and different outputs. This insertion takes place on the level of reachability graphs (as most of our considerations in this paper do). PETRIFY can also derive an STG for the modified reachability graph, and although this is not important for the synthesis of a circuit, it fits our manner-of-speaking well. We take Definition 7 of event insertion from [6]. Run with an appropriate option, PETRIFY performs a number of input proper event insertions arriving at an STG with CSC, and this we call *speed-independent CSC-solving*.[3]

Definition 7 (Event Insertion). Let N be a deterministic STG, $u\pm$ a signal transition not appearing in N for a (possibly new) internal signal u and $R \subseteq [M_N\rangle$. The *event insertion of $u\pm$ at region R into N* modifies the reachability graph RG (and results in a corresponding STG N') as follows (cf. e.g. Fig. 1):

1. For every marking $M \in R$ add a duplicate M' and add the transition $M[u\pm\rangle\rangle M'$.
2. If $M_1, M_2 \in R$ and $M_1[s\pm\rangle\rangle M_2$, add the transition $M_1'[s\pm\rangle\rangle M_2'$.
3. If $M_1 \in R$, $M_2 \notin R$ and $M_1[s\pm\rangle\rangle M_2$, remove this transition and add $M_1'[s\pm\rangle\rangle M_2$.
4. The initial marking of N' is the same as that of N. Add u to *Int*.

The insertion is called *input proper*, if there is no $M_1[a\pm\rangle\rangle M_2$ in RG with $a \in In$, $M_1 \in R$ and $M_2 \notin R$.

We define the *marking relation* $\mathcal{M}$ between the markings of N and of N' such that $(M_1, M_2) \in \mathcal{M}$ if $M_2 = M_1$ or $M_2 = M_1'$.   □

It is not hard to see that N' as above is deterministic again. The next result explains the definition of an input-proper event insertion and why we speak of speed-independent CSC-solving; the main result of this section follows.

Proposition 8. *Let N be an input proper STG and let N' be obtained by the insertion of $u\pm$ at R. Then N' is input proper if and only if the insertion is.*

Theorem 9 (Correctness of CSC Solving). *Let N be an STG and N' be obtained from N by speed-independent CSC-solving; then N' is a correct implementation of N.*

---

[3] Other methods of CSC-solving rely on timing-assumptions and are not treated here.

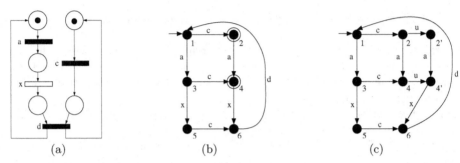

Fig. 1. Example for an event insertion. (a) A Petri net (to keep it small, transitions are labelled with signals) (b) Its reachability graph. The two marked states are the region R where the new event written u will be inserted. (c) The reachability graph with the inserted event u. The marking relation is $\mathcal{M} = \{(1, 1), (2, 2), (2, 2'), (3, 3), (4, 4), (4, 4'), \ldots\}$

Now we can conclude that speed-independent CSC-solving can be combined with decomposition. For this, we have to apply Theorems 3.1 and 9 to each component; the crucial first condition on H_K in 3.1 is satisfied since $H_K = \emptyset$ and event insertion does not change the sets of output and of input signals.

Corollary 10. *Let $(C_i)_{i \in I}$ be a correct decomposition of N when hiding H, and let C_i' be obtained from C_i by speed-independent CSC-solving for all $i \in I$. Then $(C_i')_{i \in I}$ is a correct decomposition of N when hiding H.*

5   Correctness of an ILP Approach to Decomposition

In this section we will show that the decomposition method of Carmona and Cortadella [3, 2], which has not been proven correct so far, yields components which are a correct decomposition according to our definition. For this method, it is assumed that an STG with CSC is given, where CSC can also be achieved by modifications on the STG-level, i.e. without considering the reachability graph. (It can also be given due to a suitable translation from a description in a high-level language to STGs as in [13]). As explained at the end of Section 2, we can assume that there are no internal signals.

The method of [3, 2] works roughly as follows. Starting with a deterministic STG N that already has CSC, for every output signal x a CSC support is determined; this is a set of signals, which guarantees CSC for x. Here is the formal definition:

Definition 11 (CSC Support). *Let N be an STG and $S \subseteq Sig_N$.*

1. *Let $v \in (Sig_N \pm)^*$. code_change(S, v) is defined as the vector over S, which an $s \in S$ to the difference between the numbers of $s+$ and of $s-$ in v.*
2. *S is called CSC support for the output signal x if, for all reachable markings M_1, M_2 with $M_1[v\rangle\rangle M_2$ and code_change$(S, v) = \mathbf{0}$ for some $v \in (Sig_N \pm)^*$, M_1 enables x iff M_2 does.*   □

A sufficient condition for being a CSC support used in the algorithm is that some integer linear programming (ILP) problem is infeasible. The algorithm starts for every output x with the set including the so-called *syntactical triggers* of x and x itself, and iteratively improves it – mostly by adding additional signals – until it is a CSC support for x; since the original STG has CSC, this algorithm is always successful.

After that, for every output signal the original STG is *projected* onto the corresponding CSC support: the other signals are considered as dummies, and these dummies and redundant places are removed as far as possible much as in our decomposition algorithm. If the resulting component still contains dummies, then [priv. comm.]: the reachability graph is generated and viewed as a finite automaton with dummies regarded as the empty word. Now the automaton is made deterministic with well-known methods, which in particular remove all λ-labelled edges. Finally, we can regard this automaton as an STG again, which e.g. has the edges of the automaton as transitions.

The projection part is similar to our algorithm, the difference is where backtracking is performed: the method of [3, 2] uses some form of backtracking when determining the CSC support as described above — our algorithm uses backtracking when the contraction of a dummy signal is not possible.

An advantage of the method of [3, 2] is that the components have CSC. Actually, the defining condition for a CSC support is slightly too weak to guarantee CSC in all cases,[4] but in most practical cases CSC holds, the condition and the corresponding ILP problem could easily be corrected, and most of all the given condition is sufficient for the proof of Theorem 12.

The CSC-support algorithm produces components $(C_i)_{i \in I}$ with the following properties which we need for the proof of Theorem 12.

1. Every component is deterministic.
2. The signals of every C_i are a CSC support of the only output signal.
3. $\forall i \in I : L(C_i) = L(N){\downarrow}_i$

In the last item, $L(N){\downarrow}_i$ denotes the projection of $L(N)$ onto the signals of C_i. We can now prove that $(C_i)_{i \in I}$ is a correct decomposition by our definition.

Theorem 12 (Correctness of the CSC-support algorithm). *Let N be an STG and $(C_i)_{i \in I}$ be given as above. Then, $(C_i)_{i \in I}$ is correct w.r.t. N.*

6   Conclusion

We have generalised the correctness definition for decompositions of [12, 11] to STGs with internal signals and proven that speed-independent CSC-solving as performed by PETRIFY is correct. We have shown that the new correctness is

---

[4] The condition should consider all markings with the same state vector for signals in S, and not only those where one is reachable from the other; this has already been done e.g. in [9].

preserved in a top-down decomposition, and this result has a number of consequences: now we can use step-wise decomposition in the algorithm of [12, 11] to improve efficiency, and we know that this algorithm in combination with speed-independent CSC-solving gives correct results. Applying the correctness definition to compare two STGs, we get an implementation relation, and consequences of our result are that this is a preorder and, with a small restriction, a precongruence for parallel composition, relabelling and hiding.

As another application of the correctness definition, we have shown that a decomposition method based on integer linear programming [2] is correct. It remains an open problem whether a related method in [13] is correct: while the first method checks on the original STG to be decomposed whether a set of signals is a CSC-support and in the positive case removes the other signals, the related method removes some signals and checks CSC on the remaining STG; this is in general not sufficient, but it might be sufficient under the specific circumstances of the algorithm in [13].

For a further validation of our correctness definition, it would be interesting to compare the resp. implementation relation with another one derived from the notion of I/O-compatibility in [1]. We think that the derived implementation relation holds whenever our implementation relation holds, but the reverse direction can only be true under suitable restrictions; the latter still have to be identified, but we expect that they will shed some light on the conceptual ideas behind I/O-compatibility and our correctness.

References

1. J. Carmona and J. Cortadella. Input/output compatibility of reactive systems. In *Formal Methods in Computer-Aided Design, FMCAD 2002, Portland, USA*, Lect. Notes Comp. Sci. 2517, pages 360–377. Springer, 2002.
2. J. Carmona and J. Cortadella. ILP models for the synthesis of asynchronous control circuits. In *Proc. of the IEEE/ACM International Conference on Computer Aided Design*, pages 818–825, 2003.
3. Josep Carmona. *Structural Methods for the Synthesis of Well-Formed Concurrent Specifications*. PhD thesis, Universitat Politècnica de Catalunya, 2003.
4. T.-A. Chu. *Synthesis of Self-Timed VLSI Circuits from Graph-Theoretic Specifications*. PhD thesis, MIT, 1987.
5. J. Cortadella, M. Kishinevsky, A. Kondratyev, L. Lavagno, and A. Yakovlev. Petrify: a tool for manipulating concurrent specifications and synthesis of asynchronous controllers. *IEICE Trans. Information and Systems*, E80-D, 3:315–325, 1997.
6. J. Cortadella, M. Kishinevsky, A. Kondratyev, L. Lavagno, and A. Yakovlev. *Logic Synthesis of Asynchronous Controllers and Interfaces*. Springer, 2002.
7. D. Dill. *Trace Theory for Automatic Hierarchical Verification of Speed-Independent circuits*. MIT Press, Cambridge, 1988.
8. J. Ebergen. Arbiters: an exercise in specifying and decomposing asynchronously communicating components. *Sci. of Computer Programming*, 18:223–245, 1992.
9. F. García-Vallés and J.M. Colom. Structural analysis of signal transition graphs. In *Petri Nets in System Engineering*, 1997.

10. A. Kondratyev, M. Kishinevsky, and A. Taubin. Synthesis method in self-timed design. Decompositional approach. In *IEEE Int. Conf. VLSI and CAD*, pages 324–327, 1993.
11. W. Vogler and B. Kangsah. Improved decomposition of signal transition graphs. Technical Report 2004-8, University of Augsburg, http://www.Informatik.Uni-Augsburg.DE/skripts/techreports/, 2004.
12. W. Vogler and R. Wollowski. Decomposition in asynchronous circuit design. In J. Cortadella et al., editors, *Concurrency and Hardware Design*, Lect. Notes Comp. Sci. 2549, 152 – 190. Springer, 2002.
13. T. Yoneda, H. Onda, and C. Myers. Synthesis of speed independent circuits based on decomposition. In *ASYNC 2004*, pages 135–145. IEEE, 2004.

The Complexity of Live Sequence Charts

Yves Bontemps* and Pierre-Yves Schobbens

Institut d'Informatique, University of Namur
rue Grandgagnage, 21
B5000 - Namur (Belgium)
{ybo, pys}@info.fundp.ac.be

Abstract. We are interested in implementing a fully automated software development process starting from sequence charts, which have proven their naturalness and usefulness in industry. We show in this paper that even for the simplest variants of sequence charts, there are strong impediments to the implementability of this dream. In the case of a manual development, we have to check the final implementation (the model). We show that centralized model-checking is co-NP-complete. Unfortunately, this problem is of little interest to industry. The real problem is distributed model-checking, that we show PSPACE complete, as well as several simple but interesting verification problems. The dream itself relies on program synthesis, formally called realizability. We show that the industrially relevant problem, distributed realizability, is undecidable. The less interesting problems of centralized and constrained realizability are exponential and doubly-exponential complete, respectively.

1 Introduction

Scenario-based approaches and their supporting languages, by which we mean languages such as Message Sequence Charts (MSC) [1], UML Interaction Diagrams [2] or Live Sequence Charts (LSC) [3], have shown a clear advantage on other languages, in practice [4, 5]. They are simple, with a concrete semantics, and have some graphical appeal, which gives them a steep learning curve even for non-expert users. They are specially useful for distributed reactive systems, our focus here. Their apparent simplicity made most practitioners and theoreticians believe that all problems associated to these languages would be easy. A first blow to this commonly held belief was given by Muscholl *et al.* [6] who showed that several simple problems on HMSC are undecidable.

Here, we show that many simple problems on (non-hierarchical) LSC have a surprisingly high complexity, and especially that the main tenet of the dream, the automated synthesis of a distributed algorithm, is undecidable. This may seem to render our dream unachievable, but actually it is hardly surprising that distributed software development, that requires the brains of millions of programmers worldwide and in which still today unexpected bugs are found, is

---

* FNRS Research Fellow

V. Sassone (Ed.): FOSSACS 2005, LNCS 3441, pp. 364–378, 2005.

undecidable. This means that more knowledge has to be put in the synthesis algorithms, e.g. as heuristics [7]. Thus although the dream will never be fully achieved, we can try to come close enough to it to alleviate the work of programmers of distributed systems. Thus, one can hope that synthesis will be hard in theory but usable in practice, as verification [8].

The paper is structured as follows. We present, in Sec. 2.1, the syntax and semantics of Live Sequence Charts (LSC), which is used to specify the future system behaviour. Design models of the system are given using an agent-oriented state-based formalism, here input/output automata, encoding strategies, as presented in Section 2.2. This section concludes by defining when a design model is a correct implementation of a scenario-based specification. In Sec. 3, verification problems are considered. First, checking whether a design model is a correct implementation (Sec. 3.1) and then, whether a specification refines another specification (Sec. 3.2). The question of whether a specification is implementable is investigated in Sec. 4. Sec. 5 presents various constructs that can be added to our version of LSCs, making the language more expressive, but preserving all the results of this paper. Finally, in Sec. 6, we summarize the results and put them in perspective.

2   Models

We assume that we are given a finite set of *agents* or *processes* Ag and of *message names* $\mathcal{M}$. An *event* is a triple from $Ag \times \mathcal{M} \times Ag$. The set of events is Σ. We will denote events sent (resp. received) by some agent a with Σ_a^s (resp. Σ_a^r) and let $\Sigma_a = \Sigma_a^s \cup \Sigma_a^r$. An event of the form (a_1, m, a_2) represents the fact that a_1 sends message m to a_2. We assume here, for simplicity, that communication is instantaneous. (In contrast, some undecidability proofs of [6] require the more complex FIFO communication). From agents behaviour emerge observable sequences of events. We identify behaviour and sequences of events. Σ^* represents the set of all finite sequences of events, while Σ^ω are all infinite sequences.

2.1   Live Sequence Charts

Live Sequence Charts (LSC) [3] is based on Message Sequence Charts (MSC) [1]. LSCs present agents interactions. Every agent owns a "life-line", labeled by its name, e.g. "ui", "cm", "client1" in Fig. 1. Interactions take place through events, that are shown as arrows. An occurrence of (a_1, e, a_2) is displayed as an arrow labeled by m, from a_1's life-line to a_2's life-line. MSCs are unclear with respect to the "status" of a scenario, i.e. whether a scenario represents all possible behaviours or just some of them. They are also silent about the role of messages that do not appear in a scenario, viz. whether they are forbidden by their mere absence or whether they can appear at will. We call this feature *message abstraction*. Furthermore, engineers informally assign different statuses to messages: some of them trigger the described scenario, whereas other are expected answers.

LSC clarifies this [3]. Syntactic constructs are added to MSCs to state explic-itly whether the diagram is a mere example (existential scenarios) or constrains all behaviours of the future system (universal scenarios). The former are sim-ply MSCs, surrounded by a dashed-line box. The latter are MSCs, divided in two parts: an upper part, named *prechart*, that is graphically surrounded by an hexagonal dashed-line box, and a lower-part, called *main chart*, surrounded by a solid-line rectangle. The intuitive semantics is "whenever the agents behave as in the prechart, they shall behave according to the main chart afterwards". LSC adds "message abstraction" by explicitly stating which events are *restricted*. All events appearing in the LSC are automatically restricted. Additional events can be restricted thanks to a "restricts" clause. This provides the scenario with a scope (alphabet).

Like MSCs, their semantics is based on a partial order. To be fully rigorous, the partial order is the equivalence class quotient of the preorder defined by rules (1-3) below. The temporal ordering of events is deduced from three constraints and their transitive closure: (1) life-lines induce a total ordering on their events, from top to bottom, (2) agents synchronize on shared events, i.e. two locations linked by an arrow are order-equivalent and (3) all locations in the prechart appear before main chart locations. In MSC parlance, the prechart and main chart are *strongly sequenced*. For example, combining the clauses, in Fig. 1, events "getdata" and "updating" are unordered. Clause (1) can be relaxed thanks to *co-regions*. A co-region is a sequence of locations, belonging to the same life-line, along which a dashed line is drawn, see the two "getnew" events in Fig. 1.

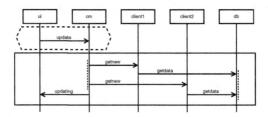

Fig. 1. Update Scenario

Live Sequence Charts have been used to model various real-life systems such as the weather synchronization logic of NASA's Center TRACON Automation System (CTAS) [9], a radio-based train system [10], virtual wrappers for PCI bus [11] and some part of the C elegans worm [12]. Examples displayed in Fig. 1 and 2(a) and (b) are based on the CTAS system. This system aims at synchro-nizing various clients that make use of weather reports. When new forecasts are available, a protocol is followed to update clients data. If some client fails to up-date, they try to roll back to the previous consistent state. The rationale is that all clients should always be using the same data. The following requirements are described by LSCs.

1. When the user asks for an update, all clients are asked to fetch the new weather reports. The user is notified of the updating process. See Fig. 1.
2. If some client fails to update its state, all clients are required to roll back to the previous state, *after* the user has been notified that the updating process is taking place. See Fig. 2(a).
3. Whenever the database refuses a download, the cm (communication manager) is notified. See Fig. 2(b).

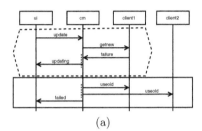 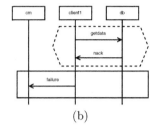

(a) (b)

Fig. 2. Failure scenarios

We now define formally the abstract syntax and the semantics of universal LSCs. It is based on labeled partial orders.

Definition 1 (Labeled partial order (LPO)). *Let V be a set of events. A V-labeled partial order (V-LPO) is a tuple $\langle L, \leq, \lambda, \Sigma' \rangle$, where*

L *is a set of* locations. *If L is finite, the LPO is called* finite.
$\leq \subseteq L \times L$ *is a partial order on L (a transitive, anti-symmetric and reflexive relation).*
$\lambda : L \to V$ *is a labeling function.*

A linearization of a finite LPO is a word of $w_1 \ldots w_n \in \Sigma^*$ such that the LPO $\langle [n], \leq, \{(i, w_i) | i \in [n]\} \rangle$, where $[n]$ is a shortcut for the set $\{1, \ldots, n\}$, is isomorphic to some linear (total) order $\langle L, \leq', \lambda \rangle$ with $\leq \subseteq \leq'$.

A labeled partial order represents an MSC. As already stated above, LSC distinguishes between examples (existential LSC) and request-reply rules (universal LSC), in which the activation part is singled out.

Definition 2 (LSC).

Universal LSC. *A universal LSC is a tuple $\langle L, \leq, \lambda, \Sigma_R, P \rangle$ such that*
1. *$\langle L, \leq, \lambda \rangle$ is a finite Σ_R-LPO. Σ_R are called the* restricted *events of the LSC;*
2. *$P \subseteq L$ is called a* prechart. *Main chart locations are all larger than prechart locations: $P \times (L \setminus P) \subseteq \leq$.*
Existential LSC. *An existential LSC is a tuple $\langle L, \leq, \lambda, \Sigma_R \rangle$ such that $\langle L, \leq, \lambda \rangle$ is a finite Σ_R-LPO.*

We will be considering infinite words $\gamma \in \Sigma^\omega$. A word γ is a model of an LSC if, at any point in γ, if the prechart is linearized, then the main chart is also linearized afterwards.

Definition 3 $(\gamma \models S)$. *For every $\gamma = e_0 e_1 \ldots \in \Sigma^\omega$, $\gamma \models S$ iff*

S **is a Universal LSC** *and* $\forall i \geq 0 :$

$$(\exists j \geq i : e_i \ldots e_j|_{\Sigma_R} \ linearizes \ P) \Rightarrow (\exists k \geq i : e_i \ldots e_k|_{\Sigma_R} \ linearizes \ L)$$

S **is an Existential LSC** *and* $\exists i \geq 0 : \exists j \geq i : (e_i \ldots e_j)|_{\Sigma_R} \ linearizes \ L$

The size of an LSC is its number of locations. An LSC specification is a set of universal LSCs, the semantics of which is defined by conjunction; a run is a model of an LSC specification iff it is a model of all its constituent scenarios. The size of a specification is the sum of the size of the conjuncted LSCs. The language defined by an LSC is its set of models: $\mathcal{L}(L) = \{\gamma \in \Sigma^\omega | \gamma \models L\}$.

Every LSC specification is equivalent to the conjunction of liveness and safety properties, *one for every event* in Σ [13]. A scenario S, with restricted events Σ_R, *forbids* $e \in \Sigma$ after a finite run $w \in \Sigma^*$ iff some suffix of $w|_{\Sigma_R}$, say w', linearizes an ideal I of the LSC, which includes P, but $w' \cdot e$ does not linearize any ideal in S. S *requires* $e \in \Sigma$ iff some suffix w' of $w|_{\Sigma_R}$ linearizes an ideal $I \supseteq P$ of S and $w' \cdot e$ *is* a linearization of some ideal in S.

An infinite run $\gamma \in \Sigma^\omega$ is e-safe iff for every prefix w of this run, if e is forbidden by some scenario after w, $w \cdot e$ is not a prefix of γ. It is e-live iff for every prefix w of γ, if some scenario requires e after w, then e eventually occurs after w.

Theorem 1 (LSC = Live + Safe). *An infinite run $\gamma \in \Sigma^\omega$ satisfies an LSC specification iff, for every $e \in \Sigma$, γ is both e-safe and e-live [13].*

2.2   Strategies

Agents are partitioned into two teams: the environment and the system. Formally, $Ag = Sys \,\dot\cup\, Env$. System-controlled events are $\Sigma_{Sys} = Sys \times \mathcal{M} \times Ag$. Engineers are not asked to construct programs for agents in Env, only agents from Sys have to be implemented. Sys implementation will be deployed among Env agents that provides thus the model-time context of the specification.

We will use Input/Output automata to describe the design-time model of agents [14]. An input-output automaton for agent $a \in Ag$ is a finite automaton the alphabet of which is Σ_a. A distinction is made between input events (Σ_a^r) and output events (Σ_a^s) Syntactically, an I/O automaton for agent a must be *input-enabled*: for every input event $e \in \Sigma_a^r$, in every state q, there is an outgoing transition labeled by e. In other words, a may never block incoming messages.

A run of an I/O automaton is an infinite path in the automaton, following the transition relation and starting from the designated initial state. A fair run is a run in which infinitely many transitions labeled by Σ_a^s events are taken. The word generated by a run is the infinite sequence of events encountered along the transitions of the run. The language of an I/O automaton $\mathcal{A}$, denoted $\mathcal{L}(\mathcal{A})$, is the set of words generated by $\mathcal{A}$'s fair runs. The composition of two I/O automata $(\mathcal{A}_1 \times \mathcal{A}_2)$ is defined as the synchronous product of $\mathcal{A}_1$ and $\mathcal{A}_2$, see [14] for details.

A finite state I/O automaton represents a finite-memory strategy for agent a. Formally, a (non-deterministic) strategy for agent a is a function $f : \Sigma^* \to 2^{(\Sigma_a^s)}$. It is of finite memory if there is an equivalence relation $\simeq$ on Σ^* such that (1) $\simeq$ is of finite index and (2) $\forall w \simeq w' : f(w) = f(w')$. The size of the memory is the index of the smallest such equivalence relation. Clearly, every finite memory strategy can be translated to an I/O automaton. Conversely, every I/O automaton can be turned into a strategy. The *outcome* of a strategy f is the set of all runs in which Σ_a^s events appear only according to the strategy. $Out(f) = \{u_0 e_0 u_1 e_1 \ldots | \forall i \geq 0 : u_i \in (\Sigma \setminus (\{a\} \times \mathcal{M} \times Ag))^* \wedge e_i \in f(u_0 e_0 \ldots u_i)\}$.

Definition 4 (Correct Implementation). *A design model M, presented as a list of strategies $(f_a)_{a \in Sys}$, is a* correct implementation *of an LSC specification iff, for every outcome $w \in \bigcap_{a \in Sys} Out(f_a)$,*

- *if w is Σ_{Env}-live, then w is Σ_{Sys}-live;*
- *and if w is Σ_{Env}-safe, then w is Σ_{Sys}-safe.*

3   Verification

3.1   Model Checking

The first problem we consider is the verification that a closed and centralized implementation is correct. This problem makes two assumptions: there are no environment agents, thus all agents described in the LSC are system agents and their behaviour is specified thanks to a single automaton.

Definition 5 (CCMC). *Closed Centralized Model Checking (CCMC) is, given an automaton $\mathcal{A}$ and an LSC specification $\{L_1, \ldots, L_n\}$, to decide whether $\mathcal{L}(\mathcal{A}) \subseteq \bigcap_{i=1}^n \mathcal{L}(L_i)$.*

This problem is co-NP complete. A first extension is to consider that some agents belong to the environment, while others are system agents. Then, we are presented with an implementation of system agents only and the question becomes: "whenever environment agents do behave correctly, does this implementation behave appropriately?". The problem becomes PSPACE-complete.

Definition 6 (OCMC). *Open Centralized Model Checking (OCMC) is, given an automaton $\mathcal{A}$, a partition of Ag into Sys and Env and an LSC specification S, to decide whether $\mathcal{A}$ is a correct implementation of Sys with respect to S (see def. 4).*

The second restriction imposes that we consider monolithic systems only, made of a single component. As it was clear from the introduction, we are mostly interested in distributed systems. The design-time specification of such systems will typically be presented as a "network" of automata, one for each agent. Every automaton prescribes how its owner shall behave, see Sec. 2.2.

Definition 7 (CLOSED DISTRIBUTED MODEL CHECKING). *Given an LSC L and a list of automata* $(\mathcal{A}_i)_{i=1,...,k}$, *decide whether* $\mathcal{L}(\prod_{i=1}^{k} \mathcal{A}_i) \subseteq \mathcal{L}(L)$.

Unfortunately, as usual in verification [15], this makes model checking more complex. The problem becomes PSPACE-complete instead of coNP-complete. Combining distribution and openness does not increase the problem complexity; it is still PSPACE-complete.

Theorem 2. CCMC *is complete for coNP.* CDMC, OCMC *and* ODMC *are PSPACE-complete.*

Proof. CCMC coNP-hardness is shown by reducing the complement of the Traveling Salesman Problem (coTSP) to CCMC. coTSP is to decide whether in a given weighted directed graph, all circuits have a total weight of larger than a given bound k. One can restrict to edge weights ≤ 2 [16]. The graph and the cost are encoded in the automaton with a counter: (1) when an edge of weight j is followed to a vertex v, the counter is incremented by j and an event v is emitted. At any point, the counter can be down-counted: if the counter is at n, n "billing" events are omitted and a final "zero" event follows. An LSC is added, the prechart of which states that all vertices should be visited once, in any order, and the main chart imposes that k "billing" events without any "stop".

PSPACE-proofs of open systems use the same technique as LSC-REACH (see below). PSPACE-proof of distributed variants rely on the fact that deadlock detection in a network of processes is PSPACE-complete [16].

All membership proofs are standard: a violating simple path is guessed in the automaton and it is checked that it actually violates the LSC. The complexity of this procedure follows from an argument on the length of simple paths in LSC tableau automata.

One can believe that this high complexity is due to the presence of automata in the problems, as sketched by the proof of Th. 2. The next section presents simple analysis problems, on LSCs only, that are also difficult. This is astonishing, as one might think that these problems can be solved by easy computations on the diagrammatic form of LSCs.

3.2   Reachability and Refinement Checking

The first problem we consider is whether an LSC specification allows some use case.

Definition 8 (LSC-REACH). *LSC Reachability (LSC-REACH) is, given an existential LSC* L^E *and an LSC specification* $\{L_1^U, \ldots, L_n^U\}$, *to decide whether* $\exists \gamma \in \bigcap_{i=1}^{n} L_i^u : \gamma \models L^E$.

LSC-REACH checks that a certain specification, together with assumptions over the domain still makes it possible to achieve a certain behaviour. This problem is PSPACE-complete.

Another natural problem on LSC only is verifying specification refinement is al. Given a certain abstract specification S, a more precise specification S' is designed and we want to verify that every behaviour induced by S' is a legal behavior of S. Logically, this boils down to verifying the validity of $S' \rightarrow S$. This problem is also PSPACE-complete.

Definition 9 (LSC-IMPL). *LSC Implication (LSC-IMPL) is, given two LSC specifications S and S', to decide whether $\mathcal{L}(S') \subseteq \mathcal{L}(S)$.*

Theorem 3. *LSC-REACH and LSC-IMPL are complete for PSPACE.*

Proof. PSPACE-hardness is obtained from reducing the halting problem of a PSPACE TM on the blank input to LSC-REACH. We sketch our encoding of a DPSPACE TM configuration, with the additional assumptions that (1) the halting configuration is never left and (2) when the halting configuration is reached, the tape head is moved to the leftmost tape cell. A TM configuration is of the form (γ, i, T) where $\gamma \in \Gamma$ is a control state, $0 \leq i \leq n$ is the tape head position (remark that at most n cells are used, this is known a priori) and $T[j] \in \{0,1\}$ $(0 \leq j \leq n)$ is the tape content. The vocabulary of our LSC specification is $(\Gamma \cup \{in, \$\} \cup \{0,1\}) \times \{0, \ldots, n\}$. The symbol in is used to initialize the TM simulation: when it occurs, an initial configuration is output and $\$$ is a technical marker, we skip its description here. A TM configuration is encoded by a word w if

1. $\exists v : w = v(\gamma, i)$
2. $\forall j : 1 \leq j \leq n : T[j] = a \Rightarrow \exists u, v : w = u(a, j)v$ and neither $(0, j)$ nor $(1, j)$ appears in v.

We have to describe the encoding of the TM transition relation. Suppose, wlog, that $C = (T, \gamma, i)$, $T[i] = 0$ and $C' = (T', \gamma', i + 1)$, where T' is like T, except that 1 has been written at the i-th position. Assume that C is encoded by some word w. By definition of configuration encoding, $w = v \cdot (\gamma, i)$, and the last occurrence of either $\{(0, i), (1, i)\}$ is $(0, i)$ in w. The transition will be encoded as the following continuation:

$$w' = v \underbrace{(\gamma, i)(0, i)(\$, i)(1, i)(\gamma', i + 1)}_{u} .$$

One can check that w' is indeed an encoding of C', by noting that

1. it ends with $(\gamma, i + 1)$;
2. in u, no event of the form $(0, j)$ or $(1, j)$ $(j \neq i)$ has been added. Hence, the tape content of the configuration encoded by w does not differ from that of C on these cells.

These rules can be described by universal LSCs and the existential LSC is simply there to ensure that, in at least one run, *in* occurs and later on in the same run, the halting location appears, too.

Harel and Marelly introduced an algorithm and an approach to the validation of LSC-based specifications, called *play-out* [17]. The specification is immediately executed, without generating any code from it, but using an animation engine instead. This animation engine uses a superstep approach: when the environment inputs some new event, by performing some action on the graphical user interface, the engine performs all system-controlled events that become required, until it reaches some stable status, in which no event is required anymore. The theorems provided in this section can be adapted to show that computing whether a finite super-step exists is PSPACE-complete. Smart play-out is a practically efficient technique that uses symbolic model checking of LTL formulae to discover such a superstep [18].

4 Realizability

In this section, we turn to the most complex class of problems considered in this paper. We want to determine automatically whether a specification is implementable. Ideally, the proof of implementability should be constructive: some state-based implementation of the specification must be built. Would this implementation be compact and readable, the burden of designing the system would be taken away from engineers.

We are interested in implementing open reactive systems. As noted by [19] and [20], realizability is not equivalent to satisfiability. Actually, the question is more accurately posed as "is there an implementation of system agents such that, no matter how environment agents behave, the specification will be respected?". We will first assume that system agents are built under the "perfect information" hypothesis. This artificial hypothesis implies that system agents may observe every event and that every system agent knows instantaneously in what state other agents are. Then, we will see that dropping this hypothesis implies undecidability of realizability.

Definition 10 (CR). Centralized Realizability *(CR) is, given an LSC specification* $\{L_1, \ldots, L_m\}$ *and a set of system agents* $Sys \subseteq Ag$, *to decide whether there is a strategy* $f : \Sigma^* \to \Sigma^s_{Sys}$, *such that* f *is a correct implementation of* $\{L_1, \ldots, L_m\}$.

In [13], we have presented an exponential time algorithm solving this problem. It constructs a two-player parity game graph, with three colors, in which player 0 has a winning strategy iff the specification is realizable. The game graph is exponentially larger than the LSC specification.

This problem is EXPTIME-complete. This proves our claim that, because LSCs are less expressive than LTL, some problems are easier on LSCs than on LTL. Actually, centralized realizability is 2EXPTIME-complete for LTL [20].

The algorithm presented in [13] is computationally expensive, yet optimal. However, it suffers from another problem: it yields design models, as automata, that are exponentially larger than the specification. This is a hindrance for readability. Nevertheless, we show below that strategies realizing LSC specifications need memories that large. Therefore, our algorithm is optimal, in the sense that every algorithm solving this problem will necessarily build exponentially large implementations.

We exhibit in Fig. 3 a family of LSC specifications $(\phi_n)_{n>0}$ the size of which grows quadratically in n but any strategy for Sys realizing ϕ_n needs at least $2^{n \log n}$ memory states.

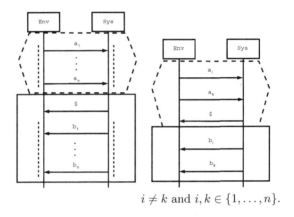

$$i \neq k \text{ and } i, k \in \{1, \ldots, n\}.$$

Fig. 3. LSC specification ϕ_n

In this game, Env controls $\{a_1, \ldots, a_n\} = \Sigma_{Env}^s = \Sigma_{Sys}^r$ and Sys controls $\{\$, b_1, \ldots, b_n\} = \Sigma_{Sys}^s = \Sigma_{Env}^r$. Env first presents Sys with a sequence of n symbols. Remark that Env *chooses* the order in which those events occur. When the whole sequence has been presented, Sys must reply with the same sequence. Hence, Sys's strategy must have at least enough memory to remember the order in which the n events have been presented, viz. n^n states. The LSC specification encoding this game is presented in Fig. 3. Along "Sys" and "Env" on the left-hand side scenario, we drew two dashed lines. This defines a *co-region*, which relaxes the ordering on the enclosed events. Therefore, $a_1 \ldots a_n$ can occur in any order, see Section 2.1. In comparison, on the right-hand side, a_i and a_k are ordered. The right-hand side scenario obliges b_i to follow b_k if a_k occurred after a_i.

Theorem 4 (Memory Lower-Bound). *There is a family of LSCs specification, namely $(\phi_n)_{n>0}$ such that any strategy realizing ϕ_n has a memory of size $2^{\Omega(n \log n)}$.*

Proof. First of all, for every n $|\phi_n| = 5n^2 + 3n + 1$. Hence, the size of ϕ_n grows only quadratically in n.

Now, consider some strategy $f : \Sigma^* \to \Sigma^s_{Sys}$ winning in this game. If f is a correct implementation, it *must* have enough memory to remember the order in which $a_1 \ldots a_n$ occurred. Otherwise, there would exist two words w and w' of $(\Sigma^s_{Env})^*$ such that every symbol of Σ^s_{Env} occurs exactly once in both w and w', $w \neq w'$, and f has not enough memory to distinguish w and w', i.e. $w \simeq w'$, and thus $f(w) = f(w')$ (see Sec. 2.2). Therefore, $w \cdot f(w) = w \cdot f(w')$ and consequently, f would not be winning, since the order of replies (b's) does not match the order of queries (a's). Contradiction.

All permutations of $a_1 \ldots a_n$ are possible, therefore there must be as many memory states in f as there are permutations of n elements, i.e. $2^{\Omega(n \log n)}$.

Remark 1 (Succinctness). Using the same family of LSC specifications and the same proof, one can show that translating LSCs to some DBA involves an exponential blow-up. Actually, it is not even possible to translate LSCs to NBA recognizing either the language of the specification or its complement without this blow-up. It follows from this fact and from the theorems in [21] that turning LSCs to equivalent ACTL^{det} formulae also involves an exponential blow-up. Indeed, for every ACTL^{det} formula, there is a nondeterministic Büchi automaton recognizing their complement, which is linear in their size.

The problem of centralized realizability is lacking some features, which lessens its applicability

1. It would be interesting to come up with an implementation that satisfies the specification and guarantees that additional requirements will be met as well. This is especially interesting if the specification is too abstract or too loosely defined to ensure the requirements, but the analyst thinks that it is possible to refine it in a way that would fulfill the requirements. The problem of deciding whether there is such a particular implementation, which we call *Constrained Realizability* is 2EXPTIME-complete, when we consider LTL as a language for expressing requirements.

2. It does not take the structural model into account, because it assumes that the "perfect information" hypothesis holds. Hence, agents are not obliged to consider only events occurring at their interfaces. It seems necessary to extend the centralized version of the problem to take this into account. This variant is called Distributed Realizability (DR). As for LTL, this problem is undecidable [22]. The proof of this theorem, given in appendix, is similar to the proof presented in [23], to show that the problem of decentralized observation is undecidable.

The problem of distributed realizability is, intuitively, to determine whether there is a network of implementations, in which every agent only senses events at its interface but the composition of which implements the specification. Distributed realizability becomes undecidable,

Definition 11 (DR). Distributed Realizability (DR) is, given an LSC specification $\{L_1, \ldots, L_m\}$, to decide whether there is a list of strategies $(f_a)_{a \in Sys}$ one for every system agent, such that

1. $f_a : \Sigma^* \to (\Sigma_a^s)$;
2. $\forall w, w' \in \Sigma^* : w|_{\Sigma_a} = w'|_{\Sigma_a} \Rightarrow f(w) = f(w')$, *i.e. if w and w' are the same, from a's point of view, then a shall behave the same way after w or w'*;
3. $\bigcap_{a \in Sys} Out(f_a)$ *is a correct implementation of* $\{L_1, \ldots, L_m\}$.

Theorem 5. CR *is EXPTIME-complete and* DR *is undecidable.*

Proof. EXPTIME-hardness of CR is obtained from the reduction of the halting problem of an alternating PSPACE TM to CR. The reduction is similar to the one provided in the proof of Th. 3. TM alternation is mapped on the statuses (antagonist vs protagonist) of the environment and the system.

Post's Correspondence Problem (PCP) can be reduced to DR, hence showing that DR is undecidable. The proof is essentially the one proposed by Tripakis [23]. Let us fix an arbitrary PCP instance $(w_1, u_1) \ldots (w_n, u_n)$ over some alphabet Θ. The alphabet of our LSC specification is $\Theta \cup \{k_1, \ldots, k_n\} \cup \{\$\} \cup \{0, 1\} \cup \{A_0, A_1\}$, plus an arbitrary finite number of events which can be exchanged between system agents, say $\{s_0, \ldots, s_q\}$. The system is made of two agents: a_1 and a_2. The first agent may observe $\Theta \cup \{\$\}$, whereas the second can observe $\{k_1, \ldots, k_m, \$\}$. All these events, but $\{A_0, A_1\}$ and the additional system events $\{s_0, \ldots s_k\}$ are controlled by the environment. A play proceeds as follows. First, the environment picks either 0 or 1. The former means that the environment chooses to read words in the first component of the pairs of words (viz. the w_i's), the latter means that it will read u_i's. Then, the environment must stick to that choice until the end of the play. Namely, the environment chooses a particular word in the list (say, w_i or u_i, depending on the "column" chosen) and indicates the index of this word to the system, by performing k_i. The environment must enumerate the letters in w_i, which are published to agent a_1. The game goes on until the environment performs \$. At this point, the system is required to output A_0 or A_1, depending on what index (0 or 1) the environment had chosen in the first place.

We claim that the PCP instance has a solution iff this specification is not implementable. Assume that PCP has a solution $i_1 \ldots i_m$ but there is a winning strategy for the system. Then, upon $0 i_1 w_1 \ldots i_m w_m \$$, the system answers with A_0. The strategy of the system shall also answer A_0 to $A_1 i_1 u_{i_1} \ldots i_m u_m \$$, because the projections of the two words on agent's alphabets are the same. Therefore, there is no winning strategy.

If the PCP instance has no solution, then, the two system agents can get together and compare the submitted run. Agent a_2 sends the sequence of indices that it has been presented with to a_1 (using some protocol on which they agreed, based on $\{s_0, \ldots, s_p\}$). This agent can then build $w_{i_1} \ldots w_{i_m}$ and compare it with the word that he has received from the environment. Since the PCP instance has no solution, either they are the same and a_1 shall answer A_0 or the two words differ and a_1 replies with A_1.

5   Extensions

The language of LSC that we have used so far was pretty simple. In this section, we present some possible extensions, that make it more expressive but does not cause any changes in the complexity of the problems investigated in this paper. Actually, all membership proofs can be simply adapted to deal with these extensions. Hardness proofs are of course not affected by adding new constructs to the language.

Alternatives: within a single LSC, one can describe several alternatives, as is done with inline constructs of MSCs or Sequence Diagrams. We need to introduce the concept of LPOs with choice, which is much heavier to manipulate. This extension does not cause any other problem, as the tableau automaton of the LSC remains simply exponential.

Conditions: it is possible to add conditions (i.e. boolean logic over some predefined set of propositions), to the language. Together with alternatives, we can embed if-then-else tests in the language. Using the concept of cold/hot conditions, one can also describe some "preconditions" and assertions: a hot condition describes a condition that must be true when it is evaluated, whereas a cold condition represents a condition that, if evaluated to false, finishes prematurely and successfully the scenario. Again, all the results of this paper remain true if we consider this extension.

Hot/Cold Locations: a cold location is a location on which the execution of the chart may stop. This provides us with a way to specify that some linearizations of the LPO may stop before reaching its end.

Modes of Communication: In our model, we assumed that communication was instantaneous. Nevertheless, we can represent other modes of communication, like asynchronous or synchronous communication in our model. Asynchronous communication means that the receiver shall not be ready for the sender to send its message. In the synchronous mode, there is a transmission delay, too, but the sender must wait for the receiver to get the message before proceeding. This represents procedure calls, in programming languages.

Unbounded loop is the only extension for which we could not prove the robustness of our constructions. With the Kleene star and alternatives, we can encode every regular expression as a basic chart. We were not able to show that the double blow up involved in the tableau method could be avoided, and we leave that problem open. Remark that Kleene star makes the language incomparable to LTL.

6   Summary and Discussion

There are two axes along which complexity increases. The distributed version of the problems is always harder than the centralized one, as in [15], while synthesis is also more complex than model checking, for it adds alternation to the problem [24].

The most interesting part is to investigate what causes such a high complexity. We identify two factors making LSCs complex.

1. LSC semantics relies on partial orders. We used this in the proof of co-NP-completeness of CCMC (Th. 2) and the lower-bound on the size of synthesized state machines (Th.4). With a chart of size n, we can thus encode a set of runs of exponential size.
2. An LSC specification is unstructured. In the PSPACE-hardness proofs, we used LSCs of constant size only and, actually, very short ones, in which events were linearly ordered. The complexity of the specification comes from the fact that many LSCs are active at the same time, describing concurrent liveness properties.

The former cause of complexity is often avoided in practice, because real-world specifications tend to consist of almost linearly ordered scenarios. The latter cause is more difficult to deal with. One shall find ways to describe the problem structure in these models and, more importantly, to rely on this additional information to get more efficient algorithms. This is all but an easy task, as it contradicts one of the basic principles of scenario-based software engineering: requirements are partial, redundant, complementary and range over several aspects of the system.

Undecidability of distributed synthesis means that we need to find other ways to cope with that problem. In [7], we propose such an algorithm, which is sound but not complete. It applies a predefined "implementation scheme" and then checks whether the distributed implementation obtained is correct.

References

1. International Telecommunication Union (ITU) Geneva: MSC-2000: ITU-T Recommendation Z.120 : Message Sequence Chart (MSC). (2000) http://www.itu.int/.
2. Object Management Group (UML Revision Task Force): OMG UML Specification (2.0). (2003) http://www.omg.org/uml.
3. Damm, W., Harel, D.: LSCs: Breathing life into message sequence charts. Formal Methods in System Design **19** (2001) 45–80
4. Weidenhaupt, K., Pohl, K., Jarke, M., Haumer, P.: Scenario Usage in System Development: A Report on Current practice. IEEE Software **15** (1998) 34–45
5. Amyot, D., Eberlein, A.: An evaluation of scenarion notations for telecommunication systems development. Telecommunications Systems Journal **24** (2003) 61–94
6. Muscholl, A., Peled, D., Su, Z.: Deciding Properties of Message Sequence Charts. Foundations of Software Science and Computer Structures (1998)
7. Bontemps, Y., Heymans, P.: As fast as sound (lightweight formal scenario synthesis and verification). In Giese, H., Krüger, I., eds.: Proc. of the 3rd Int. Workshop on "Scenarios and State Machines: Models, Algorithms and Tools" (SCESM'04), Edinburgh, IEE (2004) 27–34

8. Harel, D.: From play-in scenarios to code : An achievable dream. IEEE Computer **34** (2001) 53–60 a previous version appeared in Proc. of FASE'00, LNCS(1783), Springer-Verlag.

9. Bontemps, Y., Heymans, P., Kugler, H.: Applying LSCs to the specification of an air traffic control system. In Uchitel, S., Bordeleau, F., eds.: Proc. of the 2nd Int. Workshop on "Scenarios and State Machines: Models, Algorithms and Tools" (SCESM'03), Portland, OR, USA, IEEE (2003)

10. Bohn, J., Damm, W., Klose, J., Moik, A., Wittke, H.: Modeling and validating train system applications using statemate and live sequence charts. In Ehrig, H., Krämer, B.J., Ertas, A., eds.: Proceedings of the Conference on Integrated Design and Process Technology (IDPT2002), Society for Design and Process Science (2002)

11. Bunker, A., Gopalakrishnan, G.: Verifying a VCI Bus Interface Model Using an LSC-based Specification. In Ehrig, H., Krämer, B.J., Ertas, A., eds.: Proceedings of the Sixth Biennial World Conference on Integrated Design and Process Technology, Society of Design and Process Science (2002) 48

12. Kam, N., Harel, D., Kugler, H., Marelly, R., Pnueli, A., Hubbard, J.A., Stern, M.J.: Formal modelling of c. elegans development; a scenario-based approach. In Ciobanu, G., Rozenberg, G., eds.: Modelling in Molecular Biology. Natural Computing Series. Springer (2004) 151–173

13. Bontemps, Y., Schobbens, P.Y., Löding, C.: Synthesis of open reactive systems from scenario-based specifications. Fundamenta Informaticae **62** (2004) 139–169

14. Lynch, N.A., Tuttle, M.R.: An introduction to input/output automata. CWI Quarterly **2** (1989) 219–246

15. Harel, D., Vardi, M.Y., Kupferman, O.: On the complexity of verifying concurrent transition systems. Information and Computation **173** (2002)

16. Papadimitriou, C.H.: Computational Complexity. Addison-Wesley (1994)

17. Harel, D., Marelly, R.: Come, let's play! Scenario-based programming using LSCs and the Play-engine. Springer (2003) ISBN 3-540-00787-3.

18. Harel, D., Kugler, H., Marelly, R., Pnueli, A.: Smart Play-Out of Behavioral Requirements. In: Proc. 4th Intl. Conference on Formal Methods in Computer-Aided Design (FMCAD'02), Portland, Oregon. (2002)

19. Abadi, M., Lamport, L., Wolper, P.: Realizable and unrealizable specifications of reactive systems. In Ausiello, G., Dezani-Ciancaglini, M., Rocca, S.R.D., eds.: Automata, Languages and Programming, 16th International Colloquium, ICALP89, Stresa, Italy, July 11-15, 1989, Proceedings. Volume 372 of Lect. Notes in Comp. Sci., Springer (1989)

20. Pnueli, A., Rosner, R.: On the Synthesis of a Reactive Module. In: Proceedings of the sixteenth annual ACM symposium on Principles of programming languages. (1989) 179–190

21. Maidl, M.: The common fragment of CTL and LTL. In: Proc. 41st Annual Symposium on Foundations of Computer Science. (2000) 643–652

22. Pnueli, A., Rosner, R.: On the synthesis of an asynchronous reactive module. In Ausiello, G., Dezani-Ciancaglini, M., Rocca, S.R.D., eds.: Automata, Languages and Programming, 16th International Colloquium (ICALP). Volume 372 of Lect. Notes in Comp. Sci., Stresa, Italy, Springer-Verlag (1989) 652–671

23. Tripakis, J.: Undecidable problems of decentralized observation and control on regular languages. Information Processing Letters **90** (2004)

24. Chandra, A.K., Kozen, D.C., Stockmeyer, L.J.: Alternation. Journal of the ACM **28** (1981) 114–133

A Simpler Proof Theory for Nominal Logic

James Cheney

University of Edinburgh
jcheney@inf.ed.ac.uk

Abstract. Nominal logic is a variant of first-order logic equipped with a "fresh-name quantifier" Ɲ and other features useful for reasoning about languages with bound names. Its original presentation was as a Hilbert axiomatic theory, but several attempts have been made to provide more convenient Gentzen-style sequent or natural deduction calculi for nominal logic. Unfortunately, the rules for Ɲ in these calculi involve complicated side-conditions, so using and proving properties of these calculi is difficult. This paper presents an improved sequent calculus $NL^\Rightarrow$ for nominal logic. Basic results such as cut-elimination and conservativity with respect to nominal logic are proved. Also, $NL^\Rightarrow$ is used to solve an open problem, namely relating nominal logic's Ɲ-quantifier and the self-dual ∇-quantifier of Miller and Tiu's $FO\lambda^\nabla$.

1 Introduction

Gabbay and Pitts [8] have introduced a new way of reasoning about names and binding, in which α-equivalence and capture-avoiding substitution can be defined in terms of the basic concepts of *swapping* and *freshness*. This approach provides a cleaner treatment of α-equivalence than the classical first-order approach in which α-equivalence and capture-avoiding substitution are defined by mutual recursion. On the other hand, unlike higher-order techniques for dealing with names and binding, the semantics of this model of name-binding is relatively straightforward, so well-understood mathematical tools like structural induction can be used to reason about syntax with bound names.

These ideas have been incorporated into a logic called *nominal logic* [12]. Nominal logic is typed, first-order equational logic augmented with:

- *name-types* $\nu, \nu', \ldots$ inhabited by countably many *names* a, b, ...;
- a *swapping operation* $(- \ -) \cdot - : \nu \to \nu \to \tau \to \tau$ for each name-type ν and type τ, which acts on values by exchanging occurrences of names;
- a *freshness* relation $- \ \# \ - : \nu \to \tau \to o$[1] for each name-type ν and type τ, that holds between a name and a value independent of the name;
- an *abstraction type constructor* $\langle - \rangle -$ and *abstraction function symbol* $\langle - \rangle - : \nu \to \tau \to \langle \nu \rangle \tau$ which constructs values equal up to consistent renaming, axiomatized as follows:

$$\forall a, b, x, y. \langle a \rangle x = \langle b \rangle y \iff (a = b \wedge x = y) \vee (a \ \# \ y \wedge x = (a \ b) \cdot y) ;$$

---

[1] o is the type of propositions.

- a *some/any fresh-name quantifier* Иthat is self-dual ($\neg$Иa.$\varphi \iff$ Иa.$\neg\varphi$);
- and *freshness* and *equivariance* principles which state that *fresh names can always be chosen* and *truth is preserved by name-swapping*, respectively.

1.1   The Problem

This paper is concerned with developing simple rules for reasoning with the И-quantifier. Pitts' original formalization of nominal logic was a Hilbert-style collection of first-order axioms (which we call NL). There were no new inference rules for И. Instead, Иwas defined using the axiom scheme $\forall \overline{x}.($Иa.$\varphi \iff \exists a.a \ \# \ \overline{x} \wedge \varphi)$, where $FV(\varphi) \subseteq \{a, \overline{x}\}$. While admirable from a reductionist point of view, Hilbert systems have well-known deficiencies for modeling actual reasoning. Instead, Gentzen-style *natural deduction* and *sequent* systems provide a more intuitive approach to formal reasoning in which logical connectives are explained as *proof-search* operations. Gentzen systems are especially useful for computational applications, such as automated deduction and logic programming. A sequent calculus formalization would also be convenient for relating nominal logic with other logics by proof-theoretic translations.

Gentzen-style rules for Иhave been considered in previous work. Pitts [12] proposed sequent and natural deduction rules for Иbased on the observation that

$$\forall a.(a \ \# \ \overline{x} \supset \varphi(a, \overline{x})) \supset \text{И}a.\varphi(a, \overline{x}) \supset \exists a.(a \ \# \ \overline{x} \wedge \varphi(a, \overline{x})) \ .$$

These rules (see Figure 1(NL)) are symmetric, emphasizing И's self-duality. However, they are not closed under substitution, which greatly complicates the the proof of cut-elimination or proof-normalization properties.

Gabbay [6] introduced Fresh Logic (FL), an intuitionistic natural deduction calculus for nominal logic, and studied semantic issues including soundness and completeness as well as proving proof-normalization. Gabbay and Cheney [7] presented a similar sequent calculus called FL_{Seq}. In FL, Gabbay introduced a technical device called *slices* for obtaining rules that are closed under substitution. Technically, a slice $\varphi[a\#\overline{u}]$ of a formula φ is a decomposition of the formula as $\varphi(a, \overline{x})[\overline{u}/\overline{x}]$ for fresh variables $\overline{x}$, such that a does not appear in any of the $\overline{u}$. Slices were also used in the FL_{Seq} rules (see Figure 1(FL_{Seq})). The slice-based rules shown in Figure 1(FL_{Seq}) *are* closed under substitution, so proving cut-elimination for these rules is relatively straightforward once several technical lemmas involving slices have been proved. Noting that the FL_{Seq} rules are structurally similar to $\forall L$ and $\exists R$, respectively, Gabbay and Cheney observed that alternate rules in which ИL was similar to $\exists L$ and ИR similar to $\forall R$ were possible (see Figure 1(FL'_{Seq})). These rules seem simpler and more deterministic; however, they still involve slices.

Gabbay and Cheney presented a proof-theoretic semantics for nominal logic programming based on FL_{Seq}. However, this analysis suggested an interpretation of И-quantified formulas that was radically different from the approach used in the αProlog nominal logic programming language [2]. The proof-search interpretation of Иa.φ suggested by FL_{Seq} is "search for a slice $\varphi[a\#\overline{u}]$ of φ and substitution t for a such that $t \ \# \ \overline{u}$ and solve $\varphi(t, \overline{u})$", while in αProlog, the interpretation of Иa.φ is "generate a fresh name a' and solve $\varphi(a')$". The approach motivated by the FL_{Seq} proof-theoretic semantics seems much more complicated than experience with αProlog suggests.

$$\frac{\Gamma, a \# \bar{x} \Rightarrow \varphi, \Delta \quad (\dagger)}{\Gamma \Rightarrow \text{И}a.\varphi, \Delta} \;\text{И}R \qquad \frac{\Gamma, a \# \bar{x}, \varphi \Rightarrow \Delta \quad (\dagger)}{\Gamma, \text{И}a.\varphi \Rightarrow \Delta} \;\text{И}L \quad (NL)$$

$$\frac{\Gamma \vdash u \# \bar{t} \quad \Gamma \vdash \varphi[u/a] \quad (*)}{\Gamma \vdash \text{И}a.\varphi} \;\text{И}I \qquad \frac{\Gamma \vdash \text{И}a.\varphi \quad \Gamma \vdash u \# \bar{t} \quad \Gamma, \varphi[u/a] \vdash \psi \;\; (*)}{\Gamma \Rightarrow \psi} \;\text{И}E \quad (FL)$$

$$\frac{\Gamma, u \# \bar{t} \Rightarrow \varphi[u/a] \quad (*)}{\Gamma, u \# \bar{t} \Rightarrow \text{И}a.\varphi} \;\text{И}R \qquad \frac{\Gamma, u \# \bar{t}, \varphi[u/a] \Rightarrow \psi \quad (*)}{\Gamma, u \# \bar{t}, \text{И}a.\varphi \Rightarrow \psi} \;\text{И}L \quad (FL_{Seq})$$

$$\frac{\Gamma, a \# \bar{t} \Rightarrow \varphi \quad (*),(**)}{\Gamma \Rightarrow \text{И}a.\varphi} \;\text{И}R \qquad \frac{\Gamma, a \# \bar{t}, \varphi \Rightarrow \psi \quad (*),(**)}{\Gamma, \text{И}a.\varphi \Rightarrow \psi} \;\text{И}L \quad (FL'_{Seq})$$

$$\frac{\Sigma \# a : \Gamma \Rightarrow \varphi \quad (a \notin \Sigma)}{\Sigma : \Gamma \Rightarrow \text{И}a.\varphi} \;\text{И}R \qquad \frac{\Sigma \# a : \Gamma, \varphi \Rightarrow \psi \quad (a \notin \Sigma)}{\Sigma : \Gamma, \text{И}a.\varphi \Rightarrow \psi} \;\text{И}L \quad (NL^{\Rightarrow})$$

$$(\dagger) \; \bar{x} = FV(\Gamma, \text{И}a.\varphi, \Delta) \quad (*) \; \varphi = \varphi[a\#\bar{t}] \quad (**) \; a \notin FV(\Gamma, \psi)$$

Fig. 1. Evolution of rules for И

Gabbay and Cheney also gave a translation from $FO\lambda^{\nabla}$, a logic introduced by Miller and Tiu that also includes a self-dual quantifier, ∇ [9] into FL_{Seq}. This translation was sound (mapped derivable sequents to derivable sequents), but incomplete (mapped some non-derivable sequents to derivable ones). Gabbay and Cheney conjectured that their translation would be complete relative to $FO\lambda^{\nabla}$ extended with weakening and exchange for ∇.

In this paper we present a simplified sequent calculus for nominal logic, called $NL^{\Rightarrow}$, in which slices are not needed in the rules for И (or anywhere else), and which seems more compatible with the proof-search reading of И in αProlog. Following Urban, Pitts, and Gabbay [14, 6], we employ a new syntactic class of *name-symbols* a, b, ... Like variables, such name-symbols may be bound (by И), but unlike variables, two distinct name-symbols are always regarded as denoting distinct name values. In place of slices, we introduce variable contexts that encode information about freshness. Specifically, contexts $\Sigma\#$a:ν may be formed by adjoining a *fresh name-symbol* a which is also assumed to be semantically fresh for any value mentioned in Σ. Our rules for И (Figure 1($NL^{\Rightarrow}$)) are in the spirit of the original rules and are very simple.

Besides the sequent calculus itself, we present two applications. First, we verify that $NL^{\Rightarrow}$ and Pitts' axiomatization NL are equivalent. Second, we present and prove the soundness and completeness of a new translation from $FO\lambda^{\nabla}$ to nominal logic, solving a problem left unsolved by Gabbay and Cheney. We have also found that the original translation is complete relative to $FO\lambda^{\nabla}$ extended with ∇-weakening and contraction.

The structure of this paper is as follows: Section 2 presents the sequent calculus $NL^{\Rightarrow}$ along with proofs of structural properties and conservativity of $NL^{\Rightarrow}$ relative to NL. In Section 3, we present sound and complete translations from $FO\lambda^{\nabla}$ (with and without ∇-weakening and exchange) to $NL^{\Rightarrow}$. Section 4 discusses additional related and future work, and Section 5 concludes.

2   Sequent Calculus

The sequent calculus in this section is a generalization of the one presented in Chapter 4 of the author's dissertation [5]. Full proofs can be found there and in a companion technical report [3].

2.1   Syntax and Well-Formedness

The types τ, terms t, and formulas φ of $NL^{\Rightarrow}$ are generated by the following grammar:

$$\tau ::= o \mid \delta \mid \nu \mid \tau \rightarrow \tau' \mid \langle \nu \rangle \tau \qquad t, u ::= c \mid \mathsf{a} \mid \lambda x{:}\tau.t \mid t\,u \mid x$$

$$\varphi, \psi ::= \top \mid \bot \mid t \mid \varphi \wedge \psi \mid \varphi \vee \psi \mid \varphi \supset \psi \mid \forall x{:}\tau.\varphi \mid \exists x{:}\tau.\varphi \mid \mathsf{N}\mathsf{a}{:}\nu.\varphi$$

The base types are datatypes δ, name-types ν, and the type o of propositions; additional types are formed using the function and abstraction type constructors. Variables x, y are drawn from a countably infinite set V; also, name-symbols a, b are drawn from a disjoint countably infinite set A. The letters a, b are typically used for terms of some name-sort ν. Note that λ-terms are included in this language and are handled in a traditional fashion. In particular, terms are considered equal up to $\alpha\beta\eta$-equivalence. Similarly, $\forall, \exists$, and N-quantified formulas are identified up to α-equivalence. We assume given a signature that maps constant symbols c to types τ, and containing at least the following declarations:

$$eq_\tau : \tau{\rightarrow}\tau{\rightarrow}o \quad fresh_{\nu\tau} : \nu{\rightarrow}\tau{\rightarrow}o \quad swap_{\nu\tau} : \nu{\rightarrow}\nu{\rightarrow}\tau{\rightarrow}\tau \quad abs_{\nu\tau} : \nu{\rightarrow}\tau{\rightarrow}\langle\nu\rangle\tau$$

for all name-types ν and types τ. The notations $t \approx u$, $t \mathbin{\#} u$, $(t\,u) \cdot v$, and $\langle t \rangle u$ are syntactic sugar for $eq\,t\,u$, $fresh\,t\,u$, $swap\,t\,u\,v$, and $abs\,t\,u$, respectively.

The *contexts* used in $NL^{\Rightarrow}$ are generated by the grammar:

$$\Sigma ::= \cdot \mid \Sigma, x{:}\tau \mid \Sigma \mathbin{\#} \mathsf{a}{:}\nu$$

We often abbreviate $\cdot, x{:}\tau$ and $\cdot \mathbin{\#} \mathsf{a}{:}\nu$ to $x{:}\tau$ and $\mathsf{a}{:}\nu$ respectively, and may omit type declarations when no ambiguity ensues. We write ω for a term that may be either a name-symbol a or a variable x. The functions $FV(-), FN(-), FVN(-)$ calculate the sets of free variables, name-symbols, or both variables and name-symbols of a term or formula. Note that abstraction $\langle - \rangle -$ is just a function symbol and does not bind its first argument (which may be any term of type ν), and so $FN(\langle a \rangle t) = FN(a) \cup FN(t)$, whereas $\mathsf{N}\mathsf{a}.\varphi$ does bind a, so $FN(\mathsf{N}\mathsf{a}.\varphi) = FN(\varphi) - \{\mathsf{a}\}$. We write $\omega{:}\tau \in \Sigma$ if the binding $\omega{:}\tau$ is present in Σ. We write $\Sigma; \Sigma'$ for the result of concatenating two contexts such that $FVN(\Sigma) \cap FVN(\Sigma') = \varnothing$.

Remark 1. The inclusion of λ-terms and identification of terms and formulas with bound names up to α-equivalence may be objectionable because it appears that we are circularly attempting to define binding in terms of binding. This is not the case. A key contribution of Gabbay and Pitts' approach is that it shows how one can formally justify a traditional, informal approach to binding syntax by constructing syntax trees modulo α-equivalence as simple mathematical objects in a particularly clever way [8][5–Ch. 3–4]. We assume that this or some other standard technique for dealing with binding in nominal logic's terms and formulas is acting behind the scenes.

We write $\Sigma \vdash t : \tau$ or $\Sigma \vdash \varphi : o$ to indicate that t is a well-formed term of type τ or φ is a well-formed formula. From the point of view of typechecking, the freshness information given by the context is irrelevant. There are only two nonstandard rules for typechecking:

$$\frac{\omega{:}\tau \in \Sigma}{\Sigma \vdash \omega : \tau} \qquad \frac{\Sigma \# \mathsf{a}{:}\nu \vdash \varphi : o}{\Sigma \vdash \mathsf{N}\mathsf{a}{:}\nu.\varphi : o}$$

Terms viewed as formulas must, as usual, be of type o. Quantification using $\forall$ and $\exists$ is only allowed over types not mentioning o; N-quantification is only allowed over name-types.

Let $Tm_\Sigma = \{t \mid \Sigma \vdash t : \tau\}$ be the set of well-formed terms in context Σ. We associate a set of freshness formulas $|\Sigma|$ to each context Σ as follows:

$$|\cdot| = \varnothing \qquad |\Sigma, x : \tau| = |\Sigma| \qquad |\Sigma \# \mathsf{a} : \nu| = |\Sigma| \cup \{\mathsf{a} \# t \mid t \in Tm_\Sigma\}$$

For example, $\mathsf{a} \# x, \mathsf{b} \# \mathsf{a}$, and $\mathsf{b} \# f\, x\, y \in |x{:}\tau \# \mathsf{a}{:}\nu, y{:}\tau' \# \mathsf{b}{:}\nu'|$ (provided $f : \tau \to \tau' \to \sigma$ is a function symbol). We say that Σ is stronger than Σ' ($\Sigma' \leq \Sigma$) if $Tm_{\Sigma'} \subseteq Tm_\Sigma$ and $|\Sigma'| \subseteq |\Sigma|$. For example, $\mathsf{a}, x \leq x \# \mathsf{a}, y$.

Lemma 1 (Term Weakening). *If $\Sigma \vdash t : \tau$ and $\Sigma \leq \Sigma'$ then $\Sigma' \vdash t : \tau$.*

Lemma 2 (Term Substitution). *If $\Sigma \vdash t : \tau$ and $\Sigma, x : \tau; \Sigma' \vdash u : \tau'$ then $\Sigma; \Sigma' \vdash u[t/x] : \tau'$.*

2.2   The Rules

Judgments are of the form $\Sigma : \Gamma \Rightarrow \Delta$, where Σ is a context and Γ, Δ are multisets of formulas. We define classical and intuitionistic versions of $NL^\Rightarrow$. *Classical $NL^\Rightarrow$* is based on the classical sequent calculus **G3c** [11] (see Figure 2), whereas *Intuitionistic $NL^\Rightarrow$ ($INL^\Rightarrow$)* is based on the intuitionistic calculus **G3im** (in which $\supset$, $\forall R$, and $\exists L$-rules are restricted to a single-conclusion form). Both versions include two additional *logical rules*, $\mathsf{N}L$ and $\mathsf{N}R$, shown in Figure 1($NL^\Rightarrow$). In addition, $NL^\Rightarrow$ includes several *nonlogical rules* (Figure 4) defining the properties of swapping, equality, freshness and abstraction. Figure 5 lists some admissible rules.

Many of the nonlogical rules correspond to first-order universal axioms of nominal logic (Figure 3), which may be incorporated into sequent systems in a uniform fashion using the Ax rule without affecting cut-elimination [11]. The remaining nonlogical rules are as follows. Rule A_2 expresses an invertibility property for abstractions: two abstractions are equal only if they are structurally equal or equal by virtue of A_1. A_3 says that all values of abstraction type are formed using the abstraction function symbol. The F rule expresses the freshness principle: that a name fresh for a given context may always be chosen. Finally, the $\Sigma \#$ rule allows freshness information to be extracted from the context Σ. It states that in context Σ, any constraint in $|\Sigma|$ is valid.

2.3   Structural Properties

We now list some routinely-verified properties of $NL^\Rightarrow$ derivations. We write $\vdash_n J$ to indicate that judgment J has a derivation of height at most n.

$$\overline{\Sigma : \Gamma, p\,\bar{t} \Rightarrow p\,\bar{t}, \Delta}\ hyp$$

$$\overline{\Sigma : \Gamma \Rightarrow \top, \Delta}\ \top R \qquad\qquad \overline{\Sigma : \Gamma, \bot \Rightarrow \Delta}\ \bot L$$

$$\frac{\Sigma : \Gamma \Rightarrow \varphi, \Delta \quad \Sigma : \Gamma \Rightarrow \psi, \Delta}{\Sigma : \Gamma \Rightarrow \varphi \wedge \psi, \Delta}\ \wedge R \qquad\qquad \frac{\Sigma : \Gamma, \varphi_1, \varphi_2 \Rightarrow \Delta}{\Sigma : \Gamma, \varphi_1 \wedge \varphi_2 \Rightarrow \Delta}\ \wedge L$$

$$\frac{\Sigma : \Gamma \Rightarrow \varphi_1, \varphi_2, \Delta}{\Sigma : \Gamma \Rightarrow \varphi_1 \vee \varphi_2, \Delta}\ \vee R \qquad\qquad \frac{\Sigma : \Gamma, \varphi \Rightarrow \Delta \quad \Gamma, \psi \Rightarrow \Delta}{\Sigma : \Gamma, \varphi \vee \psi \Rightarrow \Delta}\ \vee L$$

$$\frac{\Sigma : \Gamma, \varphi \Rightarrow \psi, \Delta}{\Sigma : \Gamma \Rightarrow \varphi \supset \psi, \Delta}\ \supset R \qquad\qquad \frac{\Sigma : \Gamma \Rightarrow \varphi, \Delta \quad \Sigma : \Gamma, \psi \Rightarrow \Delta}{\Sigma : \Gamma, \varphi \supset \psi \Rightarrow \Delta}\ \supset L$$

$$\frac{\Sigma, x : \Gamma \Rightarrow \varphi, \Delta \quad (x \notin \Sigma)}{\Sigma : \Gamma \Rightarrow \forall x.\varphi, \Delta}\ \forall R \qquad\qquad \frac{\Sigma \vdash t : \sigma \quad \Sigma : \Gamma, \forall x{:}\tau.\varphi, \varphi[t/x] \Rightarrow \Delta}{\Sigma : \Gamma, \forall x{:}\tau.\varphi \Rightarrow \Delta}\ \forall L$$

$$\frac{\Sigma \vdash t : \sigma \quad \Sigma : \Gamma \Rightarrow \exists x{:}\tau.\varphi, \varphi[t/x], \Delta}{\Sigma : \Gamma \Rightarrow \exists x{:}\tau.\varphi, \Delta}\ \exists R \qquad\qquad \frac{\Sigma, x : \Gamma, \varphi \Rightarrow \Delta \quad (x \notin \Sigma)}{\Sigma : \Gamma, \exists x.\varphi \Rightarrow \Delta}\ \exists L$$

$$\frac{\Sigma : \Gamma, t \approx t \Rightarrow \Delta}{\Sigma : \Gamma \Rightarrow \Delta}\ \approx R \qquad\qquad \frac{\Sigma : \Gamma, t \approx u, P(t), P(u) \Rightarrow \Delta}{\Sigma : \Gamma, t \approx u, P(t) \Rightarrow \Delta}\ \approx S$$

Fig. 2. Classical typed first-order equational logic (**G3c**)

Lemma 3 (Weakening). *If $\vdash_n \Sigma : \Gamma \Rightarrow \Delta$ is derivable then so is $\vdash_n \Sigma : \Gamma, \varphi \Rightarrow \Delta$.*

Lemma 4 (Context Weakening). *If $\vdash_n \Sigma : \Gamma \Rightarrow \Delta$ and $\Sigma \leq \Sigma'$ then $\vdash_n \Sigma' : \Gamma \Rightarrow \Delta$*

Lemma 5 (Substitution). *If $\vdash_n \Sigma \vdash t : \tau$ and $\Sigma, x{:}\tau; \Sigma' : \Gamma \Rightarrow \Delta$ then $\vdash_n \Sigma; \Sigma' : \Gamma[t/x] \Rightarrow \Delta[t/x]$.*

The remaining structural transformations do not preserve the height of derivations. However, they do preserve the logical height of the derivation, which is defined as follows.

Definition 1. *The* logical height *of a derivation is the maximum number of logical rules in any branch of the derivation. We write $\vdash^l_n J$ to indicate that J has a derivation of logical height $\leq n$.*

Lemma 6 (Admissibility of EVL, EVR). *If $\vdash^l_n \Sigma : \Gamma, (a\ b) \cdot \varphi \Rightarrow \Delta$, then so is $\vdash^l_n \Sigma : \Gamma, \varphi \Rightarrow \Delta$. Similarly, if $\vdash^l_n \Sigma : \Gamma \Rightarrow (a\ b) \cdot \varphi, \Delta$ is derivable, then so is $\vdash^l_n \Sigma : \Gamma \Rightarrow \varphi, \Delta$.*

Lemma 7 (Admissibility of hyp^*). *The judgment $\Sigma : \Gamma, \varphi \Rightarrow \varphi, \Delta$ is derivable for any φ.*

Proof (Sketch). Induction on the construction of φ. The only new case is for $\varphi = \mathsf{N}\mathsf{a}.\psi(\mathsf{a}, \overline{x})$. By induction we know that $\Sigma\#\mathsf{a}\#\mathsf{b} : \Gamma, \psi(\mathsf{b}, \overline{x}) \Rightarrow \psi(\mathsf{b}, \overline{x})$. Using equivariance we have $\Sigma\#\mathsf{a}\#\mathsf{b} : \Gamma, (\mathsf{a}\ \mathsf{b}) \cdot \psi(\mathsf{a}, \overline{x}) \Rightarrow \psi(\mathsf{b}, \overline{x})$. Since $\overline{x} \subset FV(\Sigma)$, using

$$(S_1) \qquad\qquad (a\,a)\cdot x \approx x$$
$$(S_2) \qquad\qquad (a\,b)\cdot(a\,b)\cdot x \approx x$$
$$(S_3) \qquad\qquad (a\,b)\cdot a \approx b$$
$$(E_1) \qquad\qquad (a\,b)\cdot c \approx c$$
$$(E_2)\;(a\,b)\cdot(t\,u) \approx ((a\,b)\cdot t)\,((a\,b)\cdot u)$$
$$(E_3) \qquad\qquad p(\overline{x}) \supset p((a\,b)\cdot\overline{x})$$

$$(E_4)\;(a\,b)\cdot\lambda x.e[x] \approx \lambda x.(a\,b)\cdot e[(a\,b)\cdot x]$$
$$(F_1) \qquad a\;\#\;x \wedge b\;\#\;x \supset (a\,b)\cdot x \approx x$$
$$(F_2) \qquad a\;\#\;b \quad (a:\nu, b:\nu', \nu\not\equiv\nu')$$
$$(F_3) \qquad\qquad a\;\#\;a \supset \bot$$
$$(F_4) \qquad\qquad a\;\#\;b \vee a \approx b$$
$$(A_1)\;\; a\;\#\;y \wedge x \approx (a\,b)\cdot y \supset \langle a\rangle x \approx \langle b\rangle y$$

Fig. 3. Equational and freshness axioms

$$\dfrac{\Sigma:\Gamma,\overline{P},Q_1 \Rightarrow \Delta \quad\cdots\quad \Sigma:\Gamma,\overline{P},Q_n \Rightarrow \Delta}{\Sigma:\Gamma,\overline{P} \Rightarrow \Delta}\;Ax \qquad \bigwedge\overline{P} \supset \bigvee\overline{Q} \text{ an axiom instance}$$

$$\dfrac{\Sigma:\Gamma,\langle a\rangle t \approx \langle b\rangle u, a \approx b, t \approx u \Rightarrow \Delta \quad \Sigma:\Gamma,\langle a\rangle t \approx \langle b\rangle u, a\;\#\;u, t = (a\,b)\cdot u \Rightarrow \Delta}{\Sigma:\Gamma,\langle a\rangle t \approx \langle b\rangle u \Rightarrow \Delta}\;A_2$$

$$\dfrac{\Sigma \vdash t:\langle\nu\rangle\sigma \quad \Sigma, a{:}\nu, x{:}\sigma : \Gamma, t \approx \langle a\rangle x \Rightarrow \Delta \quad (a, x \notin \Sigma)}{\Sigma:\Gamma \Rightarrow \Delta}\;A_3$$

$$\dfrac{\Sigma\#a:\Gamma \Rightarrow \Delta \quad (a \notin \Sigma)}{\Sigma:\Gamma \Rightarrow \Delta}\;F \qquad\qquad \dfrac{\Sigma:\Gamma, t\;\#\;u \Rightarrow \Delta \quad (t\;\#\;u \in |\Sigma|)}{\Sigma:\Gamma \Rightarrow \Delta}\;\Sigma\#$$

Fig. 4. Nonlogical rules

$$\dfrac{\Sigma:\Gamma \Rightarrow \Delta}{\Sigma:\Gamma,\varphi \Rightarrow \Delta}\;W \qquad \dfrac{}{\Sigma:\Gamma,\varphi \Rightarrow \varphi,\Delta}\;hyp^* \qquad \dfrac{\Sigma:\Gamma \Rightarrow \varphi,\Delta \quad \Sigma:\Gamma',\varphi \Rightarrow \Delta'}{\Sigma:\Gamma,\Gamma' \Rightarrow \Delta,\Delta'}\;cut$$

$$\dfrac{\Sigma:\Gamma,\varphi,\varphi \Rightarrow \Delta}{\Sigma:\Gamma,\varphi \Rightarrow \Delta}\;C \qquad \dfrac{\Sigma:\Gamma,(a\,b)\cdot\varphi \Rightarrow \Delta}{\Sigma:\Gamma,\varphi \Rightarrow \Delta}\;EVL \qquad \dfrac{\Sigma:\Gamma \Rightarrow (a\,b)\cdot\varphi,\Delta}{\Sigma:\Gamma \Rightarrow \Delta,\varphi}\;EVR$$

Fig. 5. Some admissible rules of $NL^\Rightarrow$

$\Sigma\#$ we know that a $\#\;\overline{x}$, b $\#\;\overline{x}$, hence $(a\,b)\cdot\overline{x} \approx \overline{x}$, so using equational reasoning we have $(a\,b)\cdot\psi(a,\overline{x}) \approx \psi(b,\overline{x})$. Then using ⅄$L$ and ⅄R we can conclude $\Sigma:\Gamma, ⅄a.\psi \Rightarrow ⅄a.\psi, \Delta$.   □

Lemma 8 (Inversion). *The $\supset L$, $\exists L$, $\wedge L$, and $\vee L$ rules are invertible, in the sense of lemma 2.3.5 and 4.2.8 of Negri and von Plato [11]. In addition, ⅄L is invertible: if $\vdash^l_n \Sigma:\Gamma, ⅄a.\varphi \Rightarrow \Delta$ is derivable then so is $\vdash^l_n \Sigma\#a:\Gamma, \varphi \Rightarrow \Delta$ for fresh a.*

Lemma 9 (Contraction). *If $\vdash^l_n \Sigma:\Gamma, \varphi, \varphi \Rightarrow \Delta$ is derivable then so is $\vdash^l_n \Sigma:\Gamma, \varphi \Rightarrow \Delta$.*

2.4   Cut-Elimination

Lemma 10 (Admissibility of Cut). *If $\Sigma:\Gamma \Rightarrow \Delta, \varphi$ and $\Sigma:\Gamma', \varphi \Rightarrow \Delta'$ have cut-free derivations then so does $\Sigma:\Gamma, \Gamma' \Rightarrow \Delta, \Delta'$.*

Proof (Sketch). We show the most interesting case, that for principal cuts on $\mathsf{И}$-quantified formulas. In this case, the derivations are of the form

$$\frac{\overset{\Pi}{\Sigma\#\mathsf{a}:\Gamma\Rightarrow\varphi,\Delta}}{\Sigma:\Gamma\Rightarrow\mathsf{И}\mathsf{a}.\varphi,\Delta}\ \mathsf{И}R \qquad \frac{\overset{\Pi'}{\Sigma\#\mathsf{a}:\Gamma',\varphi\Rightarrow\Delta'}}{\Sigma:\Gamma',\mathsf{И}\mathsf{a}.\varphi\Rightarrow\Delta'}\ \mathsf{И}L$$

where without loss of generality we assume that the same fresh name $\mathsf{a}\notin\Sigma$ was used in both sub-derivations. Since φ is smaller than $\mathsf{И}\mathsf{a}.\varphi$, we can obtain a derivation Π'' of $\Sigma\#\mathsf{a}:\Gamma,\Gamma'\Rightarrow\Delta,\Delta'$ from Π and Π' by the induction hypothesis. Then

$$\frac{\overset{\Pi''}{\Sigma\#\mathsf{a}:\Gamma,\Gamma'\Rightarrow\Delta,\Delta'}}{\Sigma:\Gamma,\Gamma'\Rightarrow\Delta,\Delta'}\ F$$

follows using rule F. □

Theorem 1 (Cut-Elimination). *If $\Sigma:\Gamma\Rightarrow\Delta$ has any derivation then it has a cut-free derivation.*

Corollary 1 (Consistency). *There is no derivation of $\Sigma:\cdot\Rightarrow\bot$.*

Corollary 2 (Orthognality). *Suppose $\Sigma:\Gamma\Rightarrow\Delta$ and Γ,Δ have no subterms of the form $\langle a\rangle t$ (respectively, $\lambda x.t$). Then there is a derivation of $\Sigma:\Gamma\Rightarrow\Delta$ that does not use any nonlogical rules involving abstraction (respectively, λ).*

2.5 Conservativity

In this section, we show that $NL^{\Rightarrow}$ is conservative relative to Pitts' original axiomatization NL [12]. That is, every theorem of NL is provable in $NL^{\Rightarrow}$, and no new theorems become provable. For convenience, we assume that the same underlying first-order sequent calculus is used for NL and $NL^{\Rightarrow}$.

Write $\vdash_{NL}\Sigma:\Gamma\Rightarrow\Delta$ if there is a first-order equational sequent proof of $\Sigma:\Gamma,\Gamma'\Rightarrow\Delta$. for some set of NL axioms Γ'. Write $\vdash_{NL^{\Rightarrow}}\Sigma:\Gamma\Rightarrow\Delta$ if $\Sigma:\Gamma\Rightarrow\Delta$ is derivable in $NL^{\Rightarrow}$ without using any rules involving λ. Write $\vdash_{IX}$ for the intuitionistic version of provability in system X, that is, provability using only single-conclusion sequents.

We translate NL formulas φ to $NL^{\Rightarrow}$ formulas φ^* by replacing all subformulas of the form $\mathsf{И}\mathsf{a}.\varphi(a)$ with $\mathsf{И}\mathsf{a}.\varphi^*(\mathsf{a})$, for fresh name-symbols a. This translation is uniquely defined up to α-equivalence. For example, $(\mathsf{И}\mathsf{a}.\mathsf{И}\mathsf{b}.p(a,b))^* = \mathsf{И}\mathsf{a}.\mathsf{И}\mathsf{b}.p(\mathsf{a},\mathsf{b})$.

To prove the reverse direction of conservativity, it is necessary to show that $NL^{\Rightarrow}$ sequents involving fresh name-symbols and contexts $\Sigma\#\mathsf{a}$ are equivalent to sequents involving only variables.

Lemma 11 (Name-Elimination). *Suppose Σ mentions only variables and $\vdash_n^l \Sigma\#\mathsf{a}:\Gamma[\mathsf{a}]\Rightarrow\Delta[\mathsf{a}]$. Then $\vdash_n^l \Sigma,a:\Gamma[a],a\#\Sigma\Rightarrow\Delta[a]$, where $a\#\Sigma$ is an abbreviation for $\{a\#x\mid x\in\Sigma\}$.*

Theorem 2 (Conservativity). $\vdash_{(I)NL} \Sigma : \Gamma \Rightarrow \Delta$ *if and only if* $\vdash_{(I)NL^{\Rightarrow}} \Sigma : \Gamma^* \Rightarrow \Delta^*$

Remark 2 (Semantics). Conservativity justifies $NL^{\Rightarrow}$'s description as a sequent calculus for nominal logic. Although this paper focuses exclusively on proof theory at the expense of more traditional model theoretic semantics, conservativity guarantees that $NL^{\Rightarrow}$ inherits Pitts' nominal set semantics for nominal logic (as well as suffering from the same completeness problem). Space constraints preclude further discussion; however, these issues are considered in detail in Cheney's dissertation and a paper in preparation.

3   A Sound and Complete Translation of $FO\lambda^{\nabla}$

Miller and Tiu introduced a sequent calculus called $FO\lambda^{\nabla}$, which abbreviates "First-order Logic with λ-terms and the ∇-quantifier" [9]. Like ⋂, the ∇ quantifier is self-dual. However, ⋂ and ∇ have distinctly different properties. Nominal logic and $FO\lambda^{\nabla}$ have similar aims (reasoning about languages in which binding and fresh name-generation play an important role), so it is of interest to determine the relationship between $FO\lambda^{\nabla}$ and $INL^{\Rightarrow}$. Also, $FO\lambda^{\nabla}$ has only been studied using proof theory, but nominal logic has a well-understood semantics [12], so relating the two systems may also elucidate the semantics of $FO\lambda^{\nabla}$.

In $FO\lambda^{\nabla}$, formulas are generalized to *formulas-in-context* $\sigma \triangleright \varphi$, where σ is a list of *local parameters* (variables introduced by ∇) and φ is a formula built out of first-order connectives and quantifiers or $\nabla x.\psi$. We abbreviate "formula-in-context" to "c-formula". Local parameter contexts are subject to α-renaming, so that $a \triangleright p(a)$ and $b \triangleright p(b)$ are considered equal c-formulas. However, c-formulas are not considered equivalent up to reordering or extension of the contexts. Thus, $a, b \triangleright p(a)$, $a \triangleright p(a)$, and $b, a \triangleright p(a)$ are all considered different c-formulas.

The sequent calculus rules dealing with ∇ are as follows:

$$\frac{\Sigma : \Gamma \Rightarrow (\sigma, x) \triangleright \varphi}{\Sigma : \Gamma \Rightarrow \sigma \triangleright \nabla x.\varphi} \; \nabla R \qquad \frac{\Sigma : \Gamma, (\sigma, x) \triangleright \varphi \Rightarrow \mathcal{A}}{\Sigma : \Gamma, \sigma \triangleright \nabla x.\varphi \Rightarrow \mathcal{A}} \; \nabla L$$

where in either case x must not already appear in σ or Σ. However, x *may* appear in some other local context.

Most of the other sequent rules of $FO\lambda^{\nabla}$ are standard, except for the presence of local contexts. For example,

$$\frac{\Sigma : \Gamma, \sigma \triangleright \varphi, \sigma \triangleright \psi \Rightarrow \mathcal{A}}{\Sigma : \Gamma, \sigma \triangleright \varphi \wedge \psi \Rightarrow \mathcal{A}} \; \wedge L \qquad \frac{\Sigma : \Gamma \Rightarrow \sigma \triangleright \varphi \quad \Sigma : \Gamma \Rightarrow \sigma \triangleright \psi}{\Sigma : \Gamma \Rightarrow \sigma \triangleright \varphi \wedge \psi} \; \wedge R$$

are the rules dealing with $\wedge$. The only exceptions are the $\forall$ and $\exists$ rules. In $\forall R$ and $\exists L$, the bound variable is "lifted" to show its dependence on local parameters. Dually, in $\forall L$ and $\exists R$, the term substituted for the bound variable may depend on local parameters. Here are the $\forall$-rules; the rules for $\exists$ are similar.

$$\frac{\Sigma, h{:}\overline{\tau_\sigma} \to \tau : \Gamma \Rightarrow \sigma \triangleright A[h\,\overline{\sigma}/x]}{\Sigma : \Gamma \Rightarrow \sigma \triangleright \forall_\tau x.A} \; \forall R \qquad \frac{\Sigma, \sigma \vdash t : \tau \quad \Sigma : \Gamma, \sigma \triangleright A[t/x] \Rightarrow \mathcal{C}}{\Sigma : \Gamma, \sigma \triangleright \forall_\tau x.A \Rightarrow \mathcal{C}} \; \forall L$$

Although ∇ and N have some properties in common and seem to have similar motivations, the relation between them is not obvious. For example, $INL^{\Rightarrow}$ includes name-types, and N may only quantify over them; $FO\lambda^{\nabla}$ has no name-types, and ∇ may quantify over any simple type. In addition, N admits weakening ($\varphi \iff \mathsf{N}a.\varphi$ where $a \notin FN(\varphi)$) and exchange ($\mathsf{N}a.\mathsf{N}b.\varphi \iff \mathsf{N}b.\mathsf{N}a.\varphi$), and satisfies $\forall x.\varphi(x) \supset \mathsf{N}a.\varphi(a) \supset \exists x.\varphi(x)$. None of these inferences are derivable with ∇ substituted for N. On the other hand, ∇ commutes with all propositional connectives, $\forall$, and $\exists$, while N only commutes with propositional connectives.

Gabbay and Cheney studied the problem of embedding $FO\lambda^{\nabla}$ into nominal logic. They presented a translation (which we call T_{GC}) from $FO\lambda^{\nabla}$ to FL_{Seq} satisfying a soundness property: if J is derivable in $FO\lambda^{\nabla}$ then its translation $[\![J]\!]$ is derivable in FL_{Seq}. However, their translation did not satisfy the corresponding completeness property: some non-derivable judgments of $FO\lambda^{\nabla}$ were translated to derivable FL_{Seq} judgments. In particular, the translation failed to reconcile the different behavior of N and ∇ with respect to weakening and exchange principles.

In the rest of this section, we present a modified translation and prove its soundness and completeness. We also sketch a proof that the original translation is complete with respect to $FO\lambda^{\nabla}$ with ∇-weakening and exchange. Full proofs will be given in a companion technical report [4].

Our translation T departs from T_{GC} in two ways. First, T_{GC} translated c-formulas such as $x \triangleright \varphi \wedge \psi$ by first using N-quantifiers for the local context, then translating $\varphi \wedge \psi$, and finally substituting $n(a)$ for x, resulting in $\mathsf{N}a.[\![\varphi]\!][n(a)/x] \wedge [\![\psi]\!][n(a)/x]$. In this approach, the head symbol of a translated c-formula was hidden beneath a sequence of N-quantifiers, which made T_{GC} difficult to analyze. Instead, our translation delays N-quantification as long as possible and preserves the head symbol for most formulas: for example, the prior example translates to $[\![x \triangleright \varphi]\!] \wedge [\![x \triangleright \psi]\!]$. Any N-quantification is delayed as long as possible, that is, until the base case for atomic formulas.

The second change is the translation of atomic formulas. As noted earlier, the validity of c-formulas is sensitive to both the *order* and *number* of local parameters in context. To deal with this, we relativize atomic formulas to their local contexts. This is accomplished by adding an argument to each atomic formula symbol for a list of names representing the local context. Let ν^* be a type with constructors $nil : \nu^*$ and $cons : \nu \to \nu^* \to \nu^*$, that is, a type of lists of names. We use a conventional comma-separated list notation for lists: $[a, b, c] = cons(a, cons(b, cons(c, nil)))$. The translation of an atomic c-formula $\sigma \triangleright p\bar{t}$ is $\mathsf{N}\bar{a}.p^* \, [\bar{a}] \, \bar{t}[n_{\tau}(a)/\sigma]$, where if $p : \bar{\tau} \to o$ then $p^* : \nu^* \to \bar{\tau} \to o$.

Otherwise, T is similar to T_{GC}. Ordinary $\forall$ and $\exists$-quantified values are lifted to *equivariant* functions applied to lists of names. For example, $\sigma \triangleright \forall x : \tau'.p(x)$ was translated to $\mathsf{N}\bar{a}.\forall h : \tau_1 \to \cdots \tau_n \to \tau'.ev(h) \supset p(h \, n_{\tau}(a))$, where each a_i is the name representing x_i, and $ev(x) = \forall a : \nu.a \# x$.

The new translation is shown in full in Figure 6. The function $[\![\cdot]\!]$ translates judgments, contexts, and c-formulas of $FO\lambda^{\nabla}$ to judgments, formula multisets, and formulas of $INL^{\Rightarrow}$ respectively. Note that the context Σ is translated to a set of hypotheses $ev(x)$, one for each $x \in \Sigma$. Here are two examples of the new translation. The formula $\nabla x.p \iff p$ is translated to $\mathsf{N}a.p^* \, [a] \iff p^* \, []$. Likewise, we translate $\nabla x, y.p \, x \, y \iff$

$$\begin{aligned}
[\![\sigma \rhd \top]\!] &= \top \\
[\![\sigma \rhd \bot]\!] &= \bot \\
[\![\sigma \rhd p\,\overline{t}]\!] &= \mathsf{N}\overline{\mathsf{a}}.p^*\,[\overline{\mathsf{a}}]\,(\overline{t[\overline{n_\tau(\mathsf{a})}/\sigma]}) \\
[\![\sigma \rhd \varphi \wedge \psi]\!] &= [\![\sigma \rhd \varphi]\!] \wedge [\![\sigma \rhd \psi]\!] \\
[\![\cdot]\!] &= \cdot
\end{aligned}$$

$$\begin{aligned}
[\![\sigma \rhd \varphi \vee \psi]\!] &= [\![\sigma \rhd \varphi]\!] \vee [\![\sigma \rhd \psi]\!] \\
[\![\sigma \rhd \varphi \supset \psi]\!] &= [\![\sigma \rhd \varphi]\!] \supset [\![\sigma \rhd \psi]\!] \\
[\![\sigma \rhd \forall x{:}\tau.\varphi]\!] &= \forall h{:}\overline{\tau_\sigma}{\to}\tau.ev(h) \supset [\![\sigma \rhd \varphi[h\sigma/x]]\!] \\
[\![\sigma \rhd \exists x{:}\tau.\varphi]\!] &= \exists h{:}\overline{\tau_\sigma}{\to}\tau.ev(h) \wedge [\![\sigma \rhd \varphi[h\sigma/x]]\!] \\
[\![\sigma \rhd \nabla x{:}\tau.\varphi]\!] &= [\![\sigma, x{:}\tau \rhd \varphi]\!] \\
[\![\Sigma, x{:}\tau]\!] &= [\![\Sigma]\!], ev(x) \quad (ev(x) = \forall a{:}\nu.a \;\#\; x)
\end{aligned}$$

$$[\![\Sigma : \Gamma \Rightarrow \mathcal{A}]\!] = \Sigma : [\![\Sigma]\!], [\![\Gamma]\!] \Rightarrow [\![\mathcal{A}]\!]$$

Fig. 6. Translation T from $FO\lambda^\nabla$ to $INL^\Rightarrow$

$\nabla y, x.p\,x\,y$ to $\mathsf{N}a, b.p^*\,[a, b]\,(n(a))(n(b)) \iff \mathsf{N}b, a.p^*\,[b, a]\,(n(a))\,(n(b))$. Neither of these translated formulas is derivable in nominal logic.

Lemma 12. *If* $\Sigma \vdash_{FO\lambda^\nabla} t : \tau$ *then* $\Sigma \vdash_{INL^\Rightarrow} t : \tau$; *in addition,* $\Sigma : [\![\Sigma]\!] \Rightarrow ev(t)$. *Also, if* $\Sigma : \Gamma \Rightarrow \mathcal{A}$ *is well-formed then so is* $[\![\Sigma : \Gamma \Rightarrow \mathcal{A}]\!]$.

Proposition 1 (Soundness). *If* $\Sigma : \Gamma \Rightarrow \mathcal{A}$ *is derivable in* $FO\lambda^\nabla$ *then* $[\![\Sigma : \Gamma \Rightarrow \mathcal{A}]\!]$ *is derivable in* $INL^\Rightarrow$.

Proof. Similar to, but simpler than, the proof for T_{GC}. □

Theorem 3 (Completeness). *If* $[\![\Sigma : \Gamma \Rightarrow \mathcal{A}]\!]$ *is derivable in* $INL^\Rightarrow$ *then* $\Sigma : \Gamma \Rightarrow \mathcal{A}$ *is derivable in* $FO\lambda^\nabla$.

Proof (Sketch). We break the proof into the following steps:

1. Identify two normal forms for $INL^\Rightarrow$ proofs, and show that proofs of translated sequents can be normalized.
2. Show that proofs of the first normal form are proofs of initial sequents.
3. Show that proofs of the second normal form correspond to applications of $FO\lambda^\nabla$ rules.

In the analysis to follow, it simplifies matters to eliminate as many nonlogical rules as possible from derivations. By the orthogonality property, we need not consider the rules for abstraction in translated derivations, since abstractions are not used in the translation. In addition, the nonlogical rules F_3 and F_4 can also be eliminated, as we shall now show.

Lemma 13. *Suppose* Σ *has no name-variables. If* $\Sigma \vdash a : \nu$, *then for some* $\mathsf{a} \in \Sigma$, $\Sigma : \cdot \Rightarrow a \approx \mathsf{a}$.

Proposition 2. *If* $[\![\Sigma : \Gamma \Rightarrow \mathcal{A}]\!]$ *is derivable then it has a derivation that does not use* F_3 *or* F_4.

Proof. To show that F_3 cannot be used in a derivation of a translated sequent, note that $[\![\Gamma]\!]$ and $[\![\mathcal{A}]\!]$ do not mention equality or freshness, and the formulas $[\![\Sigma]\!] = \forall a.a \# x_1, \ldots, \forall a.a \# x_n$ cannot be instantiated to $x_i \# x_i$ since the variables x_i are not of name-type. We can therefore show that no sequent occurring in the derivation of a translated sequent can contain $a \# a$ using methods similar to those used for consistency and orthogonality.

Consider a subderivation ending with F_4, of the form

$$\frac{\Sigma : \Gamma, a \# b \Rightarrow \varphi \quad \Sigma : \Gamma, a \approx b \Rightarrow \varphi}{\Sigma : \Gamma \Rightarrow \varphi}$$

Name-variables are never introduced in translated derivations, so by Lemma 13, we have $\Sigma \Rightarrow a \approx a$, $\Sigma : \cdot \Rightarrow b \approx b$ for some $a, b \in \Sigma$. If $a = b$ then clearly $\Sigma : \cdot \Rightarrow a \approx b$, so we can use the second subderivation and cut to derive $\Sigma : \Gamma \Rightarrow \varphi$. On the other hand, if $a \neq b$ then clearly $\Sigma : \cdot \Rightarrow a \# b$ and also $\Sigma : \cdot \Rightarrow a \# b$. Using cut and the subderivation $\Sigma : \Gamma, a \# b$ we can derive $\Sigma : \Gamma \Rightarrow \varphi$.   □

Definition 2. *A derivation is in* first normal form *if it uses only the rules $\forall L$, $\forall R$, hyp, and nonlogical rules.*

A derivation beginning with a left- or right-rule is in second normal form *provided that if the toplevel rule is $\forall L$, $\forall R$, $\exists L$, or $\exists R$, then the next rule used is $\supset L$, $\supset R$, $\wedge L$, or $\wedge R$, respectively.*

Before proving that translated derivations always have normal forms, we need some additional technical machinery. We write $\hat{\varphi}(t)$ for the formula $ev(t) \supset \varphi(t)$; translations of universal c-formulas are always of the form $\forall x.\hat{\varphi}(x)$. We write $\hat{\Gamma}(\bar{t})$ for a set of formulas $\hat{\varphi}_1(t_n), \ldots, \hat{\varphi}_n(t_n)$ such that $\forall x.\hat{\varphi}_i(x) \in [\![\Gamma]\!]$ for each i.

Lemma 14. *If Σ is a $FO\lambda^\nabla$ context, $\Sigma\#\bar{a} \vdash t : \tau$ and $\Sigma\#\bar{a} : [\![\Sigma]\!] \Rightarrow ev(t)$ then $\Sigma \vdash t : \tau$.*

Lemma 15. *If Σ is a $FO\lambda^\nabla$ context, $\Sigma\#\bar{a} : [\![\Sigma]\!], [\![\Gamma]\!], \hat{\Gamma}(\bar{t}) \Rightarrow ev(t)$ then either $\Sigma : [\![\Gamma]\!] \Rightarrow \varphi$ has a normal derivation for any formula φ, or $\Sigma\#\bar{a} : [\![\Sigma]\!] \Rightarrow ev(t)$.*

Lemma 16. *If $\Sigma : \Gamma \Rightarrow \varphi$ has a derivation using only* nonbranching *nonlogical rules, then it has either a first normal form derivation or one that starts with F or a logical rule.*

Proposition 3. *If $[\![\Sigma : \Gamma \Rightarrow \mathcal{A}]\!]$ is derivable, then it has a normal derivation.*

Proof (Sketch). First, by Corollary 2 and Proposition 2, $[\![\Sigma : \Gamma \Rightarrow \mathcal{A}]\!]$ must have a derivation that does not use the rules A_1, A_2, A_3, F_3 or F_4.

Because of subtleties involved in the interaction between the F and $\forall L$ rule, we need a stronger induction hypothesis. We prove that if $\Sigma\#\bar{a} : [\![\Sigma]\!], [\![\Gamma]\!], \hat{\Gamma}(\bar{t}) \Rightarrow [\![\mathcal{A}]\!]$ has a derivation, then $\Sigma : [\![\Sigma]\!], [\![\Gamma]\!] \Rightarrow [\![\mathcal{A}]\!]$ has a normal derivation.

Using Lemma 16, the sequent either has a first normal form derivation (in which case we are done) or begins with F or a logical rule. If it starts with a propositional rule applied to an element of $[\![\Gamma]\!]$, then we are done. The induction steps for F and $\forall L$ are immediate. For $\exists L, \forall R$, we can use the invertibility of $\wedge L$ and $\supset R$ respectively and then use $\forall L$. This leaves the cases for $\exists R$ and for $\supset L$ applied to an element of $\hat{\Gamma}$. For $\supset L$ we must have subderivations of $\Sigma \#\bar{a} \vdash t : \tau$ and $\Sigma \#\bar{a} : [\![\Gamma]\!], \hat{\Gamma}(\bar{t}), \varphi(t) \Rightarrow [\![\mathcal{A}]\!]$. Using the lemmas we can show that the witnessing term t does not mention any names, and so we can construct a derivation starting with $\forall L$ and $\supset L$. In the similar case of $\exists R$, we also need the invertibility of $\wedge R$.   □

We next show that if the derivation is in first normal form, then the $FO\lambda^\nabla$ sequent is derivable. We need two auxiliary facts.

Lemma 17. *Suppose $\bar{x}\#\bar{a} \vdash t : \tau$ and $\pi \cdot [\bar{a}] = [\bar{b}]$. Then $\bar{x}\#\bar{a}\#\bar{b} : \cdot \Rightarrow \pi \cdot t \approx t[b_1/a_1, \dots, b_n/a_n]$*

Lemma 18. *Suppose that Σ has no name-variables and Γ consists of freshness and equality formulas only. If $\Sigma : \Gamma, p\,\bar{t} \Rightarrow p\,\bar{u}$ then for some permutation π of names in Σ, we have $\Sigma : \Gamma \Rightarrow \pi \cdot \bar{t} \approx \bar{u}$.*

Proof. The proof is by induction on the structure of the derivation. Only the hypothesis and nonbranching nonlogical rules can be involved, of these cases, only F poses a challenge. In the case for F, the π obtained by induction may mention the fresh name a introduced by F; however, a cannot appear in t or u, so $b = \pi^{-1}(a)$ must not appear in t, and so $\pi' = \pi \circ (a\ b)$ also works since $\pi' \cdot t = \pi \cdot (a\ b) \cdot t = \pi \cdot t = u$.   □

Proposition 4. *Let $[\![\Sigma : \Gamma \Rightarrow \mathcal{A}]\!]$ have a first-normal form derivation. Then $\Sigma : \Gamma \Rightarrow \mathcal{A}$ is derivable.*

Proof. If $[\![\Sigma : \Gamma \Rightarrow \mathcal{A}]\!]$ has a first normal form derivation, then $\mathcal{A}$ and some element $\mathcal{B}$ of Γ must be of the form $\sigma \triangleright \nabla \bar{x}.p\,\bar{t}$. Without loss of generality, we consider the case where no ∇-quantifiers appear. After stripping off the initial sequence of $\forall L$ and $\forall R$ rules, there must be a subderivation of

$$\Sigma \#\bar{a}\#\bar{b} : [\![\Sigma]\!], [\![\Gamma]\!], p^* [\bar{a}] \theta(\bar{t}) \Rightarrow p^* [\bar{b}] \theta'(\bar{u})$$

for some names $\bar{a}, \bar{b}$, where $\theta = [\overline{n(a)}/\sigma]$ and $\theta' = [\overline{n(b)}/\sigma']$. Note that θ and θ' are one-to-one and so invertible on on their ranges, and that $\Sigma \#a \vdash \theta(\bar{t}) : \overline{\tau}$ (that is, none of the b appear in $\theta(\bar{t})$).

By Lemma 18, there must be a ground permutation π such that $\Sigma : \cdot \Rightarrow \pi \cdot ([\bar{a}] \theta(\bar{t})) \approx [\bar{b}] \theta'(\bar{u})$. Clearly, $\pi \cdot [\bar{a}] = [\bar{b}]$, so by Lemma 17 we have $\bar{u}[\overline{n(b)}/\sigma'] = \theta'(\bar{u}) \approx \pi \cdot \theta(\bar{t}) \approx \theta(\bar{t})[b_1/a_1, \dots, b_n/a_n] = \bar{t}[\overline{n(b)}/\sigma]$. Since $[\overline{n(b)}/\sigma']$ is invertible, we have $\bar{u} \approx \bar{t}[\overline{n(b)}/\sigma][\sigma'/\overline{n(b)}] = \bar{t}[\sigma'/\sigma]$, which implies $\sigma \triangleright p\,\bar{t} \equiv_\alpha \sigma' \triangleright p\,\bar{u}$.   □

Proof (Completeness Theorem). In $FO\lambda^\nabla$, ∇ commutes with all propositional connectives, $\forall$, and $\exists$. Therefore, every judgment is equivalent to one in which ∇-quantifiers only occur around atomic formulas, that is, in subformulas of the form $\nabla \overline{x}.p \ \overline{t}$. So it suffices to consider only judgments of this form.

The proof is by induction on the complexity of the judgment $\Sigma : \Gamma \Rightarrow \mathcal{A}$. If the normalized derivation is of the first form, then by Proposition 4, the sequent is derivable. If the normalized derivation is of the second form, there are many subcases, one for each possible starting left- or right-rule. The cases for propositional rules are straightforward. The remaining cases are those for $\forall$ and $\exists$. We will show that translated sequents derived using $\forall L/R, \exists L/R$ in $INL^{\Rightarrow}$ can be derived using $\forall L/R$ and $\exists L/R$ in $FO\lambda^{\nabla}$.

If the final step of the derivation is $\forall R$, then the derivation must be of the form

$$\frac{\dfrac{\Sigma, h : [\![\Sigma]\!], ev(h), [\![\Gamma]\!] \Rightarrow [\![\sigma \triangleright \varphi[h\sigma/x]]\!]}{\Sigma, h : [\![\Sigma]\!], [\![\Gamma]\!] \Rightarrow ev(h) \supset [\![\sigma \triangleright \varphi[h\sigma/x]]\!]} \supset R}{\Sigma : [\![\Sigma]\!], [\![\Gamma]\!] \Rightarrow \forall h.ev(h) \supset [\![\sigma \triangleright \varphi[h\sigma/x]]\!]} \forall R$$

Note that $[\![\Sigma]\!], ev(h) = [\![\Sigma, h]\!]$, so the topmost sequent is of the form $[\![\Sigma, h : \Gamma \Rightarrow \sigma \triangleright \varphi[h\sigma/x]]\!]$. By induction, $\Sigma, h : \Gamma \Rightarrow \sigma \triangleright \varphi[h\sigma/x]$ is derivable, and using $\forall R$, we conclude $\Sigma : \Gamma \Rightarrow \sigma \triangleright \forall x.\varphi$. The $\exists L$ case is similar.

If the final inference is $\forall L$, then the derivation must be of the form

$$\frac{\Sigma \vdash t : \overline{\tau_\sigma} \to \tau \quad \dfrac{\Sigma : [\![\Sigma]\!], [\![\Gamma]\!] \Rightarrow ev(t) \quad \Sigma : [\![\Sigma]\!], [\![\Gamma]\!], [\![\sigma \triangleright \varphi[h\sigma/x]]\!][t/h] \Rightarrow [\![\mathcal{A}]\!]}{\Sigma : [\![\Sigma]\!], [\![\Gamma]\!], ev(t) \supset [\![\sigma \triangleright \varphi[h\sigma/x]]\!] \Rightarrow [\![\mathcal{A}]\!]} \supset L}{\Sigma : [\![\Sigma]\!], [\![\Gamma]\!], \forall h.ev(h) \supset [\![\sigma \triangleright \varphi[h\sigma/x]]\!] \Rightarrow [\![\mathcal{A}]\!]} \forall L$$

Since Σ does not mention name-constants, we have $\Sigma \vdash t : \overline{\tau_\sigma} \to \tau$ and also $\Sigma, \sigma \vdash t \ \sigma : \tau$ in $FO\lambda^{\nabla}$. Note that $[\![\sigma \triangleright \varphi[h\sigma/x]]\!][t/h] = [\![\sigma \triangleright \varphi[t \ \sigma/x]]\!]$ so we also have $\Sigma : [\![\Sigma]\!], [\![\Gamma]\!], [\![\sigma \triangleright \varphi[t \ \sigma/x]]\!] \Rightarrow [\![\mathcal{A}]\!]$, which is the same as $[\![\Sigma : \Gamma, \sigma \triangleright \varphi[t \ \sigma/x] \Rightarrow \mathcal{A}]\!]$. By induction, $\Sigma : \Gamma, \sigma \triangleright \varphi[t \ \sigma/x] \Rightarrow \mathcal{A}$ is derivable, and since $\Sigma, \sigma \vdash t \ \sigma : \tau$, we can use $\forall L$ to conclude that $\Sigma : \Gamma, \sigma \triangleright \forall x.\varphi \Rightarrow \mathcal{A}$. The $\exists R$ case is similar. □

Remark 3. If we modify the translation step for atomic formulas by defining $[\![\sigma \triangleright p \ \overline{t}]\!] = \nabla \overline{a}.p \ \overline{t}[\overline{n(a)}/\sigma]$ then we obtain a translation T_{WX} that is essentially the same as T_{GC}, and is complete with respect to $FO\lambda^{\nabla}$ with ∇-weakening and exchange principles.

We write $\theta : \sigma \hookrightarrow \sigma'$ to indicate that θ is a partial injective renaming mapping σ to σ'. We say that c-formulas are WX-equivalent ($\sigma \triangleright A \equiv_{WX} \sigma' \triangleright B$) if there is a $\theta : \sigma \hookrightarrow \sigma'$ such that $\theta(A) = B$. For example, $x, y \triangleright p(x, y) \equiv_{WX} y, x, z \triangleright p(x, y)$. Note that $\equiv_{WX}$ subsumes α-equivalence. Let $FO\lambda^{\nabla}_{WX}$ be $FO\lambda^{\nabla}$ except that atomic c-formulas are considered equal modulo $\equiv_{WX}$.

It is not difficult to show that the formulas $\nabla x.\varphi \iff \varphi$ (where $x \notin FV(\varphi)$) and $\nabla x.\nabla y.\varphi \iff \nabla y.\nabla x.\varphi$ are derivable in $FO\lambda^{\nabla}_{WX}$ for any formula φ. In addition, using the same techniques as above, we can show that the translation is sound and complete relative to $FO\lambda^{\nabla}_{WX}$. The proof is the same as that for completeness relative to $FO\lambda^{\nabla}$, except that we need to show that Proposition 4 holds for atomic c-formulas equal modulo $\equiv_{WX}$ instead of α-equivalence.

4   Related and Future Work

Besides previous formalizations of nominal logic by Pitts, Gabbay, and Cheney (surveyed in Section 1.1), several other logics and type systems have considered rules for И-quantified formulas or types. Caires and Cardelli [1] investigated a logic incorporating proof rules for И-quantified formulas based on maintaining a set of side-conditions involving freshness constraints. However, the freshness constraints are not formulas of their logic. These rules are similar in spirit to (and partly inspired) the slice-based rules of FL and FL_{Seq}. Another related system is the type system of Nanevski [10], which includes rules similar to those of FL for И-quantified types. A third closely related system is Schöpp and Stark's dependent type theory for names and binding [13], in which a bunched context is used to store freshness information. Our freshness contexts and rules for И are simpler special cases of the contexts and rules in their theory.

There are several directions for future work. $NL^{\Rightarrow}$ may be useful for developing an improved proof-theoretic semantics for nominal logic programming. Natural deduction calculi or type theories for nominal logic based on our approach could be used as the basis of proof checkers and interactive theorem provers for nominal logic. The existence of translations from $FO\lambda^{\nabla}$ to $NL^{\Rightarrow}$ suggest that $FO\lambda^{\nabla}$ can be interpreted using the semantics of nominal logic. Moreover, a semantic approach may lead to a simpler proof of the completeness of the translations.

5   Conclusions

This paper makes two contributions. First, we present a new sequent calculus for nominal logic which avoids the *slices* used in the rules for И in FL and FL_{Seq}. Instead, our calculus deals with И using *freshness contexts* that encode freshness information as well as typing information. Although this is partly a matter of taste, we believe that our approach is easier to use and analyze and provides a more transparent reading of И as a proof search operation than any previous system. In particular, the proofs of cut-elimination and conservativity relative to Pitts' axiomatization seem simpler and require fewer technical lemmas than previous attempts.

The second contribution of this paper is an improved translation from $FO\lambda^{\nabla}$ to intuitionistic nominal logic ($INL^{\Rightarrow}$), which explains the behavior of the ∇-quantifier in terms of И. We show that $FO\lambda^{\nabla}$ can be soundly and completely interpreted in $INL^{\Rightarrow}$, so any argument carried out in $FO\lambda^{\nabla}$ can also safely be carried out in $INL^{\Rightarrow}$. In addition, we argued that the translation originally proposed by Gabbay and Cheney is complete relative to $FO\lambda^{\nabla}$ with weakening and exchange for ∇.

Acknowledgments. Discussions with Ian Stark and Uli Schöpp and the anonymous reviewers' comments were of great value in improving this paper.

References

1. Luís Caires and Luca Cardelli. A spatial logic for concurrency–II. *Theoretical Computer Science*, 322(3):517–565, September 2004.

2. J. Cheney and C. Urban. Alpha-Prolog: A logic programming language with names, binding and alpha-equivalence. In *Proc. 20th Int. Conf. on Logic Programming (ICLP 2004)*, number 3132 in LNCS, pages 269–283, 2004.

3. James Cheney. A simpler proof theory for nominal logic. Technical Report EDI-INF-RR-0237, LFCS, University of Edinburgh, November 2004.

4. James Cheney. A sound and complete translation of generic judgments into nominal logic. Technical report, LFCS, University of Edinburgh, 2005. In preparation.

5. James R. Cheney. *Nominal Logic Programming*. PhD thesis, Cornell University, Ithaca, NY, August 2004.

6. M. J. Gabbay. Fresh logic: A logic of FM, 2003. Submitted.

7. M. J. Gabbay and J. Cheney. A proof theory for nominal logic. In *Proceedings of the 19th Annual IEEE Symposium on Logic in Computer Science (LICS 2004)*, pages 139–148, Turku, Finland, 2004.

8. M. J. Gabbay and A. M. Pitts. A new approach to abstract syntax with variable binding. *Formal Aspects of Computing*, 13:341–363, 2002.

9. Dale Miller and Alwen Tiu. A proof theory for generic judgments: extended abstract. In *Proc. 18th Symp. on Logic in Computer Science (LICS 2003)*, pages 118–127. IEEE Press, 2003.

10. Aleksandar Nanevski. Meta-programming with names and necessity. In *Proc. 8th ACM SIGPLAN Int. Conf. on Functional Programming*, pages 206–217. ACM Press, 2002.

11. Sara Negri and Jan von Plato. *Structural Proof Theory*. Cambridge University Press, 2001.

12. A. M. Pitts. Nominal logic, a first order theory of names and binding. *Information and Computation*, 183:165–193, 2003.

13. Ulrich Schöpp and Ian Stark. A dependent type theory with names and binding. In *Proceedings of the 2004 Computer Science Logic Conference*, number 3210 in Lecture notes in Computer Science, pages 235–249, Karpacz, Poland, 2004.

14. C. Urban, A. M. Pitts, and M. J. Gabbay. Nominal unification. *Theoretical Computer Science*, 323(1–3):473–497, 2004.

From Separation Logic to First-Order Logic

Cristiano Calcagno, Philippa Gardner, and Matthew Hague

Department of Computing
Imperial College
University of London

Abstract. Separation logic is a spatial logic for reasoning locally about heap structures. A decidable fragment of its assertion language was presented in [1], based on a bounded model property. We exploit this property to give an encoding of this fragment into a first-order logic containing only the propositional connectives, quantification over the natural numbers and equality. This result is the first translation from Separation Logic into a logic which does not depend on the heap, and provides a direct decision procedure based on well-studied algorithms for first-order logic. Moreover, our translation is compositional in the structure of formulae, whilst previous results involved enumerating either heaps or formulae arising from the bounded model property.

1 Introduction

Separation Logic [2] is a spatial logic for reasoning about mutable heap structures. It provides an elegant method for reasoning locally about separate areas of memory, and combining the results in a modular way. Its primary application is as the basis of a Hoare Logic for reasoning about memory update. An essential task is therefore to study decision procedures for validity checking, as part of a wider goal to develop verification tools for analysing C-programs.

The assertion language of Separation Logic is very expressive, due to the presence of two connectives: the separating conjunction $\phi_1 * \phi_2$ which asserts the existence of a split of the current heap into two disjoint sub-heaps that satisfy ϕ_1 and ϕ_2 respectively; and its adjunct implication $\phi_1 \mathbin{-\!\!*} \phi_2$ which asserts that, whenever a fresh heap that satisfies ϕ_1 is composed with the current heap, then the result satisfies ϕ_2. In particular, validity checking is internalizable, which means that finding decision procedures is difficult.

Validity checking for the full Separation logic is undecidable [1]. Calcagno *et al.* have therefore been studying decidable fragments of the logic [1, 3]. They have shown that the Propositional Separation Logic (no quantifiers) is decidable [1], based on a finite model property which bounds the number of heaps that need to be checked. This is a surprising result since there is an implicit existential quantification in $*$, and more significantly an implicit universal quantification over fresh heaps in $\mathbin{-\!\!*}$. However, their result does not provide a pragmatic decision procedure, since it relies on checking all the heaps of a certain size. In this paper we study a new approach. We provide a translation of Propositional Separation

V. Sassone (Ed.): FOSSACS 2005, LNCS 3441, pp. 395–409, 2005.

Logic into a decidable fragment of first-order logic, for which decision procedures have been widely studied. We avoid the inefficient enumeration of the heaps by using the universal quantification of first-order logic.

As well as the results in [1], we take inspiration from the work of Dal Zilio *et al.* [4] which provides a novel decision procedure for the Static Ambient Logic [5]. Calcagno *et al.* adapted the decidability result of Propositional Separation Logic [1] to show decidability for the Static Ambient Logic, which relied this time on a finite model property for trees. Dal Zilio spotted a more efficient decision procedure for the Ambient Logic, that used a combination of Presburger Arithmetic and automata which did not depend on tree enumeration.

We provide a translation from Propositional Separation Logic into first order logic with only the propositional connectives, quantification over the natural numbers and equality. Our results rely on the bounded model property of [1]. The main idea is that vectors of a fixed length are used to represent all the states up to a given size. This means that we can represent sets of bounded states directly as first-order formulae over a fixed number of variables. The crucial cases in our translation are the connectives $*$ and $-*$. Since the current heap is decomposed by $*$ and extended by $-*$, the vector representation must change across subformulae. We define vector operations that represent decomposition and composition of heaps, and show that they simulate $*$ and $-*$. These results are then used to give a simple proof of correctness of our translation.

The expressiveness of Separation Logic can thus be obtained in an ordinary classical logic that is independent of heap structures. This is interesting because the translation provides a more elegant decision procedure than the one in [1] (which was based on enumerating all the heaps in a finite set arising from the finite model property). Since our translation is polynomial in the length of formula, we will be able to take advantage of the maturity of existing tools for first-order logic to provide an efficient decision procedure for Propositional Separation Logic.

In [6, 7], Lozes shows a related result that the spatial connectives can be eliminated from Propositional Separation Logic. His result is obtained by using the finite model property to produce a formula that is a disjunction of (characteristic formulae of) all heaps that satisfy the given formula. Their result differs from ours in that their target logic is not independent of heap structures and the method for translating the logic requires a decision procedure for a fragment of Separation Logic. More importantly, our translation is compositional in the structure of the formulae, and is not based on an enumeration of the exponential number of satisfying heaps. An immediate consequence of our approach is that a prover can use an existing axiomatization of first-order logic to output a direct proof. A complete axiomatization for Propositional Separation Logic is still an open problem.

The structure of the paper is the following. We begin in section 2 by introducing Propositional Separation Logic and its bounded model properties. In section 3 we present our vector representation of bounded heaps and the translation into first-order logic. In section 4 we discuss the conclusions of our work and describe several avenues for further research.

2 Propositional Separation Logic

In this section we present Propositional Separation Logic. This fragment of Separation Logic has the property that formulae can be assigned a size, which bounds the size of the states that need to be considered to check validity.

We begin by defining the sets of stacks and heaps, for which we need some notation.

Definition 1 (Notation). *We use the following notation. A partial function $f : X \rightarrow_{fin} Y$ is a finite map f from X to Y. We write $f \# g$ to indicate that partial maps f and g have disjoint domains. The composition of two partial functions f and g with disjoint domains is defined as $(f * g)(x) = y$ iff $f(x) = y$ or $g(x) = y$. The empty map is denoted $[]$. We use the notation $|\_|$ to indicate the cardinality of sets (which will be overloaded to also represent the size of formulae in Definition 3).*

Values, stacks, heaps, and states are defined as follows:

$$
\begin{aligned}
v \in \quad & Val \triangleq Loc \cup \{0\} \\
s \in \quad & Stack \triangleq Var \rightarrow_{fin} Val \\
h \in \quad & Heap \triangleq Loc \rightarrow_{fin} Val \times Val \\
(s, h) \in \quad & State \triangleq Stack \times Heap
\end{aligned}
$$

where locations *Loc* are the natural numbers greater than zero. The value 0 represents the null location. A heap maps locations to binary heap cells and its domain indicates which locations are currently allocated. A stack is a partial function mapping program variables to values.

The syntax of Propositional Separation Logic is defined as follows

$E ::=$		Expressions
	x, y	Variables
	0	Nil
$\phi, \psi ::=$		Formulae
	$E = E$	Equality
	false	Falsity
	$\phi \Rightarrow \psi$	Implication
	$E \mapsto E_1, E_2$	Binary heap cell
	emp	Empty heap
	$\psi * \psi$	Composition
	$\psi \twoheadrightarrow \psi$	Composition adjunct

The binary cell formula $E \mapsto E_1, E_2$ asserts that the location denoted by the expression E is the only allocated cell, and that it contains (E_1, E_2). The formula emp asserts that the heap is empty, i.e. no location is allocated. Composition $\phi * \psi$ means that the current heap can be split into two disjoint sub-heaps satisfying ϕ and ψ respectively. Its adjunct $\phi \twoheadrightarrow \psi$ asserts that all heaps disjoint from the current heap and satisfying ϕ, when composed with the current heap satisfy ψ. The semantics is given by the satisfaction relation between formulae and states

Table 1. Semantics of formulae given a stack s and a heap h

$$J x K_s \triangleq s(x)$$
$$J 0 K_s \triangleq 0$$

$(s, h) \models E_1 = E_2$	iff $J E_1 K_s = J E_2 K_s$
$(s, h) \models$ false	never
$(s, h) \models \phi_1 \Rightarrow \phi_2$	iff $s, h \models \phi_1$ then $s, h \models \phi_2$
$(s, h) \models (E \mapsto E_1, E_2)$	iff $dom(h) = \{J E K_s\}$ and $h(J E K_s) = (J E_1 K_s, J E_2 K_s)$
$(s, h) \models$ emp	iff $dom(h) = \emptyset$
$(s, h) \models \phi_1 * \phi_2$	iff there exists h_1 and h_2 such that
	$h_1 \# h_2$; $h_1 * h_2 = h$; $s, h_1 \models \phi_1$ and $s, h_2 \models \phi_2$
$(s, h) \models \phi_1 \mathbin{-\!*} \phi_2$	iff for all h_1 such that $h \# h_1$
	and $(s, h_1 \models \phi_1)$, $(s, h * h_1) \models \phi_2$

defined in Table 1. Standard logical connectives are defined as derived operators, such as $\neg \phi \triangleq (\phi \Rightarrow \text{false})$.

Definition 2 (Validity). *A formula ϕ is valid iff $(s, h) \models \phi$ holds for all states (s, h).*

Given a fixed stack, we can use $-\!*$ to reduce satisfaction for all heaps to satisfaction for the empty heap.

Lemma 1. *Given a stack s and a formula ϕ,*

$$(\forall h. (s, h) \models \phi) \iff ((s, []) \models (\neg \phi) \mathbin{-\!*} \text{false})$$

Proof. Since $h * [] = h$, the assertion $(s, []) \models (\neg \phi) \mathbin{-\!*}$ false states that any heap that satisfies $\neg \phi$ must also satisfy false. That is, no heap satisfies $\neg \phi$ and so ϕ holds for all heaps.

We now introduce the notion of size of formulae, as in [1].

Definition 3 (Size of Formulae). *Given a formula ϕ, its size $|\phi|$ is defined by*

$$|E_1 = E_2| = 0 \qquad\qquad |\text{false}| = 0$$
$$|\phi \Rightarrow \psi| = max(|\phi|, |\psi|) \qquad |(E \mapsto E_1, E_2)| = 1$$
$$|\text{emp}| = 1 \qquad\qquad |\phi * \psi| = |\phi| + |\psi|$$
$$|\phi \mathbin{-\!*} \psi| = |\psi|$$

The size of a formula is used to determine a bound to the size of the heaps that need to be considered when checking validity, and to bound the size of new heaps needed to check satisfaction for formulae of the form $P \mathbin{-\!*} Q$. Technically, one can define an equivalence relation $\sim_n$ on states, parameterized on the size parameter n. The main property is that formulae of size n cannot distinguish between $\sim_n$-related states. For example, the size of $(x \mapsto y, z)$ is one because, in order to satisfy it or its negation, it is enough to consider heaps with at most one allocated location. The size of $\phi * \psi$ is the sum since $*$ combines subheaps together. The size of $\phi \twoheadrightarrow \psi$ is $|\psi|$ because $\sim_n$ is a congruence, and adding identical heaps in parallel (the ϕ part) does not affect the distinguishing power of formulae.

Because the semantics of $\twoheadrightarrow$ quantifies over all heaps, algorithmically determining if $(s, h) \models \phi$ for any formula ϕ is not straightforward. The following Proposition, which is an adaptation of an analogous one in [1], shows how to bound the size of new heaps that need to be considered.

Proposition 1. *For a given a state (s, h) and formulae ϕ_1 and ϕ_2, $(s, h) \models$ $\phi_1 \twoheadrightarrow \phi_2$ holds iff for all h_1 such that,*

- $h \# h_1$ *and* $(s, h_1) \models \phi_1$, *and*
- $|dom(h_1)| \leq max(|\phi_1|, |\phi_2|) + |FV(\phi_1) \cup FV(\phi_2)|$

we have that $(s, h * h_1) \models \phi_2$.

Proof. The proposition is a corollary of Proposition 1 given on page 7 of [1].

The above Proposition requires $max(|\phi_1|, |\phi_2|)$ since the observations that $\phi_1 \twoheadrightarrow \phi_2$ can make on the *current* heap depend on both ϕ_1 and ϕ_2. It is worth noting that the set of heaps satisfying the properties in Proposition 1 is infinite (the size of heaps is bounded but the values contained are arbitrary), whereas the similar proposition in [1] explicitly defines a finite set of heaps. A finite set of heaps was necessary in [1] to give a direct decision procedure enumerating those heaps. However, our translation to first-order logic only depends on the *size* of heaps, so we chose a more abstract property.

To conclude the section we define bounded states, and give a bounding property for validity of formulae, which will be used in the translation presented in the next section. Bounded stacks and heaps are defined as follows.

Definition 4 ($S^{\mathbf{X}}$). *We write $S^{\mathbf{X}}$ to denote the set of stacks such that $s \in S^{\mathbf{X}}$ iff $dom(s) = \mathbf{X}$, where $\mathbf{X} \subseteq Var$.*

Definition 5 (H_p). *Given a size $p \in \mathbb{N}$, we write H_p to denote the set of heaps such that $h \in H_p$ iff $|dom(h)| \leq p$.*

Proposition 2. *Given a formula ϕ,*

$$\left(\forall(s, h). \ (s, h) \models \phi\right) \iff \left(\forall(s, h) \in S^{\mathbf{X}} \times H_p. \ (s, h) \models \phi\right)$$

where $\mathbf{X} = FV(\phi)$ and $p = |\phi| + |FV(\phi)|$.

Proof. The proposition follows immediately from Lemma 2 and Lemma 3 below.

Lemma 2. *Given a stack s and a formula ϕ,*

$$(\forall h.\ (s, h) \models \phi) \iff \left(\forall h \in H_{|\phi| + |FV(\phi)|}.\ (s, h) \models \phi\right)$$

Proof. By Lemma 1 we know that,

$$(\forall h.\ (s, h) \models \phi) \iff ((s, []) \models (\neg \phi) \twoheadrightarrow \text{false})$$

By proposition 1, it follows that $(s, []) \models (\neg \phi) \twoheadrightarrow \text{false}$ iff for all h_1 such that,

- $[] \# h_1$ and $(s, h_1) \models \neg \phi$, and
- $|dom(h_1)| \leq max(|\neg \phi|, |\text{false}|) + |FV(\neg \phi) \cup FV(\text{false})|$

we have that $(s, [] * h_1) \models \text{false}$. Which is equivalent to,

$$\forall h_1 \in H_{|\phi| + |FV(\phi)|}.\ (s, h) \models \phi$$

since $[] \# h_1$, $h_1 = [] * h_1$ and $max(|\neg \phi|, |\text{false}|) + |FV(\neg \phi) \cup FV(\text{false})| = |\phi| + |FV(\phi)|$. Therefore,

$$(\forall h.\ (s, h) \models \phi) \iff \left(\forall h \in H_{|\phi| + |FV(\phi)|}.\ (s, h) \models \phi\right)$$

as required.

Lemma 3. *Given a formula ϕ,*

$$(\forall (s, h).\ (s, h) \models \phi) \iff \left(\forall s \in S^{FV(\phi)}.\ \forall h.\ (s, h) \models \phi\right)$$

Proof. This is immediate from the semantics of Separation Logic since the values of variables that are not in $FV(\phi)$ do not affect the truth of ϕ.

3   Translating Separation Logic to First-Order Logic

In this section we present a translation from Separation Logic to first-order logic.

3.1   Representing States as Vectors

We represent bounded stacks in $S^{\mathbf{X}}$ and heaps in H_p as vectors of fixed length. This will allow us to replace quantification over bounded states by ordinary first-order quantification using a fixed number of variables.

Given a stack $s \in S^{\mathbf{X}}$, with $\{x_1, \ldots, x_n\} = \mathbf{X}$, we assume a fixed ordering on variables and define its representation $vs(s)$ simply as the vector $(s(x_1), \ldots, s(x_n))$. Heaps in H_p are represented as vectors $\mathbf{b}$ of p triples of values. The i-th triple $(\mathbf{b}_{i,1}, \mathbf{b}_{i,2}, \mathbf{b}_{i,3})$ potentially represents a heap cell. If $\mathbf{b}_{i,1}$ is a location (not 0), then the cell is allocated and contains the pair of values $(\mathbf{b}_{i,2}, \mathbf{b}_{i,3})$. If $\mathbf{b}_{i,1} = 0$ then the i-th triple does not represent a heap cell. For example, H_2

contains the singleton heap $(1 \mapsto 2, 3)$, which can be represented by the vector $((1, 2, 3), (0, 6, 7))$ or $((0, 8, 9), (1, 2, 3))$. The values $6, 7, 8, 9$ are unimportant since they do not belong to an active cell.

Note that all heaps in H_p have several vector representations, because the order of the heap cells, and the values of cells whose location is 0, are irrelevant. Also, not all vectors represent a valid heap, since the same location could occur more than once in the vector. We formalize the representation relation as a partial function vh_p from vectors to bounded heaps, defined in Table 2. A particular vector $\mathbf{b}$ is in the domain of vh_p iff it represents a well-formed heap.

Table 2. Definition of $vh_p(\mathbf{b})$

$vh_p : (\mathbb{N} \times \mathbb{N} \times \mathbb{N})^p \rightarrow H_p$

$$vh_p(\mathbf{b}) = \begin{cases} Undef & \text{if } \exists i, j \in 1..p. \ i \neq j \wedge \mathbf{b}_{i,1} = \mathbf{b}_{j,1} \wedge \mathbf{b}_{i,1} \neq 0 \wedge \mathbf{b}_{j,1} \neq 0 \\ \{(\mathbf{b}_{i,1} \mapsto \mathbf{b}_{i,2}, \mathbf{b}_{i,3}) | \mathbf{b}_{i,1} \neq 0 \wedge i \in 1..p\} & \text{otherwise} \end{cases}$$

Lemma 4. *For all p, vh_p is surjective:*

$$\forall h \in H_p \exists \mathbf{b}. \ vh_p(\mathbf{b}) = h$$

3.2 Representing Heaps in First-Order Logic

In this section we show how to use first-order formulae to represent heaps, and operations on heap representations corresponding to $*$ and $-\!*$.

We have seen that heaps are represented as vectors of triples of values. We now show how to represent assertions about heaps as first-order formulae from the following grammar

$$A ::= E = E \mid \text{false} \mid A \Rightarrow A \mid \forall x.A$$

with free variables drawn from a vector $\mathbf{B}$ of triples of variables. We write $\forall \mathbf{B}'. \ A$ as an abbreviation for $\forall \mathbf{B}'_{1,1} \forall \mathbf{B}'_{1,2} \cdots \forall \mathbf{B}'_{p,3}. \ A$ when $\mathbf{B}'$ is a vector of p triples of variables, and similarly for $\exists \mathbf{B}'. \ A$. We use the standard notation $\bigwedge_{i \in 1..n} \cdot A$ for $A[1/i] \wedge \cdots \wedge A[n/i]$, and similarly for $\bigvee_{i \in 1..n} \cdot A$. Given a vector of values $\mathbf{b}$ and a formula A with free variables from a vector $\mathbf{B}$, we write $[\mathbf{B} \ Z\!\Rightarrow \mathbf{b}] \models A$ for the usual satisfaction relation of first-order logic, where $[\mathbf{B} \ Z\!\Rightarrow \mathbf{b}]$ is the assignment of values to the variables.

We begin by defining the derived first-order formula $heap(\mathbf{B})$ that imposes restrictions on the values of the variables in $\mathbf{B}$ to ensure that they represent a valid heap.

Definition 6. *Given a vector of variables* $\mathbf{B}$,

$$heap(\mathbf{B}) \triangleq \left(\bigwedge_{\substack{i\in 1..|\mathbf{B}| \\ j\in 1..|\mathbf{B}| \\ i\neq j}} (\mathbf{B}_{i,1} = 0 \vee \mathbf{B}_{j,1} = 0 \vee \mathbf{B}_{i,1} \neq \mathbf{B}_{j,1}) \right)$$

The following lemma states that $heap(\mathbf{B})$ holds for a vector of values $\mathbf{b}$ exactly when $\mathbf{b}$ represents a heap, that is $\mathbf{b}$ will be in the domain of $vh_{|\mathbf{b}|}$.

Lemma 5. *Given vectors* $\mathbf{B}$, $\mathbf{b}$ *such that* $|\mathbf{B}| = |\mathbf{b}|$,

$$\mathbf{b} \in dom(vh_{|\mathbf{B}|}) \iff [\mathbf{B} \, Z\Rightarrow \mathbf{b}] \models heap(\mathbf{B})$$

Proof. Immediate from the definitions of $heap(\mathbf{B})$ and $vh_{|\mathbf{B}|}$.

We present two operators on vectors for constructing and deconstructing representations of heaps. These distinct operators are required because the spatial connectives $*$ and $-\!\!*$ manipulate the heap in different ways. First consider the composition connective $*$, which splits the current heap into two disjoint subheaps whose size and contents are limited by the original heap. We use the formula $\mathbf{B} = \mathbf{B}' \circledast \mathbf{B}''$, defined below, to capture this property where the vector of variables $\mathbf{B}$ represents the current heap, and the variables $\mathbf{B}', \mathbf{B}''$ represent the two subheaps. Because we do not know exactly how the heap will be split, the size of vectors $\mathbf{B}'$ and $\mathbf{B}''$ must each equal the size of $\mathbf{B}$, as in the worst case splitting the current heap will result in the current heap on one side and the empty heap on the other.

Definition 7 (Decomposition). *For vectors of variables* $\mathbf{B}, \mathbf{B}', \mathbf{B}''$ *such that* $|\mathbf{B}| = |\mathbf{B}'| = |\mathbf{B}''|$, *define*

$$\mathbf{B} = \mathbf{B}' \circledast \mathbf{B}'' \triangleq \bigwedge_{i\in 1..|\mathbf{B}|} \left(\begin{array}{c} \left(\begin{array}{c} \mathbf{B}'_{i,1} = \mathbf{B}_{i,1} \wedge \mathbf{B}''_{i,1} = 0 \\ \wedge \mathbf{B}'_{i,2} = \mathbf{B}_{i,2} \wedge \mathbf{B}'_{i,3} = \mathbf{B}_{i,3} \end{array} \right) \\ \vee \left(\begin{array}{c} \mathbf{B}'_{i,1} = 0 \wedge \mathbf{B}''_{i,1} = \mathbf{B}_{i,1} \\ \wedge \mathbf{B}''_{i,2} = \mathbf{B}_{i,2} \wedge \mathbf{B}''_{i,3} = \mathbf{B}_{i,3} \end{array} \right) \end{array} \right)$$

The extension to vectors of values is as follows

$$\mathbf{b} = \mathbf{b}' \circledast \mathbf{b}'' \quad iff \quad [\mathbf{B} \, Z\Rightarrow \mathbf{b}, \mathbf{B}' \, Z\Rightarrow \mathbf{b}', \mathbf{B}'' \, Z\Rightarrow \mathbf{b}''] \models \mathbf{B} = \mathbf{B}' \circledast \mathbf{B}''$$

The following lemma shows that if $heap(\mathbf{B})$ holds then so does its decomposition.

Lemma 6. *For all vectors* $\mathbf{B}$, $\mathbf{B}'$, $\mathbf{B}''$, *the following is valid*

$$(\mathbf{B} = \mathbf{B}' \circledast \mathbf{B}'' \wedge heap(\mathbf{B})) \Rightarrow (heap(\mathbf{B}') \wedge heap(\mathbf{B}''))$$

Lemma 7 and Lemma 8 show that a splitting of heaps can be simulated by a corresponding splitting of representations, and vice versa.

Lemma 7. *For all* p, $\mathbf{b}$ *and* $h, h_1, h_2 \in H_p$,

$$h = h_1 * h_2 \wedge vh_p(\mathbf{b}) = h \Rightarrow \exists \mathbf{b}', \mathbf{b}''. \left(\begin{array}{c} \mathbf{b} = \mathbf{b}' \circledast \mathbf{b}'' \wedge \\ vh_p(\mathbf{b}') = h_1 \wedge vh_p(\mathbf{b}'') = h_2 \end{array} \right)$$

Lemma 8. *For all p, $\mathbf{b}$, $\mathbf{b}'$, $\mathbf{b}''$ and $h \in H_p$,*

$$\mathbf{b} = \mathbf{b}' \circledast \mathbf{b}'' \wedge vh_p(\mathbf{b}) = h \Rightarrow h = vh_p(\mathbf{b}_1) * vh_p(\mathbf{b}'')$$

The composition adjunct $\twoheadrightarrow$ requires the addition of fresh heap cells to the current heap. The heap formed by the addition of these new cells may exceed the size that can be expressed by the current set of variables, which means that new variables need to be used to represent the new cells. We introduce the derived 'append' connective $\bullet$ to capture the addition of new heap cells.

Definition 8 ($\mathbf{B}' \bullet \mathbf{B}''$). *Given vectors $\mathbf{B}'$ and $\mathbf{B}''$ we define $\mathbf{B}' \bullet \mathbf{B}''$ as vector concatenation: $|\mathbf{B}' \bullet \mathbf{B}''| = |\mathbf{B}'| + |\mathbf{B}''|$ and for all $i \in 1..|\mathbf{B}' \bullet \mathbf{B}''|$,*

$$(\mathbf{B}' \bullet \mathbf{B}'')_i = \begin{cases} \mathbf{B}'_i & \text{if } i \in 1..|\mathbf{B}'| \\ \mathbf{B}''_i & \text{if } i \in (|\mathbf{B}'| + 1)..|\mathbf{B}' \bullet \mathbf{B}''| \end{cases}$$

The following lemma shows that if the result of appending two vectors represents a valid heap, then each vector represents a valid heap.

Lemma 9. *For all vectors $\mathbf{B}$, $\mathbf{B}'$, $\mathbf{B}''$ such that $\mathbf{B} = \mathbf{B}' \bullet \mathbf{B}''$, the following is valid*

$$heap(\mathbf{B}) \Rightarrow heap(\mathbf{B}') \wedge heap(\mathbf{B}'')$$

The following lemma captures the relationship between the composition of heaps and the appending of vectors.

Lemma 10. *For all, p_1, p_2, $\mathbf{b}'$, $\mathbf{b}''$ and $h \in H_{p_1+p_2}$ such that $|\mathbf{b}'| = p_1$ and $|\mathbf{b}''| = p_2$,*

$$vh_{p_1+p_2}(\mathbf{b}' \bullet \mathbf{b}'') = h \iff h = vh_{p_1}(\mathbf{b}') * vh_{p_2}(\mathbf{b}'')$$

3.3 The Translation

We now have all the ingredients necessary to present the translation, which is defined in Table 3.

The translation $tran(\phi, \mathbf{B})$ produces a first-order formula with free variables in $\phi, \mathbf{B}$. For simplicity of notation we assume that the variables in ϕ and $\mathbf{B}$ are always disjoint (formally, we could use two syntactic categories). The translation begins with an implication, which effectively ignores all variable assignments that do not represent a heap. The bulk of the translation lies in $tran'(\phi, \mathbf{B})$.

The translations of $(E_1 = E_2)$, false, $(\phi_1 \Rightarrow \phi_2)$ and emp are fairly straightforward, but the translations of $(E \mapsto E_1, E_2)$, $(\phi_1 * \phi_2)$ and $(\phi_1 \twoheadrightarrow \phi_2)$ may benefit from an explanation.

The translation of the cell formula $E \mapsto E_1, E_2$ states that only one of the location variables $\mathbf{B}_{i,1}$ has a value that is non-zero — that is, the heap represented by the values of the variables has one cell only. Also, the values of the variables $(\mathbf{B}_{i,1}, \mathbf{B}_{i,2}, \mathbf{B}_{i,3})$ match the values of the expressions E, E_1 and E_2.

The Composition case $tran(\phi_1 * \phi_2, \mathbf{B})$ requires that we can split the current heap (the values of the variables in $\mathbf{B}$) into two parts, using $\mathbf{B} = \mathbf{B}' \circledast \mathbf{B}''$, such that the parts satisfy ϕ_1 and ϕ_2 respectively.

Table 3. Definition of $tran(\phi, \mathbf{B})$

$$tran(\phi, \mathbf{B}) \triangleq heap(\mathbf{B}) \Rightarrow tran'(\phi, \mathbf{B})$$

$$tran'(E_1 = E_2, \mathbf{B}) \triangleq E_1 = E_2$$
$$tran'(\text{false}, \mathbf{B}) \triangleq \text{false}$$
$$tran'(\phi_1 \Rightarrow \phi_2, \mathbf{B}) \triangleq tran'(\phi_1, \mathbf{B}) \Rightarrow tran'(\phi_2, \mathbf{B})$$
$$tran'(E \mapsto E_1, E_2, \mathbf{B}) \triangleq \bigvee_{i \in 1..|\mathbf{B}|} \left(\begin{array}{l} \mathbf{B}_{i,1} \neq 0 \wedge \bigwedge_{\substack{j \in 1..|\mathbf{B}| \\ i \neq j}} \left[\mathbf{B}_{j,1} = 0 \right] \\ \wedge \ \mathbf{B}_{i,1} = E \\ \wedge \ \mathbf{B}_{i,2} = E_1 \wedge \mathbf{B}_{i,3} = E_2 \end{array} \right)$$
$$tran'(\text{emp}, \mathbf{B}) \triangleq \bigwedge_{i \in 1..|\mathbf{B}|} \mathbf{B}_{i,1} = 0$$

$$tran'(\phi_1 * \phi_2, \mathbf{B}) \triangleq \exists \mathbf{B}', \mathbf{B}''. \left(\begin{array}{l} \mathbf{B} = \mathbf{B}' \circledast \mathbf{B}'' \\ \wedge \ tran'(\phi_1, \mathbf{B}') \\ \wedge \ tran'(\phi_2, \mathbf{B}'') \end{array} \right)$$

$$tran'(\phi_1 \mathbin{-\!\!*} \phi_2, \mathbf{B}) \triangleq \forall \mathbf{B}'. \left(\begin{array}{l} tran'(\phi_1, \mathbf{B}') \\ \wedge \ heap(\mathbf{B} \bullet \mathbf{B}') \\ \quad \Rightarrow tran'(\phi_2, \mathbf{B} \bullet \mathbf{B}') \end{array} \right)$$
$$\text{where}$$
$$|\mathbf{B}'| = max(|\phi_1|, |\phi_2|) + |FV(\phi_1) \cup FV(\phi_2)|$$

Finally, the translation of $\phi_1 \mathbin{-\!\!*} \phi_2$ quantifies over all heaps that satisfy ϕ_1 by universally quantifying over a new collection of heap variables — enough to represent all heaps up to the size required by Proposition 2. The formula $heap(\mathbf{B}' \bullet \mathbf{B})$ ensures that the combination of the old and new vectors still represent a heap, which implies that the new heap is disjoint from the current heap. The translation asserts that if the new heap satisfies ϕ_1 and it can be composed with the current heap, then the composition of both heaps satisfies ϕ_2, as required by the semantics of $\mathbin{-\!\!*}$.

We now prove the correctness of the translation.

The free variables of the translated formula are the original stack variables plus the variables used to represent the current heap.

Lemma 11. *For any ϕ, $\mathbf{B}$,*

$$FV(tran(\phi, \mathbf{B})) = FV(\phi) \cup FV(\mathbf{B})$$

We show that, on related states, satisfaction is preserved by the translation.

Theorem 1. *For any ϕ, p, $\mathbf{B}$, $\mathbf{X}$, $\mathbf{b}$ where $|\mathbf{B}| = p$, $FV(\phi) \subseteq \mathbf{X}$, $(s, h) \in S^{\mathbf{X}} \times H_p$ and $vh_p(\mathbf{b}) = h$,*

$$(s, h \models \phi) \iff [\mathbf{B} \mathrel{Z\!\!\Rightarrow} \mathbf{b}, \mathbf{X} \mathrel{Z\!\!\Rightarrow} vs(s)] \models tran'(\phi, \mathbf{B})$$

A consequence of the theorem above is that the formula resulting from the translation cannot distinguish between two vectors representing the same heap.

Finally, we show that a formula is valid iff its translation is valid.

Theorem 2. *For any ϕ, $\mathbf{B}$, $\mathbf{X}$ such that $|\mathbf{B}| = |\phi| + |FV(\phi)|$ and $FV(\phi) \subseteq \mathbf{X}$,*

$$(\forall (s,h).\ (s,h) \models \phi) \iff \forall (\mathbf{b}, \mathbf{v})\ [\mathbf{B}\ \mathsf{Z}\!\!\Rightarrow \mathbf{b}, \mathbf{X}\ \mathsf{Z}\!\!\Rightarrow \mathbf{v}] \models tran(\phi, \mathbf{B})$$

3.4   Decision Procedure and Complexity

Our decision procedure for Propositional Separation Logic simply consists of applying the translation followed by one of the existing decision procedures for first-order logic. The validity problem for first-order logic (on an empty signature) is a classical PSPACE-complete problem. In [1] it was proved that validity of Propositional Separation Logic is also PSPACE-complete.

Our translation into first-order logic generates a formula whose length is $\mathbf{O}(n^5)$ where n denotes the length[1] of the Separation Logic formula. This can be seen because, for each connective, the length of the vector (initially $\mathbf{O}(n)$) may increase by $\mathbf{O}(n)$ in the worst case (the $-\!\!*$ connective). Therefore, the length of the vector is always $\mathbf{O}(n^2)$. The translation of $E \mapsto E_1, E_2$ and $heap(\mathbf{B})$ are $\mathbf{O}(v^2)$, where v is the length of the vector. So, these formulae are $\mathbf{O}(n^4)$. In the worst case $\mathbf{O}(n)$ of these cases will occur, and therefore, the result of the translation will be $\mathbf{O}(n^5)$ in length.

This shows that the translation produces a limited increase in the length of formulae, therefore our decision procedure runs in polynomial space and has optimal theoretical complexity.

4   Conclusions and Future Work

In this paper we provided a translation from Propositional Separation Logic into first-order logic with only the propositional connectives, equality and quantification over the natural numbers. The translation has two main properties: a state satisfies a formula iff the state's vector encoding satisfies the translation, and a formula is valid iff its translation is valid. This translation shows that Separation Logic can be expressed in a classical logic that has no notion of a heap or spatial connectives. It also provides a new decision procedure that can utilise existing tools for first-order logic.

A natural direction for future work is implementing and evaluating the new decision procedure. In [8], we implemented the decision procedure for Tree Logic which inspired the work presented here. Using several optimisations, we found that the decision procedure was viable. We hope that, utilising possible optimisations, an implementation of this work may show similar results.

---

[1] We use 'length' with the usual meaning: the number of connectives in the formula, not the size of Definition 3.

For example, we may reduce the number of existentially quantified variables when translating $\phi_1 * \phi_2$ by only quantifying one set of variables ($\mathbf{B}'$) and calculating the second ($\mathbf{B}''$) in situ through the use of expressions rather than variables.

We may also wish to consider different fragments of Separation Logic or extensions of the fragment studied in this paper. For example, if we change the target logic of the translation to Presburger Arithmetic, we gain addition of natural numbers. This would allow us to augment the quantifier-free fragment of Separation Logic with arithmetic on stack variables. However, allowing arithmetic on the heap may invalidate the size argument on which Proposition 1 and Proposition 2 are based. Another extension is allowing quantification of variables ($\exists x. \ \phi$). The presence of full existential quantifiers also invalidates the size argument of Proposition 1 and Proposition 2. However, it is likely that restricted (e.g. guarded) forms of quantification admit a size argument. In those cases, the translation can be extended by mapping existentials to existentials, since the proofs extend trivially. We may also attempt to extend our results to the more practically motivated fragment of Separation Logic in [3], which was designed for reasoning about linked lists. That fragment presents a different technical challenge to the one presented here: there is no $-\!*$ but there is an inductive definition for linked lists. We expect our techniques to prove useful also in that setting.

A new related area of research into Spatial Logics [5, 9, 10, 11] is 'trees with pointers', which add location identifiers and cross-references to Tree Logic [12]. A practical example of this model is XML cross-references. This model combines Tree Logic and Separation Logic because the tree structures have locations on nodes, and pointers as data. Preliminary work on decision procedures for this model has identified several subtleties. First, a notion of size must be identified. A likely candidate is the maximum number of locations required at any level of the tree and the maximum depth of the tree. Secondly, a succinct method for ensuring that all locations are unique is required. At a single level of the tree this task is exactly the same as for Separation Logic. However, as the decision procedure divides the tree into independent sub-trees, enforcing the uniqueness of locations becomes a more difficult task.

Finally, we would like to study decidability properties of Context Logic [13]. This new logic uses contexts or 'trees with holes' to allow reasoning about smaller sub-trees within larger arbitrary trees. Context logic has been used to provide a Hoare logic for reasoning about tree updates, where the portion of tree left untouched by the update has the shape of a tree context. A decision procedure for this logic presents a further challenge to the 'trees with pointers' model because it would require a different notion of size.

Acknowledgments. We would like to thank the anonymous referees for their comments. This work was partially supported by EPSRC.

References

1. Calcagno, C., Yang, H., O'Hearn, P.: Computability and complexity results for a spatial assertion language for data structures. In: Foundations of Software Technology and Theoretical Computer Science (FSTTCS'01), Springer (2001) 108–119 volume 2245 of Lecture Notes in Computer Science.
2. Reynolds, J.C.: Separation logic: a logic for shared mutable data structures. In: LICS, IEEE (2002) 55–74
3. Berdine, J., Calcagno, C., O'Hearn, P.: A decidable fragment of separation logic. In: Foundations of Software Technology and Theoretical Computer Science (FSTTCS'04), Springer (2004) to appear.
4. Zilio, S.D., Lugiez, D., Meyssonnier, C.: A logic you can count on. In: Proceedings of the 31st ACM SIGPLAN-SIGACT symposium on Principles of programming languages, ACM Press (2004) 135–146
5. Cardelli, L., Gordon, A.D.: Anytime, anywhere: Modal logics for mobile ambients. In: 27th Symposium on Principles of Programming Languages (POPL'00), ACM (2000) 365–377
6. Lozes, E.: Separation logic preserves the expressive power of classical logic. As published at: http://www.diku.dk/topps/space2004/space_final/etienne.pdf (2004)
7. Lozes, E.: Elimination of spatial connectives in static spatial logics. To Appear in TCS (2004)
8. Hague, M.: Static checkers for tree structures and heaps. Master's thesis, Imperial College London, Department of Computing (2004) http://www.doc.ic.ac.uk/~ajf/Teaching/Projects/Distinguished04/MatthewHague.pdf.
9. Cardelli, L., Caires, L.: A spatial logic for concurrency (part I). Journal of Information and Computation **186(2)** (2003)
10. Cardelli, L., Caires, L.: A spatial logic for concurrency (part II). To Appear in Theoretical Computer Science (2004)
11. Cardelli, L., Gardner, P., Ghelli, G.: A spatial logic for querying graphs. Proceedings of ICALP'02 (2002)
12. Cardelli, L., Gardner, P., Ghelli., G.: Querying trees with pointers. Unpublished Notes, 2003; talk at APPSEM 2001 (2003)
13. Calcagno, C., Gardner, P., Zarfaty, U.: Context logic and tree update. To appear in POPL (2005)

A   Appendix: Selected Proofs

A.1   Proof of Theorem 1 from Section 3.3

Theorem 1 states that for any ϕ, p, $\mathbf{B}$, $\mathbf{X}$, $\mathbf{b}$ where $|\mathbf{B}| = p$, $FV(\phi) \subseteq \mathbf{X}$, $(s,h) \in S^{\mathbf{X}} \times H_p$ and $vh_p(\mathbf{b}) = h$,

$$(s, h \models \phi) \iff [\mathbf{B}\, Z\!\!\Rightarrow \mathbf{b}, \mathbf{X}\, Z\!\!\Rightarrow vs(s)] \models tran'(\phi, \mathbf{B})$$

Proof. The proof is by induction over ϕ. We only consider some interesting cases.

Case $\phi = (\phi_1 * \phi_2)$.

$\Rightarrow$: Assume $(s, h) \models \phi_1 * \phi_2$. Therefore $h = h_1 * h_2$ and $(s, h_1) \models \phi_1$ and $(s, h_2) \models \phi_2$. Therefore, by Lemma 7 there exist $\mathbf{b^1}, \mathbf{b^2}$ such that,

$$\mathbf{b} = \mathbf{b^1} \circledast \mathbf{b^2} \wedge vh_p(\mathbf{b^1}) = h_1 \wedge vh_p(\mathbf{b^2}) = h_2$$

By induction and since $vh_p(\mathbf{b^1}) = h_1$ and $vh_p(\mathbf{b^2}) = h_2$,

$$\left[\mathbf{B} \; Z\Rightarrow \mathbf{b^1}, \mathbf{X} \; Z\Rightarrow vs(s)\right] \models tran'(\phi_1, \mathbf{B})$$

and

$$\left[\mathbf{B} \; Z\Rightarrow \mathbf{b^2}, \mathbf{X} \; Z\Rightarrow vs(s)\right] \models tran'(\phi_2, \mathbf{B})$$

Therefore,

$$\left[\mathbf{B} \; Z\Rightarrow \mathbf{b}, \mathbf{X} \; Z\Rightarrow vs(s)\right] \models \exists \mathbf{B^1}, \mathbf{B^2}. \begin{pmatrix} \mathbf{B} = \mathbf{B^1} \circledast \mathbf{B^2} \\ \wedge \; tran'(\phi_1, \mathbf{B^1}) \\ \wedge \; tran'(\phi_2, \mathbf{B^2}) \end{pmatrix}$$

And so,

$$\left[\mathbf{B} \; Z\Rightarrow \mathbf{b}, \mathbf{X} \; Z\Rightarrow vs(s)\right] \models tran'(\phi, \mathbf{B})$$

$\Leftarrow$: Assume,

$$\left[\mathbf{B} \; Z\Rightarrow \mathbf{b}, \mathbf{X} \; Z\Rightarrow vs(s)\right] \models \exists \mathbf{B^1}, \mathbf{B^2}. \begin{pmatrix} \mathbf{B} = \mathbf{B^1} \circledast \mathbf{B^2} \\ \wedge \; tran'(\phi_1, \mathbf{B^1}) \\ \wedge \; tran'(\phi_2, \mathbf{B^2}) \end{pmatrix}$$

Therefore, there exists $\mathbf{b_1}, \mathbf{b_2}$ such that $\mathbf{b} = \mathbf{b_1} \circledast \mathbf{b_2}$,

$$\left[\mathbf{B} \; Z\Rightarrow \mathbf{b_1}, \mathbf{X} \; Z\Rightarrow vs(s)\right] \models tran'(\phi_1, \mathbf{B})$$

and

$$\left[\mathbf{B} \; Z\Rightarrow \mathbf{b_2}, \mathbf{X} \; Z\Rightarrow vs(s)\right] \models tran'(\phi_2, \mathbf{B})$$

By Lemma 8, letting $h_1 = vh_p(\mathbf{b_1})$ and $h_2 = vh_p(\mathbf{b_2})$, we know $h = h_1 * h_2$ and by induction $(s, h_1) \models \phi_1$ and $(s, h_2) \models \phi_2$. Therefore $(s, h) \models (\phi_1 * \phi_2)$, that is, $(s, h) \models \phi$.

Case $\phi = (\phi_1 \mathbin{-\!\!*} \phi_2)$.

$\Rightarrow$: Assume $(s, h) \models (\phi_1 \mathbin{-\!\!*} \phi_2)$. Therefore, for all h_1 such that $(s, h_1) \models \phi_1$ and $h \# h_1$, $(s, h * h_1) \models \phi_2$.

We now assume $\mathbf{b'}$ such that,

$$\left[\mathbf{B} \; Z\Rightarrow \mathbf{b}, \mathbf{B'} \; Z\Rightarrow \mathbf{b'}, \mathbf{X} \; Z\Rightarrow vs(s)\right] \models tran'(\phi_1, \mathbf{B'}) \wedge heap(\mathbf{B} \bullet \mathbf{B'})$$

By Lemma 9 we know $[\mathbf{B'} \; Z\Rightarrow \mathbf{b'}] \models heap(\mathbf{B'})$ and so $\mathbf{b'} \in dom(vh_{|\mathbf{B'}|})$ by Lemma 5. Let $vh_{|\mathbf{B'}|}(\mathbf{b'}) = h_1$, we know by induction that $(s, h_1) \models \phi_1$. By Lemma 5 $vh_{p+|\mathbf{B'}|}(\mathbf{b} \bullet \mathbf{b'})$ is defined. Therefore by Lemma 10 $h * h_1 = vh_p(\mathbf{b}) * vh_{|\mathbf{B'}|}(\mathbf{b'}) = vh_{p+|\mathbf{B'}|}(\mathbf{b} \bullet \mathbf{b'})$. By assumption $s, h * h_1 \models \phi_2$. Consequently, by induction we have,

$$\left[\mathbf{B} \; Z\Rightarrow \mathbf{b}, \mathbf{B'} \; Z\Rightarrow \mathbf{b}, \mathbf{X} \; Z\Rightarrow vs(s)\right] \models tran'(\phi_2, \mathbf{B} \bullet \mathbf{B'})$$

Therefore,

$$[\mathbf{B}\ Z\Rightarrow \mathbf{b}, \mathbf{X}\ Z\Rightarrow vs(s)] \models \forall \mathbf{B}'. \begin{pmatrix} tran'(\phi_1, \mathbf{B}') \\ \wedge\ heap(\mathbf{B}\bullet \mathbf{B}') \\ \Rightarrow tran'(\phi_2, \mathbf{B}\bullet \mathbf{B}') \end{pmatrix}$$

and

$$[\mathbf{B}\ Z\Rightarrow \mathbf{b}, \mathbf{X}\ Z\Rightarrow vs(s)] \models tran'(\phi, \mathbf{B})$$

$\Leftarrow$: Assume,

$$[\mathbf{B}\ Z\Rightarrow \mathbf{b}, \mathbf{X}\ Z\Rightarrow vs(s)] \models \forall \mathbf{B}'. \begin{pmatrix} tran'(\phi_1, \mathbf{B}') \\ \wedge\ heap(\mathbf{B}\bullet \mathbf{B}') \\ \Rightarrow tran'(\phi_2, \mathbf{B}\bullet \mathbf{B}') \end{pmatrix}$$

where $|\mathbf{B}'| = max(|\phi_1|, |\phi_2|) + |FV(\phi_1) \cup FV(\phi_2)|$.

By Proposition 1 $(s, h) \models (\phi_1 \,\text{---}\!\ast\, \phi_2)$ iff for all $h_1 \in H_q$ such that $q = max(|\phi_1|, |\phi_2|) + |FV(\phi_1) \cup FV(\phi_2)|$, $h\#h_1$ and $(s, h_1) \models \phi_1$ we have $s, h \ast h_1 \models \phi_2$. So assume we have $h_1 \in H_q$ such that $h\#h_1$ and $(s, h_1) \models \phi_1$. By Lemma 4 there exists $\mathbf{b}'$ such that $vh_q(\mathbf{b}') = h_1$. Since $h\#h_1$ we know that $h \ast h_1 \in H_{p+q}$. By Lemma 10 we know $h \ast h_1 = vh_p(\mathbf{b}) \ast vh_q(\mathbf{b}') = vh_{p+q}(\mathbf{b}\bullet \mathbf{b}')$, and so, by Lemma 5 $[\mathbf{B}\ Z\Rightarrow \mathbf{b}, \mathbf{B}'\ Z\Rightarrow \mathbf{b}'] \models heap(\mathbf{B}\bullet \mathbf{B}')$. By induction we know

$$[\mathbf{B}'\ Z\Rightarrow \mathbf{b}', \mathbf{X}\ Z\Rightarrow vs(s)] \models tran'(\phi_1, \mathbf{B}')$$

It follows then that

$$[\mathbf{B}\ Z\Rightarrow \mathbf{b}, \mathbf{B}'\ Z\Rightarrow \mathbf{b}', \mathbf{X}\ Z\Rightarrow vs(s)] \models tran'(\phi_2, \mathbf{B}\bullet \mathbf{B}')$$

And by induction $(s, h \ast h_1) \models \phi_2$ as required.

Justifying Algorithms for $\beta\eta$-Conversion

Healfdene Goguen

AT&T Labs, 180 Park Ave., Florham Park NJ 07932 USA
hhg@att.com.

Abstract. Deciding the typing judgement of type theories with dependent types such as the Logical Framework relies on deciding the equality judgement for the same theory. Implementing the conversion algorithm for $\beta\eta$-equality and justifying this algorithm is therefore an important problem for applications such as proof assistants and modules systems. This article gives a proof of decidability, correctness and completeness of the conversion algorithms for $\beta\eta$-equality defined by Coquand [3] and Harper and Pfenning [8] for the Logical Framework, relying on established metatheoretic results for the type theory. Proofs are also given of the same properties for a typed algorithm for conversion for System F, a new result.

1 Introduction

In this article we study the decidability of algorithms for $\beta\eta$-conversion for type theories. We consider two algorithms for the Logical Framework not immediately modeled by reduction to a common $\beta\eta$-normal form: Coquand's untyped algorithm relating syntactically distinct β-weak-head normal forms [3], and Harper and Pfenning's type-based algorithm [8]. We demonstrate that these algorithms can be shown correct, complete and decidable based on standard metatheoretic properties of type theory, such as strong normalization of $\beta\eta$-reduction, subject reduction, injectivity of the type constructor Π, and so on. We then apply the same technique to the polymorphic λ-calculus System F.

The focus of many existing developments of the metatheory of type theories with $\beta\eta$-equality has been on decidability of typechecking, without concern for algorithms for conversion. The fact that the standard metatheory is sufficient to justify the decidability of algorithms has never been demonstrated as far as we are aware, even for Coquand's simple syntactic algorithm. With Harper and Pfenning's definition of a more complex algorithm for equality based on type information, it has become more important to show that the traditional approach to the metatheory of type theories, justifying termination and Church–Rosser for the reduction relation, can be used to show decidability for algorithms that are more complex than the simple comparison of normal forms.

We believe that it may be more efficient and uniform to justify algorithms for $\beta\eta$-conversion through the traditional approach to metatheory than by studying the algorithm directly. As an example, our proof of the termination of the algorithm for the Logical Framework only requires a single logical relation, as

V. Sassone (Ed.): FOSSACS 2005, LNCS 3441, pp. 410–424, 2005.

opposed to the two logical relations used in [11]. Similarly, Harper and Pfenning's approach has not been extended to systems with polymorphism, whereas we are able to adapt our proof straightforwardly to System F. Any approach to the metatheory of type theory with $\beta\eta$-equality is sufficient, and several methods already exist. Geuvers [4], Goguen [6,7] and Salvesen [9] all have different approaches to the difficulties presented by η.

The key to all three proofs of decidability is a simple length measure $|-|$ on normal forms of terms, where the value of the measure for an abstraction in normal form, $|\lambda x{:}A.M|$, is greater than the value of the measure for an application to a variable in normal form, $|M(x)|$. In Coquand's algorithm, an abstraction $\lambda x{:}A.M$ and a weak-head normal term $y(N_1 \ldots N_n)$ are related if M and $y(N_1 \ldots N_n, x)$ are related; by our measure, the combined length of the conclusion, $|\lambda x{:}A.M| + |y(N_1 \ldots N_n)|$, is greater than the combined length of the premises, $|M| + |y(N_1 \ldots N_n, x)|$. This same idea can be translated to Harper and Pfenning's type-directed algorithm for conversion.

The remainder of this paper is structured as follows. Section 2 introduces the syntax and standard metatheory for the Logical Framework. Section 3 justifies Coquand's algorithm using the standard metatheory. Section 4 justifies Harper and Pfenning's algorithm using a similar approach. Section 5 presents a type-directed algorithm for conversion for System F and justifies this algorithm. We draw conclusions and discuss future work in Section 6.

2   The Logical Framework

In this section we give our presentation of the Logical Framework. Although our system includes dependent types, we do not refer to this as the Edinburgh Logical Framework or the Martin-Löf Logical Framework, because for simplicity our presentation does not include higher-order kinds and hence does not formally correspond to either system. Otherwise, our system is largely similar to Harper and Pfenning's, but we use a term structure inspired by PTS-style presentations of type theories [2] to take advantage of the similarity of rules in the algorithm.

2.1   Syntax

We assume an infinite collection of variables $x, y, z \in V$. The language of terms and contexts is defined by the following grammar.

$$\Gamma \in C ::= () \mid \Gamma, x{:}A$$
$$s \in S ::= \text{type} \mid \text{kind}$$
$$M, N, P, A, B \in T ::= s \mid x \mid \lambda x{:}A.M \mid M(N) \mid \Pi x{:}A.B$$

We say a term is basic if it is a variable x or a sort s, and a term is canonical if it is of the form $\lambda x{:}A.M$ or $\Pi x{:}A_1.A_2$. Substitution, $[N/x]M$, is defined as usual for terms, with the obvious extension to contexts. We identify terms and contexts up to α-equivalence, and write $\text{FV}(M)$ for the free variables in M. Let

$\Gamma = x_1{:}A_1, \ldots, x_n{:}A_n$; then $dom(\Gamma) \equiv \{x_1, \ldots, x_n\}$, and $\Gamma(x)$ is the partial function that returns A_i if $x = x_i$ for some $1 \leq i \leq n$.

2.2   Judgements and Derivations

Our presentation of the Logical Framework has judgements $\Gamma \vdash M : A$ and $\Gamma \vdash M = N : A$. We write $\Gamma \vdash M, N : A$ for $\Gamma \vdash M : A$ and $\Gamma \vdash N : A$, and $\Gamma \vdash J$ to denote either judgement. The rules of inference for typing are given in Figure 1; the rules of inference for the equality judgement are the evident typed compatible closure and least equivalence relation containing the rules β and Ext.

$$(\text{type}) \quad () \vdash \text{type} : \text{kind} \qquad (\text{Weak}) \ \frac{\Gamma \vdash A : \text{type}}{\Gamma, x{:}A \vdash \text{type} : \text{kind}} \ (x{:}A \notin \Gamma)$$

$$(\text{Var}) \ \frac{\Gamma \vdash \text{type} : \text{kind}}{\Gamma \vdash x : A} \ (x{:}A \in \Gamma)$$

$$(\Pi) \ \frac{\Gamma \vdash A_1 : \text{type} \qquad \Gamma, x{:}A_1 \vdash A_2 : s}{\Gamma \vdash \Pi x{:}A_1.A_2 : s} \ (s \in \{\text{type}, \text{kind}\})$$

$$(\lambda) \ \frac{\Gamma, x{:}A_1 \vdash M : A_2}{\Gamma \vdash \lambda x{:}A_1.M : \Pi x{:}A_1.A_2} \qquad (\text{App}) \ \frac{\Gamma \vdash M_1 : \Pi x{:}A_1.A_2 \qquad \Gamma \vdash M_2 : A_1}{\Gamma \vdash M_1(M_2) : [M_2/x]A_2}$$

$$(\text{Eq}) \ \frac{\Gamma \vdash M : A \qquad \Gamma \vdash A = B : s}{\Gamma \vdash M : B}$$

Fig. 1. Typing for the Logical Framework

$$(\beta) \ \frac{\Gamma \vdash \lambda x{:}A_1.M : \Pi x{:}A_1.A_2 \qquad \Gamma \vdash M_2 : A_1}{\Gamma \vdash (\lambda x{:}A_1.M)(M_2) = [M_2/x]M : [M_2/x]A_2}$$

$$(\text{Ext}) \ \frac{\Gamma, x{:}A_1 \vdash M(x) = N(x) : A_2 \qquad \Gamma \vdash M, N : \Pi x{:}A_1.A_2}{\Gamma \vdash M = N : \Pi x{:}A_1.A_2}$$

2.3   Untyped Reduction

We define reduction $M \rightarrow_{\beta\eta} N$ as the compatible closure of rules β and η:

$$(\lambda x{:}A.M)(N) \ \beta \ [N/x]M$$
$$\lambda x{:}A.(M(x)) \ \eta \ M \qquad (x \notin \text{FV}(M))$$

Weak-head reduction $\rightarrow_w$ is defined by the following rules:

$$(\beta) \ (\lambda x{:}A.M)(N) \rightarrow_w [N/x]M \qquad (\text{App}) \ \frac{M \rightarrow_w P}{M(N) \rightarrow_w P(N)}$$

Definition 1 (Normal Forms and Weak-Head Normal Forms). *The β-normal forms are defined inductively as follows: basic terms s and x are normal; abstractions $\lambda x{:}A.M$ are normal if A and M are normal; products $\Pi x{:}A_1.A_2$ are normal if A_1 and A_2 are normal; and applications $M_1(M_2)$ are normal if M_1 and M_2 are normal and M_1 is not an abstraction.*

The weak-head normal forms are presented inductively as follows: basic terms s and x are weak-head normal; canonical terms $\lambda x{:}A.M$ and $\Pi x{:}A_1.A_2$ are weak-head normal; and applications $M_1(M_2)$ are weak-head normal if M_1 is weak-head normal and not an abstraction.

We write M^{nf} for the β-normal form of M and M^{wnf} for the weak-head normal form of M.

The following definitions apply to reduction relations $\to_\beta$, $\to_{\beta\eta}$ and $\to_w$: we write $\twoheadrightarrow$ for the reflexive, transitive closure of $\to$, $M \twoheadrightarrow_! N$ if $M \twoheadrightarrow N$ and N is normal, and $M \downarrow N$ if there is a P such that $M \twoheadrightarrow P$ and $N \twoheadrightarrow P$.

Lemma 1.

- *If M is normal then there is no N such that $M \to_\beta N$.*
- *If M is weak-head normal then there is no N such that $M \to_w N$.*
- *Any term M is either weak-head normal or there is an N such that $M \to_w N$.*

2.4   Properties of the Logical Framework

We assume all of the standard properties of the Logical Framework: as we mentioned in the introduction, any approach to proving them is acceptable for the purposes of this article. We state the properties needed here for reference.

Proposition 1 (Generation). *Every derivation of a term is an application of the unique rule of inference for that term followed by a sequence of uses of Eq.*

For example, suppose $\Gamma \vdash \lambda x{:}A_1.M_0 : A$; then $\Gamma, x{:}A_1 \vdash M_0 : A_2$ and $\Gamma \vdash \Pi x{:}A_1.A_2 = A : s$ for some A_2 and s.

Proposition 2.

1. *Free Variables. If $\Gamma \vdash M : A$ then $\mathrm{FV}(M) \cup \mathrm{FV}(A) \subseteq dom(\Gamma)$.*
2. *Context Validity. If $\Gamma \vdash J$ then $\Gamma \vdash \mathrm{type} : \mathrm{kind}$.*
3. *Thinning. If $\Gamma, \Gamma' \vdash J$, $x \notin dom(\Gamma, \Gamma')$ and $\Gamma \vdash A : \mathrm{type}$ then $\Gamma, x{:}A, \Gamma' \vdash J$.*
4. *Substitution. If $\Gamma, x{:}A, \Gamma' \vdash J$ and $\Gamma \vdash N : A$ then $\Gamma, [N/x]\Gamma' \vdash [N/x]J$.*
5. *Type Correctness. If $\Gamma \vdash M : A$ then $\Gamma \vdash A : s$ for some s.*
6. *Splitting. If $\Gamma \vdash M = N : A$ then $\Gamma \vdash M, N : A$.*
7. *Uniqueness of Types. If $\Gamma \vdash M : A$ and $\Gamma \vdash M : B$ then $\Gamma \vdash A = B : s$ or $A = s$ and $B = s$ for some s.*
8. *Context Replacement. $\Gamma, x{:}A, \Gamma' \vdash J$ and $\Gamma \vdash A = B : s$ imply $\Gamma, x{:}B, \Gamma' \vdash J$.*
9. *Church–Rosser. If $\Gamma \vdash M = N : A$ then $M \downarrow_{\beta\eta} N$.*
10. *Injectivity of Π. If $\Gamma \vdash \Pi x{:}A.B = \Pi x{:}C.D : s$ then $\Gamma \vdash A = C : \mathrm{type}$ and $\Gamma, x{:}A \vdash B = D : s$.*

11. *Subject Reduction. If $\Gamma \vdash M : A$ and $M \rightarrow_{\beta\eta} N$ then $\Gamma \vdash M = N : A$.*

12. *Strong Normalization. $\Gamma \vdash M : A$ implies M is strongly normalizing under $\rightarrow_{\beta\eta}$.*

13. *Strengthening. If $\Gamma, x{:}A, \Gamma' \vdash J$ and $x \notin \mathrm{FV}(\Gamma') \cup \mathrm{FV}(J)$ then $\Gamma, \Gamma' \vdash J$.*

Lemma 2. *If $\Gamma \vdash M : A$, $\Gamma \vdash N : B$ and $M \downarrow_{\beta\eta} N$ then there is an s such that $\Gamma \vdash M = N : A$ and $\Gamma \vdash A = B : s$.*

Proof. By Subject Reduction, Splitting, Uniqueness of Types and equational reasoning.

We also observe without proof that Ext is equivalent to the following rule:

$$(\eta) \quad \frac{\Gamma \vdash M : \Pi x{:}A_1.A_2}{\Gamma \vdash \lambda x{:}A_1.M(x) = M : \Pi x{:}A_1.A_2}$$

3   Termination of Coquand's Algorithm

In this section we study properties of Coquand's algorithm, adapted to our presentation of the Logical Framework. This algorithm is based only on the syntax of the terms being compared, and contains no type information.

3.1   Definition

Coquand's algorithm is defined inductively by the inference rules in Figure 2. The algorithm $M \Longleftrightarrow N$ simply reduces its arguments M and N to weak-head normal form. The algorithm $M \longleftrightarrow N$ compares terms in weak-head normal form: the interesting cases are the non-structural rules λ-Left and λ-Right, where

$$(\text{WHRed}) \quad \frac{P \longleftrightarrow Q}{M \Longleftrightarrow N} \quad (M \twoheadrightarrow_w P \text{ and } N \twoheadrightarrow_w Q)$$

$$(\text{Var}) \quad x \longleftrightarrow x \qquad (\text{type}) \quad \text{type} \longleftrightarrow \text{type}$$

$$(\Pi) \quad \frac{A_1 \Longleftrightarrow B_1 \qquad A_2 \Longleftrightarrow B_2}{\Pi x{:}A_1.A_2 \longleftrightarrow \Pi x{:}B_1.B_2}$$

$$(\text{App}) \quad \frac{M_1 \longleftrightarrow N_1 \qquad M_2 \Longleftrightarrow N_2}{M_1(M_2) \longleftrightarrow N_1(N_2)} \quad (M_1 \text{ and } N_1 \text{ weak-head normal and not canonical})$$

$$(\lambda) \quad \frac{M \Longleftrightarrow N}{\lambda x{:}A.M \longleftrightarrow \lambda x{:}B.N}$$

$$(\lambda\text{-Left}) \quad \frac{M \Longleftrightarrow N(x)}{\lambda x{:}A.M \longleftrightarrow N} \quad (N \text{ weak-head normal and not canonical})$$

$$(\lambda\text{-Right}) \quad \frac{M(x) \Longleftrightarrow N}{M \longleftrightarrow \lambda x{:}B.N} \quad (M \text{ weak-head normal and not canonical})$$

Fig. 2. Untyped Algorithm for Conversion for the Logical Framework

the left- or right-hand side is an abstraction and two terms are equivalent after an application of Ext.

We assume implicitly that an implementation of the algorithm will examine combinations of terms and evaluate the premises given by the inference rules recursively. Axioms in the inference rules will return true, while combinations that do not appear in the inference rules will return false. Hence, the inference rules of the algorithm give us both an inductively defined relation and an algorithm yielding either true or false; clearly, the algorithm yields true iff there is a derivation using the inference rules.

Furthermore, observe that the inference rules are syntax-directed, meaning that at most one rule will apply for any pair of terms. This fact is used implicitly in the proofs below.

3.2   Termination and Completeness of Coquand's Algorithm

We now show that Coquand's algorithm terminates.

We begin by defining a measure where λ-abstractions $\lambda x{:}A.M$ are larger than applications to a variable $M(x)$. We use this measure as the base of the induction to show termination of the algorithm.

Definition 2. *Define the length of a normal term M recursively on its structure:*

$$|s| \equiv 1 \qquad |\Pi x{:}A_1.A_2| \equiv |A_1| + |A_2| + 1 \qquad |M(N)| \equiv |M| + |N| + 1$$
$$|x| \equiv 1 \qquad |\lambda x{:}A.M| \equiv |M| + 3$$

Lemma 3 (Termination). *If M and N are β-normalizing then $M \Longleftrightarrow N$ terminates.*

Proof. By nested induction on the sum of $|M^{nf}|$ and $|N^{nf}|$ and the sum of the lengths of the β-reduction sequences for M and N.

By Lemma 1 Case 1 M and N are weak-head normal or have weak-head reducts. If M or N has a weak-head reduct, then by WHRed $M \Longleftrightarrow N$ terminates if $M^{wnf} \longleftrightarrow N^{wnf}$ terminates, where the latter follows by the induction hypothesis for reduction; $M \Longleftrightarrow N$ terminates with the same result as $M^{wnf} \longleftrightarrow N^{wnf}$. Otherwise, M and N are in weak-head normal form. We perform case analysis on M and N to show that $M \longleftrightarrow N$ terminates; then $M \Longleftrightarrow N$ terminates with the same result. We consider several cases:

- M is basic and N is an application. Then $M \longleftrightarrow N$ terminates in failure.
- $M \equiv M_1(M_2)$ and $N \equiv N_1(N_2)$. If M and N are weak-head normal then M_1 and N_1 must be weak-head normal and not abstractions. If M_1 or N_1 is a product then it is canonical, so $M_1(M_2) \longleftrightarrow N_1(N_2)$ fails immediately. Otherwise, $M^{nf} \equiv M_1^{nf}(M_2^{nf})$ and $N^{nf} \equiv N_1^{nf}(N_2^{nf})$, so by induction hypothesis $M_1 \longleftrightarrow N_1$ and $M_2 \Longleftrightarrow N_2$ terminate. If both succeed then $M \longleftrightarrow N$ succeeds, and otherwise it fails.

- $M \equiv \lambda x{:}A_1.M_0$ and N is not canonical. Only rule λ-Left applies, and so $\lambda x{:}A_1.M_0 \longleftrightarrow N$ terminates if $M_0 \Longleftrightarrow N(x)$ terminates. Clearly $M^{nf} \equiv \lambda x{:}A_1^{nf}.M_0^{nf}$ and $(N(x))^{nf} \equiv N^{nf}(x)$, and $|\lambda x{:}A_1^{nf}.M_0^{nf}| + |N^{nf}| = |M_0^{nf}| + 3 + |N^{nf}| > |M_0^{nf}| + |N^{nf}| + 2 = |M_0^{nf}| + |N^{nf}(x)|$, so $M_0 \Longleftrightarrow N(x)$ terminates by induction hypothesis; if this succeeds then $\lambda x{:}A_1.M_0 \longleftrightarrow N$ succeeds, and otherwise it fails.
- $M \equiv \lambda x{:}A_1.M_0$ and $N \equiv \Pi y{:}B_1.B_2$. Then $M \longleftrightarrow N$ fails immediately.

Lemma 4 (Completeness). *If $\Gamma \vdash M = N : A$ then $M \Longleftrightarrow N$.*

Proof. By Church–Rosser and Splitting it suffices to show that if $M \downarrow_{\beta\eta} N$ and $\Gamma \vdash M : A$ and $\Gamma \vdash N : B$ then $M \Longleftrightarrow N$, which we show using the same induction principle as for Lemma 3. As in that lemma, we can distinguish two cases, depending on whether M and N are both weak-head normal. If either is not, then by Church–Rosser if $M \downarrow_{\beta\eta} N$ then $M^{wnf} \downarrow_{\beta\eta} N^{wnf}$, since M and N are well-typed, and by Subject Reduction $\Gamma \vdash M^{wnf} : A$ and $\Gamma \vdash N^{wnf} : B$. Therefore $M^{wnf} \Longleftrightarrow N^{wnf}$ follows by the induction hypothesis on reduction sequences, so $M^{wnf} \longleftrightarrow N^{wnf}$ by inversion, and so $M \Longleftrightarrow N$ by WHRed. We now consider the cases where M and N are in weak-head normal form: we show that if $M \downarrow_{\beta\eta} N$ then $M \longleftrightarrow N$, from which $M \Longleftrightarrow N$. We consider several cases where M and N are in weak-head normal form.

- M and N are basic. If $x \downarrow_{\beta\eta} y$ then $x = y$, so $x \longleftrightarrow y$. type $\longleftrightarrow$ type.
- M is basic and N is an application. $x \downarrow_{\beta\eta} N_1(N_2)$ and type $\downarrow_{\beta\eta} N_1(N_2)$ are impossible.
- $M \equiv \lambda x{:}A_1.M_0$ and N not canonical. Let $\lambda x{:}A_1.M_0 \downarrow_{\beta\eta} N$, $\Gamma \vdash \lambda x{:}A_1.M_0 : A$ and $\Gamma \vdash N : B$. Then $M_0 \twoheadrightarrow M_0'(x)$ with $x \notin \mathrm{FV}(M_0')$, and $N \twoheadrightarrow M_0'$; hence $M_0 \downarrow_{\beta\eta} N(x)$, since N is weak-head normal and not canonical. By Generation $\Gamma, x{:}A_1 \vdash M_0 : A_2$ and $\Gamma \vdash \Pi x{:}A_1.A_2 = A : s$; by Splitting $\Gamma \vdash \Pi x{:}A_1.A_2 : s$, and by Generation $\Gamma \vdash A_1 : $ type. Then by Lemma 2 $\Gamma \vdash A = B : s$, so $\Gamma \vdash N : \Pi x{:}A_1.A_2$; by Thinning $\Gamma, x{:}A_1 \vdash N : \Pi x{:}A_1.A_2$ and by App $\Gamma, x{:}A_1 \vdash N(x) : A_2$. Therefore, by induction hypothesis $M_0 \Longleftrightarrow N(x)$ implies $\lambda x{:}A_1.M_0 \longleftrightarrow N$.
- $M \equiv \lambda x{:}A_1.M_0$ and $N \equiv \Pi y{:}B_1.B_2$. Suppose $\lambda x{:}A_1.M_0 \downarrow_{\beta\eta} \Pi y{:}B_1.B_2$, $\Gamma \vdash \lambda x{:}A_1.M_0 : A$ and $\Gamma \vdash \Pi y{:}B_1.B_2 : B$. Then $\Gamma \vdash \lambda x{:}A_1.M_0 : \Pi x{:}A_1.A_2$ and $\Gamma \vdash \Pi y{:}B_1.B_2 : s$ by Generation. By Lemma 2 $\Gamma \vdash \Pi x{:}A_1.A_2 = s : s'$, and by Church–Rosser $\Pi x{:}A_1.A_2 \downarrow_{\beta\eta} s$, which is impossible.

3.3   Correctness of the Algorithm

Our proof of correctness of Coquand's algorithm is similar to his original proof, but we restate the proof because we rely on the metatheory of $\beta\eta$-reduction rather than his logical relation over the algorithm.

Lemma 5 (Correctness).

- *If $\Gamma \vdash M, N : A$ and $M \Longleftrightarrow N$ then $\Gamma \vdash M = N : A$.*

– If $M \longleftrightarrow N$, $\Gamma \vdash M : A$, $\Gamma \vdash N : B$ and M and N are not canonical then $\Gamma \vdash M = N : A$ and $\Gamma \vdash A = B : s$. If $M \longleftrightarrow N$ and $\Gamma \vdash M, N : A$ then $\Gamma \vdash M = N : A$.

Proof. By induction on the derivations of $M \Longleftrightarrow N$ and $M \longleftrightarrow N$. We consider several cases:

– WHRed. By Subject Reduction $\Gamma \vdash M = P : A$ and $\Gamma \vdash N = Q : A$, by Splitting $\Gamma \vdash P, Q : A$, and by induction hypothesis $\Gamma \vdash P = Q : A$, so $\Gamma \vdash M = N : A$ by Symmetry and Transitivity.

– Π. By Generation $\Gamma \vdash A_1, B_1 :$ type, $\Gamma, x{:}A_1 \vdash A_2 : s$ and $\Gamma, x{:}B_1 \vdash B_2 : s$; by induction hypothesis $\Gamma \vdash A_1 = B_1 :$ type, so by Context Replacement $\Gamma, x{:}A_1 \vdash B_2 : s$. By induction hypothesis again $\Gamma, x{:}A_1 \vdash A_2 = B_2 : s$.

– λ-Left. By assumption $\Gamma \vdash \lambda x{:}A_1.M_0 : C$, $\Gamma \vdash N : C$ and $M_0 \longleftrightarrow N(x)$. By Generation $\Gamma, x{:}A_1 \vdash M_0 : A_2$ and $\Gamma \vdash \Pi x{:}A_1.A_2 = C : s$. Therefore $\Gamma \vdash N : \Pi x{:}A_1.A_2$ by Sym and Eq and $\Gamma, x{:}A_1 \vdash N(x) : A_2$ by Weakening and App, and so by induction hypothesis $\Gamma, x{:}A_1 \vdash M_0 = N(x) : A_2$. Hence $\Gamma \vdash \lambda x{:}A_1.M_0 = N : \Pi x{:}A_1.A_2 = C$ by Ext.

4   Termination of Harper and Pfenning's Algorithm

Since it relies purely on the structure of terms, Coquand's algorithm cannot be used for type theories where equality may identify terms with different head variables, such as the extensional equalities on the unit type or singleton types. Such types can be important in applications, such as modules systems [1, 10], and Harper and Pfenning introduce type information into their algorithm in order to capture these types.

In this section we establish the decidability, completeness and correctness of Harper and Pfenning's algorithm for the Logical Framework.

4.1   Definition

We begin by defining a slight variant of Harper and Pfenning's algorithm.

The algorithm relies on an erasure function from the dependent types and kinds of the Logical Framework into simple types. We define our erasure into simple types formed only with constructors o and $\tau_1 \to \tau_2$, where Harper and Pfenning distinguish between sorts and constants in the Logical Framework; our approach should allow different judgements to be handled uniformly as in PTS. We use a single base type because we have used the same syntactic category for types and kinds, and it is more uniform not to distinguish between the two in the algorithm.

Formally, we define the simple types and contexts with the following BNF grammar:

$$\sigma, \tau \in S ::= o \mid \sigma \to \tau$$
$$\Delta \in X ::= () \mid \Delta, x{:}\sigma$$

The erasure is defined inductively on the structure of types and kinds in weak-head normal form as follows:

$$\text{type}^- \equiv o \qquad\qquad x^- \equiv o \qquad\qquad (A(M))^- \equiv o$$
$$\text{kind}^- \equiv o \qquad (\lambda x{:}A.M)^- \equiv o \qquad (\Pi x{:}A_1.A_2)^- \equiv A_1^- \to A_2^-$$

The definition extends in the obvious way to contexts. Erasure has the following simple properties, shown by induction on derivations.

Lemma 6. *If $\Gamma \vdash A : s$ then $([N/x]A)^- = A^-$. If $\Gamma \vdash A = B : s$ then $A^- = B^-$.*

The algorithm is defined inductively by the inference rules in Figure 3. Like Coquand's algorithm, this algorithm has a judgement $\Delta \vdash M \Longleftrightarrow N : \tau$ comparing arbitrary terms and a judgement $\Delta \vdash M \longleftrightarrow N : \tau$ comparing weak-head normal forms, but unlike Coquand's algorithm weak-head normalization in $\Longleftrightarrow$ is only performed at the base type, and terms at higher type are applied to variables and compared in the result type.

$$\text{(Base)} \quad \frac{\Delta \vdash P \longleftrightarrow Q : o}{\Delta \vdash M \Longleftrightarrow N : o} \quad (M \twoheadrightarrow_w P \text{ and } N \twoheadrightarrow_w Q)$$

$$(\to) \quad \frac{\Delta, x{:}\tau_1 \vdash M(x) \Longleftrightarrow N(x) : \tau_2}{\Delta \vdash M \Longleftrightarrow N : \tau_1 \to \tau_2} \quad (x \notin dom(\Delta))$$

$$\text{(Var)} \quad \Delta \vdash x \longleftrightarrow x : \Delta(x) \qquad \text{(type)} \quad \Delta \vdash \text{type} \longleftrightarrow \text{type} : o$$

$$(\Pi) \quad \frac{\Delta \vdash A_1 \Longleftrightarrow B_1 : o \qquad \Delta, x{:}A_1^- \vdash A_2 \Longleftrightarrow B_2 : o}{\Delta \vdash \Pi x{:}A_1.A_2 \longleftrightarrow \Pi x{:}B_1.B_2 : o}$$

$$\text{(App)} \quad \frac{\Delta \vdash M_1 \longleftrightarrow N_1 : \tau_1 \to \tau_2 \qquad \Delta \vdash M_2 \Longleftrightarrow N_2 : \tau_1}{\Delta \vdash M_1(M_2) \longleftrightarrow N_1(N_2) : \tau_2}$$

Fig. 3. Typed Algorithm for Conversion for the Logical Framework

We observe that, like Coquand's algorithm, this algorithm is syntax-directed: for $\Longleftrightarrow$ the context and type are part of the input and the algorithm returns true or false, and for $\longleftrightarrow$ the context is an input and the type is an output.

4.2   Termination and Completeness of the Algorithm

In this section we show the termination and completeness of Harper and Pfenning's type-directed algorithm for the Logical Framework.

For the following lemma, it is convenient to reason over traces of the algorithm itself, rather than the inference rules of those terms successfully related by the algorithm: we capture both success and failure of the implementation of the algorithm simultaneously. To this end, we shall write $\Delta; M; N; \tau \Rightarrow b$, for $b \in \{\text{tt}, \text{ff}\}$, to denote a trace of the algorithm for $\Delta \vdash M \Longleftrightarrow N : \tau$ yielding b as its result. Similarly, we shall write $\Delta; M; N \to v$, with $v \in S \cup \{\perp\}$, where $\Delta; M; N \to \tau$ if $\Delta \vdash M \longleftrightarrow N : \tau$ and $\Delta; M; N \to \perp$ if $\Delta \vdash M \longleftrightarrow N : \tau$ fails.

Lemma 7.

 - *If $\Delta, \Delta'; M; N; \tau \Rightarrow b$ and $x \notin dom(\Delta, \Delta')$ then $\Delta, x{:}\sigma, \Delta'; M; N; \tau \Rightarrow b$.*
 - *If $\Delta, \Delta'; M; N \to v$ and $x \notin dom(\Delta, \Delta')$ then $\Delta, x{:}\sigma, \Delta'; M; N \to v$.*

The following lemmas are by induction on types.

Lemma 8. *Let M and N be weak-head normal and not canonical. Then if $\Delta; M; N \to \tau$ then $\Delta; M; N; \tau \Rightarrow \mathsf{tt}$; if $\Delta; M; N \to \bot$ then $\Delta; M; N; \tau \Rightarrow \mathsf{ff}$ for any τ, and if $\Delta; M; N \to \tau$ then $\Delta; M; N; \tau' \Rightarrow b$ for any τ'.*

Lemma 9. *If $M \to_w P$ then $\Delta \vdash M \Longleftrightarrow N : \tau$ terminates iff $\Delta \vdash P \Longleftrightarrow N : \tau$ terminates, and with the same result, and symmetrically.*

We now prove the main results of this section.

Lemma 10 (Termination). *Suppose that M and N are β-normalizing. Then $\Delta \vdash M \Longleftrightarrow N : \tau$ is terminating for any Δ and τ, and if M and N are weak-head normal and not canonical then $\Delta \vdash M \longleftrightarrow N : \tau$ is terminating for any Δ.*

Proof. We prove this by nested induction on the sum of $|M^{nf}|$ and $|N^{nf}|$ and the sum of the lengths of the β-reduction sequences of M and N. As for Coquand's algorithm, we use Lemma 1 Case 1 to perform case analysis on whether M and N are weak-head normal or not.

We consider several cases where M and N are weak-head normal.

 - M and N basic. If $M = N = x$ and $x{:}\tau \in \Delta$ then $\Delta \vdash x \longleftrightarrow x : \tau$ succeeds. If $M = N = $ type then $\Delta \vdash$ type $\longleftrightarrow$ type $: o$ succeeds, and $\Delta \vdash$ type $\longleftrightarrow$ type $: \tau_1 \to \tau_2$ fails. Similarly, if $M \neq N$ or $M \equiv x \notin dom(\Delta)$ then $\Delta \vdash M \longleftrightarrow N : \tau$ fails. Each result lifts to $\Longleftrightarrow$ by Lemma 8.
 - $M \equiv \lambda x{:}A_1.M_0$ and N is not canonical. $\Delta \vdash M \Longleftrightarrow N : o$ fails because no rules match $\Delta \vdash \lambda x{:}A_1.M_0 \longleftrightarrow N : o$. $\Delta \vdash \lambda x{:}A_1.M_0 \Longleftrightarrow N : \tau_1 \to \tau_2$ terminates by definition iff $\Delta, x{:}\tau_1 \vdash (\lambda x{:}A_1.M_0)(x) \Longleftrightarrow N(x) : \tau_2$, which by Lemma 9 terminates iff $\Delta, x{:}\tau_1 \vdash M_0 \Longleftrightarrow N(x) : \tau_2$ terminates. But $\Delta, x{:}\tau_1 \vdash M_0 \Longleftrightarrow N(x) : \tau_2$ terminates by induction hypothesis, since $|\lambda x{:}A_1^{nf}.M_0^{nf}| + |N^{nf}| = |M_0^{nf}| + 3 + |N^{nf}| > |M_0^{nf}| + |N^{nf}| + 2 = |M_0^{nf}| + |N^{nf}(x)|$.

Lemma 11 (Completeness). *If $\Gamma \vdash M = N : A$ then $\Gamma^- \vdash M \Longleftrightarrow N : A^-$.*

Proof. By Church–Rosser and Splitting it suffices to show that if $M \downarrow_{\beta\eta} N$ and $\Gamma \vdash M : A$, $\Gamma' \vdash N : B$, $A^- = B^-$ and $\Gamma^- = \Gamma'^-$ then $\Gamma^- \vdash M \Longleftrightarrow N : A^-$; and if $M \downarrow_{\beta\eta} N$ with M and N weak-head normal and not canonical, and $\Gamma \vdash M : A$, $\Gamma' \vdash N : B$ and $\Gamma^- = \Gamma'^-$, then $A^- = B^-$ and $\Gamma^- \vdash M \longleftrightarrow N : A^-$. We use the same induction principle as in Lemma 10; we consider several cases where M and N are weak-head normal.

- M and N basic. Clearly if $M \downarrow_{\beta\eta} N$ then $M = N = x$ or $M = N = \text{type}$. If $M = x$ then $\Gamma \vdash x : A$ and $\Gamma' \vdash x : B$ imply $\Gamma \vdash \Gamma(x) = A : \text{type}$, $\Gamma' \vdash \Gamma'(x) = B : \text{type}$, and $\Gamma^-(x) \in \Gamma^-$, so $\Gamma^- \vdash x \longleftrightarrow x : \Gamma(x)$ and $\Gamma^- \vdash x \Longleftrightarrow x : \Gamma(x)$ as above. Also, $\Gamma^- = \Gamma'^-$ implies $\Gamma(x)^- = \Gamma'(x)$ implies $A^- = B^-$ by Lemma 6. If $M = \text{type}$ then $\Gamma \vdash \text{type} : A$ and $\Gamma' \vdash \text{type} : B$ imply $A = B = \text{kind}$, and $\Gamma^- \vdash \text{type} \longleftrightarrow \text{type} : o$ and $\Gamma^- \vdash \text{type} \Longleftrightarrow \text{type} : o$.

- $M \equiv \lambda x{:}A_1.M_0$ and N not canonical. Let $\lambda x{:}A_1.M_0 \downarrow_{\beta\eta} N$, $\Gamma \vdash \lambda x{:}A_1.M_0 : A$, $\Gamma \vdash N : B$, and $A^- = B^-$. Then $M_0 \twoheadrightarrow M_0'(x)$ with $x \notin \text{FV}(M_0')$, and $N \twoheadrightarrow M_0'$, and by Generation $\Gamma, x{:}A_1 \vdash M_0 : A_2$, $\Gamma \vdash \Pi x{:}A_1.A_2 = A$ and so $B \equiv \Pi x{:}B_1.B_2$ since $(\Pi x{:}A_1.A_2)^- = B^-$. Hence $M_0 \downarrow_{\beta\eta} N(x)$, since N is weak-head normal and not canonical, and $\Gamma, x{:}B_1 \vdash N(x) : B_2$ by Weakening and App, and $A_1^- = B_1^-$ implies $\Gamma^-, x{:}A_1^- = \Gamma'^-, x{:}B_1^-$, so $\Gamma^-, x{:}A_1^- \vdash M_0 \Longleftrightarrow N(x) : A_2^-$ implies $\Gamma^-, x{:}A_1^- \vdash (\lambda x{:}A_1.M_0)(x) \Longleftrightarrow N(x) : A_2^-$ by induction hypothesis implies $\Gamma^- \vdash \lambda x{:}A_1.M_0 \Longleftrightarrow N : A_1^- \to A_2^- = (\Pi x{:}A_1.A_2)^-$.

4.3   Correctness of the Algorithm

The outline of our proof of the correctness of the algorithm follows Harper and Pfenning's proof. The primary difference is that because we rely on established metatheoretic results, Subject Reduction also applies to β-reducts at the level of types by assumption.

Lemma 12 (Correctness).

- If $\Gamma^- \vdash M \Longleftrightarrow N : A^-$ and $\Gamma \vdash M, N : A$ then $\Gamma \vdash M = N : A$.
- If $\Gamma^- \vdash M \longleftrightarrow N : \tau$, $\Gamma \vdash M : A$, $\Gamma \vdash N : B$ and M and N not canonical then $\Gamma \vdash M = N : A$ and either $\Gamma \vdash A = B : s$ with $A^- = B^- = \tau$ or $A = B = \text{kind}$. If $\Gamma^- \vdash M \longleftrightarrow N : A^-$ and $\Gamma \vdash M, N : A$ then $\Gamma \vdash M = N : A$.

Proof. By induction on derivations. We consider several cases:

- Base. By Subject Reduction $\Gamma \vdash M = P : A$ and $\Gamma \vdash N = Q : A$, and by Splitting $\Gamma \vdash P, Q : A$, so by induction hypothesis $\Gamma \vdash P = Q : A$. Hence $\Gamma \vdash M = N : A$.

- Π. By assumption $\Gamma \vdash \Pi x{:}A_1.A_2, \Pi x{:}B_1.B_2 : C$, so $\Gamma \vdash A_1, B_1 : \text{type}$ by Generation, $\Gamma, x{:}A_1 \vdash A_2 : s$ and $\Gamma, x{:}B_1 \vdash B_2 : s'$, with derivations of $\Gamma \vdash C = \text{type} : \text{kind}$ or $C = \text{kind}$ from each derivation. Therefore $s = s'$, and so by induction hypothesis $\Gamma \vdash A_1 = B_1 : \text{type}$ and $\Gamma, x{:}A_1 \vdash A_2 = B_2 : s$, so $\Gamma \vdash \Pi x{:}A_1.A_2 = \Pi x{:}B_1.B_2 : s$.

5   System F

In this final technical section we show that our technique also works for a typed conversion algorithm for System F, hence extending our results beyond that of Harper and Pfenning.

5.1   Syntax

We begin by introducing the term syntax and inference rules for System F.

The following grammar presents the contexts, types, and terms of System F:

$$\Gamma \in C ::= () \mid \Gamma, x{:}A$$
$$A, B, C \in Y ::= X \mid A \to B \mid \forall X.A$$
$$M, N, P, Q \in T ::= x \mid \lambda x{:}A.M \mid M(N) \mid \Lambda X.M \mid M(A)$$

Similar to the Logical Framework, we say that a term is canonical if it is of the form $\lambda x{:}A.M$ or $\Lambda X.M$.

We use the same notations for reduction, substitution and so on as for the Logical Framework. We say that a context Γ is valid if each $x \in dom(\Gamma)$ occurs exactly once in Γ. We write $\mathrm{FTV}(A)$ for the free type variables occurring in A, and similarly for contexts.

Reduction is extended with β and η reductions for the type-level constructors:

$$(\Lambda X.M)(A) \; \beta \; [A/X]M$$
$$\Lambda X.(M(X)) \; \eta \; M \qquad (X \notin \mathrm{FTV}(M))$$

Weak-head reduction is similarly extended. The definitions of normal and weak-head normal are also extended in the natural way; observe that $(\Lambda X.M)(N)$ and $(\lambda x{:}A.M)(B)$ are normal and weak-head normal. Finally, the results of Lemma 1 exetnd to System F.

Our presentation of System F has only two judgements, $\Gamma \vdash M : A$ and $\Gamma \vdash M = N : A$; the inference rules for $\Gamma \vdash M : A$ are as follows:

$$(\text{Var}) \; \frac{\Gamma \; \text{valid}}{\Gamma \vdash x : A} \; (x{:}A \in \Gamma)$$

$$(\lambda) \; \frac{\Gamma, x{:}A \vdash M : B}{\Gamma \vdash \lambda x{:}A.M : A \to B} \qquad (\text{App}) \; \frac{\Gamma \vdash M : A \to B \qquad \Gamma \vdash N : A}{\Gamma \vdash M(N) : B}$$

$$(\Lambda) \; \frac{\Gamma \vdash M : A}{\Gamma \vdash \Lambda X.M : \forall X.A} \; (X \notin \mathrm{FTV}(\Gamma)) \qquad (\text{TyApp}) \; \frac{\Gamma \vdash M : \forall X.A}{\Gamma \vdash M(B) : [B/X]A}$$

The equality judgement is the evident typed extension of rules β and Ext for terms and types, as in Section 2.2.

System F enjoys a list of properties similar to those of Section 2.4, including Subject Reduction, Church–Rosser, Splitting, Uniqueness of Types, and so on. Due to a lack of space, we omit the full statement of these properties.

5.2   The Algorithm

The algorithm is defined by the inference rules in Figure 4.

5.3   Termination and Completeness of the Algorithm

The arguments for termination and completeness of the algorithm are very similar to the arguments for the Logical Framework, although they are simpler due to the lack of dependent types. We briefly outline the proofs here.

$$(\text{TyVar}) \quad \frac{\Gamma \vdash P \longleftrightarrow Q : X}{\Gamma \vdash M \Longleftrightarrow N : X} \quad (M \twoheadrightarrow_w P \text{ and } N \twoheadrightarrow_w Q)$$

$$(\rightarrow) \quad \frac{\Gamma, x{:}A \vdash M(x) \Longleftrightarrow N(x) : B}{\Gamma \vdash M \Longleftrightarrow N : A \rightarrow B} \quad (x \notin dom(\Gamma))$$

$$(\forall) \quad \frac{\Gamma \vdash M(X) \Longleftrightarrow N(X) : A}{\Gamma \vdash M \Longleftrightarrow N : \forall X.A} \quad (X \notin \text{FTV}(\Gamma) \cup \text{FTV}(M) \cup \text{FTV}(N))$$

$$(\text{Var}) \quad \Gamma \vdash x \longleftrightarrow x : \Gamma(x)$$

$$(\text{App}) \quad \frac{\Gamma \vdash M_1 \longleftrightarrow N_1 : A \rightarrow B \qquad \Gamma \vdash M_2 \Longleftrightarrow N_2 : A}{\Gamma \vdash M_1(M_2) \longleftrightarrow N_1(N_2) : B}$$

$$(\text{TyApp}) \quad \frac{\Gamma \vdash M \longleftrightarrow N : \forall X.A}{\Gamma \vdash M(B) \longleftrightarrow N(B) : [B/X]A}$$

Fig. 4. Algorithm for Conversion for System F

We define the length function $|M|$ in the obvious way for System F, and $\Gamma; M; N; A \Rightarrow b$ and $\Gamma; M; N \rightarrow v$ are also extended.

Lemma 13. *Let M and N be weak-head normal and not canonical. Then if $\Gamma; M; N \rightarrow A$ then $\Gamma; M; N; A \Rightarrow \text{tt}$; if $\Gamma; M; N \rightarrow \perp$ then $\Gamma; M; N; A \Rightarrow \text{ff}$ for any A, and if $\Gamma; M; N \rightarrow A$ then $\Gamma; M; N; B \Rightarrow b$ for any B.*

Lemma 14. *If $M \rightarrow_w P$ then $\Gamma \vdash M \Longleftrightarrow N : A$ terminates iff $\Gamma \vdash P \Longleftrightarrow N : A$ terminates, and with the same result, and symmetrically.*

Lemma 15 (Termination). *If M and N are β-normalizing then $\Gamma \vdash M \Longleftrightarrow N : A$ is terminating for any Γ and A; if M and N are weak-head normal and not canonical then $\Gamma \vdash M \longleftrightarrow N : A$ is terminating for any Γ.*

Proof. By nested induction on the sum of $|M^{nf}|$ and $|N^{nf}|$ and the sum of the lengths of β-reduction sequences for M and N. As in the previous sections, if M and N are not weak-head normal then the result follows by the nested induction hypothesis.

We consider several cases where M and N are weak-head normal.

- $M \equiv \Lambda X.M_0$ and N not canonical. $\Gamma \vdash \Lambda X.M_0 \Longleftrightarrow N : X$ fails immediately, and $\Gamma \vdash \Lambda X.M_0 \Longleftrightarrow N : A \rightarrow B$ fails since $\Gamma, x{:}A \vdash (\Lambda X.M_0)(x) \Longleftrightarrow N(x) : B$ fails by Lemma 13, since $\Gamma, x{:}A \vdash (\Lambda X.M_0)(x) \longleftrightarrow N(x) : B$ fails. Suppose $A \equiv \forall X.B$; then $\Gamma \vdash M_0 \Longleftrightarrow N(X) : B$ terminates by induction hypothesis on the combined length of the normal forms of $\Lambda X.M_0$ and N, $\Gamma \vdash (\Lambda X.M_0)(X) \Longleftrightarrow N(X) : B$ terminates by Lemma 14, and so $\Gamma \vdash \Lambda X.M_0 \Longleftrightarrow N : \forall X.B$ terminates.

- $M \equiv M_1(C)$ with M_1 weak-head normal and not canonical, and $N \equiv N_1(D)$ with N_1 weak-head normal and not canonical. If $C \neq D$ then the algorithm fails. Otherwise, $\Gamma \vdash M_1 \longleftrightarrow N_1 : A$ terminates: if it fails or if $A \not\equiv \forall X.B$ then $\Gamma \vdash M_1(C) \longleftrightarrow N_1(C)$ fails, and otherwise $\Gamma \vdash M_1(C) \longleftrightarrow N_1(C) : [C/X]B$ succeeds. The results lift to $\Gamma \vdash M_1(C) \Longleftrightarrow N_1(C) : D$ by Lemma 13.

Lemma 16 (Completeness). *If $\Gamma \vdash M = N : A$ then $\Gamma \vdash M \Longleftrightarrow N : A$.*

Proof. By Church–Rosser and Splitting it suffices to show that if $M \downarrow_{\beta\eta} N$ and $\Gamma \vdash M, N : A$ then $\Gamma \vdash M \Longleftrightarrow N : A$, and if M and N are weak-head normal and not canonical then $\Gamma \vdash M \longleftrightarrow N : A$. We show this by the same induction used in Lemma 15; we consider several cases here.

- $M \equiv \Lambda X.M_0$ and N not canonical. Suppose $\Lambda X.M_0 \downarrow_{\beta\eta} N$ and $\Gamma \vdash \Lambda X.M_0, N : A$. By inversion $\Gamma \vdash M_0 : B$ and $A \equiv \forall X.B$, and so $\Gamma \vdash (\Lambda X.M_0)(X), N(X) : B$ by TyApp. Hence by induction hypothesis $\Gamma \vdash M_0 \Longleftrightarrow N(X) : B$, so $\Gamma \vdash \Lambda X.M_0 \Longleftrightarrow N : \forall X.B$.

- $M \equiv M_1(C)$ with M_1 weak-head normal and not canonical, and $N \equiv N_1(D)$ with N_1 weak-head normal and not canonical. Suppose $\Gamma \vdash M_1(C), N_1(D) : A$. By inversion $\Gamma \vdash M_1 : \forall X.E$, $[C/X]E = A$, $\Gamma \vdash N_1 : \forall X.F$, and $[D/X]F = A$. Furthermore, $M_1 \twoheadrightarrow_w P_1$ and $N_1 \twoheadrightarrow_w P_1$ and $C = D$, so by Subject Reduction $\Gamma \vdash M_1 = P_1 : \forall X.E$ and $\Gamma \vdash N_1 = P_1 : \forall X.F$, so by Uniqueness of Types $\forall X.E = \forall X.F$. Therefore by induction hypothesis $\Gamma \vdash M_1 \longleftrightarrow N_1 : \forall X.E$, so $\Gamma \vdash M_1(C) \longleftrightarrow N_1(C) : [C/X]E$.

5.4 Correctness of the Algorithm

We now show that the algorithm is correct for System F.

Lemma 17 (Correctness).

- If $\Gamma \vdash M \Longleftrightarrow N : A$ and $\Gamma \vdash M, N : A$ then $\Gamma \vdash M = N : A$.
- If $\Gamma \vdash M \longleftrightarrow N : A$, $\Gamma \vdash M : B$ and $\Gamma \vdash N : C$ then $\Gamma \vdash M = N : A$ and $A = B = C$.

Proof. By induction on derivations. We consider several cases:

- $\rightarrow$. We have $\Gamma \vdash M, N : A \rightarrow B$. By Weakening $\Gamma, x{:}A \vdash M, N : A \rightarrow B$, and so by Var and App $\Gamma, x{:}A \vdash M(x), N(x) : B$, and by induction hypothesis $\Gamma, x{:}A \vdash M(x) = N(x) : B$. By λ and Ext $\Gamma \vdash M = N : A \rightarrow B$.
- Var. By inversion $\Gamma \vdash x : B$ implies $B = \Gamma(x)$, and $\Gamma \vdash x = x : \Gamma(x)$.
- TyApp. We have $\Gamma \vdash M(B) : C$, $\Gamma \vdash N(B) : D$, and $\Gamma \vdash M(B) \longleftrightarrow N(B) : [B/X]A$. By inversion $\Gamma \vdash M : \forall X.E$ and $\Gamma \vdash N : \forall X.F$. By induction hypothesis $\Gamma \vdash M = N : \forall X.A$ with $\forall X.A = \forall X.E = \forall X.F$, so $A = E = F$ and $[B/X]A = [B/X]E = [B/X]F$. Hence $\Gamma \vdash M(B) = N(B) : [B/X]A$.

6   Conclusions and Future Work

We have demonstrated that the standard metatheory for the Logical Framework and System F for $\beta\eta$-equality is sufficient to justify algorithms for conversion not immediately modeled by reduction. We used a simple inductive measure to show the completeness and decidability of the algorithms.

A natural extension of this work would be to study the algorithm for conversion for the Calculus of Constructions with $\beta\eta$-equality. We have made substantial progress towards this goal by showing how type dependency can be erased and reconstructed for the Logical Framework, and how polymorphism can be justified. Existing developments using erasure to study metatheory of dependent type theories [5] suggest that the type-directed algorithm for the non-dependent version of a calculus could be used to typecheck the dependently typed version.

One of the primary motivations for Harper and Pfenning's algorithm was singleton types, where Coquand's untyped algorithm may fail to identify equal terms. It seems that it should be possible to extend our technique given the metatheory for $\beta\eta$-equality, but one of the benefits of giving an algorithm directly is that it addresses problems with the reduction relation, such as failure of confluence. This is an interesting area for further research.

Acknowledgments

I would like to thank Bob Harper for stimulating my renewed interest in this topic, and the anonymous referees and Andreas Abel for helpful corrections and comments. I would also like to thank my wife Adriana Compagnoni for her encouragement and support as I was writing this article.

References

1. D. Aspinall. Subtyping with singleton types. In L. Pacholski and J. Tiuryn, editors, *Computer Science Logic*, pages 1–15. Springer, Berlin, 1994.
2. H. Barendregt. Lambda calculi with types. In S. Abramsky, D. M. Gabbai, and T. S. E. Maibaum, editors, *Handbook of Logic in Computer Science*, volume 2. Oxford University Press, 1991.
3. T. Coquand. An algorithm for testing conversion in type theory. In G. Huet and G. Plotkin, editors, *Logical Frameworks*. Cambridge University Press, 1991.
4. H. Geuvers. *Logics and Type Systems*. PhD thesis, Katholieke Universiteit Nijmegen, Sept. 1993.
5. H. Geuvers and M.-J. Nederhof. A modular proof of strong normalization for the calculus of constructions. *Journal of Functional Programming*, 1(2):155–189, Apr. 1991.
6. H. Goguen. *A Typed Operational Semantics for Type Theory*. PhD thesis, University of Edinburgh, Aug. 1994.
7. H. Goguen. A syntactic approach to eta equality in type theory. In *Symposium on Principles of Programming Languages*, Jan. 2005.
8. R. Harper and F. Pfenning. On equivalence and canonical forms in the LF type theory. *ACM Trans. on Computational Logic*, 2004. To appear.
9. A. Salvesen. The Church-Rosser property for pure type systems with $\beta\eta$-reduction, Nov. 1991. Unpublished manuscript.
10. C. A. Stone and R. Harper. Equivalence and singletons. *ACM Transactions on Programming Languages and Systems*, 2004. Submitted.
11. J. Vanderwaart and K. Crary. A simplified account of the metatheory of linear LF. *Electronic Notes in Theoretical Computer Science*, 70(2), 2002. Extended version available as Technical Report CMU-CS-01-154.

On Decidability Within the Arithmetic of Addition and Divisibility

Marius Bozga and Radu Iosif

Verimag/CNRS,
2 Avenue de Vignate,
38610 Gières, France
{bozga, iosif}@imag.fr

Abstract. The arithmetic of natural numbers with addition and divisibility has been shown undecidable as a consequence of the fact that multiplication of natural numbers can be interpreted into this theory, as shown by J. Robinson [14]. The most important decidable subsets of the arithmetic of addition and divisibility are the arithmetic of addition, proved by M. Presburger [13], and the purely existential subset, proved by L. Lipshitz [11]. In this paper we define a new decidable fragment of the form $QzQ_1x_1 \ldots Q_nx_n\varphi(\boldsymbol{x}, z)$ where the only variable allowed to occur to the left of the divisibility sign is z. For this form, called $\mathcal{L}_|^{(1)}$ in the paper, we show the existence of a quantifier elimination procedure which always leads to formulas of Presburger arithmetic. We generalize the $\mathcal{L}_|^{(1)}$ form to $\exists z_1, \ldots \exists z_m Q_1x_1 \ldots Q_nx_n\varphi(\boldsymbol{x}, \boldsymbol{z})$, where the only variables appearing on the left of divisibility are $z_1, \ldots, z_m$. For this form, called $\exists\mathcal{L}_|^{(*)}$, we show decidability of the positive fragment, namely by reduction to the existential theory of the arithmetic with addition and divisibility. The $\mathcal{L}_|^{(1)}$, $\exists\mathcal{L}_|^{(*)}$ fragments were inspired by a real application in the field of program verification. We considered the satisfiability problem for a program logic used for quantitative reasoning about memory shapes, in the case where each record has at most one pointer field. The reduction of this problem to the positive subset of $\exists\mathcal{L}_|^{(*)}$ is sketched in the end of the paper.

1 Introduction

The undecidability of first-order arithmetic of natural numbers occurs as a consequence of Gödel's Incompleteness Theorem [10]. The basic result has been discovered by A. Church [7], and the essential undecidability (undecidability of its every consistent extension) by B. Rosser [15], both as early as 1936. Consequences of this result are the undecidability of the theory of natural numbers with *multiplication and successor function* and with *divisibility and successor function*, both discovered by J. Robinson in [14]. To complete the picture, the existential fragment of the full arithmetic i.e., *Hilbert's Tenth Problem* was proved undecidable by Y. Matiyasevich [12]. The interested reader is further pointed to [1] for an excellent survey of the (un)decidability results in arithmetic.

V. Sassone (Ed.): FOSSACS 2005, LNCS 3441, pp. 425–439, 2005.
© Springer-Verlag Berlin Heidelberg 2005

On the positive side, the decidability of the arithmetic of natural numbers with addition and successor function has been shown by M. Presburger [13], result which has found many applications in modern computer science, especially in the field of automated reasoning. Another important result is the decidability of the *existential* theory of addition and divisibility, proved independently by A. P. Beltyukov [2] and L. Lipshitz [11]. Namely, it is shown that formulas of the form $\exists x_1 \ldots \exists x_n \bigwedge_{i=1}^{K} f_i(\boldsymbol{x})|g_i(\boldsymbol{x})$ are decidable, where f_i, g_i are linear functions over $x_1, \ldots, x_n$ and the symbol $|$ means that each f_i is an integer divisor of g_i when both are interpreted over $\mathbb{N}^n$. The decidability of formulas of the form $\exists x_1 \ldots \exists x_n \varphi(\boldsymbol{x})$, where φ is an open formula in the language $\langle +, |, 0, 1 \rangle$, is stated as a corollary in [11].

Our main result is the decidability of formulas of the form $QzQ_1x_1 \ldots Q_nx_n \varphi(\boldsymbol{x}, z)$ where $Q, Q_1, \ldots, Q_n \in \{\exists, \forall\}$, φ is quantifier-free, and all divisibility propositions are of the form $f(z)|g(\boldsymbol{x}, z)$, with f, g linear functions. This form is called $\mathcal{L}_|^{(1)}$, as there is only one variable that appears on the left of $|$. We show that any formula in this fragment can be evaluated by applying quantifier elimination to the open formula $Q_1x_1 \ldots Q_nx_n \varphi(\boldsymbol{x}, z)$, the result being a Presburger formula in which z occurs free. This fact is somewhat surprising, since the $\mathcal{L}_|^{(1)}$ fragment allows to encode queries apparently beyond the scope of Presburger arithmetic such as: given a Presburger formula φ with n free variables, is it true that all values $v_1, \ldots, v_n$ which satisfy φ, are altogether *relatively prime*?

Second, a generalization is made by allowing multiple existentially quantified variables occur to the left of the divisibility sign that is, formulas of the form $\exists z_1 \ldots \exists z_n Q_1x_1 \ldots Q_mx_m \varphi(\boldsymbol{x}, \boldsymbol{z})$, for quantifier-free φ, where the only divisibility propositions are of the form $f(\boldsymbol{z})|g(\boldsymbol{x}, \boldsymbol{z})$. Using essentially the same method as in the case of $n = 1$, we show decidability of the *positive* form of the $\exists \mathcal{L}_|^{(*)}$ subset i.e., in which no divisibility proposition occurs under negation.

However the result of quantifier elimination for the positive $\exists \mathcal{L}_|^{(*)}$ fragment cannot be expressed in Presburger arithmetic, but in the existential fragment of $\langle \mathbb{N}, +, |, 0, 1 \rangle$. This result is also the best possible in the sense that, if negation of divisibility propositions is allowed, the $\exists \mathcal{L}_|^{(*)}$ fragment is undecidable. The worst-case complexity of the quantifier elimination method is non-elementary and the decision complexity for the alternation-free fragments of $\mathcal{L}_|^{(1)}$, $\exists \mathcal{L}_|^{(*)+}$ are bounded by a triple exponential.

We applied the decidability result for the positive $\exists \mathcal{L}_|^{(*)}$ fragment to a concrete problem in the field of program verification. More precisely, we consider a specification logic used to reason about the shape of the recursive data structures generated by imperative programs that handle pointers. This logic, called *alias logic with counters* [5] is interpreted over deterministic labeled graphs. It allows to express linear arithmetic relations between the lengths of certain paths within a graph. The satisfiability problem has been shown undecidable over unrestricted dag, and implicitly, graph models, but decidability can be shown over tree models. We complete the picture by showing decidability of this logic over structures composed of an arbitrary finite number of lists. The difficulty w.r.t trees consists in the fact that lists may have loops, which introduce divisibility constraints. However, as it is shown, the problem remains within the bounds of the positive $\exists \mathcal{L}_|^{(*)}$ fragment of $\langle \mathbb{N}, +, |, 0, 1 \rangle$. Despite its catastrophic complexity upper bound, this result enables, in principle, the automatic verification of quantitative properties for an important class of programs that manipulate list structures only.

2 Preliminaries

In this paper we work with first-order logic over the language $\langle +, |, 0, 1 \rangle$. A formula in this language is interpreted over $\mathbb{N}$ in the standard way: $+$ denotes the addition of natural numbers, $|$ is the divisibility relation, and $0, 1$ are the constants zero and one. In particular, we consider that $0|0$, $0 \nmid n$ and $n|0$, for all $n \in \mathbb{N} \setminus \{0\}$. In the following we will intentionally use the same notation for a mathematical constant symbol and its interpretation, as we believe, no confusion will arise from that. For space reasons all proofs are included in [4] .

The results in this paper rely on two theorems from elementary number theory. The first one is the well-known Chinese Remainder Theorem (CRT) [9] and the second one is a (prized) conjecture proposed by P. Erdös in 1963 and proved by R. Crittenden and C. Vanden Eynden in 1969 [6]. The CRT says that: $\exists x \bigwedge_{i=1}^K m_i|(x - r_i) \leftrightarrow \bigwedge_{1 \le i,j \le K} (m_i, m_j)|(r_i - r_j)$, where $m_i \in \mathbb{N}, r_i \in \mathbb{Z}$ and (a, b) denotes the greatest common divisor of a and b [1]. The CRT can be slightly generalized as follows:

Corollary 1. *For any integers $m_i \in \mathbb{N}$ and $a_i \in \mathbb{Z} \setminus \{0\}, r_i \in \mathbb{Z}$ with $1 \le i \le K$ we have:*

$$\exists x \bigwedge_{i=1}^K m_i|(a_i x - r_i) \leftrightarrow \bigwedge_{1 \le i,j \le K} (a_i m_j, a_j m_i)|(a_i r_j - a_j r_i) \wedge \bigwedge_{i=1}^K (a_i, m_i)|r_i$$

Usually the CRT is used as a means of solving systems of linear congruences. A linear congruence is an equation of the form $ax \equiv b \mod m$, for some $a, b \in \mathbb{Z}$ and $m \in \mathbb{N} \setminus \{0\}$. Such an equation is solvable if and only if $(a, m)|b$. If the equation admits one solution y, then the solutions are given by the arithmetic progression $\{x \equiv y \mod \frac{m}{(a,m)}\}$. The second Theorem, stated as a conjecture by Erdös, is the following:

Theorem 1 ([6]). *Let $a_1, \ldots, a_n \in \mathbb{Z}, b_1, \ldots, b_n \in \mathbb{N} \setminus \{0\}$. Suppose there exists an integer x_0 satisfying none of the congruences: $\{x \equiv a_i \mod b_i\}_{i=1}^n$. Then there is such an x_0 among $1, 2, 3, \ldots, 2^n$.*

We shall use this theorem rather in its positive form i.e., n arithmetic progressions $\{a_i + b_i \mathbb{Z}\}_{i=1}^n$ cover $\mathbb{Z}$ if and only if they cover the set $1, 2, 3, \ldots, 2^n$.

---

[1] The second part of the Theorem, expressing the solutions x to the system of linear congruences on the left hand of the equivalence is not used in this paper.

If we interpret a linear congruence over $\mathbb{Z}$ instead of $\mathbb{N}$ we obtain that the solutions form a progression containing both infinitely many positive and negative numbers. In other words, $ax \equiv b \mod m$ has a solution in $\mathbb{N}$ if and only if it has a solution in $\mathbb{Z}$. The same reasoning applies to the CRT, since the solution of a system of linear congruences is the intersection of a finite number of progressions, hence a progression itself. As for Erdös' Conjecture, we can prove that it is true for positive integers only [4] . In conclusion, the above theorems hold for $\mathbb{Z}$ as well as they do for $\mathbb{N}$. In general, all results in this paper apply the same to integer and natural numbers, therefore we will not make the distinction unless necessary[2].

3   Decidability of $\mathcal{L}_|^{(1)}$

In this section we show that the $\mathcal{L}_|^{(1)}$ class can be effectively reduced to the $\langle \mathbb{N}, +, 0, 1 \rangle$ theory. Mostly for clarity, we will work first with a simplified form, in which each divisibility atomic proposition is of the form $z|f(\boldsymbol{x}, z)$, and then we generalize to propositions of the form $h(z)|f(\boldsymbol{x}, z)$, with f, h linear functions. Hence we start explaining the reduction of formulas of the following simple form:

$$Q_1 x_1 \ldots Q_n x_n \bigvee_{i=1}^{N} \left(\bigwedge_{j=1}^{M_i} z|f_{ij}(\boldsymbol{x}, z) \wedge \bigwedge_{j=1}^{P_i} z \nmid g_{ij}(\boldsymbol{x}, z) \wedge \varphi_i(\boldsymbol{x}, z) \right) \qquad (1)$$

where f_{ij} and g_{ij} are linear functions with integer coefficients and φ_i, are Presburger formulas with $\boldsymbol{x}$ and z free.

As Presburger arithmetic has quantifier elimination [13], we can assume w.l.o.g. that $\varphi_i(\boldsymbol{x}, z) \equiv \bigvee_k \bigwedge_l \exists t_{kl} \, t_{kl} \geq 0 \wedge h_{kl}(\boldsymbol{x}, z) + t_{kl} = 0 \wedge \bigwedge_l c_{kl}|h'_{kl}(\boldsymbol{x}, z)$, with h_{kl}, h'_{kl} linear functions with integer coefficients, and c_{kl} positive integer constants. Suppose now that x_m, for some $1 \leq m \leq n$, appears in some $h_{kl}(\boldsymbol{x}) = a_{kl} x_m + b_{kl}(\boldsymbol{x}, z)$ with coefficient $a_{kl} \neq 0$. We multiply through with a_{kl} by replacing all formulas of the form $h(\boldsymbol{x}, z) + t = 0$ with $a_{kl} h(\boldsymbol{x}, z) + a_{kl} t = 0$, $c|h'(\boldsymbol{x}, z)$ with $a_{kl} c|a_{kl} h'(\boldsymbol{x}, z)$, and $z|f(\boldsymbol{x}, z)$ with $a_{kl} z|a_{kl} f(\boldsymbol{x}, z)$. Then we eliminate $a_{kl} x_m$ by substituting it with $-b_{kl}(\boldsymbol{x}, z) - t_{kl}$, which does not contain x_m. We repeat the above steps until all x variables occurring within linear equations have been eliminated[3]. The resulting formula is of the form:

$$Q_1 x_1 \ldots Q_n x_n \bigvee_{i=1}^{N} \left(\bigwedge_{j=1}^{M_i} z_{ij}|f_{ij}(\boldsymbol{x}, z) \wedge \bigwedge_{j=1}^{P_i} z_{ij} \nmid g_{ij}(\boldsymbol{x}, z) \wedge \psi_i(z) \right) \qquad (2)$$

---

[2] For instance, it is not clear whether one can define the order relation in the existential fragment of $\langle \mathbb{Z}, +, |, 0, 1 \rangle$, hence we will work with $\langle \mathbb{Z}, +, |, \leq, 0, 1 \rangle$ instead of it, whenever needed.

[3] Notice that the constraint $t_{kl} \geq 0$ is trivially satisfied if we work with $\mathbb{N}$, otherwise, for $\mathbb{Z}$, we can use the fact that the solutions to a linear congruence system form a progression that contains infinitely many positive and negative numbers.

where each z_{ij} is either $a_{ij}z$, $a_{ij} \in \mathbb{N} \setminus \{0\}$, or a constant $c_{ij} \in \mathbb{N}$ and $\psi_i(z)$ are Presburger formulas in which z occurs free. In the rest of the section we show how to reduce an arbitrary formula of the form (2) to an equivalent Presburger formula in two phases: first, we successively eliminate the quantifiers $Q_n x_n, \ldots, Q_1 x_1$ and second, we define the resulting solved form into Presburger arithmetic.

Quantifier Elimination

We consider three cases, based on the type of the last quantifier Q_n ($\exists, \forall$) and the sign of the divisibility propositions occurring in the formula (positive, negative). Namely, we treat the cases existential positive, universal positive and universal mixed. The remaining case (existential mixed) can be dealt with by first negating and then applying the universal mixed case.

The Existential Positive Case. In this case the formula (2) becomes:

$$\bigvee_{i=1}^{N} \exists x_n \bigwedge_{j=1}^{M_i} z_{ij} | f_{ij}(\boldsymbol{x}, z) \wedge \psi_i(z) \tag{3}$$

W.l.o.g. we can assume that $M_i \neq 0$ for all $1 \leq i \leq N$, and that $f_{ij}(\boldsymbol{x}, z) = a_{ij}x_n + g_{ij}(\boldsymbol{x}', z)$, where $\boldsymbol{x}' = \boldsymbol{x} \setminus \{x_n\}$, and with all coefficients $a_{ij} \neq 0$. Applying Corollary 1 to the i-th disjunct, we obtain (the original i subscript has been omitted): $\bigwedge_{1 \leq k, l \leq M}(a_k z_l, a_l z_k) | (a_k g_l - a_l g_k) \wedge \bigwedge_{1 \leq k \leq M}(a_k, z_k) | g_k \wedge \psi(z)$. In the resulting formula we have three types of divisibility propositions, which we can write equivalently as:

- $(a_i a' z, a_j a'' z) | (a_i g_j - a_j g_i)$: $(a_i a', a_j a'') z | (a_i g_j - a_j g_i)$
- $(a_i, az) | g_i$: $\bigvee_{r=0}^{a_i - 1} (az \equiv r) \mod a_i \wedge (a_i, r) | g_i$
- $(a_i c_j, a_j c_i) | (a_i g_j - a_j g_i)$ and $(a_i, c_i) | g_i$ are left untouched.

We have used the equivalence $(az, c) | f \leftrightarrow \bigvee_{r=0}^{c-1} az \equiv r \mod c \wedge (r, c) | f$. Now $az \equiv r \mod c$ is a Presburger formula with z free. The formula can now be easily written back in the form (3), with $n - 1$ variables of type x_i, instead of n. The size of the resulting formula (in DNF) is at most quadratic in the size of the input.

The Universal Positive Case. It is now convenient to consider the matrix of (2) in conjunctive normal form. In this case the formula (2) becomes:

$$\bigwedge_{i=1}^{P} \forall x_n \bigvee_{j=1}^{Q_i} z_{ij} | f_{ij}(\boldsymbol{x}, z) \vee \psi_i(z) \tag{4}$$

W.l.o.g. we can assume that $f_{ij}(\boldsymbol{x}, z) = a_{ij}x_n + b_{ij}(\boldsymbol{x}', z)$, where $\boldsymbol{x}' = \boldsymbol{x} \setminus \{x_n\}$, and with all coefficients $a_{ij} \neq 0$. In each i-conjunct, the union of Q_i arithmetic progressions $\{x \mid a_{ij}x \equiv -b_{ij} \mod z_{ij}\}_{j=1}^{Q_i}$ covers $\mathbb{N}$. By Theorem 1 it is sufficient (and trivially necessary) to cover only the first 2^{Q_i} values. The equivalent form, with x_n eliminated, is the following: $\bigwedge_{i=1}^{P} \bigwedge_{t=1}^{2^{Q_i}} \bigvee_{j=1}^{Q_i} z_{ij}|a_{ij}t + b_{ij} \vee \psi_i(z)$. The size of the resulting formula (in CNF this time) is simply exponential in the size of the input.

The Universal Mixed Case. Let us consider again the formula (2) with the matrix written in conjunctive normal form:

$$\bigwedge_{i=1}^{P} \forall x_n \left(\bigvee_{j=1}^{Q_i} z_{ij}|f_{ij}(\boldsymbol{x}, z) \vee \bigvee_{j=1}^{R_i} z_{ij} \nmid g_{ij}(\boldsymbol{x}, z) \right) \vee \psi_i(z) \tag{5}$$

Again, we can assume w.l.o.g. that x_n occurs in each f_{ij}, g_{ij} with a non-zero coefficient. Also Q_i, R_i can be considered greater than zero for all $1 \leq i \leq n$, the other cases being treated in the previous. Each i-conjunct, omitting the i subscript, is: $\forall x_n \left(\bigwedge_{j=1}^{R} z_j|g_j(\boldsymbol{x}, z) \rightarrow \bigvee_{j=1}^{Q} z_j|f_j(\boldsymbol{x}, z) \right) \vee \psi(z)$. The parenthesized formula can be understood as coverage of an arithmetic progression by a finite union of arithmetic progressions. Assuming $g_j(\boldsymbol{x}, z) = a_j x_n + b_j(\boldsymbol{x}, z)$ with $a_j \neq 0$, let us compute the period of the set $\{x : \bigwedge_{j=1}^{R} z_j|g_j(\boldsymbol{x}, z)\} = \bigcap_{j=1}^{R}\{x : a_j x \equiv b_j \mod z_j\}$. Each linear congruence $a_j x \equiv b_j \mod z_j$ has a periodic solution with period $\frac{z_j}{(z_j, a_j)}$. The period of the intersection is the least common multiple of the individual periods i.e., $\left[\left\{\frac{z_j}{(z_j, a_j)}\right\}_{j=1}^{R}\right]$. Since all z_j's are either $a_j'z$, for $a_j' \in \mathbb{N}\backslash\{0\}$ or some constants c_j, we can simplify the expression of the period to the form $\frac{z k_j}{(z, l_j)}$ for some (effectively computable) constant values $k_j, l_j \in \mathbb{N} \backslash \{0\}$. Now we can apply Theorem 1 and eliminate $\forall x_n$ from the i-th conjunct of the formula (5). Supposing $f_j(\boldsymbol{x}, z) = c_j x_n + d_j(\boldsymbol{x}, z)$ for some $c_j, d_j \in \mathbb{Z}, c_j \neq 0$, the result is: $\neg \exists y \bigwedge_{j=1}^{R} z_j|a_j y + b_j(\boldsymbol{x}, z) \vee \exists y \bigwedge_{j=1}^{R} z_j|a_j y + b_j(\boldsymbol{x}, z) \wedge \bigwedge_{t=1}^{2^{Q}} \bigvee_{j=1}^{Q} z_j|c_j\left(y + \frac{z k_j t}{(z, l_j)}\right) + d_j(\boldsymbol{x}, z)$. The first disjunct is for the trivial case, in which the set $\{x : \bigwedge_{j=1}^{R} z_j|g_j(\boldsymbol{x}, z)\}$ is empty, while the second disjunct assumes the existence of an element y of this set and encodes the equivalent condition of Theorem 1, namely that the first 2^Q elements of this set, starting with y, must be covered by the union of Q progressions. Now y can be eliminated from the above formula using CRT, as in the existential positive case, treated in the previous. Notice that, in addition to the existential positive case, we have introduced a subterm of the form $\frac{z k}{(z, l)}$ within the functions f_j. This is reflected in the definition of the solved form, in the next paragraph. As in the previous case, the size of the output formula is simply exponential in the size of the input formula.

The Solved Form. The three cases from the previous section can be successively applied to eliminate all quantified variables $Q_1 x_1, \ldots Q_n x_n$ from (2). For any formula of type (2), the result of this transformation belongs to the following *solved form*:

$$\bigvee_{i=1}^{N} \bigwedge_{j=1}^{M_i} a_{ij} z | f_{ij}(z) \wedge \bigwedge_{j=1}^{P_i} b_{ij} z \nmid g_{ij}(z) \wedge \psi_i(z) \tag{6}$$

where a_{ij} and b_{ij} are positive integers, f_{ij} and g_{ij} are linear combinations of terms of the form $\frac{z}{(z,k)}$ with $k \in \mathbb{N} \setminus \{0\}^4$ and ψ_i are Presburger formulas in z.

We will consider the expressions $az|f(z)$, where a is one of a_{ij}, b_{ij} and f is one of f_{ij}, g_{ij}. Let $f(z) = \Sigma_{i=1}^n \frac{zc_i}{(z,k_i)} + c_0$. We write $az|f(z)$, equivalently as: $\bigvee_{(d_1,\ldots,d_n) \in \operatorname{div}(k_1) \times \ldots \times \operatorname{div}(k_n)} \bigwedge_{i=1}^n (z, k_i) = d_i \wedge aDz|z\Sigma_{i=1}^n c_i D_i + c_0 D$, where $D = \Pi_{i=1}^n d_i$, $D_i = \frac{D}{d_i}$ and $\operatorname{div}(k)$ denotes the set of divisors of k. Notice that the last conjunct of each clause implies that $z|c_0 D$, i.e., $z \in \operatorname{div}(c_0 D)$. The entire formula is equivalent to: $\bigvee_{(d,d_1,\ldots,d_n) \in \operatorname{div}(c_0 D) \times \operatorname{div}(k_1) \times \ldots \times \operatorname{div}(k_n)} \bigwedge_{i=1}^n (d, k_i) = d_i \wedge aDd|d\Sigma_{i=1}^n c_i D_i + c_0 D$. Each divisibility proposition of the solved form can thus be evaluated. The solved form is then either trivially false or equivalent to a disjunction of the form $\psi_{i_1} \vee \ldots \vee \psi_{i_n}$, for some $1 \leq i_1, \ldots, i_n \leq N$. The latter is obviously a Presburger formula.

Block Elimination of Universal Quantifiers

This section presents results that are used in a generalization of the universal positive and universal mixed cases, to perform the elimination of an entire *block* of successive universal quantifiers with simple exponential complexity. A set of vectors $(x_1, \ldots, x_n) \in \mathbb{Z}^n$ satisfying the linear congruence $a_1 x_1 + \ldots + a_n x_n + b \equiv 0$ mod m is called a n-dimensional arithmetic progression. The block quantifier elimination problem is equivalent to the coverage of an n-dimensional arithmetic progression by a finite union of n-dimensional progressions. The latter can be solved in simple exponential time, as shown by the following consequence of Theorem 1:

Corollary 2. *Let $a_{ij} \in \mathbb{Z}, b_i \in \mathbb{Z}, m_i \in \mathbb{N}$, $1 \leq i \leq k$, $1 \leq j \leq n$. The set of progressions $\{\Sigma_{j=1}^n a_{ij} x_j + b_i \equiv 0 \mod m_i\}_{i=1}^k$ covers $\mathbb{Z}^n$ if and only if it covers the set $\{1 \ldots 2^k\}^n$.*

This takes care of the universal positive case. In the universal mixed case we need to effectively compute the period of the intersection of any given number of n-dimensional progressions. Let $\mathcal{L}\mathbb{Z}[z]$ denote the monoid of first degree (linear) polynomials in z, with integer coefficients. Since our problem is parameterized by z, we consider a system of progressions of the form $\bigwedge_{i=1}^k \Sigma_{j=1}^n a_{ij} x_j \equiv 0 \mod z$, with solutions from $\mathcal{L}\mathbb{Z}[z]$. We need to show that this set is a finitely generated monoid, and moreover, that its base is effectively computable. The following theorem gives the result:

Theorem 2. *Let $a_i \in \mathbb{Z}$, $1 \leq i \leq n$, $n > 1$.*

1. *The set of integer solutions to the equation $\Sigma_{i=1}^n a_i x_i = 0$ is a finitely generated submonoid M of $(\mathbb{Z}^n, +)$. It is moreover possible to construct a base of M of size $n - 1$.*

---

4 Notice that we can also write z as $\frac{z}{(z,1)}$.

2. *The set of integer coefficient solutions to the congruence $\sum_{i=1}^{n} a_i x_i \equiv 0$ mod z is a finitely generated submonoid $M[z]$ of $(\mathcal{L}\mathbb{Z}^n[z], +)$. It is moreover possible to construct a base of $M[z]$ of the form $\{v_1, \ldots, v_{n-1}, z v_1, \ldots, z v_{n-1}, z v_n\}$, with $v_1, \ldots, v_n \in \mathbb{Z}^n$.*

Theorem 2 gives us the means to characterize the solution of a system of n-dimensional progressions, parameterized by z. This is done inductively. Suppose that we have already computed a base $\{v_1, \ldots, v_{n-1}, z v_1, \ldots, z v_{n-1}, z v_n\}$ for the system $\bigwedge_{i=1}^{k-1} \sum_{j=1}^{n} a_{ij} x_j \equiv 0 \mod z$, according to the second point of Theorem 2. We are now looking after a base generating the solutions to $\bigwedge_{i=1}^{k} \sum_{j=1}^{n} a_{ij} x_j \equiv 0 \mod z$. The solutions to the system are of the form $\boldsymbol{x} = \sum_{j=1}^{n-1} \alpha_j v_j + z \sum_{j=1}^{n} \beta_j v_j$ with $\alpha_j, \beta_j \in \mathbb{Z}$. Introducing those values into $\sum_{i=1}^{n} a_{ki} x_i \equiv 0 \mod z$, we obtain that $\sum_{i=1}^{n} a_{ki} \left(\sum_{j=1}^{n-1} \alpha_j v_j^{(i)} + z \sum_{j=1}^{n} \beta_j v_j^{(i)} \right) \equiv 0 \mod z$ must be the case, where $v^{(i)}$ denotes the i-th component of a vector v. This is furthermore equivalent to $\sum_{i=1}^{n} a_{ki} \sum_{j=1}^{n-1} \alpha_j v_j^{(i)} \equiv 0 \mod z$, or to the system with unknowns α_j: $\sum_{j=1}^{n-1} \left(\sum_{i=1}^{n} a_{ki} v_j^{(i)} \right) \alpha_j \equiv 0 \mod z$. According to Theorem 2, the solutions of the latter system are generated by a base $\{u_1, \ldots, u_{n-2}, z u_1, \ldots, z u_{n-1}\}$. Thus the solutions of the original system $\bigwedge_{i=1}^{k} \sum_{j=1}^{n} a_{ij} x_j \equiv 0 \mod z$ are of the form $\boldsymbol{x} = \sum_{l=1}^{n-2} \gamma_l \sum_{j=1}^{n-1} u_l^{(j)} v_j + z \sum_{l=1}^{n-1} \delta_l \sum_{j=1}^{n} u_l^{(j)} v_j$, with $\gamma_l, \delta_l \in \mathbb{Z}$. The block quantifier elimination can be now performed along the same lines of the universal mixed case, discussed in the previous.

Extending to the entire $\mathcal{L}_|^{(1)}$

Let us now revisit the quantifier elimination procedure for the general case, where the divisibility propositions are of the form $f(z)|g(\boldsymbol{x}, z)$, with f, g linear functions. The only two differences w.r.t. the case $f(z) = z$ are encountered when applying the existential positive and the universal mixed cases.

In the existential positive case, subsequent to the application of the CRT, we need to simplify formulas of the following two forms, where $a_i \in \mathbb{N}$ and $f_i(z), f_j(z), h_{ij}(\boldsymbol{x}, z), h_i(\boldsymbol{x}, z)$ are arbitrary linear functions:

1. $(f_i, f_j)|h_{ij}$. We distinguish two cases:
   - if either f_i divides f_j or f_j divides f_i in terms of polynomial division, then $(f_i, f_j) = f_i$ or $(f_i, f_j) = f_j$, respectively. Let us consider the first situation, the other one being symmetric. We obtain, equivalently, $f_i|r$, where r is the constant polynomial representing the remainder of h_{ij} divided by f_i. This can be expressed as a finite disjunction in Presburger arithmetic.
   - otherwise, (f_i, f_j) can be written equivalently as (g_{ij}, k) where g_{ij} is a linear function in z and $k \in \mathbb{Z}$, by applying Euclid's g.c.d. algorithm in the polynomial ring $\mathbb{Z}[z]$. We have reduced the problem to case 2.

2. $(f_i, a_i)|h_i$ is equivalent to $\bigvee_{0 \leq r < a_i} f_i \equiv r \mod a_i \wedge (r, a_i)|h_i$.

In the universal mixed case, subsequent to the application of Erdös Conjecture, we obtain subterms of the form $\pi = \left[\{\frac{h_j}{(h_j,a_j)}\}_{j=1}^{R}\right]$ occurring within atomic propositions of the form $h_i|a_i\pi + g_i$. where $h_i(z), h_j(z)$ and $g_i(x,z)$ are linear functions. The first step is to substitute (h_j, a_j) for constants i.e. $\pi = \left[\{\frac{h_j}{d_j}\}_{j=1}^{R}\right]$, for some $d_j \in \text{div}(a_j)$. The equivalent form is now $\pi = \frac{\left[\{D_j h_j\}_{j=1}^{R}\right]}{D} = \frac{\Pi_{j=1}^{R} D_j h_j}{D\left(\{D_j h_j\}_{j=1}^{R}\right)}$, where $D = \Pi_{j=1}^{R} d_j$ and $D_j = \frac{D}{d_j}$. Now the denominator expression is the g.c.d. of a number of linear functions in z, and can be reduced either to a linear function or to a constant, chosen from a set of divisors, like in the existential positive case above. Hence π is a polynomial from $\mathbb{Q}[z]$, of degree at most R. Every atomic proposition involving π can be put in the form $h(z)|p(z)$, where $h, p \in \mathbb{Z}[z]$ (just multiply both sides with the l.c.m of all denominators in π). We consider the following two cases:

- if z occurs in h with a non-zero coefficient, let r be the remainder of p divided by h, the degree of r being zero. Hence $h(z)|r$, which is written as a finite disjunction in Presburger arithmetic.
- otherwise, h is a constant $c \in \mathbb{Z}$. We have $p(z) \equiv 0 \mod c$, which is further equivalent to $\bigvee_{r \in \{0,\ldots,|c|-1\}} z \equiv r \mod c \wedge p(r) \equiv 0 \mod c$

Example. It is time to illustrate our method by means of an example. Let us find all positive integers z that satisfy the formula $\forall x \forall y\ z|12x + 4y \rightarrow z|3x + 12y$. To eliminate y we apply the universal mixed case and obtain:

$$\forall x \left[\neg\exists y\ z|12x + 4y \vee \exists y\ z|12x + 4y \wedge z|3x + 12y \wedge z|3x + 12(y + \frac{z}{(z,4)})\right]$$

By an application of the CRT, $\exists y\ z|12x + 4y$ is equivalent to $(z,4)|12x$ which is trivially true, since $(z,4)|4$ and $4|12x$. Moreover, if $z|3x + 12y$, then $z|3x + 12y + 12\frac{z}{(z,4)}$ is equivalent to $z|12\frac{z}{(z,4)}$, which is also trivially true. Hence, the formula can be simplified down to: $\forall x \exists y\ z|12x + 4y \wedge z|3x + 12y$ By an application of the CRT we obtain: $\forall x\ z|33x \wedge (z,4)|12x \wedge (z,12)|3x$ which, after trivial simplifications, is equivalent to $z|33 \wedge (z,12)|3$, leading to $z \in \{1, 3, 11, 33\}$.   □

Complexity Assessment. The quantifier elimination has non-elementary worst case complexity. Let φ be any formula of $\mathcal{L}_1^{(1)}$. Since the elimination of an existential quantifier in the positive case can be done in time $|\varphi|^2$, and the elimination of any block of n universal quantifiers in time $2^{n|\varphi|}$, the only reason for non-elementary blow-up lies within the alternation of existential and universal quantifiers. Even in the positive case, alternation of quantifiers causes a formula to be translated from disjunctive to conjunctive normal form or viceversa, this fact alone introducing an exponential blow-up. However it is clear that the alternation-free subset of $\mathcal{L}_1^{(1)}$ can be dealt with in at most simple exponential time. the whole decision procedure takes at most $2^{m2^{\cdot^{\cdot^{\cdot^{2^{m|\varphi|}}}}}\}2d}$ time, where d is the alternation depth of φ and m the maximum size of an alternation-free quantifier block.

4   Decidability of $\exists \mathcal{L}_|^{(*)+}$

After performing the preliminary substitution of variables x_i that occur together with some z_j in a linear constraint, we reduce a formula of the $\exists \mathcal{L}_|^{(*)}$ class to the following form:

$$\exists z_1 \ldots \exists z_n Q_1 x_1 \ldots Q_m x_m \bigvee_{i=1}^{N} \Big(\bigwedge_{j=1}^{M_i} f_{ij}(\boldsymbol{z})|g_{ij}(\boldsymbol{x},\boldsymbol{z}) \wedge \bigwedge_{j=1}^{P_i} f'_{ij}(\boldsymbol{z}) \nmid g'_{ij}(\boldsymbol{x},\boldsymbol{z}) \wedge \varphi_i(\boldsymbol{z}) \Big)$$

where $f_{ij}, g_{ij}, f'_{ij}, g'_{ij}$ are all linear functions. In this section we reduce an arbitrary *positive* $\exists \mathcal{L}_|^{(*)}$ formula to an existentially quantified formula of $\langle \mathbb{N}, +, |, 0, 1 \rangle$. In other words, we suppose that $P_i = 0$, for all $1 \leq i \leq n$.

We are going to apply essentially the same quantifier elimination method from Section 3 and analyze its outcome in case of multiple variables of type z_i. Let us have a look first at the existential case i.e., $Q_m \equiv \exists$. Application of the CRT to eliminate x_m yields atomic propositions of the form $(f_1, f_2)|g_{12}$, where $g_{12}(\boldsymbol{x}, \boldsymbol{z})$ is a linear function. On the other hand, in the universal case $(Q_m \equiv \forall)$ we just substitute x_m by a constant quantified over a finite range $\{1, \ldots, 2^{M_i}\}$ for some $1 \leq i \leq N$. Since negation does not involve divisibility propositions, the universal mixed case does not apply. The solved form is, in this case: $\bigvee_{i=1}^{N} \bigwedge_{j=1}^{M_i} (\{f_k(\boldsymbol{z})\}_{k=1}^{P_{ij}})|h_{ij}(\boldsymbol{z}) \wedge \psi_i(\boldsymbol{z})$, where f_k and h_{ij} are linear functions over $\boldsymbol{z}$. Since the g.c.d. operator is left-right associative, we can apply CRT and write each divisibility proposition $(f_1, \ldots, f_P)|h$ in the equivalent form: $\exists y_1 \ldots \exists y_{P-1} \, f_1|y_1 - h \wedge \bigwedge_{i=2}^{P-1} f_i|y_i - y_{i-1} \wedge f_P|y_{P-1}$. Since $z_1, \ldots, z_n$ occur existentially quantified, we have obtained that $\exists \mathcal{L}_|^{(*)+}$ can be reduced to $\langle \mathbb{N}, +, |, 0, 1 \rangle^{\exists}$, hence it is decidable[5]. The worst-case complexity bound for the quantifier elimination is, as in the case for $\mathcal{L}_|^{(1)}$, non-elementary. According to [11], the decision complexity for the underlying theory is bounded by $2^{(N+1)^{8N^3}}$, where N is the maximum between $|\varphi|$ and the maximum absolute value of the coefficients in φ[6].

To show the undecidability of the $\exists \mathcal{L}_|^{(*)}$ fragment with negation, we define the existential subset of the $\langle \mathbb{N}, +, [], 0, 1 \rangle$ theory into it. This is done using the classical definition of the l.c.m. relation $[x, y] = z$ [14]: $\forall t \, x|t \wedge y|t \leftrightarrow z|t$. To show undecidability of the latter, we use that, for $x \neq 0$, $x^2 = y \leftrightarrow y + x = [x, x+1]$ to define the perfect square relation[7], and $(x+y)^2 - (x-y)^2 = 4xy$ to define multiplication. The rest is an application of the undecidability of Hilbert's Tenth Problem [12].

---

[5] When interpreting $\exists \mathcal{L}_|^{(*)}$ over $\mathbb{Z}$ we assume the $\leq$ relation, since the decidability proof from [11] uses orderings of variables.

[6] Actually this expression is the result of some simplifications, the original expression being rather intricate.

[7] If we interpret over $\mathbb{Z}$, we use $-y - x = [x, x+1]$ for negative x.

5   Application to the Verification of Programs with Lists

The results in this paper are used to solve a decision problem related to the verification of programs that manipulate dynamic memory structures, specified by recursive data types. Examples include lists, trees, and, in general, graphs. We are interested in establishing *shape invariants* such as e.g. absence of cycles and data sharing, but also by *quantitative properties* involving lengths of paths within the heap of a program. For instance, consider a list reversal program that works by keeping two disjoint lists and moving pointers successively from one list to another. A shape invariant of this program is that, given a non-cyclic list as input, the two lists are always disjoint. A quantitative invariant is that the sum of their lengths must equal the length of the input list.

In order to express shape and quantitative properties of the dynamic memory of programs performing selector updating operations, we have defined a specification logic called *alias logic with counters* [5]. Formulas in this logic are interpreted over finite directed graphs with edges labeled with symbols from a finite alphabet Σ. Formally such a graph is a triple $G = \langle N, V, E \rangle$, where N is the set of nodes, $E : N \times \Sigma \to N$ is the *deterministic* edge relation, $V \subseteq N$ is a designated set of nodes called *variables* on which the requirement is that for no $n \in N, \sigma \in \Sigma$: $E(n, \sigma) \in V$. In other words, the graph is *rooted* on V. A *path* in the graph is a finite sequence $\pi = v\sigma_1\sigma_2 \ldots \in V\Sigma^*$. Since the graph is deterministic, every path may lead to at most one node. Let $\widehat{\pi}$ denote this node, if defined. We say that two paths π_1 and π_2 are *aliased* if $\widehat{\pi_1}, \widehat{\pi_2}$ are defined and $\widehat{\pi_1} = \widehat{\pi_2}$. A *quantitative path* is a sequence $\pi(\boldsymbol{x}) = v\sigma_1^{f_1}\sigma_2^{f_2} \ldots$, where $\boldsymbol{x}$ is a finite set of variables, interpreted over $\mathbb{N}$, and $f_1, f_2, \ldots$ are linear functions on $\boldsymbol{x}$. Given an interpretation of variables $\iota : \boldsymbol{x} \to \mathbb{N}$, the interpretation of a quantitative path π, denoted as $\iota(\pi)$, is the result of evaluating the functions $f_1, f_2, \ldots$ and replacing each occurrence of σ^k by the word $\sigma \ldots \sigma$, repeated k times.

The logic of *aliases with counters* is the first-order additive arithmetic of natural numbers, to which we add alias propositions of the form $\pi_1(\boldsymbol{x}) \diamond \pi_2(\boldsymbol{x})$. Given an interpretation of variables, an alias proposition $\pi_1 \diamond \pi_2$ holds in a graph if the interpretations of the quantified paths involved are defined and they "meet" in the same node: $\widehat{\iota(\pi_1)} = \widehat{\iota(\pi_2)}$. The satisfaction of a closed formula φ on a graph G, denoted as $G \models \varphi$, is defined recursively on the syntax of φ, as usual.

We have studied the satisfiability problem for this logic and found that it is undecidable on unrestricted graph and dag models, and decidable on tree models. For details, the interested reader is pointed to [5]. The problem in case of simply linked lists is surprisingly more difficult than for trees, due to the presence of loops. However, we can show decidability now, with the aid of the positive fragment of the theory $\exists \mathcal{L}_{|}^{(*)}$.

Since all memory structures considered are lists, we can assume that they are implemented using only one selector field. In other words, the label alphabet can be assumed to be a singleton $\Sigma = \{\sigma\}$. Hence we can write each quantitative path in the normal form $v\sigma^f$, with f a linear function over $\boldsymbol{x}$. Consequently, from now on we will only consider alias propositions of the form $u\sigma^f \diamond v\sigma^g$.

To decide whether a closed formula φ in alias logic with counters has a model, we use a notion of *parametric graph* $G(z)$ over a set of variables z, which is an abstraction of an infinite class of graphs. A formal definition of a parametric graph is given in the next section. The important point is that, in the case of lists with one selector, the total number of parametric graphs is finite. In fact, this number depends only on the number of program variables. Hence, the satisfiability problem is reduced to deciding whether there exists $z_1, \ldots, z_n$ such that $G(z) \models \varphi$. To solve the latter problem, we shall derive an open formula $\Psi_{G,\varphi}(z)$ in the language of $\mathcal{L}_|^{(*)}$, such that, for all interpretations $\iota : z \to \mathbb{N}$, $\Psi_{G,\varphi}(\iota(z))$ holds if and only if $G(\iota(z)) \models \varphi$. The formula φ is then satisfiable, if and only if there exists a parametric graph G such that $\exists z_1, \ldots \exists z_n \Psi_{G,\varphi}$ is satisfiable. Moreover, as it will be pointed out, $\Psi_{G,\varphi}$ is positive and the only variables occurring on the left of the divisibility are z. Hence the latter condition is decidable. The following discussion is meant only as a proof of decidability for alias logic with counters in the case $\Sigma = \{\sigma\}$, the algorithmic effectiveness of the decision procedure being left out of the scope of this paper.

A Parametric Model Checking Problem

A parametric graph over a set of variables z is a graph $G = \langle N, V, E \rangle$, the only difference w.r.t. the previous definition being the edge alphabet, which is taken to be $\Sigma \times z$, instead of Σ. In other words, each edge is of the form $n \xrightarrow{\sigma, z} m$. We assume that each edge is labeled with a different variable from z, and thus $\|E\| = \|z\|$. Given an interpretation of variables $\iota : z \to \mathbb{N}$, we define the interpretation of an edge to be the sequence of edges $n = n_1 \xrightarrow{\sigma} n_2 \xrightarrow{\sigma} \ldots n_k = m$ of length $k = \iota(z)$, with no branching along the way. The interpretation of a graph is the graph obtained by replacing each edge with its interpretation. As a convention, the values of z are assumed to be strictly greater than one. The reason is that, allowing zero length paths in the graph might contradict with the requirement that the graph is deterministic. A parametric graph is said to be in *normal form* if and only if:

- there are no two adjacent edges labeled with the same symbol e.g., $m \xrightarrow{\sigma, z_1} n \xrightarrow{\sigma, z_2} p$, such that either the indegree or the outdegree of their common node (n) is greater than one.
- each node in the graph is reachable from a root node in V.

Notice that each parametric graph can be put in normal form by replacing any pair of edges violating this condition by a single edge labeled with the same symbol. The interested reader may also consult [3] for a notion very similar to the parametric graph.

In the rest of this section we shall consider the case $\Sigma = \{\sigma\}$. For any given set V of program variables, the number of parametric graphs $\langle N, V, E \rangle$ in normal form, is finite. This fact occurs as consequence of the following lemma:

Lemma 1. *Let $G = \langle N, V, E \rangle$ be a parametric graph over a singleton alphabet, in normal form. Then $\|N\| \leq 2\|V\|$.*

Given a parametric graph and a closed formula in alias logic, we are interested in finding an open formula $\Psi_{G,\varphi}(z)$ that encodes $G(z) \models \varphi$, for all possible interpretations of z. We will define $\Psi_{G,\varphi}$ inductively on the structure of φ, by first defining characteristic formulas for the alias literals (alias propositions and negations of alias propositions). Intuitively, $\pi_1 \Diamond \pi_2$ holds on $G(z) = \langle N, V, s \rangle$ if and only if the paths π_1 and π_2 meet either in an "explicit" node $n \in N$ or in a node that does not occur in N but is "abstracted" within a parametric edge. For the latter case, we need some notation. Given an interpretation ι of variables $z \cup \{y\}$, let $d(n, y)$ denote the node situated at distance $\iota(y)$ from n in the (non-parametric) graph $G(\iota(z))$. With this notation, Figure 1 defines the characteristic formulas $\Psi_{G,l}$, for alias literals l.

$$G \models \pi_1 \Diamond \pi_2 : \bigvee_{n \in N} \widehat{\pi_1} = n \wedge \widehat{\pi_2} = n \vee \exists y \bigvee_{n \xrightarrow{z} m} \widehat{\pi_1} = d(n, y) \wedge \widehat{\pi_2} = d(n, y) \wedge y < z$$

$$G \not\models \pi_1 \Diamond \pi_2 : \exists y_1 \exists y_2 \bigvee_{\substack{n_1 \xrightarrow{z_1} m_1 \\ n_2 \xrightarrow{z_2} m_2 \\ n_1 \neq n_2}} \widehat{\pi_1} = d(n_1, y_1) \wedge \widehat{\pi_2} = d(n_2, y_2) \wedge y_1 < z_1 \wedge y_2 < z_2$$

$$\vee \bigvee_{n \xrightarrow{z} m} \widehat{\pi_1} = d(n, y_1) \wedge \widehat{\pi_2} = d(n, y_2) \wedge y_1 < z \wedge y_2 < z \wedge y_1 \neq y_2$$

Fig. 1.

Since both positive and negative literals can be encoded as positive boolean combinations of equalities of the form $\widehat{\pi} = d(n, y)$[8], it is sufficient to show how such an equality can be defined as a positive formula of $\mathcal{L}_|^{(*)}$ with the only variables occurring on the left of divisibility being the ones in z. Let $\pi = v\sigma^{f(x)}$ be a quantitative path. There are three possibilities:

1. if there is no path in G from v to n, then $\widehat{\pi} = d(n, y)$ is false.
2. if there is an acyclic path $v \xrightarrow{z_1} n_1 \xrightarrow{z_2} \ldots n_{k-1} \xrightarrow{z_k} n$ in G, then $\widehat{\pi} = d(n, y)$ is equivalent to $f(x) = \Sigma_{i=1}^{k} z_i + y$.
3. otherwise, there is a cyclic path $v \xrightarrow{z_1} \ldots n_{k-1} \xrightarrow{z_k} n_k = n \xrightarrow{z_{k+1}} n_{k+1} \ldots n_{l-1} \xrightarrow{z_l} n_l = n$ in G, and for all $1 \leq i < l$, $i \neq k$ we have $n_i \neq n$. Then $\widehat{\pi} = d(n, y)$ is equivalent to $f(x) \geq \Sigma_{i=1}^{k} z_i + y \wedge \Sigma_{i=k+1}^{l} z_i | f(x) - \Sigma_{i=1}^{k} z_i - y$, for the $v \xrightarrow{f}$ path may iterate through the $n_k, n_{k+1}, \ldots, n_l$ loop multiple times.

Example. The encoding of a query of the form $G(z) \models \widehat{\pi(x)} = n$ as a formula of $\mathcal{L}_|^{(*)}$ is better understood by means of an example. Figure 2 shows a parametric graph and three sample queries with their equivalent encodings.   □

---

[8] $\widehat{\pi} = n$ is $\widehat{\pi} = d(n, 0)$.

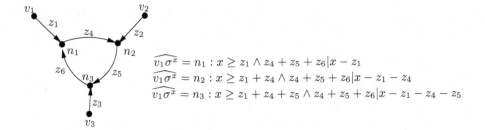

$$\widehat{v_1\sigma^x} = n_1 : x \geq z_1 \wedge z_4 + z_5 + z_6 | x - z_1$$
$$\widehat{v_1\sigma^x} = n_2 : x \geq z_1 + z_4 \wedge z_4 + z_5 + z_6 | x - z_1 - z_4$$
$$\widehat{v_1\sigma^x} = n_3 : x \geq z_1 + z_4 + z_5 \wedge z_4 + z_5 + z_6 | x - z_1 - z_4 - z_5$$

Fig. 2.

Theorem 3. *If $\|\Sigma\| = 1$, then the satisfiability problem for the logic of* aliases with counters *is decidable*.

6   Conclusion

We studied the decision problem for fragments of the arithmetic of addition and divisibility. It is known that the entire theory is undecidable [14], while its existential subset is decidable [11]. In defining our fragment we take in consideration on which side of the divisibility sign | do variables occur. Our main result is the decidability of the fragment of the form $Q z Q_1 x_1 \ldots Q_n x_n \varphi$ where the only divisibility propositions are of the form $f(z)|g(x, z)$. For this fragment we show the existence of a quantifier elimination procedure. We apply the same procedure to formulas of the form $\exists z_1, \ldots, \exists z_n Q_1 x_1, \ldots, Q_m x_m \varphi$ where the only divisibility propositions are of the form $f(z)|g(x, z)$. Here we show decidability of the positive form i.e., in which no divisibility propositions occur negated. Moreover, the full fragment of this form is shown to be undecidable. We have applied the decidability results to a problem concerning the verification of programs with mutable data structures. Having introduced a specification logic for expressing shape and quantitative properties of recursive data structures, we show that this logic is decidable on list models, by reduction to first-order formulas using addition and divisibility.

Further directions of work concern, on one hand, algorithmic aspects of the decision problem, and namely, efficient implementations of the method. On the other hand, we are investigating the possibility of applying this theory to the problem of computing loop invariants of integer counter automata. This problem has been explored using Presburger arithmetic [8], and extending the results by means of theories with divisibility seems to be a promising approach.

Acknowledgments. The authors are greatly indebted to their colleagues Yassine Lakhnech, Laurent Mazaré and Romain Janvier for the interesting discussions and enlightening suggestions concerning this paper.

References

1. Alexis Bés. A survey of arithmetical definability. *A Tribute to Maurice Boffa. Bulletin de la Société Mathématique de Belgique*, 1 - 54, 2002.
2. A. P. Beltyukov. Decidability of the universal theory of natural numbers with addition and divisibility. *Zapiski Nauch. Sem. Leningrad Otdeleniya Mathematical Institute*, 60:15 – 28, 1976.
3. S. Bardin, A. Finkel, and D. Nowak. Toward symbolic verification of programs handling pointers. In *Proc. 3rd Int. Workshop on Automated Verification of Infinite-State Systems (AVIS 2004), Barcelona, Spain*. Electronic Notes in Theoretical Computer Science, 2004.
4. Marius Bozga and Radu Iosif. On Decidability within the Arithmetic of Addition and Divisibility. Technical Report 18, Verimag, October 2004.
5. Marius Bozga, Radu Iosif, and Yassine Lakhnech. Counting aliases. Technical Report 17, Verimag, October 2004.
6. R. B. Crittenden and C. L. Vanden Eynden. A proof of a conjecture of Erdös. *Bulletin of American Mathematical Society*, (75):1326 – 1329, 1969.
7. Alonzo Church. An unsolvable problem of elementary number theory. *American Journal of Mathematics*, 58:345 – 363, 1936.
8. Hubert Comon and Yan Jurski. Multiple Counters Automata, Safety Analysis and Presburger Arithmetic. In *Proceedings of the 10th International Conference on Computer Aided Verification*, volume 1427, pages 268 – 279. Lecture Notes in Computer Science, 1998.
9. C. Ding, D. Pei, and A. Salomaa. *Chinese Remainder Theorem: Applications in Computing, Coding, Cryptography*. World Scientific Publishing Company, 1999.
10. Kurt Gödel. Über formal unentscheidbare Sätze der Principia Mathematica und verwandter Systeme I. *Monatshefte für Mathematik und Physik*, 38:173 – 198, 1931.
11. Leonard Lipshitz. The diophantine problem for addition and divisibility. *Transaction of the American Mathematical Society*, 235:271 – 283, January 1976.
12. Yuri Matiyasevich. Enumerable sets are diophantine. *Journal of Sovietic Mathematics*, (11):354 – 358, 1970.
13. Mojzesz Presburger. Über die Vollstandigkeit eines gewissen Systems der Arithmetik. *Comptes rendus du I Congrés des Pays Slaves*, Warsaw 1929.
14. Julia Robinson. Definability and decision problems in arithmetic. *The Journal of Symbolic Logic*, 14(2):98 – 114, June 1949.
15. B. Rosser. Extensions of some theorems of Gödel and Church. *The Journal of Symbolic Logic*, 1:87 – 91, 1936.

Expressivity of Coalgebraic Modal Logic: The Limits and Beyond

Lutz Schröder

BISS, Department of Computer Science, University of Bremen

Abstract. Modal logic has a good claim to being the logic of choice for describing the reactive behaviour of systems modeled as coalgebras. Logics with modal operators obtained from so-called predicate liftings have been shown to be invariant under behavioral equivalence. Expressivity results stating that, conversely, logically indistinguishable states are behaviorally equivalent depend on the existence of separating sets of predicate liftings for the signature functor at hand. Here, we provide a classification result for predicate liftings which leads to an easy criterion for the existence of such separating sets, and we give simple examples of functors that fail to admit expressive normal or monotone modal logics, respectively, or in fact an expressive (unary) modal logic at all. We then move on to polyadic modal logic, where modal operators may take more than one argument formula. We show that every accessible functor admits an expressive polyadic modal logic. Moreover, expressive polyadic modal logics are, unlike unary modal logics, compositional.

1   Introduction

Coalgebra has in recent years emerged as an appropriate framework for the treatment of reactive systems in a very general sense [24]; in particular, coalgebra provides a unifying perspective on notions such as coinduction, corecursion, and bisimulation. It has turned out that modal logic is a good candidate for being the basic logic of coalgebra in the same sense as equational logic is the basic logic of algebra. E.g., classes of coalgebras defined by modal axioms can be regarded as the dual of varieties [12, 14]. Moreover, coalgebraic modal logic as considered in [9, 13, 18, 20, 19, 22] is invariant under behavioral equivalence. Conversely, in [18, 20, 19], sufficient conditions are given for coalgebraic modal logics to be *expressive* in the sense that logically indistinguishable states are behaviorally equivalent; this is a generalization of the classical result for Hennessy-Milner logic [8]. These results depend on conditions imposed on the signature functor, i.e. the data type in which collections of successor states are organized.

Indeed, coalgebraic logic as introduced by Moss [16], which may be regarded as a somewhat extreme form of modal logic, is expressive for the (very large) class of so-called set-based functors; however, from the point of view of practical application in software specification, coalgebraic logic has the disadvantage of being rather difficult to grasp, as the syntax and the semantics of its formulae involve applications of the signature functor to the language itself and the

V. Sassone (Ed.): FOSSACS 2005, LNCS 3441, pp. 440–454, 2005.

satisfaction relation, respectively. By comparison, modal logic is rather intuitive and thus well suited for specification purposes. E.g., modal logic is used in the specification of object-oriented programs in the specification language CCSL [23] and in [13] and forms a central feature of the algebraic-coalgebraic specification language COCASL [17].

Coalgebraic modal logic as developed in [18, 20] obtains its modal operators from so-called predicate liftings, which transform predicates on X into predicates on TX, where T is the signature functor. Predicate liftings generalize the natural relations considered in [19], which may be regarded as constructions that convert coalgebras into Kripke frames. It is shown in [18, 20] that the expressivity problem for coalgebraic modal logic reduces to the existence of enough predicate liftings for the given signature functor; no general answer is given to the question of how to actually find such predicate liftings.

Here, we observe that predicate liftings are equivalent to a notion of modality used in [11]; this affords an immediate overview of all possible predicate liftings of a given functor. Moreover, one obtains easy criteria which identify so-called monotone and continuous predicate liftings, respectively. These properties of predicate liftings correspond to the validity of natural axioms in the arising modal logic; in particular, continuity corresponds to normality. It turns out that continuous predicate liftings essentially coincide with natural relations. These classification results are on the one hand helpful in designing good sets of modal operators for expressive modal logics. On the other hand, they can be used to show that certain signature functors fail to admit expressive monotone or normal modal logics, or indeed an expressive modal logic in the sense considered so far at all. Examples of the latter type include certain composite functors, e.g. the double finite powerset functor, but also single-layer datatypes such as non-repetitive lists. Typical examples of coalgebras that require non-normal modal logics are those involving some sort of weighting on the successor states, e.g. multigraphs or probabilistic automata.

We then introduce an extension of coalgebraic modal logic in which modal operators may be *polyadic*, i.e. apply to more than one formula. Both unary and polyadic modal operators may be subsumed under the abstract notion of *syntax* (or *language*) *constructor* [4, 5]. Polyadic modal logic, while hardly more complicated than unary modal logic, turns out to be expressive for a large class of functors, the so-called accessible functors. Furthermore, we show that polyadic modal logic is compositional in the sense that expressive modal logics can be combined along functor composition; differently put, polyadic modal logic is, unlike unary modal logic, closed under the composition of syntax constructors.

The material is organized as follows. Section 2 gives an overview of coalgebra and modal logic. Expressivity results for modal logic which *assume* the existence of enough predicate liftings are discussed in Section 3; in particular, we improve an expressivity result of [20] and give a simplified proof. We then proceed to discuss the classification of predicate liftings in Section 4. Finally, polyadic modal logic is treated in Section 5.

2   Preliminaries: Coalgebra and Modal Logic

We now briefly recall the paradigm of modelling reactive systems by means of coalgebras, limiting ourselves to the set-valued case, and the use of modal logic to describe reactive behavior.

Definition 1. Let $T : \mathbf{Set} \to \mathbf{Set}$ be a functor (all functors will implicitly be set functors from now on). A T-*coalgebra* $A = (X, \xi)$ consists of a set X of *states* and an *evolution map* $\xi : X \to TX$. A morphism $(X_1, \xi_1) \to (X_2, \xi_2)$ of T-coalgebras is a map $f : X_1 \to X_2$ such that $\xi_2 \circ f = Tf \circ \xi_1$. A T-coalgebra C is called *final* if there exists, for each T-coalgebra A, a unique morphism $A \to C$. Two states x and y in T-coalgebras A and B are called *behaviorally equivalent* if there exists a coalgebra C and homomorphisms $f : A \to C$, $g : B \to C$ such that $f(x) = g(y)$.

The general intuition is that the behavior map describes the successor states of a state, organized in a data structure given by T. The notion of behavioral equivalence serves to encapsulate the state space: two states are behaviorally equivalent if the observable aspects of the state evolution from the given states are identical. Thus, the reactive behavior of a state is embodied in its behavioral equivalence class. Final coalgebras are behaviorally abstract in the sense that behaviorally equivalent states are equal; the carrier set of a final coalgebra may be thought of as the set of all possible behaviors. By *Lambek's Lemma*, the evolution map of a final coalgebra is bijective.

Remark 2. Behavioral equivalence as just defined coincides in most cases with bisimilarity, and appears to be the preferable notion in cases where this fails [12]. Coalgebraic modal logic as treated here captures precisely behavioral equivalence.

Example 3.   1. Let $\mathcal{P}_\omega$ be the (covariant) finite powerset functor. Then $\mathcal{P}_\omega$-coalgebras are finitely branching graphs, thought of as (unlabeled) transition systems or indeed Kripke frames.
2. Let T be given by $TX = I \to \mathcal{P}_\omega(X)$ (equivalently $TX = \mathcal{P}_\omega(I \times X)$). Then T-coalgebras are labelled transition systems with label set I.
3. Let T be given by $TX = I \to ((O \times X) + E)$. Then T-coalgebras may be thought of as modelling *objects* with state set X, method set I, output set O, and exception set E [13]. Elements of the final T-coalgebra are finite or infinite I-branching trees with O-labelled nodes and E-labelled leaves.
4. Let $T = \mathcal{P}_\omega \circ \mathcal{P}_\omega$. Then T-coalgebras may be thought of as transition systems with two levels of non-determinism; i.e. in each step, a set of possible successors is chosen non-deterministically.
5. The *finite multiset* (or bag) functor $\mathcal{B}_\mathbb{N}$ is given as follows. The set $\mathcal{B}_\mathbb{N}(X)$ consists of the maps $B : X \to \mathbb{N}$ with finite support, where $B(x) = n$ is read 'B contains the element x with multiplicity n'. We write elements of $\mathcal{B}_\mathbb{N}X$ additively in the form $\sum n_i x_i$, thus denoting the multiset that contains x with multiplicity $\sum_{x_j = x} n_j$. For $f : X \to Y$, $\mathcal{B}_\mathbb{N}(f)(\sum n_i x_i) = \sum n_i f(x_i)$.

Coalgebras for $\mathcal{B}_\mathbb{N}$ are directed graphs with $\mathbb{N}$-weighted edges, often referred to as multigraphs [6].

6. A similar functor, denoted $\mathcal{B}_\mathbb{Z}$, is given by a slight modification of the multiset functor where we allow elements to have also *negative* multiplicities, i.e. $\mathcal{B}_\mathbb{Z}X$ consists of finite maps $X \to \mathbb{Z}$, called *generalized multisets* (this set is also familiar as the free abelian group over X).

7. Another variation of the multiset functor is the finite distribution functor D_ω, where $D_\omega X$ is the set of probability distributions on X with finite support. Coalgebras for D_ω are probabilistic transition systems (as yet without inputs).

8. Examples 5–7 above may be extended by taking into account a notion of input, with input alphabet I, as in Example 2: for $T \in \{\mathcal{B}_\mathbb{N}, \mathcal{B}_\mathbb{Z}, D_\omega\}$, one has functors S and R given by $SX = I \to TX$ and $RX = T(I \times X)$. These functors are isomorphic for $T \in \{\mathcal{B}_\mathbb{N}, \mathcal{B}_\mathbb{Z}\}$ in case I is finite, but not for $T = D_\omega$. In the latter case, S-coalgebras are reactive probabilistic automata, and R-coalgebras are generative probabilistic automata [2] (more precisely, one would usually allow for terminal states by additionally introducing the constant functor 1 as a summand), the difference being that generative probabilistic automata assign probabilities also to inputs.

All of the above examples fall into the following class of functors:

Definition 4. A functor T is called κ-*accessible*, where κ is a regular cardinal, if T preserves κ-directed colimits.

Accessible functors have final coalgebras [1, 21].

Example 5. *Parametrized algebraic datatypes* defined in terms of constructors and equations (i.e. quotients of term algebra functors) are κ-accessible functors if all constructors have arity less than κ. E.g., the multiset functors $\mathcal{B}_\mathbb{N}$ and $\mathcal{B}_\mathbb{Z}$ are ω-accessible. The finite distribution functor D_ω is ω-accessible. For each regular cardinal κ, the functor $\mathcal{P}_\kappa$ given by $\mathcal{P}_\kappa(X) = \{A \subset X \mid |A| < \kappa\}$ is κ-accessible. The class of κ-accessible functors is closed under composition; e.g. $\mathcal{P}_\omega \circ \mathcal{P}_\omega$ is ω-accessible.

Remark 6. In all results presented below, κ-accessibility can in fact be replaced by preservation of κ-directed unions. We have refrained from making this explicit in all statements, in favor of using standard terminology.

In order to specify requirements on coalgebraic systems in a way that guarantees invariance under behavioral equivalence, coalgebraic logic for so-called Kripke polynomial functors has been introduced (with variations in the syntax) e.g. in [9, 13, 22]. These results have been generalized in [18, 19, 20], where coalgebraic modal logics are defined on the basis of given *natural relations* and *predicate liftings* for the signature, respectively, as follows.

Definition 7. A *predicate lifting* for a functor T is a natural transformation

$$\lambda : 2^- \to 2^T,$$

where 2^- denotes the contravariant powerset functor $\mathbf{Set}^{op} \to \mathbf{Set}$, with $2^f(A) = f^{-1}[A]$. Explicitly, a predicate lifting assigns to each $A \subset X$ a set $\lambda_X(A) \subset TX$ such that

$$Tf^{-1}[\lambda_Y(A)] = \lambda_X(f^{-1}[A])$$

for all maps $f : X \to Y$. A predicate lifting λ is called *monotone* if $A \subset B \subset X$ implies $\lambda_X(A) \subset \lambda_X(B)$, and *continuous* if λ_X preserves intersections for each set X, i.e. $\lambda_X(\bigcap_{i \in I} A_i) = \bigcap_{i \in I} \lambda_X(A_i)$.

A predicate lifting λ is equivalently described by its *transposite* $\lambda^\flat : T \to 2^{(2^-)}$, given by $\lambda^\flat_X(t) = \{A \subset X \mid t \in \lambda_X(A)\}$. A set Λ of predicate liftings for T is called *separating* if for each set X, the source of maps

$$(\lambda^\flat_X : T \to 2^{(2^-)})_{\lambda \in \Lambda}$$

is jointly injective, in other words: $t \in TX$ is uniquely determined by the set $\{(\lambda, A) \in \Lambda \times 2^X \mid t \in \lambda_X(A)\}$; this property is called *separation at X*.

We shall need the following fact proved in [20]:

Proposition 8. *A set Λ of predicate liftings for a κ-accessible functor is separating iff separation holds at all sets X such that $|X| < \kappa$.*

Definition 9. Let T be a functor. A *language for T-coalgebras* is a set $\mathcal{L}$ of formulae, equipped with a family of satisfaction relations $\models_{(X,\xi)}$ (or just $\models$) between states of T-coalgebras (X, ξ) and formulae $\phi \in \mathcal{L}$; we define $[\![\phi]\!]_{(X,\xi)}$ (or just $[\![\phi]\!]$) as the set $\{x \in X \mid x \models_{(X,\xi)} \phi\}$.

States x and y in T-coalgebras A and B, respectively, are called *logically indistinguishable* under $\mathcal{L}$ if

$$x \models \phi \quad \text{iff} \quad y \models \phi$$

for all $\phi \in \mathcal{L}$. The language $\mathcal{L}$ is called *adequate* if behaviorally equivalent states are logically indistinguishable, equivalently: the satisfaction of formulae is invariant under T-coalgebra morphisms.

Remark 10. One can define a formula $\phi \in \mathcal{L}$ to be valid in a coalgebra (X, ξ) if $x \models \phi$ for all $x \in X$. This makes $\mathcal{L}$ into a logic for coalgebras as defined in [14]. If T has a final coalgebra, then adequacy of $\mathcal{L}$ guarantees that classes of coalgebras defined by axioms in $\mathcal{L}$ have final models [14].

Coalgebraic modal logic [18, 20] is a language $\mathcal{L}^\kappa(\Lambda)$ for T-coalgebras, parametrized by a set Λ of predicate liftings for T and a regular cardinal κ which serves as a bound for conjunctions: formulae $\phi \in \mathcal{L}^\kappa(\Lambda)$ are defined by the grammar

$$\phi ::= \; [\lambda]\,\phi \qquad\qquad (\lambda \in \Lambda)$$
$$\mid \bigwedge_{i \in I} \phi_i \qquad\qquad (|I| < \kappa)$$
$$\mid \neg\phi_0.$$

Disjunctions $\bigvee_{i \in I} \phi_i$ for $|I| < \kappa$ are then defined as usual. In the definition of satisfaction, the clauses for conjunction and negation are as expected; the clause for the modal operator $[\lambda]$ is

$$x \models_{(X,\xi)} [\lambda] \phi \iff \xi(x) \in \lambda_X [\![\phi]\!]_{(X,\xi)}.$$

The naturality equation for predicate liftings is easily seen to be precisely the condition that is needed in order to ensure adequacy of $\mathcal{L}^\kappa(\Lambda)$ [20]. The converse of this statement, i.e. the question under which conditions $\mathcal{L}^\kappa(\Lambda)$ and related logics are *expressive*, is the main subject of this paper.

The construction of $\mathcal{L}^\kappa(\Lambda)$ presupposes that a suitable set of predicate liftings for T is already given. We will discuss in Section 4 how predicate liftings may be obtained and classified in general.

Definition 11. A *natural relation* for T is a natural transformation $\mu : T \to \mathcal{P}$.

Thus, for a natural relation μ, composition with μ_X converts T-coalgebras on X into Kripke frames. A natural relation μ induces (transposites of) predicate liftings by composing with transposites of predicate liftings for $\mathcal{P}$:

$$T \to \mathcal{P} \to 2^{(2^-)}.$$

In fact, it suffices to consider the composite $(\lambda^\forall)^\flat \circ \mu$, where $\lambda_X^\forall(A) = \{B \in \mathcal{P}(X) \mid B \subset A\}$; this will be treated in more detail in Section 4.

3   Expressivity of Coalgebraic Modal Logic

We now turn to the question of when coalgebraic modal logic is strong enough to distinguish behaviorally inequivalent states.

Definition 12. A language $\mathcal{L}$ for T-coalgebras is called *expressive* if logical indistinguishability under $\mathcal{L}$ implies behavioral equivalence.

It is shown in [18] that, for T κ-accessible and Λ separating, $\mathcal{L}^\sigma(\Lambda)$ is expressive for 'sufficiently large' σ in the stronger sense that behavioral equivalence classes are characterized by single formulae. Moreover, it is shown in [20] that under the same assumptions, $\mathcal{L}^\kappa(\Lambda)$ is expressive in the sense defined above, *provided* that either $\alpha < \kappa$ implies $2^\alpha < \kappa$ (i.e. $\kappa = \omega$ or κ strongly inaccessible) or the predicate liftings in Λ are continuous. These restrictions are quite strong: even the mere existence of strongly inaccessible cardinals is unprovable in ZFC, and the next section will show that continuous predicate liftings are in fact just natural relations. The proofs in [18, 20] are by terminal sequence induction. Note that the subtle-appearing difference between the two expressiveness results is in fact rather substantial. E.g. in the case of labelled transition systems (Example 3.2), the first result concerns a modal logic with countably infinitary conjunction, while the second result asserts the expressivity of standard Hennessy-Milner logic with finitary conjunction.

We now give an improved version of the second result, in which the additional assumptions on κ and Λ, respectively, are dropped.

Theorem 13. *Let T be κ-accessible and let Λ be a separating set of predicate liftings. Then $\mathcal{L}^\kappa(\Lambda)$ is expressive.*

Proof. (Sketch) One has to show that a given T-coalgebra (X, ξ) can be quotiented by the logical indistinguishability relation R. This leads to a well-definedness problem, which may be solved using separation under Λ and the fact that on $Z \subset X$ with $|Z| < \kappa$, sets that are closed under R can be described by a $\mathcal{L}^\kappa(\Lambda)$-formula.

The above expressivity result has a partial converse:

Theorem 14. *If T is κ-accessible and the final T-coalgebra (Z, ζ) satisfies $|Z| \geq \kappa$, then expressivity of $\mathcal{L}^\sigma(\Lambda)$ for some σ implies that Λ is separating.*

Example 15. The assumption $|Z| \geq \kappa$ in the above theorem is essential. As a simple example where $|Z| < \kappa$, consider the non-empty finite powerset functor $\mathcal{P}_\omega^*$ (i.e. $\mathcal{P}_\omega^*(X) = \{A \in \mathcal{P}_\omega(X) \mid A \neq \emptyset\}$). The final coalgebra for this functor is a singleton. Thus, all states are behaviorally equivalent, so that any logic is expressive for T, including e.g. $\mathcal{L}^\omega(\emptyset)$; of course, the empty set of predicate liftings is not separating. The same holds for the functor $\mathcal{P}_\omega^* \circ \mathcal{P}_\omega^*$, which as we shall see below does not admit a separating set of predicate liftings at all.

4   Classification of Predicate Liftings

As indicated above, no general method has been given so far to actually construct predicate liftings for a given functor. The following simple fact (essentially just the Yoneda Lemma for the functor $2^T : \mathbf{Set}^{op} \to \mathbf{Set}$) gives immediate access to all predicate liftings that a functor admits.

Proposition 16. *Predicate liftings for T are in one-to-one correspondence with subsets of $T2$, where $2 = \{\top, \bot\}$. The correspondence takes a predicate lifting λ to $\lambda_2(\{\top\}) \subset T2$ and, conversely, $C \subset T2$ to the predicate lifting λ^C defined by*

$$\lambda_X^C(A) = (T\chi_A)^{-1}[C]$$

for $A \subset X$, where $\chi_A : X \to 2$ is the characteristic function of A.

Remark 17. Subsets of $T2$, i.e. T-algebras on 2, have appeared as modalities in [11]. Proposition 16 establishes that this notion of modality and the one induced by predicate liftings are equivalent.

We shall thus freely apply terminology introduced so far for predicate liftings to subsets of $T2$ as well. E.g. we say that a set of subsets of $T2$ is *separating* if the associated set of predicate liftings is separating, etc. Proposition 16 leads to a criterion for the existence of separating sets of predicate liftings, and hence of expressive modal logics.

Corollary 18. *A functor T has a separating set of predicate liftings iff the source*

$$\mathcal{S}_X = (Tf : TX \to T2)_{f:X\to 2}$$

is jointly injective at each set X. If T is κ-accessible, then joint injectivity of $\mathcal{S}_X$ for $|X| < \kappa$ is sufficient.

Example 19. 1. The (finite) powerset functor has, by Proposition 16, precisely 16 predicate liftings, generated as boolean combinations of the predicate liftings $\lambda^\forall$ and $\lambda^\exists$ corresponding to $\{\emptyset, \{\top\}\}, \{\{\top\}, \{\top, \bot\}\} \subset \mathcal{P}2$, respectively; i.e. $\lambda^\forall(A) = \{B \mid B \subset A\}$ and $\lambda^\exists(A) = \{B \mid B \cap A \neq \emptyset\}$. The predicate lifting $\lambda^\forall$ is continuous; the set $\{\lambda^\forall\}$ is separating. The modalities induced by $\lambda^\forall$ and $\lambda^\exists$ are the usual operators of modal logic.
2. A close relative of the functors $\mathcal{P}_\omega$, $\mathcal{B}_\mathbb{N}$, and the list functor list is the functor T that takes a set X to the free idempotent monoid (or *free band monoid*) over X. The set TX is obtained as the quotient of list X modulo idempotence, i.e. the equation $xx = x$. (Subsequent quotienting modulo commutativity produces $\mathcal{P}_\omega$.) By Corollary 18, T does not admit a separating set of predicate liftings: the elements of $T\{a, b, c\}$ represented by $abaca$ and $abca$, respectively, are distinct (see e.g. [25]), but identified under Tf for all $f : \{a, b, c\} \to 2$ (e.g. $T\chi_{\{b,c\}}(abaca) = \bot\top\bot\top\bot = \bot\top\bot = \bot\top\top\bot = T\chi_{\{b,c\}}(abca)$).
3. Let T be the non-repetitive list functor; i.e. TX is the set of lists over X containing every element of X at most once, and $Tf(l)$ is obtained by removing duplicates leftmost first in (list f)(l). By Corollary 18, T does not admit a separating set of predicate liftings, since $abc, bac \in T\{a, b, c\}$ are identified under Tf for all $f : \{a, b, c\} \to 2$.
4. The double finite powerset functor $T = \mathcal{P}_\omega \circ \mathcal{P}_\omega$ does not admit a separating set of predicate liftings. E.g., given a finite set X, the set $\{A \subset X \mid |A| \leq 2\}$ is identified with $\mathcal{P}_\omega(X)$ under Tf for all $f : X \to 2$. A similar argument works for $\mathcal{P}_\omega \circ$ list.

Provided the criterion of Corollary 18 is satisfied, the separation property for a given set of predicate liftings can be checked at the level of subsets of $T2$:

Theorem 20. *Let T admit a separating set of predicate liftings, and let $\mathfrak{C} \subset \mathcal{P}(T2)$. The following are equivalent:*

(i) $\mathfrak{C}$ is separating
(ii) $cl(\mathfrak{C}) = \{(Tf)^{-1}[C] \mid C \in \mathfrak{C}, f : 2 \to 2\}$ is separating
(iii) $t \in T2$ is uniquely determined by the set $\{C \in cl(\mathfrak{C}) \mid t \in C\}$.

We have seen in Example 19 that accessible functors may fail to admit an expressive (unary) modal logic. We now proceed to investigate the relationship between typical modal axioms and properties of predicate liftings, with a view to giving further separating examples.

Generally, a modal operator $\Box$ is called *monotone* [3] if it satisfies the axiom scheme $\Box(\phi \wedge \psi) \implies \Box\phi$, often referred to as axiom M. Moreover, $\Box$ is α-*normal* for a regular cardinal α if it satisfies the axiom scheme $\bigwedge_{i \in I} \Box \phi_i \iff \Box \bigwedge_{i \in I} \phi_i$ for $|I| < \alpha$. Note that ω-normality is semantically equivalent to the usual notion of normality for modal operators, i.e. the necessitation rule ('conclude $\Box \phi$ from ϕ') and the K-axiom $\Box(\phi \Rightarrow \psi) \Rightarrow (\Box \phi \Rightarrow \Box \psi)$ (equivalently: $\Box \phi \Rightarrow (\Box \psi \Rightarrow \Box(\phi \wedge \psi))$). In a nutshell, *monotone predicate liftings correspond to monotone modal logic, and continuous predicate liftings correspond to normal modal logic:*

Theorem 21. *Let T be a functor, and let λ be a predicate lifting for T. If λ is monotone then $[\lambda]$ is monotone. Conversely, if T is κ-accessible, T admits a separating set of predicate liftings, the final T-coalgebra (Z, ζ) satisfies $|Z| \geq \kappa$, and $[\lambda]$ is monotone, then λ is monotone.*

Definition 22. *For a regular cardinal β, we define $\bar{\beta}$ to be the smallest cardinal such that $2^\alpha < \bar{\beta}$ for all $\alpha < \beta$.*

E.g. $\bar{\omega} = \omega$, and $\bar{\beta} = \beta$ for β strongly inaccessible. Under GCH, $\bar{\beta}$ is either β or 2^β.

Proposition 23. *If T is κ-accessible, then a predicate lifting λ for T is continuous iff λ_X preserves intersections for $|X| < \kappa$ iff λ_X preserves intersections of less than $\bar{\kappa}$ sets.*

Corollary 24. *If T is ω-accessible, then a predicate lifting λ for T is continuous iff $\lambda_X(X) = TX$ for all X and $\lambda_X(A \cap B) = \lambda_X(A) \cap \lambda_X(B)$ for all $A, B \subset X$.*

Theorem 25. *Let T be a functor, and let λ be a predicate lifting for T. If λ is continuous, then the modal operator $[\lambda]$ is α-normal for all regular cardinals α. Conversely, if T is κ-accessible, T admits a separating set of predicate liftings, the final T-coalgebra (Z, ζ) has $|Z| \geq \kappa$, and $[\lambda]$ is $\bar{\kappa}$-normal, then λ is continuous.*

As announced above, continuous predicate liftings 'are' natural relations:

Theorem 26. *A predicate lifting λ for T is continuous iff its transposite $\lambda^\flat$ is of the form $(\lambda^\forall)^\flat \circ \mu$ (cf. Example 19) for some natural relation $\mu : T \to \mathcal{P}$.*

(A dual result holds for predicate liftings with transposites of the form $(\lambda^\exists)^\flat \circ \mu$; in pointwise form, this appears essentially already in [10].)

Corollary 27. *A functor admits a separating set of natural relations iff it admits a separating set of continuous predicate liftings.*

The slogan is thus that *normal coalgebraic modal logic is the logic of natural relations*.

We now give criteria for the monotonicity and continuity of predicate liftings at the level of subsets of $T2$. This will enable us to give examples separating modal logic, monotone modal logic, and normal modal logic w.r.t. expressive strength.

Proposition 28. *Let* 3 *denote the set* $\{\bot, *, \top\}$. *A subset* $C \subset T2$ *is monotone iff for each* $t \in T3$, $T\chi_{\{\top\}}(t) \in C$ *implies* $T\chi_{\{*,\top\}}(t) \in C$.

Remark 29. If T is a parametrized algebraic datatype (Example 5), then the condition of the above proposition informally states that C, which then consists of equivalence classes of terms in the variables $\top$ and $\bot$, is closed under replacing any number of occurrences of $\bot$ in a term by $\top$.

Proposition 30. *Let* T *be* ω-*accessible. A monotone subset* $C \subset T2$ *is continuous iff, for each* $t \in T\{\bot, a, b, \top\}$, $T\chi_{\{\top\}}(t) \in C$ *whenever* $T\chi_{\{a,\top\}}(t) \in C$ *and* $T\chi_{\{b,\top\}}(t) \in C$.

Remark 31. If T is a parametrized algebraic datatype, then the condition of the above proposition informally states that if two sets of occurrences of $\top$ in a term representing an element of $C \subset T2$ may separately be replaced by $\bot$, resulting in terms that remain in C, then replacing all occurrences in the two sets simultaneously also yields a term in C.

Example 32.   1. For the finite multiset functor $\mathcal{B}_{\mathbb{N}}$ (Example 3.5), $\mathcal{B}_{\mathbb{N}}2$ consists of elements of the form $n\top + m\bot$. By Remark 29, a subset C of $\mathcal{B}_{\mathbb{N}}2$ is monotone iff $n\top + (m+k)\bot \in C$ implies $(n+k)\top + m\bot \in C$. A separating set of monotone predicate liftings λ^k, $k \in \mathbb{N}$, is induced by the subsets of $\mathcal{B}_{\mathbb{N}}2$ of the form $C_k = \{n\top + m\bot \mid m \leq k\}$. The arising modal operators are exactly the modalities $[k]$ of *graded modal logic* (cf. e.g. [6]). Of course, $[k]$ fails to be normal unless $k = 0$.
   The functor $\mathcal{B}_{\mathbb{N}}$ does not admit a separating set of *continuous* predicate liftings, i.e. does not admit an expressive normal modal logic: using Proposition 30, one can show that all continuous predicate liftings for $\mathcal{B}_{\mathbb{N}}$ besides λ^0 are induced by $\{n\top + m\bot \mid n + m \in A\}$ for some $A \subset \mathbb{N}$.
2. The generalized multiset functor $\mathcal{B}_{\mathbb{Z}}$ (Example 3.6) even fails to admit a separating set of *monotone* predicate liftings, i.e. does not admit an expressive monotone modal logic: the description of monotone subsets $C \subset \mathcal{B}_{\mathbb{Z}}2$ is as for $\mathcal{B}_{\mathbb{N}}$ above, but with $k \in \mathbb{Z}$, so that $C = \{n\top + m\bot \mid n + m \in A\}$ for some $A \subset \mathbb{Z}$. A separating set of non-monotone predicate liftings λ^k, $k \in \mathbb{Z}$, for $\mathcal{B}_{\mathbb{Z}}$ is given by the subsets $C_k = \{n\top + m\bot \mid m \leq k\}$.
3. The finite distribution functor D_ω does not admit a separating set of continuous predicate liftings; this is shown in the same way as for $\mathcal{B}_{\mathbb{N}}$. A separating set of monotone predicate liftings is given by the sets $C_p = \{P \in D_\omega 2 \mid P\{\top\} \geq p\}$. These predicate liftings give rise to probabilistic modal operators $[p]$, where $[p]\,\phi$ reads 'ϕ holds in the next step with probability at least p' (this modal operator appears in [4]; similar operators are used e.g. in [15]).
4. When the above examples are extended with inputs from a set I as laid out in Example 3.8, one obtains essentially the same modalities as above, indexed over $a \in I$ in the form $[\_]_a$. In the case $T = D_\omega$, the meaning of $[p]_a\,\phi$ in reactive probabilistic automata is that on input a, ϕ holds in the next step with probability at least p, and in generative probabilistic automata that with probability at least p, the input is a and ϕ holds in the next step.

There is a canonical way to produce predicate liftings which often leads to useful modal operators: one can just apply T to subsets of 2. In particular, the predicate lifting given by $T\{\top\}$ is often important; in fact, this is the principle which is currently used for the definition of modal operators in CoCASL [17].

5   Polyadic Coalgebraic Modal Logic

Having seen in the preceding section that accessible functors may fail to admit separating sets of predicate liftings, we now proceed to develop a slightly generalized framework that yields expressive logics for all accessible functors. Essentially, all one has to do is to move on from unary modal operators to polyadic modal operators. Polyadic modal operators for coalgebras rely on the following notion of polyadic predicate lifting.

Definition 33. An α-*ary predicate lifting* for a functor T, where α is a cardinal, is a natural transformation

$$\lambda : (2^-)^\alpha \to 2^{T^{op}}.$$

A set Λ of such *polyadic predicate liftings* is called κ-*bounded* if all predicate lifings in Λ have arity properly smaller than κ (in particular Λ is ω-bounded if all predicate liftings in Λ are finitary). Moreover, Λ is called *separating* if the associated source of transposites

$$(\lambda^\flat : T \to 2^{((2^-)^\alpha)})_{\lambda \in \Lambda},$$

formed analogously to the unary case, is injective at each set X.

Explicitly, the naturality condition states that, for each map $f : X \to Y$ and each family $(A_i)_{i \in \alpha}$ of α subsets $A_i \subset Y$,

$$Tf^{-1}[\lambda_Y(A_i)_{i \in \alpha}] = \lambda_X(f^{-1}[A_i])_{i \in \alpha}.$$

The polyadic modal language is then defined as follows.

Definition 34. Let T be a functor, let Λ be a set of polyadic predicate liftings for T, and let κ be a cardinal. The language $\mathcal{L}^\kappa(\Lambda)$ is defined as in the unary case (cf. Section 2), except for application of modal operators: an α-ary predicate lifting $\lambda \in \Lambda$ gives rise to an α-ary modal operator $[\lambda]$, i.e. we have formulae of the form

$$[\lambda] (\phi_i)_{i \in \alpha}$$

where $(\phi_i)_{i \in \alpha}$ is a family of formulae in $\mathcal{L}^\kappa(\Lambda)$.

The satisfaction relation over a T-coalgebra (X, ξ) is given by the generalized clause

$$x \models [\lambda] (\phi_i)_{i \in \alpha} \quad \text{iff} \quad \xi(x) \in \lambda_X([\![\phi_i]\!])_{i \in \alpha}.$$

It is easy to see that $\mathcal{L}^\kappa(\Lambda)$ *is adequate.* The expressivity results discussed in Section 3 generalize in a straightforward manner (essentially by inspection of the proofs given above and in [18]), i.e. if T is accessible, Λ is a separating set of polyadic predicate liftings, and σ is 'sufficiently large', then $\mathcal{L}^\sigma(\Lambda)$ has characterizing formulae for behavioral equivalence classes, and

Theorem 35. *Let* T *be* κ*-accessible and let* Λ *be a separating set of polyadic predicate liftings for* T*. Then* $\mathcal{L}^\kappa(\Lambda)$ *is expressive.*

One has the same simple classification result as for unary predicate liftings:

Proposition 36. *For* α *a cardinal,* α*-ary predicate liftings for* T *are in one-to-one correspondence to subsets of* $T(2^\alpha)$*. The correspondence works by taking a predicate lifting* λ *to* $\lambda_{2^\alpha}(\pi_i^{-1}\{\top\})_{i\in\alpha} \subset T(2^\alpha)$*, where* $\pi_i : 2^\alpha \to 2$ *is the* i*-th projection, and, conversely,* $C \subset T(2^\alpha)$ *to the predicate lifting* λ^C *defined by*

$$\lambda_X^C(A_i)_{i\in\alpha} = (T\langle\chi_{A_i}\rangle_{i\in\alpha})^{-1}[C]$$

for $A_i \subset X$ *(*$i \in \alpha$*), where angle brackets are used to denote tupling of functions.*

Corollary 37. *The functor* T *admits a separating* κ*-bounded set of polyadic predicate liftings iff the the source*

$$\mathcal{S}_X = (Tf : TX \to T(2^\alpha))_{\alpha<\kappa, f:X\to 2^\alpha}$$

is injective for each set X*.*

Unlike for unary predicate liftings, we now obtain that *all accessible functors admit expressive polyadic modal logics:*

Corollary 38. *If* T *is* κ*-accessible, then* T *admits a separating* κ*-bounded set of polyadic predicate liftings.*

A further issue in coalgebraic modal logic is the modular construction of logics. It has been shown in [18] that separating sets of unary predicate liftings can be propagated along small products of functors, subfunctors (hence along small limits), and small coproducts; by Example 19, however, unary predicate liftings can *not* be combined along functor composition. Modularity results for expressive languages for accessible functors are proved at a more abstract level in [4,5], using notions of *syntax* (or *language*) constructor and *one-step semantics*. These results include combinations of syntax constructors and their one-step semantics, respectively, along functor composition.

We now show that separating sets of *polyadic* predicate liftings can be combined along composition of κ-accessible functors for arbitrary κ (of course, the *existence* of separating sets for such composites is clear by Corollary 38). The arising modal logic can then be seen to be equivalent, via a simple syntactic transformation, to a multi-sorted modal logic obtained by composing the associated syntax constructors and their one-step semantics according to [4,5].

Thus, polyadic modal logic is essentially closed under the composition operation of [4, 5] — i.e. for purposes of the meta-theory, one never has to go beyond the polyadic modal language defined above.

We begin by observing that predicate liftings can be composed:

Proposition and Definition 39. *Let T and S be functors, let λ be an α-ary predicate lifting for T, and let $(\nu^i)_{i \in \alpha}$ be a family of predicate liftings for S, where ν^i has arity β_i. Then*

$$(\lambda \circledast (\nu^i)_{i \in \alpha})_X (A_{ij})_{i \in \alpha, j \in \beta_i} = \lambda_{SX}(\nu_X^i (A_{ij})_{j \in \beta_i})_{i \in \alpha}$$

defines a $\sum_{i \in \alpha} \beta_i$-ary predicate lifting for $T \circ S$.

Next we note that (possibly infinitary) boolean combinations of polyadic predicate liftings are again predicate liftings:

Proposition and Definition 40. *Let Λ be a set of polyadic predicate liftings. Then each of the following equations defines a polyadic predicate lifting ν:*

(i) $\nu_X(A_i)_{i \in \beta} = \lambda_X(A_{\Phi(j)})_{j \in \alpha}$, where β is a cardinal, $\lambda \in \Lambda$ has arity α, and Φ is a map $\alpha \to \beta$;

(ii) $\nu_X(A_i)_{i \in \alpha} = TX - \lambda_X(A_i)_{i \in \alpha}$, where $\lambda \in \Lambda$ has arity α;

(iii) $\nu_X(A_i)_{i \in \alpha} = \bigcap_{j \in \gamma} \lambda_X^j(A_i)_{i \in \alpha}$, where γ is a cardinal and for each j, $\lambda^j \in \Lambda$ has arity α.

The closure of Λ under these constructions, with (i) and (iii) restricted to $\beta < \kappa$ and $\gamma < \kappa$, respectively, is called the κ-boolean closure of Λ, denoted $\mathrm{bcl}_\kappa(\Lambda)$. The elements of this set are called κ-boolean combinations of Λ.

The announced compositionality result for separating sets of predicate liftings is the following.

Theorem 41. *Let S and T be functors, where T is κ-accessible for a regular cardinal κ, and let Λ_S and Λ_T be κ-bounded separating sets of predicate liftings for S and T, respectively. Then*

$$\Lambda_T \circledast \mathrm{bcl}_\kappa(\Lambda_S) = \{\lambda \circledast (\nu^i)_{i \in \alpha} \mid \alpha \text{ cardinal}, \lambda \in \Lambda_T \ \alpha\text{-ary}, \nu^i \in \mathrm{bcl}_\kappa(\Lambda_S) \text{ for all } i\}$$

is a κ-bounded separating set of predicate liftings for $T \circ S$.

If, in the notation of the above theorem, S is κ-accessible, then it follows from Theorem 35 that $\mathcal{L}^\kappa(\Lambda_T \circledast \mathrm{bcl}_\kappa(\Lambda_S))$ is an expressive logic for $T \circ S$-coalgebras. Such an expressive logic can also be obtained by the methods of [4, 5], i.e. by composing the syntax constructors associated to Λ_T and Λ_S, along with their one-step semantics. The result is a multi-sorted modal logic where Λ_T-modalities and Λ_S-modalities appear in alternating layers, with Λ_T-modalities in the outermost layer. This logic can easily be seen to be equivalent to $\mathcal{L}^\kappa(\Lambda_T \circledast \mathrm{bcl}_\kappa(\Lambda_S))$; in the translation, boolean operators on formulae are turned into boolean operations on predicate liftings, and two layers of modal syntax in $\mathcal{L}^\kappa(\Lambda_T)$ and $\mathcal{L}^\kappa(\Lambda_S)$, respectively, are combined into one layer of modal syntax in $\mathcal{L}^\kappa(\Lambda_T \circledast \mathrm{bcl}_\kappa(\Lambda_S))$. E.g., if $\lambda \in \Lambda_T$ is α-ary and $\nu_i \in \Lambda_S$ for all i, then the multi-sorted formula $[\lambda][\nu^i](\phi_{ij})$ becomes the formula $[\lambda \circledast (\nu^i)](\phi_{ij})$ of $\mathcal{L}^\kappa(\Lambda_T \circledast \mathrm{bcl}_\kappa(\Lambda_S))$. In other words, composites of polyadic modal logics in the sense of [4, 5] can always be flattened into a polyadic modal logic.

6   Conclusion

We have studied expressivity issues in the modal logic of coalgebras based on the notion of predicate lifting, following [18, 20]. In [20], an expressivity result for coalgebraic modal logic has been proved under the assumption that the signature functor admits a separating set of predicate liftings. We have improved this result by dropping restrictions on the accessibility degree of the signature functor. Moreover, we have given a simple classification of predicate liftings which has lead to a necessary and sufficient criterion for the existence of separating sets of predicate liftings, and by means of this criterion we have identified examples of functors that fail to admit an expressive unary modal logic.

We have also related monotonicity and continuity of predicate liftings to monotonicity and normality, respectively, of the induced modal operators. The above-mentioned classification of predicate liftings has then allowed us to give examples separating the coalgebraic expressiveness of modal logic, monotone modal logic, and normal modal logic. Furthermore, we have identified normal modal logic as the modal logic of natural relations as introduced in [19]. Since natural relations convert coalgebras into Kripke frames, the latter result lends precision to the claim that normal modal logics describe exactly Kripke frames. More generally, reversing the original viewpoint that modal logic serves as a specification language for coalgebras, our results show that coalgebra constitutes a good semantic framework also for non-normal and even non-monotone modal systems (for non-normal systems cf. also [7]).

Finally, we have proposed to generalize coalgebraic modal logic to include polyadic modal operators based on polyadic predicate liftings. We have shown that all accessible functors admit an expressive polyadic modal logic. Moreover, we have proved a compositionality result stating essentially that polyadic modal logic is stable under the composition of languages described in [5].

Future work will include the exploitation of these results in the practical specification of reactive systems. In particular, modal operators specified in terms of our classification result will be integrated into the design of CoCASL.

Acknowledgements. The author wishes to thank Till Mossakowski, Markus Roggenbach, and Horst Reichel for collaboration on CoCASL, and Alexander Kurz, Bartek Klin, and the anonymous referees for useful suggestions for improvement.

References

[1] M. Barr, *Terminal coalgebras in well-founded set theory*, Theoret. Comput. Sci. **114** (1993), 299–315.

[2] F. Bartels, A. Sokolova, and E. de Vink, *A hierarchy of probabilistic system types*, Coalgebraic Methods in Computer Science, ENTCS, vol. 82, Elsevier, 2003.

[3] B. Chellas, *Modal logic*, Cambridge, 1980.

[4] C. Cîrstea, *A compositional approach to defining logics for coalgebras*, Theoret. Comput. Sci. **327** (2004), 45–69.

[5] C. Cîrstea and D. Pattinson, *Modular construction of modal logics*, Concurrency Theory, LNCS, vol. 3170, Springer, 2004, pp. 258–275.

[6] G. D'Agostino and A. Visser, *Finality regained: A coalgebraic study of Scott-sets and multisets*, Arch. Math. Logic **41** (2002), 267–298.

[7] H. H. Hansen and C. Kupke, *A coalgebraic perspective on monotone modal logic*, Coalgebraic Methods in Computer Science (J. Adámek and S. Milius, eds.), ENTCS, vol. 106, Elsevier, 2004, pp. 121–143.

[8] M. Hennessy and R. Milner, *Algebraic laws for non-determinism and concurrency*, J. ACM **32** (1985), 137–161.

[9] B. Jacobs, *Towards a duality result in the modal logic of coalgebras*, Coalgebraic Methods in Computer Science, ENTCS, vol. 33, Elsevier, 2000.

[10] B. Jónnson and A. Tarski, *Boolean algebras with operators I*, Amer. J. Math. **73** (1951), 891–939.

[11] B. Klin, *A coalgebraic approach to process equivalence and a coinduction principle for traces*, Coalgebraic Methods in Computer Science, ENTCS, vol. 106, Elsevier, 2004, pp. 201–218.

[12] A. Kurz, *Logics for coalgebras and applications to computer science*, Ph.D. thesis, Universität München, 2000.

[13] ———, *Specifying coalgebras with modal logic*, Theoret. Comput. Sci. **260** (2001), 119–138.

[14] ———, *Logics admitting final semantics*, Foundations of Software Science and Computation Structures, LNCS, vol. 2303, Springer, 2002, pp. 238–249.

[15] K. Larsen and A. Skou, *Bisimulation through probabilistic testing*, Inform. Comput. **94** (1991), 1–28.

[16] L. Moss, *Coalgebraic logic*, Ann. Pure Appl. Logic **96** (1999), 277–317.

[17] T. Mossakowski, L. Schröder, M. Roggenbach, and H. Reichel, *Algebraic-coalgebraic specification in* CoCASL, J. Logic Algebraic Programming, to appear.

[18] D. Pattinson, *Expressivity results in the modal logic of coalgebras*, Ph.D. thesis, Universität München, 2001.

[19] ———, *Semantical principles in the modal logic of coalgebras*, Symposium on Theoretical Aspects of Computer Science, LNCS, vol. 2010, Springer, 2001, pp. 514–526.

[20] ———, *Expressive logics for coalgebras via terminal sequence induction*, Notre Dame J. Formal Logic **45** (2004), 19–33.

[21] J. Power and H. Watanabe, *An axiomatics for categories of coalgebras*, Coalgebraic Methods in Computer Science, ENTCS, vol. 11, Elsevier, 2000.

[22] M. Rößiger, *Coalgebras and modal logic*, Coalgebraic Methods in Computer Science, ENTCS, vol. 33, Elsevier, 2000.

[23] J. Rothe, H. Tews, and B. Jacobs, *The Coalgebraic Class Specification Language CCSL*, J. Universal Comput. Sci. **7** (2001), 175–193.

[24] J. Rutten, *Universal coalgebra: A theory of systems*, Theoret. Comput. Sci. **249** (2000), 3–80.

[25] J. Siekmann and P. Szabo, *A noetherian and confluent rewrite system for idempotent semigroups*, Semigroup Forum **25** (1982), 83–110.

Duality for Logics of Transition Systems

Marcello M. Bonsangue[1,*] and Alexander Kurz[2,**]

[1] LIACS, Leiden University, The Netherlands
[2] Department of Computer Science, University of Leicester, UK

Abstract. We present a general framework for logics of transition systems based on Stone duality. Transition systems are modelled as coalgebras for a functor T on a category $\mathcal{X}$. The propositional logic used to reason about state spaces from $\mathcal{X}$ is modelled by the Stone dual $\mathcal{A}$ of $\mathcal{X}$ (e.g. if $\mathcal{X}$ is Stone spaces then $\mathcal{A}$ is Boolean algebras and the propositional logic is the classical one). In order to obtain a modal logic for transition systems (i.e. for T-coalgebras) we consider the functor L on $\mathcal{A}$ that is dual to T. An adequate modal logic for T-coalgebras is then obtained from the category of L-algebras which is, by construction, dual to the category of T-coalgebras. The logical meaning of the duality is that the logic is sound and complete and expressive (or fully abstract) in the sense that non-bisimilar states are distinguished by some formula.

We apply the framework to Vietoris coalgebras on topological spaces, using the duality between spaces and observation frames, to obtain adequate logics for transition systems on posets, sets, spectral spaces and Stone spaces.

Keywords: transition systems, coalgebras, Stone duality, topological dualities, modal logic

1 Introduction

The framework presented in this paper aims at a general theory of logics for transition systems built on Stone duality. The relationship between these notions can be displayed as follows.

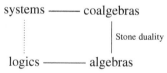

The upper row refers to the theory of coalgebras as laid out by Rutten [22] which proposes coalgebras as a general framework allowing to treat a large variety of different (transition) systems in a uniform way.

The lower row refers to the connection between logics and algebras as familiar from propositional logic/Boolean algebras or intuitionistic logic/Heyting algebras. The

---

* The research of Dr. Bonsangue has been made possible by a fellowship of the Royal Netherlands Academy of Arts and Sciences
** Partially supported by NWO/British Council.

V. Sassone (Ed.): FOSSACS 2005, LNCS 3441, pp. 455–469, 2005.

modal logics that are the basis for most logics of transition systems have similar algebraic counterparts [3].

The connection between the two rows will be provided by Stone duality (Johnstone [13]). Stone duality provides set-theoretic representations of algebras, or, in other words, provides a state-based semantics for the logics described as algebras. It has been used, for example, in the ground breaking work of Jónnson and Tarski [15] and Goldblatt [11] in modal logic and Abramsky [1, 2] in domain theory.

Lifting a Stone Duality via Dual Functors. In this paper we show that there is a simple general principle underlying all these works. It can be formalised in a framework parametric in the basic duality and the type of the transition structure. The key role in this framework will be provided by a suitable duality between a category $\mathcal{X}$ (e.g. Stone spaces [13]) and a category of algebras $\mathcal{A}$ (e.g. Boolean algebras). This duality extends to a duality between relational structures on $\mathcal{X}$ (e.g. descriptive general frames [11]) and modal algebras on $\mathcal{A}$ whenever there are dual endofunctors $T:\mathcal{X} \to \mathcal{X}$ and $L:\mathcal{A} \to \mathcal{A}$.

The relational semantics is given by T-coalgebras and the algebraic semantics is given by L-algebras. The respective categories $\mathsf{Coalg}(T)$ and $\mathsf{Alg}(L)$ are dually equivalent by construction. Informally speaking, T encodes the possible next-step transitions a T-coalgebra may engage in; and L describes how to construct, up to logical equivalence, modal formulae of depth 1 from propositional formulae. We show in Theorem 5 that under fairly general circumstances dual functors on dual categories automatically give rise to a modal logic and an adequate relational semantics (i.e. the logic is sound, complete, and expressive).

Instantiating the Framework with a Powerdomain for T_0-Spaces. We instantiate the above framework to show that a number of modal logics arise in a uniform way if we take $\mathcal{X}$ above to be a suitable category of topological spaces and T to be a variant of the powerset functor. In particular, we want to be able to characterise the relational structure providing an adequate semantics to positive modal logic with infinite joins and infinite meets. This builds on the work of [6] since such a characterisation will require a duality between T_0 topological spaces and so-called spatial observation frames. As a novel result, we present a functor L defining the modal algebras dual to the relational structures induced by T. It is a non-trivial extension of the Vietoris functor on locales as defined in [14].

By considering suitable subcategories of topological spaces we obtain modal logics with an adequate relational semantics on transition systems over posets, sets, spectral spaces, and Stone spaces. The last two cases give us well known modal logics, namely the positive and the classical ones, with $\mathsf{Alg}(L)$ being positive modal algebras and Boolean algebras with operators, respectively, and $\mathsf{Coalg}(T)$ being the $\mathbf{K}^+$-spaces of [8] and the descriptive general frames of [11], respectively. This unifies and extends recent work [21, 17] showing that $\mathbf{K}^+$-spaces and descriptive general frames can be described as $\mathsf{Coalg}(T)$ for an appropriate functor T. Compared to [21], which uses Priestley spaces, our description of $\mathbf{K}^+$-spaces as coalgebras is simpler in that the definition of the Vietoris functor on spectral spaces avoids taking a quotient identifying indistinguishable subsets.

Related Work. The idea of relating constructions on algebras and topological spaces is extensively discussed in [23] and, for a specific class of topological spaces, in [1]. Our approach is more general since it also treats logics with infinitary conjunctions. Moreover, the models we are interested in are not only the solutions of recursive domain equations (final coalgebras) but any coalgebras. On the other hand, we only deal here with categories that do not accommodate the function spaces important in domain theory.

Our algebraic description of the Vietoris construction is a generalisation of that presented in [13, 14], since it allows for equations involving infinite conjunctions. However, when these are not necessary, the two constructions coincide. The equations for spectral spaces of Section 5, for example, are the same as those presented in [14].

Soundness and completeness of an infinitary modal logic for transition systems has been proved in [7] using a topological duality. Completeness, however, is obtained by significantly restricting the class of transition systems under consideration. For example, they form a subclass of the descriptive general frames. Our result here incorporates the above as a special case, obtained by considering a specific category of topological spaces. Furthermore, by applying our framework to the category of posets, we obtain completeness for a larger class of transition systems *including* the descriptive general frames. To our knowledge, this is the first such result for a positive infinitary modal logic.

Overview. We proceed as follows. The next section introduces some basic notions on coalgebras, algebras and their presentation by generators and relations. In Section 3 we describe the framework for the use of dualities for a coalgebraic semantics of modal logic. In Section 4, we introduce a duality for topological spaces and set up, in Section 5, the necessary ingredients for finally applying in Section 6 the above framework to obtain sound, complete, and expressive modal logics for transition systems. We conclude with a discussion on possible future directions in Section 7.

2   Preliminaries

Although category theory does not play a major role in this paper, we will have to assume some basic notions. As usual, *Set* denotes the category of sets and functions.

Algebras and Coalgebras for a Functor. Roughly speaking, coalgebras for a functor generalise transition systems, whereas algebras for a functor generalise the ordinary algebras for a signature where carriers are not sets but taken from some category. Further, (co-)algebras for a functor give rise to the principle of (co-)induction [22].

Given a functor $T:\mathcal{X} \to \mathcal{X}$ on a category $\mathcal{X}$, a *T-coalgebra* (X,ξ) consists of an object $X \in \mathcal{X}$ and an arrow $\xi:X \to TX$. A coalgebra morphism $f:(X,\xi) \to (X',\xi')$ is an arrow $f:X \to X'$ such that $\xi' \circ f = Tf \circ \xi$. Dually, an *L-algebra* on a category $\mathcal{A}$ is given by an arrow $\alpha:LA \to A$, and an algebra morphism $f:(A,\alpha) \to (A',\alpha')$ is an arrow $f:A \to A'$ such that $\alpha' \circ Lf = f \circ \alpha$. The respective categories are denoted by $\mathsf{Coalg}(T)$ and $\mathsf{Alg}(L)$.

If the category $\mathcal{X}$ has a forgetful (i.e. faithful) functor $V:\mathcal{X} \to Set$ then we can talk about the elements of a coalgebra. In particular, we have a canonical notion of behavioural equivalence (or bisimulation). Explicitly, given T-coalgebras $(X, \xi), (X', \xi')$ and elements $x \in VX$, $x' \in VX'$, we say that x and x' are **behaviourally equivalent** or **bisimilar**, denoted $x \simeq x'$, if there is a coalgebra (Y, ν) and there are coalgebra morphisms $f:(X, \xi) \to (Y, \nu)$ and $f':(X', \xi') \to (Y, \nu)$ such that $Vf(x) = Vf'(x')$.

Example 1. If $\mathcal{X}$ is the category Set of sets and functions and $T = \mathcal{P}$ is the powerset functor (mapping a set to its powerset and a function to the direct image function), then $\mathsf{Coalg}(T)$ is the category of Kripke frames with bounded morphisms (also called p-morphisms [11]). Kripke models w.r.t. a given set $Prop$ of atomic propositions are $(\mathcal{P}(Prop) \times \mathcal{P})$-coalgebras. Behavioural equivalence yields the standard notion of bisimulation in both cases.

The Final and Initial Sequences. The intuition that T describes the possible next-step transitions can be made precise using the final (coalgebra) sequence. Moreover, in cases were the final coalgebra does not exist, one can still work with the final sequence. We just outline the basics, for further information see e.g. [25].

The **final sequence** (or terminal sequence) of $T:\mathcal{X} \to \mathcal{X}$

$$ T_0 \xleftarrow{\; p_0^1 \;} T_1 \longleftarrow \cdots \qquad T_n \xleftarrow{\; p_n^{n+1} \;} T_{n+1} \longleftarrow \cdots $$

is an ordinal indexed sequence of objects T_n in $\mathcal{X}$ together with a family $(p_m^n)_{m \leq n}$ of arrows $p_m^n : T_n \to T_m$ for all ordinals $m \leq n$ such that

- $T_{n+1} = T(T_n)$ and $p_{m+1}^{n+1} = T(p_m^n)$ for all $m \leq n$,
- $p_n^n = id_{T_n}$ and $p_k^n = p_k^m \circ p_m^n$ for $k \leq m \leq n$,
- the cone $(T_n, (p_m^n))_{m<n}$ is limiting whenever n is a limit ordinal.

Here we are assuming that $\mathcal{X}$ has the necessary limits (in particular, a final object T_0). The **initial sequence** of an endofunctor is defined dually.

Intuitively, T_n represents behaviours that can be observed in n steps. This can be formalised by observing that, for every coalgebra (X, ξ), there are arrows

$$ \xi_n : X \to T_n $$

where $\xi_n : X \to T_n$ is $T(\xi_m) \circ \xi$ if $n = m + 1$ and ξ_n is the unique map satisfying $\xi_m = p_m^n \circ \xi_n$ for all $m < n$ if n is a limit ordinal. If $V:\mathcal{X} \to Set$ is the forgetful functor we now consider $V\xi_n$ as the map assigning to each state x its n-step behaviour, that is, for $(X, \xi), (X', \xi')$ and $x \in VX$, $x' \in VX'$ define x, x' to be n-**step equivalent**, denoted $x \simeq_n x'$, if $\xi_n(x) = \xi'_n(x')$.

The final sequence is said to converge if there is an ordinal n for which p_n^{n+1} is iso. Then the inverse $(p_n^{n+1})^{-1}$ is the final T-coalgebra. In this case, two states are behaviourally equivalent if and only if they are identified by the (unique) morphisms into the final coalgebra, that is, $x \simeq_n x'$ for all ordinals n.

Example 2. Let $\mathcal{X} = Set$. If TX is the powerset $\mathcal{P}X$ of X, then n-step equivalence coincides with the notion of bounded bisimulation as e.g. in [10]. The final coalgebra does not exist (as an object in $\mathsf{Coalg}(T)$) since its carrier is not a set but a proper class.

Presenting Algebras by Generators and Relations. A category $\mathcal{A}$ is *algebraic* when it comes with a monadic functor $U{:}\mathcal{A} \to Set$ [18]. In this case, the functor U has a left adjoint $F{:}Set \to \mathcal{A}$, mapping every set S to the *free algebra* FS. Furthermore, every object of $\mathcal{A}$ can be presented by generators and relations, that is, for each $A \in \mathcal{A}$ we can find a set S (the elements of which are called *generators* in this context) and a set $R \subseteq FS \times FS$ (the elements of which are called *relations* in this context) such that A is the quotient FS/R. Algebraically speaking, objects of $\mathcal{A}$ can be identified with algebras of an (infinitary) algebraic theory[1]. Clearly, every *presentation* $\mathcal{A}\langle S|R\rangle$ by generators S and relations R defines an algebra in $\mathcal{A}$.

Example 3. A *frame* is a complete lattice L that satisfies the infinite distributive law $a \wedge \bigvee C = \bigvee\{a \wedge c \mid c \in C\}$ for all $a \in L$ and all subsets $C \subseteq L$. Frames with functions preserving arbitrary joins and finite meets form a category called Frm. The forgetful functor from Frm to Set mapping each frame to its underlying set is monadic. Hence the infinitary algebra $Frm\langle S|R\rangle$ presented by a set of generators S and a set of relations R presents a frame and every frame can be presented by generators and relations. In particular, the free frame over a set S can be presented as $Frm\langle S|\emptyset\rangle$.

A model of a presentation $\mathcal{A}\langle S|R\rangle$ is a pair $\langle B, f{:}S \to UB\rangle$ such that $B \in \mathcal{A}$ and $f^\dagger(e_l) = f^\dagger(e_r)$, where $(e_l, e_r) \in R$ and $f^\dagger{:}FS \to B$ is the unique extension of f such that $f^\dagger(\eta(s)) = f(s)$ for each $s \in S$, with η the unit of the adjunction between F and U. It follows that presentations are canonical: if $\mathcal{A}\langle S|R\rangle$ is a presentation of $A \in \mathcal{A}$ then it comes equipped with a function $[\![-]\!]_A{:}S \to UA$ such that for every other model $\langle B, f{:}S \to UB\rangle$ there exists a unique function $f^\ddagger{:}A \to B$ with the property that $f^\ddagger([\![s]\!]_A) = f(s)$ for each $s \in S$.

Example 4. A complete lattice L is a ***completely distributive lattice (cdl)*** if, for all sets $\mathcal{C}$ of subsets of L, it holds that $\bigwedge\{\bigvee C \mid C \in \mathcal{C}\} = \bigvee\{\bigwedge f(\mathcal{C}) \mid f \in \Phi(\mathcal{C})\}$, where $f(\mathcal{C})$ denotes the set $\{f(C) \mid C \in \mathcal{C}\}$ and $\Phi(\mathcal{C})$ is the set of all functions $f : \mathcal{C} \to \bigcup\mathcal{C}$ such that $f(C) \in C$ for all $C \in \mathcal{C}$. Completely distributive lattices with functions preserving both arbitrary meets and arbitrary joins form a category, denoted by CDL. Also the forgetful functor from CDL to Set mapping each completely distributive lattice to its underlying set is monadic.

Since every cdl is a frame we have that $CDL\langle S|R\rangle$ together with the function $[\![-]\!]_F$ is a model of $F = Frm\langle S|R\rangle$. Therefore, the identity function over a set S can be uniquely extended to a frame morphism from $Frm\langle S|R\rangle$ to $CDL\langle S|R\rangle$ for each set of frame relations R. In other words, $CDL\langle S|R\rangle$ is the presentation of the free cdl over the frame presented by $Frm\langle S|R\rangle$.

---

[1] The converse is, in general, false. For example, there is no free complete Boolean algebra over a set of two generators.

3   The Framework: Dualities for Modal Logic

This section describes a general framework for the use of dualities in modal logic. Consider the following situation

$$
T \overset{\curvearrowright}{} \mathcal{X} \underset{Pt}{\overset{\mathcal{O}}{\rightleftarrows}} \mathcal{A} \overset{\curvearrowleft}{} L
$$

$$
V \downarrow \qquad F \big(\big) U
$$

$$
Set \qquad Set
$$

where $\mathcal{O}$ and Pt are a dual equivalence (or duality, for short) between the categories $\mathcal{X}$ and $\mathcal{A}$, i.e. $\mathcal{O}$ and Pt are contravariant functors and there are isomorphisms $X \to Pt\mathcal{O}X$, $A \to \mathcal{O}PtA$, for all $X \in \mathcal{X}, A \in \mathcal{A}$. Further, V is a faithful functor from $\mathcal{X}$ to Set, and L and T are **dual functors** in the sense that there is an isomorphism $PtL \to T^{op} Pt$. Clearly, $\mathsf{Alg}(L)$ and $\mathsf{Coalg}(T)$ are dual categories.

We assume that $\mathcal{A}$ is a category of algebras over Set, that is, categorically speaking, the functor $U{:}\mathcal{A} \to Set$ is monadic. In particular, for any set $Prop$ the free algebra $F(Prop) \in \mathcal{A}$ exists. We call $UF(Prop)$ the set of propositional formulae in variables (or atomic propositions) $Prop$. Since algebras can be represented by generators and relations we can find, for each algebra A, a set of generators GA and a surjective algebra morphism $\tau_A{:}FGA \to LA$. We assume G to be a functor from $\mathcal{A} \to Set$ and τ_A to be natural in A.[2]

These ingredients allow us to define modal formulae and their algebraic semantics. Consider the diagram

$$
\begin{array}{ccccc}
L'_0 & \longrightarrow & FGL'_0 & \longrightarrow & \cdots \\
\downarrow{\scriptstyle q_0} & & \downarrow{\scriptstyle q_1} & & \\
L'_0 & \longrightarrow & L'_1 & \longrightarrow & \cdots
\end{array}
\qquad
\begin{array}{ccc}
FGL'_n & \longrightarrow & \cdots \\
\downarrow{\scriptstyle q_{n+1}} & & \\
L'_{n+1} & \longrightarrow & \cdots
\end{array}
$$

where the lower row is the initial sequence (Section 2) of the functor $L' = L + F(Prop)$, that is, L'_0 is the initial object in $\mathcal{A}$, $L'_{n+1} = L(L'_n) + F(Prop)$. The elements of FGL'_n are the modal formulae of depth $n + 1$. The horizontal arrows allow us to consider a formula of depth n as a formula of depth m for any $m \geq n$. The vertical arrows q_n assign to each formula of depth n its algebraic semantics (which is an equivalence class of modal formulae) and are given by $\tau_{L'_n}$ composed with the left injection into $L(L'_n) + F(Prop)$. By naturality of τ, the above diagram commutes. If the sequence converges, the colimit of FGL'_n is the set of all modal formulas and the colimit of the L'_n is the Lindenbaum-Tarski algebra of the logic. In many interesting cases, the sequence will converge (even after ω steps), but since we also want to cover infinitary logics we can not assume this.

---

[2] For example, we can take $G{:}\mathcal{A} \to Set$ to be the functor $GA = \coprod_{B \in \mathcal{A}} ULFUB \times \mathcal{A}(FUB, A)$ and $\tau_A(f, g) = ULg(f)$. But often, as in the case studied in this paper, a much more economical presentation is possible.

In this paper, the objects of $\mathcal{A}$ will always be (distributive) lattices, that is, although all objects are equipped with a partial order $\leq$ they may lack implication. This means that we cannot reduce consequence $\phi \vdash \psi$ to theoremhood $\vdash \phi \to \psi$. We define

$$\phi \vdash \psi \quad \Leftrightarrow \quad q_n(\phi) \leq q_n(\psi) \text{ for some ordinal } n, \ n \geq \text{depth of } \phi, \psi$$

On the semantic side, in this paper, the objects of $\mathcal{X}$ will be $\mathcal{T}_0$-spaces and $\mathcal{O}$ maps continuous functions to their inverse image functions. We can now describe the coalgebraic semantics for the logic. Let $\xi:X \to TX$ be a coalgebra and x in X. Due to the duality, L'_n is dual to T'_n where $T' = T \times Pt(F(Prop))$, that is, there are isomorphisms $j_n:L'_n \to \mathcal{O}(T'_n)$. Note that a T'-coalgebra $(X, \langle \xi, v \rangle)$ is a T-coalgebra (X, ξ) together with a valuation $v:X \to Pt(F(Prop))$. That is, for each T-coalgebra (X, ξ) together with a valuation $v:X \to Pt(F(Prop))$ there are arrows $\langle \xi, v \rangle_n:X \to T'_n$ (see Section 2). The situation is summarised in

$$FGL'_{n-1} \xrightarrow{\ q_n\ } L'_n \xrightarrow{\ j_n\ } \mathcal{O}(T'_n) \xrightarrow[\langle \xi, v \rangle_n^{-1}]{} \mathcal{O}X$$

We define the semantics $\Vdash$ of $\vdash$ w.r.t. a coalgebra $\langle \xi, v \rangle$ as follows. $\phi \Vdash_{\langle \xi, v \rangle} \psi$ if for some ordinal n, $n \geq$ depth of ϕ, ψ,

$$\langle \xi, v \rangle_n^{-1}(j_n(q_n(\phi))) \subseteq \langle \xi, v \rangle_n^{-1}(j_n(q_n(\psi))) \tag{1}$$

Intuitively, $\langle \xi, v \rangle_n^{-1}(j_n(q_n(\phi)))$ is the set of elements of X that satisfy the formula ϕ under valuation v. As usual, $\phi \Vdash \psi$ means $\phi \Vdash_{\langle \xi, v \rangle} \psi$ for all coalgebras ξ and valuations v. We can now prove soundness, completeness, invariance under bisimilarity and expressiveness.

The theorem can be proved under two different assumptions. This paper employs the theorem under the first assumption, the second assumption will be useful to treat the non-compact powerspace.

Theorem 5. *In the situation described above assume that either*

1. *the final T'-coalgebra exists or* •
2. *T' weakly preserves limits of n-chains for all limit ordinals n.*

Then the modal logic is sound and complete w.r.t. its coalgebraic semantics, that is, $\phi \Vdash \psi \Leftrightarrow \phi \vdash \psi$. Moreover, formulae are invariant under behavioural equivalence and the logic is expressive in the sense that any non-bisimilar points are separated by some formula.

Proof. We first sketch the proof under *Assumption 2* which means that all arrows in the final sequence of T' are surjective (split epi). *Soundness:* Assume $\phi \vdash \psi$, i.e. $q_n(\phi) \leq q_n(\psi)$. Since $\langle \xi, v \rangle_n^{-1} \circ j_n$ is a morphism and therefore monotone it follows $\phi \Vdash \psi$. *Completeness:* Assume $\phi \nvdash \psi$, i.e. $q_n(\phi) \not\leq q_n(\psi)$. Since $j_n:L'_n \to \mathcal{O}(T'_n)$ is an injective morphism, there is $t \in j_n(\phi))$ such that $t \notin j_n(\psi)$. It follows from assumption 2 that each arrow $p_n^{n+1}:T'(T'_n) \to T'_n$ in the final sequence has a right-inverse ζ. ζ is a T'-coalgebra for which $\phi \nVdash_\zeta \psi$, the (counter)example being t. *Invariance:* It is immediate from the definition that formulae are invariant under $\simeq_n$.

Expressiveness: If $\langle \xi, v \rangle, \langle \xi', v' \rangle$ are two coalgebras and x, x' are two elements with $\langle \xi, v \rangle_n(x) \neq \langle \xi', v' \rangle_n(x')$ then, by surjectivity of j_n (and the spaces being $\mathcal{T}_0$), there must be some ϕ such that $j_n(q_n(\phi))$ contains one of $\{x, x'\}$ but not the other. Hence ϕ separates x and x'.

Under *Assumption 1*, the proof is essentially the same. One replaces q_n by the morphism to the initial L'-algebra, $\langle \xi, v \rangle_n$ by the morphism to the final T'-coalgebra and ζ by the final coalgebra itself.

Remark 6. Expressiveness of the logic can also be considered as full abstractness of the final semantics.

Example 7. We briefly illustrate the notions with a well-known example. Let $\mathcal{A}$ be the category of Boolean algebras and $\mathcal{X}$ the category of Stone spaces. $VPtA = \mathcal{A}(A, \mathbf{2})$ is the set of ultrafilters over A. (Similarly, writing $2_{\mathcal{X}}$ for the two-element Stone space, we have that $U\mathcal{O}X = \mathcal{X}(X, 2_{\mathcal{X}})$ is the set of clopens of X.) If we take $GA = A$ and $\tau_A(a) = \square a$ and LA to be the quotient of FGA defined by the equations expressing that $\square$ preserves meets, then $\mathsf{Alg}(L)$ is the category of modal algebras (Boolean algebras with operators). $GL'_n = \{\square \phi \mid \phi \in L'_n\}$ and FGL'_n is the closure of GL'_n under propositional operations (modulo Boolean equations). The functor T dual to L is the Vietoris functor and $\mathsf{Coalg}(T)$ is the category of descriptive general frames. The continuity of a valuation $v:X \to Pt(F(Prop)) \cong \prod_{Prop} 2_{\mathcal{X}}$ means that the extension of a propositional variable in $Prop$ has to be a clopen set. See [17] for details.

4   Topological Duality

In this section we set up the necessary ingredients for applying the above framework. In particular we will briefly introduce a duality for topological spaces, generalising the Stone duality considered in the previous example.

Recall that a *topological space* is a set X together with a collection of subsets of X, called opens, closed under arbitrary unions and finite intersections. A function between two sets X and Y is continuous if its inverse maps opens of Y to opens of X.

Each topological space X induces a *closure operator* mapping each subset S of X to the least (w.r.t. subset inclusion) subset $\overline{X}$ such that $X \setminus \overline{X}$ is open. Each topological space induces also a *pre-order* on X defined by $x \leq y$ if and only if $x \in o$ implies $y \in o$ for each open o of X. A space X is said to be $\mathcal{T}_0$ when the above pre-order is a partial order. We denote by Top_0 the category of all $\mathcal{T}_0$ topological spaces with continuous functions as morphisms.

For the category of algebras we consider the category $OFrm$ of observation frames, a structure introduced in [6] for representing topological spaces abstractly. An *observation frame* is an order-reflecting frame morphisms $\alpha:F \to L$ between a frame F and a completely distributive lattice L such that

$$q = \bigwedge \{o \in \alpha(F) \mid q \leq o\}$$

for every element q of L. A morphism between two observation frames $\alpha:F \to L$ and $\beta:G \to H$ is a pair $\langle f, g \rangle$ consisting of a frame morphism $f:F \to G$ and a cdl-morphism $g:L \to H$ such that $g \circ \alpha = \beta \circ f$.

Example 8. Each topological space X defines an observation frame $\mathcal{O}X$ as the inclusion map between the frame $O(X)$ of all open subsets of X and the cdl $Q(X)$ of all upclosed subsets of X. Furthermore, $\mathcal{O}$ can be extended to a functor by mapping a continuous function $f\colon X \to Y$ to $\langle f^{-1}\colon O(Y) \to O(X), f^{-1}\colon Q(Y) \to Q(X)\rangle$.

The functor $U\colon OFrm \to Set$ mapping an observation frame $\alpha\colon F \to L$ to $\alpha(F)$ is monadic [5]. Therefore every observation frame $\alpha\colon F \to L$ can be presented as $OFrm\langle S|R\rangle$ for some set S of generators and set R of relations $e_l = e_r$. Here e_l and e_r are expressions formed by applying the infinite meet operator $\bigwedge$ to expressions formed from the generators in S by applying the infinite join operator $\bigvee$ and finite meet operator $\wedge$. In particular, L is isomorphic in CDL to $CDL\langle S|R\rangle$, whereas F is isomorphic in Frm to $Frm\langle S|R^-\rangle$, where R^- is the subset of R obtained by considering relations involving only finite meet and infinite join operators. Since $\langle L, [\![-]\!]_L\rangle$ is a model for the presentation of F, the frame morphism $\alpha\colon F \to L$ is obtained as the canonical extension of the identity on S. Similarly, every presentation $OFrm\langle S|R\rangle$ presents an observation frame.

Next we show that the functor $\mathcal{O}\colon Top_0 \to OFrm^{op}$ has a right adjoint. Let 2 be the two-element cdl with $\top_2$ as top element and $\bot_2$ as bottom one, and **2** be the identity morphism on 2. For an observation frame $\alpha\colon F \to L$ we denote by $Pt(\alpha)$ the topological space given by the set $OFrm(\alpha, \mathbf{2})$ together with a topology with open sets defined, for every $x \in F$, by $\triangle(x) = \{\langle f, g\rangle\colon\alpha \to \mathbf{2} \mid f(x) = \top_2\}$.

Theorem 9 ([6]). *For every observation frame α, the assignment $\alpha \mapsto Pt(\alpha)$ can be extended to a functor from $OFrm^{op}$ to Top_0 which is right adjoint of $\mathcal{O}$.*

For every T_0 topological space X, the unit $\eta_X\colon X \to Pt(O(X))$ of the above adjunction is an isomorphism, whereas for each observation frame $\alpha\colon F \to L$ the counit $\triangle(-)\colon F \to O(Pt(\alpha))$ is injective. We say that α is *spatial* when $\triangle$ is an isomorphism. The above adjunction thus restricts to an equivalence between Top_0 and the full subcategory $SOFrm$ of spatial observation frames [6].

5   Two Vietoris Functors

In order to apply the duality framework introduced in Section 3 we define two endofunctors $\mathcal{P}_c$ and $\mathcal{V}$ on Top_0 and $OFrm$, respectively, and prove that they are dual functors using the duality introduced in the previous section.

We call a subset c of a topological space X *convex* if $c = c{\uparrow} \cap \overline{c}$, where $c{\uparrow}$ is the upclosure of c w.r.t. the pre-order induced by X whereas $\overline{c}$ is its topological closure.

Definition 10. Given a space X, define the Vietoris hyperspace $\mathcal{P}_c(X)$ to be the set of all convex compact subsets of X equipped with the topology generated by the sub-basic sets

$$\{c \in \mathcal{P}_c(X) \mid c \subseteq o\} \text{ and } \{c \in \mathcal{P}_c(X) \mid c \cap o \neq \emptyset\}$$

for each $o \in O(X)$.

The restriction to convex subsets in the definition of $\mathcal{P}_c(X)$ guarantees that the hyperspace $\mathcal{P}_c(X)$ is $\mathcal{T}_0$ if X is a $\mathcal{T}_0$ space [19]. $\mathcal{P}_c$ extends to an endofunctor on Top_0.

Example 11. If X is a set, i.e. a discrete topological space, then $\mathcal{P}_c(X)$ is the set of all finite subsets of X taken with the discrete topology. Also, if X is an ω-algebraic complete partial order equipped with the Scott topology, then $\mathcal{P}_c(X)$ coincides with the Plotkin powerdomain.

For the definition of the endofunctor $\mathcal{V}$ on $OFrm$ it is enough to define a presentation of $\mathcal{V}(\alpha)$ for each observation frame α. Its set of generators is

$$G(\alpha) = \{\Box a \mid a \in \alpha(F)\} \cup \{\Diamond a \mid a \in \alpha(F)\}$$

and the relations are given by the following rule schemes

$$(\Box - \textstyle\bigwedge) \quad \frac{\bigwedge_I a_i \leq b}{\bigwedge_I \Box a_i \leq \Box b} \qquad\qquad (\Diamond - \textstyle\bigvee) \quad \Diamond \bigvee_I a_i = \bigvee_I \Diamond a_i$$

$$(\Box - \vee) \quad \Box(a \vee b) \leq \Box a \vee \Diamond b \qquad (\Diamond - \textstyle\bigwedge) \quad \frac{\bigwedge_I a_i \wedge b \leq c}{\bigwedge_I \Box a_i \wedge \Diamond b \leq \Diamond c}$$

$$(COM) \quad \Box \bigvee_I a_i = \bigvee_{J \in Fin(I)} \Box \bigvee_J a_i \,,$$

where $Fin(I)$ is the set of all finite subsets of I. Rules $(\Box - \bigwedge)$ and $(\Diamond - \bigwedge)$ generalise corresponding rules for the Vietoris locale [14] basically by imposing the $\Box$ operator to distribute over all meets of F which are preserved by α as meet of L. The scheme (COM) corresponds to restricting to compact subsets in the definition of $\mathcal{P}_c$ as in [14, 23] and states that $\Box$ distributes over directed joins.

Theorem 12. *For every $\mathcal{T}_0$ space X, $Pt\mathcal{V}\mathcal{O}X \cong \mathcal{P}_c X$.*

If α is a spatial observation frame then $\alpha \cong \mathcal{O}Pt\alpha$ and it follows $Pt\mathcal{V}\alpha \cong \mathcal{P}_c Pt\alpha$. Hence the functors $\mathcal{P}_c$ and $\mathcal{V}$ were dual if $SOFrm$ was closed under $\mathcal{V}$. This is not the case in general [14], but we will see below that it is true for many important subcategories of $SOFrm$ to which we then apply the framework of Section 3.

Posets. The category $PoSet$ of posets with monotone functions can be characterised as the full subcategory of Top_0 that has as objects those topological spaces where open sets are closed under arbitrary intersections (the Alexandroff topology). The category $PoSet$ is closed under the Vietoris functor $\mathcal{P}_c$. The adjunction in Theorem 9 restricts to a duality between the category $PoSet$ and $AlgCDL$, the category of algebraic cdl's. $AlgCDL$ is equivalent to the full sub-category of $OFrm$ whose objects are observation frames $\alpha: F \to L$ with $\alpha(F) = L$ and L algebraic [5]. The duality implies that these observation frames are spatial.

The category $AlgCDL$ is closed under the Vietoris functor $\mathcal{V}$. To see this one can first note that because $\alpha(F) = L$ the presentation of $\mathcal{V}\alpha$ can be simplified by replacing the schemes $(\Box - \bigwedge)$ and $(\Diamond - \bigwedge)$ with the following two:

$$(\Box - \textstyle\bigwedge') \quad \bigwedge_I \Box a_i = \Box \bigwedge_I a_i \qquad (\Diamond - \wedge) \quad \Box a \wedge \Diamond b \leq \Diamond(a \wedge b) \,.$$

That the cdl presented by $\mathcal{V}\alpha$ is algebraic (and hence spatial) follows from the following lemma, similar to one in [2, 24].

Lemma 13. Let $\alpha: F \to L$ be an observation frame and X a subset of $\alpha(F)$. In the observation frame $\mathcal{V}\alpha$ we have $\Box \bigvee_I a_i = \bigvee_{J \in Fin(I)} (\Box \bigvee_J a_i \wedge \bigwedge_J \Diamond a_i)$.

Summarising, the categories $PoSet$ and $AlgCDL$ are dual and closed under the two Vietoris functors $\mathcal{P}_c$ and $\mathcal{V}$, respectively. Furthermore, the two functors are also dual, and the category $AlgCDL$ is algebraic.

Sets. The category Set of sets and functions is a full subcategory of $PoSet$. It can be characterised as the full subcategory of Top_0 with as objects the topological spaces with open sets closed under arbitrary intersections and complement (the discrete topology). We have already seen that Set is closed under the Vietoris functor $\mathcal{P}_c$. The duality between the categories $PoSet$ and $AlgCDL$ restricts to a duality between Set and $CABool$ the full sub-category of $AlgCDL$ with objects equivalent to observation frames $\alpha: F \to L$ with $\alpha(F) = L$ and L an algebraic boolean algebra. Note that algebraic complete boolean algebras are just complete atomic boolean algebras.

If $\alpha: F \to L$ is an observation frame as above then in the observation frame $\mathcal{V}\alpha$ it holds

$$(\Box - \neg) \quad \Box a \vee \Diamond \neg a = \top \quad \text{and} \quad (\Diamond - \neg) \quad \Box a \wedge \Diamond \neg a = \bot .$$

for each $a \in \alpha(F)$ with complement $\neg a \in \alpha(F)$. Hence $\Diamond \neg a$ is the complement of $\Box a$. The presentation of $\mathcal{V}\alpha$ can thus be simplified by replacing the schemes $(\Box - \bigwedge)$, $(\Box - \vee)$ and $(\Diamond - \bigwedge)$ with $(\Box - \bigwedge')$, $(\Box - \neg)$ and $(\Diamond - \neg)$. By applying the framework described in Section 3 we obtain an infinitary modal logic (with negation) that is sound and complete w.r.t. its coalgebraic semantics.

Spectral Spaces. The category $Spec$ of spectral spaces is a subcategory of Top_0 with as objects topological spaces with compact open sets closed under finite intersections and forming a base for the topology. Morphisms in $Spec$ are continuous functions with inverse preserving compact opens. As for the other categories above, $Spec$ is closed under the Vietoris functor $\mathcal{P}_c$ [13, 23]. The adjunction in Theorem 9 restricts to a duality between the category $Spec$ and $DLat$, the category of distributive lattices, equivalent to the full sub-category of $OFrm$ whose objects are observation frames $\alpha: F \to L$ with F an algebraic arithmetic frame and L the free completely distributive lattice over F. Equivalently, observation frames in $DLat$ can be presented by relations using only finite meet and finite join operators, because they are equivalent to distributive lattices. It follows that observation frames in $DLat$ are spatial.

The category $DLat$ is closed under the Vietoris functor $\mathcal{V}$, because if $\alpha: F \to L$ is an observation frame in $DLat$, then the presentation of $\mathcal{V}\alpha$ can be simplified by using the following relations:

$$(\Box - \wedge) \quad \Box(a \wedge b) = \Box a \wedge \Box b \qquad (\Box - \top) \quad \Box \top = \top$$
$$(\Diamond - \vee) \quad \Diamond(a \vee b) = \Diamond a \vee \Diamond b \qquad (\Diamond - \bot) \quad \Diamond \bot = \bot$$
$$(\Box - \vee) \quad \Box(a \vee b) \leq \Box a \vee \Diamond b \qquad (\Diamond - \wedge) \quad \Box a \wedge \Diamond b \leq \Diamond(a \wedge b) .$$

Note that these axioms are precisely those which have to be added to distributive lattices to define positive modal algebras, see e.g. [8]. It follows that $\mathsf{Alg}(\mathcal{V})$, with $\mathcal{V}$ restricted to $DLat$, is (isomorphic to) the category of positive modal algebras. From Section 3, it follows that $\mathsf{Coalg}(\mathcal{P}_c)$, with $\mathcal{P}_c$ restricted to spectral spaces, provides an adequate relational semantics for positive modal logic. Compared to [21] this yields an alternative description of $\mathbf{K}^+$-spaces ([8]) as coalgebras.

Stone Spaces. Stone spaces are spectral spaces with compact opens closed under complement. Let *Stone* be the full subcategory of *Spec* with Stone spaces as objects. We can restrict the duality between *Spec* and *DLat* to a duality between *Stone* and *Bool*, the full subcategory of *DLat* with as object boolean algebras. If $\alpha{:}F \to L$ is an observation frame equivalent to a boolean algebra then in the observation frame $\mathcal{V}\alpha$ both $(\Box - \neg)$ and $(\Diamond - \neg)$ hold. Hence the presentation of $\mathcal{V}\alpha$ for *DLat* can be simplified by replacing the schemes $(\Box - \vee)$ and $(\Diamond - \wedge)$ with $(\Box - \neg)$ and $(\Diamond - \neg)$. We can further simplify by reducing the set of generators to $G(\alpha) = \{\Box a \mid a \in \alpha(F)\}$ and the relations to

$$(\Box - \wedge) \quad \Box(a \wedge b) = \Box a \wedge \Box b \qquad (\Box - \top) \quad \Box\top = \top$$

Note that these axioms are precisely those which have to be added to Boolean algebras to define modal algebras (Boolean algebras with operator). It follows that $\mathrm{Alg}(\mathcal{V})$, with $\mathcal{V}$ restricted to *Bool*, is (isomorphic to) the category of modal algebras. The category $\mathrm{Coalg}(\mathcal{P}_c)$, with $\mathcal{P}_c$ restricted to *Stone*, is isomorphic to the category of descriptive general frame and has also been described in [17].

6   Modal Logics for Transition Systems

In order to obtain sound, complete, and expressive modal logics, we now apply the framework of Section 3 to the dualities obtained in the previous section. For all four dualities

$$\mathcal{P}_c \bigcirc \mathcal{X} \xrightleftharpoons{\hspace{1cm}} \mathcal{A} \bigcirc \mathcal{V}$$

the final coalgebra of the functor $\mathcal{P}_c$ exists, so that we can apply Theorem 5. The corresponding propositional logic is obtained in the following way.

For a description of $\mathcal{A}$ via signature Σ and equations E take the formulae to be the terms built from the signature Σ plus the two unary operation symbols $\Box$ and $\Diamond$. The calculus is given by the calculus for equational logic plus the equations E plus the rules describing the functor $\mathcal{V}$ (some of the rules have been given as inequations, but $\phi \leq \psi$ can be considered a shorthand for $\phi \wedge \psi = \psi$).

As it is well-known, such an equational calculus can be translated into a propositional modal calculus. Since our algebras are lattices we can use inequations instead of equations. We write $\phi \vdash \psi$ for $\phi \leq \psi$. That is, $\phi \vdash \psi$ corresponds to the equation $\phi \wedge \psi = \psi$ and, conversely, an equation $\phi = \psi$ to inequations $\phi \vdash \psi, \psi \vdash \phi$.

As it is apparent from (1) in Section 3, the semantics of $\phi \vdash \psi$ is the so-called local consequence of modal logic. In classical modal logic, local consequence can be formulated as theorem-hood because $\phi \vdash \psi$ is equivalent to $\vdash \phi \to \psi$. But as in e.g. [1, 7, 8], not all our logics have '$\to$'. We will detail below the modal calculi arising in the way just described from the four dualities of the previous section.

Posets and Spectral Spaces. The first is the infinitary version of the second. In both cases, the modal operators will obey the rule schemes

$$\frac{\phi \vdash \psi}{\Box\phi \vdash \Box\psi} \qquad\qquad \frac{\phi \vdash \psi}{\Diamond\phi \vdash \Diamond\psi} \qquad\qquad (2)$$

Posets The signature Σ is $\{\bigvee, \bigwedge\}$ and these operators are axiomatised according to the laws of completely distributive lattices (i.e. , negation free infinitary propositional logic).[3] The axiom schemes for the modal operators are the following.

$$\bigwedge_I \Box\phi_i \vdash \Box\bigwedge_I \Box\phi_i \qquad\qquad \Diamond\bigvee_I \phi_i \vdash \bigvee_I \Diamond\phi_i$$
$$\Box(\phi \vee \psi) \vdash \Box\phi \vee \Diamond\psi \qquad\qquad \Box\phi \wedge \Diamond\psi \vdash \Diamond(\phi \wedge \psi)$$
$$\Box\bigvee_I \phi_i \vdash \bigvee_{J \in Fin(I)} \Box\bigvee_J \phi_i$$

Spectral Spaces The signature Σ is $\{\top, \bot, \vee, \wedge\}$ and these operators are axiomatised according to the laws of distributive lattices (i.e. , negation free propositional logic). The axiom schemes for the modal operators are the following.

$$\Box(a \wedge b) \vdash \Box a \wedge \Box b \qquad \top \vdash \Box\top$$
$$\Diamond a \vee \Diamond b \vdash \Diamond(a \vee b) \qquad \Diamond\bot \vdash \bot$$
$$\Box(a \vee b) \vdash \Box a \vee \Diamond b \qquad \Box a \wedge \Diamond b \vdash \Diamond(a \wedge b).$$

In the previous section some of the inequalities above are presented as equalities. The 'missing' directions follow from the monotonicity rules (2).

Sets and Stone spaces. The first is the infinitary version of the second. Since we have classical implication, we only need to axiomatise $\top \vdash \phi$ which we abbreviate by $\vdash \phi$. Since we have negation, we need only one modal operator, say $\Box$.

Sets The signature Σ is $\{\bigwedge, \neg\}$ and these operators are axiomatised according to the laws of completely distributive lattices with negation (i.e. , classical propositional logic). In order to stay close to the equational axiomatisation it is convenient to choose as a rule scheme

$$\frac{\vdash \phi \leftrightarrow \psi}{\vdash \Box\phi \leftrightarrow \Box\psi} \qquad\qquad (3)$$

(which is the congruence rule of equational logic for $\Box$) and as axiom schemes

$$\vdash \bigwedge \Box\phi_i \leftrightarrow \Box\bigwedge \phi_i \qquad\qquad \vdash \top \leftrightarrow \Box\top$$
$$\vdash \Box\bigvee_I \phi_i \leftrightarrow \bigvee_{J \in Fin(I)} \Box\bigvee_J \phi_i$$

Stone Spaces The signature Σ consists of the operators $\top, \vee, \neg$ which are axiomatised according to the laws of boolean algebra (i.e. classical propositional logic). In order

---

[3] The category $\mathcal{A}$ of Section 3 is $AlgCDL$ whereas the category described by the signature is CDL. But since $\mathcal{V}$ preserves algebraic cdls, the initial sequence for $\mathcal{V}$ remains in $AlgCDL$.

to stay close to the standard calculus of modal logic, it is convenient to choose the following rule and axiom scheme

$$\frac{\vdash \phi}{\vdash \Box \phi} \qquad \qquad \vdash \Box(\phi \to \psi) \to (\Box \phi \to \Box \psi)$$

These schemes correspond to the equations from the previous section because they are equivalent to the rule 3 together with $\vdash \Box(\phi \wedge \psi) \leftrightarrow \Box \phi \wedge \Box \psi$ and $\vdash \Box \top \leftrightarrow \top$.

7   Conclusion and Further Work

We have presented a general framework relating modal logics and their relational (i.e. coalgebraic) semantics. It can be read in two directions: describe a given logic as a functor L and work out the adequate relational semantics by describing the dual functor T; or, for a given notion of transitions systems as T-coalgebras, work out the adequate logic by describing the dual of T via generators and relations. To apply this idea and equip the coalgebraic logic of Moss [20] with modal operators (given by the generators) and a complete axiomatisation is one of many directions for future research.

Another one is to look at other functors T than the compact hyperspace. An obvious candidate is the non-compact hyperspace which is expected to give interesting infinitary logics for the categories of posets and sets (the infinitary counterparts of spectral and Stone spaces, respectively). Further candidates are the Kripke-polynomial functors of Jacobs [12].

Furthermore, it would be interesting to determine the range of the framework of Section 3. Apart from generalising some of the specific assumptions, there is also the question which logics can be described by categories of algebras that admit a duality, leading to connections with algebraic logic [9].

References

1. S. Abramsky. Domain theory in logical form. *Annals of Pure and Applied Logic*, 5:1–77, 1991.
2. S. Abramsky. A domain equation for bisimulation. *Inf. and Comp.*, 92, 1991.
3. J. van Benthem, J. van Eijck, and V. Stebletsova. Modal Logic, Transition Systems and Processes. *Journal of Logic and Computation*, 4:811–855, 1994.
4. P. Blackburn, M. de Rijke, and Y. Venema. *Modal Logic*. CSLI, 2001.
5. M.M. Bonsangue. *Topological Dualities in Semantics*. Vol. 8 of ENTCS, Elsevier, 1996.
6. M.M. Bonsangue, B. Jacobs, and J.N. Kok. Duality beyond sober spaces: topological spaces and observation frames. *Theor. Comp. Sci.* 15(1):79–124, 1995.
7. M.M. Bonsangue and J.N. Kok. Towards an infinitary logic of domains: Abramsky logic for transition systems. *Inf. and Comp.* 155:170–201, 1999.
8. S. Celani and R. Jansana. Priestley duality, a Sahlqvist theorem and a Goldblatt-Thomason theorem for positive modal logic. *Logic Journ. of the IGPL*, 7:683–715, 1999.
9. J.M. Font, R. Jansana, and D. Pigozzi. A Survey of Abstract Algebraic Logic. *Studia Logica*, 74:13–97, 2003.

10. J. Gerbrandy. *Bisimulations on Planet Kripke*. PhD thesis, Univ. of Amsterdam, 1999.
11. R.I. Goldblatt. Metamathematics of modal logic I. *Rep. on Math. Logic*, 6, 1976.
12. B. Jacobs. Many-sorted coalgebraic modal logic: a model-theoretic study. *Theoretical Informatics and Applications*, 35(1):31–59, 2001.
13. P.T. Johnstone. *Stone Spaces*. Cambridge University Press, 1982.
14. P.T. Johnstone. The Vietoris monad on the category of locales. In *Continuous Lattices and Related Topics*, pp. 162–179, 1982.
15. B. Jónsson and A. Tarski, Boolean algebras with operators, part I. *American Journal of Mathematics*, 73:891–939, 1951.
16. M. Kracht. *Tools and Techniques in Modal Logic*. Vol. 142 of *Studies in Logic*, Elsevier, 1999.
17. C. Kupke, A. Kurz, and Y. Venema. Stone coalgebras. *Theoret. Comput. Sci.*, 327:109–134, 2004.
18. E.G. Manes. *Algebraic Theories*. Springer-Verlag, 1976.
19. E. Michael. Topologies on spaces of subsets. *Trans. Amer. Math. Soc.*, 71, 1951
20. L. Moss. Coalgebraic logic. *Annals of Pure and Applied Logic*, 96:277–317, 1999.
21. A. Palmigiano. A coalgebraic semantics for positive modal logic. *Theoret. Comput. Sci.*, 327:175–195, 2004.
22. J.J.M.M. Rutten. Universal coalgebra: A theory of systems. *Theoret. Comput. Sci.*, 249:3–80, 2000.
23. S. Vickers. *Topology via Logic*. Cambridge University Press, 1989.
24. S. Vickers. Information systems for continuous posets. *Theoret. Comp. Sci.*, 114, 1993.
25. J. Worrell. Terminal sequences for accessible endofunctors. In *Coalgebraic Methods in Computer Science (CMCS'99)*, vol. 19 of *ENTCS*, Elsevier, 1999.

Confluence of Right Ground Term Rewriting Systems Is Decidable

Lukasz Kaiser

Mathematische Grundlagen der Informatik, RWTH Aachen

Abstract. Term rewriting systems provide a versatile model of computation. An important property which allows to abstract from potential nondeterminism of parallel execution of the modelled program is confluence. In this paper we prove that confluence of a fairly large class of systems, namely right ground term rewriting systems, is decidable. We introduce a labelling of variables with colours and constrain substitutions according to these colours. We show how right ground rewriting systems can be reduced to simple systems with coloured variables. Such systems can be analysed using reduction-automata techniques which leads to an interesting decision procedure for confluence.

1 Introduction

Term rewriting systems (TRS) were developed from mathematical logic and are used in many contexts in computer science. They serve as models for computer programs, abstract mathematical structures and are used in equational reasoning. Such systems consist of sets of rewriting rules that can be applied to transform one term into another. There are many interesting properties of TRS and algorithms working on them used in different fields including functional programming languages, where properties like confluence and termination of TRS are investigated.

Confluence, also called the Church-Rosser property, is a very important property of TRS and programs that contain some kind of nondeterminism, for example parallel or probabilistic programs. It states that after any possible rewritings of a term or after a number of steps of program execution on different execution paths there is always a way to rewrite to a common term or follow the program execution to the same result, which can eliminate the problem of nondeterminism.

Confluence is known to be undecidable for general TRS. Oyamaguchi studied confluence of a simple class of ground TRS already in 1987 and showed it to be decidable [11]. Dauchet et. al. gave a decision procedure for the first order theory of ground rewrite systems in 1990 [5] using methods related to tree automata and tree transducers. In 2001, Comon, Godoy and Nieuwenhuis showed that confluence of ground TRS can be decided in polynomial time [1] and they were the first to use new methods like analysing top stable symbols to attack the problem. This line of research was continued by Tiwari [13].

V. Sassone (Ed.): FOSSACS 2005, LNCS 3441, pp. 470–489, 2005.

Ordered term rewriting systems were also analysed and Comon, Narendran, Nieuwenhuis and Rusinowitch proved the decidability of confluence of such systems for wide classes of orderings [3, 4].

In recent years, there was an active development in the theory of wider classes of TRS, right ground systems and linear shallow systems. Godoy, Tiwari, and Verma showed that the confluence of linear shallow term rewrite systems can be decided in polynomial time [7]. Their article not only extended the methods of [1] but also simplified and clarified the proofs. Finally the proofs of [7] were again redone and presented in a clarified form in [6].

When we go outside linear systems, things become undecidable quite fast. Marcinkowski proved in 1997 that the first order theory of right ground rewriting is undecidable even for one step rewriting [10]. Also in 2003 Jacquemard proved that reachability and confluence are undecidable for general flat term rewriting systems [8].

When we consider the natural syntactic division of rewriting systems based on whether the rules are ground, linear of flat and we want to analyse reachability, joinability, confluence and first order theory of such systems then the results mentioned before, together with the reductions in [15] answer all decidability questions except for the one we want to investigate here, the confluence of right ground systems. This was a long standing open problem [16] solved in [9] and also recently in an independent work by Tiwari, Godoy and Verma in [14], where authors further developed stability and rewrite closure methods used in [1, 7].

We extend the right ground rewriting system to a system with constraints, analyse the constrained system and look for constrained substitutions. This allows us to see the methods used before in a different context and use reduction automata techniques (see [2]) to complete the proof. Combining automata techniques and analysis of rewriting properties has already proved successful many times and goes back to [5, 11], conditional rewriting systems are also well known and widely used. Moreover, methods using automata techniques and constrained rewriting have often been used in different contexts, so we hope that the presented methods not only give the decision procedure for confluence but can also be extended to other problems and used in program analysis.

The Organisation. of this article follows the outline of the proof that confluence of RGTRS is decidable and the reductions done to the system. First we define the basic notions and tools that will be used for right ground systems and reduce the rewriting system by naming all ground terms in the rules by new constants and then by taking a limited rewrite closure. This reduction has already become a standard starting point when analysing right ground rewriting systems. Then we prove a technical lemma and reduce the non-confluence problem to the problem of deep non-joinability of constants and semi non-confluence, which is also a variation of a well known method.

Later we introduce colour constraints and coloured substitutions and show how standard unification can be extended to the coloured case. We analyse stability of terms and reduce semi non-confluence to the existence of stable terms fulfilling some constraints. We then show how to decide the existence of such terms by reducing it to emptiness of reduction automata which is known to be decidable. Also the deep joinability of constants is reduced to emptiness of reduction automata, which completes the proof.

Acknowledgement. The result proved in the paper was first proved as a part of the authors masters thesis [9] written under the direction of *Leszek Pacholski*. We also want to thank *Jerzy Marcinkowski* for helpful comments and revision. Later *Dietmar Berwanger* and *Erich Grädel* helped to prepare the current version. We also want to thank *Christof Löding* for references about tree automata that made it possible to clarify and simplify the proofs a lot.

2   Basic Notions

2.1   Terms and Positions in Terms

Let us assume that we are given a finite set of symbols Σ called the *signature* and a function $arity : \Sigma \to \mathbb{N}$. Symbols with arity 0 will be called constants ($\Gamma = \{c \in \Sigma : \text{arity}(c) = 0\}$) and denoted by letters a, b, c. The other symbols will be called function symbols and denoted by letters f, g, h. We also assume that there is an infinite set of variables V which will be denoted by letters x, y, z. Throughout the paper the signature will be assumed to be constant, also in all algorithmic problems the maximal arity of function symbols is assumed to be a constant and not an input parameter.

Terms over Σ are defined inductively as the smallest set $\mathcal{T}$ such that:

- $\mathcal{T} \supseteq V$,
- if $f \in \Sigma$ with arity n and $t_1, \ldots, t_n \in \mathcal{T}$ then $f(t_1, \ldots, t_n) \in \mathcal{T}$.

The set $\text{Var}(t)$ of variables occurring in a term t is also defined inductively by $\text{Var}(c) := \emptyset$, $\text{Var}(x) := \{x\}$ and $\text{Var}(f(t_1, \ldots, t_n)) = \text{Var}(t_1) \cup \cdots \cup \text{Var}(t_n)$. When $\text{Var}(t) = \emptyset$ then the term t is called *ground*.

The usual intuition behind terms is to view them as labelled trees, therefore we introduce the notion of positions in terms. The set P of *positions* in terms is the set of sequences of positive natural numbers. By $\lambda \in P$ we will denote the empty sequence or the top (root) position in the term.

For a given term t and position p we either say that p does not exist in t or define the term at position p in t (denoted by $t|_p$) in the following inductive way:

- λ exists in each term and $t|_\lambda = t$,
- $p = (n, q)$ exists in $t = f(t_1, \ldots, t_m)$ if $m \geq n$ and q exists in t_n and in such case $t|_p = t_n|_q$.

A position p is *above* some position q if there exists a sequence r of numbers such that $q = (p, r)$. In this case we also say that q is *below* p. The height of a position is its length. The height of a term is the maximal height of a position existing in this term.

For example in the term $f(a, f(b, c))$ position $2, 1$ exists and $f(a, f(b, c))|_{2,1} = b$, but neither the position 3 nor the position $1, 2$ exists. The height of $f(a, f(b, c))$ is 2, the height of $f(b, c)$ is 1 and the height of a constant is 0.

2.2   Substitutions and Rewritings

Substituting term s in term t at position p yields the term $r = t[s]_p$ such that for all positions q not below p that exist in t, it holds that $r|_q = t|_q$ and $r|_p = s$. Less formally r is just t with the subtree at position p replaced by s, for example substituting $f(a,b)$ at position 1 in $f(a, f(b, c))$ yields the term $f(f(a,b), f(b,c))$.

Substituting term s in term t *for a variable* x is defined as substituting s in t at all positions p where $t|_p = x$. A *substitution* (usually denoted with letters σ, τ, ρ) is a set of pairs, each consisting of a variable and a term (such pairs are denoted by $x \leftarrow t$). Applying a substitution $\sigma = \{x_1 \leftarrow t_1; \ldots; x_n \leftarrow t_n\}$ to a term t, we obtain a term $r = t\sigma$ which is the result of substituting each x_i by t_i in t. As an example, let us take the term $t = f(x,y)$ and the substitution $\sigma = \{x \leftarrow a, y \leftarrow f(b,c)\}$. Then $t\sigma = f(x,y)\sigma = f(a, f(b,c))$.

A *rewriting rule* is a pair of terms t and s denoted by $t \rightarrow s$ such that $\text{Var}(t) \supseteq \text{Var}(s)$. The rule is called *ground* if both t and s are ground and *right ground* if s is ground.

A rewriting rule $l \rightarrow r$ can be *applied* to a term t at position p, if there exists a substitution σ of variables in l such that $t|_p = l\sigma$. The result of applying the rule is $t[r\sigma]_p$ - term t rewritten at position p. You should note that there is only one possible result of applying a rule to a term at a given position and that since $\text{Var}(l) \supseteq \text{Var}(r)$, a ground term remains ground after applying a rule to it at any position. For example we can apply a right ground rule $f(x,x) \rightarrow c$ to the term $f(c, f(a,a))$ at position 2 and obtain the term $f(c,c)$.

A *term rewriting system* (TRS) is a set of term rewriting rules and throughout this article we consider only systems with finitely many rules. The system is ground (GTRS) or right ground (RGTRS), if all rules in the system are ground or respectively right ground. We say that a term t rewrites to a term r with respect to a given TRS T, if there is a rule in T and a position p in t such that r is the result of applying the rule to t at p and we denote it by $t \rightarrow_T r$. The relation $\twoheadrightarrow_T$ is the transitive and reflexive closure of the relation $\rightarrow_T$, where $t \twoheadrightarrow_T s$ means that t rewrites to s in a finite number of steps. We will often talk about successive rewriting steps $t \rightarrow_T t_1 \rightarrow_T t_2 \rightarrow_T \ldots \rightarrow_T t_n \rightarrow_T s$ forming a rewriting path $t \twoheadrightarrow s$. When the system is clear from the context we will omit the index T.

Continuing our previous example, if we take a RGTRS with only one rule $T = \{f(x,x) \rightarrow c\}$ then $f(c, f(a,a)) \rightarrow_T f(c,c)$ and since $f(c,c) \rightarrow_T c$, we can say that $f(c, f(a,a)) \twoheadrightarrow_T c$ on the rewriting path $f(c, f(a,a)) \rightarrow f(c,c) \rightarrow c$.

Given a term rewriting system T and two terms s and t we will say that s is *reachable* from t if $t \twoheadrightarrow_T s$ and that s is *joinable* with t if there exists a term u such that both $s \twoheadrightarrow_T u$ and $t \twoheadrightarrow_T u$. Any such term u that both $s \twoheadrightarrow_T u$ and $t \twoheadrightarrow_T u$ will be called a *joinability witness* for s and t. In our example $f(c, f(a,a))$ and $f(b,b)$ are joinable, since both can be rewritten to c, and c is the only joinability witness of these two terms.

We say that t and s are *deeply joinable*, if all pairs of terms to which these two respectively rewrite are joinable. More formally when $t \twoheadrightarrow_T t_1$ and $s \twoheadrightarrow_T s_1$ then t_1 and s_1 have to be joinable. If the two terms are not deeply joinable then there exist two non-joinable terms t_1 and s_1 such that $t \twoheadrightarrow_T t_1$ and $s \twoheadrightarrow_T s_1$ which will be called *witnesses of deep non-joinability*. A term t is *confluent* with respect to T, if it is deeply joinable with itself and the witnesses of deep non-joinability of t with t will then be called the *witnesses of non-confluence*. A TRS T is confluent if all terms are confluent with respect to T.

Example 1. Let us take a right ground rewriting system

$$R = \{c \rightarrow f(c,c), c \rightarrow g(c,c), f(x, f(x,x)) \rightarrow c\}.$$

Let us now look at the term $t = f(c,c)$. We can rewrite it at position 2 to $s = f(c, g(c,c))$ and it is easy to see that s can not be rewritten to c, since the g symbol at position 2 will not be reduced by any of the rewriting rules as it is too near to the root position to be destroyed inside the variable in the third rule.

Also please note that $t = f(c,c)$ can be rewritten also as position 2 but with a different rewrite rule obtaining $f(c, f(c,c))$, which can be further reduced to c. So t is not confluent with respect to R and one possible pair of witnesses of non-confluence is $f(c, g(c,c))$ and c.

All mentioned properties (reachability, joinability, deep-joinability, confluence of a term and of a TRS) can also be analysed as algorithmic decision problems: given the TRS and possibly the terms as arguments, decide if the property holds or not.

3   Basic Tools for Right Ground TRS

It is a well known (see [12]) fact that reachability and joinability are decidable for right ground TRS.

Fact 1. *Reachability and joinability problems are decidable for RGTRS.*

3.1   Naming Ground Terms with Constants

We consider an arbitrary RGTRS

$$R = \{l_1 \rightarrow r_1, l_2 \rightarrow r_2, \ldots, l_n \rightarrow r_n\}.$$

Let us now take any ground term of height one $f(c_1, \ldots, c_n)$ appearing as a sub-term of any right side r_i and introduce a constant to name it. So for the term $f(c_1, \ldots, c_n)$ we add a new constant $c_{f(c_1, \ldots, c_n)}$ and two new rewrite rules

$$c_{f(c_1, \ldots, c_n)} \rightarrow f(c_1, \ldots, c_n),$$

$$f(c_1, \ldots, c_n) \rightarrow c_{f(c_1, \ldots, c_n)}.$$

Then we replace each occurrence of $f(c_1, \ldots, c_n)$ in R with $c_{f(c_1, \ldots, c_n)}$.

Let us notice that the new term rewriting system R_1 obtained in this way is confluent if, and only if, R is confluent, since the relations $\twoheadrightarrow_R$ and $\twoheadrightarrow_{R_1}$ are identical on terms without the constant $c_{f(c_1, \ldots, c_n)}$ and this constant can always be replaced with $f(c_1, \ldots, c_n)$. Therefore we can repeat this procedure until the resulting RGTRS R' has only the following types of rules:

>: rules in the form $c \rightarrow f(c_1, \ldots, c_n)$,

$\leq$: rules $t \rightarrow c$, where t is any term.

Of course, here f stands for different function symbols and c for different constants. Further, we will call the rules of type $>$ *increasing*, those of type $\leq$ *non-increasing*, since the first ones increase the height of the term and the second ones do not. This extension allows us to restrict our attention to RGTRS that have only the two types of rules given above, and for a given RGTRS T with such rules we will denote by $T^>$ the rules of the first kind in T and by $T^\leq$ the rules of the second kind. More detailed description of this method and the proof that it preserves confluence can be found in [1].

Since we know that reachability for right ground systems is decidable, we can extend R' to a new system R'' in the following way: for each constants c and c' and each term $f(c_1, \ldots, c_n)$ of height one, we have

$$c \rightarrow c' \in R'' \text{ if } c \twoheadrightarrow_{R'} c',$$

$$c \rightarrow f(c_1, \ldots, c_n) \in R'' \text{ if } c \twoheadrightarrow_{R'} f(c_1, \ldots, c_n),$$

$$f(c_1, \ldots, c_n) \rightarrow c \in R'' \text{ if } f(c_1, \ldots, c_n) \twoheadrightarrow_{R'} c.$$

Therefore, if a constant rewrites to a term of height one or a term of height one rewrites to a constant, or constant rewrites to another constant, then the rewriting can be done in one step. If RGTRS is in this form, we will call it *reduced*.

The following simple lemma will be used very often.

Lemma 1. *For ground terms $t_1, t_2, \ldots, t_n, s$ and reduced RGTRS T we have*

$$t := f(t_1, \ldots, t_n) \twoheadrightarrow_T s$$

if and only if one of the following conditions holds:

(1) $s = f(s_1, \ldots, s_n)$ and for each i we have $t_i \twoheadrightarrow_T s_i$,

(2) there is a constant c such that $t \twoheadrightarrow_T c$ and $c \twoheadrightarrow_{T^>} s$.

Proof. In any TRS, if any of these two conditions hold, then obviously $t \twoheadrightarrow_T s$. The converse is true in any reduced RGTRS since if there is a rewriting at the root position in t somewhere on the path $t \twoheadrightarrow_T s$, then it has to go through a constant because all non-increasing rules rewrite to a constant. Also, when rewriting from a constant we do not need to use the decreasing rules any more since, if a constant rewrites to a term of height one, then the rewriting can be done in one step without decreasing rules. ∎

Definition 1. *A ground term t is* stable *with respect to a rewriting system T if no sub-term of t that is not a constant rewrites (is in $\twoheadrightarrow_T$ relation) to a constant.*

Stability is a very important property in connection with Lemma 1, since intuitively in stable terms the rewriting needs to be done only at leaf positions. One can think of stability as a normal form with respect only to non-increasing rules. Stability is also useful when analysing joinability, which is expressed by the following lemma.

Lemma 2. *A stable term $f(t_1, \ldots, t_n)$ is not joinable with a constant c with respect to a reduced RGTRS T if and only if for any term $f(c_1, \ldots, c_n)$ such that $c \xrightarrow{*}_T f(c_1, \ldots, c_n)$ there is some sub-term t_i not joinable with c_i.*

Proof. Indeed, the term $f(t_1, \ldots, t_n)$ is stable, so it does not rewrite to any constant and it can be joined with c only if $c \xrightarrow{*}_T f(c_1, \ldots, c_n)$ and $f(c_1, \ldots, c_n)$ will be joined with $f(t_1, \ldots, t_n)$ without rewriting to a constant, so each constant c_i must be joined with the appropriate sub-term t_i. ∎

3.2   Reduction of the Confluence Problem

Let us now reduce the problem of confluence to a more tractable problem. First we have to define when a RGTRS T is *semi non-confluent*.

Definition 2. *Rewriting system T is semi non-confluent if there exists a term s and a constant c such that s is an instance of the left hand side of some rule $l \to c \in R$ and on the other hand s can be rewritten to a term r and r is not joinable with c.*

Please note that if T is semi non-confluent then it clearly is not confluent, but there can also be other reasons for a system not to be confluent. The following lemma reduces the general confluence case for reduced RGTRS to semi non-confluence and the confluence of constants.

Lemma 3. *If a reduced right ground term rewriting system T is not confluent then either there exists a constant that is not confluent or T is semi non-confluent.*

The prove this lemma, we look at the smallest term that is not confluent with respect to T and analyse possible rewriting paths to the witnesses of non-confluence relying on Lemma 1. The proof is given in detail in appendix A.

4   Coloured Terms

Let us now define a set of constraints that we will call colours and show some basic properties of coloured terms and coloured rewritings. This can be interpreted as a simple form of conditional rewriting systems, but we will not introduce the general definitions of conditional systems and only concentrate on our simple case.

The colour constraints are defined in a very simple way, a *colour* K is a set of constants $K = \{c_1, \ldots, c_m\}$. We say that a ground term t has colour K with respect to a TRS T if each $c_i \xrightarrow{*}_T t$. We will omit the TRS T if it is fixed in the context. Please note that with this definition each term t has a number of colours, actually one biggest colour

$$K(t) := \{c \; : \; c \xrightarrow{*}_T t\}$$

and all its sub-colours. Each term has $\emptyset$ as its colour.

Definition 3. *A coloured term is a term t with each variable $x \in \text{Var}(t)$ labelled with a colour C_x. A correct ground substitution for a coloured term with respect to a TRS T is a substitution σ such that only ground terms are substituted for variables and a ground term s is substituted for a given variable x only if C_x is a colour of s w.r.t T, i.e. $C_x \subseteq K(s)$.*

Definition 4. *A coloured (right ground) rewrite rule is a pair consisting of a coloured term and a constant. A coloured rewrite rule $l \to c$ can be applied to a ground term t at position p if there exists a correct ground substitution σ for l such that $t|_p = l\sigma$.*

We will now fix a reduced RGTRS with respect to which the colourings are defined and extend it with a set of coloured rewrite rules so that on any rewriting path of a ground term the increasing rewritings can take place only at the end.

Example 2. Let us continue our example for

$$R = \{c \to f(c,c), c \to g(c,c), f(x, f(x,x)) \to c\}$$

and the colour $K = \{c\}$. Let us take any term t such that $c \xrightarrow{*} t$ and look at the rewriting path

$$f(t, c) \to f(t, f(c,c)) \xrightarrow{*} f(t, f(t,t)) \to c. \tag{1}$$

Please note that using the second rewrite rule in the last step was possible because $c \xrightarrow{*} t$, e.g. for $t = f(c,c)$. Also please note that such rewriting could be done for each term t with colour K.

This suggests a new coloured rewriting rule

$$f(x : K, f(c,c)) \to c,$$

where $x : K$ denotes that the variable x is coloured with K. Looking at the rewriting (1) it is also evident that the coloured rule

$$f(x : K, c) \to c \tag{2}$$

can also be added to the system without changing the semantics or rewriting.

What we will do next is to show how using coloured rules we can eliminate the need to change increasing and non-increasing rules on a rewriting path with respect to a reduced RGTRS.

Please look at the rewriting (1) and follow it again for $t = f(c,c)$, so

$$f(f(c,c),c) \xrightarrow{*}_{R>} f(f(c,c), f(f(c,c), f(c,c))) \to_{R\leq} c.$$

As you can see we have to interchange rewriting with $R^>$ and with $R^\leq$ to rewrite the term to c. But if we add the rule (2) to the non-increasing rules ($R^\leq$) then we do not have to use the increasing rules any more.

We will generalise this example to an arbitrary reduced RGTRS T by taking all possible positions in the left sides of rewriting rules in T and substituting there all possible constants and looking if appropriate colouring for the remaining variables can be found. First let us introduce a notation and define what an appropriate colouring is.

We will say that a term s *grows from* a term t if $t \xrightarrow{*}_{T>} s$. Please note that in such case all rewritings on the rewriting path take place in the leafs of the term (viewed as a tree).

Let us now take a term l (possibly a left side of a rewriting rule) and a sequence of different positions $P = p_1, \ldots, p_n$ existing in l and a sequence of constants $A = c_1, \ldots, c_n$. We will be interested in the term l with each constant c_i substituted at the corresponding position p_i and we will use the notation

$$l(A, P) := (((l[c_1]_{p_1})[c_2]_{p_2}) \ldots)[c_n]_{p_n}.$$

Definition 5. *Given a term l a sequence P of positions in l and a sequence A of constants with the same length as P we will say that a colouring*

$$\{x_1 : K_1, \ldots, x_n : K_n\}$$

of variables in l is appropriate w.r.t. A and P if there exists a term s that fulfils the following properties. The term s grows from $l(A, P)$ and contains exactly the same positions as l and at all positions where there is no variable in l it has the same symbols as l. Then the colouring is appropriate if for each variable x_i the assigned colour K_i is equal to the set of constants that appear in s at the positions at which x_i appears in l.

Please note that in this definition we assume that the positions P are incomparable with the prefix ordering of positions, so all constants can be put in parallel and the order of positions in P does not matter.

Let us analyse this definition looking at the example presented before. We can take the term $l = f(x, f(x, x))$ and choose to insert the constant c at position 2, so $A = c$ and $P = 2$ and $l(A, P) = f(x, c)$. Although $f(x, c)$ can grow either to $f(x, g(c, c))$ or to $f(x, f(c, c))$, according to the definition we will consider only the second case, as the first one has g at position 1, which is different from f at position 1 in l. We can see that $x : \{c\}$ is the appropriate colouring in this case.

Let us now take all possible rules $l \to c \in T^{\leq}$, all possible sequences of different positions P in l and for each P take all sequences of constants A with the same length.

Let us now colour each rewrite rule

$$l(A, P) \to c.$$

Let us take all possible appropriate colourings of the variables from l with respect to A and P. To obtain colourings of variables from $l(A, P)$ we can just cast each colouring of variables of l, but we will exclude some of them. Namely, if in a colouring of variables of l there are coloured variables that does not appear in $l(A, P)$ and they are coloured with $K_1, \ldots, K_m$ then we will allow the cast of this colouring only if each colour K_i is satisfiable, i.e. there exists a term u such that all constants in K_i rewrite to u. Please note that it is decidable whether a colour is satisfiable as it is a simple extension of joinability (see [12]) and we will call u the satisfiability witness for K_i.

Let us denote the set of all coloured rewrite rules obtained in this way with respect to T coloured with all allowed colourings by T^c. Since we have defined correct ground substitutions for coloured rewrite rules we define the relation $\rightarrow_{T^c}$ and $\overset{*}{\rightarrow}_{T^c}$ on ground terms in the same way as we did for uncoloured rewrite rules, only using correct ground substitutions.

Lemma 4. *For any reduced RGTRS T with T^c defined as above and for any two terms t and s if $t \overset{*}{\rightarrow}_{T^c} s$ then also $t \overset{*}{\rightarrow}_T s$.*

The proof of this lemma follows the construction presented above and is given in detail in appendix B. As we see from the above lemma the extension of T with coloured rules is correct in the sense that it does not change the semantic of rewriting. Moreover, we do not need any more to grow constants in order to match a sub-term in a rewriting rule, since a coloured rule can be used instead, as stated in the following lemma, which is proved in similar way in appendix B.

Definition 6. *Term s grows from a term t in bounds of a term l with respect to a reduced RGTRS T if $t \overset{*}{\rightarrow}_{T>} s$ and all rewritings either take place on the positions that exist in l or at (new) positions that do not exist in t.*

Lemma 5. *Given a reduced RGTRS T let us take a rule $l \rightarrow c \in T$ and two ground terms u and w such that w grows from u in bounds of l and w is an instance of l. Then any rewriting path in T in the form*

$$u \overset{*}{\rightarrow}_{T>} w \rightarrow_{\{l \rightarrow c\}} c$$

can be reduced to one step rewriting in the system T^c defined above, so $u \rightarrow_{T^c} c$.

The construction of such coloured closure of the rewriting system will be later used to show that stability of a term with respect to a reduced RGTRS t can be replaced by a property analogous to being a normal form with respect to T^c and therefore that stable terms can be recognised by a reduction automaton.

Before we proceed to analyse confluence we need one more tool to handle unification in the coloured case. Let us assume that we are given a coloured term t and a coloured rewrite rule $l \rightarrow c$ and we want to describe the set of substitutions σ for variables of t such that $t\sigma$ is an instance of l, i.e. there is a correct substitution τ for l such that $t\sigma = l\tau$.

If we forget about colours then we can take the most general unifier α of t and l and denote $u = t\alpha = l\alpha$. As the colours are only constrains on the non-coloured case then obviously all substitutions σ we are looking for will just constrain the most general unifier α. It can also be noted that the right substitutions σ impose exactly such constraints, that guarantee, that on positions where coloured variables appeared in t and l, there will only appear ground terms with the right colour in u. Unluckily, to propagate the constraints from positions in u where there were coloured variables in t and l down to the variables in u we will have to increase the number of unifiers with colour constraints. Let us fix a reduced RGTRS T and state the following lemma.

Lemma 6. *For two coloured terms t and s with disjoint variables there exists a set $u_1, \ldots, u_l$ of terms such that for correct ground substitutions σ, ρ it holds $t\sigma = s\rho$ if, and only if, there exists an i and a correct ground substitution τ for which*

$$t\sigma = u_i\tau = s\rho.$$

Moreover, for each i there exists a coloured substitution μ_i (substituting coloured terms for variables) such that $u_i = t\mu_i = s\mu_i$. The set $\{\mu_1, \ldots, \mu_l\}$ is called the most general unifier of t and s and is computable.

Proof. Let α be the most general unifier of t and s forgetting about the colour constraints and let $u = t\alpha = s\alpha$. It should be noted that there are correct ground substitution σ and ρ such that $t\sigma = s\rho$ exactly then, when there is a ground substitution β for variables in u for which

$$u\beta = t\sigma = s\rho$$

and if there was a variable coloured with colour K at position p in t or in s, then the term substituted at this position has the colour K.

As we see we can describe all the substitutions we are looking for by giving the term u and the set of constraints consisting of a position and a colour. Such constraints can be propagated to lower positions and finally be checked for constants and set as new colours for variables, but for the price of creating multiple copies of u with different constraint sets. The details of how the constraints are propagated are given in appendix B.

5   Stability of Coloured Terms

According to Lemma 3 we know that we only need to decide deep non-joinability of constants and the semi non-confluence property. We will reduce semi non-confluence to a set of instances of the coloured stability problem. We assume that a reduced RGTRS T is fixed.

Definition 7. *The coloured stability problem asks given a coloured term t and a constant c to decide if there exists a correct substitution σ such that $t\sigma$ is stable and not joinable with c.*

Lemma 7. *The problem to decide for a given term s and a constant c if there exists a substitution σ and a stable term t such that $s\sigma \twoheadrightarrow t$ and t is not joinable with c, can be reduced to a finite set of instances of the coloured stability problem.*

Please note that if there exists any such term t then there also exists a stable one. Hence, we can assume that t is stable.

Proof. Let us analyse the reduction path $s\sigma \twoheadrightarrow t$. We can restrict our attention to substitutions σ such that there are no rewritings in the substituted variables, since if there is a need to rewrite, we could have substituted already the rewritten form. Therefore we can also assume that the rewritings are done in the appropriate bounds and use Lemma 5 to describe the rewriting path. First let us divide the rewritings on the path into segments of increasing and non-increasing rewritings (the increasing segments may have length 0)

$$s\sigma = s_1 \overset{*}{\to}_{T>} s'_2 \to_{T\leq} s_2 \overset{*}{\to}_{T>} s'_3 \to_{T\leq} s_3 \ldots \to_{T\leq} s_n \overset{*}{\to}_{T>} s'_{n+1} = t.$$

Then using Lemma 5 we can describe this path with coloured rewritings in the following way:

$$s\sigma = s_1 \to_{T^c} s_2 \to_{T^c} \ldots \to_{T^c} s_n \overset{*}{\to}_{T>} t.$$

Since s is given and the number of positions in s is bounded, we can enumerate all positions in s at which these non-increasing rewritings take place together with the rules applied there. Let us denote these positions by $p_1, \ldots, p_n$ and the coloured rules used at these positions by $l_1 \to c_1, \ldots, l_n \to c_n$. For given positions and rules we will enumerate all coloured terms $t_1, \ldots, t_m$ such that if there exists a ground substitution σ satisfying

$$s\sigma = s_1 \to_{\{l_1 \to c_1\}} s_2 \to_{\{l_2 \to c_2\}} \cdots \to_{\{l_n \to c_n\}} s_n$$

then there exists a correct ground substitution ρ for some t_i such that $s_n = t_i\rho$.

If we find such terms t_i then we can substitute for each constant a in t_i a new variable coloured with $\{a\}$ obtaining a terms t'_i and then we will know that $t = t'_i\rho$ for some correct ground substitution ρ and in this way the problem will be reduced.

We will now show how to enumerate the requested coloured terms t_i using the unifiers we defined before. We will proceed inductively with respect to n (the length of the rewriting path $s_1 \twoheadrightarrow s_n$) starting with s and we will show how to proceed one step, generating for one coloured term the appropriate set of coloured terms.

In an intermediate step let us consider the coloured term u such that $s_i = u\rho$ for some correct ground substitution ρ and let s_i be rewritten to s_{i+1} by the coloured non-increasing rule $l_i \to c_i$ used at position p in u. It is now enough to enumerate the terms $v_1, \ldots, v_m$ such that if for some correct ground substitution σ the term $u\sigma$ can be rewritten with $l_i \to c_i$ at position p, then $v = v_j\rho$ for some $1 \leq j \leq m$ and some correct substitution ρ. In such case $u|_p\sigma = l_i\tau$ for some correct τ and from Lemma 6 we know that there exists the set

$$\{\mu_1, \ldots, \mu_m\} = \mathrm{mgu}(u|_p, l_i).$$

Then it is sufficient to take $v_i = u\mu_i[c_i]_p$ to get the desired terms. ∎

6   Reduction Automata

We have reduced the confluence problem to the coloured stability problem and to the problem of confluence of constants. We will now show how to solve these problems using reduction automata. The definitions, facts and theorems presented here can be found in [2] in the chapter about automata with equality and disequality constraints. Since we are using exactly the same objects as presented in that chapter, we do not present all the terminology with the same level of detail as presented there.

Reduction automata are a special kind of automata with equality and disequality constraints (AWEDC). An *equality (disequality) constraint* is an expression $p_1 = p_2$ ($p_1 \neq p_2$), where p_1 and p_2 are positions and is satisfied by a term t if $t|_{p_1} = t|_{p_2}$ ($t|_{p_1} \neq t|_{p_2}$). An *automaton with equality and disequality constraints* is a tuple

$$(Q, \Sigma, Q_f, \Delta),$$

where Σ is the signature, Q is a finite set of states, $Q_f \subseteq Q$ and Δ is a set of rewrite rules in the form

$$f(q_1, \ldots, q_n) \to^\alpha q,$$

where $q_1, \ldots, q_n, q \in Q$ and α is a boolean combination of equality and disequality constraints.

The language accepted by an automaton and the run of an automaton on a term is defined in an analogous way to the standard automata, only by each application of a rule the corresponding constraint must hold. The automaton is *deterministic* if for every term t there is at most one state q such that there exists a run of the automaton on t ending in the state q, and it is *complete* if there is at least one such state.

A *reduction automata* is a member of AWEDC such that there is a ordering on Q such that for each rule $f(q_1, \ldots, q_n) \to^\alpha q$, where α is not trivial (empty) the state q is strictly smaller than each state q_i. The most important facts about reduction automata (see [2]) that we will use are the following.

Fact 2. *The class of reduction automata is closed under union and intersection. There is a construction for the union that preserves determinism.*

Fact 3. *With each reduction automaton we can associate a complete reduction automaton that accepts the same language. This construction preserves determinism. The class of complete deterministic reduction automata is closed under complement.*

Fact 4. *The emptiness of a language accepted by a reduction automata is decidable.*

Fact 5. *It is possible to construct a deterministic complete reduction automaton accepting the set of terms that are correct ground substitutions of a given term with coloured variables. It is also possible to construct a deterministic complete reduction automaton encompassing such correct ground substitutions.*

From these facts only Fact 5 is not a literal copy of facts from [2], since there the construction is presented for uncoloured terms. But since colour constraints can be expressed as tree automata, deterministic and without constraints, we can use the same construction as presented in [2] for uncoloured terms only adding the states of automata recognising coloured constraints and substituting accepting states of these automata for $q_\top$ used in the uncoloured construction to denote all non-special terms.

Using these facts and the relation between stability with respect to T and being a normal form with respect to T^c that is proved in Lemma 5 we can prove the following lemma (see appendix C for details).

Lemma 8. *The coloured stability problem for a term t and constant c with respect to a reduced RGTRS T is decidable.*

The analysis of deep joinability of constants relies on a technical lemma similar to Lemma 2 that concerns joinability. To use reduction automata for deep joinability of constants we have to analyse pairs and construct the automaton for terms with signature extended to cope with pairs. The technical details are given in appendix C together with the proof of the following lemma.

Lemma 9. *Deep joinability of constants with respect to a RGTRS is decidable.*

From the results proved in lemmas 3, 7, and 8 and 9 follows our main theorem.

Theorem 1. *Confluence of right ground term rewriting systems is decidable.*

7   Conclusions and Remarks

We showed how to analyse confluence of right ground term rewriting systems. Our results provide a method to reduce confluence to satisfiability of a constrained stability of terms. Although the presented techniques rely heavily on the fact that the analysed TRS is right ground, it could be interesting to try to extend them to other classes of TRS. The use of reduction automata for solving constrained stability and its extension to deep joinability of constants might be transferred to other cases. It might also be used to prove more refined results concerning right ground or non-increasing systems.

These methods might also be used to analyse special classes of RGTRS in order to get complexity results. Finding an optimised algorithm for coloured stability for linear TRS would open the way to show that left linear right ground TRS are in coNP. If there is no such algorithm then due to the tight integration with automata methods there is a chance that the strict complexity bounds for automata might be translated to show that this problem is not in coNP.

The presented technique of colouring variables with automatic constraints and using more powerful automata to analyse the resulting constrained programs can certainly be used also in other contexts for program analysis.

References

1. H. Comon, G. Godoy, R. Nieuwenhuis, *The Confluence of Ground Term Rewrite Systems is Decidable in Polynomial Time*, 42nd Annual IEEE Symposium on Foundations of Computer Science, Las Vegas, NV, USA, 2001.

2. H. Comon, F. Jacquemard, M. Dauchet, D. Lugiez, R. Gilleron, S. Tison, M. Tomassi, *Tree Automata Techniques and Applications*, available on internet under http://www.grappa.univ-lille3.fr/tata/

3. H. Comon, P. Narendran, R. Nieuwenhuis, M. Rusinowitch, *Decision Problems in Ordered Rewriting*, IEEE Symposium on Logic in Computer Science, Indianapolis, IN, USA, 1998.

4. H. Comon, P. Narendran, R. Nieuwenhuis, M. Rusinowitch, *Deciding the Confluence of Ordered Term Rewrite Systems*, ACM Transactions on Computational Logic 33 - 55, ACM Press, New York, NY, USA, 2003.

5. M. Dauchet, S. Tison, *The Theory of Ground Rewrite Systems is Decidable*, IEEE Symposium on Logic in Computer Science, Philadelphia, PA, 1990.

6. G. Godoy, R. Nieuwenhuis, A. Tiwari, *Classes of Term Rewrite Systems with Polynomial Confluence Problems*, ACM Transactions on Computational Logic Vol. 5 No. 2, pp. 321-331, 2004.

7. G. Godoy, A. Tiwari, R. Verma, *On the Confluence of Linear Shallow Term Rewrite Systems*, Symposium on Theoretical Aspects of Computer Science, Berlin, Germany, 2003.

8. F. Jacquemard, *Reachability and Confluence are Undecidable for Flat Term Rewriting Systems*, Information Processing Letters, 87 (5) pp.265-270, 2003.

9. L. Kaiser *Confluence of Right Ground Term Rewriting Systems is Decidable*, Masters Thesis, University of Wroclaw, June 2003.

10. J. Marcinkowski *Undecidability of the First Order Theory of One-Step Right Ground Rewriting*, Intl. Conference on Rewriting Techniques and Applications, Sitges, Spain, 1997.

11. M. Oyamaguchi, *The Church-Rosser Property for Ground Term Rewriting Systems is Decidable*, Theoretical Computer Science, 49 (1) pp.43-79, 1987.

12. M. Oyamaguchi, *The Reachability and Joinability Problems for Right-Ground Term-Rewriting Systems*, Journal of Information Processing, 13 (3) pp.347-354, 1990.

13. A. Tiwari, *Polynomial time Algorithms for Deciding Confluence of Certain Term Rewrite Systems*, IEEE Symposium on Logic in Computer Science, Copenhagen, Denmark, 2002.

14. A. Tiwari, G. Godoy, R. Verma, *Confluence Characterization Using Rewrite Closure with Application to Right Ground Systems*, Applicable Algebra in Engeneering, Communication and Computing Vol. 15 No. 1, pp. 13-36, 2004.

15. R. Verma, M. Rusinowitch, D. Lugiez *Algorithms and Reductions for Rewriting Problems*, Intl. Conference on Rewriting Techniques and Applications, Tsukuba, Japan, 1998.

16. RTA list of open problems, available on internet under http://www.lsv.ens-cachan.fr/~treinen/rtaloop/problems/

A   Proof of Reduction of Confluence

Lemma 10. *If a right ground term rewriting system R is not confluent then either there exists a constant that is not confluent or the following semi non-confluence property is fulfilled. A RGTRS R is* semi non-confluent *if there exists a term s and a constant c such that s is an instance of a left hand side of a rule $l \rightarrow c \in R$ and on the other hand s can be rewritten to a term r and r is not joinable with c.*

Proof. Let us assume that R is not confluent, so there exists a lowest term t that is not confluent. If there exist a few such lowest witnesses of non-confluence with equal height, we can take any of them. If t is a constant then the proof is complete. Assume $t = f(t_1, \ldots, t_n)$. Since t is not confluent, we know that there exist witnesses u, v of non-confluence, so $t \twoheadrightarrow u$, $t \twoheadrightarrow v$ and u and v are not joinable. We can assume that u is the first term on the rewriting path $t \twoheadrightarrow u$ that is not joinable with v and v is the first on the path $t \twoheadrightarrow v$ not joinable with u, otherwise we could just take the terms appearing before on the paths.

Let us now show that there has to be a constant on the rewriting path $t \twoheadrightarrow u$ or $t \twoheadrightarrow v$. Indeed, if there was no constant on these paths then we know by Lemma 1 that $u = f(u_1, \ldots, u_n)$ and $v = f(v_1, \ldots, v_n)$ and for each i $t_i \twoheadrightarrow u_i$ and $t_i \twoheadrightarrow v_i$. But since u and v are not joinable so there exists an i such that u_i and v_i are not joinable, and for this i the term t_i would not be confluent itself, which contradicts the assumption that t was the lowest not confluent term. We can now assume without loss of generality, that there is a constant c on the rewriting path $t \twoheadrightarrow u$. Even more, we can assume that this is the first constant on this path and that each term on the path before c is joinable with v, since any term on the path before u was joinable with v.

We know that

$$t \twoheadrightarrow s \rightarrow c \twoheadrightarrow u$$

and that $t \twoheadrightarrow v$ and u is not joinable with v. Let us assume that v and c are joinable and let v_1 be a joinability witness for v and c. Then $c \twoheadrightarrow v_1$, $c \twoheadrightarrow u$ and v_1 is not joinable with u hence c is not confluent, which contradicts the assumption that all constants are confluent. Therefore we know that not v is not joinable with c. Also since s is on the rewriting path before c we know that s is joinable with v and we can denote a witness of their joinability by r. Then we have all the terms required in our assertion, since $s \twoheadrightarrow r$ and r is not joinable with c because v is not joinable with c and $v \twoheadrightarrow r$. ∎

B   Proofs of Properties of Coloured Closure

Lemma 11. *For any reduced RGTRS T with T^c defined before and for any two terms t and s if $t \twoheadrightarrow_{T^c} s$ then also $t \twoheadrightarrow_T s$.*

Proof. Let a rule $l(A, P) \rightarrow c \in T^c$ be applied to some ground term w at position p with $w|_p = u$. So there is a correct substitution σ such that $u = l(A, P)\sigma$.

Since $l(A, P)$ in the rule is appropriately coloured so there exists the term s that witnesses that the colouring is appropriate and s grows with respect to T from $l(A, P)$ and differs from l only at positions with variables. We can rewrite u in the same way as $l(A, P)$ grows since u is an instance of $l(A, P)$. Therefore we obtain a term v such that $u \xrightarrow{*}_{T>} v$ and at all positions p in l where there are no variables $v|_p = l|_p$.

Let us now take a variable x appearing in l and consider all terms appearing in v at positions where x appears in l. At positions that also appear in $l(A, P)$ there is the term $x\sigma$ and at the other we have some constants $c_1, c_2, \ldots, c_n$. But since the colouring is appropriate, then x is coloured with $K = \{c_1, \ldots, c_n\}$ and since σ is correct then for each c_i we have $c_i \xrightarrow{*}_T x\sigma$. If we do this rewriting for each variable in l, it becomes clear that $v \xrightarrow{*}_T l\sigma$ and therefore $u \xrightarrow{*}_T c$. You should note that if the variable x does not appear in $l(A, P)$ then we have to rewrite each c_i to the satisfiability witness for K instead of rewriting to $x\sigma$. ∎

Lemma 12. *Given a reduced RGTRS T let us take a rule $l \to c \in T$ and two ground terms u and w such that w grows from u in bounds of l and w is an instance of l. Then any rewriting path in T in the form*

$$u \xrightarrow{*}_{T>} w \to_{\{l \to c\}} c$$

can be reduced to one step rewriting in the system T^c defined before, so $u \to_{T^c} c$.

Proof. Since u grows to an instance of l, there is a sequence of positions in u where there are constants and these positions can grow first to a term s that is identical to l except for the positions where l has variables and later to w being an instance of l. Let us denote the sequence of positions in u mentioned above by P and the sequence constant appearing at respective positions in u by A.

Let us then consider the rule $l(A, P) \to c \in T^c$ with the appropriate colouring for variables of l that comes from s. Please note that since s grows to an instance of l then in the appropriate colouring all colours of variables of l that are not variables of $l(A, P)$ must be satisfiable as the witnesses appear in w, so the mentioned rule indeed is in T^c with the casted colouring. Then it is clear that u rewrites with this rule to c, since the colour constraints are fulfilled in u as they were in w. ∎

We will now repeat literally a part of the proof presented in the paper to be sure that the notation is consistent.

Lemma 13. *For two coloured terms t and s with disjoint variables there exists a set $u_1, \ldots, u_l$ of terms such that for correct ground substitutions σ, ρ it holds $t\sigma = s\rho$ if, and only if, there exists an i and a correct ground substitution τ for which*

$$t\sigma = u_i\tau = s\rho.$$

Moreover, for each i there exists a coloured substitution μ_i (substituting coloured terms for variables) such that $u_i = t\mu_i = s\mu_i$. The set $\{\mu_1, \ldots, \mu_l\}$ is called the most general unifier of t and s and is computable.

Proof. Let α be the most general unifier of t and s forgetting about the colour constraints and let $u = t\alpha = s\alpha$. It should be noted that there are correct ground substitution σ and ρ such that $t\sigma = s\rho$ exactly then, when there is a ground substitution β for variables in u for which

$$u\beta = t\sigma = s\rho$$

and if there was a variable coloured with colour K at position p in t or in s, then the term substituted at this position has the colour K.

As we see we can describe all the substitutions we are looking for by giving the term u and the set of constraints consisting of a position and a colour. We will now show how such constraint can be propagated to lower positions but for the price of creating multiple copies of u with different constraint sets.

If we have a colour

$$K = \{c_1, \ldots, c_m\}$$

at a position in u where the sub-term at this position is $f(w_1, \ldots, w_n)$ then the constraint can be satisfied only if for each $c_i \in K$ there is at least one rule in the form

$$c_i \to f(a_1^i, \ldots, a_n^i) \in T.$$

Let us now take all possible ways to choose one such rule for each $c_i \in K$. Then for each w_j we have a new colour constraint defined by

$$K_j = \{a_j^1, a_j^2, \ldots, a_j^m\}.$$

In this way we reduced a colour constraint to lower positions, but for each way of choosing the rules from the system we had to create a separate instance of the term u with coloured positions. Since for all constants we took into account all possible ways to satisfy the colour constraint, all possible correct substitutions will be taken into account.

If we repeat the above procedure then all colours will be propagated to constants, where they can be checked for satisfiability and either accepted or rejected, and to variables. Taking into account only the cases where the colour constraints were accepted at positions with constants we are left with a set of coloured terms $u_1, \ldots u_l$ that we were looking for and since these are just differently coloured copies of u then we can define μ_i to be the most general unifier β with the same colours as the variables in u_i.

C   Reduction Automata Constructions and Proofs

Let us first concentrate on the coloured stability problem and start with a simple fact about possible automata construction.

Fact 6. *There is a reduction automata accepting all the normal forms with respect to a given set of coloured rewrite rules.*

Proof. Construct the sum of the automata encompassing the coloured rewrite rules which have a deterministic reduction automata by Fact 5. This construction can be done so that the resulting automata is deterministic (see Fact 2 or [2]) and according to Fact 3 it can also be made complete. Therefore we can construct it's complement using Fact 3. ∎

Lemma 14. *The coloured stability problem for a term t and constant c with respect to a reduced RGTRS T is decidable.*

Proof. According to Lemma 5 we can check the stability of a given term t by creating a reduction automata accepting all normal forms with respect to the coloured rewrite system T^c. When we know that the term is stable we can use Lemma 2 to construct a tree automaton without constraints that will accept only terms that are not joinable with the constant c. This automata works in the described way only on stable terms, but stability is assured by intersecting it with the reduction automata recognising stable terms. Intersecting it again with the automata that accepts only correct ground substitutions of t and checking the emptiness yields a decision procedure according to Fact 4. ∎

We will start analysing deep joinability of constants by exhaustively checking if any two constants have deep non-joinability witnesses of depth zero (other constants). For other cases we will observe the following lemma.

Lemma 15. *Two constants a, b are deeply non-joinable if, and only if, they have witnesses of deep non-joinability of height zero or one of the following holds:*

(1) *There exists a term t for which $b \twoheadrightarrow t$ and t is not joinable with a or a constant c such such that $a \rightarrow c$, or vice versa (swapping a and b).*

(2) *There exist terms of height one $f(c_1, \ldots, c_n)$ and $g(d_1, \ldots, d_m)$ with $f \neq g$ for which $a \rightarrow f(c_1, \ldots, c_n)$ and $b \rightarrow g(d_1, \ldots, d_m)$. Moreover, there exist stable terms $f(u_1, \ldots, u_n)$ and $g(v_1, \ldots, v_m)$ with each u_i having colour $\{c_i\}$ and each v_j having colour $\{d_j\}$.*

(3) *There exist terms $f(a_1, \ldots, a_n)$ and $f(b_1, \ldots, b_n)$ for which $a \twoheadrightarrow f(a_1, \ldots, a_n)$ and $b \twoheadrightarrow f(b_1, \ldots, b_n)$. Moreover, stable terms $u = f(u_1, \ldots, u_n)$ and $v = f(v_1, \ldots, v_n)$ exist with each u_i having colour $\{c_i\}$ and each v_j having colour $\{d_i\}$ and for some $1 \leq i \leq n$ the terms u_i and v_i are witnesses of deep non-joinability of the constants a_i and b_i.*

Proof. It is evident that if any of these conditions holds then the constants are deeply non-joinable.

For the converse we need to look at the paths from constants to the witnesses of deep non-joinability of which at least one is of height at least one. If one of the witnesses is of height one then it is covered by the first case taking into account the the fact that the considered RGTRS is reduced

In the other case you note that there exist stable witnesses of deep non-joinability. If these have different function symbols at the root position then stability is enough for them to be witnesses of deep non-joinability. If they have the same function symbol in the head then since they are stable and not joinable then according to lemma 2 they have to have some non-joinable children, which are then witnesses of deep non-joinability for other constants. ∎

Since we are now analysing pairs of terms let us extend our signature by new function symbols P, P_l, P_r with arity two. We will later say that $P(t, s)$ *denotes* t and s, $P_l(t, s)$ denotes the left term t and $P_r(t, s)$ the right term s. Let us also extend our set of coloured rewrite rules so that for each rule $l \to c$ and each position p in l we add the rules

(1) $l[P(l|_p, x)]_p \to c$,
(2) $l[P(x, l|_p)]_p \to c$,
(3) $l[P_r(x, l|_p)]_p \to c$,
(4) $l[P_l(l|_p, x)]_p \to c$,

where x is a new variable $x \notin \mathrm{Var}(l)$. We repeat this process as long as possible without having two $P's$ one after another on any path in the term l considered as a tree. Please note that a term t with a P symbol is stable with respect to the new set of rules if all terms that it denotes are stable.

Fact 7. *For each pair of constants a and b there exists a tree automaton $A_{[a,b]}$ that accepts a stable term if it denotes the pair of witnesses of deep non-joinability of a and b.*

Proof. For constants a, b we will denote by q_a the state for all terms with the extended signature for which the denoted term is reachable from a, and by $q_{a,b}$ the state when the denoted term is reachable from a and not joinable with b.

We will denote the state which is reached by a stable term if the term denotes a pair of deep non-joinability witnesses of a and b by $q_{[a,b]}$ and we will also use $q_{l[a,b]}$ and $q_{r[a,b]}$ for the left and right witness. This defines our set of states and by Lemma 15 we can construct $A_{[a,b]}$ with the following rules:

(1) $P(q_a, q_{b,a}) \to q_{[a,b]}$ and $P(q_{a,b}, q_b) \to q_{[a,b]}$,
(2)
$$P(f(q_{a_1}, \ldots, q_{a_n}), g(q_{b_1}, \ldots, q_{b_m})) \to q_{[a,b]}$$
for each $f(a_1, \ldots, a_n) \xleftarrow{} a$ and $g(b_1, \ldots, b_m) \xleftarrow{} b$ with $f \neq g$,
(3)
$$P(f(q_{a_1}, \ldots, q_{l[a_j,b_j]}, \ldots, q_{a_n}), f(q_{b_1}, \ldots, q_{r[a_j,b_j]}, \ldots, q_{b_n})) \to q_{[a,b]}$$
for each $f(a_1, \ldots, a_n) \xleftarrow{} a$ and $f(b_1, \ldots, b_n) \xleftarrow{} b$,
(4) all above items repeated with P_l or P_r instead of the first P on the left side and $q_{l[]}$ or $q_{r[]}$ on the right side accordingly,
(5) ϵ-transitions from $q_{a,b}$ to q_a.

The correctness of the construction follows from Lemma 15. ∎

Lemma 16. *Deep joinability of constants with respect to a RGTRS is decidable.*

Proof. We showed that we can construct an automaton accepting the witnesses of deep non-joinability of two constants when the terms are stable and we showed before that we can construct an reduction automaton accepting only stable terms (only now we use an extended signature and other set of coloured rewrite rules). Then we can use Fact 4 to decide the emptiness of intersection of these automata.

Safety Is not a Restriction at Level 2 for String Languages[*]

K. Aehlig[**], J.G. de Miranda, and C.-H.L. Ong

Oxford University Computing Laboratory

Abstract. Recent work by Knapik, Niwiński and Urzyczyn (in FOS-SACS 2002) has revived interest in the connexions between higher-order grammars and higher-order pushdown automata. Both devices can be viewed as definitions for term trees as well as string languages. In the latter setting we recall the extensive study by Damm (1982), and Damm and Goerdt (1986). There it was shown that a language is accepted by a level-n pushdown automaton if and only if the language is generated by a *safe* level-n grammar. We show that at level 2 the safety assumption may be removed. It follows that there are no *inherently* unsafe string languages at level 2.

1   Introduction

Higher-order pushdown automata and higher-order grammars were originally introduced as definitional devices for string languages by Maslov [10] and Damm [4] respectively. Damm defined an infinite hierarchy of languages, the OI Hierarchy, the nth level of which is generated by level-n grammars that satisfy a syntactic constraint called *safety*[1]. Similarly, Maslov defined an infinite hierarchy, the nth level of which is generated by level-n pushdown automata (or nPDA). It was then shown [5] that the OI and Maslov hierarchies coincide: a language is generated by a level-n *safe* grammar if and only if it is accepted by a level-n pushdown automaton.

Recently, Knapik *et al.* [7,8] have re-introduced higher-order grammars and higher-order pushdown automata as definitional devices for *term trees*. Not surprisingly, safety is, again, key to connecting the two. They show that a term tree is generated by a safe level-n grammar if and only if it is accepted by a level-n pushdown automaton. Furthermore, if a term tree is generated by a safe grammar it enjoys a decidable monadic second order (MSO) theory. This latter result has sparked much interest among communities interested in the verification of infinite-state systems.

---

[*] This is an extended abstract of a longer paper [2] complete with proofs, which is downloadable from the authors' web pages.

[**] On leave from Mathematisches Institut, Ludwig-Maximilians-Universität München. Supported by a postdoctoral fellowship of the German Academic Exchange Organisation (DAAD).

[1] Formerly referred to as the restriction of "derived types".

V. Sassone (Ed.): FOSSACS 2005, LNCS 3441, pp. 490–504, 2005.

In light of Knapik *et al.*'s result, it seems important to investigate why safety *appears* to be key to such good algorithmic behaviour and desirable properties. To date, no results concerning unsafe grammars (whether in the string-language or term-tree setting) exist. We recall two questions raised by Knapik *et al.* [8]. First, is safety required to guarantee MSO decidability of term trees? Secondly, is safety required (whether in the string-language or term-tree setting) for the equivalence between higher-order grammars and higher-order pushdown automata?

In this paper we make a first attempt at tackling the second of the above problems. We analyse the string-language case and show that at level 2 the restriction is redundant. Precisely we show that every string language generated by a level-2 *unsafe* grammar can be generated by a level-2 *safe* grammar. Hence we arrive at the title of our paper. We conjecture that this is not the case for the term-tree setting.

We briefly sketch a proof of our main result (Theorem 1). By examining why Knapik *et al.*'s translation [8] of higher-order grammars to PDAs fails for unsafe grammars, we discover an important relationship between items in the higher-order store of the PDA in question. To formalise the idea, we introduce a new kind of machine, called *2PDA with links* (2PDAL for short), which is just a 2PDA such that each 1-store that is pushed has a *fresh* link to the item below that has "caused" the push_2 action. When performing a pop_2 subsequently, these links serve as a means of determining the number of 1-stores to pop off. We show that a 2PDAL can implement (i.e. accept the same language as that generated by) a level-2 grammar, whether safe or not. Unfortunately there is no a priori bound on the number of links required, so it is not obvious how a 2PDAL can be directly translated to a 2PDA. However, by a careful analysis of the way links behave, one can use a *non-deterministic* 2PDA to simulate a 2PDAL. Thus we have a way of transforming a (possibly unsafe) level-2 grammar to an equivalent 2PDA.

Related Work. In [1] we address another question concerning safety: we show that the MSO theory for all string and tree-languages defined by level-2 grammars is decidable (previously this could only be asserted if the grammar was safe). An independent proof of the same decidability result has also been given by Knapik, Niwiński, Urzyczyn and Walukiewicz [9].

2   Definitions

In this section we introduce higher-order grammars and higher-order pushdown automata as definitional devices for string languages. However, in Section 6 we will relate our result to the term-tree setting [7, 8].

2.1   Higher-Order Grammars and Safety

Types and Terms. *Simple types* (ranged over by A, B, etc.) are defined by the grammar: $A ::= o \mid (A \to B)$. Each type A can be uniquely written as

$(A_1, \cdots, A_n, o)$ for some $n \geq 0$, which is a shorthand for $A_1 \to \cdots \to A_n \to o$ (by convention $\to$ associates to the right). We define the *level* of a type by $\mathsf{level}(o) = 0$ and $\mathsf{level}(A \to B) = \max(\mathsf{level}(A)+1, \mathsf{level}(B))$. We say that $A = (A_1, \cdots, A_n, o)$ is *homogeneous* just if $\mathsf{level}(A_1) \geq \mathsf{level}(A_2) \geq \cdots \geq \mathsf{level}(A_n)$, and each A_i is homogeneous.

A *typed* alphabet is a set Δ of simply-typed symbols. We denote by Δ^A the subset of Δ containing precisely those elements of type A. The set of *applicative terms of type A* over Δ, denoted by $\mathcal{T}^A(\Delta)$, is defined by induction over the rules: (1) $\Delta^A \subseteq \mathcal{T}^A(\Delta)$; (2) if $t \in \mathcal{T}^{A \to B}(\Delta)$ and $s \in \mathcal{T}^A(\Delta)$ then $(ts) \in \mathcal{T}^B(\Delta)$. Finally, we write $t : A$ to mean $t \in \mathcal{T}^A$ and we define $\mathsf{level}(t)$ to be $\mathsf{level}(A)$.

Higher-Order Grammars and Safety. A *higher-order grammar* is a tuple $G = \langle N, V, \Sigma, \mathcal{R}, S, e \rangle$ such that N is a finite set of homogeneously-typed non-terminals, and S, the *start symbol*, is a distinguished element of N of type o; V is a finite set of typed variables; Σ is a finite alphabet; $\mathcal{R}$ is a finite set of triples, called *rewrite rules* (also referred to as *production rules*), of the form

$$F x_1 \cdots x_m \xrightarrow{\alpha} E$$

where $\alpha \in (\Sigma \cup \{\epsilon\})$, $F : (A_1, \cdots, A_m, o) \in N$, each $x_i : A_i \in V$, and E is either a term in $\mathcal{T}^o(N \cup \{x_1, \cdots, x_m\})$ or is $e : o$. We say that F has *formal parameters* $x_1, \cdots, x_m$. In the case where the grammar has two or more rules with the non-terminal F on the lefthand side, then we assume (w.l.o.g.) both rules have the same formal parameters in the same order. Following Knapik *et al.* [7] we assume that if $F \in N$ has type $(A_1, \cdots, A_m, o)$ and $m \geq 1$, then $A_m = o$. Thus, each non-terminal has at least one level-0 variable. Note that this is not really a restriction – as this variable need not occur on the righthand side.

We say that G is a *level-n grammar* (*n-grammar* for short) just in case n is the level of the non-terminal that has the highest level. We say that G is *deterministic* just if whenever $F x_1 \cdots x_m \xrightarrow{\alpha} E$ and $F x_1 \cdots x_m \xrightarrow{\alpha'} E'$ are both in $\mathcal{R}$, then (1) if $\alpha = \alpha'$ then $E = E'$ and (2) if $\alpha = \epsilon$ and $E \neq e$ then $\alpha' = \epsilon$ and $E = E'$.

We extend $\mathcal{R}$ to a family of binary relations $\xrightarrow{\alpha}$ over $\mathcal{T}^o(N) \cup \{e\}$, where α ranges over $\Sigma \cup \{\epsilon\}$, by the rule: if $F x_1 \cdots x_m \xrightarrow{\alpha} E$ is a rule in $\mathcal{R}$ where $x_i : A_i$ then for each $M_i \in \mathcal{T}^{A_i}(N)$ we have $F M_1 \cdots M_m \xrightarrow{\alpha} E[M_i/x_i]$.

A *derivation* of $w \in \Sigma^*$ is a sequence $P_1, P_2, \cdots, P_k$ of terms in $\mathcal{T}^o(N)$, and a corresponding sequence $\alpha_1, \cdots, \alpha_k$ of elements in $\Sigma \cup \{\epsilon\}$ such that

$$S = P_1 \xrightarrow{\alpha_1} P_2 \xrightarrow{\alpha_2} P_3 \xrightarrow{\alpha_3} \quad \cdots \quad \xrightarrow{\alpha_{k-1}} P_k \xrightarrow{\alpha_k} e$$

and $w = \alpha_1 \cdots \alpha_k$. The *language* generated by G, written $L(G)$, is the set of words over Σ that have derivations in G. We say that two grammars are *equivalent* if they generate the same language.

A grammar is said to be *unsafe* if there exists a rewrite rule $F x_1 \cdots x_m \xrightarrow{\alpha} E$ such that E contains a subterm t (say) in an operand position (i.e. (st) is a subterm of E, for some s), and t contains an occurrence of x_i for some $1 \leq i \leq n$

such that $\text{level}(t) > \text{level}(x_i)$. Otherwise, the grammar is *safe*. It follows from the definition that all grammars of levels 0 and 1 are safe. This definition of safety follows the one presented by Knapik *et al.* [7, 8]. In our technical report [2] we present an alternative definition of safety based on the *safe λ-calculus*. We make no use of this alternative characterisation here, but offer it to the interested reader as a natural way to understand the restriction and how it arises. For an example of an unsafe grammar, see Example 1.

The OI Hierarchy. Damm [4] introduced the OI Hierarchy. The nth level of the hierarchy is generated by level-n grammars (defined differently from our grammars). Furthermore, each level is strictly contained in the one above it. The first three levels correspond to the regular, the context-free, and the indexed languages [3]. Damm's grammars are rewrite relations over expressions that are required to be objects of "derived types". An analysis of his definition reveals that the constraint of "derived types" is equivalent to the requirement that all types be *homogeneous* and the grammar be *safe*, both in the sense of Knapik *et al.* Assuming the grammar makes use of only homogeneous types (which all definitions in the literature do), it follows that safety and derived types are equivalent. In particular, it is routine to show that a level-n grammar using his definition corresponds to a *safe* n-grammar in our definition (and the converse holds too). For a comparison of the two (ours and Damm's) we point the reader to a note [6]. This note also motivates our preference for our definition.

Example 1. Consider the following *deterministic* and unsafe (because of the underlined expressions) grammar, where $\Sigma = \{h_1, h_2, h_3, f_1, f_2, g_1, a, b\}$, with typed non-terminals $D : ((o,o), o, o, o)$, $H : ((o,o), o, o)$, $F : (o, o, o)$, $G : (o, o)$, $A, B : o$, variables φ, x, y and with rules:

$$S \xrightarrow{\epsilon} DGAB \qquad H\varphi x \xrightarrow{\epsilon} \varphi x \qquad A \xrightarrow{a} e$$
$$D\varphi xy \xrightarrow{h_1} D(\underline{D\varphi x})y(\varphi y) \qquad Gx \xrightarrow{g_1} x \qquad B \xrightarrow{b} e$$
$$D\varphi xy \xrightarrow{h_2} H(\underline{Fy})x \qquad Fxy \xrightarrow{f_1} x$$
$$D\varphi xy \xrightarrow{h_3} \varphi B \qquad Fxy \xrightarrow{f_2} y$$

As this grammar is deterministic [6] each word in the language has a unique derivation. Hence, the reader can easily verify that the word $h_1 h_3 h_2 f_1 b$ is in the language, whereas $h_1 h_3 h_2 f_1 a$ is not.

2.2   Higher-Order Pushdown Automata

Fix a finite set Γ of *store symbols*, including a distinguished bottom-of-store symbol $\bot$. A *1-store* is a finite non-empty sequence $[a_1, \cdots, a_m]$ of Γ-symbols such that $a_i = \bot$ iff $i = m$. For $n \geq 1$, an $(n+1)$-*store* is a non-empty sequence of n-stores. Inductively we define the *empty* $(n+1)$-*store* $\bot_{n+1}$ to be $[\bot_n]$ where we set $\bot_0 = \bot$. (Note that n-store is sometimes called n-stack in the literature.) Recall the following standard operations on 1-stores:

- $\text{push}_1(a)\ [a_1, \cdots, a_m] = [a, a_1, \cdots, a_m]$ for $a \in \Gamma - \{\bot\}$
- $\text{pop}_1\ [a_1, a_2, \cdots, a_m] = [a_2, \cdots, a_m]$

For $n \geq 2$, the following set Op_n of *level-n operations* are defined over n-stores:

- $\text{push}_n\ [s_1, \cdots, s_l] = [s_1, s_1, \cdots, s_l]$
- $\text{push}_k\ [s_1, \cdots, s_l] = [\text{push}_k\ s_1, s_2, \cdots, s_l],\quad 2 \leq k < n$
- $\text{push}_1(a)\ [s_1, \cdots, s_l] = [\text{push}_1(a)\ s_1, s_2, \cdots, s_l]$ for $a \in \Gamma - \{\bot\}$
- $\text{pop}_n\ [s_1, \cdots, s_l] = [s_2, \cdots, s_l]$
- $\text{pop}_k\ [s_1, \cdots, s_l] = [\text{pop}_k\ s_1, s_2, \cdots, s_l],\quad 1 \leq k < n$

In addition we define $\text{top}_n\ [s_1, \cdots, s_l] = s_1$ and $\text{top}_k\ [s_1, \cdots, s_l] = \text{top}_k\ s_1, 1 \leq k < n$. Note that $\text{pop}_k\ s$ is undefined if the top k-store consists of only one element.

A *level-n pushdown automaton* (nPDA for short) is a tuple $\langle Q, \Sigma, \Gamma, \delta, q_0, F \rangle$ where Q is a finite set of states; $q_0 \in Q$ is the start state; $F \subseteq Q$ is a set of accepting states; Σ the finite input alphabet; Γ the finite store alphabet (which is assumed to contain $\bot$); and $\delta \subseteq Q \times (\Sigma \cup \{\epsilon\}) \times \Gamma \times Q \times Op_n$ is the transition relation.

A *configuration* of an nPDA is given by a triple (q, w, s) where q is the current state, $w \in \Sigma^*$ is the remaining input, and s is an n-store over Γ.

Given a configuration (q, aw, s) (where $a \in \Sigma$ or $a = \epsilon$, and $w \in \Sigma^*$), we say that $(q, aw, s) \to (p, w, s')$ if $(q, a, \text{top}_1(s), p, \theta) \in \delta$ and $s' = \theta(s)$. The transitive closure of $\to$ is denoted by $\to^+$, whereas the reflexive and transitive closure is denoted by $\to^*$. We say that the input w is *accepted* by the above nPDA if $(q_0, w, \bot_n) \to^* (q_f, \epsilon, s)$ for some pushdown store s and some $q_f \in F$.

3 Relating nPDAs and n-Grammars

3.1 The Main Result

Damm and Goerdt [5] showed that a string language is generated by a safe n-grammar if and only if it is accepted by an nPDA. To our knowledge, no results exist for *unsafe* n-grammars. In particular if G is an unsafe n-grammar, it is not known whether $L(G)$ is accepted by an nPDA, or perhaps a PDA of a higher level. Our main result is a first step towards solving this problem.

Theorem 1. *For any 2-grammar that is not assumed to be safe, there exists a non-deterministic 2PDA the accepts the language generated by the grammar. Moreover the conversion is effective.*

Our proof is split into two parts. Given a 2-grammar we first show that it can be implemented by a 2PDAL, where 2PDAL is a machine that has yet to be introduced (Section 4); we then show that a 2PDAL can be simulated by a non-deterministic 2PDA (Section 5). Combining our result with Damm and Goerdt's, we have:

Corollary 1. *Every string language that is generated by an unsafe 2-grammar can also be generated by some safe (non-deterministic) 2-grammar.*

3.2   An Example: Urzyczyn's Language

Before we explain our result and sketch a proof, we present an example of a deterministic but unsafe 2-grammar that generates a string language, which we shall call Urzyczyn's language, or simply U. We then show, via a "bespoke" proof, that U can be accepted by a 2PDA. We shall have occasion to revisit U later in Section 6 in the form of a conjecture.

The language U consists of words of the form $w *^n$ where w is a proper prefix of a well-bracketed word such that no prefix of w is a well-bracketed expression; each parenthesis in w is implicitly labelled with a number, and n is the label of the last parenthesis. The two labelling rules are:

I. The label of the opening (is one; the label of any subsequent (is that of the preceding (plus one.
II. The label of) is the label of the parenthesis that precedes the matching (.

For example, the following word is in U:

$$(((( )) (( ) (( ))) (( )) * *$$
$$1\ 2\ 3\ 4\ 3\ 2\ 5\ 6\ 5\ 7\ 8\ 7\ 5\ 2\ 9\ 10\ 9\ 2$$

We shall first give an unsafe 2-grammar – call it G_U – that generates the language and then show that it is accepted by a 2PDA.

$$D\,\varphi\,x\,y\,z \xrightarrow{\ (\ } D\,(D\,\varphi\,x)\,z\,(F\,y)\,(F\,y) \qquad S \xrightarrow{\ (\ } D\,G\,E\,E\,E$$
$$D\,\varphi\,x\,y\,z \xrightarrow{\ )\ } \varphi\,y\,x \qquad\qquad\qquad F\,x \xrightarrow{\ *\ } x$$
$$D\,\varphi\,x\,y\,z \xrightarrow{\ *\ } z \qquad\qquad\qquad\quad E \xrightarrow{\ \epsilon\ } e$$

Remark 1. The language U [12] was motivated by a term tree that is conjectured in [8–p. 213] to be inherently unsafe.

Accepting U with a 2PDA. In order to show that U is accepted by a 2PDA we make use of the following observation.

Proposition 1. *Let $y \in \{(,),*\}^*$. Then $y \in U$ if an only if it has a unique decomposition into $wx*^n$ where w is a proper prefix of a well-bracketed word such that no prefix of it (including itself) is well-bracketed and w ends in (; x is a (possibly empty) well-bracketed word; and n (the number of stars) is the number of ('s in w.*

In the preceding example, $w = (($ and $x = (( )) (( ) (( ))) (( ))$.

Thanks to the decomposition in Proposition 1, the construction of a 2PDA that accepts U is very simple. We guess the prefix of the input that constitutes w and process w as though checking for a proper prefix of a well-bracketed expression (using the power of a 1PDA). At the same time we perform a push_2 for every (found. Thus, the number of 1-stores is equal to the number of ('s in w. After reading w we check that x is well-bracketed. When we first meet a $*$, if x was indeed well-bracketed, then we perform a pop_2 for each $*$ found.

$$(q_0, a, Dt_1 \cdots t_n) \rightarrow (q_0, \mathsf{push}_1(E)) \text{ if } Dx_1 \cdots x_m \xrightarrow{a} E \text{ and } n \leq m \qquad \text{(R1)}$$

$$(q_0, \epsilon, e) \rightarrow \mathsf{accept} \qquad \text{(R2)}$$

$$(q_0, \epsilon, x_j) \rightarrow (q_j, \mathsf{pop}_1) \text{ if } x_j : o \qquad \text{(R3)}$$

$$(q_0, \epsilon, x_j t_1 \cdots t_n) \rightarrow (q_j, \mathsf{push}_2 \,;\, \mathsf{pop}_1) \text{ if } x_j \text{ has level} > 0 \qquad \text{(R4)}$$

$$_{1 \leq j \leq n}, (q_j, \epsilon, \$ t_1 \cdots t_n) \rightarrow (q_0, \mathsf{pop}_1 \,;\, \mathsf{push}_1(t_j)) \qquad \text{(R5)}$$

$$_{j > n}, (q_j, \epsilon, \$ t_1 \cdots t_n) \rightarrow (q_{j-n}, \mathsf{pop}_2) \qquad \text{(R6)}$$

Fig. 1. Adapted transition rules from Knapik *et al.* [8]

Convention. In the Figure x_j means the j-th formal parameter of the relevant non-terminal. Furthermore, $\$ \in N \cup V$.

4   Simulating Higher-Order Grammars by 2PDALs

4.1   Understanding KNU's Proof

Knapik *et al.* [8] have shown that a term tree generated by a safe n-grammar is accepted by an nPDA. Their proof, based on a transformation of n-grammars to their corresponding nPDAs, can easily be adapted to work in the string-language setting.

Theorem 2. *Let G be a safe 2-grammar that generates a string language. Then $L(G)$ is accepted by some 2PDA.*

Proof. We use the same setup as Knapik *et al.* [8–Sect. 5.2], but now we incorporate an input string over the alphabet Σ. The transition function is given in Fig. 1.

Let us examine why the construction fails if we attempt to apply it (blindly) to an unsafe 2-grammar. As an example, we consider the grammar given in Example 1. Recall that the word $h_1 h_3 h_2 f_1 a$ is *not* in the language.

The automaton starts off in the configuration $(q_0, h_1 h_3 h_2 f_1 a, [[S]])$, after a few steps we reach the following configuration:

$$(q_0, h_2 f_1 a, [[\varphi B, D(D\varphi x)y(\varphi y), DGAB, S]])$$

As the topmost item, φB, is headed by a level-1 variable, we need to find out what φ is in order to proceed. Note that φ is the 1st formal parameter of the preceding item: $D(D\varphi x)y(\varphi y)$, i.e., it refers to $D\varphi x$. To this end, we perform a push_2 and then perform a pop_1, and replace the topmost item with $D\varphi x$. In other words, we have applied rule R4 followed by R5 to arrive at:

$$(q_0, h_2 f_1 a, [[(D\varphi x)^{\langle 1-\rangle}, DGAB, S],$$

$$[\varphi B^{\langle 1+\rangle}, D(D\varphi x)y(\varphi y), DGAB, S]])$$

Here we have labelled two store items, one with a $1-$ and the other with a $1+$. These labels are not part of the store alphabet, they have been added so that we may identify these two store items later on.

The crux behind their construction is the following. Suppose we meet the item $D\varphi x^{\langle 1-\rangle}$ later on in the computation, and suppose that we would like to request its third argument, meaning we would be in state q_3. Note, however, that D in $D\varphi x^{\langle 1-\rangle}$ has only 2 arguments. The missing argument can be found by visiting the item $\varphi B^{\langle 1+\rangle}$. Hence the labelling. We need to ensure that there is a systematic way to get from $D\varphi x^{\langle 1-\rangle}$ to $\varphi B^{\langle 1+\rangle}$ whenever we are in a state q_j for $j > 2$ and we have $D\varphi x^{\langle 1-\rangle}$ as our topmost symbol. This systematic way suggested by Knapik *et al.* is embodied by rule R6 of Fig. 1. It says that all we need to do is perform a pop_2, followed by a change in state to q_{j-2}, and to repeat if necessary.

After a few more steps of the 2PDA we will arrive at another configuration where the topmost symbol is headed by a level-1 variable:

$$(q_0, f_1 a, \ [[\varphi x, H(Fy)x, (D\varphi x)^{\langle 1-\rangle}, DGAB, S],$$
$$[\varphi B^{\langle 1+\rangle}, D(D\varphi x)y(\varphi y), DGAB, S]])$$

Therefore, we next get:

$$(q_0, f_1 a, \ [[Fy^{\langle 2-\rangle}, (D\varphi x)^{\langle 1-\rangle}, DGAB, S],$$
$$[\varphi x^{\langle 2+\rangle}, H(Fy)x, (D\varphi x)^{\langle 1-\rangle}, DGAB, S],$$
$$[\varphi B^{\langle 1+\rangle}, D(D\varphi x)y(\varphi y), DGAB, S]])$$

Again we have labelled a new pair of store items, so that the same principle applies: if we want the missing argument of $Fy^{\langle 2-\rangle}$, then we will be able to find it at $\varphi x^{\langle 2+\rangle}$. After a few more steps we eventually reach the following crucial configuration:

$$(q_3, a, \ [[(D\varphi x)^{\langle 1-\rangle}, DGAB, S],$$
$$[\varphi x^{\langle 2+\rangle}, H(Fy)x, (D\varphi x)^{\langle 1-\rangle}, DGAB, S], \qquad (1)$$
$$[\varphi B^{\langle 1+\rangle}, D(D\varphi x)y(\varphi y), DGAB, S]])$$

Intuitively, here we want the third argument of D in the expression $D\varphi x$. By rule R6 we arrive at: (in the following $\to_n$ means n steps of $\to$)

$$(q_1, a, \ [[\varphi x^{\langle 2+\rangle}, H(Fy)x, (D\varphi x)^{\langle 1-\rangle}, DGAB, S],$$
$$[\varphi B^{\langle 1+\rangle}, D(D\varphi x)y(\varphi y), DGAB, S]])$$
$$\to_2 (q_2, a, \ [[H(Fy)x, (D\varphi x)^{\langle 1-\rangle}, DGAB, S],$$
$$[\varphi B^{\langle 1+\rangle}, D(D\varphi x)y(\varphi y), DGAB, S]])$$
$$\to_2 (q_2, a, \ [[(D\varphi x)^{\langle 1-\rangle}, DGAB, S],$$
$$[\varphi B^{\langle 1+\rangle}, D(D\varphi x)y(\varphi y), DGAB, S]])$$
$$\to_2 (q_2, a, \ [[DGAB, S],$$
$$[\varphi B^{\langle 1+\rangle}, D(D\varphi x)y(\varphi y), DGAB, S]])$$

$$\to_2 (q_0, \epsilon, [[e, A, S],$$
$$[\varphi B^{\langle 1+\rangle}, D(D\varphi x)y(\varphi y), DGAB, S]])$$

Note that we have accepted $h_1 h_3 h_2 f_1 a$ which is incorrect! The construction only works under the assumption that the grammar is safe. However, the labels we have used lead us to the construction of a new kind of machine which can remedy this problem.

Provided that each time we create a new pair of labels (the $+$ and $-$ part), we ensure they are unique, then these labels provide a way of always jumping to the correct 1-store when we are looking for missing arguments. Why? Because each time we want the missing argument of an item labelled with $n-$, we would simply perform as many pop_2's as necessary until our topmost symbol was labelled with the corresponding $n+$. To see how this would work, let us backtrack to configuration (1) in the above example. Applying this idea of a parameterised pop_2, this brings us to:

$$(q_1, a, [[\varphi B^{\langle 1+\rangle}, D(D\varphi x)y(\varphi y), DGAB, S]])$$

which is indeed what we wanted, and it is easy to see the word will be rejected. This idea of using pairs of labels, which we call *links* is formalised in a new kind of machine called level-2 *pushdown automaton with links*, or simply 2PDAL.

4.2   Formal Definition of 2PDAL

Formally, a 2PDAL is a 2PDA with the added feature that each item can be decorated with labels from the set $\{n+ : n \geq 1\} \cup \{n- : n \geq 1\}$. It is possible for an item to have zero, one or two labels – no other possibilities exist. We write labels as superscripts, as in $a^{\langle\rangle}$ (or simply a), $a^{\langle 3+\rangle}$ and $a^{\langle 3+,4-\rangle}$. These superscripts are sets of at most two elements, ranged over by λ; thus we have $\langle 3+\rangle \cup \langle 4-\rangle = \langle 3+, 4-\rangle = \langle 4-, 3+\rangle$. In the case where an item has two labels, one of these will always be a $+$ and the other a $-$. These labels come in matching pairs. Thus, if there exists an item in the store labelled by $m-$ and another labelled by $m+$, together they are said to form an *instance* of the *link* m. We refer to the item that gains the $-$ as the *start point* and that which gains the $+$, the *end point*.

In addition to the usual operations of a 2PDA, a 2PDAL has an iterated form of pop_2, parameterised over links m, defined as follows: for s ranging over 2-stores

$$\mathsf{pop}_2(m)\, s = \begin{cases} s & \text{if } \mathsf{top}_1(s) \text{ has label } m+ \\ \mathsf{pop}_2(m)(\mathsf{pop}_2(s)) & \text{otherwise} \end{cases}$$

Given a 2-grammar G (not assumed to be safe) transitions of the corresponding 2PDAL, written 2PDAL$_G$, are defined by induction over the set of rules in Fig. 2. For convenience we have written $\mathsf{repl}_1(a)$ as a shorthand for $\mathsf{pop}_1;\mathsf{push}_1(a)$. The store alphabet, Γ, is comprised of the start symbol S (as the bottom-of-store symbol) and a subset of the (finite) set of all subexpressions of the right

$$(q_0, a, Dt_1 \cdots t_n{}^\lambda) \rightarrow (q_0, \mathsf{push}_1(E)) \text{ if } Dx_1 \cdots x_m \xrightarrow{a} E \text{ and } n \le m$$

$$(q_0, \epsilon, e) \rightarrow \text{accept}$$

$$(q_0, \epsilon, x_j) \rightarrow (q_j, \mathsf{pop}_1)$$

$$(q_0, \epsilon, \varphi_j t_1 \cdots t_n{}^\lambda) \rightarrow (q_0, \mathsf{repl}_1(\varphi_j t_1 \cdots t_n{}^{\lambda \cup \langle m+ \rangle})\,;\, \mathsf{push}_2\,;\, \mathsf{pop}_1\,;\, \mathsf{repl}_1(s_j{}^{\langle m- \rangle}))$$

$$\text{where } m \text{ is fresh and } Ds_1 \cdots s_{n'}{}^{\lambda'} \text{ precedes } \varphi_j t_1 \cdots t_n{}^\lambda.$$

$$_{1 \le j \le n,}\, (q_j, \epsilon, \$t_1 \cdots t_n{}^\lambda) \rightarrow (q_0, \mathsf{repl}_1(t_j))$$

$$_{j > n,}\, (q_j, \epsilon, \$t_1 \cdots t_n{}^\lambda) \rightarrow (q_{j-n}, \mathsf{pop}_2(m)) \text{ if } m- \in \lambda$$

Fig. 2. Transition rules of the 2PDAL, 2PDAL$_G$

hand sides of the productions in G. We assume that each production rule of the grammar assumes the following format:

$$F \varphi_1 \cdots \varphi_m x_{m+1} \cdots x_{m+n} \xrightarrow{a} E \tag{2}$$

where the φ's are used for level-1 parameters, and the x's are used for level-0 parameters. As in Knapik $et\ al.$, the set of states includes $\{q_i : 0 \le i \le M\}$, where M is the maximum of the arities[2] of any non-terminal or variable occurring in the grammar. As can be seen from Fig. 2 the automaton works in phases beginning and ending in distinguished states q_i with some auxiliary states in between.

Proposition 2. *The language of a (possibly unsafe) 2-grammar G is accepted by 2PDAL$_G$.*

Proof. (Sketch) Intuitively the correctness of this proposition should be clear. For a formal proof we find it useful to appeal to a new model of computation for higher-order grammars due to Stirling [11] called *pointer machines*. We show that a pointer machine for a grammar G can be simulated by 2PDAL$_G$. Unfortunately, owing to space constraints, we cannot give details of pointer machines here, but we point the interested reader to the technical report [2].

Remark 2. In an e-mail [12], Urzyczyn sketches a model of computation for evaluating (possibly unsafe) grammars called a "panic automaton". We understand that it can be shown that a level-2 panic automaton can be simulated by a 3PDA. However, only after our submission to FOSSACS'05 did a full account [9] of this new automaton become available. A preliminary reading of this account suggests that panic automata and PDALs are similar in many respects, but a detailed analysis of their relationships awaits further investigation. It should be mentioned that in [9] panic automata are used to give a proof of the MSO decidability of all *term trees* generated by level-2 grammars (as was mentioned at the end of Section 1).

---

[2] A term of type $A_1 \rightarrow \cdots \rightarrow A_n \rightarrow o$ is said to have arity n.

5   Simulating 2PDALs by Non-deterministic 2PDAs

The incorporation of labels (as names of links) into the store alphabet will, in general, lead to an infinite alphabet. Here we show how these links and the way in which they are manipulated can be simulated by a *non-deterministic* 2PDA.

5.1   Intuition

Note that in the running example of Section 4, only the link labelled by 1 was "followed", in the sense that we jumped from the 1− to the 1+. The link labelled by 2, on the other hand, did not serve any purpose in this run.

The intuition behind simulating 2PDAL$_G$ with a 2PDA relies on guessing which links are "useful" and *only* labelling those. We will see that "useful" links interact with one another in a very consistent and well-behaved way that will allow us to label them anonymously. We formalise this here.

We say that a link m is *queried* if we are in a configuration (q_i, w, s) where $i > 0$ and $\mathsf{top}_1(s) = \$t_1 \cdots t_n^{\lambda}$ with $m- \in \lambda$. Intuitively, querying a link m formalises the notion of "asking for a level-0 argument" from an item labelled with $m-$. We say that a link m is *followed* if the link m is queried (as above) and $i > n$. The following lemma is crucial:

Lemma 1. *Given a link m, m is queried at most once during the run of a 2PDAL$_G$ for a 2-grammar G.*

The simulating non-deterministic 2PDA will follow the rules in Fig. 2 almost exactly. The difference is that each time we are about to generate a link we guess whether it will ever be followed in the future or not. We have the luxury of doing this precisely because of Lemma 1. Thus, we label the start and end points of the link if and only if we guess that it will be followed. Furthermore, instead of a fresh label m, we simply mark the start point with a − and the end point with a +. Our non-deterministic 2PDA will thus have a finite store alphabet: $\Gamma \cup \{a^+ : a \in \Gamma\} \cup \{a^- : a \in \Gamma\} \cup \{a^{+/-} : a \in \Gamma\}$ where Γ is the store alphabet of the preceding section.

A Controlled Form of Guessing. Now this presents a problem of ambiguity. Suppose we find ourselves in a configuration (q, w, s) where $\mathsf{top}_1(s)$ is labelled by −, how can we tell which of the store items labelled by a + is the *true* end point of this link? (True in the sense that if we did have the ability to name our links as with 2PDAL$_G$, the topmost item would have label $m-$ for some m, and the *real* end point would have label $m+$ for the same m.) The answer lies in the use of a *controlled* form of guessing: when guessing whether a link will be followed in the future we require the guess to be subject to some constraints. We shall see that as a consequence the following invariant can be maintained:

Assume that the topmost 1-store has at least one item labelled by −. For the leftmost (closest to the top) of these, the corresponding end point can always be found in the first 1-store beneath it whose topmost item is marked with a $+$.[3]

Before formalising the controlled form of guessing, we introduce a definition. Let (q_0, w, s) be a reachable configuration of 2PDAL$_G$ such that

$$\text{top}_2(s) = [\varphi_{j_1} t_1 \cdots t_n^\lambda, A_1, \cdots, A_k, \cdots, A_N]$$

where $N \geq 2$. We say that φ_{j_1} *ultimately refers to* A_k just if:

(i) For $i = 1, \cdots, k - 1$, the j_ith argument of A_i (where A_i is of the form $Ds_1 \cdots s_l$ for some $D \in N$ and some $l \geq j_i$) is a variable $\varphi_{j_{i+1}}$. We remind the reader of the notational convention set out in (2).
(ii) The j_kth argument of A_k is an application or a non-terminal.

Suppose that we are in a configuration (q_0, w, s) of the non-deterministic 2PDA where $\text{top}_2(s) = [\varphi t_1 \cdots t_n^?, A_1, \cdots, A_k, \cdots, A_N]$ where ? may either denote a $-$ or no label at all. Furthermore, suppose that φ ultimately refers to A_k. Two possibilities exist:

A. None of the store items $\varphi t_1 \cdots t_n^?, A_1, \cdots, A_k$ are labelled by a $-$; or
B. There exists a store item in $\varphi t_1 \cdots t_n^?, A_1, \cdots, A_k$ labelled by a $-$.

In the first case we leave it up to the 2PDA to guess whether this link will be followed or not. In the second case, we *force* it to label $\varphi t_1 \cdots t_n$ (with $+$) as well as its matching partner (with $-$), thus committing it to following this link in the future.

We illustrate why this maintains the above invariant with an example. Consider:

$$\begin{bmatrix} [\varphi x_1 x_2, D\varphi x^-, F(F\varphi x)y, G\varphi x^-, \cdots] \\ [A^+, \cdots] \\ [B^+, \cdots] \end{bmatrix}$$

Note that the topmost store has two items labelled with a $-$, $D\varphi x$ and $G\varphi x$. By our invariant we know that $D\varphi x$ has end point A^+. And let us suppose that $G\varphi x$ points to B^+. Suppose that the φ of the topmost item ultimately refers to $F(F\varphi x)y$. Furthermore, suppose we go against our controlled form of guessing and allow the machine *not* to label $\varphi x_1 x_2$ and its matching partner. Thus we arrive at

$$\begin{bmatrix} [\varphi, F(F\varphi x)y, G\varphi x^-, \cdots] \\ [\varphi x_1 x_2, D\varphi x^-, F(F\varphi x)y, G\varphi x^-, \cdots] \\ [A^+, \cdots] \\ [B^+, \cdots] \end{bmatrix}$$

Now $G\varphi x$ is the leftmost item labelled with a $-$. Our invariant has been violated as the real end point of $G\varphi x$ is not A^+.

---

[3] The invariant is actually stronger than this, but this is sufficient to ensure that the simulation works correctly.

$$(q_0, a, Dt_1 \cdots t_n^\lambda) \to (q_0, \mathsf{push}_1(E)) \text{ if } Dx_1 \cdots x_m \xrightarrow{a} E \text{ and } n \le m$$

$$(q_0, \epsilon, e) \to \mathsf{accept}$$

$$(q_0, \epsilon, x_j) \to (q_j, \mathsf{pop}_1)$$

$$(q_0, \epsilon, \varphi_j t_1 \cdots t_n) \to \begin{cases} (q_0, \mathsf{repl}_1(\varphi_j t_1 \cdots t_n^+) \,;\, \mathsf{push}_2 \,;\, \mathsf{pop}_1 \,;\, \mathsf{repl}_1(s_j^-)) \\ (q_0, \mathsf{push}_2 \,;\, \mathsf{pop}_1 \,;\, \mathsf{repl}_1(s_j)) \end{cases}$$

$$\text{if Situation A holds and } Ds_1 \cdots s_{n'}{}^{\lambda'} \text{ precedes } \varphi_j t_1 \cdots t_n$$

$$(q_0, \epsilon, \varphi_j t_1 \cdots t_n^\lambda) \to (q_0, \mathsf{repl}_1(\varphi_j t_1 \cdots t_n^{+\cup\lambda}) \,;\, \mathsf{push}_2 \,;\, \mathsf{pop}_1 \,;\, \mathsf{repl}_1(s_j^-))$$

$$\text{if Situation B holds and } Ds_1 \cdots s_{n'}{}^{\lambda'} \text{ precedes } \varphi_j t_1 \cdots t_n^\lambda$$

$$1 \le j \le n, (q_j, \epsilon, \$t_1 \cdots t_n^\lambda) \to \begin{cases} (q_0, \mathsf{repl}_1(t_j)) \text{ if } - \notin \lambda \\ \mathsf{abort} \qquad\quad \text{if } - \in \lambda \end{cases}$$

$$j > n, (q_j, \epsilon, \$t_1 \cdots t_n^\lambda) \to \begin{cases} \mathsf{abort} \qquad\quad \text{if } - \notin \lambda \\ (q_{j-n}, \mathsf{pop}_2^+) \text{ if } - \in \lambda \end{cases}$$

Fig. 3. Transition rules of the non-deterministic 2PDA, 2PDA$_G$
In the above, Situations A and B refer to the two possibilities outlined in the preceding page regarding ultimate referral.

Penalty for Guessing Wrongly. The cost of using non-determinism is that we commit ourselves to following our guesses. When we find out that we have guessed wrongly, we shall have to abort the run. There are two cases. Suppose we find ourselves in a configuration (q_j, w, s) where $\mathsf{top}_1(s) = \$x_1 \cdots x_n^-$ and $j \le n$. The fact that the topmost item is labelled by $-$ means that we guessed that we would follow this link. We have guessed wrongly and we abort. Symmetrically if we reach (q_j, w, s) where $\mathsf{top}_1(s) = \$x_1 \cdots x_n$ and $j > n$, then we also abort. Why? The absence of a $-$ label means that we guessed that we would *not* follow this link, but we are now about to turn against our original guess.

5.2   Definition of the Non-deterministic 2PDA, 2PDA$_G$

Let G be a (possibly unsafe) 2-grammar. The transition rules of the corresponding non-deterministic 2PDA, 2PDA$_G$, are given in Fig. 3.

Note that we assume that production rules of the grammar assume the format given in rule (2). Let s range over 2-stores, we define $\mathsf{pop}_2^+(s) = p(\mathsf{pop}_2(s))$ where

$$p(s) = \begin{cases} s & \text{if } \mathsf{top}_1(s) \text{ has label } + \\ p(\mathsf{pop}_2(s)) & \text{otherwise} \end{cases}$$

Remark 3. In the definition of the transition rules (Fig. 3), in case the top_1 item of the 2-store is headed by a level-1 variable, the 2PDA has to work out whether situation A or B holds. This can be achieved by a little scratch work on the side: do a push_2, inspect the topmost 1-store for as deep as necessary, followed by a pop$_2$. Alternatively we could ask the oracle to tell us whether it is A or B, taking care to ensure that a wrong pronouncement will lead to an abort.

Proposition 3. *Given a 2-grammar G, 2PDAL$_G$ can be simulated by 2PDA$_G$.*

Proof. (Sketch) It should be quite clear from Fig. 3 that 2PDA$_G$ behaves like a "crippled" 2PDAL$_G$. Thus, we can expect that if w is accepted by 2PDA$_G$, then w is accepted by 2PDAL$_G$. To show the converse requires a more delicate analysis of the behaviour of 2PDALs which we do not have space to contain here. Roughly, we assume the existence of an all-knowing oracle that can tell us whether or not a link will be followed in the future. All we then need to show is that the controlled form of guessing does not restrict the choices of the oracle – which it does not (i.e the controlled form of guessing is actually "sensible"). Full proofs of both directions are given in the technical report [2].

6   Urzyczyn's Language: A Conjecture About Term Trees

We have shown that the language U is accepted by a non-deterministic 2PDA. Based on the grammar G_U for Urzyczyn's language, we can construct the following term-tree generating grammar[4] over signature $\Sigma = \{(\ :(o,o),\ )\ :(o,o),\ *\ :(o,o),\ 3\ :(o,o,o,o),\ e:o,\ r:o\}$ and with the following rewrite rules.

$$S \to (DGEEE$$
$$D\varphi xyz \to 3((D(D\varphi x)z(Fy)(Fy))()\varphi yx)(*z)$$

$$Fx \to *x$$
$$E \to e$$
$$G \to r$$

Proposition 4. *Suppose that the term tree generated by the above grammar can be generated by a safe (term-tree generating-) 2-grammar. Then the language U can be accepted by a deterministic 2PDA.*

Conjecture 1. U cannot be accepted by a deterministic 2PDA.

Conjecture 1 is closely related to a conjecture of Knapik *et al.*; see Remark 1. Thanks to Proposition 4, provided Conjecture 1 is true, we will have an example of an *inherently unsafe* term tree i.e. an unsafe 2-grammar whose term tree cannot be generated by a safe 2-grammar.

7   Further Directions

Let us recall our main result. We have shown that the string language of every level-2 grammar (whether safe of unsafe) can be accepted by a 2PDA. Combining

---

[4] See [7, 8] for the term-tree definitions of grammars and PDAs.

this with earlier results [5] we have that there are no *inherently* unsafe string languages at level 2. This was a first attempt at understanding safety. However, our result leaves many questions unanswered:

- Does our result extend to levels 3 and beyond?
- What is the relationship between deterministic unsafe grammars and deterministic safe grammars? In particular, Conjecture 1.
- Is safety a requirement for MSO decidability? (An easy corollary of the result we have presented here is that LTL model-checking [13] is decidable for term trees generated by level-2 unsafe grammars – see technical report [2] for details. This has recently been superseded [1, 9].)
- It would be useful to have a "pumping lemma" for higher-order PDAs. We understand that Blumensath has a promising argument involving intricate surgeries on runs on an automaton; his ideas gives conditions under which such runs can be "pumped".

References

1. K. Aehlig, J. G. de Miranda, and C. H. L. Ong. The monadic second order theory of trees given by arbitrary level-two recursion schemes is decidable. *TLCA'05 (to appear)*.
2. K. Aehlig, J. G. de Miranda, and C. H. L. Ong. Safety is not a restriction at level 2 for string languages. Technical Report PRG-RR-04-23, OUCL, 2004.
3. A. Aho. Indexed grammars - an extension of context-free grammars. *J. ACM*, 15:647–671, 1968.
4. W. Damm. The IO- and OI-hierarchy. *TCS*, 20:95–207, 1982.
5. W. Damm and A. Goerdt. An automata-theoretical characterization of the OI-hierarchy. *Information and Control*, 71:1–32, 1986.
6. J. G. de Miranda and C. H. L. Ong. A note on deterministic pushdown languages. Available at http://web.comlab.ox.ac.uk/oucl/work/jolie.de.miranda, 2004.
7. T. Knapik, D. Niwiński, and P. Urzyczyn. Deciding monadic theories of hyperalgebraic trees. In *TLCA'01*, pages 253–267. Springer, 2001. LNCS Vol. 2044.
8. T. Knapik, D. Niwiński, and P. Urzyczyn. Higher-order pushdown trees are easy. In *FOSSACS'02*, pages 205–222. Springer, 2002. LNCS Vol. 2303.
9. T. Knapik, D. Niwiński, P. Urzyczyn, and I. Walukiewicz. Unsafe grammars, panic automata, and decidability. 25 October, 2004.
10. A. N. Maslov. The hierarchy of indexed languages of an arbitrary level. *Soviet Math. Dokl.*, 15:1170–1174, 1974.
11. C. Stirling. Personal email communication. 15 October, 2002.
12. P. Urzyczyn. Personal email communication. 26 July, 2003.
13. M. Y. Vardi. An automata-theoretic approach to linear temporal logic. In *Banff Higher Order Workshop*, pages 238–266. Springer-Verlag, 1995.

Author Index

Lecture Notes in Computer Science

For information about Vols. 1–3334

please contact your bookseller or Springer